THE COOK'S ENCYCLOPAEDIA

Ingredients and Processes

Tom Stobart

THE COOK'S ENCYCLOPAEDIA

Ingredients and Processes

Tom Stobart

Grub Street • London

Published by Grub Street
4 Rainham Close
London SW11 6SS
Email: food@grubstreet.co.uk
Web: www.grubstreet.co.uk
Twitter. @grub_street
Facebook: Grub Street Publishing

First published by BT Batsford, 1980

The moral right of the author, Tom Stobart has been asserted

A CIP record for this title is available from The British Library

ISBN 978-1-910690-09-3

Printed and bound in India

Publisher's Note

This book was first published in 1980 so some entries may seem dated or out of date but the text has not been amended to preserve the integrity of what is considered by many to be a classic work.

Acknowledgements

The information contained in this encyclopaedia came from many people and many books. Indeed, it is in the very nature of an encyclopaedia that it gathers together what other people have discovered. They cannot all be named, but they must not be forgotten; the agriculturists, economic botanists, food scientists and cookery writers have all, in their various ways, contributed towards our daily bread and have often made it more enjoyable. What better work is there than that? However, the people, firms and organisations listed in the credits have contributed directly to this book, and special thanks are due to them.

It requires a very special type of person to keep calm and avoid panic when faced with an office piled with scribbled-all-over paper full of an author's spelling mistakes and fantasies. Those who remain sane during the editing of an encyclopaedia deserve particular praise, as I do not think that many people realize just what a shattering amount of very meticulous work is involved.

Ian Cameron, thank you for going through the text personally. Bettina Tayleur, thank you for coping with masses of questions and keeping everything in order. Mimi Errington, thank you for research, shopping and unstinting help. Betty Leslie, thank you for the careful typing of over 300,000 words of untidy manuscript.

And to the publishers, thank you for so much faith and patience.

Tom Stobart

Introduction

Ingredients are the fundamentals of cookery, and every cook who hopes to excel should know about them. Great chefs and restaurateurs are likely to pay just as much attention to choosing their ingredients as they do to choosing their recipes – the two are inseparable.

When I was making films on European cooking, I got to know a number of distinguished chefs from various countries. Many of them worked in towns with good open-air markets. As I have always been fascinated by markets (and my love for them is one of the reasons why this book came to be written), I would visit them as soon as they opened, which was well before even an early breakfast. In the beginning, I was surprised to see a certain master chef, one of that exclusive body, the *Maîtres Cuisiniers de France*, was at the market before me. He was not young and was certainly wealthy enough to take it easy, but still he had come himself to prod the strawberries, smell the melons and squeeze the onions. Later, I came to accept this keenness as normal, as I observed chefs doing the same in country after country.

Great chefs become marvellously choosy and dogmatic. They are likely to tell us that *coq au vin* absolutely requires a real Bresse chicken and thyme from Provence, so that any idea of making it in America or Australia is absurd. In many ways, that is the right approach, even if it is a little chauvinistic. We might equally ask if a Frenchman in France could bake a proper New England Johnnycake or a Yorkshire pudding.

Of course, some ingredients – olive oil, for instance – are more critical than others – but even seemingly mundane things, like salt, are worthy of close attention. The very air can come into the equation. It is not just that local dishes do not taste right or that recipes do not work with the wrong ingredients – using the right ones is among the secrets of good cooking.

There is, of course, a no-nonsense view that holds that if a recipe calls for a Bresse chicken, the operative word is chicken and any chicken, even a broiler, will do. This is a sure route to mediocrity as it will inevitably eliminate the subtleties that are the mark of fine cooking. The more 'nonsense', then, the better. Why waste effort trying to imitate classic recipes with only substitutes for the ingredients they demand? Surely it is better to discover the virtues of what is actually available. We should remember, too, that inspired improvisation by cooks in circumstances where only a limited range of ingredients were obtainable led to the invention of some of the world's great dishes.

No book can list every ingredient that is locally available or discuss every nuance. Nor can it be totally objective about such subjective qualities as taste. Personal judgement cannot be avoided – in any case, there is no such thing as a good but impersonal cookery book. What I have tried to do is to list as wide a range of ingredients as possible, to give some of their background and to identify their particular characteristics. They should have an individuality and an identity beyond mere appearance – a brown root or a white powder. It is the specific qualities of ingredients that give the cook something to build on.

While I hope that this book will provide entertainment for people who like to browse in cookery books (as I do), my aim has been to offer practical advice to cooks who buy unfamiliar ingredients and try to use them. Today, shops and markets offer the most staggering variety of produce. In them, you can drool over anything from bottled insects to dried duck's feet and long for advice. 'Oh, those!' the shopkeeper may well say. 'Some Tibetans or Koreans from up the road come in for them, but God knows how they cook them. We just get them from the wholesaler.' It is possible that, after boiling the things for several hours, you will find that they are pan scourers.

With the jet age, the world's food has entered a phase of explosive evolution, and anyone who is essentially curious is likely to have a hard time keeping up. Indeed, while writing this book, I have sometimes felt like a hunter tracking the Yeti; it became evident that the Yeti was walking faster than I was. New ingredients crop up faster than they can be tried out – which should not be a cause for despair but rather of rejoicing at the richness that is available to us. At least by mastering the usual ingredients and processes, we can have more time to devote to the unusual.

This is not a recipe book, but recipes have been included for a variety of reasons. In some cases, they have been chosen simply to illustrate the use of an ingredient, or how to prepare it in ways other than those commonly used in British or American cooking. For instance, nuts are not just for eating at Christmas but can make subtle additions to the consistency and flavour of every course. Recipes are also given so that expatriates can make basic ingredients for themselves when they are living out of reach of suitable suppliers. Others are there because showing how something is made may be the best way of defining or describing it. The rest are there just because I felt like putting them in or because one of the many people who have helped with the book wanted some particular recipe. The same freedom has been taken with the methods and the science. In general, I have put in what I remember that I once did not know myself and what I still have to look up, often in books on agricultural botany or geography or biochemistry or nutrition rather than on cookery. I have also tried to straighten out old confusions. Again, even though the book has grown far beyond its intended size, there has had to be selection, as the subject is infinite.

I am frequently asked why someone who has spent so much time travelling and 'exploring' should want to write books about food instead of concentrating on such excitements as man-eating tigers. Food, though, is one of the greatest of all travel subjects – people who fly around the globe but never eat outside the international hotels are hardly to be described as travellers. Their only contact with foreign lands is through the soles of their shoes; they never become involved. Anthropologists, on the other hand, sometimes go as far as to marry a girl of the country they want to study, which is hardly a practical solution for the traveller, who is unlikely to spend more than a few months in any country (it is also liable to create little problems).Visiting a place and eating the food that the people there enjoy at home or on their feast days is also a way of becoming involved in local life. Those who have smelled the aroma of garlic and Gauloises, eaten *tapas* or *meze*, or chewed grilled meat wrapped in entrails will understand why, as a traveller, I became interested in cooking. They are the kindred souls that I had particularly

in mind when I was writing this book. My aim has been to provide a reference source for cooks who are adventurous in spirit, whether they are able to travel widely or must find their culinary adventures at home.

About this book

Contents. The majority of the entries in this book deal with the ingredients and processes used in cooking. The ingredients that I have included are in general of sufficient culinary importance to be sold somewhere in the world. Very many things that grow wild can also be eaten or at least made edible and used in cooking to an extent that depends on the cook's determination and ingenuity (or sometimes eccentricity). Although there are various books, like Richard Mabey's *Food for Free* (Collins), about edible wild things, these can relate only to a particular country or area. A similar effort on a worldwide scale would be endless; on the whole, the wild animals and plants covered here are, at least locally, objects of commerce. Even so, I have been rather sparing in the number of entries allotted to one category of wild food that is very widely sold: fish and shellfish come in such a multitude of species, many of them rather restricted in distribution, that I have dealt only with the main edible groups. Finally among the list of intentional exclusions, I should mention that I have not gone into cuts of meat. Again, regional variation is the reason. Because not just the names but the actual cuts can differ even between different areas of the same country, any straightforward translation tables are likely to be misleadingly oversimplified. In any case, those outlines of carcasses divided up with neat lines into named areas are moderately uninformative. The best way of learning about the cuts of meat you can buy is from the butcher who actually produces them.

Arrangement. The entries are arranged alphabetically and cross-referenced. Words preceded by asterisks can be looked up for further information relevant to the entry in which they appear. However, the absence of an asterisk does not mean the absence of an entry for the word, merely that looking it up will not yield much that is germane to the matter in hand.

Foodstuffs often go under so many different names that it would have been easy to swamp the whole book with cross-references for every imaginable synonym. Two restrictions have been applied to save the day here. First, only the most important dialect names, archaic names and spelling variants have been included (a particularly rich source of cross-references could have been alternative transliterations from, say, Arabic). Second, I have taken advantage of the undoubted intelligence of my readers by doing away with cross-references from the whole of a name to its second word. Thus, you will not be given a cross-reference to take you from brown sugar to sugar or from red mullet to mullet. Where the destination is not the second word of the name, a cross-reference is, of course, provided, as from green bean to kidney bean.

Units. Much of the English-speaking world is at present in an awkward stage of partial metrication. A large part of the population, especially its older members, can cope only with the traditional units, while school leavers now emerge into society thinking entirely metric. The rest of us switch uneasily back and forth between the old units and the metric ones. At present, and probably for some years to come, the only sensible course in a cookbook is to include both units.

In the British edition of this book, metric units are given first, followed by their Imperial equivalents in parentheses. Anyone who cares to check the conversions will quickly find that they vary considerably in their accuracy. The rule here is a very simple one: conversions have been made only as accurate as they need to be, which is to say pretty accurate for baking, where quantities are often critical, and often quite approximate elsewhere. The abbreviations that have been used for the various units are the conventional ones with the exception of litres, for which the Italian abbreviation lt has been chosen as being less confusing typographically than the more usual l. The various units are covered in some detail in the entry on weights and measures.

Scientific names. Popular names for plants or animals can often be confusing, with the same thing having a variety of names or, worse still, the same name applying to a variety of things. Scientific names are supposed to sort out the confusion by being internationally accepted. Unfortunately, though, the scientists have managed to create some muddles of their own and have had to ape the College of Heralds in unscrambling confusions in nomenclature. For example, two biologists may independently have given a name to what later turns out to be the same species; the older of the two names is the one that sticks (unless, of course, it has previously been used by someone else as a name for another species altogether). Groupings

into genera, families and so on are meant to reflect relationships and to make up a sort of genealogical table. But since there are no church registers in evolution, taxonomists have to work on the available evidence, so that generic names (the first word in the name of any species) tend to be changed. To make a biological name unambiguous, you have to add the name of the person who first described the species (and ideally the date of the description).You will then know that when you are talking about White mustard as *Sinapis alba Linnaeus*, you are referring to the same species that other authorities have called *Brassica alba* or *Brassica hirta*, which is all very clear for a scientist. For the purposes of this book, such extremes of scientific pedantry seem unnecessary and the scientific name that seems to be most commonly used has been adopted without the name of its author. For the most part, scientific names are there either for precision or just as an extra piece of information that might be useful. There are, however, some things such as edible fungi and exotic fish and shellfish that have no popular names in English. Where a number of species of the same genus have been referred to in the same entry, the convention has been adopted of abbreviating the generic name on its second and subsequent appearances, as in *Brassica napus* and *B. rapa*.

Translations. Entries for the more usual ingredients and processes give translations in French, German, Italian and Spanish. For processes the translation is always the infinitive i.e. the French for boiling is given as *bouillir* – literally 'to boil'.

Sources. Books that have been important as sources of information have been acknowledged in the particular entries for which they have been used, and the British publisher has been given for the edition that was consulted. Some books, such as Alan Davidson's invaluable works on seafood, therefore receive quite a number of mentions. There are, however, a number of titles that have been consulted for a large number of entries. Five that have been at hand throughout the editing of this book are *Food Science – A Chemical Approach* by Brian A. Fox and Allan G. Cameron (University of London Press, 1970), *Success in Nutrition* by Magnus Pyke (John Murray, 1975), *Teaching Nutrition and Food Science* by Margaret Knight (Batsford, 1976), *The Oxford Book of Food Plants* by S.G. Harrison, G.B. Masefield and Michael Wallace (Oxford University Press, 1969) and my own *Herbs, Spices and Flavourings* (Grub Street, 1998).

Cookery adviser..Elizabeth David
Cookery editor...Mimi Errington
Copy editor..Ian Cameron
Organisation ....Bettina Tayleur

Research ....Victoria Burgess
....Jill Hollis
....Alice Macnab
....Corinne Molesworth
....Mrinalini Srivastava
....Marijke Taylor

Consultants...A.M.C.K. Bannerman, M.B.E.
....Gordon G. Birch, D.Sc.
....Maggie Black
....The British Turkey Federation
....The British Waterfowl Association
....H.P. Bulmer Ltd
....C.A.M.R.A.
....J.G. Davis O.B.E., D.Sc., Ph.D.
....Percy Fox & Co. Ltd
....Freezer Family
....Fyffes Group Ltd
....Good Housekeeping
....H.J. Green & Co. Ltd
....Wendy Godfrey
....Harrods Ltd
....Irish Distillers International Ltd
....Robert Jackson & Son Ltd
....Leon Jaeggi & Son Ltd
....Jardox Concentrated Products Ltd
....R.A. Knight
....Norman Kolpas
....The Metal Box Company Ltd
....National College of Food Technology
....The Prestige Group Ltd
....Duncan Rayner Ltd
....The Scotch Whisky Association
....The Earl of Selborne
....Janet Simpson
....Tate & Lyle Ltd
....Margaret Trotter
....Thompson & Morgan
....Van den Berghs
....Hiram Walker & Sons Ltd

a

ABALONE and **ORMER**. These flattened molluscs of the genus *Haliotis*, the sea-ears, are best known for their ornamental shells, which have a row of holes and a fine mother-of-pearl lining. They have almost lost their spiral shape and creep around in a limpet-like way eating the algae on rocks below the low tide mark. The edible part is the muscular foot which serves the creature for both anchorage and locomotion. After the animal has been taken out of its shell, the dark-coloured visceral hump (the guts) must be removed. The remaining foot should be beaten soundly to break up the muscle fibres. Otherwise it will be exceedingly tough.

Ormers are small European abalones which are found as far north as Guernsey, although they have become very scarce; they are very rare in Jersey (which is too far from the Gulf Stream) and are almost absent from Britain. The name is a Channel Islands corruption of the French *ormeau* or *oreille de mer*. Ormers may be gathered from the rocks at spring low tides. They are out of season in the summer, when they are at their toughest. Some authorities distinguish the slightly smaller Mediterranean ormer (*Haliotis lamellosa*) from the Atlantic ormer (*H. tuberculata*).

Abalone is the Californian Spanish name for the species of *Haliotis* found in warm seas; they are commonly much larger and finer in flavour than ormers. The true abalone is the Red abalone (*H. rufescens*), which is fished in southern California and traditionally prepared for market by Japanese girls whose forebears would have eaten them in their own country. Other species, such as the Black abalone (*H. cracherodii*), are popular in Mexico. Indeed, abalone are eaten wherever they occur in sufficient numbers. In Australia, they are known as mutton fish. In Japan, they are famous as *awabi* or *turbo*, and the fishing was done traditionally by almost naked girls, called *ama*, who went down to a depth of 12 m (40 ft), wearing no more than a G-string and carrying a large stone to help them sink.

In countries where abalone is found, the foot, cleaned and pounded, is sold by weight, fresh and sliced. It can be eaten raw or cooked. Fresh or frozen slices may be covered with breadcrumbs and fried like cutlets, but they must be cooked on each side for no more than a minute or they will become tough. Recipes can be found in American, Japanese and Chinese cookery books. In China, abalone is often dried; it is then called *pao yü* and must be soaked for four days in fresh water before use. In Europe, canned abalone is available. The cream-coloured foot should be sliced; it may be served in a salad or as part of an *hors d'oeuvre*.

[*Ormer* – French: *oreille de mer*, *ormeau* German: *Seeohr*, *Ohrmuschel* Italian: *orecchia marina*, *orecchia di San Pietro* Spanish: *oreja de mar*]

ABELMUSK. *See* mallow.

ABUTILON. *See* mallow.

ACETIC ACID (CH_3COOH). This, the acid of *vinegar and of spoiled wine, is an important organic acid formed when alcohol is oxidized by acetic-acid producing bacteria. These are aerobic – they require oxygen from the air – and so cannot spoil a properly corked bottle of wine, but can turn it sour after it has been opened. Natural wine vinegar will contain 5-10% acetic acid. Acetic acid is an important flavouring, and traces of it are responsible for a pleasant tang in yoghurt and cheese.

As acetic acid is volatile, the strength of vinegar can be increased by distillation or conversely weakened by long boiling. Industrially, acetic acid can be made from coal and limestone. (They are heated together to make calcium carbide. This, slaked, makes acetylene gas, which in turn is converted to acetic acid.) Pure acetic acid looks a little like a mixture of ice and water, which is why it is known as glacial acetic acid. Being a highly-corrosive substance, it is not one to keep in the kitchen, but suitably diluted (to 5%), and often coloured with burnt sugar, it is used in cheap pickles and as a vinegar substitute, which turns up in fish and chip shops labelled Non-Brewed Condiment.

It also is added to natural vinegar (like fortifying wine with alcohol) to make it keep better, since dilute vinegar is open to attack by bacteria which change acetic acid into carbon dioxide and water. Acetic acid is a stronger preservative than other kitchen acids (citric, lactic and tartaric), and even at the same *pH is more toxic to spoilage organisms, though less so than benzoic acid (see preservation). Even a 1% solution strongly inhibits most bacteria, though not moulds. These qualities make vinegar effective in pickling.

[*Acetic Acid* – French: *acide acétique* German: *Essigsäure* Italian: *acido acetic* Spanish: *ácido acético*]

ACIDS. From the Latin *acidus* (sour) – all sour foods contain acids. Sourness is an important taste and is supplied by acids in many natural ingredients, such as *acetic acid in vinegar, *citric acid in lemon juice, *tartaric acid in wine and unripe fruit, *malic acid in sour apples, *lactic acid in sour milk, and *oxalic acid in sorrel and rhubarb.

Although naturally-occurring sour ingredients are the ones most commonly used in cooking, there is sometimes a need for pure acids such as citric and tartaric, which may be bought as crystalline powders. Even *hydrochloric and *sulphuric acids, which are highly corrosive and dangerous, have some relevance to food.

Acids are highly active chemicals: even rather weak ones will attack iron, zinc (on galvanized articles) and, more slowly, lead and copper in the circumstances in which they may occur in the kitchen. The resulting salts of zinc, copper and, above all, lead are poisonous. On the other hand, for practical purposes, organic acids do not attack enamel, stainless steel, tin (on cans or tinned pans of brass or copper), aluminium, silver or gold. Wooden tubs, china, stoneware, enamel and plastics are also resistant, but acids should not be kept in marble mortars, which they will dissolve, in earthenware vessels with low-fired glazes that are high in lead content, or in high-lead crystal glass bottles – the last two are potentially dangerous. Acids dissolve carbonates (marble, limestone, chalk, washing soda) and bicarbonates (baking soda), giving off a fizz of carbon-dioxide gas. This property is used in sherbets, fruit salts and baking powders. Acids are always neutralized by *alkalis, and the two cannot exist together. It is no good mixing fuming hydrochloric acid and caustic soda together to make a double-acting cleaner – one will neutralize the other with some violence. In theory, fruits can be made less sour by adding soda or lime. Home winemakers sometimes temper rhubarb by adding chalk, which is quite logical, but the salts formed can taste nasty and may be purgative. Sugar, on the other hand, does not neutralize acids but produces a pleasant sweet-sour sensation in the mouth.

Adjustment of acidity, and therefore of sourness, is a fundamental operation in cooking, which is why a last-minute squeeze of lemon juice can be so important in finishing a dish. Fruits with insufficient acidity are insipid. A wine with less than 0.2% acid will be uninteresting and moreover will not keep, while one with more than 1.5% will be too sour.

Acids above a certain strength are *preservatives (though some are more toxic to bacteria than others), which is why Viking relics are pickled in peat bogs and vegetables are preserved in vinegar.

Acid and alkaline solutions can be distinguished with litmus papers, which are turned red by acid and blue by alkalis. Many of the natural colours of food behave in a similar manner. Acid vinegar will turn beetroot or red cabbage a bright red, while cabbage boiled in acid water turns an unappetizing yellow.

Weight for weight, some acids are much stronger than others. For instance a 1% solution of hydrochloric acid is much stronger than a 1% solution of citric acid, in that it is sourer and able to neutralize a greater amount of soda, attack metals faster and so on. In fact, it is more acid. The essential acidity of solutions, irrespective of which acids are present, can be compared by means of the *pH scale.

[*Acids* – French: *acides* German: *Säuren* Italian: *acidi* Spanish: *ácidos*]

ACIDULATED WATER is water that has been made slightly acid with a teaspoon or so of vinegar or lemon juice to each half litre or pint of water. It is used for briefly holding cut fruit or vegetables which would otherwise darken quite quickly when their cut surfaces come into contact with the air. It is effective for fruit such as apples and pears and for vegetables such as globe and Jerusalem artichokes and salsify. It can also be used as a cooking medium – cauliflower cooked in acidulated water will be beautifully white even if the curd was rather yellow when raw.

ACITRÓN. A candied substance made in Mexico from the large cushion-like Biznaga cactus (*Echinocactus grandis*). It is shaped into bars and is used for meat stuffings. Any sweet candied fruit may be used as a substitute if it is not too strongly flavoured.

ACKEE or **akee**. A tropical fruit (*Blighia sapida*) belonging to the same family as the lychee but very different to look at. It was introduced from West Africa to Jamaica, where it has become particularly popular. The fruit, some 8 mm (3 in) in diameter, is bright red. When ripe, it bursts open to reveal three large shiny black seeds and the creamy aril which is well described by the name 'vegetable brain'. This is all that is eaten, because the pink parts of the fruit are very poisonous, as are both the unripe and over ripe fruits. The flavour of ackee as a fruit is delicate, but its most famous use is cooked in the West Indian 'salt fish and ackee'. As canned ackees are available outside the West Indies, anyone could attempt the following recipe:

Salt Fish and Ackee

Soak 450 g (1 lb) salt cod and cook it in water. Fifteen minutes before the fish is cooked, add the creamy part of 24 ackees. Drain, skin and bone the fish, flake it and mix with the ackee. Dice 100 g (4 oz) salt pork and fry it until crisp and brown.

Remove the pork, and in the fat fry 2 finely-chopped medium onions and a chopped sweet pepper until very lightly browned. Then add 1 or 2 chopped chillies, 4 chopped spring onions, 3 peeled and coarsely-chopped tomatoes, and a sprig of thyme. Fry this gently for about 5 minutes, and finally put in the salt cod and ackee, together with the fried salt pork, to warm through. Serve seasoned with pepper and garnished with crisply fried slices of bacon, a few tomato wedges and parsley or watercress for decoration. If canned ackees are used, a 450 g (1 lb) tin will suffice. They do not require cooking, but should be drained and added with the fish and pork near the end of cooking.

Those interested in further recipes should consult Elisabeth Lambert Ortiz's *Caribbean Cookery* (Penguin) on which this salt fish and ackee recipe is based.

ACORN. One of the original foods of man, acorns are still used extensively in some parts of Europe and also by North American Indians. Acorns from all species of oak are edible but those (e.g. of the English oak, *Quercus robur*) that taste very astringent should first be ground and washed or boiled in water until the water-soluble tannins, which could cause stomach upsets, are dissolved out. However, a number of oak species bear acorns which are sweet and edible without treatment.

Among the best is the evergreen Holm oak or Ilex (*Quercus ilex*), which grows on the stony hillsides of Mediterranean countries and has plump brown acorns. The cultivated sweet varieties (var. *ballota*) are sold in the markets of Spain, Algeria and Morocco in January, and fetch the same price as chestnuts which in many ways they resemble. They become sweeter with keeping, but may acquire a winey flavour.

Other sweet acorns commonly eaten in Europe are those of the Valonia oak (*Q. macrolepis*) from Italy, Greece and the eastern Mediterranean, and of the Manna oak (*Q. persica*) and the Kermes oak (*Q. coccifera*), also from Mediterranean hillsides. In North America, the best are from the White oak (*Q. alba*) and the Live oak (*Q. virginiana*). Acorns are also eaten in China (*Q. cornea*) and in Japan (*Q. cuspidata*).

Acorns are usually eaten roasted like chestnuts, but I have also found them useful as a substitute for water chestnuts, as they do not disintegrate quickly on boiling. It is possible to make use of any acorns by shelling and boiling them until they are sweet and dark brown, or by pounding and washing them for a day in running water, after which the residue can be dried and be used in cakes, like other nuts. Roasted acorns are sometimes used as a coffee substitute, and acorn flour can be made into bread.

[*Acorn* – French: *gland* German: *Eichel* Italian: *ghianda* Spanish: *bellota*]

ADULTERATION is the trader's dirty trick of padding foods, especially expensive ones, with cheaper materials of similar appearance to cheat the customer. Because adulteration of this sort is difficult to detect and needs the trained investigator with microscope and laboratory, we all depend on the vigilance of food inspectors. As individuals we can protect ourselves only by avoiding incredible bargains (nobody is going to sell saffron cheaply if it is real saffron) and by buying items like spices whole – it is only too easy to fake ground pepper with ground date-stones. In other cases, the adulteration is done quite openly: thus ground almonds are commonly padded with biscuit meal and almond flavouring. The confectioner knows he is buying a substitute – he is continually visited by salesmen selling substitutes for eggs, cherries, chocolate, cream and other ingredients, and there is often no concealment. As for the tradesmen involved – most have long ago stopped being concerned that such things as genuine ground almonds ever existed. That, one may say, is not quite the same as selling salami made of plastic, as was done when I lived in Italy. (After an official inquiry, the local river was suddenly flooded with large sausages bobbing their way to pollute the Mediterranean.)

Although dictionaries do not do so, I have made a distinction in this book between adulteration and the much more worrying question of additives which are put into manufactured foodstuffs – often, though not always, with good intentions. Additives are there to improve texture, colour and appearance, to prolong shelf-life or to bring out flavour. They might be acceptable, if they were not so often substances which in quantity might prove a health hazard.

[Adulteration – French: freletage
German: Nahrungsmittelverfälschung
Italian:adulterazione Spanish: adulteración]

ADZUKI BEAN. A small reddish brown bean (Phaseolus angularis), easily cooked and with a very pleasant, sweet flavour. Adzuki beans are much grown in China and Japan, and have now become generally available outside the Orient. In Japanese cooking, the boiled beans, mashed and sweetened, are an important base for various cakes (e.g. yonkan) and sweets, and in red rice. The beans are also sold powdered (azukisarashien) – a short cut. I have found adzuki beans tender and palatable when used in place of other small beans in non-Oriental recipes.

AGAR-AGAR, **kanten**, **Japanese gelatine** or **vegetable gelatine**. Available as a powder, in sticks or in shreds, agar-agar is obtained from a number of seaweeds by boiling them in water, then filtering and drying the resultant jelly. It is a complex carbohydrate, unlike gelatine which is a protein. Agar-agar melts at about 90°C (194°F) and sets at about 45°C (112°F); gelatine melts at about 27°C (80°F) and sets at 20°C (68°F).

Agar-agar can be obtained from pharmacists, because it is the usual medium for cultures of bacteria. It does not melt at blood heat and so can be incubated. This characteristic suits the bacteriologist, but makes agar-agar unpopular in the kitchen, as it does not melt in the mouth like other jellies. Also, the texture is peculiarly short and brittle.

Agar-agar will dissolve only in boiling water. Like gelatine, it varies in jellying power from sample to sample, but 1 teaspoon to ¾ lt (1 ⅓ pt) of water would be a sensible point to start from. As agar-agar jelly sets at 40-44°C (104-111°F) – which

is lukewarm – it is not too long a job to learn by experiment. Do not, however, boil agar-agar for long with an acid, or it will change its character and fail to set at all. On the other hand, one can make fresh pineapple or papaya juice into jellies with agar-agar, but not with gelatine, as they contain substances which attack the protein in gelatine.

As kanten, agar-agar is an ingredient of Japanese cooking and is often used to make a very stiff, coloured jelly from which decorative shapes – leaves or fruits – are cut. For this purpose, kanten, which often comes in cakes, is heated rather gently in water until it melts; then it is seasoned, coloured and set in sheets of the required thickness. Kanten is also an ingredient of fake bird's-nest soup, in which it provides the viscous texture.

AJOWAN, **bishop's weed** or **omum**. A spice seed (Carum ajowan), closely related to caraway, but with a strong taste of thyme and containing thymol; it therefore has antiseptic properties. It is used in Indian cooking, but dried thyme is a very fair substitute.

AKAVIT. See liqueurs and cordials.

AKEE. See ackee.

ALBACORE. See tuna.

ALBUMIN. Member of a class of proteins once thought to make up almost the entire protein content of egg white which was called albumen. In fact, the protein of egg white is only about 70% ovalbumin and 9% conalbumin. Albumins are an important constituent of seeds, a stored food for the embryo to use for a start in life. They are also a constituent of milk and of meat, as well as being the main protein in blood plasma, which is why egg-white substitutes used by commercial confectioners are often made from blood. During World War II, certain jokers used to make meringues from plasma filched from the field hospitals. Like many proteins, albumin coagulates and hardens when heated. Ovalbumin starts to coagulate at 60°C (140°F); it is also partially coagulated if beaten into a foam (see whipping). Because this process is slowed down at low temperatures, it is slower work to beat the whites of eggs that have come straight out of the refrigerator than it is with them at room temperature.

[Albumin – French: albumine German: Albumin
Italian: albumina Spanish: albúmina]

ALCOHOL. Chemically, there are dozens of alcohols, several ranges of them, but popularly (and in our context) by alcohol we mean, unless otherwise qualified, only potable alcohol, silent alcohol or neutral spirit, which are all names for ethyl alcohol mixed with water. Ethyl alcohol or ethanol is one of a series of alcohols of which the simplest members are:

methyl alcohol CH_3OH boils at 55°C (149°F)
ethyl alcohol C_2H_5OH boils at 78°C (173°F)
propyl alcohol C_3H_7OH boils at 98°C (208°F)
butyl alcohol C_4H_9OH boils at 118°C (244°F)

Each member of the series has one carbon and two hydrogen atoms more than its predecessor and has a higher boiling point; from this list the would-be moonshiner, who wishes to distil ethyl alcohol without too many of its more poisonous relations, may get some idea of his problems. Methyl alcohol, also known as wood alcohol or methanol, is the most volatile. It is the stuff that sends methylated-spirits drinkers blind. Other series of alcohols include such substances as glycerine and are well represented in the higher boiling point mixture of congenerics known as *fusel oil, which comes over towards the end of distillation. Ethyl alcohol is produced when sugars are fermented by yeasts, but the raw materials usually used for making alcoholic drinks – grapes, malted grain, potatoes, rice, fruit juices – contain much more than just sugars, so that many reactions take place, and other substances – the congenerics – are formed in fermentation. Many people regard ethyl alcohol itself as a poison, but some of the other substances are far more poisonous and are largely responsible for hangover headaches (*see* distillation).

The Properties of Ethyl Alcohol. At ordinary atmospheric pressure, pure alcohol boils at 78°C (173°F). Since pure water boils at 100°C (212°F), a mixture of water and alcohol will boil somewhere between these two extremes, depending on the relative amounts of each. *Proof spirit boils at 82°C (180°F). Of course, the alcohol does not all boil away suddenly when the temperature of wine, for example, reaches the boiling point of alcohol, but the higher the temperature of hot punch or spiced wine, the more alcohol is lost, until finally at 100°C (212°F) it is gone altogether.

Alcohol freezes at a much lower temperature than water, which is why thermometers for low temperatures are frequently filled with coloured spirit. Every winter there are fatal accidents in the Arctic when thirsty travellers swig vodka or akavit which has been left in sub-zero weather. This causes internal burns from frostbite and caustic burns from the alcohol being strengthened as the water freezes out of the original mixture.

Pure ethyl alcohol is known as absolute alcohol; it is clear, inflammable and exceedingly caustic. The strongest alcohol normally sold in shops is 90-95% and is found in countries where the duty is not prohibitive, such as Spain (as *alcohol para licores*) or Italy (as *alcool puro grado*). It is used in home-made liqueurs and for preserving fruits such as grapes and cherries. This alcohol must be cut with an equal quantity of water before it is in any way comparable to ordinary spirits, such as gin and whisky. Taken neat, it will skin the mouth and possibly have fatal consequences. When water is added to such strong alcohol, the total volume shrinks slightly and heat is generated. It is best to dilute it with ice water.

The Effects of Alcohol. Alcohol depresses, but as it depresses first those parts of the brain which cause depression and inhibition, it appears to act as a stimulant. Later effects are impaired efficiency, slow reactions, recklessness, self-pity, bad temper, aggressiveness and falling flat on your face. Alcohol also increases the circulation in the skin, which may make you feel warmer but will, in reality, lead to cooling. Thus, a Planter's Punch on a hot day is sensible, but the idea of a St Bernard bringing help with the brandy keg is sheer lunacy. Brandy makes the avalanche victim feel warmer, but increases his heat loss and reduces his chance of survival. A man who is cold must get into a warm place before having his whisky and hot water.

Absorption of alcohol into the blood-stream starts soon after a drink has been swallowed and is especially rapid once the drink has entered the small intestine. This happens quickly if the drink is diluted and is taken on an empty stomach. The absorption occurs more slowly if you are eating as well as drinking especially when the food is fatty, oily or heavy. There is some sense in taking a spoonful of oil or a slice of bread thickly spread with *pâté* before a drinking party. Similar wisdom lies behind the Russian *zakousky*, the Spanish *tapas* or the Levantine *meze*. Elimination of alcohol from the blood goes on much more slowly than its absorption, particularly if drinks have been taken which are rich in the higher alcohols (fusel oil). It is a scientific fact, and not an advertising gimmick, that people will sober up far more quickly after a session on highly-rectified vodka than after the same quantities of brandy or whisky. The trouble with mixing drinks is not the alcohol but the congenerics.

Germicidal effect. Tests have shown that the germicidal effect of alcohol is greatest at a 50% concentration (i.e. at American proof). Some people disinfect jam papers with spirits, but such treatment, as usually carried out, is probably not effective. Stronger or weaker mixtures are even less effective. At a concentration over 18%, alcohol will stop the fermenting action of yeasts and will not be turned to acetic acid by bacteria. At this sort of strength it is used to preserve fruit syrups (e.g. *crème de cassis*). When preserving fruit such as grapes or cherries in alcohol, you should remember that it will be diluted by the juices of the fruit. You therefore have to start with a good, strong spirit.

....

Italian Cherry Liqueur

Wash 450 g (1 lb) ripe bitter black cherries. Put 300 g (11 oz) sugar, 2 cloves, a 5 cm (2 in) of stick cinnamon, and 150 ml (¼ pt) water in a pan, bring to the boil and cool. Mix the cooled syrup with 300 ml (½ pt) 90% alcohol. Pack the cherries into the jars without breaking them, but include a couple of cracked stones if you like. Fill the jars until the fruit is covered. Seal. Put the jars daily in the sun, turning and shaking them gently each day. After some weeks, the bottles are ready. The liquid may be drained off and bottled (adjust with boiled syrup if necessary). You can eat the cherries.

[*Alcohol* – French: *alcool* German: *Alkohol* Italian: *alcool* Spanish: *alcohol*]

....

ALE. Alcoholic drink brewed from a cereal. Now more or less synonymous with *beer, a term which used to refer to hopped ale.

[*Ale* – French: *ale, bière* German: *englisches Bier, Ale* Italian: *birra* Spanish: *cerveza*]

ALECOST. *See* costmary.

ALEXANDERS. A heavily-built, strong-smelling umbelliferous herb, with yellow-green flowers, indigenous to Mediterranean Europe but naturalized in Britain. Alexanders (*Smyrnium olusatrum*) was once important as a vegetable, with a flavour between celery and parsley. Today, celery has superseded it.

[*Alexanders* – French: *ombrelle jaune* Italian: *macerone* Spanish: *esmirnio*]

ALFALFA. Probably the world's most important forage legume, alfalfa (*Medicago sativa*) is a native of the Mediterranean region. It was grown by the ancient Persians, Greeks and Romans, and spread into China and the whole of Europe. It is fashionable at the moment to sprout alfalfa seeds as a salad food. The flavour is mild and pleasant.

ALKERMES. An old-fashioned French and Italian sweet red cordial made with *kermes.

ALKALIS are, in many ways, the opposites or antagonists of *acids. The word comes from the old Arab alchemists and referred to the white ashes of wood; these were mostly carbonates of potassium and sodium and were used in experiments as well as for cleaning and making soap. Today we would use the much stronger *caustic soda and *washing soda. When dissolved in water, and perhaps filtered, the wood-ash solution was known as *lye. Other common alkalis are *bicarbonate of soda (the one alkali commonly used in cooking), *lime and *ammonia. Substances which neutralize acids and combine with them to form salts are known in chemistry as bases; alkalis are bases that are soluble in water. The alkalinity of a solution is measured by its *pH.

Many alkalis are dangerously caustic when strong. Even when highly diluted, they feel slimy on the fingers and often have an unpleasant soda taste, although an alkaline flavour is sometimes liked in soda bread, scones and girdle cakes, or as the ash on bonfire-roasted potatoes or on the bottom of old-fashioned, brick-oven bread.

Alkalis turn litmus paper blue and likewise affect beetroot and red cabbage, turning them an unappetizing purple; on the other hand, they intensify the green of green cabbage. Also they soften the skins of seeds, which is why bicarbonate of soda is frequently added to the water in which beans or chickpeas are cooked. They can even be used to remove skins entirely. In some places, bicarbonate of soda is also used to tenderize meat. *Lime-water and lye are required in some pickle recipes, and dilute caustic soda enters into quick commercial cures for green olives.

[*Alkalis* – French: *alcalis* German: *Alkalien* Italian: *alcali* Spanish: *álcalis*]

ALKALOIDS. Nitrogenous organic substances

which are basic (alkaline, hence the name) and often poisonous and bitter, alkaloids are found in certain plants. Many of them are used as drugs. Examples are morphine in the gum of unripe poppy capsules, belladonna (*atropine*) in the leaves and roots of deadly nightshade, cocaine in coca leaves and strychnine from the seeds of the East Indian *nux vomica* tree. Perhaps the instinctive dislike we have of bitter tastes could be an archaic survival trait. Quinine in very dilute form is used in the Indian tonic water of gin and tonic. In larger quantities, it is a powerful and dangerous drug, but in amounts likely to be immediately harmful, the bitterness would be intolerable. *Caffeine is a common alkaloid present in coffee, tea and cola nuts. Another alkaloid associated with caffeine is theobromine, which does not stimulate the brain, but dilates the arteries.

[*Alkaloids* – French: *alcaloides* German: *Alkaloide* Italian: *alcaloidi* Spanish: *alcaloides*]

ALKANNA, **anchusa**, or **dyers' alkanet**. A plant of the borage family (*Alkanna tinctoria*), native to the Mediterranean and south-east Europe. It has bright blue flowers, and the roots contain a powerful red dye, soluble in oil, alcohol and water (in the last giving a brownish colour). Alkanna is used to colour wine, drinks, ices, sausage skins, margarine, etc. As a colouring for meat dishes, it is frequently mentioned in 14th century recipes.

[*Alkanna* – French: *orcanette* German: *Alkanna* Italian: *alcanna* Spanish: *alcoma, orcaneta*]

ALL-GOOD. *See* spinach (Good King Henry).

ALLIGATOR PEAR. *See* avocado.

ALLSPICE, **Jamaica pepper**, or **myrtle pepper**. The dried berry of a tree (*Pimento dioica*) native to tropical America. Although it is grown in other tropical countries, the bulk comes from Jamaica. The name allspice describes its taste, which resembles a mixture of several Old World spices, in which cloves predominate. However, it really cannot be imitated exactly.

Whole allspice looks like large peppercorns. They are often included in pickle-spice mixtures and in marinades and brines for herring and beef. In Arab countries, although it is not normally used in curries, it has been adopted for pilaus and is very popular. Ground, preferably freshly, it is a usual spice in fruit cakes, mince pies and plum pudding. It can be used with discretion in many places where

a hint, but no more, of cloves might be nice, for instance with tomatoes and beetroot or, for those who like it, with cooked apples and pears. In fact, allspice is rather liked in northern Europe, but surprisingly in view of historical connections, it is not much used in Spain. In recipes from Yorkshire, allspice is often referred to as sweet pepper, which can be confusing.

[*Allspice* – French: *quatre-épices, piment de la Jamaïque* German: *Allgewürz, Jamaikapfeffer, Nelkenpfeffer* Italian: *pimento* Spanish: *pimiento de Jamaica*]

ALMOND. From a gastronomic point of view, undoubtedly the world's most important nut. Almonds come from the kernel of a fruit closely related to the apricot and like it in many ways, except that the fruit of the ripe almond is leathery, dusky green and quite inedible. Only when they are very young, before the nut is formed, is it possible to enjoy the sour, hard little fruits as a rough sort of *hors d'oeuvre*, for which they are eaten occasionally in the places where they grow. They have the same internal effects as sour apples.

Almond trees (*Prunus amygdalus*) are essentially Mediterranean, and indeed are probably indigenous to the eastern Mediterranean (they are mentioned in the Old Testament), although it has been claimed that they came from further east. They were spread by the Romans and later by the Arabs, but can be grown profitably only in the warm climate liked by the rather hardier lemon and olive. The almond is the first orchard tree to flower in the spring, often in January, which makes the young fruit exceedingly vulnerable to frost. It flowers well further north, but the results are too uncertain to make it a commercial crop. The decorative blossom often seen in English gardens is usually of hard-stoned, bitter varieties, which rarely get nuts, not just because of the frost but because almonds are self-sterile and need another almond of a compatible variety growing nearby.

Today almonds are grown extensively in South Africa and Australia, but do not like the tropics, where the so-called tropical almonds (which are not almonds at all) have to take their place. The bulk of the world's supply comes from Spain, Italy and California, and almonds are also grown in Provence (especially around Aix), Languedoc, Portugal, the Canary Islands, North Africa (especially in Algeria and Morocco), Greece, Turkey, Persia, Afghanistan and Kashmir. This distribution means that almonds are traditional in the cooking of Europe, the Middle

East and as far away as northern India, where they are commonly used in the more elaborate Mogul food.

Bitter Almonds (*Prunus amygdalus* var. *amara*), grown mainly in Sicily, Sardinia, North Africa and southern France, are small with very hard shiny shells. The kernels are usually less oily than those of sweet almonds, but the important distinguishing characteristic is the strong taste of bitter almond which develops when mixed with water (or saliva). They contain a glucoside (a nitrogenous substance related to sugar) which, when acted on by an enzyme, reacts with water to form prussic (hydrocyanic) acid and benzaldehyde. Prussic acid is lethal in very small doses, which is why it is unsafe to eat more than one or two bitter almonds, peach stones or other bitter-almond flavoured nuts or leaves. Fortunately, this acid is highly volatile and vanishes into the air on heating, leaving behind only the bitter-almond flavoured benzaldehyde, which is relatively harmless in small quantities. Roasting fruit kernels will also destroy the enzyme system. Those who like the taste of bitter almonds will find it in confections like *amaretti* (but not in *amaretti di Saronno* which contain apricot kernels), macaroons and some pastes; there is also *noyau. With more delicacy, the flavour pleases most people in plum, cherry and apricot jam, to which it is imparted by adding a few crushed stones. An almost unrecognizable waft of it is delicious with pork, too. But almond essence, as bought in bottles, is almost always a fairly nasty substance, and since it is used heavily in the average multi-storey wedding cake, people with discriminating palates may be encouraged to live in sin. When the flavour is wanted in emergency, then cherry laurel (*Prunus laurocerasus*) or peach leaves may be used provided that, after maceration in water, the liquid is heated. Ratafia, orgeat, noyau and other almond-flavoured liqueurs may also be pressed into service. Bitter almonds are illegal as a commercial ingredient in the US.

Amaretti

Blanch 100 g (4 oz) each of sweet almonds and bitter almonds. Dry them in a cool oven and pound them with 225 g (8 oz) sugar. Beat 2 egg whites until they are stiff and gently fold in the almond mixture to form a medium-soft paste. Pipe blobs of this on to rice paper. Sprinkle them with icing sugar and let them stand for a few hours. Then bake for 40 minutes in a moderate oven.

Sweet Almonds. When the type of almond is not specified in a recipe, one should use sweet almonds. They have a delicate flavour with no trace of benzaldehyde. The many varieties differ in size, shape, oil content and shell hardness (important in dessert almonds).There are paper-shell and soft-shell types, which can be cracked with the fingers, and famous varieties like the Jordan (*jardin*) almond and the Italian *premice* with fine, large, flat, regular-shaped nuts. You should suspect round nuts, especially if they have close-textured, shiny shells, as these are usually commercial types intended to be cracked by machine and may not be sweet almonds at all. For purposes other than dessert, most people will prefer to buy shelled almonds, which keep well and can be bought whole, either in the skin or blanched, in halves (for cake decoration), sliced, shaved, chopped or ground. They are also available roasted and salted for snacks. Ground almond is easy to adulterate and, since almonds are expensive, this is frequently done (though in most countries will be indicated in the ingredients listed on the label).When buying ground almonds or almond flour, check to make sure that it has not been padded with cheap nut flour, biscuit meal and sugar, and flavoured with bitter almonds. If it is, avoid it because it will ruin any recipe and the result will taste like a nasty product from some third rate shop.

The use of almonds in confectionery is well known. They are used in almost every country, in *panforte* from Siena, in *Schokoladetorte mit Mandeln* from Austria and in Bakewell tarts from Derbyshire. There are also sugared almonds and rich sweetmeats such as *torrone* (Italy), *turrón* (Spain) or *tourron* (France) and marzipan, marchpane, *massepain* (France), *marzapani* (Italy) or *mazapán* (Spain), which are of ancient origin. Less well known outside the almond-producing countries of the Middle East and Mediterranean are the various forms of almond milk; for instance, the popular *leche de almendras* of Spain, which, with sugar, becomes an *almendrada* or a *horchata de almendras* (and is made like *horchata de chufas). In the Spanish supermarkets, there is *miel de almendras* (literally, honey of almonds) in jars.

Of the savoury uses of almonds, everyone knows *truite aux amandes*, a universal restaurant dish. Oriental countries, from Turkey to India, use almonds with rice in stuffings for poultry and in pilau. Chinese chicken or pork with almonds is widely known. Raw or toasted almonds are used in salads for nourishment or texture, as in *salade forestière* (where sliced raw mushrooms, bound lightly with mayonnaise, are covered with a layer of almond shavings) or the *nougada* of the Middle East (which, like *homous*, is more of a dip than a salad: a cream of pounded almonds, garlic, parsley and lemon juice). In the *sopa blanca* of Andalusia, an emulsion is made by pounding together a small handful of blanched almonds with an equal volume of peeled broad beans and a clove of garlic. Into this, olive oil is gradually worked; finally, the emulsion is diluted with the juice of a lemon and 1 lt (1¾ pt) of cold water, salted to taste, and strained over bread cubes in a tureen.

Dishes containing toasted almonds have a rather different flavour. Such almonds are used particularly in Catalan cooking. A paste of toasted almonds (sometimes with pine nuts) pounded with garlic, fried bread cubes, parsley and saffron is added to many dishes. One may see a bottle labelled *picada* (made by liquidizing olive oil, saffron, almonds, parsley and water) standing near the stove in restaurants from the Costa Brava to Tarragona. Examples of dishes using this combination are *mero a la costa brava, langosta del ampurdán* (a casserole of langouste with snails, onion, tomato and wine) and *gallina tibidado* (chicken). Spain has many almond recipes including those for eels and other fish in almond sauce, artichokes stuffed with almonds, and kidneys with almonds. Other countries do not so far seem to be so prolific in this respect.

Ajo Blanco

Soak 1 or 2 crustless slices of bread in water and squeeze them dry. Pound them to a paste with 100 g (4 oz) blanched almonds and 2 large cloves of garlic. Work the mixture to a cream, slowly adding olive oil and wine vinegar. Beat well and add salt to taste. This can be eaten, diluted, as a cold soup, as a seasoning or as a sauce with fish, vegetables or anything with which its smooth garlicky flavour will blend.

Salted Almonds

Many recipes advise frying almonds, but this leaves them rather oily. It is better to roast them very slowly, watching all the time, till they go a pale biscuit colour and can be snapped. Cool them and, when they are almost cold, shake them first with egg white and then with very fine salt. Some people put them into saturated brine before drying.

[*Almond* – French: *amande* German: *Mandel* Italian: *mandorla* Spanish: *almendra*.

Bitter almond – French: *amande amère* German: *Bittermandel* Italian: *mandorla amara* Spanish: *almendra amarga*]

ALTITUDE. The effects of altitude on cooking are considerable, because the higher the altitude, the greater the drop in atmospheric pressure and the lower the temperature at which water boils. For those who live at around 4000 m (13,000 ft), it is impossible to cook a potato or a cabbage properly without a pressure cooker. Such effects are felt not only in places like La Paz, Bolivia, at 3590 m (11,800 ft) but even in Johannesburg – at about half that altitude. In particular, the lowered boiling point critically affects things like sterilization and canning. Camping on the shores of the Dead Sea, 395m (1,296 ft) below sea level, one can notice a slight shortening of cooking times. In canning and bottling, temperatures and pressures should be adjusted as follows:

Altitude		Water boil		To Sterilize	
m	ft	°C	°F	Extra or Extra minutes pressure kg/cm²	lb / in²
Sea level		100	212		
150	500	99.4	211	2	1
305	1000	98.9	210	4 }0.07{	1
610	2000	97.8	208	8	1
914	3000	96.7	206	12	2
1219	4000	95.6	304	16 }0.14{	2
1524	5000	94.4	202	20	3
1829	6000	93.9	201	25 }0.21{	3
2134	7000	92.8	199	30 0.28	4

In rough terms, the boiling point of water drops 1°C (about 2°F) for every 300 m (1,000 ft) of altitude.

[*Altitude* – French: *altitude* German: *Höhe* Italian: *altitudine* Spanish: *altitud*]

ALUM. The alum which has most commonly

been used in the kitchen is potash alum, potassium aluminium sulphate, $K_2SO_4.Al_2(SO_4)_3.2H_2O$. Like all alums, it is a double salt, and is made by mixing solution of potassium sulphate and aluminium sulphate and crystallizing out the alum. It also occurs naturally (as in the Yorkshire alum shales, which have been worked since 1600) and in 18th century recipes was called rock alum. It was used by the Arabs as a mordant for dyes and used to be a common household remedy: being very astringent, it was used to treat piles, gumboils and sore gums caused by ill-fitting false teeth; it also formed the basis of an invalid drink called alum whey.

In cooking, alum had various uses (I have an old recipe for curd cheese cakes which used it) and was not thought harmful. Today, it is largely banned from commercial products (although it is permitted in glace cherries). It is also used in some baking powders, but this, too, is forbidden in Britain.

[*Alum* – French: *alun* German: *Alaun* Italian: *allume* Spanish: *alumbre*]

ALUMINIUM or **aluminum** (US). The most abundant metal in the earth's crust, aluminium cannot be smelted from its ore by simple means so was one of the last of our common metals to be discovered (in 1825). Even then, there was no way of making it in quantity until 1886, when the electrolytic process was invented. For many years more, it remained expensive, but in this century, with the arrival of plentiful electric power, it has become the cheap everyday metal of kitchen utensils, while the iron pots have become more costly.

Aluminium, when exposed to the air, gets a thin coating of oxide which protects it. It is dissolved by strong alkalis, such as caustic soda, but only to a small extent by fruit and kitchen acids, although these are likely to strip off the film of oxide. In any case, after extensive research, no harm has been found to come from using aluminium pans, and taste changes are much less than with iron saucepans. (The violent antipathy that some people have to aluminium utensils has no known scientific basis.) Aluminium is an excellent conductor of heat, better than iron, though not as good as copper – as long as pans are fairly thick and heavy, they do not develop hot spots. Some foods have a tendency to stick to aluminium, especially when the pan bottom becomes pitted. Unlike cast iron, aluminium is not porous, so does not trap fat and develop its own non-stick surface, nor can it be coated with tin. It may be treated with a non-stick plastic, but that is all too vulnerable to scratching.

Foils made of aluminium have happily replaced lead foil for most purposes. They have also come into general kitchen use for wrapping meat for the oven, for pit barbecues, covering pans, sealing sandwiches and a host of other purposes. The foil does not burn, and, being shiny, reflects radiant heat (which is why it must be removed to allow meat to brown). However, it does not absorb fat, so in that respect is inferior to the old-fashioned paper for oven wrapping. Heavy gauge aluminium wire is easily bent and makes excellent small skewers for kebabs. To make them, nothing more is needed than a small pair of half-round pliers.

[*Aluminium* – French: *aluminium* German: *Aluminium* Italian: *alluminio* Spanish: *aluminino*]

AMARANTH. *See* spinach.

AMBER ACID. *See* succinic acid.

AMCHUR or **amchoor**. Dried *mango powder.

AMINO ACIDS. These weak organic acids containing the nitrogenous amino group are the bricks from which proteins are made and into which they are broken down during digestion. Of about twenty amino acids required by the body only eight cannot be made by it. They are: tryptophan, lysine, methionine, phenylalanine, threonine, valine, leucine and isoleucine. The others are: glycine, alanine, glutamic acid, proline, aspartic acid, serine, tyrosine, cysteine, cystine, asparagine, glutamine, histidine and arginine. Although the latter can all be made by the body, children sometimes cannot make enough histidine and arginine to meet their requirements. Protein foods which contain the full range of amino acids are egg yolk, fresh milk, liver and kidney. Meat is low in some essential amino acids and the much-vaunted calf's-foot jelly, the invalid food of Victorian days, is sadly lacking. There is some evidence that if the whole lot are not present in a meal – all together – then much or all of the others consumed are wasted. Vegetarian complete sources are brewer's yeast, soya beans and wheat germ. Other pulses, on which much of the world depends for protein, are deficient unless eaten with good wholemeal bread or other complementary proteins.

[*Amino acid* – French: *acide aminé* German: *Aminobenzoesäure* Italian: *amminoacido* Spanish: *amino ácido*]

AMMONIA (NH₃). Once called spirits of hartshorn (as it was made from the antlers of deer), ammonia is an exceedingly pungent gas with a characteristic smell. Household ammonia is a dilute solution of the gas in water. Ammonia is sometimes released by certain sorts of baking powder, but it is highly volatile and passes off during cooking. Ammoniacal smells are produced in the breakdown of amino acids (from proteins) by bacteria, and, for instance, in Camembert cheese which has been wrongly handled, the smell is a warning of decomposition.

[*Ammonia* – French: *ammoniaque* German: *Ammoniak* Italian: *ammoniaco* Spanish: *amoníaco*]

AMMONIUM BICARBONATE (NH₄HCO₃). A colourless, crystalline substance with some smell of ammonia. At 60°C (140°F) it slowly decomposes into carbon dioxide, water and ammonia, and can thus be used as a baking powder, since the ammonia is lost into the atmosphere.

AMMONIUM CARBONATE is actually a mixture of carbonate, (NH₄)₂CO₃, and bicarbonate since the carbonate is unstable and decomposes in air, becoming the bicarbonate. It smells strongly of the ammonia it is giving off, but was used in baking powders.

AMONTILLADO. *See* sherry.

AMYLASE. *See* diastase.

ANAR DANA. *See* pomegranate.

ANCHOVY. All over the world there are species of small fish locally known as anchovies (and many are species of the same genus *Engraulis*) but they do not when cured, develop the flavour of the true anchovy (*Engraulis encrasicolus*), which comes mainly from the Mediterranean and from the coasts of southern Europe but extends as far north as the English Channel. When the fish is bought fresh in the market (as commonly seen in Spain and Italy), it is 8-16 cm (3-6 in) long and bright silver, except for the back which is green when freshly caught but finally almost to black. This is a barometer to freshness. Anchovies move in large shoals which are attracted to the fishermen's lights at night. Although caught from March to September, anchovies are most plentiful in summer, when the bulk of the catch is treated commercially. Anchovies, incidentally, can always be distinguished from sardines (which may also be in the market) because, in the anchovy, the mouth is very large indeed, extending to the back of the head, and when opened it gives the fish a spectacular gape. (The Spanish call the fish *boquerón* which one might translate as big-mouth.)

Fresh anchovies are delicious, but they have white flesh and none of the special anchovy taste. This, together with the red colour, develops by fermentative changes under alkaline conditions after salting and leaving for at least a month. In many places on the European coasts where anchovies are caught, it is usual for housewives to cure their own. The salting of anchovies goes back thousands of years, into antiquity. Later, in Victorian times, they were often used for larding meat. Anchovy sauce was served with beef steaks and on fish, while anchovy butter on hot toast was a simple, popular savoury. Bottled anchovy essence was a usual kitchen ingredient, and plain salted anchovies were to be bought. Today, these are difficult to obtain because, as the Portuguese *Instituto de conservas de peixe* told me: 'A long time ago we exported anchovied fish in brine, which is not done any more because it represents the raw material for our fillets industry.' In fact, anchovy fillets in oil do quite well for most cooking purposes. Canned fillets are not cooked in the can, and are thus not sterile, but are preserved by the oil and the salt. Chemical preservatives are unnecessary and, in most countries, are not allowed by law. Anchovy essence, a rather Edwardian taste, is still obtainable as now are anchovy paste, anchovy spread and anchovy butter in tubes.

Acciuga in salamoia

This is the way of salting anchovies used in Italy, where special straight-sided glass jars are sold for the purpose. However, any wide-mouthed jar big enough to get your hand into will do. You also need a clean, flat stone to act as a weight in the jar. The anchovies must be quite fresh and firm.

To clean them, hold the fish in the left hand and, with the right, pinch behind the head, through the backbone and pull, in one movement, bringing out the guts, still attached to the head. Do not wash the fish, but pack them in layers in the jar, sprinkling each layer well with salt (start with salt at the bottom). When the jar is nearly full, but not filled to the top, finish with a good sprinkle of salt and put the clean stone on top. Cover to keep out dust. Shortly, the liquid extracted from the fish by the salt will come up to cover them as the stone sinks. If mould grows, remove it and sprinkle on a little more salt. After 3 months, the fish should be ready. Before use they will need to be soaked for a short time in water to remove some of the salt, especially if they have been oversalted – 100 g (4 oz) salt will do for 1 kg (2¼ lb) anchovies.

The red colour develops naturally. Some books say that brick dust or a red clay called Armenian bole were used, but I have certainly seen no evidence of this practice being continued today.

Anchovies are particularly used for flavouring in Austrian cooking and the garnish *à la viennoise* contains anchovies. They are perhaps used even more in Italy, where they are often mixed with garlic as a flavouring, as in the sauce used for dipping vegetable pieces in *bagna cauda* and in many sauces for pasta. In Spain, anchovies are eaten as *boquerones,* which have none of the anchovy flavour.

Spaghetti con alici e pomodori

Chop, peel and de-seed 400 g (14 oz) tomatoes and fry them slowly for 20 minutes in 2 tablespoons good olive oil together with 8 chopped (canned) anchovy fillets and a clove of garlic (whole). Meanwhile, put 450 g (1 lb) spaghetti to cook in fast-boiling salted water. Heat a serving dish. Chop up a handful each of fresh basil and parsley and add them, plus plenty of freshly-ground pepper, to the sauce a minute and a half before the spaghetti is cooked. Drain the pasta. Mix it immediately with 4 tablespoons grated parmesan and 5 tablespoons olive oil. Pour the sauce over and mix again. Rush it to the table where it will feed four people as a main course and more as a starter.

[*Anchovy* – French: *anchois* German: *Anschovis, Sardelle* Italian: *acciuga, alice* Spanish: *anchoa, boquerón*]

ANCHUSA. *See* alkanna.

ANDOUILLE. Type of thick, French sausage, originally from Normandy and Brittany, made of pig's gut, tripe, and a little belly, salted, cut in strips and packed into convenient lengths of large intestine. The sausages are cooked by boiling in a marinade (which often contains white wine varying with local practice), then treated for two days in salt brine and finally smoked for about three days. *Andouille* is not a keeping sausage: it lasts about

a week and is usually bought sliced and ready for eating cold as part of an *hors d'oeuvre*. Some small local varieties are made to be sold whole. *Andouilles* from Vire in Normandy are the most famous. Generally not a very elegant-looking sausage, the *andouille* is black or brown from the smoke and wrinkled and knobbly from the bits of tripe. When cut, it has an interesting section, with thick whitish squiggles of tripe embedded like fossils in a matrix. The taste, however, is excellent.

ANDOUILLETTE. Virtually the same in contents as an *andouille* but much smaller, being packed into the small intestine of the pig. *Andouillettes* are often not smoked and are intended for grilling, although they can be eaten cold as they are already cooked. They are sold either glazed with fat or wrapped in paper, and have sometimes been pressed while cooling, which improves their appearance, but they may also be left in their original knobbly state. In either case, they will keep only for a couple of days. They are usually slashed and grilled or fried. There are some fancy local varieties, such as those from Nancy which contain truffles and Madeira wine. *Andouillettes* are a delicious French speciality, and easy to make, so anyone who has access to pig's tripes should possess Jane Grigson's *Charcuterie and French Pork Cookery* (Grub Street), which gives full directions on how to make these and other pork products at home.

ANGEL FISH or **angel shark**. *See* shark.

ANGELICA. A giant umbelliferous plant standing as high as a man. A native of Scandinavia and most countries north-east of the Alps, it has white flowers, a thick, hollow stem and a distinctive musky smell. Angelica (*Angelica archangelica*) is best known for its green, candied stems, which are used in confectionery and for decorating sweets. It is now little grown in gardens and impossible to buy fresh. Nevertheless, the leaves and stems of angelica have many uses – as a herb for flavouring fish, in salads, with stewed rhubarb, or in marmalade. The roots are mainly used in herbal medicine. The seeds may be harvested and used as a flavouring. Angelica is sometimes said to have certain flavour similarities with juniper (although not to my palate), and it may be used in flavouring gin and liqueurs.

Candied Angelica

Cut the young stems towards the end of June. Boil them in water till tender, then strip off the outer skin. Put the stems back in the water and simmer until they are green. Dry and weigh. Cover with an equal weight of sugar and leave for 2 days to make a syrup in which they should be boiled well, then taken out and drained. Concentrate the syrup by further boiling or by adding more sugar, being careful not to let it caramelize (brush down the sides of the pan with water). Put back the angelica. Allow it to cool in the syrup, then drain and dry in a cool oven with the door ajar.

[*Angelica* – French: *angélique* German: *Angelika* Italian: *angelica* Spanish: *angélica*]

ANGOSTURA BITTERS. Named after the Venezuelan town on the Orinoco, now called Ciudad Bolivar, Angostura bitters were originally formulated by a Doctor Siegert as medicine for fever, but are today (like Indian Tonic Water which also contains quinine) used with gin for fun. The formula is secret, but the contents are said to be cloves, mace, cinnamon and nutmeg, with orange and lemon peel, prunes, quinine and rum. Angostura bitters may be used in creams and cups as well as in cocktails.

Hiccup Cure

Cut a thin slice of lemon. Heap ½ – 1 teaspoon sugar on it. Moisten the sugar with plenty of Angostura bitters. Eat the whole thing in one mouthful. Cures even the most stubborn cases.

ANISE or **aniseed**. From an umbelliferous plant (*Pimpinella anisum*) native to the Middle East and cultivated at least since the days of the Pharaohs, this seed was used by the Romans to flavour cakes. Today its most important use is in certain Mediterranean and Aegean drinks: *pastis, ouzo, arrack* and *anisette*.

Many people do not like its flavour. Although anise blends delightfully with dried figs, I cannot approve the Spanish habit of using it to flavour bran for a breakfast cereal. In savoury dishes, it gives a new dimension when traces are used in fish soup, as it blends well with garlic, and its perfume suits *langouste* and prawns of various kinds. There are, too, speciality dishes in which it is used with chicken, partridge and other birds.

In France, anise is usually introduced in the form of *pastis*, which is a mixture of flavours with anise predominant. In South East Asia, and to a lesser extent in India, the seed is ground as one of the spice ingredients in certain curries, and the seeds are often chewed as a digestive and to sweeten the breath after a meal. The flavour also plays its part in Chinese cooking, but there it usually comes from *star anise. The appearance, size and taste of aniseed varies greatly from country to country. As a flavouring for use in difficult-to-recognize amounts, anise is neglected and repays experiment.

[*Anise* – French: *anis* German: *Anis* Italian: *anice* Spanish: *anís*]

ANISE PEPPER. *See* Chinese pepper.

ANNATTO. A bright, orange-yellow dye, virtually tasteless and long used for colouring butter (which is often naturally white), margarine, cheese (like Cheshire) and smoked fish. It comes from a small evergreen tree (*Bixa orellana*), locally called *urucú* by the Indians of tropical South America. The spiny pods are full of seeds surrounded by bright red arils. The arils are scraped out and made into a paste for commercial annatto. The seeds are ground whole and used as a spice in parts of Latin America.

ANU. *See* yam (*ysaño*).

APOLLINARIS. *See* water (mineral water).

APOTHECARIES' WEIGHTS are sometimes used in old recipes where substances were sold by the chemist. The apothecaries' dram is not the same as the avoirdupois dram.

20 grains (gr.) = 1 scruple (s.ap.) = 1.3 g
3 scruples   = 1 dram* (dr.ap.) = 3.9 g

Before 1864:
8 drams   = 1 ounce (oz.ap.) = 31.1 g
12 ounces = 1 pound (lb.ap.) = 373.2 g

In Britain the scales were changed in 1864 to make 16 ounces (oz.ap.) = 1 pound (lb.ap.), and the apothecaries' ounce and apothecaries' pound were made identical to the avoirdupois ounce and pound. The new apothecaries' ounce therefore also equals 437.5 grains (instead of 480) and the pound 7000 grains (instead of 5760).

APPLE. The apple (*Malus sylvestris*) is the world's

most important temperate zone fruit. The wild crab apple is a native of Europe, and apples have been cultivated for at least 3,000 years. Over twenty distinct varieties were known and grown even in Roman times. Since apples are highly variable and the trees cross easily when flowers are pollinated from one variety to another, there are said to be at least six thousand named British varieties known today. However, the number that are widely grown has decreased with the emergence of types which are outstanding in either commercial or gastronomic qualities, such as the Cox's Orange Pippin in Britain and the Golden Delicious, first in Europe, then almost everywhere. Reduction in breeds is a modern tendency; you find the same thing with sheep and cattle.

Apples grow anywhere in the Northern hemisphere south of latitude 65°N (and in similar climates in the Southern hemisphere), provided they get an adequately cold resting period in winter (and are not nipped by frost during flowering). Apples will not grow naturally in the tropics, although a resting period can be induced by root pruning, and then two crops can be had in a year. They are a cool country fruit and a modern innovation in tropical cooking.

As apples store well for many months, they were at one time the only fresh fruit to be had at all during the winter (and were among the first items planted by the colonists in America).Today, with winter apples brought from the Southern hemisphere, and the techniques of chilling and gas storage (by which apples can be kept in good condition for up to a year), we have forgotten what it was like to be dependent on the seasons. Few people still bother to lay down apples at home.

Don't bother to store early or mid-season varieties as they will keep for only a short period. However, late varieties which mature only after gathering need to be stored for from four weeks to several months. Select apples which are not damaged or bruised in any way and then wrap them singly in newspaper or put them individually into small polythene bags, making sure that they are not sealed. You may prick the bags to make air holes for the necessary ventilation. Wrapping prolongs the life of an apple, helps prevent it shrivelling and stops the spread of rot from one apple to another. Once wrapped, the apples can be stored in boxes, bread crocks or metal bins and left in a cool, frost-free place such as a cellar or garden shed. Keep apples which ripen at different times in separate containers. They shouldn't be left in a loft or attic where the air tends to be too warm and dry.

British cooks have long divided apples into cookers and eaters, a bad tradition. Cookers (Bramley's Seedling, Grenadier, Newton Wonder and so on) are usually too sour (though not always) to be used as a dessert apple, but their main characteristic is that they cook to a purée. Most eating apples do not; they stay in their individual pieces unless stewed to rags and are therefore better cooked in some dishes (e.g. flans and chutney) than those labelled cookers. Many of them also have an excellent, though different, cooked flavour. Cox's Orange Pippin is an excellent variety for cooking, as are Ribston Pippin, Crispin and Idared.It would be far better to think of apples in the way we do floury or waxy potatoes, and not to label them eaters and cookers. Every place has its own varieties, which are available at different times of the year (as well as unidentified ones inherited in orchards and gardens). Anyone who wants to cook superlative apple dishes should try to study them. The variety of apple is also important in cider-making – the special cider types provide some bitterness. Experience will soon show that crab apples differ in their quality for making jelly; country people know the best hedgerow trees and ignore those that make insipid jelly.

Products made from apples include dried apple rings (*see* drying), *pectin (from cores and skins) and apple butter (which the Dutch took to America) for spreading on bread. Apple sauce and apple butter were laid down in large quantities in the autumn to see the American colonists through the winter. An early recipe for apple butter gives some idea of the quantities involved: '10 gallons sweet cider. 3 pecks (i.e. 6 gallons) of cored and quartered apples (do a few at a time). Cook slowly Add 10 lb of sugar, 5 oz of cinnamon. Stir for 5-6 hours with a wooden paddle.'

From *cider we get cider *vinegar (on which some health cures are based) as well as apple-jack and calvados (on which they are not).

To prevent apples turning brown when cut (because of exposure to the oxygen in the air) lemon juice can be effective, but for large amounts, or where the lemon might be unsuitable, cover them for 10 minutes with a solution containing 1 *Camden tablet per 100 ml (3½ fl oz) water.

[*Apple* – French: *pomme* German: *Apfel* Italian: *mela* Spanish: *manzana*]

APRICOT. The apricot (*Prunus armeniaca*) has been cultivated for so long (it has been grown in

China for some 4,000 years) that it is impossible to be quite certain of its natural home, which is probably somewhere in Asia. It is a staple fruit in Middle Eastern valleys – those flat parcels of alluvial soil irrigated by a river, shaded by poplars and surrounded by barren mountains. In fact, apricots thrive in the sort of climate where the pomegranate and almond grow. They do not like the tropics, save in exceptional situations. Apricots are extensively grown in Iran, Afghanistan, the western Himalayas, China, Japan, California, South Africa and Australia, as well as the warmer areas near the Mediterranean, notably North Africa and Spain (Murcia, Valencia and the Balearic Islands).

There are many varieties, differing in hardness, texture and size. Colours range from pale yellow to deep reddish-orange, and some are sun-freckled with brick or carmine, even with rosy patches. Inside, the apricot flesh is usually a shade of yellow or orange, but some are white-fleshed. Apricots do not peel easily – anyway, some of the flavour lies in the skin – but they can be pulled into two halves and the stone is always free. A fresh, perfectly ripe apricot of a good variety, picked warm off the tree, has an incomparable smell and a delicious taste. Imported apricots, though, will have been picked rather unripe – though with full colour – and the flavour is never the same. Unlike peaches, apricots are best eaten at the temperature of a summer's day, not chilled.

Apricots are cooked with meat in Iran and the Middle East, going especially well with lamb (the staple meat of the area). From there, by a roundabout route, apricots have got into the sauce for *sassaties* (kebabs) in South Africa. In sweet dishes, they are much more interesting in flavour than peaches when cooked. Usually an apricot dish should be very sweet. Syrups that apricots are poached in should be heavy. Stuffed with almonds or almond paste, apricots are Allah's gift to the Arab sweet tooth, but one of the simplest and most delicious ways of eating them is in the Austrian *Marillenknödel*, an apricot dumpling of diet-shattering splendour (an apricot, stuffed with a lump of sugar, sealed in a thin coat of light dumpling mixture, poached, and finished in crispy, butter-fried breadcrumbs and sugar).

As apricots travel badly and do not keep, many are canned or dried, or are made into jam. Canned apricots are very often disappointing; they do not take on a new dimension as do canned peaches. Dried apricots are made by splitting them and leaving them out on mats to dry in the sun. To prevent browning, the halves are usually treated with burning sulphur fumes. More modern methods of treatment produce a softer, more pliable and sweeter product – nice even to chew raw – but those who suspect the use of chemicals will prefer whole dried apricots, which are untreated chemically.

Apricots and their kernels have recently come in for attention following the discovery that the people of Gilgit, where apricots are staple food, do not suffer from many of our common Western diseases, and cancer is virtually unknown there. Apricots are particularly rich in Vitamin A compared to both peaches and apples.

Apricots are easily made into jam, and apricot jam – with its pleasant but not assertive taste – is much used in confectionery for fillings and glazes. With fresh apricots, jam is usually made with equal weights of sugar and fruit, but with dried apricots, the sugar must be three times the weight of the fruit.

Apricot liqueurs are produced in most countries – apricot brandy, *apry*, *abricota*, *abricotine*, *capricot*, etc. Some taste rather too strongly of bitter almonds, while others are very sweet. However, the Hungarian *barackpálinka* (made by distilling a fermented apricot mash) is my favourite spirit; it may with advantage be used either before or after a meal. The flavour is nothing like apricots, being rather reminiscent of a very fine *mirabelle*. The kernels of apricot stones may be poisonous for the same reason as bitter *almonds are poisonous, and can equally be made safe by roasting. A delicious liqueur, *noyau, can easily be made from them, and they are the traditional ingredient of the famous *amaretti di Saronno*. Apricot kernels are exported in bulk from Australia and are important in commercial baking and confectionery, particularly in the US where bitter almonds are banned.

Apricots in Syrup

Wash 1 kg (2 lb) very fine, ripe apricots, put them in a pan of cold water and bring them to the boil. Immediately refresh the fruit in ice-cold water and leave it for 3 hours to cool thoroughly. Put the apricots in a cold syrup made by dissolving 1 kg (2 lb) sugar in 600 ml (1 pt) water. Bring them to the boil and cook until they are tender. Cool the fruit in the syrup.

[*Apricot* – French: *abricot* German: *Aprikose*, *Marille* (Austria) Italian: *albicocca* Spanish: *albaricoque*]

APRY. *See* liqueurs and cordials.

ARBUTUS. *See* cranberry

ARGOL or **winestone**. The name for the hard, crusty deposit in casks or tanks of maturing wine. It is dried and exported from wine-growing areas as hard, shiny scales and is the raw material from which *cream of tartar and *tartaric acid are made. The semi-purified form is called tartar. To remove impurities, the argol is dissolved in boiling water and mixed with absorbent clay and blood charcoal to take up colour and other unwanted material. It is then filtered, and the pure cream of tartar is crystallized out.

[*Argol* – French: *tartre brut* German: *Weinstein* Italian: *tartaro* Spanish: *tátaro*]

ARCHIL. *See* cudbear.

ARECA NUT. *See* betel nut.

ARHAR. *See* pigeon pea.

ARMAGNAC. French brandy, second only to cognac and with its own marked, individual character. Armagnac comes from Gascony, in the vicinity of Condom, a town south-east of Bordeaux. It is made from the poor acid wine of the *picpoul* grape (a variety of the *folle blanche*), which must, by law, be grown, fermented and distilled in the Bas-Armagnac, Haut-Armagnac or Ténarèze districts (that from the Bas-Armagnac and Ténarèze is the best). Like cognac, armagnac is aged in oak casks for up to 40 years. It is empty to argue whether cognac or armagnac is the better, because they are different, and it is a matter of each person's taste. However, in cooking, armagnac is sometimes specified and then the recipe must be followed. For example, a *bécasse à l'armagnac* (woodcock cooked with armagnac) would be distinguished from the same bird cooked *à la fine champagne* (cognac).

ARROWROOT. This is an old-fashioned ingredient, a fine white powder consisting of over 80% starch. The original arrowroot plant is from Central and South America and is named after the *aru* root of the Aruac Indians, but other sources of starch have been used and given the name arrowroot. True West Indian or Bermuda arrowroot is made from the young rhizomes of tropical species of *Maranta*, mainly *M. arundinacea*, and supplies mainly come from St Vincent in the Caribbean. The rhizomes are dealt with in the usual way for starch preparation. They are first pulverized (originally in wooden mortars but now by machinery); the pulp is then mixed with water, the fibre removed and the milky liquid strained into settling tanks. For further purification, the water is drained off, the white sludge is again mixed with water and again settled. It is finally drained and dried to a powder of starch grains with very little other debris. Because of the small size of the grains, it is easily digestible and has always been regarded as an invalid food. It is thus available from chemists rather than from supermarkets, though it may be found in a few grocers. As a thickening, it is superior to cornflour in clarity, appearance and the absence of any taste of its own. West Indian arrowroot forms a firm, clear starch jelly when heated with syrup or water, it is particularly good for fruit glazes and for flans and puddings. Arrowroot can be made to substitute for other starchy substances: arrowroot noodles, which are made in China, differ from other pasta in being completely transparent.

Other arrowroots include Florida arrowroot (from *Zamia floridana*), East Indian arrowroot (from *Curcuma angustifolia*) and Tous-les-mois, Tulema or Queensland arrowroot (from *Canna edulis*).Queensland arrowroot, in spite of its name, comes from a plant native to South America and there called *achira*. Brazilian arrowroot is from the cassava, and Oswega arrowroot is an American product made from maize. Portland arrowroot is made from the poisonous cuckoo pint or lords-and-ladies (*Arum maculatum*) but is acrid, despite many washings, and so is only survival food in an emergency. There are others.

[*Arrowroot* – French: *arrow-root* German: *Pfeilwurz* Italian: *maranta, tubero edule* Spanish: *arrurruz*]

ARSENIC. This non-metallic element is a deadly poison, but is also an essential trace element normally circulating in human blood to a concentration of six parts per million. Arsenic eaters in Austria and Hungary, at least by tradition, can gradually get used to consuming quantities that would kill an average person. It is supposed to give them long life and a youthful complexion. Most of us get sufficient in our diet; indeed, in a month we normally take in a quantity that would kill us if eaten in a single dose. Arsenic salts occur in seawater to the extent of 20 mg per 1000 lt, and some natural salt deposits contain dangerous amounts of it.

[*Arsenic* – French: *arsenic* German: *Arsenik* Italian: *arsenico* Spanish: *arsénico*]

ARTICHOKE. A name shared by three unrelated plants, *Chinese artichoke, *globe artichoke and *Jerusalem artichoke.

ARVI. *See* yam (dasheen).

ASAFOETIDA. A gum obtained from the root of a giant fennel-like plant, *Ferula asafoetida*, which is grown in Iran, Afghanistan and India. It is usually bought ground. Although it has a horrible, garlicky smell, it is a useful spice in small quantities, with fish for instance, and is quite essential in many Indian vegetarian dishes.

[*Asafoetida* – French: *assafoetida, férule perisque* German: *Teufelsdreck* Italian: *assafetida* Spanish: *asafétida*]

ASCORBIC ACID. *See* Vitamin C.

ASPARAGUS is a cultivated form of the wild *Asparagus officinalis*, a member of the lily family which grows quite plentifully in some parts of Europe and Russia and is naturalized elsewhere, for instance in the eastern states of the US and in irrigated parts of the American West. A subspecies, *prostratus*, is a rare native of the coasts of Dorset, Cornwall, South Wales and Ireland. The wild asparagus often seen in spring in Spanish markets – bunches of very spindly green stalks – is a different species (*Asparagus aphyllus*), in which leaves have become strong spines. It grows in dry, rocky situations in the hotter parts of the Mediterranean region – Spain and the Balearic Islands, Sardinia (but not Corsica), Sicily, Greece, Cyprus and North Africa. It is much gathered as a local speciality and has a strong, rather bitter flavour which comes through when it is mixed with other vegetables. Asparagus fern is a decorative species of asparagus and not a fern.

Cultivated asparagus has been prized in Europe for over 2,000 years, although in Britain it was not much grown until Elizabethan times. We eat the only part of the plant that is not impossibly tough and woody, the young shoot just before or just after it leaves the ground. Asparagus is expensive because it takes several years to establish a good bed, and although the bed will last and improve for many years, the crop occupies the ground continually and does not produce a heavy yield of food. It also demands a lot of hand work, as each spear must be harvested individually with a long asparagus knife probing beneath the soil. Its merit is its deliciousness.

There is much controversy as to which type of asparagus is the best: white, green or purple. The white is more popular in Belgium, Germany and parts of France, the green or purple in Britain, the US and most of Italy. Essentially, white asparagus consists of shoots which have never seen the light, and it is claimed that they are more tender in texture and more delicate in taste as a result. The spears are usually thick, with almost no scales, but only a short part of the length is young enough to be edible. Early varieties, too, tend to be white, as also is out-of-season asparagus which is obtained by forcing roots artificially.

Green and purple types, however, are cut when the shoots are well clear of the soil, and advocates say that having seen the sun they have a better flavour. They have a more pointed tip, and are more open, sometimes loose and 'scaly', usually with the tender, edible part of the spear longer. These tend to be main crop or later varieties.

May and June mark the high season for asparagus in the Northern hemisphere, but forced or imported spears may be available at other times. Asparagus keeps well in the deep freeze and may even be eaten raw after freezing, as the process tenderizes it.

When buying asparagus, first look for freshness, since stale asparagus is bitter. Stale spears look dry or wrinkled and are often dirty-coloured; also the cut ends may be soggy where the bundles have been stood in water. Spears should be of even size (not a few large ones on the outside of the bunch concealing the poor ones in the middle). Asparagus may be freshened up at home by standing the cut ends for a short time in water, but the sooner it is eaten the better. The points, which are very brittle in good asparagus, should be intact, and only the base of the stem should feel woody. Bargain asparagus must always be suspected except when the reason for the low price is that the spears are mis-shapen or thin, in which case they are called 'sprue'. Such asparagus is excellent for soups, with eggs, and in other made-up dishes.

Asparagus spears should be peeled – you can use a sharp potato peeler – from the base of the scaly tip down to the cut end. They are then tied in small bunches and put into boiling, salted water (10 g of salt per 1 lt or 2 teaspoons per 2 pt) and boiled fast for usually (depending on size of spear) 15 to 25 minutes. You can also stand the bunches upright so that the tips steam clear of the water. There are special asparagus boilers, some rather like small, rectangular fish kettles, with a perforated plate on which the asparagus is laid, and others in which the spears stand upright. After draining, put the asparagus on a folded napkin or, if it is to be served cold, chill it immediately in ice-cold water. Some consider that asparagus is best eaten luke-warm. There are dozens of sauces to go with it. In Britain, it is usually served hot with melted butter, but other preferences include vinaigrette, mayonnaise (especially if combined with orange juice and cooked peel, or bitter orange juice), hollandaise, mousseline, and mornay sauces. In fact, asparagus goes very well with cheese, and is often eaten combined with or sprinkled with parmesan cheese in Italy (*asparagi all parmigiana, risotto di asparagi, ris e spargit*).The many classic asparagus dishes range from soup and *asperges frites* to *soufflé aux pointes d'asperges*.

In America, asparagus is commonly served as a vegetable, rather than as a starter. The raw stalks are then often broken, and the tough bit discarded, leaving only the edible end, which is eaten with a fork, rather than the fingers. Asparagus is rich in vitamin A as well as in vitamins B_1, B_2, and C. Slimmers may gorge on it (but not on most of its standard accompaniments), as it offers only 15 to 18 calories per 100 g (4 oz). Asparagus is diuretic. Canned or bottled asparagus is good when not too soft, as are frozen asparagus spears, though they are still inferior to fresh ones.

[*Asparagus* – French: *asperge* German: *Spargel* Italian: *asparago* Spanish: *espárrago*]

ASPARAGUS BEAN or **yard-long bean**. (*Vigna sesquipedalis*) is a close relative, if not a variety of, the *cowpea. It is used both as a pulse and as a green vegetable in India and elsewhere in the tropics. The beans, though thin, can grow up to nearly 1 m (3 ft) long.

ASPARAGUS PEA. A vetch-like wild legume (*Lotus tetragonolobus*) of Mediterranean Europe, with dark red flowers like small sweet-peas, and hairy leaves and stems. Although it is uncommon as a cultivated vegetable, the young pods, when they are about 3 cm (1-1½ in) long and still tender, can be eaten steamed or stir-fried in butter. Although called asparagus peas, they are more like peas than asparagus in taste.

ASPIC. A clear, light savoury jelly used for embedding or glazing cold dishes of eggs, fish and meat. It may be bought as a powder (in which case follow the instructions), faked up from gelatine and stock cubes or made from basic ingredients in the traditional manner. Unlike calf's-foot jelly, it is a garnish: a way of serving and improving cold dishes rather than a food. It may be cubed and used to surround cold meats, or even chopped finely and piped. Its main use, though, is as the basis of savoury moulds, which can be a decorative part of a buffet if they include in their outer layers carefully arranged patterns made up of such colourful ingredients as pieces of red pepper.

[*Aspic* – French: *aspic* German: *Aspik* Italian: *aspic* Spanish: *áspic*]

AUBERGINE or **eggplant** (US). The plant (*Solanum melongena*) belongs to the tomato family and is native to tropical Asia, probably to India, where it has been cultivated since antiquity. Aubergines are an important vegetable in all warm countries, but can be grown only under glass in Britain. They are exported in quantity from Spain and Italy. Although available for most of the year, they are expensive and unsatisfactory after Christmas, but cheap and good in August and September.

The first aubergine I ever saw growing was in my garden in India. It was of a poor local variety but did look exactly like an egg in size, shape and colour. As such varieties are rarely grown today, the origin of the name eggplant is not usually so obvious. Modern varieties, when ripe, are mostly large and coloured violet or purple. Some are streaked with white and mauve, even with green. They may be round, oval-football shaped, or elongated like clubs. The last are necessary for certain dishes; the footballs are preferred for others. Poor aubergines have rather many seeds and may be bitter, but modern varieties rarely need the salting and draining of juice which was once essential. The flesh of aubergines is always white and a little spongy. It discolours badly when exposed to the air and should preferably be cut with a stainless steel knife. Experts advocate mashing cooked aubergine with a wooden fork rather than with one of metal.

Aubergines are almost always eaten cooked – boiled, baked or fried. Their spongy texture does incline them to mop up too much fat in frying, especially if they have not been salted, and they are best dipped first in a light batter. On the other hand, they take up spices and flavourings excellently. Famous aubergine dishes include *ratatouille niçoise* from Provence, *melanzane ripieni* (stuffed aubergines baked in tomato sauce) from Italy, *moussaka* from Greece, *imam bayeldi* from Turkey and another Levantine speciality, the smoky-flavoured 'poor man's caviar', of which probably the best is made in Romania. In India they are called *brinjals* and are the basis for the delicious hot *brinjal kassaundi* or pickle.

Poor Man's Caviar

Cut the stems off 3 medium aubergines and grill them, turning them occasionally, until the skin is black and cracking, and the aubergines are soft to the touch. Take them from the grill, let them cool a bit, then peel off the skin (or halve them lengthwise and spoon out the flesh). Put the pulp, cleaned of all bits of skin, into the blender with 1-2 cloves of garlic and 3-4 tablespoons of olive oil. Blend until it is a purée, then add the juice of ½ -1 lemon (or more to taste) and season it with salt. Stir in 2 tablespoons of chopped parsley and serve it with hot pitta or other bread. Poor man's caviar also makes a delicious dressing for a tomato salad.

[*Aubergine* – French: *aubergine* German: *Eierfrucht* Italian: *melanzana* Spanish: *berenjena*]

AURUM. *See* liqueurs and cordials.

AUSTRALIAN BARRACUDA. *See* snoek.

AUTOLYSIS is the destruction of cells by their own enzymes; one sees autolysed yeast on the labels of yeast extracts. The process also takes place when meat is hung. *See* yeast extract.

AVOCADO, avocado pear, or alligator pear (US, but archaic). A fruit borne on a tropical and sub-tropical evergreen tree (*Persea americana*) of the laurel family. Behind the strikingly different types in shops and markets, are three races. The Mexican, with small fruits and anise-scented leaves, is the hardiest; the Guatemalan, from the highlands of Central America, has medium to large fruits with a thick, woody skin; the West Indian grows only in a properly tropical climate and often has very large fruits. There are plenty of crosses between these races, and varieties (now over five hundred of them) are easily propagated by layering, budding or grafting. The avocado was used by the Aztecs, who called it *ahuacatl*, from which the modern name is derived via the Spanish *aguacate*. Although the fruit had been noted by the Spaniards as long ago as 1519, and it was planted in the Botanical Gardens in Bangalore, India, in 1819, the general opinion used to be that it was tasteless (as poor varieties

certainly are), and its value went unrecognized. It has come into its own, only rather recently, mainly through the work of American breeders; it is still not really popular in the Orient, where it could make a significant contribution to the local diet in many places. However, it is now grown in most tropical and sub-tropical countries, although it will not tolerate winds or too dry a climate. Avocados thrive in Central and South America, Florida and California, Hawaii and the South Pacific, Australia, South Africa, West Africa, Israel, Madeira and the Canary Islands, as well as in the Mediterranean regions, where they grow in a similar climate to the orange.

Avocados may be round or pear-shaped, smooth or rough-skinned, green, flecked with yellow, reddish, crimson, purple or almost black. In size, they vary from that of a hen's egg in small Mexican varieties to huge fruits weighing several pounds each, which can be grown in the West Indies and have no doubt given rise to the name 'poor man's breakfast'. The avocado, which in many places is an expensive luxury, is a very cheap food in others. It has the highest protein content of any fruit and contains at least 25% fat as well as vitamins A and B.

In nature, avocados drop before they are ripe; as they are clipped as soon as they begin to colour, they must be given time to ripen. (Till ripe, they need a warm place and must not be put in the refrigerator.) The ripe fruit yields to gentle pressure; you are aware that you could squash it. The single stone comes out cleanly in good varieties. The flesh is creamy, yellowish or greenish and, when ripe, has a smooth, buttery texture.

Avocados may be cut in half lengthwise and eaten straight out of the skin with a spoon, and the hole left by the stone will conveniently accommodate the dressing – pepper, salt, oil and vinegar is the simplest of many – but it can also be filled with shrimps or other delicacies. Avocados may be peeled easily if the skin is first cut through in narrow strips. Chopped or cubed avocados are used in salads. There is avocado soup and even avocado ice cream, but perhaps the most famous avocado dish is *guacamole*, a favourite dish of the Aztecs long before the Spanish conquest. Once just a smooth purée of avocado with tomato (or tomatillo) and chilli, it has, with the introduction of onions, coriander, olive oil, vinegar, and other ingredients from Europe, been elaborated into many versions.

Guacamole

In Mexico, where avocado trees can be grown in the back yard, the fruit is a staple food and guacamole is not an elegant party dish but everyday fare. Therefore guacamole becomes a 'go-as-you-please' dish; there are dozens of recipes, which vary from one part of the country to another and can also depend on what is to hand. In the north, for instance, the tomatillo is an ingredient while in the south the ordinary tomato is commoner. Other recipes do not include tomato at all. Essentially, guacamole is only mashed, ripe avocado flesh seasoned with salt, and flavoured with the ubiquitous hot, green chilli and green coriander. Outside Mexico, canned *serrano*, *jalapeño* or other very hot chillis can be substituted for fresh ones without much alteration from the original – even hot chilli sauce or cayenne will do if there is nothing else – but the substitution of parsley for green coriander (which is used like parsley in Mexico) will remove an essential taste.

(It is not much trouble to grow a pot of coriander on the window sill. Many Americans can buy it as cilantro in specialist stores, and in Britain it can be obtained from Greek and oriental shops.) To the essentials are frequently added peeled, seeded and chopped ripe tomato, finely chopped onion, garlic, and lemon or lime juice. A typical recipe is as follows:

Mash roughly 2 large, ripe avocados. Add 1 peeled, seeded and chopped ripe tomato (not too large), 2 teaspoons of very finely-chopped mild onion, a trace of garlic, 2-3 finely-chopped, seeded green chillis (the amount depends on their hotness), and a small handful of green coriander leaves, finely chopped. Mix and season with salt and lemon juice to taste.

In some parts of Mexico, avocado leaves are used either fresh or dried as a flavouring (at last, a use for plants raised from stones sprouted in a jar). The leaves should be toasted lightly on a hotplate. When ground, they have an aroma which has been described as 'mixed anise and hazel', although this will be mild if they have been grown in a cold climate.

[*Avocado pear* – French: *avocat*, *poire d'avocat* German: *Advokatbirne* Italian: *avocado* Spanish: *aguacate*]

AVOIRDUPOIS. *See* weight and measures.

AWABI. *See* abalone.

AZEROLE. *See* rowan.

b

BACALAO. *See* salt cod.

BACON. The cured sides of the pig, from which traditionally the back legs have first been detached for separate curing as *hams. In modern industrial bacon-making, the whole side is cured, including the back leg which is then referred to as gammon. Bacon was originally the form in which the meat of the cottager's pig, which had been fattened during the summer, could be made to last over the winter. It would have been very dry and salty, with little resemblance to the modern supermarket rasher.

Curing the pig is not difficult, providing that you are not intimidated by the vast technology which has been built up by the bacon industry and is needed only for mass-producing a uniform product without waste. Bacon-making was a yearly task on every farm not so long ago. Indeed, the first bacon factory in Britain was not opened until 1770, after a man called John Harris had watched pigs being rested at Calne in Wiltshire on their way from Ireland to London. (They had presumably been shipped from Cork to Bristol.) He had the idea of slaughtering the pigs and curing them on the spot, thus saving the long and damaging journey. Half the bacon eaten in Britain comes from Denmark, which has been exporting it for over a century.

The Danes have built up their trade through efficient production based on their bacon pig breed, the Danish Landrace, which has been bred to combine leanness and length of back to the exclusion of all else. The result is a creature that requires the carefully controlled environment provided by industrialized pig farming.

The Landrace may have reached perfection of design for bacon production but it is no longer too good as a pig. In his book *The Chance to Survive* (David & Charles), Lawrence Alderson suggests that 'maybe the body has become so long that in some pigs the hind legs no longer function efficiently,' and that 'the extreme emphasis on the animal's shape has led to deterioration in meat quality.' This expresses itself in a tendency to disintegrate under high-speed slicing (and the Landrace is also one of the breeds with a tendency to produce pork with a particularly unattractive defect called PSE – pale, soft and exudative – meat which will lose weight by oozing fluid if it is left to stand). If the Landrace shows the danger of taking selective breeding too far, it does embody the commercial ideal of a good bacon pig, with a high proportion of the best cuts (i.e. more backside than shoulder) and a nice balance between lean meat and fat. Feeding is also important in bacon production as it determines the quality of the fat, which can be firm or sloppy. Bacon pigs are sent to the factory when 6-7 months old and weighing about 90 kg (just under 200 lb).

Farm bacon. The carcass, after scalding and scraping to remove the bristles, is hung in a cool place to harden. It is split down the back, and the backbone (chine) is removed. The fillets are also taken out as they do not cure well, and usually the hams and shoulders are taken for separate treatment, leaving the side (flitch) to be cured. The *dry-salting method is the most usual on farms. Here, the sides are rubbed with a mixture of salt, saltpetre and sugar over a period of about 2 weeks. This method gives the best bacon with the highest keeping quality.

Simple Curing

First clean the side well, soaking and washing it for half an hour in cold brine (28 g of salt per lt or 1 oz per 1¾ pt) with a pinch of saltpetre. Dry the side with a clean cloth and weigh it. You will need 8% of this weight in salting mixture, which should consist of coarse salt containing 3-4% saltpetre and some sugar – best is light brown sugar – which is optional, but may be from 5% to as much as 33% of the cure. The temperature should be cool, but not icy (4-10°c or 40-50°F), such as one would find in a cold larder in winter. To begin with, rub the skin-side well with the dry-salting mixture until it begins to sweat. Turn it over and rub the meat side a little, having carefully given all pockets a little saltpetre for safety before salting. Put the side, skin downwards, on a bed of salt, and cover it with more salt. Add more the next day, and every day afterwards (as it gets wet) with some inspection and rubbing in any suspicious places – for the first 4-5 days. After that, leave the side until it is cured – about 14 days on average. Finally, wipe off the adhering salt with a cloth dipped in boiled water and hang the bacon to dry in a current of cold air, unless you prefer to smoke it. As it matures, bacon may need protecting from flies; common coverings include pepper, paraffin wax and stockinette bags. Well-cured farm bacon hung in a cool dry place will keep for a year.

Factory bacon is mostly cured in brine (sometimes after an initial dry-salting), because brine cures give more even results with less hard work The carcasses can be quickly chilled by refrigeration, which makes it possible to make good bacon all the year and not just in winter.

Mild brine is pumped into the arteries or directly into the muscles by a sort of embalming process. This is so efficient that the curing solution often goes right into the bones. Pumping is an excellent technique if the manufacturer can resist the temptation of making 'instant' bacon (some modern methods have produced something approximating to bacon within hours). Such cures often use nitrites instead of saltpetre and load the injection fluids with monosodium glutamate and flavourings to replace the natural hammy tastes which have no time to develop. Artificial sweeteners can also replace sugar. The general use of refrigeration has made possible a very lightly-cured green (unsmoked) bacon which will survive no more than a few days at room temperature and would have been unthinkable under farm conditions. In factories, it is usual to cure the whole Wiltshire side – with ham and shoulder intact. The farm practice of detaching the legs from the flitches and curing them separately as hams is still predominant in countries which eat more ham than bacon.

British Cuts of Bacon

Back. (Prime back, Top back, Long back.) This may be cut in rashers or chops, or rolled and used as a joint. In the north of Britain, the back is rolled before slicing, which gives the rounded shape of the back rashers there.

Bacon chops. Back rashers cut very thick, like chops, and used for grilling.

Collar. The whole collar weighs about 4 kg (9 lb) and is usually cut into smaller joints or sliced into rather square rashers. Collar has more fat and is somewhat coarser meat than that from the back or from gammon.

Corner. Part of a gammon (*see below*).

Flank. The fattiest and least valuable part of the belly of the pig. This can sometimes be bought very cheaply, but is nowadays often sliced with the back above it to give the more economical through-cut rashers. If the cook cuts off the flank part and uses it for cooking, this may well be less of an economy for him or her than it is for the butcher, who is unloading the bits that might otherwise be difficult to sell.

Flitch. The side of bacon minus the shoulder and ham.

Fore-end. Shoulder and neck part of the pig; shoulder is inferior to the gammon. The meat is coarser and more fatty.

Forehock. Whole, this weighs about 3½ kg (7-8 lb). It can be boned and used for roasting or boiling either as a large joint or cut into smaller joints.

Gammon. Same word as the French *jambon* (ham), but cured as part of a Wiltshire side of bacon and not given a stronger, longer ham cure. It is the finest part of the pig. Gammon is cooked whole to make a very mild ham, used as bacon joints or cut into gammon rashers. Corner is a triangular joint of 1½ kg (3½ lb) or a smaller joint plus corner fillet steaks. Middle gammon, also called prime gammon, is cut from the centre of the backside, a lean, fine textured and well-flavoured joint which weighs 3½ kg (8 lb); it is also cut into gammon steaks for grilling. Slipper, a small joint of only ½ kg (1¼ lb), is very lean but not quite so good as the middle gammon. Gammon hock, 6 kg (13 lb), is more or less the whole gammon, apart from the narrowest part, the knuckle. This is mostly bone, with some well-flavoured, rather stringy meat. It is mainly used for soups and some European dishes.

Knuckle, may be either gammon knuckle (*see above*) or fore (fore hock) knuckle, which is used similarly.

Loin. The section behind the oyster and in front of the gammon. When cut right through it may be called long back or long loin.

Middle. The middle of the pig is what you would expect it to be: the part behind the collar and in front of the gammon. It corresponds roughly to the rib cage and belly and can be divided horizontally into the back and the streaky. A whole middle would weigh about 12¼ kg (27 lb) and is the part providing most of the breakfast bacon rashers. Back rashers have a good area of lean and less fat than the streaky rashers (*see below*). Middle cut or through cut rashers are cut right through (after boning) and are long rashers which include both back and streaky or flank (*see above*). Middle is also the best part of gammon (*see above*).

Oyster. A small fist-shaped piece which nestles between the long back and the short back. It may be rashered or boiled.

Rasher. Any thin slice of bacon. Very thin slices are preferred in Scotland, while further south and in Wales they are usually cut thicker. Thin slices are best for those who prefer crispy-fried bacon, and the thickness to which rashers are cut is important in some dishes.

Slipper. Part of a gammon (*see above*).

Streaky. The belly part of the pig, with alternating streaks of fat and lean. In many European countries, this is the only part turned into bacon. It is nearly always rashered and fried, and for many is the nicest of all for breakfast. The front part, which is leaner, is called prime streaky, while the hind part is thin streaky. The bit right at the rear is called flank (*see above*). The whole piece of streaky weighs about 3 kg (6½ lb).

European Bacon

Guanciale. A speciality from southern Italy and usually translated as a bacon, although it is the cured jaw of the pig and thus more similar to *Bath chap in origin. It has a special type of fat and is the correct 'bacon' to use in *spaghetti alla carbonara* and *all'amatriciana*, two well-known Italian dishes.

Lard. French for bacon, although the French often use the word *bacon* in the English sense. (*Bacon* is originally a French word meaning any sort of pork, as indeed it was in English until after Shakespeare's time.) The French for lard is *saindoux*.

Panchetta. Italian salted pig's belly. When smoked it is called *bacon*.

Poitrine fumée. Literally smoked breast, the French for bacon.

Selschcarée. Perhaps this just comes in the category of bacon. It is carefully-trimmed back, cured in spiced brine for only 3 days, lightly smoked (cold) for 24 hours, and usually eaten boiled with *sauerkraut*.

Speck. German for bacon but covers items which would hardly come under the same heading in other countries, such as *zigeuner Speck* which is little more than cured and smoked fat rolled in paprika; you can eat it raw on cold days when skiing or climbing in the Alps.

Tocino. Spanish salted fat belly or other fat pork. Often covered with a layer of crystalline salt, it is not smoked and bears little resemblance to bacon. Smoked, cured belly in Spain is known as *bacon*.

[*Bacon* – French: *lard* German: *Speck* Italian: *lardo* Spanish: *jamón*]

BACTERIA. These microscopic organisms are smaller than *yeasts and are found everywhere in astronomical numbers. Even though processes involving them were managed by mankind long before bacteria were discovered, some knowledge about them can be useful in the kitchen.

There are thousands of different bacteria, just as there are thousands of different animals and plants, but bacteria have to be distinguished, not by their appearance (there are only a few shapes and many look alike), but by what they do. This is possible because each species operates in a specific way and in specific conditions. For instance, *Lactobacillus bulgaricus* (bacteria have no popular names, though they may be referred to by the name of the process or disease which involves them) will always turn milk sugar into lactic acid, but it cannot utilize cane sugar or produce alcohol.

Each single bacterium has an infinitesimally small effect on its surroundings, but we are normally dealing with millions of millions. Bacteria can multiply at a startling rate by simply splitting into two; they can split twice – even three times – in an hour when conditions are exactly right. This accounts for the surprising fact that a single teaspoon of starter will *clabber 2 lt (3½ pt) of milk in five hours – it would set three times that amount if conditions were perfect, which they never are. Twelve hours later it would, in theory, have clabbered over 100,000 lt (175,000 pt). It has been calculated that the offspring from a single bacterium could theoretically cover the entire surface of the earth in two or three days. However, bacteria rapidly use up the available food or pollute their environment with their own waste products – they overwhelm themselves with their unbridled breeding, a solemn thought for humans.

In nature, it is rare to find one sort of bacteria growing alone; they are always in mixtures. Indeed, some will not grow at all except in association. Certain kinds are habitually found together in a particular situation (in milk, for instance), and they work together to produce an end product in a way that none of them could do singly. They feed on each other's waste products and follow one another in logical order. It is such a chain of events (which also includes yeasts and fungi) rather than the effect of one organism which we have to deal with in the kitchen. A good example is the ripening of cheese. People were making cheese long before they knew that it was a living process they were controlling. This is comforting because it taxes the best dairy bacteriologists to follow the sequence of events in any detail, but at least we can now understand why the accepted procedures must be followed exactly and why short cuts or variations may lead to disaster. If the book says boil for 20 minutes, then the substance must boil for 20 minutes and not for 10 minutes.

Bacterial processes can be controlled first of all by temperature. Yoghurt-producing bacteria grow at around 40°C (104°F), but will be beaten out of the race by other organisms when the temperature is lower. Acidity, type of food, moisture, salt, light or dark, air or no air, the presence or absence of certain other types of organism and the presence of antibiotics or antiseptics – all these are factors influencing the growth of bacteria.

Certain rod-shaped bacteria can produce spores, which create a special problem. There are only about 150 kinds of these: 100 aerobes (which need air) and 50 anaerobes (which do not need air). Unlike the spores of fungi (but like the spores of yeasts), bacterial spores are not produced for purposes of multiplication, but so that the organism can survive tough conditions. Spores usually form only when the community or culture becomes old, the environment is polluted by waste or food is scarce. It takes 24 hours for bacteria to form spores (but only 4-6 hours to start germination again). Spores are very difficult to kill. Some can lie doggo for up to 10 years and survive hours of boiling. See pasteurization, poisoning.

[*Bacteria* – French: *bactérie* German: *Bakterie* Italian: *batteri* Spanish: *bacteria*]

BADOIT. *See* water (mineral water).

BAGACEIRA. *See* marc.

BAJRA. *See* millet.

BAKING. In English, this somewhat inexact term usually means cooking bread or cakes in an oven. The Germans have the word *backen* too, from the same source, but in French, Italian and Spanish one has to be specific and say 'cook in an oven'. Baking can also mean almost any method of cooking in which the food comes into contact with dry heat, or is otherwise parcelled and cooked in ashes. Girdle cakes, muffins, *chapatties* and similar breads are baked on an iron plate or girdle, and potatoes may be baked in the ashes of a camp fire. For a clam bake, the shellfish is steamed in seaweed, but the seaweed is in contact with hot ashes and stones in a pit – a variation on the most primitive method of baking there is.

In the Orient, a traditional way of baking is to wrap food in banana leaves and cover it in hot ashes. The modern variant is to wrap the food first in foil and then bury it in a pit in which a fire has burned for many hours. (Sheep-stealers bake their stolen lamb *under* the fire.) The supposed gypsy way of cooking a hedgehog encased in clay is baking. So also, perhaps, is the even more basic method used by some Australian aborigines whom I have seen throw a wallaby, skin and all, into the camp fire. The skin and fur char to form a protective shell of carbon inside which the meat is beautifully baked.

The most primitive form of oven for baking is no doubt the *tandoor*, which in its simplest form is a large pot sunk into the earth. This is a Middle Eastern device – you find it much used in Iran – and it has spilled eastwards into the Punjab, where it is the common way of cooking. In more sophisticated versions, the pot is raised above ground and built into a sort of stove, which is well insulated with plaster and mud. There may be a means of letting air in at the bottom of the pot to adjust the heat. The fire of wood or dried dung is lit some two hours before cooking time, and fuel is controlled so that it will have burned down to ashes by the time the *tandoor* is hot. Breads are slapped on to the hot sides near the top (beginners will burn their arms and drop the bread into the coals), and meat is threaded on a sword or metal spit and thrust down into the heat. (People with gardens will find a square *tandoor* easy to construct with fire bricks.)

The *tandoor* type of oven is limited, and an advance is the brick oven with a side opening which was once common in Britain and America and is still used in rural parts of Europe and in the Middle East. The usual form has a flat bottom, an arched or domed top, and a chimney at the back. The door is closed with an iron sheet which also provides the means of controlling the rate of burning by the amount of air let in – the oven is heated by burning brushwood *in* it, not underneath. The heat permeates the brickwork to give an oven which cools slowly as it is being used; in some ovens a bank of pebbles is heated up. The time taken to heat is several hours, depending on when the oven was last used. When the wood is reduced to ashes, these can be either drawn out or pushed to the back, and the chimney is blocked with a stone. Experts judge the heat of the oven by rubbing a piece of charred stick on the brickwork and noting the sparks formed. There are other tests, such as the time taken to char paper. To work with this type of oven, one must get used to baking on a falling heat, but as bread cooked in such an old-fashioned brick oven has an incomparable taste, it is worth the little practice (and some disasters) needed to master the technique. Flat bread, pizzas and *nan* – or other doughs – should be put straight on to the hot, ashy brick to bake. They never stick.

[*Baking* – French: *cuire au four* German: *backen, im Ofen braten* Italian: *cuocere al forno* Spanish: *cocer al horno*]

BAKING POWDER is a mixture of acid and alkaline substances which, when moistened and/or heated, react together to produce carbon dioxide gas, which in baking makes cakes rise. It is a relative newcomer to cooking. Until the end of the 18th century, *leavening was managed only with *yeast, although lightness in cake-making could be produced by beating in air – some recipes suggested 'beating for an hour or two' – or by adding spirits, which, being volatile, would expand into a gaseous state when heated.

In 1790, in America, it was found that a refined form of wood ash called pearl ash (a carbonate of potash) could be used in baking cakes to make them rise. Two years later, some 8,000 tons were exported to Europe. However, as pearl ash produces a soapy taste in baked goods, its use was limited to highly-spiced cakes such as gingerbread. Pearl ash was followed by *bicarbonate of soda which was also called saleratus (aerating salt). One writer remarked that 'it was said to be responsible for much of the dyspepsia common in the USA'.

By the mid-19th century, baking powder had been introduced. This was a mixture of bicarbonate of soda with a mild acid, usually *cream of tartar or *tartaric acid, and rice flour. Modern baking powder still contains bicarbonate of soda as its alkaline ingredient, plus a combination of acids to provide a double action with the bicarbonate – an acid such as tartaric acid which reacts on moistening (releasing gas to aid in the mixing), and a slower-acting acid such as acid sodium pyrophosphate which releases very little gas until it is heated in the oven. Dried starch or flour is added to baking powder as a filler which also absorbs any moisture in the atmosphere and thus prevents any reaction taking place during storage.

In the absence of a bought baking powder, you may use bicarbonate of soda in a mixture containing an acid, such as *buttermilk. An alternative is to make up your own simple baking powder by mixing a tablespoon of bicarbonate of soda with 2 tablespoons of cream of tartar – both of which must be very dry. A drawback in this preparation is that it starts to fizz as soon as it is mixed with liquid; the cake should therefore be baked as soon as possible and not kept hanging about, or the powder may have exhausted its potential before the cake is heated through enough to set it.

The quantity of baking powder required varies from recipe to recipe, but a good general rule is that the plainer the cake mixture the more baking powder is required; the richer the cake the less baking powder is needed. Too much or too little baking powder upsets the balance of the ingredients, so it is always worth measuring baking powder carefully and making minor adjustments to recipes after assessing your results.

[*Baking powder* – French: *levure chimique* German: *Backenpulver* Italian: *lievito* Spanish: *levadura*]

BAKING SODA. *See* bicarbonate of soda.

BALACHAN, **balachong**, or **blachan** (and various other spellings) is a very important flavouring in the cooking of Malaysia, Indonesia (where it is called *trasi*) and other South East Asian countries. It is made of shrimps or prawns, which are caught in huge numbers in the tropical creeks and salted, dried, pounded and allowed to mature in a humid heat until a ripe smell and taste develop. One might describe it as gamey, but it is quite essential in the dishes of the region and is not the same as Indian *balachong.

It may be coloured from pink to dark brick, and may be caked, powdered or in the form of a pinkish paste. There is no real substitute, although anchovy paste has been suggested as the nearest thing outside the Orient. It keeps almost indefinitely in the refrigerator, provided it is kept dry in a closed jar. Balachan is never eaten raw, but is fried with the spices in a recipe, or is roasted dry, then ground and added. You would be well advised to wrap the piece to be roasted in foil, as this helps to prevent the smell from pervading the house.

BALACHONG, **balichow**, or **balachow** is a pickle made in South India of salted prawns, mangoes or even dried duck eggs and eaten as a relish with curry (compare *balachan), It is hot and strongly flavoured, for though fresh prawns are used, the tropical sun has usually given them a ripe taste before the pickle is made. This relish can be bought, or you can make it as follows:

Prawn Balachow

Clean and shell 450 g (1 lb) prawns, and put them through a mincer. Heat 600 ml (1 pt) of oil and fry in it 300 g (11 oz) minced onion, 300 g (11 oz) skinned, seeded and chopped tomato. Add a paste made of 50 g (2 oz) garlic, 50 g (2 oz) fresh ginger, 1 teaspoon cumin, 1 tablespoon peppercorns, 15 g (½ oz) turmeric and 125 g (5 oz) hot chilli, which have been moistened during pounding with a little vinegar. Fry this paste and then add the minced prawn with a small handful of curry leaves (if available). Fry for another minute or so, then add salt and vinegar – up to 600 ml (1 pt) – to obtain a nice taste and consistency for a relish. Simmer gently till cooked, allow to cool a little, bottle and seal in screwtop jars.

Basic Cake Recipes

This table shows the proportion of baking powder and plain flour to other ingredients. Eggs used are size 4 (55 to 60 g). Teaspoons should be standard size.

Basic Recipe	Flour (plain)	Fats	Sugar	Eggs	Fruit	Liquid Milk	Baking Powder (level tsp)
Scone mix	8 oz 225 g	1½ oz 38 g	as required		optional	approx ¼ pt approx 125 ml	4
Plain mix	8 oz 225 g	3 oz 75 g	3 oz	1	3-3½ oz 75-100 g	approx ¼ pt approx 125 ml	3
Rich mix	8 oz 225 g	6 oz 150 g	6 oz 150 g	3	6-8 oz 150-225 g	a little	1
Very rich mix	8 oz 225 g	8 oz 225 g	8 oz 225 g	4	8-12 oz 225-325 g	a little	–
Victoria Sandwich	4 oz 100 g	4 oz 100 g	4 oz 100 g	2	–	a little	1

BALM, lemon balm or **melissa**. A labiate plant native to southern Europe, balm (*Melissa officinalis*) was first introduced to Britain by the Romans. It has a strong lemony scent and can make a change as a flavouring where a little lemon zest might be nice; it is useful as a substitute for lemon grass and particularly as a flavouring in liqueurs.

[*Balm* – French: *amélisse, eau de mélisse* German: *Bienenkraut, Melisse, Zitronenmelisse* Italian: *melisa, melissa* Spanish: *balsamita mayor, toronjil, toronjiña*]

BALSAM APPLE and **BALSAM PEAR**. *See* marrow (*Momordica charantia*).

BAMBOO SHOOTS. Bamboo is a huge grass. There are many different species, some of which grow to 30 m (100 ft) with a width of 50 cm (20 in) at the base. Bamboo is one of the characteristic plants of eastern Asia, where it has an important role in the economy. The shoots of those species used for food are dug just before they come above the ground. They can be up to 10 cm (4 in) in diameter and 30 cm (1 ft) long, looking in that case rather like giant asparagus spears. Hungry travellers should not experiment with bamboo without guidance. Not all species of bamboo are edible, and those that are include some that have a hard outer coat or irritant hairs which must be removed; others contain the exceedingly poisonous prussic (hydrocyanic) acid, which is volatile and thus dissipated when the shoots are boiled. The season when the shoots can be dug is also variable. In northern countries, such as China and Japan, there is a definite spring and autumn, but in the monsoon tropical regions further south the season for bamboo is dictated by the rains. There are also great differences in the way in which the various sorts of bamboo shoots must be prepared. Some need only to have the scales removed and to be boiled for 10 minutes; others need boiling for several hours.

Bamboo shoots dry and conserve very well.They retain their flavour and crispness when canned. In fact, canned bamboo shoots are often used in the Orient in preference to fresh ones, as they are already cooked and ready for use. Canned bamboo shoots are exported from China and Japan (where they are called *takenoko*), canned either in water (usually best) or brine, in pieces or whole (best). They look like ivory-coloured spinning tops. If the whole can is not to be used at once, the shoots will keep in the refrigerator for up to 10 days if put in a jar of fresh water which is changed daily. Canned bamboo shoots are ready for use in Chinese or Japanese dishes. In most cases, they are cooked for 5 minutes, which just warms them through, but they may also be eaten cold.

Dried bamboo shoots have been dried in the sun and are even tastier than the canned shoots, but they require more preparation. Their colour varies from white to yellow and black. The thin, dark shoots are better flavoured than white ones. The white need to be boiled for an hour, cut up and cooked for a further half hour. The yellow must be soaked for 3 hours in water, then cooked for at least 2 hours before they become tender, but they are worth it for the taste.

Pickled bamboo shoots are steamed with beef or pork.

[*Bamboo shoot* – French: *pousse de bambou* German: *Bambusprosse* Italian: *germoglio di bambù* Spanish: *caña de bambu*]

BANANA and **PLANTAIN**. Originally from India and southern Asia, the banana (*Musa sapientum*) is now cultivated all over the world in frost-free climates. In the warm, humid, windless tropics, it is both the most important commercial fruit and a home-grown staple for poor, subsistence-level farmers. The banana is said to be one of the first fruits to have been brought into cultivation. Documentary evidence suggests that it was being grown in the Middle East (e.g. in Assyria) over 3,000 years ago, but it must then have died out, as the armies of Alexander the Great were surprised at the sight of the strange fruit growing in the Indus Valley in 327 BC. A thousand years later, the Arabs brought bananas into Egypt and Palestine. In the 15th century, Portuguese navigators found bananas on the Guinea coast of Africa and established them in the Canary Islands, which had been discovered and colonized in 1402. They were taken to the West Indies by a Dominican friar in 1516 and within 25 years had spread throughout the West Indies and tropical America, now the world's main banana-producing area. They had also, it seems, travelled in the opposite direction from Asia across the Pacific, because they were already growing in Hawaii when Captain Cook arrived in 1778. Bananas remained a luxury in northern Europe until the Imperial Direct Line started operations in the West Indies in 1901. Before the days of refrigeration and fast steam ships Europe had depended on the Canary Islands for bananas (and Canary bananas were the only bananas accepted by my grandmother who despised the rest as 'plantains').

The 'hands' of a dozen or so fruit ('fingers'), in

which bananas are usually marketed, are part of a larger bunch – up to a dozen hands arranged around a central stem – which grows on a plant which may be up to 10 m (30 ft) high, but is botanically a herb rather than a tree.

Bananas to be transported are cut when they are fully plumped but still green, and the bunches are packed carefully in cartons. They are kept at a temperature of 12-13°C (53-56°F) – never colder, as cold turns bananas black – during shipment; when needed, the bunches are hung to ripen in warmed rooms. Good though such bananas are, they are never quite as excellent as those sun ripened on the plant. The food value of bananas is high – from a nutritional point of view, they are better than apples.

Some species of the genus *Musa* are cultivated for fibre and not for fruit (the Manila rope used by mountaineers was made from these). There are some four hundred varieties of banana; in India and South East Asia, the multitude of different sorts in markets may be bewildering. Not only are there varieties grown to withstand transport or for climatic reasons (some will survive several degrees of frost), but some are grown for their fine leaves, which are used to wrap food for cooking (this gives the contents a special taste) or as throw-away plates for serving food. The leaves are used as a wrapping for food in Mexico as well as India. Passing the half leaf (with the midrib removed) over a flame to warm it thoroughly will make it more flexible.

Of the bananas grown for eating, some are intended for consumption raw, while others require cooking. There are even very nasty varieties with stony black seeds, on which you can break your teeth. Small bananas are often the most tasty and sweet (one of these is called Lady's Fingers and is not to be confused with *okra). Fat, red bananas are particularly used as offerings in Hindu ceremonies. Cooking varieties, which are often referred to as plantains (*M. paradisiaca*), are not sweet at all, very firm, and excellent finely sliced and fried as chips. In India, bananas are frequently curried with their skins on.

In European and North American cooking, the role of bananas is much more restricted, being limited to sweet dishes (and those chunks embedded in imitation custard for school trifle). In the Caribbean, where bananas are used much more in cooking, a great favourite on the Spanish-speaking islands is *tostones*, slices of green plantain, partly fried, then squashed down and fried again until crisp. They are served as a vegetable and as an appetizer with cocktails. On the French-speaking islands, plantains are called *banane*, while the sweet, eating varieties are known as *figues* and are popular in a wide range of exotic puddings, usually flavoured with rum.

Dried bananas, which are also known as banana figs, have been peeled, spread out to dry in the sun, and turned daily until they are desiccated. Treated in this simple way, the bananas may darken very much and are inclined to be attacked by insects. A more sophisticated method is to treat the peeled bananas with sulphur dioxide (from burning sulphur) for 20 minutes, or to dip them in 1% citric acid solution, before sun-drying. Even more successful is artificial drying at 54-60°C (129-140°F) for 15-20 hours, after first soaking the bananas in a 1% sodium carbonate (washing soda) solution for 15 minutes, and dipping them in a solution of 1 *Camden tablet per 100 ml (3½ fl oz) water.

Cooking varieties are also dried in a similar manner and ground to make banana flour (plantain meal, *pisang* starch, banana meal etc.) which is very digestible, a good invalid food, and very sustaining. (The famous African explorer, Stanley, is reputed to have used it.) Finally, part of the flower, or the heart of the flower before it opens, is used as a vegetable, as also is the central part of the stem. Banana jam, banana wine and banana-flavoured liqueurs (often reinforced with synthetic flavourings) are made, but I have yet to meet anyone who likes them.

[*Banana* – French: *banane* German: *Banane* Italian: *banana* Spanish: *plátano*

Plantain – French: *plantain, banane des Antilles* German: *Wegerich* Italian: *piantaggine, petacciuola* Spanish: *llantén*]

BARACKPÁLINKA. *See* fruit brandy.

BARBARY PEAR. *See* prickly pear.

BARBE. *See* chicory.

BARBECUE SAUCE. The word barbecue comes from the Mexican Spanish *barbacoa* (*barbacua*), which originally described the grilling of meat over a fire on bars of green wood. Today it has come to mean almost any open-air party at which meat is grilled, and equivalent to the South African *braivleis*. This is perhaps the most primitive method of cooking, but delicious for all that. Barbecue sauces are spread on the meat before cooking, or used for basting. Many ready-made barbecue sauces are on sale. Home-made ones are usually based on minced onion, tomato purée, paste or ketchup, sugar and Worcestershire sauce. Many such sauces are apt to add a cloying flavour to the meat, and the simplest mixture, with probably the best of all tastes, is sea salt and lemon juice.

BARBERRY (*Berberis vulgaris*) is a shrub that may be native in parts of England as it is over much of Europe. It used to be cultivated for its elongated, bright red berries. They were candied, made into jellies or pickled for use as a garnish. Barberry is much less common than it was, because the discovery that it is an intermediate host of a cereal fungus, Black rust, led to its eradication in many areas.

[*Barberry* – French: *épine-vinette* German: *Berberitze, Berbesbeere* Italian: *berbero, crespino* Spanish: *berberis, bérbero, agracejo, arlo*]

BARCELONA NUT. *See* hazel nut.

BARDING. A bard was an armoured breastplate for a horse. In cooking, it is a breastplate of fat, salted fat or bacon, a thin slice of which is tied around meat or fowl to protect and moisten it during roasting. This is particularly necessary when the meat lacks its own fat; the bard also helps to keep rolled meat neatly in place.It is usually removed when the retaining string is cut before sending to table.

BARLEY (*Hordeum vulgare*) was one of the first cereals to be cultivated by man and it was used even before wheat in making bread. A very hardy plant, it used to be the staple grain in many northern countries and still is in parts of the Near East. It was used in the form of unleavened barley cakes because it has insufficient gluten to be leavened like wheaten bread. The main culinary use of barley today is as pearl barley, which is the grain with the husk ground off. Barley with most but not all of the outside removed is known as pot barley.

Barley has an attractive and individual taste which goes well in soups and stews, but it is also excellent when boiled and mixed with plenty of thick cream, a taste I remember well from childhood. Most barley is used as animal feed. Much, however, goes for brewing, and for this purpose, what is most important to the farmer is its malting quality, which decides the price he gets for it (*see* malt). A high-starch grain is superior in this respect and looks white when it is cut in half. Poor quality malting barley looks flinty, but is the more nutritious food.

Barley meal is wholemeal ground barley, and can be made into a porridge or into simple barley cakes baked on a girdle. Barley water, usually flavoured with the zest of a lemon, is made by infusing pearl barley in boiling water and allowing it to get cold before straining off the liquid. (I part by volume of washed pearl barley needs to be boiled in 10 parts of water for 20 minutes.) It is a famous and very soothing drink for invalids. Patent barley is ground pearl barley. Barley sugar was originally made of lemon, barley water and sugar, now it is simply sugar boiled to crack and acidified, a sweet for children.

[*Barley* – French: *orge* German: *Gerste* Italian: *orzo* Spanish: *cebada*]

[*Pearl barley* – French: *orge perlée* German: *Perlgraupen* Italian: *orzo perlato* Spanish: *cebada perlada*]

BARM. Brewer's *yeast.

BARNACLE. Although the barnacles that are common on rocks on the seashore may look like molluscs, they are actually crustaceans. They are something like lazy shrimps which have taken to lying on their backs and kicking food into their mouths with their feet. The famous *percebe*, so popular in tapas bars in Spain, is the goose barnacle (*Pollicipes cornucopia*) found on the Atlantic coast (but not in the Mediterranean).It has a long, flexible 'stalk', which is the part that is eaten. *Percebes* are washed thoroughly, put into boiling brine – 2 teaspoons salt per lit (2 pt) of water – and cooked for 15 minutes, timed from the moment the water reboils. They are eaten cold, with or without a squeeze of lemon; the technique is to draw the stalk through your teeth and eat what squeezes out, discarding not only the hard shell but the tough skin of the stalk. They are expensive, much sought after in Spain and also eaten in South American countries. They taste a little like shrimps.

[*Goose barnacle* – French: *pouce-pìed* German: *Entenmuschel* Spanish: *percebe*]

BASES. *See* alkalis.

BASIL or **sweet basil**. A very aromatic labiate plant (*Ocimum basilicum*) with white flowers and tender, light green leaves. Basil is extremely variable; the leaves may be small or half the size of a hand, but this herb is always recognizable by its smell, which is very scented and rather like sweet cloves. Basil is one of the most worthwhile herbs to grow at home, but it is a warm country plant, a native of India, and in temperate climates is better started in a heated glasshouse. Even on the Italian Riviera, it is forced in glasshouses with a high humidity, even in the summer's heat. That produces the most tender, delicately scented leaves. Basil is much grown in Spain and Greece, but mainly to keep flies away. Its greatest importance is in Italy, where it is the basis of the fabulous Ligurian spaghetti sauce with pine nuts, *pesto alla genovese*, and other delicious local specialities. It is also the basis of the French *pistou*, and is recommended as the best herb for tomatoes, salads and various sauces. In this context, it is sometimes used to excess.

To preserve basil for winter use, it is best to deep-freeze it after dipping it quickly into boiling water. It may alternatively be preserved in the Italian way, packed in jars with each layer of leaves sprinkled with salt, and covered with oil. The jar is best kept in the refrigerator. The leaves go black, but the taste remains almost unimpaired. The same cannot be said for dried basil, which acquires a curry-like taste. Bush basil has much smaller leaves and an inferior taste.

[*Basil* – French: *basilic* German: *Basilienkraut* Italian: *basilico* Spanish: *albahaca*]

BASS. The word has no exact meaning and is applied to different fish in different parts of the world; cookery writers sometimes fail to specify which bass should be used. Many forms of bass are sporting anglers' rather than cooks' fish – for instance, the Large-mouthed black bass (*Micropterus salmonoides*), a fine freshwater sporting fish of up to 10 kg (22 lb) introduced from the US into Europe, will not be seen on fishmongers' slabs. There are a great many species of American freshwater bass, which are known locally but would merely cause confusion if listed here.

The various sea bass are gastronomically more important. The Black sea bass of the US east coast (*Centropristes striatus*) is an important food fish, as is the Striped bass or Rockfish (*Roccus saxatilis*), which occurs on both sea-boards and often weighs 10 kg (22 lb) but can reach 50 kg (110 lb). But the most famous of all to gastronomes is the Common bass (*Dicentrarchus labrax*) under its French name of *bar* or *loup (de mer)*. This is among the best of all fish, with firm, delicately-flavoured flesh and no trouble from bones. It is fished in the Mediterranean and on the Atlantic coast of Europe as far north as the English Channel; in France, it is sufficiently valued to be the subject of fish farming in the

maritime part of the Vendée. The Mediterranean name of *loup* (wolf) does not indicate relationship with the wolf-fish (*Anarhichas lupus*) of northern seas which the French call *loup marin* – an ugly and savage relative of the blenny, excellent eating but not to be compared with the Common bass.

Although always costly, Common bass are most plentiful from January to May and in September and October. They should be handled with care as they bruise easily. Gut them through the gills and by a small incision in the belly. Do not scale them if they are to be poached. If they must be scaled, do so gently to avoid tearing the skin.

Closely related to sea bass are the groupers, of which there are many species, some of them reaching an enormous size. We used to catch 250 kg (550 lb) monsters with shark-hook and rope in the Gulf of Carpentaria in Northern Australia, but only for crocodile bait, as the flesh was far too tough to be palatable. However, the Mediterranean grouper or *mérou* (*Epinephelus guaza*), often shot in caves by spear fishermen, is delicious. Though it does not go outside warm waters, it is sometimes imported into Britain.

[*Bass* – French: *bar, loup (de mer)* German: *Seebarsch* Italian: *spigola, branzino* Spanish: *lubzna, róbalo*

Grouper – French: *mérou* Italian: *cernia* Spanish: *mero*]

BASSWOOD. *See* lime.

BASTING. The main purpose of basting is to prevent the surface of food from drying out during cooking, as when basting meat while it roasts and becomes hard. It may also be a method of coating surfaces with flavouring substances or juices, as when basting foods with a marinade.

[*Basting* – French: *arroser* German: *begiessen* Italian: *spruzzare* Spanish: *pringar*]

BATAVIA ENDIVE. *See* chicory.

BATH CHAP. A chap is the fleshy part of the jaw – the jowl – and a Bath chap consists of half the lower jaw meat of a pig, salt-cured, boiled, boned and rolled into the shape of a miniature ham. Bath chaps are usually served cold, cut in slices, but sometimes are eaten hot. Being fatty, they are best when combined with other cold meats. They must be taken from a lean, long-snouted breed of pig. Although they are usually bought ready cooked, Bath chaps can be prepared at home.

Bath Chap

Take the lower jaw of a pig and split it into two. Salt the halves for 3 days in *brine. If chaps are bought ready salted, soak them in 600 ml (1 pt) water, skin side downwards, overnight. Simmer them gently for 3-4 hours, depending on size. Remove the skin and bones, trim the meat and tie it up in a bandage, thus setting it into a nice shape as it cools. Then remove the bandage and cover the Bath chap with toasted breadcrumbs.

BATHING. *See* soaking.

BAUMÉ. Antoine Baumé (1728-1804) was a French chemist who produced scales for a *hydrometer to measure brine strengths – a *brinometer – and for a saccharometer to measure the strengths of sugar syrups.

BAY, **sweet bay** or **sweet laurel**. The aromatic leaves of this bush (*Laurus nobilis*) or small tree – it can grow up to about 18 m (60 ft) – are an essential and absolutely basic flavouring in any self-respecting European kitchen. The tree came originally from Asia Minor, but became known generally around the Mediterranean at a very early date. It was not only a culinary and medicinal herb, but also one of magical significance, used for the victor's crown of laurel in ancient Greece and Rome.

Bay leaves can be used fresh or dried. They have a strong balsamic scent which fades with age, so that old dried leaves are quite flavourless. Bay is always part of a *bouquet garni*: It is used with fish, meat and fowl, especially when wine is included in the recipe; it also goes into marinades, pickles and preserves. Bay is a humble, everyday, cheap flavouring, but it can also be used grandly, as when thick veal fillets are skewered with a wreath of bay and fried in butter. It is sometimes called for in sweet dishes and is the leaf in the box of dried figs, put there to keep away the weevils.

Bay should not be confused with other types of laurel, such as the Mountain laurel and the Cherry laurel, which has a bitter-almond flavour, or with the two important leaves of Indian cooking – which might be thought to have a very superficial resemblance – the *cassia leaf and the *curry leaf.

[*Bay* – French: *laurier* German: *Lorbeer* Italian: *lauro* Spanish: *laurel*]

BAY SALT. Coarse *salt from seawater evaporated in bays.

BEAN CURD, a pressed purée of *soya beans, is a very common and nourishing ingredient of Chinese cooking (and Japanese, where it is known as *tofu*). It is available from Chinese shops, fresh, canned or dried. The last must be soaked before being added to vegetable soups, stir-fried dishes and so on. There are also sweet bean-curd sticks, used with fish and vegetables, as well as sheets of bean-curd skin for egg rolls and vegetable dishes.

BEAN-CURD CHEESE. White bean-curd cheese slightly resembles Camembert and is made from small squares of bean curd, which are salted and matured in rice wine. It is eaten raw with a little oil or sugar as an accompaniment to rice, but it is mainly used as a flavouring in Chinese pasta dishes or with chicken, pork or fish. Red cheese, too, is made from bean curd and is fermented with salt, wine and spices. It is more strongly flavoured than the white and goes well with duck, chicken or pork. Both are available canned or in jars.

BEAN PASTE and **BEAN SAUCE**. Pastes of red and yellow beans are important in Chinese cooking. Red bean paste is sweet and is made from *adzuki beans. The yellow variety is made from *soya beans and is salty and pungent – it can be used as a flavouring and, like the red paste, can be bought in cans. Fermented salted black beans, made from a black variety of soya beans and known as black bean sauce, are a flavouring in fish, lobster, chicken and pork dishes. The sauce is heavily salted and, once opened, will therefore keep well in the refrigerator. Brown bean sauce is a thick paste of salted brown or yellowish beans and is also used as a flavouring with fish, fowl, vegetables or *bean curd. It is rather like a thick soy sauce and is more or less interchangeable with black bean sauce in some dishes; it is also available in cans or jars.

BEANS. Originally a bean was a broad bean or a field bean, and a pea was what is now called a garden pea. When other beans were introduced, mainly from America, the meaning of bean was broadened to include any legume with a kidney-shaped seed (and pea to include any pea-shaped one).There is no longer any precise meaning to either term – there is even a pea-bean. *See* legume, pulse.

[*Beans* – French: *haricots* German: *Bohnen* Italian: *fagnoli, fagioli, fave* Spanish: *habas*]

BEARBERRY. *See* cranberry.

BEARD. The beard of an oyster is its gills. Some people like to have the beard removed; others do not. The byssus of a mussel (the fibrous extrusion which attaches the mussel to the rock) is also sometimes called the beard.

BEATING. *See* whipping.

BÊCHE DE MER. *See* sea cucumber.

BEECH NUT or **beechmast**. The small triangular nuts of various species of beech, such as *Fagus sylvatica* in Europe and *F. grandifolia* in North America, are edible. They were important in the past, not only as food for pigs which were allowed to forage in the forest, but also for humans and as a source of oil. Beech nuts vary in size: many years, in Britain, you will find most of the nuts empty, but sometimes you may come upon a tree bearing well-filled nuts that are worth gathering.

The nuts should be heated gently in an oven until the husk becomes brittle. It can then be broken by rubbing and winnowed off. The inner seed-coat can be removed after blanching or frying. The flavour of beech nuts is excellent, but they were most commonly used as a source of beech-nut oil (especially in France). This was extracted by grinding the nuts, preferably with the skins removed, in a little water, then pressing the slurry in stout linen bags. The oil can be drawn off because it floats on the water. After the impurities have been allowed to settle, the oil is again siphoned off and is ready for storage. It improves with keeping and is said to be best after 6 years. If you can find beech-nut oil, it is an excellent salad oil. Beech nuts are rich in oil and protein but low in carbohydrate. The seed-coat (and to a small extent the nut) contains a poisonous substance, fagin, which is harmless to us in any quantity we are likely to take but poisonous to horses.

In North America, the indigenous beech bears slightly smaller but oilier nuts than its similar European brother. There are huge beech forests in the eastern states, but the nuts are of importance only to hogs and to children.

[*Beech nut* – French: *faîne* German: *Bucheichel* Italian: *faggiuola* Spanish: *hayuco*]

BEECHWHEAT. *See* buckwheat.

BEEF and **VEAL**. Beef is the meat of the ox, while veal is that of the young ox, preferably one that has fed exclusively on milk. Oxen were originally domesticated for pulling carts and ploughs. Only in the past 200 years have they been systematically selected for either milk or beef, and since the invention of artificial insemination, there has been great change in this direction. In the last century, the preference was for large joints, well marbled with fat and from not too young animals. Well-hung, these give the most flavourful yet tender meat, yet with families getting smaller, costs going up and dire warnings being issued against saturated fats and calories, the modern tendency has been towards joints that are small and lean. Farm economics are a dominant factor here: an animal that grows quickly to a reasonable size brings in more cash to the producer. It may be fattened in a stall, which saves on food but does not give the best flavour. Beef is now usually eaten fairly fresh. That bought from the butcher will rarely have been hung for more than a week, as proper hanging occupies storage space and thus raises the price of the meat. Large restaurants, though, can buy their steak in great hunks and hang it for 2-3 weeks in a cool, fly-proof place, but it grows mould on the surface, which must be cut off and thrown away. This matters little in restaurant castings, but does make a difference at home when the piece is small – so hanging one's own meat is scarcely practicable.

The best beef comes from bullocks bred for the purpose. Bull's meat is tough and strong. (In Spain, after bullfights, it is commonly sold to the poor and to those who think it gives them virility.) Cow meat is also good if the animal is young, but it usually comes from old cows which have run out of milk and are stringy and tough (cow meat, sometimes acknowledged as such, tends to go into cheap supermarket mince).

Veal also varies greatly. Young, unwanted calves, which it would be unprofitable to rear, give tasteless, watery meat. The best veal, such as is for instance produced in Holland, is from animals several months old and finished on dried milk. It is white, firm and delicious. Older animals which have eaten some solid food should be known as 'baby beef'; their meat, intermediate between beef and veal, can be unsatisfactorily made to do duty for either – their appeal is to the farmer, not the cook. Alpine countries, like Austria and Italy made great use of veal in the past, because calves necessarily born to ensure the cow's lactation could not be fattened over winter when the mountain pastures were covered in snow. Because good veal is expensive and is used more for made-up dishes than for roasting joints, the butchery is elaborate and involves dissecting out particular muscles. From these, slices can be cut for schnitzels, veal birds, escallops, etc.

[*Beef* – French: *boeuf* German: *Ochsenfleisch* Italian: *manzo* Spanish: *carne de vaca*

Veal – French: *veau* German: *Kalbfleisch* Italian: *vitello* Spanish: *ternera*]

BEER. Alcoholic drinks have been made by *brewing from cereals since the very earliest times. For instance, a Babylonian inscribed clay tablet from the 6th century BC shows brewing. Many different types of ale were made in ancient Egypt, and the techniques were passed on by the Greeks to the Romans. The Britons were already brewing ale when the Romans invaded in 55 BC. Indeed, brewing is not a very difficult discovery to make: if a porridge of grain and water is left standing, it will ferment into a sour, alcoholic brew which can have nice effects when drunk, even if its taste is rather nasty. Any grain may be used: barley, wheat, rice, millet, maize, etc. Primitive brews which are still made today are Zulu beer and Tibetan *chang*. Rice wine, which is important in the cooking of China and Japan, would more correctly be called rice ale.

The great advances were the malting of barley and, later, the introduction of *hops. Although ale and beer are now almost synonymous, the old word was ale, and beer referred to hopped ale. Herbs such as madder, alecost, ground ivy or ale-hoof, spruce and nettles had long been used to flavour ale, as unflavoured ales are rather insipid. The use of hops for this purpose first gained favour in Germany, and a taste for hopped ale is said to have been brought to Britain by soldiers returning from Flanders during the Hundred Years War. By the middle of the 15th century, hops were being cultivated in Britain, and a bitter controversy was raging between those who liked hopped ale and those who considered it good only for foreigners. It seems incredible that, in 1464, London brewers even petitioned the Lord Mayor to forbid altogether the use of hops and herbs of any kind. Real ale should be made from just malted barley, yeast and water, they said. But in the end, hopped ale won, and today beer is universal. People liked the refreshing, bitter taste of hops, and hopped ale was cheaper because an interesting drink could be made with half the quantity of malt required to produce a passable unhopped ale. It would also keep a month, as compared with two weeks for the unhopped brews. The economic significance of this was vast, because in those days, and for a century to come,

there was neither tea nor coffee – ale was the drink for man, woman and child at every meal.

The various types of beer are determined mainly by the types of yeast and malt that are used. Lager and American beers use the most lightly cured malt and a yeast that works slowly on the bottom of the vat; lager (which is from the German *Largerbier*, meaning beer kept in store) should be stored for up to three months, although some is kept even longer. British beers are brewed with faster working yeasts that live mainly on the surface. Bitter is made with lightly cured malt and is thus pale in colour and has a dry, rather bitter taste; bottled, gassy versions of ordinary and best bitter are usually known respectively as light ale and pale ale. Mild is made in the same way as bitter but with darker, more highly cured malts, extra sugar or caramel and less hops; it is less bitter in taste and usually somewhat weaker. Brown ale is bottled mild. Stout, the darkest beer, is made with black malt, which has a burnt taste.

The occasional use of ale and beer in the kitchen must be of some antiquity, although it is only in Belgium and neighbouring parts of France that it has become classic – in the dishes known as *carbonnades*. Belgian cooks are insistent that the correct type of beer must be used, as well as the strong local onions. Authentic *carbonnade à la flamande* is beef cooked in the strongly-hopped Belgian beer, *lambic de gueuze* or simply *La Gueuze*. The same beer is used as a liquid in which to cook pike (*brochet à la gueuze*). On the other hand, with *carbonnade à la wallonne*, which is sweet and black with prunes, the beer used must be *diest noire*.

Locally, in Britain, people cook shin of beef in mild beer, and there are a number of recipes using Guinness stout, one of which, Mr Guinness's Cake, is a popular version of the older porter cake of Ireland and the West Country. Beer is also used in many cures for ham and as a medium in which ham is cooked. Some of the famous German sweet soups, which are served either hot or cold, are made from beer or beer and milk; a mild, sweetish beer is usually best for these.

Beer is a relatively cheap and handy ingredient with which to experiment in the kitchen, although as a cooking medium it is not greatly admired by most French chefs.

In Britain, the home brewing of beer for personal consumption was freed from tax and restriction in 1963 and, once more, many people brew their own beer. A similar development may be expected in the US where excise duty on home brewing was not lifted until 1979.

Carbonnade à la Flamande

Trim a 1.5 kg (¾ lb) piece of stewing beef and cut it into 5 cm (2 in) cubes. Thinly slice 5-6 medium onions and cook them gently in fat or oil until they become opaque but not brown. Remove them from the pan. Now heat the fat until it is almost smoking. Dredge the cubes of meat in flour seasoned with salt and pepper, and quickly brown them, a handful at a time, in the fat, adding more fat if needed. Return all the meat to the pan, put the onions back on top of the beef, and add 0.5 lt (scant 1 pt) each of beef broth and beer, 2-3 cloves of crushed garlic and a *bouquet garni* of thyme, parsley and bay leaves. (The more flavourful the beer, the richer the gravy will be.)

Simmer the stew for 1-1½ hours, or until the meat is tender. Remove the *bouquet garni*, add 2 teaspoons each of sugar and vinegar, and continue the simmering for a further few minutes. If there is too much gravy at this stage, pour it, without the meat or onions, into a saucepan and boil it up until there is enough to half-cover the stew. Pour it over the meat and onions, adjust the seasoning and serve with boiled potatoes.

Mr Guinness's Cake

Cream together 225 g (8 oz) each of butter and soft brown sugar until they are light and creamy. Gradually beat in 4 lightly beaten eggs. Sieve together 350 g (10 oz) plain flour with 2 level teaspoons of mixed spices and fold this into the butter mixture. Stir in 225 g (8 oz) each of seedless raisins and sultanas, and 100 g (4 oz) each of mixed peel and chopped walnuts. Mix together well. Stir in 4 tablespoons of Guinness and mix all to a soft, dropping consistency. Grease and flour an 18 cm (7 in) round deep tin and turn the batter into it. Bake it at 160°C (325°F, Gas Mark 3) for 1 hour. Then reduce the heat to 150°C (300°F, Gas Mark 2) and cook it for another 1½ hours. When the cake is done, allow it to become cold before taking it from the tin. Prick the base of the cake with a skewer and spoon a further 4-8 tablespoons of Guinness over it. Keep the cake for a week before eating it.

[*Beer* – French: *bière* German: *Bier* Italian: *birra* Spanish: *cerveza*]

BEESTINGS, **biestings** or **colostrum**. The thick, albuminous milk produced by the newly-calved cow. It is quite unlike normal milk and sets (or clots) when heated, rather like a custard. Beestings is traditional in farm recipes for making special curds and puddings, even a baked, fresh cheese. It is not normally sold, but might be obtained direct from a dairy farm. Recipes for using beestings can be found in *Farmhouse Fare*, a collection of recipes from The Farmer's Weekly (Hulton Press).

[*Beestings* – French: *amouille* German: *Biestmilch* Italian: *colostro* Spanish: *calostro*]

BEETS belong to the family Chenopodiaceae, which include some important edible plants, such as spinach, orache, Good King Henry and *quinoa* (grown for its seed and a staple in Ecuador, Bolivia and Peru). The beets are all varieties of one species, *Beta vulgaris*, of which the wild one, subspecies *maritima*, grows on seashores in many places from Britain through to Asia. This is known locally as sea spinach; its leaves, gathered from clean shores and cooked like spinach, are delicious. It is from Mediterranean, North African stock of subspecies *valgaris* that our cultivated types seem to have been derived. One of them, sugar beet, is of no gastronomic value, but of immense importance industrially in the production of sugar.

Beetroot. Although beets (var. *esculenta*) have been selected for their roots for over a thousand years, it is only in the last 150 that we have had the tender, uniform roots we know today. The 1633 edition of Gerard's *Herbal* illustrates some very rough specimens and says that red beets brought into England from abroad were then treated with grave suspicion, so most of them were presumably white. It was not until the early years of the 19th century that Vilmorin, the famous French plant breeder, put beetroot properly on the gastronomic map. Even today, in Spain and other places where the seed is not always good, it is possible to experience what those old beetroots must have been like – anything from orange to white, with a tough, fibrous core and a nasty, earthy, over-sweet taste like sugar beet. Beetroots are an important bulk vegetable in Poland and Russia, but elsewhere are consumed only in small quantities. Nutritionally, they are rich in sugar, in potassium and in betain, a substance which the body seems to be able to use to replace choline, and which has been claimed to have some beneficial effect against cancer. There are a number of different shapes – spherical, top-shaped or cylindrical – and choice is merely a matter of preference.

When handling and cooking beetroot, do

everything you can to minimize their bleeding. Tops should be twisted off, not cut, and the beetroots should be washed gently to avoid breaking off rootlets or damaging the skin. Some prefer to bake them in a moderate oven, but they may be boiled or steamed; perhaps they are most conveniently cooked in a pressure cooker. A dash of vinegar (1 tablespoon per 1 lt – 2 pt – of water) helps keep the colour red. It is best to remove the skin when the beetroots are hot, after dipping them in cold water to make them possible to handle. The skins will then slip off. Raw, grated beetroot has a pleasant, nutty taste. Cooked beetroot is commonly dressed with something sour, such as vinegar or lemon juice, or mixed with apple, sour grapes or sour cream, as sourness counteracts the rather earthy taste. Other combinations are sweet-sour (e.g. with red currant jelly). Beetroot goes with allspice, cloves, caraway, mustard, horseradish, celery, onion, chives, garlic and capers. If it is simply dressed as a salad, a good olive oil with the vinegar makes all the difference, but is frequently neglected in Britain. In the US, two popular ways of serving beetroots are hot with melted butter, and cold in a sweet-sour sauce (Harvard Beets). As beetroot bleeds, some aesthetic consideration should be given before combining it with other ingredients in salads.

The red juice can be used as a dye, even in icing for cakes. For that purpose, grate the beets raw, soak them in lemon juice and squeeze the juice out in a cloth. If the juice is extracted this way, then concentrate by boiling (not too long, or the colour will go brown) and well soured, its earthy taste is not noticed.

To store beetroots, put them in a box, right way up, and cover them with dry sand, soil or peat. They must be kept dry or they will sprout or become mildewed.

Spinach Beet. This plant (var. *cicla*) is the form grown for its leaves. There are also well-known varieties developed for their thick stalks and midribs and known as chard, Swiss chard or seakale beet (the leaf stalks look vaguely like those of seakale and are often eaten separately as a vegetable in their own right). Dark green types with red ribs and stalks are called rhubarb chard in the US. The common leafy form is a popular vegetable in the Mediterranean countries, as it produces a continuous heavy crop of green leaves during the winter and spring; it is often seen growing wild (as an escape) on building sites near the sea. Like all beets with a seashore ancestry, it likes salty soil. Beet

leaves contain much less oxalic acid that do those of their near relative, spinach, so are probably more beneficial as food. Although spinach appears good when analysed, the oxalic acid tends to lock up the iron. Children who detest any sort of spinach can occasionally be induced to eat spinach beet but real spinach is generally regarded by adults as tasting better. Raw beet leaves do not taste very nice, though they are wholesome enough. The leaves of beetroot can also be cooked and eaten.

[*Beet* – French: *betterave, navet* German: *Rübe, Runkelrübe* Italian: *bietola* Spanish: *betarraga*

Beetroot – French: *bette rouge* German: *rote Rübe* Italian: *barbabietola* Spanish: *remolacha*

Spinach beet – French: *carde* German: *Mangold* Italian: *bietola da coste* Spanish: *acelgo*]

BELL PEPPER. *See* sweet pepper.

BELUGA. *See* caviar.

BENGAL GRAM. *See* channa.

BENZOIC ACID. *See* preservatives.

BERGAMOT. *See* orange.

BESAN FLOUR. In Indian cookery, fine flour made by grinding *channa. It can be bought from shops which specialize in Indian foodstuffs or made at home by grinding chickpeas and sieving out the husks. If you are trying to do the grinding in a whirling-type coffee mill, the chickpeas must be crushed first or they may break the blades. *Besan* flour is a pale creamy yellow. It is high in protein and very nutritious. Mixed with water, it forms a batter much used in India for coating food for frying, to make such dishes as *bhajias* (or their North Indian equivalents, *pakoras*) and *bondas* (spiced potato balls coated in *besan* batter and fried). It also appears in *dahi* (sour curd or yoghurt) curries as a stabilizer and thickener, in spicy snacks such as *murukas*, and in various sweetmeats. Although a stranger to non Indian kitchens, *besan* has a number of uses, for example in thickening soups.

Bhajias

Make a thick batter with *besan* flour (or half *besan*, half rice flour) and water, flavouring it with salt, chilli powder and a pinch of asafoetida. Other mixtures contain garlic, fresh ginger, chilli, cloves and cinnamon. Into the batter dip lightly-salted onion rings, whole seeded fresh green chillies, strips of sweet pepper, potato slices, salted aubergine slices, spinach leaves – and any other bits of vegetable you wish. Deep fry them until they are crisp. Drain on absorbent paper and serve hot as an appetizer.

BETEL LEAF is the leaf of the betel vine (*Piper betel*), a very close relation of the pepper vine (*P. nigrum*) that produces black pepper. Although sometimes the cassia leaf (related to cinnamon) is chewed in the Orient, it is the betel leaf that is the usual wrapping of *pan and the selection of the leaf is of social as well as gastronomic significance in India.

BETEL NUT or **areca nut**. The astringency in a *pan or betel chewing is provided by betel nuts, which come from tall, very slender palms (*Areca catechu*). Originally from Malaysia, this palm is common enough in most tropical areas today. To get the nuts, which grow in bunches of a hundred or more, a man has to climb the trees – an acrobatic feat. The nuts may be harvested when green for tender nuts (*chikni* in India) or when ripe (*chali*) and orange or scarlet. The nut is encased in a husk and is about the size and shape of a nutmeg, with ivory-white meat veined with intricate folds of brown. The tender nuts are shelled, boiled to extract the tannin, and dried in the sun. The ripe nuts are dried in the husk without boiling and then shelled. Betel nut whole, cracked or as a paste can be bought in Indian food shops. It may be chewed alone or mixed with sugar and spices in the absence of *betel leaf.

[*Betel nut* – French: *noix d'arec* German: *Arecanuss* Italian: *noce di areca* Spain: *nuez de areca*]

BEURRE MANIÉ. *See* binding.

BHANG. *See* religious food laws (Hindus).

BHARTI. *See* millet.

BIANCO DI SPAGNA. A variety of *kidney bean.

BIBLELEAF. *See* costmary.

BICARBONATE OF SODA, **sodium bicarbonate**, or **baking soda** ($NaHCO_3$). In old books, this common kitchen chemical is often called 'carbonate of soda', which, strictly speaking,

is *washing soda. When strongly heated to 270°C (518°F), it gives off water and carbon dioxide to change to the carbonate, but such temperatures are not usually reached in cooking. It also effervesces strongly, giving off a fizz of carbon dioxide gas, when mixed with an acid solution. This is the reaction which enables bicarbonate of soda to be used as a leavening agent, the acid being sometimes supplied by buttermilk, lemon juice or cream of tartar (*see* baking powder).

In every case, the bicarbonate of soda should be mixed in just before baking as otherwise the gas is lost. It effervesces rather slowly with cream of tartar, but much more quickly with lemon juice or an acid like tartaric acid. A strong reaction of this sort occurs, for instance, in Eno's Fruit Salts which I have seen being used as a baking powder in India.

As an *alkali, bicarbonate of soda can be used instead of lime in softening the skin of maize for making *masa, or added to the water in which chickpeas and other pulses are cooked or soaked in order to soften the skins and to make them more digestible. A pinch may be added to the water for cooking cabbage or cabbage greens, as it gives them an attractive green colour. It does, however, neutralize and destroy the vitamins B, and C. One less-known use of bicarbonate of soda is in the Romanian skinless sausages called *mititei*, which are flavoured also with ground caraway seed and garlic.

The bicarbonate tenderizes the meat, puffs it up a little and gives a strong, unusual and slightly ammoniac taste to the sausage. The use of bicarbonate of soda in water as a remedy for acid indigestion is not much recommended, but in an emergency does little harm to healthy people.

[*Bicarbonate of soda* – French: *bicarbonate de soude* German: *doppelkohlensaures Salz, Bikarbonat* Italian: *bicarbonato* Spanish: *bicarbonato de soda*]

BIERWURST is a German slicing sausage which should be rather coarse in texture. It may be spiced with juniper berries and cardamom and sometimes flavoured with garlic. A common component in selections of German cold cuts, it derives its name (literally 'beer sausage') from the fact that it was once made with ham that had been marinated in beer. *Bierschinken* is similar but contains pieces of ham.

BIESTINGS. *See* beestings.

BILBERRY. *See* cranberry.

BILTONG. This dried meat (from the Dutch *bil* =

buttock, *tong* = tongue) was originally a food of the South African pioneers as they trekked northwards from the Cape. It consisted of dried strips of meat cut from game, ostriches, even failing draught oxen. The American equivalent is *charqui* or jerked beef.

To make *biltong*, lean meat is cut in long strips 2.5 x 5 cm (1 x 2 in) along the grain of the muscle. It is salted, often well spiced with pepper and hung to dry in a current of air, away from flies and in a shady place. Sometimes it is hung so that it is touched by the smoke of the camp fire. It may be marinated for 3 days in a dry-salting mixture of 450 g (1 lb) salt, 50 g (2 oz) sugar and 25 g (1 oz) saltpetre before rubbing with spices and drying. The surface is often wiped with vinegar. The quality of *biltong* varies from deliciously meaty and with the consistency of good plug tobacco to a dry, fibrous material like old shoe leather. It is best cut in very thin slices and chewed with the sundowner.

BINDING. In cooking, materials are bound together by substances which set when heated, or occasionally by jellies, which set when cold. In the first category come protein substances which are coagulated by heat – egg, blood and the gluten of flour would be examples – while the second includes gelatine, agar-agar and starch jellies which set on cooling.

Excessive use of binding agents results in a tough, heavy, leathery, sometimes barely edible product, and the skill of the cook lies in sailing as close to the wind as possible – too little binding and the structure disintegrates. An Austrian chef once advised me: 'If your bread dumpling falls to pieces when you poach it [as a test], you can always add some flour. That is what they do in *Gasthaus* kitchens where they can't cook, if they add too much flour, they make little cannon balls – to throw at the chef.' Adding too much binding agent is a common error in hotel kitchens. On one occasion when I had rather foolishly undertaken to make a *kofta* (meatball) curry for 150 people, I expressed concern to the Spanish chef who was helping me that with such a quantity the meatballs would collapse and we would finish with a mess. He looked at me patronizingly, grabbed the flour bin and tipped several kilos into the mixture. 'Now they will remain whole,' he said confidently. He was certainly right. But the most feather-weight and delicious *quenelles*, meatballs, *pâtés* and other creations which need binders are made by cooks who with subtlety and skill are able to reduce

binding substances to almost nothing.

The word 'binding' is also used to describe the thickening of sauces, as with *beurre manié* (an intimate mixture of flour and butter which chefs keep at hand to bind sauces quickly), egg, blood or cornflour.

BINDONE. *See* salame.

BINGLEBERRY. *See* raspberry.

BIRDS. (Domestic and game birds have individual entries, as have peacock, ostrich, swan and pigeon.) Wild birds of many other kinds were commonly eaten in the past. Eating them was a necessity to colonists in the New World and to the poor in Europe. In places like St Kilda, survival without a harvest of sea birds would have been impossible. In British markets, a variety of birds were sold, especially water birds and species that were easily shot or netted. Amongst them were bitterns, whimbrels, curlews, lapwings and other plovers, spoonbills, herons, redshanks, knots, greenshanks, godwits, ruffs, stints, dunlins, dotterels, moorhens, coots, corncrakes, water rails, cormorants, fulmars, gannets, herring gulls, black-headed gulls, puffins, rooks, jays, starlings, blackbirds, thrushes, wheatears, fieldfares, larks – and many more. As food, some were nice and some were not. A few, if kept on an artificial diet for a while, would improve in flavour. Seagulls kept on bread and scraps lost their fishy taste. Others had first to be skinned. It was even claimed that certain birds – wild geese for instance – would lose their fishy taste if buried in the ground for a few hours. (Some friends advise that a cock capercaillie is much improved by this treatment, especially if you forget where you buried it.)

Today, many birds which were once eaten freely, have become rare and are protected. Others are still used as food in some countries but not in others. Few will see harm in a *salmis* of moorhen served in some country restaurant in the Camargue, but it is another matter when birds are sent in thousands to town markets. If larger grain-eating, running or swimming birds are seriously wanted for the table, then some enterprising person will start to breed them. But this does not happen with the smaller birds, especially if they eat insects. Most notable amongst the wild birds regarded as delicacies are thrushes, ortolans, warblers and larks. These are birds which flock together in autumn or migrate southwards to winter quarters in Africa. In either case, they are then in large groups and are easily netted or caught with bird lime. They are caught either as they come southwards through France and Italy, or when they land to rest on Mediterranean islands such as Cyprus, Sardinia, Sicily and the Balearics. Such small birds have to be consumed in quantity as each bird is little more than a mouthful.

Choosing to eat game birds – grouse, pheasant or partridge – but not lark or thrush, is not merely a question of sentiment. Game birds are controlled, encouraged and even bred for shooting, but every adult male from Biscay to the Adriatic seems to be armed with a shotgun, and blasts away at everything that moves (including his own kind). The birds are decimated every year. It is heartbreaking to see a sack of small birds, which have been shot indiscriminately, dumped on a kitchen table. One may watch the wife sorting them through, discarding a crossbill here and a rare warbler there among the assortment of kinds she does not recognize or relish.

Garden warblers (*Sylvia borin*) and Lesser whitethroats (*Sylvia curruca*) are the main warblers among the victims but other species get caught on bird lime or nets. These little birds migrate southwards in autumn and are caught particularly in the South of France, Corsica, Sardinia, Sicily, Cyprus and Greece. They are plucked and singed, sometimes drawn and sometimes not, but the feet are usually cut off. They are then cooked in various ways and eaten whole, beak and all. In France, they are brushed with butter and wrapped in vine leaves for cooking. Elizabeth David (*Italian Food*) mentions them put inside *ovole* (*Amanita caesarea*), those beautiful orange mushrooms related to the death cap. In Sicily, they are sometimes cooked inside hollowed-out onions, with the top put back so that they are steamed in an atmosphere of onion vapour. In northern Italy, they are generally served with polenta, usually after grilling on skewers (in the company of robins and other small birds); in Cyprus and Greece, they are even pickled. One is expected to chomp the whole bird, head, beak and all.

Skylarks (*Alauda arvensis*) flock together in autumn, when the birds are very fat. Thousands used to be netted each year and sold in markets both in Britain and in continental Europe. The flesh of larks is excellent. They are probably best known these days as the basis for the famous Pithiviers lark *pâté*.

Song thrushes (*Turdus philomelos*) and Mistle thrushes (*Turdus viscivorus*) are netted in huge numbers each autumn when they run the Mediterranean bird gauntlet on their way south. In Majorca, for instance, people start out before dawn with huge V-shaped clap nets to go to the tops of the mountains. At dawn, they are in position with nets spread, waiting for the flights of migrating thrushes to come in. Thrushes are still commonly sold in the market. In Spain they are stuffed with sweet white grapes, wrapped in cabbage leaves and braised. Thrushes taste good, but not sensational, and surely only a deaf man could ever prefer a thrush on a plate or in a *pâté de grives*.

The Ortolan bunting (*Emberiza hortulana*) is widely celebrated for the delicacy of its flesh, while its fat is, in the opinion of many gourmets, almost the equal of that of the green turtle. The birds were once netted annually with a decoy in many thousands, put in dark rooms (which kept them quiet) and fattened on millet and oatmeal, until, in the words of one old author, they became 'mere lumps of fat weighing three ounces'. At this point, they were killed. Today, they are a particular speciality of the Landes and are sometimes to be found in cages behind the restaurants that serve them. Sometimes ortolans are merely beheaded and have only the crop removed before being cooked with the insides (trail) intact; they may also be drawn and stuffed with *foie gras* or a delicate forcemeat, or threaded on skewers between slices of toast (to catch their fat) before being grilled. There are also very elaborate recipes in which ortolans are cooked in hollowed-out black truffles and served with a Madeira sauce. Like warblers, they are eaten beak and all if they are whole, merely cut into two by the diner 'like a sausage and just as tender'. They may even be boned and stuffed, a job requiring total dedication to gastronomic art.

[*Birds* – French: *oiseaux* German: *Vogel* Italian: *uccelli* Spanish: *pájaros*]

BIRD'S NEST. 'Among the many travellers' tales which called forth such ridicule from sceptical readers of early voyages, the accounts of the Chinese cuisine were held to be amongst the most extravagant ... that the Chinese should make soup out of birds' nests, was an absurdity so self-evident that it destroyed all possibility of faith... the reader having no conception of the possibility that a bird's nest could be made of anything but sticks, moss, mud and feathers.' (The Revd J.G. Wood's *Natural History*, 1861.)

The birds (of the genus *Collocalia*) that make the nests used for soup are similar to swifts. One of the species was named the Edible swallow, as if it were the bird one ate. The birds nest in colonies in stupendous caverns in South East Asia – Java, Malaya, Thailand, the Philippines – and, like swallows, stick their nests to the rocky walls and ceilings. They make them, however, not of mud but of a gelatinous spit which they secrete for the purpose. Collecting the nests in semi-darkness and the stink from the droppings that cover the cavern floor is dangerous work. It is like scraping a cathedral roof while balancing on a sweep's pole. There are two main categories of nest, black and white. Black nests are the cheaper, but are full of debris and need a lot of cleaning to make them edible. The white nests are clean and are more expensive. There are numerous grades, the best being the most absorbent and therefore swelling more when soaked. First-grade nests are whole, almost white cups with little in the way of feathers and foreign matter. Second grade, or Dragon's teeth, are bits of broken nest, and the third grade is made of fragments pressed into cakes. Nests from different areas are also assessed on their own merits by experts and are even used for distinct purposes.

Basic preparation depends on what the nests are to be used for – soup, stuffings or sweets – but one method is to clean them, soak them overnight, remove any feathers, then boil them for 10 minutes and rinse. To most of us, however, birds' nests are fragments of translucent material, a bit like dried seaweed, bought ready prepared in a packet from a Chinese provision shop. Exhortations such as 'use half a nest per person' or 'one should use nests in the year in which they are gathered' are superfluous when directions are printed on the pack. The sense of adventure has gone, but the results are probably better for it.

[Bird's nest – French: *nid d'oiseau* German: *Vögelnest* Italian: *nido di uccello* Spanish: *nido de pájaro*]

BISCUIT. In Britain, this is the general collective word for all sorts of flat, thin, dryish baked goods, and it causes some confusion when people try to translate it into other languages, in which it cannot be rendered by a single word. Even Americans have the words cookie and cracker to cover the field. What appear at first sight to be the equivalents in French, Italian and Spanish are not so except in the original meaning of the word.

The word biscuit came from the French, and meant 'twice cooked', as also did the Italian *biscotto*, the Spanish *bizcocho* and the German *Zwieback*. It referred to what we might call ship's biscuits – army biscuits, hard tack, *biscuits de guerre*

– the very dry, bone-hard, little slabs of cooked flour and water paste made to keep for ever and ever (unless destroyed by seawater or weevils) on voyages in old sailing ships. So hard were biscuits that they had to be soaked before use, and many an ancient mariner has broken his teeth on them. Ship's biscuits have long been extinct (I used to buy them with difficulty from the Army and Navy Stores to take climbing) and would cause a mutiny on a modern ship. In French, *biscuit* is now used for several sorts of baked goods, including some we would call sponge cake (so a cake tin is *un moulard de biscuit*). The Italian equivalent is *biscoccia*, while the word *biscotto* (and the French *biscotte*) often indicates a sort of rusk, though there are biscuit-like cakes from Genoa and Sardinia that bear that name (*biscotti sardi, biscotti di san martino, biscotti del lagaccio* – or simply *lagaccio*), often covered with fennel or anise seeds and intended for long keeping in a tin. In Spanish, *bizcocho* can mean a rusk or toasted bread, but is also applied to mixtures of flour, eggs and sugar cooked in the oven which are in some cases a kind of biscuit (*bizcochos de avellanas* with hazel nuts), but equally a sort of cake (*bizcocho de chocolate*) to be served with cream, or even something like a sponge (the Cuban *bizcocho relleno al ron* filled with jam and sprinkled with rum). The German *Zwieback* is a very popular kind of rusk. In 17th-century English recipes, references to French biscuit indicate sponge cake.

BISHOP'S WEED. *See* ajowan.

BIVALVES. The *oysters, *mussels, *cockles, *clams, *razor shells, *scallops and so on – molluscs with two shells hinged together and closed by strong muscles. They may bury themselves in sand or mud and move laboriously by a foot, attach themselves to rocks with threads like the mussel, bore into rocks like the sea date or even swim by flapping their shells like scallops. Most bivalves are edible, but they are sometimes responsible for poisoning or spreading infections, as they feed by filtering out particles from the water and may pick up pathogenic bacteria from sewage or poisonous plankton. Undisturbed shells gape to allow entry of food and oxygenated water, but if a bivalve still gapes when it is disturbed, do not eat it because it is dead or dying. A healthy bivalve indeed closes tight as a clam.

[Bivalves – French: *bivalves* German: *zweischalige Muscheln* Italian: *bivalvi* Spanish: *bivalvos*]

BLACHAN. *See* balachong.

BLACK BEAN. *See* kidney bean.

BLACKBERRY or **bramble**. Blackberries and the very similar dewberries (which are less prickly and have fruit with the same bluish lustre as black plums) belong to the genus *Rubus*, in the rose family. The genus also includes the raspberry. The dewberry is *Rubus caesius*, and botanists originally called the blackberry *R. fructicosus*. A recent monograph, however, distinguishes 386 species of blackberry and there is a similarly complicated situation in North America. Even the distinction between blackberry and raspberry becomes clouded outside Europe, where the names originated to describe the fruit growing there. There is even a black raspberry in eastern Canada and the US. Other relatives do not look exactly like blackberries or raspberries – the cloudberry (*R. chamaemorus*), for example, is orange.

A berry which I came on one day when hot and thirsty in the Himalayas (and which has stayed in my mind as one of the most delicious fruits I have ever eaten) was beyond question a *Rubus*, but I have never discovered exactly what it was.

There is considerable natural hybridization between the species. The best-known hybrid is the loganberry, a natural hybrid between a blackberry and a raspberry, which was first found in California. The cultivated varieties of blackberry are large, juicy and often seedless. It is doubtful whether they can ever become very popular because they command the same price as raspberries in the shops and are equally perishable, so most people will prefer the raspberry's more delicious flavour. Cultivated blackberries also suffer in popularity from being no better than the best wild ones, which can be gathered free from the hedgerows in summer. However, wild ones can be so seedy as to be fit only for jelly. Seedy blackberry and apple pie is one of the supreme horrors of British cooking. A linguistic warning: the same word is used in French, Spanish and Italian for both blackberries and black mulberries (which are of course a different fruit altogether).

[*Blackberry* – French: *mûre* German: *Brombeer* Italian: *mora selvatica* Spanish: *mora, zarzamora*]

BLACK CURRANT. *See* currant.

BLACK-EYED PEA or **black-eyed bean**. *See* cowpea.

BLACK GRAM, **urd**, or **mash** (*Phaseolus mungo*) is a pulse about half the size of a pea, and usually has a black seedcoat, though this is sometimes green, which can lead to confusion with the green gram or *mung bean. However, when split for *dal*, the mung bean is yellow while the flesh of the black gram is white. This is especially obvious in the expensive *dhuli urd* from which any black flecks of husk have been washed out. It is exceedingly important in Indian cooking and is grown and used all over the sub-continent, but especially in the north-west, the Punjab, where in winter it is eaten as a daily food. It is very nutritious – 'heating', they say in South India – and so is more suitable for cold weather, though a bit stodgy and difficult to digest. Black gram is best cooked without prior soaking. It takes longer to soften than either *mung bean or *pigeon pea (*tur*), and it does not mix readily into its water. Usually the most costly pulse, black gram is nonetheless essential in a number of important dishes. Roasted, it goes into the mixtures for flavouring vegetarian curries. Soaked and ground to a paste, it is one of the ingredients of the classic *idlis* and *dosas* of South India, and is also the usual basis for poppadoms.

BLACK JACK. *See* browning.

BLACK PUDDING, **blood pudding** or **blood sausage**. 'Yet who would have thought the old man to have so much blood in him', Macbeth, Act IV, Scene 1. Anyone who has attended a village *matanza* (pig-killing feast) in Spain, a survival of something which in medieval times went on all over Europe, will not easily forget this quotation. The wretched pig, cherished lovingly through the summer and the autumn nut season, is suddenly betrayed to enable its owners to survive during the coming winter. Every part is precious; nothing can be wasted. The blood does not keep well, but drained and mixed with cereal, onion, fat, salt and spices it can be made into blood sausages or black puddings.

Variations on this theme exist in every country in Europe and have emigrated to America. In Britain, commercial black puddings are often too heavily padded with cereal – barley, oatmeal, flour and rusk. Their flavouring is undistinguished, and in most places the results are deservedly not very popular, although better may be had from individual butchers in the north of England, where the blood puddings are traditionally flavoured with pennyroyal. Sometimes in Scotland they are made with sheep's blood. The *boudins noirs* of France, those glossy black sausages one sees in the *charcutier*, which are cheap only in comparison to most of the other pork butcher's products, are made with finer ingredients than their English counterparts. They contain a smaller proportion of cereal and usually some cream. They are correspondingly more delicious, although, as a north-countryman, I like to make blood sausages with the French materials and the distinctive English pennyroyal flavouring. Black puddings keep only a few days in the refrigerator but may be frozen. Although cooked when made, most versions are intended to be eaten sliced and fried, or cooked according to local recipes.

Black pudding

Mix together pig's blood (which has been salted and stirred until cold) and oatmeal (which has been soaked overnight in water), in the proportion 1 lt (1¾ pt) blood to 1 lt (1¾ pt) oatmeal. Grate 1.5 kg (scant 3½ lb), or a bit less, of bread, soak it well in 1.75 lt (3 pt) of hot milk, and add it to the blood mixture. Add 800 g (1¾ lb) chopped suet, 400 g (14 oz) *flair fat and a seasoning of onion (grated), thyme, pennyroyal, and 1 teaspoon each ground spices (allspice and ginger), 5 cloves, and half a small nutmeg (grated).

Half-fill large sausage skins (which leaves room for the oatmeal to swell) and simmer them gently for an hour. The skins must be pricked occasionally to let out trapped air. When the puddings are done, the juice which comes out on pricking is clear. Take them out of the pan and allow them to cool. Commercial black puddings are dyed black, so home-made black puddings do not have the same slick appearance as commercial ones.

Boudin noir. Apart from pig's blood, this contains varying amounts of fat, cream, onion, and maybe *quatre épices*. There are many local variants, e.g. *de Poitou* containing spinach, *de Lyon* with herbs and brandy, *aux pommes, aux marrons, à l'ail* containing apple, chestnut and garlic respectively, as well as many other additions to the basic mixture.

Blutwurst. German blood sausage is made of blood with pork and bacon fat, which show when it is cut, and flavoured with marjoram and allspice. Unlike other blood sausages, it is intended for eating cold in slices, but is also good fried.

Sanguinaccio is the Italian blood sausage. It is large, rounded and tied in a net of thread.

BLACKSTRAP. Another name for *molasses.

BLADDER CHERRY. *See* physalis fruit.

BLAEBERRY. *See* cranberry.

BLANCHING. To blanch something, put it into boiling water, or bring water with the ingredient in it to the boil for a relatively short time. In practice, the name is given to several rather different operations. Blanching can mean:

1. To whiten and harden meat and temper its flavour, as when slices of bacon are blanched before adding to a delicately-flavoured dish, when rabbit is blanched to whiten the meat or joints are blanched to harden them before larding.

2. To set the colour and partly cook vegetables in the French method: vegetables are first cooked for a short time in boiling water, then refreshed in ice-cold water to cool them quickly, drained and finally heated again in butter or cream.

3. To dip vegetables or bundles of herbs into boiling water for various lengths of time before freezing in order to destroy and inactivate enzymes and to set colour.

4. To make it easy to remove skins. Peaches and tomatoes should be dipped in boiling water for a few seconds only; oranges, for ½ -1 minute. Nuts, like almonds and hazels, are usually covered with boiling water and left to soak only for long enough for the skins to become soft and easy to slip off. Chickens' feet can be peeled after leaving in boiling water for 10 seconds – no more. The skin of tongue and salt pork requires much longer to loosen it, and the operation is usually begun in cold water which is brought to the boil. Onions for pickling need 12-14 seconds blanching, then cooling in cold water, before skinning.

When boiling water is poured over something, this is known as scalding, but the word also describes bringing milk or cream almost to the boil. To a gardener, blanching means whitening vegetables (e.g. celery) by depriving them of light, for example by banking up earth over them.

[*Blanching* – French: *blanchir* German: *abkochen*

Italian: *imbiancare* Spanish: *emblanquecer*]

BLENDING. The dictionary definition is 'mixing together, especially intimately and harmoniously', and that applies in cooking. But the word has other specialized meanings – a blended, as opposed to straight whisky; a blend, as in 'our own blend of tea', meaning a formula. The word is also applied to operations carried out by the modern electric blender, and in that case implies reducing ingredients to a fine state of suspension in a liquid, even to an emulsion.

[*Blending* – French: *mélanger* German: *mischen* Italian: *mischiare* Spanish: *mezclar*]

BLOATER. *See* herring.

BLOOD. The Masai tribe might be called the vampires of East Africa; they drink fresh blood (sometimes mixed with milk) warm from the cow, and it is partly to this diet that they owe their marvellous, slender figures. It is also a very humane practice as it involves no killing. They take blood by tying a cord round the neck of one of their cattle, just tight enough to cause the jugular vein to swell, but not to cause distress, and then shoot, at point-blank range, a small arrow with a blunt end armed with two pins into the vein. They have a tiny bow especially for the purpose. From the two small punctures thus made (I doubt Dracula was so neat), a pint or so of blood is collected. Afterwards, mud is rubbed on the puncture to stop the bleeding, and the animal is released with no more harm than is suffered by a human donor to the blood bank. One might recommend the practice to vegetarians who eat eggs and cheese or drink milk. As blood coagulates very quickly, it must be well stirred or beaten with twigs immediately it is drawn.

Blood is much used in traditional country cooking. Pigs' blood, not to be wasted, goes into *black pudding and related sausages. For really hearty food, it can be substituted for egg in a batter to make blood pancakes which few, other than Scandinavians, can tolerate. (The Norwegian cook on the Antarctic expedition I was with years ago used to make excruciating pancakes out of seals' blood.) Chickens' blood is the correct medium for thickening the sauce of a *coq au vin*. It needs careful collecting in a vessel which contains a little brandy and vinegar to prevent coagulation. There is really no substitute for blood in a *coq au vin* as other thickeners do not give the proper black, ointment-like sauce of a *coq au chambertin* as made in Dijon. Because sauces thickened with blood behave like sauces thickened with egg, they are likely to curdle if boiled.

In some European countries, especially in districts where there is still a robust, old-fashioned peasant style of cooking, blood which has been coagulated by boiling or baking is sold in shallow earthenware pans in the market. Even coagulated chickens' blood is offered for sale in small pots. Although some people try to reconstitute such coagulated blood by liquidizing it in the blender, it will not thicken sauces properly, as it is already coagulated. Baked blood – sold by weight – is mainly used in fried dishes of which the Spanish *sangre con cebolla* (blood with onion) or *sangre con pimientos* (blood with peppers) are typical examples. It is also put into the well-known *fritos mallorquine*.

....

Sangre con Cebolla

Put some oil in a frying pan with a few crushed cloves of garlic and plenty of onion which has been sliced lengthwise so that it retains its identity. When this is cooked to your liking, add some finely-chopped fennel, some small potato chips (already fried) and some pieces of baked blood. Mix together and continue frying until the blood and chips are nicely hot. Serve with grilled pork chops.

[*Blood* – French: *sang* German: *Blut* Italian: *sangue* Spanish: *sangre*]
....

BLOOD SAUSAGE or **blood pudding**. *See* black pudding.

BLUEBERRY. *See* cranberry.

BLUEPOINT. *See* oyster.

BLUTWURST. *See* black pudding.

BOAR. The wild pig (*Sus scropha*) occurs in deciduous and mixed forests and in scrub in many parts of Europe and Asia, but became extinct in Britain in the 17th century. European Boars grow to about 155 cm (5 ft), in Europe, but in some places, such as Kashmir, they grow to weigh over 300 kg (660 lb); at that size, one is capable of taking on a tiger. As wild boar is not bled like pork, the meat is dark. There is little fat, and the flesh can be dry and tough unless marinated and larded, but the flavour is excellent.

A Classic French Marinade for Boar

Take 100 g (4 oz) each of sliced onions and carrots, 2 shallots, a clove of garlic, a small stick of chopped celery and 4 sprigs of parsley. Colour all lightly in oil, then add 4 glasses of red wine, 1 glass of good wine vinegar, 1 teaspoon of salt, a few peppercorns, a large sprig of thyme and several bay leaves. Simmer this gently for 45 minutes, then strain it over the meat. After marinating for 24 hours, the meat can be cooked in any way liked. This marinade also suits hare and venison.

[*Boar* – French: *sanglier* German: *wildes Schwein* Italian: *cinghiale* Spanish: *jabalí*]

BOCKWURST. *See* frankfurter.

BOG MYRTLE or **sweet gale** (*Myrica gale*). Well known to all who tramp northern moors, and an important aromatic herb in the past, this is vaguely like bay, and possibly called for in old country recipes.

[*Bog myrtle* – French: *myrte des marais* German: *Gagel, Sumpfmyrte* Italian: *mirto* Spanish: *mirto holandés, arrayán*]

BOILING is an easily recognized reference point: it is the hottest water can get in an open pot. Go on boiling it over the fire and the extra heat is used up in changing the water into steam. Water boils – and stays boiling – at 100°C (212°F). The only way in which the temperature of boiling water can be raised above this is by adding sugar or salt (which will push it up a few degrees), by increasing the pressure (in a pressure cooker) or perhaps by carrying the cooking pot down to the Dead Sea. Conversely water boils at a lower temperature when pressure is reduced at a higher *altitude. (Himalayan climbers take pressure cookers with them. At about 6000 m or 20,000 ft, with less atmospheric pressure, water boils at only 80°C (176°F), ideal for simmering yak, but hopeless for making a decent cup of tea.) The effect of pressure on boiling point is made use of when water is extracted from delicate foodstuffs by evaporating under reduced pressure.

Although boiling is a common operation in cooking (because it is easily recognized without a thermometer), the temperature is often not ideal for cooking. For the proteins of fish or meat it is too high, and for vegetables not high enough. A quick blast of a higher temperature for vegetables preserves colour and vitamins better. Pressure cookers would undoubtedly be used more if they allowed the cook to prod, stir and observe the food while it cooked.

[*Boiling* – French: *bouillir* German: *sieden* Italian: *fare bollire* Spanish: *hacer hervir*]

Boiling points of water under pressure		°C	°F
1.05	kg/cm2 (15 lb/in²)	121°	250°
0.7	kg/cm2 (10 lb/in²)	155.5°	240°
0.35	kg/cm2 (5 lb/in²)	109°	228°
Atmospheric pressure (sea level)		100°	212°

BOLETUS. *See* cèpe.

BOLOGNA is the home of the *mortadella, but the name of the city is also used, particularly in the US, to mean a sausage of finely ground pork and beef that has been smoked and sometimes also simmered.

BOMBAY DUCK or **bummalo** (*Harpodon neherius*) are small, semi-transparent, peculiarly-shaped fishes, which live mainly in the Arabian Sea off the west coast of India, although they migrate elsewhere in search of food. They are fished from the end of the monsoon (October) to the end of January and are so plentiful (second only to mackerel) that only some 20% of the catch is eaten fresh. The rest is hung on racks on the beaches to dry in the hot tropical sun. The smell (mingled with drying ribbon fish and sandy mixtures of whitebait and prawns spread on mats) is like a fish-glue factory in full spate. It blows through the fishing villages of the Bombay coast: you can smell it on the breeze amongst the coconut palms or across the black mud of mangrove-bordered creeks. And this picturesque smell invades the kitchens of curry addicts the world over because Bombay duck is not only eaten around Bombay, but is exported. The dried fish is usually sold abroad in flat tins or packets. It keeps for a long time, provided it is kept dry and is usually eaten as a curry adjunct, either crisped in the oven or fried to the point where it can be crumbled over the rice. Some even like it as a cocktail snack with drinks. An excellent product for the many who like a high-fish taste.

BONAVIST BEAN. *See* lablab bean.

BONDIOLA. *See* coppo.

BONE forms the skeleton of vertebrate animals, apart from some fish, such as *sharks, which have skeletons of cartilage. Over half the weight of bones consists of calcium phosphate, an insoluble substance which is not broken down by boiling. The other main component of bone is collagen, a fibrous protein which gives it tensile strength. Boiling turns collagen into soluble gelatine, which will form a jelly on cooling. *Marrow bones of mammals are tubular, with soft marrow in the middle – they are limb bones, which need to resist bending, against which a tubular structure is mechanically the most effective. Many of the bones in birds have their cavities connected to the lungs so that they are filled with air, which makes for more efficient breathing and a lighter skeleton, both important in flying.

Closely attached to bone is a tough sheath, the periosteum, to which the tendons are attached. Bones, together with their accompanying cartilage and connective tissue (gristle), are used in cooking to make *stock. Bone is very dense, although it does contain canals connecting the cells and holes through which nerves and blood vessels pass. Extraction of soluble substances in stock making is therefore helped if the bones are well broken up with a hammer before boiling.

An important and often neglected use for bones is to keep food away from the bottom of the pan; this prevents sticking and at the same time makes a contribution to the flavour. For instance, chopped bones are used to cover the bottom of the pan under a pork roast in Austria and under stuffed vine leaves in Lebanon. This is a most useful practice, with many applications.

[Bone – French: *os* German: *Knochen* Italian: *osso* Spanish: *hueso*]

BONITO. Cooks and zoologists often fail to agree on the classification of fishes. Thus, the name bonito covers a number of distinct species, of which two are of culinary importance. The bonito or Atlantic bonito (*Sarda sarda*) is a larger relative of the mackerel – up to 70 cm (27 in) long and thus big enough to be sold cut into steaks for grilling. It has stripes along its back and is found in the Black Sea, the Mediterranean and both sides of the Atlantic. The skipjack (*Katsuwonus pelamis*), otherwise known as the Oceanic, California or Pacific bonito, is a smaller relative of the tuna – up to 80 cm (31 in) long. It has stripes along the belly and occurs in both the Atlantic and the Pacific; in the Mediterranean, it is mainly caught on the North African coast. It is cooked in the same way as other species of *tuna and emanates from Pacific canneries as tuna (or more precisely as skipjack tuna). In Japan, the skipjack is called *katsuo*, and dried fillets (*katsuobushi*) are a basic necessity in the preparation of foundation stocks or *dashi* which are made from *seaweed (*kombu*), shavings of *katsuobushi* and *monosodium glutamate (*ajino-moto*).

BOQUERONES. *Anchovies in Spanish, but usually referring to the fillets pickled in salt and vinegar – a popular Spanish snack. They are white and are commonly sold in boxes or loose by weight in markets. Anyone who likes roll-mops will like *boquerones*.

BORAGE (*Baraga officinalis*) is a herb that gives its name to a whole family, the Boraginaceae. It has a beautiful blue flower and is easily grown (it self-seeds) in any warm situation. A common wild flower of southern Europe, it is also found on chalk downs in southern England (where it was introduced by the Romans). Borage has a cucumber flavour and is a traditional part of the decorative garden put into a Pimms. It can be used in other drinks, but, to be frank, it will, if grown, be used mainly as decoration. The plant is very hairy, can hurt fingers and must be finely chopped if used in salads; it is considerably more trouble than cucumber. The best use for it is to boil it like spinach to make a stuffing for ravioli (as they do in Liguria) or to dip it in batter and fry it; both ways get rid of the prickly hairs. The flowers can be candied. Borage is reputed by herbalists to be very healthy and to give one courage, which, if true, could sometimes be useful.

[Borage – French: *bourrache* German: *Boretsch, Gurkenkraut* Italian: *borraggine, borana* Spanish: *borraja*]

BORECOLE. *See* kale.

BORIC ACID. *See* preservatives.

BORLOTTI BEAN. A variety of *kidney bean.

BORNHOLMERE. *See* herring.

BOTARGO, **botarega**, **botargue** or **poutarg**. *Botargo*, from the Arab *batarkhah* or *batarekh*, is the salted, pressed, dried female roe of either the tunny or the Striped Grey mullet. It is an old eastern Mediterranean delicacy, known even in ancient Egypt and still popular in that country; it is also a favourite in Italy; the Greek *tarama is virtually the same. In Britain, though it was popular in the 17th century, mentioned in Pepys' *Diary* (he was eating it with bread as a blotting paper during a heavy night's drinking) and served at James II's coronation, it is not well known today. In Victorian times, they called it *poutarg* (from the French). Today it is usually *botargo* and may be bought from shops which sell Levantine or Italian foods. If it is made from tunny roes, the pieces can weigh up to 7 kg (about 16 lb) – though usually from 2 to 5 kg (4½ to 11 lb) – and they look like large, square-sectioned sausages. When made from mullet roe, the pieces are much smaller, and usually each piece is squashed flat to only a few centimetres thick. The roes are in pairs, each one in its original membrane, and have usually been dipped in preservative wax. The colour varies between rose pink, dirty brown and translucent amber. *Botargo* is expensive and may be bought in the piece, by weight, sliced or packed as slices in oil. It is eaten as an *hors d'oeuvre*, *meze*, or snack with drinks. It can be served alone or with oil, which may be combined with a little vinegar or lemon juice plus freshly-ground black pepper or a pinch of finely-chopped parsley or cayenne pepper, according to taste. In Italy it is also grated over pasta or rice.

Botargo from tuna. This, as an example, is the Sicilian method. The roes are carefully removed, so as not to damage the membrane around them and they are put on a long table, covered with salt and left there for 2 days. Then a funnel is inserted into the duct and the sacs containing the roes are filled and irrigated several times with saturated brine. After that the roes are put into dry salt and left for another 2 days. When the salt is changed the next time, a clean board is placed on top and lightly weighted with stones. From then on, the salt is changed every day and the weight gradually increased, the only variation being that, after the first day, the sacs are pricked with beechwood skewers to promote drainage. The daily change of salt and increase in pressure is continued until the roe is completely impregnated, a period which varies according to size. When judged ready, the roes are washed in water and hung in a current of air to dry.

Botargo from grey mullet. The species of Grey mullet used for *botargo* is not usual in British waters, but in the US it is called the Striped or Black mullet (*Mugil cephalus*). *Botargo* from mullet is mainly made in Corsica, Sardinia and Tunisia, as well as in Egypt and Turkey. The following method is used in Sardinian homes. The roes are removed in pairs without breaking or puncturing the sacs. The pairs of roe are then well salted, pressed between boards and left for 2-3 days under a 5 kg (11 lb) weight. The roes, when pressed, are about 18 cm (7 in) long and 2 cm (¾ in) thick. After salting, they are hung in the shade to dry and when ready are dipped for an instant in molten wax. They must not be dried so much that they become powdery. In *A Book of Middle Eastern Food* (Penguin), Claudia Roden gives details of a *botargo* made from the frozen mullet roes which are sold out of barrels in Canada. As always, the membrane must be free from holes. The roes are rolled in fine kitchen salt and laid on absorbent paper. The salt is changed and the roes are turned whenever the papers become wet. This process continues until weeping stops altogether. Drying in air and dipping in wax is as before, or the *botargo* may be kept in the refrigerator in polythene bags.

BOTTLED SAUCES. Certain bottled sauces are commonly used as ingredients and flavourings in cooking, among them *tabasco, *tomato and *Worcestershire sauces. Most of the recipes for commercial sauces are trade secrets and may depend on the special quality of ingredients. It is not difficult to make good bottled table sauces at home (*see* ketchups). Those based on vinegar, salt and spices improve with maturation and keep almost indefinitely.

BOTTLING. The word covers filling bottles with liquids such as wine and preserving foodstuffs in glass jars under sterile conditions.

Filling bottles (mainly for wine). Try to get hold of the right bottles for the job. To force wine corks into bottles made without suitably strong necks is asking for trouble. Red wine should be put into dark bottles, unless it is certain to be kept in the dark. Uniform and correct bottles, properly labelled, also have aesthetic appeal. Bottles must be scrupulously clean inside. Stubborn deposits at the bottom may be removed by swishing round lead shot, fine gravel or sand with water, and a bottle brush deals with the neck. After cleaning, bottles must be thoroughly rinsed and inspected by holding them to the light and peering down the neck. Some advocate a final rinse in a sterilizing solution made with *Campden tablets, but this is hardly necessary. After washing, bottles should be stacked neck down to drain and dry. This keeps out bacteria, yeasts and dust. Bottles should be filled to leave only a small space between the surface and the cork (2 cm or ¾ in). New corks of good quality are best and should first be soaked in boiled water for 24 hours to soften them. If old corks have to be used, they must be in good condition – not pierced by the corkscrew – and should be boiled to sterilize them. Plastic stoppers are likely to pop out. Corks and stoppers may be tied down with string or wired. Bottles should be stored on their sides to keep the corks wet and swollen, so that they will not dry out and admit air and bacteria.

Preserving food in jars is essentially the same as canning and depends on complete sterilization by heat, and hermetic sealing. Bottling is a more expensive method than canning (manufacturers prefer cans where possible), but it is the popular home method as it requires a minimum of apparatus, and the bottles can be used over again indefinitely. As a technique, it is not very old – there is little mention of bottling in cookery books even as late as the turn of this century, when the older methods of preservation were still popular – salting, potting under fat, drying, and conserving with sugar. In fact, bottling followed on the work of Nicolas Appert (1749-1841) who was the first – under the spur of the Napoleonic Wars – to patent a method of preserving foods by heating and sealing them in cans or jars. The technique was improved around 1850 by Chevalier Appert, who added heating in a water bath under pressure to the existing technique. One cannot call it sterilization as the word was not yet invented – it was not until 1854 that Louis Pasteur began his famous work on fermentation, which demonstrated the role of *micro-organisms. Thereafter, progress was rapid. Before home-bottling could become popular, suitable jars with reliable seals had to be available at a reasonable price. This did not happen overnight. Today there are several alternative methods of closure – screw tops, clip tops, wired tops – and the seal of rubber or plastic makes an air-tight joint with the glass. Yet there are still countries, even in Europe, where jars for bottling are not commonly available or are imported at a price which prohibits their use by the poorer people who would most benefit from them.

Packing. There are two methods used in bottling, the hot pack and the cold pack. In the hot pack, which is the older method, the foods are cooked first, then put into heated sterilized jars and sealed immediately. The jars may sometimes need heat treatment after that. As the hot-pack method is liable to damage the form and texture of the food, the cold-pack method is generally preferred today. In foods where the form does not matter, such as purées, sauces and creamed corn, the hot-pack method may actually be preferable. Heat travels to the centre of jars of solidly-packed, dense or viscous food rather slowly, and it may therefore be better to do the cooking in an open pan where the product can be stirred.It seems silly to let purées, which have to pass through a sieve after cooking, get cold and then heat them up again for sterilization.

In the cold-pack method, the fruit or vegetables are arranged in the jar raw (or at most partly cooked if they are inclined to shrink with heat), then cooked and sterilized in one operation in the sealed jar. In practice, jars with a lid held by a screw ring – which is not flexible – must be screwed tight and loosened half a turn to allow any pressure build-up to escape. They are tightened again after being taken out of the sterilizing bath.

Liquids in bottling. Fruits are usually packed in syrup. As a general rule, a strong syrup helps preserve taste, colour and texture (obviously also, more sugar is necessary for very sour fruit). In commercial practice, the best grades are packed in 40-60% syrups, the cheap grades in as low as 10%. A few fruits, which may be wanted sour, can be packed in plain water. Sugar syrups are prepared as a percentage sugar to water by weight. (100 g or 4 oz of sugar in lt or 2 pt of water is a 10% syrup. So also is 450 g or 1 lb of sugar in 4½ lt or 8 pt.) Anyone who does a lot of bottling will find a Brix *hydrometer useful. A rough home system is to use equal volume measures (e.g. cups) of sugar and water for a heavy syrup, 1:2 of sugar to water for a medium syrup and 1:3 of sugar to water for a light one.

Vegetables, on the other hand, are commonly packed in a very light brine (2% is usual), but some are packed in water. A home method is to add a teaspoon of salt to each litre (or quart) jar before filling with water.

Preparation. Fruits and vegetables for bottling (or canning) should be in good condition – fresh, undamaged and unbruised. They need to be cleaned, de-stalked, peeled, cut in bits, stoned, blanched, parboiled or otherwise prepared. It is best to use a stainless steel knife. Fruits which tend to discolour in the air on cut surfaces should be put in some form of anti-oxidant solution, such as water with a *Campden tablet, lemon juice or vinegar and salt (30 g salt and 30 ml vinegar per 4 lt or 2 tablespoons of each per 4 qt) until ready to fill the bottles. Peaches and tomatoes can be peeled easily after dunking in boiling water, the trade often uses boiling 1% caustic soda solution for peaches, but they have to be well washed afterwards.

Sterilization temperatures. Boiling will rapidly kill all organisms, including the heat-resistant spores of botulism if the foodstuff is sufficiently acid. This is the case with most fruits and tomatoes. In fact, sour fruit juices can be rendered sterile merely by *pasteurizing at 50-65°C (120-150°F). Not so vegetables, which are usually slightly alkaline. They cannot be sterilized by boiling, unless an acid such as lemon juice or vinegar is first added. To sterilize them without an acid, a higher temperature, such as can be reached in an autoclave or pressure cooker, is necessary. The usual pressure chosen is 0.7 kg/cm² (10 lb/in²), which gives a temperature of 115°C (240°F) at sea level, but some vegetables, such as spinach and Swiss chard, are more usually sterilized at 1.05 kg/cm² (15 lb/in²) (122°C or 250°F) because of the time they take at the lower pressure.

Sterilization times. The object is to raise the temperature in the middle of the jar to the point where, if it is held for an appropriate time, all organisms are killed. In the cold-pack method, the food also has to be cooked. As it is not very practical to stick a thermometer into a sealed jar, we have to depend on times worked out by food scientists. For most cold-packed fruits, 30 minutes processing submerged in a boiling water-bath is necessary for 1 kg jars (2 pt). Half-kilogram jars (1 pt) take 5 minutes less. Vegetables (with the exception of tomatoes) are much more critical in their requirements and must always be sterilized in a pressure cooker. Only if directions are followed to the letter and the bottles are in good condition with new rings is home bottling of vegetables foolproof and safe. Cutting corners is risky.

Testing and storage. When bottles are heated, the contents expand a little (in some cases, as with peas and corn, there is also swelling during cooking), and some air is driven out. On cooling,

there is contraction, and if the seal is good, a partial vacuum is formed which sucks the lid on tightly. In this condition, no organisms can get in to infect the contents. Jars should be tested, because if the lid is not sucked on properly, air will continually go in and out with the changes in atmospheric pressure, and spoilage organisms may enter. Although we are always told to store bottled fruit in a dry place, anywhere will do, although preferably it should be dark (unless the jar is wrapped). Light promotes bleaching, and after a time the appearance of the product is spoiled. Naturally. the jars should be labelled with contents and date.

BOTULISM. *See* poisoning.

BOUDIN BLANC. Not like the British white pudding but a delicate, costly, smooth, creamy sausage about 15 cm (6 in) long. It is made of finely-minced white pork with chicken – and sometimes rabbit or other meat – milk or cream, eggs, sometimes a little bland cereal, and a light flavouring of salt, spice and onion. Though poached in the making, they are best brushed with melted butter and grilled. *Boudin blanc de Paris* contains chicken breasts, and *du Mans* does not, but the exact make up is local. *Boudins blancs* do not keep.

BOUDIN NOIR. *See* black pudding.

BOUFFI. *See* herring.

BOUILLON. *See* broth.

BOUQUET GARNI. A bundle or faggot of herbs. The herbs are tied together or enclosed in a muslin bag, so that they can be removed at any time, either at the end of cooking or when they have given sufficient flavour to the dish. The basic bouquet consists of a bay leaf, a sprig of thyme and three sprigs of parsley, but there are endless variants and bouquets may contain marjoram, lemon thyme, basil, chervil, savoury, tarragon, chillies, mace, cinnamon sticks, bitter orange peel and anything else that the cook thinks will improve flavour. The *bouquet garni* is absolutely essential to good European cooking. It should be kept simple to begin with and elaborated by experience.

BOURGOURI. *See* burghul.

BOYSENBERRY. *See* raspberry.

BRACKEN. *See* fern.

BRAIN has a soft and creamy texture when cooked. Although the brains of all the main meat animals are eaten, calf brain is the most used as a dish in its own right. All brains should be soaked in cold water for anything from 1 hour (calf brain) to 4 hours (ox brain). The surrounding membranes are then removed together with any traces of blood that are still visible. The first stage in most recipes for brain is simmering for about 20 minutes in a *court bouillon* that has been slightly acidified with vinegar. Brain may then, for example, be browned in butter or dipped in batter and deep fried.

[*Brain* – French: *cervelle* German: *Gehirn* Italian: *cervelli* (pl) Spanish: *cerebro*]

BRAISING. A combined roasting and stewing technique applied to meat, fish or vegetables. The food is put in a pan with a closely-fitting lid (which stops evaporation and keeps in the aromas) and cooked very slowly on top of the stove or in the oven. Very little liquid is added, and the meat or fish is usually laid on a *mirepoix* of chopped or diced vegetables, chopped bones, or blanched pork rind to protect it from the hot pan bottom. The correct utensil to use is a *braisière*, and the best are made of tinned copper.

[*Braising* – French: *braiser* German: *Schmoren* Italian: *brasare* Spanish: *cocer en cazuela con poca agua*]

BRAMBLE. *See* blackberry.

BRAN is the fibrous skin of the *wheat grain which is separated in milling. It is mainly used for feeding animals. Bran may be fine or coarse and varies in colour from yellowish to dark reddish brown. When sold as animal feed, it is often known as wheatfeed or middlings.

As bran provides roughage, which is useful in alleviating constipation, it has long been sold as a health food, although not everyone will like the flavour, which in some cases seems to have been developed on the principle that what tastes nasty must do you good. Much bran is therefore toasted and made into breakfast cereals. Bran contains a high proportion of B vitamins as well as about half of the mineral content of the grain. Most of its weight, though, is made up of cellulose, which humans cannot digest. Bran is now valued by many dieticians as a source of fibre in the diet to compensate for the general over-refinement of our food. A diet that is rich in fibre is said to have the result of reducing the cholesterol level in the blood

and might thus be a factor in helping to prevent heart disease. The idea that such an inexpensive item as bran might actually be health-giving inevitably excited the food manufacturers, with the result that proprietary brands of bread and crispbread are now promoted in bran-enriched versions.

During milling, bran is deliberately kept in flakes so that it can be separated easily. Where wholewheat flour is unobtainable, you can grind up bran finely in a coffee grinder and add it to white flour. This cheating will produce something with the grittiness of *atta*, the Indian wholemeal flour which makes the best *parathas* and other unleavened breads.

[*Bran* – French: *son* German: *Kleie* Italian: *crusca* Spanish: *salvado*]

BRANDY (from the Dutch *brandewijn*, burnt wine) is distilled from wine (unlike *marc*) and is found in every country where there are vineyards. Brandy was originally an expensive remedy sold by apothecaries. As it is made from many types of wine and hence from many different grapes, brandy is an exceedingly variable product. Every country produces its own range, and there are strong local preferences and tastes. In France, the finest brandies are *cognac and *armagnac. A good, lesser brandy is usually called a *fine*, with possibly the area of origin tacked on. If recipes specify *un verre à liqueur de fine bourgogne*, it would probably (to anyone other than a Burgundian) be permissible to use another *fine*, but never cooking brandy, and certainly not a brandy from another country which might be muscat flavoured or over-sweet to French tastes.

Spain produces brandies of its own which are not imitations of French brandies; indeed, the Spanish probably first learned the technique of distillation from the Arabs. Popular Spanish brands vary greatly, and there are also fine Spanish liqueur brandies long aged in the wood. In cooking Spanish dishes, such as *zarzuela* of fish, the selection of the right local brandy is necessary for the authentic dockside taste (if that is what you want), especially as cheaper brandies are often faked up with vanilla or sassafras.

Where Spain is addicted to brandy for both cooking and drinking, Italy is not, and brandy is not a common ingredient in Italian food. When used, it tends to be in sophisticated recipes, for which cognac is often specified.

In Germany, people often refer to *Weinbrand* as cognac without implying that it is the genuine article from France. For a country that produces such superb wines, the brandy is usually fiery stuff, but then the Germans are *Schnapps* drinkers and prefer it like that; otherwise they wouldn't make it that way. In German recipes containing brandy, however, nothing is to be gained by searching for a German brandy as a French one can be used. In Greece, brandy is a popular drink and has its own peculiar taste which is derived from the local grapes. It is not much used in Greek cooking.

Outside Europe, important producers are the US, which manufactures enormous quantities of brandy in continuous stills, South Africa – another country where brandy is a very popular drink – and Australia, where the home market is limited as Australians prefer beer. In the past, South African brandies were noted for their over-strong, raisiny taste, as they were made from muscat grapes. There, as in many countries, *folle blanche* and other special brandy grapes have recently been introduced from France and a great improvement has been the result. (I must say, though, that hard-boiled penguin eggs, without that raisiny brandy, will never taste so memorably horrible again.) South America also makes a great deal of brandy which follows the usual pattern, but *pisco*, a brandy from Peru, has a highly characteristic taste, which was originally derived from the bees' wax used in pioneer days to waterproof earthenware amphorae, which had to serve instead of oak casks. Naturally, if a recipe calls for *pisco* you have to use *pisco*, but use one made in Peru, as there are imitations made elsewhere which are little like the brandy they purport to imitate.

[*Brandy* – French: *cognac, eau de vie* German: *Weinbrand, Branntwein, Kognak, Schnapps* (colloquial) Italian: *acquavite, cognac* Spanish: *aguardiente, coñac*]

BRANK. *See* buckwheat.

BRASS is an alloy of copper and zinc, which was probably first known to the Romans at about the time of Christ. An earlier alloy (probably that referred to as brass in the Bible) was bronze, a mixture of copper and tin. In the Orient, brass is still much used for utensils though, it is, alas, fast being replaced by aluminium – aesthetically less pleasing, but cheaper. The coppersmiths in the bazaars beat brass, as it can be worked cold if it contains over 64% copper.

Naked brass is used for making those beautiful water vessels village girls in India carry on their heads. The vessels are kept scrupulously clean by scouring with ashes inside and out. Naked brass is also traditionally used for drinking mugs for water or milk. For cooking, however, brass pots are usually tinned inside; the exceptions are preserving pans and the pans used for heating jam glaze. Heavy tinned brass pans can still be bought in the Orient, and although it takes much work to keep them clean (they are not as easy to clean as copper), they are durable, beautiful and excellent for cooking. My kitchen is full of them. However, these pans should be retinned as the original tinning is likely to contain lead.

[*Brass* – French: *cuivre* German: *Messing* Italian: *ottone* Spanish: *cobre amarillo*]

BRATHERINGE. *See* herring.

BRATWURST is a German sausage for grilling or frying. It is pale in colour and made of finely ground pork or veal. There are also smoked varieties which should be cooked only for a short time.

BRAWN. Usually pig's head, salted and cured very briefly, boiled with seasonings, boned and chopped, then moulded with some of the gelatinous broth formed during boiling. In this form, it is equivalent to the French *fromage de tête* or *fromage de cochon*; indeed, in the US, brawn is usually known as head cheese. Sheep and cow heads may also be used, and brawn was even made from baby rabbits by the hard-hearted farmer's wives where I lived as a child.

Although most modern brawn recipes call for the head to be chopped and the brawn set in a mould, there are also recipes which leave the outside of the head, the skin and the cheeks intact to serve as a covering. After removal of the bones, and arrangement of tongue and other bits, the whole is rolled and tied in a cloth in a sausage shape before being given a final boiling. In France, this form of brawn might be called *hûre* (head, as in *hûre de sanglier*, boar's head). Refined versions of brawn, in which the broth is clarified and used to coat a mould (often with cut-out vegetable decorations), merge with galantine, although this was usually made from chicken or veal. Brawn is eaten cold (otherwise the jelly would melt), and needs mustard and pickles or, better, Dijon mustard with it.

Brawn

Brawn (in my opinion) is best when made from a

young pig, the head lightly dry-cured, and cooked very simply without flavourings. The following is based on a Sussex recipe. For half a head, well cleaned and washed in cold water, you will need 25 g (1 oz) saltpetre, 100 g (4 oz) sugar and 225 g (8 oz) salt, with ¼ lt (½ pt) of vinegar. Have the brains removed by the butcher and possibly also the tongue; but traditionally the latter is included in the brawn.

Cut off the ear, cut it open and clean it well. Scald the head and scrape off any bristles a careless butcher may have left. Dry the meat and ear well and rub all over with half of the salt. Leave it overnight. Next day, throw out the accumulated liquid and rub the meat with a mixture of the saltpetre, sugar and remaining salt. Make quite sure that this mixture is poked into every hole and cranny. Leave until next day. Then pour on the vinegar and turn all the bits round in the brine that has been formed until they are well wetted. Turn the meat (I always drain off the brine and pour it back over again) daily for at least another 2 days (you can continue for up to a week).Then wash the head, tongue and ear, and put them to soak in plain water for 2 hours to remove some of the salt. Put them into a pan of cold water, bring to the boil, skim and simmer until the tongue can be skinned and the bones removed. Do this as soon as the meat is cool enough to handle. Check that everything is tender and sufficiently cooked (the tongue or ear gristle occasionally need a little longer than the rest). When they are ready, cut the cheek (the main piece of meat) into 3 slices, parallel to the skin. Line a basin with 2 of these slices, and fill the centre with the bits of muscle, ear and cut-up tongue. Cover with the third slice of cheek. Press down. (I like to use a basin which is just overflowing and press the brawn down into it with a weighted board, but others wrap the brawn in a cloth, or bandage it, and then press it down under a board.) When cold, unmould the brawn and, if possible, keep it in the refrigerator to mature for 2 days before use. Brawn may be flavoured with onion, pepper, nutmeg, *bouquet garni* or lemon juice, but if is well made, the meat can stand on its own. Some brawns are made by cutting the meat into small bits and incorporating it into the jelly. The choice is open and the results range from a delicately flavoured, pale pink, tender brawn, to a tough, greyish jelly with bits of chopped gristle embedded in it.

[Brawn – French: *fromage de tête, galantine de porc, pâté de cochon* German: *Schweinesülze* Italian: *salome di porco, sminuzzato* Spanish: *carne en gelatine*]

BRAZIL NUT, para nut or **cream nut**. This nut is the seed of a giant tree (*Bertholettia excelsa*) which grows wild in the tropical South American jungle. Although domestication has begun and the tree has been tried in other tropical places, the odds are still that the nuts one buys have come from some remote tributary of the Amazon. They grow packed together like the sections of an orange inside a large, spherical woody fruit. The tree itself grows to a great height, and, with its long unbranched trunk, thrusts its head far above the general green canopy of thick forest. When the nuts are ripe, the whole fruit comes crashing to the ground. Since each one weighs several pounds and falls from such a height, collecting is a dangerous occupation. It goes on from November to June. The fruit are broken open with a *machete* and the nuts washed in the nearest creek (bad nuts tend to float away). They are then dried on mats, taken downstream by canoe during the rainy season and finally transported to market by river steamer.

Brazil nuts are graded. The largest come mainly from the higher forest of the upper Amazon. Most common are the average-sized nuts. The small ones go to the chocolate makers.

Apart from the whole dessert nuts, which have become traditional at Christmas, it is usual, for cooking purposes, to buy nuts already cracked, because extracting the kernel in a whole state is difficult with ordinary nutcrackers. Commercially, they are cracked by rollers. As Brazils become rancid fairly soon after exposure to the air, you need to be careful when buying cracked ones. They are easy to grate or grind.

As Brazil nuts contain 60-65% oils and up to 20% protein, they are very nutritious. They are high in cobalt and even higher in calories than almonds which, in analysis, they rather resemble. Even the oil pressed from Brazils is like almond oil. When fresh, it is pale yellow, almost odourless and pleasantly nutty. It is sometimes used in Brazil as an olive oil substitute.

Brazil nuts are used in modern vegetarian or health food recipes, but are otherwise neglected. When freshly cracked, they have a delicious and individual flavour, so the field is wide open for experiment.

Paradise or **Sapucaya nut** (*Lecythis sabucajo*). A near relative of the Brazil, and rather like it, but more rounded and with deep grooves running from end to end. The shell is so fragile that it can often be broken with the fingers. The creamy-white kernel is sweeter than that of the Brazil and has a more delicate flavour. It is used mainly in tropical South America, but is increasingly exported.

[*Brazil nut* – French: *noix du Brésil* German: *Paranuss* Italian: *noce del Brasile, noce del Para* Spanish: *nuez del Brasil*]

BREAD. Unleavened bread has been a staple food for many thousands of years. In Europe and Asia, it was mainly made of wheat, barley or millet, but in America up to the time of Columbus, bread was baked from maize, the only cereal known on that side of the Atlantic. It is interesting that rice was usually boiled and not baked into a bread (although such exists), while in northern China (where wheat, not rice, is the staple), the wheat is traditionally eaten steamed as dumplings or made into pasta, rather than being baked into bread.

Although leavened bread with yeast was well known in the Middle East of the Old Testament among poor people, especially nomads, this bread would usually have been baked on a flat iron plate or stone; an oven is more costly to construct and cannot be conveniently moved about. The old brick ovens in which the hot fuel had to be raked out before the bread was put in were ideal, as they provided a falling heat and the fuels added flavour to the bread. Compared to modern ovens, though, they are tricky to manage. Some think that the bread tastes better if the oven has been fired with wood. Modern bakeries use ovens heated by gas, oil or electricity, and the bread is often baked on conveyor belts.

Until the middle of the 19th century, bread was always leavened by yeast, but then various forms of baking powder were tried. This leavening is still used for scones, girdle cakes and soda bread (as well as for cakes).The so-called aerated bread was also invented and introduced in Victorian times. This contained no yeast, but had the dough artificially inflated by gas. It never became really popular because of its uncharacteristic flavour. Today, in some developed countries, much bread is made in factories, and new, shorter methods of making bread have been introduced. One of their advantages is that they allow a higher proportion of low-gluten flour to be used. Also, partly because fermentation losses are smaller, more loaves can be made from the same quantity of flour. In the Chorleywood Bread Process, the gluten fibres are 'developed' during a few minutes of high-power mixing. Bread made in this way contains a proportion of yeast to allow it to mature quickly. Another method, Activated Dough Development, relies mainly on chemicals to work on the gluten; the additives include Vitamin C, potassium bromate and the amino acid, cysteine.

Many people today, brought up on the sliced, wrapped product, have never tasted an old-fashioned baker's loaf. Those who have may consider that modern technology has not made better bread, but worse. The craft sector of the bakery trade in Britain now represents only about a quarter of the total, since many small bakers have been forced out of business. For this reason, those who like decent bread may have to make it themselves.

Part of the attraction of commercial, wrapped bread is its long shelf life. It can hang about in the shop for days, so there is less waste, and it is now baked in such a way as to have a soft crust, which allows it to be sliced easily at the factory. Such bread is even gaining ground in France, Italy and Spain. Bread is sometimes sold part-baked. The dough has been baked to set it and to make a very pale, soft crust. The baking is then finished in the home. Such bread is very popular in the US and is becoming so elsewhere.

Toast is sliced bread held in radiant heat until brown caramel and dextrins are formed on the surface. Toasting destroys some of the B vitamin, thiamine, and toast is no more slimming than the same quantity of untoasted bread. Packaged toast is usually made from bread containing a slightly higher proportion of sugar, and may be browned right through.

Baked bread keeps well when frozen, especially if it has a soft crust. Hard crusts are likely to separate from loaves which have been kept frozen for more than a few weeks. To minimize staling, which occurs fastest at temperatures just above freezing point, freeze and thaw bread as quickly as possible.

With home-baked bread, faults may occur, but these are usually easily corrected. Bread which has not been baked long enough will have a doughy, sticky consistency. If it has not proved (i.e. risen) thoroughly, it will have very small holes, and if it has proved too long, it may have developed a gas pocket between the crust and the loaf. If it is not kneaded properly, it may have lumps of dry flour in it, a streaky crumb and over-sized air holes.

There are a bewildering number of breads, many of which show national and local variations. In addition, there are baked products which are difficult to categorize as breads, pastries or cakes. What, for instance, are those specialities made with currants, from the Welsh *bara brith* to the Italian *panettone*? Do we consider *croissants* as bread rolls? And what about the Spanish *ensaimadas*? *Brioches* and *Gugelhupfen* are other doubtful cases. Almond breads, fig breads and spiced breads are not bread in the usual sense. And unleavened mixtures, such as *chapatties*, are also not considered to be bread. Scandinavian rye breads, such as *knäkkebrød*, verge on biscuits. The following are some basic categories of bread.

Wholewheat bread, **wholemeal bread**, **Graham bread**, **pain integral**, and **pan negro** should be made from the whole, ground wheat kernel, including the germ and the bran, with nothing else except yeast, salt, and a little fat and sugar added. This is the ideal bread of the health-food enthusiast and for those who like the flavour of the whole grain. It contains fibrous bran as well as more vitamins and mineral elements than white bread. It also contains more of the organic phosphorus compound, phytic acid, which may reduce the absorption of calcium, iron and zinc (although it is partly broken down by the action of enzymes during the fermentation of the dough). Tests carried out with children did not show that wholewheat bread was superior to white in terms of the growth of the children studied.

Brown bread is intermediate between whole-wheat and white breads, since it contains some wheat bran, with the germ extracted. It is made with brown flour containing some bran and may also contain caramel. There are also brown breads with added wheat germ which has had its enzymes inactivated by heat so that it will keep. There is probably little or no dietary advantage in eating brown bread instead of white.

Granary bread is made with a proprietary meal containing malted flour and pieces of whole cereal or coarsely-ground flour. It may have a fake, rough, country-baked appearance but is not the same as wholewheat bread.

White bread is made from white flour which contains little bran and germ. It is significant that throughout history, when people could afford it, they have always preferred bread made from low-extraction (white) flour. Unless it is fortified, this is much less rich in B vitamins and minerals, such as iron, than wholewheat flour. In some countries (including Britain), Vitamin B, and nicotinic acid are added as supplements, together with iron and calcium compounds.

Rye bread. Rye flour by itself makes very heavy bread (it does not have the coherence as dough to aerate properly – the dough tends to crack) and is usually mixed with wheat flour. The original rye bread, popular in Scandinavia, Germany and through into Russia, was made by a sour-dough process, which helped to give it a special flavour. Unfortunately, the magnificent rye bread which was available before World War II has largely disappeared, and some modern rye breads contain only a small quantity of rye and are soured by added acid.

Soda bread is leavened with bicarbonate of soda or baking powder. The alkali destroys some of the vitamin value, but the bread can be made quickly, and some like the taste.

Diet bread and **starch-reduced bread**. The latter are made by various means to have a much higher percentage of protein than normal bread. They may be made by adding high-protein soya flour or extra gluten to the flour or by removing some of the starch from the flour. Ordinary bread contains 12–13% protein, gluten bread 16%, high-protein bread 22%, and extra-high-protein or starch-reduced bread around 50% (all of these figures being expressed on a dry basis). As the percentage of protein is increased, the percentage of starch becomes less. Other diet breads depend on extra aeration of the loaf. Each slice therefore weighs less than a slice of ordinary bread, although weight for weight the energy value would be the same.

Bread in cooking is a very versatile ingredient. It was used as a thickener for sauces in medieval recipes. According to Jane Grigson in her *English Food* (Penguin), it was needed because the sauces had to be solid enough to stay on the bread trenchers that served as plates. Achieving the same thickness with flour would have turned the sauces to glue. Today, it gives flavour as well as texture to bread sauce and thickens soups such as *gazpacho*. Slices of bread or *croûtons* give the eater something to get a purchase on in the very thin broths of garlic soups and French onion soup.

   *Crumbs or *croûtons* on top of casseroles or

gratins absorb the juices, butter and oil from the ingredients below and form a crust. If the recipe includes herbs, these can be mixed with the breadcrumbs to make the crust even better, while the herbs still give their flavour to the rest of the dish.

Bread is often the main ingredient in stuffings and is added to oily ingredients, such as the roe in *taramasalata*, to lighten the texture. It is also called for in many meat loaf recipes and in some for items described (presumably on grounds of shape) as hamburgers – in such recipes, the bread is often meant to stretch the meat and make it go further, if the bread is used to excess and underseasoned, the intention will be only too obvious.

Bread can also become a container, as when a large *brioche* is hollowed out and filled with *pâté*, or when rectangles of bread dipped in melted butter line a tin which is then filled with thickened, spiced apple purée – baked, the result is Apple Charlotte. Bread is a main ingredient in summer pudding and, in winter, in steamed puddings (including Christmas pudding) and in baked bread and butter pudding. Breadcrumbs appear in cake recipes, notably from North Africa, often in combination with ground nuts. The cakes are moist, pudding-like and delicious.

[*Bread* – French: *pain* German: *Brot* Italian: *pane* Spanish: *pan.*

Brown bread – French: *pain noir* German: *Weizenbrot* Italian: *pane scuro* Spanish: *pan moreno.*

Rye bread – French: *pain de seigle* German: *Roggenbrot* Italian: *pane de segala* Spanish: *pan de centeno.*

White bread – French: *pain blanc* German: *Weissbrot* Italian: *pane bianco* Spanish: *pan bianco*]

BREADCRUMBS. *See* crumbs.

BREADFRUIT. Related to the *jack fruit, this belongs to the same family as mulberries and figs. The fruits are borne on a large tropical tree (*Artocarpus communis*) and are yellow-brown when ripe. The average size is about that of a small soccer ball, but there are over a hundred varieties, which vary a great deal. The original home of the breadfruit is South East Asia and the Pacific, where it is the staple starchy food. It was introduced to other countries (among others by Captain Bligh of the *Bounty*), but has not achieved equal importance elsewhere.

Breadfruit are easy to cultivate. Once established (after 8 years), they yield 700-800 fruits annually over most of the year. These can be baked, roasted, boiled, sliced and fried, ground to a paste, dried into a sort of flour, stored and baked into bread. Some varieties have seeds, which are also edible. Canned breadfruit can be bought in Britain. The breadfruit seems to make possible that fortunate state of complete idleness for which many have longed.

[*Breadfruit* – French: *fruit de l'arbre à pain* German: *Frucht des Brotbaumes* Italian: *frutto del albero del pane* Spanish: *fruta del árbol del pan*]

BREAM is a name given to several quite distinct types of fish. The freshwater bream (*Abramis brama*), a handsome fish of little gastronomic value, is related to the carp, while the marine Ray's bream (*Brama brama*) belongs to quite a different family. Fishmongers used sometimes to sell the very ordinary redfish (*Sebastes marinus*) and Norway haddock (*Sebastes viviparus*) – both scorpion fish related to the *rascasse* which is an important item in *bouillabaisse* – as Red bream, which it is not.

The bream of real gastronomic importance belong to yet another family, the Sparidae, which are mostly warm water fish, plentiful in the Mediterranean but with a single member that is common around northern Europe, the genuine Red bream (*Pagellus centrodontus*). Over a dozen species of sea bream live off the coast of the US, where they are known as porgy. Sea bream is one of the most popular fish in Japan, raw in *sashimi* or cooked by grilling or poaching. The species there is *Chrysophrys major*, which is closely related to the Gilthead bream, the French *daurade* (*Chrysophrys aurata*), probably the best of the breams found in European waters. The Black bream or Old wife (*Spondiliosoma cantharus*), which is caught in the Mediterranean and around British coasts as far north as the Tyne, also makes good eating. Among my own favourites in this group is the dentex (*Dentex dentex*), not a British fish but one which will be known to package-holiday customers under its Spanish name, *dentón*.

Most of the fish labelled as bream are stocky-looking fish with Roman noses and one long fin right down the back. As they usually live on shellfish, they have grinding teeth rather than the sharp teeth of hunting fish. Bream are not generally large fish, but the biggest, such as the dentex, can reach 1 m (39 in) long and weigh 30 kg (66 lb). Recipes will be found in Jane Grigson's *Fish Book* (Penguin), and the species are clearly differentiated and illustrated in Alan Davidson's *North Atlantic*

Seafood (Penguin) and *Mediterranean Seafood* (Penguin), essential books for everyone interested in cooking fish. In general, though, Sea bream can be baked or grilled for excellent results.

[*Gilthead bream* – French: *daurade* Italian: *orata* Spanish: *dorada*

Red bream – French: *daurade commune* German: *nordische Meerbrassen* Italian: *occhialone* Spanish: *besugo.*

Black bream – French: *griset, brème (des rochers)* German: *Seekarpfen* Italian: *tanuta* Spanish: *chopa.*

Ray's bream – French: *brème de mer.* German: *Brachsenmakrele* Italian: *pesce castagna* Spanish: *palometa, japuta*]

BRESAOLA. Dried beef fillet or other tender lean cuts, matured for about 2 months to a dark red colour, it is somewhat similar to *Bundnerfleisch* and a speciality of the Valtellina in the Italian Alps. *Bresaola* is usually served finely sliced and seasoned with olive oil (as it is costly, it deserves the best), a little lemon juice and freshly-milled black pepper. It is better if left to marinate for half an hour before serving as an appetizer with drinks.

BREWING. The brewing of ale has prehistoric origins. It would not have been a difficult discovery; if pounded grain is mixed with water and allowed to stand for a time in warm weather, it ferments and produces alcohol. Even animals sometimes get drunk from eating fruit which has fermented naturally, so we may conclude that alcoholic beverages of some sort were inevitable. Primitive ales do not taste nice to sophisticated palates, but still have their effect. *Chang* (rice beer) from Nepal, Kaffir beer or Zulu beer (made with maize and millet) from Africa, and no doubt other brews which I have not personally suffered, taste like sour, watery porridge, but can be much improved if flavoured with herbs and clarified. Even the ancient Egyptians knew a bit about brewing. They used herbs and even, some claim, hops, which would bring their brew close to *beer.

Modern beer is brewed by fermenting a hop-flavoured *wort with a suitable strain of *yeast. In home-brewing, beer may be made from malt extract (powder or syrup) or directly from *malt by mashing, a process that is rather difficult to manage at home. Canned, concentrated, ready-to-use worts can also be bought, and they are simply diluted with a specified amount of warm water, and put – with yeast – to ferment.

The type of ale or beer brewed depends on the type of malt, the quantity of sugar (maltose, sucrose, glucose), the quantity and quality of *hops, the strain of yeast and whether top or bottom fermentation is used, as well as on physical conditions such as temperature. There are now many excellent books on home-brewing. Recommended is W.H.T. Tayleur's *Penguin Book of Home-Brewing and Winemaking.*

Beer spends, on average, 5 days fermenting, though lager takes much longer, and for British beers, modern conical fermenters which are used commercially enable the job to be done in 2-3 days, a fact liked by the brewers, but possibly less so by consumers. As fermentation declines, the yeast tends to fall to the bottom of the vessel, a process speeded up by cooling until only a small amount is left in suspension. The newly-brewed beer is generally called green beer. This can be, and once was, put straight into casks, matured for a few days, then sent to the pub. Today, the beer is put into conditioning tanks. The rising bubbles of carbon dioxide from the fermentation, which is still continuing slowly, carry away some of the strongly flavoured substances which are responsible for harshness in green beer. Most of the yeast can be removed by *fining. Once, finings (isinglass) were added to casks in pub cellars. Sometimes sugar syrup is added to promote a natural sparkle by secondary fermentation.

The best draught beer comes from casks kept in the bar, but this may be impossible, because of space limitations or an unsuitable temperature, in which case the beer has to be drawn up from the cellars, most often by pumping through pipes. The ideal storage temperature for British beer is 14°C (57°F).

Bottled beers are almost always filtered, pasteurized and gassed, although a few aristocrats are bottled in their natural condition with yeast still living in the bottles. They contain some sediment, so need careful pouring – like wine. The dregs should be left in the bottle.

Canned beers, essentially similar to bottled ones, have become increasingly popular for their convenience, although they are often over-gassed and of poor flavour.

Keg beers have been filtered and usually pasteurized. They are flat, clear and free of yeasts capable of initiating a secondary fermentation. It is gassed in stainless steel containers at the brewery, and is effectively bottled in a large metal bottle. Keg beer is served from taps in the bar (forced out by the pressure) and is often very fizzy. Pubs with a large sale may have the same sterile beer delivered by tanker into cellar tanks. The beer is gassed with cylinders of carbon dioxide. Again, top pressure forces the beer up to the bar, but it is not quite as gassy as beer gassed at the brewery.

[*Brewing* – French: *brasser* German: *brauen* Italian: *fare la birra* Spanish: *bracear de cerveza*]

BRILL. *See* flatfish.

BRINE. Brines of salt dissolved in water are used for curing meat (ham, bacon, tongue, beef and even sausages) and fish (the brine is formed from water extracted from the fish after dry-salting), and for holding vegetables and fruits from times of glut until it is possible to turn them into pickles or otherwise process them.

For all practical purposes, bacteria cease to function in 25% salt solutions, and most spoilage organisms give up even in a 10% solution. Some, however, are exceedingly sensitive to salt and a few are salt lovers. Practical methods of using brines for preservation have been developed over the centuries by simple trial and error.

Cleanliness. Sterility is not essential, and may be actually detrimental to the working of a cure, but all crocks, tubs, and utensils should be very clean and well rinsed before they are used for brining.

Boiling. Brines are boiled to help dissolve the salt, to extract the flavour from the spice-bag and to reduce the number of micro-organisms. Some vegetables are put into brine when it is boiling, but usually (always for meat) brine should be cooled till it is stone cold before it is used.

Storage temperature can be critical, because a brine strong enough to preserve in cool conditions may not work in warm ones. Recipes for preserving vegetables through a north German winter will probably be wrong if they are tried without adaptation in a Mediterranean summer.

Scum. Various air-loving organisms form a scum on top of the brine tub. Though not harmful themselves, they should be skimmed off regularly as they create musty flavours when they die and decompose.

Immersion. Whatever is to be preserved in brine must be kept well below the surface. Otherwise, spoilage of the whole tub is certain. A slate, a board weighted by a stone, or even a plastic bag or box filled with salt and sealed will serve the purpose.

Injection brines. In modern curing, the brine for hams and other large pieces of meat is usually injected, like embalming fluid, with a syringe plugged into the arteries (not veins, which have valves to prevent reverse flow). Brines for this purpose can be weaker. The results are quick and certain but there is not the same development of flavour.

Basting with brine is a technique halfway between immersion and dry salting; it is useful for home-curing where space is limited. Such brines are strongly acidified with vinegar and do not give delicate cures.

Additives. *Saltpetre, *Chile saltpetre, *sal prunella, sodium or potassium nitrite (see nitrites) – any of these may be added to brines, especially to those for meat and fish, not only for their cosmetic action of turning meat pink, but also for their preservative effect.

Sugar is added to meat cures because it counteracts the hardening effect of saltpetre and makes the meat taste sweeter and less salty. If brown sugars, molasses or syrups are used, they add their flavour. An important action of sugar is to encourage the growth of bacteria which create a little acidity, helping preservation and improving the flavour. Vinegar is used particularly in basting cures for meat but is also usual with vegetables. Spices used for flavour have also some preservative action. The most common in brines are black pepper, allspice, juniper berries, ginger, mace, cloves, cinnamon and bay leaves.

Brine strength. The preservative effect of brine is related to its strength. Because fluids diffuse out of the foods being preserved, it may be necessary to fortify them with more salt, and some method of checking becomes necessary, especially if the brine is to be used more than once. The easiest way to think of brine strength is as a straight percentage by weight, because that is the way we make it up. 100 g salt in 1 lt water is 10% brine. Since an Imperial gallon of water weighs 10 lb, 1lb (450 g) of salt in 8 pt (4.5 lt) is also 10%. Old recipes call for brine strong enough 'to float an egg'. It must be a fresh egg, which lies on the bottom of fresh water and not one already starting to take off. It should just rise to the surface of the brine, not float proud. Although pretty inaccurate, this method has served farmers' wives for centuries (a potato is another object they used), but any hydrometer, even a home-made one, will do a better job. *See* brinometer.

Saturated brine is the strongest brine it is possible to make. At room temperature, water will dissolve about 35% salt (350 g per 1 lt or 3½ lb per 8 pt), but as solubility increases with temperature, boiling water will dissolve 40% (400 g per 1 lt or 4 lb per 8 pt). Excess will crystallize out again on cooling. Saturated brine is too strong and crude for most purposes (as the art of all salting is to use no more than is necessary and so make a delicate product), but it is used for preserving limes and lemons.

Indian Brined limes

Wash and dry the fruit, and cut into quarters but not completely through. Boil it in saturated brine for 5 minutes. Pack the fruit in hot bottles and fill them with boiling brine. Seal immediately.

A Standard Butcher's Brine for Tongue, Bacon and Meat

This is a 20% brine, which contains 25 lt (40 pt) water, 5 kg (11 lb) salt, 100 g (3½ oz) saltpetre, 300 g (11 oz) sugar and a spice-bag. Boil the ingredients for 20 minutes, adding a spice-bag towards the end. (A good spice-bag used by butchers is made of equal weights of coriander and allspice with a half weight of juniper berries. Use 25 g per 4.5 lt (1 oz per 8 pt), but do not follow the formula slavishly, to allow for individual taste and the quality of the spices.) Cool the brine, remove the spice-bag, throw in a slice of bacon (to start the denitrifying bacteria) and sink the meat under the pickle. An old rule of thumb says you should leave the meat in the pickle 1 day for every 500 g (1 lb) of meat, but thin pieces obviously take less time than thick ones of the same weight.

Brine for Holding Vegetables

This is a 15% brine, which contains 25 lt (40 pt) water (soft water or rain water for preference),

3.75 kg (8¼ lb) sea salt or cooking salt and 1.5 lt (2½ pt) vinegar. Boil the water with the salt for 20 minutes and then add the vinegar. Boil it for a minute or so and then let it cool. The vegetables which are put into this brine must be fresh and free from blemishes. Keep them below the surface of the liquid and remove any trapped pockets of air. Later, because the brine strength will be reduced by water extracted from the vegetables, check the solution and raise it once more back to strength by adding extra salt. Roughly 2 kg (4½ lb) of salt per 10 kg (22 lb) of vegetables will be required (though it is better to measure); it may be added as saturated brine or simply put on the board covering the vegetables to diffuse slowly into the pickle. (If the salt is tipped in, it sinks to the bottom, leaving the top layers under strength.) Vegetables brined this way need soaking to remove salt before they are cooked, but may be made directly into pickles. This brine is suitable for holding large pieces of vegetables, such as cauliflower and for small carrots, green beans, etc.

Brine for Fermented Vegetable Pickle

This is a 5% brine, which contains 25 lt (40 pt) water, 1.25 kg (2½ lb) salt and 1.5 lt (2½ pt) vinegar. Into this brine, made in the same way as the last, put cauliflower divided into florets, French beans, small carrots, beetroots, or cucumbers, turnip slices or greens. Pack the vegetables tightly, remove air bubbles, and weight the contents under the surface. A lactic acid fermentation will take place, and the acidity will increase. Aerobic organisms will form a flor (or white scum) on the surface which must be skimmed off daily. The pickle will be ready in about 10 days, depending on the kind of vegetables and on the temperature. Naturally the process takes less time in hot weather.

If it is not to be eaten immediately (it can be held for a few days in the refrigerator), the pickle should be packed in preserving jars, covered with the brine and sealed (if the jars have screw caps, loosen them half a turn for safety). Immerse them in cold water, bring them to the boil and hold them at boiling point for 30 minutes to sterilize them (screw caps then need to be tightened). This pickle does not need desalting but may be rinsed if it is too acid.

[*Brine* – French: *saumure* German: *Salzwasser*, *Salzbrühe* Italian: *salamoia* Spanish: *salmuera*]

BRINJAL. Indian name for *aubergine.

BRINOMETER. A special type of *hydrometer

used by butchers to measure the percentage saturation of brine. On this scale, fresh water is 0° and saturated brine is 100°. The older *Baume scale, still often used by European butchers, takes 0° for fresh water but 20° for saturated brine. So 1° on the brinometer scale is 5° Baumé. Thus we have the following set of approximate conversions:

	Salt in gl/t or lb/gallon	Hydrometer	Baumé
Fresh water	0	0°	0°
5% brine	5	14°	2.9°
10% brine	10	29°	5.7°
15% brine	15	43°	8.6°
20% brine	20	57°	11.4°
Saturated brine (at room temperature)	35	100°	20°

BRISLING. The Scandinavian name for *sprat. Brisling are often canned and treated as a substitute for sardines to which they are inferior.

BRISTOL MILK and **BRISTOL CREAM.** *See* sherry.

BRITISH GUM. *See* dextrin.

BROAD BEAN, shell bean (US), **Windsor bean** (US), **field bean, fava bean** or **horse bean** (*Vicia faba*). The field bean was the original bean and has been cultivated in Europe and Asia since the Stone Age. The modern broad bean is merely an improved variety. Field beans are still commonly grown as farm crops and, except for their size, are gastronomically indistinguishable from broad beans. It is easy to see why they were one of the first plants to be taken into cultivation by early man: they have a large seed (to dry and keep over the winter) and will grow almost anywhere, in any poor soil, as long as there is a suitable climate. You still see them in the more primitive places around the Mediterranean, *il carne del povero*, the meat of the poor.

Broad beans are the first beans for picking in spring. In Mediterranean climates, they are ready from March (having been sown the previous autumn), but in Britain they start in May, coming in a flush in June. Very young pods can be eaten whole, though the texture is a bit slimy. Young beans, which are bright green, are delicious raw with coarse salt or *prosciutto crudo*. After a few more days, when the skin begins to turn a greyish-pink (some varieties remain green and are considered superior), they are better boiled until tender (about 15 minutes) and eaten with chopped parsley and butter, or with a sauce made with plenty of parsley, as the flavours of beans and parsley seem to be complementary. The French combine broad beans with savory as do the Germans, but this taste is not shared by everybody.

Broad beans are disliked by most children, and in some people they cause favism (*see* poisoning).

When old broad beans become tough, they are hardly worth eating, even skinned, and are better left on the plant to ripen. They can then be dried and used in winter. In Spain, dried broad beans (*habas secas*) are particularly popular and are sold both whole and peeled (often sliced) in the market. Whole beans must be soaked and the skins removed before using, but the sliced beans cook quickly to a purée when simply boiled in water. The Spanish also make much use of canned broad or field beans, as bean dishes are served as an 'appetite stopper' (although they might not admit it) at the beginning of a meal.

Habas con Longanizas

Longanizas or *longanizas blancas* are the long, white, low-fat pork sausages of Cataluña, but any not-too-fatty pork sausage will do. The beans can be fresh, shelled broad beans or canned broad beans, drained. Heat ½ cup oil till it spits and then cool it a little before putting in 1 kg (2 lb) beans, a bay leaf and salt, otherwise the beans may split. Cook them on a slow fire until the beans are half cooked – about 5 minutes. Then add ½ cup water and 250 g (about ½ lb) sausage. Continue to cook on a slow fire until all the liquid has been absorbed and the sausages are ready.

[*Broad bean* – French: *haricot large* German: *grosse Bohne* Italian: *fava* Spanish: *haba*]

BROCCOLI. *See* cauliflower.

BROILING. In Victorian kitchens, one broiled a steak on a broiler, but today the word broil has fallen into disuse in Britain and has been replaced by the word grill. In America one still broils.

[*Broiling* – French: *griller* German: *rösten* Italian: *arrostire sulla graticula* Spanish: *asar*]

BROTH. The liquid in which any bones, meat or vegetables have been boiled. It is usually concentrated, flavoured and salted to make a soup, but is always unclarified. *Bouillon* (French for broth) is concentrated, also usually unclarified, and likely to be made from beef or veal. Consommé is both concentrated and clarified. *Stock is also made by boiling bones, meat, fish or vegetables in water. It is never a finished dish, but only a basic material from which soups or sauces are made.

[Broth – French: bouillon German: Fleischbrühe Italian: brodo Spanish: caldo]

BROWNING, black jack or **kitchen caramel.** This was previously considered a kitchen essential, when roasts and brown gravies to go with them were more common than now; it can still be bought ready made. It consisted of caramelized sugar and water. When badly made, it was nasty and bitter. To make it, melt 225 g (½ lb) of sugar in a thick pan with just a little water (a tablespoon) over a very low flame. Take off any scum and leave the mixture on the lowest flame for several hours until it has become a dark brown colour – when the bubbles have turned from red to blue – then add about 500 ml (1 pt) water. Let the liquid boil on the fire until a solution has been formed. Bottle it for use. Browning should have little taste; it is a kitchen cosmetic.

BRUSSELS SPROUT. Sprouts are a variety of the *cabbage species (Brassica oleracea, var. gemmifera) which originated, as far as is known, in the early 13th century near Brussels, but did not become popular in Britain until the 19th century. They are only gradually becoming a common winter vegetable in Spain and Italy. Modern varieties of Brussels sprouts produce regular and tight buds which require little trimming. The small 'cabbage' at the top of the long, sprout-bearing stem is used as greens (sprout tops). It is generally believed in Britain that a frost is necessary to make sprouts sweet, but certainly with modern varieties this is not necessary. Some types are naturally sweeter than others. The purple-red sprouts often taste as sweet as the chestnuts with which they are sometimes cooked. Loose, blown sprouts are cheap, but often take a lot of cleaning and are therefore wasteful. If sprouts are yellowish, they will be stale, have a horrible smell and taste, and should not be bought under any circumstances.

[Brussels sprout – French: chou de Bruxelles German: Rosenkohl Italian: cavolino di Brusselle Spanish: col de Bruselas]

BUAL. See madeira.

BUCKLING. See herring.

BUCKWHEAT, beechwheat, brank or **Saracen corn.** Being the seed of a starch plant (Fagopyrum esculentum) which belongs to the same family as rhubarb, sorrel and dock (Polygonaceae), buckwheat is not a true cereal, although it is treated as such. The plant has pink or white flowers (which are good for honey), reddish stems and long, pointed, heart-shaped leaves. It is a native of Asiatic Russia, where it is still found growing wild in its original form (which usually means that it has been taken into cultivation very late in history – it is said, under 1,000 years ago); it did not reach Europe until the 15th century. It grows very rapidly, even on poor soil, and so will smother weeds.

Buckwheat gets its name through the Dutch boek-weit, meaning beech wheat, because the grain is shaped like a beechnut, though smaller. It is an important staple in Russia, but is also grown extensively both for its grain and as green fodder in the US, Germany, France, Japan and elsewhere. It can now be found on sale in health-food shops as a result of the discovery that buckwheat contains rutin, a glucoside first isolated from rue (and named after it), which is beneficial in some cases of high blood pressure.

As a food, buckwheat has a distinctive flavour. Buckwheat flour, either plain or mixed with wheat flour, is the basis for buckwheat pancakes, a well-known winter breakfast favourite in parts of the US. Recipes vary from a simple type of girdle cake leavened with baking powder to more elaborate versions based on yeast. The famous Russian, yeast-leavened pancakes, blinis, are also often made with a mixture containing buckwheat flour, and savoury crêpes are made wholly or partly with buckwheat. Whole, husked buckwheat is the basis for kasha in Russian cookery. It can be made into a porridge or cakes, or cooked in loose grains, when it may be compared to rice. Traditionally, buckwheat goes with borstch and with shchi (thick vegetable soups). It is used as a stuffing for both fish (like carp and trout) and meat (including pork and goose). Many prefer it to rice with beef Stroganoff, gulash, or other meats cooked in a sauce.

Kasha

Measure the required amount of husked buckwheat grain and pick it over to remove husks and any unhusked grains. Roast the grain with care in an ungreased frying pan, stirring and shaking it continually, until the grain begins to pop. Now turn it into an ovenproof dish with a lid, or into a double boiler, and add 1½-2 times the volume of boiling, salted water. Cook in the oven at moderate heat (180°C, 350°F Gas Mark 4) or in a double boiler, for about ¾ hour, or until the grains are soft but not soggy. Add plenty of butter, fluff it with a fork and serve.

[Buckwheat – French: sarrasin, blé noir German: Buchweizen Italian: grana saraceno Spanish: trigo negro]

BULGAR WHEAT. See burghul.

BULLACE. A small wild variety of the European *plum (Prunus domestica, ssp. insititia), the bullace tree looks very like the blackthorn, but the bark of the twigs is brown, not black, and the tree is less thorny. The fruits also look very like sloes, though they are a little larger, they have the same blue bloom, but there are also yellow varieties. Wild bullaces are locally common in hedgerows and at the edges of woods in England.

Bullaces, though less sour and astringent than sloes, are of greatest use for similar purposes – to make bullace wine and bullace gin. They can also be made into jam and even, given enough sugar, used as stewed fruit. Although gastronomically intermediate between sloes and damsons, they lack the incomparable flavour of the latter. Bullace is not often planted nowadays, although cultivated varieties are very prolific and fairly sweet, especially if they are left on the trees well into the autumn, after the leaves have fallen.

[Bullace – French: crèque German: Pflaumenschlehe Italian: susmo selvatico Spanish: endrina grande]

BULLOCK'S HEART. See custard apple.

BULLY BEEF. Canned *corned beef.

BUMMALO. See Bombay duck.

BUNDNERFLEISCH. Swiss cured and dried beef, similar to the *bresaola from neighbouring districts of Italy, and traditionally made in the Grisons in winter. In other areas, such as the Bernese-Oberland, the beef is smoked, but not in the Grisons. It is an expensive delicacy, which is served in very thin slices as an appetizer.

A Swiss woman, whose mother used to make it at home, says that a pickle was made with all sorts of chopped vegetables, mountain herbs, onions, chives, parsley, thyme and so on mixed with coarse salt (gros sel). First the meat was dipped in white wine, then rubbed with the salt mixture (and very little saltpetre for colour), and put in a barrel in a cool cellar. The juice extracted by the salt was drained off, and the meat again rubbed with the mixture, a process which was repeated until no more juice flowed out. After that, the pieces of meat were hung to dry in an attic 'where we had a little tower, la tournalette, for the purpose'. The windows, covered with wire mesh to keep out the flies, were left open, but if it was cold at night someone had to go up to shut them and prevent the meat from freezing. The finished bundnerfleisch was taken down when thoroughly dried.

In a more cynical modern vein, a butcher says that it used to be made in the Grisons in winter, but that now, with air conditioning, any salami manufacturer can make it all the year round.

BURGHUL, **bulgar wheat**, **bourgouri** or **pourgouri**. Often described as cracked wheat, burghul is cracked by boiling, not mechanically. It is a staple in the Middle East, especially in Syria and in the Lebanon, and is the essential basis of tabbouleh and kibbeh. It can be bought ready-made from specialist shops or made at home as follows:

Burghul

Take good-quality wholewheat and, if necessary, pick it over and wash it. Put the wheat in a saucepan and cover it with water. Boil it until it is somewhat soft and begins to crack open. Then drain well and dry in the sun or in a very low oven. The dried burghul must then be ground in a hand grinder (or coffee mill if only small quantities are needed) and sieved. The fine burghul is used for kibbeh and tabbouleh, the coarse for other dishes (kishk and pilau).

Tabbouleh

Soak 225 g (8 oz) burghul for about an hour in cold water, until it has softened but gives a little resistance to the bite. Drain the water from it thoroughly, then spread it on a tea towel and press further moisture out of it. Put the wheat in a bowl and add 4-6 dessertspoons olive oil and 1 medium onion, several sprigs of mint, a large handful of parsley, all finely chopped. Stir everything together, keeping the mixture light, and season it with the juice of a juicy lemon, salt and pepper. If you wish, add shredded lettuce and pieces of cucumber.

BURNET. Several plants are called burnet, but the one that is relevant to the kitchen is the salad burnet (*Poterium sanguisorba*).This plant, a member of the rose family, is a native of most of Europe, growing on limey soil, and is a common plant of downland in Britain. It was taken to North America by the early colonists. The plant grows 15-30 cm (6-12 in) high, and the insignificant flower head looks like a greenish bobble with a few purple wisps sticking out of it. The leaves, which are eaten, have small, round leaflets with regularly toothed edges. When crushed, they have a smell of cucumber, which gives a final identification, but salad burnet would not be easily confused with anything poisonous. It is grown in some herb gardens, and is collected together with shoots of wild chicory in many southern European countries as a winter or spring *salad. It is an ingredient of *ravigote* and *chivry* sauces as well as of various butters.

[Burnet – French: *grande pimprenelle, pimprenelle commune des prés* German: *Pimpinelle, grosser Weisenkopf* Italian: *pimpinello* Spanish: *pimpinelo, salvastrella*]

BUSH BEAN. *See* kidney bean.

BUTTER is an ancient invention of herdsmen, one of the original, simple ways of preserving milk. If butter is rendered to a form of pure fat, it will keep for many weeks. The milk of most mammals (except that of the *camel) can be made into butter by shaking it until the fat globules come together into more or less solid butter-fat. This would be done, for instance, in skins – the bedouins' *mirjahah* and others like it are still seen among nomadic tribes in North Africa and the Middle East. An earthen pot with a whirling wooden paddle is a device that is still used in Indian villages. Because we are used to butter from cow's milk, we must not forget that it is also made from buffalo milk, yak milk and, in arid regions, from ewe milk (e.g. the Syrian yellow butter).

Home-made Butter

Few people these days possess a wooden barrel churn or even one of those glass jars fitted with revolving paddles. Butter can, however, be made in a large screw-topped jar of any sort by anyone with the energy to shake it for long enough, or with willing children.

First, the fat must be concentrated as cream, by letting the milk stand in a refrigerator and then skimming it off (homogenized milk is obviously no use for this) – or cream may be bought. For the most flavourful butter, a starter should be added and the cream should be ripened for 2-3 days; a temperature of 25°C (77°F) is the best. Bacterial action produces butter aroma (particularly a substance called diacetyl); butter made from unripened sweet cream is relatively tasteless, but keeps better. Churning is best done at 15-16°C (60°F). If the weather is very cold, churning can take longer.

During churning, the cream first goes thick, like custard, but it soon becomes grainy with tiny flecks of butter. This is the time to add a cup of cold water, which helps the butter to separate. As churning proceeds, the flecks become larger, and finally coalesce into blobs of butter. Strain these out of the watery whey and beat them together into a lump with wooden paddles. Finally, wash the butter several times in cold water to remove the sour *buttermilk. When clean and well compacted, add salt or leave the butter unsalted, as wished. Salted butter keeps better.

In addition to butter flavours produced by lactic bacteria in maturing cream, there are flavours derived from the milk itself. They come from the pastures on which the cows are fed. In modern farming practice, pastures are no longer natural and lack the flowers and herbs that give the finest butters their incomparable taste. However, you can still find good butters such as those from Normandy and, even better, from herds kept on meadows in the Alps.

Clarified Butter

For frying, clarified butter (that is, pure butter fat) is best; otherwise the small percentage of milk protein and sugars that ordinary butter contains will precipitate and burn. Traces of water also need to be removed from the fat. To clarify butter, heat it gently until the sediment comes down and frothing ceases, then strain it.

Ghee

Indian ghee is much the same as clarified butter,

but has a much stronger taste. It starts with butter made perhaps from well soured buffalo milk (or cow's milk) and is kept on a very low heat for up to ¾ hour. By this time, the sediment will have browned slightly, and the oily ghee will have acquired a very special taste, which some describe as 'nutty', and which makes the most delicious food.

[*Butter* – French: *beurre* German: *Butter* Italian: *burro* Spanish: *mantequilla*]

BUTTER BEAN, **Lima bean** (US) or **Madagascar bean** (*Phaseolus limensus*). A native of tropical America (opinions range from Guatemala to Brazil), whose wild ancestors have disappeared – the bean has been in cultivation for thousands of years (remains were found in prehistoric Peruvian graves). Some botanists regard the Sieva bean (*P. lunatus*) as a smaller variety of the same species.

The beans require a warm, moist climate and will not grow in northern countries, where they are known only as the dried large and flat butter beans, rather than as the fresh Lima beans. However, in the US and other countries where they are grown, they are eaten fresh as shell beans – though not in the pod – and are also available frozen or canned.

There are many varieties, some with large fat beans (known as potato types) and in a range of sizes and colours, usually white or pale green. Some types contain a significant amount of hydrocyanic acid and so are poisonous until they are cooked. Dried butter beans are usually covered with cold water and soaked until they are plump, the time depending on the age and variety of bean. The cooking time is roughly 45 minutes. Butter beans are one of the best-flavoured of all beans and are excellent cold as an *hors d'oeuvre*. In some places, wax-pod beans are known locally as butter beans.

[*Butter bean* – French: *haricot beurre* German: *Wachsbohne* Italian: *fagiolo asciabola, fagiolo di Lima* Spanish: *judia*]

BUTTERMILK is what is left over when milk is churned to butter – that is, milk with most of the fat and some of the other milk solids taken out. It differs from skimmed milk, though, in that it is sour. Churning used to take place only two or three times a week on the farm, and milk was kept and allowed to gather its cream long enough for it to sour naturally. The buttermilk which was effectively sour, skimmed milk was often fed to the pigs. It is a useful emulsifying agent and is now recognized as a health promoting product, which is sold in cartons in many supermarkets, often homogenized and doctored in the way the trade knows best. In cooking, it is used with bicarbonate of soda to leaven scones, cakes and soda breads. However, modern 'buttermilk' and 'cultured buttermilk' are respectively skim milk and soured skim milk.

[*Buttermilk* – French: *petit lait, babeurre* German: *Buttermilch* Italian: *siero di latte* Spanish: *leche de manteca*]

BUTTERNUT is the name commonly given to the American White *walnut (*Juglans cinerea*) and also to the Nara nut or butter pit (*Acanthosicyos horrida*) which is found growing wild in the deserts of south-west Africa. The latter looks like a large melon seed, and is in fact the oily seed of a gourd, the fruit of a spiny shrub.

C

CABBAGE. All types of cabbage – with the exception of the various forms of *Chinese cabbage – are probably derived from a wild species, *Brassica oleracea*, which still grows in a few places on the coasts of Britain, France, Spain and Italy. This plant takes the prize for having produced the most weirdly different varieties: it does not just come as open and ball cabbages – red and green at that – but is the forerunner of *kale, *Brussels sprouts, *cauliflower, broccoli and probably *kohlrabi. Cabbage has a certain taste similarity to other plants of the same family (Cruciferae), to turnips and their tops, to mustard greens, and even to cress and rocket. (Perhaps this is a reason why mustard goes well with cabbage.)

Greens, collards and *kale (var. *acephala* – 'without a head').These are the nearest to the original wild cabbage. However, tender young greens may come from genuinely unhearting varieties or from hearting varieties taken very young, or they may even be young shoots from old cabbage plants, cauliflowers or sprouts. Kale is commonly grown as food for sheep in northern Britain, and in places as food; curly kale, with frizzy leaves, is most often eaten. While all cabbage greens must be young and tender to be nice, this particularly applies to kale, which can be very tough and bitter.

Hearted cabbage (var. *capitata* – 'with a head'). This, the common cabbage, is very old. It was introduced into Britain by the Romans and into America by the first settlers. There are many types, of which some form exceedingly dense hearts, others only loose ones. There are varieties which make hearts at different times of the year, so that fresh cabbage can be had at all seasons.

A few special cabbages should be noted by the cook. The very tight white cabbages, which are grown particularly in Holland and widely exported, keep for many weeks (which other types of cabbage do not), are easily shredded and good for salads and for *sauerkraut*, but are not very nice when cooked. For that, the best is undoubtedly the Savoy, a winter variety with wrinkled leaves, which was developed in Savoy during the Middle Ages and brought to Britain during the 17th century. A Savoy compares with an ordinary cabbage as a sole with a whiting. On one occasion, a fussy Italian arrived at my home just as I was sitting down to a very frugal dinner – a Savoy – and had nothing more to offer. Crazy English and their cabbage! I could see it on his face. Yet, when he saw it, a lovely green on the dish, he wanted to try some. He ate two helpings.

Boiled Savoy

Take a sparkling fresh Savoy, remove the outer leaves and wash only if necessary. Cut out the thick stalks of the core without disturbing the shape. Plunge it into a large amount of water which is boiling fast over a high flame and has been carefully salted by tasting. Put on a well-fitting lid with a weight on top (this will raise the temperature slightly, a sort of primitive pressure cooker). Watch, test, and remove the cabbage the moment it is tender enough, but slightly crisp. It is better to undercook than overcook it. Drain very thoroughly, bottom downwards, so that the water can run out, helping with light pressure. Serve immediately with good salt, freshly-ground pepper and, if possible, a fine Alpine or Normandy butter.

Red cabbage is traditionally pickled in Britain, but is very decorative raw in salads. Also, in a sweet-sour form – sometimes with apple and caraway seeds – it is one of the best-loved vegetables in Germany, Denmark and Holland.

Røkaal

Shred the raw cabbage. Put it in a heavy pan (not iron) with a very little water and, for each 1 kg (2 lb) of cabbage, a tablespoon of sugar, 2 of butter, and a little vinegar. Stew gently for 2-3 hours; when it is nearly cooked, add ½ cup (roughly) of the juice squeezed from red currants, and more vinegar and sugar to taste. This red cabbage is better made the day before and reheated.

Jersey cabbage. A tall type of kale from the Channel Islands; in its second year it grows up to 3 m (10 ft) high, and the stalks make good walking sticks. This cabbage was much prized by my grandmother for making soup, but is not commonly met with.

Portugal cabbage, couve tronchuda, or Braganza cabbage. A distinct variety of cabbage with long, coarse stems. The white midribs of the leaves are sometimes cooked and eaten like *sea kale. The leaf can also be cooked as ordinary cabbage, and there is a frizzy type. This very hardy cabbage was introduced into Britain in the 19th century, but has not become popular, although, like the Jersey cabbage, it has a good flavour and is excellent in soups.

Portuguese Caldo Verde

A green soup, popular in Portugal. Brown a chopped onion in oil with a handful of lentils. Boil 2 potatoes, then purée them in 1 lt (1¾ pt) of milk. Add to the fried onion and lentils and simmer until cooked (about 30 minutes). Five minutes before serving, add 3 cups of the finely-shredded heart of Portugal cabbage.
[Cabbage – French: *chou* German: *Kohl* Italian: *cavolo* Spanish: *col*]

CABBAGE PALM. *See* palm cabbage.

CACAO. *See* chocolate.

CACTUS PEAR. *See* prickly pear.

CAFFEINE. The principal *alkaloid found in tea, coffee, cocoa and cola. Its effects are to stimulate the nervous system, to stop feelings of sleepiness and to clear the brain. It also increases the flow of urine. The amount necessary to have an effect varies between 100 and 300 mg. A cup of tea has 50 to 100 mg, coffee 100 to 150 mg and cocoa 50 mg. Cola drinks contain 35 to 55 mg per bottle.
[Caffeine – French: *caféine* German: *Kaffeestoff* Italian: *caffeina* Spanish: *cafeína*]

CALABRESE. *See* cauliflower.

CALALOO. *See* callaloo.

CALAMARE. *See* squid.

CALAMONDIN. *See* orange.

CALAMUS or sweet flag. A common marsh plant of the Northern hemisphere, native in the US and Asia but introduced to Europe. The plant (*Acorus calamus*),which grows wild in shallow water, is aromatic and the roots were at one time candied. Calamus is a flavouring used in liqueurs, but rarely in other contexts.
[Calamus – French: *roseau, jonc odorant, lis des marais* German: *gemeiner Kalmus* Italian: *calamo aromatico* Spanish: *cálamo*]

CALCIUM (Ca). A metallic element that makes up nearly 3.5% of the earth's crust yet cannot exist as a metal in nature because it reacts instantly with water. It occurs mainly as a carbonate in limestone, chalk and marble, but also as a sulphate in gypsum and as a phosphate (apatite). Calcium chloride occurs in seawater. Calcium makes up 5% of the weight of the human body and is an element of extreme biological importance, because calcium phosphate is a main constituent of bones and is essential in smaller amounts for the health of nerves and muscles, and for the blood clotting mechanism. Adequate calcium in assimilable form is essential in the diet, and must be accompanied by vitamin D, which aids in its absorption. Whole or skimmed milk, yoghurt and cheese are outstandingly rich in calcium, but not those milk products, like cream, cream cheese and butter, in which the fat is concentrated. Cauliflower, broccoli, cabbage and other *Brassica* greens are good sources, as are other vegetables including beans, leeks, watercress and lettuce. Small fish, which you eat complete with bones, such as whitebait and sardines in oil, are another. It is thought that an adult needs to take in 500 mg of calcium a day (others say double that or over) to be really healthy. In practice, much calcium is thrown away with the vegetable water.
[Calcium – French: *calcium* German: *Kalzium* Italian: *calcio* Spanish: *calcio*]

CALCIUM CARBONATE. *See* chalk.

CALF'S FOOT JELLY was once considered a wonderful restorative after sickness. I remember having it forced down my throat as a child after the 1918 influenza epidemic. Today it is treated with less enthusiasm.

71

CALLALOO or **calaloo** (though there seem to be almost as many spellings as there are Caribbean islands) is a West Indian soup and also the green leaves that are the soup's main ingredient. These are the young leaves of various *yams belonging to the arum family, notably those of dasheen and yautia. Also used as (and in) callaloo are local species of Amaranth *spinach; this is sold in cans in shops that sell Caribbean produce. According to Elisabeth Lambert Ortiz, who gives several callaloo recipes in her *Caribbean Cooking* (Deutsch), ordinary spinach or Swiss chard taste much the same and can be used as substitutes.

CALORIES. The Calorie of biology, medicine and the diet sheets is the large calorie or kilocalorie and is usually spelled with a capital C. It is 1,000 times the basic calorie of the physics lab, which is too small to be of use as a measurement in matters of eating. The Calorie is the amount of heat necessary to raise the temperature of 1 litre of water by 1 °C. It is necessary to think of it also as the way of expressing the quantity of heat produced when a substance is burned, i.e. as a measure of the energy a food contains. Since heat is a form of energy and energy is expended as work, we can also use calories to measure what we use up in being alive (metabolism) and what we need to do our chores, have fun and take exercise. This enables a balance to be struck between what we need and what we eat. If we eat more than we need, then either we must burn away the surplus food or store it as fat. Since there are many other considerations, such as whether the food is absorbed into the blood, the Calorie way of looking at diet gives us only a rather crude and basic sum, in particular, it takes no notice of the types of food, the proteins, oils, vitamins and trace elements, necessary for health. But it does provide an indication and is something to base a weight-watching diet on. Calories are now being replaced by *joules.

[*Calories* – French: *calories* German: *Kalorien* Italian: *calorie* Spanish: *calorías*]

CALVADOS. *See* fruit brandy.

CAMEL. There are two sorts of camel: the one-humped dromedary and the heavier, two-humped bactrian. Camels were first domesticated in deep south-eastern Arabia around 1300 BC. There are many recognized strains, some good for hauling loads, some for swift riding and yet others for giving milk. As they are precious animals and their meat

is a bit coarse and beefy, the people of the deserts generally prefer to eat goat or sheep, the other livestock which survive in all but the most arid regions. However, young camels are at times killed for feast days, and camel meat is quite commonly eaten in some places during the winter, especially in November and December when the sheep are bags of bones from the shortage of grass. The camel's hump is considered the best eating, and the meat is supposed to be 'warming'.

Camel milk is commonly drunk in desert regions and in towns with a desert hinterland. Together with dates, it is the main source of food for the poor, nomadic bedouin herdsmen. It is nourishing, but inclined to be purgative. Because the fat globules are in a finely-divided state (homogenized by nature, so to speak), no cream will rise, and it is profitless to try churning it to butter. It is, however, soured and churned to make *leben* (a kind of yoghurt), although more commonly it is drunk plain.

[*Camel* – French: *chameau* German: *Kamel* Italian: *cammello* Spanish: *camello*]

CAMOMILE or **chamomile**. Camomile tea is a well-known calming drink. It can be made from either of two herbs, both belonging to the composite family and claimed to be equally effective. They are the Sweet camomile (*Chamaemelum nobile*), a native of England, Western Europe and North Africa, and the Wild camomile or German camomile (*Matricaria recutica*), which grows wild over much of Europe, including Britain, and has been introduced in North America and Australia. Camomile can be bought in packets, dried and ready for making into camomile tea, which is brewed by pouring boiling water on the dried herb and infusing like any other tea.

[*Camomile* – French: *camomille* German: *Kamille* Italian: *camomilla* Spanish: *camomila, manzanilla*]

CAMPDEN TABLETS are a handy form of sodium metabisulphite ($Na_2S_2O_5$) and were originally made up for use in preserving fruit. Each tablet contains 0.44 g (7 grains) of sodium metabisulphite in a sugar base. Campden tablets are now much used by home wine and beer makers. The metabisulphites of both sodium and potassium are convenient sources of sulphur dioxide, very low concentrations of which will inhibit or destroy micro-organisms. Sulphite, as the winemakers call these compounds, is much less toxic to wine yeasts, some of which are actually encouraged if there are minute quantities of it still around. In any case, the action of the metabisulphite is largely finished after 24 hours, which is normally recommended as the time that should elapse before the wine yeast is added.

In wine must and other fruit juices, 50 ppm (parts per million) of sulphur dioxide will suffice to kill undesirable bacteria and stop the action of yeasts and moulds. If over-ripe or damaged fruit has been used, 100 or even 150 ppm of sulphur dioxide will be needed. These three concentrations are achieved by adding one, two or three Campden tablets for every 4.5 lt (1 gallon) of liquid – one Campden tablet per gallon gives 50 ppm of sulphur dioxide.

If you are going to have much use for metabisulphite, you will find it a lot cheaper and no less convenient to buy sodium (or potassium) metabisulphite from the chemist and make up your own stock solution. You can do this by completely dissolving 100 g metabisulphite in 500 ml hot water (or 4 oz in 1 pt) and diluting the solution to 1 lt (or 2 pt) with cold water. This 10% metabisulphite solution will keep for 4-6 months in a well stoppered bottle. This solution is said to contain 5% by weight of available sulphur dioxide, but, more important, 5 ml (1 teaspoon) of it is equivalent to one Campden tablet.

This 10% stock solution is also invaluable for sterilizing glass jars, bottles and equipment. If you keep a separate bottle of the solution for rinsing equipment, you can use it over and over again. The equipment should be cleaned before the sterilizing solution is poured in and swirled around; it should then drain for half an hour before use (or be swilled out with boiled water).

As the stock solution gives off a choking smell of sulphur dioxide, avoid working with it in very confined or ill-ventilated places. Weaker stock solutions, right down to 1%, have been recommended as a less smelly alternative, but they do not have the keeping qualities of the 10% solution. Their effectiveness can be increased by the addition of citric or tartaric acid, but the resulting brew will last for only a few days. One such recipe uses 2 Campden tablets (or 10 ml or 2 teaspoons stock solution) plus ¼ teaspoon citric acid in 500 ml (1 pt) water. This is an effective rinsing solution but should be thrown away after use.

Metabisulphites are something of a panacea for the home winemaker. Not only are they used to treat the must and sterilize the equipment, but they are also added to the wine at later stages to discourage new yeast growths and prevent browning that may be caused by the absorption of oxygen. The latter action depends on another quality of a metabisulphite – it is a reducing agent, which is to say that it combines eagerly with any free oxygen. For this reason, it will also prevent cut apples from going brown. The main uses of metabisulphites in the kitchen are in *bottling, *drying and making *candied fruit.

CANDIED FRUIT, fruit confit, crystallized fruit and preserved fruit. Candied fruit is fruit or pieces of fruit (e.g. candied peel) impregnated with sugar (which acts as a preservative), then washed and dried on the surface. The surface is covered with crystalline sugar in crystallized fruits; a glazed surface characterizes *fruit confit* (e.g. glace cherries and *marrons glacés*). Preserved fruit (e.g. preserved ginger), will be packed in a dense syrup, unless otherwise stated.

Essentially, the technique leading up to all of these products is the same. The fruits (and certain vegetables, like carrots, as well as angelica stalks) are prepared – peeled, cored, scraped, cut in suitable sized pieces, etc. A few items, like marrow, demand special techniques, such as an initial soaking of the pieces in *lime water overnight, and fruit which discolours when cut up must be kept in water in which a *Campden tablet has been dissolved or which has been laced with ascorbic acid (*vitamin C) or lemon juice. After preparation, the fruit must be boiled until it is just tender and, if it is in large pieces, pricked all over with a needle to aid sugar penetration.

The methods used in preserving fruit to be packed in syrup and to be candied differ in some details. In preserved fruit, some of the juices can flavour the syrup, but in candied fruit, the juices should stay in the fruit. Preserving fruit in syrup is a less critical process; the sugar concentration can be raised fairly rapidly, and the syrup can be made with pure cane sugar. Candying needs more care: the sugar concentration must be raised slowly and (for best results) the sugar should be mixed with glucose.

Fruit Preserved in Syrup

Stack the prepared fruit in layers in a container, and cover each layer well with sugar to a total of half the weight of the fruit. After 24 hours, juice will have run from the fruit to make a syrup, usually of about 30-35% sugar. Add more sugar to bring the strength up to 60%. To calculate how much sugar is necessary to do this, you should ideally use a syrup-measuring *hydrometer, but alternatively you may rely on adding the same weight of sugar as used previously.

Now bring the pot of fruit to the boil and boil it for 4-5 minutes. Leave it to cool and let it stand for 24 hours. Next day, repeat the process, and add more sugar, bringing it up to 68% and do it again the following day, in a final boiling to raise the sugar to 70%. Leave the fruit in this syrup for 4-5 days until it is thoroughly impregnated. It is then ready to be packed into jars, covered with the syrup and sealed to prevent evaporation.

Candied Fruits

For candied, crystallized or *confit* fruit, a sugar mixture of 2 parts cane sugar to 1 part glucose gives better results than pure cane sugar. The glucose stops the fruit going hard. Make a 30% syrup with 300 g (11 oz) sugar mixture per litre (1¾ pt) water, and boil the prepared fruit in it for 2 minutes. Then allow it to cool and leave it for a day or so, during which time the fruit must be kept submerged in the syrup. Repeat the same process every day, adding sugar to increase its strength by no more than 10% each time (and for the very best results only 5%) until a 70% syrup (or thereabouts) is reached. Leave the fruit in this concentrated syrup for a week, so that it becomes completely impregnated with sugar, after which it can be very quickly rinsed in boiling water and dried off on a tray at not more than 48°C (120°F).If the fruit is to be crystallized, do not wash it, but dip it into coarse sugar before drying. For a *glacé* effect, wash and dry the fruit, then dip it into crack-boiled sugar for a moment or soak it in a dilute (1%) pectin solution and dry it for 2-3 hours at a low temperature (48°C or 119°F).This gives the fruit a shiny glaze.

Candied peel is the peel of various citrus fruit (oranges, bitter oranges, lemons and citrons) preserved by impregnating with sugar. During the glut seasons of winter and spring, the fruits are cut into two and held in brine until wanted. The salt is then soaked out, and the peel is cooked and soaked in syrups of increasing strengths as described above. Candied peel varies enormously in quality; it may be succulent or hard. These days, it is very often chopped in the factory and sold as mixed peel. Many people who like the taste of candied peel do not like the hard bits, which are rather indigestible, and prefer to put peel through the mincer.

[*Candied fruit* – French: *fruit confit* German: *kandierte Frucht* Italian: *frutta candita* Spanish: *fruta azucarada*

Candied peel – French: *zeste confit, zeste d'Italie* German: *Zitronat*]

CANDLE NUT. This tropical nut (*Aleurites moluccana*), a member of the spurge family, is so oily that it can be burned like a candle. Under the name of *kemiri* or *buah keras* (kras), it is used in Malay and Indonesian cooking, crushed in soups, ground with other ingredients for *saté* and curry pastes. When fresh and raw, the nuts are violently purgative, indeed poisonous, but the poison dissipates after they have been kept for some time, and the nuts can be used, often first roasted, in cooking. *Macadamia nuts are recommended as a substitute, as also are the less oily almonds, the latter even being preferred in South East Asia by those who can afford them.

CANELLINI. *See* kidney bean.

CANNING. Canned foods, something we take for granted, are derived from the heat-sterilized bottled foods, which are supposed to have been invented by Nicolas Appert early in the 19th century to help feed Napoleon's armies. Before canned food could replace bottled food, tin plate had to be invented. Today, canning is a huge industry, and since certain varieties of fruit and vegetable respond to canning better than others, huge acreages of produce are grown near the canneries by farmers working under contract and often using seeds or plants developed and provided by the canners. Crops have also to be harvested at exactly the right stage, which demands close collaboration between farmer and canner.

Canning is mainly done in containers made of plain or lacquered tin plate. Although the materials used pass under human inspection, the processes of selection, grading and cleaning in large factories are done almost entirely by machinery. So also is the filling of the cans with the food.The cans are usually exhausted and sealed before sterilization, in contrast to the old methods in which the food was sealed in the container immediately after heating, to remove as much air as possible. Fruit is usually sterilized at a temperature near boiling, 94°C (202°F) or thereabouts, depending on the product, and vegetables at well over boiling temperature in an autoclave for 20-45 minutes, which is necessary to ensure the destruction of all bacterial spores that could cause spoilage or health risks.

There is little point in home canning and there are strong reasons against it. Where canning or bottling acid fruit may be safe, the home canning of vegetables is not, unless the person doing it is very careful, very expert and very well equipped. Statistics show that most outbreaks of botulism (*see* poisoning) can be traced to home canning. As this disease is so often fatal, do-it-yourself canning is best forgotten. An expert from the Metal Box Company whom I consulted, advised: 'Don't do it!' However, in spite of a very few highly publicized scares, food poisoning from commercially-canned foods is so rare as to be negligible, because of the scientific control which has been perfected over the years by engineers and scientists in the canners' laboratories.

[*Canning* – French: *mettre en boite* German: *eindosen* Italian: *conservare in iscatola* Spanish: *enlatar*]

CAN SIZES. *See* weights and measures.

CANTALOUPE. *See* melon.

CAPE BUTTERCUP. *See* yam (*Oxalis* tubers).

CAPE GOOSEBERRY. *See* physalis fruit.

CAPER. Capers (*Capparis spinosa*, spiny; *Capperis inermis*, spineless), which grow wild all round the Mediterranean, have been used as a condiment for thousands of years. Plants may often be seen hanging down over old walls and growing on building sites or on the rough ground at the edges of roads. They can be recognized by their flowers, which look a little like large wild roses with tassels of long purple stamens. Caper flowers have a very short life – they open in the morning and are wilted by lunch time – but if a spray is cut and put in water in the house, the unopened buds will burst into flower – and last for a day or more. Capers are the small, immature flower buds (the cucumber-like fruit, which have annoying small seeds inside, are sometimes pickled in country areas). Raw capers have none of the interesting goaty taste, which develops only when they have been pickled.

Although capers are very easy to grow in a dry warm climate, they are expensive because of the great amount of hand work necessary in picking them. This is especially the case with the best capers, which are made from the very small hard buds. The plant has to be picked over almost every morning, just as the buds reach the proper size, and it takes a long time to gather a worthwhile quantity. Raw capers may sometimes be bought in Mediterranean country markets, or you can pick your own, as I do each year.

The capers should be washed well to remove dust and then spread out in the sun to dry and wilt for a day. They can then be put into jars of strongly salted wine vinegar. The best pickled capers (*non-pareilles*) can be bought packed in bottles, and their quality is shown by the price; but in the countries around the Mediterranean where capers are an everyday ingredient, they are also sold in the markets, loose, by weight. Some are even dry-salted (but are not very nice). In either case, the loose capers should be covered with well-salted vinegar at home if they are not to be used within a few days. Capers should always be kept covered with liquid, as otherwise they develop a nasty taste. A well-known use of capers is in the caper sauce which is eaten with boiled mutton, but they also go into many other sauces. Grated lemon rind and garlic combine exceptionally well with capers, and I always use them together. Capers are used with fish, in salads and *hors d'oeuvre*, for decoration, and for special accent (as in liptauer cheese). Addicts eat them on bread and butter when nobody is looking.

Other buds and seeds which look superficially rather like capers are sometimes advocated as substitutes, particularly the caper spurge (*Euphorbia lathyrus*) and the young fruit of the nasturtium. Spurges are best avoided, as most species are poisonous. Pickled nasturtium fruit have a very interesting mustard overtone and may be regarded as a condiment in their own right. They are wilted and put into salted vinegar in exactly the same way as capers.

[*Caper* – French: *câpre* German: *Kaper* Italian: *cappero* Spanish: *alcaparra*]

CAPERCAILLIE. *See* grouse.

CAPOCOLLA. *See* coppa.

CAPSICUM. A genus of plants in the Solanaceae, the potato, tomato and nightshade family, which are native to tropical America and the West Indies. The two gastronomically important species are *chilli pepper (*Capsicum frutescens*), which is also sold dried and ground as red pepper or cayenne pepper, and *sweet pepper (*Capsicum annuum*), which, dried and ground, forms the spices, *paprika and *pimentón.

[*Capsicum* – French: *capsicum* German: *spanischer Pfeffer* Italian: *peperone* Spanish: *pimiento*]

CARAMBOLA (*Averrhoa carambola*). A tropical fruit belonging to the Oxalidaceae, the wood-sorrel family, and native to Indonesia. The fruits, borne on a small tree, are a delicate, translucent yellow or greenish-yellow, and 7-12 cm (3-5 in) long, with a characteristic lobed shape. When sweet, this can be a nice juicy fruit; it is popular in China. It is used in fruit salads, jellies, drinks and preserves. When sour, it makes a useful souring agent and is used in South India, where it is a substitute for tamarind. The carambola prefers a hot humid climate. The Indian name is *kamrakh*.

CARAMEL. If sugar is heated through the various stages to hard crack and extra-hard crack, further heating will produce caramel. Caramelization begins when the sugar starts to turn amber, it then goes red-brown and finally black. This occurs at around 180°C (356°F), although, in practice, sugar may begin to caramelize before then, during boiling. In the process, sugar breaks down into other substances and a characteristic flavour develops.

Caramel to be used as a flavouring or to coat moulds is easily made by heating sugar with a very little water to melt it, then continuing to heat it, watching carefully, until the desired degree of caramelization is reached. Over-heating results in burning and a bitter taste. The unwanted caramelization that takes place during jam-making or when boiling sugar for sweets is usually due to local over-heating on the bottom of the pan, or on the sides where sugar has splashed. It may be prevented by careful stirring to make sure that sugar never sticks to the bottom and by washing down the sides of the pan with a brush dipped in water.

Caramel also tends to form when sugar is cooked for too long. It is responsible for giving over-cooked jam its brownish colour and poor flavour. As a schoolboy, I used to work at making butterscotch for pocket money. The aim, I was told, was to get it as light coloured as possible, with no hint of a caramel taste. The quicker the temperature could be raced up without burning, the less caramelization there would be, and the paler and more delicate the result. In the end, I became so proficient that my aunt (who kept a rather famous tea shop) was no longer able to sell it. 'It doesn't look home-made,' the customers complained.

[*Caramel* – French: *caramel* German: *Karamel* Italian: *caramella* Spanish: *caramelo*]

CARAWAY. This spice seed comes from an umbelliferous plant (*Carum carvi*) which grows wild in many parts of Europe and Asia. The young green leaves of caraway are sometimes used as a green herb and have a flavour somewhere between parsley and dill. However, it is the ripe seeds that are important, particularly in German and Austrian cooking. It lies often unrecognized in the characteristic flavour of Austrian food – with meat as well as in sweet dishes. Caraway seeds are used with cheese, with cabbage, in *sauerkraut*, sprinkled over roast pork, ground in sausages, with paprika in *gulash*, and on bread. In Britain, however, caraway seeds are now mainly associated with seed cake, although they were used much more in the past.

[*Caraway* – French: *carvi, cumin des prés* German: *Kümmel* Italian: *carvi, comino dei prati* Spanish: *alcaravea*]

CARBOHYDRATES get their name because they contain carbon combined with hydrogen and oxygen in the same 2:1 proportion as in water. Among carbohydrates are starch, sugar, glucose, pectin and cellulose. They are synthesized out of carbon dioxide and water by green plants which use the energy from sunlight for the purpose. The process is called photosynthesis. Carbohydrates are used as fuel by animals. Total or almost total removal of carbohydrate from the diet (the basis of the Atkins diet) forces the body to mobilize and use its fat reserves to make its own carbohydrate.

[*Carbohydrates* – French: *hydrates de carbone* German: *Kohlenhydrat* Italian: *idrati di carbonio* Spanish: *hidratos de carbone*]

CARBONATED WATER. *See* soda water.

CARBON DIOXIDE or **carbonic acid gas** (CO_2). The gas of soda water exists in small amounts in the air and is a necessary food for green plant life. It is formed when there is a fire – whenever organic matter is burned with adequate air (with insufficient air the very poisonous carbon monoxide, CO, is formed instead). Carbon dioxide gas is denser than air. It dissolves in water to give a weak acid – carbonic acid – which in nature slowly dissolves limestone and chalk, making the water hard and causing caverns in the rock. Carbon dioxide can be solidified by cold and high pressure; blocks of carbon dioxide snow or 'dry ice' are often used in ice cream carts – the blocks evaporating to gas at atmospheric pressure have a temperature of -78°C (-108°F). Carbon dioxide is the gas formed during the fermentation of wine and beer. If it is prevented from escaping (say in a screw-top bottle), its pressure builds up. Under pressure, carbon dioxide dissolves in water to a greater extent than under normal atmospheric pressure; it comes out again as a fizz when the pressure is released. Dissolved carbon dioxide gives a pleasant prickle in the throat, which is why drinks with a natural fizz, which have been known since ancient times, were later joined by drinks artificially gassed under pressure. Carbon dioxide under high pressure stops fermentation, a quality utilised to hold fruit juices (e.g. apple) in bulk before filtration to remove yeast cells. This technique has made possible the bottling of certain non-alcoholic fruit juices without pasteurization or preservatives.

[*Carbon dioxide* – French: *gaz carbonique* German: *Kohlensäuregas, Kohlendioxyd* Italian: *biossido di carbonio* Spanish: *dióxido de carbono*]

CARDAMOM. A highly aromatic spice seed which tastes vaguely like eucalyptus but is far sweeter and richer. The plant *Elettaria cardamomum* is related to ginger. A native of the wet, tropical jungles of southern India, it is now grown in many other places in the tropics. The small, dark brown or black seeds are borne inside capsules which may, as they reach us, be creamy, brownish, pale green or white. Much larger, dark brown, often hairy seed capsules of another cardamom species are commonly sold as black cardamoms. They are less aromatic, but cheaper. Cardamom is an expensive spice, one good reason why it should not be bought ready-ground – adulteration is too tempting. The other reason is that ground cardamom rapidly loses its best essential oils. It is better to break open the capsules and use the fresh seeds. Cardamom is important in Indian cooking. It is also much used in Scandinavia and Germany in cakes, in meat dishes (like *Sauerbraten*) and in pickled herrings. A seed dropped into coffee gives a strange taste (well known to anyone who has travelled in the Middle East) which most people will enjoy and which guests inquire about.

[*Cardamom* – French: *cardamome* German: *Kardamome* Italian: *cardamomo* Spanish: *cardamomo*]

CARDOON. A native of the Mediterranean region, the cardoon (*Cynara cardunculus*) is a close relative of the globe artichoke. However, it is not eaten for its thistle heads, but for its leaf stalks (which are like very large sticks of celery). Cardoons are best when blanched; otherwise they are too bitter. To prepare them, scrape the tender ribs and strip off the fibres and prickles on the outside. Then cut the ribs into suitable lengths. The simplest way to cook them is in boiling salted water until they are tender (25-30 minutes).They may then be served with butter, a rich white sauce or a cheese sauce; other methods are described in French and Italian cookbooks. Raw cardoon is eaten with the *bagna cauda* in Piedmont. The tender leaf part may also be eaten if it is treated in the same way as spinach. The flower buds can be used like artichokes. The flavour of cardoon is delicate and only vaguely like artichoke. It comes into season in Mediterranean climates at the end of summer and lasts into early winter.

[*Cardoon* – French: *cardon* German: *Kardone* Italian: *cardone* Spanish: *cardo silvestre*]

CAROB or **locust bean**. A leguminous tree (*Ceratonio siliqua*) which is said to have its origin in Syria, though it has been grown around the Mediterranean for so long that it is one of the commonest sights amongst the pines on stony, dry hillsides, where few other trees can gain a footing. The pods, which turn dark brown in the autumn, have a very sweet pulp (50% sugar) and are sometimes sold as sweets for children. But they have a peculiar taste, which is not very pleasant perhaps, especially after you have smelled a stack of them fermenting on the quayside of a Mediterranean island, as they wait for shipment as cattle food. They are supposed to be the locusts eaten by John the Baptist, but why not the insects which are also eaten in many countries? Carob beans have recently come into fashion as a health food, but I have never succeeded in making anything very nice out of them (I have tried, as they are going begging). In the countries where they grow, carob beans are often not gathered. In Majorca, a thick, brown, treacly aperitif called *palo* is made from them and is much prized locally for its good effect on the stomach. The leathery leaves are used to stuff into the tops of jars of olives to keep them under the brine.

[*Carob* – French: *caroube* German: *Johannisbrot* Italian: *carruba* Spanish: *algarroba*]

CARMINE. *See* cochineal.

CARP. There are hundreds of species of carp, mostly fish of fresh or brackish water, ranging from the goldfish to huge, active fish like the *mahseer*, a famous game fish of the northern hill streams of India. Surprisingly, the Common carp (*Cyprinus carpio*) is not native to Europe; it was introduced from further east during the Middle Ages and was soon widely established in rivers and fish ponds. It was taken onwards to North America in the latter half of the 19th century and became naturalized, particularly in the Mid-West. Carp are plentiful in the great inland seas of Russia, in the Sea of Azov and the Caspian, where they are fished along with the sturgeon. Even there, they may have been introduced and their natural home may be the rivers of China.

The importance of the Common carp is that it can so easily be farmed – as can many of its close relatives, which are often much larger. Because carp live on plankton, they live peacefully with other fish, and their food can be encouraged to proliferate by fertilizing the water with measured amounts of manure or purified sewage. They can, however, acquire a muddy taste when they live in stagnant ponds – which perhaps accounts for the poor reputation they had in Britain before the Industrial Revolution when the streams and rivers still held a profusion of fine fish. Carp are not only very hardy, standing considerable variation in conditions, but can even survive for a long time – up to a week – out of water if they are packed in wet moss. They are very long lived, reaching at least 50 years and weighing as much as 20 kg (44 lb) in exceptional circumstances. In parks, they become very tame, as they regard people as a source of food, not as a danger, whereas in the wild state they have become very cunning and have earned the title of 'fox of the waters' from anglers.

As food fish, carp are inclined to be coarse even when young; they need a good sauce. Their flavour also depends very much on their food, although some of their occasional muddy taste can be removed by soaking in brine or in vinegar and water. Nevertheless, the only thing to do with a really muddy carp is throw it away. On the other hand, with its firm flesh and easy bones, the carp is highly esteemed in many countries. It is a versatile fish and can be cooked in almost any way, even *au bleu* – many national cookbooks give regional recipes. Normal sizes range from 1 kg (2 lb) to fine specimens of 4 kg (9 lb), above which the fish becomes increasingly coarse. Specimens from carp farms are normally around 1 kg (2 lb), a weight they reach at the end of their third summer. The typical carp has large, strong scales, which can be left on if the fish is to be skinned after cooking. Otherwise, they have to be removed, an operation which is made easier by quickly dunking the fish in boiling water. The gills should generally be removed

as they can be a source of the muddy taste, and the gall sac must be extracted carefully.

There are two artificially-bred varieties, the Mirror carp, which has a few very large scales, and the Leather carp, which has a leathery skin and almost no scales at all. Carp are said to be in season from 17th June to 13th March, when they are not breeding. The soft roe is a delicacy which is often cooked separately.

Many important Chinese dishes are built around carp, and a sweet-sour sauce of some kind is also popular with this fish in Europe.

[*Carp* – French: *carpe* German: *Karpfen* Italian: *carpio, carpione* Spanish: *carpa*]

CARRAGEEN, **Irish moss**, **sea-moss** or **pearl moss**. One of the red algae, a tufted and fan-like seaweed, carrageen (*Chondrus crispus*) is found on rocky coasts of Northern Europe – notably in Ireland and Brittany – and across the Atlantic from Maine to North Carolina. This weed is collected especially in New England and commercially in Massachusetts, where it is spread out to dry and bleach on the beaches. It is moistened with seawater and allowed to dry again four or five times until the pale yellow, horny material called 'moss' results. This material contains a mucilaginous substance, carrageenin, which is much used in the preparation of commercial ice cream, soups and salad dressings. Carrageen can be gathered and sun dried by anyone interested enough, but can be bought as well. Typically, soak the dried material – after careful washing – for 20-30 minutes, then boil it in water or milk for a quarter of an hour or so. Strain off the liquid, which can be sweetened with sugar or honey. Add flavourings, such as fruit juice or sherry. When the liquid begins to set, fold in cream or beaten egg white. Jellies and drinks made with carrageen were in the past considered good for invalids.

[*Carrageen* – French: *carragheen, mousse perlée d'Irlande* German: *irländisches Moos, Perlmoos* Italian: *lichene d'Irlanda* Spanish: *musgo de Irlanda, carragahen*]

CARROT. One of the world's most important root vegetables. The wild carrot (*Daucus carota*), which grows all over Europe, looks very unpromising food, and the garden carrot, which has been cultivated for two or three thousand years, is regarded as a distinct subspecies (ssp. *sativus*).The shape of the root ranges from conical to almost cylindrical and even globular. Orange varieties are the most commonly cultivated, but there are others with dark purple roots and usually a paler or greenish core. The latter are cultivated mostly in the warmer countries, such as Spain, Italy and India. Poor varieties may have a woody central core, especially when old. Carrots have an incomparable flavour when freshly pulled and cooked without scraping, since most of the flavour is in the skin. Unfortunately, they are now usually washed with high-pressure hoses to remove mud before marketing, and this ruins them. The outside quickly goes slushy and, after this has been removed, the usual tasteless vegetable results. Some recipes use herbs or add caramelized sugar and butter to produce a toffee flavour, but such expedients should not be necessary, as carrots are a flavouring in themselves. As such, they are frequently used in marinades, *court-bouillons*, *fumets* and stocks, occasionally browned to caramelize their sugar.

Although carrots are rich in vitamins and in substances from which the body can make vitamin A, relatively little is absorbed by the human body from raw carrot which, however, especially when lightly perfumed with lemon zest, is an excellent part of salads or *crudités*. Many umbelliferous herbs (e.g. chervil, parsley, anise, fennel) go well with carrot, which is also an umbellifer.

[*Carrot* – French: *carotte* German: *Möhre* Italian: *corota* Spanish: *zanahoria*]

CASEIN. A heat-stable, insoluble substance containing phosphorus and calcium, casein is the main protein that can be extracted from milk. The tiny protein particles which are in colloidal suspension in milk are precipitated by dilute mineral acids – like the hydrochloric acid in the stomach – and by the lactic acid which is formed when milk sours, as in yoghurt. It is digested by the enzymes in the stomach (pepsin) and the large intestine (pancreatin) and by similar enzymes which are produced by micro-organisms, such as the bacteria in hard cheese and the moulds in blue-veined cheese.

[*Casein* – French: *caséine* German: *Kasein* Italian: *caseina* Spanish: *caseína*]

CASHEW. The nut of the cashew (*Anacardium occidentale*) grows out of the end of the fruit in a most peculiar and distinctive manner. The tree belongs to the same family as the mango and pistachio and comes from Brazil, where the native Indian name was *acaju*. As *cajú*, it was taken to Goa in India by the Portuguese and planted there

in the 16th century; today, South India is one of the world's largest exporters of nuts, on a level with Brazil itself. The cashew is also grown around the African coasts, in Malaya, the West Indies and elsewhere.

The tree will grow in poor sandy soil with a low rainfall, but is at its best in the tropics near the sea. The fruit turns from green to yellow or orange with reddish tints when ripe. It is edible, but somewhat tart, fibrous and astringent from its tannin content. When this has been removed by boiling (3-4 minutes in slightly salty water) or pressure cooking for 5 minutes, it makes a very nice drink. Sugar must be added as the malic acid in the fruit makes it sour. Both in Brazil and in India (especially in Goa), the cashew fruit, or 'apple', is fermented to make a wine and is the basis also for vinegar.

Cashew nuts are green or pinkish when tender, becoming grey when fully ripe. They can be eaten green and, in South India, are considered a delicacy when fried in various dishes. However, the shell is hard and oozes a dangerously blistering oily substance containing cardol and anacardic acid, even when the nuts are fully ripe. Green nuts must therefore be removed and washed with great care, without getting this oil on the skin. Wood ashes will help neutralize the oil, which is also dissipated by heating. Commercially, nuts are roasted in the shell in a rotating kiln. If doing the job by hand use care, as they easily burn. The acrid fumes are nasty. The shells used to be cracked by hand, but machines have been recently devised to do this delicate job.

Good cashews are white, plump and sweet. The best quality nuts are sold whole or as halves; they are rather brittle, with a 'short' texture, unlike that of other nuts. Containing 47% oils, 21% protein and 22% carbohydrate, with considerable vitamin and mineral value, they are a good food. It is better to buy cashew nuts as required and not attempt to store them for very long at home.

For a long time, they have been roasted and salted to serve with drinks in the tropics. When I first went to India, I was advised that eating too many would make me sick, but I have never found this to be the case and have frequently eaten more than a reasonable amount. Cashew nuts are much used in the cooking of South India, particularly in dishes from Kerala. They may be used whole or ground and are usually added late in the cooking, sometimes just before the dish is taken off the fire.

[*Cashew nut* – French: *noix d'acajou* German: *Elefantenlaus* Italian: *noce d'anacardo* Spanish: *nuez de anacardo*]

CASSAREEP. A dark, almost black, syrupy substance, essential for pepperpot, a Caribbean stew which originated in Guyana. To make cassareep, grate peeled bitter *cassava root, mixing it with about 100 ml (about 4 fl oz) cold water per kg (2 lb) of root, leaving it to soak for some minutes, then squeezing out the juice. To this, add about 2 teaspoons of brown sugar per kg (2 lb), cassava and a pinch each of cloves and cinnamon (although these spices came from the East and must not have figured in original pre-Columbian recipes); simmer the liquid until a syrupy consistency is reached. Bottled, prepared cassareep can be bought in shops that specialize in West Indian food. It can be very good.

CASSAVA, **manioc** or **yuca**. The large, starchy tubers of the cassava plant (*Manihot utilissima*) are a staple in some tropical countries, notably in Central America and West Africa. The plant is easy to grow – it shoots up to some 3 m (10 ft) in nine months – and the tubers are easy to harvest. In fact, it is a good, lazy, hot-country crop.

There are some 150 varieties, which fall broadly into two classes – sweet and bitter. Cassavas belong to the spurge family (Euphorbiaceae); they are often poisonous, and tubers of many varieties contain a glucoside which, when acted on by enzymes, produces quantities of deadly hydrocyanic acid (*see* bitter *almonds). This is exceedingly volatile and is driven off on cooking, but bitter cassavas must not be eaten raw as they are poisonous unless cooked.

Cassava tubers are typically 25-30 cm (about 12 in) long and as thick as your wrist. They are covered with a scaly, rather hairy, bark which has to be peeled off (best do it under a tap). After this, the flesh can be grated, the juice squeezed out in a cloth (*cassareep can be made from that) and the pulp baked as flat cakes. It is also chipped, soaked, dried and deep fried (exactly as for potato chips), or made into a dried meal (*farhina* or *farine de manioc*). Outside the tropics though, most people know cassava best as *tapioca.

A correspondent from the West Indies writes: 'Cassava bread is not a taste teaser. We used to pour a rough Spanish red wine over it, and call it "wetdish-rag" in Cuba and the Dominican Republic, the presumption being a wet dish-rag would have tasted better, soap and all.' As a food, cassava is particularly low in protein and high in starch; a diet in which it predominates can lead to malnutrition.

[*Cassava* – French: *cassave, manioc* German: *Maniok (Brotwurzle)* Italian: *cassava manioca* Spanish: *canabe, mandioca*]

CASTOR OIL Some idiot once told my small daughter that the seeds of the castor oil plant (*Ricinus communis* and allied species) were good to eat. Luckily, she did not eat many as they contain not only the well-known oil, but also some very poisonous substances (one of which, ricin, came to prominence as a means of political assassination). I have, however, one reference to castor oil being used in India to grease the *tava* (the circular iron plate, rather like a girdle) with ghee for frying chillies for a mutton pilau. 'The castor oil will counteract the heating effect of the green chillies (its pungency disappears on cooking).'

[*Castor oil* – French: *huile de ricin* German: *Rizmusöl* Italian: *olio di ricino* Spanish: *aceite de ricino*]

CASSIA. *See* cinnamon.

CATCHUP. *See* ketchup.

CATECHU or **cutch** is the gummy substance which forms when chips of wood from the Indian tree, *Acacia catechu*, are boiled in water and the resulting solution is evaporated by further boiling. Catechu, very astringent and rich in tannin, is used in *pan for chewing. It is also the red-brown dye with which the sails of fishing boats were once preserved, and, suitably mordanted, was also used to dye khaki.

CATMINT or **catnip** (*Nepeta cataria*). Growing wild over much of Europe, this typical labiate is well known as a garden plant loved by bees and cats. It is sometimes used as a culinary herb, but was more popular in the past and was used in Roman times. Dried, it can be used on pork roasted on a spit over an open fire. Rub on as much as will stick to the meat, and use no other seasoning. Dried catmint, intended as a medicinal tea, can be bought from health-food shops.

[*Catmint* – French: *cataire, herbe aux chats* German: *Katzenminze* Italian: *erba dei gatti* Spanish: *calaminta, calamento*]

CATSUP. *See* ketchup.

CATTLEY. *See* guava.

CAUL. A membranous cap that covers the heads of some babies at birth. Also the name often used for the omentum, the mesenteries and even the peritoneum of mammals. Caul is a strong, nearly-transparent membrane with islands of fat, which give it a lacy appearance. It is strong because it has to suspend the various organs inside the abdominal cavity. Butchers once used it to cover legs of mutton, to make them look attractive. By the cook, it is used as a covering for faggots, *crépinettes* and *gayettes*. Before trying to use caul, put it in warm water with a little salt or vinegar to soften the fat and unstick the layers of membrane; otherwise it tears easily.

CAULIFLOWER. The original cauliflower (*cavoli a fiore* or 'flower cabbage') appears to have come from the Orient – where it goes back to ancient times – and is variously said to have come into Spain with the Arabs in the 12th century, and into Italy in the 16th. At any rate, as a vegetable it became established in Europe fairly late. It was being grown in Britain by the 18th century. The cauliflower does not particularly like the British climate, so will only thrive in summer.

A late arrival from Italy is broccoli, which matures in the winter and is only a type of cauliflower, but distinguished by gardeners who must be conscious of the seasons. The cook, buying in the market, calls all white varieties cauliflowers, and distinguishes the winter ones from the summer only by the leaves which curl over to protect the curd in the latter. 'Broccoli' has come to be applied only to the open-sprouted forms, such as calabrese and purple sprouting broccoli, particularly since 'broccoli' has become familiar as a frozen vegetable. The gardeners' distinction between summer cauliflower and winter broccoli is now largely disregarded.

The cauliflower and its brothers are, incredibly, all varieties of the same species as *cabbage. The flower stalks of the cauliflower have become thickened into storage organs, producing the curd-like 'flower'. Perhaps the fact that it is a converted flower accounts for the nutritive richness of cauliflower, which contains, as well as the more usual vegetable vitamins (ascorbic acid, riboflavine,thiamine and niacin), considerable amounts of folic acid, one of the B vitamins, which is not found in such quantity in other vegetables. Since lack of folic acid causes certain types of anaemia, cauliflower has been christened 'vegetable liver' by some health-food enthusiasts. As it also contains considerable amounts of calcium in an assimilable form, as well as useful iron, it is very helpful to anyone who cannot take milk.

Types of cauliflower vary somewhat in their cooking quality, and beauty is not always the best guide when shopping, since some cauliflowers which do not have the aesthetically ideal tight curd and white colour may prove excellent for eating. But a cauliflower should look and feel really fresh and firm, with no wilted bits. The leaves should not have been trimmed away, as that is done by retailers to fool the customer. Moreover, cauliflowers will not keep after trimming; old cauliflowers are horrid.

Broccoli – in the modern usage of the word – has no compact curd. It may be white but is more usually green or purple. Most familiar is calabrese (the Italian *broccoli calabrese* means broccoli from Calabria). In calabrese, when the central head is cut out, the plant goes mad and produces delicious side shoots. Although these shoots remain quite good even when they are beginning to flower, you must be sure they are fresh and not flowering because they have been picked for several days. Sprouting broccoli and calabrese deserve care in cooking, even if they are no longer luxury vegetables. All except the large cauliflower-shaped varieties should be tied in small bundles before plunging into fast-boiling salted water. They should be cooked for a minimum time, just to make them tender, and in general treated with the same respect as asparagus. There are a number of unusual kinds of broccoli, such as the perennial variety which produces a succession of 'cauliflowers', or sprouts and broccoli, on one plant, but as yet these are only garden curiosities.

[*Cauliflower* – French: *chou-fleur* German: *Blumenkohl* Italian: *cavolfiore* Spanish: *coliflor*

Broccoli – French: *chou-broccoli* German: *Spargelkohl* Italian: *broccoli* Spanish: *bróculi; brécol*]

CAUSTIC SODA or sodium hydroxide (NaOH). As the name suggests, this is highly caustic and dangerous; it should be kept in an airtight container (or it loses its strength) and well out of reach of children. Caustic soda dissolves readily in water, getting very hot in the process, to form an alkaline solution which, when strong, will dissolve paper and other vegetable matter, and react with fats to form soap. The solution must not be kept in a glass stoppered bottle, as the stopper will refuse to come out. It must be handled with rubber gloves, as it will seriously blister the skin and, even when dilute, will soften the nails. Like other alkalis, it feels slimy (the slimy feeling can be removed with an acid like vinegar). Caustic soda was once a common household ingredient, because people saved fat and made their own kitchen soap. Today it is used commercially in dilute solution for various purposes (for instance to speed the cure of green olives by removing their bitterness, and for treating the skins of peaches before canning), especially as a substitute for *lye.

[Caustic soda – French: soude caustique, hydrate de soude German: Ätznatron Italian: soda caustic Spanish: sosa cáustica]

CAVALANCE. See cowpea.

CAVEACH. The word comes through the Spanish from the Arab sakbay, meaning meat or fish pickled in vinegar. It is usually fish that is preserved in this way, but the method is sometimes used for meat, brains or tongue. Caveach differs from soused fish in being fried before pickling and having extra oil added to cover it if the fish is to be preserved. Escabeche, the Spanish and Provençal version, is used mainly as an hors d'oeuvre. It can be bought by weight or packed in jars at delicatessen stores, but is very easy and rewarding to make at home and will keep for some months in a cool place.

Most fish can be caveached – cod, salmon, mackerel, smelts, whiting, red mullet, sardines, tunny, anchovies, etc. are all recommended.

Fried fish preserved in vinegar was a Roman dish. The famous South African pickled fish, which was my favourite summer breakfast when I worked there, is really a form of caveach. Variations on the theme are also popular in Northern Italy (the Veneto), Romania, Turkey and the Balkans; the method is always the same.

Escabeche

Gut and clean 1 kg (2 lb) fish, leaving small ones whole but cutting large ones into fillets or pieces. Flour the fish and fry it a pale brown in plenty of oil. Take out the fish and in the same oil fry 1 large sliced onion and 6 cloves of crushed garlic until they just start to colour. Take off the heat, add a bouquet garni of parsley, bay and thyme, 1 teaspoon paprika or pimentón, stir and immediately add 250 ml (8 fl oz) vinegar, a little water and (optional) a finely-sliced lemon. Cook the mixture slowly for 15 minutes, salt to taste, then put in the fish and bring back to the boil. Arrange the fish in a suitable dish and cover with the liquid. Leave it for 2 days in a cool place. If the fried fish is fully covered with the marinade (which in turn is covered with a layer of oil) and packed in a jar with the top tied down, it will keep for some months. The vinegar can be more heavily spiced, as is usual in Britain.

South African Pickled Fish

Flour and fry fish fillets. Make a marinade using for each 450 g (1 lb) of fish fillets, 425 ml (¾ pt) of vinegar, a sliced onion, a bay leaf, a good pinch of peppercorns and another of coriander seeds, plus 1 clove. Boil until the onion is soft. Then stir together about 25 g (1 oz) of curry powder and 25 g (1 oz) of flour (that is about 3-4 dessertspoons of each, but this depends on the strength of the curry powder and the type of flour) and make them into a paste with a little cold vinegar. When you have a smooth liquid sauce, salt it to taste and then pour it hot over the fried fish, which has been arranged in a dish. Leave it for 2 days or more before eating. It will keep at least a week in the refrigerator, or longer if covered with oil and sealed in a jar. There are also more sophisticated versions.

Original Indian varieties of pickled fish are many. Naturally, they use fresh spices, not curry powder, and very often the pieces of fish are rubbed with salt and turmeric powder and left to drain for an hour or more to get out some of the water from the fish. It keeps better if you do this. The spicing in India is heavy (which helps preservation), and the pickles are also well saturated with oil in addition to the vinegar. Mustard oil in particular seems to have special preservative properties. Such Indian pickles are, however, used as a relish with curry and rice and not eaten as a separate dish like South African pickled fish.

CAVIAR. Although we associate caviar with Russia, the word comes from the Italian caviale or cavia via the Turkish khavyar. The Russians call it ikra. Real caviar is made only from the ripe eggs of various species of sturgeon – primitive fish of rather shark-like appearance. When I first disturbed one while wading across an Iranian river and saw a shark's tail lashing out of the water, I did find myself wondering whether freshwater sharks existed. However, sturgeon are quite inoffensive and actually toothless; they feed by sucking up detritus.

The two dozen species of sturgeon are found only in the Northern hemisphere. The smallest is the sterlet (Acipenser ruthenus) from eastern Europe; the largest is the beluga (Huso huso), an enormous fish which lives to be 100 years old and can then weigh over 1000 kg (2200 lb) – even 1600 kg (3500 lb). This fish should not be confused with the White whale, a mammal which is also called *beluga*. Other well-known sturgeon species used for caviar are the Common sturgeon (*Acipenser sturio*) of the Atlantic and the Mediterranean (rarely caught in British waters these days), the *sevruga* (*Acipenser stellatus*) and the *osciotre* (*Acipenser guldenstädti*), both of the Caspian Sea and weighing 10 kg (22 lb) and 18 kg (40 lb) respectively.

The centre for sturgeon is in the area of the Black and Caspian seas. The world's largest sturgeon fisheries are in Russia and, since 1950, in Iran. The Romanian fishery at the mouth of the Danube is of lesser importance. Some sturgeon are also fished in North America and caviar is made from them – there are species found, for instance, in the Great Lakes, and in the St Lawrence and Delaware rivers. There is now a problem with pollution, which the Russians have also had to face in the northern Caspian Sea and the Volga, and one of their responses has been to introduce sturgeon into new and unpolluted habitats.

Sturgeon are fished with gill nets laid off the mouths of the rivers up which they will spawn. The riper the eggs, the better the caviar, so it follows that the best comes from sturgeon caught off the mouths of short rivers, such as those arising in the Elburz Mountains of northern Iran. Here, with little distance to travel, the fish can wait until the last moment before going upstream. Only about one in every fifteen fish caught contains eggs suitable for making into caviar. A *beluga* will produce 17-20 kg (38-45 lb) of caviar, *osciotre* 4-7 kg (9-17 lb) and *sevruga* only 1½-2 kg (3½ -5 lb).

Caviar can be made only from the roes of perfectly fresh fish: once taken out of the net, they must reach the processing station within an hour or two. The stations are sited near the mouths of the rivers, sometimes on wooden artificial islands in particularly shallow areas of the Caspian. The sturgeon roes have to be removed with the greatest care so that the eggs do not get smeared with blood. If roe has to be washed, it does not make good caviar. Roes are cut in pieces the size of a fist, and rubbed gently on a string sieve to free the eggs from the membranes. The mass of eggs, which has fallen through the sieve into a basin, is now drained, accurately weighed and mixed by hand with fine salt (50-80 g/2-3 oz per kg/2 lb according to the judgement of the highly-skilled caviar maker). In caviar destined for most countries of Europe, a small percentage of boric acid is also added. This preservative improves the flavour by giving a slight acidity and preventing the growth of fishy flavours; it is not legally permitted in caviar for the US.

The caviar is later packed in the special tins, and the lid is sealed with a rubber band. This is, therefore, not a sterile product, so must be kept chilled (never frozen) and handled carefully until it reaches the table. Caviar is at it best 3 days after making. It is then totally devoid of any fishy taste (as I know from having spent a morning tasting with the chief Iranian caviar grader). It is unfortunate that by the time caviar reaches the restaurants, its price is astronomical and it is often not worth eating. The taste is fishy, which perhaps explains why many people who have tried it once do not like it, and why it is so often served with lemon or onion.

The best caviar is lightly salted. Russian tins are marked *malassol* (from *malo*, little, and *ssoleny*, salted). The eggs should be separate and not squashed together. They will, of course, vary in size according to the species of sturgeon from which they come. The largest, from the *beluga*, are usually the most expensive, but probably not the best, as *beluga* caviar does not travel as well as some of the others. Caviar from the sterlet (*sterlyad*) was once reserved for the Tsars and the Emperors of Austria, just as the golden caviar from Iran was reserved for the Shah. The excellence of golden caviar, however, is entirely in its appearance; the colour of caviar has no bearing on flavour. Because appearance is important, caviar from different fish is not mixed – the result would be speckled. Colours vary from black, through shades of grey to almost white, and from golden to orange-brown and even greenish.

Caviar should be served in its tin, surrounded by crushed ice and accompanied by lightly-toasted, fresh white bread and fine butter. Etceteras like chopped hard-boiled eggs are added merely to make it go further. While it is traditional outside Russia to drink champagne with caviar, you eat it with a spoon out of grease proof paper and wash it down with vodka on a Caspian caviar station. This (the vodka not the paper) is also the norm at Soviet diplomatic parties, but you may think the spirits kill the delicate flavour. It is sometimes served in small tarts, or with sour cream stuffed into *blinis*, but should never be cooked or heated itself.

....

Pressed caviar or **payousnaya** is a cheaper product made from sturgeon eggs which are not quite mature. After being separated from the membranes in the usual way, the slushy, half-formed eggs are treated with hot brine which coagulates them. The mass of eggs is then pressed into small wooden tubs. Pressed caviar has a sticky, waxy texture and is always rather salty. It is usually served spread on squares of toast, or in small tarts or *barquettes*.

Red caviar or **ketovaia** is, strictly speaking, not caviar, as it is made from the eggs of the *keta* or dog salmon (*Onchorynchus keta*) found in the rivers of Siberia which drain into the Pacific and of the west coast of Canada. The eggs are very large, red and almost transparent. Red caviar is much more salty than the true caviar and has a different flavour, which some people even prefer.

Imitation caviar. Salted fish eggs of other kinds are a popular delicacy in many fish-eating countries, but unfortunately there are also many such products which are artificially coloured grey or black and sold at inflated prices to simulate caviar and provide snob appeal. These substitutes are heavily salted, with a hard and grainy texture. They are commonly sold in glass jars with a sealed metal lid and have such names as 'German caviar'.

Salted roe of this type can be made at home if hard (female) roes are taken from fish just before spawning, cleared of fibre, washed if necessary in cold water, drained and mixed with salt: 1 part by weight to every 6 of roe. (For good caviar the proportion is only 1:20.) After being kept for 2 days in a cool place and being turned occasionally in the brine that is formed, the eggs can be drained, spread on a board 1 m (3 ft) from a fire and dried thoroughly for 10-12 hours before being pressed into jars.

Lumpfish caviar. The lumpfish (*Cyclopterus lumpus*) is also called lump-sucker, sea-owl or cock-paddle, because its dorsal fin is reminiscent of a cock's comb. It is fished in the North Atlantic, and the main source of supply is Iceland, but it is also found off the coasts of Scotland. Its flesh is not regarded highly, except smoked, but in spring the females are stuffed with eggs, which are used to make lumpfish caviar.

Salted roes can be made at home if ripe roes are taken from fish just before they spawn. The method is that given above for imitation caviar, before final drying, the eggs can be slightly acidified with powdered citric acid (to taste).The product, though without black grains and concomitant snob appeal, is tasty. It can be kept in the refrigerator for some days.

Synthetic caviar. It had to come. The Russians, after years of research, are making synthetic caviar for the common man. They do this by blowing little bubbles of protein, flavouring them, and adding salt. The result is said to be a bit slushy, though better than feared. As the price is right, it is immediately snapped up, for only a small quantity is at present being made.

Egyptian caviar is a name for *botargo,while 'poor man's caviar' is a dip made of puréed *aubergines.
   [*Caviar* – French: *caviar* German: *Kaviar* Italian: *caviale* Spanish: *caviar*]

CAYENNE PEPPER. *See* chilli.

CELERIAC. *See* celery.

CELERY (*Apium graveolens*) is a strong-smelling umbellifer that grows wild through much of the temperate world. The cultivated variety (var. *dulce*) is grown as both a herb and a vegetable. As a herb, it has thinnish green stems; bundles, complete with leaves, are sold as a flavouring in European markets. It is much used in soups and tends to be rather bitter. Varieties selected for use as a vegetable have thick stems and a good heart. Some types are earthed up to make the stems white; others are self blanching. While green celery stems are generally bitter, there are also varieties which are green and sweet. Celery is eaten raw in *crudités*, with cheese or chopped in mixed salads, and it may be braised as a wonderful vegetable.

Turnip-rooted celery or celeriac (var. *rapaceum*) is a variety selected for its bulbous root. The skin is very fibrous and is covered with roots, so needs to be peeled deeply. Celeriac can be cooked – it is excellent in a purée with potato – but it is more often shredded and, either raw or lightly cooked, marinated in mustardy French dressing for a few hours to make a favourite *hors d'oeuvre*.

Celery seed is commonly used as a flavouring, but is rather bitter. When combined with salt, it makes celery salt, a popular flavouring with eggs.
   [*Celery* – French: *céleri* German: *Sellerie* Italian: *sedona* Spanish: *apio*.
   Celeriac – French: *céleri-rave* German: *Knollensellerie* Italian: *sedano-rapa* Spanish: *apio-nabo*]

CELERY CABBAGE. *See* Chinese cabbage.

CELSIUS. In 1742, Anders Celsius, a Swedish

astronomer, described a scale for *temperature measurement which took the melting point of ice (or freezing point of water) as 0° and the boiling point of water as 100°. Measurements on this scale are known as degrees Celsius or centigrade (either way, °C). Apart from the convenience of having two easy-to-check reference points (although the boiling point of water varies with the atmospheric pressure), the Celsius scale became linked with the metric system in scientific definitions and, as a result, the Fahrenheit scale is gradually becoming obsolete. To convert Celsius to Fahrenheit, multiply by 9, divide by 5 and add 32. To convert Fahrenheit to centigrade, subtract 32 then multiply by 5 and divide by 9.

CENTIGRADE. *See* Celsius.

CÈPE or cep (*Boletus edulis*) is the most delicious member of a largely edible genus of fungi which are characterized by having tubes rather than gills under their caps. The *cèpe* has a brownish cap and a pale brown, usually very swollen stalk. It is found particularly in beech woods. It keeps its flavour better than any other fungus in drying or prolonged cooking. The Italians produce large quantities of sliced and dried *cèpes*, which they call *funghi porcini* (*see* mushrooms).

CEPHALOPODS. The most advanced molluscs, including the *squid, *cuttlefish and *octopus. They are all marine and range over every ocean. Their common characteristic is that they have arms with suckers which surround the mouth, a beak like a parrot (but with the larger half below) and well-developed eyes, which give them a savage, baleful glare. They all have ink sacs. A further characteristic, which has had an influence on cooks, is that their gills and internal organs are all contained in a hollow, muscular sac called the mantle (which the animals fill with water and contract to jet themselves backwards). It just asks to be filled with stuffing. Although these animals are much eaten in southern Europe and were relished by the Romans, who spread so many gastronomic habits about, they have never become popular in Britain or indeed in North America, except among people of Spanish, Italian or Greek stock. The Japanese probably eat more cephalopods than any other nation: about a fifth of their seafood consumption (including shellfish and seaweeds) is cephalopod.

CERAMIC GLAZES. Most ceramics, particularly *earthenware, are to some extent porous. Except where the porousness does not matter (as in flower pots) or is actually an advantage (as in old-fashioned milk coolers), pots are normally given an impermeable surface by firing them with a glaze. The reason that glazes are of concern to the cook is that they come into direct contact with food and drink but can contain such poisonous elements as selenium, chromium, cadmium, antimony and – commonest of all – *lead.

Glazes consist of substances that fuse together during firing to form, in effect, a glass. Lead oxides are excellent fluxes which work at relatively low temperatures to produce a fine, shiny surface. Unfortunately, glazes with a high lead content, especially if they have been fired at low temperatures, may have some of their lead still in a form that is soluble in weak acids. The danger here is not immediate lead poisoning, but something rather more insidious: lead is a cumulative poison. Improved techniques have made modern glazes almost entirely safe, and in Britain, the US and many other countries, there are strict regulations about the soluble lead content of glazes.

It is the interesting peasant pots, notably the low-fired ones which can be used on a naked flame, that must be treated with some care. They should be reserved for braising and frying, which is what they are intended for, and for which they are perfectly safe. On the other hand, sour fruit, vinegar, wine and cider should not be left standing in them as the acid content will attack under-fired lead glazes – brewing and storing drinks in lead-glazed vessels used to cause many cases of poisoning.

Salt glaze is highly resistant to acids and was once used for pipes to carry chemicals. It is commonly used on *stoneware, producing a semi-matt, orange peel surface texture. Salt-glazed vessels are ideal, among other things, for brewing.

CERASELLA. *See* liqueurs and cordials.

CEREALS (from Ceres, the Roman name for the Greek goddess of the corn, Demeter) include any sort of grain derived from a grass. From the Old World come *wheat, *barley, *oats, *rye, *rice and *millets of many kinds; *buckwheat, though not from a grass, is usually included as a cereal crop. In the New World, only *maize was known to the civilizations before Columbus.

[*Cereals* – French: *céréales* German: *Getreide* Italian: *cereali* Spanish: *cereales*]

CERIMAN. *See* Monstera.

CERVELAS may once, from its name, have been made with brain. The English saveloy is descended from the same word in Old French. French *cervelas* is normally a rather short sausage made of pork and usually flavoured with garlic. It is usually slightly dried and is eaten hot after being poached in water. One variety is *saucisson (-cervelas) de Paris*.

CERVELAT is a large German sausage of minced pork and beef, usually smoked. It is a rather different item from the French *cervelas and is sliced and eaten cold. It can be rather like a very mild, fine-textured salame.

CEVICHE or **SEVICHE** is a South American way of preparing white fish by marinating the fish in lime or lemon juice (or a mixture of both); the action of the acid in the juices 'cooks' the fish. The juice is poured over thin, raw pieces of very fresh white fish and is seasoned with a little salt and rather more pepper (or chillies) according to how piquant it is to be. Thinly sliced onions and finely chopped garlic are added, and the fish marinates in the juices for several hours; it will become opaque, like ordinary cooked fish. Ceviche is served with slices of tomato, sweet peppers, sections of hard-boiled egg, sweet corn, etc. See caveach.

CHALK or **calcium carbonate** ($CaCO_3$). Calcium carbonate is a white, odourless and tasteless substance, insoluble in plain water but soluble in acids. It dissolves in water which contains carbon dioxide, forming calcium bicarbonate, a reaction which is reversed by heating – hence the chalky scale which is deposited in kettles and hot-water pipes in places with hard water. Impure forms of calcium carbonate occur naturally as chalk, marble or limestone. Pure chalk (such as precipitated chalk, drop chalk, whiting or English whites) is sometimes used in the kitchen. In Britain, a pure form is compulsorily added to white flour. Chalk can be used to neutralize acids (such as fruit acids and acids used for hydrolysis) and forms a calcium salt of the acid concerned (e.g. calcium chloride, calcium citrate).
[*Chalk* – French: *craie* German: *Kreide* Italian: *creta* Spanish: *creta*]

CHAMOMILE. *See* camomile.

CHANNA, **chana**, **Bengal gram** or **gram**. A small Indian variety of *chickpea, and the most common pulse food of the masses there. Millions of tons are grown, making up more than half of the total pulse production of India. The *dal made from it is yellow, somewhat oval and rather larger than other *dals*. (A split pea, with which it is most easily confused, is round.) Much of the crop is roasted or parched, and some is ground into *besan* flour. *Channa* is nutritious and easily digested, but does not have an exceptional flavour.

CHANTERELLE or **girolle** (*Cantharellus cibarius*) is a fungus of deciduous woodlands. It is distinguished by its funnel shape and the fact that it is not just apricot yellow in colour but smells of apricots as well. Fried in butter with onion or garlic and parsley, it is one of the very best of wild fungi. In *The Mushroom Feast* (Grub Street), Jane Grigson points out that *chanterelles* are always slightly chewy; they are toughened by overcooking. They can be bought dried or canned. (*See* mushrooms.)

CHAR. *See* trout.

CHARCUTERIE. Literally and mainly the products of the pork butcher, the *charcutier* – hams, sausages, *terrines*, galantines, *crépinettes*, *gayettes*, *boulettes*, pies, *boudins* – or the shop itself. The *charcutiers* in France were first formed into a body by royal edict in 1476, a measure to protect the public from fraud and from bad meat. At that time, they were allowed to sell only cooked pork and raw pork fat, but not to slaughter the animals themselves. At the beginning of the 17th century, they gained the right to sell uncooked pork as well. From these beginnings has developed the French *charcuterie* of today, where sausages made of veal and *terrines* of game may be found in addition to the pork products. In English, the word *charcuterie* embraces all these things. Readers are referred to Jane Grigson's *Charcuterie & French Pork Cookery* (Grub Street) for full information and recipes.

CHARD. *See* beet.

CHARQUI or **jerked beef**. The American equivalent of *biltong: beef cut in strips and sun-dried.

CHASOBA. *See* noodles.

CHAYOTE, **custard marrow**, **pepinello**, **choko** or **vegetable pear** (*Sechium edule*) is a squash from tropical America; it was a food of the Aztecs and the Mayas. The fruits, borne on a trailing vine, are irregularly ridged, pear-shaped, and often covered with prickly hairs. The colour varies from creamy white to dark green. In Mexico, three main types are grown – the small and light green, the cream, and the large, spiny dark green variety – of which the last is reckoned to be superior. Chayotes have begun to gain commercial importance in recent years. They need a warm climate and grow well in the southern states of the US, in Australia, and in Italy, Spain, Algeria and other Mediterranean countries. The fruit, the size of a large pear, contains one big seed. The flesh is firm, and the taste delicate. We usually peel the fruits, slice them thinly, dip them in batter and fry them.

This is a most useful plant because the shoots, when young, can be boiled and served like asparagus, the leaves can be eaten as greens, and the huge tuberous roots, which can weigh 10 kg (22 lb), are similar to yams in appearance and use. The chayote is a vigorous and heavy-yielding plant, growing in all sorts of conditions when asked to; no doubt it will be increasingly popular as it becomes better known.

CHEESE was an early discovery in the Old World the Sumerians are known to have made it 6000 years ago – but it was never discovered by the American civilizations, perhaps because they lacked sheep, oxen and horses. The story of David and Goliath begins with David being sent by his father, Jesse, to take parched grain and bread to his brothers, who were camped with the army confronting the Philistines. At the same time, he was charged to deliver 'ten cheeses to the commander of their thousand'. We may speculate on what those cheeses were like. Possibly they resembled the Bedouin *igt*, which sounds like an exclamation of disgust, but is actually a sort of cheese made by boiling down sour curds until they are almost dry, then mixing the paste with desert herbs.

The ancient Greeks made cheese, and Aristotle wrote about it; the Romans were also cheese-makers, and Virgil wrote about it. Indeed, the Romans were quite sophisticated about cheese and used it in cooking, perhaps starting the passion that Italians have for it to this day. Romans made a number of different types of cheese which were sold in the *velabrum*, the dairy market in Rome, and no doubt also in Britain, since the Roman soldiers carried cheese on the march whenever they were lucky enough to get it. Large Roman houses of the period had cheese rooms where the cheese was made, and other rooms for storage and maturation.

Smoked cheese was also popular, larger towns had centres where the populace could take their home-made cheeses to be smoked. Some of the cheeses known today have been made for centuries. Gorgonzola, for instance, has been made since before AD 879. Italy remained the cheese-making centre of the world until after the Renaissance, but has now been overtaken by France, which heads the world, at least in the number of different cheeses and the interest taken in them. Italy still makes more use of cheese in cooking than any other country, and it sometimes seems that Italians put grated Parmesan, just for luck, into everything.

Cheese depends for its existence on a property of milk that the protein in it will coagulate and form a curd of casein when it is treated with acids, rennets, certain plant extracts or alum. It depends for its incomparable array of tastes on the combined effects of rennet and of the bacteria and (for some types of cheese) the moulds which attack it and cause chemical changes of unbelievable complexity, processes not understood until recently. During the last 100 years, cheese-making has gradually moved from the farmhouse to the factory, and a complicated technology has grown up around it. This need not intimidate the amateur cheese-maker. The technology is necessary to turn out thousands of uniform, average cheeses, without waste or failure, but the amateur, filled with enthusiasm, may make some bad cheeses, but with some basic knowledge and care, has the chance of making some splendid ones.

The simplest cheese is exemplified by ordinary soft or cottage cheese, in which milk curdled by natural souring is hung in a cloth to drain. Although the curd is acid and mixed with salt, the cheese is very moist and so will not keep well. An even more elementary cheese is the Indian *panir, which is almost tasteless and has a rubbery texture but can be cut into cubes, fried and made into curry (usually in combination with fresh peas). Similar cheeses are made in many countries (e.g. *requeson* in Spain); they may be eaten with quince paste (*membrillo*) or used in cakes.

For what we might call 'real' cheese, milk is soured to develop acidity and the curd is ripened with the help of bacteria and sometimes moulds. If milk is pasteurized (and usually also when it is not), the souring bacteria are added as a starter culture. This contains the correct proportions of organisms needed for the cheese being made. A cheese is to be looked on as a developing community. If the rind is thick, it may be almost a closed community, but in a small cheese, such as a Camembert, the centre is ripened by enzymes diffusing in from aerobic moulds which need oxygen and thus grow on the surface. When first made, the young cheese is acid, but later bacteria which feed on the acid come into prominence, and the cheese becomes sweeter. At the same time, organisms attack and break down the casein. These protein-splitting organisms make the curd into a digestible substance which melts when heated. Concurrently, certain compounds are formed which give flavour. In cheeses such as Emmentaler, special bacteria form gas which cannot escape and so make 'eyes'.

The important thing to realize is that a cheese contains living organisms; the various operations of the cheese-maker are intended to guide its evolution. Development is influenced by temperature, since there is an optimum temperature for each type of micro-organism. It is influenced in surface mould types by the humidity of the air, which controls the drying of the rind on which the moulds are growing. Some types are washed with beer or wine, or treated by scraping, oiling and so on. Size and shape determine whether or not enzymes produced by organisms in the rind can diffuse to the middle. Major factors in the ripening are the amount of moisture in the curd and the quantity of salt.

At each stage in making a cheese, there are a large number of choices, and many combinations of factors are possible, which is why there are some thousand named cheeses, with more being constantly invented.

The milk. In theory, cheese can be made from any sort of milk, but in practice, cows, goats, sheep and water buffalos are the most usual sources, although perhaps some of the earliest 'cheese' was made from ass's milk or mare's milk. The composition of the milk from different animals varies considerably in the amounts of protein, sugar and fat. Cow's milk usually contains some 4% of butter fat, but the fat level can be adjusted to anything from skimmed milk to thick cream and used as a basis for cheese. Since the cow is now the most common source of milk, it is used in many cases to make types of cheese that were once made from the milk of sheep or goats. While the cheeses are roughly the same, they lack the flavour of the original, since the fat of sheep's milk and that of goat's milk are different from cow-milk fat. A Mozzarella made from buffalo's milk, as it was originally, no doubt tastes richer than a modern cow's-milk version.

The composition and flavour of milk also depend on the time of year and the sort of pasture on which the animals have grazed. An animal fed artificially in winter and one fed on grass leys or a summer Alpine pasture full of flowers cannot be expected to produce the same milk

Pasteurization. All factory and much farmhouse cheese is now made from pasteurized milk. This makes sure that any disease organisms are destroyed, and enables the cheese-maker to start with a more or less clean slate, although the milk is not sterile. To sterilize milk, it would have to be heated to boiling point at least, and this would make the calcium salts insoluble. Since soluble calcium and some acidity are necessary for rennet to act, cheese cannot be made from boiled milk in the usual way. Even pasteurization destroys some of the enzymes which are present in raw milk and so influences the final result.

The starter. Carefully devised cultures or starters are now always used to introduce the right types of micro-organism in the right proportion. This removes some of the chance factors. The starter is added when the milk is warm and contains special souring organisms, because the first consideration is to develop acidity. This is necessary for good curd formation by the rennet. The acidity and the rennet act together to shrink the curd, to promote drainage, to prevent the growth of putrefying organisms, to encourage the matting of the curd and to affect its elasticity.

Curdling. In most types of cheese, the curd is set milk with a strong cheese rennet. There are also a few in which curdling is brought about purely by natural souring, and others in which the curd is set with certain plant juices. Variations are produced by the amount of rennet used, the point in souring at which it is added, the temperature etc. When the rennet coagulates the milk, casein, fat globules and most of the micro-organisms are trapped; a little of these drains away in the whey.

Cutting the curd. When the curd is set, it must be cut or broken up to allow the whey to drain out. This is one of the most important operations in cheese-making, as the fineness of the curd particles and the amount of whey left in the cheese will determine its type. In the simplest, old-fashioned methods, the curd is simply broken up and stirred with the hand; the amount of heat which the hand can tolerate then limits the temperatures at which such cheeses can be made. I have watched shepherds in Sardinia making their sheep's-milk cheese (*pecorino sardo*) by this simple method, with the pot kept warm by the wood fire and the curd stirred with the bare hand and gradually kneaded into a lump which is then scooped into the mould. However, the curd is usually cut into cubes with a knife or an arrangement of knives and, if it is for heated or 'scalded' curd cheese, the curd is heated further and stirred to make the granules finer and to cause them to shrink, thus ensuring that even more whey can be drained out. As the size of grain is vital, the cutting is often done with a device of wires strung on a frame (a harp).

Cheddaring is one of the essential stages in making Cheddar cheese. Here, the curd, when firm enough to be turned without breaking, is cut in slabs, drained by stacking and finally milled in a curd mill before being mixed with salt, allowed to drain once more and finally pressed into hoops.

Cooking the curd. For the harder types of cheese, the curd is usually warmed to up to about 54°C (130°F), which is rather more than can be endured by the bare hand. This shrinks the curd and hardens it making it easier to get the whey out. These cooked types of cheese, such as Emmentaler or Parmesan, are therefore harder than, say, Cheddar, just how hard will also depend on other factors as well, but in general the higher the cooking temperature, the harder the cheese. The usual limit to which the curds are 'cooked' is 54-55°C (130 -132°F), though higher temperatures are used in making plastic curd cheese and Scandinavian sweet cheeses.

Draining the curd. Whether the curd has been cooked or not, it has now to be drained. In the soft cheeses, where quite a lot of whey will be left, the cut curd, stirred or unstirred, is ladled directly from the vat into the forms, but there are many variations. For instance, in the very simple types of cheese made in some parts of the Carpathians, the curd is simply squeezed into lumps in the hands and eventually cured in brine. In making Pont l'Evêque, the curd is first drained slightly on straw mats, gently squeezed by the cheese-maker by rolling up the mat, and then ladled into square wooden forms (careful and even packing being part of the skill) and the forms left to drain on straw mats. The curd compacts under its own weight. Other types

of cheese are drained in baskets or in tall perforated moulds.

Pressing the curd. For the harder types of cheese, pressure is applied to help the whey drain out. This may be no more than a matter of putting a brick on top, or it may involve a hydraulic press. For instance, in the making of Emmentaler, after cutting, cooking and stirring in giant steam-heated kettles, the huge mass of curd is scooped into a cloth which is drawn under it and lifted with a block and tackle into an adjustable wooden form positioned under a hydraulic press. The press squeezes it into the huge cartwheel shapes. The pressure applied is an important factor in cheese-making.

Salt in cheese is not only necessary for taste, but also has a great influence on micro-organisms; some are very sensitive to it. For instance, one of the heat-loving, milk-souring bacteria, *Streptococcus thermophilus* (used as starter for Emmentaler) will not grow in as little, even, as 2% salt (which, in effect, means in most cheeses except fresh curd cheese). Some types of cheese are salted by rubbing with dry salt or washing in brine. This also discourages the growth of moulds. Some cheeses, such as the Greek *feta*, are packed in salt in barrels, and a brine soon forms which preserves the cheese. Other additives are colours (most commonly annatto), spices (such as caraway or cloves in Leyden), pepper, wine, sage, etc.

Ripening or **maturing**. There are unripened cheeses which are eaten fresh, such as cottage cheese, *boursin* (with pepper or garlic and herbs), *petit Suisse, demi-sel, fromage blanc* and so on. They do not keep for more than a few days and are known as *fromages a pâté fraîche* in France. The softcurd types (*pâtés molles*) are matured for a short time and are soft and perishable, because of their high whey or moisture content.

They can be broadly divided into two types: those like Camembert, Brie and Coulommiers, in which moulds are encouraged to grow on the surface, and the others, such as Maroilles and Munster, in which surface moulds are deliberately discouraged by washing and salting. Some, like Pont l'Evêque, come in between: some mould is wanted, but not too much.

Surface moulds ripen cheeses by means of enzymes which diffuse inwards from them; hence you may get a Camembert that is soft and ripe throughout, but for a small white layer in the centre, where the enzymes have not yet reached. Cheeses ripened by moulds which grow only on the surface where they have sufficient air are small or, if large in diameter, like a Brie, are at least thin. Other cheeses are ripened internally by green moulds, among them Stilton, Gorgonzola and Roquefort. The curd for such cheeses has to be packed loosely to leave cracks for the mould to grow in; today, however, the cheeses are stabbed to let air in. Other cheeses are ripened by the action of bacteria working within and are not limited in size, although a really soft cheese is likely to be small, if only for mechanical reasons.

The hard-pressed cheeses are made by cooking or 'scalding' the curd, so more whey is taken out and the cheeses are harder. They include the Dutch Gouda and Edam, and the French Port Salut, Cantal and Saint Paulin; the more strongly cooked types are represented by Emmentaler, Gruyère and Parmesan. These are large cheeses, ripened only by bacteria and enzymes. Their surfaces are often washed, scraped, salted, oiled, waxed or covered in various compounds to stop moulds from growing on the surface and create a thick, tough, impervious rind. Today, hard cheeses are often wrapped in moisture-proof film so that no rind is formed.

Since ripening involves micro-organisms and enzymes, the control of temperature and humidity is of the greatest importance. Cheeses may be stacked in ripening rooms or in natural caves and cellars. Most cheeses are frequently turned and inspected, and in the case of the cheeses that come in huge cartwheels, the work is so heavy that the turning is done these days by machinery.

Although the details of each type of cheese are different, maturation is characterized in general by a reduction of the acidity by bacteria which feed on the acid. At the start, the strong acidity gives elasticity to the curd. If the curd is washed to reduce its calcium content, it can be drawn out into strings, a factor made use of in making plastic curd cheeses. Cheeses like Camembert are initially very acid, and become hard as they dry out. They are then softened by enzymes in the moulds. Immature cheese, like fresh Cheddar, will go very stringy if cooked – like a mixture of chewing gum and butter, as one author described it.

The cook needs to know about ripening cheese only to be aware of the stages of ripeness when buying it. A maturation period of a year or more, as is needed for hard Italian *grana* like Parmesan, explains to some extent why it is so expensive. Cheeses are best bought when ripe, and the ripening should not be attempted at home. At most, a Camembert should be kept until the next day, but it is bought almost ready; if the cheesemonger tries to foist off a leathery Camembert on the grounds that it will be ripe in a day or so, it is best not to buy it. The odds are that, because of mishandling, it will never ripen properly. In general, cheeses are best ripened in their proper environment. Thus, you can never get a perfect Gorgonzola far from the caves of northern Italy, where they are matured, for, unless removed early (like fruit), they will not stand up to travel, being large and, when ripe, rather squashy.

Buying cheese. Most cheese today is sold pre-packed in plastic film. If, however, you are lucky enough to have access to a cheese merchant who still cuts pieces to order, always ask to taste a sliver before buying, and get fully-ripe cheese in manageable quantities. Since it is impossible to describe tastes with any accuracy, try to build up over a period of time a working knowledge of cheese available locally.

Keeping cheese. Ideally, cheese should not be kept, as it starts to deteriorate once cut. However, some storage is usually inevitable. One may wrap cheese in greaseproof paper or foil and put it in a cool larder (if anyone possesses such a thing these days). The cold of a refrigerator slows down the growth of ripening micro-organisms, but may encourage others that prefer low temperatures and so spoil the cheese. Never forget that a cheese is a living community of organisms; if you destroy the balance, then the cheese is likely never to recover. Only processed cheese, which is 'dead' and designed for a long shelf-life, will keep, but it is not noted for its character.

Cheese rinds. The rind and what grows on it has a profound effect on the cheese. The rind may be bathed in wine or beer to encourage micro-organisms, or coated with lamp black, burnt umber, gum, even (at least in the past) varnish bitumen to discourage them. Some cheeses are smoked, others wrapped in leaves or coated with grapeskins, pepper, dried thyme or plastics. The question sometimes asked is whether or not one should eat the rind. Added coatings should obviously not be eaten, and in general, even natural rinds are best removed. As one maker of Pont l'Evêque told me, 'We spend a lot of effort making sure that the cheese is not bitter, and then some idiots go and eat the rind as if it were Camembert'. I have even known people to eat the grape pips on *tôme au raisin*.

Plastic curd cheeses are characteristic of southern Italy, the best known being the sausage-shaped provolone. To make these cheeses, the soured curd is heated in water to 57°C (137°F) until it becomes plastic and can be stretched and kneaded; it is then shaped and moulded while still hot.

Classification of cheeses. As there are at least a thousand named cheeses, it would be useful to be able to classify and group them for purposes of description. Unfortunately, this has so far defeated even the experts. According to the writers of *Cheeses of the World* (US Department of Agriculture), there are probably only eighteen distinct types of cheese, which are typified as follows: Brick, Camembert, Cheddar, Cream, Edam, Gouda, Hand, Limburger, Neufchâtel, Parmesan, Provolone, Romano, Roquefort, Sapsago, Swiss (Emmentaler), Trappist, Mysost, Ricotta.

One basic characteristic used for description is consistency: very hard (grating), hard, semi-hard, semi-soft, soft, or very soft and runny. These groups may be subdivided into those ripened by bacteria only, by moulds (external and internal) and by organisms growing on the surface and their enzymes – or by a combination – as well as the fresh cheeses which are unripened.

Very hard	*Ripened by bacteria*: Asiago (old), Parmesan, Romano, Sapsago, Spalen.
Hard	*Ripened by bacteria and with no eyes*: Cheddar, Provolone *Ripened by bacteria and with eyes*: Emmentaler, Gruyère
Semi-hard and semi-soft	*Ripened by bacteria*: Brick, Munster *Ripened by both bacteria and surface organisms*: Limburger, Port-Salut, Trappist *Ripened by interior blue mould*: Danblu, Gorgonzola, Roquefort, Stilton
Soft	*Ripened*: Bel Paese, Brie, Camembert, Hand, Neufchatel *Unripened*: Cottage, Cream, Fromage Blanc, Petit Suisse, Ricotta
Very soft	Many cheeses could be described as very soft or runny when fully ripe, such as Vacherin.

It is part of the problem of classification that the texture of many cheeses changes as they ripen: some are table cheeses or grating cheeses according to their age and dryness. To the consumer, the questions of whether a cheese is ripened by moulds or by bacteria are largely academic, though interesting. Of more importance are the following considerations. Do you buy by weight or must you buy the whole cheese? What does it look like when ripe? How is the genuine cheese marked and packed? Is it strong or mild? Is it for eating, cooking or grating?

Cheese in cooking. Wherever cheese is made, it figures in the local cooking. Thus, when trying traditional recipes, you must use the correct cheese if you want the dish to taste as it is meant to. When it is impossible to find the right cheese, though, trial and error with other cheeses becomes necessary. If you are aiming at authenticity, try to use cheese of the right type and age. Avoid using too young a cheese for melting, as it is likely to become stringy when heated.

Certain types of cheese have distinctive characteristics which either make them highly suitable for some dishes or give a particular flavour to a cuisine. For British cooking, Lancashire and Cheshire cheeses melt best, although others, such as Cheddar types, melt well too. Americans have discovered that blue cheeses, in addition to giving a fine flavour to a *vinaigrette* or a mayonnaise, melt well on the ubiquitous hamburger. In Italy, where cheese is a basic culinary flavour, the *grana* cheeses such as Parmesan are grated into and over innumerable dishes. The elastic *mozzarella* melts beautifully, while the whey cheese *ricotta* is found in both savoury and sweet dishes. French cooking frequently uses Gruyère and Emmentaler in savoury dishes and soft cream cheeses in sweets such as *fromage à la crème* and *tourteau fromagé*. In Greece, *feta* cheese is found not only in salads but also layered between sheets of *phyllo* pastry with spinach or other ingredients. Generally, curd and cream cheeses bake well; they are the basis of some Danish pastry fillings and of endless cheesecake recipes. Simple cottage cheeses are a very useful basic ingredient in *cuisine minceur* and for diets. For such purposes, they are often processed in a blender to make light temporary emulsions.

[*Cheese* – French: *fromage* German: *Kase* Italian: *formaggio* Spanish: *queso*]

CHERIMOYA. *See* custard apple.

CHERRY. Like plums, cherries are members of the genus *Prunus*. There are well over a thousand varieties, some of them almost unchanged since Roman times. Most of the important ones are derived from two species, the sour cherries (pie or Morello cherries) coming from *P. cerasus*, a shrub or small tree, and the sweet cherries from the gean or mazzard (*P. avium*), a larger tree. Both are native to Europe, though sweet cherries probably originated in a form of *P. avium* from Asia Minor. There are hydrids between the two species which go under the name of Duke cherries (*Royale* in France, where they originated). In addition, there are a number of wild cherries indigenous to both Europe and North America, none of which is cultivated. In Europe, there is the Bird cherry (*P. padus*), a hardy northern species with small bitter-sweet black berries which can be fermented to make a fruit brandy, and the Mahaleb or St Lucie's cherry (*P. mahaleb*), with wood that is prized for making pipes and fruits that are sometimes used for liqueurs. Another European species, the Cherry laurel (*P. laurocerasus*) smells of the *hydrocyanic acid it contains; it is very poisonous. The Cornelian cherry or cornel (*Cornus mas*) of central and southern Europe (excluding the Iberian Peninsula) has edible fruit, although it is related not to the cherry but to the dogwood (*C. sanguinea*). In North America, both the sweet cherry and the sour cherry have escaped and gone wild. None of the indigenous American cherries is cultivated, but the Rum cherry (*Prunus serotina*) was used by the early New Englanders to turn raw rum into a fine cherry liqueur and also to make Cherry Bounce (by a similar technique to that used for sloe gin, with brandy instead of gin, suitably sweetened with sugar).Then there is the common chokecherry (*P. virginiana*) with astringent, pea-sized cherries

which make good jelly, and the very similar *P. melanocarpa*, which is less astringent. In the US, the name of Bird cherry or Pin cherry is given to *P. pennsylvanica*, which is sour and not much utilized, but which can also make a good jelly.

The sweet cherries are rather particular about the soil and climate and are very prone to diseases – one reason why they are expensive. They are also highly perishable and have to be packed very carefully and refrigerated. Old cherries can usually be recognized by their stalks, which are dark, not crisp and green like those of freshly-picked cherries. There are some 600 varieties in cultivation. At one time, they were classified into the *bigarreaux* with firm dryish flesh, and the *guignes* or geans with soft and juicy flesh – a distinction that no longer works because of the many intermediate forms. Their colour varies from dark red to almost white or yellow, the meat from white to dark red, and the hearts white and black. Sweet cherry varieties are usually sweet, but some can be bitter, veering towards the wild gean. The great majority of varieties are intended for eating as dessert and are not of much interest when cooked.

The Sour or Morello cherry has some 300 cultivated varieties and is the one for cooking. The Morello itself is dark, almost black, but there are red varieties called *amarelles*. This is the species for cherry pie, liqueurs and cherry brandy. Few varieties are good to eat from the hand. However, the hybrid Duke cherries, which may be black or red include varieties both for eating and for cooking. Some 65 kinds are grown.

Special uses of cherries are in making fruit brandies and liqueurs. Kirsch, which comes from the area including Alsace, the Black Forest and north-east Switzerland, is a dry, white spirit with a very characteristic flavour, but tasting nothing of cherries. In cooking, it is used with fruit (e.g. with pineapple), in some cakes and in a cheese fondue, which it also accompanies in the glass. It is a totally different drink to maraschino, which is sweet and again often used as a flavouring with fruits and sweets. Maraschino is said to have originated in Dalmatia, but it now comes equally from Italy on the other side of the Adriatic. Apart from being made from a different variety of cherry, the stones are crushed for maraschino (but not for kirsch), and honey is added to make the fermentable mash. The taste of maraschino contains a dash of bitter almond from the stones and is quite unlike that of kirsch. It is also sweet. Cherry brandy, of which the finest is probably Grants, an old English make, has a strong taste of cherries and is made by infusion, not by fermenting and distilling the cherries. Its use in cooking would be original rather than classical. *Glacé* cherries (*see* candied fruit), which appear much in cakes and in cake decoration, are often faked. The cherries are stoned, hardened with chemicals, and most often dyed (sometimes green) with synthetic dyes. Occasionally they are not even made out of cherries.

[*Cherry* – French: *cerise* German: *Kirsche* Italian: *ciliegia* Spanish: *cereza*]

CHERRYSTONE. American hard-shell *clam.

CHERVIL (*Anthriscus cerefolium*) is a feathery umbelliferous herb with a delicate taste that is somewhere between parsley and anise. It came originally from the Balkans and the Middle East. In Britain, where it was probably introduced by the Romans, it is widely naturalized. It has also been introduced into North America and New Zealand. Although it is not often available in markets outside France, it can easily be grown in any garden or window box where conditions are not too hot and dry. It is a standard component of *fines herbes*, for example in omelettes, as well as being a classic ingredient of Ravigote sauce. The Belgians use it as a major ingredient in soups. However it is used, though, it should not be boiled as this will destroy its flavour; it is normally added to hot dishes just before serving.

[*Chervil* – French: *cerfeuil* German: *Kerbel* Italian: *cerfoglio* Spanish: *perifollo*]

CHESTNUT, sweet chestnut or Spanish chestnut. There are some ten species of chestnut. The sweet chestnut (*Castanea sativa*) has been cultivated in southern Europe for several thousand years. Today, there are hundreds of varieties propagated by grafting. They are particularly grown in France (around the Massif Central), Italy, Spain and Portugal, and are very important in the regional cooking of such places as Corsica (where, alas, property developments are ousting the chestnut plantations). In more northerly countries, like Britain (where chestnuts were probably introduced by – inevitably – the Romans), the crop is uncertain and quality nuts are not produced. In North America, there are good local varieties of sweet chestnut, although the nuts are not so generally familiar as in Europe. They were introduced by the early colonists, who also used the indigenous American chestnut (*C. dentata*), which has an excellent nut

but has now almost been wiped out by a blight. It is often replaced by the Japanese chestnut, *C. crenata*, which has a large but inferior nut. There are other sweet chestnuts, all edible, and some are of excellent quality.

Sweet chestnuts are borne on a fine tree and formed inside very prickly capsules which split open when ripe to release the nuts. In this, they are similar to the unrelated horse chestnut (*Aesculus hippocastanum*), an ornamental tree with inedible nuts (though *in extremis*, these may be made edible by grinding and washing in many changes of water to leach out the astringent substances, leaving a flour which can be dried and roasted). According to the locality, chestnuts start to ripen from September onwards, but there are early, late and mid-season varieties. Chestnuts are sugary and starchy, but contain little oil. Many varieties are distinctly astringent, especially when freshly gathered, and they are rarely eaten raw. In the great chestnut forests, such as those of the Apennines, the semi-wild trees produce the small rounded *castagne* used for feeding animals or for drying and grinding into flour. These normally have three nuts to a capsule. The more expensive eating varieties, the *marroni*, are produced from grafted trees which bear nuts that are much larger, usually only one to a capsule, and often square. Although there is some variation in flavour and sweetness, the consideration of greatest practical importance to the cook is whether or not the chestnuts are easy to peel, which here means removing the brown inner skin of the nut, not the outside husk. In some small or wild nuts, the inner skin may be folded into the meat, which makes skinning almost impossible. Even with a good variety, you may have difficulty unless the correct methods are employed.

Peeling Chestnuts

Cut each chestnut through the outer husk along the convex face. Then a) bake them for 7-8 minutes on the tray at the bottom of the oven, moistening them with a few spoons of water, or b) put them in a pan of cold water, bring to the boil and boil for 1 minute, or c) throw the chestnuts into boiling water and boil them for 5 minutes. With any of these methods it is easy to peel off the outer husk of the chestnut.

Now, to remove the brown inner skin. Put the husked chestnuts into cold water with a little cooking oil and bring them to the boil. Then turn down the heat to the lowest possible. When the skins start to come off, take out a few at a time (they must be peeled hot) and rub them with a cloth, while holding the chestnut with another cloth to avoid burning your fingers. Since there are some very stubborn varieties, an alternative method is to put the husked chestnuts into a frying pan and fry them in a little sweet oil or butter until the skins become crisp. They can then easily be rubbed off.

When buying whole nuts, examine them carefully for spoilage from insects or fungus. As it is not easy to tell from the outside, try to cut a few open. Carry a penknife when buying them in quantity. Really fresh nuts are firm and feel solid. Nuts which give when pressed have been dried out somewhat, but may be excellent and even sweeter from the storage.

In Britain, chestnuts are mostly eaten roasted in the husk or used for stuffing the Christmas turkey. Roasting may be done in a hot oven, but the flavour is much better if they are roasted very quickly and 'shown the fire'. In France and Italy, one can buy special pans (like a frying pan with large holes in the bottom) for roasting chestnuts over the flames. (These pans have been used in Britain since Tudor times, and imported ones are available from specialist shops.) Every child knows that the husk must be pierced before roasting or the nut will explode. Some people advocate boiling the nuts before roasting, which makes them soft but does not give the best flavour. Roasted chestnuts are probably nicest eaten by the fireside – with a little salt handy – but if sent to table they must be hot, and it is correct to serve them in a napkin.

Although British recipes for chestnuts are normally limited to chestnut stuffing, chestnuts with Brussels sprouts, and perhaps a chestnut pudding, recipes abound in other countries, where in the past these nuts were a winter staple, taking the place of potatoes. Even forms of bread and polenta were made from them (although chestnuts, like maize, are unsuitable for making proper bread, as they contain insufficient glutinous substances for binding). The everyday peasant recipes would often have been no more than rustic porridges.

Among the more sophisticated chestnut-based dishes, France offers soups like *potage de marrons dauphinois*, *soufflé aux marrons et potiron* (chestnut and pumpkin soufflé), and purées of chestnuts to be eaten with mutton and pork or game like boar, hare and venison. There are also various chestnut gateaux, and the world-famous *marrons glacés*, as well as the Lucullan *marrons au kirsch* (poached in a thick syrup and flavoured with kirsch). The chestnuts which are canned either in syrup or as purée come from the Ardèche region, which is the main source of chestnuts in France. In Italy, we have the delectable *monte blanco* (cooked chestnuts riced into a mountain and given an alpine look with fine sugar and avalanches of beaten cream) and the various forms of *castagnaccio* (a blend of chestnut, sultanas and pine nuts, which may be flavoured with fennel, rosemary or vanilla according to locality). More modern dishes include the *dolce di castagne*, the *semifreddo di castagne* and the *budino di castagne al savoiardi*. The Austrians have their Nesselrode pudding, a chestnut ice. Any of these rich chestnut dishes would put a delicious but firm stop to any meal. In Spain, you might eat *castañas con mantequilla* (with butter), *con jaraba* (in syrup) and *helado de castañas* (ice cream). Similarly, there are many chestnut dishes from the Balkans, Greece and further east. They are often flavoured with anise.

Dried chestnuts are commonly on sale in all Mediterranean countries. As *secchielli*, they may be bought from Italian grocers. Chestnut flour is also available, and the best quality contains little of the red skin. Commercially-made chestnut jams and spreads are all hideously suitable for children. Canned chestnut purée is useful and available in many countries.

Castañas con mantequilla

Peel 1 kg (2 lb) chestnuts. Put them with a stick of celery, 25 g (1 oz) butter and a pinch each of salt and sugar in a saucepan with hot water barely to cover. Put the lid on and simmer without stirring for about 40 minutes. Remove the stick of celery, drain and add another 25 g (1 oz) butter. Reheat and serve very hot.

Castagne all'ubriaco

A simple Italian peasant dish (literally 'drunk chestnuts') for the fireside. Roast chestnuts, preferably in a chestnut roaster (*see above*) and peel them. Put them in a dish by the fire, cover them with a clean cloth soaked in red wine, and leave them for half an hour to absorb the wine flavour, keeping them hot. You can eat these drunken wine-flavoured chestnuts as they are or cover them with honey and again serve hot.

Minestra di castagne secche

Wash and then soak 300 g (11 oz) dried chestnuts for 24 hours, and then boil them in water for 2-3 hours. Add 300 g (11 oz) rice, and, when it is half cooked, 1 lt (1¾ pt) milk and 50 g (2 oz) butter, salt to taste. The soup should be creamy.

Castagnaccio

Pour boiling water over 100 g (4 oz) sultanas and leave them until they are cool enough to take out with the fingers. Put them to dry. Sieve 450 g (1 lb) chestnut flour with a good pinch of salt, and add water, mixing to a soft paste. Pour into a well-oiled baking tray. Sprinkle with 1 teaspoon fennel seed, 50 g (2 oz) pine nuts and the sultanas. Dribble a little olive oil on top and bake in the oven until a crust is formed. Eat hot or cold.

[*Chestnut* – French: *marron, châtaigne* German: *Edelkastanie* Italian: *castagna, marrone* Spanish: *castaña, marrona*]

CHICKEN. The original domestication of the chicken probably took place in South East Asia. Among its many breeds was the great Cochin China fowl, of enormous size and ungainly form, which took England by storm in the middle of the last century.

It was in such demand that, according to a contemporary, people paid huge sums of money for a bird, and talked almost about nothing else. Indeed, the prices paid would have bought three or four good cows or a reasonable flock of sheep.

If you go into the jungles of the Sundarbans, at the mouth of the Ganges and Brahmaputra rivers, you will hear the hens clucking and the cocks crowing from the treetops at dawn every morning. The jungle fowl there are small birds, almost bantam size, but there is little doubt that these are pretty much what the first chickens must have looked like. From some such ancestors are descended our modern hens, the White Leghorn, Light Sussex, New Hampshire and Rhode Island Red – poor, egg-laying machines of the modern world – and the heavy, quick-maturing table birds, like White Cornish and White Rock, which have been computer-selected to gain the most weight on the least food in the shortest time. It is these that have done for us what Henry IV of France (1553-1610) failed to do – to put a chicken in every Frenchman's Sunday pot.

Anything outside mass production will be more difficult to get and more expensive. It will also probably taste better. Top restaurants in France still insist on a Bresse or Le Mans, and a bird with black or white feet, but never yellow. If choosing a bird in a market, where you are probably not allowed to handle it, look at the legs. If they are coarse, scaly and battered, the bird is old. Then look for bruises. Those inflicted during life showing as dark red marks. In European markets, be careful that the butcher does not chop up your chicken into pieces before you can tell him not to. The British, who expect chickens with white fat, are often surprised to find that the chickens sold elsewhere, for instance in France and the US, often have yellow fat, and are none the worse for it. The size of bird depends more on breed and feeding than on age.

Poussin, **baby chicken** or **broiler** (US). 4-6 weeks old. 350-600 g (¾-1¼ lb). Usually grilled. Very tender but with little taste.

Coquelet (French). Very young cock. Around 1 kg (2 lb).

Poulet or **spring chicken**. 1-2 kg (2-4½ lb).

Poularde or **fat fowl**. 1.5-2 kg (3¼-4½ lb) plus.

Poule or **boiling fowl**. 2 kg (4½ lb) plus. Often with much fat. Can be roasted if less than 8 months old. Fowl over a year old cannot be roasted, but have to be boiled. Real barnyard fowl may be expensive, but full of flavour.

Coq, **cock** or **cockerel**. 1.5-2 kg (3¼-4½ lb). Not as good eating as hens and usually killed at 6 months.

Chapon or **capon**. A castrated cock, or one in which the administration of female hormones has had a similar effect. Capons are very large, 2.5-3.5 kg (6-7¾ lb), and can approach the size of a small turkey.

Some idea of a chicken's anatomy is a help when cutting it up or boning it. Points to notice are that the foot is cut off below (and not through) the joint to prevent the drumstick contracting during cooking. The tips of the wings are usually removed, and they join the bones for stock.

There are many ways of cutting up a chicken for cooking. The usual way is to cut off both legs, not through the joint as in carving, but by breaking and cutting off the strip of back which contains the oyster and leaving it attached to the leg. The oyster muscle, after all, is a part of the leg's musculature. Then cut off each wing with a diagonal cut made from the centre of the wishbone, so that a good piece of breast goes with each wing. Finally, cut away what is left of the breast on either side from the carcass. This gives five portions of more or less equal size and leaves the back and trimmings to go into the stockpot, or to be used in any other way to add flavour, although there is little meat on the bones.

A quicker and easier method, which is often used in French restaurants, is to cut off both legs, being careful to scoop out the oyster still attached as part of the leg, before severing the joint as in carving. Then find the shoulder joint, hold the wing against the body to present the joint and cut through the tip of the joint. If you find the right spot, you do not have to cut through anything harder than cartilage. Sever the tendons around it with the knife point, put your fingers inside (there is a pocket in which to put it) and rip backwards. This pulls off the wing and outer breast in one piece. After doing this on both sides, cut the back of the breastbone free from the ribs and grasp the breastbone. Pull it forwards to break it free and pull away together with the wishbone, which should then be removed, as it is somewhat unsightly. This gives five pieces, two legs as before, two side breasts with wing attached and a double fillet of inner breast attached to the breastbone.

Boning a chicken requires a modicum of patience and practice, but is a skill worth learning. The easiest way is to cut through the skin right down the back and to dissect the meat away on each side, cutting through the joints as you come to them. When all of the body bones are free, the bones of legs and wings can be removed with little difficulty, first freeing the joint and then scraping down the bone while holding the joint and gradually drawing out the bone. When you reach the knee joint, that must in turn be freed and the next bone drawn out; the leg meat will all turn inside out in the process. Finally when you reach the end point, it is easiest to snip off the rest with a pair of scissors. You take only the first bone out of the wing, as boning the whole lot would demand more skill and patience than the results would justify. When the boned chicken is laid flat, meat side up, the stuffing can be put on top and the chicken rolled up around it and sewn with needle and thread into something which usually

looks like a cross between a chicken and a sausage but when cooked can be cut into elegant slices.

The alternative method is to start from the rear with the back and gradually free and roll back the skin and meat, treating the legs and wings as already described. To do this you need a thin, sharp knife, and a bit more patience. The finished product looks a little more like a chicken.

[*Chicken* – French: *poulet* German: *Huhn* Italian: *pollo* Spanish: *gallina, polio*]

CHICKLING VETCH. *See* lath.

CHICKPEA, channa, Egyptian bean, garbanzo, or **ram's-head pea**. Chickpeas (*Cicer arietinum*) are one of the most important legumes. They are sometimes eaten green but mostly dried as a pulse. The plant is indigenous to the Levant and the Near East, where it has been cultivated since antiquity. Later, chickpeas, which are exceedingly nutritious, were the food of the Arab armies in their conquest of North Africa and Spain. As they will not stand frost, growing them is confined to the belt stretching eastwards from the Mediterranean countries, through Romania, southern Russia and the Middle East, extending to India and onwards. Nowadays, they are also grown extensively in the Americas, South Africa and Australia. The plants are a striking grey-green colour and stand about 40 cm (18 in) high. The pods are short, fat and hairy, containing two or three large seeds. They are sticky and secrete so much oxalic acid that walking through the crop can spoil your shoes. In the countries where they grow and the seeds are frequently eaten green, the pulling must be done with gloves to protect the hands from the acid.

Legend has it that the plant was cursed by the Virgin Mary because it refused to hide the Holy Family when they were pursued by Herod's soldiers. The name 'ram's-head pea' or 'ram's-head chiche' comes from the fact that seeds of the larger varieties, when seen from the side, suggest a ram's head with large curly horns. Other, smaller varieties have round seeds not much bigger than a pea. Though usually creamy or biscuit-coloured, they can also be pale green, brown or even black. Chickpeas are especially important in Arab cooking and hence in Spanish cooking and in the countries of Spanish America. They are an essential part of many poor-man's 'stews' with meat and vegetables – in couscous, for instance. Then there is that famous Arab purée of chickpeas called *homous*, which usually contains *tahina (and sometimes yoghurt), and is used as a 'dip' for bread. Further East, in India, a smaller chickpea is grown called *channa.

Chickpeas must be soaked before being boiled as, unlike other pulses, they are almost impossible to cook otherwise, soaking is usually done overnight. Many cooks add a teaspoon of bicarbonate of soda per kg (2 lb) to the soaking water to help to soften the skins, although this does not improve the flavour and is not always necessary with modern varieties. Old-fashioned ones may need to be boiled for up to 4 hours in an open pan, or blitzed for an hour in a pressure cooker, but new types will be cooked in as little as 20 minutes in a pressure cooker. Since it is almost impossible to overcook chickpeas, it is best always to err on the generous side. If the skins have to be removed, this may be done by soaking the peas for an hour in a strong solution of bicarbonate of soda – say 2 teaspoons per 225 g (½ lb) of chickpeas – and then giving them a quick boil in the solution. After that the peas may be drained and put into cold water, rubbed hard between the hands, and the skins washed off. The skinned chickpeas should be rinsed in several waters. In Mediterranean countries, cooked chickpeas may be found in the markets. Chickpeas are also available canned, a great saving in time and effort. *Besan flour can always be found in Indian shops but, if it is not available, chickpeas can be ground at home; it is, however, necessary to put them through the grinder twice, once to break them coarsely and again to grind the broken bits to a flour. The bits of husk have to be sieved out. (An ordinary coffee grinder is unsuitable as chickpeas are so hard that they will break the machine.) Roasted chickpeas used to be added to coffee with chicory, not to adulterate it but because some people liked the flavour.

Chickpeas have always been common in Spanish cooking, despite criticisms of them. 'As for garbanzos,' said Théophile Gautier, 'they sounded in our bellies like pieces of lead in a Basque drum'. And Alexandre Dumas, in his great Dictionnaire Gastronomique, claimed that they are 'bullet-sized peas quite beyond the powers of digestion'. But whatever these Frenchmen may say, chickpeas are excellent and an essential part of Spanish cooking. For instance, a Castillian cocido consists of ham, stewing beef, chorizo sausage and chickpeas simmered for 3-4 hours in water with some olive oil, a piece of fat and a bone. Vegetables (cabbages, leeks, onion and garlic) are cooked separately and seasoned with a little pimentón. The liquid is served first as a soup with some pasta cooked in it, then the meat, chickpeas and other vegetables are eaten

with a salad of lettuce and tomato dressed with oil and lemon. Plenty of coarse salt is essential. Other versions are more elaborate.

At the simpler end of the scale are the Spanish potajes de garbanzos, in which, after cooking, a few of the chickpeas are crushed to thicken the juice, and perhaps a handful of spinach or some potato is added. The soup may be seasoned with olive oil (in which several cloves of garlic have been fried and some red pimentón stirred in), or alternatively with a sofrito of garlic and tomato fried in oil. To this, a little chopped raw garlic, cumin seed and black pepper may be added, following the common Spanish custom of combining raw and cooked garlic. For a more nourishing dish, chopped hard-boiled eggs, meatballs, minced salt fish (bacalao) or even a pasta may be included. These are comforting winter dishes, best not demanded by tourists in August.

[Chickpea – French: pois chiche German: Kichererbse Italian: cece Spanish: garbanzo]

CHICORY and ENDIVE. There is a great deal of popular confusion between these two plants, which is not surprising as both wild and cultivated forms are very much alike, belonging to the same genus of the composite family. In any case, from the culinary point of view, it is more important to distinguish between the various types of chicory than between chicory and endive in a botanical sense.

Chicory or succory (Chicoria intybus) grows wild throughout much of Europe and is a common escape in the US. It is recognized by its pale blue flowers and does not look promising to eat. However, the very young shoots, hardly appearing above the ground, have been used as a salad since at least Roman times, and are still eagerly grubbed out in Mediterranean countries and sold in winter and early spring.

Endive (Chicoria endivia) comes originally from eastern Asia and has gone wild in places in Mediterranean countries. It came into Europe as a salad plant at a much later date.

Both chicory and endive need to be blanched by the grower, as they are very bitter when green (and still rather bitter when blanched). Commercially, they are always blanched. Greenness is thus not a sign of freshness but of age. They are even best kept in the dark at home until eaten.

The true endives fall into two general types. Firstly there is the frizzly form, called moss curled or stagshorn endive. Rarely is it seen perfectly white; more often, a tile or slate has been put on the plant so that only the centre is properly blanched – the rest will be somewhat bitter and the outer leaves tough. There is also a well-known form with broad, slightly curled leaves, known as Batavia endive or *escarole*. It looks more like a curly lettuce. In chicory also there are similar leafy forms such as the Italian *spadona*, in which the leaves are bunched, and the form with long narrow leaves, the *puntarelle* of the Roman markets (also called *cicoria asparagio* or *di Brindisi*, or *catalogna*). Again in Italy there are the exotics, for *fiori commestibile* (edible flowers) which, when blanched, are red or variegated pink, orange or yellow, instead of white. The chicory which looks like a red-leaved brush – the root being the handle – is called *radicchio di Treviso*, while the pink flower-like chicory, which is sometimes almost like a vegetable rose, is *radicchio di Castelfranco Veneto* and *rosso di Verona*, *radicchio* being an alternative Italian word for chicory. These flower types have almost no bitterness and give colour to winter salads.

The well-known Brussels chicory or Belgian endive is a true chicory with the tight spindle-shaped hearts (*chicons*) forced and blanched. Even in the US, these come mainly from Belgium. The alternative name for this is *witloof* (white leaf). Like other chicories, it is slightly bitter, it can be eaten raw or cooked.

There are also varieties grown for their large tap roots, of which the best known is Magdeburg chicory. In the second half of the 18th century, the roasted root began to be used to flavour coffee – and soon to adulterate it. Cheating became so rife that in Britain the use of chicory in coffee was banned altogether in 1832, but eight years later – because those who liked chicory in their coffee protested – it was once more allowed, provided it was marked on the label.

To make chicory for coffee, the tap roots are washed, cut in bits and dried in gentle heat. Then the dry pieces are broken into nibs, roasted brown and ground. Chicory in coffee has a characteristic taste and is liked in France and in some of the southern states in America.

Yet more unwanted confusion about names can be caused by using *barbe* (beard) for chicory and other related salad plants and vegetables. *Barbe-de-bouc* (Goat's beard) is Brussels chicory (forced *chicons*) in Belgium. In France, *barbe-de-cupucin* is the shoots of wild chicory, as also in Italy is *barba di cappuccine di campo* (Capuchin friar's beard); Italian *barba di becco* (Billy goat's beard) is white *salsify and *barba di frate* or *di prete* (priest's beard) is another relative of salsify which is used

as a salad plant and vegetable in Italy. In England it is called Jack-go-to-bed-at-noon or goat's beard (*Tragopogon pratensis*).

[*Chicory* and *endive* – French: *chicorée*, *endive* German: *Endivie*, *Zichorie*, *Wegwarte* Italian: *cicoria*, *indivia*, *radicchio* Spanish: *achicoria*, *endibia*, *escarola*]

CHIHLI. *See* Chinese cabbage.

CHIKU. *See* sapodilla.

CHILE SALTPETRE or sodium nitrate ($NaNO_3$) is used as an alternative to *saltpetre (potassium nitrate), as it is cheaper. It is roughly one-sixth stronger in its action on meat, so quantities should be scaled down accordingly.

CHILLI, **chili** or even **chilly**. Chillies and *sweet peppers belong in the same genus and mostly perhaps in the same species (*Capsicum annuum*). However, the tiny, very pungent chillies at least can be referred to another species, *C. frutescens*, which is a perennial, unlike *C. annuum*, and cannot survive frost. Two other chilli species are cultivated in South America. Some long, pointed forms with the classic chilli outline are sweet and mild, while certain large kinds, especially those from Peru, look as if they ought to be mild, but are blistering. Even colour is nothing to go by. Most chillies start green and turn red when ripe. Some may first be yellow, and then red, and others turn chocolate, brown or even black. In size, there are varieties 30 cm (12 in) or more long and others no bigger than a pea. To many people, a chilli is merely a source of painful hotness, the raw material for cayenne pepper, but in Mexico, Spain, India and South America, the selection of exactly the right chilli for a particular purpose is a matter of gastronomic importance. Chillies vary not only in hotness but also in flavour – and in intensity of flavour. The hotness can be adjusted, with added cayenne perhaps, but the flavour cannot.

Chillies are natives of tropical America. They have been found in prehistoric Inca remains from Peru and were in common use by the Aztecs before the arrival of the Spanish in Mexico. It is difficult to imagine how Asiatic countries like India (which today is the largest producer of chillies) managed before they were introduced. Chillies are the flavouring above all used by poor people the world over, since a little goes a long way and they make almost anything palatable. People who use chillies at every meal become used to their burning principle and need increasingly larger doses and hotter chillies to obtain any impact.

It is therefore quite wrong to make Mexican or Indian food blindingly hot on the grounds that it is authentic. That is not how it tastes to the people of those countries. Very hot chilli, especially if the dish contains seeds or bits of the fruit, is not very good for the insides when suddenly sprung upon them and can even cause internal blisters. You must wash your hands carefully after handling chillies, as any residual juice on the fingers can burn the eyes if they are rubbed by accident. Chillies of many types are canned, and they freeze fairly well. Fresh green chillies, which cannot be replaced by dried ones, are now to be found in Britain (often imported from Kenya) thanks to the demand created by the immigrant population. In the US green chillies are available in markets, especially where there are customers who enjoy Mexican food, for which they are essential.

....

Mexican chillies

The use of chillies is more sophisticated in Mexico than anywhere else in the world. It has been estimated that there are about two hundred types of chilli, half of which are used in Mexico, including those listed below. When the hottest Mexican chillies are not obtainable, fresh cayenne pepper makes an acceptable substitute.

Cascabel. Dried. A small, plum-shaped chilli which has a nutty flavour after roasting. It makes the not over-hot *salsa de chile cascabel*.

Chilaca. Fresh, this is a long, thin, almost black chilli, which is very hot and well flavoured. *Chilacas* are roasted and skinned before use. When dried, they are *pasillas* which, toasted and ground, are used particularly in sauce for seafood.

Guajillo. Dried and exceedingly hot, this average-shaped, slender, pointed chilli is smooth, red-brown and sometimes sold as the much milder and rounder *cascabel*.

Güero. Fresh, this is a pale yellow chilli of variable size and typical long shape. It may be lightly grilled and used as a salad or added to sauces; it is hot and has a distinctive flavour.

Habanero. This tiny, light green, irregular chilli is possibly the hottest of them all. It is the one Mexican chilli that probably belongs to a separate species, *Capsicum sinense*.

Jalapeño. A short, fat, green chilli that is top-shaped with a rounded end. It is also fairly well known in the US, where it is put into processed cheese. This is a fairly hot chilli if the seeds and septa are included. It is the basis for the common, *chiles jalapeños en escabeche*, a Mexican table condiment which is also used in cooking. *Jalapeños* are sometimes available frozen as well as in cans. Dried, smoked *jalapeño* is *chipotle*, which is used to flavour soups and stews; it is obtainable canned in vinegar or red *adobo* sauce.

Poblano. This top-shaped, very dark green chilli is usually rather mild but has a rich flavour. It is roasted and skinned and is used particularly for stuffing. The dried, ripe *poblano* is an *ancho*, the dried chilli that is most used in Mexico; it is dark brown, becoming brick red when soaked. The *mulato* is another brown dried chilli which is very like the *ancho* but is sweeter in flavour.

Serrano. These small green chillies have very piquant seeds and septa. They are used fresh or toasted, often in green sauces, and are among the commonest types of Mexican chilli, being also available canned and in *escabeche* with other vegetables.

....

In the US, chillies are produced particularly in Florida, Louisiana, Texas and California. Best known is the Anaheim or Californian Green chilli, which is about 20 cm (8 in) long. This is a fairly mild, sometimes even sweet, chilli which is often stuffed with cheese or other filling and fried in batter (*chiles rellenos*).

The *fresno* is a small, conical chilli something like the *jalapeño*, but not so hot. Among yellow types, Banana chillies are mild and sweet, while the yellow wax *caribe* and *güero* are pretty hot. (You should approach all chillies warily.) The hot cayenne peppers, dried and ground to a hot, red powder, are used as a condiment. Tabasco peppers, small and red, are grown mainly in Louisiana for sauce.

The use of chillies in parts of the US is influenced by traditional Mexican dishes. The same Mexican influence has also travelled to Spain, where chillies are valued. Hot chillies, called *guindillas*, are used notably to add a kick to the dishes cooked *al ajillo* (fried with garlic), and green chillies are in the markets, but only in small quantities, from summer to autumn. Substituting *guindillas*, as some foreign books do, for the Romesco peppers, which are mild *sweet peppers, in Romesco sauce is disastrous.

Indians make wonderful fresh chutney, a thick purée of ground green chilli, green coriander, salt, lemon juice and coconut. Many varieties of chilli are grown in the east, mainly chosen for yield in a given climate and soil. They are dried by the thousands of tons, and used whole or ground to make chilli powder, often after a mild roasting which improves the flavour. Chilli powder is pure chilli, hot, but not as hot as cayenne. The chilli powder sold in the US and used for chilli beans or *chili con carne* is usually mixed with cumin or oregano. The most famous chilli condiment is *tabasco sauce; other chilli sauces are often highly-flavoured unsieved ketchups. Nepal pepper – not much seen these days – is merely a variety of chilli, and the *harissa* of North Africa is a mixture of chilli and cumin.

CHINE. The chine of a small pig consists of two undivided loins (the same cut as saddle of mutton), but from larger pigs, especially bacon pigs, the chine is the backbone with some meat between the wings of the vertebrae attached to it. The word is applied to similar parts of other animals.

Chining a loin of lamb or pork is sawing close alongside the backbone from the inner surface, cutting through the bases of the ribs and/or the wings of the vertebrae, but leaving the backbone attached to the meat. It is then easily removed when the loin is cooked, to make carving very much easier.

[*Chine* – French: *échine* German: *Rückenstuck* Italian: *coppa* Spanish: *espinazo*]

CHINESE ARTICHOKE or **chorogi**. These small tubers from a labiate plant, *Stachys sieboldii*, an exotic relative of the common hedgerow woundworts, get their name from a slight resemblance in flavour to *globe and *Jerusalem artichokes. They are popular in winter in France, as well as in the Far East from where they came. The French name, *crosnes*, is from Crosnes, where they were first grown in Europe in 1882. (They were sent to a Monsieur Pailleux by the doctor to the Russian ambassador in Peking.) It is essential that Chinese artichokes be fresh, as they rapidly lose flavour when dug out of the ground. (They can safely be left and dug as required.) After washing them well, remove the skin by shaking the tubers

in a cloth with coarse salt or by blanching them in boiling water and rubbing the skin. Some leave the skin on. There are many ways of cooking them, but they may simply be boiled for a quarter of an hour in salted water, drained and finished in butter with chopped parsley, or heated in gravy or a creamy sauce.

CHINESE BEAN. *See* cow pea.

CHINESE CABBAGE. There is a lot of confusion about the two Chinese species of *Brassica* and their variants, partly because the original 'Chinese cabbages' were much improved in the US after World War I and returned to their former country in a greatly changed form. The Chinese cabbage or *pe-tsai* (*Brassica pekinensis*) is also wrongly called 'celery cabbage'; the variety that is usually sold by British greengrocers looks a little like a cos lettuce with large white midribs, but others look almost like Swiss chard. So, too, does Chinese mustard or *pak choi* (*B. chinensis*), which is also known as mustard greens; two other varieties of this species are known as *wong bok* and *chihli*. According to some authorities, *B. chinensis* is only a variety of rape (*B. napus* var. *chinensis*).

The pickle which is often known as Chinese *sauerkraut* is made from *pak choi* fermented in salt; it is used in stir-fried dishes or steamed with meat and fish. This is available in cans and sometimes also from the barrel in Chinese stores. It is generally rinsed in water and squeezed dry, just like ordinary *sauerkraut*, before use. Dried, salted cabbage, which is usually sold tied in bundles, needs to be soaked in warm water until it is soft (about 15 minutes). It can be used as a particularly interesting flavouring in soups.

CHINESE CHIVE. *See* onion.

CHINESE FIVE SPICES consists of equal parts of star anise, cassia (or cinnamon), cloves, fennel seed and Chinese pepper. It may be bought ready ground from shops which specialize in Chinese foods or made at home, although the spices are difficult to grind finely. As you will have to visit the Chinese suppliers for the Chinese pepper, you might as well buy the five spices. Apart from being essential in certain Chinese dishes (e.g. *porc laqué*), it is also most useful flavouring with pork.

[*Chinese five spices* – Chinese: *heung new fun, hung-liu, ngung heung* French: *cinq épices chinoises* German: *fünf Gewürze* Italian: *cinque spezie cinese*

Spanish: *cinco especias chinas*]

CHINESE LANTERN PLANT. *See* physalis fruit.

CHINESE MUSTARD. *See* Chinese cabbage.

CHINESE PARSLEY. *See* coriander.

CHINESE PEPPER, **Japanese pepper**, **anise pepper**, or **Szechwan pepper**. This useful spice – which, despite its peppery taste, is no relation to ordinary black pepper – is the dried berry of a shrub (*Zanthoxylum piperitum*) belonging to the same family, the Rutaceae, as citruses and rue. Among its close relatives are satinwood (once commonly used for furniture), and the prickly ashes of North America, which have medicinal barks. The Chinese pepper bush can be grown in any temperate climate.

In China, this spice is commonly mixed with salt and used as a table condiment. For this, it is first gently roasted until crisp, then ground and mixed with a little salt (a teaspoon to 2 tablespoons of the powdered spice). Chinese pepper is also an ingredient of *Chinese five spices. When allowed to get stale, it develops a nasty scent.

[*Chinese pepper* – Chinese: *hua chiao*]

CHINING. *See* chine.

CHIPOLATA may be derived from the Italian for an onion (*cipolla*), but in Britain it simply means a small but otherwise ordinary sausage (16 instead of 8 to the pound).

CHITTERLINGS. This name is given to sausages made of bits of intestine, usually pig's. They may be bought from butchers ready prepared (cleaned, scraped inside, freed of fat, washed, soaked in salt water, and simmered in water and milk with spices, herbs and onion for several hours). In some places (e.g. Wiltshire) they are plaited. Grill and serve them with a vinaigrette dressing. To butchers making sausages, chitterlings would refer to the frilly part of the large intestine of the pig. And in the US, chitterlings are the odd scraps of a newly-killed pig, and are cut in squares and cooked in broth.

CHIVE. An onion with pretty purple flowers (superficially rather like those of thrift) and very fine, tubular, grass-like leaves, which are the part of the plant used in the kitchen. They are chopped finely and should be added to hot dishes at the last moment. Native to most of Europe, chives (*Allium*

schoenoprasum) have long been used as a flavouring in soups, omelettes and sauces, with cream cheese and in salads, particularly in Germany, Austria and Switzerland. Although the flavour of chives is unmistakably onion, it is subtly different. Anyone with green fingers but no garden should be able to grow a supply of fresh chives (which are infinitely superior to the dried variety) by growing them in a window box or flower pot. Remove any flower buds as they appear.

[*Chive* – French: *ciboulette* German: *Schnittlauch* Italian: *erba cipollina* Spanish: *cebollino*]

CHLORINE (Cl). A poisonous yellow-green gas, found on earth mainly in the form of its sodium salt (sodium chloride, or common salt) in seawater. Chlorine is an important element in life processes, but is chemically too active ever to be found in its uncombined state in nature.

First discovered in 1774, it has long been used for bleaching and disinfecting, as it dissolves in water to form a powerful oxidizing agent, hypochlorous acid. Its smell and taste are well known in over-chlorinated tap water. To get rid of this, add a very little hypo (sodium hyposulphite), a common chemical known to all photographers. Hypochlorous acid is lethal to all forms of micro-organisms, but as it also reacts with dead organic matter (such as you find in ponds and streams), unfiltered water needs much more chlorinating than clear water.

[*Chlorine* – French: *chlore* German: *Chlor* Italian: *cloro* Spanish: *cloro*]

CHLOROPHYLL The green pigment of plants, the means by which they use the energy of sunlight to build complex carbohydrates from carbon dioxide and water molecules. Chlorophyll, which contains magnesium, is often mixed with other pigments – yellow, red, or brown – to produce the range of leaf colours we see in nature. Chlorophyll is used as a green food colouring, but synthetic green dyes are more often used.

[*Chlorophyll* – French: *chlorophylle* German: *Chlorophyll* Italian: *clorofilla* Spanish: *clorofila*]

CHOCOLATE, from the Aztec, *chocolatl*, was used as a drink long before the Spaniards arrived in Mexico. Columbus noticed it on his fourth voyage, when it was found in an Indian trading boat in the Gulf of Honduras, but it was first brought to Spain by Cortes in 1528. The Spanish tried to keep its existence a secret, and for a good while, few people north of the Pyrenees had any idea of its value or use. Dutch and English pirates, for instance, threw cocoa (or cacao) beans overboard when they captured a cargo, calling them 'sheep shit'. The first chocolate house opened in London in 1657, but the high customs duty imposed on cocoa kept it as rich man's beverage until as late as 1828. The tree (*Theobroma cacao* – the generic name means 'food of the gods') which provides chocolate is native to tropical America, but to satisfy world demand, it was soon being cultivated in other countries – notably West Africa – between 20° north and south of the equator.

The 'beans' from which chocolate is made grow inside fat, spindle-shaped pods which are borne directly on the main branches and trunk of the tree. The beans are scooped out of the pod with the adhering pulp and are fermented to develop their flavour. They are then dried in the sun. After shipping to the factory, the beans are roasted and broken into small nibs, and the shell is winnowed away. The grinding and refining of the nibs is a long and skilled process, on which the fineness of the finished chocolate depends. The pressure of the refining mills liquefies the cocoa nibs as they are ground, turning them into what is called chocolate liquor, and this emerges from the mill as a solidified block.

Drinking chocolate (as opposed to *cocoa) is chocolate with much of the fat (which is known as cocoa butter) pressed out, leaving a dry cake which is then pulverized. If you add extra cocoa butter to the chocolate and refine it by 'conching' (rolling the chocolate liquor back and forth in a curved trough by a mechanical roller), you get fondant chocolate, which usually has sugar added to make it bitter-sweet or semi-sweet. The longer conching continues – it can last from less than a day or as long as 7 days – the finer the chocolate. Fondant chocolate was invented by Rodolphe Lindt. The adding of condensed milk to chocolate, which was first done by M. Peter in Switzerland in 1875, produces milk chocolate.

The quality of chocolate you get depends to a large extent on the price you pay. It seems obvious (but has to be said) that chocolate varies enormously in flavour and that you cannot expect to make a good chocolate dish with inferior chocolate. The problem today is finding good chocolate – for example, in the US, chocolate may be totally defatted, then reconstituted with inferior fat; careful inspection of the label is advisable. The best chocolate for cooking is the very finest eating chocolate such as Lindt or Bendick's Sporting and Military. Perhaps it is because chocolate is usually

sweetened commercially that people find it so extraordinary that it is used in savoury dishes – with meat, game, octopus and so on – but unsweetened chocolate does appear in this role in Mexico, Spain and Italy. Bitter chocolate goes well with onion and tomato, for instance, as a base for a dish of fish or meat. In Mexico, it is added to chilli powder. For sweet dishes, it combines especially well with vanilla, another Central American discovery, and also with cinnamon. There are chocolate-based liqueurs, too, which are usually unbearably sweet.

[*Chocolate* – French: *chocolat* German: *Schokolade* Italian: *cioccolata* Spanish: *chocolate*]

CHOKO. Australian name for *chayote.

CHORIZO is the most famous Spanish sausage and comes in many regional varieties. They are all smoked and combine chopped pork with *pimentón*. *Chorizos* are made in other countries, including France and, particularly, Mexico, which took the tradition of making them from northern Spain. Mexican varieties, of which there are said to be 124, each with its own balance of chillies, herbs and spices, are generally less tough than the Spanish ones. *Chorizos* are very good grilled (preferably over charcoal) until they are crisp on the outside and cooked right through. They are also an important ingredient in Spanish and Mexican cooking; for some recipes they are skinned before being added.

CHOROGI. *See* Chinese artichoke.

CHOW-CHOW. No doubt derived from the Chinese, this now means a mainly American pickle of mixed vegetables, which is rather rich with yellow mustard seed. The following is a typical recipe.

Chow-chow

Cut into small pieces 1 kg (2 lb) green tomatoes, 1 large bunch of celery, 450 g (1 lb) each green beans and green peppers, 1 kg (2 lb) firm cucumbers, 1 small cauliflower and 400 g (14 oz) onions. Sprinkle well with kitchen salt. Leave overnight. Next day bring to the boil 2 lt (3½ pt) vinegar plus 60 g (2½ oz) white mustard seed, 25 g (1 oz) ground turmeric and 1 tablespoon each ground cloves, allspice and black pepper. Drain and squeeze the vegetables to remove some of the water and throw them into the boiling vinegar. Cook gently until the vegetables are tender, then bottle.

The chow-chow that can be bought in Britain in jars for use as a relish is mainly made of fruit and is sweet-hot in taste.

··

CHROMIUM (Cr). A very shiny, silvery metal often used for plating, usually over a film of nickel. Chromium is corrosion resistant, because of the film of its oxide which forms on the surface. It is an important constituent of stainless steel, and also a trace element present in an available form in raw vegetables and unrefined foods. Good sources are brewer's yeast, wheat germ, mushrooms, even beer and pepper, but the metal is made unavailable by temperatures over 120°C (248°F), which means that food sterilized in an autoclave or cooked in a pressure cooker – which for practical purposes means canned goods – is lacking in chromium. Deficiency is claimed by some authorities to be a contributory factor in heart disease.

[Chromium – French: chrome German: Chrom Italian: cromo Spanish: cromo]

CHRYSANTHEMUM. This genus of the daisy family (Compositae) has about 150 species ranging from the ordinary wild ox-eye daisy to the enormous varieties sold by florists. Among its members are *costmary (Chrysanthemum balsamita), *tansy (C. vulgare), pyrethrum (C. cinerariifolium) and *chrysanthemum greens (C. coronarium). They may be annuals or perennials. The chrysanthemum varieties grown as flowers belong to a number of species, and since they are not poisonous – though not necessarily nice to eat – they can be safely used as decoration in food.

[Chrysanthemum – French: chrysanthème German: Chrysanthemum Italian: crisantemo Spanish: crisantemo]

CHRYSANTHEMUM GREENS or shungiku. Although this annual is sometimes thought to be a separate species (Chrysanthemum spatiosum), it may well be a cultivated variety, with larger leaves, of the Crown daisy (C. coronanum), also called Garland chrysanthemum. The wild form of the Crown daisy which is so common in Mediterranean countries, has feathery leaves that are strong in taste and less worth eating. Japanese chrysanthemum greens can easily be grown in Britain or the US. They should be young and tender, old leaves are not worth eating. Shungiku is called for in Japanese recipes and may be used raw in salads.

CHUFA, tiger nut, earthnut, earth almond, yellow nut grass, pignut, or rush nut.
The chufa is the small tuber of a sedge (Cyperus esculentus) which is native to Mediterranean Europe and Portugal. The plant is related to Cyperus papyrus, from which the ancient Egyptians made a precursor of paper. Chufas have certainly been eaten for several thousand years, but though cultivated in a number of countries, it is in Spain that they are of most importance. As bought, chufas are knobbly, shrivelled little objects about the size of the thumbnail, and with a sweetish taste. They are better when shrivelled than when fresh, as keeping makes them sweeter. Although eaten as nuts, mainly by children, and used occasionally for ice cream, their gastronomic importance is in the preparation of horchata de chufas, a milky drink much loved in Spain.

··

Horchata de Chufas

Soak 225g (½ lb) of chufas in water overnight and wash them very carefully. Put them in a liquidizer with a little water and reduce to a fine state. Add a bit of cinnamon stick (bruised), a little grated lemon rind, about 150 g (5 oz) sugar, to taste, and 1 lt (1¾ pt) of water. Stir well and leave to stand for another 4-5 hours. Then strain through muslin and bottle. Chill in the refrigerator. (A horchata of almonds is made in the same way.) Horchata is drunk as a cool, refreshing drink on a hot day. Horchatas are also made with melon seeds and with other nuts.

··

CHUMP. Means the end of something – wood, meat, etc. The term is applied by butchers to chump chops, which are the chops at the hind end of the rack, not exactly like the other chops and so often sold more cheaply.

CHUTNEY. A chutney is a piquant Indian relish, eaten in small amounts to add an accent to a meal. The correct pronunciation is more like 'chatni', but in old books it is often written 'chutnee'. There is a great difference in what is understood to be chutney in the East and the West.

A chutney in India is almost invariably a mixture ground fresh on a curry stone, and consists of a paste of raw ingredients, such as fresh ginger, fresh green chilli, onion, garlic, mint, green coriander, sour fruits, coconut – in fact, anything considered tasty, stimulating or refreshing to the palate. Within wide limits, the cook is free to create from what he happens to have available.

The sweet, bottled chutney sold elsewhere is very different. Though it is of Indian inspiration, and quite often manufactured there, most people in India would call it a sweet pickle rather than a chutney. This chutney is always cooked and always combines sugar and vinegar with spices and fruit. The fruit is mango, but the British home substitute, well known on stalls at craft sales and church jumbles, is based on apples and raisins. More rarely, other fruits, such as apricots, are used.

Mint Chutney

Take a handful of mint leaves, a medium-small onion,1 teaspoon salt, 5 fresh green chillies and the juice of about half a lemon (to taste). Chop and blend with about ½ cup water. The remaining component is freshly grated or desiccated coconut. If you are using desiccated coconut and a blender, first grind the coconut dry to a powder. Finally add the coconut to the other ingredients, a little at a time, until you have a smooth, soft paste. Quantities are flexible.

Green Coriander Chutney

Make as above with a handful of green coriander leaves, 2-6 fresh green chillies, salt, lemon juice and water.

Mrs Luck's Bengal Chutnee

The following comes from Spellow House near Harrogate in Yorkshire. Mrs Luck was my grandfather's cook and must have been born about 1850 – a real Victorian. Her method of dealing with holes in her stockings (as reported by my father) is interesting. She would draw the stocking together round the hole, tie it with a piece of string and cut off the surplus tuft with a pair of scissors. After which, as she forced the stocking on again, she would remark: 'It's a bad foot indeed that won't shape its own stocking.'

Dissolve 225 g (½ lb) salt and 900 g (2 lb) brown sugar in 3.5 lt (6 pt) cold brown vinegar. Add 3 dozen peeled and cored apples, 100 g (4 oz) sultanas and 225 g (½ lb) crystallized ginger of cooking quality cut into small pieces. Slice up 5 Spanish onions and add them together with 25

g (1 oz) mustard seed, 6 shallots, and 40 g (1½ oz) chillies – bird chillies are best. Boil everything together until the apples are tender. Bottle. Keep for some months before use.

Sweet Mango Chutney

This is an Indian recipe, which needs ripe, but not soft, mangoes – washed, peeled and sliced. Heat in a very little water until they are soft. For each kg (2 lb) of mango slices, add 1 kg (2 lb) sugar, 60 g (2½ oz) salt, and, pounded and tied in a muslin bag, the following flavourings: 25 g (1 oz) mixed spices (equal parts of cumin, cardamom, cinnamon), 15 g (½ oz) ground chilli, 50 g (2 oz) onion, 2-3 cloves garlic, and 125 g (4½ oz) green ginger. Cook the whole to a jammy consistency before putting in 100-125 ml (4-4½ fl oz) vinegar, depending on strength, per kg (2 lb) of mango slices. Then cook for 5 minutes, remove the spice-bag and bottle the chutney.

CIDER is an ancient drink, although exactly how ancient is a matter for argument. it has certainly been made for over 1,000 years, and it is possible that the Romans were the first to introduce sweet apples, suitable for cider-making, into Britain. By the 17th century, when the British cider apples were classified by the first Viscount Scudamore, there were over three hundred varieties grown, with splendid names like Handsome Maud's, Slack-my-Girdle, and Skryme's Kerne. Cider-making had become a traditional cottage industry in the west of England (in Somerset, Devon, Dorset and Herefordshire); in the 19th century it was not uncommon for farm labourers to get part of their wages in cider, just as the Scottish farm workers got part of theirs in oatmeal. The West Country colonists also took their knowledge of cider-making to America and cider was the usual drink of the early settlers, (with the applejack they learned to distil from it). In the old days, cider varied enormously from place to place and from year to year, because of the wild yeasts which made fermentation an uncertain process. At the end of the 19th century, the isolation of good yeasts made reliable cider-making possible on a bulk scale. Today, the best cider is made from blends of cider apples, which give a fine balance between astringency, acidity and sugar, but cheap, run-of-the-mill ciders are sweet and uninteresting.

In making cider, the apples are milled to a pulp

and the juice pressed out of them. It is fermented in barrels or, commercially, in large tanks, in the same way as grape juice is fermented in a winery. The residue is used as a source of *pectin. What remains after that goes into animal foodstuffs. Cider can vary between a fine dry drink of champagne-like quality, to a sweet, child's drink, or from something smooth to a rough farm cider, suitable for scaling a boiler. 'Old Scrumpy' will still dissolve rats, as it was said to in the past, (and as my father's cider used to do), although, as PR men are quick to point out, this no longer happens in the factories.

Obviously, the type and quality of cider is of great importance if one is cooking with it. Recipes for using cider come from all the American 'apple states', as well as from Normandy and the west of England. Northern Spain, in the main, produces sweet cider, and does not seem to use it much in cooking. Opinions are sharply divided as to the merits of cider in meat and fish dishes, where it has often been advocated merely as a cheap substitute for wine. French chefs, who, like most good cooks, are apt to have definite opinions, do not look on it as a particularly notable ingredient unless they are Norman – you have to make up your own mind. The dishes in the classic cuisine which use cider are all Norman; they include *tripes à la mode de Caen* and *l'oie en daube à la Normande* (goose cooked slowly in a closed pot with onion, celery, leek, carrot, with apples and cider). They usually contain *calvados (which is to Normans what applejack is to Americans). Indeed, calvados is a more frequent cooking ingredient than cider.

....

Pork Chops in Cider

Score 4 pork chops on one side and ease them away from the bone. Slit the fat diagonally in several places on the outside to prevent the chop curling up when it is cooking. Chop 2 tablespoons of fresh herbs and use them to fill the slits in the meat. Crush 8 juniper berries and place them in the meat, 2 to a chop. Marinate the chops in 300 ml (½ pt) cider for an hour. Remove the chops and season them with salt and pepper on the opposite side to the herbs. Heat the grill to the maximum heat and grill the chops, in the grill pan (not on the rack) for about 2 minutes on each side. Turn down the grill and, after about 10 minutes, drain off the excess fat. Add the marinade and cook for a further 5 minutes or until no pink shows in the chops. Serve them garnished with 1 tablespoon each of chopped capers and gherkins.

....

Cider Cake

Heat the oven to 180°C/350°F/Gas Mark 4. Grease and line a 17 cm (7 in) cake pan. Grate the peel of an orange and squeeze it. Make up the juice to 300 ml (½ pt) with sweet cider. Cream 100 g (4 oz) butter and 175 g (6 oz) caster sugar with the orange rind until the mixture is light and fluffy. Beat in 2 eggs, one at a time. Sift 225 g (8 oz) flour with ½ teaspoon each powdered cinnamon and allspice; stir into the butter mixture alternately with the cider, beating until smooth after each addition. Turn the batter into the pan. Bake for about 1 hour, or until the cake feels firm to the touch and a warmed skewer inserted into the centre comes out clean. Leave the cake to cool for 10 minutes, then turn it out. Serve it with apple purée and whipped cream.

[*Cider* – French: *cidre* German: *Apfelwein, Apfelmost* Italian: *sidro* Spanish: *sidra*]

....

CILANTRO. *See* coriander.

CINNAMON and CASSIA. Cinnamon, which many only know as a powdered spice, is the dried bark of a tree (*Cinnamomum zeylanicum*), a native of Ceylon and adjacent parts of South India. When cinnamon trees are 2-3 years old, cutting begins. The bark is stripped off and flattened; after the corky outside is planed away, it is ready to be dried. It rolls up into a scroll and is known as a quill. Several quills are usually packed together, one inside the other.

In the related cassia (*Cinnamomum cassia*), the bark is thicker, it is not usually planed clean on the outside or packed quill inside quill. Cassia is rather more pungent than true cinnamon and has a less delicate taste. In many countries, the two are sold as one, but in others (including Britain) this is now not allowed, although much confusion remains.

Cinnamon is one of the most important spices; it is very common in sweet dishes, for which it is best bought ground (in small quantities, as ground cinnamon quickly loses its aroma and becomes stale). It is anyway difficult to grind to atomic fineness at home. In savoury meat dishes – and there are many in which cinnamon is used, especially in mutton dishes influenced by the cooking of the Middle East – the spice can be added in whole pieces or ground in a simple coffee mill (which is kept for grinding spices). Like all spices, it keeps its flavour best when whole. However, cinnamon sticks are thin and inclined to break up into small splinters, which are a nuisance in food. This is one reason for using cassia, which breaks up less easily, in pilaus. In Indian dishes, cassia is also more correct. Cinnamon, though, is better for sweet dishes. The powerfully antiseptic essential oils in cinnamon help to preserve food. The leaves of the cassia, under their Indian name of *tej pat*, are also used in Indian cooking.

[*Cinnamon* – French: *cannelle* German: *Zimt* Italian: *cannella* Spanish: *canela*.

Cassia – French: *casse* German: *Kassie* Italian: *cassia* Spanish: *casia*]

CITRIC ACID. A fairly weak organic acid, which occurs particularly in the juice of lemons and other citrus fruits, as well as in many other fruits, in wine and even cheese. One of the few acids used in the kitchen in pure, crystalline form, it is included in recipes for home-made soft drinks and in yeast nutrients for home-made wine. It is a useful standby souring agent, can be made to do in place of lemon juice and is perhaps preferable to bottled lemon juice, which sometimes has a nasty flavour. Commercially, it is made by a fermentation involving citric acid producing organisms. Citric acid has anti-oxidant properties and, in dilute solution, will prevent cut vegetable surfaces browning. It is also preservative, but less so than the acetic acid of vinegar.

[*Citric acid* – French: *acide citrique* German: *Zitronensäure* Italian: *acido citrio* Spanish: *ácido cítrico*]

CITRON. A citrus fruit which looks like a large, warty lemon with very thick peel. They can sometimes be found on sale in Italy. The citron was the first citrus fruit to reach Europe (it probably originated in India), and the ancient Greeks found them growing in the land of the Medes and Persians (hence its botanical name, *Citrus medica*). It was later cultivated in the famous Hanging Gardens of Babylon and used to perfume toilet waters.

The main use for citron in the kitchen is as a candied peel. It has a resinous taste and is thicker than other candied peels. Citron is made into a liqueur in some parts of the Mediterranean – this is called *Kitrinos* in the Cyclades and *cédratine* in Corsica.

[*Citron* – French: *citron* German: *Zitron* Italian: *cedro* Spanish: *cidra*]

CITRUS FRUIT are a very closely related group, all coming from shrubs or small trees of the genus *Citrus*, which grows from the tropics to warm but temperate regions such as southern Europe. They are all rich in vitamin C. Their sweetness or sourness depends on the balance between the sugars and fruit acids which together form 80-90% of the solid matter that is dissolved in the juice. The main sweet species are the Sweet *orange (C. sinensis)*, and tangerine or mandarin (*C. reticulata*); the *grapefruit (C. paradisi)*, Seville *orange (C. aurantium)*, *lemon (C. limon)* and *lime (C. aurantifolia)* range from less sweet to definitely acid. Other species are the *citron (C. medica)*, *shaddock (C. grandis)* and papeda (*C. hystrix*).The bergamot (*C. bergamia*) is used mainly in perfumery – its skin, like that of other citrus fruits, contains aromatic essential oils. A related genus, *Fortunella*, includes the *kumquats. There are also hybrids (such as tangelos, e.g. the ugli, which are grapefruit X tangerine), varieties and forms which are known in their own right (such as the ortanique, a flattened, thin-skinned Sweet orange, which might be a hybrid) and one or two types of uncertain origin, such as the clementine (which could either be tangerine X Sweet orange or a variety of tangerine).

CLABBER. Thick, sour milk which has not separated into curds and whey. Clabbering is souring milk until it reaches this point.

CLAM. A term applied to various types of bivalve mollusc. The British tend to think of them as American – clam chowder, clam bakes, clam juice and canned clam broth. 'A kind of cockle', says a Victorian cookery book, 'to be found on the west coast of Ireland and Scotland, and in Devonshire and Cornwall, and some parts of Wales. Though they figure largely in American cookery they are not much used in England.' Clam is an old English word for a fetter, clamped to arms and wrists, and then for any gripping tool. Hence clam shell, a shell that grips tight. It is a useful word without exact definition: almost any bivalve may be called a clam if it does not have a special name of its own.

There are said to be over twenty thousand species of bivalve in the world, all of them probably edible, although the number of clam species that are commonly eaten is probably no more than fifty. They range in size up to the Giant clams of tropical reefs, which have shells weighing 250 kg (550 lb) and 10 kg (22 lb) of meat inside, enough to feed a large party. Clams vary greatly in flavour and toughness. Alexis Soyer is said to have claimed that clams the same size as oysters should be eaten raw, larger ones cooked. Such sweeping statements without reference to species or locality are valueless, but the *praire* of Brittany and Normandy is indeed very fine.

The recognition of unknown clams in strange markets is for shell collectors, hardly for cooks. About ten years ago, after being bewildered by fish markets in Normandy. Italy and Spain, all within the space of two months, I decided to start buying and identifying samples of clams in markets wherever I went. Very soon, I concluded that there are so many local differences, so many sizes, so many local names, and even so many scientific names given to the same species, that clam collecting, taken seriously, would become a lifetime hobby. Nevertheless, there are certain basic facts about clams which the consumer needs to know thoroughly.

Clams very often live buried in sand or mud. Some are dug or ploughed up on beaches near the low tide mark, while others have to be dredged from under the water. Clams feed and breathe by drawing a current of water through their bodies; they filter food particles out of the stream of water. It is important to understand this because it explains why clams that have grown in dirty places can be infected with harmful organisms – disease germs like typhoid or even poisonous plankton (*see* poisoning). It also explains why clams will clean themselves of grit if they are left in clear water. Commercially dredged or farmed clams are kept for some days in tanks of clear seawater under ultra-violet light (which kills bacteria but not plankton) and are therefore sand-free and safe to eat.

Clams bought in markets from local fishermen need to be cleaned. First they should be well scrubbed and picked over for dead or damaged specimens – dead ones will gape open. Then they should be put, not too many together, in a wide shallow basin filled with clean seawater (if you are near the sea) and kept quietly in a cool place for a couple of days with frequent changes of seawater – if the clams die from lack of oxygen in the water, it will be worse than not bothering to wash them. If you are not near the sea, the clams should be put into cold water in which has been dissolved about 100 g (4 oz) of salt (preferably sea-salt) per 4 lt (7 pt) of water. Clams will clean themselves in this, at least partially, if left quietly for 2-3 hours. They will live up to a week when kept cool and packed in seaweed.

Clams are eaten either cooked or raw. If cooked, they can be opened by heat, like mussels. Many types may benefit by being opened by hand before cooking, which should be short or the flesh will toughen. A clam which may take some time to steam open can be cooked in a minute under the grill if it has already been opened.

Clams are often more difficult to open raw than oysters. The best implement for the purpose is a short, thin-bladed, double-edged stainless steel knife. Insert it between the shells or drive the point in near the hinge, depending on the type of clam. Move the knife close to the uppermost shell, being careful not to puncture the animal's body, and cut the two muscles – one at each end – which hold the valves together. Then pull the top shell off and free the animal from the bottom shell by cutting underneath it. If the clam is held flat, the juice may be preserved – or the job can be done over a bowl. As when opening oysters, you should wear some protection on the hand holding the clam; otherwise, if the knife slips, there can be blood all over the kitchen. A trick advocated by American friends is to put the clams in the freezer for a couple of hours before opening. After a short thawing, the clams are in no condition to resist the cook's designs upon them. The treatment does not alter their quality.

With canning and freezing, clams now come from all over the world. They can be put into a freezer without any preparation other than cleaning and still eaten raw for up to two months afterwards. If kept longer, they are good only for cooking. In many cases, the commercial exploitation of clam beds by mechanical methods of digging (which are over efficient), have made formerly plentiful clams come to the verge of extinction. A good example is the New Zealand *toheroa*, which makes one of the world's most delicious soups. Another now-scarce clam is the Pismo clam of California. In recent years, however, the farming of clams has gained momentum, and fine clams are now cultivated where they formerly did not exist. France is a pioneer in this business. *Palourdes* have long been tended near the estuary of the Loire, and American hard-shell clams were introduced into the mouth of the Charente at the time of World War I. Britons can feel pleased that since the 1940s the same type of clam (probably brought from America on liners using Southampton) has established itself in the Solent, in waters warmed by the coolers of the Fawley petroleum refinery. After the disastrous freeze in the winter of 1962-63, when so many oyster beds were ruined, American clams were taken from these waters and left to fatten and cleanse in the Newtown River on the Isle of Wight where oysters had previously been growing. These clams are hardier than oysters, and, with the lessons learned from bitter necessity, the cultivation of American hard-shell clams alongside oysters is now an established industry in Britain, although most are exported to France and Belgium, since the British (as suspicious of shellfish as they are of toadstools) are only just learning to eat them.

This is perhaps why, although the Americans have names for their clams, often taken from the indigenous Indian languages, there are no popular clam names in Britain, though there are a few in Ireland. Invented names like 'carpet shell' and 'warty venus' are not gastronomically inviting, and it would be better to use the French words as we do in so many culinary matters. France is lucky in having both an Atlantic and Mediterranean seaboard. The most important indigenous clams in France are the *palourde*, the *clovisse* and the *praire*. In Spain, also blessed with a northern and Mediterranean coast, a common snack is the *almeja*. These are much canned in northern Spain, and it is not always easy to know what kind you are eating, since *almeja* seems to cover many species. So also does the Italian word *vongola*. *Spaghetti alla vongole* must be one of the most internationally-known Italian dishes. Clams of all kinds are particularly fished and eaten around Naples and Venice. The following are the best known clams in Europe.

Palourde (*Venerupis decussata*). Carpet shell. French: *palourde*. Italian: *vongola nera* or *vongola verace*. Spanish: *almeja* Palourdes are often also called *vongole napoletane* (Neapolitan). This is the largest of the European 'gastronomic' clams, reaching 8 cm (3 in), and one of the best. Found both in the Atlantic and Mediterranean, it is cultivated in the sandy muds north and south of the Loire estuary, and is common in Brittany, both in Morbihan and on the north coast around Roscoff. They are also fished off the Gulf Stream warmed coasts of Southern Ireland (where they are called *ruacan* or *kirkeen*) and exported to France. In Britain, they are found only locally in warm waters. *Palourdes* are the classic clams for *spaghetti con vongole*, the sauce for which is made from small ones. These clams have tender meat and a fine flavour. They are eaten raw or cooked. Raw ones can have a bitter aftertaste, but they have many devotees. They are also superb stuffed with garlic butter, or with a herb butter containing shallots, tarragon and parsley.

Clovisse (*Venerupis geographica*, grey, and *V. aurea*, yellow.) French: *clovisse* and *clovisse jaune*. Italian: *vongola grigia* and *vongola gialla*. Spanish: *amarguela* and *margarita*. These two very similar species of clam are mainly from the Mediterranean (they are scarce in the Atlantic and not so tasty) and are commonly eaten in the South of France. They are fished all the year, but are best in summer and autumn when they are larger and fatter. These are common types of *vongole* used in Italy, but considered inferior to the *vongola nero*, and are usually referred to as *vongola commune*.

Praire (*Venus verrucosa*). Warty Venus. French: *praire*. Italian: *tartufo di mare* (sea truffle). Spanish: *verigüeto*. A very heavy concentrically ridged shell about 5 cm (2 in) wide which occurs both in the Mediterranean and Atlantic (e.g. Brittany coasts); it is common in Britain, though neglected as a food and with no popular English name. Elsewhere *praires* are regarded as delicious – usually eaten raw – and one of the more expensive bivalves; they are also cooked, with garlic butter and in other ways.

Venus gallina. French: *galinette*. Italian: *poveracce*, or similar, in Veneto and northern Adriatic, *lupino*, or similar, in Naples and the south. Spanish: *chirla*.

Smaller than *Venus verrucosa*, 3-4 cm (1¼ -1½ in), and much fished in the Mediterranean where it is one of the cheapest bivalves. Though available all year, it is most abundant in winter and spring. Not very well flavoured and rather tough, it is commonly used in soups and sauces. It is often referred to as *vongola*, sometimes *arsella*.

Wedge shell (*Donax trunculus*). French: *olive de mer* Italian: *tellina* Spanish: *coquina*. This bivalve is small, 3-4 cm (1¼-1½ in), and wedge shaped. It is tender and the taste is fine and sweet. In Italy, it ranks with the *vongola nera*, and many Italians consider it the very finest for making soup, or to go into sauces for spaghetti and risotto. It is also delicious eaten raw but, being so small, can only be a *passa tempo*, like sunflower or melon seeds. *Telline* are available all the year round in Mediterranean countries.

Smooth venus (*Callisto chaine*). French: *verni*, *grosse palourde* Italian: *cappa liscia*, *issolon* in the Veneto, *fasulara* in Naples. Spanish: *savenna*. This is a large, smooth clam, up to 12 cm (5 in), which will attract attention in Mediterranean markets by its beautiful appearance. Its meat is inclined to be tough.

In North America (in sharp contrast to Britain), clams are a popular food on both coasts; they are eagerly sought after both fresh and canned. In times past, they were a favourite food of the Indians, not only around the coasts but also inland where various freshwater clams were eaten. Most famous of the American clams are:

Hard-shell clam (*Mercenaria mercenaria*). Alternatively, round-shell clam, quahaug or quahog (from the Algonquin Indian name). This and a very similar species with a more southerly distribution (*M. campechiensis*) are both indigenous to the East Coast of North America and are found in shallow estuarine waters. These are delicious shellfish. When large (about 11 cm/4½ in) they are known as chowder clams, when smaller (about 7.5 cm/3 in) as cherrystones, and when smaller still (about 6 cm/2½ in) as littlenecks; the last two are generally eaten raw.

Soft-shell clam (*Mya arenaria*). Alternatively, long-shell clam, soft clam, oval clam or sand gaper. This is another East Coast clam, but occurs on both sides of the Atlantic and was introduced accidentally to the West Coast in the 19th century, probably with oysters. It lives in sandy mud and has a fragile shell, from which it gets its name. This is the best clam for steaming – it is sometimes called steamer clam. It cooks in about 15 minutes.

Pismo clam (*Tivela stultorum*). The Pismo clam is a very large (up to 450 g or 1 lb) species of hard-shell from the coasts of southern California, famous for making an excellent chowder, but now becoming rare.

Giant West Coast clams. *Schizothaerus nuttalli*, the great Washington clam, from the West Coast is very large and lives 60 cm (2 ft) deep in muddy sand; it makes an excellent chowder. It is commonly confused with the Giant saxidome (*Saxidomus giganteus*) which is found all the way from the Aleutians to San Diego. Another large West Coast clam with a strange Indian name, is the geoduck (*Panope generosa*), which may weigh over 2 kg (4½ lb).

Eastern surf clam (*Spisula solidissima*). A large clam 18 cm (7 in) with a smooth, tan coloured, oval shell. This clam is found from Maine to South Carolina and is the clam most common in the US. It is too big to eat raw and is best minced in clam chowder.

[*Clam* – French: *palourde* German: *essbare Muschel* Italian: *vongola verace* Spanish: *almeja, telina*]

CLARIFYING and **CLEARING**. Clarifying, as applied to fats rendered from meat or chicken, consists of washing out the impurities. This can be done by boiling the fat for a few minutes with a largish volume of water, pouring it off the top into a basin, letting it cool, refrigerating it until solid, then removing and cleaning the underside of the fat. If the fat is still not clear enough, repeat the operation. There are also gadgets which enable liquid fat or oil to be separated from water. Clarifying, as applied to butter or margarine, consists of heating the butter (preferably unsalted) or margarine until all the solids come down as a sediment which can be strained out with muslin. Indian clarified butter, ghee, is cooked over a low heat for longer until it gets a special nutty taste.

Clarifying is also used synonymously with clearing when applied to things like wine and aspic. Two techniques are used. In the first, a substance is added which dissolves or changes the substance causing the cloudiness. This is done with wine when an enzyme, a pectinase, is added to remove cloudiness caused by pectin. The second, and more usual, technique is to add something which will bring down the offending cloud to the bottom of the vessel. With wine, this is known as fining. In the kitchen, we are mostly concerned with clearing stocks and aspic. Details of the methods are given under these headings.

[*Clarifying* – French: *clarifier* German: *abklaren* Italian: *chiarificare* Spanish: *clarificar*]

CLARY. A labiate herb (*Salvia sclarea*), native to southern Europe and closely related to sage. As a culinary herb, it was more used in the past than today; it is bitter and aromatic, and can be used fresh or dried in omelettes, or for any other purpose if you like it.

[*Clary* – French: *orvale, sauge sclarée, toute-bonne* German: *Schlarlachkraut, Muskateller-salbei* Italian: *erba moscatella* Spanish: *amaro, esclarea*]

CLEARING. *See* clarifying.

CLEMENTINE. *See* orange.

CLOTTED CREAM, Devonshire cream or **Cornish cream**. This delicious thick cream, with its characteristic 'boiled-milk' taste, was made from the rich milk of Devon cows on lush pastures, and was at one time used on farms in south-west England as others use butter. Clotted cream is about 60% fat – the legal minimum is 55%. It was traditionally made in special, shallow, glazed earthenware pans holding about 9 lt (16 pt) of milk. The milk was strained into these pans while still warm from the cow. Sometimes a little water was added to help separate the cream, and the pans were then put into a cool dairy, where the cream would rise. In summer, this would take 12 hours or less but in winter 24 hours, even more, would be needed. After this, the pans were moved very carefully (so as not to disturb the cream) on to the back of the stove, or put over hot water, to raise the temperature to 80-85°C (176-185°F) over a period of about half an hour, and certainly not less than 20 minutes. The cream is ready when a ring the size of the base of the bowl appears on the surface.(For amateurs it is best to heat the pan over hot water, if the heating is done too quickly, the cream goes greasy and lacks the special, delicious taste.) The pan was then cooled quickly and the cream removed. Naturally, the yield of clotted cream would depend on the richness of the milk. Jersey milk gave more than would the now common Friesian milk. Clotted cream made from machine-separated milk lacks some of the fine flavour, but is still good with home-made raspberry jam and Devon splits.

CLOVES. With black pepper, cinnamon and nutmeg, cloves rank as one of the world's most important spices. Cloves are native to the 'Spice Islands' of South East Asia (and were traded into Europe even in Roman times), but in the 18th century, plantations were established in many other tropical countries, notably Zanzibar (now the most important producer), Madagascar and the West Indies. The tall evergreen clove trees (*Eugema aromatica*) flourish only near the sea. Cloves are the flower buds, picked when they are pink and spread out to dry on mats. They contain an essential oil (eugenol), which is powerfully antiseptic and has a preservative action. Cloves are well known in pickle spice, hot bottled sauces and chutneys, and are stuck into an onion for bread sauce. They go into apple pie, mixed spice and the caramelized brown-sugar glazing for boiled bacon and pork. A little less well known is the clove in beef stock, or in a stew, where it gives a richness without being identified. Used wrongly, clove flavour is crude – a reminder of the dentist (who uses clove oil as a penetrating antiseptic). It should be used with care (and that

may mean using no more than a tiny crumble of the clove head) so that it becomes part of the background. As a flavouring, cloves are best when kept below the level of recognition.

[*Clove* – French: *clou de girofle* German: *Nelke* Italian: *chiòdo di garafono* Spanish: *clavo*]

CLUSTER BEAN. See gaur.

COAL FISH. See cod.

COATING. Food to be fried is coated with egg and breadcrumbs, batter, flour, oatmeal, egg white and so on. There are two important considerations whatever coating is used: that it should stick to the food being coated, and that it should not be thick and stodgy. Reasons for stodginess include having too thick a batter, pressing the breadcrumbs on to the egg instead of shaking them off, or using fine toasted breadcrumbs instead of coarser untoasted ones. As to adhesion, if food is wet and the least bit slimy – whether it is fish or meat – then egg will not make a sufficiently intimate contact for it to stick. The surface must be lightly floured first. Egg should be beaten a little and may be thinned with a little milk or water so that it does not form too thick a layer. The very lightest batter coating is made on the food, not separately in a bowl. For instance, food may be simply dipped in flour or cornflour and then in egg diluted with milk, or in white of egg diluted with a very little water. After coating, the food should go quickly into hot fat and not be left to go soggy. If the coating is to keep fat from soaking into the preparation, then a quick dip into egg white is often sufficient. An interesting batter for coating is the Indian one made simply of water and **besan* flour with salt and some spices. The Chinese usually make batter of egg and cornflour.

COB. See hazelnut.

COCA. The chewing of coca leaves, which contain the alkaloid cocaine, is traditional in the Andes and nearby parts of the Amazon basin, where the plant (*Erythroxylon coca* and other species) grows wild. Coca chewing was common amongst the ancient Incas, and Pizarro found it in general use in 1553. The effect of cocaine is highly stimulating (as we know from Sherlock Holmes), and it enables its users to travel or to work for long periods without food. Coca chewers, who consume some 25-50 g (1-2 oz) per day, get hooked on the habit, become addicts and run the risk of sickness, even death, from anorexia, as the drug destroys the appetite for food. Coca leaves are not used outside the tropical areas where the plant can be grown – after picking, the drug is rapidly lost. As a masticatory, like *betel leaves, coca leaves are chewed with lime or wood ash. Coca is mentioned here in case it might be confused with the *cola nut, which is used in soft drinks.

COCHINEAL. A natural food colouring first brought to Europe in 1518, cochineal is made from the dried bodies of the female cochineal bug, as also are artists' carmine lake. The insect (Coccus cacti) is a native of Central America. It is bred in specially grown plantations of cactus (e.g., on Tenerife). The cochineal bug is one of the scale insects, a close relative of the mealy bug that infuriates gardeners, of the kermes scale insect (Coccus ilicis), which also produces a colouring, and of the lac insect, which produces lac for lacquer. The extraordinary thing about these scale insects is that the female, who starts as a normal, active, girl insect, goes peculiar as soon as she is fertilized, attaches herself permanently to the food plant, loses her limbs, swells and changes shape until she looks just like a gall, a mere part of the plant itself. There is nothing in outward appearance to suggest that she is an insect, which is why both cochineal and kermes were originally thought to be of vegetable origin.

To make cochineal, the scale insects are brushed off and either heated for a moment on trays in an oven or dunked into boiling water before being thoroughly dried. The result is in the form of greyish grains which can later be pulverized and extracted to give the bottled cochineal essence that is familiar in the kitchen. It is said to be tasteless, but as a child I did not think so.

[Cochineal – French: cochenille German: Koschenille Italian: rosso di cocciniglia Spanish: cochinilla]

COCKLES. Heart-shaped bivalves with thickly-ribbed shells. In some species, the ribs are ornamented with knobs or spines. Several species of cockle, including the Common cockle, Cerastoderma edule, and Acanthocardia aculeata (spiny), A. Echinata (prickly), and A. tuberculata (tuberculate), are found commonly round the coasts of Britain and Europe. Cockles were an important food in the past; witness the following written over 100 years ago. 'A crowd of the more youthful description of peasantry are collected every spring

tide to gather Cockles on the sands by daylight when the tide overruns. The quantities of these shellfish thus procured would almost exceed belief; and I have frequently seen more than would load a donkey collected in one tide by the children of a single cabin. They form a valuable and wholesome addition to the limited variety that the Irish peasant boasts at this humble board; and afford children, too young for other tasks, a safe and useful employment.' One wishes that the beaches were as clean and wholesome these days.

All cockles live buried in sand, usually around low tide mark. They are therefore liable to be gritty unless allowed to clean themselves in clear seawater, or water with some salt added (100 g/4 oz per 4 lb/7 pt) for several hours, after first washing them well in several waters and scrubbing each one with a hard brush. Throw out any that are broken or do not close tightly when handled. Cockles are often eaten raw or roasted on a stove top until they open; they are popularly seasoned with pepper and vinegar, and accompanied by buttered brown bread. They may be opened like mussels, by putting them in a saucepan with a dash of water and, with the lid on tight, heating and shaking the pan. As soon as they open, they are done. Like other shellfish, overcooking will make them tough. Cockles are sometimes covered with sauce or cooked in more elaborate ways. They are also canned.

[Cockle – French: coque German: Herzmuschel Italian: cuore edule, cocciola Spanish: berberecho]

COCOA. The cocoa bean, from which *chocolate is made, contains an unpalatable amount of fat. In Holland, Conrad van Houten, following his early work in pressing out part of this fat to make an improved drinking chocolate (1828), went on to treat drinking chocolate with an alkali which darkened it and destroyed part of the flavour, but saponified the fats, leaving traces of soap. This is cocoa. It blends more easily with milk but has not the fine taste of a good drinking chocolate.

[Cocoa – French: cacao German: Kakao Italian: cacao Spanish: cacao]

COCONUT palms (Cocos nucifera) lean out over tropical beaches in both the Old and New Worlds, and nobody knows whether they got there through the nuts being carried on ocean currents or by the agency of man. Indeed, it is not absolutely sure that South East Asia was the coconut's original home, though it probably was. Certainly it is in parts of southern Asia that it is most important in cooking. Coconuts do not only grow on the coast; in many places, there are plantations hundreds of miles inland, but the palms prefer sandy soil. There are many cultivated varieties.

Coconut juice. Unhusked green nuts are opened by cutting off the top with a sharp *machete* or *panga*, and the juice, which is always cool and pure, is drunk straight out of the nut. This is a welcome and life-saving drink for travellers in the tropics. It should not be confused with the heavy, sweet liquid (milk or cream) that is contained in ripe coconuts.

Unripe or **green nuts**. The flesh of unripe coconuts is gelatinous and may be scraped off the inside of the nut after you have drunk the juice. There are a few recipes for its use in puddings.

Toddy. The coconut palm, like several other species of palm, is often tapped for its juice. The flowering shoots are cut off and earthenware pots are hung to catch the sap, which flows copiously. In the hot tropical sun, sap caught during the day has usually fermented by the evening. That caught during the night may have only just started to turn. Unfermented juice is a pleasant drink, much liked by teetotal Hindus. During prohibition in India, it became common to put preservatives in the catching pots to prevent natural fermentation. Drinking toddy was illegal. In fact, toddy is usually a crude, sour drink and has a very unpleasant smell on the breath. It is used sometimes instead of brewer's yeast in Indian cooking, and gives a distinctive and unusual taste to the South Indian rice preparations leavened with it.

Palm sugar is made by boiling down the juice (*see* sugar).

Choosing coconuts. A good coconut is heavy, and you should be able to hear the juice when the nut is shaken. If the nut has dried out or leaked, it may be bad. It is also important that the eyes should be dry and not smell mouldy, as they are the weak point in an otherwise impervious shell and the point of entry for spoilage organisms. In particular, beware of nuts with fibre still covering the eyes. It may hide the mould.

Opening the nuts. Pierce two of the eyes with a skewer. Drain out the liquid into a glass. Now hold the nut horizontally in both hands and bang it

down hard on one of its three ridges against a stone or a concrete floor. It should split into two halves. If you want to free the kernel, after draining and before splitting put the nut in a hot (200°C/400°F/ Gas Mark 6) oven for 20 minutes and bang it all over.

Shredding the nut. In countries where coconut is much used in the cooking, there are devices available for scraping shreds out of the shell. For occasional needs, it is enough to remove the flesh, pare off the thin brown skin, and grate or liquidize the flesh. A medium nut gives 3-4 cups of grated coconut.

Keeping nut pieces fresh. A trick from fairgrounds: put the nut pieces in the liquid you drained from the nut and keep in the refrigerator. After all, it is this liquid that keeps the nut fresh till you open it.

Desiccated coconut. Modern desiccated coconut is a high-quality product made by shredding the coconut and drying it in a vacuum at 70°C (158°F) for an hour. The result has none of the slight rancidity of the sun-dried nut. It is sold in flakes of varying fineness. It can be more finely ground by giving it a whirl in a coffee grinder. Although it lacks some of the delicate flavour of the fresh nut, desiccated coconut commends itself for being cheap and easy to use (500 g or 18 oz roughly equals 3 nuts). Desiccated coconut will keep in a closed jar in the refrigerator for several weeks without drying out.

Coconut milk and **coconut cream**. Not to be confused with the juice of the nuts. It is necessary for many Indian and South East Asian dishes. Boiling water is poured over grated (or desiccated) coconut and left to cool somewhat before the milk is squeezed out with the hands or in a cloth. A thinner milk is made by pouring a second lot of boiling water over the partly-spent nut shreds. For thick milk, take 2 cups of boiling water to 1 cup shredded nut (gives 3 cups). Half that amount of water makes thick cream (but naturally it depends on the size and quality of the nut). It is best to err in making it thick and thinning it down later with water or second pressing thin milk. A somewhat improved yield can be obtained by using a liquidizer. 'Cream of coconut' and 'coconut cream' are names given to several products, sold in cakes or frozen, which may be used to make coconut milk. Both coconut milk and coconut cream are also canned. Such products should never be used if they taste rancid.

....

Fish Molee

Molees are essentially dishes from the coconut-growing areas of India but are enjoyed everywhere in that country. Heat a little cooking oil in a pan and add to it in turn 1 large chopped onion, 4 cloves chopped garlic, 3-4 chopped green chillies and a 2.5 cm (1 in) piece of fresh ginger, chopped. The mixture should not be allowed to brown but should cook gently until the onion is soft. Allow the pan to cool slightly to avoid burning the spices which are now added: 1 teaspoon ground turmeric, I pinch red chilli powder (to taste), 4 cloves, 4 cardamoms and a 2.5 cm (1 in) cinnamon stick. Fry for 30 seconds, mixing the turmeric into the oil, then add, little by little, 2-3 cups thick coconut milk (from 1 grated coconut), letting it amalgamate into a sauce. Cook this for a further 15 minutes uncovered, without letting it boil. Put in the fish fillets and shake the pan to cover them with the sauce. Continue to cook without boiling until the fish is ready. (Add some thin coconut milk if the sauce becomes too dry.) Adjust the salt and add a few drops of lemon juice if it is needed. Sprinkle with chopped coriander leaves, if you have them, and serve with rice.

....

Coconut oil. This is a usual cooking fat in parts of South India, Ceylon, Malaysia and elsewhere in coconut areas, although there has been a tendency to replace it with hydrogenated vegetable cooking fats. Some people find food cooked with coconut oil difficult to digest. In South India, the oil was made at home by grating the kernel, soaking it in water, and then boiling it until the oil floated to the surface. The oil was then skimmed off and strained. This oil tastes of fresh coconut. Villages had their *chekku* or oil press.

Other coconut products. Coconut syrup is a product made by evaporating expressed coconut juices with invert sugar. Coconut honey is a thicker, darker product made in a similar way but with longer cooking. These and other coconut products are modern commercial ingredients to be judged on their individual merits.

[*Coconut* – French: *noix de coco* German: *Kokosnuss* Italian: *noce di cocco* Spanish: *nuez de coco*]

COCOYAM. *See* yam (dasheen, yautia).

COD (*Gadus morhua*) and its family (Gadidae) are particularly important to the countries bordering on the North Atlantic, cod having been one of the major food fishes for centuries. First fished with lines and later with trawls, it had great value, as it could be salted and dried, and so gave significance to distant fishing grounds, such as the Grand Banks, which would not have been so valuable for perishable fish. (*See* salt cod.)

Coal fish, **saithe**, **coley** or **pollock** (US) (*Pollachius virens*) is a poor relation of the cod, particularly caught in northern waters. It is usually one of the cheapest fish and is very ordinary in gastronomic quality, although its nutritive value is as high as that of the cod. The skin of the coal fish is darker than the cod's, and the flesh is a bit darker when raw, but quite white when cooked.

Haddock (*Melanogrammus aeglefinus*) averages 40-60 cm (16-24 in) in length and is easily distinguished from the usually larger cod because it has a black lateral line rather than a white one and also has a conspicuous black spot on each side below the front dorsal fin. Unlike the usually smaller whiting, it has a barbel on its lower lip. It is found on both sides of the Atlantic as well as in the North Sea. It is at least as delicious as the cod and is smoked to make that great British delicacy, *Finnan haddock.

Hake (*Merluccius merluccius*), which grows up to 1 m (39 in) long, is generally regarded as the best of the cod family in Europe, although there are others, like the Silver hake (*Merluccius bilinearis*) on the northern coasts of America, which are good or better. On the Pacific coast of America, the most plentiful hake is *Merluccius productus*. The hake is the easiest of the cod family to bone, and so is particularly suitable for children. It is abundant from May to September, and is excellent poached whole or used for *ceviche; the head is good for soup.

Ling (*Molva molva*) lives in the North Atlantic as far south as the Bay of Biscay. It is a prolific fish, caught in large quantities in trawls and, by many, not distinguished from cod. It grows up to 2 m (78 in) long and is salted like cod, differing from it in shape, rather than in quality.

Pollack (*Pollachius pollachius*) is a good sporting fish for sea anglers, as it grows up to 10 kg (22 lb). Distinguished from the coal fish (*see above*) by its projecting lower jaw with no barbel and its almost square tail, it is little liked as a food fish, being rather watery; it is best baked. The insides have a notoriously unpleasant smell.

Whiting (*Merlangus merlangus*) ranges from Norway to the Mediterranean, but is very common in the North Sea. Whiting are small fish, rarely over 30 cm (12 in) long, and at most 2 kg (4½ lb) in weight. The flesh is rather dry, but is considered wholesome and digestible. The fish has a black mark on its side, but no barbel, which distinguishes it from the haddock. They are smoked, as butterfly fillets, and like small haddocks, are sold as cutlets. This is the fish which always used to be served with its tail bent round in a loop and held in its mouth. Many related species are called 'whiting' in the US, such as the Carolina whiting (*Merluccius americanus*) and the California whiting (*Merluccius undulatus*).

Other species of the cod family, such as the pout or bib (*Trisopterus luscus*), are of more interest to anglers than to cooks. The pout could be mistaken for a haddock, as it has a black blob on the bottom of its pectoral fin and a barbel, but its colour is rather bronze and the body is deeper.

[*Cod* – French: *morue, cabillaud* German: *Kabeljau, Dorsch* Italian: *merluzzo* Spanish: *bocalao, abadejo.*

Haddock – French: *aiglefin* German: *Schellfisch*

Hake – French: *merluche, merlu* German: *Hechtdorsch, Seehecht* Italian: *nasello, merluzzo* Spanish: *merluza.*

Whiting – French: *merlan* German: *Weissfisch, Wittling* Italian: *merlano* Spanish: *plegonero, merlan*]

COFFEE probably came first from Ethiopia, where it is still to be seen growing in a semi-wild state, although it is possible that it originated in the mountains of the Yemen on the other side of the Red Sea. In the 16th century, it was brought up the Red Sea to Egypt, and coffee houses began to open in London and Paris from 1650 onwards. The plants were introduced to both the East and West Indies, and reached Brazil in 1727. Of the many different species of *Coffea*, the most important is still the original one to be cultivated, *C. arabica*. A second species, the prolific *C. canephora* produces a type of 'robusta' coffee, which is cheaper and used for blending.

Coffee plants are small trees, but are cultivated as bushes. Their fruits, called cherries, grow in clusters and, when ripe, are red and the size of a cherry. Each cherry normally contains two 'beans', flat sides together, in a parchment-like skin. (The few varieties

with a single rounded berry give peaberry coffee, which roasts more evenly.) The flesh of the beans is sweet but without value and is removed by stacking the beans until they begin to rot (ferment is the usual word), then by washing it off with water. The seeds are separated, cleaned, dried and graded. Fresh, unroasted beans are anything from grey-green to yellow-brown and have no trace of coffee flavour.

Coffee varies enormously in appearance and in quality. It is very much a field for experts, especially as blending is usual. Few unblended coffees are used, because it is rare to find a coffee which is perfectly balanced in flavour, acidity and strength. Some people make their own blends, but for most of us it is best to leave this to the professionals, who have made a life study of the subject, know the thousands of different types available and have developed a palate. With the present high price of coffee, it is a costly business to start from scratch. The roasting which gives the coffee beans their flavour may be light, medium or dark. Fine coffees would rarely, if ever, be heavily roasted, because this would spoil their subtle flavour. Once roasted, coffee beans must be cooled as rapidly as possible because, as long as they are hot, they are rapidly losing the most delicious and ethereal essential oils. These oils are continually dissipating, though not so fast, even when the beans are cold. Thus, the sooner the beans are used, the better – anyone who cares about coffee will always look for freshly-roasted beans.

As a mechanical roaster is not a common item of domestic equipment, roasting beans at home would have to be done in a pan on the stove or in a heatproof dish in the oven. Old Boer farmers in South Africa always insisted that their wives roasted the coffee freshly in the mornings, but these days, few people will bother to do that except on special occasions, as once when I was given a sack of beautiful coffee on one of my visits to South India. The coffee beans must be continually but gently turned over in a dry pan; to stop turning them for even a second burns them. Roasting will take some 15 minutes of undivided attention; in the oven, it would take slightly longer. At the end you may put in a little sugar to melt and coat the beans, thus helping to seal in the flavour, but I find that this gives a caramel flavour – which some, I suppose, may like.

Although it may be argued that the imperfections of home-roasting are likely to cancel out the advantages of freshness, there can be no question of the superiority of home-ground coffee. It repays the effort overwhelmingly, quite as much – perhaps even more – than using freshly-ground pepper from the mill. Ground coffee deteriorates in flavour noticeably in half an hour. Manufacturers minimize losses by packing ground coffee in a vacuum or an inert gas, but once the tin is opened, deterioration begins just as quickly. As small electric grinders are cheap and efficient, there is really no reason for buying ground coffee.

Each of the many methods of making coffee has its advocates. Those who like a strong, bitter espresso like a strong, bitter espresso, and it is useless to argue that other coffees are better. Fine coffees are best made by putting a generous amount of the ground coffee into a warmed earthenware jug and pouring on boiling water. After stirring, then letting the coffee stand for some minutes, you may put a teaspoon of cold water gently over the top to help settle the grains, but filtration is not usually necessary. Also popular are filter methods in which the ground coffee is put in a paper filter in a funnel of some sort which rests over the top of the coffee pot. Water, which has come to the boil, is then poured over the coffee and drips through to the pot.

Good coffees are produced in many countries. The famous Mocha coffee, originally from Arabia, is very aromatic and, at best, tastes like the smell that wafts down the street from the shop with the roaster. Blue Mountain is another familiar name and is properly from Jamaica. However, most Blue Mountain is exported straight to Japan and so it is hard to find true Blue Mountain in coffee shops. Fine coffees also come from Central and South America. Coffee from other sources (Kenya, for instance) are continually improving in quality.

Turkish coffee (or Greek coffee, depending on where you are drinking it) is served throughout the Levant. To make it, coffee beans are ground to a powder in a mortar or in a special hand grinder, and the drink is made by boiling the powdered coffee with a little water and sugar in a special, long-handled pot (an *ibrik*). It is boiled up several times to get exactly the right froth on top, and is offered in several degrees of sweetness. In Arab countries, coffee is part of the traditional hospitality and its serving can be almost as much a ritual as the Japanese tea ceremony. Arab coffee pots have a peaked spout into which can be put some vegetable fibre for straining; opened cardamom seeds or even cloves can be used for added flavour.

With good coffee, additives such as salt and mustard are unnecessary. Instant coffee is popular for its convenience. Flavour varies from brand to brand, but connoisseurs are unlikely to find it delicious, though many now use it as a flavouring in cooking.

Exhaustive medical tests have been made, and nobody has shown that coffee in ordinary amounts is harmful. Excess, especially when coupled with bad eating habits, is another matter. As coffee is expensive, it is open to adulteration and imitation. *Chicory root, roasted and broken into nibs, is the most common additive, and its use has become hallowed by tradition so that some people prefer blends that contain it. Coffee substitutes include roasted barley (sometimes malted), which is also used as a cheap additive to 'stretch' coffee and produce a less expensive drink, roasted dandelion root (which is something like chicory) and roasted sugar beet. *See* caffeine.

[*Coffee* – French: *café* German: *Kaffee* Italian: *caffè* Spanish: *café*]

COGNAC is a particular type of *brandy made in a legally specified area around the town of Cognac about 100 km (60 miles) north of Bordeaux, but the word is popularly used in many countries as a synonym for brandy. Cognac is distilled in old-fashioned pot stills from a thin, sourish white wine which is made traditionally from the *folle blanche* grape, but today also from other less frost-prone varieties. The wine is undrinkable, but the brandy is superb. After distillation, the cognac is matured for periods of up to 40 years in casks of local oak. For sale, cognac is almost always blended. A *fine champagne* must contain at least 51% from the central Grande Champagne region of the Cognac area and the remainder from the adjacent Petite Champagne. (In this case, 'Champagne' means countryside and has nothing to do with the sparkling wine from near Rheims.) There is a shorthand, which is not legally defined but is generally accepted, for indicating the quality of cognac and the length of time it has been matured in the cask. One star * has been matured for at least 3 years, ** at least 4, *** at least 5. Older brandies are denoted by initials starting with VO, very old; then VSO, very superior old (12-17 years in cask); VSOP, very superior old pale (20 years); WSOP, very, very superior old pale: XO, extra old (30 years). After, at most, 40 years, the quality begins to decline.

In cooking, unless otherwise specified, use a three-star cognac for 'brandy' wherever the spirit is to be used cold or sprinkled in towards the end of cooking. A cheaper spirit might be used when it is to be burned.

COINTREAU. *See* liqueurs and cordials.

COLA NUTS or kola nuts are used for chewing, as they contain relatively large amounts of *caffeine and other stimulating alkaloids. The tree (*Cola nitida*) is native to the forests of tropical West Africa, but today is grown in many other parts of the tropics. The taste is at first bitter, then sweet, and a simple drink can be made by boiling the powdered nuts in water. Prepared drinks containing cola are today almost, if not quite, universal.

COLCHESTER PYEFLEET. *See* oyster.

COLE or coleseed. *See* rape.

COLEY. *See* cod (coal fish).

COLLAR. *See* bacon.

COLLARD. *See* cabbage, kale.

COLLOP. A fairly thick slice of meat, but alternatively an egg fried with bacon.

COLOCASIA. *See* yam (dasheen).

COLOSTRUM. *See* beestings.

COLOURINGS. Most countries have their own lists of approved food colourings and synthetic dyes which are thought by the pundits to be harmless and therefore allowed in foods. Some countries are more cautious than others, and experts do not always agree. Harmful and even carcinogenic substances have, in the past, got through the net, and as nobody can be sure of long-term effects until substances have been used over a period of time, we are no doubt going to find other wolves among the lambs. Having said that, one should also say that there is no *a priori* reason for thinking that synthetic substances are more toxic than natural ones. Dyes are very often active chemicals and so likely to be harmful, but the food industry knows that the public buys by sight. Yellow butter must be rich, and the Spaniard must offer yellow paella to the tourist (and to himself) for even though there is no taste of saffron, the yellow colour fools the tourists into thinking there is; such is the power of suggestion that the Spanish may even imagine the missing taste. I would always leave dyes out.

Natural food colours which have been in use for a long time are: *cochineal (crimson), *kermes (purple red), *annatto (yellow), *safflower (yellow), *chlorophyll (green), *alkanna (crimson and violet), *cudbear (red) and the juices of various berries and roots. Coloured substances often have strong flavours which limit their application as simple colouring agents – examples are saffron and turmeric.

In cake decoration, I use: for red, the juice expressed from raw, grated beetroot mixed with plenty of lemon juice and concentrated by boiling (not much or it goes brown) to reduce the volume; for green, spinach, blanched and pounded and the juice squeezed out; for brown, instant coffee or chocolate. With these simple materials, it is possible to make beautiful floral decorations on cakes.

[*Colouring* – French: *colorant* German: *Farbmittel* Italian: *colorito* Spanish: *colorante*]

COMMON BEAN. *See* kidney bean.

COMPOSITE. Member of the plant family Compositae, which includes such common flowers as thistles, daisies and dandelions. The common feature of composites is that what we might think of as their flowers are in fact groups of tiny flowers (florets). The composites are the largest family of flowering plants with more than 14,000 species ranging from annuals to trees. Among them are many plants of culinary significance. The seeds of sunflower and safflower yield fine oils. The most important salad greens – lettuce, endive and chicory – are composites, as are some root vegetables, notably salsify, scorzonera and Jerusalem artichoke. Other composite vegetables are the globe artichoke, of which the young flower-heads are eaten, and cardoon, which is grown for its leaf stalks. Composite herbs include tarragon, tansy, camomile and wormwood.

COMPRESSED YEAST. A cake of American compressed *yeast equals roughly 15 g fresh yeast.

CONDENSED MILK. When people speak of condensed milk they usually mean sweetened condensed milk. (They refer to the unsweetened as *evaporated milk. The two have different characteristics and are preserved by different methods.)

The idea of concentrating milk by boiling is ancient. Indian *khoa* or *mawa* (often used in Indian sweets) is made by boiling and concentrating milk – originally buffalo milk – right down to a paste. Modern canned condensed milk is made after first pasteurizing the milk at just below boiling (80-90°C/176-194°F) for a minute and then adding sugar. After that, the pressure is lowered until the milk boils at 50-60°C (122-140°F). It is reduced by boiling to about a third of its original volume. This leaves the sweet sticky condensed milk; it consists of 40-45% cane sugar with 28% milk solids and the rest water. The preliminary pasteurization destroys the enzymes (which, if left, might cause undesirable changes) and kills most bacteria, but sweetened condensed milk is not sterile and, when canned and sealed, it is not sterilized by heat. Sweetened condensed milk nevertheless keeps well, just like jam, because of its high sugar content. For the same reason, sweetened condensed milk also keeps for some time after it is opened. If, as occasionally happens, one finds a blown or bad-tasting tin, the contents are harmless though unpleasant. In cooking, it is mainly used as a short cut in making some simple puddings and salad dressings, and it is useful for making Indian sweetmeats to offer after a curry.

Indian Coconut Sweets

Grate some coconut. (If fresh coconut is not available then desiccated coconut can be used, though it is not quite so good.) Mix the grated coconut with condensed milk until a paste is formed of such a consistency that it can be rolled into balls. As each ball is made, roll it in more coconut and set it on a plate to dry a little.

[Condensed milk – French: lait condensé German: Kondensmilch Italian: latte condensato Spanish: leche condensada]

CONDIMENT. Salt, pepper, mustard, vinegar, spice, pickle or relish. The word, from the Latin condimentum (pickle or seasoning), has very little exact meaning, except that we understand condiments to be taken to table rather than added in the kitchen. (Seasoning is what the cook does in the kitchen.) Condiments are also always salty, spicy, piquant or stimulating. We would not usually call sugar a condiment nor redcurrant jelly, but we would include horseradish and mustard, and we may certainly copy the French and include *nuoc-nam. We also include ketchups and bottled sauces. Powdered dried lime or *sumac are other possibles, and I often feel the need for such sour powders as

are used in some countries of the Middle East for sprinkling on rice; their use might well be more widely adopted.

[Condiment – French: condiment German: Wurze Italian: condimento Spanish: condimento]

CONGER EEL (Conger conger) is a marine fish which is widely distributed throughout the world. Congers grow to a very large size – monsters are 3 m (9 ft) long and weigh over 70 kg (160 lb). They are gifted with the same tenacity of life as common eels. Large ones are formidable creatures and give a very severe bite. Fishermen usually kill them in the boat. Congers have some superficial resemblance to the adult common eel as caught in the sea, but the eyes and gill openings are much larger, and the conger is without scales, while the common eel has scales embedded in the skin. Although the conger is a good fish and not bony, it lacks the richness and oiliness of the common eel and is not regarded as a delicacy. Conger is much used in soups, for instance in the Genoese burrida, in French bouillabaisse, cotriade and so on. Its flesh is firm but avoid using the bony tail end which is particularly unpleasant. It is abundant off rocky coasts in the winter months from September to April.

[Conger eel – French: congre German: Seeaal, Meeraal Italian: grongo Spanish: congrio]

CONSOMMÉ. See broth.

CONTREXÉVILLE. See water (mineral water).

CONVERSIONS. Although official tables offer conversions between units that are accurate to six places of decimals, the inaccuracy of most kitchen-measuring equipment will invalidate any pretensions to scientific accuracy. The conversions given below are quite accurate enough for the kitchen and are, I hope, reasonably easy to handle.

Temperature

Fahrenheit to Centigrade (Celsius): subtract 32, multiply by 5 and divide by 9. Centigrade (Celsius) to Fahrenheit multiply by 9, divide by 5 and add 32.

Weight

Pounds to kilograms: multiply by 5 and divide by 11. Kilograms to pounds: multiply by 11 and divide by 5. Ounces to grams: multiply by 25 or 30 (the exact conversion is 28.3). Grams to ounces: divide by 25 or 30.

Volume: British/Metric

Gallons to litres: multiply by 9 and divide by 2. Litres to gallons: multiply by 2 and divide by 9. Pints to litres: multiply by 4 and divide by 7. Litres to pints: multiply by 7 and divide by 4. Fluid ounces to millilitres: multiply by 25 or 30. Millilitres to fluid ounces: divide by 25 or 30.

Volume: American/Metric

Gallons to litres: multiply by 4. Litres to gallons: divide by 4. Liquid pints to litres: divide by 2. Litre to liquid pints: multiply by 2. Fluid ounces to millilitres: multiply by 30. Millilitres to fluid ounces: divide by 30.

Volume: British/American

There are rich possibilities for confusion here because the US dry pint and the US liquid pint represent different volumes. Effectively the US dry pint is the same as the UK pint, while the US liquid pint is smaller (16 fluid ounces instead of 20). Thus: Liquid pint and gallon, UK to US: multiply by 5 and divide by 6. Liquid pint and gallon, US to UK: multiply by 6 and divide by 5. UK and US fluid ounces are effectively the same (though the US fluid ounce actually equals 1.04 UK fluid ounces).

Volume: US Cups & Spoons/ British

US cups to fluid ounces: multiply by 8. Fluid ounces to US cups: divide by 8. Tablespoons to fluid ounces: divide by 2. Fluid ounces to tablespoons: multiply by 2. Teaspoons to fluid ounces: divide by 6. Fluid ounces to teaspoons: divide by 6.

Volume: US Cups & Spoons/ Metric

US cups to litres: divide by 4. Litres to US cups: multiply by 4. US tablespoons to millilitres: multiply by 15. Millilitres to US tablespoons: divide by 15. US teaspoons to millilitres: multiply by 5. Millilitres to US teaspoons: divide by 5.

Length

Inches to centimetres: multiply by 10 and divide by 4. Centimetres to inches: multiply by 4 and divide by 10. Feet to metres: multiply by 3 and divide by 10. Metres to feet: multiply by 10 and divide by 3.

COPPA. This is usually *coppa cruda* (raw), but there is also *coppa cotta* (cooked) which is of less gastronomic importance.

Coppa cruda consists of cured collar (neck) of pig, pressed raw – whole or in large pieces – into sausage skins (bladder or large gut) and hung to dry and mature for 2-4 months. Although it is a typical product of Emilia-Romagna from around Piacenza, Parma and Langhirano, it is also made traditionally in neighbouring Tuscany and Umbria – there is a version from Perugia. It may also be known as *bondiola* or *capocolla*. Thin slices of *coppa cruda* are a classic part of an Italian *antipasto* (*hors d'oeuvre*) of cold meats. *Coppa* is also made in Corsica.

Coppa cotta is typical of central Italy, where it is made of the cooked and pressed meat of pig's head and tongue, flavoured with pepper, bay and spices. In Rome, it is something like brawn, though more solid, but in Venice it may be more like a mould of cooked ham and tongue. It is not usually enclosed in a skin.

COPPER (Cu) is a necessary element in the diet, and lack of it causes serious health problems. It is needed, for instance, for the formation of red blood cells. The daily intake for most people is adequate but not handsomely so.

The richest dietary sources of copper are oysters and crustaceans, which can contain as much as 400 parts per million, but ordinary fish are low in copper. Other good sources are yeast (50-100 ppm), liver (50-100 ppm), gelatine (25 ppm), cocoa, chocolate, tea and coffee (10-20 ppm), currants (17 ppm) and nuts (10 ppm). Meat, eggs, milk, cheese, fruit and vegetables are all low in copper. Copper salts in large quantities are poisonous to animals and plants.

Unlined copper vessels were once common, and they served well as long as they were in continual use and kept scrupulously clean. A copper water jug even had the advantage that since copper is lethal for bacteria, even in tiny quantities, it made the water safer to drink. However, when copper pots were used spasmodically and verdigris (a green coating of copper carbonate) was allowed to develop or when common kitchen acids, such as vinegar, were stood or boiled in copper pans, there were cases of poisoning. This led to the lining of copper pots with other metals, first lead or a 50:50 mixture of tin and lead, and finally tin with only a little lead. This last was used until quite recently and still is in some countries, but in the last few years pure tin with lead present only as a trace is usually specified by law. As such pure tin is very costly, it is one of the reasons why tinned copper utensils are so expensive. (Tinning these days seems to be done better in France than in England.) Tinned copper is unsuitable only for cooking curry, as this pits and discolours the tin lining. Untinned copper pans are still used for bowls for beating egg whites – French chefs insist on it when they can – for sugar-boiling pans (tin would be on the verge of melting at the temperatures that may have to be reached) and for jam pans.

There are two reasons for the excellence of copper pans, which far offsets the bother of keeping them clean. One is that copper is a superb conductor of heat. Copper pans heat evenly over their whole surface and do not burn (pans of stainless steel – a bad conductor of heat – are often given copper bottoms to spread the heat). The other reason is that copper has a low specific heat which means that copper pans heat up quickly and, conversely, quickly cool down. It is therefore easy to control the rate of cooking. Also, there is little damage that can be done to a copper pan that cannot be repaired. They can be re-tinned, and hammered into shape if dented; handles can be re-riveted if they become loose, and splits in the copper can be sealed.

In air, copper becomes dull, and when moist will develop the green coating of copper carbonate. To clean copper, rub it with a mixture of vinegar (or lemon juice) and salt rinsing it thoroughly afterwards. Never use an abrasive cleaner on the tin lining, as it will wear the tin away. Above all, do not overheat the pan; it will melt the tin.

[*Copper* – French: *cuivre* German: *Kupfer* Italian: *rame* Spanish: *cobre*]

CORIANDER (*Coriandrum sativum*), also called Chinese and Japanese parsley and cilantro (US), is the world's most commonly used herb in spite of the fact that the name comes from the Greek, *koris* – a bug. There is a supposed similarity between the smell of the green leaves and the smell of bed bugs. A green umbelliferous herb, it takes the place of parsley, not only in China and Japan, but also in South East Asia, India, the Middle East, Mexico and Spanish America. Its peculiar taste grows on one until it is difficult to do without it. It combines especially well with green chilli. The seed is also an important spice seed. 'And the house of Israel called the name thereof manna and it was like coriander seed, white; and the taste of it was like wafers made with honey.' (Exodus XVI: 31).

It is a native of southern Europe and its use is very ancient. For Mexican or Indian cooking, it is sufficient to sow the seed you buy as a spice; provided it is fresh, it will germinate. The plants can be used chopped as soon as they are a few centimetres high. Not only is green coriander delicious, but it is also highly nutritious.

The seeds have a flavour somewhat reminiscent of oranges, and quite unlike that of the green leaves. They are round and easily split in two, but are difficult to grind finely unless they have first been slightly dry-roasted to be crisp, but not to spoil the delicate taste. The seed, unlike the green leaf, is much used in European cooking, in anything *à la grecque*, in pickles and on roast meat; it is the secret of a fine steak and kidney pudding. In the Middle East, *taklia*, an Arab flavouring for spinach, chickpeas, meatballs, etc., is made by gently frying 3 cloves of garlic which have been crushed with salt together with a teaspoon of ground coriander until the mixture gives off an aromatic smell. The *taklia* is added to the dish at the end of cooking. In India, coriander is one of the foundation spices of curry. It is an essential spice to have on the shelf and has even been used in sweet dishes.

Although coriander is used both as seed and, above all, as a green herb in South East Asian food, it is the use of the root as a flavouring that is a unique feature of Thai cooking, as is described in Rosemary Brissenden's *South East Asian Food* (Penguin). In Costa Rica and Dominica, *cilantro* is used as the name for another herb with a rather similar flavour which has the scientific name *Geringium foetidum*; this is also used in southern Mexico.

[*Coriander* – French: *coriandre* German: *Koriander* Italian: *coriandolo* Spanish: *coriandro*]

CORN means grain – any grain – depending where you are, and what is the common cereal in the region. Thus, in England it means *wheat (to farmers at least) and in Scotland, *oats. In the US, it means *maize. To add to the possible confusion, the British have adopted American usage of sweetcorn and corn on the cob.

[*Corn – French*: *grain* German: *Korn, Getreide* Italian: *grano* Spanish: *grano*]

CORNED BEEF is beef that has been cured – with salt, sugar and saltpetre – and is so named probably because coarse grains or 'corns' of salt were in the past used in the cure. In Britain, corned beef is normally understood to be cured, cooked pieces of beef held together by their gelatinous material and fat when pressed or moulded in a tin and allowed to go cold. It is more or less synonymous with bully beef. In America, as it used to be in Britain, corned beef is whole pieces of salted meat, such as the corned beef used in the New England boiled dinner. It is what the British would now call salt beef.

Pressed beef is another similar preparation, a piece – usually of brisket – cured, boiled and, while it cools, pressed. Afterwards it is usually glazed, and, of course, served cold. Bully beef is canned corned beef, and its name (a corruption of the French *bouilli*; boiled) we owe to the British Army. It was a ration for the French Army in the Franco-Prussian war of 1870-71 and was used extensively by British troops in World Wars I and II. Until recently, when it became expensive, it was a great standby for everyone who could afford to keep a tin in the cupboard. Corned beef can be made from the most hard-bitten Queensland cattle and a lot of animals that could scarcely be eaten in any other form. A Belgian friend, who worked in a corned beef factory in France just after the war, almost put me off eating it, although, on expeditions, I have depended on it for months on end. True, in the early days, when cans were sealed with blobs of solder, there were many bad ones, and even lead poisoning came from some. Today, bad cans are rare, and it is kept as an emergency store even in France.

Corned Beef

Cures vary a great deal. As an example, a dry cure might be made of 1 kg (2 lb) salt, 25 g (1 oz) saltpetre, 150 g (5 oz) brown sugar and 1 teaspoon black pepper, the mixture should be rubbed into the piece of beef twice a day for 8 days.

To make a brine pickle, add to each 10 lt (18 pt) water, 2 kg (4½ lb) salt, 1 kg (2 lb) sugar and 60 g (2¼ oz) saltpetre. The meat should remain in the pickle for about 2 days per kg (1 day per pound). To cook it, boil it in unsalted water for about 40 minutes per kg (20 mins per lb).

Gimmer Bully

Among the dozens of desperation recipes for disguising canned corned beef is this one which I invented in Langdale many years ago. After a day's climbing on Gimmer Crag (from the name it should have been made of Cumberland mutton), it tasted good, and ways of varying outdoor rations are sometimes useful.

Slice corned beef generously and make neat sandwiches, sprinkling the inside of each sandwich with some mixed herbs.

Make a white sauce with flour, good butter and good milk from the farm. Season it well with pepper and cook until the raw taste goes. Then put it aside. Quickly fry the sandwiches on both sides in butter till the bread is crisp. Put on the plates, smother with the sauce. Eat at once while there is the contrasting texture between the crisp fried bread and the unctuous sauce. For variation the sauce can be flavoured with mustard pickles, capers, mustard, or cheese, but with good ingredients the herbs and good butter are enough.

CORNFLOUR or **cornstarch** (US). Commercially, cornflour is made as follows. Maize is soaked in water with a small percentage of sulphurous acid to prevent fermentation and to soften the maize kernels, which facilitates easy separation of the components. The soaked corn is then ground in such a way as to keep the germ intact and the bran in flakes, as these must be separated from the starch. Finally the very finely ground, starchy part of the grain is mixed with water and the milky liquid run on to inclined trays, where the starch settles and the water is run off. The starch can then be collected and dried in kilns. Cornflour is therefore almost pure starch and in this respect differs from corn meal (*polenta*) and *masa*.

Cornflour differs from ordinary flour in containing no gluten. Because this decreases its tendency to form lumps, it makes a better thickener than flour. When mixed into a cream with water, and boiled, it forms a gelatinous, rather clear jelly – though not as clear as *arrowroot. Like arrowroot, cornflour has little taste.

[*Cornflour – French*: *farine de maïs* German: *Maismehl* Italian: *farina di granturco* Spanish: *harina de maíz*]

CORN HUSKS. *See* maize.

CORNISH CREAM. *See* clotted cream.

CORN SALAD. *See* salad.

CORNSTARCH. *See* cornflour.

CORN SUGAR. *See* glucose.

CORN SYRUP is a sweet, *glucose syrup made commercially by heating cornstarch and water under pressure with a little sulphuric acid or hydrochloric acid to convert the starch to simple sugars. Hydrolysis may also be achieved by the use of enzymes or by a combination of enzyme and acid treatments. The acid is subsequently neutralized by adding an alkali, and the syrup is then decolourized with charcoal. (In Europe, glucose is mainly made from potato starch.) Corn syrup is much used in the US for commercial purposes (brewing and confectionery), and also as a table syrup, sometimes flavoured or mixed with maple syrup, brown sugar, honey or molasses.

COSTMARY, **alecost** or **bibleleaf** (US). A perennial, hardy herb (*Chrysanthemum balsamita*) of the daisy family, with yellow button-like flowers; a close relative of tansy. This plant was well known to the ancients, and the name alecost was given it because it was one of the herbs used to flavour beer. It can be used as a flavouring herb in soups and in stuffings for poultry, veal, etc. Although I have come across it in recipes from northern Italy, it is not a commonly-used herb in these days.
[*Costmary* – French: *balsamite* German: *Balsamkraut* Italian: *balsamite* Spanish: *balsamita*]

COTECHINO. A speciality of Emilia-Romagna, a *cotechino* is a large succulent sausage with a filling similar to *zampone, which includes pork skin – mainly the soft rind of head and snout, this is what makes the sausage gelatinous after boiling. (*Cotenna*, – as the French *couenne*, – means pig skin, hence *cotechino*.) Normally, this sausage is flavoured with salt and pepper, but there are varieties with garlic and even vanilla, moistened with white wine. *Cotechino* is eaten boiled (soak, prick, and cook very slowly for about 2 hours) – never raw – and is usually served with a purée of lentils or as part of a *bollito misto* (mixed boiled meats). The *bondiane* and *malette* are similar, but of different shape. The most famous *cotechini* are made in Modena and Reggio Emilia.

COTIGNAC. *See* quince.

COTTON-SEED OIL. A good vegetable oil. However, up to 1880, the cotton seeds from which the oil is expressed, were treated as waste. Today huge amounts of cotton-seed oil are made in all cotton-producing countries, particularly the US. Cotton seed is hulled, crushed, heated and pressed to obtain the oil which, when refined, is a good cooking and salad oil. Most of it goes as an important raw material for margarine and hydrogenated cooking fats, for salad dressings and creams, as an olive oil substitute in packing sardines, and for the commercial frying of potato chips and doughnuts. Although known to cause allergies, it is wholesome to most people. Cotton-seed oil is much used in Egypt as a cooking oil and, like all except highly refined cooking oils and fats, gives a regional flavour to food cooked in it.
[*Cotton-seed oil* – French: *huile de graine de cotton* German: *Baumwollöl* Italian: *olio di cotone* Spanish: *aceite de algodón*]

COURGETTE. *See* marrow.

COURT-BOUILLON. Any previously prepared liquid in which something is to be boiled or poached, is called a *court-bouillon*. Its purpose is to improve the flavour, aromatize or perfume, even improve the colour of the ingredient. Fish and shellfish are the items most often cooked in a *court-bouillon*, which is salted and acidified with lemon juice, white wine or vinegar, and aromatized with onion, garlic, carrot, herbs (such as parsley, thyme and bay) and spices (such as peppercorns and coriander). Cooks soon arrive at their own formulae, and there is a lot of national prejudice. (For instance, Danes insist on sugar in the water when they cook lobsters.)

Meats and vegetables are less often cooked in *court-bouillon* for an obvious reason. A *court-bouillon* is prepared in advance by boiling the flavouring ingredients before the food is put in to cook. This is necessary with fish, and shell fish, as they spend only a short time in the cooking liquid. But with meats and vegetables, which take longer to cook, the flavouring materials can usually be boiled while the food is cooking. *Court-bouillon* is very easily over flavoured in a fit of enthusiasm; it can swamp, instead of enhance, natural flavours, and be quite unsuitable for use in a sauce. When the food is to be cooked in the liquid and marinated (as in pickled fish), one is dealing with a different dimension.

COUSCOUS is a dish of Berber origin and a staple of North African Mediterranean countries – Tunisia, Morocco and Algeria. Now adopted in France it is traditional also in Sicily, as an Arab introduction long ago. The dish consists of a stew, spiced with red pepper and usually made of mutton with vegetables and chickpeas, over which, in a perforated bowl, is cooked a special type of semolina preparation which in Europe is referred to as couscous. Couscous may also be turned into a sweet dish – a versatile product. In the Sicilian version, the basis for the stew is fish.

Couscous can be bought in packets, ready to be cooked and with instructions and recipes on the packet. It is on sale everywhere in France and there are 'instant' forms of couscous for non-cooks to play with. There are many ways of making the basic material, which the Italians regard as a form of pasta, as minute gnocchi – gnocchettini di semola, in fact. You need a 50:50 mixture of coarse and fine semolina, preferably from hard wheat, but it can be made from one grade of hard semolina.

The simplest way is to have ready a basin of water, a shallow dish of the semolina and a clean cloth spread on the table. Touch the palm of the right hand into the water to wet it slightly, then lay it on the semolina mixture so that some of it sticks to the palm and rub one palm against the other, finishing with a circular movement to roughly round the grains. Then let the grains fall on the cloth. Naturally the touch must be light or the grains will become dough. The fine particles of semolina are of course necessary to make the coarser ones stick together. The final operation is to sieve out any surplus flour or fine bits, and then to let the couscous dry. In Sicily, where it is called cùscusu, it is made using water with saffron – as is appropriate with a fish dish – and the mixture of fine and coarse semolina is rubbed on a special dish known as a mafaradda. A spoonful of the saffron water is put into the dish to wet it, and a handful of the semolina mixture put on top and then rubbed gently into a granular form with the fingers. It is essentially the same process, but for beginners the hand system is probably easier. There are other forms of couscous made by using a little mutton fat as a binder instead of water. To cook, couscous is first moistened by sprinkling with a little water and mixing gently to allow the grains to swell. Then when the 'stew', over which the couscous pan fits, is about an hour from being ready, the couscous is put into the steaming pan sprinkled with a little more water, and put to steam. There is no lid to a couscousière, and the couscous is not covered. A tip, which was given to me, is to pack the junction of the steamer and the pan below with a damp rag so that no steam can escape.

COUVE TRONCHUDA. See cabbage.

COWBERRY. See cranberry.

COWPEA, cow-gram, yard-long bean and asparagus bean. We are dealing here with three beans of the genus Vigna which may be regarded as different species or as varieties of the same species. From our point of view, it is easier to consider them as different species. The genus Vigna is mostly tropical and forty or fifty species are known of which only three or four are cultivated.

The name cowpea originated in the US; the earlier English name of cavalance was first used in the West Indies. The cowpea (Vigna unguiculata) is much used in India, where it has been cultivated since ancient times, although its original home may have been Africa, where wild varieties of the plant can still be found. The pods are about the thickness of a pencil and up to 30 cm (12 in) long, but often less. They hang downwards on the plant. The young pods are used in curries or are boiled as a vegetable, some varieties being better than others for this purpose. The seed of the ripe bean, which may be coloured anything from maroon to red, blue, brown, black, pink or white, plain or speckled according to variety, is used whole, split as dal or even ground to a flour. Although, in India, the cowpea is generally considered inferior to green *mung or *black gram, it can grow in dry areas and so is an important food, not only in India (as lobya), but also in Africa and parts of tropical America.

Cowpeas, particularly varieties with a black area around the hilum (the attachment to the pod), are known in northern states of the US as black-eyed peas and in Britain as black-eyed beans. In the southern states of the US, they may be known as southern peas or simply as peas. In that case, garden peas are called English peas to distinguish them. Black-eyed peas figure in Creole dishes, but are also a generally useful and, because of the health food vogue, a widely available pulse.

Catjang bean (Vigna catjang) is less often grown. It is included in case someone should be puzzled to see what looks like a cowpea but with pods about half the length and standing upright on the plant instead of drooping. Catjang beans have otherwise the same uses.

Yard-long bean, **asparagus bean**, or **Chinese bean** (*Vigna sesquipedalis*) has pods which grow very long and thin – up to 1 m (39 in) – hence its name. As you might guess, such long beans droop on the plant. The taste of the young pods is delicate, hence the alternative name *asparagus bean*, and the young beans are soft and flabby. This characteristic has been made use of in a dish called *lambchi* and *boonchi* (*boonchi* being the local name for these beans in the Dutch West Indies), which is described fully by Elisabeth Lambert-Ortiz in her excellent *Caribbean Cooking* (André Deutsch). In this dish, the long flabby beans are wound spirally round skewers of lamb (which have been previously marinated in spices) and the whole brochette is grilled over charcoal. *Vigna* beans do not grow further north than latitude 40°N (i.e. the southern half of the Mediterranean), even in a warm summer.

COWSLIP. A common primula (*Primula veris*) of the fields, its yellow flowers once covered the pastures in Britain, but now no more, as there is so little permanent pasture. The flowers were once candied or made into wine. Like primroses, which are a close relation, their flowers can make a pretty yet edible addition to salads and puddings. They ought not to be picked indiscriminately as they are now so scarce.

[*Cowslip* – French: *primevère commune, fleur de coucou* German: *Primel, Schlüsselblume* Italian: *primaverina* Spanish: *vellorita*]

CRAB. A decapod crustacean related to lobsters, crayfish and shrimps, but distinguished from them by the large flattened body and small tail, which is kept tucked underneath, serving as a flap to hold the eggs but not much else. Even in swimming, the crab's propulsion is by the back legs, which are modified into paddles, and not by the tail. The internal anatomy of crabs is basically similar to that of lobsters, but crabs are more highly evolved creatures. Their nerve cord (which as in all crustaceans is situated underneath) is concentrated in two centres and not (as in lobsters) diffuse. Thus, it is claimed that crabs can be killed humanely by piercing through the shell from underneath with a pin or bodkin to destroy the cerebral ganglion (which lies just under the shell between the base of the eyes and the mouth) and the thoracic ganglion (which lies just under the shell in the mid-line and opposite the base of the front legs). For the operation, the crab must be laid on its back. It is doubtful whether the job can be done efficiently without some practice.

The RSPCA method, (described more fully in the section on lobsters) is to put the animal into cold salted water and gradually raise the temperature to boiling. The creature gradually loses consciousness. The time taken to cook a crab depends on its size, of course, but there is great difference between the recommendations of various authors. This suggests that, within reason, it is not very critical. French experts, for instance, may advocate a short cooking time and allow the crabs to cool in the cooking liquid. Crabs are plunged into boiling *court-bouillon* and cooked (after being brought back to a gentle boil) for the following times: 10 minutes for 300-500 g (up to about 1 lb); 12 minutes for up to 600 g (a bit under 1½ lb); 18 minutes for 700-800 g (1½-1¾ lb); 25-30 minutes for 900g to 1 kg (about 2 lb); 30-35 minutes for 1.5-2 kg (3½-4½ lb). These times apply to all large crustaceans, including lobsters and *langoustes,* cooled in the *court-bouillon*.

At the opposite end of the scale, American methods may call for the immediate cooling of cooked crabs in cold water, and in that case they must be cooked for somewhat longer. If crabs are killed by the RSPCA method, and raised to boiling point from cold brine, then 15 minutes for the first 450 g (1 lb) and 10 minutes for each additional 450 g (1 lb) is recommended; the crabs are taken out and allowed to cool in the larder.

The legs and claws of a cooked crab can be twisted off and cracked, and the meat pulled or poked out. One must make sure that no bits of shell or internal septum are left in the meat. The job is fussy, and small legs are best sucked at table. The body is opened along the suture at the back, and usually the two halves can be simply forced apart by thumb pressure with the crab laid on its back. Some types of crab may need a strong knife point and some leverage. Pressure on the mouth parts will snap them inwards, and the whole of the stomach and intestine – parts to be discarded – can then be lifted out still attached and in one piece. The only other parts to be discarded are the gills – called devil's fingers or dead man's fingers. In spite of their name, these are harmless, but would be impossibly chewy and indigestible if you tried to eat them. The meat in the bases of the legs can be got at most simply by breaking the lower part of the crab in two down the middle line, and then digging the meat out with a marrow scoop or other implement.

Crabs may, or course, be bought ready-boiled, and indeed that is the way they usually come nowadays, but where possible it is still better to buy a live crab and cook it yourself.

In choosing a live crab, pick one that is active and not already half dead. Look for one that is heavy for its size, and then shake it. Do not buy it if there is any suspicion of water swishing about, as this means the crab has recently moulted; it will be watery and out of condition. In buying cooked crabs, you naturally buy only those that smell fresh and avoid ones in which the joints have become flaccid or floppy. A crab of decent size should yield just under half its weight of meat (about 40% in a good one). If crabs are to be served in the shell, then the shells should be well cleaned, scrubbed (some even boil them in water with washing soda) and then rubbed with a little fat or oil to make them shine. The edges may need to be trimmed. When small crabs are served whole, as they often are in France for an hors d'oeuvre, finger bowls are essential.

An enormous number of different species of crab are eaten around the world. They range from the tiny pea crabs which live inside oyster shells to gigantic Alaskan king crabs weighing 10 kg (22 lb) and with legs spanning up to 3½ m (11 ft). Crabs are found in both icy and tropical seas. In North Queensland, I once subsisted for several days on Horlicks Malted Milk tablets and the Giant Mud crabs, a diet which is not recommended. However, they are very nutritious, and I do not know of any crabs that are poisonous to eat when they are fresh and in good health. Many species are now eaten which were formerly despised in days when there were fewer people, less over-fishing and more seafood at reasonable prices. When I was on a trawler north of the Shetlands in 1935, octopus, cuttlefish and spider crabs that came up in the trawl were simply thrown back, and the Aberdeen fishermen laughed when I said they were good eating.

In Britain, the crab most often eaten is the Common Edible crab (Cancer pagurus), a large, smooth-shelled, clean-looking creature, with pinkish brown colouring and exceedingly powerful pincers. It lives on rocky coasts, and a big one can be dangerous. The first reaction of a crab when disturbed is to close up, but very soon its response changes to attack. (Fishermen in the part of Wales where I lived as a child used to quieten crabs by spitting in their faces.) Never hold a crab where it can reach you with its claws, which it is best to tie up. Crabs are cannibals and will eat each other, so do not put two together. The spider crab (Mala squinado), a popular delicacy around Venice and

elsewhere in the Mediterranean, is fished off the south coast of England and exported live to Spain, although it is also beginning to be accepted in Britain as well.

In France (but not in Britain), the Swimming crab (Macropipus puber), the étrille, is commonly eaten. This is found both in the Atlantic and the Mediterranean, where there are five other related smaller species. These crabs (of which there are many other species) are 5-10 cm (2-4 in) across the shell and never grow very big.

The little Shore crabs (Carcinus maenas) are also found in the Mediterranean. In spring and autumn, when they moult, they have a particular gastronomic importance in Venice (where they abound in the lagoons on the Adriatic coast) and are known as moleche 'soft-shells' in America. In one method, moleche ripiene (stuffed), small soft-shell crabs are put alive into beaten egg and left there for a couple of hours, by which time they will be dead and have absorbed some of the egg (which is why they are called stuffed), after which they are floured and fried. In Italy, soft-shelled crabs are traditionally eaten with polenta or a salad of finely-sliced leeks. Another method is to drown them in milk, and some even claim that they taste best when raw. Traditionally, small crabs are hung up, tied in strings far enough apart to keep them out of claw range of each other. Shore crabs, being closely related to land crabs, will stay alive out of water for long periods (several weeks) in a cool damp place.

In Mediterranean countries particularly, many other small crabs are eaten. They give an excellent taste to fish soup. The hairy ériphie (Eriphia verrucosa) is perhaps the most treasured crab on the Côte d'Azur because of its exquisite flavour. A Mediterranean curiosity which visitors may wonder at sometimes in Spanish markets is the Box-crab (Calappa granulata), a handsome pink crab about the size and shape of a clenched fist, with red spots, which is striking because the claws are designed to fit snugly over the face, and it can box itself in (becoming like a ball) for protection. When the claws are apart, it looks out with a peculiarly bulldog expression and once seen, is never forgotten. Box or no box, it is eaten.

North American crabs are far from being the same as those in Europe. The most important of all and comprising nearly three-quarters of the total crab catch in America, is the Blue crab (Callinectes sapidus), which is confined to the East Coast, going as far south as the Gulf of Mexico. The Blue crab is characterized by its colour and by the shape, which might be described as pointed sideways. Even the claws are rather pointed. Blue crabs weigh 150-450 g (5 oz to 1 lb), much smaller than the Common crab of Britain. In normal times, they may be known as Eastern hard-shells, but at the moult they become soft-shells or 'softies', although at various stages they may be 'busters' or 'shedders', – when the old shell is loose but not yet shed, later 'peelers' and 'paper shell', the latter being the state when the new shell has just begun to harden. Epicures consider that 'busters' are the finest. Soft-shell crabs packed in ice and seaweed can live long enough in good condition to be air-freighted to any part of the US, but they are famous as an Atlantic Coast delicacy. Unlike the Italian *moleche*, the soft-shelled Blue crab must be cleaned before cooking. The front of the crab, enough to include eyes, mouthparts and the stomach (sandbag) which lie behind them, is snipped off with scissors. Then the tail (apron) is removed and the points on either side are lifted up and the spongy material underneath is discarded. Some also remove the gut before cooking. There are recipes for soft-shelled crabs in every American cookery book. The Red crab, which belongs to another genus (*Geryon quinquedens*) is exploited off the East Coast of the US. In UK waters, there are apparently stocks of it at 500-600 m (1666-2000 ft) depth off Rockall.

On the Pacific coast of the US, the Dungeness crab (*Cancer magister*) looks rather like the Common crab of Britain, but its colour is greenish and its claws are not so massive. It ranges from Alaska to Mexico, and is an excellent crab. State laws prohibit its use as a soft-shell. The meat of the Dungeness crab is slightly pink, in contrast to that of the Rock crabs from both the Atlantic (*Cancer irroratus*) and the Pacific (*C. autennarius and magister*) which is brownish. Rock crabs are eaten locally as soft-shells. There are also many local North American crabs which are highly valued where they occur. the Jonah crabs (*Cancer borealis*) of New England, the Stone crabs (*Menippe mercenaria*) of Florida, and the minute Oyster or Pea crabs (of the Pinnotheridae family) of New England. The last live in oyster shells for protection, but nevertheless get stewed in cream and flavoured with Madeira to be eaten whole as a local delicacy. The Alaskan King crab or *taraba gani* (*Paralithodes camtschatica*), which ranges across the Pacific to Japanese and Russian waters, is a monster deep-water Spider crab with a huge claw-span. Its meat is of excellent quality, and it is much used as canned or frozen crab meat, often being processed on factory ships

within a very short time of catching.

Hermit crabs, although not strictly crabs, belong to the same group (Decapoda). They are often on sale in Mediterranean markets and are mainly used in soups, as they are too small for other purposes. They are boiled and cleaned like any other crustaceans – they are not hard to get out of the shells they inhabit once they have been cooked – but gastronomically are largely neglected. Perhaps they would be good as 'softies'.

[*Crab* – French: *crabe, cancre* German: *Krabbe, Krebs* Italian: *granchio* Spanish: *cangrejo*.

Common crab – French: *tourteau, dormeur* German: *Taschenkrebs* Italian: *granciporro* Spanish: *buey*.

Shore Crab – French: *crabe vert* German: *Strandkrabbe* Italian: *granchio commune* Spanish: *cangrejo de mar*.

Eriphia verrucosa – French: *ériphie* Italian: *favollo* Spanish: *cangrejo moruno*.

Spider crab – French: *araignée* German: *Troldkrabbe* Italian: *grancevola* Spanish: *centola*.

Hermit crab – French: *Bernard-l'ermite* German: *Einsledlerkrebs* Italian: *paguro* Spanish: *ermitaño*]

CRACKER. Dry biscuit, usually unsweetened, sometimes also unsalted and sometimes made of wholemeal flour (Graham cracker). Crackers have considerable importance in American cookery in the form of cracker crumbs which can be made by crushing the biscuits or can be bought ready prepared in packets. Crackers are used as topping, to make 'crumb' pie shells (which are also made from other types of biscuit), for coating and many other purposes.

CRACKLING. The British name for the crisp, roasted skin of a pig. In Mediterranean countries, where roasted pork and suckling pig is popular, the skin is not usually scored before roasting, and it may even be removed for other uses. There are only a few rules for producing good crackling. First, score the skin with a sharp knife yourself – the butcher has not the time to do it carefully. Cut just through the skin in neat ½-1 cm (¼-½ in) wide strips. For this, you need a very sharp knife or a razor blade. Rub the cut surface with salt just before putting the meat into the oven. Make sure that the crackling never gets into the fat. Baste with water if basting is necessary; the Danes, for instance, brush the crackling with water just before it is ready; which makes the crackling bubble. The oven must be hot enough, but if in spite of all efforts the crackling refuses to crisp, then brush it with water and finish it under the grill (a small electric grill is ideal for this).

[*Crackling* – French: *rissollé (porc)* German: *knusprige Kruste* Italian: *pelle di porco arrostito* Spanish: *chicharrón*]

CRANBERRY and related berries are all members of the heather family (Ericaceae) which thrive in the acid soil of bogs, moorlands and mountains. The same family includes the rhododendrons, all of which, from the lovely Alpenrose to the huge crimson-flowered tree rhododendrons of the Himalayan gorges, are very poisonous – even honey from the flowers is toxic (which certainly sets them apart from the heathers). On the other hand, the 130 or so species of the genus *Vaccinium*, including cranberries, bilberries, blueberries and cowberries, all bear edible (though not necessarily appetizing) fruits, as do some related genera, notably *Gaylussacia* (huckleberries) and *Arctostaphylos* (bearberries), as well as the similar genus *Empetrum* (crowberries), which belongs to another family. Of these, a few, such as the American cranberry and the low-bush and high-bush blueberries, are cultivated, but most are gathered wild. They fruit in summer and autumn, and are particularly favourites in mountain country where the berries are plentiful. The hands and mouths of children in the Alps are stained black with bilberry juice from July until the season is over. The fruits of the heather family are of special importance in all sorts of traditional fruit dishes and pies both all over Europe and in America.

Bearberry (*Arctostaphylus uva-ursi*) grows on moors and mountains of Europe. Its red fruits are of little culinary interest.

Bilberry, blaeberry, or whortleberry (*Vaccinium myrtillus*) is the common blue berry of moors, mountains and open woodlands in Britain, Europe and northern Asia. The juicy blue-black fruits, about 8 mm (⅓ in) in diameter and with a cup-shaped depression in the top, are ripe from July to September. Although bilberries are rather neglected in most parts of Britain because of the bother of picking them, they are an excellent fruit and worthy of more attention. Their commercial possibilities are overshadowed by the American blueberries which are very similar but larger.

Blueberry. Blueberries are North American species of *Vaccinium*, and the many species range from

above the Arctic circle to as far south as Florida. High-bush blueberries (*V. atrococcum* and *V. corymbosum*) grow usually to 3 m (10 ft) high, while dwarf forms of blueberry, such as *V. pennsylvanicum*, may be as small as 15 cm (6 in). Blueberries are also commonly confused with huckleberries, but since there are no poisonous kinds of either and they mix well, there is no problem, although some kinds do taste better than others. Good blueberries, whether the large cultivated sort or the smaller wild ones, are plump. If shrivelled, squashy or leaking purple juice through the box, they will be stale and tasteless. While they are the second most important berries, after strawberries, in the US, they are certainly the most versatile for cooking. Delicious raw, with just cream and sugar, they also make wonderful pies, cakes, puddings, muffins, pancakes, ice cream and fruit soup. When stewed, they make a medium for cooking dumplings which are served with cream or ice cream and the hot berries and juice on top. They can be frozen just as they are, with no washing or other preparation needed.

Blueberry Muffins

Sift 250 g (9 oz) plain flour with 2 tablespoons sugar, ½ teaspoon salt, 2 teaspoons baking powder, and almost a teaspoon of bicarbonate of soda. Wash a cup of blueberries, drain them and, when they are still slightly wet, shake them carefully into the flour mixture and turn it gently so they are coated. Now add 1 lightly beaten egg, 2 tablespoons of melted butter and 175 ml (6 fl oz) of buttermilk. Stir gently until just mixed, no more, and then half fill greased muffin tins with the thick mixture. Bake at 200°C/400°F/Gas Mark 6 for 18 minutes.

Cowberry or Mountain cranberry (*Vaccinium vitis-idaea*). These grow wild in the mountains of the Northern hemisphere, over the whole of Europe except the Iberian Peninsula. The dark red, globular berries are about 1 cm (½ in) in diameter, so it might be confused with the bearberry, but not with the cranberry (which has very small leaves in relation to the size of fruit). It is popular in Scandinavian countries, and the taste is spicier than the cranberry's.

Cranberry. There are two main sorts of cranberry; the European cranberry (*Vaccinium oxycoccus*) which grows wild on moors all over northern Europe and Asia, as well as in North America, and the American or Large cranberry (*Vaccinium macrocarpon*) which is naturalized locally in Europe, including parts of Britain. In America, it grows wild from Newfoundland, south to North Carolina and westwards to Saskatchewan. It is the American cranberry which is cultivated, because it has larger fruits, up to 2 cm (¾ in) in diameter compared to the 8 mm (⅓ in) of the European species. Cranberry growing is centred in Massachusetts, with Cape Cod producing 70% of the total. Two hundred years ago, there were laws in America against picking cranberries before September, and the season is from September to December, peaking in November. American cranberries used to be exported to Europe in the days of sailing ships. They were simply packed in barrels and covered with water, in which condition they would remain good for the long sea voyage. Even today, some people keep cranberries in jars covered with water, in this way, the berries remain good for months in the refrigerator. They can, of course, be frozen. (In view of the fantastic keeping qualities of cranberries, it is interesting to note that they naturally contain benzoic acid which is a preservative and is used in tomato sauce, for instance, in the form of sodium benzoate.) Cranberries can be preserved in jars by boiling them with a little water and sugar until they burst – about 10 minutes – and then bottling them in sterile jars. No heat treatment is necessary. Proportions for cranberry sauce are 2 cups of cranberries to 1 cup of water and 1 cup of sugar.

Cranberries are known as 'bouncing berries' because good ones bounce. In the old days, they were tipped down steps; the bad ones remained on the steps because they did not bounce. Modern grading machines use the same principle, each berry having seven chances to bounce over a 10 cm (4 in) barrier. Cranberries are fool-proof to buy and will keep up to 8 months in a refrigerator. They have a refreshing sourness, and recipes for other uses than cranberry sauce will be found in American cookery books.

Crowberry (*Empetrum nigrum*) grows on moors, bogs and mountains over most of Europe. It has very different leaves to the bilberry and black rather than blue-black fruits. While not of great culinary importance, crowberries are welcome to climbers.

Huckleberry (*Gaylussacia baccata*) is North American. There are many other species, including the inferior Bear huckleberry or buckberry (*Gaylussacia ursina*), which should not be confused

with the bearberry (*see above*). Huckleberries are so similar to blueberries that there is considerable popular confusion. American Indians depended greatly on both for food and dried them for use in winter. The different species give a long season, and they are found from the Arctic Circle to Florida, as are blueberries.

Strawberry tree or arbutus (*Arbutus unedo*). This is a Mediterranean bush of rather a dark-leaved, almost rhododendron-like appearance, which also grows in Ireland. It is found among the vegetation on the rough hillsides, often in the gullies where there is a little more water. It flowers one year and the berries form the next. Though very decorative, the fruits, which are dark red, rough and the size of a strawberry, are very disappointing to eat. The outside is covered with tiny, woody warts and the inside is soft and flavourless. The French make a liqueur out of the berries, but it is not commonly available.

[*Cranberry* – French: *canneberge* German: *Moosebeere* Italian: *mortella di palude* Spanish: *arándano agrio*.

Bilberry – French: *airelle, myrtille* German: *Heidelbeere, Blaubeere* Italian: *mirtillo* Spanish: *arándano*]

CRAQUELOT. *See* herring.

CRAWFISH. A confusing name that is perhaps better avoided. Particularly in the US, it is a synonym for the freshwater *crayfish, while in Britain it normally refers to a marine variety of lobster, which is perhaps best called by its unambiguous French name of *langouste*.

CRAYFISH. Small, freshwater crustaceans, *Astacus astacus* (red-clawed) and *Astacus pallipes* (white-clawed), which are very like tiny lobsters in both appearance and habits. The red-clawed are larger. They are sometimes abundant in streams and lakes both in Europe and in North America, although disease and pollution have made them much less common than they used to be. Though not too well known in Britain, they are considered a great delicacy in France (which imports them from Czech Republic, Poland and Turkey). The Norwegians even have a late summer festival dedicated to eating *kraftor*.

Crayfish live in the holes in river banks and can be caught in traps like small lobster pots or fished with nets stretched in hoops. These are baited in the centre with meat and sunk flat on the bottom of the water. After lying there for an hour, the net is pulled up quickly, and the crayfish will usually be surprised before they can escape. They can be kept alive in a bucket with about 2.5 cm (1 in) of water or covered with wet grass or nettles. In winter, they will live for up to a week in a cool place. Crayfish must always be alive when prepared. There are several species, but all are to be treated the same. It is likely that there are local differences, and local lore should be respected.

Crayfish can be eaten at any time between April and October, but are best during a short season at the end of summer. At other times they are edible but tasteless and soft. Females are reckoned to be better than males, and egg roe, when found, is made into crayfish butter. The thread-like gut of crayfish should be removed, as it tastes bitter, although some cooks starve the animals for two days instead. The classic method of removing the gut is to move the centre two blades of the tail to either side, which breaks the articulation, and then pull gently. The gut should come out as a fine string. Alternatively, the job can be done by finding the anal opening at the base of the tail, sticking a sharp knife point beneath it and pulling out the gut. The animals are then thrown straight into boiling *court-bouillon* or hot butter. This is cruel. They may be killed instantly by piercing through the top of the head, behind the beak, and on a level with the back of the eyes, where the cerebral ganglion, which does duty for a brain, is situated. Great emphasis is always placed on the necessity for crayfish to be alive when cooking begins, and they must be cooked quickly for 10 minutes, no more, in a very little liquid, 120 ml (4½ fl oz) for 24 crayfish (which is enough to serve 4).They should never be cooked in red wine, which turns them black. There are dozens of ways of preparing crayfish. I give one typical recipe from the Hôtel de la Poste, Chevillot, Beaune.

Écrevisses à la crème

Put the crayfish in a casserole in a little hot butter, salt and pepper, sauté and flame them with cognac. Add a mixture of chopped parsley and shallot, half a bottle of dry white wine, 2 dessertspoons of skinned, seeded and crushed tomato, and 4 dessertspoons of double cream. Cook for 10 minutes. Take out the crayfish and reduce the sauce. Bind it with a little *beurre manié*. Taste and

adjust the seasoning. Add a pinch of finely-chopped tarragon, a few drops of cognac and several nuts of good butter. Cover the crayfish with the sauce and serve very hot.

[*Crayfish* – French: *écrevisse* German: *Flusskrebs* Italian: *gamberi di fiume* Spanish: *congrejo de rio*]

CREAM is a concentration of the fatty part which collects on top when milk is stood. The amount depends on the breed and breeding of the cow, on when it calved and on its food; the colour depends mainly on the pastures on which the cow was fed and on the season. Cream consists of the larger fat globules which float because they are less dense than water. (Such large globules and clusters are broken up by homogenization, which makes them small and evenly dispersed.) In the old days, cream used to be obtained by letting milk stand for 8-10 hours, then skimming the cream off the top, leaving skimmed milk. Double cream came from standing the milk for 24 hours before skimming. The milk would be stood in a wide earthenware pan, covered with muslin in a cool larder at about 11°C (52°F) in winter and 15-16°C (60°F) in summer. However, since the beginning of this century, cream has been generally removed with a separator, which spins the milk and concentrates the cream by centrifugal force. Single or double cream can be obtained with this machine merely by an adjustment. Such cream, unless deliberately matured to allow favourable bacteria to multiply, lacks the flavour of naturally skimmed cream.

If it has not come straight from a farm, bought cream will always be pasteurized – which takes out some flavour-producing organisms. (The addition of preservatives is not permitted in Britain, but may be in some other countries.) Pasteurized cream will keep for some days in the refrigerator before going nasty – not sour, as souring organisms do not operate at low temperatures and other bacteria become predominant. They work on the fat and protein content to produce an unpleasant taste. However, when unpasteurized cream is held at room temperature, lactic bacilli become predominant and the cream develops a sour taste (*see* sour cream).

When using cream to enrich sauces, you should avoid boiling them after adding the cream, which would be likely to curdle. In using well-matured cream, always add the hot liquid to it, as cream poured into hot liquid (including coffee) is also liable to curdle.

British legal standards for cream specify the fat

content as follows:

Half cream (homogenized)	12%
Single cream (homogenized)	18%
Canned or sterilized cream (homogenized)	23%
Whipping cream	35%
Whipped cream	35%
Double cream	48%
*Clotted cream	55%

As the fat content increases, the solids-not-fat content decreases.

Whipped cream. Cream whips best at about 5°C (40°F) but can be whipped at 10°C (50°F). It will not fluff so much if it is taken straight out of the refrigerator or if it is allowed to reach the temperature of a warm room – over 18°C (65°F). If beaten too hard and long, especially in summer, it is likely to start turning to butter, as soon as cream starts to stick to the whisk or beater, it is time to stop. Equal quantities of single and double cream form a mixture suitable for whipping.

Artificial cream. There are many versions of artificial cream on the market, as well as devices for making it by reconstituting cream from milk and unsalted butter. In the latter, milk and butter are warmed together until all the butter is melted to a yellow oil, and the two are then forced together through a small hole (a machine for the purpose can be bought). This breaks up the fat into tiny globules and forms an emulsion. At its best, reconstituted cream is very like real cream – it has the same constituents – but it is usually more oily. Imitation creams do not have the constituents of real cream but merely simulate it. They consist of an emulsified fat, which is not butter fat, with substances to improve texture and flavour. Imitation cream is usually sweetened. Skimmed milk, lard, and alginates (from seaweed) are the sort of things that commonly go into them, together with sugar, colour, perhaps, and flavourings.

Canned cream usually has a pleasant, slightly-cooked but detectable flavour. Evaporated milk – which differs from cream in that it contains the milk solids as well as the fat and is thickened by loss of water – can be used as cream, although it has a much stronger boiled-milk flavour and is often slightly salty. It can even be whipped if the unopened tin is boiled for 20 minutes and cooled

beforehand.
    [*Cream* – French: *crème* German: *Sahne* Italian: *panna* Spanish: *crema, nata*]

CREAM NUT. *See* Brazil nut.

CREAM OF TARTAR. Purified form of tartar which, in crude form, is obtained from the encrusted *argol and *lees in wine. It is essentially acid potassium tartrate, a white crystalline powder with a slightly sour taste. Cream of tartar is only sparingly soluble in water, and hardly at all when the water is cold. One of the main reasons for keeping wine cool in the cellar is to get the tartar to crystallize out and fall to the bottom of the tank. Cream of tartar is used in baking powders, but is rather an old-fashioned ingredient in the modern kitchen. Three teaspoons of cream of tartar to 1 teaspoon of *bicarbonate of soda in a cake mixture (with the two ingredients mixed in separately) can be used as a substitute for baking powder. Cream of tartar used also to be put into soft drinks.

....

Lemonade

To 2¼ lt (4 pt) boiling water add 25 g (1 oz) cream of tartar, 100 g (4 oz) sugar and the juice and rind of 2 lemons. Mix all together and drink when cold.
    [*Cream of tartar* – French: *crème de tartre* German: *gereinigter Weinstein* Italian: *cremore di tartaro* Spanish: *crémor*]

....

CRÈME DE CACAO and **CRÈME DE CASSIS**. *See* liqueurs and cordials.

CRÉPINETTE in French charcuterie is any mixture of minced meat, usually pork, but also lamb, veal, chicken or liver, with fat, herbs, spices and seasonings, sometimes with a slice of truffle, parcelled up in a piece of mesentery or caul (*crépin*), and usually given a round, slightly flattened shape. *Gayettes*, from Southern France, are similar but ball-shaped and stuffed with lights – liver, lungs, spleen, etc. – very like English faggots. Sometimes *crépinettes* can be bought already cooked, in which case they can be eaten cold, but otherwise they should be dipped in melted butter (or butter and bread-crumbs) and grilled, or roasted, sautéed, or fried, or even poached in gravy or sauce.

CRESPONE. *See* salame.

CRESS. A number of plants, mostly crucifers, are called cress if they have pungent or peppery leaves.

Watercress is a plant of shallow water. It is native to Europe and western Asia and naturalized in many other countries – it is a serious weed of rivers in New Zealand. Commercially, it is cultivated in shallow tanks fed by natural springs or boreholes because of the danger that it may carry typhoid or other diseases if it is grown in river water (or gathered wild from streams). If you are in any doubt about the cleanliness of the source, it is best to cook the watercress as soup.

Two basic types are cultivated in Britain: Green or Summer cress (Rorippa nasturtium-aquaticum), which stays green in autumn but is damaged by frost, and Brown or Winter cress (R. microphylla X nasturtium-aquaticum), a hybrid with the other wild species and less affected by frost. Like the wild One-rowed watercress (R. microphylla), its leaves turn purplish brown in autumn. The cultivated strains of watercress range from green to bronze or almost black. The last is considered the best. Watercress may be almost too pungent to eat or so mild as to be uninteresting. It should preferably be moderately free from small roots.

To keep it fresh, the bunch can be immersed in cold water right up to the base of the leaves. Freshly gathered watercress, if it is unbruised, will keep for some days in a plastic bag in the refrigerator (away from the freezer compartment); you should first pick off any roots and dead or battered leaves, wash it gently but thoroughly in several changes of water, and drain it.

Cress, Garden cress, Pepper cress or Peppergrass (Lepidum sotivum). Native in Egypt and western Asia but naturalized as a wild plant in Europe and North America, this is the cress of 'mustard and cress', which should be a mixture of the seedlings of this and mustard (Sinapis alba). Home growers of mustard and cress will know that the cress has to be planted first, as its feathery-leaved seedlings take 3-4 days longer to sprout, which is undoubtedly why commercially grown punnets described as mustard and cress tend to deliver only half their promise, containing nothing but the quicker-growing mustard or *rape. As a garden salad plant, cress has the advantage of needing little water and not developing small roots along its stems. It is not as fine in taste as the best watercress.

Winter cress or Yellow rocket (Barbarea vulgaris) and Land cress or Early flowering yellow rocket (B. verna) both grow wild in Britain, though only the former is a native. These and probably other species of Barbarea go under various names, including American cress and Belle Isle cress. They are pungent in taste and are a useful winter salad as they can be picked for much of the winter if they are protected by a cloche or frame.

*Rocket (Eruco sativa) is another crucifer that is sometimes grown as a salad.

Indian cress is better known as the garden flower, *nasturtium (Tropaeolum majus).
[Cress – French: cresson de ruisseau German: Brunnekress Italian: crescione di fonte Spanish: berro.
Garden cress – French: cresson cultivé German: Gartenkresse Italian: crescione di giardino Spanish: mastuerzo de Jardin.
American cress – French: cresson alénois German: Barbarakraut]

CRIMPING. In cooking, this means making gashes (as transversely in the sides of a fish) to allow penetration of marinade, and to make for quicker grilling, with more flavour. Crimping also means to corrugate in small pleats, and so is applied to shaping the edge of a flan or pie crust. However, a crimping iron is for hair.

CRISPBREAD. See flatbread.

CROSNES. See Chinese artichoke.

CROWBERRY. See cranberry.

CRUCIFER. Member of the plant family Cruciferae, which has about 1900 species, mainly in the temperate regions of the Northern hemisphere. The family is characterized by the four-petalled, usually white or yellow flowers and a seed capsule that opens on two sides, starting at the stalk end (it may be short and flat as in honesty or long and thin as in rocket).The most important food plants in the family belong to the genus Brassica, which includes both leaf and root vegetables: B. oleracea (cabbage, cauliflower, kale, broccoli, kohlrabi and brussels sprouts), B. napus (rape and swede) and B. rapa (turnip). Two more species, B. nigra and B.juncea provide mustard seed, as does the white mustard (Sinapis alba). Both mustard and rape seeds are sources of oil. The leaves of many species, both wild and cultivated, are eaten as salad, notably watercress and other cresses as well as rocket. Horseradish root is used, not as a vegetable, but as a flavouring.

CRUMBS. Anyone who thinks that crumbs are not worthy of attention may well ruin a lot of food as a result, for crumbs have a taste as well as a texture. They are an important ingredient and not a way of using up bits of stale, otherwise inedible, bread.

Dried breadcrumbs can be bought ready prepared. Bakers find them a way of using up unsold bread and may or may not make them well. They can also be bought in packets from supermarkets, and are often artificially coloured, which may make food look equally artificial. Fried breadcrumbs are easily made by drying crustless left-over bread, in a very cool oven until it is crisp and pale coloured. This can be reduced to crumbs with a rolling pin or in a blender. Crumbs should be sieved and stored, bone dry, in a screw-topped jar. It is best to replace them every few weeks and not expect them to keep sweet for ever. Such crumbs are for sprinkling on food which has been covered with sauce and put in the oven, or under the grill, to be browned. With the dots of butter and perhaps grated cheese, they sop up the fat to form a crust. They are also used to cover the fatty nakedness of a boiled ham or *Bath chaps. They should not be used for coating food to be fried, or for stuffings. For such purposes, fresh white breadcrumbs are best.

Fresh, white breadcrumbs will not keep (unless frozen), but can be quickly made with a fast blender. Day-old bread is sliced and the crust cut off, ideally some hours before it is used, so that it can dry a little. Then it can be roughly broken into the hopper of the blender and reduced to crumbs. If they are not fine enough after the first go, they can be spread out on a tray and left in a warm place to dry a little before being given another whirl. For coating fried food, such fresh breadcrumbs are greatly superior to the dried, brown crumbs that are so frequently used. They do not get over-fried or give a rank taste. For stuffings and bread sauce, it is better to use very finely-cubed bread, not breadcrumbs, as a lighter texture can be achieved that way, but if breadcrumbs are used they should be coarse.

Cake crumbs, from plain cake, and biscuit crumbs are used for some dishes. American recipes frequently call for cracker crumbs or Graham cracker crumbs, which confuses British cooks. For savoury crackers, any salted one is used in America, and a British equivalent would be the TUC biscuit. Where Graham crackers are called for, digestives provide an approximate, if not exact, substitute.

[Crumbs – French: miette German: Brotkrume Italian: briciola Spanish: miga]

CRUSTACEANS. Nearly always aquatic creatures, crustaceans have a hard, jointed outside skeleton – the *shrimps, *lobsters, *crayfish, *crabs and *barnacles – and include, amongst the inedible kinds, woodlice and water fleas. The meat of crustacea is rather slowly digested, and, after dining on lobster or prawns, you will be sustained for a considerable period.

[Crustaceans – French: crustacés German: Krustentieren, Krebstieren Italian: crostacei Spanish: crustáceos]

CRYSTALLIZED FRUIT. See candied fruit.

CRYSTALS. Examples of crystalline substances used in the kitchen are cane sugar, salt and washing soda. The geometrical shape of a crystal is due to the regular way in which the molecules arrange themselves when it forms. Crystals may form either when a suitable molten substance cools and becomes solid or when a saturated solution is cooled or allowed to evaporate. Large crystals form when the liquid is cooled or evaporated very slowly, small crystals when the liquid is chilled rapidly. They do not have time to grow. That is why foods must be frozen quickly. Large crystals would break cell walls and spoil the texture.

Crystals are sometimes grown for decoration. The sugar crystals grown on those twigs in liqueur bottles indicate that the liqueur is saturated with sugar and very sweet.

[Crystals – French: cristaux German: Kristalle Italian: cristalli Spanish: cristales]

CUCKOO FLOWER. See lady's smock.

CUCUMBER (Cucumis sativus). One of the oldest cultivated vegetables, cucumbers have been grown for some 4000 years. They possibly came from southern India originally, but this is not certain. It is recorded that the Emperor Tiberius demanded a continuous supply of them, so they were even forced in winter. In Britain, cucumbers were commonly grown at the time of Edward III (1327), but then went out of favour, not to be revived until the days of Henry VIII. They became general in the mid-17th century. They were introduced by Columbus to Haiti in 1494 and soon spread all over the North American mainland, as they were liked by the Indian tribes. The popularity of the cucumber depends on its refreshing taste – it is 96% water and a gift for anyone on a slimming diet.

The many varieties may be divided into fairly distinct groups. In Britain, the best known is the long, smooth greenhouse type, which, when not fertilized, is seedless and rarely if ever bitter (fertilized, it can be). It is grown under high humidity and heat. Varieties of what in Britain are called ridge cucumbers (which may be prickly, warty or smooth) are commoner in countries warm enough to grow cucumbers over a long period in the fields, in Mediterranean countries for instance, and in the US where a distinction is made between eating and pickling types. Eating varieties can be pickled but are liable to go hollow, while pickling varieties can be eaten but may be bitter. Varieties of cucumber which are stubby and yellow are known as lemon cucumbers. They taste fine but have a tough skin. Those from the Middle East and northern India are selected to stand some drought and are much grown in pits in the sand in half-dry river beds. A long, very pale type, with a finely-ridged and very tender skin, is the one commonly seen in markets from Turkey to the Indus valley. This I take to be similar to the variety Americans call Armenian, Turkish or Syrian cucumber. These cucumbers have rather dry flesh, no seeds to matter when young, and a strong, excellent taste. You will see them (well sprinkled with dirty water) in a Pakistani town like Dera Ghazi Khan, where the market is thronged with wild, bearded, hook-nosed characters swathed in black turbans. It is the common cucumber of that sort of market in Muslim countries. Chinese and Japanese cucumbers are long outdoor varieties, which may be smooth, ribbed or prickly and have recently been grown in Europe and America.

In buying cucumbers, always look for young ones. Older outdoor types are likely to have seeds and, at best, can only be used for stuffing after the seeds have been scraped out with a spoon. Out of season, imported commercial cucumbers have sometimes been dipped in wax, which is unpleasant for anyone who likes to eat cucumber with the skin on. In countries where ridge cucumbers are commonly eaten and there are some bitter ones, peeling is done from the flower end towards the stalk, because it is the stalk end that is bitter. A sliver is tasted, as a cucumber can sometimes have a

bitter end which must be detected and cut off. Old-fashioned varieties had to be salted to remove some of the bitter juice, a habit that has persisted. Some people still like to remove part of the water, but the long salting advocated in old books is unnecessary. Simply slice, sprinkle generously with salt, leave no more than a minute, tip the cucumber into a clean cloth and gently squeeze out as much of the juice as you like. Cucumber is often dressed with yoghurt and a touch of vinegar, it goes particularly well with yoghurt – dishes range from the Indian cucumber *raita* to the Turkish *cacik* and Greek *zaziki*. Cooked cucumbers are also excellent and have a better flavour than marrows or courgettes. Cucumber halves stuffed with meat and served with sour cream were one of my favourite dishes when I was in Romania long ago.

[*Cucumber* – French: *concombre* German: *Gurke* Italian: *cetriolo* Spanish: *pepino*]

CUDBEAR, archil, orchil, or orseille. Lichens were much used in the past as dyes. For instance, the browns of Scottish tweeds – and some of their strange smell – came from a lichen. Other species, notably the Mediterranean *Rocella tinctoria*, produce a blue, red or purple dye. One form is litmus, the common acid-alkali indicator of the school laboratory. Another form – extracted in a slightly different way – is the dye cudbear, which is used for colouring sauces and bitters. To make this dye, the lichens are macerated in water and ammonia is added, after which the mixture is exposed to the air. The blue liquor turns red when it is heated to drive off the ammonia, and the result is cudbear.

CULATELLO. This is one of the finest raw ham products of Italy. It consists of lean meat only, cut from the backside of a pig (*culo*, vulgarly, means arse), cured as for a ham, soaked in wine, packed in a bladder and hung to mature. It has a fine, rosy colour and a delicate taste. A speciality of Zibello, Busseto and Soragna, between Parma and Piacenza (in Emilia), *culatello* is one of the best, and so most expensive, Italian raw ham products, and quite exceptional. It is sliced thinly and served as *antipasto*.

CUMIN. This close relative of caraway is a vital spice in Indian and Middle Eastern cooking and important enough all over the world. It came originally from the Orient but was being grown in the Mediterranean regions well over 2000 years ago. The Romans used it as a substitute for pepper and even ground it to a paste for spreading on bread. Much confusion is caused in European markets by shops muddling the names of cumin and caraway. For instance the alternative name for caraway in France is *cumin des prés* while in Spain caraway is often known as *comino holandese* (Dutch cumin). Worse still, Indian cookery books often translate cumin as caraway. There is very little taste resemblance.

Cumin (*Cuminum cyminum*) is little used in European cooking (except in Portugal and Spain), but it is important in North Africa and through to the Far East, in Mexico and South America, and in any place where there are sizeable numbers of Indian colonists. Americans may use it in *chili con carne*. Its taste is both strong and assertive. There are two forms commonly used in Indian cooking – black (*kala zeera*) and white *zeera* (*safed zeero*), *zeera* or *jeera* being the usual word for cumin. If cumin is dry-roasted in an old pan until it is just too hot to touch (it has gone very slightly brown), much of its raucous flavour is turned to a more nutty one.

[*Cumin* – French: *cumin* German: *Kreuzkümmel* Italian: *cumino* Spanish: *comino*]

CURDLING AGENTS. *See* rennet.

CURDS. When milk is coagulated by acids, natural souring, rennet or crushed herbs, the solid part is known as curds, and the liquid as whey. ('Curd' is also used to describe the curdy-looking white part of a cauliflower and the soft material that forms between the flakes of really fresh salmon when it is cooked.) Milk curd is basically casein and fat.

To make curds, rennet essence is added to lukewarm milk, and the milk kept warm until the curd is solid and the whey is clear. Lemon juice or any other acid food will hasten the process.

Curds are usually drained of the whey before being eaten (except in junket, Miss Muffet's curds and whey) or used in cooking. A pinch of salt stirred into the curdled milk will assist the separation, and the whey is usually strained off through muslin. The classic way to eat curds is with an equal amount of cream and with wine as a flavouring. Curd is used to make cheesecake, mixed with egg and fried as fritters, or used in various puddings that were more popular in the past than they are today. They are also, of course, the starting point in making *cheese.

[*Curds* – French: *lait caillé* German: *Quark* Italian:

gluncata Spanish: *cuajada*]

CURLY KALE. *See* cabbage, kale.

CURING means preserving by drying, brining and so on. *See* brine, drying, dry-salting.

CURRANT. The term originally applied to a small, black, dried grape, originally imported from the Levant and taking its name from Corinth in Greece. The grapes from which currants are made are of a tiny black variety which has been known for at least 2000 years. To this day, Greece is a prime producer and exporter of currants, although other countries, such as Australia, have taken a large share of the market.

Red currant (and white currant, which is a variety of the same thing) is bred from *Ribes rubrum*, which grows wild in Europe and can still sometimes be found in damp woods, stream banks and hedges in Britain, although its ancestry probably involves crossing with other European species. The name currant came from a fancied resemblance to the Corinth currant, although red currants belong to the same family as gooseberries and are not related to grapes. Currants are so well known in Britain, Germany and northern Europe generally that it is surprising to find they are almost unheard of in the Mediterranean countries. The Italians and Spanish do not even have a word for this fruit (they use the Latin). Even the French lump it with the gooseberry, although currants have long been grown in the northern part of the country. Red-currant juice was a popular drink in Paris in the mid-18th century; the fruit was formerly called *groseille d'outre mer* and thus considered foreign. Many people will agree that red-currant jelly, especially if it is rather tart, is an almost indispensable kitchen ingredient. It is necessary for Cumberland sauce, of course, but also in other contexts to counteract oversweetness. Red currants are, with rowan berries, the best fruity souring agent that grows in northern Europe and are our natural equivalent of sumac, pomegranate and even tamarind if we wish to use them as such.

Red-currant Jelly

Put the fruit in a jar and stand the jar in cold water. Heat gently until the juice begins to flow, then turn the currants into a jelly bag and collect the juice. (Do not squeeze the bag or the jelly will be cloudy.)

Allow 1.25 kg (2¾ lb) of sugar per 1 lt (1¾ pt) of juice. Warm the sugar and dissolve it in the juice. Boil until the jellying point is reached, and put in jars in the usual way.

Black currant (*Ribes nigrum*) is a close relative of the red currant and grows wild in northern Europe and Asia. It has increased in importance as a commercial crop since it was found to be rich in vitamin C, but has always been in demand as a medicine for soothing sore throats. It is not very nice raw, but makes delicious jam. In France, black currants are particularly grown in Burgundy, where they are used to make the alcoholic cordial *crème de cassis*, which is mixed with white wine to make one of the best of all summer aperitifs, *vin blanc cassis* or *kir* named after its famous inventor, the Resistance hero, Abbé Kir. Like red currants, black currants are rarely to be seen in any Mediterranean country.

[*Currant* – French: *raisin de Corinthe* German: *Korinthe* Italian: *uva passa, uva seca* Spanish: *uva, paso de Corinto*

Red currant – French: *groseille rouge* German: *rote Johannisbeere* Italian: *ribes ross* Spanish: *grosella colorada*

Black currant – French: *cassis* German: *Johannisbeere* Italian: *ribes nero* Spanish: *grosella negra*]

CURRY LEAF. This is one of the most important flavourings of Indian vegetarian cooking, but is almost unknown in Europe. The plant is native to southern Asia and grows wild profusely in the forests of the Himalayan foothills. In the Corbett National Park, the smell is overpowering as your elephant bursts through thickets of this plant. The scientific name is *Murraya koenigii*, and it belongs to the citrus-rue family (Rutaceae). In fact, citrus fruits have even been grafted on to it. To make a typical seasoning for South Indian food, take a good pinch of black mustard seed, a small pinch of asafoetida, and half a dozen curry leaves. Fry these briefly in oil or ghee in a large spoon or ladle, until the mustard seeds start to splutter, then quench the whole in the dish (*dal* for instance, or a curry of yoghurt with spices).There is no substitute for curry leaves or for this seasoning. Nothing else will give its very special taste, and since a large number of Indians have come to live in Britain, fairly fresh curry leaves can be bought in shops which specialize in Indian foods. If the leaves offered do not smell strongly of curry, do not buy them, as curry leaves quickly lose their virtue. Curry leaf is also used in Malay and Indonesian cooking.

CURRY PASTE. Frying the spices is the most difficult part of making any curry, and when you add to that the undoubted fact that curry improves and matures with keeping, you have one *raison d'être* for curry pastes. In addition, it is not always possible to get fresh ginger and fresh green chillies – two items necessary for many types of curry and difficult to incorporate in a powder. Many types of curry paste are on the market, but the name of E.P. Veeraswamy is associated with this type of product which, in the past, was necessary to introduce Indian cooking to the West. Anyone who makes curry can easily make curry pastes when fresh ingredients are handy, and, because of the preservative action of spices, it is not difficult to devise formulae which will keep for many months. Easiest, perhaps, is vindaloo paste which contains *vinegar and so keeps without difficulty.

Vindaloo Paste

Use 20-25 g (1 oz) hot red chillies – or double even treble that. Vindaloo should be hot, but chillies vary as do tastes. If they are dried, soak them in ¼ lt (½ pt) of vinegar for 3 hours or until soft. Put them in a liquidizer with 20 cloves of garlic and 35 g (1½ oz) fresh ginger, scraped and cut in bits. Liquidize. Grind in a coffee grinder, a pinch of cumin, a big pinch of black mustard seed, 50 g (2 oz) coriander seed, and add to it 5 g (1 teaspoon) ground turmeric. Mix everything to a paste and fry in 1 lt (½ pt) of oil for about 10 minutes or until the oil separates. Add a dessertspoon of salt (which helps to preserve it) and bottle when cool enough.

To use the paste, fry an onion, add paste (according to your taste), mix into the fat and fry a moment; then add meat. Fry for a moment more (but do not burn) and then add a little water. Cook till the meat is tender. Adjust the salt.

CURRY POWDER. Curry comes from the Tamil (South Indian) word *kari*, meaning a sauce. To Europeans, it covers any hot, spicy Indian stew, but in India there are hundreds of dishes that would qualify under this definition, each quite distinct and with its own name. These dishes use varying combinations from a list of two dozen spicy ingredients. Hoping to reduce Indian cooking to 'curry powder' is like hoping for a ready-mix 'cake powder' to make all European cakes. It can't be done. Curry powder, in fact, is a European convenience food, invented by Indians for our use, but there is no agreed mixture. Unfortunately, many European recipes call for curry powder, treating it almost as if it were a natural spice or a definite substance. It is not, so when one reads 'mijoter dans une bonne sauce currie' in a recipe for lobster à la Créole, one feels that the famous chef who wrote it was leaving much in doubt.

Books commonly say that Indians do not use curry powder. This may have been largely true in the days when even servants had servants. In those days, the masala of fresh ginger, garlic, onion, coconut, green chilli and spices was ground on the stone freshly for each dish. But today, a First-World cost of servants has caught up with Third-World households, and ready-ground convenience spice mixtures are no longer beyond the pale. However, they do not so much use 'curry powder' as a variety of mixtures (which they may have formulated and have had specially ground in the bazar), including traditional garam masalas (hot mixtures), but also powders for particular types of curry: sambar, kolumbu, rasam or dhansak masala, to name but a few, and the mixtures are always fresh.

Alerted to the fact that curry powders are not standard, cooks have a wide choice of what they will use in recipes. Trial is the only way to choose. The chef has expressed no opinion, so we are back to the cook's personal taste. When choosing a recipe for home-made curry powder (and all serious cooks make their own), keep the following points in mind. One may want to vary the hotness, and a light hand with the chilli in the powder and a jar of pure chilli powder on the shelf enables any degree of hotness to be achieved. Turmeric makes

curries yellow but does not necessarily have to go into them. Although it is not very spicy, its taste is assertive, penetrating and rather banal. It is best not to overdo it. Fenugreek can also very easily be overdone, and its flavour gets stronger with time. Cumin is a taste some people do not like, especially if it is rank because it has not been properly roasted. Ginger makes you sweat. Some do not like the taste of dried ginger very much and others, often those who tolerate chilli, find its peculiar hotness overpowering. In India, ginger in curries is usually fresh and thus has a kinder taste. Volatile, oily spices, such as cloves, cinnamon, cardamom and mace are needed, particularly in powders for very aromatic meat curries or as a flavouring for raw or lightly-cooked dishes, such as stuffed eggs and sauces, but for best results curry powders should be fried a little (not burned), and it is worth making up your own *curry pastes and bottling them. There are also many ready-made pastes.

The spices most commonly used in curry powders are dealt with separately in this book. They are: chilli, turmeric, ginger, coriander, cumin (black and white) fenugreek, cloves, cinnamon, cardamom, mace, black pepper, mustard, asafoetida, cassia leaves, curry leaves, poppy seeds and various dals. Other spices, such as ajowan, pomegranate seeds, kalonji, anise and mango powder are used for special purposes. Curries from further south and east may include zedoary, lemon grass, galangal and other less-known ingredients.

Making curry powder at home. Before grinding, certain whole spices should be roasted, an operation which has to be learned by experience. Roasting partly dries the spice and helps to

	a	b	c	d	e	f	g	h	i	j	k	l	m
Black pepper	1	1	4	1	1	1⅓	2	2	½	1	1¼	8	4
Chilli	1	2	–	1	8	1	3	2	6	8	4	–	–
Cloves	1	1	4	–	–	–	–	–	–	–	½	2	2
Cinnamon	–	2	1	–	–	–	–	–	–	1	½	2	2
Cardamom	1	1	1	–	–	–	–	–	–	1	½	2	2
Coriander	8	6	–	8	6	8	8	8	8	8	8	8	8
Cumin	–	2	4	2	1	–	1	1	½	4	2	6	4
Curry leaves	–	–	½	–	½	–	–	–	–	–	–	–	–
Fenugreek	–	½	–	2	1	–	1	–	1½	–	1	–	–
Ginger	1	–	–	1	–	2	–	1	–	–	–	–	–
Mace, Nutmeg, Allspice	–	1	1	–	–	–	–	–	–	–	–	–	–
Mustard seed	–	–	–	½	1	–	–	2	–	–	–	–	–
Poppy seed, Lentils	–	–	–	1	–	–	–	–	–	–	–	–	–
Turmeric	10	–	–	5	–	10	4	2	2	3	2½	–	–

develop and change the flavour. It is done in a dry pan (such as an old iron frying-pan) on top of the stove, and the spice must be stirred and lifted constantly to prevent burning. Whole dry chillies may be roasted in a cool oven. Each spice should be roasted separately and receive individual attention. Chillies should be brittle, but not burned. Coriander seed should be heated slowly until it gives off a lovely orange scent and is just too hot to touch comfortably. If it is not roasted and dried long enough, it will be difficult to grind. Cumin is roasted until the crude smell disappears and the aroma becomes slightly nutty. The colour taken is very slight. Black peppercorns are roasted a little, just until they begin to smell. Most tricky of all is fenugreek seed which must just begin to colour a brown-yellow; if it is roasted too much, so that it starts to turn red, the spice becomes impossibly bitter. The more volatile and oily spices such as cloves, cinnamon, cardamom and mace are not usually roasted, but some recipes call for roasting various *dals* as well as mustard seeds and asafoetida. *Dals* go biscuit coloured and develop special tastes necessary to the background in vegetarian curries. Mustard seeds lose their ability to produce hot flavours with water and develop a nutty taste when roasted until they splutter (the enzymes are destroyed). Asafoetida mellows but should be heated very little or it will lose its special flavour.

Spices are easily ground in a small whirling-blade electric coffee grinder. The exceptions are ginger and turmeric which are the better for a preliminary bashing with a hammer, as they are apt to break the blades of the mill. Thus, roast and grind the whole spices separately, sieve them into a bowl (grinding the residue, if there is any, a second time) and then mix well together. Pack the powder immediately into bottles, excluding as much air as possible, and seal. Exposure to air destroys flavour, or it is lost into the atmosphere. Damp also destroys curry powder.

Curry Powder Formulae

The thirteen formulae given on page 135 are from my book *Herbs, Spices and Flavourings* (Grub Street). They give some idea of the enormous variations possible in curry powder recipes. The numbers indicate parts by weight.

[*Curry powder* – French: *poudre de curry* German: *indisches Ragoutpulver* Italian: *polvere di curry* Spanish: *carí*]

CURUBA. *See* passion fruit.

CUSTARD APPLE is an American tropical fruit of the family Anonaceae, which is represented in the temperate zone only by the *papaw from the US. The other edible fruits of this family are rarely seen outside the tropics; some have been cultivated in tropical Asia as well as America. They are multiple fruits made up of many divisions, each containing a seed, and vary in taste from acid to sweet. One of the most acid is the Sour sop (*Anona muricata*), which is also the largest – its fruits, which are green and have rows of spines, typically weigh up to 2.7 kg (6 lb) and may reach 3.6 kg (8 lb); they are popular in Cuba, where they are used to make drinks and ices. The Sweet sop or Sugar apple (*A. squamosa*) is also popular in the Caribbean and is the one which you are most likely to find being referred to simply as the custard apple. It is eaten as a fruit as well as being used as pulp in drinks and ices. Sweet sops are picked when they are firm but after the skin between the segments has turned creamy yellow; they are kept in straw for a few days until they are soft, with rather custard-like flesh. In this state, they must be handled with great care – they are difficult to transport over any distance. Bullock's heart or ramphal (*A. reticulata*) has more solid and granular flesh and can be heart-shaped and reddish brown or buff. The cherimoya (*A. cherimolia*) has a scaly surface and a flavour not unlike pineapple; it is a species of tropical highlands, while the similar ilama (*A. diversifolia*) grows in lowland areas. The soncoya (*A. purpurea*) has particularly large fruit and is restricted to Mexico and Central America.

CUSTARD MARROW. *See* chayote.

CUSTARD POWDER. One of the first ready-mix convenience foods was custard powder. Invented by Birds in 1846, it became a standard food of school and nursery. It is cheap, being made of cornflour with dye, salt and flavourings, but the exact composition is a trade secret. Combined with hot milk, it is meant to produce an approximation to real custard, which is made with eggs and milk. The word custard or custade is a corruption of 'crustade', meaning a pie with a crust.

[*Custard powder* – French: *poudre à flan* German: *Puddingpulver*]

CUTCH. *See* catechu.

CUTTING IN. In making pastry, it was once usual to rub the fat lightly into the flour with the fingers, an operation which needed cold hands and a sensitive touch. These days, it is more usual to cut the fat into the flour, using two knives, one knife, a pastry blender, blending fork or other device, according to the skill and taste of the pastry-maker, but the newer food processors such as the Magimix do the job superlatively even for the novice. Light pastry can thus be made by the hot and heavy handed.

CUTTLEFISH. Cuttles are *cephalopods with a stiffening 'bone', a familiar white porous object which is washed up on beaches and used to provide grit for cage-birds. The living cuttle is a free-swimming, savage animal with eight arms and two tentacles. The latter are kept retracted ready to shoot out and grab the prey. Living cuttlefish should be handled with care – they bite if given a chance, as a rather important lady, who once picked up one I had speared, discovered to her cost. The common cuttlefish of Europe (*Sepzia officinalis*) is 30-40 cm (12-16 in) long but is best at 25 cm (10 in). The smaller *Sepia elegans* is only 20 cm (8 in) long, but only people in places like Naples will be able to tell the species apart. The very tiny *seppiola* (*Sepiala rondoleti*), only 3-6 cm (1¼-2½ in) long, is commonly seen in Mediterranean fish markets. Very often *seppiole* are mixed with the young of the larger species, which are even better, being very tender. The *seppiole* have fins like little ears sticking out at the sides, but the tender young have fins running almost from end to end.

To prepare cuttlefish, first make a slit in one end and remove the bone through the slit. Turn the animal inside out and remove the guts (reserving the ink sac if needed). Cut off the head and remove the parrot-like beak. Skin the cuttlefish and wash it well before cooking. The body is the best part and is very often stuffed, but cuttles are in general inferior to squids.

[*Cuttlefish* – French: *seiche* German: *Tintenfisch, gemeine Sepie* Italian: *seppia* Spanish: *jibia*]

CYANOCOBALAMIN. *See* vitamin B12.

CYCLAMATES. In the 1960s sodium and calcium cyclamate were much used as artificial sweeteners in soft drinks, ice cream and food products generally. They are about thirty times as sweet as ordinary sugar, are not fattening and do not have the unpleasant lingering sweetness and bitterness of *saccharine. During 1969 and 1970, they were removed from the permitted lists of many countries, when American tests showed that artificial sweetening mixtures of cyclamates and saccharine caused a significant increase in bladder cancer when fed to rats. Some people have said that the scare over artificial sweeteners was promoted by sugar interests, that the amount of cyclamates consumed even by American children in soft drinks was insignificant, that in any case the bladder cancer was provoked in rats and not in humans. Others have said that the harm was done by impurities and not by the substance itself.

CYMLING. *See* marrow.

d

DAB. *See* flatfish.

DAIKON. *See* radish.

DAL, dhal or **dholl** is the Indian term for a split gram of any kind, including split lentils. In Central and South India, the gram is soaked and re-dried before it is split, which is economical because it gives a maximum yield of clean, whole grains. In North India, Gujarat and Maharashtra, the gram is not soaked before splitting. This method leaves more waste and makes the *dal* more expensive, but the flavour is better. Such *dal* is always smooth on the outer (curved) face, but wet-split *dal* has the face rather flattened, with a depression in the middle due to shrinkage. Good *dal* is all of one colour, with few bits, husks or shrivelled grains. It should also be free from rogue seeds and stones, though for safety it is always a good idea to spread the *dal* out and pick it over. *Dal* stored for long is prone to attack by weevils.

Dal cooks best in soft water, without salt (which is added at the end) and without prior soaking. It is soaked only when it is to be ground raw to a paste, as for some Indian preparations (e.g. *dosas* and *idlis*). *Dal* is vital in Indian cooking and in the cooking of the South East Asian countries, not only because it is the main source of protein for many people – and almost the only one for some poor vegetarians – but also because it is the basis on which many vegetarian flavours are created (it is even the basis for sweet dishes). For this reason, it is important to use the type specified in the recipe, as the *dals* are very different, and it will frequently spoil or change the dish if you try to use substitutes without knowing what you are doing. The types of *dal* are best called by their Indian names; even when they are varieties of species well known elsewhere, they are often rather different.

*Channa. Large textured and yellowish. Can be made into a simple purée (sar) but is very often eaten parched or ground into *besan flour.

Tur or *arhar* (*tuvaram* in the South of India).

This is *pigeon pea or red gram. It is usually fairly small and orange-red, but bits of skin may be red or brown, even cream. It is little used in dishes from North India, where it will not grow well on account of frost, but it is the type of *dal* most used in the south and west, in Gujarat and Bombay. When people from Bombay write about *dal*, they mean *tur*. *Tur* mixes easily with water when cooked, and is light and easily digested. It is the *dal* of Parsi *dhansak* and also of the *rasam* and *sambhar* of the South.

Urd, ulutham or *mash* is *black gram, and a close relative of *mung*. The grain is small, and the colour white with flecks of black, even of green skin, according to the variety. *Dhuli urd*, the expensive washed type, is dead white.

Mung or *mug*. Green *dal*. The split *mung bean is cream or yellow, not white; the flecks of seed coat in it may be black or green. It is very digestible, perhaps the most digestible of all the *dals*, and is often given to invalids.

Masur or *masoor*. Lentils. This is regarded as the most humble *dal*, but it is much eaten in Bengal and by Muslims. The *masur* of India differs somewhat from the lentils of the Middle East (such as the small, orange Egyptian lentils) and European varieties, but is regarded as a variety of the same thing. Some varieties cook to a mush, and others do not.

There are *dals* made from other pulses such as *dal moth* from the *moth bean, from the cowpea (lobya), the *lath*, *khesari* or *teora*, but they are only of local importance – often in drought areas.

DAMSON. (*Prunus damascena*). Both the popular name and the specific name of this small *plum go back to the Latin *prunum damascenum* – Damascus plum. The Middle English name was damascene.

Damsons are small, deep purple fruit with a rich, slightly bitter flavour. Of all plums they make the finest stewed fruit and jam. The traditional damson cheese is a solid conserve of damsons and sugar. Although damsons are not a favourite with commercial growers today, they were a popular fruit in English kitchens in the days before World War II. Some damson trees that grow more or less wild produce outstanding fruit (there was one such in a handy hedgerow when I was a child), but 'improved' cultivated varieties are often disappointing.

[*Damson* – French: *prune de Damas* German: *Damaszenerpflaume* Italian: *damaschina, susina damaschina* Spanish: *ciruela damascena*]

DANDELION. Cultivated varieties of dandelion (*Taraxacum officinale*) have larger, tenderer, less bitter leaves than wild ones. Dandelion leaves resemble chicory and make an excellent winter salad, while the roasted, dried root is used as a coffee substitute, like chicory, and may be bought from health-food shops.

[*Dandelion* – French: *pissenlit* German: *Löwenzahn* Italian: *dente di leone* Spanish: *diente de léon, amargón*]

DASHEEN. *See* yam (dasheen).

DASHI. A basic Japanese stock, based upon dried *bonito, seaweed, monosodium glutamate and water.

DATE. The sticky objects that reach temperate countries are dried dates; fresh ones are paler, firm and not wrinkled. Date palms were among the earliest trees to be cultivated, having been grown in the ancient civilizations of the Middle East. Iraq is still the most important date-growing country, but the fruit is grown in other suitably dry and hot climates, including parts of the US. The male and female flowers grow on separate trees, and one male is allotted by growers to 50 or 100 females.

There are three important classes of date: soft, which are usually sold in compressed blocks and are intensely sweet; semi-dry, such as those sold in boxes with a stalk (or a plastic replica of one) down the middle; and dry, which are hard and ideal for carrying by travellers or for storage. Containing some 54% sugar and 7% protein when fresh, and higher concentrations when dried, dates are good high energy food, splendid for iron rations on climbs or walks. In the days before oil transformed their lives, the Bedouins of Arabia virtually lived on dates and on the products from their camels and flocks of sheep. H.R.P. Dickson, in *The Arabs of the Desert* (Allen and Unwin, 1949), describes a sheik's banquet which included bowls of *leben* (buttermilk) with lumps of rather dirty looking butter floating in it and dates. After the meal of a whole sheep

or lamb (with the eyes and tail fat as the guest's particular right), the guest drinks the buttermilk and eats the dates with the bits of butter. If you care to try, you will find that dates actually do go well with butter and with yoghurt.

[*Date* – French: *datte* German: *Dattel* Italian: *dattero* Spanish: *dátil*]

DATE MUSSEL or **date shell**. *See* sea date.

DEAD-NETTLE. *See* spinach.

DECANTING. Red wines, very old wines even if they are white, and vintage port should be decanted. Ordinary red plonk, and wines in restaurants, are normally served from the bottle. In the latter case, you want to see what you are buying. Decanting gets rid of sediment, which spoils a wine's appearance, and helps the wine breathe by getting air to it and so allowing it to lose any mustiness or 'bottle stink'.

Decanting is simple for anyone with a steady hand. The bottle should be stood upright for 12 hours or so to let any sediment sink to the bottom. Red wines should be decanted about an hour before serving. There is no rule of thumb here, as the optimum time varies with the type of wine and its year, it is a question for experts to argue about. After wiping the top of the bottle, draw the cork, taking care not to disturb the sediment. Then wipe the inside of the neck and decant the wine slowly into a scrupulously clean decanter. To make this easier, a funnel can be used and the bottle should be viewed against the light so that you can see exactly when the sediment is in danger of coming out of the bottle. Wine does not keep in the decanter, and although port can be kept for a week or more, it gradually loses its best aromas.

[*Decanting* – French: *décanter* German: *dekantieren, abklären* Italian: *versare, travasare* Spanish: *decantar, trasegar*]

DEHYDRATION. *See* drying.

DEMI-DOUX. *See* herring.

DENTEX. *See* bream.

DEVONSHIRE CREAM. *See* clotted cream.

DEWBERRY. *See* blackberry.

DEXTRIN or **British gum**. A white or yellowish powder, first prepared from starch in 1833. It is

139

formed either by incomplete hydrolysis when starch is treated with a dilute acid or by the effect of heat on dry starch. Dextrin dissolves in boiling water – less easily in cold – to make a gummy solution which can be used to glaze bread and rolls in baking. The proportion of dextrin in *malt is an important factor in brewing.

[Dextrin – French: dextrine German: Dextrin Italian: destrina Spanish: dextrina]

DIASTASE or **amylase**. Class of *enzymes which break down starch to sugar (*maltose). Such enzymes occur in many micro-organisms, especially in yeasts and moulds, and also are formed in quantity when grain germinates as part of the mechanism by which the growing embryo gets at the stored starch. The diastase content gradually increases in sprouting barley, for instance, and this is used to produce *malt. Diastases are also the means by which we digest starch: there is one (ptyalin) in human saliva and a more efficient one which is produced by the pancreas of adults and works in the small intestine. Very little of it is produced by babies – which is why starchy gruel is not very good as baby food.

DEXTROSE. *See* glucose.

DHAL or **dhol**. *See dal.*

DIBS. A household syrup made in the Middle East by dissolving out the sugar from raisins, carob beans or sweet grapes, and boiling down the solution until it forms a thick syrup which can be used as a sweetener.

DILL. The dill plant (*Anethum graveolens*) looks very like fennel, with the same yellow umbelliferous flowers and feathery leaves, but it is smaller and an annual, not a perennial. When crushed, dill has a quite distinctive aroma with nothing of the anise background of fennel. It is a native of Asia, but has been grown in Mediterranean countries since ancient times and is now naturalized over most of Europe. As a green herb, it is very popular in Scandinavia (e.g. in *gravlax), Russia, Germany, central and south-eastern Europe, Iran and Turkey. It is not so well known further west, in Italy and Spain, or further east, in India. In Britain, the use of dill (along with most other herbs) almost died out until recently, surviving mainly in dill water for babies. In the US, it is strongly associated with pickled cucumbers – dill pickles. The seed is also used as a spice and has a taste reminiscent of caraway. Good brands of dried dill leaf (dill weed) are quite adequate when fresh but soon lose flavour if open to the air.

[Dill – French: aneth German: Dill Italian: aneto Spanish: eneldo]

DISACCHARIDES. *See* sugar.

DISINFECTANTS, **germicides** and **antiseptics** are almost synonymous; they prevent micro-organisms from multiplying, may reduce their numbers by killing them, and occasionally kill their spores. Disinfection should not be confused with *sterilization, which is the total destruction of all living organisms, including spores; disinfection is certainly not that.

In the kitchen, household disinfectants are used for cleaning. There are special disinfectants for treating bottles, casks and jars for home preserving and wine making. In unhygienic places, particularly in the tropics, it may be necessary to disinfect water or vegetables that are to be eaten raw. Occasionally small quantities are added to food. Kitchen disinfectants must be harmless in the amounts used; they must either be flavourless and odourless, or have odours that are quickly dispelled by heat. Disinfectants overlap with *preservatives, as in the case of *alcohol and acids.

Formaldehyde. Formalin is a 40% solution of formaldehyde gas in water and is very active against any organisms, including growing cells and spores. Although it has a strong smell, it was formerly used in minute concentrations as a preservative in milk and cream, but it is now generally forbidden by law.

It makes the eyes water and is potentially dangerous, so if used it should be handled in well ventilated places. But it is much too nasty to find a place among the regular kitchen disinfectants.

Oxidizing Agents. Powerful oxidizing agents are very active in killing germs, especially when they contain chlorine. Well-known substances in this category are hypochlorous acid, hypochlorites such as sodium hypochlorite (bleaching powder), chloramine, which is used in water-sterilizing tablets, and dichloramine. Among the oxidizing disinfectants which do not contain chlorine is potassium permanganate which gives a bright purple-red solution when dissolved in water. It is a powerful germ-killer, especially when combined with an acid (a 1% solution of permanganate containing 1.1% hydrochloric acid will kill anthrax spores in 30 seconds). In the old days, travellers in the Third World always used permanganate to rinse salads, though a quick rinse in very dilute solution was doubtfully effective. In contact with organic matter, hydrogen peroxide (H_2O_2) gives off its extra oxygen atom to become water. It is a good cleaner, because the froth of oxygen it gives off dislodges dirt and gets behind it, but it is not commonly used for kitchen disinfection.

Salt. Brine is not normally thought of as a disinfectant, but salt stops bacteria growing in solutions of 25% and over, and it inhibits many bacteria in considerably smaller concentration.

Soap is an antiseptic as well as a cleaning agent. I was taught by the head of British Army medical services in India in World War II that a pure soap, free from perfume, can with advantage be used to wash the skins of fruit and vegetables when they are to be eaten raw. For fruit, this is probably more effective than washing in dilute permanganate because soap removes grease, a prime protector of bacteria. Naturally, the fruit must be well rinsed, after soaping, in pure water.

Use *Campden tablets in bottling and wine-making, *sodium hypochlorite for swabbing surfaces. A proprietary disinfectant, Milton, includes two disinfecting substances: it contains 1% sodium hypochlorite and 16.5% common salt. Its makers recommend it in various dilutions for cleaning in the kitchen, for use on salads and fruit and for adding to spring and well water. Soap and hot water should be used first on utensils, wherever possible, to remove grease.

[Disinfectant – French: désinfectant German: Desinfektionsmittel Italian: disinfettante Spanish: desinfectante]

DISTILLATION (from the Latin, stilla, a drop) is a method of separating or refining volatile substances by heating them until they vaporize and then cooling (condensing) the vapour back to the original state; the apparatus used is called a still. The ancient Greeks knew how to get fresh water by distilling seawater (that was easy, since the dry salt was left behind) but separating *alcohol from the water in wine or a fermented mash was more difficult, and the technique is probably no more than a thousand years old, if that. When introduced into Europe, spirits were first called by names such as eaux-de-vie, or uisge-beath (whisky), which mean 'waters of life', because they were medicinal, and sold by apothecaries, not publicans.

The separation of alcohol from water is possible because it is more volatile than water and boils at a lower temperature: 78°C (172°F) as opposed to 100°C (212°F). A mixture boils at an intermediate temperature (depending on the relative proportion of water and alcohol), and the vapours contain both alcohol and water. The first run-through with a simple still will produce a distillate of between 20-40% alcohol. Distilling this a second time may increase the alcohol content to 70% depending on the spirits being made and the distiller's technique. Further distillation can increase the alcohol strength to 97.2% (by volume) but never more, as this mixture boils at a lower temperature than does 100% alcohol. The only uses related to cooking for alcohol of great strength are in making liqueurs and alcohol-preserved fruits. It is dangerous and highly inflammable stuff.

In spirits for drinking, such as whisky, brandy, rum, fruit brandies and gin, there are important considerations other than strength. Fermented mashes contain varying amounts of other volatile substances. One such is methyl alcohol, of which very little is produced in the fermentation of sugar solution (or sugar from starch), but some will be formed from woody cell walls and pectin (in stalks and pips) when fruit mashes are fermented. Methyl alcohol is poisonous and can cause blindness, but it will come over in the first runnings (heads or foreshots), which is why these are discarded. At the other end of the scale are the congenerics, which make up *fusel oil. This is a mixture of higher alcohols and other substances, which are less volatile and mainly come over last in distillation. Although the congenerics are removed almost entirely from vodka, some are retained for flavour in other spirits. It is the distiller's art to leave in exactly enough; with too little there is a poor flavour, while too much produces nasty hangovers.

An important consideration is the type of still. Very fine quality spirits are mostly made in variants of the old-fashioned pot stills, which are essentially boiling pots sealed with a bulbous head and leading over into condensing coils. In these, each batch is distilled individually. More ordinary spirits are made in continuous stills which are complicated in design but cheaper to operate.

In many countries, governments have made laws forbidding the citizen to distil his own liquor, an infringement of liberty which often goes unnoticed. It was, until recently, also illegal to brew beer or make wine at home in Britain, although the law was ignored until even Parliament finally decided it could not be enforced and made home brewing legal. However, if the Briton makes his own gin or whisky, the revenue men will no doubt come elbowing into his castle.

Oil men working in 'dry' Arab countries have devised simple rules for making 'silent spirits' which have even less hangover effects than bought brandy or whisky. They ferment solutions of sugar, so that only traces of methyl alcohol are formed, and distil the spirit two or three times to eliminate the unpleasant yeasty taste. At each distillation the first and last runnings are of course discarded.

In places where distillation at home is not legal, shops cannot sell safe, properly made home stills. The distillation of over-proof alcohol is just about as dangerous as distilling petrol, and any leak in the system is likely to cause an explosion. It is best to do it outdoors and never to leave the still unattended or drink while it is in operation. Like eating toadstools or driving a car, distillation has to be done with a lot of knowledge and good sense or not at all. Oil men have demonstrated that the main danger lies not in blindness, or in revenue officers, but in blowing up the kitchen.

[*Distillation* – French: *distillation* German: *Brennen* Italian: *distillazione* Spanish: *destilación*]

DISTILLED WATER. Water which, after distillation, is virtually free from mineral matter and contains very little dissolved air. Although it tastes flat, it is safe to drink, but will need mineralizing if it is to be used for long periods. Water distilled from seawater is increasingly used in waterless but oil-rich regions and on ships (like nuclear submarines) which have to stay at sea for long periods. The only usual use for distilled water in the home – apart from car batteries – is in steam irons. The water ice melted in defrosting the refrigerator can be used for both purposes.

DOGFISH. *See* shark.

DRAMBUIE. Liqueur based on whisky.

DRAWING. The process of extracting the entrails of birds. Make sure that the bird has been properly plucked and singed. Some Italians advocate washing the skin of chickens with plain soap and water, and they claim that this makes a significant improvement to the flavour. (It could be a sensible precaution.)

The head is retained only in very small birds. Otherwise, cut it off. Heads and combs are used in country cooking, but *most* people throw them away.

The feet should be cut off just below the joint. If they are cut above the joint, the thigh muscle attachments are severed and the meat shrinks, exposing the bone on cooking. Remove the claws and dip the feet into boiling water while you count to ten. (If they are kept in the water too long, the job is more difficult.) Immediately, scrape off the fine skin. The cleaned feet are then ready for the stock-pot.

The neck is chopped off near, but not too near, the body; remove the gullet and windpipe. The neck usually goes into the stock-pot, but the neck skin can be used for stuffing, like a sausage.

The crop is joined to the gullet and is the thin bag at the base of the throat. The crop lies just under the skin; it may be freed by blunt dissection with the fingers, then severed from the rest of the gullet where it passes into the main body cavity. There is no use for the crop. Discard it.

The vent. Birds have a common vent situated beneath the tail stump or parson's (or pope's) nose. Make a slit below the vent (in fact above it, because you will have the bird breast upper-most); I always enlarge the slit by snipping right round the vent and freeing it entirely. Put two fingers inside the bird and free the viscera from the cavity walls by blunt dissection. When they are free, gently pull out all the guts – first the gizzard, then the liver, and finally the heart and remains of the gullet.

The liver. In most birds (but not, for instance, in pigeons), there is a gall bladder. This is a small green sac closely applied to the liver. Locate it and snip it out without breaking it, as the gall inside is intensely bitter. Wash the liver and set it aside.

The heart. One of the giblets. Separate and wash it.

The gizzard is a large muscular sac, part of the digestive canal, where the food is ground up with grit. Cut it free from the rest of the guts (which are discarded) and slice carefully into it until the knife feels the surface of the horny lining (there is a gristly lining to be snicked through first). If this is done properly, the gizzard can now be pulled open and the horny lining separated and discarded as a complete bag with the contents enclosed in it. Wash the gizzard, which usually goes into the stock-pot.

Other internal organs include the lungs, which are spongy and closely stuck to the top of the body cavity, the testes or oviducts and ovaries (which may contain partly-formed eggs, sometimes used in cooking) and the kidneys. They can be left in or not, according to preference. Rinse out the cavity (and dry it) only if necessary.

Skin. To skin a chicken, cut through the skin along the breastbone and, with a knife, free it from the muscles underneath. Using fingers as instruments for blunt dissection, free the skin at the sides of the breast and around the base of the thigh. Pull the skin inside out over the whole leg. When one leg is completely skinned, do the same for the other. Now get the fingers under the skin and push them right across the back to the other side. Run the fingers along, tearing the skin free up to the parson's nose. Cut off the nose and skin it in one stroke of the knife. Now pull the skin forwards, blunt dissecting with the fingers around the base of the wings and up to the neck. Pull the skin off, inside out, over the base of the wings. It will tear but do not bother, as the skin on the wings is almost impossible to remove entirely.

[Drawing – French: *vider* German: *ausnehmen* Italian: *estrarre* Spanish: *destripar*]

DRAWN BUTTER. In America, this is simply *clarified butter. In Britain, melted butter sauce is thickened with flour, drawn butter is melted butter to which either water or vinegar has been added and which is then beaten until it is thick. Or, as Elizabeth David says in *Spices, Salt and Aromatics in the English Kitchen* (Grub Street), it can simply be melted butter.

DREDGING. Sprinkling heavily with sugar or flour – more than a light sprinkling or dusting and less than a coating.

DRESSING. *See* salad dressing.

DRIED BEAN. *See* kidney bean.

DRIED MEAT. Many countries have ancient types of dried meat. *Drying has a preservative action because spoilage organisms cannot multiply without water. Salting, *smoking and even spicing are adjuncts. *Dry-salting in particular works by extracting water from meat, as well as through the preservative action of the salt. Equally, drying is essential for hams and sausages which are mainly preserved by salt, saltpetre and smoke. It is difficult (and pointless) to try to draw any line between hams and dried meats except one of convenience. However, in recent years, the introduction of scientific methods of desiccation under reduced pressure, freeze-drying and so on, have resulted in thoroughly dehydrated foods, which are a logical extension of the same processes, and these are a thing apart.

The primitive method of drying is hanging strips of lean meat in the sun. Such a product is the *dendang* of South East Asia, made of buffalo or game. In Africa, I have often seen strips of game meat hung to dry in the smoke of the camp fire (which I suspect was how smoking meat was discovered, not as is usually claimed, through hanging it in the roofs of caves with their damp and stagnant air).The camp-fire smoke exerts a preservative action, but, perhaps even more important, it keeps away flies which would otherwise lay their eggs on the meat and walk about on it with their filthy, contaminated feet.

The best-known dried meats include the *biltong of South Africa, the *tassajo* or *charqui* of Spanish America, the more sophisticated *bundnerfleish of the Grisons in Switzerland and the *bresaola from just over the border in the Adda valley region (Valtellina) of northern Italy. Beef is the meat most commonly dried, plus game in the jungle, sheep (the *chalona* of Latin America and also a horrible dried mutton in Tibet), goat, and even dolphin meat (*musciame*) in Sardinia and on the Ligurian coast of Italy.

DRIPPING. The fat that dripped from roasting joints, in the days when meat really had fat on it, was called dripping. When cold and solidified, some brown meat jelly was usually trapped and preserved under the fat. When the fat (especially of beef dripping) was mixed with the jelly, salted, and spread on toast, it used to be a standard – and delicious – appetite stopper for farm workers and children at tea time on raw evenings in winter or after skating. Dripping was also commonly clarified and used as a cooking fat. In that case, the distinction between dripping and rendered fat is mainly one of usage. Chicken fat, so much a part of

Jewish cooking, is not called 'chicken dripping'.

[*Dripping* – French: *graisse de rôti* German: *Bratenfett, Schmalz* Italian: *grasso d'arrosto* Spanish: *pringue*]

DRUMSTICK. Not just the lower part of the legs of chickens, turkeys or other fowl, but also the name of a tree, *Moringa oleifera*, which is used as a vegetable. It is also called horseradish tree (because its roots taste like horseradish and are used as a flavouring) and ben tree (the seeds – ben nuts – give oil of ben which is used commercially). It is a native of India, but is planted in southern parts of the US, and has gone wild in the West Indies. The drumstick tree is important in Indian cooking, where the flowers, leaves and even the twigs are cooked. The leaves are pounded with onion and sour pomegranate seeds to make a chutney. Most important of all are the unripe pods, which are long (up to 0.5 m or 19 in) and though often rather fibrous, have a delicious taste (sometimes compared with asparagus). Particularly in Madras and Bengal, they are often used in vegetarian curries to which they give an incomparable, almost meaty flavour. Drumsticks can occasionally be found in Britain in shops which specialize in Indian foods, or may be acquired locally in Florida and southern California.

DRYING is the oldest method of preserving food, and in its modern form of dehydration is of great industrial importance. It works because dry food is not spoiled by yeasts, moulds and bacteria – or even by enzymes – as long as the amount of water left in it is not enough to support life processes. Since micro-organisms are not necessarily killed by drying, dried foods which get damp spoil very quickly; dry, though, they will keep for long periods. Even such highly perishable items as fish and shellfish can be preserved by natural drying.

Drying depends on relative humidity, the quantity of water vapour in the air in relation to the amount it will hold. But as the amount of water the air will hold increases with temperature, warming air drops the relative humidity, not by removing water vapour but by increasing the quantity that the air can potentially hold. That is why, even on the dampest day, things will dry in a low oven or in an airing cupboard.

In deserts, the relative humidity is often naturally low, so drying is easy, even in the shade, but on humid tropical beaches the relative humidity is often very high, in spite of the heat, and the drying of shrimps, fish or octopus must be done in the sun

– which raises the temperature. In such conditions, rapid drying is necessary to forestall decomposition. Even so, the products – Bombay duck is typical – develop a gamey flavour. (In Arctic regions, fish may be laid on rocks or hung in rigging to dry slowly, as in the preparation of stockfish.) Sun-drying is not the method for most foods. True, the ultra-violet rays help kill surface bacteria, but they also increase the effects of oxygen and so tend to destroy colour and flavour. Drying in the shade is therefore usually preferable if low relative humidity makes it possible.

A breeze helps drying because it continually changes the air, in stagnant conditions, the air is quickly saturated with moisture from the objects that are drying. Reduced pressure also promotes drying – at high altitudes, evaporation directly from ice produces the strange pinnacled glaciers around Mount Everest. Cold, in itself, does not prevent drying.

Dried food is convenient because it is light in weight and takes up little space. With modern high-speed techniques such as drying under reduced pressure, spray drying and freeze drying, the end products are often almost indistinguishable from those made with fresh ingredients. However, dried foods usually need to be soaked before use, and if this is not properly done the results may be unsatisfactory. Over-soaking can lead to decomposition, and living products, such as pulses, should not be soaked if they can be cooked without it.

The simplest dried foods are grain, pulses and nuts, all of which require very little drying. Fruit mostly dries well, although large species like apples need to be sliced. Some fruit discolours when cut and needs to be treated chemically if appearance is important. Vegetables must be blanched before drying. Drying fish, meat, eggs and milk is normally a commercial undertaking (*see* dried meat).

Drying fruit. Fruit, provided it is not too watery, can be dried in the sun (as tomatoes are in southern Italy). Figs need no treatment, other than gentle squashing, but apricots must be split and stoned, while apples and pears have to be peeled, cored and cut in rings or pieces about 0.5 cm (¼ in) thick. To keep them from going brown, soak them briefly (10 minutes) in a solution of one *Campden tablet per 100 ml (3½ fl oz) water before spreading them out on mats or muslin trays to dry. The time taken will depend on the type of fruit and the amount of sun, as well as on the relative humidity. Naturally, the trays should be taken in or covered at night or when there is a possibility of rain.

More certain results are obtained by drying in ovens or in special driers in which everything is under control. A cool oven, with the door ajar for ventilation, is difficult to regulate exactly. Driers can be bought and are not difficult to construct, the requirements being an easily-controlled source of heat and a means of creating ventilation.

[Drying – French: sécher German: trocknen Italian: seccare Spanish: secar]

DRY-SALTING, curing meat by salting and drying, involves rubbing the surface with mixtures of salt, sugar and saltpetre, so there is more hand-work than when curing in brine, but the dry-salting cure penetrates more slowly and produces a better flavour. Ham, bacon and other cured meats can be produced by brining (see brine), by dry-salting or by a mixture of both. Dry-salting, though, is used for the most expensive products. The delicious Cumberland hams, for instance, which were cured in every farm and provided the fabled ham and egg teas in the Lake District, were dry-salted. The following (given merely as an example) is from *Farmhouse Fare*, a splendid collection of country recipes first published by *The Farmer's Weekly* in 1946.

Cumberland Cure

For a 125 kg (20 stone) pig, you will need 225 g (½ lb) saltpetre, 9.5 kg (1½ stone) salt – preferably Cheshire Block Salt – and 450 g (1 lb) brown sugar. Lay the hams, flitches and shoulders on a stone slab, with the rind to the top. Rub salt into the rind until moisture forms. Turn it over, take out all the blood veins and sprinkle all over with 225 g (½ lb) saltpetre and 450 g (1 lb) brown sugar (more so about the bones and veins), then cover with salt. Leave it a day; when the salt will have moistened. Cover again with salt, and do so each day for 3-4 days. Take out the flitches at the end of 14 days, the shoulders and hams at the end of 21 days. Wash all pieces with a cloth dipped in lukewarm water and hang them to dry. Curing time from November to March. (From Mrs. T. Fox, Cumberland).

When salt is rubbed dry on meat, there can be no penetration by salt until some of it has dissolved in liquid extracted from the tissues. From then on, as water flows out of the meat, the salt solution diffuses in, a process that takes place rather slowly. Very finely ground salt (or sugar) is never recommended for curing because it sops up liquid like blotting paper, thus increasing the rate at which the meat loses water while slowing down the penetration of the salt. In dry-salting, the greatest care must be taken to see that all pockets in the meat and places near the bones are in contact with salt and saltpetre, as they may otherwise become centres of putrefaction.

DUBLIN BAY PRAWN. *See* scampi.

DUCK. Like geese and swans, ducks belong to the family Anatidae. Wild ducks are found all over the world, and some of the many species are excellent to eat, while others are horrible. Within a species, palatability also depends on the time of year and on the duck's age and diet. Almost all the domesticated ducks have been derived from the mallard, which is widely distributed throughout the world, but ducks have been domesticated for so long that breeding has changed them enormously from their original form, as they have been selected for special characteristics. (For instance, Indian Runners and Khaki Campbells were bred for laying.) Domesticating ducklings does not take much effort. They don't even need to be on water, but they appreciate a trough or bucket of water in which they can wash their beaks and heads. Ducks have been eaten in Europe and China for many thousands of years. The Greeks and the Romans ate them (gourmets only the breasts and brains) and, in China, the duck is highly prized. In fact, the trouble the Chinese take with ducks – removing the oil glands in the tail, inflating the animal to separate the skin from the flesh to get a better crackle, or stuffing it with wild mixtures of stir-fried pork, water chestnuts, ginkgo nuts, ham, shrimps and rice wine – makes even pressed Rouen duck seem simple. The Chinese also value ducks for their beauty, especially the Mandarin, which is commonplace today, but was not so a little more than a hundred years ago. The Chinese took, according to a 19th-century naturalist 'a singular dislike to seeing their birds pass into the hands of Europeans.' Another writer in the mid-19th century reported: 'A gentleman very recently wrote from Sydney to China requesting some of these birds sent to him. The reply was that from the present disturbed state of China it would be easier to send him a pair of mandarins than a pair of Mandarin ducks.' Nevertheless, shortly after that, nine white Peking ducks, which had previously been bred only in the Imperial Palace, arrived in the US, and it is claimed that these are the ancestors of today's Long Island ducklings. With time, the number of common breeds has reduced to those regarded as best – or most profitable. In Europe and the US, these include:

Aylesbury is the most important English breed. White, with some similarity to Rouen ducks, Aylesburies put on weight rapidly and have dark, tender and tasty flesh. They run to about 2 kg (4-5 lb) when dressed. The British have a preference for roast duck and green peas, but there are other interesting dishes, such as the excellent boiled duck of North Wales. Many British restaurants go in for a sloppy version of the French *Caneton à l'orange*, which too often means duck with a dollop of marmalade in the gravy.

Long Island ducklings of Chinese ancestry are said to be produced in greater numbers than any other breed in the world. They are excellent and run almost to 3 kg (5-6 lb) as ducks, and something under 2 kg (3½-4 lb) as ducklings. In the US, apple sauce is traditional with roast duckling.

Nantes ducks, famous in France, are smaller than Rouen ducks but have a fine texture and flavour. At 4 months, they are usually a little over 1.5 kg (3½ lb). Nantes ducks, unlike Rouens, are always bled when they are killed. The easiest way to do this is to chop off the head and to hang up the duck by the feet to drain off the blood.

Rouen ducks from Normandy, are large. They reach about 3 kg (6 lb) in 4 months and are never bled when killed. Instead, they are suffocated or strangled so that they do not lose any blood. This gives a very dark meat and a special taste. Once killed, a Rouen duck must be eaten within 24 hours. The most famous dish is *Caneton à la rouennaise*. While the duck is still warm, the breast must be plucked so that the blood flows into it. In drawing the bird, care is taken to lose as little blood as possible from the duck, and any that does escape is caught in a bowl. The gall bladder is separated from the liver and the liver returned to the cavity. The bird is trussed and roasted on a spit for only 15-30 minutes, depending on its size; it is then skinned. Legs and wings are cut off for separate treatment.

The thigh bone is removed from the leg, which is then marked with a hot skewer, brushed with melted butter, grilled and, finally, sprinkled with coarse salt. The wing tips are rolled in breadcrumbs and grilled. These are put on the hot serving dish with the breast, pink and sliced, and are covered with a sauce made with Bordeaux wine in which shallots have been simmered. The juices from the carcass are pressed in a special press – although a Mouli will do – and the liver and heart are sieved. Full details of this classic dish are given in that book of marvellous recipes, *Les Recettes Secrètes des meilleurs restaurants de France*, by Louisette Bertholle (an abridged version in English is *Secrets of the Great French Restaurants*, published by Sphere).

The other domesticated species of note apart from the mallard and its descendants is the grotesque-looking Muscovy duck (*Cairina moschata*), which hails not from Muscovy (Russia) but from South America. It is the favourite table duck in Australia and is also eaten in the US and Britain. The flesh is musky unless the ducks are very young. Because they are so big, their livers are sometimes used to make *pâté de foie gras*.

Although ducks are so valued in France, they are much less so in Spain and Italy, where recipes are relatively few. Perhaps one reason is that the French roast duck for rather a short time (as the British do with wild duck) and eat it pink, though not bloody (15 minutes per 450 g/1 lb is the rule of thumb), whereas Spanish recipes advocate roasting a duck for 2 hours. They also say that the meat is dry and inferior to chicken, which is not surprising. In Italy, the Venetians have several original recipes for stuffed duck (*anara col pien*), including in the stuffing veal, sausage, bread soaked in Marsala, bitter-almond biscuits and the inevitable Parmesan cheese, and basting, for example, with wine and rosemary.

Choosing domestic ducks – or ducklings – is not difficult, as it is fairly obvious from the look of a duck if it is old and in any case, commercially-produced birds are killed when quite young. It may be less easy in some remote market or with wild ducks, and the following rules will help. Ducks should be fresh, without smell, and plump, particularly on the breast, which is the important part. The bottom half of the beak should be flexible, and you should be able to bend it back easily. The webs of the feet should be soft – in old ducks they are hard – and the wing pinions should also be flexible. To carve a duck, remove the legs and carve the breast in long, thin slices fore and aft, more or less vertically, down to the bone.

In Europe, the US and Asia, wild ducks of various species come in from further north to winter, settling in large numbers in estuaries and lakes, or feeding inland in fields according to their habit. Thousands of birds were netted or shot by wildfowlers with great punt guns which were fired into the massed birds. In Britain, the mallard is the commonest wild duck (it is the *canard sauvage* of France) and the one most eaten everywhere, since it is abundant and of excellent table quality. It is at its best in November and December. In southern France, it is preserved in brine.

Other ducks commonly eaten in Britain are the pintail (*Anas acuta*), the teal (*Anas crecca*), which is small, the scaup (*Aythya marila*), the shoveler (*Spatula clypeata*), the widgeon (*Anas penelope*) and the pochard (*Aythya ferina*). Others, like the shelduck (*Tadorna tadorna*), and the Tufted duck (*Aythya fuligula*), are protected or avoided. Nature-lovers get more pleasure from flights of ducks over the water than from wild duck on the table.

In North America, the most prized wild duck is the Canvasback (*Aythya valisineria*), so-called for its light canvas-coloured back; it is said to take its delicious flavour from the 'wild celery' it gets by diving. In addition to the pintail, teal, scaup, shoveler and widgeon, other ducks which are highly-prized in North America are the Redhead (*Nyroca americana*),the Black duck (*Anas rubripes*),of which the Cayuga is a domesticated version, the colourful Carolina or Wood duck (*Aix sponsa*),the Ring-neck (*Aythya colloris*), and, further south, the Dominican Masked duck (*Nomonyx dominicus*), as well as many others of less quality. There are also favourite wild ducks in Asia, Africa, Australia and New Zealand, and some gastronomic oddities like the dried Fray duck (*Anas zonorhyncha*) of China. Opinions vary as to the respective merits of ducks; some are good when young, but horrid when old. Old ducks of edible species make good game stock, though.

Wild ducks should not be hung, though some recipes call for them to be marinated to tenderize them and rid them of any fishy flavour. Plucking out the down is tedious; one solution is dunking the bird in scalding water for a couple of minutes and then rubbing it with finely-powdered resin, which brings off the down by sticking to it. After plucking, the duck needs singeing. Cut off the head and draw and wipe out the ducks in the normal manner. In the old days, wild duck were usually trussed with the feet left on, and the feet were scalded and skinned, but people today are more squeamish and don't like to be reminded of what they are eating. Wild duck is usually served rare – the old saying was that a mallard should walk through the kitchen,

a widgeon should run slowly through and a teal should rush through. Most experts recommend about 20 minutes in a hot oven, but such short cooking might be inadvisable with frozen game or with any that might be infected with *Salmonella*. See eggs.

[*Duck* – French: *canard* German: *Ente* Italian: *anitra* Spanish: *pato*]

DURIAN or **durion** (*Durio zibethinus*) is a well-known tropical fruit, a native of Malaysia which looks something like a *jack fruit but is not related. The fruits, which are green, rugby ball shaped and have a hard shell with pointed warts or spines, weigh about 2 kg (4½ lb).When they are ripe, they go yellowish and may fall, making it inadvisable to walk underneath the trees, which may reach 30 m (100 ft). Many people find the fruit delicious, although it has a dreadful stench of stale vomit. Optimists say that this can be removed if the pieces of fruit are soaked in coconut milk for a day. The flesh has the consistency of custard; the taste is rich, aromatic and sweet, with a strange balsamic background.

DULSE. *See* seaweed.

DURRA. *See* millet.

DWARF CAPE GOOSEBERRY. *See* physalis fruit.

DYERS' ALKANET. *See* alkanna.

DYES. Nearly 90% of food colourings sold are synthetic dyes and have to be certified as safe by the responsible authorities. The first coal-tar dye, aniline purple, was discovered by the British chemist, Sir William H. Perkin, in 1856, and by the beginning of this century, dye chemists had developed dozens of these synthetic colourings, any one of which could be added to food, provided there was no obvious and immediate harmful effect. At that time, nobody had registered that dyes could also have long-term ill effects. Gradually, over the years, the more obviously harmful dyes have been weeded out and banned, but it has recently become clear that the control and selection has not been done well enough. Even more alarming is the situation when authorities such as the World Health Organization, the Federal Drug Administration and the responsible agencies of the various European governments do not agree on the dyes which should be considered safe, in spite of the pressure they are under to standardize, because differences upset international trade. Such a situation arose, for example over the colour amaranth. When this was provisionally banned on suspicion in the US, the authorities in Britain (where it is most commonly used for colouring jams and other foods that tend to be eaten by children) did nothing about it, on the grounds that the tests were inconclusive. Most parents would consider it more sensible to take the attitude that any chemical is guilty until proved innocent, rather than waiting for cast-iron proof of harmfulness before taking action. Children, who eat most of these dyes, are also most vulnerable. Dyes, amongst other things, can cause cancer, allergies, and damage to unborn babies.

However, in fairness, it is a mistake to think that every natural substance is harmless and every synthetic one harmful. All cooking, all life, is chemical. Naturally charred substances used to colour gravies could be carcinogenic. One concludes it is best to use food colours only on special occasions and to keep the children's soft drinks and sweets to a minimum. Making them at home is not only more wholesome but also cheaper. Flowers, fresh or crystallized, nuts and fruits can be used for colour and decoration.

e

EAR SHELL. *See* abalone.

EARTHENWARE. This is the simplest and most primitive form of pottery. It is soft, porous and fragile. Although easily broken by a knock, it is comparatively resistant to thermal shock; that is, it is not so easily cracked by sudden changes of temperature. Pouring cold liquid into a hot, dry earthenware pot is, however, likely to crack it. Earthenware does not heat evenly like a metal, but good quality earthenware cooking pots can often be put straight on the open fire or gas flame without harm, especially when the bottom of the pot is rounded.

Unglazed earthenware is the classic material for water pots. The water soaks through, evaporates and so cools the contents. For wine, it was more usual to use skins, gourds or other less permeable containers, with good reason. Nobody wants to lose wine by evaporation, and glazed earthenware in the past was dangerous if used for storing acid substances (see ceramic glazes).

Earthenware pots, such as the Spanish *ollas* or *graxioneras* and Italian *padellas* are splendid to cook in, if you understand their characteristics. Some dishes, like the pot-roasted rabbit with herbs and black olives of Liguria (*coniglio alla sanremese*), even taste better when cooked in earthenware, although I have not been able to work out the reason.

However, if food is allowed to burn in earthenware, it burns badly. The glaze of an earthenware pot which has been used regularly on a fierce fire or on naked gas for some months may crack or craze. The exposed earthenware can then give an unpleasant taste to the food and the pot must be replaced with a new one.

Earthenware has a high specific heat, which means that it needs to absorb a lot of heat to raise the temperature. Earthenware pots warm and cool slowly. Food brought to table in the pot in which it was cooked will stay hot – and may even go on cooking. Should the instability of pots with a rounded bottom be an embarrassment, then a mat of straw or wood, shaped like a ring, is the traditional rustic solution for the table; a metal flan-ring will solve the problem on the stove.

[*Earthenware* – French: *terre cuite* German: *Töpferware, Steingut* Italian: *terraglie, stoviglie* Spanish: *loza de barro*]

EAU-DE-VIE. *See* fruit brandy.

EAU-DE-VIE DE MARC. *See* marc.

EDDO. *See* yam (dasheen).

EELS are fish which show a resemblance to snakes in shape. This makes them repugnant to some people, but they are all good eating, and the common eel has become an expensive delicacy. The large marine eels, the *conger and *moray belong to different but related families.

The Common eel of Europe and North Africa (*Anguilla anguilla*) used to be a most mysterious creature. Every spring, about March, baby eels (or elvers), tiny worm-like animals only 6-8 cm (2¼-3¼ in) long and 2-3 mm (1½-1⅛ in) thick came wriggling up rivers in a massive migration known as an eel-fare. The elvers pushed on into every tiny stream and even crossed fields to reach ponds and ditches. Every autumn, large silvery eels left those ponds and ditches, reached the streams and headed down river to the sea. Old books carry descriptions of silver and yellow eels, of sharp and broad-nosed eels which were thought to be of different species. In the days when even mice were thought to arise from fermenting grain, there were bizarre notions about the origin of eels. In 1905, the International Council for the Study of the Sea assigned to Denmark the task of unravelling the life history of the eel, and Dr Johannes Schmidt of the Carlsberg Laboratory in Copenhagen was chosen to head the team. It took almost twenty years and the co-operation of countless ship's captains before the mystery was unravelled. Eels were found to breed 275 m (900 ft) down in the depths of the Atlantic to the south-west of Bermuda, not far from the Sargasso Sea. The eel larvae – very small, almost transparent leaf-like objects – drift about 5000 km (3000 miles) in the Gulf Stream until they reach the shores of Europe – a journey which takes three years. They then change their shape and turn into elvers, which swim up the rivers (a large proportion of males stay in the estuaries). They live in fresh water for eight to ten years, feeding voraciously and growing. These eels are yellow. Then they change: their eyes get larger, their lips thinner, their noses more pointed, and their colour goes from yellow to silvery before they start to migrate in autumn, crawling like snakes through the grass on wet nights, knowing where to go by some incredible instinct. Once back in the sea, they swim for their breeding ground, a journey which takes them six months to complete. The following spring, they are ready to lay their eggs in the place they left as minute larvae. After breeding, they die or so it is presumed – because they never return to their rivers. The American eel (*Anguilla rostrata*), which is closely related, breeds not far away from its European cousin and so has a shorter distance to travel. Eels in Japan (*A.japonica*), Australasia (*A.*

australis) and elsewhere have similar habits and closer breeding grounds, so they do not travel the same vast distances as the European species.

In the past, elvers were a common seasonal delicacy. In Britain, they were boiled and pressed into eel-cakes. Today, the high price of eels means that most of the elvers caught go to stock eel farms, but they can still sometimes be obtained locally, for instance, at the mouth of the Severn. Elvers are usually bought ready for cooking. As soon as they have been brought home, they should be well washed in salted water.

In Spain, elvers (*angulas*) are a popular and expensive spring treat. They are usually cooked *à la bilbaina*, quickly boiled in oil with chilli and garlic. For 300 g (11 oz) of elvers, fry 8 cloves of garlic and a red chilli in oil until the garlic begins to colour. Then put in the elvers and continue to fry for a couple of minutes. The elvers are still soft and white (they look unfortunately like parasitic worms).They are usually cooked in individual earthenware dishes, to be fished out of bubbling hot oil and eaten with a wooden spoon.

Fully grown eels are another sort of delicacy. They need to be mature; when yellow they are poor eating. The best size is under 1 kg (2 lb), although females sometimes grow to a monstrous 1½ m (5 ft) and 6 to 7 kg (about a stone). Mature silver eels are caught in nets as they migrate towards the sea in autumn. They are also fattened on eel farms. Near Venice, eels from the *valli*, as the salt-water lagoons in that part of the Adriatic are called, are kept in huge, half-sunken baskets called *bolaghe* and left to fatten until they are ready for eating.

It is a shame that pollution and modern drainage have led to drastic reduction in the numbers of eels. At one time, canals were full of eels, and barge men carried a trident-like eel-spear for jabbing at the muddy banks as they went past – eels disclose their presence by tell-tale bubbles. Even in those days, there was a pollution problem: the Dutch eel boats (there were so many that they had even their own mission in the East End of London) would not come above Gravesend for fear that the live eels, carried in perforated 'wells' open to the sea, would be poisoned.

Eels should be bought live. It is best to get the fishmonger to kill and skin your eel for you (but cook it immediately). However, it is quite easy to kill eels by banging the heads against a hard object; the trouble is they go on wriggling after they are dead. To skin an eel, cut a ring in the skin round the neck with a sharp knife. Get someone to hold the head (a skewer passed through it helps the grip) and pull the skin back, inside out, like peeling off a glove. A pair of pliers helps in gripping the skin; so also do wood ashes or coarse salt. Eels may be grilled, baked or cooked in dozens of ways. In Germany, it may be eels in dill sauce; in Britain, jellied eel is famous. Shops selling this speciality were once common in the East End of London, and there were jellied eel stalls on the streets. Eels were popular, too, in most seaside resorts. But now, alas, price has turned eels from poor man's food into a rich man's delicacy (like salmon and oysters). Eels are popular in almost every other European country from Norway, through Holland, to France, Spain and Italy. Frozen eel is imported from as far away as Japan and New Zealand (but is not as good as the freshly-killed article).

Smoked eel is also a great delicacy and an excellent, if expensive, start to a meal. The skin, dried by smoke, is easily peeled off and the fillets are removed from the backbone. Smoked eel is usually served with brown bread and butter, and lemon wedges. The finest smoked eel comes from Holland.

[Eel – French: anguille German: Aal Italian: anguilla Spanish: anguila]

EGGPLANT. See aubergine.

EGGS. It is generally stated that all fresh eggs are edible, though possibly not nice. I do not know if this bold statement is intended to cover reptile eggs – although turtle and alligator eggs are certainly good to eat; what about snake eggs? With birds' eggs, though, I feel inclined to accept the generalization. (Having climbed several times to vultures' nests, I will leave the trial of their smelly offerings to someone else.)

However, the eating of wild birds' eggs, once prevalent, has now become a matter of conscience because of our dwindling wildlife. It is also often a matter of what is allowed by law, even though, with some species, taking eggs expertly might do no harm. The nests must be found before the bird has finished laying her clutch. If only one or two eggs are now quietly taken when the bird is away feeding, she will usually go on laying to make good the loss. With management – an egg being taken every day – a continuous supply can be arranged over a period of a week or more, and yet the bird in the end can be left to hatch out a full clutch. This benefits the robber. He is following the pattern of the good parasite which does not exterminate its host. It is quite immoral to grab a whole nest of

eggs or through ignorance to cause birds to desert the nest.

Eggs have superlative food value (containing about 12% fat and 12% protein). While hens' eggs in particular are excellent value for money, they are also a promoter of good health, although in recent years some medical opinion has denigrated them. Eggs contain cholesterol, the stuff that they say clogs up the arteries. But eggs also contain lecithin – which unclogs arteries – and the sulphur-rich amino acid, methionine, which also helps in this.

As eggs are also rich in iron, in vitamin B, and in vitamin A, it is not surprising that there are doctors who greatly approve of them and advise eating up to four a day; they say that excluding eggs is a disaster, especially for people with defective circulation and heart, for whom an egg-free diet is often prescribed. One day, no doubt, the truth will be known. When people are allergic to eggs, the trouble is almost always due to the white, especially if it is raw or lightly cooked. Raw white, in fact, is said to contain traces of a harmful substance, but in practice this can be ignored. For most people, who are outside the controversy, eggs for breakfast, or with oil in mayonnaise, are probably a passport to good health.

Hen eggs. 'Egg', without qualification, always means the egg of the domestic fowl. It is an article of food produced yearly by the billion. There is scarcely a village in the whole world, outside the high Arctic, perhaps, where hens cannot be found. Indeed, eggs are probably the most universally known food of man. The domestic hen is descended from a species of jungle fowl and was domesticated in India or Indonesia, where wild jungle fowl are still common in places. Domestication took place quite early in history; and the practice of keeping hens soon spread from the East over the Old World. The Romans noted them in Britain when they arrived, but they did not reach America until they were taken there by Columbus on his second voyage.

The shell of a hen's egg is usually under 0.5 mm thick (1/50 in) and weighs roughly one-eighth of the total weight of the egg; it is made up largely of calcium carbonate. The strength of the shell varies with breed and with the hen's food and health. Battery hens often lay eggs with fragile shells. Colour may vary from dead white through cream to brown, even speckled. Brown eggs are more expensive than white eggs because they look nice, but apart from their use as boiled eggs in the shell they have only one advantage to offset their greater price – they have slightly less porous shells and so may possibly keep longer. The shells of all eggs have to be porous to some extent, to allow air to enter for the developing chick (which, we sometimes forget, was what the egg was designed for). This porosity means that aromas can enter (an advantage only if you are keeping eggs in a bag with truffles), as can micro-organisms. One in ten eggs contains harmless bacteria even when freshly laid, but less harmless kinds can get in subsequently; especially when the shell is dirty and wet. That is why, if an egg has to be washed, it should be used at once.

Lining the shell is a flexible double membrane, the two layers of which are virtually stuck together except at the large end of the egg where they separate to enclose an air space. This pocket grows bigger as the egg gets older, until after some days it gets big enough to cause the egg to float, or at least for the large end to lift off the bottom of a basin of water. It is on this that the tests for freshness are based.

The white of an egg is layered, the outer layer being more watery than the inner. Egg white consists of on average 9% protein and 88% water, and makes up a little over half the total weight of the egg. Egg white mixes with water when raw, but coagulates when heated to about 70°C (160°F) and becomes very hard and indigestible when heated to still higher temperatures. However, like meat protein, it becomes soft again when boiled for several hours, as in Chinese tea-leaf eggs and the *hamine* eggs of Egypt, for which see Claudia Roden's *A Book of Middle Eastern Food* (Penguin).

Tea-leaf eggs are boiled for 2-3 hours in water containing tea leaves and star anise, with various other additions – salt, monosodium glutamate, soy sauce, sugar, onion, etc. – according to the recipe. These eggs have pale brown marbling which is produced by cracking the shell after the first 20-30 minutes cooking, a smoother tender texture which comes from the long boiling, and flavour that has seeped in from the anise and other substances in the water. Tea-leaf eggs are served cold as *hors d'oeuvre* or with salads.

Egg white dries into a hard, shiny coat – something like varnish – and can, of course, be whipped to a firm froth (*see* whipping). In stale eggs, the white becomes watery.

The yolk is contained in a sac – the vitelline membrane – and is suspended at either end by a stringy chalaza or balancer. The chalaza is attached to the yolk so firmly that it clings to it as a tail when the egg is separated. Yolk makes up about a third of the weight of an egg and consists of 16% protein, 51% water and 30% fat. It is the most nutritious part of the egg. The colour of the yolk depends upon the food eaten by the hen.

Blemishes in commercially-packed eggs are rare because they have been examined against a light (candled) at the packing station. Blood spots, unless very large, can be ignored as they merely indicate that a tiny blood vessel was ruptured while the egg was being formed. Commercially-produced eggs are rarely fertile, but in fertile eggs a minute spot can be seen on the upper surface of the yolk. This is the germ from which the chick would develop if the egg were to be incubated. Some say that fertile eggs are better than infertile ones, an opinion not shared by vegetarians, who prefer unfertilized eggs because eating them does not involve taking life. Battery produced eggs are avoided by many people because they lack flavour and possibly some of the more subtle nutrient qualities of free-range eggs, but here the question of price is also involved.

There is, however, universal agreement that an egg is best when fresh. A simple test is to put the egg in water. If it lies flat on its side on the bottom, it is fresh; if it shows a tendency to get up at the broad end, eventually standing vertical, it is stale; if it floats under water, it is 2-3 weeks old; if it floats on the surface, it may have been laid for several months and be bad. A more sensitive test is to put the egg into 12% salt solution (which can be kept in a bottle and used many times). Fresh eggs will lie flat on the bottom, but they will get up at the broad end after only 2-3 days and will eventually hang suspended in balance when they have the same specific gravity as the brine.

At only four days, the eggs will come to the surface and float vertically with the broad end peeping out; thereafter they will float higher each day. After fifteen days, the egg will topple and lie flat, floating on the surface of the brine. This test is depressing. Most of the eggs you buy in the shops are at least a week old, good but not excellent. When broken on to a flat surface, really fresh eggs stand up in a convex mound, but as they get older the convexity decreases. In really stale eggs, the white is watery and the vitelline membrane so weakened that yolk and white mix. Such eggs may still be tolerable in cakes but are not much use for anything else.

The average egg weighs about 60 g (2 oz), large eggs 70 g (2¾ oz) or more, and small ones go down to 45 g (1½ oz); even smaller are pullet's eggs. In the poorer countries, eggs are almost always smaller than the European or American average and allowances should be made for this when following recipes from such countries.

EEC egg sizes are:

Size		
	1	over 70 g
	2	65-70 g
	3	60-65 g
	4	55-60 g
	5	50-55 g
	6	45-50 g
	7	under 45 g

These do not correspond exactly to the grades of the previous British system, in which the main sizes were large (over 62 g or 2³⁄₁₆ oz), standard (over 53 g or 1⅞ oz), medium (over 46 g or 1⅝ oz) and small (under 46 g or 1⅝ oz).

Coagulation. The white of an egg coagulates at about 60-65°C (140-149°F) and the yolk at the slightly higher temperature of 62-70°C (144-158°F). When yolk and white are mixed the coagulation takes place at about 69°C (156°F). The coagulation temperature is even higher when milk, water or sugar are added, so that custard coagulates at around 80-85°C (175-185°F). Those making custard or sauces thickened with eggs may also find it useful to know that coagulation will begin at a lower temperature – though only slightly so – when the temperature is raised slowly than it does when the temperature is raised fast, and that while the custard is thickening the temperature in it does not continue to rise because – put simply – heat is used up in the thickening process. Once the temperature starts to rise again it means that coagulation is completed. If the heating is continued, the sauce will curdle (at around 88°C/190°F). Of course, the sauce must be stirred because otherwise it will set solid, like baked custard.

Smoked eggs from China are lightly hard-boiled eggs which have been shelled, marinated and smoked. They are served as *hors d'oeuvre* or as part of a cold plate. A similar result can be obtained by marinating hard-boiled eggs in soy sauce seasoned with smoked salt and slightly sweetened with sugar.

Preserving eggs. You need to use new-laid, clean eggs. Even so, you can expect one in ten to be contaminated by bacteria. This means that a few

may go off, though they will not be dangerous, only unpleasant. Preserved eggs should always be broken one at a time into a separate container. There are many methods of preservation to choose from, some old fashioned, as follows:

Preserving eggs in lime

Make a mixture of 200-250 g (7-9 oz) slaked lime, 30-40 g (1-1½ oz) salt and 1 teaspoon cream of tartar to each 1 lt (1¾ pt) of water. Boil the mixture, but do not put the eggs in until it is stone cold. Keep in a cold cellar.

Preserving Eggs in Waterglass

Waterglass is a clear, syrupy substance, which, as bought, is a 50% solution of sodium silicate in water. Prepare according to the instructions on the tin. If there are none, try diluting it with 5-10 times the volume of water.

A 3% solution of sodium silicate is enough to preserve eggs, but 5% is really safe. Stronger solutions make the eggs taste nasty. Eggs may be dipped in waterglass, allowed to dry and stored in dry sawdust to prevent breakage. (This may be a convenient method for yachtsmen on a long voyage.) However, it is better and more usual to leave the eggs in the liquid. They must be kept between 7°C (45°F) and freezing (but not below) – e.g. in a cold cellar. If the temperature rises, even for a few hours, deterioration is rapid. Waterglass eggs should be well rinsed in fresh water before use. It is interesting to know that although the purpose of storing eggs is usually to preserve them from the spring (when there may be too many) to the autumn and winter (when the hens moult and stop laying), they can, if necessary, be kept for very much longer periods. At six months, waterglass eggs are merely a bit stale but good for most purposes. At a year, the extra storage time can scarcely be noticed. At two years, it is obvious; at three, the white starts to turn pink and become very watery, and at four years…! Nevertheless, the eggs are still quite edible, the white will still coagulate when heated, and the taste is not unpleasant.

The effect of lime or waterglass is to seal the pores in the eggshell. Other methods of doing this are also effective. Shells may be rubbed with clarified butter, dipped in molten wax or painted with gum arabic; the eggs are then stored in bone-dry sawdust, bran, charcoal or ashes. Another way is simply to pack the eggs tightly in dry salt. (They are packed thus to exclude air.) An interesting way – which relies on a thin coagulated layer – is to plunge the eggs for 20 seconds into boiling water before drying and packing them in dry bran. Some people even store eggs for shorter periods by wrapping in greaseproof paper.

Eggs will stay good for a long time if they are chilled – stored at 6°C (43°F) but not below this.

Eggs cannot be frozen in the shell. To freeze eggs, first crack them, then either separate the yolks and whites or stir the two together. Mix with either salt or sugar (according to the purpose for which they will later be used) at the rate of 1 teaspoon per dozen eggs and freeze as usual in containers. Frozen white does not return to normal after unfreezing but it can be whipped and used in cooking.

Dried egg. The idea of drying eggs was thought up in the 19th century, but was first successfully undertaken by German engineers in China in the present one. China was the principal source of dried egg for the world until the 1930s, when production became viable in the US and Britain. Dried egg production reached a peak during World War II, and immediately afterwards dropped sharply, no doubt because of a general aversion to anything to do with rationing and war-time shortages. Since then, intensive research has improved the product, and the commercial use of dried egg has grown steadily. Eggs to be dried may be separated into yolk and white or mixed up and dried whole. They are generally spray-dried and pasteurized. Drying causes little or no loss to the nutritional value of eggs, but the flavour does alter. However, dried eggs usually taste much the same as fresh eggs in custards or scrambled. The whipping qualities which are largely lost in drying can be restored by the addition of certain chemical compounds and carbohydrates such as sugar. Dried-egg products are principally used in the baking industry and in sweet manufacture (e.g. in the fondant filling for chocolates). Dried egg is now of little interest outside the food industry except to the nostalgia prone who want to follow wartime recipes and to campers in remote places.

Duck eggs have a chalky white or very pale blue shell. Many people prefer them to hen eggs for flavour. They have a distinctive taste, and a somewhat gelatinous, blue-tinted white. Some varieties of duck beat all records for egg laying – almost one a day for the whole year – but the eggs are not so popular as hen's, because ducks,

being messy and none too disciplined, may drop their eggs in dirty and contaminated places. Not all producers are fussy about what they sell, and so duck eggs have a bad reputation with the general public. Occasionally, they have become infected with *Salmonella* bacteria and have caused food poisoning.

However, duck eggs are very popular in the Far East and are the basis for the famous Chinese thousand year eggs (*trúng-den*).They are in fact ready to eat in something under two months and become solid by a maturation process – ripened as if they were cheese. The egg inside is variable in colour from greenish yellow to malachite green and black, usually in concentric rings, following the pattern of the original egg layers. The texture is smooth and creamy, the flavour original and unlike anything else, although overtones of bad egg are detectable when they are first broached. Thousand year eggs are served at the start of a meal, usually quartered and served as an appetizer, perhaps with lime and fresh ginger. They can be bought at shops which specialize in Chinese foods, but it is probably better to be introduced to them by Chinese friends who know what a good bad egg should taste like.

Salted eggs are another Chinese speciality. These duck eggs preserved in strong brine may be bought from Chinese provision shops and are very salty. Keep them in a refrigerator.

Thousand Year Eggs

For a couple of dozen absolutely clean and fresh duck eggs, mix up a paste of 120 g (4½ oz) each of salt and wood ash, and 100 g (3½ oz) slaked lime, with about ½ lt (1 pt) of water. Wash the eggs in hot water and roll each one in a handful of the 'paste', coating each about 1 cm (½ in) thick. Roll each coated egg in chaff to give it a non-stick coating. Pile the eggs in a crack and cover with a lid. After 3 days turn the pile over, eggs on top to the bottom, and do this every 3 days for 15 days. After that, seal the jar and leave it for a month. The eggs are now ready to eat. Remove paste and shell, and cut the cheesy egg into pieces for serving.

Goose eggs are something like a very large duck egg, but rather milder in flavour.

Guinea-fowl eggs look something like small hen eggs and are of excellent quality with a mild flavour.

Black-headed gull eggs have now replaced

plover eggs. They have a somewhat similar appearance (brownish olive-green with dark brown spots) and are not much larger. They are good, but not quite equal to plover eggs, like which they are usually eaten hard boiled. The eggs of the herring gull and other seabirds (e.g. the gannet) were – and still are in places – harvested off the cliffs. I remember from my childhood the egg-gatherers arriving yearly with ropes at the great red sandstone cliffs of St Bees Head. After gathering eggs, they boiled great buckets of them on the beach below. This was a wasteful process, as many of the eggs already had chicks half developed inside them. The eggs of herring gulls are tolerable if fresh, though stronger than those of the black-headed gull. In the past, they were an essential food to many islanders, but their collection is no longer necessary, and it is hardly worth risking your neck to get them.

Moorhen eggs. The eggs of this common bird are good and were once much taken by country people. Provided eggs are removed quietly, a few at a time, moorhens will go on laying for many weeks.

Ostrich eggs are available only in South Africa and other places where ostriches are farmed. These enormous eggs are equivalent to one to two dozen hen eggs. They have a rather eggy taste, but are excellent for cooking and are sometimes sold as dried egg.

Partridge and **pheasant eggs** are sometimes available where game birds are bred. They are smaller than hen eggs and are excellent.

Penguin eggs. Penguins nest in huge rookeries, so the eggs just beg to be gathered and eaten. Eggs of the Cape or jackass penguin are officially taken in modest numbers from the islands off Cape Province, in South Africa. They fetch a high price. Penguin eggs are peculiar, in that the whites remain clear even when they are hard boiled (so they look like eyes on the plate), but since they are usually eaten well laced with Worcestershire sauce, I cannot help feeling that motives for eating them are more snobbish than gastronomic.

Pigeon eggs. Small and delicious, pinkish-white eggs, most often served hard boiled. As the author of the Time-Life publication *The Cooking of China* says, it is something of a chore to eat a hard boiled pigeon's egg with chopsticks, and anyone who has mastered the art can justly claim to be an expert.

Plover eggs. In the past, these were considered a great delicacy, and there are recipes for them, not only hard boiled, but also cooked in other ways. Unfortunately, the population of plovers has declined (mainly because of changes in agricultural methods), and it is now against the law to gather the eggs in Britain. Plovers must have been very plentiful in the past – because their nests are hard to find – and gathering was done by professionals with the care necessary to induce the birds to go on laying over a period and subsequently to hatch their normal setting.

Quail eggs. Very small eggs, usually eaten hard boiled. They have become available in recent years as a by-product of quail farming. For a long time, they have been highly regarded as a delicacy in the Far East.

Turkey eggs. Large, brown, spotted eggs of excellent quality. The smaller eggs of young birds – paler than those of older birds – are good boiled, the others are used for cooking. They taste rather like hen eggs and make splendid omelettes.

[*Egg* – French: *oeuf* German: *Ei* Italian: *uovo* Spanish: *huevo*]

EGUSI MELON. *See* marrow (*Cucumeropsis edulis*).

EGYPTIAN PEA. *See* chickpea.

EGYPTIAN BEAN. *See* chickpea, lablab bean.

ELDER. There are many species of elder in Europe, Asia and North America. Both the European common elder (*Sambucus nigra*) and the American elder (*S. canadensis*) have clusters of white flowers followed by dark purple to black berries. The flowers have a sickly smell, supposed to be like muscatel grapes, and bunches are stirred into wine, jam, jelly or stewed fruit (particularly gooseberries) to impart their aroma. The flowers are edible and may even be fried in batter. The berries are used for making wine, for colouring jellies, and for preserves, fruit soups and ketchup, they are also dried. However, their strange taste limits their use.

[*Elder* – French: *sureau* German: *Holunder* Italian: *sambuco* Spanish: *saúco*]

ELEPHANT'S EAR. *See* yam (dasheen).

ELVER. Baby *eel.

EMULSIONS. An emulsion is a mixture of two liquids which are not mutually soluble, for example, oil and water. Instead, one liquid is dispersed as tiny globules in the other. The emulsions which mainly concern us in cooking are of oil and water. Milk is an emulsion, and so is mayonnaise. Emulsions can be made by forcing oil and water together through a fine nozzle, or by using emulsifying agents such as egg yolk or some mustards. Emulsions break when the globules of like substances come together and amalgamate.

[*Emulsion* – French: *émulsion* German: *Emulsion* Italian: *emusione* Spanish: *emulsión*]

ENDIVE. *See* chicory.

ENO'S FRUIT SALTS. This famous old nursery indigestion remedy, which fizzes violently when water is added, consists of bicarbonate of soda (55.58%) with tartaric acid (36.61%) and anhydrous citric acid (7.81%).To use it as a substitute leavening agent, you have to mix it in pretty quickly, or the carbon dioxide gas will be gone before it can be effective.

ENZYMES, which were also called ferments, are organic catalysts fabricated by living cells. Catalysts are substances which cause or accelerate chemical changes without themselves being used up or permanently altered in the process. In nature, there are countless numbers of enzymes, each of which is responsible for its own reaction or group of reactions. Enzymes, in other words, are specific. They control and initiate most of the chemical reactions making up the life processes. Some operate only inside living cells. Others can also function outside the cell or after the organism that created them has died. Enzymes are sensitive to temperature; many will be killed by heat or strong chemicals, almost as if they were living. They may also be prevented from working by substances such as salt and vinegar. Enzymes produced by yeasts, fungi and bacteria are responsible for many natural food processes such as fermentation, ripening of cheese, souring of milk and vinegar production. Plant enzymes play their part in such diverse operations as producing a bitter-almond flavour in peach stones (or bitter almonds), a bite in mustard, or the spoilage of unblanched vegetables in the deep freezer. The names of enzymes end in -ase. For instance, an enzyme which oxidises is an oxidase, and one that hydrolyses carbohydrates is a carbohydrase. Pectinase acts on pectin.

Invertase (produced by most yeasts and moulds) inverts sugar. There are proteinases, phosphatases, glycerophos-phatases, and polysaccharidases, even penicillinases. This is the specialist world of the biochemist, the cheese technologist and the brewer, but we should register the simple fact that most things we handle in the kitchen are subject to alteration by enzymes and that changes, one after another in patterns of astronomical complexity, are constantly going on in foods we keep (except in those that have been treated to prolong their shelf life).

[*Enzyme* – French: *enzyme* German: *Enzym* Italian: *enzima* Spanish: *enzima*]

EPAZOTE, Mexican tea, or wormseed. This is a strongly-flavoured herb, native to tropical America. It is best fresh, but can also be dried. The plant (*Chenopodium ambrosloides*) belongs to the same family as goosefoot and spinach. It grows wild as an escape in parks and backyards in New York City, although it does not have such a strong flavour there as it does further south. It is not available in Britain, where it would presumably grow – it can be wintered in a pot indoors. The flavour is strong (the name comes from Nahuatl *epatl* and *tzotl* meaning an animal smelling like a skunk, something dirty). It is used in soups, with beans, in tortilla dishes, etc.

ERGOT. *See* moulds.

ESCABECHE. *See* caveach.

ESCARGOT. *See* snail.

ESCAROLE. *See* chicory.

ESSENCES. An essence should contain the fundamental quality of a substance in a concentrated form, but in cooking the word is given many loose meanings. Flavoured waters, like orange-flower water, rosewater and *kewra* water are sometimes called essences because they are liquids in bottles, as are coffee essences and *sirops*. The French use of the word implies the natural, concentrated juices which run from food during cooking – the juices from roasting meat, for instance. However, with these exceptions – and a few concentrated products like essence of rennet – we are dealing with flavourings in bottles; they may be extracts, essential oils (natural or synthetic) or new chemical compounds created by the chemists. Powders, produced by drying under reduced pressure, may strictly speaking be essences but are not usually so regarded. It is best to forget definitions and to discuss the whole complex together.

Essences may be made by extracting with a solvent. If the solvent is harmless, like water or alcohol, the essential flavourings may be left in solution (a tincture), but other solvents such as hydrocarbons or ether have subsequently to be removed by evaporation. On the other hand, essential oils, which are found in aromatic herbs and spices, are usually volatile and can be obtained from the natural source by distillation (usually by steam distillation as they are often fragile). Rose oil (attar of roses), for instance, has been made for many hundreds of years by simple distillation from a watery mash.

Modern techniques can separate and purify the various essential oils. For instance, the aroma and taste of dill or sage can be extracted and split up into its various components, even though it is usual for something to be lost in the process. Manufacturers like these essential oils, and we cannot entirely blame them. The public expects a particular product always to taste the same, something that is very difficult to achieve using natural (and thus highly variable) herbs and spices. It is much easier to reconstitute the components to a fixed formula. However, out of the two thousand or so flavourings currently available to the food industry, only some five hundred are in any way natural; the balance is entirely the brain-children of chemists and are not known to occur in plants in nature. Artificial flavourings are imitations of natural ones, perhaps, and may contain twenty or more separate substances in carefully formulated proportion. Since the food industry employs very expert 'cooks', who conduct thousands of tests, the products they come up with are often exceedingly popular. However much purists may denigrate the food industry (and not without reason), the fact remains that sales of a food do not depend entirely on appearance and advertising, but also on whether people like the product. One cannot even claim that what is natural is harmless and what is synthetic is harmful. Essential oils from household flavourings like nutmeg, cloves, cinnamon, pennyroyal and even peppermint are harmful in quantity, and so also must these herbs and spices be if you eat enough of them, while no doubt many of the synthetics are harmless. The problem is to know it, while we are checking their long-term safety, we may be at risk.

And how many of this bewildering range of substances are really necessary? One thing cooks can learn from the food trade is that small, unrecognizable quantities of very unlikely flavourings can be used in improbable contexts. You might be astounded to know that the oil distilled from rue (a nasty smelling herb) is used, for instance, in raspberry and blueberry flavourings. It is even used in rum and peach flavourings. Asafoetida (another horrid smell) goes into ice cream and candy (what sort is not specified), eucalyptus into ginger-ale flavour. All this should encourage us to experiment.

[*Essence* – French: *essence* German: *Extrakt* Italian: *essenza* Spanish: *esencia*]

ESSENTIAL OIL Volatile oil containing substances which provide flavour and aroma. Essential oils may be extracted (e.g. from the skins of *citrus fruits) and used in perfumery or as *essences.

EVAPORATED MILK is unsweetened whole milk which has been evaporated to half its original volume, homogenized, canned and sterilized by heat (unlike *condensed milk which has sugar added as a preservative). Diluted with an equal quantity of water, it can be a substitute for fresh milk in all recipes that do not involve the use of rennet. Undiluted, it can make a substitute for cream, although it has a boiled milk taste. It can be whipped if the unopened can is first heated in boiling water for 20 minutes and then cooled before opening or, more simply, if it is put into the refrigerator for 12 hours and then mixed with 2½ tablespoons of lemon juice before whipping.

EXTRACTS in cooking are flavourings which have been dissolved out and concentrated. They thus include natural *essences, which are extracts, for example, of spices and fruit peels, usually made with ethyl alcohol. Also classified as extracts are meat concentrates, which are effectively clarified *stocks that have been boiled down to a fraction of their initial volume and stored for use in sauces and gravies. Commercial beef extracts such as Bovril and Oxo contain salt, yeast extract and various other flavouring ingredients.

f

FAGGOT. An old English way of using the insides of the pig, very similar in concept to the French *gayette* and *crépinette*. All are made of minced meats with flavourings parcelled up in *caul. Much less time is needed to make faggots than to make sausages, at least if you are doing it from scratch. Traditionally liver, lungs, spleen, and scraps are minced with fat, usually a filler such as breadcrumbs. and flavourings such as onion, sage (or other herbs), spices (mainly pepper and nutmeg or mace) and salt. The mixture is rolled in squares of caul, packed in a tin and baked brown on top. Faggots are available locally at butchers in Britain, particularly in the Midlands and north of England, and in parts of Wales. An old-fashioned convenience food which can be eaten hot with gravy or cold, they are also available frozen. These and other widely distributed versions may contain a less enterprising range of ingredients than the traditional faggot.

FAHRENHEIT. Named after German physicist, Gabriel Daniel Fahrenheit (1686-1736), this system of measuring temperature is only just being phased out of use. Fahrenheit took as zero the temperature of an equal mixture of snow and salt and, as 100, the temperature of the human body. This put the freezing point of water at 32°F and its boiling point at 212°F – a difference of 180. Improved instruments later showed that the temperature of the human body was not exactly 100°F. Although the Fahrenheit scale was satisfactory for all daily purposes, it was not used by science because the *Celsius scale was linked with metric definitions.

FARINA. Although this word is applied to any flour (for instance, *farina dolce* is chestnut flour in Italy), it is most often applied to potato flour. This mixes easily with water and absorbs it quickly. It is a good binder, so is used commercially as a filler in cooked sausages, where a compact texture is needed. Farina made from wheat, another common type, would not produce the same result, so one cannot necessarily substitute one farina for another.

Fecula is much the same as farina, but with the starch separated from the source (potato, corn or arrowroot) by washing with water, it is then allowed to settle out and is dried. *Cornflour and *arrowroot are typical feculas.

FATS and **OILS** are essentially similar substances, fats being solid and oils being liquid at ordinary room temperatures. Mutton fat will melt in places as hot as Death Valley and sunflower oil will solidify when the Fahrenheit thermometer reads zero (-18°C). A little simple chemistry is necessary to show what is meant by words such as saturated and polyunsaturated, which are much bandied about in discussions on diet and health. Fats and oils are formed by the combination of a fatty acid with an *alcohol (usually glycerine).There are dozens of fatty acids, of which the simplest is *formic acid ($HCOOH$) and the next *acetic acid (CH_3COOH).

The fatty acids form a series of ascending complexity which goes on through butyric acid (C_3H_7COOH), which is found in rancid butter, and caproic acid ($C_5H_{11}COOH$), the smell of billy goats, to the very much larger molecules involved in most of the fats. The molecules are composed of carbon, and hydrogen atoms in chains, and when these chains contain only carbon atoms with their fullest possible complement of hydrogen atoms attached, then the fatty acid and any fat formed from it are said to be saturated – their molecules can take no more hydrogen. But in some fatty acid molecules, there are extra linkages between adjacent pairs of carbon atoms in the chain and each of the two carbon atoms involved in such a double bond consequently has one less hydrogen atom linked to it. The fatty acid is then unsaturated – monounsaturated if it has one double bond, polyunsaturated if it has more than one.

The double bond represents a potentially active point in the chain, and unsaturated fats are thus less stable and more easily changed. For instance, it is relatively easy for the oxygen in the air to attack the double bonds. The oxidation products have an unpleasant smell and taste – we say the oil has gone rancid. But if the double bonds are replaced by extra hydrogen atoms – a process known as hydrogenation – then the slow oxidation is prevented.

Hydrogenation also raises the melting point, and the unsaturated oil becomes a saturated fat – the basis of margarine production.

As an industrial process, hydrogenation involves heating oil with hydrogen under pressure, using nickel as a catalyst. Any unsaturated oil can be hydrogenated – fish oil, whale oil or vegetable oil (even mineral oils, but they are not used in food). Saturated fats keep well, but if they are consumed in large quantities, they are often associated with raised serum cholesterol levels and may be involved in the development of atherosclerosis, a condition in which arteries, such as coronary arteries, become clogged with a fatty deposit. Monounsaturated fats are relatively neutral in this respect, but people who switch to eating less saturated fat and more polyunsaturated fat can benefit from the lowering of their serum cholesterol level. The value of partially substituting polyunsaturates for saturated fat is still a controversial issue, but it is recommended by several well-known medical bodies throughout the world.

Of the vegetable oils regarded as suitable in a low-cholesterol diet, safflower, sunflower, soya, cottonseed, corn and sesame are best, but wheat-germ oil has exceptional qualities when raw and fresh. Olive oil and peanut oil are in the middle category, as are the oils in some nuts and in avocado pears. Oils in fish are generally good – some, like herring oil, very good – and chicken fat is tolerable. But coconut oil or fat, ordinary commercial hydrogenated peanut butter, palm oil, butter, pork, mutton and beef dripping are medium to high in saturated fats, as also are hard margarines and vegetable shortening.

A few fatty acids are suspected of being potential health hazards. One such is erucic acid, which when used experimentally in large quantities has been suspected of causing damage to heart muscle in animals. Significant quantities have been found only in rapeseed oil but new strains of rape now yield fats with little or no erucic acid content. Within the EEC, consumers are protected by a directive which fixes the maximum permitted level of erucic acid in oils and fats intended for human consumption. The allied mustard oil is much used in Indian cooking in various areas, particularly in Bengal, and might be suspect.

We should not worry unduly about this, but remember that over the centuries man has evolved a physiology to deal with a wide variety of different foods. He is likely to get into trouble only when he takes a lot of any one thing continuously, without a change.

The best oils gastronomically are cold pressed and retain some of the flavour of their origin. Some oils that come from oilseeds have tastes which are thought displeasing or interfere with the purposes for which they will be used. This is particularly so when the oils have been heat treated or extracted with solvents. These oils are decolourized and stripped of their flavours by heating with steam under reduced pressure. Such treatment will remove nasty – indeed almost any – tastes.

In normal conditions, fats and oils exposed to the air gradually go rancid because of oxidation. This can be arrested only by extreme measures, such as removing the air (as when nuts are sealed in a vacuum). Polyunsaturated oils, being more reactive than saturated fats, go rancid more quickly. The process is encouraged by traces of metals (molybdenum, nickel, copper) which act as catalysts, by ultra-violet light (so oils are best stored in the dark), by the presence of free fatty acids (present as impurities or produced by heating) and by warmth (since it makes chemical reactions go faster).

Common sense therefore dictates keeping oils in a cool place, decanting from large containers into small ones for use and keeping bottles full. Many fresh cold-pressed oils naturally contain vitamin E, an anti-oxidant which helps protect the oil from going rancid. In some countries manufacturers may add synthetic anti-oxidants (even vitamin E sometimes) and sequestrants. The latter are chemicals that hijack stray ions and attach themselves to metals. They render inactive the substances that encourage changes. Sequestrants are much used to maintain colour, flavour and texture in commercial products, from beverages to canned crab.

Oil that has been continually heated in the deep fryer is prone to rancidity, because of the accumulation of free fatty acids; its polyunsaturated fat and vitamin content are slowly reduced, and it may acquire an unpleasant flavour. There is even the possibility of harmful substances eventually being produced if the oil is overheated. Frying oil should be discarded if it smells objectionable, foams excessively, smokes easily and darkens in colour. Fat for deep frying lasts longer if it is kept clean by straining between fryings. It should be used at a temperature below its smoke point; and at other times should be kept carefully covered, cool and away from air and light. The metal from which the cooking utensil is made is important. Iron pans and, worse still, untinned brass or copper pans, encourage fats to break down, but stainless steel or chromium-plated pans do not have this effect.

Some frying fats can stand heating to about 280°C (450°F) before they break down. In general, the more saturated the fat, the higher the temperature it will tolerate. Unsaturated fats break down at lower temperatures, although their performance in this respect can be improved by refining.

The type of oil or fat used in the kitchen is immensely important. Fats give flavour and character and even the most careful stripping does not render them entirely neutral. Even if tasteless, they each have their own quality of 'greasiness' and produce quite different results when mixed with flour in a sauce, boiled in a pudding or used in a pastry. Recipe instructions which just call for 'oil' or 'shortening' should be more specific – the difference between mayonnaise made with olive oil and maize oil will be only too obvious.

It is common knowledge that Normandy cooks with butter, Provence with oil, eastern France with lard and south-western France with goose fat – not always, of course, but often enough to give a regional flavour. Pastry is usually made with butter, margarine, lard, or a mixture; or it may be made with a modern hydrogenated fat. Each gives a different result. My neighbour makes her pastry with olive oil; the result is very rich and crumbly.

There is an incredible difference between a curry made with *ghee*, coconut oil, *til* (sesame seed oil), or *Dalda* (hydrogenated fat), and this comes through any amount of spice and chilli. The Chinese do not use butter. The lard that is much used in Chinese cooking is not the tasteless steam-stripped version that comes in packets, but the more flavourful rendered pork fat. Chinese cooking also uses oils such as sesame and peanut, but the sesame oil which is employed as a flavouring is a virgin one which has not been stripped of its natural taste.

These few examples are mentioned here only to show the enormous significance of the choice of oil or fat in cooking. The most important fats and oils in the alphabetical list below have their own entries elsewhere in this book.

Almond oil is sweet and is made by pressing milled sweet *almonds (the less shapely varieties) or from bitter almonds. In bitter almond oil, traces of hydrocyanic acid and benzaldehyde have to be eliminated. Almond oil is expensive, and may be bought from chemists. Its main use is in confectionery, both on moulds to stop boiled sugar sticking and on the marble slabs where hot sugar is to be worked or toffee kneaded. It is valuable in the kitchen to coat moulds for sweet things.

Animal fats tend to be entirely saturated (containing on average over 40% saturated fatty acids) and so are used less than they used to be in days before cholesterol was considered to be a health factor. However, they are vital flavours in regional cooking. Many are dealt with below.

Arachide. Peanut oil (*see* below).

Avocado oil. The *avocado has a high fat content, around 30% and is sometimes used as a source of oil. In this, 20% of the fatty acids are saturated, 65% are monounsaturated, and some 15% are polyunsaturated.

Beef fat is suitable for frying, but is rarely available in modern families which eat small, lean joints. It contains more saturated fatty acids than any other fat in general use, but farmers in the north of England where I lived as a boy regularly ate bread and *dripping and lived long and active lives. In Yorkshire, beef dripping is still used for frying chips, and alternatives are despised.

***Butter** consists mainly of butterfat. It has 40% of saturated fatty acids and very few polyunsaturated fatty acids (4%). It remains the most delicious cooking fat, but may need to be clarified before use.

Candlenut oil is used somewhat locally in South East Asia, where *candlenuts grow.

***Castor oil** is medicinal, as well as nasty. I have heard of it being used to grease the iron plate used for baking in India.

Chicken fat is not too saturated for an animal fat, with 35% saturated fatty acids, 50% mono-unsaturated (i.e. neutral) and 15% polyunsaturated, depending on what the chicken has eaten. Chicken fat is softer and nearer in consistency to oil than other animal fats. When clarified, it fries well and can be heated to 200°C (392°F) without burning. It is much used in south-western France and in Jewish cooking, perhaps because it is the nearest thing to butter which they can use with meat, as dietary laws forbid meat and dairy products being used together.

Coconut oil is one of the most saturated of vegetable fats and has an almost buttery consistency. Saturated fatty acids form about 75% of the total. However, the taste of *coconut is necessary in much tropical cooking, though it is often added in the form of coconut milk or cream. Coconut oil itself may be needed in the cooking of India, South East Asia, the West Indies, and the Pacific. It is a common constituent of vegetable cooking fats and margarines and is good for frying as it can be heated to 250°C (482°F) before it burns. It is not, however, very easily digested.

Cocoa butter is the fat which is pressed out of cocoa beans. White or yellowish and with a chocolate smell, it is full of highly saturated fatty acids and is firm at room temperature. It is a main constituent of bar chocolate and is not usually a kitchen ingredient.

Cod-liver oil is very rich in vitamins, like other fish liver oils. It is especially so in vitamin D (which may be lacking in the diets of the less sunny northern countries) and is used as a diet supplement.

Colza oil is extracted by cold-pressing the seeds of *Brassica napus* (rape) and *B. campestris* (field mustard). It is used in salad oils and cooking oil mixtures in Europe.

Corn oil is expressed from the germ of maize (which in some is 50% oil). It contains 15% saturated fatty acids, but 35% monounsaturated and 50% polyunsaturated. From the cook's point of view, it is all right for frying, but not in the top bracket as a raw oil. You can make mayonnaise with it very easily, as it readily emulsifies, but the result is rather nasty. Some people also detect unpleasant flavours in corn oil.

*Cotton-seed oil. A good oil for cooking and salads. It contains 25% saturated fatty acids, 20% monounsaturated and 50% polyunsaturated.

*Dripping usually means beef fat (*see* above).

Fish oils generally have a low saturated fat content. Herring oil, for instance, has 20%

saturated fatty acids, 45% monounsaturated and 50% polyunsaturated. Oily fish may be as much as 30% fat and are likely to be high in the fat-soluble vitamins.

Frying oils. Oils that are marketed as frying oils may have a cotton-seed oil base or be a mixture of vegetable oils; they will normally be cheaper than those labelled as salad oils. They are sometimes perfumed with lemon, but essentially are highly-stripped oils with little or no taste of their own. When they are used for deep frying, it matters little from a dietary viewpoint what oils are in the mixture.

Ghee. Indian clarified *butter.

Goose fat is a good cooking fat, with some of the characteristics of chicken fat. It is soft and can be heated to around 200°C (390°F) before it burns. It imparts a characteristic taste to any food cooked with it.

Grape-pip oil. An oil extracted from the residues of grapes.

Groundnut oil. Peanut oil (*see* below).

Horse fat, claimed by a few to be the best for deep frying and used in some restaurants, may be obtained from the horse butchers, which are common in European countries.

Hydrogenated fats. Many brands of cooking fat, such as Crisco, Spry, Trex and Dalda are made by hydrogenating oils from various sources; they look approximately like lard. Though lacking in flavour, these products can be very useful in everyday cooking.

*Lard is purified pork fat.

Linseed oil is pressed from the seed of the flax plant (*Linum usitatissimum*). It is an important ingredient in paints and varnishes, for which it is extracted with heat and pressure or with solvents. However, such oils are only for painting. Cold-pressed linseed oil, on the other hand, is used as a food oil, and has very healthy qualities. It is particularly rich in one of the essential fatty acids, linoleic acid.

*Margarine is made from oils which may be partly

hardened by hydrogenation and emulsified with water containing salt and whey or skimmed milk.

Mineral oils. In general, these are very undesirable in foods, and there are horrific stories of the effects produced when unscrupulous vendors have sold them for frying. However, highly purified mineral oil of the type which is used medicinally under the name of liquid paraffin is common in food production. A little of the mineral oil used to lubricate machinery, such as choppers and mincers, gets into food. Mineral oil is used as a defoaming compound, to coat and give a shine to dried fruit and, in confectionery, to seal and moisture-proof surfaces. Although it is an inert substance, its power of coating and isolating interferes with the body's absorption of vitamins A and D. Although the quantities eaten with food are probably too small to matter, liquid paraffin in quantity can cause severe medical problems, so it is best avoided. Petroleum jelly (such as Vaseline) and paraffin wax are similar mineral hydrocarbons, though with larger molecules. Paraffin wax is solid at body temperature and is inert. It is used for sealing surfaces of preserves to exclude organisms and moisture, but it is slightly permeable to oxygen. It is also used in chewing gums. Vaseline is sometimes used in the kitchen for coating iron utensils to stop them rusting. It should be cleaned away completely before a utensil is used on the stove.

Mowra butter, also known as bassia fat and illipe butter (Tamil: *illupai*), is a fat extracted from the *mohwa* or Indian butter tree (*Madhuca indica* and *M. longifolia*), which grows wild in the jungles in the dry, hilly regions of Central India. In spring, the flowers, with their long sweet tubes, attract peacocks, bears and other wild creatures, while the villagers sweep the ground clean under the trees and harvest the flowers, which they use to make a wine or dry for food. Later, the greenish-yellow fruits, about the size of an egg, are gathered. The seeds contain 55-65% of a soft yellow oil. In India, it is used locally for cooking and also exported to be made into margarine.

Mustard oil. An important cooking oil in India, where it is a generic term covering *sarson* oil (from varieties of turnip, *Brassica rapa*, which are grown for oil seed and not for fat tap-roots), *toria* (from another variety of turnip), *taramira* or *tara* (from *rocket, Eruca sativa*) and *rai* (from Indian mustard, *Brassica juncea*). In the food trade, all these are described as rapeseed or colza oil, except *rai*, which is known as mustard oil.

Mustard oil is much used in Indian cooking. It may have a strong mustard flavour (which vanishes on heating), and the oil is not, to my knowledge, ever used raw. Although there is some difference in taste when curries are made with mustard oil rather than other oils, the great value of mustard oil is in making Indian pickles which then never seem to go bad, even when opened. (A home-made aubergine pickle left for three years after opening was still in perfect condition.) Mustard oil is available in Indian shops, but is rather expensive. It is worth trying.

Mutton fat or **lamb fat**. This is the least used common fat in Western cooking. It is hard and has a flavour which many find incompatible with other foods. Those who fear fat for health reasons avoid it as it is highly saturated, containing about 50% saturated fatty acids, 45% monosaturated and only 5% polyunsaturated. However, in the Middle East, with its hard people and hard lands, fat-tailed sheep and mutton fat are prized foods. Meat is preserved in mutton fat (*qwwrama*) and eggs are fried in it, which gives them a characteristic taste.

Niger oil. The niger plant (*Guizotia abyssinica*) is a composite which is a native of tropical Africa and especially of Ethiopia. It is grown as an oil seed in many areas, although India is the largest producer. The seeds contain up to 50% oil and are sometimes ground into a chutney. The oil is pale yellow, with a nice, nutty taste. By the time it reaches the shops, it has usually been blended with other oils for cooking.

Nut oils. Oils expressed from nuts such as pecans, filberts, pistachios, brazils and cashews are expensive but are a way of using nuts which are too small or broken to be sold without processing. These oils are used for confectionery or cosmetics. Locally, there are also nut oils of varieties so local that they scarcely get outside their native jungles. The only oils from temperate zone nuts that are in common kitchen use are almond oil and walnut oil.

*Olive oil. The original oil, and the word 'oil' even comes from the same root as 'olive'. The Spanish word for oil, *aceite* (not to be confused with *aceto*, the Italian for vinegar), comes from the Arab word, *az-zait*, meaning fruit of the olive. It contains 15% saturated fatty acids, 75% monounsaturated and 10% polyunsaturated. Olive oil and seed oils are often custom-mixed, on demand, in village shops in Europe.

161

Palm oil comes from the fruit of the African Oil palm (*Elais gutneensis*), which is native to West Africa, though cultivated elsewhere in the tropics. In Honduras, it is called *dendê* oil. Palm-kernel oil is a more delicate white oil expressed from just the kernels rather than from the whole pulp. It has a pleasant flavour and is much used by margarine and candy manufacturers. There are many other palm oils which come from Brazilian species of palm, notably *babassu, cohune, licuri, tucum* and *murumuru* palm oils. Anyone who stays in a West African household will meet the special and rather nice oily taste of palm oil (which is characteristic of the food there) the first time there are fried eggs for breakfast. Palm oil is rich in saturated fatty acids – 40% – with 40% monounsaturates and only 10% polyunsaturates.

Paraffin oil. A mineral oil (*see* above).

Peanut oil or **groundnut oil**. One of the most important cooking oils and preferred on salads by those who do not like olive oil. It congeals at 5°C (23°F) and can be heated to 218°C (424°F) before it reaches its smoke point and starts to deteriorate. It contains about 20% saturated fatty acids, 50% monounsaturates, and 30% polyunsaturates. The biggest *peanut producers are India and China, but the main exporters are the US, Senegal and the Sudan. Processing facilities tend to be near ports such as Liverpool, Hamburg or Marseilles.

Perilla oil is an oil from the seeds of the perilla (*Perilla frutescens*), a labiate plant which is native to northern India, China and Japan. An edible oil can be got by crushing the roasted seeds, and this has been used in oriental food from very early times.

Poppy seed oil is expressed from opium *poppy seeds. The first pressing gives a fine oil which can be used as a salad oil, but the reddish oil from a second pressing with heat is inedible and used as a medium by painters. Poppy seed oil – *huile blanche* – is well known in northern France.

Pork fat is marginally less saturated than that of mutton or beef (saturated fatty acids 28%, monosaturated 50%, polyunsaturated 8%) but cooks use it because they like it. Purified pork fat is *lard.

Rape seed oil. According to some authorities, rape (*Brassica napus*) is another cultivated variety of the same species as the swede. It can be found growing wild over most of Europe. The green tops are poisonous to cattle, and large quantities of rape seed oil should not be used because of the high erucic acid content. It contains 5% saturated fatty acids, 15% monounsaturated and 15% polyunsaturated. It is used a lot in Indian cooking and may be referred to as colza or mustard oil (*see* above).

Safflower oil comes from the seed of a kind of thistle (*Carthamus tinctorius*), which is possibly native to the mountains of Abyssinia and Afghanistan, but has escaped in southern Europe. It is cultivated in Egypt, Iran, India and China as well as in the US. At one time, it was also grown for the yellow dye which can be extracted from the dried flower petals. The oil content of the seeds is 24-36%, and the seeds can be roasted and eaten, but more usually the oil, which is golden yellow, is used for cooking and to adulterate *ghee*. It is an oil high in polyunsaturated fatty acids (75%) and low in saturated ones (10%). Pure safflower oil can sometimes be bought in health-food shops; it is a good source of vitamin E.

Salad oils. The salad oil *par excellence* is *olive oil, if it is light and delicately flavoured, but heavy, fruity olive oils are not liked by most people. If good olive oil is not available, it is best to copy the French and use peanut oil, poppy oil, or other delicate oil to replace it. Strongly flavoured oils, like walnut oil, are favoured in some parts of France, but again it is a matter of taste. Commercial salad oils are usually a mixture, and are adequate but never sensational. Since oil should make up three-quarters of a French dressing, its quality is of the first importance in salads.

Sesame oil. The *sesame plant (*Sesamum indicum*) is probably native to India, which ranks first in production, but it is also grown over a wide area of the Orient. Sesame oil is much used in South Indian cooking, and its nutty flavour makes it excellent for many purposes if it can be found unmixed with other oils.

Shortening. Originally this was fat which made pastry short or brittle, but it is now a general American term for fat or oil of any sort.

Soya oil. The *soya bean is now one of the world's most important sources of vegetable oil. Soya is the cheapest vegetable oil in many places. It is nutritionally excellent, but often has a slightly fishy smell. Soya oil is high in polyunsaturated fatty acids – 55% against 10% saturated and 25% monounsaturated. Most people would probably rate this oil lower than most of the other important ones for flavour.

*Suet is the hard fat from around the kidneys of an ox. It has a very definite flavour which is necessary in suet crust for steak and kidney puddings and for suet pudding. Commercial suet contains quite a lot of flour or starch (15%) which is needed to keep the chopped fat pieces separate.

Sunflower oil. The oil extracted from the seeds of the sunflower (Helianthus annuus) is of ever-growing importance. The seeds contain up to 45% of a pale golden oil which has an excellent taste and very high nutritive and dietary value. The percentage of saturated fatty acid is only 5%, of the neutral monounsaturates 25% and of the polyunsaturates as much as 65%. It is a pity to use sunflower oil for deep frying, but for all other kitchen uses, including making mayonnaise and dressing salads, it is excellent.

Sweet oil may mean a nut oil like almond oil, although oils are not actually sweet. It can also mean oils that are not rancid.

Tallow is any coarse, hard fat. In the past, tallow was used for candles. Occasionally, in old books, you are told to smear something with tallow, or to use tallow for some kitchen purpose.

Triglycerides. Fats and oils are esters of the alcohol glycerol (glycerine) with long-chain fatty acids. A triglyceride molecule is made up of one molecule of glycerol combined with three fatty acid molecules. Triglycerides are the ordinary fats. You may come on the term in diet books relating to the triglycerides in the blood.

Walnut oil. Oil expressed from *walnuts is used in parts of France as a salad oil, although it is expensive. Walnut oil from the Dordogne, but not that from Jura or the Loire, is strong tasting and thus will not be liked by everyone.

Whale oil. I remember being taken down into the bowels of a whaling factory-ship somewhere south of South Georgia, and shown a clear, water-white oil that came out of a tap. It was totally odourless, surprisingly so in relation to the ghastly stink on deck. The clear oil was *whale oil destined for margarine. Despite the work of the International Whaling Commission, who were supposed to husband the world's whales, the animals are rapidly becoming scarce, and whaling from most civilized countries has stopped. At present whale oil is likely to be found in margarine only in the Soviet Union and Japan.

Wheat-germ oil. The oil expressed from the germ of wheat has outstanding medicinal qualities, but its dietary value is rapidly destroyed on heating or on exposure to air. It is also very expensive, and has at best an interesting taste which is halfway between wholewheat bread and varnish. It might perhaps be used as a flavouring, but at present is only for diet. High in vitamin E as well as in polyunsaturated fatty acids, it occasionally seems to have almost miraculous curative effects.

[Cotton seed oil – French: huile de coton German: Baumwollöl Italian: olio di cotone Spanish: aceite de algodón.

Rape seed oil – French: huile de colza German: Rapsöl Italian: olio di colza Spanish: aceite de colza.

Sunflower oil – French: huile de tournesol German: Sonnenblumenöl Italian: olio di girasole Spanish: aceite de girasol

Walnut oil – French: huile de noix German: Nussöl Italian: olio di noce]

FAVA BEAN. See broad bean.

FECULA. See farina.

FENNEL (Foeniculum vulgare) is a tall, strong, umbelliferous perennial with yellow flowers and feathery foliage. Looking very much like a large version of dill, but with a quite different taste, it is grown all over the world in suitable climates for its seed. This varies from the slightly bitter wild type to some cultivated kinds which have little bitterness and are not always easy to distinguish from anise. A very common wayside plant in Mediterranean Europe, especially near the sea, it has gone wild in the Californian climate since it was introduced there and has become one of the most prevalent weeds.

As a green herb, fennel has been used in European cooking since ancient times – it was well established in Britain before the Norman Conquest and almost certainly used there in Roman times. Although traditionally used with fish, it has countless other uses, especially in Mediterranean cookery, as it is so readily to hand. It is used for flavouring everything from pork to olives and snails. The dried seed makes a useful spice and appears in items ranging from the Florentine salami, *finocchiona*, to various types of curry. It is particularly popular in Italian cooking. A variety with thick, bulbous leaf stalks (*finocchio* or Florence fennel) is much grown in Italy and is becoming increasingly popular elsewhere. It is eaten either cooked or raw, like celery. The tough outer leaf bases should always be taken off. The flavour is similar to anise. Fennel is also used in cordials and liqueurs, often predominating in the *hierbas* that is sometimes drunk after a meal in Spain.

[*Fennel* – French: *fenouil* German: *Fenchel* Italian: *finoccheo* Spanish: *hinojo*]

FENUGREEK. A native of Europe and Asia, related to clover. The name means 'Greek hay', and the plant is grown as fodder in seed mixtures, often where virtually unknown as a spice.

Fenugreek (*Trigonella foenum-graecum*) is used to a small extent in countries bordering the eastern Mediterranean, but is overwhelmingly important in India, where the seed is a flavouring in curries (and many other dishes) and the leaves, usually of special varieties, are used as a vegetable. In Hindi, fenugreek is called *methi*. In recent years, many people in the West have taken to sprouting it or sowing it in boxes, for use in the same way as mustard and cress, as the flavour is pleasantly bitter. Leaves of the fully-grown plant (which are curried in India) vary from shatteringly bitter to only moderately so, depending on the type. They may have an exceedingly aromatic smell and can be bought fresh or dried in Indian and Pakistani shops. The seed is equally variable in its aromatic quality. It should be gently roasted to develop its flavour before being ground, but roasting must be done with extreme care. If fenugreek is over-heated (when it turns red), the taste becomes indescribably bitter, and it has to be thrown away. Some Indian cooks roast fenugreek seed until it becomes almost black, when it loses its bitterness again. Many people do not like the taste of fenugreek, which is associated with cheap curry powders. Those who like the traditional English curry powder will find they know the taste of fenugreek very well.

[*Fenugreek* – French: *fenugrec* German: *Bockshornklee, griechisches Heu* Italian: *fieno greco* Spanish: *fenogreco, alholva*]

FERMENTATION. The origin of the word relates to boiling because of the bubbles of gas evolved during alcoholic fermentation. However, fermentation is used as a general term for any process of change induced by living organisms and their enzymes (e.g. alcoholic fermentation, lactic acid fermentation); ferment is a synonym for enzyme. The organisms producing fermentation can be bacteria and moulds as well as yeasts. We use fermentative processes, for instance, in brewing and in making wine, cheese, yoghurt, *sauerkraut* and bread. Control depends on so adjusting the environment (food material, acidity, saltiness, temperature, etc.) that the organism or organisms whose effects are wanted grow at their best – or that unwanted organisms grow slowest or not at all. In practice, we are rarely dealing with one type of organism by itself but with a mixture, often of interdependent types which produce an effect no one of them could do alone. Making a good fermented product therefore means achieving the correct balance of types, and this is particularly important in creating flavour. For instance, certain bacteria produce small quantities of flavouring substances, such as those giving a creamy taste in milk products. Since the balance is affected by quite slight changes in conditions, recipes for any fermented products should be followed to the letter.

[*Fermentation* – French: *fermentation* German: *Gärungsprozess* Italian: *fermentazione* Spanish: *fermentación*]

FERNS. The young, half-coiled shoots of various fern species are eaten, particularly in North America and the Orient, in Japan for instance (as *warabi*), but rather rarely in Europe. The first ones I ate were roasted over a camp fire peeled to remove the furry outside and sprinkled with salt. The young shoots of bracken (*Pteridium aquilinum*) are edible and plentiful, as farm animals will not eat them. Bracken has a very wide distribution, and even the roots are edible. Of more gastronomic significance are the shoots of the ostrich fern, *Matteuccia struthiopteris*, which are known as fiddleheads because the opening shoots look like the scroll on a violin. This fern grows in damp places and beside streams over much of the eastern side of North America, and is particularly plentiful in New Brunswick. Fiddleheads can be gathered only over a brief season – no more than three weeks in early May – when the plants are shooting. They would be a very short-lived delicacy were it not for the ease with which they can be frozen or canned; they are readily available from supermarkets in Canada.

All fern shoots can be treated in the same way as asparagus, boiled or steamed until tender. They are served hot with hollandaise sauce or melted butter, or cold with mayonnaise or *vinaigrette*. Species with scaly or hairy skins have to be scraped or peeled before cooking. Since some ferns are poisonous and some have been considered carcinogenic, it is best not to experiment with unknown species. The flavour of fern shoots is rather strong, but those who like them consider them a delicacy.

[*Fern* – French: *fougère* German: *Farnkraut* Italian: *felce* Spanish: *helecho*]

FETTUCINE. *See* pasta.

FIDDLEHEAD. *See* ferns.

FIELD BEAN. *See* broad bean.

FIG. A very ancient cultivated fruit, the fig (*Ficus carica*) is often mentioned in the Bible and presumably grew in the Garden of Eden. More scientifically, figs were probably found wild somewhere in Arabia in ancient times. They have been growing in all Mediterranean countries long enough to go wild; they spring up wherever someone has dropped a seed between two rocks – a favourite place for figs to get a hold. Figs belong to the family Moraceae (together with mulberries and breadfruit), and there are dozens of wild species, such as the famous banyan and pipal trees (*Ficus religiosa*), under which the *sadhus* sit in India. Figs grow in the same climates as almonds, olives and oranges.

But figs are not fruit in the usual sense – the flowers are actually inside the fruit – and they have a most complicated life history. There are several basic types – Common figs, Smyrna figs, San Pedro figs and caprifigs. Common figs need no pollination and have no seeds. There are some hundreds of different varieties, both white and black. They are propagated by cuttings and the varieties thus tend to be regional; they form a wide spectrum of flavour, sweetness and tenderness – not to mention size and colour.

In the Mediterranean regions, fig trees bear two crops. In Italy, first crop figs are known as *fioroni* and arrive in June and July. *Fioroni* are usually large but not as sweet as the second crop figs. (In some varieties, only one crop ripens.) Second crop figs, the most plentiful, are smaller in size, juicy and full of sugar. They are produced in August, September

and even into October and November. These second-crop figs, though eaten fresh, are also dried. To my taste, they are usually too sweet – especially the black ones which can have a strong wild taste – and they do not go with *prosciutto* as well as those that ripened earlier.

Smyrna figs are varieties which need to be pollinated and thus produce seeds. This is said to give them a more nutty flavour. They are pollinated by a small wasp (*Blastophaga psenes*), which is hatched in caprifigs (otherwise useless, semi-wild types), so caprifigs must be grown near Smyrna figs; otherwise there will be no crop. In fact, branches of caprifigs are actually suspended in the Smyrna fig trees to make sure of this caprification. Smyrna figs are the most important type for drying and are grown in Turkey, Greece, North Africa and California (where the caprifigs and wasps had to be introduced). San Pedro figs are intermediate between Smyrna and Common figs; they give a first crop without caprification but must be caprified for the second.

Ripe figs are highly perishable, and the varieties that reach the market are the more durable ones, which are usually picked rather unripe. Figs are incomparably better picked straight from the tree at the desired state of ripeness and eaten either hot from the sun or chilled in the refrigerator. In most Mediterranean countries, it is a tradition that the traveller may help himself to a fig as he passes, but not, of course, pick them into a basket. Dried figs combine especially well with the flavours of anise and fennel. The bay leaf in a box of Smyrna figs is there to keep away weevils.

[*Fig* – French: *figue* German: *Feife* Italian: *fico* Spanish: *higo*]

FILBERT. *See* hazelnut.

FILE POWDER or **filet powder**. Young leaves of *sassafras (Sassafras albidum)* have a very mucilaginous quality and a nice, spicy taste. They are thoroughly dried, then rubbed to a powder. The result, after sieving to remove bits of stalk, is *filé* powder. An important ingredient in Creole cooking and essential for *gumbo filé*; it gives a special flavour and a smooth, mucilaginous texture to dishes in which it is used. It can also be used as a table condiment.

FILLING. *See* stuffing.

FILLET. From the French *filet*, a diminutive

of *fil* (thread). As applied to cooking, without qualification, it means a beef fillet, the undercut of the sirloin. Pork fillet, veal fillet, mutton fillet and so on are usually specified. Fillets of chicken and turkey are generally fairly thin slices cut from the breast. Fillets of fish are slices or whole boned sides of fish, depending on size. *Filet mignon* is a steak taken from the small end of the fillet.

[*Fillet* – French: *filet* German: *Filet, Lendenstück* Italian: *filetto* Spanish: *filete*]

FILLETING. See fish.

FINES HERBES. Finely chopped fresh herbs, a mixture which may include parsley, tarragon, chervil, chives and so on, according to choice – or even parsley alone. The pundits say that *fines herbes* could once have included such things as mushrooms and shallots. In Britain and the US, unless one grows them oneself, many of the ingredients are fairly difficult to obtain except dried and *omelettes fines herbes* are, alas, often made with ready mixed dried herbs.

FINING means removing cloudiness and sediment, as in the clarifying of beer or wine, though the clearing of aspic is essentially the same. The usual method is the mechanical one of adding something which will stick to the minute particles that cause the cloudiness. (They may be so fine that they would take months to settle naturally.) Substances used for the purpose include egg white (often with the shell to make it sink more quickly), isinglass, gelatine, alkaline alginates, blood, milk, casein, bentonite (an earth), kiesel-guhr (diatomaceous earth) and kaolin (china clay). Amateur winemakers can buy packaged fining agents with instructions. For home use, the simplest is egg white.

Filtration through a filter paper or a porcelain filter (commercially filtration is done in huge filter presses) is another mechanical method of fining. Chemical methods rely on altering the substances causing the cloudiness. A pectin cloud, often developed in home-made wines that have been boiled, is dispelled by the enzyme pectinase.

Home winemakers sometimes add a few drops of milk to clear white wine. If this fails, the white of one egg and a tiny pinch of salt beaten up in a small quantity of the wine (250 ml or ½ pt) will clear up to 45 lt (80 pt). Gelatine, softened and dissolved in hot water, is frequently used to clear red wine, but it reacts with tannin in the wine to form an insoluble precipitate and so to some extent changes the character of the wine. The use of asbestos pulp, advocated by some authorities, now seems a dubious practice as asbestos is carcinogenic when inhaled as dust.

FINNAN HADDOCK. Named after the village of Findon, near Aberdeen, this, in pre-Victorian times, was a haddock, split open, dry-salted and heavily smoked over peat or seaweed to withstand the journey to London by stage-coach. However, the popularity of Finnan haddock has been decreasing over the last 20 years, as has that of most fish with bones in.

Finnan haddocks are now prepared with beheaded, gutted and cleaned fish. They are split open from the belly, leaving the bone on one side, put in strong brine for 5-15 minutes (depending on size) and speared through the lug flaps with stainless steel rods, several fish to a rod. They are then left to drain for 2-3 hours. The longer the draining period, the higher the gloss. The haddocks are finally smoked over oak sawdust or over peat or whitewood sawdust, which imparts a colour fairly quickly, so that the fish are still moist when the required shade is reached. The finished item has a golden-brown colour with a good gloss and should feel dry to the touch – hence the London fishmongers' expression 'a dry haddock'.

To produce Finnan haddock at home, clean and split the fish. Dry-salt them for a few hours – overnight if you want to keep them for more than a week. Hang them to dry in the breeze and cold-smoke them (not above 27°C/80°F) over oak sawdust started with a hot iron bar. They are smoked to a 'fine yellow', a process which takes at most 12 hours.

They are cooked by skinning, rubbing with butter, grilling and serving with pats of cold butter – the best method according to the late André Simon.

The Scottish dish is prepared by lightly poaching the Finnan in water and serving it with a poached egg on top.

Glasgow pales are another type of smoked split haddock, smaller than the Finnan and given less smoke to bring about a barely-visible colour change. Golden cutlets are double or 'butterfly' fillets of either small haddock or whiting. They are lightly brined in a salt solution containing a lemon-coloured dye and are either hung on hooks by the tail or laid in trays for smoking over white-wood sawdust.

Any of the smoked haddock or whiting products can be shallow-fried, or poached in water or milk with a little butter. The cooked, boned flesh of smoked haddock is the base for the English kedgeree.

FINO. *See* sherry.

FINOCCHIETTO and **FINOCCHIONA**. *See* salame.

FISH is the only important type of food animal that is not fully domesticated. It is true that fish ponds have been maintained at least since classical times (and there are some tall stories about Romans feeding Moray eels on slaves), but we still depend mainly on wild fish caught in nets. Battery-reared sole and salmon have arrived, but we should eat the types of fish that are caught in the proportions in which they are available. Anyone who has the luck to watch the 'cod end' being undone to let the catch of a North Sea trawler on to the deck will see a marvellous selection of seafood, although certain fish, like ling or cod, will predominate, according to the season and the area. By the time this catch is sold, the variety will have been severely reduced; many types will be skinned and beheaded or tidied up and sold as fish fingers, fish cakes or fish balls. Many shoppers undoubtedly prefer fish fillets to be square, and others would not like to see the head of an Angler fish or Wolf fish in all their natural ugliness (even though they are two of the nicest of all fish to eat). Some lucky people can still visit fish markets near the sea, where the fish will be locally caught and the number of species on sale will run into dozens, but where some knowledge of the quality of the local fish is necessary.

Some countries depend to a large extent on fish for their protein. Japan, the world's premier fishing nation, once ate no red meat at all (meat-eating was introduced by foreign visitors).The poor of tropical South East Asia depend on fish, not only along their coasts, but inland where fish abound in rivers, ponds, creeks and artificial tanks. Even the water flooding the rice fields is alive with small fish, which may be bony and taste of mud, but are still nutritious enough. Fish markets in unfamiliar or exotic places are bewildering; you will have to depend on the dealers for identification of the fish. Not only is the number of different species in the world enormous, but identification from books is not at all easy. Books intended for sportsmen are often good, but tend to deal with the few fish that offer the finest sport rather than with those that are best to eat. Advice should also be sought on cooking and edibility; although most fish are good

in all their parts, some do have poisonous organs or are purgative. Care should always be taken in handling fish, as many have spines (on the back, fins or gill covers) which at very least can inflict a nasty wound and at worst may be rankly poisonous. A fish that is not quite dead may suddenly become galvanized into thrashing the fisherman with a thorny tail, or even biting the hand about to feed on it.

All fish, no matter how strangely shaped, share the same basic anatomy. Knowing this can be a help when you have to deal with a fish that you have never seen before.

Skin may be smooth, soft and scaleless, in which case it can be left as it is and cooked without problems, or it may be rough like a dogfish's or covered with scales overlapping like tiles on a roof. Dogfish or skate (*see* sharks) may be skinned or alternatively blanched in boiling water and then rubbed with a cloth to remove the roughness. Remove scales from other fish by scraping them against their grain, from tail to head, unless they are so firmly fixed that you can only start by scraping off a few at the front and gradually working backward, taking off a strip at a time, as too vigorous scraping from the tail may just tear the skin. In the stubbornest cases, quickly dunking the fish into boiling water will loosen the scales.

Head and **gills** are usually removed and are either given to the cat or used for soup or stock. They are sometimes left on for the sake of appearance when the whole fish is served, and discarded at table. With a few fish, the head is a delicacy, as, for instance, is that of some large species of sturgeon, which are supposed to have seven different types of meat in the head to be picked out by *aficionados*. In Norway, whole, gutted cod with the head left on is steamed with the tongue (like sheep's eyes in Arab countries) offered to the guest as a delicacy. Large cod have 'cheeks' which can be cut out and are sometimes sold by fishmongers or retained by the filleters as 'fry'.

Fins. There are two paired sets, pectoral (front) and pelvic (back).These fins are anchored to structures of bones which are rarely extensive and can usually be taken out with little difficulty. In many fish, the pectoral fins and their associated bones are situated so far forward that they can be removed with the head and gills in one cut. The single fins along the back and the underside (the dorsal and ventral fins – which may sometimes be reduced to no more than spines) can often be removed by cutting down on either side to free them and then pulling them out.

Bones. In some fish, the spine and bones present few problems. The spine has 'ribs' which lie in the wall of the gut cavity, but there is little else to worry about. With such fish (most catfish, for instance), the bones are easy to remove. However, other fish have a second set of bones extending from the spine at each side, above the 'ribs'. These are a particular nuisance, as they may be cut through in filleting and left embedded in the flesh. Many fish go even further and have intermuscular bones between the muscles. Really bony fish like these are best used for soup. Another solution is to pickle them in vinegar, which will soften small bones to the point where they will not be noticed within a day or so.

Gutting. The simplest method is to put the point of the kitchen scissors into the vent and to snip forward as far as the gills, opening the body cavity along the belly. With some fish it is then enough to cut through the spine behind the head and to pull the head forward and downwards, which will also bring the bony pectoral girdle and the gills away together, followed by the guts. With small fish, such as anchovies, all you have to do is pinch through the spine behind the head and pull.

Among the guts can be recognized the two roes (male roe or milt is soft and female is hard with eggs) and the liver. In a few fish, such as skate, the liver is a delicacy. The swim bladder, a shiny, elongated sausage shape which lies just under the backbone, is the source of *isinglass. Sharks and rays do not have a swim bladder and sink if they stop swimming. The rest of the gut is normally thrown away, although the Chinese dry and eat the stomach of the shark. Perhaps this is the point at which to mention that although roes and livers are sometimes delicacies, they may be poisonous in some otherwise edible fish (deadly in the case of the puffer fish and definitely harmful in others), so these parts of unfamiliar fish should not be eaten.

If fish have to be washed, they are best washed quickly just before they are cooked, and they should never be put into water unless this is necessary to soak out blood.

Filleting. It is difficult to learn how to fillet fish from a book and much better to watch someone doing it. Because fish vary enormously, the best

technique for filleting one species does not necessarily work for another. Fish with many intermuscular bones should rarely be filleted, as this might lead the unsuspecting diner to think that the fish is boneless when it is not. Few things are worse to eat than fillets with bones in them, especially if these are well concealed by a sauce. Short of getting your fingers into the dish and feeling, like a surgeon, there is no possible remedy.

In the absence of precise instructions, use the following general method for filleting. First cut diagonally behind the head and gills, and then down the back beside the dorsal fins. Then following the dorsal spines of the backbone, with the knife always cutting and scraping along the direction of the bones, dissect the flesh away until you reach the vertebral column itself. Next, still moving the flesh away from the bones, separate the flesh from the rib cage and ventral spines until the fillet comes free. After that, the fish is turned over and the method repeated on the other side. In some fish, two fillets are taken from each side; a cut made down to the backbone on each side before filleting is started will simplify the operation. Filleting many fish is quite easy if it is done with a sharp, flexible knife, such as the sort made for the purpose. On fishing trips, we used to fillet perch with a penknife in the boat, and drop the fillets into vinegar and water, so that they were ready to cook for breakfast the moment we landed.

If fish is to be flaked, it is best to cook it first on the bone, as this produces better fish and easier boning.

Cooking. The simplest way to serve fish is raw, as is done in Holland and Indonesia as well as in Japan. It may be 'cooked' without heat by salting (as with anchovies), by salting and marinating (as with Scandinavian salt herring) or by simply marinating in lemon juice or lime juice (as with seviche) or in vinegar (as in roll-mops) until the protein coagulates. Fish may be simmered or poached in a court-bouillon, then eaten hot or cold, or they may be steamed, baked, planked or roasted beside the heat of a wood fire (especially trout), or cooked in hot smoke. What is important is that fish should be just cooked and no more. Although there are rough rules for timing – such as 8 minutes steaming for the first 1 cm of thickness and 5 minutes for each additional one (10 minutes for the first ½ in and 6 minutes for each additional ½ in) – the factors involved vary so much that one cannot rely on formulae, and it is best to test the fish frequently as it approaches doneness. You can then snatch it away from the heat at the exact moment that it is ready. For baking in a medium oven of 180°C/350°F/Gas Mark 4, allow about 5-6 minutes per 1 cm thickness (13-15 minutes per 1 in) and then start to check on progress. When the fish is just coming away from the bone or has become flaky right through, it is done. In general, fish cooked with skin and bones still intact loses less moisture and is therefore more succulent. It is difficult to cook a very large fish to perfection without getting the outside overdone by the time the inside is just right.

Freshness. Skate and sole are exceptions to the rule that fish should be eaten as fresh as possible. Perfectly fresh fish have virtually no fishy smell (though some, like pike, have an odour of their own). The eyes are bright, shiny and transparent, never cloudy. If the mouth is gaping and the gill flaps open, then the fish has just died. Other checks, such as the colour of the gills, do not always work. If scales are being shed, then the fish is probably not quite fresh, but there is enormous variation in the ease with which scales are shed in different species. With many fish, skin colour is an important indication. Signs of staleness are when silveriness fades, iridescent blue or green lights disappear, and black or brown fish turn grey. Sunken eyes or an unpleasant smell mean that when the fish is opened at home, the flesh will look yellow or dull, the guts will have softened, the blood will be thin and watery, and the 'ribs' will have started to come loose through the wall of the body cavity. Such fish is not fit for consumption. White fish may not go off as quickly as oily fish, but it can be equally unpleasant.

Frozen fish. I once attended a lunch organized by some fish freezers in which fish bought from a fishmonger by an independent expert and as fresh as possible was matched against the highest quality frozen fish of the same species. Dishes using both were cooked in identical ways, so that one could be compared with the other. While, ideally, there should have been virtually no difference between fresh and frozen, the general opinion of the guests was that the fresh fish had the better texture, but the frozen fish had the better flavour. Neither would compare with fish landed straight out of the water, but nobody claimed that. Frozen fish is at present only the best possible solution for handling a commodity that is so very perishable. On the old trawlers, the fish, though immediately gutted, were packed down on ice. But even on ice, a week or more's storage on trawlers fishing in far northern waters left the fish far from fresh when they were landed. Today, most fish is deep-frozen on board ship very shortly after netting. Frozen fish may need to be thawed if it is to be fried, grilled, filleted, rolled or stuffed, but not if it is to be baked, simmered or poached. Thaw it in the refrigerator. This may take 24 hours.

[*Fish* – French: *poisson* German: *Fisch* Italian: *pesce* Spanish: *pez*]

FLAGEOLET. A type of *kidney bean, the *flageolet* is a rather special and expensive French variety of haricot, with a pale green, tender skin and fine flavour. *Flageolets* are not soaked before cooking and are often cooked in fancier ways than those applied to the average bean, for instance with fresh cream.

[*Flageolet* – French: *flageolet* German: *Flageolett* Italian: *fagiolino* Spanish: *judía verde*]

FLAIR FAT. The interior fatty lining of the loin of the pig, also covering the kidneys.

FLAMING. Spirits, unlike wine, can be set alight and used for flaming (although only the very strongest will burn without prior warming). The massive use of spirits in cooking is a modern innovation and, in recipes from the last century, the use of brandy, even as a flavouring, was limited. Cooks relied more on wine, port or madeira, and rum was the most important kitchen spirit. When brandy was added to cakes and batters, it was largely to promote lightness of texture; the volatile alcohol turned to gas and acted as a leavening when heated. In older French cookery books, it is rare to find the word *flambé* (and the verb *flamber* usually referred to cingeing the fluff off chickens before roasting).

The question of whether spirits should or should not be ignited is calculated to start an argument. It is claimed that flaming will burn off excess fat or take the raw taste off the spirits. However, the heat generated is mainly above the flame and not under it. Expert opinions vary. In Burgundy, one famous *maître cuisinier de France* does not flame his *coq au vin* but sprinkles it with a *fine champagne* cognac just before the dish is ready; and he does this himself in the kitchen. On the other hand, another Burgundy chef I talked to (a local traditionalist) was quite belligerent in his insistence that spirits must be ignited. Raymond Oliver says that burning spirits is risky as it can make the food bitter. These people have highly refined palates, but I do not agree with the English restaurateur who wrote in *The Journal of the International Wine and Food Society* that you can leave the brandy out of a *coq au vin* altogether as nobody will notice the difference.

Certainly it is a new notion that pyromaniac waiters, who are not cooks, should take time off serving to flood the food with alcohol and set fire to it. As a Danish friend said (and he must be right because his many restaurants in Copenhagen have made him wealthy), 'The customers want to see a show'. He forgets that some of us go to restaurants to eat.

FLATBREAD. The anglicized version of the Norwegian word *flatbrød*, also called crispbread (*knakkebrød*.) Many forms of these biscuit-like breads are made in Scandinavia, not necessarily the elegant rectangles we get in packets but also great rough sheets, usually based on rye flour but sometimes mixed with up to three times the weight of wheat flour or potato. One wonders why this type of bread and its many commercial variants should be so popular in slimming diets.

....

A Flatbread

Mix 500 g (18 oz) rye flour with 1,500 g (3¼ lb) mashed potato or 500 g (18 oz) rye flour with 750 g (26 oz) plain flour and knead into a dough with water. It is usual to incorporate a little fat, salt or sugar, and often some baking powder (or allow a day to stand in a warm place for some fermentation). The dough is rolled out thin and baked to crispness in a slow oven.

....

FLATFISH (the plaices, soles, halibuts and flounders) are all members of a single zoological order which has one outstanding common denominator: back in their evolutionary past, they elected to lie lazily on their side on the bottom of the sea and wait for their prey to come within range. The heads of the adults have become twisted round so that both eyes are now on the side which is on top, while the side on which they lie has become white. They rely on camouflage and have developed a capacity to change colour to match the seabed on which they lurk. Colour is therefore not a reliable guide to the identification of flatfish. Some flatfish lie on their right side and look left, while others lie on their left side and look right. Although mirror-image fish do turn up very occasionally, the distinction between dextral species, with the eyes on the right, and sinistral (left-looking) species is important in identifying flatfish.

Skates and rays are also white underneath and adapted to lie on the sea bed, but they lie on their belly, not on their side, and are cartilaginous fish related to sharks. Narrow fish of various sorts, such as the John Dory and the pomfret, swim around upright but sometimes get called flatfish and treated as such by the cook.

With the exception of the halibut, which is a powerful swimmer and often pursues its prey, the flatfish are lazy and do not move about very much. Perhaps that is why some, like soles, tend to develop local variations even in quite a small distance. The French say of soles that they differ between Boulogne, Dover and Ostend. From the cook's point of view, the species vary greatly in quality from Black or Dover sole, which is a gastronomic prince of fishes, to the megrim, which is not. But they all have one feature which makes them acceptable – an easily removed set of bones.

To fillet a flatfish, you merely make a cut along the length of the spine, cutting down to the bone, then, with sweeping strokes of the knife, lift the two fillets. The fish can now be turned over and the other two fillets removed. Flatfish have soft skins and do not need to be scaled, but some, in particular the sole, are usually skinned. If you make a transverse cut through the skin, just short of the tail, and loosen a large enough flap to get a grip on, the skin can be pulled off towards the head. An alternative is to lay the fillets on a board, skin-side down, and to slice the skin off with a very sharp knife.

The naming of the less well-known flatfish is confused, particularly because of the transplantation of names like flounder and sole from Britain, where they have an exact meaning, to other parts of the world, where they do not. This unavoidable process has caused considerable misunderstanding when one country reads another country's cookery books. The original British fish from which the names have been taken are as follows.

Brill (*Scophthalmus rhombus*) is a fairly large sinistral flatfish, up to 3-4 kg (6½-9 lb) in weight and distinguished from turbot by both its oval shape and the lack of knobs on its upper side. The flesh is delicate, but more easily broken than that of the turbot, and brill is generally considered inferior to it. Brill are found from the Mediterranean to the east Atlantic, north to Scandinavia.

[*Brill* – French: *barbue* German: *Kleist, Glattbutt* Italian: *rombo liscio* Spanish: *rémol*]

Dab (*Limanda limanda*) are small, lozenge-shaped dextral flatfish, usually not more than 30-38 cm (12-15 in) long. The dab has a rough skin to which its scientific name refers (Latin, *lima*, file). They occur in north European waters but not in the Mediterranean or in the west Atlantic where there is a related species, the Yellowtail dab (*L. ferruginea*). As food, they are good rather than exceptional.
 [*Dab* – French: *limande* German: *Kliesche* Italian: *pianuzza, limanda* Spanish: *lenguado, platija*]

Flounder. In Britain, a flounder is a species of small dextral flatfish (*Platichthys flesus*), the next most common after the dab, and is distinguished by a rough patch on its head. It is found in the English Channel, the Mediterranean and Black Seas and on the muddy bottoms of estuaries and creeks. The flesh is also about bottom, as European flatfish go.
 In the US, flounder has become the common general term for any flatfish, referring to, among others, Yellowtail dab, Grey sole and fluke, as well as lending its name to the Summer flounder (*Paralichthys dentatus*) and the Blackback or Winter flounder (*Pseudopleuronectes americanus*).
 [*Flounder* – French: *flet* German: *Flunder* Italian: *passera pianuzza* Spanish: *platija*]

Halibut (*Hippoglossus hippoglossus*) is dextral and the largest of the flatfish; it can be over 4.5 m (about 15 ft) long and weigh 600 kg (1320 lb). Small ones are often called chicken halibut. Large ones are naturally sold in cut pieces and not whole. The meat is very white and of good flavour, but inclined to be coarse, dry and lacking in firm consistency. It is more popular in Britain than in France, and fishermen of the two nations have been known to exchange fish at sea. Halibut ranges north from Biscay to Spitzbergen, Iceland and Greenland and west to New England, but is not found in the Mediterranean.
 The Pacific halibut (*Hippoglossus stenolepis*) is very similar, but the Californian halibut (*Paralichthys californicus*) is a sinistral fish which belongs to the same family as the brill and the turbot. The Greenland halibut (*Reinhardtius hippoglossoides*) is a much smaller fish which grows up to only 1 m (39 in) and is also known as the Black halibut in Germany and France.
 [*Halibut* – French: *flétan* German: *Heilbutt* Italian: *grosso rombo, ippoglosso* Spanish: *hipogloso, halibut*]

Lemon sole (*Microstomus kitt*) gets its name from the French *limande* (which comes, like the biological name of the dab, from the Latin, *lima*, file). It is dextral and is distinguished notably by its small head and its oval shape. Lemon sole is a well-flavoured flatfish and is often unjustly despised because it is compared to *sole; it is not a sole or even a substitute for it. Found from the Bay of Biscay to the North Sea, Iceland and the White and Arctic Seas, it can grow to 60 cm (2 ft) in length, but 40 cm (16 in) is more common. Two similar flatfish are the scald (*Arnoglossus laterna*) and the megrim or whiff (*Lepidorhombus whiffiagonis*). Both are inferior to the Lemon sole and may be easily distinguished from it as they are both sinistral.
 [*Lemon sole* – French: *sole limande* German: *Rotzunge* Italian: *sogliola limanda* Spanish: *mendo limon*
 Scald – French: *fausse limande* German: *Lammzunge* Italian: *suacia* Spanish: *serrandell*
 Megrim, whiff – French: *cardine* Italian: *rombo giallo* Spanish: *lliseria*]

Plaice (*Pleuronectes platessa*) come mainly from the North Sea, the Atlantic coasts of Europe and the Baltic; they are not much found in the Mediterranean. In Britain, they are the best-known and most important flatfish, and are the most common fish sold in restaurants. The flesh is nice-tasting, lean and easily digested; plaice is the flatfish that most people who cannot afford sole will choose as next best. It is a dextral fish and can be identified by its red or orange spots. Plaice grow to 75 cm (29 in), but are more usually around 40 cm (16 in).
 [*Plaice* – French: *carrelet, plie* German: *Plattfisch, Scholle* Italian: *passerino* Spanish: *platija*]

Sole (*Solea solea*) is often called Dover sole in Britain to distinguish it from the Lemon sole, and even the French admit that the best ones are caught near Dover and not on the French coast, an admission which has to be true, as torture would otherwise be needed to wring such an opinion from French chefs. This fish is usually skinned (a trick that Carême apparently learned in England), preferably on both sides. Sole is found from the Mediterranean to Norway, but not on the west side of the Atlantic, although some are shipped to the US from Europe.
 Soles are dextral and reach 40-70 cm (16-28 in) and face right.
 There are many other species of sole, such as the Sand or French sole (*Soleo lascaris*) and the Thickback sole (*Soleo variegata*), but most are

somewhat inferior to the real thing.

[Sole – French: *sole* German: *Seezunge* Italian: *sogliola* Spanish: *lenguado*]

Turbot (*Scophthalmus maximus*) comes close to sole at the top of the flatfish league. It is a larger fish at 70-100 cm (28-39 in), with lean, white, very well flavoured flesh and a firm consistency. Turbot are found in waters from the Mediterranean to Norway, though not on the western side of the Atlantic. A related species is found in Canadian waters and on the Pacific coast. The turbot is a sinistral fish and can be distinguished immediately by the bony knobs on its top side. Since the fish weigh up to 20 kg (45 lb), a special rhomboid kettle (*turbotière*) is necessary for cooking them whole. This was used more in the past; today, in a less lavish age, we have to be content with *turbotin* weighing 1-2 kg (2¼-4½ lb) or with pieces.

[*Turbot* – French: *turbot* German: *Steinbutt* Italian: *rombo chiodato* Spanish: *rodaballo*]

Witch (*Glyptocephalus cynoglossus*), also called Torbay sole, is a small elongated flatfish (30-50 cm/12-20 in long), common in the trawls. When I was on a trawler, witches were the fish the cook picked out and flung, still nipping, into the frying pan to feed the crew. They had less commercial value than the other fish in the trawls. However, they are well flavoured and are found plentifully on the Atlantic coasts of Europe, but not in the Mediterranean.

FLAVOURINGS. Apart from natural herbs, vegetables, spices, and condiments, there are a number of flavourings which cooks find useful in the kitchen. True, many commercial *essences (particularly bitter almond and synthetic vanilla) can be horrid, but I suppose everyone would allow oil of peppermint (which has a taste that is difficult to get from the fresh or dried herb). There are also a whole range of chemicals supposed to simulate anything from bananas to cherries, of which the best known is the amyl acetate of old-fashioned peardrops. Such things are to be avoided where possible, because they lack subtlety.

Other substances like maple syrup flavouring (because real maple syrup is difficult to come by) and Bisto (because of its Pied Piper effect on children) must be kept out of sight of purists, but every cook is entitled to some secret ingredients; a box of tricks with which to tart up the tasteless and disguise the failures is fine so long as you do not

depend on it too much.

[*Flavouring* – French: *saveur artificielle* German: *künstliches Schmackmittel* Italian: *aroma artificial* Spanish: *artificial sabor*]

FLIES. Among the thousands of different kinds of flies, the ones that mainly bother the cook are blow flies and house flies.

House flies are filthy creatures, which breed in refuse and excreta. They not only bring possibly pathogenic bacteria to food on their feet but actually vomit part of their last meal on to it. The famous old French naturalist Henri Fabre once put the body of a bird in a paper bag and hung it up. It did not go bad but became dry and mummified. Had flies walked on it, the result would have been putrefaction. Moral: food should always be kept covered and not left lying exposed for flies to walk on.

Blow flies, bluebottles, greenbottles and grey flesh flies all lay their eggs on meat, and the eggs hatch to maggots, which feed and grow before turning into pupae, and eventually adult flies. Some species do not 'lay' eggs but tiny maggots which have already hatched in the mother, and some are able to shoot their maggots or eggs sideways, so that meat near the edge of a meat-safe is liable to be reached. Meat should be hung away from the sides of a meat-safe, which should have a solid top.

[*Flies* – French: *mouches* German: *Fliegen* Italian: *mosche* Spanish: *moscas*]

FLITCH. *See* bacon.

FLOTØST. *See* whey.

FLOUNDER. *See* flatfish.

FLOUR means wheat flour, unless otherwise qualified as rice flour, maize flour, barley flour, *besan* flour, pea flour and so on.
White flour is usually ground in roller mills (*see* milling), during which almost all the *bran and *wheatgerm are separated out, leaving mainly the starchy endosperm, the inside of the wheat (which makes up about 85% of the grain). This endosperm is ground to the required fineness and separated by sieving through woven wire, silk or nylon screens in plansifters (vertical nests of horizontal sieves which gyrate in a horizontal plane). Stone-ground flour, which has been ground between old-fashioned mill-stones, contains much more of the bran and germ than does white flour.

Flour improves both in bread-making quality and in whiteness if it is stored for several months. These improvements develop more rapidly if the flour is exposed to the air and are caused by the oxidation of components of the protein. It was found that certain substances would bleach and 'improve' flour very quickly. This made storage for long periods unnecessary and reduced the risk of spoilage; the public demand for white flour and bread could thus more easily be satisfied. Chlorine gas was patented as a flour bleach as long ago as 1879, although its use for this purpose seems not to have been commercially exploited until much later. In the early 1900s, nitrogen peroxide was introduced; by 1920, other oxidizing agents, including benzoyl peroxide, potassium bromate and Agene (nitrogen trichloride) were in use as bleaching and/or improving agents. Agene continued to be widely used until it was shown that heavily-treated flour caused hysteria in dogs. Although Agene-treated flour was never shown to be harmful to human health, its use was voluntarily discontinued by British millers in 1955. It was replaced by another bleacher/improver, chlorine dioxide. In Britain, white flour is fortified with certain nutrients lost during milling (thiamine, nicotinic acid, iron). It must also, by law, contain between 2.35-3.9 g of chalk per kilo, although wheat is not an important source of calcium, and the need for the addition of chalk has been questioned.

Extraction rate is the percentage of the whole grain that is produced as flour during milling. Wholewheat flour has a 100% extraction rate, but what are known as brown or wheatmeal flours contain 80-90% of the wheat grain (thus have an 80-90% extraction rate). Flour of 85% extraction rate still contains much of the germ, but the bulk of the bran has been removed. White flours contain mainly the endosperm and have a 70-75% extraction rate because, although the endosperm makes up about 85% of the grain, some of it always remains attached to the bran and the germ. Even white flours will contain a trace of bran, as separation is never perfect. Patent flours, which are the whitest of all, have an extraction rate of about 40-50% and are used only for special purposes as they are expensive.

Flour varies in granularity and also in strength. Strong flours are often from *wheat with a high *gluten content and are best for bread and other yeast-raised goods. Softer flours are good for cakes and biscuits. Coarsely-ground flours, especially if they are wholewheat, do not rise so much as fine

flour and bake to a closer texture. Biscuits, which should have a very short texture, may even have *rice flour or *cornflour – ingredients with no gluten and much starch – added.

Self-raising flour contains chemical leaveners, usually added at the mill. The mechanical mixing methods used are more efficient than the blending done by hand in the kitchen. The raising agents are formulated in such a way that doughs and batters made from self-raising flour can be left standing for short periods in a cool place with little loss of performance.

High-ratio cake flours are specially treated flours which are common in America as 'cake flour', but are not generally available in Britain, except in bought cake mixes. They are snow-white, low in gluten, starchy, soft and finely ground. When combined with specially emulsified fat, they take up high quantities of liquid and sugar. Cake batters which are made with this flour have a pouring consistency; the cakes are of a melting quality – sweet, rich and moist.

Super-sifted flours. Modified methods of grinding and sifting have enabled millers to produce a flour which is free-flowing. Particles do not cling together into lumps and they mix smoothly with liquids. This makes the flour easier to use and is a convenience for the cook.

Proprietary flours and meals. In addition to the usual grades of white, brown and wholewheat flour, some flours are available for special purposes. They may contain ingredients such as wheatgerm, bran, soya flour, malt flour, rye and barley. They are for making special types of bread and are available mainly to professional bakers, but also in health-food shops. In the more famous patent wheatgerm flours, the germ has been heat-treated to improve its keeping qualities and much of its value may thus have been destroyed.

Storing and keeping. Experts recommend keeping flour in its bag on a cool, dry, airy shelf, but if the kitchen is damp or steamy the bag should be put into an airtight container. Fresh flour should not be added to old, and containers should always be carefully cleaned and washed, then thoroughly dried before refilling. Plain flour can keep for 4-6 months (white flour much longer than that), and self-raising flour for 2-3 months, but wholewheat flour, which contains the germ, should only be kept for 2 months in ordinary circumstances, because the oil in the germ tends to go rancid.

[*Flour* – French: *farine* German: *Mehl* Italian: *farina* Spanish: *harina*]

FLUORINE (F). This element, which does not exist in an uncombined state in nature, is a yellow gas, very similar to chlorine but even more active and toxic. It is used industrially in making PTFE (polytetrafluoroethylene) non-stick plastic, and the fluoro- and chlorofluoro-carbons such as freon for refrigerators and propellants for aerosols. Fluorine has become noticed in recent years as a trace element because of its effect in preventing decay in teeth, although the whole subject is still extremely controversial, and feelings run very high over the merits and demerits of fluoridating water supplies. Nevertheless, many water supplies are now fluoridated with fluorine salts (e.g. sodium fluoride or sodium fluorosilicate) to a level of 1 part per million. Too much fluorine, however, is definitely bad and will produce mottled teeth. Sea-fish contain 5 to 10 parts per million and tea some 80 (China tea even 100), but you would have to eat a lot of fish and drink a lot of tea to make up for tap water being deficient in the element.

[*Fluorine* – French: *fluor* German: *Fluor* Italian: *fluorina* Spanish: *flúor*]

FOIE GRAS is goose-liver *pâte*, one of the great French delicacies. Large breeds of geese (Toulouse or Strasbourg) are fattened on a rich diet, which includes hard-boiled eggs and skimmed milk as well as barley and potato. They are finished by force-feeding with boiled maize through a funnel. Geese are naturally greedy, but this force-feeding, combined with total lack of exercise (they are kept in tiny cages) causes the livers to become huge (reaching 1.5 kg/3¼ lb) and bloated with fat. In France, such livers are mainly produced in Alsace, in the Périgord region and in the south-west. The livers are fat from mid-November until January. Most convenient for the amateur are medium-sized livers of 500-750 g (1-1½ lb) which should be pink, without hard nodules or spots. Most people will prefer to buy their *foie gras* ready made, but serious French cookery books offer recipes.

For a start, any parts stained yellow with gall will have to be cut off. Livers may be soaked overnight in anything from cold water to spices and port, or simply salted and peppered and allowed to 'rest'. The livers are often kneaded first and any threads

of connective tissue are removed, then perhaps placed overnight in a marinade of armagnac, kirsch, pepper and allspice, but the treatment varies with the chef. Finally the livers are slit, pieces of black truffle are put in, and some salt sprinkled on. This done, the livers are squashed into *terrines*, and the lids are sealed on with flour and water paste. They are cooked in an oven in a *bain-marie* for periods of 30-80 minutes for a 500 g (1 lb) liver, according to the type of terrine and the ideas of the chef. Certainly the water in the *bain-marie* must never come to the boil. When cooked, the *foie gras* is chilled, although a version from the Landes is served hot. Alsatian *foie gras* is pinker than the *foie gras* of Périgord, but opinions differ as to which is better. Those who are rich enough can spend many happy hours trying to decide. Outside France, you are usually limited to the *foie gras* from a can. It may be in one piece or sliced. The black bits are the truffle.

Cans labelled *pâté de foie gras* must, by law, contain 80% goose liver. *Mousse de foie gras* must contain over 55%. This latter is only slightly inferior and is difficult to tell from the real thing, but it cannot be used as a garnish on hot dishes (like *tournedos Rossini*), because it will melt. However, mousse and purée are excellent for sauces. *Foie gras en croûte*, in which the liver is cooked in a pastry case is sometimes to be found, but is a very expensive delicacy.

Although *foie gras* is usually served at the start of a meal, it can also be a second course, as it sometimes is in France. As it is very rich, not much is required for each serving. It should be well chilled (but not frozen) and should be cut in slices or served in curls scooped with a spoon. (Dip the spoon or knife in hot water to prevent it sticking.) *Foie gras* deserves a good wine. Dry Champagne, Alsatian Riesling, dry or sweet white Bordeaux, even a light red Bordeaux all have their advocates.

Foie gras de canard, made from duck liver, has devotees who think that it is even better than the more usual goose version. It comes from the Landes and the Dordogne.

FOOTS. *See* sugars.

FORCEMEAT. *See* stuffing.

FORMALDEHYDE (HCHO). A simple organic gas made by the partial oxidation of methyl alcohol. Formaldehyde is best known as a 40% solution in water called formalin. Even when greatly diluted, it has a strong and distinctive smell. Because of its powerful action against bacteria, yeasts and fungi, it is used as a *disinfectant for barrels and in other situations when sterilization by heat is impossible. Formalin is poisonous. It damages the eyes and lungs, and will harden the skin of the hands, so needs to be used with care in well-ventilated places or in the open air. Once dissipated, however, it leaves no harmful residues.

FORMIC ACID (HCOOH).The acid of ants and the simplest organic acid, formed when the simplest alcohol, methyl alcohol, is oxidized. A sharp, blistering acid and very toxic to micro-organisms, it is used sometimes for disinfecting wine barrels, but is too unpleasant for general use in the household. A strong solution (55%) in water is sold under proprietary names for removing hard-water scale from kettles.

FOULE MEDAMES. *See ful medames.*

FRAISE. *See* fruit brandy.

FRAMBOISE. *See* fruit brandy.

FRANKFURTER. Smoked sausage of German origin made, in its original form, of very finely ground lean pork with a small amount of salted bacon fat. Other versions contain varying proportions of beef and other meat, while some American frankfurters (and all Kosher ones) contain no meat other than beef.

Knackwurst look like fat frankfurters and are similarly smoked and sold in pairs. They contain finely ground pork beef and pork fat, pinked with saltpetre and seasoned with cumin, garlic and salt. *Bockwurst*, at least in Frankfurt, look like large frankfurters, and are dispensed singly in snack bars which deal out the smaller fellows in pairs.

Sausages of this sort should be poached, but must never be boiled, or they will split. Frankfurters have a claim to be the original hot dog sausage, but so have *Wienerwurst*.

FREEZING. The American, Clarence Birdseye, who is regarded as the father of deep freezing, thought up his revolutionary ideas between 1912 and 1916 when he was living in Labrador, where in winter the fish froze as soon as it was caught in temperatures that hovered around -45°C (-50°F). He experimented with fish, seal and caribou meat, and had a special shipment of cabbages sent to him – probably the first-ever frozen vegetables. In 1924,

Birdseye built his first automatic quick-freezing machine, but the general introduction of frozen foods depended on the foods being conveniently packed and display freezers being installed in the stores. In the US, this innovation began in the late 1930s but in Britain packaged frozen food was not generally sold until after World War II.

Now, however, the frozen food business is vast, and even the home freezer is becoming standard equipment. A freezer, though rarely a means of saving money, at least enables people to live better on the same money. It is a boon to the cook who can now have many items, which were previously unobtainable out of season, at least in passable condition if not quite as good as they would be if fresh. In comparison with commercial quick-freezing methods, the slower action of a home freezer is relatively inefficient. However, this should not deter you. If all the proper steps are taken in preparing it, frozen food at least has the same nutritive value as fresh food.

All spoilage organisms and enzyme processes are slowed and finally brought to a standstill if the temperature is lowered sufficiently. A few specialized micro-organisms can grow in Arctic cold, and some moulds can carry on when yeasts and bacteria have given up, but as a general rule 10°C (14°F) halts biological and bio-chemical processes, which is the basis of deep-freeze storage. Snow, ice and natural freezing have always been taken advantage of in northern countries and in areas with snow on the mountains, but modern freezing techniques were impossible until after the invention of mechanical freezers, and were first tried out only in the middle of the 19th century. The first frozen meat came to Britain from Australia around 1880.

The storage temperature in a freezer should be -18°C (0°F). Frozen food does not improve in quality with keeping; the time for which it can be held in a freezer depends on the kind of food. Bought frozen foods are code-marked on the package for their keeping quality. It varies from a week or so to a year, but there is no rule of thumb. Correct preparation and packing are essential when freezing food. Anyone who wants to do it should have one of the many books on the subject. Excellent general guides are *Fresh From The Freezer* by Marye Cameron-Smith (Penguin) and *The Basic Basics Home Freezing Handbook* by Carol Bowen (Grub Street).

Vegetables. Use only very fresh, young vegetables. On the whole, those vegetables which are normally cooked freeze well, while salad vegetables with a high water content, such as lettuces, radishes, green and red peppers, and celery, lose their crispness when frozen.

To prepare vegetables, wash, trim and slice them as for cooking, then blanch them. *Blanching is a very important step, as it inactivates the enzymes which are likely to cause deterioration and checks the natural loss of flavour and colour. It also helps to retain vitamins. Blanching times vary from 1½ minutes for peas to 10 minutes for large corn on the cob, but most vegetables need 2-4 minutes.

There are two methods of blanching:
a) Immersion in boiling water. Place a small quantity of the vegetables in a wire basket and immerse them in a pan of boiling water. Bring back to the boil and count the blanching time from the moment the water returns to the boil. Shake the basket to ensure that all the vegetables are blanched. Remove the basket and plunge it into iced water for 1-2 minutes. Drain well, dry the vegetables on kitchen paper and pack.

b) Steam blanching. This is especially good for French green beans, diced turnip and cut kernel corn. The method conserves vitamins and minerals better than immersion in boiling water. Bring 2.5 cm (1 in) of water to the boil in a pan, place the vegetables in a wire basket above water level and cover the pan tightly. Dry the vegetables and pack them in rigid containers or polythene bags, which should be sealed so that they are completely airtight. Always remove the air from polythene bags before sealing.

Frozen vegetables require about half the normal cooking time because they have already been blanched. Most are best cooked, still frozen, in a minimum of lightly salted, boiling water. However, corn on the cob should be completely thawed before cooking. Vegetables will keep for 9-12 months, except onions, which keep for only 2-3 months.

Fruit. Nearly all fruit, except bananas, freezes well. Use fresh and ripe, though not over-ripe, fruit. Do not wash fruit (especially soft fruit, such as strawberries, raspberries, currants, blackberries) as this tends to make it mushy.

Three ways of freezing fruit are as follows:
a) Open freezing is generally best for soft fruit. Spread the fruit on trays and freeze at the lowest possible temperature until it is solid (30-60 minutes). Then place it in rigid containers and seal for storage in the freezer.

b) With sugar. This is suitable for harder fruit, such as gooseberries, rhubarb and citrus fruit. Pack in rigid containers, alternating a layer of fruit with a layer of sugar. Allow 1 cm (½ in) headspace for expansion, seal and freeze.

c) With sugar syrup. This is good for such fruit as pears and peaches, which discolour when peeled, and for fruit salads (do not include banana). An average syrup contains 275 g (10 oz) of sugar to 500 ml (1 pt) of water. Place the sugar and water in a pan, and add 1 tablespoon of lemon juice or ¼ teaspoon of ascorbic acid (*vitamin C). Bring the syrup to the boil, stirring occasionally, then simmer for 5 minutes. Leave it to cool before adding the peeled, chopped or sliced fruit. Pack in a rigid container, allowing 1 cm (½ in) headspace. Seal, label and freeze.

Cooked and puréed fruit may be prepared in the usual way, packed in cartons and frozen.

Frozen fruit should be allowed to thaw at room temperature for 3-4 hours, but should not be allowed to become too warm. It should keep in the freezer for 9-12 months.

Dairy products. Butter, margarine, lard and cheese all freeze very well. You should overwrap the packets in polythene bags before storing them in the freezer. These products should keep for up to 6 months, except soft cheese which will keep for 4 months. Double, clotted and whipped cream can be frozen, but the fat content in single cream is not high enough to allow it to freeze. Adding a tablespoon of sugar per 500 ml (1 pt) of cream helps to increase its storage life. Cream can be frozen in its original container, wrapped in polythene, and will keep for up to 3 months. Frozen yoghurt can be bought. The home-made variety does not freeze very well.

Fish. Prepare fish as for cooking. The fresher it is, the longer will be its storage life. Wrap each fish, fillet or steak in waxed paper or foil and pack in polythene bags. Once frozen, white fish will store for 6-9 months, while oily fish, such as mackerel and trout, will keep for 4 months.

Shellfish. If possible, buy lobster, crab and crayfish live and cook them by plunging them into boiling water for 10-15 minutes. Let them cool, then remove the meat from the shells and claws, pack it into rigid containers, seal and freeze. Prawns and shrimps should preferably be frozen uncooked in their shells but with the heads and tails removed. Wash them in cold salted water before freezing them.

Oysters, clams and scallops are best frozen uncooked. Remove them from their shells, taking care to keep any natural juices. Discard any that have already opened. Pack them in rigid containers with their juices. Fill any headspace with crumpled foil, seal and freeze.

Shellfish does not have the storage life of other fish and will keep for only about 2 months. Shellfish and whole fish should be allowed to thaw in the refrigerator for about 14 hours before cooking. Small fish, fillets and steaks may be cooked while still frozen, allowing extra cooking time.

Poultry and game. Game should be hung before freezing. Game birds and poultry should be plucked and gutted, the head and tail removed, and the insides washed out with cold water. They may be frozen whole or jointed, either way, they should be wrapped in airtight polythene bags. It is not advisable to stuff birds before freezing, as the stuffing will keep for only a month, while the bird can be frozen for up to a year. The liver and giblets may be washed, packed separately and frozen in polythene bags. Birds must be thoroughly thawed overnight in the refrigerator before cooking. Venison should be hung for 5-8 days and then frozen as you would meat.

Hare may be hung for 5-6 days, then skinned and gutted. Freeze it whole or jointed, packed in airtight polythene bags. The blood, which is often required in recipes such as jugged hare, can be frozen in ice-cube moulds. Rabbit, which does not need to be hung, can otherwise be treated in the same way as hare.

Meat. Before freezing meat, remove as much bone as possible, as it wastes freezer space. Care should be taken when packing meat for freezing, as it is particularly susceptible to 'freezer burn'. This is unsightly, but not harmful. Wipe joints clean and prepare them as for cooking; wrap them in polythene, seal and freeze.

Prepare stews and casseroles as for cooking and pack in small quantities in polythene bags. Steak, chops and cutlets should be trimmed, separated with pieces of foil and packed in polythene bags for freezing. Prepare offal as if for cooking and pack in small quantities in polythene bags. Sausages and sausage meat should also be packed in polythene bags.

Meat is best thawed overnight in the refrigerator, joints then cook more evenly.

Bread and cakes. Bread, buns and cakes freeze very successfully and can be stored for up to 6 months. Cakes are better frozen before they are iced, as the icing tends to smudge when it is packed. Pack bread and cakes in polythene bags. Wrap sandwiches in foil or plastic film and then in polythene bags.

Pastry. Uncooked pastry freezes very well indeed and will keep for up to 6 months. Shape the pastry into a block, wrap it in plastic film and put into a polythene bag. Cooked pastry, such as flan cases, is very fragile and should be packed carefully in rigid containers.

General tips. The quicker food is frozen the better. If it is frozen slowly, large crystals of ice form in it and rupture the cells. On the other hand, the slower food is thawed the better. Hot or warm food should never be put into a freezer, as this will raise the temperature in the freezer and may cause damage to its other contents. It is sensible to freeze food in small quantities, as this avoids the temptation to refreeze it, which is inadvisable. When labelling packages, always give the date of freezing so that you can be sure that the food has not outlived its freezer life. It is also a good idea to note how many people a packet will serve. When preparing dishes for the freezer, take care not to overcook them, as they will continue to cook when you heat them for use. It is best to leave most of the seasoning until then as tastes change during freezing. For example, cloves, garlic, pepper and sage become much more pronounced, while salt and onions lose their flavour.

Foods that do not freeze well or should be avoided are hard-boiled eggs (they quickly become tough and rubbery), single and sour cream (as the fat content prevents freezing), bananas (which become black in the cold), mayonnaise and custard (which separate if frozen), and cooked potato (which goes hard and discolours).

If you know in advance that there is going to be a power cut, switch on to 'fast freeze' for 4 hours beforehand, having filled any space in the freezer with crumpled newspaper (to help keep the food cold for longer). Do not on any account open the freezer. Cover the top of the freezer with heavy blankets to provide extra insulation. After the power cut has ended, switch on to 'fast freeze' again for a further 4 hours and keep the lid firmly shut for at least 6 hours. If you are taken by surprise and have no time to make these preparations, remember that the food will keep for 24 hours if you do not open the freezer.

If the worst comes to the worst and your food thaws, there are a few points to bear in mind. All uncooked vegetables, meat, poultry and fish must be cooked before refreezing. All ice cream and puddings made with fresh cream should be eaten immediately or thrown away, as should all pre-cooked dishes. Most fruit can be refrozen, but it will probably lose some of its flavour and colour. Bread and cakes may safely be refrozen.

FRENCH BEAN. *See* kidney bean.

FROG, '*que les Anglais nous reprochent de consommer*', says one of my French cookery books sadly (since when have the French been so sensitive to British opinion on food?). It is probable that all frogs are wholesome to eat, although many are too small to bother with, and some no doubt taste better than others. The European Edible frog (*Rana esculenta*) is found in ponds and streams from southern Sweden to northern Italy and eastwards through Hungary and Romania; there are small colonies, probably introduced, in southern England. It is rather larger than the common frog and usually greenish with black markings. However, frogs vary greatly in colour, so it is useful to know that green frogs such as the European Edible frog do not have the conspicuous black mark behind each eye which is characteristic of brown frogs such as the common frog. The Edible frog is closely related to other species and may be a hybrid between them; they are the larger Marsh frog (*R. ridibunda*) and the smaller Pool frog (*R. lessonae*), both of which are edible and have been introduced in southern England. European Edible frogs grow to 12 cm (5 in) for a really big female (they are larger than the males), but American bullfrogs grow to 40 cm (16 in) and in the US there is no inhibition about eating frogs' legs. There are frog farms, particularly in Florida and Louisiana, and frozen frogs' legs are also imported from Japan.

It is common to compare frog with chicken – one writer says they taste like 'smelt with breast of chicken' – while in Dominica in the Caribbean, the large hill frogs are called 'mountain chicken'. Dr Livingstone wrote that when cooked the African bullfrog looked 'exactly like chicken'.

Frogs are eaten all over the world – they can be seen in markets in the Orient – although throughout history the fashion for them has been spasmodic. It seems that they were not favoured by the Romans, but at other periods they have been an expensive luxury. The Revd J.G.Wood, writing in 1863, described how poachers used to steal frogs from the fenced-off ponds or froggeries around Paris. 'Poaching was done over the fence, without entering, by a curious mode of angling, something like "bobbing" for eels. They get a very long fishing rod, tie a line of sufficient length to the tip, and at the end of the line they fasten, in place of hook and bait, a simple piece of scarlet cloth. Thus prepared they push the rod over the fence, let the scarlet rag just touch the surface of the water, and shake the rod so as to make the cloth quiver and jump about. The frog, thinking it has found a savoury morsel, leaps at the rag, closes its mouth firmly upon it, and is neatly tossed over the hedge before it can make up its mind to loosen its hold.'

Frogs are at their best in spring. It is usual to eat only the back legs, as there is little meat on the rest of the body, although there are recipes for whole frogs, which are, for example, stuffed with spinach in Italy. Unfortunately, the back legs are often chopped off living frogs and the animals thrown into a waste tub to bleed slowly to death. Most people will buy frogs' legs already prepared – they are often sold skewered together for cooking *en brochette* – but if they are fresh, they must be skinned and have the feet cut off.

Frogs' legs are usually soaked in cold water or milk for an hour to plump the meat before cooking. (Frogs dry out very quickly even when alive, but equally quickly absorb water through the skin when put in damp surroundings.) With frozen frogs' legs, follow the packagers' instructions. The simplest way to cook frogs' legs is to fry them gently in butter for 5 minutes. However, there are many recipes including those for *nymphes*, a euphemism optimistically used by Escoffier in an effort to overcome British prejudice.

[*Frog* – French: *grenouille* German: *Frosch* Italian: *rana* Spanish: *rana*]

FROMAGE DE TÊTE. *See* brawn.

FRUCTOSE, fruit sugar, laevulose, or levulose is a monosaccharide *sugar that is found in fruit juices, honey and the nectar of flowers, usually with *glucose and *sucrose. When sucrose (cane or beet sugar) is hydrolysed (inverted), the resulting invert sugar contains equal quantities of fructose and glucose. Fructose alone is formed by the hydrolysis of inulin which is found in the roots of composite plants such as chicory and dahlia. Fructose is more soluble in water than glucose and has a much sweeter taste. Like glucose it is fermented by yeasts to form alcohol and carbon dioxide.

FRUIT BRANDY or **eau-de-vie**. As the name suggests, fruit brandies are distilled from fruit wines. They are usually drunk as aperitifs or Schnapps, but sometimes also as liqueurs. Undoubtedly the most important fruit brandies used in cooking are calvados (from apples) and kirsch (from cherries). However, some of the others may be found in regional recipes and, for this reason, they are listed here.

Barackpálinka. A Hungarian *eau-de-vie* made of apricots, usually clear and at most a pale straw colour. Often very strong and, when matured, an excellent spirit with a flavour something between apricots and slivovitz, but distinctive.

Calvados. Distilled, fermented apple juice from Calvados, Normandy. Pot stills are used, and the calvados is aged for varying periods. As a drink, a bad calvados (or applejack for that matter) is one of the most excruciating spirits known to man. In cooking, calvados is often used in Norman dishes, with fish, as in *truite à la normande*, with pork, veal or chicken, and of course in the classic version of *tripes à la mode de Caen*. In some recipes, the calvados is ignited and in others not. Calvados gives a special taste to the Norman dishes in which it is used. If calvados is not available, whisky is suggested as the best substitute by Elizabeth David in *French Provincial Cooking* (Grub Street).

Fraise and **Framboise**. Made respectively from strawberries and raspberries in Alsace, correctly from wild fruit. Expensive *eaux-de-vie*, clear and colourless.

Kirsch or **Kirschwasser**. Distilled from fermented crushed *cherries of types which vary from place to place, kirsch is a spirit of the area which includes Alsace, the Vosges mountains, the part of Switzerland south of Zurich and Basle, as well as the Black Forest in Germany across the Rhine. In French, but not German or Swiss kirsch, a proportion of the kernels are crushed with the fruit, which gives a trace of bitter-almond flavour. To be good,

kirsch has to be distilled in pot stills and aged; it is matured in glass, not in the wood, and is said to improve when kept in the bottle. It is much used in cooking, for instance with fruit (e.g. with apricots, or with pineapple in *ananas au kirsch*) and in creams and cakes. Kirsch is also considered indispensable for cheese *fondue*, both in the fondue and to drink, and adds great distinction to Alsatian *Sauerkraut*, to which Elizabeth David in *French Provincial Cooking* recommends that it should be added as a last touch before serving. Neither kirsch nor the equally colourless maraschino should be confused with the thick and garnet-red cherry brandy, which is made by infusion (like sloe gin).

Maraschino. Made from Dalmatian *marasco* *cherries and usually very much sweetened, this liqueur is slightly redolent of the bitter-almond taste from crushed stones. It is much used as a flavouring in sweet dishes and with fruit compôtes.

Mirabelle. Distilled from the small yellow mirabelle plums, which are sweet and strongly flavoured, this Alsatian *eau-de-vie* has similarities to quetsch and slivovitz. It is colourless and matured in the bottle.

Quetsch. Distilled from the quetsch plum, like mirabelle it is an Alsatian *eau-de-vie*, clear, colourless and matured in the bottle.

Slivovitz. Distilled from plums in Yugoslavia, Hungary and Bulgaria. In Romania, the same drink is *tuica* (pronounced tsuika). A clear colourless spirit, rather similar to mirabelle and quetsch, it may or may not have a bitter-almond taste from crushed plum stones.

FRUIT SUGAR. *See* fructose.

FRYING is cooking in fat or oil which is at a temperature well above 100°C (212°F), the boiling point of water. Fats and oils can be made very hot without vaporizing, although they do eventually burn or decompose. The temperature is different for each particular fat or oil, but most vegetable oils stand temperatures well over 200°C (392°F), which is far above the 165°C (374°F) usually needed for frying.

The effect of putting food (which contains water even if it looks dry) into hot fat is to cause the water on the surface, and progressively inwards, to be converted in a flash into steam. There is a violent bubbling and a coagulation of protein, and fat cannot enter the food through the pores that are left because of the rush of steam coming out. Very shortly, as the temperature rises (having dropped when the food was put in), starches and sugars in the outside layers become dried and caramelized. The food acquires a brown and crisp coating. The coating is important, and great attention is given to it by competent cooks. Those who cannot judge when the fat is at the correct temperature should use a thermometer. If the fat is heated too much, it burns (and never heat it to smoking, as some books advise, because when it smokes, it is burning) and its temperature is such that the food may well carbonize before the centre is cooked. On the other hand, if food is put into fat which is not hot enough, then the instantaneous coagulation and outflow of steam does not take place; the fat gets into the food and makes it soggy. A similar effect is produced when too much food is put into the fat; the food causes the temperature to drop, and may lower it too much.

Egg is a very good coating for things to be fried because it coagulates quickly and forms a more or less impenetrable skin. Egg batters also have a sealing effect, but dusting the food with flour or cornflour alone, though it absorbs surface moisture, will not make surfaces impervious, although it may help crisp them. For shallow frying, fat should come halfway up the food; otherwise, when the food is turned over, a strip all round it will either be uncooked or twice cooked. For deep frying, there must be enough fat for the food to be totally immersed. When frying is done properly, the fat should not pick up tastes from the foods fried in it. Fat used for deep frying should be strained frequently through a fine cloth to remove any crumbs or bits, otherwise they will burn and spoil the flavour of the next food cooked in the fat. As oils tend to go rancid more easily after they have been heated, it would be ideal to keep fat or oil for deep-frying in the refrigerator between uses. It is also healthy to avoid using the same fat for too long.

FUL MEDAMES or **foule medames**. A brown broad bean which is the basic ingredient of the Egyptian dish of the same name. For this, the beans are soaked overnight, then cooked until tender (or they can be bought canned) and mixed with garlic. *Hamine* eggs, which have been simmered with onion skins for some hours until they have stopped being hard and have become creamy, are the usual accompaniment to *ful medames*, together with a seasoning of parsley, olive oil, lemon juice and black pepper.

FUMET. *See* stock.

FUNGHI PORCINI. *See* cèpe.

FUNGI. *See* mushrooms, truffles, moulds.

FUSEL OIL. Towards the end of alcoholic distillation, an oily, high boiling-point fraction comes over, this is fusel oil. It consists largely of damyl and isoamyl alcohols plus other alcohols such as glycerine and aromatic ethers. In all naturally flavoured spirits – such as brandy, whisky and rum – some of these substances are necessary as they give the drink its character. This is unfortunate, because it is the fusel oil which is the prime cause of hangover headaches, and it also delays the sobering-up process (which is why there is less hangover and quicker recovery from vodka which contains very little fusel oil). Good distillers, such as those making cognac, manage to keep the maximum flavour and yet lose the worst of the fusel-oil components. Bad distillers do not. One glass of bad moonshine whisky can make you feel as if you have been hit on the head with a steam hammer.

Home distillers should know that the quantity of fusel oil formed during fermentation depends both on the type of yeast and on whether it has sufficient nitrogen for its needs without having to depend on the amino acids isoleucine and leucine in the dead yeast cells. The less the amino acids are broken down, the less amyl alcohols are formed.

g

GAGE. *See* plum.

GALACTOSE ($C_6H_{12}O_6$). A white, crystalline monosaccharide sugar, which, with glucose, is obtained by the hydrolysis of *lactose (milk sugar). During the digestion of milk, lactose is split down into these two component sugars, both of which are absorbed through the gut and handled by the liver.

Some babies with defective metabolism are unable to handle galactose and therefore ordinary milk. They have a hereditary disease called galactosaemia and must be fed on lactose-free milks if they are to survive. Even later in life, they must avoid all milk products, such as cheese and yoghurt, as well as cakes and biscuits, soups and anything else which contains milk. *Agar-agar, *carrageen moss, beetroot and molasses must also be avoided as they contain a sugar called raffinose, which is broken down by bacteria in the gut giving a mixture of glucose, fructose and galactose. Unlike glucose and fructose, galactose is not fermented by baker's yeast, although it is by some other yeasts.

GALANGAL There are two galangals, both members of the ginger family. Greater galangal (*Alpinia galanga*) is a native of Indonesia. Its knobbly roots are gingery and are used for flavouring the curries of the region. Lesser galangal (*Alpinia officinarum*) is native to South China and is mentioned in ancient Chinese and Indian manuscripts. The roots are small, red-brown on the outside and pale inside. The flavour is something between ginger and pepper. It is known as *laos* or *leuqkuas* in Malay and Indonesian cooking and is used in Russian cooking for flavouring vinegar and the liqueur *nastoika*. Galangal is used fresh in South East Asia, but is also dried for sale in shops.
[*Galangal* – French: *souchet long, souchet odorant* German: *Galangawurzel, Galantwurzel* Italian: *galanga* Spanish: *galanaga*]

GAME originally meant any animal killed for game or sport. In the kitchen, it means any edible animal brought home by hunters; or indeed any species which has not been domesticated for food. Most countries have close and open seasons for hunting, and game on sale may have to carry an official tag. You can get into trouble parading out-of-season game through the streets, even though it has come from the freezer.

Big game. Bear, hippopotamus, elephant (or at least elephant foot), ibex and wild sheep, even lion, are all eaten somewhere. They cannot be given individual coverage here, but the following observations are worth noting:
a) Consult local people about edibility and always cook the game thoroughly, as some wild animals suffer from parasites that can be passed on to humans.
b) Either cook big game when it is still warm or hang it well, unless local knowledge tells you otherwise.
c) In the bush, your retainers will usually try to make off with the animal's liver. It may be the only part you can get your teeth into. Polar bear liver is poisonous, except to the Eskimos and others who are used to it.
d) Immature antelopes are inclined to be tasteless. Young but mature animals are best.
[*Game* – French: *gibier* German: *Wildbret, Hochwild, Federwild* Italian: *selvaggina* Spanish: *caza*]

GAMMON. *See* bacon.

GARAM MASALA is a mixture of ground spices used as seasoning in Indian food and usually added at the end of cooking or even sprinkled on food when served. It is neither the same as curry powder nor a complete spicing. There are hundreds of formulae, and some bought ones are very elaborate, although the basic ingredients are commonly the same. In the table overleaf, the figures represent quantities by weight, but if you are using ground spices, for a start you can take the figures as teaspoons and work from there until you reach the proportions you like.

Black pepper	2	4	4
Coriander seeds	4	4	4
Cumin seeds	4	3½	3
Cloves	1	1½	2
Cinnamon	2	1	2

If you are making *garam masala* at home from whole spices, as is best, the spices should be ground finely in a coffee mill and sieved. You can, if you wish, gently roast the cumin, coriander and black pepper before grinding them.

GARBANZO. *See* chickpea.

GARLIC (*Allium sativum*) is a member of the same genus as leeks and onions and is probably a native of Central Asia. There are dozens of varieties, differing in size of bulb, pungency and skin colour. In Britain, which has returned to using garlic again in the last 30 years, supplies come mainly from Italy, Spain and France. In the US, garlic is grown commercially in California, Louisiana and Texas, but it is also imported from Mexico, Italy, France and elsewhere.

There are three common types: the white-skinned American or Creole has a strong taste, the Mexican or Italian has a pink or purple skin, and the large Tahitian has enormous bulbs. In Europe, garlic is plentiful and fairly cheap in the summer and autumn. At the start of the summer, it is fresh and difficult to peel, but as time goes on, it gradually dries out. In early winter, the price starts to rise. By spring, much of the garlic has dried out, leaving empty husks or cloves gone brown in patches, and care must be taken in buying it in Mediterranean markets, as the price has gone sky high and the new crop will also have come in, harvested before it is ready, hard to peel and rank. It is then difficult to know what to buy. The types of garlic with very small cloves are the ones for the timid, who use only a little in the cooking. Other types have large cloves, some quite enormous cloves, and are the ones for people who use a lot or who have to peel it by the pound to make chutney. There is at least a twenty-fold difference in size between a small and a large clove.

Garlic has a strong flavour from its oil, which is excreted through the lungs and so perfumes the breath. This is an irritant – though harmless and even healthful in the quantities used in food – but it will cause severe blisters on fingers if a lot of garlic – say a pound or so – has to be peeled. This process is made easier if the bulbs of garlic are split into cloves and then put in the sun for an hour or so to dry. The skin comes free. On the other hand, skinning garlic is often an unnecessary chore; the cloves can be crushed with the skin on (it is removed in due course), or the whole can be liquidized, depending on what the garlic is to be used for. Cloves can be crushed by putting them under the flat of a kitchen knife and banging it with your fist; or by putting the clove, concave side down, on a plate and leaning on it with the ball of your thumb. A little is best got by rubbing the clove against the prongs of a fork pressed flat on a plate. A garlic press is a crude and unnecessary device. In some places, garlic is fried to 'temper' the oil, and the cloves, after being fried brown, are thrown out. Garlic salt is easily made by pounding a few cloves of garlic with bone-dry salt – previously dried in the oven – and can be kept in a closed jar for quick use. However, garlic salt and garlicked foods that have been stored for any length of time can smell horrid and taste worse.

The quantity of garlic in cooking is a highly personal matter, though it should not be allowed to overwhelm delicate foods. The cautious will interpret 'a clove' as a small one, *aficionados* will add more than is called for and addicts will need more still to satisfy their palates. Generally, though, if the flavouring is to be light, just rub the food or the inside of the mixing bowl or salad bowl with a peeled clove of garlic. Chopping, pounding or pressing the garlic clove will give a stronger result. Some dishes call for roasted garlic; it is roasted in a dry pan or on a stove top before peeling. This treatment changes the flavour. Roasted and unroasted garlic are sometimes mixed together.

[Garlic – French: *ail* German: *Knoblauch* Italian: *aglio* Spanish: *ajo*]

GAS MARK. *See* regulo.

GASTROPODS. One of the three main classes of molluscs, the gastropods include the *snails and slugs, the marine shellfish that look like them such as *whelks and *periwinkles, the large and extravagant variations on this theme that are found in tropical seas and coral reefs, the conch shells, cowries, and spider shells, as well the *limpets and *abalones which have shells with the spiral form lost (or obscured) in the course of evolution.

Small gastropods such as snails and winkles are eaten whole (after removal from the shell) but the larger ones – from the Burgundy snail upwards – should first have the visceral spiral (the dark-coloured part deep in the shell) removed. This consists of the liver and digestive organs. It may taste bitter or contain partly-digested poisonous food as well as grit. Gastropods in general tend to be edible though tough. Some cone shells (*Conus*) from warm waters contain a poisonous dart which is shot out through the narrow end and can in some cases kill.

Unlike the bivalves, which includes oysters, clams and mussels, there are no great gastronomic treats among the gastropods, even snails and abalones are hardly in the same class. However, a large number are eaten. Apart from the commonplace whelks and periwinkles, other marine gastropods that are eaten include the horn shells, of which the common Mediterranean species is called *torricella* (*Cerithium vulgatum*). In Italy it is used in soups. The Top shells (notably *Monodonta turbinata*) occupy the place of the periwinkle in the Mediterranean world. Above all, there are the various species of *Murex*, sea snails which were the source of the dye Tyrian purple. The animals are tough, but the beauty of their shells ensures them a place in many a collection of seafood, and lovers of Mediterranean seafood restaurants are bound to come on them. The local people like them, but some will eat almost anything that comes from the sea. Others think that the best place for sea snails is in a soup.

GAUR or *cluster bean*. Until recently, *gaur* (*Cyamopsis psoraloides*) was little known outside India, where the name comes from and where it has been cultivated for countless years. The long, pencil-like green pods with pointed ends are commonly seen in the markets of Bombay and the south of the subcontinent, less so in the north. While some varieties are for green manure or forage, others are eaten as green beans and make an excellent hot-country vegetable. They are cut in bits and mixed with potato or included in vegetable curries of various kinds. *Gaur* is not usually used as a dried pulse. Commercially, it is the source of a gum which is used to stabilize or give viscosity to ice creams, processed cheese, salad dressings and canned fruit.

GAYETTE. *See crépinette.*

GELATINE or **gelatin**. From the Latin *gelare*, to freeze. A protein substance obtained commercially from cattle bones (though skin, tendons, gristle and connective tissue can all be used) by digesting them in hot water. It is basically the same as old-fashioned glue and, in the last century, when it was first made commercially, gelatine apparently often tasted gluey.

Today, it is highly refined and virtually tasteless. It may be made by either an acid or an alkaline process; the product of the latter is stronger and more expensive, but is also less clear. The cook is mainly concerned with finding a reliable brand and sticking to it. Gelatine may be bought as a powder, cubed, diced, kibbled or in transparent sheets. It should be clear, not yellowish and with virtually no taste of its own. Quality is also related to the amount needed to make a good gel and the firmness with which it sets. Gelatine is a variable product, and recipes cannot therefore be dogmatic about the proportion of gelatine and liquid to use. In any case, jellies of different stiffness are needed for different purposes. Stiff jellies are easy to turn out and handle, but light jellies are more pleasant to eat. As a starting point, in the complete absence of other information, you might try 15 g (1 packet, 1 tablespoon or ½ oz) to 500 ml (1 pt) of liquid.

Gelatine is used to make fruit jellies (it is in the ready flavoured, sweetened and coloured jelly cubes that are on the market – or in the US in powdered form), but it is also put into ice cream, as it helps to prevent the growth of ice crystals, and also into soups and syrups to give them a thicker consistency. It is used in glazes to protect meat products and for fake *aspic. Gelatine was once thought to be a useful food, but has little nutritive value in comparison with many other proteins as it lacks tryptophan, one of the essential *amino acids.

Gelatine should first be soaked for half an hour or more to allow it to absorb water and swell. A gelatine jelly melts at about 27°C (80°F) and sets at about 20°C (68°F), but varies. Boiling it, especially with acids, tends to reduce its jellying power, but if necessary it may be pasteurized at 71°C (160°F) for 20 minutes. Alternatives to gelatine in various circumstances include *agar-agar, *carrageen and *isinglass.

[*Gelatine* – French: *gélatine* German: *Gallert* Italian: *gelatina* Spanish: *gelatina*]

GENDARME. *See herring.*

GENTIAN. The excruciatingly bitter root of the yellow gentian (*Gentiana lutea*), which is native to the mountains of Europe, is used in aperitifs such as the French *suze* and the Austrian *enzian*, but rarely in the kitchen.

[*Gentian* – French: *gentiane* German: *Enzian* Italian: *genziana* Spanish: *genciana*]

GERANIUM. Garden geraniums, which are

natives of South Africa and more correctly called pelargoniums (*Pelargonium capitatum* and *P. ororatissimum*), are much grown for the perfume of their leaves – rose, orange, lemon, apple, nutmeg – according to variety. Like most herbs, the plants reach maximum fragrance just before flowering, and the leaves can be used to perfume jams and jellies.

[*Geranium* – French: *géranium, pélargonium* German: *Storchschnabel, Geranie* Italian: *geranio, pelargonio* Spanish: *geranio*]

GHEE. *See* butter.

GHERKINS. True gherkins are not very small cucumbers, or even a special dwarf variety of cucumber, but a separate plant, *Cucumis anguria*, a native of the Caribbean and much grown in America. However, small varieties of cucumber are also grown for making pickles. Good varieties must remain firm yet have a tender skin. Pickled gherkins are a classic garnish and accompaniment to cold meats and pork *pâtés*.

[*Gherkins* – French: *cornichon* German: *Pfeffergurke, Essigurke* Italian: *cetriolino* Spanish: *pepinello, cohombrillo*]

GIBLETS. The neck, ends of wings (pinions), liver, heart and gizzard of chickens and other birds. The feet, which, when trimmed and peeled, make such an excellent stock, are for some reason usually not included in the definition. The giblets, with the exception of the liver, are used for stock and gravy.

[*Giblets* – French: *abatis* German: *Gänseklein, Innereien* Italian: *rigaglie, frattaglie* Spanish: *menudillos*]

GIN is occasionally used as an ingredient in the cooking, though more frequently in the cook. The name is a corruption of *jenever* from *genièvre* meaning juniper, and it was first distilled as a medicine by the doctors at Leyden University in Holland towards the end of the 18th century. Shortly afterwards, it was being distilled in London, Bristol and Plymouth. To begin with, gin was generally sweet, but as time went on different places evolved their own style. Dutch gin is now very different from London Dry Gin, which in turn is unlike the Plymouth Gin so traditional in the Royal Navy. London Dry Gin is, with whisky, the most popular spirit in the world today and is made in all countries, although the best still comes from London.

Recipes for gin were even left behind as a legacy of the British occupation of Minorca (1708–1756), and again at the time of Nelson), and today are still made on the island to ancient formulae. In spite of its popularity, until well into this century gin remained rather naughty, mother's ruin, the rot-gut of the poor and very much 'down-market'. (However, I am amazed at the number of recipes for sloe gin collected by my aunts around the turn of this century.)

The flavour of gin is based on juniper berries. Cheap gin may be made with alcohol flavoured by having the 'botanicals' (the berries and other flavouring plants) steeped in it, while the better gins are redistilled so that essential oils and other volatile substances are refined in the process. Gin is usually a rather unsatisfactory spirit for use in cooking and for flaming, but there are some good modern recipes that use it (such as *rognons à la liégoise*).

Sloe Gin

Pick the sloes on a dry day when they have been mellowed by an early frost. Remove the stalks and prick the fruit all over with a darning needle. For each 225 g (½ lb) of sloes allow 450 ml (¾ pt) of gin, 50 g (2 oz) sugar and 6-10 blanched, bruised almonds. Bottle and leave for 3 months, then strain off the liquid and re-bottle it.

[*Gin* – French: *gin* German: *Genever, Wachholderschnaps* Italian: *gin, liquore di ginepro* Spanish: *ginebra*]

GINGELLY OIL. *See* sesame.

GINGER (*Zingiber officinale*) is indigenous to the tropical jungles of southern Asia, but has also been used in China for thousands of years. It was coming along the trade route into Europe long before Roman times. Today it is grown all over the world in suitably warm climates. A few years ago, most people in Britain knew it only dried, powdered or crystallized, or as Chinese ginger preserved in syrup. Today, it is easy to buy fresh ginger, a benefit brought by immigrants from India and the Caribbean, where ginger is in everyday use. Americans have it because of the popularity in the US of Chinese food, and it is grown in Florida. Further north, if sprouting rhizomes are planted in good, humus-rich soil, they will grow into a plant, but even in a Mediterranean climate the yield of ginger at the end of the growing period will be negligible. Perhaps it would give more rewarding results if grown in a heated glasshouse. Fresh ginger rhizomes bought in the autumn, when they are resting, keep well for a long time in a dry place. I used to keep them in sherry in the refrigerator, but they are then less good than fresh ginger, so there is no point in preserving ginger this way except in summertime when it has sprouted and will not keep. A method of keeping ginger which is recommended by Elizabeth David and is particularly useful if you have a damp kitchen, is to wrap the rhizome in foil and keep it in the freezer. You can take it out to grate off what you want and then put it back.

Dried ginger comes in two varieties: black, also known as green, which is simply dried, and white, which is parboiled, bleached and skinned. The flavour depends more on where the ginger has originated, but dried ginger has a markedly different taste to fresh ginger and cannot accurately replace it in Asian dishes.

[*Ginger* – French: *gingembre* German: *Ingwer* Italian: *zenzero* Spanish: *jengibre*]

GINGER BEER. A drink made by fermenting a solution of sugar in water with added lemon juice, ground ginger and sometimes other flavourings. The so-called 'ginger beer plant' is a mixture of yeasts fed with ginger and sugar. Real ginger beer is alcoholic; how alcoholic depends on the strain of yeast used, the amount of sugar and the length of fermentation. Ginger beer has been used in cooking as the liquid in which to cook ham.

GINGERBREAD, as sold in Paris as early as the 14th century, was a highly spiced, hard cake sweetened with honey and very elaborately decorated, even gilded with gold leaf, as it was used as a medicine. It may have been made in Britain in medieval times, and its ingredients in 16th and 17th century England included honey and almonds. After 1660, treacle, which is now accepted as a traditional component of gingerbread, became available. The French version, *pain d'épices*, is made with honey and rye flour instead of treacle and wheat flour as in the British version; it is an ingredient in *carpe à la polonaise*, in which, with onion, shallots, caramel and wine, it goes to make up the sauce. Similarly, ginger biscuits are used in various ways in modern quick recipes both for meat dishes and for sweets.

[*Gingerbread* – French: *pain d'épices* German: *Pfefferkuchen, Lebkuchen* Italian: *pane pepato* Spanish: *bizcocho melado*]

GINKGO or **maidenhair tree**. The ginkgo tree (*Ginkgo biloba*) is probably native to Western China, although it has been grown for many centuries in Japan, and is called the maidenhair tree because the leaves are shaped like those of the maidenhair fern. It is the last representative of a plant order which was very important in prehistoric times, a sort of living fossil. There are separate male and female trees. Ginkgo trees were first planted in Europe in 1780. They fruit well in Mediterranean countries such as Italy, but more rarely in Britain. (A specimen planted by my grandmother in Sussex in 1921 bore a few small fruits in 1977, but that was unusual.) The fruit resembles a small greenish-yellow plum 2.5-4 cm (1-1½ in) long. The flesh smells beastly, like vomit, but the nut inside is an important ingredient in Japanese cooking, and is also eaten on its own, roasted. Ginkgo nuts will keep in a covered pan for some weeks, if refrigerated.

GIROLLE. *See* chanterelle.

GJETOST. *See* whey.

GLACÉ FRUIT. *See* candied fruit.

GLASGOW PALE. *See* Finnan haddock.

GLASSWORT. *See* samphire.

GLAYVA. Liqueur based on whisky.

GLAZING is covering with a thin film of anything that looks like glass, so includes *ceramic glazing. Food glazing has several meanings. For instance, to brown a dish quickly under the grill is to glaze it, especially when the dish is sprinkled with fine sugar that caramelizes to make a shiny topping. Egg white, milk or *dextrin brushed on buns glazes them. In other contexts, glazing can mean brushing with melted jelly or jam.

Cold meat dishes are often glazed with a jelly that is traditionally made by boiling down the more cartilaginous parts of animals – knuckle of veal, shin of beef, mutton shank – to produce a clear, fat-free stock, and then reducing it by further boiling until a strong jelly forms. However, most people these days will use gelatine as a basis for glaze and make a very firm jelly (9-14% gelatine). Since the gelatine itself should be tasteless, it is salted and flavoured with meat extract or, better, the jelly that has formed under roasted meat. Vinegar, lemon juice, or other flavourings may be added as well, and the glaze can be coloured with caramel, whitened with a little cornflour or left clear. It is always melted in a *bain-marie* (like an old-fashioned glue-pot), never on an open flame, and lightly brushed on the meat when it is almost cool enough to set. Once it has set, a second or even third coat can be given. While glaze is usually applied for the sake of appearance, it is also used commercially to protect meat products and in that case may contain sodium benzoate as a preservative.

GLOBE ARTICHOKE. The original artichoke, a thistle (*Cynara scolymus*) is related to the *cardoon (*Cynara cardunculus*). Both come from the Mediterranean region, where the cardoon can still be seen growing wild, unlike the artichoke, which has been in cultivation for thousands of years.

The part of the globe artichoke eaten is the young flower bud, most of which is tough. Only the bases of the scales are tender enough to eat; also, the spiny filaments of the central choke (which will eventually become the purple part of the flower) must be discarded. The meatiest parts are the flower base or *fond* and the top of the stalk. The latter only needs peeling to remove the fibrous outer part. Blanched shoots and tender leaf midribs are also sometimes eaten in the same way as the cardoon. They must be carefully peeled to remove the stringy parts before cooking.

In Mediterranean regions, globe artichokes are a common and cheap winter and spring vegetable. There are a number of distinct varieties propagated by suckers, since seed does not run true. The plant is perennial, and each year the flower buds are cut when they are young and tender. In Britain, artichokes are not well understood; although some are imported, they are usually expensive and often hang around the shops until they are stale and have a rank taste. Greengrocers know that they can be revived several times by trimming the stalk and standing them in water, but this cosmetic treatment improves only the looks. Artichokes from British gardens can be eaten in early summer, but they are often of spiny types and left too long on the plant. Artichokes will stand very little, if any, frost, and in Britain the plants need protecting with straw in winter.

Globe artichokes are most commonly prepared simply by boiling them in plenty of salted water (a pinch of bicarbonate of soda will keep them green) and then serving, hot or cold, with melted butter, *vinaigrette*, mayonnaise or other appropriate sauces. They have to be eaten with the fingers, the scales are pulled off one at a time, the base of each dipped in the sauce and the flesh scraped off between the teeth. The spiky choke must be scooped out and discarded before the base is eaten. Tender stems, after trimming, are delicious boiled in salted water and served with a béchamel or mornay sauce. Very young and tender artichokes are also excellent raw, and are commonly eaten this way in Spain and Italy.

For more elaborate dishes, the tough parts of the scales are pared away and the unpleasant choke removed, so that everything that remains is edible. Experience shows how much must be cut away – to begin with it is best to bite a piece to test it. It is a serious mistake to be mean and leave fibrous bits. Better to throw away too much than too little. To prevent the artichokes going black on cut surfaces, rub them with a slice of lemon or keep them submerged in acidulated water until they are ready to cook. Once cooked, artichokes should not be kept for more than a day, as toxins develop which can be upsetting.

Globe artichokes are regarded as being medicinal and having a boosting effect on flagging livers. They are the basis of the well-known aperitif, Cynar.

Alcachofas a la romana

A delicious way to eat young artichokes. After paring them, slice them vertically. The slices are then dipped in flour and egg to coat them lightly and fried in deep oil. Eat them with a squeeze of lemon juice.

[*Globe artichoke* – French: *artichaut* German: *Artischocke* Italian: *carciofo* Spanish: *alcachofa*]

GLUCOSE ($C_6H_{12}O_6$) is the best known of the monosaccharide *sugars and is often referred to as dextrose which is, more specifically, the name given to the naturally occurring form of glucose. It can be said to be the most abundant organic compound in nature, as cellulose, starch and the carbohydrate storage material of animals, glycogen, are all built up from it (and can be broken down into it). It occurs in its own right, along with *fructose, in sweet fruits and honey.

What we know as glucose in the kitchen is not usually a pure sugar but a mixture of dextrose with *maltose and *dextrins made by the hydrolysis of starch with dilute mineral acids. It is sold in bulk as irregular chips or, more often, as a pale-coloured, heavy syrup (*corn syrup in the US). Pure glucose, which is sold by pharmacists, is a fine white powder.

Glucose will not crystallize and is used to prevent graining during sugar boiling. Commercial glucose is used largely in confectionery and jam manufacture, in canning and sometimes to supplement the natural sugars of the grapes in wine-making. Although glucose is sometimes advertised as a source of 'instant energy' in glucose drinks, it is worth noting that sucrose is converted to glucose in the body and absorbed almost as quickly.

[*Glucose* – French: *glucose* German: *Glukose, Glykose* Italian: *glucosio* Spanish: *glucosa*]

GLUTEN is a mixture of proteins which occurs especially in wheat and to a lesser extent in some other cereals. Its two main constituents are proteins called gliadin and glutenin, which absorb water and form elastic strands when flour is kneaded with water. If a small ball of dough is soaked in water for half an hour, the starch can be washed out of it by kneading under a running tap. The sticky material, something like chewing gum, which is left behind, is the gluten. This is the constituent of flour which makes possible the light structure of leavened bread. The proportion of gluten varies with the type of wheat from which the flour is made, as well as with its variety and where it was grown.

When a dough is leavened with yeast or baking powder, tiny bubbles of carbon dioxide gas are trapped in the gluten. These bubbles expand when the dough is baked to give a light, open texture. Gluten with a tough quality is hard to blow up, but soft gluten, although it blows up easily, also collapses easily. It should thus be sufficiently elastic to blow up into bubbles of the right size, but should also hold its shape until set by baking. Gluten is toughened by kneading and mixing, by salt (dough without salt goes sticky) or by acid (sour milk in scones or lemon juice in puff pastry), but it is made softer by fat, sugar, yeast enzymes, malt enzymes, bran and germ (as in wholewheat flours). Gluten absorbs water – the greater the gluten content of flour, the more water it will hold and the larger the mass of dough that can be made from a given quantity. A strong flour usually has a high gluten content and a high-rising, high water-absorbing quality; it can make a large volume of dough with a light, open texture, such as is needed in bread. A low-gluten, soft, starchy flour usually makes the best cakes and biscuits. Variation in gluten content and in other water-absorbing constituents often makes it impossible for cookery writers to specify exactly the

quantity of liquid required in a mixture.

Low-density, highly-aerated starch-reduced rolls are made from flour from which almost all the starch has been taken, leaving mainly gluten.

People who suffer from coeliac disease – an intolerance of gluten – require a gluten-free diet to protect them from the harmful effects produced by eating wheat, rye and, to a lesser extent, certain other cereals.

[*Gluten* – French: *gluten* German: *Gluten* Italian: *glutine* Spanish: *gluten*]

GLYCERINE or **glycerol** ($CH_2OH.CHOH.CH_2OH$) is an alcohol, traces of which are produced during several types of bacterial and other fermentations. It is present in *fusel oil and is rather bad for the liver. As it is one of the substances formed when fats are treated with caustic soda, it is also present in home-made soap. Most people know it is a sweet, water-clear syrup which can be obtained from pharmacists. In the past, it was regarded as a soothing remedy for softening the hands or for doctoring sore throats on account of its moisturizing qualities. For the same reason, it was put into commercial cherry cake to stop it going stale too quickly. Glycerine is, however, a wolf in sheep's clothing because (like other alcohols) it grabs and holds on to water, and so while it seems to be moistening the dry throat it is actually taking water from the tissues. A substance best avoided.

[*Glycerine* – French: *glycérine* German: *Glyzerin* Italian: *glicerina* Spanish: *glicerina*]

GNOCCHI. *See* pasta.

GOA BEAN (*Psophocarpus tetragonolobus*). Used as a green bean in tropical Asia and West Africa, this *legume is characterized by its four-angled pods. These are cooked whole. The roots are also edible.

GOAT is closely related to sheep. It is sometimes quite difficult to tell them apart when faced by goat-like sheep or sheep-like goats amongst the many breeds, especially in the Middle East. Goats have horns which are more or less flattened or rounded behind and with a keel in front, although the keel may only be represented by knobs. Some goats, though, are hornless. Billy-goats have beards and a strong smell, but rams do not. The meat of old goats is tough and worse, if possible, than old mutton. I was once forced to subsist for a week on the meat of an elderly ibex – a species that is so close a relative of the goat that they freely interbreed – and do not recommend its tough, goaty-flavoured meat. However, young kid is excellent and is regarded in Mediterranean countries as the equal of young lamb. It is especially popular in Italy, where *capretto* or better still the *capretto di latte* (milk-fed kid) is a delicacy, roasted in a number of ways, often with garlic and rosemary. In the US, kid is called chevron. In Britain, however, goat has never been popular, although it was traditional to keep the animals in and about stables, as (to quote from the Revd J. G. Wood's *Natural History* of 1860) 'there is a prevalent idea that the rank smell of the goat is beneficial to horses.' He goes on to say that 'a very firm friendship often arises between the goat and one of the horses. Sometimes it gets so petted by the frequenters of the stables, that it becomes presumptuous and assaults anyone whom it may not happen to recognize as a friend. Happily, a goat, however belligerent he may be, is easily conquered if his beard can only be grasped...' It was said that the goat was the only animal that would boldly face fire, and that its chief use in stables was to lead the horses to safety. Because goats, when they are allowed to roam, destroy trees and eventually cause erosion, they are now much less plentiful than they were. However, they are useful to smallholders as a source of *milk, which also makes wonderful cheese.

[*Goat* – French: *chèvre* German: *Ziege* Italian: *capra, capro* Spanish: *cabra, cabrón*]

GOAT'S BEARD. *See* salsify.

GOFIO. A flour made of toasted cereal – wheat, maize or barley – and a speciality of the Canary Islands. It is sold as a health food throughout Spain. The flavour is nutty, and in many ways it is very similar to *tsampa* and *satu* of the Himalayas and Tibet. In the Canaries it is commonly eaten as a gruel or fried in cakes and used as a substitute for bread.

GOLD. Generally regarded as a rather useless metal except to give in exchange for something else, it is nonetheless remarkable in its resistance to corrosion, being unaffected by air, water, acids or alkalis and so requiring no cleaning. It is, therefore, an excellent metal for plating. Although pure 24 carat gold is too soft to be practical, lower carat gold, often laced with copper, is harder and more useful. Gold was a component of early medicines, and its use to decorate gingerbread was a survival from medieval days when gingerbread was also

considered medicinal. In cooking, it was a part of the Italian Renaissance extravagance. Both gold leaf and silver leaf were harmlessly used by the cooks to Mogul emperors and wealthy maharajas in India as a food decoration. They are still used on occasion in Indian *tandoori* kitchens. Elizabeth David remembers a wedding in Delhi at which the food was literally smothered in gold leaf. In Indian cookery, the use of gold and silver leaf today is mainly in sweetmeats. The only time I used silver leaf on a party pilau, most of the guests thought I had been careless with a foil wrapper. Tiny flakes of gold leaf are also put into *Danziger Goldwasser* and other liqueurs for show.

[*Gold* – French: *or* German: *Gold* Italian: *oro* Spanish: *oro*]

GOLDENBERRY. Synonym for Cape gooseberry. *See* physalis fruit.

GOLDEN CUTLET. *See* Finnan haddock.

GOLDEN SYRUP is a thick syrup or pale, golden treacle, famous as the accompaniment to British suet pudding and, in its way, as important to Britons as maple syrup is to Americans. This syrup is a trade secret of Tate & Lyle and was devised by Abram Lyle, a sugar refiner from Scotland, in the 1880s. At that time, a by-product of sugar refining was an uncrystallizable syrup, which was thrown away, as no use was known for it. After some experiment, Lyle found that further refining would produce a delicious golden syrup. He sold this locally and it immediately became popular. However, Lyle was not yet satisfied and continued to experiment and to refine the product still further. Ten years later, he had produced a syrup so clear that one dissatisfied customer described it as looking like castor oil. He had to backtrack.

It is actually the impurities in the syrup which give it both colour and taste – a lesson to all technicians. The basic analysis is 24% glucose, 23% fructose and 33% sucrose. There are no starch-conversion products, such as dextrins, which are found in *corn syrup but there are small amounts of inorganic compounds of calcium, iron and phosphoric acid. The high sugar content makes it impossible for any spoilage organisms to grow.

A tip worth knowing is that if Golden Syrup is applied quickly to burns, it reduces the pain and disperses the blisters. (*British Medical Journal*, 4th May 1935).

GOLDWASSER. *See* liqueurs and cordials.

GOMOST. *See* whey.

GOOD KING HENRY. *See* spinach.

GOOSE. The goose is the adult female, the gander the adult male, and the young up to six months are goslings. The Greylag goose (*Anser anser*), from which present day breeds are descended, was reared in numbers by the Romans, who even force-fed them to fatten the livers, as is done today for *foie gras. The goose has never become domesticated and tamed to the extent of the duck or the domestic hen. Geese do not adapt to modern intensive rearing and do not produce eggs endlessly. Even the best-laying Chinese geese do not lay more than a hundred eggs a year, while most table breeds lay no more than 30 or 40. Geese like to forage for themselves on green grass in fields – another problem, as they make a nasty mess, and other animals do not like to graze with them.

In Britain, farmyards used always to have a few geese, but they are now less commonly kept. You can still see them *en masse* in the parts of France where *pâté de foie gras* is made, in parts of Germany where they still like goose for Christmas, and in Yugoslavia, Hungary and Romania. There can be few more picturesque sights than children minding a flock of geese, something that takes you straight back to the old fairy-story books.

Apart from its bloody-minded attitude to being mechanized, the goose for modern tastes, is considered rather fat. That surely is the whole joy of it, but to enjoy it demands a healthy appetite and a cold winter's day. Geese are anyway at their best from the autumn through to February. Goose fat is the preferred and traditional cooking medium of the Landes and other parts of south-western France, but even so, the goose does not have great dishes based on it (to complement those based on its liver). *Confit d'oie* is, however, an excellent way to preserve it in its fat, and is essential to a perfect *cassoulet de Toulouse*.

In Britain, goose is customarily roasted with a sage and onion stuffing; in France, the stuffing is of apples or chestnuts; in Germany, the Christmas goose is traditionally stuffed with apples and prunes, with an accompaniment of red cabbage. However, Germany has many stuffings for goose, and some include a sprig of mugwort or wormwood, a medieval custom. A sausage is made in Germany and France (where it is called *cou d'oie farci*) from the goose's liver enclosed in the skin of the neck.

Wild goose. Many species of wild goose come south in winter. Although wildfowlers have shot them as they have ducks, in Britain wild geese are generally considered poor eating compared to other game.

North Americans cannot be of the same opinion, since over a million geese are shot every year in the US, mainly Brent, Canada, Snow and White-fronted geese, which come south to winter. The meat is dark and lean (unlike the domesticated goose). Ganders weigh 3.5-6 kg (7¾ to 13¼ lb) and the females would be a kilo (2 lb) lighter. Only those that are less than a year old are said to be good to eat.

[*Goose* – French: *oie* German: *Gans* Italian: *oca* Spanish: *ganso*.

Gosling – French: *oison* German: *Gänschen* Italian: *paperino* Spanish: *ansarino*]

GOOSEBERRY. Gooseberries (*Ribes uva-crispa*) belong to the same genus as red currants. They are native to Europe and their natural habitat is damp woods and valleys. Although they have been cultivated for a long time, they are essentially plants of the north, thriving in cold damp climates and not much grown or even known in southern France. Gooseberries are not very popular in the US, where the plants do not thrive particularly well because of pests, especially the American gooseberry mildew, which is also now rife in Europe. American varieties are usually crosses of European gooseberries with local species, notably the Currant gooseberry (*Ribes hirtellum*) with small purple fruits and the Worcesterberry (*Ribes divaricatum*). The latter was at one time wrongly thought to be a cross between a black currant and a gooseberry. Neither is as yet of much importance commercially. Varieties range when ripe from green through white to yellow and red. The old rule that green varieties taste better than red and hairy ones better than smooth is not always correct. Dessert varieties are larger and sweeter than cookers; they are fine to eat raw, but when cooked do not have the same 'gooseberry' flavour as the cookers. Gooseberries are popular in Britain and in Germany, but in France they are mainly used in the north-west – Normandy and Brittany – and then largely in a sauce for mackerel (hence the French name, *groseilles à maquereau*). They are little known in Spain and Italy, and rarely seen in the markets there. In addition to being used in fools, tarts, and jam, they can be made into gooseberry jelly, gooseberry wine and gooseberry vinegar. There are old recipes for crystallized gooseberries and a dried sweet gooseberry paste on the lines of quince paste. In Germany, gooseberries have been dried as a raisin substitute.

Chinese gooseberries or **kiwi fruit** (*Actinidia sinensis*) were first grown commercially in New Zealand and are now being cultivated in America. The fruit is covered with a furry, brown skin, inside which is a pleasant, firm, lime-green pulp. The taste is slightly acid, and not much like gooseberry. The fruit is supposed to have a tenderizing effect when it is rubbed onto meat, and contains ten times the vitamin C of a lemon. Opinions vary as to its gastronomic merit, probably because people do not understand it. Some find the fruit delicious and some rather insipid. I do not find kiwis very exciting – possibly I abandoned them before finding a good variety. Cape gooseberries are *physalis fruits.

[*Gooseberry* – French: *groseille à maquereau* German: *Stachelbeere* Italian: *uva spina, ribes* Spanish: *grosella blanco o verde*]

GOOSEFOOT. *See* spinach.

GOURD. *See* marrow.

GRAHAM FLOUR. The American name for wholewheat flour, and the name 'Graham' indicates that the food (for instance, Graham crackers), are made from wholewheat flour – at least in theory. The Revd Sylvester Graham (1794-1851) was a Connecticut parson and an early health-food nut, who preached 'brown bread and the Bible' and said that spices caused insanity and meat inflamed the baser passions. Even tea was claimed to cause DT's. He is said to have expected to live to 100 but was actually called to his Maker at the age of 57, having proved or disproved nothing.

GRAINS OF PARADISE, Guinea grains or **Melegueta pepper.** The plant from which these come, *Aframomum melegueta*, is a relation of the cardamom that is found only on the coast and islands of tropical West Africa. The grains, which are used as a spice and as a substitute for pepper, are its seeds. With ginger and cinnamon, they went in the past into the spiced wine which was called hippocras. Today, they are very little used but might just be found in specialist shops.

GRAM. From the Latin *granum* (a grain), via the Portuguese *grao*, to become, in India, the general term for small pulses other than those now called peas and beans. *Gram*, in Indian cooking, always means *channa, a variety of chickpea, unless otherwise indicated, as in *black gram.

GRANA. *See* parmesan.

GRANADILLA. *See* passion fruit.

GRAND MARNIER. *See* liqueurs and cordials.

GRAPE. The majority of grapes are varieties of the European grape (*Vitis vinifera*), which is one of the oldest cultivated plants. However, there are plenty of other species – little-known ones grow wild in the Himalayas, for instance, while those of North America are important because famous cultivated varieties like Concord, Catawba and Niagara are descended from them (notably from the northern Fox grape, *V. labrusca*) but also from the Muscadine grape (*V. rotundifolia*). Grapes descended from American native vines tend to be large and watery in comparison with those from the European vines, and often have a foxy tang to them, but do have thin skins which slip off easily. European vines were taken to America by the early colonists (for example in 1616 by Lord Baltimore), but none did well as the East Coast climate is rather unsuitable for them and the vines could not stand the local pests. Indeed, one of these, the root louse *Phylloxera*, when introduced into Europe accidentally in the last century, almost completely wiped out the European grapes. They were saved only by grafting them on to resistant American root stocks. However, the European grape varieties do thrive west of the Rockies and are grown in huge quantities in California. Of the myriad numbers of grape varieties, a rough division is made between wine grapes and dessert grapes. In general, wine grapes are small, often tough skinned and very sweet. They may be black, red or white, and they strongly influence the character of the wine made from them. In the newer wine-producing countries, which have few if any traditional names for their wines, the wines may be called after the grape – *cabernet, sauvignon* or *reisling* – and the practice, which is also usual in Alsace and Germany, is being adopted increasingly elsewhere, for example in northern Italy. Because the grape is a *pineau noir*, it does not follow, of course, that a wine made from it will be burgundy. It also takes the soil and climate of the Côte d'Or and generations of experience. Dessert grapes also come in hundreds of varieties, ranging over a wide spectrum of colour and quality, from the meaty muscat-flavoured Hanepoot grapes of South Africa to the wild-flavoured black Concords from the eastern US. Even the same grape variety tastes different when grown in different countries. Most grapes have seeds, but seedless grapes are becoming more popular, even though the number of varieties available is limited. In California, half the grape acreage is devoted to Thompson Seedless, a type of sultana grape. Seedless grapes are the most convenient to use in cooking (as in *sole veronique*); varieties with seeds must be halved and seeded, a process that is worth the trouble in the case of Muscats, which give the best flavour. Unripe sour grapes are an excellent souring agent, and the classic source of *verjuice, although that used in mustards today is often synthetic. The juice of sweet grapes is available sterilized and bottled.

Grapes are made into jam and jelly, which can be good but often lacks flavour and acidity. Sweet grape juice can with advantage replace sugar in certain dishes, and it is in some countries boiled down to a sweet syrup, *dibs.

Dessert grapes should be bought with care. Grapes are best when they have ripened on the vine, although bunches that have ripened in transit may improve a bit if they are hung in the sun. The fruit is perishable and should be put into the refrigerator if it is not to be eaten immediately. For full flavour, a grape should be sun-warm and not icy, though on a hot day, cold grapes can be delicious. In Europe most people wash grapes by dunking them at the table. They know that the fruit has been sprayed and the spray has possibly not been cleaned off by rain. But wet grapes are of doubtful gastronomic value, and it is better to wash the grapes and let them dry beforehand. A pair of scissors or clippers should accompany grapes which are served as dessert so that small bunches can be clipped off, or the division into manageable bunches can be accomplished less elegantly in the kitchen. Bunches of grapes are often offered for sale enclosed in bags to prevent dropping and damage in handling. They are among the few fruits that may benefit from such packaging, as grapes tend to drop badly when they have been fully ripened on the vine. Grapes for export are picked when barely ripe, packed carefully in boxes and refrigerated, which is why northern countries can enjoy grapes grown in the Southern hemisphere. Dried grapes are *raisins, *sultanas and *currants.

From the culinary point of view perhaps the most important part of the vine is not the grape (except for wine) but the *vine leaves. Even the prunings of vine are used for making a flavourful fire for a barbecue, or for grilling spring onions. Grape seed oil is used for frying.

[*Grape* – French: *raisin* German: *Traube* Italian: *uva* Spanish: *uva*]

GRAPEFRUIT. When you contemplate that most dreary of all openings to a meal, you may sometimes wish that the grapefruit had never been invented. After oranges, grapefruit (*Citrus paradisi*) are the most grown citrus fruit in the world today. Their origin is still in doubt, but it is thought they arose as a mutation from the *shaddock in the West Indies. The first mention was in the 18th century, when they were referred to as the 'Forbidden Fruit of Barbados', and it was not until 1814 that the word 'grapefruit' first appeared (in Lunan's *Hortus Jamaicensis*). Grapefruit travelled from the West Indies to Florida in 1809 and were grown there by one Odet Philippe, a surgeon who had served with Napoleon and whose name is remembered by growers to this day. Florida is now by far the world's largest producer of grapefruit, although a lot are grown in Texas, California and Arizona. Outside the US, the West Indies, South Africa and South America are large producers. Grapefruit also grow well in Mediterranean countries – Cyprus and Israel produce a lot, for instance – and in parts of India.

The tree is large for a citrus and the fruits vary in size, sweetness and flesh colour. Some varieties have pink flesh and some are seedless. Skins are yellow, sometimes flushed, and may be smooth or slightly rough. They are often waxed and polished for sale. Grapefruit did not come into commercial production until 1885 and were not generally known except in Florida until well into this century. Cookery books written at the end of Victorian times may mention the shaddock but not the grapefruit. Today, however, the fresh fruit is available all the year round, the sections are canned, and the juice is canned, frozen and condensed. The fruit are not very perishable and can be kept for some time in the refrigerator. They can remain on the tree for months like lemons, gradually getting sweeter.

Grapefruit is a dangerous fruit to mix with others in fruit salads as it is assertive, and most of the 'starters' in which grapefruit segments are mixed with shrimps, mayonnaise, and almost anything the magazine cookery writer can devise, are better forgotten. Grapefruit does not go with wine, which hardly matters at breakfast. It freshens a furred palate and it is supposed to be healthy and slimming.

When buying grapefruit, look for dense, heavy fruit which are likely to be juicy and not to be dried out or to have a thick and pithy skin. Avoid rough skins and shrivelled fruit.

[*Grapefruit* – French: *pamplemousse* German: *Pampelmuse* Italian: *pompelmo* Spanish: *pomelo, toronja*]

GRAPPA is the Italian equivalent of *marc, distilled from the refuse left after pressing out the wine grapes. It is the great speciality of Bassano in the province of Treviso. Grappa has a strong, individual flavour, a taste for which one could say is acquired rather than bestowed by Providence. *Con ruta* on the bottle and a leafy sprig inside means that the grappa is flavoured with rue. Some Italian recipes, mainly from the northern provinces, call for grappa. For instance, *faraona al vino rosso* (guinea fowl in red wine) from the Veneto, uses it, as do such sweets and cakes as the *zelten* of Trentino and *fave dei morti* of Lombardy, and the small cheese fritters known as *sciatt* from the Valtellina.

GRAS DOUBLE. The fatter outer layer of the ox stomach, usually sold cooked in France, otherwise simmer it for five hours in slightly salted water. In England, it is not distinguished from other forms of *tripe.

GRASS PEA. *See* lath.

GRAVLAX, gravadlax (Swedish), or **gravlaks** (Norwegian). Literally 'grave salmon', this treated salmon is one of the world's great food specialities. Methods of making it vary from one country to another, but basically the salmon is boned into two fillets, rubbed on the cut faces with a mixture of salt, saltpetre, sugar, ground black pepper and finely-chopped dill, put back together and pressed under a weight for 24-36 hours. *Gravlax* is usually eaten raw – it has been 'cured' by the salt – with a sauce. Occasionally, it is grilled or lightly baked in foil with dill. *Gravlax* is expensive, but well worth trying for a treat.

Each 30th April (Walpurgis Night), Sweden celebrates the end of winter and the arrival of spring. The main dish is usually *gravlax*, with the following mustard sauce.

Mustard Sauce for Gravlax

Mix together in a bowl 2 tablespoons mustard and 1 tablespoon each of vinegar and sugar. Then add 6 tablespoons oil, a little at a time, until well blended. The sauce will thicken rapidly and must be stirred vigorously. Finally, add 6 tablespoons sour cream and plenty of finely-chopped dill.

GREEN ALMOND. *See* pistachio nut.

GREEN BEAN. *See* *kidney bean.

GREENGAGE. *See* plum.

GREEN GRAM. *See* mung bean.

GREEN LAVER. *See* seaweed.

GREENS. *See* cabbage.

GREENSAUCE. *See* sorrel.

GRENADINE. A French fruit syrup made from pomegranates and sugar.

GRILLING or **broiling**. In the old days, this always was done on an iron grill over red hot charcoal and was distinguished from roasting which was done beside the fire. Grilling therefore was a combination of radiant and rising heat, while roasting was almost entirely done by radiant heat, and the meat did not get so much taste from the fire. Also, since the heat of grilling was more intense, it was a method suitable for smaller bits of meat – steaks, chops and so on. The modern electric or gas grill is in a sense more like roasting since the cooking is by radiant and not by rising heat. The meat, of course, does not get the taste of the fire or of burning drippings. In barbecue grilling, it is important that the grill be really clean, something that cooks often neglect. Before use, the grill should be heated and rubbed with fat so that the meat does not stick. The grill should preferably be slightly inclined to encourage the fat to run down the bars and so to minimize dripping into the fire. Dry meats should be brushed over with oil before being cooked. Salt should be sprinkled on the meat only at the last moment before it is put on the heat, as it will otherwise make the juices run. In the US grilling is still called broiling, an old English term.

[*Grilling* – French: *griller* German: *auf dem Rost braten, rösten* Italian: *cuocere alla graticola* Spanish:

asar a la parrilla]

GRILSE. *See* salmon.

GRINDING. Sometimes it is useful to be able to grind things in the kitchen. For those wishing to grind their own wheat or chickpeas, small hand grinders can be bought. With chickpeas, it will be necessary to put them through twice. Grinding spices is best done in a small whirling-blade coffee grinder kept for this purpose. Very hard, large pieces, such as dried ginger and whole turmeric need to be cracked with a hammer first or they may break the blades. In making spice mixtures, oily materials like cloves and mace are best ground with non-oily spices such as ginger, turmeric or chilli if possible. The difference between freshly-ground spices, coffee and even flours and the commercially-milled, bought versions is immense – more than you will imagine until you have tried.

[*Grinding* – French: *moudre, émoudre* German: *mahlen* Italian: *macinare* Spanish: *moler*]

GRISKIN. In cutting up pigs (especially for bacon), when the spine is separated from the sides, some 5 cm (2 in) of meat are left attached to it, and this is known as the griskin. The word is also used for bits of loin. In small pigs, the griskin is left attached to the top of the spare ribs. *See* chine.

[*Griskin* – French: *grillade de porc* German: *Schweinsrücken, Rippenstück* Italian: *coscia di maiale*]

GRISSINI. Finger-thick, crisp bread sticks, a speciality of Piedmont, especially Turin, but now made commercially and distributed throughout the world. The excellence of *grissini* was noted in writings in the 17th century. Napoleon was partial to the *petits bâtons de Turin*, and an attempt was made to make them in Paris, with two Torinese experts brought in for the purpose. The result was a disaster. tough sticks of pale bread instead of the crisp, light and beautiful *grissini* of Italy. *Grissini* are extremely difficult to make by hand and require great dexterity. They are formed by taking strips of dough about 1 cm (⅓ in) thick and 7 cm (3 in) long and pulling it out into a thin filament almost 1 m (about 3 ft) long, then swinging it to shape it and laying it out on a sheet sprinkled with rice flour. In Piedmont, Lombardy and a few other places in Italy, it is still possible to get the authentic *grissino stirato torinese*, which is preferred by some to the factory-made *grissino*. However, commercial *grissini* are often excellent and, properly packaged, have the advantage of keeping crisp and good for two weeks,

while the hand-made article keeps for at most a day. *Grissini* are very digestible, very dry – they contain only 12% moisture compared to 25-40% in bread – and are baked at a high temperature, usually 250°C (480°F).

GRITS. Grain which has had the hull removed and has been ground into a coarse meal. In Britain, the grain is usually oats, but in the US, usually maize (i.e., hominy grits). Groats, which are mixed with hot milk as an infant food, are oat grits.

[*Grits* – French: *gruau d'avoine* German: *Grütze* Italian: *tritello d'avena* Spanish: *avena a medio moler*]

GROATS. *See* grits.

GROENE HARING. *See* herring.

GROS SEL. *See* salt.

GROUND CHERRY. *See* physalis fruit.

GROUNDNUT. *See* peanut.

GROUSE, PTARMIGAN and **CAPER-CAILLIE.** The grouse family are game birds of the cold North and mountain regions, and are characterized by their feathered legs and feet. Its members include the ptarmigan (*Lagopus mutus*) from Europe and North America, and the caper-caillie (*Tetrao urogallus*) of Scandinavia, northern Russia, the Alps and the Carpathians, which clings to the north of Scotland (after having become extinct there and been reintroduced). It also includes the hazelhen (*Tetrastes bonasia*) of Scandinavia and Eastern Europe and the Black grouse (*Lyrurus tetrix*), which is also called the blackcock (male) and greyhen (female). One of the many American species, the Sage grouse (*Centrocercus urophasianus*), feeds on sage buds; it needs to have the crop removed as soon as it is shot, but even then does not have a very pleasing flavour on account of its diet.

None of these relatives approaches the Red or Scottish grouse (*Lagopus lagopus scoticus*) – usually just known as grouse – for quality. Indeed, many gastronomes have said that grouse is the finest game bird in the world. The Red grouse is a subspecies of the Willow grouse (*Lagopus lagopus*) of Scandinavia and North Russia, a bird which, like a ptarmigan, has a lot of white on it and goes almost completely white in winter. The Red grouse is ruddy brown and does not go white in winter. Probably because of its diet of heather buds and berries on the moors, it has an incomparable flavour. Such is the cult of the grouse that experts claim to distinguish between the flavour of birds from one part of Britain and another, and say it also varies from year to year, like a wine vintage. Red grouse are found only in the north and west of Britain and in Ireland; they live only on moors. The shooting season starts on 12th August and lasts until 10th December. Visitors to Britain at that time may have a unique experience. The best grouse are those born the same year and eaten before mid-October.

Young grouse will have clean, fresh-looking claws and a flexible tip to the breastbone – like other young birds. They are hung as long as possible – a week in warm weather and considerably longer in cold (unless they have been badly shot) – and are then plucked, wiped (never washed), drawn, trussed neatly either without the head (or with the head tucked under the wing) and roasted. They are best done very simply, perhaps stuffed with a spoonful of butter mixed with a few rowan berries. Older grouse may be made into pies or *pâtés*, but grouse recipes are never elaborate as the bird needs little added flavour.

[*Grouse* – French: *tétras* German: *Birkhuhn, schotisches Moorhuhn* Italian: *starna di montagna* Spanish: *gallo de bosque, lagópodo escocés, ortega*.

Ptarmigan – French: *lagopède* German: *Alpenschneehuhn* Italian: *pernice di montagna* Spanish: *perdiz blanca*]

GUANCIALE. *See* bacon.

GUAVA. The guava (*Psidium guajava*) is a tropical and subtropical fruit, originally from central America but now grown all over the world in warm climates, though not greatly in the Mediterranean region or in the US. It is important in India, South East Asia, Hawaii and Cuba. In many places, it is a poor man's fruit, as it runs wild, even becoming a pest and producing poor quality fruit, which is nonetheless useful as it contains about ten times as much vitamin C as an orange, and vitamin C is a frequent deficiency in tropical diets.

The name guava comes from the Spanish-American *guayaba*. The plant is a small tree of the myrtle family, which includes such important plants as eucalyptus, and the spices allspice and cloves. The fruit looks superficially something like a quince (though no relation), being greenish, yellowish or creamy in colour, round or pear shaped, with a smooth or rough thin skin, according to variety. The whole fruit is edible. Inside, it is divided into two zones, an outer seedless one and an inner pulp which usually contains minute gritty seeds (although there are seedless varieties). Good guavas are acid-sweet, with a strange exotic flavour. The smell is very strong, especially when the fruit is over-ripe, and it drowns all others in Asian fruit markets during the guava season.

Unripe fruits are so astringent that they are inedible. The best fruit are plucked perfectly ripe, but commercially they are picked when the colour is just turning from green to yellow, so that they will be ready about 24 hours later. Guavas go off rapidly. Though they can be kept in cold store for up to a week, the results are not really satisfactory. Guavas are therefore rarely available outside the warm countries unless they have been flown in as a luxury. They make excellent jelly and guava cheese (a stiff fruit butter).They are also canned, and the better brands are worth eating, although the flavour is not quite the same as in the fresh fruit.

The related cattley or Strawberry guava (*Psidium cattleianum*) is native to Brazil and is sometimes cultivated. It is reddish purple, smaller than the guava, and good to eat.

[*Guava* – French: *goyave* Italian: *guaiva* Spanish: *guayaba*]

GUINEA FOWL. There are a number of species of guinea fowl which make up the small family Numididae. They come from Africa, where they are plentiful in some places. I once stayed for a month with a Kenya farmer whose wife served guinea fowl for lunch and dinner every day, and never any other meat. After a while, I became interested and made enquiries. From other guests I discovered that guinea fowl were so plentiful in the area that the farmer had probably eaten no other meat for at least eight years, possibly longer. Since guinea fowl run and rarely take to the wing where they can be shot, the technique was to go out in the evening with a pack of assorted dogs who compelled the birds to take to the trees where they could be picked off with a .22 rifle. Getting the day's supply took no more than a few minutes.

The handsome speckled bird we know was domesticated from West Africa long ago. It was known to the Romans as Carthage or Numidian hen. Until after Shakespeare's time what we now call guinea fowl were known as turkeys in English – people thought they had come from Turkey (the place everything from foreign parts seems to have been ascribed to in the old days). It was only later that the name was transferred to the American turkey. Presumably the early colonists called their new-found birds after the smaller, but in some respects similar, bird they knew at home. To confuse things further, the old French name for guinea fowl was *poule dinde*. Guinea fowls are smaller than chickens and were often hung and used as substitutes for pheasants in Victorian times to cover the months when real pheasant was out of season.

The flesh of young guinea fowl is excellent, though rather dry. As domestic birds, guinea fowl have the snag that they are inveterate wanderers, almost always trying to hide their nests and never quite liking captivity. The eggs, smaller than hens, are slightly speckled, with very thick shells, so that when boiled they take some cracking. They are excellent when hard boiled and are used as a substitute for plover's eggs. Roasted guinea fowl tends to be rather dry, so the bird needs to be larded, or at least barded. There are also some excellent casserole recipes in British, French and Italian cookery books, and guinea fowl, under the guise of Bohemian pheasants have even had a place at banquets, though they are in general neglected.

[*Guinea fowl* – French: *pintade* German: *Perlhuhn* Italian: *faraona, gallina di Faraone* Spanish: *gallina de Guinea*]

GUINEA GRAINS. *See* grains of paradise.

GUITAR FISH. *See* shark.

GUM is used more by industry or by professional cooks and sweet-makers than in the home. British gum is another name for *dextrin. Of the true gums, gum arabic and gum tragacanth are the best known. These, like most other gums, are chemically closely related to *pectin. Gums are colloids, which usually dissolve completely in water, but not in alcohol, and they can be obtained by wounding various plants, mainly trees, and collecting the sticky stuff that exudes. In this, gums may seem similar to resins such as *mastic, but in other respects they are quite different. (Resins contain essential oils and do not dissolve in water.) Both gum arabic and gum tragacanth were known in pre-Christian times. In ancient Egypt, for instance, gum arabic was used in paint as long ago as 2000 BC. It is still largely produced and shipped from Egypt, although nowadays Senegal, India and other parts of the world including the southern US have an important production. Gum tragacanth comes mainly from Iran, Turkey and Syria. Both these gums are exuded from small leguminous trees, gum arabic from

a small acacia, *Acacia senegal*, and tragacanth from *Astragalus gummifer* of the milk-vetch genus. Acacias are well known to flower lovers and include the 'mimosas' which flower so profusely in Mediterranean countries in January, although they are Australian trees more correctly called 'wattles' (the flowers are candied for cake decoration). Another acacia, *Acacia farnesiana*, originally from the West Indies and abundant in the Jordan Valley, produces a gum as fine as gum arabic.

Gum arabic. Strips of bark are removed from the acacia in spring (February to May). After about three weeks, the tears of gum can be removed. These are dried and bleached in the sun; after cleaning they are ready for export. Gum arabic is colourless and without taste or smell. Although there are a few people who are allergic to it, it is generally considered harmless. In food manufacturing, it is a stabilizer used in the soft drinks and brewing industries, in chewing gums, jellies, jujubes, marshmallows and various food mixtures. In ices, it retards the crystallization of sugar. Gum arabic can usually be bought from chemists (it was used in making pills). When melted in a little hot water, it makes a gum useful for sticking and varnishing in cake decoration. It can be coloured and used as a paint on marzipan. Artificial frost for cakes can be made by painting a thin layer of the gum on a clean glazed surface and allowing it to dry until it crazes, after which it is scraped off and roughly powdered.

Gum tragacanth. Collected in the same way as gum arabic, it can be bought in tears or flakes. A commonly used, and cheaper, substitute is Karaya or sterculia gum (from a plant of the cocoa family), which can be bought as a powder. Gum tragacanth has a faintly gluey taste, but is harmless. Allergies to it are very rare, and it is one of the oldest known emulsifiers. Commercially, it is used in water ices, salad dressings, jellies and candies. Gum tragacanth can be used to make small cake ornaments if it is soaked in water, and then mixed into a paste with icing sugar, the mixture can be coloured and moulded into shapes.

[*Gum* – French: *gomme* German: *Gummi* Italian: *gomma* Spanish: *goma*.

Gum arabic – French: *gomme arabique* German: *Gummiarabikum* Italian: *gomma arabica* Spanish: *goma arábiga*]

GUMBO. *See* okra.

GUR. See jaggery.

GUTTING. See drawing (for birds), fish.

GYPSUM, calcium sulphate ($CaSO_4$), a common mineral. It is to some extent soluble in water and in tap water causes the 'permanent' hardness which is not removed as a precipitate by boiling. Plaster of Paris is gypsum that has been heated in a furnace.

Adding gypsum to wine is known as plastering, an ancient technique for increasing acidity, already known – and complained about – by the Romans. Hot-country grapes (unless picked early so that a percentage of them are unripe) are liable to lack the acidity that is necessary for the preservation and flavour of good wine. If gypsum is added, it reacts with the *cream of tartar that is naturally present to produce tarraric acid plus calcium tartrate and potassium sulphate. Calcium tartrate is not soluble in water, so is precipitated as a sludge, which settles out. Unfortunately, the potassium sulphate remains in the wine, and this is unwelcome. Plastering is always done in making sherry because the *palomino* grape is always short on acid. Apart from that, in most wine-producing countries, the use of gypsum has been discontinued. The modern alternative is to add tartaric acid instead of gypsum.

[*Gypsum* – French: *gypse* German: *Gips* Italian: *gesso* Spanish: *yeso*]

h

HADDOCK. See cod.

HAGGIS. A type of sausage consisting of minced sheep's liver, heart and lungs, mixed with toasted or plain oatmeal, onion and fat (usually suet), seasoned with salt, pepper and nutmeg, packed in a sheep's stomach and simmered in salted water for 4 hours. (Haggamuggie is similarly prepared from the liver of a fish.) There is much argument as to the origin of this, the Scottish national dish, some saying it was introduced by the Romans, others that it came from France. Why shouldn't it have come from Scotland? On a farm north of the Cairngorms, where I worked one winter, two things were plentiful besides the snow: oatmeal – the farm workers had part of their wages paid in it – and sheep. Given those two ingredients, and the bleak cold to keep out, it is difficult to see how the invention of haggis could have been avoided. Ever since then, whenever we killed a sheep on expeditions, I have made haggis (with wild onions and porridge oats). Apart from being tasty and filling, sheeps, innards dealt with in that way would keep for up to two weeks, even when being carried about from place to place. Haggis, indeed, is not a Burns Night speciality, but an economical, basic food of hard-living people.

Haggis

Carefully wash a sheep's stomach, soak it in the burn for an hour, turn it inside out and scrape it, then scald it. Meanwhile boil the sheep's liver and heart (and the lungs, if you like) to harden the meat before chopping it finely with a knife. Add 2 cups oatmeal (which has been lightly toasted in a dry pan), some chopped fat or suet – 2-3 handfuls – plenty of salt, pepper and nutmeg, and a couple of chopped onions. Mix all together with some water to make a paste. Stuff it into the cleaned stomach, not too full or the oatmeal will burst the bag when it swells. Sew up the openings and any weak places, and secure in loops of string for easy handling. Pop the haggis into boiling, salted water and cook it slowly for 4 hours. Hang it up to dry. When you are ready to eat it, cook it again in salt water until it is thoroughly hot. Dish. Slash through the stomach wall and spoon out the savoury contents. Drink whisky with it. The traditional Burns Night accompaniment is mashed swede.

HAKE. See cod.

HALAL. See religious food laws (Muslims).

HALIBUT. See flatfish.

HAM. From the old English word *hamm*, a thigh, ham is the salted and aged back leg of the pig, unless otherwise specified, as in, say, mutton hams or badger hams. Commercially cured and pressed pork shoulder is also referred to as 'ham', which strictly speaking it is not. A close relative is gammon, which is the leg cured as part of a Wiltshire side of *bacon. It is not therefore matured for long enough to get much of a hammy taste, and does not keep. However, gammon is often boiled or baked and used as a mild ham, although it is most frequently sliced into rashers or cut into bacon joints.

It is probable that ham curing was originally perfected by the Gauls, who exported hams to Rome over two thousand years ago. Their products cannot have been very different from the best hams of today, as they raised pigs of the old, semi-wild ridgeback type in the forests that then covered most of France. They salted the hams for two or three days, smoked them, and finally rubbed them with oil and vinegar before hanging them up to dry. Lean, rangy, forest-fed hogs make the best-flavoured ham to this day.

Ham, like cheese, comes in a host of different types according to the way in which it is made and matured. Of first importance is the breed of pig, its age and the food it has eaten. It also matters whether the pig has been living a sedentary or energetic life, and whether it was killed without exhaustion or fear. Pigs which have been chased round and frightened are thought everywhere to make bad ham and bacon. Experts can tell by the smell of the meat if the pig has been tired or disturbed. For once, humanity and commercial practice are in agreement. Curing may be done with many mixtures, although all are based on salt. Usually saltpetre is in the mixture and often sugar. For the rest, there is a choice of molasses, vinegar, herbs, spices, paprika and no doubt secret ingredients. The curing may be done with dry salt or brine, or a combination of the two, with varying strengths and times. Commercial hams are now usually 'pumped'; that is, brine is forced directly into the meat through the femoral artery before the more traditional curing processes begin. Hams may be dried off in fresh air or smoked with oak, beech, pine, juniper berries, hickory, apple, sage, bay, heather, peat and even seaweed. Combinations of these will give quite different smoky tastes.

Finally there is variation in the ageing and maturation – in the length of time, the conditions and temperature involved. During this period, which may be from a few months to two years, the ham develops its hammy taste by complicated and incompletely understood processes. At best,

the subtlety is like that of wine-making, and some districts excel in making superb hams just as some produce superb wines. They say it is due to the drying effect – and even purity – of the air, although one might think that both were easy to duplicate by artificial means; it is more likely the tradition of expert knowledge, love and care.

Some hams are intended to be eaten raw; others, cooked. There are also dual-purpose hams. Any ham is safe to eat raw after it has hung for several months (if not, it will also be unfit to eat cooked), but most dual-purpose hams are better cooked. The finest raw ham can equally be cooked, though it is a crime to do so except where small amounts are used as a flavouring (for instance, *prosciutto crudo* goes into some of the best stuffings for *tortellini*).

To keep whole hams at home, simply hang them in free air in a cool, dry place. The temperature should be between 0°C (32°F) and 15°C (60°F).The problem in most houses is finding a suitable spot, since cellars are too damp and attics vary from too hot to too cold. In old farms, the best place was the kitchen ceiling, away from the stove. Whole hams for long ageing are best hung where an eye can be kept on them. Cracks may be filled with a mixture of salt, fat and pepper – the last helps to keep away flies. A white powdering of mould is part of the normal ripening process – like the rind of a cheese – but if the ham grows long whiskers or green mould, it is too damp. Hams are sometimes wrapped in calico, which is coated with several layers of limewash, or they are enclosed in stockinette, or even packed in boxes filled with dry wood ash and kept above floor level. Once the ham has been started, the cut surface should be kept covered with paper. Ham that has been bought sliced must be kept in the cool part of the refrigerator and well wrapped to prevent drying out. It does not improve with keeping.

Before cooking, all hams – except ready-to-bake commercial hams and very lightly-salted hams like *Jambon blanc* – need to be soaked in cool fresh water to remove some of the salt. The soaking time varies with the saltiness of the ham and its size, which may be from 2 kg (4½ lb) to 12 kg (27 lb). There may be manufacturer's recommendations to follow, or the shopkeeper may offer good advice. If you have to guess, you should taste the water after 15 minutes of cooking, and if it is too salty for comfort start again with fresh cold water. Although some correction is possible, a bad error of over-saltiness, especially with a big ham, may be beyond recall. Home-cured hams, farm hams, Smithfield and Virginia hams – hams made by old methods –

are soaked overnight. It is easier to bone ham after soaking than before.

Before cooking, hams should be trimmed, which, in practice, means cutting off any bits you would not like to eat. Hams are always started in cold water and brought slowly up to temperature, which should be ideally 77°C (171 °F), at which there is least shrinkage. They may go 5°C (9°F), even 10°C (18°F) higher, but *must never boil*. Average cooking time is around 50 minutes per kg (25 minutes per lb), but it may be more or less according to the size and type of ham. You should cook the ham until the small bit of chump bone can easily be pulled out, or, more precisely, until you get a meat thermometer reading of around 65°C (150°F) in the centre of the thickest part. Ham should be allowed to cool in its liquid until it is easy to handle; the skin should then be pulled off. The fatty surface may be covered with breadcrumbs or glazed, according to preference, though ham is widely thought to taste better without a covering. Part of the fat is sometimes pared away, but as some people like the fat, it is best to leave it on.

Some 20% of the weight of a ham consists of inedible bone and trimmings, while 20% is often lost in cooking. As a further 20% is sometimes lost by evaporation during long ageing, the amount of cooked ham you finish with might be only 40% of the weight of the original leg – one reason why ham can be an expensive food. Even the pumped, under-aged hams of ordinary commerce usually give only 60-70% of their original weight in cooked meat.

British and Irish Hams

There are many traditional cures – almost every county has its own. They range from hams, like Cumberland hams, which are simply dry-salted for three weeks and then hung in the kitchen rafters to mature, to hams with sweet Suffolk and Devonshire treacle cures, in which vinegar or beer are used.

Many country hams are only locally available. The now famous collection of recipes made by *Farmer's Weekly, Farmhouse Fare*, contains details of many of these, as they are still made on some farms up and down the country. Britain lacks the habit of eating raw ham. Irish hams are usually peat-smoked, which gives them a characteristic flavour.

Bradenham ham. Made at Chippenham, Wiltshire and cured by a secret recipe dating from 1781, it can be recognized by its coal-black outside with the name branded on it. Bradenham ham undergoes a six-month cure, during which time it absorbs flavour from molasses, juniper berries and spices, so that it has a sweet, unusual flavour. A delicacy, with its own character, and not a ham for routine consumption.

Wiltshire ham or **gammon**. If the ham (gammon) is removed from a Wiltshire side of bacon, it may be boiled to produce a mild-flavoured joint. It will lack the strong ham taste that is obtained by long maturation. Gammons of this sort are made from young, quickly-grown bacon pigs, and although tender, lack flavour. The mild cure makes them unsuitable for hanging and keeping; they are really bacon rather than ham.

York ham has a dry salt cure; it is matured 3-4 months and may be lightly or heavily smoked. A mild, pale pink ham, always cooked and, at its best, regarded everywhere as the finest type of cooked ham. York hams are not made in York – the cure is a popular one which is used all over the world. Unless otherwise instructed, soak the ham for 6-24 hours and cook it 15 minutes per 450 g (1 lb). Epicure ham is similar to York ham; No. 1 is heavily smoked and No.2 is lightly smoked.

American Hams

The best hams in the US are reckoned to come from Kentucky, Georgia, Tennessee, North Carolina and, above all, Virginia, where the famous Smithfield ham is made. Run-of-the-mill ham, however, is made by the quick-cure injection method and is not very noteworthy. Hams of all types, ready to boil or bake, can be bought complete with instructions on the pack.

Kentucky ham. Made from Hampshire hogs, range-fed on acorns, beans and clover, and finished on grain, these have a high reputation. They are dry-salted and smoked over apple and hickory for 30 days, after which they are aged for 10-12 months.

Smithfield ham is defined as being made from peanut-fed hogs from the peanut belt of Virginia and North Carolina, cured and processed in Smithfield, a small town on the James River estuary in Virginia. The pigs, at best, are allowed to range in the woods for some months and are turned into the peanut fields to root before being finished on corn. Smithfield hams are dry-salted with a mixture which includes pepper, and then heavily smoked with apple and hickory. They are aged for a year or more. Smithfield ham is eaten baked or boiled (rarely, if ever, raw), served hot or cold and often glazed with a sweet glaze such as jam, sugar or honey. Unless otherwise instructed, soak the ham overnight and cook 20-30 minutes per 450 g (1 lb). Virginia hams are traditionally made from razor-back hogs. Queen Victoria used to have six hams per week sent to her from Smithfield – or were they for Albert?

Tenderized hams and **precooked hams**. To be baked at 160°C (325°F) for 20 minutes per kg (10 minutes per lb).

French Hams

France produces excellent hams with many regional types of *jambons de campagne* (country hams) both unsmoked and smoked. *Jambon d'York* is also made and sold all over the country. Cheaper 'hams' are made by boning, rolling and pressing the shoulder (*épaule roulée*) or salting the forehock (*jambonneau*).

Jambon blanc, jambon de Paris or **jambon glacé**. Unsmoked ham, lightly cured in brine, always eaten boiled and usually cold. Cook for about 40 minutes per kg (20 minutes per lb) without prior soaking.

Jambon de Bayonne. The centre for this most famous French regional ham is at Orthez, about 40 miles east of Bayonne. This ham is always eaten raw, never boiled, but is sometimes used as an ingredient and flavouring in cooked dishes. As it is smoked (at a low temperature) to a golden brown colour, it has a smoky flavour, though not aggressively so, and in this respect is unlike the raw hams of Spain and Italy which are unsmoked.

Jambon de campagne. Local ham, made all over France. These hams may be smoked or unsmoked, and many are eaten raw as well as cooked, or used as an ingredient in cooking. Often mentioned in French cookery books, is the ham from Morvan (south-east of Auxerre) and those of the Auvergne and of Alsace and Lorraine. Such hams should still be made by honest salting or brining, and not by the injection method, although this is increasingly used in France as elsewhere for the sake of economy. Injected hams do not need such long soaking as traditionally made ones.

Jambon de Toulouse. A fine, unsmoked ham eaten raw or cooked, or used as an ingredient in cooking.

Italian Hams

Ham, especially raw ham, is very popular in Italy, and the best Parma ham is probably the finest of all raw hams, unless you prefer a smoky flavour. It is the Italians who created what is perhaps the world's finest summer *hors d'oeuvre*: raw ham with green figs.

In addition, Italy produces good cooked ham (*prosciutto cotto*), often boned and pressed into shape, as well as the redder and less tasty pressed shoulder (*spalla*), which is forced into a rectangular mould. Other Italian ham products include *coppa and *culatello.

Prosciutto crudo. Traditionally, the hams of Parma were made from pigs at least eight months old and were salted only in the winter. Before slaughter, pigs for the best ham must be rested for some 24 hours, especially if they have made a long journey. The hams are dry-salted with sea salt for 25-30 days, then wiped clean and hung in the crowded curing rooms so that fresh air reaches the hams from all sides. (Curers are continually opening and closing windows according to the weather and the breezes.) If the skin dries too much, or the hams crack, repairs are made by rubbing them with a little fat or plugging cracks with a paste of fat and pepper. The maturation must be for at least 8-9 months and may be as long as two years in exceptional cases. The average ham (cured in winter) is ready in the following July and August (when figs and melons are ready to eat with it). So much attention and the great loss of weight from evaporation during hanging make *prosciutto crudo* expensive. The most famous comes from Langhirano near Parma, but that of San Daniele in Friuli, near Udine, has its own cure and is almost equally famous. (In Sardinia and Maremma, hams are made from wild boar, these are easy to recognize because they are black and bristly.) Raw ham is eaten finely sliced as an *hors d'oeuvre* with good butter or green figs or melon.

German Hams

Germany makes some delicious hams, and is especially renowned for types which are subtly, yet strongly, smoked. The most famous is Westphalian ham, but there are many other excellent local hams, mostly named after their town or district: Hamburg, Mainz, Stuttgart, etc.

Lachsschinken. Literally 'salmon ham', so-called from its salmon-pink colour, this expensive German smoked-pork product is not strictly a ham, as it is made by lightly curing and smoking the loin of pork, which is cut into joints and rolled in sheets of bacon fat to conserve moisture and flavour. It is always eaten raw, cut in thin slices and served as an *hors d'oeuvre* with brown bread and butter, accompanied by horseradish sauce. In French *charcuterie*, it is called *filet de saxe*. A similar product is made in Poland and widely exported.

Westphalian hams are taken from mature pigs which have been well rested before slaughter. The hams are cooled and the blood massaged out before they are dry-salted (with an 8:1 mixture of salt and saltpetre) for up to two weeks. They are then put in a 20% brine for another two weeks, washed and packed down to ripen for yet another two weeks, and sometimes for as long as a month. Finally, they are scrubbed in lukewarm water and hung up to smoke and dry, a process which traditionally takes several weeks, but which commercially is nowadays often cut to little more than a week. Smoking is done at a very low temperature over beechwood sawdust mixed with juniper twigs, with juniper berries thrown in from time to time. The finished Westphalian ham has a lovely dark chestnut colour and a strong, but subtle, smoky taste. It is eaten raw in thin slices either alone or, at most, with brown bread and butter, and fresh black pepper. Some recommend it with melon or green figs in the Italian manner, but the smoky taste is better without such accompaniments.

Spanish Hams

Some of the cheaper commercial types of Spanish cooked and pressed ham are gelatinous, tasteless and best avoided. Hams of slightly better quality may be labelled *jamón de York, jamon cocido* (cooked ham) or *jamón en dulce* (sweet), but they are not the best that the country has to offer. Of much greater importance is the *jamón serrano* (mountain ham) which is eaten raw in sandwiches or as an *hors d'oeuvre*. In fact, it is in many ways similar to Italian raw ham, though with a character of its own. Correctly, and at its best, *jamón serrano* is made from hams taken from the black Iberian (*Ibérico negro*) pig, which has been allowed to run free in the forests, getting plenty of exercise and staying lean. The Red Iberian pig (*Ibérico colorado*) runs the Black a close second, but is slightly lazier (and so fatter). Experiments have also been made at crossing other breeds of pig with wild boars in order to produce little fat and fine flavour, but the modern tendency to make cheaper (though far from cheap) *jamón serrano* from white hybrid pigs is increasing. It is frowned on because fat has to be cut off, which it never is when hams are made from traditional breeds – and because curing is also reduced to 4-6 months. The result is very naturally not so fine tasting. A real *jamón serrano* from an Iberian pig will weigh 6-8 kg (13¼-17½ lb), while a fake usually runs only 4-5 kg (9-11 lb).

Typically, the Iberian pig is killed in autumn and the hams are put in salt, without saltpetre, for 8-10 days. They are sometimes brined for three weeks, but it is important that the hams are not over-salted. They are then scrubbed clean and hung in the rafters through the winter. When the weather starts to warm up in May, the hams begin to sweat (cups are hung underneath to catch the drips) and they are allowed to do so for 7-10 days, after which they are moved to cool cellars (where the stink of ripening ham becomes overpowering) to be ready for eating in autumn that is, a year after they were first salted. Most famous *jamón serrano* is from Jabugo (Huelva) and Montánchez (Cáceres), where the air is pure and good for drying, but close runners are Trévelez (Granada), Sotoserrano and Candelario (Salamanca). Although Spanish raw ham is liable to be tough (being from well exercised pigs), its flavour is very fine.

Embuchado de lomo. Cured pork loin, enclosed in a skin like a sausage, and preserved in a bath of olive oil. An excellent and expensive Spanish speciality.

Other Hams

Belgian. Belgian hams are excellent and *jambon d'Ardennes* has an international reputation.

Pragerschinken. In spite of its German name, this ham comes from Czech Republic. The hams are salted and brined for several months before being smoked over beech sawdust and matured in cool cellars. *Pragerschinken* is often cooked whole and served hot, and is considered by many to be the finest ham for serving hot, just as York ham is the finest cooked ham for serving cold. (Soak it for 6-24 hours and cook it about 30 minutes per kg or 15 minutes per lb.)

[*Ham* – French: *jambon* German: *Schinken* Italian: *prosciutto* Spanish: *jamón*]

....

HAND. In pork butchery, the front leg and adjacent meat.

HANGING. When an animal is freshly killed, the muscles are soft and relaxed, but after an hour or so (as every reader of detective stories knows) *rigor mortis* sets in and the muscles become hard. Animals eaten completely fresh are usually tender, but are likely to be tasteless. With *rigor*, the flesh becomes tough; later, after a variable time (depending on temperature and other factors), the *rigor* passes off. The flesh starts once more to become tender. This tenderizing process is due to autolysis by enzymes in the meat, not to bacterial decomposition, although that will later play a part. At the same time, as the meat becomes tenderer, it gains in flavour and eventually becomes 'gamey'. The cycle is very obvious in a fish, which passes through the changes quickly. A mackerel, to take an example, is flexible when landed but soon becomes stiff. Pick one up by the tail in the fish market. If it sticks out horizontally and is nice and stiff, then it is fresh enough and good to eat. But if it flops, *rigor mortis* has already passed off, and the mackerel when opened will be found to have started deteriorating. Fish is usually eaten fresh, although skate may be better slightly hung. The length of time a mammal or bird should be hung for best tenderness and taste is very variable – getting it right is a matter of judgement and experience.

Only a few definite instructions can be given. Meat should always be hung in a dry, cool, airy place, away from a wall, and kept entirely clear of *flies. In many cases, butcher's meat has not been hung long enough when you buy it, but it would be inadvisable, if only for economic reasons, to hang small cuts of, say, *beef after you have bought them. The length of time that game is hung is discussed under individual entries. Long-hung

meat very often gets a mould growing on it, but this is harmless and is cut off before the piece is prepared. Indeed meat can be stinking high and full of maggots, as long as it is to be cooked. The main problem over really high game is not that it is bad to eat when cooked but that it is likely to be very unpleasant for the cook who has to prepare it. The danger of food *poisoning lies in meats that have been left lying around after they have been cooked. Certain peoples, like the Turkana tribe in northern Kenya, are used to eating really rotten meat. They will eat it when it smells so bad that other people feel sick; they even eat vultures on occasion. Because the Turkana have iron constitutions, which have adapted over the centuries to their diet, they are able to eat putrid meat raw without apparent harm – which would not be wise for the rest of us.

HARE. *See* rabbit and hare.

HARENG SAUR. *See* herring.

HARICOT. *See* kidney bean.

HARISSA. A very hot chilli-based mixture of spices used in North African cooking, with couscous and so on. It can contain up to twenty spices and might be likened to a curry powder or *garam masala*, though it tastes nothing like either. Harissa can be bought in specialist shops and formulae are often secret. It is also available as a paste in small cans. You can use a pinch of cayenne or some chilli if *harissa* is not available. Paula Wolfert in her *Moroccan Cuisine* (Grub Street 1998) suggests another chilli-based preparation, Indonesian *sambal oelek*, as a substitute. Her recipe for *harissa* is as follows:

....

Harissa

Cover 30 g (1 oz) dried red chillies with hot water. Soak for 1 hour, then drain and cut into small pieces. Make into a purée by pounding in a mortar or grinding in an electric spice mill with 1 clove garlic and 2 teaspoons caraway seeds (or 1 teaspoon caraway seeds plus ½ teaspoon each ground cumin and coriander seeds). Sprinkle with a little salt before spooning the purée into a clean jar and covering it with a layer of olive oil. Covered tightly and refrigerated, this *harissa* keeps for 2-3 months.

....

HARUSAME. *See* noodles.

HASLET or **harslet** is the edible innards – the pluck – usually of a pig, or these parts prepared and spiced in the caul and cooked as a sort of jumbo *faggot which can be sliced and eaten cold. More refined (which does not mean better) versions replace the innards with pork meat and rusk.

HAWTHORN. *See* rowan.

HAZEL NUT, **cob nut**, **filbert** or **Barcelona nut**. There are a dozen species of wild hazel found in the temperate woods of Europe, Asia and America. The trees bear nuts of varying sizes and excellence which were no doubt eaten by our ancestors even before *Homo sapiens* became human. Apart from the familiar hazel nuts, there are good species of local importance in China and Japan, as well as hazels in Tibet and the Himalayas which have the nuts in strange prickly clusters.

The cultivated nuts we know are derived from *Corylus avellana* (the cob, which grows wild in Britain), *C. maxima* (the filbert, a larger nut from warmer southern Europe and countries bordering the Mediterranean) and *C. colurna* (the Turkish hazel, which overlaps the filbert in the Middle East, especially in Turkey). It need not bother us that the first two are sometimes claimed to be mere varieties of the same species. You can tell the difference between cobs and filberts when the nuts are growing (in the filbert the husk completely covers the nut and extends beyond it, while in the cob it does not – you can usually see the nut peeping out), but it is almost impossible to tell them apart when they are shelled or even in the shell. The Kentish cob, which is grown in Kent, is not a cob but a filbert.

The most important producers of hazel nuts are Italy, Spain, Turkey and France. In Italy, hazel is grown particularly in Campania (around Naples), Liguria, Piedmont and Sicily, as well as everywhere in the hilly regions of the Apennines. In Spain, hazel nuts come especially from the Catalan provinces of Tarragona, Barcelona (hence Barcelona nuts) and Gerona, but also from Asturias and Galicia in the north-west. Spain makes the most original use of nuts in its regional cooking. Turkish nuts tend to be cheaper and smaller than the good Italian and Spanish nuts, but are excellent nonetheless. Going under names like Messina cobs and Trebizond nuts, they are much grown, especially on the lower slopes of the mountains fringing the southern shores of the Black Sea – not far from Trebizond, in fact. France has large quantities of hazels from Brittany and around Le Mans, in the Vendee south of Nantes, in parts of the south and the foothills of the Pyrenees.

Portugal, Greece, Tunisia, Algeria and Morocco also grow hazels in quantity. Other countries tend to produce them only for local consumption. In North America, little use is made of varieties of the largest indigenous hazel (*Corylus americana*), but European varieties are grown in Oregon. They do not do well in the eastern states.

In Germany, immature hazel nuts are sometimes preserved in brine or used in salads. Very young, fresh hazels are delicious. These are local specialities. Ripe nuts in the shell for dessert purposes keep well and are usually of the larger varieties. Hazels with very dark, almost mahogany-coloured shells have been kiln-dried. For most cooking, nuts can be bought ready shelled or even ground into a flour because shelled hazels, like almonds, keep better than most nuts and do not go rancid so rapidly.

Although hazels have been in use for so long (they were certainly collected and stored in the Bronze Age), in most countries they seem primarily to have been eaten as fresh nuts and not used in the cooking. When they are, it is usually in cakes and sweet dishes. They are especially popular in the confectioner's creations of Switzerland and Austria (in which they are often mixed with almonds), less so in France and Italy, though they appear in some versions of *torrone* (Italian nougat) and in *gianduia*, a hazel nut spread from Turin. From Italy, one should mention *torta alle nocciole* and the many versions of *torrone*. Indeed, many people seem to prefer them to almonds in cakes as they are more easily digested and have a lovely texture and flavour. Although the French have *beurre de noisette* (lightly roasted hazel nuts pounded with butter used as a garnish for *hors d'oeuvre*), it is only in Spain that the full possibilities of the hazel nut in savoury dishes have been realized, as in the Castilian *higado a la molinera* (liver cooked with onion, white wine and pounded hazel nuts) or the famous *salsa romesco* from Tarragona, which is used with fish or vegetables, or especially in a *calcotada* (a feast of spring onions grilled over vine clippings).

To remove the husk from the freshly-picked nuts, leave them in a layer about 25 cm (10 in) deep for a day or so until the nuts separate from the husk. Dry the nuts in a cool oven or in the sun for better keeping and store them in sawdust or sand.

To blanch and remove the inner skins, pour a kettle of boiling water over the shelled nuts. Let them stand for six minutes and remove the skins with the aid of a knife. Dry.

....

Higado a la molinera

Cut 500 g (1 lb) liver, preferably calf's, in pieces and coat it in flour. Fry the pieces in hot oil until they are just cooked and put them aside to keep warm. Bruise 2 cloves of garlic, put them in the hot oil, add a chopped onion and cook until they are golden. Return the cooked liver. Add a little flour to thicken the juice (plus a dash of water if needed), a handful of chopped, roasted hazel nuts and a handful of parsley. Adjust the seasoning with pepper, salt and a squeeze of lemon juice, if necessary, before serving.

....

Salsa romesco

There are many versions of this sauce, and a competition is held in Tarragona to establish who is the current Master of Romesco. Correctly the *sweet peppers in the sauce should be the highly-flavoured Romesco peppers grown in the locality and not available elsewhere in Spain. A reasonable alternative are ñoras or any other variety of dried, sweet pepper, but not chillies, which would make the sauce hot. Almonds are sometimes used as an alternative to hazel nuts.

Take 3 medium-sized ripe tomatoes; roast 1 tomato whole and keep the other 2 raw. Peel and remove the seeds from all the tomatoes and chop them roughly.

Roast one large clove of garlic in its skin on a hot iron pan (in Spain they use the stove top). When it is soft, skin it and add it to another unroasted clove. Roasting the tomato and garlic gives greater depth of flavour.

Fry a slice of bread without crust in a little oil until it is golden. Add the 2 dried ñoras with seeds and stalk removed and fry a little. Pound 12 roasted hazel nuts and all the other ingredients to a paste, and add 250 ml (8 fl oz) oil. Adjust the seasoning with about 1 tablespoon vinegar, salt, pepper and a little chilli if necessary, and balance with either a little more vinegar or with a trace of sugar. Use the sauce cold on vegetables or fish. It can be made in a blender, which produces a more emulsified texture.

[Hazel nut – French: noisette German: Haselnuss Italian: nocciola Spanish: avellana]

....

HEAD CHEESE. See brawn.

HEART, unlike most other offal, is made up largely of muscle, and very hard-working muscle at that, as it has spent the animal's entire life pumping away, circulating the blood around the body. Not surprisingly, it is inclined to be tough. The most tender (and tasteless) is calf's heart, which it is possible to grill or fry gently, but heart in general benefits from long, slow, moist cooking. Small lambs' hearts are usually stuffed and served whole, while large, tough ox heart is best cut in slices and stewed. All heart needs to be prepared for cooking by washing in water and removing fat, arteries, veins and any remaining clots of blood.

[Heart – French: coeur German: Herz Italian: cuore Spanish: corazón]

HEMLOCK. See spruce.

HERB PATIENCE. See sorrel.

HERBS. Essentially, in the context of cooking, a herb is a plant with aromatic leaves used as a flavouring. In the past, when the range of foodstuffs was narrow, and the quality probably poor, herbs were of enormous importance in the kitchen; they were also the basis of medicine. Indeed, many of the herbs used as flavourings were originally brought into use medicinally – some even for magical reasons.

In Elizabethan times, the herb garden was a most elaborate affair. At the opposite end of the scale, earlier in this century, herbs were reduced in Britain to mint (in bottled mint sauce and jelly), sage (dried in ready-mixed stuffing) and thyme (also dried in ready-mixed stuffing). Parsley was used only for decoration and an occasional bay leaf would be seen in the more advanced kitchens. Cookery books continued to mention chervil, tarragon and burnet, but who could get them? For years, virtually no one. But the use of herbs is coming back, partly because of greatly improved modern methods of drying (and even of deep freezing), partly because people have hybridized a greater interest in cooking with the realization that the days when British food was 'so good it would be a shame to mess it up' are long over. They have learned from gifted romantics like Elizabeth David that herbs – even garlic – are a part of the delicious and economical country cooking of Europe, and that if the greengrocer is not interested there is always the possibility of a box of earth on the kitchen window-sill. So now once more we find people with bay leaves and thyme, fresh marjoram and basil, chives and tarragon, mint and even lovage. The next lesson to learn is not to mix them all together, in delight.

There are no rules laying down which herb must be used with what dish, but certain herbs or combinations of herbs are used in particular national or local styles of cooking. For instance, French cooking uses bay, thyme and parsley in the *bouquet garni*, and chervil and tarragon are popular. In Italy, rosemary, sage, oregano and basil occur alone or in various combinations. Chives and dill are more commonly used in northern or eastern European cooking. To cook in regional style you must select the right palate of flavourings.

[*Herbs* – French: *fines herbes* German: *Kräuter* Italian: *erbe* Spanish: *hierbas*]

HERRING (*Clupea harengus*) is one of the group (including the sprat, sardine and pilchard) which have been possibly the most important of all fish, both for human consumption and, dried, for animal feed and oil. The herring shoaling off the coast of Britain were caught from Shetland down to East Anglia on the east coast and from the Minch to the Isle of Man on the west coast. As the shoals appeared at different times of the year on the fishing grounds, it was presumed that the same herring which were off Shetland in May slowly moved round the coast – June to August off Peterhead and Fraserburgh, August to September off Yorkshire and October to December off East Anglia. They were actually separate lots of herring which matured and spawned at different times of the year. The herring found off the Yorkshire coast and in the Clyde estuary are smaller than the others. Stocks, which once seemed inexhaustible are now so depleted by over-fishing that such extreme measures as a total ban on East Coast herring fishing have become necessary to allow the fish population to recover.

Before World War II, the herring was looked upon as a poor man's food – in 1928 they were offered wholesale at 6 kg (14 lb) for a penny. Until 1939, they were hawked from barrows in the street for six a penny. Nowadays you would be lucky to get three for a pound. Fresh herrings are delicious, full of flavour, oily and rich. They are perhaps best cooked in simple, traditional ways, either slashed and grilled, or rolled in oatmeal and fried. A fresh herring can be boned by removing the head and gut, and massaging the flesh for a couple of minutes. Then grip the exposed top of the vertebrae and pull. The herring will be turned inside out. Break off the bone near the tail end and turn the

herring back, skin side out. The open cavity is ready for stuffing, and the fish is practically bone-free, apart from the very fine floating rib bones which are left in. The *roes are often packed and sold separately as a by-product of the kipper industry. Before refrigeration, the catching of herring in glut quantity when the shoals arrived off the coast, led to the use of many preserving methods, such as salting, smoking and pickling. The products have become a part of tradition and are now made for their own sake rather than from necessity.

Whenever possible, use fresh herrings and bloaters the day you buy them. Otherwise, store them in a closed container in the refrigerator for as short a time as possible. Kippers will keep for one or two days after purchase, but the sooner they are eaten the better they taste. If they are to be stored, keep them in an airy place in a container lined with greaseproof paper.

Baltic herring. There are herrings in the Baltic, a small species (*Opisthonema oginum*). In France, the name Bismarck herring was changed to Baltic after the Franco-Prussian war of 1870, when Bismarck was naturally not very popular.

Bismarck herring. Boned herring fillets marinated in vinegar (or vinegar and white wine), with onion and spices ranging from red peppers to juniper berries. To prepare them, soak fresh herring fillets in vinegar for 6 hours, then pack them into jars in layers, between each of which is a sprinkle of salt, sliced onion, a pinch of chilli and a few juniper berries. Leave 24 hours and they are ready for eating.

Bloater. A speciality of Great Yarmouth in Norfolk, this type of smoked herring has been made for about 300 years. The herrings are sprinkled with dry salt and left overnight. The surplus salt is washed off and the fish is dried for several hours, then lightly smoked (at one time they were dried over a coke brazier). Bloaters are not gutted and so develop a somewhat gamey flavour. They do not keep for much more than a day unless refrigerated and were originally eaten locally in East Anglia, where – supply permitting – they are still popular. They are at their best in October and November, depending on the date when the herring shoals arrive off the coast. To prepare bloaters, open them down the back, bone them, butter the inside, refold them and grill. Bloater paste is a famous English delicacy, a favourite for tea time sandwiches. The soft roes of bloaters, dusted with cayenne pepper and fried in butter, were served on toast as a well-known Victorian savoury.

Bornholmere. Alternative French name for buckling *(see below)*. Bornholm is the Danish island at the entrance to the Baltic.

Bouffi. From the French *bouffi* meaning puffed or bloated. They are also called *craquelots* or *demi-doux*. The French equivalent of the bloater, very lightly salted and smoked. Like Norfolk bloaters, *bouffis* do not keep. They are eaten both grilled and raw.

Bratheringe. A German delicacy of boned herrings, floured and fried, then marinated in vinegar with onion slices, bay, peppercorns and mustard seed.

Buckling. Originally a German speciality from the Baltic (the alternative French name is *Bornholmere*), this type of smoked herring is now produced in Holland and Britain. At one time, the Jewish population of London would accept these only if the box felt hot, so that the fish were still warm from the kiln.

After a light salting, the fish are hot-smoked and so are cooked. The skin is toughened and should easily lift off to disclose the moist flesh underneath. In this respect, buckling are rather like smoked trout. They are usually eaten without further preparation, accompanied by buttered brown bread, lemon, red pepper, and sometimes horseradish. Skinned, filleted and cut in pieces, they may be used in salads.

A sauce served with smoked fish in Sweden is sour cream spiced with one or more finely-chopped fresh herbs, such as chives or dill, parsley and maybe some chopped spinach.

Craquelot. French bloater – *bouffi* (*see above*).

Demi-doux. Alternative French name for *bouffi* (*see above*).

Gendarme. Popular name in France for a *hareng saur* (*see below*), but the name is also used for a type of dry smoked sausage made in Switzerland.

Groene haring. Dutch for 'green herring', in other words a *matjes* herring (*see below*).

Hareng saur. The French equivalent of a red herring, *saur* referring to the colour and derived from the same old French as our word 'sorrel', which is still used to describe the red-brown colour of horses. Unlike the British red herring, the *hareng saur* is still popular in France today, and the fish may be bought by the piece from the barrel. These, at least originally, were salted on board the fishing boats and later cold-smoked. Before being eaten, *hareng saur* are de-salted by soaking in milk, tea or white wine for a couple of hours and then cooked – usually filleted, buttered and grilled. The French also put the fillets to marinate in oil, and such marinated fillets can be bought in plastic packets, loose or in cans. They are used as part of an *hors d'oeuvre*. The smoked hard and soft roes are sold separately, often packed in wooden boxes, and used for the same purposes.

Kipper is, classically, a herring which has been split down the back, gutted, salted in brine for about 10-15 minutes, and then cold-smoked over oak sawdust for 6-18 hours. However, as oak sawdust is now practically impossible to obtain, mixed hardwoods are used instead. A kipper was originally a male salmon after spawning, or a smoked salmon, and not a smoked herring. The method was then applied to herring by John Woodger of Seahouses in Northumberland in 1840. Splitting before smoking made possible a less salty product which compared favourably with red herring (*see below*). However, the kipper does not keep so well and would perhaps not have replaced the red herring had it not been for railways and refrigeration. In any case, replacement was gradual. In books published around the turn of the century, there are many recipes for preparing red herrings, but few for kippers. Kippers should not have a gamey smell and should be fat and pale. Excellent kippers, such as those from Loch Fyne and Craster (Northumberland), can be bought outside their areas, and the difference between them and the ordinary run-of-the-mill, commercial kipper is enormous. Fine kippers should be put, head down, in a jug which is then filled with boiling water. After leaving them for 10 minutes, they are cooked. They may also be grilled. My uncle's method is good for the more usual quality: butter the kippers, refold them, wrap them in greaseproof paper and bake the packets in the oven. Modern methods of selling kippers include packing fillets with butter in a plastic wrapper and also canning them. As with canned salmon, the bones are softened and the kippers can be broken up with a fork, spread on toast and lightly grilled.

Marinated herring of various kinds are especially popular in all the Scandinavian countries, where they are used in open sandwiches and, it often seems, as a starter for every meal. Great inventiveness has resulted in dozens of recipes, often secret, for herring fillets, which may be dark red, grey or pink, and in sauces that range from cream to mustard and wine. Denmark makes dozens of kinds of marinated salt herring, and many excellent ones are canned or packed in plastic and available as an export. Versions come in sauces including sweet-sour, tarragon, cherry, mustard, sherry and curry. These preparations are ready to eat without cooking, and usually need to be kept cool or in the refrigerator.

Swedish Marinated Salt Herring

The herrings recommended (by a housekeeper in Degafors) are the fat, wet, salted herrings that are exported from Iceland in barrels, but any good salted herrings will do. They are filleted and the fillets soaked in water overnight to remove most of the salt.

A marinade is prepared by boiling 300 ml (½ pt) water with a cup (or more to taste) of sugar, a good pinch of peppercorns and allspice, and a few bay leaves. When this is cold, add 1 cup vinegar with some sliced onion and carrot. Marinate the herring fillets in this for 2 days. Although the recipe is simple, the result is excellent.

Marinated Fresh Herring

Skin and fillet the herrings, sprinkle them with cooking salt, pack them in a dish and leave them 2-3 hours, then drain and dry. Pack them into a wide-mouthed jar and cover with the following marinade: To 300 ml (½ pt) each of white wine and vinegar add 4 onions cut in rings, 1 teaspoon peppercorns, 1 teaspoon coriander seeds, 6 cloves and 2 tablespoons salt. (The spices are an individual matter. You can use allspice berries, juniper berries, bay leaves, or what you will.) Leave at least 24 hours. This product will keep some 10 days in the refrigerator. The ideal quantities will vary with the ingredients used. A simple mixture of vinegar and water, when salted and softened with a little sugar, gives excellent results if it is formulated by taste before pouring over the fish.

Matie or **Matjeshering** is a herring in which the roe is not yet fully developed and is the first of the season's herring. Maties are very lightly salted in a brine of salt, saltpetre and sugar. They are eaten raw with chopped onion and boiled green beans and are available in May. They are also salted in the normal way and are often used to make red herrings with a rather cheesy flavour. This is a German speciality which is also eaten in Belgium and Holland (where they are called *groene haring* – green herring and where, by tradition, the first barrel is offered to the queen). Elsewhere, maties are a rather expensive import.

Matjessill is a sweet pickled herring and is the traditional lunch for Midsummer's Day in Sweden.

Red herring. In the Middle Ages, red herrings became an important product. After gutting, herrings were heavily salted and heavily smoked. This produced an article which would keep for some time, and which was tough, dry and easily transported inland. Red herrings were common until the beginning of this century, but were replaced by the kipper, which is less salty and needs no soaking. They are still produced in England (in Great Yarmouth) and are exported – Greeks eat them raw with bread and wine for lunch. Red herrings need several hours in lukewarm water or milk before they are ready for cooking. The exact time depends on the saltiness of the herring and on personal taste. They can then be slashed – the simplest method – or split down the back, boned, buttered and refolded, before being grilled. Red herrings are to be found with difficulty in Britain but the French *hareng saur* (*see above*), while not identical, is similar.

Rollmop. Butterfly fillets of herring, rolled around a stuffing of onion, gherkin and spices, held with a wooden splinter, and marinated in vinegar and salt solution. The fish is not cooked and is hardened instead by the salt and the acetic acid of the vinegar. Commercial rollmops can be bought loose or in jars.

Rollmops

Take 4 salted herrings and soak them for 12-24

hours in water – the time depends on the saltiness. Fillet them and strip the skin from them. Place skin side down and spread with German mustard. Put on top a teaspoon of mixed sliced onion, pickled gherkin and capers. Roll up and skewer with a toothpick. Pack the rolls in a glass jar.

Make a marinade of 1 cup white vinegar diluted with 3½ cups water (taste to get the right sourness as the exact quantities depend on the strength of the vinegar). Add 2 sliced carrots, 2 sliced onions, 1 teaspoon peppercorns, 8 juniper berries, 1 teaspoon white mustard seed, 2 bay leaves. Bring this to the boil and allow it to cool. Pour this marinade to cover the rolls of fish and fill the jars. Leave for a week before using. Some recipes use a mixture of vinegar and white wine, and some stuff the rollmops with other mixtures which may include sliced peppers and even chillies. In others, the prepared mustard is omitted.

Salt herring. Before the days of refrigeration, herrings had to be salted down in barrels, on board ship or ashore, and formed the starting point for all the herring products. In some cases, the fish rested temporarily in the salt or in brine and were then smoked; in others, they were heavily salted and packed for shipment in sealed casks. Scandinavians argue about which is the best salt herring, but for most people the argument is academic as they have to use whatever salted herring they can get. If salt herrings are not available, they can be made at home. Scale and gut the fish, leaving the roes in. Then soak them in brine (strong enough just to float an egg) for 14-16 hours; drain them well and pack them into jars with a layer of salt between each herring layer. Keep them tightly covered and below the surface of the liquid that forms, otherwise they will develop rancid flavours. A quick method given in Jane Grigson's *Fish Cookery* (Penguin) is to soak boned herring in a 10% brine for 3 hours. Herrings may also be salted with the addition of spices such as pepper, allspice and bay. Anyone interested should consult Mrs Grigson's admirable book.

Smoked herring. Types include bloater, buckling, *hareng saur* and kipper (*see above*).

[*Herring* – French: *hareng* German: *Hering* Italian: *aringa* Spanish: *arenque*]

HICKORY is closely related to the walnut. Most species are indigenous to North America; the most famous is the *pecan. Other species have been neglected by breeders in spite of their excellent

nuts, because the relatively thick shells make the nuts difficult to crack. So, in general, hickory nuts have been collected from wild trees in the forest and sold in local markets. They have rarely been exported, and in general are known only by name outside America. However, with improved commercial varieties and hybrids, this situation may alter. Hickory nuts keep well and many have an excellent flavour.

Shagbark hickory (*Carya ovata*) is the best of the hickories and is found particularly around the Great Lakes and in the Ohio River Valley. Its nuts were an important food of the North American Indians, who pounded them (apparently not bothering to shell them) with water to make a nut milk. This was added to corn cakes, soup and sweet potatoes. It was also evaporated to a thick cream for storage in jars or fermented to make a drink called *pawcohickora*. Hickory-nut oil was also important to the early settlers.

Big Shell-bark hickory (*C. laciniosa*) has a slightly coarser flavour than the Shagbark, but runs it a close second for quality. It is common in bottom lands of the Ohio and Mississippi river basins. The nut is rather large and has a thick, spongy husk.

The Pignut or Switchbred hickory (*C. glabra*) and Mockernut or Common hickory (*C. tornentosa*) both produce good nuts, though much inferior to those mentioned before. Other hickories may be eaten locally, but they are mainly too small or too hard to be worth cracking. Some, like the Small-fruited hickory (*C. microcarpa*) are sweet, but others like the bitternut (*C. cordiformis*) are full of tannin. Hickory sawdust is important in the US for smoking hams, etc.

[*Hickory* – French: *carya* German: *Hickorynuss* Italian: *noce bianco Americana* Spanish: *nuez americana*]

HOMINY or **hulled corn**. Hulled maize, one of the staples of the South and North American Indians, was adopted from them by the pioneers. Taking its name from the Algonquin, *rocka-hominy*, it was originally made by soaking and boiling maize in wood lye (ashes and water) until the outer skin of the grain could be rubbed off. Boiled whole, it was used as a starchy food instead of potatoes and, when dried, could be ground into coarse grits – hominy grits.

Hominy is particularly a food of the southern states. Although available canned, it is not difficult to make from maize, but all varieties are by no means equally good. American seedsmen sell hominy corn with a white kernel for those who like to start even earlier in the process and grow their own.

Hominy grits may be boiled in salted water, served as a breakfast food with milk and a lump of butter, or may be made into puddings and breads, like other ground cereals.

....

Hominy

Prepare a solution of bicarbonate of soda, 1 teaspoon to a litre (2 pints) of water, and soak the maize in it overnight. Next morning, boil it rapidly for about an hour until the hulls start to loosen and slough off. Rinse the maize in cold water, rubbing it to free the skins. Wash the skins away in clean water (which will also remove any remaining soda), put the hominy in fresh water and boil it until it is tender. The hominy may be dried in the sun or a very cool oven. When thoroughly dry, it will keep like any other grain. It may be ground into grits in a mill and may also be frozen.

....

HOMOGENIZING. A process applied to milk, which breaks down the fat globules to roughly the same small size and so stops the cream rising to the top. It is done by forcing the milk through small nozzles. (A similar technique is used to make emulsions like fake mayonnaise and reconstituted cream.) Homogenized milk is more digestible than ordinary milk, as it does not form tough curd in the stomach, but cooks would usually like to have the practice of homogenizing milk stopped, disliking the dead quality of the liquid and missing the useful creamy top.

[*Homogenizing* – French: *homogénéiser* German: *homogenisieren*]

HONEY is the most ancient sweetening substance and, in the past, was the basis of the confectioner's art. A complete Roman confectioner's shop was excavated at Herculaneum together with all its moulds, pans and implements, which proved very similar to those used to this day. In those days honey was boiled, but unlike cane sugar (which came much later) it contains large amounts of glucose and fructose, formed when the sucrose, the sugar in nectar of flowers, is broken down by the saliva of the bees. An average honey contains 38% fructose, 31% glucose, and 7% maltose with other substances as well. Honey will granulate easily if the percentage of glucose in it is high (as in alfalfa,

clover or buckwheat honeys), and almost always if kept long enough. The crystals are mainly glucose and the liquid fructose. It will become runny again (and will not easily regranulate) if kept for half an hour at 60-65°C (140-150°F), as the tiny glucose crystals dissolve and do not easily form again. On the other hand, stirring honey encourages it to granulate. (Granulation is not due to added sugar as some suspect.)

Honeys vary a great deal, according to the flowers from which they come. A bee-keeper can take out what is gathered from each honey-flow, thus getting honey with a preponderance of flavour from a single flower. There are several hundred different honeys available in the US alone, and they vary in colour from white or cream, to brown, purple or even black. A few are red or green. The flavours also vary greatly. Some are even poisonous (if, for instance, the bees have been taking the nectar from a lot of oleander trees). A very special honey is heather honey from the ling (*Colluna vulgoris*). It is gelatinous in texture, full of air bubbles and does not flow when the comb is cut. (Honey from other heathers flows normally.) Heather honey contains a lot of protein and so granulation is slow – it takes two years even to start. If honey is heated in cooking, then the heat drives off its special aromatics, and the sugars begin to caramelize, so delicate honey is spoiled. (Heather honey also stiffens.)

Fine honeys should always be kept for eating raw and for sweets that do not need to be cooked. A delicious one which will be acceptable to the most dedicated health food fan, is thick creamy yoghurt, honey and wheatgerm. Honey is the basis for several liqueurs, including those made from Scotch whisky, and, of course, the famous Atholl Brose. A turn-of the-century cookbook gives the following recipe:

'Upon virgin honeycomb pour the oldest procurable French Brandy and the best old Scotch Whisky in equal proportions. Allow this mixture to stand for five or six days in a large earthen pipkin in a cool place, strain it, and it is ready for drinking.' Other recipes incorporate oatmeal and cream.

[*Honey* – French: *miel* German: *Honig* Italian: *miele* Spanish: *miel*]

HOPS. The hop plant (*Humulus lupulus*) belongs to the same family as hemp (cannabis) and is a perennial climber native to both Europe (including Britain) and North America. It can sometimes be seen growing wild in its natural state, sprawling over hedges and bushes. The use of wild hops for flavouring and preserving *beer seems to have started in Germany some thousand years ago; records show that they were being cultivated on a small scale at least as early as 1079. Hopped ale gradually increased in popularity in Europe and, by the middle of the 14th century, it was being brewed commercially in Holland. Hops not only give a refreshing, bitter taste to ale, but they are also a preservative; a hopped ale keeps about twice as long as ale brewed without them. Substances in the hop also have a calming and sleep-promoting effect on the human system, according to the herbalists.

Under cultivation, the hop plants are encouraged to grow up strings or wires in hop yards or gardens. They are grown to some extent in most countries outside the tropics. The hop has separate male and female plants; it is the cone-shaped female flower that is dried and used in brewing. British hops have traditionally been fertilized, and the cones then produce seeds, but this is not the practice in Europe. Fertilization apparently is necessary to produce large cones from the traditional British varieties known as Geldings and Fuggles. (The demands of lager brewers have now made it necessary to have some areas in Britain in which all male hops have been eradicated.) Geldings, with a delicate flavour, are used particularly in pale ales and bitters, while Fuggles are better in general for mild ale and stout.

Since British home brewing became legally freed of restrictions, dried hops of many named varieties can now be bought in specialist shops. In buying hops, always look for samples warranted to be from the latest crop, and avoid old stuff. Like all dried herbs, hops tend to lose flavour with storage, especially if they have been exposed to the light. When freshly dried, hops have a pale yellow colour, and rubbing them between the palms of the hand makes them emit a bright, intensely aromatic smell, and particles of a waxy substance, lupulin (which gives the flavour), should stick to the fingers.

Hop-picking used to be an annual event for East End Londoners who travelled in thousands to the hop gardens of Kent, but today the work is mechanized. The cones are quickly removed from the vines and spread in a layer up to 60 cm (2 ft) thick on the cast house floor which is made of an open mesh – traditionally of horsehair – to allow hot air to rise through the hops. An exit for the now humid air is produced by a wind cowl, a well-known silhouette in hop growing areas. The drying heat is gradually increased for three hours and then kept constant until the hops are ready, about six hours later. In Britain, dried hops are traditionally stored in long sacks called 'pockets', but nowadays they may be powdered and compressed into small pellets. Hop extracts and hop oil are used by some brewers. Such essences reduce the skill the brewer needs to the minimum, but do not make the finest beers.

In hop-growing areas, young shoots are used in spring as a vegetable, but they can rarely be found in markets. Hop shoots are popular in Belgium and northern France, where they are known as *jets* or *pointes de houblon*. Basic preparation is to scrape the tender, young shoots lightly, rinse and plunge them into fast boiling, salted and slightly acidulated water. After being cooked until just tender, they are drained, heated in cream or butter, or used in the many recipes *à l'anversoise* (with eggs and so on). Wild hop shoots are eaten in Italy, particularly in a Venetian risotto, but they may be misleadingly described as wild asparagus. If the shoots are to be eaten cold as salad – as in Germany – they are best cooked tied in bundles like calabrese or asparagus. There are also old English recipes for hop shoots, particularly in 17th and 18th century books.

[*Hops* – French: *houblon* German: *Hopfen* Italian: *luppolo* Spanish: *lúpulo*]

HORSE. There are few recipes for horse meat in British or American cookery books, and many of the standard works do not even mention it. On the other hand, most European countries admit it, although only in Belgium and northern France with any enthusiasm, but there are certainly restaurants in Italy (e.g. in Modena) where horse appears on the menu alongside the more usual meats. In Italy, horse meat is prescribed raw for invalids. Since the horse is so far removed from the usual human food cycle, there are few parasites or diseases which man and horse have in common – horse is one of the safest of all raw meats.

The British love horses to the extent that they would rather eat the rider than eat the horse. Even the unsentimental Belgians, though, would have to admit that horses are less often bred for food, than for riding. Horse meat is rather sweet – which one does not notice in *cheval bourguignon* but would in other dishes. In Britain, horse butchers are synonymous with knackers and the meat they are selling is for dogs; in France, Italy and Spain there are horse-meat stalls and shops which offer respectable horse meat at about the same price as beef.

The word horse, applied to any foodstuff, means

strong, big or coarse. Horse mackerel, for instance, are a large, inferior species of mackerel; horse mushrooms, a large, tough species of mushroom (*Agaricus arvensis*); horseradish is large, tough and exceedingly pungent in comparison to the ordinary salad radish.

[*Horse* – French: *cheval* German: *Pferd* Italian: *cavallo* Spanish: *caballo*]

HORSE BEAN. Alternative name for *broad bean and *jack bean.

HORSE GRAM, **Madras gram** or **kulthi bean**. Much grown as a pulse and eaten by the poor, especially in southern India. Its scientific name, *Dolichos biflorus*, shows it as a close relative of the *lablab bean. It is eaten both green and as a pulse. The seeds are red, white, mottled or black, but most frequently reddish-brown. The bean is smaller and flatter than a pea. Horse gram is rarely if ever split, but is used whole. It may be soaked overnight, but the flavour is better if it is cooked without a prior soaking, although this takes longer – three hours or more. In India, this pulse is regarded as 'heating' and not very digestible.

HORSERADISH (*Armoracia rusticana*) is a cruciferous plant with large, usually wavy-edged leaves. A native of south-eastern Europe and western Asia which now grows wild in Britain, Europe, North America and New Zealand, it is cultivated for its pungently flavoured tap-root. For use, this is scrubbed clean and any discoloured bits are cut out before the outer part, which has the strongest taste, is finely grated or scraped off; the core is discarded. Horseradish is used as a cold garnish or flavouring and is added to mayonnaise to go with fish or salads. Horseradish sauces, which are usually uncooked or at most cooked or warmed very gently, tend to contain cream and vinegar or (in France) lemon juice. The flavour of horseradish depends entirely on volatile essential oils, which quickly disappear in cooking. Grated horseradish does not retain its pungency for very long, but sliced horseradish can be dried in an oven at the lowest temperature setting – commercially dried horseradish has a much better flavour than the bottled horseradish sauces.

Although its main use in Britain these days is as sauce with beef and smoked fish, horseradish used to be more popular and goes well with other things, notably chicken and hard-boiled eggs.

[*Horseradish* – French: *raifort* German:

Meerrettich Italian: *rafano* Spanish: *rábano picante*]

HUCKLEBERRY. *See* cranberry.

HUITALACOCHE is a Mexican fungus (*Ustilago maydis*) which grows on the ears of maize and makes the kernels swell and become deformed. The skin of the kernels turns silver-grey; the inside is black. In cooking, a black juice with a delicious fungus flavour is given out. There is no substitute for the fungus, which can be obtained only by growing it on fresh maize.

HULLED CORN. *See* hominy.

HUNGRY RICE. *See* millet.

HYACINTH BEAN. *See* lablab bean.

HYDROGENATION. *See* margarine.

HYDROGEN PEROXIDE. *See* disinfectants.

HYDROCHLORIC ACID (HCl). A very strong mineral acid, which is found in a very dilute form in human stomach juices. Strong fuming hydrochloric acid is highly dangerous and no kitchen product. A few drops of the dilute acid shaken up in a cane sugar syrup and allowed to stand in a warm place for several days, will convert the cane sugar to glucose and fructose. The acid can be neutralized with a pinch of chalk or bicarbonate of soda.

[*Hydrochloric acid* – French: *acide chlorhydrique* German: *Chlorwasserstoff* Italian: *acido idroclorico* Spanish: *ácido hidroclórico*]

HYDROLYSED PROTEIN has been broken down by acid hydrolysis and is used as a flavouring by the food industry. Hydrolysed vegetable protein (from wheat, maize or soya beans) has a rather meaty taste and is the basis of, for example, Maggi as well as being a component of various meat cubes, stock cubes and meat extracts.

HYDROLYSIS. The breaking down of complex substances into simpler ones by the addition of hydrogen and oxygen atoms in the proportion in which they occur in water – 2:1. Hydrolysis may be achieved by warming with dilute acids, as when starch is hydrolysed to maltose and dextrose, cane sugar to glucose, or proteins to amino acids. It often happens as a result of the activity of enzymes (e.g. in *malt) and also with alkalis.

[*Hydrolysis* – French: *hydrolyse* German: *Hydrolyse* Spanish: *hidrólisis*]

HYDROMETER. An instrument for measuring the density of liquids. A hydrometer floats higher in a dense liquid than in a lighter one (as people can float high enough in the Dead Sea to read a newspaper), and the exact degree to which they float or sink can be read off on a scale graduated on the long neck. Because the denser the liquid the higher the gadget floats, the scale has the smaller figures at the top and the larger ones near the bottom. For accuracy, the hydrometer should be clean and dry, and readings should be taken with the eye held as near as possible on a level with the surface of the liquid. The point where the surface cuts the scale is the reading to take. The liquid must be at the temperature for which the hydrometer is graduated, because liquids expand and become less dense when warmed.

The principle on which the hydrometer is based was discovered (it is said) by Archimedes in his bath. Cooks are in the same business when they make a brine 'to float an egg', which would be fine apart from the fact that the density of eggs varies with their freshness. There are hydrometers manufactured with specialist scales designed for many purposes – brinometers reading brine strengths, saccharometers measuring the strength of sugar solutions, alcoholometers indicating alcohol strength in beers and wines – just as there are for determining the state of car batteries. They may be graduated in various units, from Baumé, Brix or Balling to straight SG (specific gravity). There are also simplified versions for home use, such as those graduated to predict the strength of alcohol to be hoped for from fermenting out a particular sugar solution.

Specific gravity, also called relative density, is the density of a substance measured in terms of that of water. Liquids denser than water (such as sugar syrups or brines) have an SG greater than 1, while liquids lighter than water (such as alcohol) have an SG less than 1. Practice is sometimes confusing because hydrometers are mostly graduated to omit the 1 and the decimal point. Thus an SG of 1.050 becomes SG 50 (and one of 1.150 becomes 150) on the graduated scale.

The Baumé scale (°B or °Bé). Antoine Baumé (1728-1804) was professor of chemistry in the *Collège de Pharmacie* in Paris from around 1752

onwards, a time when people were trying to devise scales to put science on a footing of comparison by exact measurement. What was done then is clumsy by modern standards, but somehow the Baumé scale – which ought to be obsolete – has stayed with us in a number of industrial uses (from molasses to sulphuric acid) in spite of better scales having been devised subsequently. 0° on the scale, which is for liquids denser than water, was the point to which Baumé's hydrometer sank in distilled water (at 12.5°C). At the other end of the scale, 15° was the mark the hydrometer floated to in 15% salt brine. The trouble is that the early work was not very accurate, and Baumé kept on revising his scales, making other scales based on other substances. Hence confusion. Baumé scales are not greatly loved by Bureaux of Standards, but the Belgian butcher up at the corner near my home in Mallorca still uses a Baumé brinometer. For practical purposes, you can take the Baumé scale as indicating a straight percentage by weight of salt in a brine. Very nice, but it does not work out quite so conveniently when applied to sugar syrups.

Brix or **Balling**. In the first half of the 19th century, Balling produced a scale for graduating hydrometers on the basis of a percentage by weight of sugar (sucrose) dissolved in distilled water. In 1854, this scale was revised by Brix but it remains basically the same. Brix hydrometers are calibrated in °Brix, which are a straight percentage of sugar (by weight) usually at 20°C (68°F) although it was originally calculated at 17.5°C (63.5°F). Brix degrees are often quoted in recipes for bottling in syrup.

Alcohol potential. Various types of hydrometer are sold by shops that cater for the home brewer and winemaker. They may be designed specially for the amateur covering a range of specific gravities from 0.990 to 1.170 and marked also in potential alcoholic strengths; more accurate ones will cover only a part of the scale. The hydrometers are used not only to measure the original gravity of the liquid before fermentation, enabling the correct amount of sugar to be added to produce the required alcohol strength, but also to check how fermentation is progressing, to decide when it is finished or if it is stuck, and to calculate the alcohol content of the finished beer or wine, from the drop in specific gravity that has taken place. A rough method of calculating the final alcohol percentage by volume from the gravity drop is given by W. H.T. Tayleur in his *Penguin Book of Home Brewing & Wine-*

Making, which should be read by anyone seriously interested in this subject.

[*Hydrometer* – French: *hydromètre* German: *Hydrometer* Italian: *idrometro* Spanish: *hidrómetro*]

HYGIENE is a system of principles evolved to maintain good health and is not synonymous with cleanliness. Indeed, on a strict definition many convenience foods of impeccable sterilization but doubtful content are unhygienic, and most country kitchens full of ash and soil from fresh vegetables are quite as hygienic as the soulless palaces of stainless steel and white enamel. The latter have the advantage that if they are dirty they look it, and so are more work to maintain, but rarely does the best food come from them. Hygiene begins with government vets and inspectors who are supposed to see that food, milk and water is fresh, wholesome and free from disease when it comes to us. They are also supposed to see that what is sold as food is food, and not just an exercise in advertising, consumer research and shelf-life.

In the kitchen, few rules are necessarily observed, but the following are important. Always wash your hands before starting to cook. Surfaces used for cutting or chopping need to be kept clean especially if they are made of wood, which is porous. A good scrub with soap and a rinse in really hot water is all that is needed. Knives and surfaces used for cutting raw meat must be washed before cutting cooked meat. In general, raw and cooked foods should be kept apart. Pans, plates, bowls and cutlery must be well washed and properly rinsed. (The long-term effect of synthetic detergents on the guts has not yet been determined.) If the washing water is really hot, then no disease organisms will be passed from one person to another on glasses, cups or forks, the key points for cross-infection. Crockery and cutlery are better left to drain dry than to be dried with a towel. Foods should not be left lying about in the kitchen or kept for long periods forgotten at the back of the refrigerator. *Copper pans should be properly tinned, or at least used and emptied immediately, and any earthenware covered with lead glaze should be kept for foods that are not acid. *Flies are public enemy number one; they are filthy and should not come in contact with food – all food should be kept covered if it is not in the refrigerator.

Finally it is worth looking at the question of washing fruits and salads. In the developed countries the main reason for this is to remove insecticidal or fungicidal sprays, and preservatives, the bad effects, if any, of which are long term and sometimes cumulative. In developing countries, where sewage disposal is dicey, the skins of fruit and tomatoes to be eaten raw should be washed carefully with water containing unscented soap as a *disinfectant. Alternatively, you can dip the fruit in boiling water, count to 15, take it out and skin it. Citrus fruits are effectively protected by their skins but in some areas might need scrubbing if you are going to use the peel and not just the contents. Green salads in such areas can never be certainly safe if they have been bought in the market and are best replaced by home sprouted seed – mustard and cress or sprouted fenugreek. Anything cooked or pasteurized is safe if it is not recontaminated.

[*Hygiene* – French: *hygiène* German: *Hygiene* Italian: *igiene* Spanish: *higiene*]

HYSSOP (*Hyssopus officinalis*). A beautiful, decorative labiate herb of the thyme family which grows wild in Mediterranean Europe from the Alps across to Russia (but not in Greece or Turkey). Hyssop has long been used for its warm, aromatic smell, but it has no firm place in cooking, although it is sometimes used as a flavouring. More commonly, it is an ingredient of liqueurs (e.g. chartreuse), because it is soothing to the stomach; the taste is slightly minty but bitter. It is recommended for the herb garden.

[*Hyssop* – French: *hysope* German: *Ysop, Eisop* Italian: *issopo* Spanish: *hisopo*]

i

ICE. The freezing point of water and the melting point of ice are at the same temperature, 0°C or 32°F. This does not mean that if you cool water to 0°C it will suddenly solidify or that if you raise the temperature of ice to 0°C it will suddenly melt. To freeze water at zero, it is necessary to go on taking out heat, or to melt ice at zero it is necessary to go on supplying heat. In fact, it is necessary to put in or take out heat in order to cause a change of state just as it is to change water to steam), and during this period the temperature remains the same. Thirsty Himalayan climbers must sit for hours melting snow, and all the snow has to melt before the water can be heated to make a hot drink. A drink with ice floating in it (once it has settled down) will be at roughly 0°C, with both the ice and the water at the same temperature in it. The temperature of ice can, of course, be reduced below zero. It becomes crisp and the cubes do not stick together, but they do stick to the fingers.

Before the invention of refrigerators, winter snow was stored in pits or ice-houses insulated with straw for use later in the year. There is even a huge ice-house in the middle of the great Persian salt desert, a building the size (and rather the shape) of a tennis stadium, where snow was once packed to help people survive the summer's awful heat. When water freezes to ice, it expands – which is why bottles of beer will crack in the deep freeze, and why, being less dense than water, ice floats. It will melt under pressure, as anyone who has left a bottle standing on a block of ice will have noticed – the bottle sinks in. Ice also melts when salt is put on it, but the heat consumption in the change of state from solid to liquid makes the temperature drop. This is the basis for the use of ice and salt in old-fashioned methods of freezing ice cream.

[*Ice* – French: *glace* German: *Eis* Italian: *ghiaccio* Spanish: *hielo*]

ICE CREAM, WATER ICE and **SORBET**. Ice creams were probably invented in China, or at least somewhere in the East. At any rate, ices spread to the rest of Europe from northern Italy; it was one of the cooks who went to France with Catherine de Medici in 1533 who introduced them to the French court. Some hundred years later, another Italian chef brought them to the court of Charles I. In that same century, Italians opened cafes to sell ices in Paris (the first in 1670), at first selling sorbets and later ice creams. It was Italians once more who introduced ice cream into the US early in the 19th century. At that time ice cream was a real luxury, and nobody could have foreseen the enormous profits which would be made in the 20th century from selling frozen froth. True, the machines that make the drums of coloured mixture into ices are rather expensive, but the products can then be sold at a quite remarkable profit. If ices were cheaper and more certainly harmless, they would have to be praised as (*pace* the dental profession) they are undoubtedly fun, especially for children. However, as a vehicle for synthetic dyes, sugar, synthetic flavourings, emulsifiers, stabilizers and lard, they are not above suspicion. Ices are very easily made at home, if you do not find it too much trouble. The primitive method (and still the best to use) is an ice cream churn, consisting of a metal drum with a lid. Into this are put the materials to be frozen, the drum is surrounded with a freezing mixture of ice and salt, and is fitted with spring-loaded paddles which keep the ice cream mixture continually stirred and pressed against the sides. Such a machine can be laboriously worked by hand or can have an electric motor. There are also electric *sorbétières* with stirring paddles, which make ice cream in the freezer or freezing compartment of the refrigerator. Many people use recipes containing gelatine or egg white which need little stirring. There are two basic types of ice: water ices (*sorbet*, *granita* or *frappé*) and cream ices. In the former, fruit juices or purées are sweetened with sugar. This family of ices is expected to be granular, and so is suitably made in the freezer compartment of the refrigerator. Water ices should be stirred four or five times, or beaten with egg white while freezing to keep them from being too solid. Gelatine is another substance which helps to minimize the formation of ice crystals.

Total freezing time is 4-6 hours, depending on circumstances. Sorbets and water ices should be light and refreshing. Cream ices, on the other hand, are rich and delicious. The cream and egg yolks have also a decided effect in preventing the growth of ice crystals. Again, there are many successful recipes for making ices in the freezer, with no more than an occasional stir while freezing, although the best texture, and exactly the right temperature results from using an ice cream churn.

[Ice cream – French: *glace, crème glacée* German: *Eis, Speiseeis* Italian: *gelato* Spanish: *helado*]

ICELAND MOSS (*Cetraria islandica*) is not a moss but a lichen, almost the only one that is used as a food (although the genus *Roccella*, which grows on coastal cliffs, yields dyes such as *cudbear and litmus). It is a moorland and mountain plant with a bitter taste which needs to be removed by thorough soaking in numerous changes of water. It can then be boiled to produce an edible jelly or dried and ground to a flour which is used in the Arctic to make bread.

ILAMA. *See* custard apple.

INDIAN CORN. *See* maize.

INDIAN CRESS. *See* nasturtium.

INDIAN DATE. *See* tamarind.

INDIAN FIG or **Indian pear**. *See* prickly pear.

INDIAN RICE. *See* wild rice.

INSECTS. Marine crustaceans like shrimps, crabs and lobsters are forbidden to Orthodox Jews, so it is interesting to read in the Bible (*Leviticus 11: 21-22*) that Moses allowed four different kinds of insects as food, while the Islamic food laws, which have a common origin, allow the eating of locusts, though not of grasshoppers. Insects are a traditional food in many countries: in Africa, in parts of South East Asia (where spiders and scorpions are also sometimes put in the pot), in China (where silkworms are eaten) and by the Aborigines in Australia. Locusts were also liked in ancient Greece, but the tradition of eating them was never carried on into European and American cooking.

Indeed, the very idea of eating insects is repulsive to most people, even though they eat honey (which we forget has been swallowed and regurgitated by insects) and put *cochineal into cake icing. If the comb containing bee larvae is blanched and the grubs removed, dried and then dry fried in a little salt, the result is an excellent appetizer. In fact, insects generally have a good taste. The witchity grub I once ate in North Queensland tasted like fish cooked in cream, while fried locusts have been described as tasting like roasted chestnuts. Many people I know like fried termites, and there are various combinations of insects and chocolate on the market. The insects used for food are much cleaner feeders than prawns and shrimps, but of course the reader should not rush off in a burst of enthusiasm and eat any sort of insect. Some probably taste horrible, and others, like the Spanish fly, a beetle used in the past as an aphrodisiac, are dangerously poisonous.

A great many, though, are known locally as good food and a valuable source of protein when the insects swarm or can be collected in sufficient numbers. The Red or Carmine locust (*Nomadacris septemfasciata*) is the one most commonly eaten in Arabia. Only the females are eaten. They are boiled for about 5 minutes, have legs and wings removed, and are then fried in butter. Termites, species of *Macrotermes*, are often eaten in Africa when they swarm at the beginning of the rainy season. They are dry-fried, dried in the sun, have the wings winnowed away, and are then re-fried with a little salt and fat. Crickets, grasshoppers, shield bugs, flying ants and even some caterpillars are eaten. They may need to have the gut removed before they are cooked, just like some crustaceans, and it is necessary to follow local practice. One of the most interesting insect foods is provided by the Lake fly (*Chaoboro edulis*), which swarms at the new moon over Lake Nyasa. Though this is a tiny insect, it occurs in such numbers that the black clouds of countless millions can be seen for a considerable distance. The insects, when caught and dried in cakes, are a useful food. The cake is broken into bits, boiled in a little salt water till soft, and then incorporated with tomato, onion and pounded fried peanuts to make a sauce to go with rice or maize-meal porridge. I have no doubt that as the problem of feeding the world grows, the question of insects as a source of food will receive increasing attention.

[Insects – French: *Insectes* German: *Insekten* Italian: *insetti* Spanish: *insectos*]

INVERT SUGAR. A mixture of simple *sugars, *glucose and *fructose, which occurs naturally in many fruits, but is also made when cane sugar is warmed with a dilute acid ('inverted').

[*Invert sugar* – French: *sucre inverti* German: *Invertzucker* Italian: *zucchero inverso* Spanish: *azúcar inverto*]

IODINE (I). An element that belongs to the same group as fluorine and chlorine. Small quantities in a combined form are essential in the human body, and shortage of iodine causes goitre, a condition that used to be very prevalent in mountainous country far from the sea, which is the major source of the element in nature. The iodine content of foods varies widely from place to place, but most people get enough in their diet. Good sources of iodine are seafish, shell fish, kelp, agar-agar, laver and other seaweed products or iodized salt, which is common salt to which 25 parts per million of potassium iodide have been added. In some seaweeds, as much as 0.2% of the living plant is iodine.

[*Iodine* – French: *iode* German: *Jod* Italian: *iodio* Spanish: *yodo*]

IRISH MOSS. *See* carrageen.

IRON (Fe). A metal that makes up 4.7% of the earth's crust (and almost certainly is one of the main constituents of its molten core), yet some soils are deficient in it. Iron is an essential element for human nutrition, as it is vital for the formation of the haemoglobin of red blood cells and pigment in muscles. We need to assimilate about 10 mg per day. Although iron is in an available form in many unrefined foods – liver, wholewheat, fruits and vegetables – it is often not absorbed as well as it might be, particularly when oxalic acid is present, and it is absent, or short, in milk, white bread and sugar. (Iron is added in Britain to all bread flour other than 100% wholewheat to give it an iron content of 1.65 mg per 100 g); in the US, 'enriched' bread flour has 2.9 mg iron per 100 g. It is better to get iron from food than by taking supplements, and ferrous sulphate or chloride are best avoided.

The Iron Age is the most recent archaeological age. As far as is known, iron was first worked in the Middle East about 2500 BC, but it was not until about 1200 BC that iron smelting became common. It is a very suitable metal for pots, grills, knives and other cooking utensils, being harmless (though not ideal with sour fruits or other acids). Early vessels were of beaten iron, much later came cast iron which was cheap, brittle and porous. Cast-iron frying-pans actually benefit from being porous – they become saturated with fat and so get a good, non-stick surface. Iron surfaces are best 'cured' with fat and then rubbed with paper to remove excess fat. Girdles, *tavas* for making *chapatties* and iron plates for cooking *a la plancha* may be so cleaned and treated.

Steel is iron with a little carbon and often other metals such as nickel or vanadium added. Mild steel is easily bent and makes excellent kebab skewers. Stainless steel contains chromium and other metals in alloy – chromium protects the surface so that it does not rust or stain but knives made of it do not take such a keen edge as those made of carbon steel. Some modern steels are stainless and sharpen reasonably well.

[*Iron* – French: *fer* German: *Eisen* Italian: *ferro* Spanish: *hierro*]

ISINGLASS. Originally, an equivalent of *gelatine made from the swim bladders of sturgeon (Dutch: *huysenblas*, from *huso*, the beluga), though more recently the swim bladders of cod, ling, carp and other fish have been used. The swim bladders were removed from the sturgeon, washed in fresh water and hung to dry for a couple of days until it was possible to peel away the outer membrane. The bladders were then cut into strips. The best isinglass was in long staples, dull and hard. You may still sometimes see these dried strips, but in general the crude isinglass has been replaced by refined forms or by *gelatine. To use isinglass, it must be boiled until dissolved in an appropriate amount of water. The best will take a long time to dissolve completely – around a half hour. It is said to set a hundred times its weight of liquid, but isinglass varies in quality, and ordinarily you should allow a proportion by weight of 1 in 30, say 35 g to 1 lt (or ¾ oz to 1 pt), but this depends on the stiffness of jelly that is required. Isinglass is also used for clarifying vinegar, wine and, particularly, beer.

[*Isinglass* – French: *colle de poisson* German: *Hausenblase, Fischleim* Italian: *colla di pesce* Spanish: *colapez, cola de pescado*]

j

JACK BEAN or **horse bean** (*Canavalia ensiformis*) is a native of tropical America. A related species of large bean is the Sword bean or Sabre bean (*Canavalia gladiata*) from tropical areas of Asia. The two species are sufficiently similar to be confused, although the Sword bean has red, pink or brown seeds and the Jack has white ones. The pod of the Sword bean is curved like a sabre. Both beans are used green as vegetables. The Sword bean at least is also eaten ripe as a pulse, but ripe Jack beans may possibly be slightly poisonous.

In India, both beans are known as *bara sem*. The plant is a perennial, and there is a dwarf variety for small gardens. Jack beans, under the name of Horse beans, are grown to a considerable extent in the southern parts of the US.

JACK FRUIT or **jak fruit** (*Artocarpus integrifolia*). You are not likely to see this fruit unless you go to the tropics where it grows, as it is amongst the world's largest fruits – weighing sometimes 40 kg (89 lb) – and not the sort of thing greengrocers would like to handle. It is, however, available canned in syrup. As the immature fruit (as well as the flowers and seeds) are used in curries, some may well occasionally be exported from the growing areas. The tree belongs to the mulberry family (Moraceae) and to the same genus as the bread-fruit. The Jack tree is a native of the Western Ghats in India, but is today grown in most tropical countries, particularly in South East Asia, Brazil and parts of Africa.

The enormous fruits are green and carried on short stems hanging strangely from the main trunk and large branches. There are two types of fruit, one with a firm, sweet meat and the other softer and more acid. There are also some wild relatives. The fruit should not be confused with the *durian.

JACK-GO-TO-BED-AT-NOON. *See* salsify.

JAGGERY or **gur**. Crude, dark sugar from India. The name is often used for palm sugar, but is also applicable to cane sugar. Jaggery has an aromatic, winey smell overlying the molasses smell of unrefined sugar. It may be sold very unhygienically in Indian bazaars, shaped into large, sticky balls the size of a coconut and sometimes wrapped in leaves. It looks unappetizing, but has a delicious taste and is an extremely important part of the flavouring of vegetarian curries. In India, it sweetens the hot milk that may be offered in hospitality when a traveller visits a village.

JAK FRUIT. *See* jack fruit.

JAMAICA FLOWER, **roselle** or **red sorrel**. The acid flower of a *mallow, *Hibiscus sabdariffa* is popular in Mexico as a basis for a refreshing drink, and in the form of a syrup for making punches. The flower is available dried, as dark red sepals, and tastes rather like *sumac water. The flower sepals should be put into a saucepan, boiled for three minutes and then left in a china jug for some hours, preferably overnight. The syrup is sugared and made to taste.

JAMAICA PEPPER. *See* allspice.

JAMBERRY. *See* physalis fruit.

JAM, JELLY and **MARMALADE**. In British usage, jam is a conserve of fruit boiled with sugar, jelly is the juice only boiled with sugar, and the term marmalade is normally reserved for jams made from citrus fruits – orange, lemon, grapefruit, lime. A thick paste of boiled-down quinces was an early sweetmeat all round the Mediterranean and the term marmalade comes via French from the Portuguese *marmelada* which in turn comes from the word for quince, *marmela*. Quince and other fruit marmalades long preceded orange marmalade in English parlance; 16th and 17th century recipe books abound with recipes for marmalades, particularly quince.

There are three basic problems in making jams. The first is making sure that it contains sufficient sugar to make it keep. Organisms cannot grow when the sugar percentage is over 50-55%. In early days, honey or the natural sugars in the fruits themselves were used, but today sugar is added to bring the content up to 50%. You can then add acid juice (e.g. lemon) if the jam is too sweet, or more sugar if the jam is too sour. However, as cane sugar will crystallize, there is an upper limit to the amount that can be added. The fact that the boiling point of water is raised by adding sugar makes it possible to know roughly what the concentration of sugar is by taking the temperature at any time. Jams are usually cooked until they reach 113°C (235°F). The old rule for jelly – 1 lb of sugar to 1 pt of juice (or 475 g of sugar to 600 ml of juice) – will, when the evaporation that takes place during boiling is allowed for, give a jelly that will keep.

The second problem is whether the jelly or jam will set. Setting depends on the formation of a *pectin jelly, for which there must be sufficient pectin, sugar and acidity. Fruits lacking in pectin may be made to set by adding pectin extracted from citrus peel (one of the richest sources) or apples, and a similar result can be obtained by mixing in a pectin-rich fruit to make a compound jelly.

The third problem is flavour. Many fruits lose flavour when they are boiled for a long time; some – like strawberries and raspberries – can hardly survive being boiled at all. Moreover, long boiling causes sugars to caramelize, which spoils the jam's colour, and gives an underlying bitter caramel taste. To reduce the time jam is on the heat, the sugar is made hot before it is added to the fruit, or it is added as a syrup boiled to soft-ball stage – 116°C (240°F) – while added liquid is kept to a minimum. Because efficient heating of jam is so important, it is necessary to use pans of aluminium or untinned brass and copper. Iron pans cannot be used because of the acids in the fruit and enamel pans do not conduct heat fast enough and burn easily. Tin may melt.

Although the British regard jam as something to be used in tarts or spread on bread, in the Middle East and the Balkans, as well as at times in France, it is something to be eaten as a sweetmeat with a spoon. In houses from Bulgaria to Egypt, and from Greece to Iran, you can experience those awful social arrivals when you sit stiffly in the best room and accept the offered token of hospitality, a glass of water and a spoon of incredibly sweet jam. That is the minimum. A cup of Turkish coffee usually goes with it. It is the equivalent of the biscuit and cup of tea, the brandy or sweet liqueur, the madeira and piece of cake. Nowadays the ritual offering is often replaced by a Coke.

Jams are made of many things which would be unfamiliar at a vicarage tea-party. So we can have rose petal and orange flower jam, fig and date jam, jams made of whole green oranges and jam of chestnuts. One of the oddest is *cabello de ángel* (angel's hair), a speciality of parts of Spain, a tasteless jam made from the 'stringy bits' surrounding the seeds of a special type of marrow bred to be almost all stringy bits and little use for anything else (though it is grown and sold in Britain as 'spaghetti marrow'). The jam is much prized and is used in cakes, but few foreigners like it.

[*Jam* – French: *confiture* German: *Marmelade, Eingemachte* Italian: *marmellata, conserva di frutta* Spanish: *mermelada*]

JAPANESE GELATINE. *See* agar-agar.

JAPANESE MEDLAR. *See* loquat.

JAPANESE PARSLEY. *See* coriander.

JAPANESE PEPPER. *See* Chinese pepper.

JELLY. In the United States, jelly is the equivalent of British jam, and what the British call jelly is called jello. Substances turning liquids into jellies can be imagined as having long, thread-like molecules (too small to be seen through the microscope) which tangle up and bind the liquids in which they are dissolved. If there is insufficient jellying substance to make a jelly, then it at least makes the liquid very viscous. Jellying substances used in the kitchen are: *gelatine, *isinglass, *pectin, *agar-agar, *carrageen moss and other *seaweed extracts. Bones, hooves and cartilage can be boiled down effectively to gelatine.

Natural fruit jellies (i.e. home-made jello) set with pectin are made by extracting the juice (by boiling the fruit and tying it up in a bag to drip, or by pressing), adding extra pectin and acid if necessary, and finally boiling for a short time (10 minutes) with sugar until setting consistency is reached. With fruit of good pectin content, 800 g (1¾ lb) of sugar is added per 1 lt (1¾ pt) of juice; with moderate pectin content, the sugar has to be reduced to 600 g (1 lb 5 oz) per 1 lt (1¾ pt).

The cubes of concentrated jelly and the jello powders, with natural or synthetic fruit flavourings and colouring to match the fruits they imitate, are based on gelatine. Those flavoured with lemon or lime are sometimes used as ingredients in salads and mousses, but you will probably prefer to make your own with *gelatine, sugar and juice, unless you are desperately short of time.

[Jelly – French: gelée German: Gallerte Italian: gelatina Spanish: jalea, gelatina]

JERKED BEEF. See biltong.

JERUSALEM ARTICHOKE (Helianthus tuberosus) is related to the sunflower, not to the thistle (the *globe artichoke). It is said that the name Jerusalem is a corruption of the Spanish girasol (turning with the sun), i.e. sunflower. Both plants are said to have originated in North America, although some authorities say the sunflower originated in Peru. John Goodyer, who revised Gerard's Herbal, wrote on 17th October 1621 that he did not know whether Jerusalem artichokes originated in Peru, Brazil or Canada, but placed them next to the sunflower (which he called 'marigold of Peru'), so the kinship had been observed. Goodyer is so scathing about the culinary quality of Jerusalem artichokes that he is worth quoting:

'These roots are dressed in divers ways; some boil them in water, and after stew them with sack and butter, adding a little ginger, others bake them in pies, putting marrow, dates, ginger, raisins of the sun, sack & etc. Others some other way, as they are led by their skill in cookery. But in my judgement, which way soever they be dressed and eaten, they stir and cause a filthy loathsome stinking wind within the body, thereby causing the belly to be pained and tormented, and are a meat more fit for swine than men; yet some say they have usually eaten them, and have found no such windy quality in them.'

The name artichoke, of course, was given because of some fancied likeness in taste to the globe artichoke. The similarity is not strong. The original varieties were irregular and difficult to peel (although the skin slips off easily if they are first parboiled) but modern varieties are more potato-like in shape. Jerusalem artichokes can be eaten raw – they have a sweet nutty taste and crisp texture – but are more usually boiled. They are cooked when they can be easily pierced with a knife point. They are also delicious roasted. In France, they are often boiled in milk flavoured with an onion stuck with a clove, then drained, dipped in batter and fried.

[Jerusalem artichoke – French: topinambour German: Erdartischocke Italian: topinambur carciofo di Giudea Spanish: cotufa, pataca, aguaturna]

JESUIT'S BREAD. See water chestnut.

JET. See hop.

JEW'S EAR. See mushrooms.

JICANA. See water chestnut.

JOB'S TEARS. See millet.

JOULES and **KILOJOULES** (Kj.) The joule, named after British physicist James Prescott Joule (1818-1889), is a unit of energy and is therefore considered by scientists more apt than the calorie (which is a unit of heat) as a means of comparing the crude fuel values of foods. At any rate, it has been adopted internationally and the slogan is now: 'Watch your kilojoules!' It is kilojoules and not joules because, like the ordinary calorie, the joule itself is too small a unit to be practical in measuring what we eat. So just as we used to use 1000 ordinary calories, i.e. a Calorie with a capital C (or a kilocalorie), as our unit, now we are taking 1000 joules and using the kilojoule. You multiply calories by 4.2 to get them approximately into the new terms.

JOWAR. See millet.

JUJUBE is the name given to small trees and shrubs of the genus Zizyphus which are found in hot, dry areas around the world. Their fruits are generally candied or preserved in sugar or honey. Some, such as the North African and Middle Eastern Christ's thorn or crown of thorns (Z. spina-christi), are eaten dried. The fruits of the Mauritanian jujube (Z. mauritiana) are known as Chinese dates or tsa. The berries of an Andean species, the mistol or Argentinian jujube (Z. Mistol), form the basis of a Bolivian drink, chicha. Perhaps the most important species is the Common jujube or Chinese jujube (Z. jujuba), a native of eastern India and Malaysia that has been introduced elsewhere in Asia and around the Mediterranean; its ovoid fruits are about the size of an olive. According to James Sholto Douglas in Alternative Foods (Pelham Books), 'they may be eaten fresh or dried like dates, cooked with rice or millet or in honey or syrup, stewed boiled or baked, made into glacé fruit or jujube bread.' The fruits of the Lotus jujube (Z. lotus) of North Africa were what were consumed by the lotus eaters mentioned by Homer.

JUNEBERRY. *See* rowan.

JUNGLE TREE. *See* ngapi.

JUNIPER. There are 40-50 species of juniper, but *Juniperus communis*, the species used for flavouring, is distributed over much of the Northern hemisphere. The ripe berries, fresh or dried, are used. These are usually ripe in autumn, but the berries take three years to develop, and several stages are found on one bush. There are separate male and female bushes. Since the juniper is exceedingly prickly, it is best to wear gloves for gathering the berries and to use a fork for stripping them from the bush. Apart from flavouring gin, juniper berries are much used in brines for pickling meat, in marinades for game and in stuffings for various birds, including chicken. They go well with most herbs, and a jar of dried juniper berries should be in every well-stocked kitchen.

[*Juniper* – French: *genièvre* German: *Wachholder* Italian: *ginepro* Spanish: *enebro, junípero*]

JUNKET. *See* rennet.

k

KAFFIR CORN. *See* millet.

KAHLUA. *See* liqueurs and cordials.

KAKI. *See* persimmon.

KALE, **kail**, **collards** or **borecole**. 'Kale' is the northern form of 'cole', an old name for cabbage. 'Borecole' comes from the Dutch *boerenkool* (farmer's cabbage). Kales are *cabbages which do not heart, including a specific variety of cabbage (*Brassica oleracea*, var. *acephala*) and often Rape kale (*B. napus*) a variety of turnip greens which produce leaves from January to April. The purpose of kales is suggested by one variety name – Hungry Gap. Kale played an important part in the old domestic economy, keeping cottagers alive at the back end of winter. Perhaps most famous of all is the Scottish kale, with its curly leaves. When young, it is good (cooked for at most 20 minutes in fast-boiling water), but the flavour is strong; when old, it is better left to the sheep. A clue to the place of kale in the old economy – when part of a farm worker's pay was in oatmeal – is suggested by the following recipe:

Kale Brose

Clean an ox-heel, put it in 2-3 lt (5 pt) of water, bring it to the boil, and skim and simmer it for 4 hours. Put 2 large handfuls of finely-shredded kale into the broth, and when it is cooked stir in 275 ml (½ pt) of toasted oatmeal. Salt and pepper to taste, boil till the oatmeal is cooked and serve as hot as possible.

[*Kale* – French: *chou frisé* German: *Krauskohl, Winterkohl* Italian: *cavolo riccio* Spanish: *col rizada*]

KALONJI. *See* nigella.

KANTEN. *See* agar-agar.

KASHA. *See* buckwheat.

KATSUOBUSHI. Dried, boned *bonito. With *kombu, one of the main ingredients of *dashi*, the foundation broth of Japanese cooking.

KÉFIR. A sour-milk product originating in the Caucasus, it is made from cow's milk, using *kéfir* grains, a special starter. They are yellow and may be anything from the size of small seeds to that of almonds. For use, they are soaked in water at 20-30°C (68-86°F) for a day, then washed, and soaked in water at the same temperature for another day, until they have swollen to three or four times their original volume. They are then taken out of the water and put into pasteurized milk at about 20°C (68°F) and kept there for a day.

If they are washed after use, the grains can be

kept and re-used half a dozen times. *Kéfir* is slightly alcoholic and has a creamy texture.

KELT. Spent *salmon.

KENTJOER or **kentjur**. *See* zedoary.

KERMES. An ancient red dye, made from the dried bodies of a female scale insect, *Coccus ilicis*, which lives on the Kermes oak (also called Holly oak or Grain tree). Chaucer refers to it as 'the grain of Portugal'. There is also a similar dye-producing bug, *Coccus polonicus*, the Polish scarlet grain. The best known today of these insect dyes is *cochineal, which has the finest colour.

Kermes was used as a food colouring and gave its name to the old-fashioned French cordial, alkermes. The al- is presumably Arab and kermes comes from the Arabic *qirmiz*. Alkermes is crimson red and very sweet. It contains distilled extracts of nutmeg, cinnamon, cloves and bay leaves, sugared and coloured.

[*Kermes* – French: *kermès* German: *Kermes* Spanish: *quermes*]

KETCHUP, **catchup** or **catsup**. A ketchup is a kind of sauce – the word came into English from the Orient, perhaps from Malay or Chinese. In fact, it is still used there to describe various salty sauces, often of fish, products which vary from country to country. If *katjap* is called for in a recipe from Indonesia, or *kéchap* in a Malay one, then it must be the right sort. Javanese *katjap*, for example, is a very sweet *soy sauce. In the West, *ketchup*, without qualification, has come to mean tomato ketchup, although the word originally referred to a host of salty, spiced condiment liquids made from fish, shell fish, fruit, vegetables, mushrooms, etc. The cookery books of the last century abound with recipes – oyster ketchup (oysters with white wine, brandy, sherry, shallots and spices), mussel ketchup (mussels and cider), pontac or pontack ketchup (elderberries), Windermere ketchup (mushrooms and horse radish), wolfram ketchup (beer, anchovies and mushrooms) and ketchups based on walnuts, cucumbers and all manner of other items that caught the cook's imagination.

....

Mushroom Ketchup

In the days when transport depended on horses, when there were permanent pastures and no artificial fertilizers, mushrooms used to whiten the fields in August and September. As the glut of mushrooms could not be preserved easily by primitive methods, mushroom ketchup was a way in which their flavour could be kept for use all round the year.

Use the large, open mushrooms if possible. Clean, but do not wash them. Chop or crush them in your hands and fill a container (such as a plastic bucket or aluminium pan) with layers of the chopped or crushed mushrooms sprinkled with salt – about 90 g (3½ oz) salt per kg (2 lb). Leave the salt to extract the juice overnight (or longer) and then put the lot in a pan and bring slowly to the boil. Boil the mixture for about 5 minutes and stand it aside to cool. Strain out the debris, squeezing out any remaining juice in a cloth, and bring the liquid to the boil again. You may now add a spice-bag – allspice, cloves, mace and ginger in various combinations can be used as you wish – with black peppercorns and cayenne. Brandy is often added as well. If the mushroom ketchup is to be used for flavouring, it is best to keep the spices to a minimum so that they do not mask the mushroom taste (I use only black pepper and a trace of garlic). As mushroom ketchup contains no acid, it must depend on the salt for preservation or needs a half-hour boil in a pressure cooker before bottling hot in sterile bottles. Long boiling destroys the flavour, and can produce a ketchup that makes dishes become over-salted before enough has been added to enhance their taste.

....

Pontac Ketchup

Strip ripe elderberries from their stalks. For 1 lt (1¼ pt) of fruit, heat 700 ml (1¼ pt) of vinegar. Put the elderberries in a jar that will go into the oven, pour the boiling vinegar over, and put in a low to medium oven for 2½-3 hours or until the juice has come out of the berries. Strain off the liquid without squeezing the fruit, and put the juice in a saucepan with a small piece of bruised ginger, 2 blades of mace, a teaspoon of peppercorns, 5 cloves, 8 shallots and 225 g (½ lb) boned, salted anchovy fillets. Bring to the boil and cook until the anchovies have disintegrated. Add salt if necessary. Strain and bottle.

....

Tomato Ketchup

Make up a spice-bag containing (for each 4 kg or

9 lb of tomatoes): 1 teaspoon bruised celery seed, 1 teaspoon cloves, a 5 cm (2 in) piece of cinnamon stick broken in pieces, a 3 cm (1¼ in) piece of bruised ginger, ½ teaspoon allspice berries, and 1 teaspoon peppercorns. Put it in 250 ml (½ pt) of boiling vinegar and allow to cool.

Take well-flavoured ripe tomatoes the quality matters – peel them and squeeze out the pips into a strainer. Discard the pips (which make the ketchup bitter), but save the juice. Put the tomato and any juice on a low heat with ¼ clove of garlic and a little olive oil. Cook slowly for 30 minutes or until soft and put through a fine sieve or mouli. Return to the pan and add 100 g (4 oz) of sugar and a pinch of cayenne. Simmer uncovered until the volume is reduced by about half (which will take about 1¼ hours),and then gradually add the spiced vinegar and about 4 teaspoons salt, tasting as you go to get the balance right. It may be necessary to add more or less vinegar – according to the sourness or sweetness of the tomatoes – and more or less salt. Continue the boiling until the right consistency is reached. Pour the ketchup immediately into hot sterile bottles and seal at once. The addition of 1 g per kg (2¼ lb) of *salicylic acid – as done by Italian housewives – will make sure that the ketchup keeps and does not ferment when opened. (The trade uses benzoic acid.) Store in the dark and wrap each bottle in brown paper to exclude light and so preserve the colour.

[Ketchup – French: *sauce relevée/ketchup* German: *kalte pikante Sosse* Italian: *salsa* Spanish: *salsa*]

KETJAP. *See* soy sauce.

KETOVAIA. *See* caviar.

KEWRA or **screwpine** (*Pandanus tectorius* and other species) is a tree which forms umbrellas of aerial roots in humid, swampy areas of tropical Asia. Its male flowers have an exquisite perfume. *Kewra* is used as a flavouring with *betel. Outside the tropics, it is possible to obtain *kewra* flavour in the form of *kewra* water and in syrups and cordials. *Kewra* is used in sweet dishes and is often included in *birianis*. Pieces of dried *kewra* may be put into curries, notably in Sri Lanka. The soft, sweet fruit, which are said to taste like pineapple, are also eaten.

KHAS-KHAS or **vetiver** (*Vetiveria zizanioides*) is an Indian aromatic grass also grown in the tropics and in Louisiana. It is used in Indian cooking as a flavouring, and its roots yield vetiver oil which is used in perfumes. *Khas* syrup and *khas* water may be bought from shops specializing in Indian products.

KHESARI. *See* lath.

KID. *See* goat.

KIDNEY. Although the kidneys of different mammals vary in shape, they all have roughly the same structure: a soft outside part and a tough central core surrounding a cavity from which runs a tube that drains the urine into the bladder. This central core is tough and gristly; it should be cut out and discarded. Kidneys should also be examined to make sure that they do not contain 'gravel' (sharp kidney stones), as man is not the only mammal to suffer from this complaint.

Lamb kidneys are the sort cooked for the traditional Englishman's breakfast, while veal (calf's) kidneys are used for more elegant dishes and ox kidneys for homelier ones.

[Kidney – French: *rognon* German: *Niere* Italian: *rognone* Spanish: *riñón*]

KIDNEY BEAN, **French bean**, **haricot bean** or **common bean**. This is the type of bean most usual in European and American cooking today and has largely replaced the old bean, which was the broad bean. The plant, *Phaseolus vulgaris*, was unknown in Europe and Asia before Columbus sailed west. Kidney beans are almost certainly native to Guatemala and southern Mexico, and were domesticated in ancient times and grown as a supplement to maize by the Aztecs and other civilized American peoples, who had many types in cultivation by the time that the first Europeans set foot on their continent. As is often the case when plants have been domesticated for a long time, there are no longer any recognizable wild ancestors. The first name given to the new bean in Britain was 'kidney bean', as early specimens were dark red and shaped like a kidney. (The word *haricot*, incidentally, is a corruption of the Aztec word for kidney bean, *ayecotl*, and has no connection with the haricots of beef, game or mutton. That *haricot* comes from the old French *harigoter*, to cut up into fine bits.)

From the outset, the new kidney bean was eaten green in Europe. In Britain, immature green beans (eaten with their pods) are today usually called French beans; in the US, snap or string beans. For some reason difficult to understand, the British do not usually eat freshly-matured beans although these are delicious and are a prized and expensive article in other countries. Mature dried kidney beans are usually called haricot beans in Britain, dried beans in the US.

There are a bewildering number of bean varieties, some grown mainly for their green pods and others for the shell or dried beans. Some of the more important ones follow:

Bianco de Spagna. A large, tender, white bean, in popularity in Italy, second only to the *borlotti*.

Black bean or **Mexican black bean.** Black beans from a yellow pod. They have a strong and delicious meaty – some say mushroom – taste and produce a thick black sauce. They are needed in some Mexican dishes (*frijoles negros*) and for the American black bean soup, and may be found in specialist shops. Substitution by *pintos* or other beans does not produce quite the same rich flavour, as these black beans are highly distinctive. They are also much used in Spain.

Borlotti. By far the most popular variety in Italy striated with red and very similar to the Spanish *pinto*. They are usually soaked overnight in Italy, but this is not usually necessary.

Canellini. Generic names for Italian white beans, particularly large ones such as *bianco de Spagna* (*see above*). *Canellini* would be the usual accompaniment to *cotechino* or a *bollito misto*.

Dried bean or **haricot sec.** Unless the beans are very old, the modern opinion is that they have a better flavour and are more digestible if they are not soaked, although traditionally and in old recipes they always are. It was usual to soak them overnight; the chef who gave me the recipe for Serbian bean soup (*see below*) claimed that the beans ought to be soaked for three days, though in very cold water. Modern authorities say that beans should be soaked for only a few hours at most. The objection to soaking is that it starts enzyme changes which would lead to germination; in warm weather, it may also start fermentation by micro-organisms. This is obviated by putting the beans into boiling water, blanching them for 2 minutes – which upsets the enzymes, kills the beans and most of the organisms – and then soaking them for 1 or 2 hours. (Softening the skins in tough varieties can be helped with a pinch of bicarbonate of soda.)

However, in most cases it is sufficient to put the beans into cold water and bring them gradually to the boil. Mature beans should always be cooked slowly – according to size and variety, they will need cooking for 3 hours or more. Many recipes leave them in a low oven overnight. One of the best ways is to do them in a pressure cooker. Wash the beans, put them in the pressure cooker without salt and cover them with cold water. Seal, bring up to the boil and cook for 5 minutes. Cool the cooker under the tap, open it and drain the beans. Now put them back with suitable flavourings (onion, cloves, *bouquet garni*, garlic and other seasoning if necessary) and salt. Cover them with boiling water, seal and bring up to pressure. Cook for 40 minutes (according to size). This method produces very digestible beans.

Serbian Bean Soup

This is a dish to warm you after skiing. Select large white dried beans and soak them in icy mountain water for 3 days. Boil them for 3-4 hours (preferably in water in which bacon has been boiled). Now brown an onion in oil with some chopped fat bacon, and add some canned red peppers with a little of their water, tomato purée and paprika with enough water for soup. Add salt and pepper, a little caraway seed, some *Maggi and the beans. Let the soup cook slowly for several hours. Thicken if necessary with a little flour, and continue cooking until the raw flour taste goes. Adjust the seasoning – the soup should be very slightly sour – and serve with sour cream. Bean soup is even nicer if a little minced beef is added to it.

---

*Flageolet. Small, pale creamy-green bean, a very delicate variety, greatly prized in France.

Fresh shell bean. The beans are ripe and the pods have turned to parchment, usually yellowish and perhaps splashed with scarlet. According to variety, the beans may be large or small, red, white, purple, black and yellow, either in one colour or eyed (with a dark spot round the hilum, where the bean is attached to the pod) or mottled, streaked, squiggled or splotched in brown or reds. Beans are as pretty as bird's eggs, but the patterns are destroyed by cooking. Appearance is no indication of flavour or of cooking quality. Some strains throw a high proportion of hard seeds, others have thick, tough seed-coats. A bean is not necessarily tender because it is small. (One of the reasons why it is so difficult to duplicate the good brands of baked beans at home is that the canners have developed their own tender-skinned varieties, which are probably better than any you can buy in the open market.) Fresh ripe beans cook without soaking. Put them into boiling water (which most people salt) and cook gently until they are tender.

After boiling, beans are dressed in many ways, some of those preferred by bean-lovers are very simple. In Spain, a meal may be begun with a plate of boiled beans into which each person mixes chopped parsley, chopped onion, *pimentón*, olive oil and vinegar according to his taste. In Venice, a dressing is made by warming some parsley and anchovy in garlic-flavoured oil and adjusting with a little vinegar. This sauce is mixed with the beans and left to mature for 10 minutes before serving.

Green bean or **haricot vert**. The pods may be large or small, flat or cylindrical, green, yellow, waxy (wax-pods are also referred to as butter beans in some places just to cause confusion), blue, purple, or green streaked with purple.

For gardeners, it matters whether the beans are dwarf (US, bush beans) or climbing (US, pole beans) and, in warm countries, where more than one crop can be grown in a year, whether they are long-day, short-day or day-neutral varieties, and cooks need to know if the beans are stringless. Kidney beans are very sensitive to frost, so in northern countries can be grown only in summer, although they are available out of season as imports. In the past, they were preserved for winter by salting, but now that frozen and canned beans are so commonly available, salting is rarely undertaken except by those who have a glut in the garden and no freezer. Salted beans never had gastronomic qualities in their own right, like salted and fermented cabbage (*sauerkraut*).

Before cooking, green beans are topped and tailed, and, if they are not stringless, the strings pulled out. The beans are then dropped into boiling water. Whether or not this should be salted is a matter of argument. Some French experts consider that the salt is best added towards the end of boiling, which should be fast. Beans cook in 10-20 minutes on average, depending on the size – some of the thin varieties cook very quickly – and also on whether you like beans well cooked or *al dente*, still a little crisp. Of course, they need less cooking if they are to be cooked again in butter. Some varieties have a much better flavour than others.

Navy bean. Small, white American bean, the type often recommended for Boston baked beans.

Pea bean. Californian or New York pea beans are small white beans often used for baked beans.

Pinto bean, from the Spanish for painted. *Pintos* and white beans are the most common in Spain and in many other countries; *pintos* have bright red markings.

KIMCHI. This staple Korean relish, served at every meal, is highly characteristic of Korean food. There are dozens of different types, but essentially *kimchi* is made from sliced or shredded vegetables – cabbage, cucumbers, onions, radishes, garlic, chillies – and sometimes fruit, all fermented in brine by lactic-acid-producing organisms and often with added spices and fresh ginger. This method of preserving food for the winter is an ancient one and is still an annual task for which all the family have to be mobilized each autumn. In warm weather, the fermentation takes little more than a day, but in the cold it takes longer.

The jar of *kimchi* for the winter is buried under the ground and taken out as necessary; it usually has a very bad smell. Emasculated *kimchi* sterilized in jars, is sometimes found in specialist shops.

Kimchi

Cut 450 g (1 lb) of white cabbage into 2½ cm (1 in) squares, and salt them for 15 minutes using about 2 tablespoons of salt. Wash the salt off the wilted cabbage with fresh water, drain and mix with 4 shredded spring onions – the green part included – 2-3 chopped cloves of garlic and a small, chopped fresh chilli. Add a small piece of fresh ginger, finely sliced, and a tablespoon of salt. Put the mixture into a jar and cover with cold water. Shake the jar to dissolve the salt and stand it in the sun for a day. If the weather is warm, fermentation may be completed in 24 hours but in cold weather it will take considerably longer, perhaps 5 days. When the fermentation is completed, the jar of *kimchi* may be kept in a refrigerator for several weeks.

KINGCUP. *See* marigold.

KIPPER. *See* herring.

KIRSCH or **kirschwasser**. *See* cherry, fruit brandy.

KIRSEBOER. *See* liqueurs and cordials.

KISHK is a Lebanese and Syrian staple food which is made in autumn after the harvest has been gathered and thrashed for use in the winter. Milk, yoghurt and *burghul* are mixed and allowed to ferment. Each day, for a period of nine days, the mass is kneaded, after which the fermentation is complete and the product is spread out to dry, usually on clean cloths on the flat roofs. When it is completely dry, the *kishk* is rubbed to a powder between the palms of the hands and stored in a dry place. Its usual use is as a porridge, made by frying several cloves of garlic in a tablespoon of *qawwrama* (preserved sheep fat) and then adding 2 tablespoons of the *kishk*. Frying is continued for several minutes. Finally, a cup of water is put in with some salt and the whole is boiled to the consistency of a porridge.

KITCHEN CARAMEL. *See* browning.

KIWI FRUIT or **Chinese gooseberry**. *See* gooseberry.

KNACKWURST. *See* frankfurter.

KNEADING. A process known and carried out ever since man learned to make bread. Flour, mixed with water, has to be worked hard to turn it into a dough, whether the dough contains yeast or is intended for such simple unleavened breads as the *chapatti*. Kneading not only mixes the ingredients but develops the elasticity of the *gluten in the flour, the quality that is responsible for the structure of the bread, particularly when the loaf is expected to rise and stand up. It is difficult to describe the point to which kneading should be taken – words often used to describe the dough are 'springy' and 'silky'. Average times for kneading would be 5-7 minutes, depending on the energy and weight that are put into it.
[Kneading – French: *pétrir* German: *kneten* Italian: *impastare* Spanish: *amasar*]

KNOL-KHOL. *See* kohlrabi.

KNOTTED MARJORAM. *See* sweet marjoram.

KNUCKLE. In veal and pork butchery, the knuckle is the lower part of the back leg.
[Knuckle – French: *jarret* German: *Kniestück* (veal), *Eisenbein* (pork) Italian: *garretto* Spanish: *jarrete*]

KOHLRABI or **knol-kohl**. One of the many forms of cabbage, *Brassica oleracea* var. *gongylodes*, but is sometimes elevated to a separate species, *B. caulorapa*. It has the stem swollen into a bulb from which the leaf stalks arise. There are greenish-white and purple varieties. An excellent vegetable, something like a turnip but with its own individuality, popular in Europe and the Orient, less so in Britain and the US.
[Kohlrabi – French: *chou-rave* German: *Kohlrabi* Italian: *cavolrapa*]

KOLA NUT. *See* cola nut.

KOKUM. The kokum of Indian cooking comes from a tree (*Garcinia indica*),which grows wild in the Western Ghats and is closely related to the mangosteen (*G. mangostana*). It bears deep purple fruits, with four to five large seeds (from which kokum butter is extracted), and the pulp of the fruit, though much inferior to the mangosteen, has a pleasant, sour taste. It is dried – sometimes the fruit is sliced and dried, but sometimes only the skin with attached pulp – and used as a souring agent in South Indian cooking. It is slightly laxative (like tamarind, which it resembles, though tamarind is much sourer). Thoroughly dried samples can be ground to a powder and used as a condiment.

KOMBU *seaweed is an essential ingredient, with *katsuobushi* (dried bonito), of the Japanese basic stock, *dashi*.

KOSHER. From the Hebrew *kasher* meaning *right*, kosher food has been prepared (or, with meat, killed) by Jews and approved by the rabbi for consumption by orthodox Jews in accordance with their *religious food laws.
[Kosher – French: *casher* German: *Koscher*]

KOUMISS. A sour-milk drink originally made from mare's milk by tribes in the eastern part of Russia (Uzbek, Bashkir, Kirghiz) and containing as much as 2-2½% alcohol, the strength of very weak beer. According to Marco Polo, it was drunk by Genghis Khan. Today, less glamorously it is in great demand in Soviet sanitoria. Because mare's milk contains less *casein than cow's milk, it forms a much finer and weaker curd particle and so is exceedingly digestible. Though originally made in skins, it is now prepared in wooden pails as follows: To 2.5-3 lt (4½-5¼ pt) of mare's milk are added 1.72-2 lt (3-3½ pt) of sour cow's milk, and the two well stirred together. The temperature should be 25-26°C (59°F) at which temperature it is kept for further fermentation and the production of gas and alcohol.

KRUPEK or **krupuk**. A large crisp made from dried prawns, a favourite Indonesian accompaniment to a meal. These crisps are bought ready-made even in Indonesia and need only to be fried in deep oil and well drained. If they are not available, the smaller Chinese prawn crisps are an acceptable substitute.

KULTHI BEAN. *See* horse grain.

KÜMMEL. The German word for *caraway* and also for the caraway-flavoured liqueur, said to have originated in Riga (in Latvia), but which has for long been made in Germany, Denmark and Holland.

Different makes vary in sweetness, aroma and strength.

KUMQUAT, a native of China, is smaller than the citrus fruits, to which it is closely related, only 2-4 cm (1-1⅗ in) in diameter. They are juicy and acid, with few seeds and a sweet, edible rind. Although often grown for ornament, they are also candied or canned whole. Two species, the oval kumquat (*Fortunella margarita*) and the round kumquat (*F. japonica*) are the most important.

KYRYNGA. A Central-Asian sour milk product, made from cow's milk, and slightly gassy and alcoholic. The method of preparation is very like that used for *koumiss* and involves wooden vessels which have become impregnated with the necessary organisms and so provide a natural starter, as long as they are not cleaned out.

I

LABIATES are members of the plant family Labiatae, which includes lavender and dead-nettles. They have stems that are square in cross-section and characteristic flowers with the petals joined to form a tube usually with two lips. The fruit is a cluster of four nutlets. The labiates often have aromatic leaves and are the most important family of herbs as they include, among others, basil, marjoram, mint, oregano, pennyroyal, rosemary, sage, savoury and thyme. A labiate vegetable is the Chinese artichoke.

LABLAB BEAN, **Hyacinth bean**, **bonavist bean**, or **Egyptian bean**. This small bean (*Dolichos lablab*) is much cultivated in warm countries – South and Central America, the West Indies, China, Africa and South East Asia. It is a native of India, a twining, attractive bean which is used dried or green. Even the leaves are edible and the green pods are often pickled in India, where it is called *wal* or *val*. The dried beans are usually brown with a white central hilum.

LACTIC ACID ($CH_3.CHOH.COOH$) is the acid of

sour milk. As a chemical, it is used in the laboratory but never in the kitchen. Nevertheless, it is an important preservative and is commonly found in foods, in particular where lactic-acid-producing bacteria have been at work on sugars.

The formation of lactic acid goes on not only in the souring of milk but also in the making of *sauerkraut*, dill pickles and *kimchi* – in fact, in all pickles that depend on acid fermentation (rather than on the addition of vinegar).The lactic acid formed when milk sours stops putrefactive organisms; if these are allowed to multiply they not only produce nasty tastes and bad smells but some are dangerous. This is why lactic acid bacteria are used as cheese starters (curd that isn't soured goes bad very quickly) and why yoghurt can be kept for many days in the refrigerator. Preparations in which fish is fermented with sour cream or milk also depend on lactic acid fermentation for their preservation. With time, the lactic acid is itself attacked by other types of micro-organism and is broken down, so that mould-ripened cheeses which are sharply acid when young become sweet

225

when matured. Lactic acid is formed in the working muscles of living animals. In animals that have been killed, it appears in muscles when meat first hardens and plays an important part, with enzymes, in the maturation and tenderization process during *hanging.

[Lactic acid – French: acide lactique German: Milchsäure Italian: acido lattica Spanish: àcido làctico]

LACTOSE or milk sugar is the natural *sugar of milk. Like sucrose (cane sugar), it is a disaccharide which forms hard crystals, but it is much the least sweet of naturally occurring sugars and is not normally used in a pure form. It is present in the whey of coagulated milk and is the food of the bacteria which sour milk by making lactic acid. During digestion, lactose is broken down into glucose and galactose.

[Lactose – French: lactose German: Milchzucker Italian: lattosio Spanish: lactosa]

LADIES' FINGERS. See okra.

LADY'S BEDSTRAW. A wild plant (Galium verum) of the madder family with tiny yellow flowers. It grows all over Europe (except Russia) and in Western Asia. In the past, the flowers were much used as a vegetable *rennet to curdle milk.

[Lady's bedstraw – French: gaillet German: Labkraut Italian: caglio Spanish: gaglio]

LADY'S FINGERS. See banana.

LADY'S SMOCK or **cuckoo flower** (Cardamine pratensis) is a crucifer which is a common meadow plant of Europe and North America. It has four-petalled, pale mauve or white flowers. Though not as plentiful as it was (because of the ploughing up of pasture), it is one of the first plants each year that is sufficiently common to be worth including in a spring salad. It has a cress-like flavour.

[Lady's smock – French: cardamine, cresson des prés German: Wiesenschaumkraut Italian: billeri, cardamine, crescione dei prati Spanish: cardamine]

LAEVULOSE. See fructose.

LAMB. See mutton.

LAMB'S LETTUCE. See salad.

LAND JÄGER. See sausage.

LANGOSTINO. See shrimp.

LANGOUSTE, spiny lobster, or **southern lobster**. This is the French name for the spiny lobster (Palinurus elephas and other species) which is also confusingly referred to as the crawfish (in contrast to *crayfish), an artificial distinction since the two are alternative spellings of the same thing. The Revd J.G. Wood called Astacus fluviatilis 'the common cray-fish or craw-fish of our rivers' in his Natural History of 1863. He calls the langouste the Spiny lobster, sea cray-fish or red crab. It was not then much esteemed in Britain and it is still not seriously fished in many areas (its habits are not identical with those of the lobster). It is confined to the warmer waters of the southern and west coasts, but is better known on the coasts of France and in the Mediterranean, where it is avidly sought. There are similar creatures on the other side of the Atlantic and other oceans – those of South Africa's Cape Province are particularly well known. Langoustes are essentially like lobsters, but without the big claws. It would be best to steal the French word langouste – as we have stolen and exchanged so many others (especially as they are called langosta in Spanish and Languste in German). In Italy, where the langouste is much more common than the lobster, it is called aragosta. The langouste grows to about 50 cm (20 in) maximum in length, but there are other larger species, variously coloured but not much different in other respects. Preparation is generally as for lobster. Commercially available frozen crayfish tails are the abdomens of marine langoustes.

LANGOUSTINE. See scampi.

LAOS. See galangal.

LAPWING. See plover.

LARD is purified pig's fat (but lard is also French for *bacon). Readily available, wrapped in blocks, the commercial product is white, with only the slightest porky taste. It is the usual cooking fat in some districts, for instance in parts of south-western France. A combination of circumstances including the introduction of vegetable cooking fats and the saturated fatty-acid scare have reduced its popularity, but it still gives a wonderful texture in pastry and a 50:50 mixture of lard and butter (for flavour) is traditional for flaky pastry. It is used in lardy cakes and delicious, though rich, sweet specialities.

Where pigs are home-cured, lard is usually made of the fat that surrounds the kidneys, as this has the highest proportion of fat to tissue. (Back fat is sometimes used too.) After washing and if necessary soaking to remove all traces of blood, the fat is minced to break up the cells, and rendered at a very low temperature, no more than 50°C (122°F) being best. This really needs to be done in a double boiler or *bain-marie* (though some mix the fat with water); with direct rendering, even over low heat, the lard is easily coloured. The liquid fat is tipped off from time to time, filtered through muslin to remove any bits, and poured straight into the warmed glass jars in which it is to be kept. The whole process is likely to take 1-2 hours. The lard keeps for a month or more if properly sealed and stored in a cool place.

[*Lard* – French: *saindoux, graisse de porc, panne* German: *Schweinefett, Schmalz* Italian: *strutto, sugna* Spanish: *manteca de cerdo*]

LARDING. The process of introducing ribbons of pork fat (lardoons) into meat which lacks fat and would otherwise cook dry (venison, veal, pigeons are examples). 'This operation is great fun to do, and most soothing... and looks sensational', says Jane Grigson. In French cookery books of the last century, almost every joint looks like a hedgehog. Fat, usually back fat, is cut in strips, pinched into the clip of the larding needle, and gently inserted in the meat. A modern gadget, rather on the lines of a surgeon's trocar (a tube cut diagonally and sharpened at one end) enables you to lard with frozen butter (or herb butter). Slaves to poly-unsaturated oils can do a somewhat similar job with a hypodermic syringe, though one large enough for a horse is best.

[*Larding* – French: *larder* German: *spicken* Italian: *lardellare* Spanish: *mechar*]

LARK. *See* birds.

LASAGNA. *See* pasta.

LATH, chickling vetch or **grass pea**. In India, **khesari**. This plant (*Lathyrus sativa*) is a legume closely related to the sweet-pea (*L. odorata*) and grown as a fodder crop and pulse, often in the rice fields in Asia. As food, its use is mainly confined to the poor – although it is sometimes used to adulterate other pulses such as *pigeon peas. It was long suspected of being poisonous in quantity and of causing lathyrism, which mainly attacked men who had been cold and wet while working in the fields, causing their legs to become paralysed, at least temporarily. The poisoning is now thought to be mainly, if not entirely, due to seeds of the common vetch *Vicia sativa*, a true vetch (which lath is not) and related to the *broad bean. The vetch seeds become mixed with the lath seeds and are eaten with them.

LAUREL. *See* bay.

LAVER, laver-weed, red laver, or **tangle**, is a rosette-shaped *seaweed, pinkish purple (sometimes turning greenish brown) and growing near the low-tide mark on rocky coasts of northern Europe. As a food, it is particularly famous in South Wales – it grows plentifully on the Gower coast – and similar species (*nori*) are used and even cultivated in Japan. In Scotland, laver (*Porphyra umbilicalis*) is called slake, slouk or slokum; in Ireland, stoke. A very similar species, Pink laver (*P. lacinata*), is also known as tangle and (in Orkney) redware. It is mainly a winter food, although it is in season from June to March. After gathering, the weed must be thoroughly washed to free it of sand and soaked for 2-3 hours in running water (or changes of water) to remove the salt. It must then be boiled until it is quite soft. This will normally take anything from 5-6 hours up to 12 hours, but in winter, when laver is tender, it may take as little as 2 hours. The water is then drained off and the laver may be sieved. This thick purée, which is usually mixed with oatmeal, is now called laver bread (Welsh: *bara lawr, bara* being bread). Ready prepared laver bread is sold in the markets in South Wales out of wooden tubs lined with white cloths or in small cakes. It should be used as soon as possible, as it does not keep.

Laver

For 4, take 450 g (1 lb) laver bread, divide it into 4 equal cakes, roll them in oatmeal and fry them for 5-6 minutes. Serve very hot with bacon and eggs, sprinkling the laver, if you like, with a little vinegar. Or: Laver is also the classic Welsh accompaniment to mutton. To 450 g (1 lb) of laver bread, add 100 g (4 oz) of butter and stir over a flame (with a wooden fork) until it is very hot. Season to taste with a squeeze of lemon juice or bitter orange juice. Serve in a hot dish preferably over a table heater to keep it hot. Serves 4.

LEAD is an exceedingly poisonous element and a

cumulative poison, which means that apparently harmless amounts tend to remain in the body until they eventually reach a dangerous level. Tolerance to lead varies from person to person, so that levels of lead which may not affect one may cause serious symptoms of poisoning in another.

In the past, lead poisoning was much more common that it is today. Paints were very often based on lead oxides, and painters often suffered from 'painter's colic'. Lead pipes were, however, the commonest danger, for lead got into soft water, aerated water, beer and, above all, cider. Lead pipes were used in pubs – there was nothing else suitable – and rough cider in particular caused 'Devonshire colic'. Tea shipped in chests lined with lead foil, and milk bottles topped with lead foil caps were other sources of contamination. Nowadays lead foil is rare; aluminium foil is used instead. And plastic and stainless steel pipes have replaced lead pipes in pubs.

Pewter is a mixture of tin and lead, as also is solder. The tin used to line old copper pans contained lead as it still does today in some countries, but in most modern pans, the tin is very pure. Crystal glass, in which lead replaced lime, was developed in the 17th century because of its high refractive index and brilliance for cut glass, and this lead could contaminate the contents of decanters. As lead oxides are highly efficient fluxes, they make *ceramic glazes run at low temperatures, and so were used for old-fashioned traditional earthenware. Although glazes for earthenware no longer contain potentially dangerous amounts of lead, at least on pots made or bought in Britain, France, Italy, and Germany, it is better not to use such pots for acid substances at all. Never use earthenware vessels for marinating – use stoneware, glass, enamel or plastic.

[Lead – French: plomb German: Blei Italian: piombo Spanish: plomo]

LEAVENING. To leaven is to lighten, in this case to lighten a bread or cake by introducing bubbles of gas which expand during cooking. This requires a means of supplying the gas bubbles and also an elastic substance which can first be blown up and then set (like egg white or gluten). Undoubtedly the first breads were unleavened and probably flat, like matzos, chappattis or tortillas. If dough is left for a few hours in warm weather, the organisms that are naturally present, including yeasts, will cause fermentation. This sort of simple, natural leavening is still used in India, for instance, when batters are left overnight to ferment (as when making idlis and dosas). Such methods depend on the chance that suitable organisms are in the dough. In many countries, it became the practice to make sure by keeping back a piece of one batch of dough in order to inoculate the next. Such a starter was known as leaven; as the dough became sour (from the activity of *lactic-acid organisms) the product was called sour-dough bread. Today yeast is usually added as a separate ingredient. As it is not always convenient to use yeast – it requires warmth and time to produce sufficient gas – chemicals to do a similar job (*baking powders) were immediately popular when introduced to the public. Other possible methods of leavening are the addition of soda water or beaten egg.

[Leavening – French: faire lever German: säuern Italian: lievitare Spanish: leudar]

LEBERWURST. German for *liver sausage.

LEEK. Cultivated leeks (Allium porrum) are possibly derived from the wild leek (A. ampeloprasum), which is very rare in Britain but grows in Mediterranean and south-eastern Europe; yet we cannot be certain because leeks have been cultivated for so long that their origins have become clouded. In Britain, leeks tend to be regarded as only a vegetable (and there are Freudian competitions to see who can grow the largest specimen) while in the US, in spite of vichyssoise being so popular, leeks are rather neglected. Not so in France, or in Spain and Italy, where leeks of small and tender types, quite unlike those monstrous competition specimens, are a necessary and all-year-round ingredient. They are the sweetest of the onion tribe, which is perhaps why Nero thought that eating them improved his oratory.

Before using leeks, it is important to make sure they are cleaned properly because, especially after rain, mud splashes up on to leeks (which are earthed up to make them white) and gets down between the leaf sheaths. After cutting off the roots and most of the green tops, and removing the tough outer sheaths, the leek should be washed under a running tap – it must be held head down all the time (it may or may not be necessary to slit the top to open up the sheath) so that any grit is washed not inwards but outwards. Each layer of leaf should be examined and rubbed clean of any mud. After that, the leeks can be stood upside-down in clean water until they are put to cook. They should never, on any account, be thrown into a basin of water. When buying leeks, look for fresh-looking, young specimens, devoid of a central hard core, untrimmed, unwilted, and with a large proportion of white. Do not buy large, coarse-looking specimens. Fresh, young leeks are magnificent: old or stale leeks are bitter and horrid.

Leeks are boiled in salted water for about 30 minutes (best tied in bunches to help them keep shape) or parboiled and braised in butter or fried in batter (after parboiling); they are served with many sauces. As an *hors d'oeuvre,* either *à la grecque,* in a *vinaigrette* or served in the Romanian way with olives in a sweet-sour, oily, tomato sauce, they are excellent. They go into soups of all sorts as a flavouring and are sometimes included in the *bouquet garni.* Young and tender leeks can be shredded raw into salads – a use that goes back to the Romans.

[*Leek* – French: *poireau* German: *Lauch* Italian: *porro* Spanish: *puerro*]

LEGUME. Member of the botanical group Leguminosae, a plant that bears seeds in a pod which splits open down both seams when ripe. Among the legumes are peas, beans, lentils, clovers, vetches, alfalfa, lucerne, tamarind, acacia, mimosa and wattle. This very large group includes about 12,000 known species. Legumes are found in all types of climate and soil. They may be herbs, shrubs, trees, climbers, desert plants or water plants. They are of crucial importance because many have root nodules containing bacteria which fix nitrogen from the air, and because they provide the bulk of the world's protein both for people and livestock. Some, such as soya and peanuts, also provide important oils. Others like tamarind, fenugreek and carobs are sources of flavour, sourness or sweetness, while gum arabic and gum tragacanth are also from legumes. Dried legume seeds are *pulses.

Because legumes play such a widespread and important part in man's food, many of them have acquired a baffling collection of alternative names, some of which are dealt with in cross-references in this book. The main types of legume with entries of their own are adzuki bean, alfalfa, asparagus bean, asparagus pea, black gram, broad bean, butter bean, carob bean, *channa,* chickpea, cowpea, fenugreek, *ful medames, gaur,* goa bean, gums, horse gram, jack bean, kidney bean, lablab, lath, lentil, liquorice, moth bean, mung bean, pea, peanut, pigeon pea, rice bean, runner bean, soya bean, tamarind, tepary bean. A large number of the familiar legumes of Europe and America from

haricots to Mexican black beans are varieties of the kidney bean. The legumes which are dealt with here are only the ones which are widely eaten; a multitude of other legumes are eaten locally around the world. Not all legume seeds are edible, however, and poisonous ones include laburnum and some vetches.

[*Legume* – French: *légume* German: *Hülse, Hülsenfrucht* Italian: *legume* Spanish: *legumbre*]

LEMON (*Citrus limon*) is, with orange, the most important citrus fruit. However, it did not come into Europe from the East until at least the 1st century AD, and possibly not until the 10th century – if it was there at the earlier date, it was probably not at all common. Nobody is sure of the lemon's country of origin; some experts say it is India, but others point out that lemons are much less common there than limes. It is unfortunate that in early writings citrons (the earliest citrus to reach Europe) and limes and lemons are confused.

Today, lemons are grown in all the countries of the Mediterranean basin – and Portugal – but not further north, because they stand no frost and need a warm climate to thrive. In the US (which now produces a gigantic quantity), lemons are mainly grown commercially in California and Arizona, for even Florida was found to have too much frost. Lemon trees are thorny, but their pale leaves and yellow fruit make them the most beautiful of the citrus trees. By using several varieties, it has been possible to provide fresh lemons all the year round – just. They also store well, but are cheapest in spring and early summer, most expensive in the autumn. So that they will travel, lemons are picked slightly green and not allowed to ripen on the tree, which is a pity because they then never develop their full scent. English lemon curd, for instance, made with freshly-picked lemons in a Mediterranean country (where it is unknown) is a revelation to anyone in England who has had to depend on imported lemons from the local fruit shop. In some cases, bought lemons have been treated with sprays, dyes or wax, which can make the skin unappetizing. Growers forget that from lemons we get two separate items, the sourness of the juice and the lemon-oil taste from the zest.

Lemon juice is rich in citric acid and is the most commonly used *souring agent in Western cooking, as it has little flavour to interfere with other tastes. As lemons can at a pinch be kept for up to a month in the vegetable tray of the fridge, there is no excuse for being without 'a squeeze of lemon'. I carry a tube of citric acid on expeditions, because there is no alternative, but the lemon juice sold in bottles (or in plastic lemons) is a pale imitation of the real thing.

Lemon zest is much used in cakes and sweets, but is neglected as a flavouring in savoury dishes. Yet grated lemon rind can sometimes make a huge difference not only to stuffings, but also to sauces flavoured with herbs, and particularly to those containing capers with which lemon seems to have a special affinity.

Lemon leaves are occasionally used, but do not have a very strong flavour. Lemon flavours also come from lemon *balm, lemon-scented *verbena and lemon grass, as well, of course, as lemon oil and lemon extract.

The bioflavinoid citrin (once called vitamin P), which is present in lemon pith, does not seem to have the effect on the common cold it was once credited with, but I am still convinced that lemon and honey is an excellent home treatment. While it is generally believed to have been limes which the British navy once provided for their sailors as a defence against scurvy, it was, in fact, lemons.

[Lemon – French: citron German: Zitrone Italian: limone Spanish: limón]

LEMON GRASS, sereh, or serei. A grass Cymbopogon citratus and Cymbopogon flexuesus, with a bulbous base, smelling rankly of lemon (it contains citral as does the zest of lemon). It is much used in the cooking of Ceylon and South East Asia, and is available dried as sereh powder from specialist shops. It is not difficult to grow lemon grass where it can be provided with warmth. Lemon *balm or lemon scented *verbena are usually considered a better lemon grass substitute than zest of lemon. The oil extracted from lemon grass is poisonous.

[Lemon grass – French: citronnelle Italian: cimbopogone]

LEMON SOLE. See flatfish.

LENTIL (Lens culinaris) is a pulse that came originally from the Middle East. The plant is small, 40-50 cm (16-20 in) high, something like a vetch, with short, broad pods. There are many cultivated varieties, some with large and some with quite small seeds; colours are also variable, but the seeds are most often brown or green when whole. Inside, they are yellow, cream, orange or red. Lentils are much grown in Egypt and North Africa, over

the whole of southern Europe and in many other warm countries. In Britain, they can be grown in a sheltered position by anyone who wishes to eat them as a green vegetable. In India, masoor or masur is a variety of lentil that is popular with the Muslim community, but is otherwise regarded as a poor man's pulse, except in Bihar and Bengal. The food value of lentils is high, and they are one of the three most popular pulses eaten in Europe. In Britain, lentils were until recently the only available pulse other than beans and split peas; the lentils sold were mostly the peeled, red, so-called Egyptian lentils and not the whole green or brown German lentils of Victorian books. These whole lentils are the type known on the Continent and to be used in all Continental recipes. In France, the tiny, green, expensive lentilles vertes du Puy are a delicacy used, amongst other things, for salads and hors d'oeuvre.

Lentils taste best when they are not soaked before cooking; if soaking is felt to be necessary, it should be for a short time and certainly not overnight. As a preliminary, all lentils should be washed. Seeds that float may contain grubs. Whole lentils should be examined to see if there are stones among them, as these are common in samples of whole lentils badly cleaned by machine. Stones that are actually bits of dried earth will be removed by washing in several waters, but if the stones are real (and tiny like the lentils), the lentils must be shaken in water in a tilted pan until the stones (which are denser than the lentils) have slid down into the bottom corner. They can be left behind when the clean lentils are scooped, not tipped, out.

In the Orient, lentils and other dried seeds bought in the bazaars are often very dirty and cooks become expert at removing stones and rogue seeds by tossing them in baskets or mats. Whole lentils take ¾-1½ hours to cook, depending on age and variety. They should be watched, as they absorb a surprising amount of water. The water in which lentils are cooked makes good stock, so save the remaining water. In a pressure cooker, all except the toughest lentils can be cooked in 15-20 minutes.

Lentils are mainly a winter dish, popular in Germany as Linsensuppe (lentil soup) or saures Linsengemüse (savoury lentil purée) which is served with Rotwurst (red sausage from Thuringia), Schweinerippchen (pork ribs) and Blutwurst. In northern Italy, lenticchie in umido (boiled) are eaten with *zampone or *cotechino; zuppa di lenticchie (lentil soup), may be flavoured with sage or mixed with chestnuts and flavoured with thyme, basil and marjoram as in the Abruzzi. In France, there are also substantial lentil dishes, *lentilles au lard, à la Dijonnaise* or *à la Picarde*, but also more refined treats such as:

Lentilles du Puy à la crème

Put 300 g (11 oz) *lentilles du Puy* (washed but not soaked) in 1½ lt (2¾ pt) cold water on the lowest possible flame. They should take at least 45 minutes to come to the boil, during which time they soak and swell. When they come to the boil, turn up the heat slightly and cook until they are tender – another 45 minutes. Add a little salt just before the water is all absorbed (as it should be).When the lentils are ready, add a large knob of butter and plenty of cream (keeping them hot but not letting them boil). Season with freshly-ground black pepper and celery salt.

In Spain, both whole, unpeeled lentils (which remain whole when cooked) and peeled lentils (*lentejas peladas)*, which cook to a purée, are used. Dishes include *lentejas* with potato, raw ham and smoked bacon, flavoured with tomato, bay, thyme and parsley and *lentejas con arroz* (lentils with rice) flavoured with onion, garlic, bay, parsley, *pimentón* and vinegar. In this connection, it is interesting to note that *masoor dal* is the correct pulse to use in a *kichri*, the Indian dish which gave rise to kedgeree, because the lentils retain their shape and do not go to a purée. If they did, lentil and rice dishes would be very stodgy indeed.

[*Lentil* – French: *lentille* German: *Linse* Italian: *lenticchia* Spanish: *lenteja*]

LENTISK. *See* mastic.

LETTUCE (*Lactuca sativa*) has been cultivated from Europe to China for so long that its wild origin is uncertain, although there are a number of wild relatives. The pale yellow flowers of plants that have bolted show that they are composites – members of the daisy family. The smell of lettuce is rather like that of opium because of certain alkaloids. Indeed, the milky latex from another species of lettuce (*L. virosa*) is dried like opium and used as a raw material in drug manufacture, and all the species of lettuce are narcotic to a greater or lesser extent. Even the stems of bolted garden lettuces, if eaten in quantity, have been known to make people drowsy, even unconscious. In normal amounts, lettuce is only calming and sedative. A concoction made with lettuce is a country way of relieving coughs and soothing painful skin.

Garden lettuces are grown by the million in almost every country. Cabbage lettuces (var. *capitata*) range from the thin-leaved types to the thick, solid ones such as Webb's Wonderful; they may be green or tinged with red or bronze. As lettuces are rather sensitive to soil type and climate, the varieties grown anywhere are likely to be determined by their success in the particular place. Different varieties come into season at different times of the year. Selecting lettuce for salad requires attention to variety as well as to freshness. Very thin-leafed types, for example, need a light dressing as they easily collapse when mixed with a heavy one or crowded with other vegetables in mixed salads. On the other hand, many of the thick, juicy lettuce types have a strong 'opium' flavour which may go well with a stronger dressing, and is good just with salt in a sandwich. In the hot countries, the Cos or Romaine type of lettuce (var. *crispa*) is the most common. Cos lettuce, with its large elongated leaves, can be very tough. In Egypt, people commonly tear off the leaf part and eat only the sweet, juicy mid-rib. Living in Spain, I find it necessary to tear the leaf part into pieces, and then chop the mid-rib. Mixed together again, they give in effect two vegetables in one salad. (Cooks should in general be alert to texture in salads – then perhaps we would get fewer of those mixtures of lettuce and ill-considered chunks of tomato, or claggy mixtures stained red with beetroot.) Lettuce can be kept briefly in the refrigerator, but optimistic restaurants, especially in America, keep it until it goes transparent. No amount of 'crisping' in the refrigerator will revive a tired lettuce. Because lettuces have at best a minimal food value and are mainly there because they are nice, there seems little point in serving an old one; even its vitamins are defunct. And, of course, lettuce for salads must be bone dry. Only the outer of the inner leaves need washing. Each leaf needs drying with a clean cloth for a perfect salad.

Cooked lettuce is not greatly popular and tends to go slimy, but there are many recipes for lettuce boiled, stewed, braised, puréed, stuffed or cooked with peas, and wrappings of lettuce are used in *cuisine minceur*. Large outer leaves of Cos are useful to lay over fish in the oven and are better than foil to prevent over-browning. The stems of bolted lettuce are sometimes preserved in a ginger-flavoured syrup, and some people even eat lettuce with sugar.

[*Lettuce* – French: *laitue* German: *Lattich*,

Gartensalat, Kopfsalat Italian: *lattuga* Spanish: *lechuga*]

LETTUCE LAVER. *See* seaweed.

LEUQKUAS. *See* galangal.

LEVULOSE. *See* fructose.

LIEBIG. The great German chemist, Baron Justus von Liebig (1803-1873), turned his attention from pure chemistry to apply it to the relief of human suffering when he was about 40. That was the time of the Tiny Tims that Dickens wrote about in his *Christmas Carol*, a time when malnutrition was rife. In addition to his work on chemical fertilizers, Liebig is remembered for his development of meat extract.

Before there were refrigerator ships, it was impossible for South American beef to be brought to Europe in the way that it is today. Liebig ground raw beef with cold water and, when the soluble elements in the meat had had time to dissolve, filtered and squeezed out the liquid, which contained 15-25% of the meat in solution. This liquid was then boiled to coagulate the albuminous substances, leaving a clear soup which could be evaporated over gentle heat until it left a brown extract that smelled like roast beef: Liebig's Beef Extract. A factory was set up in 1847 at Fray Bentos in Uruguay. Real Liebig's Meat Extract is now very expensive, as lean meat is rendered down to only about one-thirtieth of its weight of extract. Variations on the method can usefully be applied in making stock, and, in an emergency, it can be made for very ill people.

LIGHTS are lungs. They go into various meat preparations such as some *pâtés* and into traditional *faggots. Larousse Gastronomique* offers half a dozen recipes for dealing with pig's lights. Most cooks, however, are likely to buy lights only for feeding the dog – if the dog will eat them.

LIMA BEAN. *See* butter bean.

LIME. When limestone, chalk or marble (calcium carbonate) is strongly heated, quicklime (calcium oxide) is formed, a caustic and potentially dangerous substance. When water is added, the quicklime gets very hot and turns into a crumbly mass of slaked lime – calcium hydroxide. If quicklime is exposed to the air, natural humidity will produce the same result in a few days. Slaked

lime is dissolved rather sparingly in water to give *limewater. Very fine lime (*chuna*) is a natural part of the mixture used to make *pan. Slaked lime can be bought from chemists.

[*Lime* – French: *chaux* German: *Kalk* Italian: *calce* Spanish: *cal*]

LIME (*Citrus aurantifolia*) is a small, sour, citrus fruit which has much in common with the lemon. Limes are used in the same way and for similar purposes. Like lemons, they can stand no frost; in fact, they are even fussier about climate. Like lemon trees, lime trees are also very prickly, but are typically smaller and bushier. Limes probably originated somewhere in South East Asia, and were brought west, eventually reaching southern Spain with the Arabs. Columbus took them to America on his second voyage, in 1493. In Europe, limes are little known – they have a foothold in places like southern Italy and Sicily – and lemons are dominant. However, in very hot and tropical countries lemons do not do so well (they have a tender skin) and limes take over.

There are a number of types. The common lime in India and southern Asia, for instance, is more yellow than green, rounded, oval and rarely with a nipple. It is also quite small. The maximum diameter is about 5 cm (2 in) and the average is not much bigger than a table tennis ball. The skin is thin, and the flesh very sour and juicy. The flavour is characteristic, with nothing of the citron taste of lime cordial.

On the other hand, in Europe and America, the limes are mainly of the type of the Tahiti lime, which originated by chance, although it has been claimed to be a hybrid. It is a markedly larger fruit than the Indian variety, green rather than yellow, and with a more citrony flavour. In Britain, both Indian and Caribbean limes turn up as imports; in the US, the Tahiti type is grown in Florida and California, as well as being imported. In Florida, the so-called Persian variety is much grown. It has large, oval fruits with a few seeds, and is very acid. Maximum production is in thirsty August – in that respect it beats the lemon, which gets scarcer as summer advances. California comes a little later than Florida, mainly with the Bearss variety, which is smaller and seedless. There is considerable difference in the flavour of the limes. A caveach of raw fish as made in Peru requires the juice of Persian limes to have the authentic flavour. It is very inferior when made with the juice of lemons, just as a lemon curd flavoured with lime peel would hardly pass as pukka

in the vicarage garden. Indian lime pickle does
not have the authentic taste when it is made with
Caribbean limes, and is quite a different substance
when it is made with lemons. In some parts of
the Middle East, limes are dried and ground as a
condiment. The acid powder is delicious sprinkled,
for instance, on rice.

Sweet limes (*Citrus limettioides*) were once much
planted in India because they are heavy bearers and
hardy. The fruit looks like a greenish orange; the
skin is thin, but the juice is very insipid. However,
sweet limes arrive towards the end of the monsoon
when other and better citruses are not available.
Limes, like other citruses, hybridize easily to such
creations as the limequat (lime X kumquat).The
citrus lime should not be confused with lime, linden
or basswood tree.

[*Lime* – French: *lime, limette, citron vert* German:
süsse limone Italian: *cedro, lima* Spanish: *lima*]

LIME, **linden**, or **basswood** (US).The lime trees
which are planted in so many European towns are
usually a hybrid form (*Tilia* X *europaea*). Both it and
its two ancestors, *T. cordata* and *T. platyphyllos*,
have beautifully scented, yellowish flowers, which
can be dried and used as a calming tisane or tea.
They can also be used as a flavouring and go into
home-made liqueurs. These trees are not related to
the citrus limes.

[*Lime* – French: *tilleul* German: *Linden* Italian: *tilo*
Spanish: *tiglio*]

LIMEWATER can be made by stirring 2-3
tablespoons of slaked *lime in hot water, leaving
it to get cold and then filtering it (although for
most purposes filtering is not really necessary). In
Belgium, Holland and Germany, dried fish (*stock
fish) is soaked in it. Some people crisp watermelon
rind by soaking it in limewater for 3 hours before
pickling. Limewater is also the liquid in which maize
is traditionally boiled to remove the horny yellow
skin in making Mexican *mixtamal*, the first stage
in producing *masa for *tortillas, tamales*, etc. The
limewater softens the seed-coat to the point where
it can be rubbed off. Limewater, being alkaline, will
neutralize an acid. In emergency, I have also found
limewater a soothing liquid to pour over minor
burns.

[*Limewater* – French: *eau de chaux* German:
Kalkwasser Italian: *acqua di calce* Spanish: *agua de
cal*]

LIMPET (species of *Patella*) are the conical shells
that stick to rocks between the tide marks. They are
tough but tasty. A former director of the National
Gallery in London used to scoop them out of their
shells with his thumb and eat them raw on the
beach. If you plan to do the same, be sure the area
is not polluted. More usually, they are made into
soup.

[*Limpet* – French: *patelle* German: *Napfschnecke*
Italian: *patella* Spanish: *lapa*]

LINDEN. *See* lime.

LING. *See* cod.

LING. *See* chestnut.

LIQUEURS and **CORDIALS** – the distinction is
blurred – are often made by infusing flavouring
substances (which may be fruits, herbs, spices
and other aromatics) in alcohol. Such straight
infusions are called ratafias. In some cases, there
is subsequent distillation, and for the sake of
uniformity, there is a modern tendency to use
essential oils and extracts. In cheaper liqueurs,
synthetics provide the flavour. Ratafias and cordials
differ from *fruit brandies (*eaux-de-vie*), which are
distillations of fermented fruit mashes and may also
be called liqueurs.

Nobody knows exactly what goes into most of
the famous liqueurs or the methods by which they
are made, because these are closely-guarded trade
secrets. Indeed, there is such secrecy that, to take
an extreme case like the making of Chartreuse, no
one monk (it is made by the Carthusians) knows all
the formula. It is entrusted only in parts to brothers
who specialize in its manufacture.

Originally, liqueurs were medicines. Even today
many are looked on as digestives. They are still
often made to family formulae in countries, such
as Spain and Italy, where spirits can be generally
afforded. These liqueurs are ratafias, made by simple
infusion. As with commercial liqueurs, the alcoholic
base can be a highly-rectified spirit of any origin or
a brandy, rum or whisky. Some are mixtures. There
is nothing particularly difficult about making your
own liqueurs, which can, for instance, contain both
rum and brandy (or *gin – as in the case of sloe
gin).

Liqueurs are very useful flavourings in the kitchen,
and a range of miniatures can be kept for the
purpose. Modern cookery books and magazines
abound with recipes, and practically every liqueur
ever heard of is favoured by someone. No liqueur
represents the pure taste of the main flavouring
ingredient. Cointreau, Grand Marnier and Curacao

all taste more or less of orange, but are different. Other liqueurs, such as Van der Hum and Unicum, have an orangey ingredient, which is masked with spices. Cooks feel that they are safe putting like with like – say an orange liqueur with oranges, a cherry liqueur with cherries and so on – expecting there to be a natural unity. Fair enough, but from there the adventurous can depart to try complementary flavours, like the tradition-hallowed pineapple and kirsch. And liqueurs do not have to be used singly; they can be combined and mixed like cocktails. In addition to the flavourings listed below, there are fruit cordials made from blackberries, raspberries and strawberries, with some unusual ones from northern Europe. These include the Polish Jarziebiak from rowan berries and the Finnish Karpi from cranberries and Suomuurian from cloudberries.

Apricot flavours Apry and other apricot brandies. These are sweet liqueurs, tasting of apricots, but often also of bitter almonds (from the apricot stones). Hungarian *barackpálinka*, however, has a totally different flavour and is dealt with under fruit brandies.

Banana is the predominant flavour of *crème de banane* and other such liqueurs. Most are very sweet and have a ripe banana flavour.

Bitter almond. A number of ratafias, made from *Prunus* fruit kernels (apricot, peach, plum, etc.), as well as from bitter almonds, are on the market and the name for such preparations is *noyau*. They are more kindly than the synthetic almond essence of commerce, and I regularly make my own from apricot stones.

Black currant. There is black currant rum, but the best known is *crème de cassis*, with only 18% alcohol – just enough to preserve it. It has a strong, clear flavour of black currants and is an excellent flavouring for creams or topping for ices.

Cherry. Grant's Morello Cherry Brandy has a bite from the morello cherry, while other cherry brandies, such as Kirseboer or Cherry Heering, are sweeter. There are cherry whiskys such as Chesky, and Cerasella is an Italian cherry liqueur with herbs from the Abruzzi mountains. Maraschino is important in cooking, a sweet white fruit brandy made from maraschino cherries and their crushed kernels. Traditionally in a square, straw-covered bottle, it has been made for several centuries.

Chocolate. Chocolate-flavoured liqueurs are very sweet, with a taste of vanilla. *Crème de cacao* is one.

Coffee. Tia Maria is the best known and is based on rum, as is Kahlua.

Flowers. *Crème de rose* and the Bulgarian rose liqueur taste something like roses smell, but are very sweet. There are violet-flavoured liqueurs, and Parfait Amour is supposed to taste of violets and vanilla. Mille Fiore is equally meant to taste of a thousand Alpine flowers; the bottles contain a sprig of a bush covered with sugar crystals. All these liqueurs are sweet and scented.

Herbs. A combination of herbs goes into many of the classic liqueurs; single-herb liqueurs are rare. Mint or peppermint is one of these though, with most liqueur houses producing some form of *crème de menthe*, as well as mixtures like Royal Mint Chocolate Liqueur. There is also an angelica liqueur.

Herb seeds. As a flavouring, caraway is well represented in Kummel, Akavit and Goldwasser. Very often, it is combined with anise. The flavour of the latter can be clear, sweet and strong, as in Anis del Mono of Spain, and the Anisette, Anisetta and Stellata of Italy. It may also be introduced into cooking through the dry *pastio* drinks, such as Ricard and Pernod, which can be used, for instance, with fish. The flavour of liquorice is often confused with anise; the Italian Sambuca is made with liquorice and elder.

Honey is used with whisky in Scottish liqueurs, and its taste is recognizable in Glen Mist.

Orange, from the cook's point of view, is the most important of the fruit flavours in liqueurs. Orange Curaçao, Triple Sec, Cointreau and Grand Marnier are the ones most usually found in the kitchen. Other liqueurs with orange connections are the spicy Aurum from Italy, Unicum from Hungary and Van der Hum from South Africa. The American Forbidden Fruit is based on shaddock or grapefruit. Grand Marnier is a good liqueur for the beginner, being slightly sweeter than Cointreau and not quite so strong.

Pineapple. Rum and pineapple liqueurs often have a somewhat synthetic flavour.

Plum, sloe and **damson**. Best known in this group

are sloe gin and prunelle. There is also damson gin. Quite different are the flavours of quetsch, mirabelle and slivovitz (which are all fruit brandies).

Spices, herbs and **mixtures**. Into this category must come the great monastic liqueurs, Benedictine and Chartreuse (green and yellow), as well as Izarra, Trapestine, Drambuie, Raspail, Cuaranta-y-tres, Glayva, Bronte, Strega, Vieille cure, Escorial, Calisay, Galliano, Mentuccio, Herbias, Elixir d'Anvers and even Chu Yeh Ching Chien, the green bamboo-leaf liqueur from China.

Walnut is the flavouring for a liqueur made in France and Italy, but it is mostly home-made.

Wine-based liqueurs include Cordial Medoc (sweetish and highly aromatized) and Ponche Soto, with sherry and spices.
[*Liqueur* – French: *liqueur* German: *Likör* Italian: *liquore* Spanish: *licor*]

LIQUID SMOKE. *See* pyroligneous acid.

LIQUORICE (*Glycyrrhiza glabra* and other species) is a legume which looks something like a purple-flowered bean. It grows wild in southern Europe and was once cultivated in Yorkshire, near Pontefract, which is still the centre for making liquorice confectionery (e.g. Pontefract cakes) in Britain, although its raw material is now imported. Black liquorice is made by extracting the root with water and concentrating the sweet liquid by boiling. It is occasionally used by home brewers. In the 16th and 17th century, it was an important ingredient of gingerbread and was used mainly to darken it.
[*Liquorice* – French: *réglisse* German: *Süssholz* Italian: *liquirizia* Spanish: *orozuz, regaliz*]

LITCHI. *See* lychee.

LITTLENECK. An American *clam.

LIVER. School meals of thick gravy containing dry textured lumps that grew in size with chewing have done more than their share to create a widespread dislike of liver. Properly cooked, though, liver – particularly calf's liver – is moist and tender, almost melting. It is also more adaptable than the British habits of grilling or frying calf's and lamb's liver and of stewing ox liver would suggest. Liver is delicious not only with fried onions or bacon but also flavoured with sherry, marsala, Worcestershire

sauce or other piquant sauces. In Tuscany, for example, cubes of pig's liver are seasoned with salt, pepper and herbs, wrapped in caul fat and grilled or fried. Chicken livers may be sautéed in butter and served on toast, but they may also be used in risotto and are one of the correct ingredients for *ragù* or Bolognese sauce, as well as being an important ingredient in Jewish cooking. Livers may be major or minor ingredients in *pâté de *foie gras*. Although the main use of fish livers is for their oil content, the livers of turbot and of some rays are eaten. They may be poached in a good broth, sliced and served on buttered toast. Some fish livers, though, are poisonous.

When buying calf's liver, look for paleness. Avoid liver of any sort that has a greenish tinge. Make sure, too, that it is cut in even slices – variation in thickness will matter most if the liver is to be grilled or fried. It is best to remove the thick membrane that covers the liver. With chicken liver, cut out any greenish yellow spots of bile before cooking; otherwise the bitterness will permeate the entire dish. Ox liver is best soaked in milk for an hour before cooking to remove any undesirable flavours.
[*Liver* – French: *foie* German: *Leber* Italian: *fegato* Spanish: *hígado*]

LIVER SAUSAGE comes in a plethora of forms and textures from most European countries and hence in the US (which has produced the bastard term liverwurst). Pig liver is the usual basis for liver sausages, but there are kosher versions, and goose liver is used, sometimes with truffles in the German *Gänslebewurst*. Other parts of the pig – meat, snout, lights, etc. – may be added, and flavourings include various herbs and spices, onion and anchovy. Liver sausage may or may not be smoked but is always cooked and ready to serve cold. Some varieties are coarsely chopped and may contain flecks or lumps of fat, but the most widely marketed sorts are fine and even in texture and may be more suitable for spreading than for slicing, in which case they are effectively *pâtés*. Recipes can be found in *The Book of the Sausage* by Antony and Araminta Hippisley Coxe (Pan, 1978).

LOBSTER (*Homarus gammarus*). A decapod, ten-legged crustacean, like *shrimps and prawns, *crayfish, *langoustes and *crabs. The lobster has eight legs plus two pincers which are modified legs. Lobsters are frequently confused with Spiny lobsters, the Southern lobsters of the US, the *langoustes* of France. The *langouste* has ten legs, but no pincers;

when alive, it is speckled pink or brown – in some species greenish – but the lobster is rarely greenish, and almost always dark blue to nearly black. It goes red when cooked. Lobsters have smoothish shells, at most knobbly, while *langoustes* are well armed with blunt spines. Lobsters mainly inhabit the colder waters of the Northern hemisphere, although they are found as far south as the Mediterranean and North African coasts. *Langoustes*, on the other hand prefer warmer waters, and various species are found all over the world in tropical and subtropical seas. In North America, lobsters are found as far south as North Carolina. From Florida and southern California southwards, the Southern lobsters are *langoustes*. There is a huge world-wide business in frozen tails of many species of *langouste*, which are generally called 'crawfish tails'. They come from many countries including South Africa, Brazil, Australia and New Zealand. This trade does not exist with lobsters, which are much rarer beasts.

Lobsters can grow to an enormous size, and the claws then become disproportionately vast. Record specimens have been almost 1 m (over 3 ft) long and have weighed 15 kg (33 lb). Some huge ones may be 40-50 years old and are reputedly very tough. However, a friend recently caught one of these giants with the grab on his mini-sub – he was inspecting a pipeline in the North Sea – and he said it made excellent eating, although it was big enough to furnish lobster for the entire rig.

Like other crustaceans, lobsters must moult their hard shell in order to grow. They do this some seven times in the first growing season, but less often after that and, after four years, moulting normally happens only once a year. It takes about six years to produce a 500 g (1 lb) lobster. Very small lobsters are delicious, but many countries now have conservation laws regulating the minimum size allowed to be sold.

Lobsters are caught in creels or pots – traps which allow the lobster to enter, but impede its exit. The pots are baited with fish or meat, which can be bad and stinking for lobsters; crabs will eat only fresh bait. Lobsters are very belligerent and when two or more get into a pot they fight. A damaged lobster can bleed to death; the remedy is to break off the whole limb, as lobsters regenerate lost limbs and have a mechanism for sealing off injury at the joint. Damaged lobsters are no problem if they are to be cut up and then cooked, but if they are to be poached, they should be uninjured, or any holes should be plugged with kneaded bread or dough. When handling live lobsters, never hold them

round the middle, as they can close up suddenly and wound your hand. Large lobsters can be quite dangerous – so always grasp the creatures from above, just behind the head, with fingers and thumb on either side of the body, where the pincers cannot reach.

To choose a live lobster, which is essential for many dishes, look for specimens around 500 g (1 lb) in weight. Although the large lobsters are cheaper, weight for weight they are not so good. Lobsters should not be half-dead but full of life, with the tail tucked under the body and plenty of movement in the legs. When picked up, a lobster should feel heavy for its size and the carapace should feel hard between the fingers and thumb, with no give. Softness shows that the lobster has recently moulted and will be out of condition, because crustaceans hide and do not emerge to feed during this danger period in their lives. Hen (female) lobsters are reckoned by some to be slightly superior to the cocks (males).They have a slightly wider body, though smaller claws, and may have eggs (coral) under the tail. Other experts like big claws, and think the claw meat is the best, but there is really no significant difference between the cock and hen. At home, lobsters can be kept alive for some time in damp seaweed, but if several are put together, their claws should be tied up or taped shut to prevent fights (and for safety, if curious children are about).

To choose a cooked lobster. Although it is preferable to buy living lobsters, you may not want to face killing them. If you are buying a cooked lobster, see that it smells fresh and that the tail springs back when it is opened out. If it stays open or the lobster feels floppy, then it is not fresh. You can tell if the lobster has not been cooked properly or has been dead some time before being cooked. In either case, the gut is broken down by very active enzymes and the liquified gut discolours the meat at the front end of the tail so that it becomes dark green to black.

Anatomy. Lobsters are not vertebrates, and their main nerve cord runs down the underside and not the back, so exhortations to kill a lobster by severing its spinal cord are way off. The cerebral ganglion – which is probably not comparable to a brain – lies more or less between the eyes, and is connected with the main cord by two branches running on either side of the stomach. This stomach, which is in the head, is full of grit and is sometimes called the grit sac. It is easily removed and discarded when the lobster is cleaned. From this, the gut runs straight between the muscles to open underneath the tail. The gut looks like a black cord or thread and is discarded. The digestive gland, liver or tomally, is a feathery organ situated just behind the stomach and on either side of the gut. It is one of the tastiest parts and is usually scraped out separately for use in the sauce. The gills, equivalent to the 'dead man's fingers' in crabs, are situated in cavities on either side of the body and can be ignored. When a lobster is split from head to tail, it is easy to pick out the gut and stomach. Another method of preparation is to remove the tail by cutting it off the body, then to cut off the fan. This makes it easy to poke the meat out in one piece; the gut must also be removed.

Killing. The old way was to plunge the lobster head first into boiling brine and then to clap on the lid to prevent it jumping out. This seemed cruel, and the RSPCA gave its opinion that it took the lobster 38-72 seconds to die – at least lobsters could be active for this sort of time. Instead, the RSPCA advocated putting the animal into cold water and gradually raising the temperature. By the time around 40°C (100°F) or human body heat was reached, the lobster had lost consciousness. However, more recently the Universities Federation for Animal Welfare (UFAW) has given its opinion, based on experimental evidence, that lobsters plunged into boiling water remain alive for at most 15 seconds, and it considers this method the most humane. Since some people claim that lobsters lose flavour when brought slowly to the boil, it would seem that plunging into boiling water is once again 'the method of choice' as the surgeons would say. They then emit a sound that has been thought of as a scream but is actually the noise of air being forced out from inside the shell by the sudden change in temperature.

When lobster meat is needed for the more elaborate dishes, it is needed raw, not cooked. The lobster is a very primitive creature, more so than the crab, for instance, and it has no brain, only a long nerve cord with various swellings (ganglia) along its course, and it cannot be killed instantly by a knife thrust. Only those who can split a lobster into two down the middle line in one blow can claim to kill it instantly. Others say you should stun it with a blow on the head, and that seems at least to immobilize the creature. After that, as Pellaprat advises: 'Les

découper sans hesitation ni attendrissement en morceaux ...' (Cut them in pieces without hesitation or compassion), and this boldness surely kills a lobster quicker and more humanely than any other way.

Cooking. A lobster should be cooked in sea-water strengthened with salt to the point where the brine will float an egg. If you are using fresh water, between 100-150 g (4-5 oz) salt per 1 lt (1¾ pt) is correct. Cook lobsters for 12 minutes per 500 g (11 minutes per lb), although small ones of 450 g (1 lb) may need a little longer. As soon as the lobster is cooked, plunge it into ice-water if it is wanted cold; alternatively, merely strain it and put it into a cool larder.

[*Lobster* – French: *homard* German: *Hummer* Italian: *astice* Spanish: *bogavante*]

LOCUST. *See* insects.

LOCUST BEAN. *See* carob bean.

LOGANBERRY. *See* raspberry.

LONGAN. *See* lychee.

LOQUAT or **Japanese medlar**. From the moth-eaten examples in Mediterranean markets in early spring, you would hardly realize that the loquat is a delicious subtropical fruit. The loquat (*Eriobotrya japonica*) came originally from central China but has also been cultivated in Japan for many centuries. It has considerable importance in both countries, which have developed many superior varieties. The loquat is a relative of the European *medlar, but the quality of their fruit is totally different. The tree is evergreen, decorative, tropical-looking and about 7½ m (25 ft) high. It is grown in the US, South America, Australia, South Africa, India and wherever the climate is warm enough. Introduced into the Mediterranean by the French in 1874, it is the only fruit in the rose family (which includes most of our temperate fruits) which can stand both considerable frost and intense heat. Unfortunately, the fruit does not travel well, because the loquat must be ripened on the tree, the duration of the harvest is short, and the fruits must be picked daily. Commercially, it has everything against it.

The ripe fruit is yellow or apricot coloured, with a thin, slightly downy skin, a pleasant slightly crunchy texture, and exceedingly juicy yellow pulp which tastes both acid and sweet. The large, black shiny stones come free easily. It is worth looking for good varieties, because poor loquats are good only for making jelly, chutney or jam, for which they have ample pectin. Best of all is to steal a few fruits off the trees while taking a springtime Riviera walk.

LOTUS. There are only about a hundred species in the lotus family, and they are popularly known as water-lilies. The common White water-lily of Europe (*Nymphaea alba*) has edible underwater rhizomes which are eaten in some places. So have most species of water-lily, including the giant Victoria water-lily (*Victoria regia*), which has leaves big enough to float a baby. Its seeds are eaten roasted in its native Brazil. Egyptian lotuses (*Nymphaea lotus*) and others related to it are called *chota kamal* (little lotus in India) and are important in hungry times. Their beautiful flowers grace the tanks around temples and palaces in many places. Water-lilies are world-wide and, if it were a matter of survival, it would be a fair bet to risk eating any of them. The true lotus (*Nelumbium nuciferum*), which appears in stylized form in Hindu and Buddhist sculpture, belongs to a different genus in the family. It is another beautiful flower, differing from the water-lily in that the leaves stand up and do not float on the water. The plant has been cultivated since antiquity, and was grown in ancient Egypt but is no longer wild there. The rhizomes and seeds, even the leaves, are important in the cooking of the whole of Asia, and particularly so in Japan and China.

As a cultivated vegetable, the lotus looks like a succession of 5 cm (2 in) thick turnips stuck top to bottom like a string of sausages. When cut in two, it has a concentric pattern of air spaces which give a lace-like impression. It can sometimes be bought fresh from Chinese shops, and canned lotus is readily available. The seeds, harvested from boats with large nets, are eaten cooked or raw. The leaves are used as wrappers. Recipes for using lotus roots will be found in most Chinese and Japanese cookery books. After peeling, they can be sliced, scalded and used in salads, or grated and eaten raw. In Japanese cooking, the lacy form of the lotus root is made use of for cutting decorative shapes. Since lotus root goes brown when cut, it should be put straight into acidulated water. Slices of lotus root, boiled until just tender in acidulated water, may be marinated in a dressing of 4 tablespoons vinegar to I tablespoon sugar with a pinch of MSG and a pinch of salt to give a Japanese *hors d'oeuvre*. In India (called *bhain*), they are boiled, mashed and used in vegetarian *koftas* (vegetarian meatballs) or mixed with lentils and curried.

Dried lotus roots can be bought in Chinese supermarkets and need soaking before use. Dried lotus leaves, also after soaking, are used as an aromatic wrapping in which fish or pieces of pork are steamed. These are also sold in Chinese markets. The seeds are oblong, black and about 2 cm (¾ in) long. If gathered before they are fully ripe, they have a nice nutty taste, but when mature they need to be roasted or boiled, and the bitter germ should be removed. In Chinese cooking, they are used, for example, in soups.

Lotus Seed Sweet

Put a pinch of wood ash on the seeds (a pinch of bicarbonate of soda might do as a substitute) and pour boiling water over. Cover and leave to stand till the skins can be peeled off easily. Break the seeds in half and take out the bitter germ. Wash and boil in water with sugar added according to taste. When the seeds are soft, eat hot or cold or, if you like, add beaten eggs.

[*Lotus* – French: *lotus, lotos* German: *Lotos, Lotusblume* Italian: *Loto* Spanish: *loto, ninfea*]

LOVAGE. An umbelliferous plant (*Levisticum officinale*) rather like celery, with strong-smelling leaves and a taste like lemony celery, but with distinctive musky overtones. It grows wild all over Europe and on America's North Atlantic coast. This is one of the most rewarding of all herbs, though neglected these days. It is particularly useful in soups, but should be added sparingly as the flavour is strong. Scottish lovage (*Ligusticum scoticum*) – which is, of course, just known as lovage in Scotland – grows wild on rocky coasts there; its aromatic leaves can be added to salads and are sometimes used as a pot herb.

[*Lovage* – French: *livèche* German: *Liebstückel* Italian: *levistico* Spanish: *ligústico*]

LUGANEGA. *See salsiccia.*

LUMPFISH. *See caviar.*

LYCHEE, litchi, or other spellings. The lychee (*Litchi chinensis*) is native to subtropical areas of southern China and Thailand. The fruit is borne in clusters on small trees. Typically – but varying from type to type – ripe lychees are about the size of a plum, with a beautiful red, leathery, knobbly or spiny skin. Very shortly, the skin goes brown and becomes rather brittle. Lychees are gathered at once in whole bunches – they keep better that way. If they are for export, this is done when they just begin to turn red and are not fully ripe. The skin is very thin and easily separates, and inside is a juicy fruit, looking like a jumbo peeled grape. It even tastes something like a grape, though it is much more scented. There is a single, large, dark (and bitter) pip. Lychees will keep for up to three months in the refrigerator at around 5°C (40°F) and are best eaten chilled. The fruit cans well, and canned lychees taste remarkably like fresh ones. Dried lychees – Chinese nuts – have been either dried in the sun or kiln dried, and rattle when shaken. They are a common product and taste like raisins. Lychees also deep-freeze well and will no doubt become more available in the future.

The lychee was certainly being cultivated in China 2000 years ago, and there is a possible reference 1500 years before that. It was tried in Europe in the 19th century, but the climate is not right, for though it seems possible to grow lychees in some Mediterranean areas, the fruit needs heat and high humidity to come to perfection. In the dry conditions of a southern European summer they crack open and go bad while ripening. In fact, the lychee is choosy. However, it thrives in parts of South Africa (from where lychees come to Britain), and has been tried in southern Florida and California.

Closely related to the lychee is the longan (*Euphoria longana*), commonly grown along with it in China. Though a smaller and inferior fruit, it has the virtue of ripening later, when the lychees are over. Tropical fruits of the same family are the rambutan (*Nephelium lappaceum*), native to South East Asia and something like a lychee but with dense tendrils instead of warts covering the fruits, and the pulasan (*Nephelium mutabile*), with red or yellow tubercles. In both the tropical species, the edible flesh adheres to the seed. All these fruits belong to the soapberry family (*Sapindaceae*) which also includes the *ackee, but few other edible fruits.

LYE. Originally an alkaline solution made by boiling white, calcined wood ashes in water, then filtering and concentrating by further boiling. It consisted largely of carbonates of potassium and sodium. Soap was originally made by boiling lye with fat, lye and lime being the only alkalis available until fairly late in history. Almost any task now performed by caustic *soda was performed in the past by lye. One such process is the accelerated removal of bitterness from green olives. Today the word has dropped out of use in Britain, but in the US it has come to mean a dilute solution of caustic soda.

[*Lye* – French: *lessive* German: *Lauge* Italian: *lisciva* Spanish: *lejía*]

m

MABOLO. A close relative of the *persimmon.

MACADAMIA NUT or **Queensland nut**. *Macadamia ternifolia* (hard shell) and *M. integrifolia* (easier to crack) are native to the coastal forests of Queensland and New South Wales, where they grow wild along the edges of rivers and creeks. The value of the nuts was first noticed about a hundred years ago, and the trees are now cultivated in the southern US, South Africa and even in the Caribbean and Mediterranean regions.

An important production centre is Hawaii, which exports roasted and vacuum-packed macadamias. The nut is rounded, with a kernel shaped something like a hazel, but with no skin. It is white, sweetish and very oily. In fact, a salad oil is expressed from macadamias and they make an excellent nut butter. Some sorts of macadamia nut are very difficult to crack, but they will keep in the shell for several months. Kernels which have been removed will keep only if dried and cold-stored at 4°C (39°F) in sealed containers.

Macadamias are recommended as a substitute for the *candle nut in Indonesian cooking, and they will no doubt find other uses as their popularity grows. They are a delicious dessert nut.

MACARONI. See pasta.

MACCHERONI. See pasta.

MACE is the dried aril – a sort of cage – surrounding the seed of the nutmeg (*Myristica fragrans*). It is bright red when fresh, but is pressed flat and dried until it looks like creamy-brown seaweed. It has a taste something like nutmeg, but subtly different, and is more expensive. Mace is difficult to grind as it is very oily, but *grinding is easier if you are able to mix less oily spices, a little raw rice, or even flour with the mace.

[Mace – French: *macis, fleur de muscade* German: *Muskatblüte* Italian: *macis* Spanish: *macia, macis*]

MACERATION. Soaking materials in liquid, usually water or watery solutions, to soften them. The effect can be mechanical or physical – as when dried tissues reabsorb water and swell, or when gummy substances cementing cells together are leached out. The softening can also be brought about by chemical changes (due, for instance, to acids or alkalis) or to the action of micro-organisms or enzymes, which have been encouraged by water. See soaking.

[Maceration – French: *macération* German: *Einweichung* Italian: *macerozione* Spanish: *maceración*]

MACKEREL (*Scomber scombrus*), a small relative of the Atlantic bonito, is found on both sides of the Atlantic, in the Mediterranean and the Black Sea. Mackerel, which come in shoals, are caught in large numbers and are an important food fish. In Britain, they are in season all the year, but are best in April, May and June. They should be eaten as fresh as possible; it has been claimed that they can cause poisoning when stale, but in fact they are merely unpleasant. In eastern Mediterranean countries mackerels are salted in brine and dried. Hot-smoked mackerel is a delicacy in its own right. In Britain, mackerel is soused, like herring, in vinegar and water, but there are superior French methods of pickling in white wine. Like most oily fish, mackerel is excellent grilled and has bones which are easily dealt with. It needs a sour sauce, which in France is often made with gooseberries.

[Mackerel – French: *maquereau* German: *Makrele* Italian: *sgombro* Spanish: *caballa*]

MADAGASCAR BEAN. See butter bean.

MADEIRA. The Portuguese introduced vines into Madeira in the early 15th century, and by Tudor times sweet madeira wines had become popular in Britain; *malvoisie* or malmsey wine was particularly famous. Madeiras are blended wines fortified with cane spirit and are distinguished from other fortified wines by the heating they undergo during maturation, which is said to duplicate the temperature changes of a voyage around the world in the hold of a ship.

Madeira is heated very gradually – either in the cask or in large tanks – taking a month to reach a temperature which may be as high as 50°C (122°F); it is then kept hot for 4-6 months and cooled equally slowly. Madeiras are shipped in four main types:

Sercial. The driest and lightest blend, with a unique flavour often described as nutty. Sercial is an aperitif wine and, as the driest madeira, is the one best used in cooking as a flavouring.

Verdelho is darker and rather sweeter than sercial. It is the madeira to be taken with cake (hence Madeira cake) and is excellent to drink with soup.

Bual or Boal. Rather sweet, with a delicate taste, this is the lighter of the two dessert Madeiras.

Malmsey, dark, sweet, fruity and very fragrant, is a fine dessert wine with almost the qualities of a liqueur. Its use in cooking would be limited by its sweetness.

Madeira is internationally used as a flavouring in many dishes; in soup (particularly turtle), in aspic, in sauces for meat and ham (e.g. *jamon asado al vino de Madera*), for *sauce au madère* and in cakes and jellies. It is also sometimes used with carrots and gives a strong, rather characteristic vinous flavour. Madeira is an excellent item for the kitchen shelf – if it is recorked after opening, it keeps almost indefinitely. As a drink, it is rather neglected in these days except in Scandinavian countries.

Possibly confusable with Madeira are wines called *malvasia* in Italy and elsewhere. The name comes from Monemvasia, the port in southern Greece through which the sweet wines of the Aegean Islands were shipped in ancient times, and from the *malvasia* grape brought from there and introduced to Italy, Madeira and elsewhere. A *malvasia*, whether from Frascati near Rome, from Sardinia, from Stromboli or Salina (the Lipari Islands), or elsewhere, is a strong, golden-yellow dessert wine, which is sweet and usually best served cold. It has not been given the *estufa* heat treatment of a Madeira malmsey.

[*Madeira* – French: *madère* German: *Maderawein* Italian: *vino di Madera* Spanish: *vino de Madera*]

MADRAS GRAM. *See* horsegram.

MAGGI is the proprietary name of a hydrolysed vegetable protein preparation which is sold for use as a 'meaty' flavouring.

MAGNESIUM (Mg) is a silvery metal which burns giving a brilliant light, leaving white magnesium oxide. It occurs naturally in dolomite, magnesite and seawater, its sulphate is Epsom salts. Magnesium is an essential element in chlorophyll, and so is present in all green plants. It is also one of the important elements in the human body, and a deficiency can be a cause of ill health.

Amongst the rich sources are almonds and Brazil nuts, soya beans, whole-grain oats and wheat – and therefore wholemeal bread – cocoa and shrimps. The diet of people living on convenience foods, refined sugar, fats and soft drinks (as is sometimes the case in the 'civilized' world) is likely to be deficient in magnesium, and there is some evidence, although not conclusive, that this deficiency may be a contributory factor in heart disease.

[*Magnesium* – French: *magnésium* German: *Magnesium* Italian: *magnesio* Spanish: *magnesio*]

MAIDENHAIR FERN. This feathery fern (*Adiantum capillus-veneris*) can be found growing wild in shady, damp places in Europe and America. It was used as a decoration on wedding cakes in the pre-plastic era, and it can be boiled to make a mucilaginous liquid, even a jelly. This has little taste of its own, but often has flavour added, and commercial syrups, known by their French name as *capillaire*, can taste like scented soap. According to Boswell, Doctor Johnson liked to add *capillaire* to his port.

[*Maidenhair fern* – French: *capillaire commun, cheveux de Vénus adranthe* German: *Frauenhaar, Venushaar* Italian: *capelvenere, adianto* Spanish: *culantrillo*]

MAIDENHAIR TREE. *See* ginkgo.

MAIZE, **corn** (US), or **Indian corn** (*Zea mays*) has

been cultivated in both North and South America for at least 3000 years, according to radio carbon dating of remains found in caves; it was the only cereal of the Aztec, Maya and Inca civilizations – the name maize is from the American Indian *má-his*. Maize was brought to Europe by the Spanish in the late 15th century, and was later taken by the Portuguese to Asia. In the early days there seems to have been popular confusion as to where it came from, because the British, French and Dutch called it 'Turkey' corn, (the Turks, 'Egyptian' corn, the Egyptians, 'Syrian').

Today, maize grows in every country with sufficient warmth and water, if not for human food then at least for animal fodder. About half of the world's crop, though, is grown in the corn belt of the Mississippi basin – Illinois, Indiana, Missouri, Iowa, Kansas and Nebraska. No wild forms of maize exist today.

Maize is a heavy-yielding crop, but is not very satisfactory as a staple for humans. It does not have the gluten needed for leavened bread and is also lacking in available niacin, a deficiency of which causes pellagra. This problem is made worse by the fact that maize is mostly eaten by poor people who cannot make up their vitamin requirements from other sources (e.g. in Central and Southern Africa where it is called 'mealies'). Gerard demonstrates a sound knowledge when he writes: 'Turkey wheat doth nourish far less than either wheat, rye, barley or otes. The bread made thereof is mealy white without bran: it is hard and dry as Bisket, and hath in it no clamminess at all: for which case it is hard of digestion, and yealdeth to the body little or no nourishment; it slowly descendeth and bindeth the belly as that doth which is made of Mill' [millet]. And with prophetic insight he goes on: 'We have no certaine proofe or experience concerning the virtues of this kind of corn, although the barbarous Indians which knoweth no better, are constrained to make a virtue of necessitie, and think it good food; whereas we may judge that it is more convenient food for swine than for men.' It is true that Benjamin Franklin, writing in 1766, was stung to rise in its defence: 'Indian corn, take it for all in all, is one of the most agreeable and wholesome grains in the world – johnny and hoecake hot from the fire is better than a Yorkshire muffin.' But although maize is certainly good, the verdict of history is that, given the choice, people prefer wheat.

There are hundreds of types of maize, ranging from tiny popcorn varieties smaller than a finger to the enormous 50-75 cm (2 ft) long cobs of the Jala valley in Mexico. The colour ranges from yellow and white to red, blue, brown and variegated. The main types and products are as follows:

Corn husks are sold ready-prepared for making *tamales*. Otherwise, the point and bottom parts of these outer coverings of the ears of corn must be cut off. If they are dry and not flexible, pour a kettle of boiling water over them and leave them to soak for several hours until they are pliable. They must then be drained and dried on a cloth before filling, as directed in Mexican cookery books.

Cornmeal. Early American settlers adopted the Indian ways of using maize and adapted them for their own cooking. The meal they used was ground from locally grown varieties of corn. Thus, southern cornpone, ashcake, hoecake and spoonbread were made of dent (*see below*), while Rhode Island johnnycakes and cornbreads were made from the less starchy flint (*see below*).There was a general preference for white varieties of both types, although yellow meal was preferred for a few purposes, such as mixing with pork bits to make scrapple. The most primitive indigenous use was to make cakes out of meal and water, then bake them in the ashes of the campfire. When they were cooked and still hot, the ash could be quickly washed off and they would dry instantly, ready for eating. Settlers, of course, used iron sheets and ovens. Modern meal, ground in roller mills by several methods (and usually with the germ extracted to make it keep better) does not make the authentic, rough article. For this, it is necessary to find meal ground by stones in the few remaining old grist mills, which are usually powered by water.

Dent. This is the most commonly grown commercial corn, the type of the American corn belt. In this grain, the hard coat covers only the sides of the grain, so that a dent forms at the top. Dent corn may be yellow or white. It is starchier than flint corn.

Flint. The grains are entirely surrounded by a flinty, hard skin. As flint varieties mature early, they were grown in the more northerly parts of the US. However, growing flint today is unprofitable as yields are low, and thus flint varieties are less grown than formerly.

Hulled corn. *Hominy.

Mamaliga. The Romanian equivalent of polenta,

this is a maize flour dish which is no doubt descended from the gruels of other cereals made by the Romans in their colony of Dacia Felix. Although it is a simple peasant dish, there are gourmet versions dripping with butter and melted cheese.

Polenta. Maize is extensively grown in northern Italy. It is a staple food north of the River Po, in a strip south of the Alps and running through Piedmont, Lombardy, Trentino and the Veneto. Ground maize, *farma gialla*, may be coarse or fine. To cook it, water is brought to a boil and salted before maize flour is stirred in. The proportion varies according to the dish and the quality of the maize flour, but 300 g (11 oz) to a litre (1¾ pt) of water is average. Polenta becomes very thick and should be cooked for about 40 minutes (20 is the absolute minimum), so it is quite likely to stick and burn, which is why it was traditionally cooked in a copper cauldron hung over the fire. The taste of polenta is strong, and many people do not like it. However, it can be excellent with cheese and rough red wine; it is even better, if allowed to cool, then sliced and grilled.

Popcorn. The grains may be pointed or round, but are always small, hard, and flinty. When they are heated, the starchy interior swells, but is confined at first by the hard skin. When pressure builds up, the grain suddenly bursts – pops, in fact – and turns inside out. Popcorn is nothing new; it was known to the Incas.

Soft corn, **flour corn**, or **squaw corn**. This has soft, mealy grains and is preferred by the Indians and by people in Bolivia, Ecuador and Peru. It will not normally be met with by the cook elsewhere.

Sweetcorn has a relatively high sugar content. It is grown mainly in the cooler areas and is eaten fresh and unripe as a vegetable. There are over 60 varieties from which to choose. To be at its best, sweetcorn should be picked and put into boiling water within minutes, which means that really perfect sweetcorn can never be bought in a shop. Boiling should be only for a few minutes as longer cooking, far from making it tender makes it tougher.

Waxy corn has the carbohydrate almost all as a waxy substance called amylopectin, and it is used commercially for various purposes but not normally in cooking.

[*Maize* – French: *Maïs* German: *Mais* Italian:

granturco Spanish: *maíz*]

MALABAR NIGHTSHADE. *See* spinach.

MALAGA. Wines from the mountain hinterland of Malaga in southern Spain are handled through that port and bear its name. Malagas are sweet wines, made mainly from the Pedro Ximenez sherry grape. In the making, malagas have similarities to *marsala in that they are sweetened with evaporated grape juice (in Spain, called *arrope*, in Italy, *mosto cotta*). They usually also contain *color* (literally colour) or *pantomina*, similar to *arrope* but evaporated down still further to a very dark, thick, pasty mass. Sugar is further increased in the wine by drying muscatel grapes on mats in the sun for one or two days (wine from these is called *vino tierno*) and by stopping fermentation before it is complete by adding alcohol (*calebre* or *vino maestro*). Varying the proportions of these elements before maturing them in casks for two years or more produces a great variety of malagas: *seco*, dry; *palido*, pale; *dulce*, sweet; *semi-dulce*, semi-sweet; *oscuro*, dark; *negro*, black (very dark).

Malagas are drunk as dessert wines and may be of great age (I once was allowed a sip of one that was nearly two hundred years old). Malaga may be used as a flavouring in cooking – there are some dishes such as *jamon dulce con vino de Malaga* (sweet ham with Malaga wine) which demand it. The effect is somewhat similar to port but *jamon dulce al porto* is rather different. As there are some quite horrible 'malagas' on the market (although the name is now controlled), do not go for the cheapest on the grounds that it is only for cooking.

[*Malaga* – French: *vin de Malaga* German: *Malagawein* Italian: *vino di Malaga* Spanish: *vino de Malaga*]

MALDIVE FISH. Dried fish of several species, crumbled, pounded or powdered, is much used in the cooking of Sri Lanka. There is no substitute, although Bombay duck is often given as one. The importance of dried fish is one of several ways in which Sri Lankan cooking shows its connections with South East Asia.

MALIC ACID. A sharply sour organic acid which takes its name from the apple (*Malus*). Besides being present in sour apples, malic acid is an important acid in grapes, especially in those produced in the cooler and less sunny wine regions. The change from malic to the less sour lactic acid, which takes place in wine, is brought about by bacteria and is

known as the malo-lactic fermentation. Malic acid can be bought as a white, crystalline powder and is occasionally used by those who make fruit wines.

MALLOW. Many members of the mallow family, even hollyhocks at a pinch, are edible. The leaves of various species of wild mallows are commonly eaten. In the Jordan valley, for instance, I had some as they are popular with Arab farmers, but they are not very enjoyable. The *abelmusk* (*Hibiscus abelmoschus*) is a musk-like flavouring seed. The *Jamaica flower, roselle or red sorrel (*H. sabdariffa*) is another interesting plant. Its deep red calices have a sharp, fruity flavour and are used in tarts and jams, and for refreshing drinks. The green leaves are also edible. Another mallow, abutilon (*Abutilon esculentum* and other species), has leaves that are used as a spinach; it is cultivated for this purpose in countries from India (*ranghi*) to Brazil. *Melokhïa* or *molokhia*, a soup that is an Egyptian national dish, is made from the leaves of a mallow, *Corchorus olitorius*; dried *melokhia* leaves, which are obtainable from Greek shops, according to Claudia Roden in *A Book of Middle Eastern Food* (Penguin) are very acceptable in place of fresh ones. Other mallows are *Marsh mallow, *okra and cotton which is significant in cooking as the source of *cotton-seed oil.

[*Mallow* – French: *mauve* German: *Malve*, *Pappelkraut* Italian: *malva* Spanish: *morado*]

MALMSEY. *See* madeira.

MALT. Any cereal can be malted, but by 'malt' we understand malted barley unless otherwise specified. Malt is the raw material from which beer and malt *whisky are made.

In fresh grain, the food on which the tiny sprout will have to subsist when it starts life is stored in the form of starch. Once sprouting begins, enzymes (known generically as diastase) start to break down the starch into, mainly, maltose (a sugar) and dextrins (gums).To make malt, *barley (preferably a variety rich in starch) is first soaked in water for two days and then spread out to sprout, being kept moist and turned occasionally to prevent heating. After about a week – the time varies with the temperature, the variety of barley and its age – when the tiny first shoot is nearly, but not quite, as long as the grain, the barley is very gradually heated and dried, with the temperature rising over a period of several days. The final temperature is critical, determining the type of malt that is produced. After the rootlets have been rubbed off, the malted grain is stored for a week or so to mature and is then ready to be milled or crushed to grist for use.

The palest malt (lager malt) is heated to about 93°C (200°F). Higher temperatures will produce (in ascending order) pale malt, amber malt, crystal malt, brown malt, black malt and patent black malt, the last being a substance in which the sugars are charred – it was originally used only for colouring. Naturally, the flavour changes as the malt is heated and more and more of the enzymes are put out of action. Black malts have a burnt taste and are used for stouts. Crystal malt is toffee-coloured, has a strong flavour and contains quite a proportion of sweet, unfermentable dextrins which make it a popular addition to brown ales, as these need to be smooth and slightly sweet.

Before they can be used in fermentation, malts must be mashed to develop the sugars and extract them in solution. The grist of milled malt is mixed with warm water and kept at a suitable temperature. At 54°C (130°F) and a pH of 4.7, a maximum amount of malt sugar is formed, but if the temperature is increased to 65°C (149°F) and the acidity reduced to pH 5.7, the conditions favour maximum production of dextrins for the sweeter, more full-bodied beers. The temperature must be maintained for at least two hours, but longer times are usual in brewing.

The liquid which is filtered off is known as wort. This has to be boiled to sterilize it and to destroy the enzymes before the yeast is added for brewing beer. If wort is evaporated to a thick syrup by boiling under reduced pressure, the mixture of malt sugar, dextrins and flavour compounds is known as malt extract. The extract may also be dried. Extracts of the various types of malt can be bought from shops which specialize in materials for home-made beers and wines. A sweet, darkish malt extract is also sold in jars by chemists, though you have to be careful not to get the type mixed with cod-liver oil.

In cooking, malt was once added to various porridges and simple puddings for children and invalids. It was supposed to be especially effective in building up people with tuberculosis and other wasting diseases. Malt bread is a sticky, sweet, dark bread, often with currants, raisins and sultanas. As malt extract is sweet, and has a pleasant, distinctive taste, it is probably worth a little experiment.

Proprietary granary flour for breadmaking contains malted wheat kernels. Malted wheat-meal flour is sometimes to be found in health food stores. Malt is highly regarded in the bakery trade as a dough improver to improve volume, bloom, crust,

etc.

[*Malt* – French: *malt* German: *Malz* Italian: *malto* Spanish: *malta*]

MALTOSE or **malt sugar** ($C_{12}H_{22}O_{11}$) is a crystalline disaccharide *sugar which is the main sugar in malt and is also formed in the digestion of starch with enzymes produced by the salivary glands and, more importantly, the pancreas. Although it is not used in its pure form in the kitchen, it is of immense importance as it is keenly fermented by yeasts to produce alcohol (the basis of brewing) and carbon dioxide (which makes bread rise).

MALVASIA. *See* madeira.

MAMALIGA. *See* maize.

MANDARIN. *See* orange.

MANGANESE (Mn) is an unattractive grey metal which is an essential trace element in food but is toxic in any larger amount. Tea is particularly rich in manganese, containing from 150-1000 parts per million, depending on where it comes from. Cloves contain 450 ppm. Bran, wholemeal flour and liver are also common and good sources.

[*Manganese* – French: *manganèse* German: *Mangan* Italian: *manganese* Spanish: *manganeso*]

MANGE-TOUT. *See* peas.

MANGO (*Mangifera indica*). At their best, mangoes can well claim to be the world's most delicious fruit, although another school of thought awards *mangosteens that place. A fine eating mango, such as the famous Alphonso variety, will have fine-textured, orange flesh surrounding a flattened central stone and enclosed in a leathery skin. The taste is acid-sweet and perfectly balanced, and the aroma is that of a pine wood in spring – if it is possible to describe at all the unique mango taste.

Such eating varieties are best chilled (they keep some days in the refrigerator).To eat a mango, cut off both sides of the fruit, on either side of the stone, and scoop the flesh out of the skin with a spoon. Afterwards, strip the skin off the remaining central part and suck the stone clean. (This is messy, but mangoes are so delicious that even the most fastidious will not mind being smeared with juice. After eating a good mango, you need a bath.) At the other end of the scale, there are semi-wild varieties with small, fibrous fruits that taste strongly of turpentine. Intermediate types make specially delicious pickle or chutney. There is also a tremendous range of stringy but juicy mangoes which are supposed to be sucked, but these are often over-sweet. People who say that mangoes are over-rated have almost always got hold of a poor variety or of one grown in unsuitable soil or climate – many such inferior mangoes are produced.

The mango is a tree of the Indian region and has certainly been in cultivation there for over 4000 years. Alexander the Great's men saw trees growing in the Indus Valley in 327 BC. In the last few hundred years, mangoes have been introduced to suitably warm climates all round the world: Florida, California, Queensland, the Azores, the Canary Islands during the 19th century, for instance, and southern Italy early in the last century. Countries which now grow and export them include Egypt, Israel and Kenya. Some mangoes were even grown under glass in England in 1690, and one tree fruited in Kew Gardens in 1818. In fact, mango trees can exist in a wide variety of conditions as long as they have sun and no frost during the flowering season, but those fruiting in any but perfect climates will rarely give good table fruits.

Commercially, mangoes are always picked just before they are ripe; if wrapped carefully and chilled at 5-10°C (41-50°F), they can be shipped by air as far as from India to Britain. Mangoes are best placed carefully in straw to ripen. Once ripe, they will keep for up to ten days at room temperature and up to two weeks in the refrigerator. Unfortunately, mangoes are expensive; good ones are expensive even where they are grown.

The mango belongs to the same family (Anocardiaceae) as the cashew and pistachio nuts. Mango trees grow to an enormous size, often covering 30 m (100 ft) with the dense shade of their elongated, dark green, shiny leaves. The tree is evergreen and characteristic of the landscape over large parts of India, where it is of great economic importance.

Mango *chutney, in India, may be made fresh from raw ground mango, herbs and spices, but sweet cooked mango chutney is a common commercial item elsewhere. In Britain, it is often eaten with cold meat, and goes with cheese in pub sandwiches. A typical commercial recipe is as follows.

Sweet Mango Chutney

Take ripe but firm mangoes. Wash, peel and slice. For 1 kg (2¼ lb) of sliced mango, add 1 kg (2 lb) sugar, 50 g (2 oz) salt and a very little water, boil for a short time until the mango is just tender. Put 25 g (1 oz) mixed spice (equal weight of black pepper, cumin, cloves, cinnamon and cardamom), 15 g (½ oz) ground chilli, 100 g (4 oz) bruised ginger, 50 g (2 oz) chopped onion, and 15 g (½ oz) crushed garlic in a muslin bag and add to the boiling mango. Add 150 ml (¼ pt) vinegar – the quantity needed to achieve a good balance will depend on the sweetness of the mangoes and the strength of the vinegar. Adjust the salt if necessary. Cook for five minutes or until the desired consistency is reached. Bottle and seal.

Dried mango powder is known in India as *amchur* or *amchoor* (*am* means mango in North India). It is an ingredient needed for certain Indian dishes and can be bought at most shops that specialize in Indian products.

Mango leather (*amavat*) is made in India when there is a glut of mangoes. The juice is squeezed on trays or plates and put in the hot sun to dry. As the juice dries, more is squeezed out until a leathery material about 1 cm (½ in) thick has been made. This is usually rolled and cut into strips. It makes a nourishing sweet. Commercially, mango leather is made by adding a trace of potassium metabisulphite (or *Campden tablets) to the juice and then drying it at 60-65°C (140-150°F) on oiled wooden trays.

Mango pickle, of varying degrees of hotness, is a popular accompaniment to curries in India and quite a different article to the mango chutney used in the West, being salty, sour, spicy, and not at all sweet. A defining recipe is as follows:

Mango Pickle

Use unripe but plump green mangoes. Wash and slice them and put the slices temporarily into brine to prevent them blackening. Drain before using. For each 1 kg (2¼ lb) of mango slices, mix in 250 g (9 oz) salt. Stand them in the sun for 3-5 days depending on the weather. Now add 25 g (1 oz) each of ground, very lightly roasted fenugreek seed and bruised nigella seed, and the same quantity of ground turmeric, aniseed and black pepper, with enough mustard oil to cover the mango surfaces and lubricate the mass. Stir well and pack tightly in jars, filling each with oil to cover.

It is claimed that some varieties of mango are excellent when canned, but most people who have enjoyed mangoes where they grow will probably agree that canned ones are a very poor substitute. They do not change and take on a new dimension as do peaches, but rather acquire an over-sweet and sickly aspect. Canned mango pulp may be used to make mango fool and mango leather. Canned mango juice is also available.

[*Mango* – French: *mangue* German: *Mango* Italian: *mango* Spanish: *mango, manguey*]

MANGOSTEEN. Tropical fruit from a tree, *Garcinia mangostana*, that is native to Malaysia and rarely, if ever, met with outside the tropics. It has a tough brownish rind around delicious white flesh which is divided into segments. It is eaten raw but the related *kokum is used in Indian cooking.

MANIOC. *See* cassava.

MANTIS SHRIMP (*Squilla mantis*) is a curious crustacean with front legs superficially like those of a praying mantis and a general shape like a shrimp or lobster with a rather large abdomen. Mantis shrimps, which reach 25 cm (10 in) long and lurk in mud or sand below low-tide mark, are a good ingredient for fish soup. They can also be boiled and dealt with much in the same way as prawns (the tails may be served cold with the upper part of the shell removed to expose the flesh).They are popular in Italy, particularly in Romagna and the Veneto, and elsewhere around the Mediterranean. A related species, *S. empusa*, is found on the East coast of the US.

[*Mantis shrimp* – French: *squille* Italian: *pannocchia cannocchia* Spanish: *galera*]

MANZANILLA. *See* sherry.

MAPLE SYRUP and **MAPLE SUGAR** are the boiled-down sap of the Rock or Sugar maple (*Acer saccharum*) and of the Black maple (*A. nigrum*). These grow in south-eastern Canada and the north-eastern US, from Pennsylvania north and west to Wisconsin.

The early colonists were taught by the Indians to tap the maples and to evaporate the sap to syrup or sugar. While the materials now used may be different (with galvanized tin or plastic replacing wood for the pails, and metal spiles instead of hand-carved sumac ones), the 'sugaring-off' ritual is relatively unchanged.

The sap starts to rise in late February or early March, when the worst of winter is over. This is the beginning of sugaring or sapping time; the farmer or syrup-maker bores a hole about 1 cm (½ in) wide and 5 cm (2 in) deep into the trunk of the maple, where the sap runs, and inserts the spile, hanging a loosely covered pail under the spile to catch the sap. Suitable maples have either trunks at least 25 cm (10 in) in diameter or are 40 or more years old. Large trees may make up to five buckets.

Until about mid-April, the buckets are emptied regularly and the watery, virtually tasteless sap is evaporated to syrup or sugar in huge pans over a fierce fire. On average, it takes about nine gallons of sap to produce one of syrup. As a single tree produces about 8-16 Imperial gallons (10-20 US gallons or 37-75 lt) of sap, maple syrup and maple sugar can only emerge as expensive products. A further reduction by a quarter makes the syrup into maple sugar, which in Colonial days was a general sweetener and accepted in part-payment of wages, but today is just a moulded candy.

While maple syrup and sugar are delicious in a very sweet way and the syrup is often the best part of a plate of pancakes or waffles, a heavy hand with the syrup in cooking will overwhelm everything else in the dish with a cloying sweetness. Maple syrup can be used to glaze carrots, at the end of cooking; it can be mixed with mustard and vinegar, instead of molasses, for the sweet coating on baked ham; used to flavour mousses and ice cream, or poured over ice cream and other puddings.

A traditional use of maple syrup is to turn it into a candy by pouring it on to snow. Boil up a quantity of maple syrup until it reaches the soft-ball stage (when a bit dropped into cold water forms a ball, but loses its shape when touched).You will need a patch of packed clean snow out of doors or a baking tin full of it in the kitchen. Pour the hot, thickened syrup on the snow in swirls and designs; it will immediately harden into a chewy candy. For a harder sweet, boil the syrup longer before pouring.

The quality of maple syrup is variable, and a liking for the best pure maple syrup is usually coupled with a dislike of any of the combinations of it with other syrups (corn syrup, honey, etc.) that are commercially available. Pure maple syrup is designated by a maple leaf on the label. Synthetic maple syrup flavouring added to sugar syrup is a common but crude substitute for the real thing.

[*Maple syrup* – French: *sirop d'érable* German: *Ahornsaft* Italian: *sciroppo d'acero* Spanish: *amilbar de arce*]

MARASCHINO. *See* cherry, fruit brandy, liqueurs.

MARC or **eau-de-vie de marc**. This is not strictly speaking a *brandy, although they are often confused. For instance, *dop* brandy (Cape smoke) is a South African *marc*. Brandy is, or should be, made from wine, but *marc* is made by fermenting the mess of sludge, skins, pips and stalks left over after the juice for wine-making has been pressed out. The *marc* must therefore always be highly rectified to get rid of the methyl alcohol and other hangover-promoting congenerics. It is less delicate and less expensive than brandy and varies greatly from region to region. Some *marcs* are excellent and are much drunk in France; others are firewater. In local recipes, *eau-de vie de marc* is sometimes specified and it should really, if one is sufficiently fussy, be a *marc* from the region of the recipe. Other countries distil *marc*. In Italy, the equivalent is *grappa; in Portugal, *bagaceira*; and in Germany, *Tresterbrantwein*.

MARGARINE. Margarine was invented in France during the 1860s by Mèges-Mouriés, a chemist, who patented it towards the end of the decade. At first, it was made largely of beef suet and skimmed milk and was nothing like the sophisticated product of the present day. Although it was variously called 'oleo', 'oleo margarine' or 'butterine', the Margarine Act of 1887 made the name 'margarine' compulsory in Britain and put an end to confusing designations. Today, margarine is almost universally regarded not as a cheap butter substitute but as a product in its own right.

The main ingredient of margarine today is a blend of edible oils. A proportion of the oils may have to be hardened to produce a fat suitable for spreading on bread. The hardening method commonly used is hydrogenation. Oils which are liquid at room temperature contain a higher proportion of unsaturated fatty acids than fats which are solid at room temperature. Hydrogenation is the addition of hydrogen to unsaturated fatty acids in the oil with the aid of a nickel catalyst (which is recovered later). The unsaturated fatty acids become saturated, raising the melting point of the oil so that it becomes a solid fat at room temperature. The proportions of saturated and unsaturated fat vary according to the type of margarine. The ones containing most unsaturated fat are marked 'high in polyunsaturates'. This kind, which is recommended by doctors for lowering serum cholesterol levels, contains an oil blend of which normally less than

20% is saturated and the level of polyunsaturates is of the order of 50% or more. Other soft margarines which 'spread straight from the fridge' contain less unsaturated fat and more saturated fat. However, they are still soft enough in texture to require packing in tubs. The hard margarines can be packed in foil or greaseproof paper.

The other ingredients which go into margarine can include salt, skimmed milk or whey, emulsifiers, lecithin, synthetic flavours such as lactones, colour such as *annatto and vitamins A and D. Today, the consumer has a wide range of margarines to choose from. All can be used for spreading, cooking and baking. In addition, there are low calorie alternatives to butter or margarine such as Outline, a low-fat spread which has half the fat content of margarine.

Margarines can be clarified to produce a cooking fat resembling ghee, but the fat does not have the same flavour. Ghee made from vegetable oils is available in cans.

MARIGOLD. It is the Pot marigold (*Calendula officinalis*), the common plant in gardens almost all over the world, which can be used in the kitchen. (Seeds of plants used in Tibetan monastery gardens which I collected and sent to Kew turned out to be nothing more exciting than marigolds.) The petals were used as long ago as Roman times as an edible yellow colouring (when extracted in milk) and are still sometimes passed off as saffron. But the flavour is no more than slightly bitter and the colour is weak. The petals were much used in 17th century English cooking, in salads and stuffings, as a pot herb, and later to colour cheese and butter. Marigold leaves are said to be good in salads, but they must be very young or they are rough fare, rather nasty and tough. Buds of the marsh marigold or kingcup (*Caltha palustris*) were once pickled and used as capers.
[*Marigold* – French: *souci* German: *Ringelblume* Italian: *calendula* Spanish: *caléndula*]

MARINATING. Marinades, pickles and brines are aromatized liquids into which food is put for various purposes. A *brine always has salt as its most important ingredient and is almost always intended to preserve, although of course in the process it alters flavour. A *pickle may be a brine or it may be based on vinegar, lemon juice or any other sour fruit juice, or verjuice, and it is also preservative. A marinade, however, is intended primarily to change the ingredient (meat, fish or vegetable or fruit) in some way and is only incidentally a short-term preservative. It may be intended to allow flavours to soak in, to aromatize, to impregnate meats with juice and oil if they would otherwise be dry, or to create less usual effects, such as to coagulate the protein in fish which is to be eaten raw – a sort of chemical cooking. Above all, perhaps, marinades are intended to tenderize, but one function cannot be isolated from the others. Meats like wild boar, hare and venison are so tough as to be almost inedible unless the animals are very young. They also tend to be dry, since animals that rush madly about the countryside never have much fat on them. Even long, slow, overnight cooking on a dying fire will hardly tenderize a boar. *Hanging, that other tenderizing process, may not be possible, especially in hot weather. Turning in wine, vinegar or yoghurt checks immediate decomposition and allows the acids to begin breaking down the muscle fibres into less tough proteins. The inclusion of aromatics – spices, bay leaves, garlic, onion, and herbs like thyme – perfumes the meat being marinated. If oil is used, it soaks into meat and so adds fat to keep it soft during cooking – a sort of liquid larding.

[*Marinating* – French: *mariner* German: *marinieren* Italian: *marinare* Spanish: *marinar*]

MARJORAM. *See* oregano, sweet marjoram.

MARLIN. *See* swordfish.

MARMALADE. *See* jam.

MARMITE. *See* yeast extract.

MARROW, SQUASH, PUMPKIN and **GOURD** are overlapping terms for members of the family Cucurbitaceae which also includes *cucumber, *gherkin, *melon and *chayote. They all have a fruit which, however variable, is built on the same general plan. In general, they like a fairly warm climate and will stand little if any frost. The fruits are watery and mild. Squash – which comes from the Red Indian *askoot-asquash* – is a word not usually understood in Britain, where summer squash is called vegetable marrow. Dwarf varieties are courgettes from France or zucchini from Italy, which have been adopted on both sides of the Atlantic; in general usage, the two words are synonymous. Crookneck, pattypan and acorn squashes and so on are so-named from their shapes. Marrows and squashes are often stuffed and can be hollowed out to act as vessels in which to serve soup, and even carved with patterns, a nice party decoration which

is made in China.

Many warm-country gourds can be bought in Indian shops in Britain, and some are cultivated in the southern states of the US. Many of these are essential for Indian vegetarian cooking, some are needed for Chinese dishes, and they are often worth trying cooked in European styles. Sometimes there is a huge difference between varieties of the same species, just as much as there is between cabbages, cauliflowers and kohl-rabi. Who would suspect at first sight that a pumpkin, a courgette and an ornamental gourd were blood brothers? In fact, from the cook's point of view, the species to which a plant belongs is mainly of academic interest, but it makes sense here to use the biological names as a way of sorting out the mass of popular names.

Cucurbita pepo includes the pumpkins, marrows, summer squashes, courgettes, custard marrows, scalloped summer squashes, pattypans, cymlings and ornamental gourds. There are trailing and bush varieties used in different conditions, and some, like courgettes, are dwarf *Pepo* forms distinguished from *maxima* forms (*see below*) by their roughly bristled stems and leaves, by their short, deeply grooved and slightly swollen fruit stalks, and deeply lobed leaves. This is a North American species, cultivated by the Indians before the arrival of Columbus, but not known in Europe until later. In fact, even a hundred years ago the vegetable marrow was thought to be a sort of pumpkin which had originated in Persia. In spite of the giant marrows that are paraded at village shows, people everywhere, even before the arrival of courgettes, preferred specimens only 15 cm (6 in) long, although mature specimens were kept for the winter. While the British marrow, swimming in its water and thin white sauce, is no doubt selected as food for the damned in the place where the devil rewards his followers, a dish like *courgettes à l'angoumise* (slices cooked slowly with garlic, oil and butter) is worthy of heaven to garlic lovers. Such summer squashes as crooknecks and pattypans should be eaten very young and never overcooked; they are too old for eating when a fingernail does not easily go through the skin without pressure. When buying, look always for fruit that is firm and turgid, without any sign of shrivelling at the end of the stalk.

Pumpkins also belong to this species. In Europe, they are often club shaped and are usually cut and sold by weight. Their peculiar earthy taste is not greatly valued. In their native America, pumpkins are appreciated more; they provide pumpkin-pie filling and the basis for the Halloween jack-o'lantern. If hung in a net or rested on straw, pumpkins will keep over most of the winter. The seeds, which contain a good percentage of oil, are washed, dried and salted for eating. (Heat them in a pan with a little oil until they swell – a matter of seconds – dry them on absorbent paper and salt them.) There are even special varieties developed for their seeds which are without a hull and can be eaten whole and unshelled. Another squash, with very long strings inside, is sometimes called vegetable spaghetti or spaghetti marrow. In Spain, these soft fibres are boiled in sugar to make a sort of tasteless jam called *cabello de ángel* (angel's hair).

Cucurbita maxima includes the winter squashes which are little known in Europe. Best known among them are Hubbard, turban, butternut and mammoth squashes. The species is also of American origin, and the plants can be distinguished from the *pepo* summer squashes because the hairs are soft, the stalk of the fruit is not strongly ribbed, but is swollen, and the leaves are not deeply lobed. Winter squashes take longer to mature than summer squashes and make hard shells; they are allowed to mature and are stored for use in winter, although they are also excellent when immature. For keeping, they need to be picked when fully mature, leaving some stalk attached. Colour can be from yellow or orange to green or blue-grey, and shapes vary from club to acorn, often heavily ribbed.

Cucurbita moschata includes the cushaw and the winter crookneck or Canada crookneck, all little known outside America, where this species originated.

Citrullus vulgaris var. *fistulosus*. The Round gourd or *tinda* is a tiny variety of the watermelon, and is sometimes also called the squash melon. (Large watermelons, which are eaten as fruit are dealt with in the melon entry.) This variety is thought to have originated in India, where it is one of the most important summer vegetables, especially in the Punjab. It is also found where there are Indian communities abroad. There are two types, light and dark green, of which the light is reckoned the better. The first flush of fruit is removed by growers to make way for the larger second flush. The fruit are slightly hairy and are harvested before the seeds become hard.

Tricosanthes cucumerina. The Snake gourd

appears to be a native of India, where it is called *chichinda*. It is very important in South India and South East Asia, and is useful in vegetarian cookery, as it has a firm, smooth texture as well as a fine taste. The Snake gourd, although subtropical, grows very well in a Mediterranean climate. It is a quick-growing climber with white, lacy-petalled flowers. The gourds are long and thin, up to 120 cm (4 ft) long, around 5 cm (2 in) thick and usually slightly curved (although Indian gardeners sometimes hang weights on them to make them grow straight). The gourds turn a brilliant orange when mature, but are eaten young and light or dark green. They have a strange, foxy smell and are covered with a powdery white down which is removed before cooking by rubbing with salt. It is not necessary to peel snake gourds. Both ends of snake gourds are pointed, which distinguishes them from snake-like varieties of the bottle gourd with which they are sometimes confused, even in books. This vegetable can be seen in Indian shops and is very good indeed, either in vegetable curries or as a vegetable dressed in Western ways.

Trichosanthes dioica is a close relative of the snake gourd, called the *parwal* in India. It is much grown in Assam (where it is probably native) and in Bengal and Bihar, as well as throughout South East Asia. This needs a hotter, more humid climate than the snake gourd. The fruits are rather like small cucumbers and are eaten young and immature. There are light green and dark green varieties, and some are striped. This again is a vegetable that is likely to be imported and found in Indian shops. It is regarded as one of the best Indian vegetables and is very digestible.

Momordica charantia. The Bitter gourd or Balsam pear and its close relative, the Balsam apple (*Momordica muricata*) or *ucche*, are important vegetables in the Orient, occurring in both Indian and Chinese cooking. They are available canned and sometimes also fresh from Chinese or Indian stores. The Bitter gourd is harvested when fully grown but still green, the Balsam apple when young, small and with immature seeds. In China, these gourds are used in soup or in stir-fried vegetable dishes. Usually the pulp is removed and the flesh sliced. The slices are then boiled for three minutes to remove some of the bitterness. In India, the gourds are often stuffed or put into curries. They need to be cut up and salted for at least an hour so that some of the bitter juice can be squeezed out. Alternatively cut in pieces and fried with spices. In India, the Bitter gourd is called *karela*.

Benincasa hispida. The Ash gourd or Wax gourd is important in tropical countries. In India, it is known as *petha*. It is harvested when immature and is largely used for sweet dishes. It is a round or oblong gourd sometimes reaching 10 kg (22 lb). Said to have originated in Japan, it has been used since ancient times in China and is now eaten widely in Asia.

Luffa cylindrica. The Sponge gourd, when ripe, develops a tough skeleton which, after maceration to remove the flesh, is dried to make the well-known bath loofah; it is also a good vegetable when unripe. The plant is a spreading climber, which is often grown up trees. It has probably been taken into cultivation in Asia fairly recently in history as it does not vary much (as do plants that have been cultivated for a long time) and it has no Sanskrit name. It is commonly used in South Indian vegetable curries, called *kali, tori* or *nenna*.

Luffa acutangula. Closely related to the Sponge gourd is the Ridged gourd or Club gourd, an important warm-country vegetable, which has long green fruits with sharp ribs. Varieties range in size from a few centimetres (1-2 in) to 1 m (3¼ ft) long. It is known as *kali, tori* or *jhingli* in India and *ketola* in Malaya. This vegetable is very important in South Indian vegetarian cooking. It has to be harvested before it becomes spongy.

Lagenaria siceraria. The Bottle gourd, when mature, develops a very hard, woody shell which is used to make bottles, spoons, bowls and musical instruments. The shape is often modified by binding during growth. The plant has been used since ancient times – there is evidence from Egyptian tombs dated around 3500 BC and from Mexican caves as long ago as 7000 BC. Perhaps it originated in Africa and the seeds drifted on the sea to America. Immature bottle gourds make an excellent vegetable, with firm and tender flesh, and a nice taste. Indeed the snake-like form, *Lagenaria longissima* (sometimes confused with the snake gourd), which grows in Italy and can be seen in Riviera markets, is possibly the best of all gourds, and is superior to courgettes when young. When old, they become bitter, purgative and, indeed, poisonous. Bottle gourds are much used as food in India, where they are called *lokhi*.

Cucumeropsis edulis and other species (e.g. *C. manii*) are Egusi melons, grown in West Africa for their oily seeds, as are also other species of gourd, such as the *Acanthosicyos horrida*, which produces the butter-pits of south-west Africa.

MARROW BONE. Some bones are strengthened inside with a cross lattice, but others – the long bones of the limbs – are hollow and are a good source of bone marrow. Marrow, especially marrow from beef bones, is fatty and tasty and marrow bones have long been a delicacy. Even bones found in prehistoric-man's caves have often been cracked so that the marrow could be sucked out. More elegantly, it can be extracted with the aid of long, narrow marrow scoops. In Victorian times, marrow on toast was a common savoury. Marrow is used in sauces such as *sauce bordelaise* (wine, demi-glace sauce and marrow) or *sauce à la moelle*, and as a garnish. It is also used to enrich dishes, including risotto. As a preliminary, marrow bones, sawn into suitable lengths, are usually sealed at the ends with a flour paste, tied in a cloth for safety, and poached for an hour, but they may be treated much more simply.

Marrow on Toast

This is the very quick recipe that I use. Take the marrow out of the bones and poach it briefly – a minute or so is enough – in salted water. Drain well and put it on hot toast. Sprinkle it with salt, pepper, plenty of lemon juice and chopped parsley. I often rub the toast with garlic, and some people like cayenne pepper to season the marrow.

[*Marrow bone* – French: *os à moelle* German: *Markknochen* Italian: *ossobuco* Spanish: *caña medular, hueso medular*]

MARSALA. In the second half of the 18th century, an Englishman, John Woodehouse, who was in Sicily on business, noticed that there was a large production of sweet wine in the western part of the island, behind the port of Marsala. He thought that it would be possible to introduce to Sicily the methods used to make the dessert wines of Spain and Portugal, which were at that time so popular in Britain. He opened his business in 1773, and flourished to such an extent that a second Englishman, a Mr Ingham, founded a rival business in 1813. This was followed in 1832 by the Italian house of Florio, which swallowed the two English firms in 1929 and is to this day the most famous producer of Marsala.

Marsala is made by a process similar to that used for making *malaga. The white wine which forms the basis of marsala is made from local Sicilian grapes from a delimited area and is very strong, running to 15-17°C of alcohol. With this is mixed *sifone*, sweet grape juice that has been prevented from fermenting by the addition of 20% alcohol (to prevent the yeasts from working), as well as *cotto*, a liquid made by boiling down grape juice to a syrup. (Incidentally, a syrup made from boiled grape juice – *mosto cotto*, cooked must – or boiled ripe figs, is still made as a sweetener in southern Italy, and with honey, must have been the basis of all sweet dishes in the days before sugar from sugar cane was introduced from the Orient.)

Sifone gives marsala sweetness and softness, while the slightly caramelized *cotto* give colour, bitterness and a trace of almond flavour. The ingredients are mixed in various proportions to produce different types of marsala, reinforced with more alcohol if necessary, cleared – usually with ox blood – and put to mature in the cask for several years. After that, they may be blended to produce the finished product. Marsalas can be *fini* (fine), *superiori* (superior), dry or *virgini*, or very sweet. There are also special ones such as *marsala all'uovo* (with egg), *marsala-crema* (cream) and *marsala-mandorla* (almond). The alcoholic strength varies between 17° and 21°, the stronger being mainly for export to northern Europe. The sugar content is 5-12%. This was the wine that was once drunk in Italy by *mamma, nonna* and *zia* when they got together to gossip over a piece of cake, but today marsala has lost most of its popularity there. However, it is an important wine in the battery of kitchen flavourings and has the advantage that it will keep indefinitely as long as the bottle is re-corked. A dry one is preferable as it has more uses. Marsala is particularly used in the more sophisticated dishes of northern Italy: with veal, e.g. *scaloppine di vitello alla bolognese* (veal scallops as cooked in Bologna), *costolette alia modenese* (the marsala flavour combined with truffles), *ossibuchi alla reggiana* (veal knuckle as cooked in Reggia); with chicken (*pollo alla cacciatora*); with game, *pernici in salmi* (partridges cooked with butter, carrot, celery, onion, olive oil, rosemary, bay, dry marsala and white truffles) from Piedmont, and *salmi alla toscana* (hare, rabbit or chicken cooked with chicken livers, butter, olive oil, carrot, onion, celery, bay, tomato purée and dry marsala) from Tuscany. However, it is rarely, if ever, traditionally used with fish, although I have found one recipe from Liguria in which marsala is used with brandy and white wine in the stuffing for squid (*totani ripieni*). The only vegetables with which it is commonly used are carrots (in Sicily itself) and truffles. Marsala is the classic wine for *zabaglione* or *zabaione* (although in some parts of Italy they use it mixed with sweet wine, and in Sardinia they prefer a sweet *vernaccia* wine), but the many other Italian sweet dishes and cakes in which it is used are unknown in other countries.

MARSHMALLOW is an ingredient in American cooking. The original marshmallow sweet or *pâte de guimauve*, though, was a thick decoction of the roots of the marshmallow plant, sweetened with sugar and flavoured with orange flower water. The Marshmallow (*Althaea officinalis*), which is native to most of Europe and was used as a vegetable in Roman times, is a downy-looking, greyish-white plant with pink flowers, a member of the *mallow family. It was boiled and eaten as a vegetable in the eastern counties of Britain until fairly recent times; a syrup made from it was a remedy for coughs. The modern marshmallow no longer contains the mucilage from the mallow root. It is a spongy sweet made from gum arabic, white of egg, sugar, orange flower water and pure water. Other recipes replace the orange flower water by vanilla or fruit flavour.

···

Marshmallows

Dissolve 50 g (2 oz) of gum arabic in 150 ml (¼ pt) of water, strain it and put into a clean pan with 1½ teaspoons of sugar. Heat, stirring continuously until the sugar has dissolved, then boil until it reaches the firm ball stage (when a bit dropped into cold water forms a sturdy but pliable ball). Have ready the stiffly beaten whites of two small eggs. Flavour the sugar and gum mixture with orange flower water and work in the egg whites. Spread in a layer – as thick as the marshmallows are to be – on a bed of cornflour, cover the layer with coating of cornflour and leave to set till next day. Disinter and cut the layer in pieces. If they are to be used in recipes, marshmallows are most easily cut up with wet scissors.

[*Marshmallow* – French: *guimauve, bonbon à la guimauve* German: *Lederzucker* Italian: *altea, bismalva* Spanish: *malvavisco*]

···

MARZIPAN or **marchpane** might have got its name from *panis martius* (March bread), a confection of almonds made even in Roman times as an offering to the gods, but the derivation is dubious. There are many recipes. Essentially, marzipan consists of pounded blanched almonds and sugar, but egg white, whole egg, and gum arabic are often added, together with various flavourings. Decorative flowers and fruits may be modelled from it, and sometimes it is lightly baked. Here is a simple recipe from Italy:

Marzipan

Pound 500 g (18 oz) of blanched almonds to a paste with 2 eggs and 450 g (1 lb) sugar. Work in a little vanilla and the grated zest of 2 tangerines. Roll into small fruit shapes, sugar the outsides and bake at a low temperature for 20 minutes on a floured baking sheet.

[*Marzipan* – French: *massepain* German: *Marzipan* Italian: *marzapane* Spanish: *mazapán*]

MASA. A Spanish word for dough, especially the hulled maize dough used in Mexico for making *tortillas, tamales* and *enchiladas*. A modern dried version is sold in America as *masa harina*, instant *masa, tortilla* or *tamale* flour. It is made by first simmering maize in *limewater until the skin begins to flake off – for each 1 kg (2¼ lb) of maize, use 2 lt (3½ pt) of water and 60 g or about 2 oz of slaked lime. The skins are rubbed off and what remains is washed white in fresh water. This is called *nixtamal*, which is pounded to a flour in a stone mortar (*metate*), slapped into a paste from which the *tortillas* are shaped, and baked on a terracotta girdle called a *comal*. Though *nixtamal* is not identical to *hominy, it makes a good substitute.

MASH. *See* black gram.

MASOOR or *masur*. *See* lentil.

MASTIC is a resin from various bushes of the genus *Pistacia* (to which the pistachio nut belongs). The best known is the lentisk (*Pistacia lentiscus*), a straggly bush with red berries, one of the most common plants of dry Mediterranean hillsides. When slashed, it produces a clear, gummy substance, sticky like pure resin and with a strange aromatic smell. This, and the gum from other species, is used for flavouring some dishes in Greece and the islands of the eastern Mediterranean, in Turkish delight – *rahat lokum* – and for the Greek

liqueur, *mastika*.

[*Mastic* – French: *mastic* German: *Mastix* Italian: *mastice, lentischio* Spanish: *almáciga, mastice, lentisco*]

MATÉ, Paraguay tea, yerba maté, or **yerba**. Maté is, after tea and coffee, the most important hot, stimulating drink, with the possible exception of cocoa. Although not much used in other parts of the world, it is the most common drink over much of South America, having been adopted by the colonists from the Indians who used it in pre-Columbian times. The plant is a species of holly (*Ilex paraguayensis*), and other species (*I. gongonha* and *I. theezans*) are also used in parts of South America for the same purpose. People have even used the leaves of holly (*I. aquifolium*) in Europe during wartime, and roasted the berries, which are emetic when raw, for coffee.

Maté leaves are oval or lance shaped, with rather toothed edges. The branches are first dried over a fire. The leaves are then beaten off with sticks, dried in ovens and finally powdered. Maté makes a greenish-coloured tea, slightly bitter and refreshing, when boiling water is poured over it. (There are darker double-baked versions for export.)

Methods of making and serving vary, but the traditional vessel is a gourd (the *maté*), which is passed round, and the tea is sucked through a hollow tube or *bombilla* which has a perforated bulb at the end to act as a strainer and may be made of silver, brass or straw, according to the wealth of the person. Maté is often drunk with lemon and sugar, sometimes with burnt sugar. Though it is a universal drink in South America, it is not popular in North America and is hardly known in Europe, although some drink it in the mistaken belief that it is caffeine or theine free, which it is not. Maté is a stimulant, but has less tannin than tea.

MATIE or **Matjeshering**. *See* herring.

MATJESSILL. *See* herring.

MATSUTAKE. *See* mushrooms.

MATZO. A thin, unleavened Jewish bread made of flour and water only. Although used by orthodox Jews, especially during Passover, it has recently become popular as a biscuit, in place of water biscuits, which it somewhat resembles. It is also available ground as the matzo meal of Jewish cooking. This meal comes in two degrees of fineness: medium, which has about the consistency of burghul and is used, for example, for breading foods to be fried and in matzo balls (*knaidlach*), and fine, which is called for in potato dishes, to bind *gefüllte* fish and in Passover cakes. It can also be used to thicken soups, as it sometimes is in southern Spain.

MAYONNAISE is an emulsion of oil and vinegar stabilized with egg yolk. There are many theories about the origin of its name. 1) That it originated in Mahon (in Minorca and in sailing days regarded as the finest port in the Mediterranean) or may have been given the name by the Duc de Richelieu after he defeated the British there in 1756. 2) That it was named after Napoleon's Irish General MacMahon by the General's chef. 3) That it was derived from the French *magnonaise* (*manier*, to stir). 4) From the old French *moyeu* (yolk). 5) After the town of Bayonne in the Basses-Pyrénées – i.e., it was originally *bayonnaise*.

Whatever the origin of the French name, it is not likely that the sauce itself was created suddenly by an 18th-century chef, and if you see crowds of Catalans making *ali-oli* at a communal picnic (using the special glazed earthenware or china mortars they have for the purpose), you get the feeling that mayonnaise was invented south of the Pyrénées and worked northwards into France. Some old people in Spain say that *ali-oli* is correctly made with oil and garlic alone, without any egg yolk at all, and although it is rather difficult to make an emulsion hold without the egg, *alioli* means 'garlic and oil' as also does *aioli*. It seems most likely that mayonnaise was invented by peasants near the Mediterranean where the olive grows.

For some reason, mayonnaise has a reputation for being difficult to make. I remember asking a young chef, who was on his way to work at La Réserve, the famous restaurant at Beaulieu-sur-Mer on the Côte d'Azur, what job a beginner was given and was surprised when he said, 'making the mayonnaise'. When I asked 'Isn't that supposed to be difficult?' he answered, 'Yes, but it's easy when you start with 20 egg yolks. He had put his finger on the point. With 20 yolks, a beginner could afford to be careless in adding and working in the first few drops of oil, but with one or two yolks one cannot. (I do not know why it is that once the mayonnaise emulsion is started one can afford to be progressively generous with the additions of oil, but it is so.) Mayonnaise may also be difficult to make in very cold winter weather, and certainly neither eggs nor oil should have come straight out of the refrigerator. They should preferably both be at room temperature. A little vinegar or lemon juice should also be added to acidify the yolks before any oil is added. Powdered mustard contains an emulsifying agent and is also a help, though not everyone approves of its use. There are many opinions as to the type of oil and the type of souring agent that should be used in mayonnaise – lemon juice, spirit vinegar and so on. Some oils emulsify more easily than others, but poor olive oil, and maize oil, give a nasty taste.

An old lady in Majorca, known to my family as 'Madame at the shop' showed me how to make mayonnaise in the local way. It involved beating with a rotary whisk until I dropped. This makes a fluffy mayonnaise. Those who use mayonnaise regularly become opinionated and with practice become so adept that... well, I used to make mayonnaise in 60 seconds with a thing like a Horlicks Mixer – a perforated plunger in a cylinder. The oil floated on top and it required a delicate hand to mix in the first few drops, but when the mayonnaise began to thicken – one could feel it – the stroke could be increased. However, if anyone spoke while I was making it, the mayonnaise would curdle, so now I use an electric gadget which is fool-proof, but takes more washing up. To make *aioli* quickly, liquidize the garlic with oil first. Since (with practice) making mayonnaise is so easy, it horrifies me that many families prefer the sort bought in jars from the supermarket. The chefs employed by the manufacturers are experts at the art of flavouring, and add essential oils – such as rue – in minute and unrecognizable amounts to beguile the palate. Other permitted additives include spices, sugar, milk and milk products, mustard, edible gums and edible starch. The creaminess of commercial products may be obtained at home by beating a teaspoon of water into each 300 ml (½ pt) of mayonnaise.

MEAT is not an essential part of the human diet; the Japanese used to get along very well on fish. But for human beings, complete vegetarianism, in the sense of eating no animal product at all, is risky. A diet without even milk or eggs, results in a likelihood of vitamin B12 deficiency and consequently of anaemia or of nervous disorders. Especially in the rich countries of the West, far more meat is eaten than is necessary for health, because once people have acquired the meat habit, they find a diet containing little meat rather boring.

The ox and the ass were the first animals to be domesticated, but not for food; they were the beasts of burden for ancient Middle Eastern civilizations. Sheep and goats provided milk and clothing, and were sometimes eaten, though usually in connection with a sacrifice or festival. Day-to-day meat consisted of game, when it could be hunted. Later, the horse came down into the Mediterranean from Central Asia, and it was after this that the camel was domesticated. These animals were for the work of ploughing, pulling carts and carrying loads, and for riding – during several periods it was a serious matter, punishable even by death, to kill an ox or a horse for food.

Meat now effectively means the flesh of ox, sheep and pig, while camels, reindeer, horses, goats and even llamas are local foods; other animals are categorized as game, even if they are kept by man and no longer wild.

To begin with, methods of butchering were no doubt primitive. I am not talking about cutting the animal's throat with a prayer, but about chopping it into joints. Even 25 years ago, village butchers in Spain more or less hacked sheep to pieces with an axe. It paid to reach the market early, because the butcher sold all the lumps, whether bone or meat, at the same price. Rather more knowledge was displayed in cutting up pigs at the autumn slaughter, when the hams, sausages and bacon were prepared for winter. There were professional pork butchers in ancient Rome, using equipment and cuts strikingly similar to modern ones. The way in which animals are cut up has evolved gradually, and is different in each country and even from area to area. And it is still constantly changing, because public demand does. Stock breeders produce smaller or leaner animals to satisfy fashion, but ultimately it falls on the butcher to market the meat in forms that suit his public. At the same time, he must cut with economy to make a living. With all the variations, simple translation from one language or country to another is impossible; cuts are rarely equivalent.

Suppose that many people have some idea of the cuts of meat in their own country; it is when they try to reproduce foreign dishes, as is the fashion now, that they are in trouble. If they happen to be within range of a butcher who caters for French or Italian clients, then there is no problem. Some of the great food stores, like Harrods in London, employ butchers who can cut in the styles of several countries. But without such resources, cooks must turn to those puzzle pages, where British, American and French cuts are compared. Here, the impression is given that butchers cut the carcass up in straight lines with a band-saw (as they do these days in freezer centres). You should not take these diagrams too literally. They show only the general area from which the cuts are made, and are more to make the names meaningful than to be taken as serious indications.

Butchery depends on anatomy, and the cuts can be defined in anatomical terms. Travellers do best, I think, to forget what they did at home, and to accept the local cuts at face value. Only a few dishes, such as *ossobuco*, owe their existence to a special cut, and cannot be made with an approximation. While some parts of an animal are generally accepted to be better than others, a bad cut from a good animal is better than a good cut from a bad one. As for the quality of meat, whatever you may read, you finally have to rely on finding a good butcher. He alone knows the history of the animal. Butchers vary in the trouble they take to prepare the meat properly, and in the neatness with which they do it. (In France, bad butchers scarcely make a living.) Although it may cost a little more to buy meat in which the fascia and gristle have been carefully trimmed off, it is worth it.

The cook needs a good general idea of the anatomy of the three meat animals, and of the different types of tissue. You can get an idea of mammalian anatomy by looking in the bathroom mirror. Human and meat – animal general plans are similar. The neck, the shoulder blades, the ribs, which are attached to the back at one end and the breastbone at the other, are obvious. Below the ribs and down to the pelvic girdle is the loin (with the fillet lying underneath it), while in front is the belly, which is thin walled and – in the bathroom mirror view – preferably not too obvious. Finally, there is the pelvic bone and the hips, with the legs (the hind legs of a meat animal) and the large muscles of the thigh and buttocks.

Meat, red meat or butcher's meat, is muscle. All red muscles have a fibrous structure, with the fibres running lengthwise. The more work the muscle has to do, the tougher and more fibrous it has to become. Muscles are often spindle shaped, fatter in the middle and with the ends attached by tendons to the bones they move. These splay out into the ends of the muscles and are built into them to take the strain. Therefore, the middle of a muscle is usually the tenderest part. In general, the muscles of the fore part of the animal are coarser and tougher than those of the hind part. The tenderest muscle is the fillet, but it is not the one with the best flavour.

Muscles are enclosed in fascia, tough elastic bags or sheaths which hold them in shape and allow one muscle to move on another. Fascia, tendons and connective tissue, form the gristle, which is rich in jellying substances, but needs long cooking to make it tender. The cartilage, which lines the bone joints, and the fibrous bursas and capsules, which hold the joints together, are also full of jellying substances. So are the skin and hooves. Pork rind gives *zampone its lusciousness. Knuckles and feet are used for aspics and jellies. Bones contain marrow, a fatty and tasty soft substance, and are either hollow tubes, like the thigh bone, or are filled with spongy bone for strengthening purposes, like the pelvic girdle or hip bone. The glandular organs – liver, kidneys, sweetbreads, etc – have no fibrous structure, but may be enclosed in tough, protective sacs and have mesenteries from which they hang in the body cavity and ducts or tubes of tough material which may have to be removed by dissection. Stomach (tripe) and intestines are glandular, muscular and tough. They need long cooking. Heart is muscle tissue of a special sort, which is tough, because hearts work hard; they contain valves which need cutting out. Lungs, which tend to disappear from sight in Britain and the US, are tough, elastic and full of air, they need special cooking. Nerve tissue, like brain and spinal cord, is soft, even when coagulated by strong heat which would toughen other tissues. Fat, which is deposited particularly around the internal organs (e.g. *suet), varies in quality from one part of the body to another and is much influenced by the animal's feeding.

Meat has two kinds of connective tissue – collagen, which is white, and elastin, which is yellow. Meat from old animals and muscles that have had hard exercise contain a lot of elastin, which is not softened by cooking but can only be broken up by bashing. But collagen can be changed to gelatine by the combined action of heat and water, the process is hastened by acids, which is why marinating is effective.

[Meat – French: viande German: Fleisch Italian: carne Spanish: carne]

MEDLAR. The medlar (Mespilus germanica), which originated in southern central Europe and the Caucasus, has the merit of being exceedingly hardy; it grows wild over much of Europe and has been introduced into North America. The wild trees are thorny, but the cultivated ones are usually not. Although they were doubtless useful when the only winter fruit was stored apples, medlars are now among the least popular fruit. Even when ripe, medlars look like young apples, with russet-brown skin and a large calyx surrounding a cup-shaped depression in which the five seed vessels can be seen, and they are so hard and astringent as to be inedible. They are picked from the end of October onwards, when they are ripe, but must then be kept on straw until they are 'bletted' – soft, brown and acidly aromatic. Fermentation has taken place, and you could be forgiven for saying they were rotten. At this point they are ready to eat. There are people who love them, and dons at the ancient universities are likely to enjoy eating them as they sip the college port. In Victorian times, it was usual to keep medlars in a silver dish of moist sawdust on the sideboard.

Many authors say that the medlar ripens in Italy and is eaten there as a fresh fruit, but they confuse the common medlar with the *loquat. In fact, medlars are grown in Italy and are found wild in much of southern Europe, but the fruits there are also allowed to rot until they are bletted. They are little loved fruit in a country rich in fruit but they are liked in Piedmont, where they are called piciu. They are also unpopular in the US. However, they do make a delicious jelly. The Naples medlar (Crataegus azarolus) is more closely related to the hawthorn (see rowan).

Medlar Jelly

Simmer ripe medlars in water just to cover and, when they can be pulped, strain off the juice through a jelly bag. Take 1¼ lt (2¼ pt) of juice to every 1 kg (2¼ lb) of sugar, boil rapidly, keeping the liquid skimmed until it reaches jelling point. Pour it into moulds to be turned out and served with cream as a sweet.

[Medlar – French: nèfle German: Mispel Italian: nespola Spanish: níspola]

MEGRIM. See flatfish (lemon sole).

MELEGUETA PEPPER. See grains of paradise.

MELILOT. Leguminous plant sometimes grown as a fodder crop. The melilots (Melilotus) have the strong aromatic smell of new-mown hay because they contain coumarin. The leaves of the Common melilot (M. officinalis), which has yellow flowers, are sometimes used for stuffing, wrapping or marinating rabbits to give them a sweet flavour. A paste of melilot is an ingredient of Schabzeiger cheese (US, sapsago), made in Glarus, at the eastern end of Lake Zurich. Melilots abound in Swiss pastures, but today the Blue melilot (Melilotus coeruleus), introduced from Turkey, is the one used to grind and mix with the curd. Schabzeiger cheese, which is hard and pale green, is grated and pounded with butter for spreading or used as a flavouring and sprinkled in soups. The melilot gives it a taste that is unique.

[Melilot – French: mélilot German: Honigklee, Steinklee Italian: meliloto Spanish: mililoto, trébol dulce]

MELOKHIA. See mallow.

MELON (Cucumis melo) and watermelon (Citrullus vulgaris) were both grown by the ancients. Today, they are important commercial fruits, which are vital in the summer in the hot, dry countries of the Mediterranean and the Middle East (where the best melons, if not the best watermelons, are grown). In more northern climates, both have to be grown under glass. Melons are difficult fruit, because dozens of varieties and types span a wide range in quality, and to be really good, any melon must be exactly ripe, a difficult moment to judge.

Melon seeds, which are largely wasted, are very oily and contain some 35-40% of fats. They are dried and are eaten as nibbles or are used in cooking in China, Greece, Central and South America, and in other places where people cannot afford waste. Watermelon seeds are highly valued by the tribes of Nigeria.

Cantaloupe melon. The real cantaloupe is popular in Europe. What is called a cantaloupe in the US is the Netted melon (see below). Cantaloupes are usually rather small and rounded. Many varieties have a heavily netted skin and broad ribs, which seem to show where the melon might be sliced into portions. The most famous variety is probably the French charentais, which is small, very highly scented and orange fleshed, as is the Tiger melon. There are also green-fleshed cantaloupes, like the Ogen, and even ones with bright scarlet flesh, such as the Sweetheart. Cantaloupes are reckoned to be ready when gentle pressure at the stalk end shows some give. There will also be a fine scent. They need a day in the refrigerator to cool properly for eating. Good cantaloupes should not be gilded with ginger or pepper and, at most, benefit from a slight squeeze of lemon if they are not acid enough.

Casaba melon, generally larger than cantaloupes and musk melons, is mainly green, which, in a musk melon, would suggest unripeness. Casabas, with

Honeydew melons, are classed as winter melons in Britain because they have a long growing season, are ready at the end of the summer, keep to some extent and ripen a bit off the vine. They are ripe when there is a little give at the opposite end to the stem. The flesh is creamy or golden yellow, orange, green or white, according to variety.

Musk melon, Netted melon, Nutmeg melon, or Sweet melon. It is recorded that the first melons in the Americas were planted by Columbus's men on 29th March 1494. Musk melons are popular summer melons in the US, where they are often referred to as cantaloupes, but there are so many hybrids that the cook – and probably also the gardener – is lost. However, this type of melon is usually covered with a creamy netting and has orange flesh. It may or may not be segmented very clearly. They are ripe when there is a slight give at the stem end. Persian melons are of the same type, but are larger and have a finer netting. Cranshaw melons are hybrids between the Persian and the Casaba; they have no net.

Honeydew melon. These, in general, are shaped like a rugby ball and have either a smooth skin or a very slight and irregular net on a tough, heavily-wrinkled outside. They are often dusky green, but may also be white and yellow. The flesh is greenish white. These melons appear at the end of the season and are available well into the winter, as they store well and ripen in storage. Although not comparable to the cantaloupe, they are very good when properly ripe.

Snap melon. In Asia, melons are often grown in the sand along river beds. As pathogenic organisms can live inside melons, especially if they are injected with dirty water, melons often cost the traveller a bellyache. The Snap melon or phooti (var. momordica) of India bursts open when ripe and is used unripe as a vegetable, as also is the Long melon or kakri.

Watermelon belongs to a different genus of the cucumber family. It is thought to have originated in Africa, but as there is a Sanskrit name for it, the fruit must have been cultivated thousands of years ago in India. Today, there are many varieties, differing in shape and size from melon-sized ones and almost spherical ones to monstrous blimp-shaped ones so heavy that only a strong man can lift them.

The skin is smooth and glossy; it may be, for

example, dark green with paler green stripes and blotches or pale green with dark green netted marks. There is even a golden-skinned variety. Most watermelons have black seeds, but some have almost white ones, even when ripe, and there are seedless hybrids. Though the flesh is usually red to purplish, there are watermelons with creamy yellow flesh (e.g. 'Yellow Baby').The names are sometimes a bit flattering, like 'Sweet Princess' and 'You Sweet Thing'.

It is not easy to judge when a watermelon is ripe, and some experts say that cutting it in two is the only sure way. Since the fruit is apt to be too large for the average household, and in particular for chilling in the refrigerator, watermelons are often sold in halves, which enables you to judge ripeness and to avoid any with white streaks or core, immature seeds or a granular, pale look in the middle. Never buy cut melon slices in Oriental markets or from street vendors in exotic places. This is the quick way to get ill, because flies get on cut surfaces, and there is insufficient acidity to kill unpleasant organisms. The vendors are likely to splash dirty water on their wares to keep them looking fresh. When buying a whole watermelon, look for one with a matt surface; it is usually better than a shiny one. The standard way to tell if a watermelon is ripe is to hold it near the ear and to press the ends together sharply. If it cracks, it is ripe. If you are a regular customer, it would also be as well to consult the greengrocer, as there are years when many watermelons are of poor quality, and a kind greengrocer might advise you to buy something else.

Watermelons are harvested when ripe, but travel well, because of their tough skin. They will keep uncut for at least a week in the refrigerator. Large ones may need to be kept in the cold for up to 24 hours before they are ready to eat. Watermelon experts like to separate large melons into core and outer part along the line of the seeds by cutting in just so far, but not right through. Some people prefer the outer part and others the core, and these sections are offered separately at table. The white rind underlying the skin is often made into pickle. There are dozens of recipes in American cookery books, and special varieties of watermelon for pickle are grown (with all or nearly all white part), and they are sometimes eaten immature as a vegetable in the Orient.

Watermelons contain valuable minerals and trace elements. As they need a long hot summer, they are not grown in Britain, but if harvested when ripe,

they keep for up to three weeks chilled at around 3°C (37°F) with 85% relative humidity, so can be shipped. After picking, they never become sweeter, just softer.

Watermelon Pickle

Soak 2 kg (4½ lb) cubed watermelon rind with all skin and red parts removed overnight in a 3% salt solution (30 g of salt per 1 lt of water or a good 2 tablespoons per pt). Next day, make a pickle from the rest of the ingredients. Tie 2 tablespoons of whole cloves, a few allspice berries and a dozen 2.5 cm (1 in) pieces of stick cinnamon together in a spice-bag. Boil 2.2 lt (4 pt) vinegar, 600 ml (1 pt) water and 1.8 kg (4 lb) sugar, plus the spice-bag for five minutes, drain the watermelon cubes and add them to the pickling liquid. Simmer it until the rind becomes transparent. Bottle and seal the pickle immediately while it is hot.

[Melon – French: *melon, cantaloupe* German: *Melone, Beutelmelone* Italian: *mellone, popone* Spanish: *melon.*

Watermelon – French: *pastèque* German: *Wassermelone* Italian: *cocomero* Spanish: *sandia*]

MERCURY. *See* spinach (Good King Henry).

MERGUEZ. *See* sausage.

MERSINE. Smoked *swordfish.

METAL. Common metals and alloys such as iron, copper, aluminium, brass, tin, lead, zinc, silver and gold have sections to themselves. As pans, jugs, other utensils and pipes, they can all come into contact with our food and drink. Metals themselves are not soluble in water, but their various salts often are and may be poisonous in any quantity. On the other hand, many metals are necessary for health as *trace elements, even when poisonous in larger quantities. Apart from this aspect, the conductivity of metals is of importance. Food cooks well in a copper pan because copper is an excellent conductor of heat, but that same quality makes it impossible to drink hot liquids from a copper mug without burning your mouth. Food does not cook well in stainless steel, which is a poor conductor of heat (unless the bottom of the pan is copper coated), but you can drink with reasonable comfort from a stainless steel mug.

[Metal – French: *métal* German: *Metall* Italian:

metallo Spanish: *metal*]

METRIC SYSTEM. The metric system was first introduced into France at the end of the 18th century as one of the changes of the revolution, although comprehensive decimal systems of measurement had been devised by scientists over a century earlier. The basic unit is the metre, which is a ten millionth part of the distance between the pole and the equator, measured along the meridian running through Paris. In practice, it is the length of a platinum bar kept near Paris. The unit of volume derived from this is the litre which is the volume of a cube with 10 centimetre sides, i.e. 10 x 10 x 10 = 1000 cubic centimetres. The unit of weight is the gram, which was originally the weight of a cubic centimetre of pure water (at 4°C) but is now based on a standard Kilogram (1000 grams), which is also kept near Paris. See weights and measures, conversions.

Five hundred grams is known in France as a *livre* (pound). In the mind's eye, a gram can be pictured as 15 grains of wheat. Metric shoppers think in terms of a kilo or in hundreds of grams, sometimes in a half or a quarter of a kilo. Small items like spices would be bought in 25, 50 or 100 grams. Household scales do not measure accurately under 10 grams and rarely under 25 grams, so spoons are used. In nutrition, the daily requirements of minerals and vitamins are measured in milligrams. The mind's eye picture of 10 milligrams is a large grain of wheat.

MEXICAN BLACK BEAN. A variety of *kidney bean.

MEXICAN TEA. *See* epazote.

MICRO-ORGANISMS or **microbes**. Readers of old cookery books should remember that it was not until about the middle of the last century that Louis Pasteur (1822-1895) recognized that fermentation, the souring of milk, putrefaction, and, of course, diseases were caused by tiny living organisms. Their effects are felt because of their vast numbers. It is a sobering thought that in 28 g (1 oz) of grubby hamburger mince, the number of micro-organisms is greater than that of the entire human population of the world, and in warm weather this could double inside half an hour. Microbiology is now an advanced science – in the sphere of food, it is involved in the making of such products as bread, beer, wine, vinegar, cheese, butter, yoghurt, *Sauerkraut*, pickles, ham, sausages, anchovies and soy sauce as well as in processes like canning, bottling, freezing and drying. Since micro-organisms are everywhere and cause food spoilage, it is useful to know something about them, even for those who only buy foods ready made in the supermarket.

There are five important groups of micro-organisms that can affect food: *bacteria, *moulds, *yeasts, *protozoans and *viruses. Methods of preventing their activity are dealt with under preservation, pasteurization, sterilization, freezing and drying.

All organisms require water or moisture, which is why drying is preservative. Bacteria and yeasts need more water than moulds, which can often manage on a small quantity of condensation. Organisms cannot grab water from strong solutions of salt or sugar, which are therefore preservative in effect. A 60-70% sugar solution effectively stops organisms from growing, and 25% of salt stops all but special, salt-loving organisms.

Some sorts of organism, described as aerobic, need air to live. All moulds are aerobic, which is why they grow only on the surface of jam and not at the bottom of the jar, though some can manage with very little air and are micro-aerobic (e.g. the blue moulds in cheeses). Other organisms are anaerobic and refuse to grow except in the total absence of oxygen. In between, there are all sorts of intermediate preferences, and many organisms can grow equally well both with oxygen and without it. These can be important considerations. For instance, anaerobes can thrive in canned food. Sometimes oxygen may get used up by aerobic organisms and in the resulting conditions anaerobes can operate, as happens inside large, hard-rinded, maturing cheeses.

Some organisms are very sensitive to temperature and others less so, but they all have a temperature range within which they will grow, as well as an optimum. For convenience, they are divided into three categories as follows:

1) Cold-loving (psychrophilic) organisms do not grow well in a warm kitchen, but prefer the larder and the warmer parts of the refrigerator. They will, of course, also grow when food passes through their favoured range of temperature. They do not multiply in the deep freeze. Temperature range for multiplication: lowest, -11°C (12°F); optimum, 10°C (50°F); highest, 30°C (86°F).

2) Medium-range (mesophilic) organisms grow best at normal, summer's-day temperatures, more

slowly in winter or in a cool larder and hardly at all in a refrigerator. The majority of organisms fall into this category, including the disease-producers, which prefer the precise temperature of the human body, and the yeasts which like it comfortably warm but not very hot or very cold. Temperature range: lowest, 0°C (32°F); optimum, 25-35°C (77-95°F); highest, 40-50°C (104-122°F).

3) Heat-loving (thermophilic) organisms are hot weather microbes. In nature, they like hot springs, compost heaps and the temperatures of blazing deserts. This group also includes the organisms responsible for *yoghurt. Temperature range: lowest, 30°C (86°F); optimum, 50-65°C (122-149°F): highest, 70-80°C (158-176°F).

Most organisms are killed by boiling for one minute (but see pasturization and sterilization). Naturally, the thermophilic organisms tend to withstand more heat than the others, but certain bacteria – not too many – can form resistant spores. One, perhaps the world's most common organism, is the hay bacillus (Bacillus subtilis), which has spores that can stand fast boiling for three hours. Those of the deadly botulism organism (see poisoning) can stand six. Spores have also been known to remain alive for as long as ten years. They form when food starts to run out and waste products accumulate (i.e. in old cultures).They take about 24 hours to form, but are killed by boiling for five minutes during that vulnerable period. When conditions improve, the spores germinate much more quickly – usually in five or six hours.

On the other hand, the effect of extreme cold is merely to prevent the multiplication of organisms rather than to kill them. For instance, the typhoid germ can live up to a week in ice cream, and some organisms have been known to survive the shattering cold of liquid hydrogen at -252°C (-421°F). Deep freezing does not sterilize food.

For many micro-organisms, the *pH is critical. Yeasts prefer acid conditions (pH 3.0-6.0) and so do moulds, although some can be found to thrive at almost anything from pH 1.0 to pH 11.0. On the other hand most bacteria prefer more or less neutral conditions (pH 6.5-8.0) and very few (and certainly not the harmful ones) will grow or even survive for long in acidity below pH 4.0 (or in really alkaline conditions over pH 9.0).You can get an idea of what this means from the fact that lemon juice is about pH 2.3. Even sour milk, which is pH 4.4, is inimical to many bacteria.

However, the activity of acids in stopping bacteria from growing is not entirely dependent on the pH.

Some acids are more toxic to micro-organisms than others and, therefore, more preservative. If we gave sulphuric acid an effectiveness of one, then the relative effectiveness of the other commonly-used *preservatives would be as follows: tartaric acid 3; hydrochloric acid 6; sulphurous acid (sulphur dioxide in water) 9; citric acid 13; formic acid 16; benzoic acid 21 and salicylic acid 33. Chemicals which either stop micro-organisms from multiplying or kill them are *disinfectants.

Ultra-violet light will kill micro-organisms, although some are more susceptible than others. There is ultra-violet in sunlight, and ultra-violet lamps are sometimes installed in operating theatres, factories and food stores. If they are switched on when the rooms are not being used, they serve to reduce the number of organisms in the air.

MILK has been a source of food and drink since early herdsmen first learned to take milk from their animals. However, milk and milk products (such as butter and cheese) are less common in China (though butter is popular in Tibet), and they were quite unknown to the ancient civilizations of America. Milk today is normally cow's milk, but in ancient times there were no dairy cows, and oxen were beasts of burden. Milk mainly came from sheep, goats, asses and horses. Camels were domesticated much later – their milk is purgative but is used by Bedouin tribes. (Pigs cannot be induced to give milk.)

Milk evolved as a complete diet for suckling mammals, but is a very good food for children and adults. It contains good quality protein, digestible fat and a sugar as well as minerals and vitamins; composition varies enormously from species to species. The main constituent of milk is water (87% by weight) in which are dissolved lactose (milk sugar), an albumin, citrates and chlorides of sodium and potassium, and vitamins B_1, B_2, and C. Partly in solution and partly in suspension are phosphates of calcium and magnesium while caseinogen, the chief protein, is in colloidal suspension. The minute fat droplets contain the fat-soluble vitamins A and D. The yellow colour of the fat in summer milk in some breeds is caused by carotene which is a precursor of vitamin A, and comes from the grass and herbs the animal eats. The *pH value of fresh cow milk lies between 6.5 and 6.8 (i.e. it is very slightly acid) but is most commonly about 6.6. Milk is an ideal food for many bacteria. Many of them can convert the lactose into lactic acid, making the milk gradually go sour. Souring can first be detected by taste at around pH 6.2; milk that is slightly more sour may curdle when heated. You should note that it is particularly liable to do so when given a sudden heat shock, for example by being poured into hot tea; when it is treated more gently (and the tea is gradually poured into the milk), it may not do so.

When milk curdles, the main protein, which has been held in colloidal suspension, is precipitated as casein. Heat encourages curdling, as also does salt. This explains why some soups and sauces need careful handling to avoid curdling, and why they may need stabilizers such as the starch gel used in white sauces. Milk may curdle either with or without setting to a clabber. Bacterial action, mild acids and rennet will cause milk to clabber, but strong acidity and salts like alum will curdle milk without producing a clabber. Acid curdling takes place when the pH reaches about 4.8, but happens at higher pH values (i.e. lower acidities) when the milk is heated. Raw milk usually goes sour if it is kept at room temperature, but pasteurized milk and boiled milk in which the acid-forming bacteria have been destroyed, usually develop a bitter taste and unpleasant flavours.

The composition of milk varies appreciably not just between species but between different breeds of the same species, between animals in the same breed and even in each individual animal around the year. The figures given in the table are average ones.

Composition of milks of various mammals

Average% of	Fat	Protein	Lactose	Minerals	Water
Cow	3.8	3.3	4.8	0.72	87.40
Zebu (Eastern Humped Cattle)	4.92	3.21	4.58	0.75	86.56
Water Buffalo	7.16	3.77	4.81	0.76	83.56
Goat	4.1	3.6	4.6	0.85	86.85
Sheep	6.7	5.8	4.6	0.82	82.08
Camel	4.5	3.5	4-9	0.70	86.40
Mare	1	2	6.7	0.30	90.00
Human	3.5	1.7	6.7	0.20	87.00

Several interesting points emerge from these figures. Cow's milk is richer in protein and contains less sugar than human milk; some adjustment is advisable when cow's milk is used to feed babies. Mare's milk is high in milk sugar, in Asia, it is fermented to make alcoholic drinks such as *koumiss*. Camel's milk, which is rather low in fat, has very small fat globules and cannot readily be churned to make butter. Buffalo milk, on the other hand, is very rich in fat and protein, and so makes splendid cheese and butter.

In an emergency, a suitable milk for feeding babies can be made up of one part water to one part cow's milk, with a level teaspoon of sugar per 100 cc (3½ oz) of feed, provided it is heated nearly to boiling and then cooled to blood heat. Feeding of cow's milk to babies can sometimes cause trouble – a form of allergy to cow's milk is thought to be a possible cause of 'cot deaths' in babies. If you have to feed other suckling animals, you should find out the composition of milk in the species concerned, and cow milk should then be adjusted with cream, water, and sugar. Having brought up many animals, from wolves to gazelles and wild rabbits, on a bottle, I know that care over the composition of the milk makes all the difference to their survival.

Grades of milk in Britain are distinguished by colour-coded bottle tops, although much milk is now sold in cartons or even polythene bags on which the description of the contents can be printed. The colour code for bottle tops is as follows:

Raw, untreated	Green top
Pasteurized	Silver top
Homogenized	Red top
Sterilized	Crown cap or blue foil top
UHT	Pink top (date stamped)
Channel Islands	Green top with gold stripe if raw or bottled on farm. Gold top if pasteurized

Only TB-free or TT milk is now allowed to be sold in Britain.

Channel Islands milk comes from Jersey or Guernsey cows, small animals which produce especially rich milk – by law, this must contain a minimum of 4% butter fat.

Pasteurized milk has been heated to 71°C (160°F) for 15 seconds and quickly cooled to 10°C (50°F).It keeps for 1-2 days in a cold larder, 2-3 days in the refrigerator.

Homogenized milk has been mechanically treated – *homogenized – so that the cream no longer rises when the milk is left to stand. The even nature of the product is an advantage in the catering business, but not to the cook.

Sterilized milk is homogenized and sterilized

in bottles at 108-115°C (226-239°F) for 20-30 minutes. Now usually has a preliminary high temperature treatment. Unopened keeps fresh for at least a week and often for several weeks without refrigeration.

UHT milk or **long life milk**. UHT means Ultra High Temperature: homogenized milk is heated to 132°C (270°F) for 1-2 seconds, then rapidly cooled and packed in sterile conditions. It will keep for several months unopened, but behaves like other milk once it has been opened.

Skimmed milk has had practically all the fat removed by separation. It is often no cheaper than full cream milk, but is much used by people on diets or with a cholesterol problem.

Dried milk, **powdered milk**, or **dehydrated milk**. Spray-dried milk is made by spraying whole or skimmed milk into a large chamber of hot dry air, the powder which is formed falls to the bottom of the chamber. It is almost 100% soluble in water. Roller-dried milk is made by putting a film of concentrated milk on a heated steel roller and scraping it off when it has dried. Reconstituted roller dried milk contains small insoluble particles, which fall to the bottom. Milk powder, whether whole or skimmed, contains about 4% moisture. Because of changes which take place on heating and exposure to the air, it is nutritionally slightly inferior to fresh milk. To reconstitute it, mix it to a thin paste with a little cold water, and then dilute with hot water. 10 parts water to one part of dried milk is a usual mixture. The fat – 26% in full-cream powdered milk – becomes partly oxidized in drying; this produces the characteristic, not very nice, flavour of dried milk. Skimmed milk powder, with very little fat (1%) tastes better. At a pinch, melted butter, even oil or margarine, can be emulsified in a blender with water and skimmed milk powder, and the result is better flavoured than that of reconstituted whole milk powder.

Frozen milk. If milk is frozen slowly, it will keep but does not return to normal when thawed. It can be used only for cooking. If milk is held just above freezing, its life is lengthened, but after a week, it can begin to putrefy without souring, and poisons can accumulate, which make it dangerous. Do not keep milk refrigerated for over ten days (get sterilized or UHT milk as a standby). UHT milk can be frozen and drunk as milk after it has thawed (which can be useful in the tropics).

Milk products include *cream, *evaporated milk *condensed milk, *buttermilk, *yoghurt and *sour milk products.

Milk substitutes are the filled milks and non-dairy creamers which are made with skim milk solids, fats or oils (such as lard or hydrogenated vegetable oils), emulsifiers and anti-oxidants. Those made with vegetable oils may have a higher unsaturated fatty acid content than ordinary milk and no cholesterol.

Vegetable milk can be the milky sap of plants such as that of *Galactodendron*, which is used in Colombia as a drink and in cooking; it can be an emulsion made with oil-rich nuts, such as milk of almonds or the coconut milk and cream which are used in Indian cooking. It can also be made from soya beans – soya milk.

[*Milk* – French: *lait* German: *Milch* Italian: *latte* Spanish: *leche*]

MILK SUGAR. *See* lactose.

MILLE FIORE. *See* liqueurs and cordials.

MILLET and **SORGHUM**. Various grasses, with small edible grains, are known as millets, a word derived from the Latin *milium*, the common millet which was grown by the Romans. Millets vary greatly in the quality of their grain, and none is as good as wheat, but they are grown because they produce a crop, often a good crop, even in the poorest soils, both waterlogged and in drought. Some, like the Bulrush millet, make it just possible for people to exist in areas of extreme aridity and heat.

Most people in Britain see millet only as bird seed – sometimes the whole ears are hung up in cages. The seeds will often sprout and grow on waste dumps – and even ripen in a good year. In the US, millets are grown extensively as animal feed, and the sweet variety is used for sorghum syrup. Otherwise, millets are foods of the world's poor – they are rough, but healthy. The common millet contains about 10-13% protein and about 4% oil, although millets are considered as carbohydrate cereals. Millets are quite commonly fermented and made into beers, both the crude 'native beers', and more sophisticated brews, in which case the grain is malted. Millets do not make gourmet foods; they are mostly ground and boiled into porridges or made into unleavened bread. Recipes for other millet dishes are few, but one for *ragi* (finger millet) *dosas* is offered as an example.

Ragi Dosas

Dosas might be described as South-Indian pancakes, usually made of a fermented batter of soaked and pounded black *dal* and rice (though modern short cuts use rice flour). *Dosas* are often rolled and stuffed with vegetable curry as a breakfast dish. *Ragi dosas* are not so good to look at, but are still delicious.

Take 2½ cups of ground finger millet, add a teaspoon of salt, and mix with water into a stiff paste. Soak 7½ tablespoons of black gram *dal* for an hour, then put it in the liquidizer and grind it to a thin, frothy paste. Mix the two pastes together into a batter of thick pouring consistency. Cook by putting a large spoonful on to a hot iron girdle or plate (which has been smeared with a little oil) and spreading it quickly into a thin, round plate-sized pancake with the back of a spoon. When the underside is golden brown, turn it over and cook the other side rather more lightly. Put a spoon of filling on it and roll it up, or eat it with butter and honey (and some fresh coriander-green chilli chutney for perfection).

Barnyard millet or **bharti** (*Echinochloa crusgalli*) which grows as a naturalized weed in Britain and the US, is grown as a crop in the Orient, but mainly for fodder. The Japanese millet or *sanwa* (*Echinochloa frumenlacea*) and the smaller *shama* millet (*Echinochloa colona*) are eaten as a porridge or with rice.

Bulrush millet, **bajra**, **cattail**, or **reedmace** (*Pennisetum typhoideum*) is a tropical millet that is important in India, Nigeria and the Sudan; it grows quickly and stands drought. Under the name of *bajra*, it is one of the most important Indian millets (although it is native to Africa) and is used by the poor to make flour and unleavened bread. It gets its popular name because its head is like that of reedmace, commonly called bulrush. It is not to be confused with foxtail millet, which is more hairy. Its white-seeded variety is known as pearl millet.

Common millet, **broom-corn**, **proso**, **Indian millet**, or **Hog-millet** (US), *Panicum miliaceum*, is a temperate millet, which is grown in Russia, China, Japan, North America and southern Europe. In the US and southern Europe, it is rarely used today as human food – for long it has been grown only for chickens and other livestock – but its use as human food is prehistoric, and it makes good unleavened bread. The grain of common millet is oval and varies from white to straw-coloured, red or brown. It is often used as a bird seed.

Finger millet or **ragi** (*Eleusine coracana*) is of Indian origin. Although it grows in many forms, it gets its name from a common type in which the head looks like five stubby, outwardly-curved fingers. It is a staple in India, not only because it can grow in poor soils but also because it gives a heavy yield and the grain stores particularly well. In Africa, it is grown from Rhodesia to the Sudan. Coarse when compared to wheat, it has a good taste and is made into breads and other cereal preparations. It is also fermented into beers and is even malted.

Foxtail millet, **German millet**, **Hungarian millet**, **Italian millet**, or **Siberian millet** (*Setaria italica*) is a warm temperate millet, which came originally from the Orient. It was used in China in 2700 BC, and also by the Lake Dwellers in prehistoric Europe. It is still reaped in Russia to a considerable extent for beer. The grain may be white, yellow, red, brown or even black. It is grown in southern Europe and the US for chicken food and fodder. It can be used boiled or parched as human food but is not particularly nice.

Hungry rice (*Digitaria exilis*) is a grain that is locally important in dry West Africa.

Job's tears (*Ciox lachryma-jobi*) is not really a millet, as the seeds are large. A tropical and subtropical crop, native to India, it can also be found growing in southern Europe as an ornamental plant. The pearly fruits are used for necklaces, and it is claimed that the seeds contain more protein than any other cereal. This is eaten mostly in South East Asia and the Philippines (where it is called *adley*). It is sometimes used medicinally, as well as for sustenance.

Little millet (*Panicum miliare*) is like the common millet but smaller. It gives a moderate yield on very poor soils. In India, it is known as the poor man's crop (which there means really poor).

Sorghum (*Sorghum vulgare*) is often a tropical

crop, and in India and Africa is a staple for the poor. Varieties differ considerably and may be grouped into categories based on their uses as well as on their characteristics.

Sweet sorghum or Sugar sorghum (var. *saccharatum*) has a stem rich in sugars and is crushed to obtain the juice which is boiled down and evaporated in shallow pans to make sorghum syrup (which is a thinner and sourer equivalent of molasses). Millions of gallons of this are used in cooking in the US every year, but elsewhere sorghum syrup is less known.

Durra or Great millet is called *jawor* in India. It is a staple food for millions around the world and is one of the world's most vital crops. There are two main types: white-grained sorghum, which is favoured for bread, and red-grained, which is bitter and mainly used for brewing beer. In India, *jowar* is ground daily in most poor homes and used to make flat unleavened bread which is not so refined as the *chapattis* or *rotis* made from wheat flour (*atta*), but which makes a satisfying meal. This, not wheat or rice, is the main food in the dry areas of the subcontinent.

Kaffir corn (var. *caffrorum*) and milo (var. *subglabrescens*) are of African origin and are essentially the same from the gastronomic, if not the cultivator's, point of view, as is the Chinese kaoliang.

Teff (*Eragrostis abyssinica*) is the most widely grown cereal in Ethiopia. It is ground to form the basis of the fermented flat bread called *injura*, which is eaten with the hot curry-like stew called *wot*. *Injura* is full of bubbles and has the texture of tripe. The taste is sour. It is rather nice, once you are used to it.

[*Millet* – French: *millet* German: *Hirse* Italian: *miglio* Spanish: *mijo*]

MILLING is reducing to a powder or paste. The most primitive method is pounding, and since such creatures as different as otters and vultures have learned to use stones as tools, it is probable that man learned to pound grain even before he could grow it. Today, in the more primitive tropical countries, you can still see grain being pounded in large mortars hollowed out of stones or tree trunks. Primitive grinding with stones, the precursor of milling, is done daily by countless Indians when they grind their fresh curry spices with a roller on a stone slab.

A more sophisticated grinder is the quern, which is typically constructed of two round stones, the top one revolving on a peg set in the lower. The peg must be shaped to allow grain to fall round it down between the stones. The top stone is rotated by hand. Portable querns are still used today – for instance, by the nomadic tribes in Baluchistan – and were common enough everywhere in the past, and there were even special mini-querns for mustard.

It is only a step from the hand quern to some sort of mechanization. The simplest powered mills are still to be seen in remote mountain regions, such as the Himalayas (where people have even harnessed water power to say their prayers for them). Almost every village has at least one diminutive water-mill housed in a stone hut that is little bigger than a dog kennel and is built across a side-stream of the river. The stones are less than a metre (3¼ feet) across; the bottom one is driven, without any gears, by an arrangement of inclined wooden paddles. More complicated and bigger arrangements, such as those found in windmills or the old water-powered grist mills, require gears, which usually turn the top stone.

The stones used in old-fashioned mills had to be abrasive, long-wearing, and sharp. Various types of rock were used; some were highly prized, such as buhrstones, which were finely-pitted quartzite stones. These were even shipped to the US from France. Stones were dressed so that the ridges in them both ground the flour and moved it outwards from the centre. Heat is generated by the friction of grinding, but skilled millers managed to keep the flour from getting too hot.

Progress in milling was aimed mainly towards obtaining a whiter, finer flour. Special bolting cloth was woven for fine sifting, but that only separated the large particles from the small. However, a machine called a purifier, invented in the early years of the 19th century, enabled particles of the same size but different weights to be separated, as was possible by winnowing; it depended, like winnowing, on currents of air. It allowed a greater proportion of the husk (bran) to be taken out of flour in large-scale milling.

Another radical development was roller milling, which was widely adopted in the latter years of the 19th century, and is still in use today. Passing the wheat between fluted rollers revolving at slightly different speeds and with diminishing clearance literally scrapes the white starchy inside of the grain (the endosperm) off the skin, leaving the flakes of almost pure bran which can then be removed by sifting. The particles of endosperm are then reduced in size by smooth reduction rollers. This process, perfected over the years, enables the modern miller to separate endosperm, bran and germ fairly completely. The white flours that result are preferred by the public. They undoubtedly make better cakes and fine white bread, but there is increasing evidence that a long-term shortage of bran in the diet may contribute towards some diseases that are prevalent in modern societies.

Milling or grinding at home can be easily done in a hand mill, of which several types are on the market. Mills which grind between two cutters or grooved plates will easily reduce even hard seeds, such as maize or chickpeas, to a flour (though it is hard work and there are now electric grain mills on the market for domestic use). Flour will have to be sifted and the coarser particles returned to the mill for further grinding.

A whirling-blade electric coffee grinder can deal only with small quantities of grain but is useful for spices, though the hardest seeds and dried roots (such as turmeric and ginger) need to be cracked first by hammering.

[Milling – French: moudre German: mahlen Italian: macinare Spanish: moler]

MILO. See millet.

MILT. Male *roe.

MILTON. See disinfectants.

MINT. Mints (species of Mentha) are among the most important culinary herbs. They are mostly native to the temperate regions of the Old World, and the ease with which the 25 or so species cross, even in the wild, has resulted in a baffling range of hybrids. Peppermint (M. X piperita) is not a separate species, but a hybrid between Water mint (M. aquatica) and spearmint (M. spicata). Mints produce a wide range of flavours – some, like eau-de-cologne mint (M. citrata), have very scented overtones. Spearmint is the type that is normally cultivated for use in cooking, but cooks must decide for themselves what mint they prefer and will doubtless be influenced by the choice available locally or easily grown in the garden. The juicy leaves of apple mint (M. rotundifolia) are ideal for mint sauce, which was used by the Romans and is delicious when properly made. Even when the British had given up most other herbs, they still habitually used fresh mint in cooking new potatoes and garden peas. Dried mint is a common

flavouring in Mid-Eastern cooking. Fresh mint *chutney is a very Indian taste that is worth trying. Peppermint is rarely used as a herb in cooking, but its oil is important in confectionery. Another species of the genus is *pennyroyal.

[Mint – French: menthe German: Minze Italian: menta Spanish: hierbabuena, menta]

MIRABELLE. See fruit brandy, plum.

MIRIN. See sake.

MISO. See soya.

MIXED SPICE for use in plum puddings, cakes, etc., is often bought ready-ground, but can be stale and lacking in flavour, since it is ground very fine and loses its aromatic oils very quickly. It may be made by mixing, say, one part (by weight) of cloves, two parts ginger, four parts cinnamon and four parts nutmeg – for practical purposes you can measure the spices in teaspoons, but the difficulty at home lies in grinding the spices finely enough, unless you use an electric coffee grinder. Some mixed spices are much more elaborate and include touches of star anise, for instance. With experience, you can please yourself

MOCHA. Variety of *coffee.

MOLASSES is the liquid residue in sugar-making which is separated by centrifuge from the crystals of crude brown sugar. While most molasses is made from sugar cane, some may come from specially processed sugar beet, although molasses produced from beet in normal sugar production is inedible to humans.

Baking molasses still contains a large amount of crystallizable sugar, while blackstrap molasses is the lowest grade of all and has lost all the sugar that can economically be extracted. *Treacle is partly decolourized molasses, and is usually sweeter than molasses.

[Molasses – French: mélasse German: Melasse Italian: melassa Spanish: melaza]

MOLLUSCS include gastropods (such as slugs and *snails, *limpets and *abalones), bivalves (such as *mussels, *clams, *oysters and *cockles), and cephalopods (*octopuses, *cuttlefish and *squids). The word comes from the Latin mollis (soft) or molluscus (softish), perhaps.

[Mollusc – French: molusque German: Molluske,

Weichtier Italian: *mollusco* Spanish: *molusco*]

MOLOKHIA. *See* mallow.

MONKFISH. *See* shark.

MONKEY NUT. *See* peanut.

MONOSACCHARIDES. *See* sugars.

MONOSODIUM GLUTAMATE, **MSG**, **taste powder**, **gourmet powder**, **p'sst**, or **ve-tsin**. This is the sodium salt of glutamic acid, one of the amino acids, and can be bought as a white, crystalline substance. It occurs naturally in soy sauce and can be made from wheat (as it was originally) or, as now, from glutamic acid recovered from sugar beet molasses or by bacterial fermentation of solutions of glucose and simple nitrogen compounds. Although MSG has very little taste of its own, it has the property of bringing out the taste of other ingredients, particularly of meat, but also of vegetables and mushrooms. It is commonly used in commercial products, canned goods and stock cubes and in Chinese and Japanese cooking.

[*Monosodium glutamate* – French: *glutamate de soude* German: *Mononatriumglutamat* Italian: *glutiminato di soda* Spanish: *glutamato de sodio*]

MONSTERA or **ceriman** (*Monstera deliciosa*) has a fruit that looks like an elongated green pinecone. The plant, a favourite of the indoor horticulturist, has natural slashes in the leaves; it is an epiphyte from tropical America which belongs to the Arum lily family. I have found the fruit in London as an import from Portugal. it is ripe when the cone begins to break up; you can then take off the outer segments, with the green surface attached. Inside are white, creamy segments reminiscent of a custard apple, with black flakes and a central core. The flavour is acid-sweet and refreshing, vaguely like a pineapple. It is liable to make the mouth sore, especially if it is not quite ripe.

MONTILLA. *See* sherry.

MORAY EEL (*Muraena helena*) is a sinister looking creature that is common in warm seas but rare further north. Morays used to be plentiful in the Mediterranean until pollution took charge. Their heads, teeth bared, were a familiar sight to skin divers who probed under rocks. The moray is brown or purple-brown, mottled with yellow spots, up to 150 cm (5 ft) long and exceedingly aggressive. Its bite, though not venomous, is very painful. It is said that the moray can also live in fresh water – though it prefers the sea – and that it was kept and fattened in ponds by wealthy Romans who even, legend has it, fed the eels on recalcitrant slaves. The taste of the moray is excellent – it reminds me of sole – but it is full of bones. There is supposed to be a local way of removing the bones by rubbing the fish with ashes and pulling it through a noose, but I have never found anyone who can demonstrate this. Moray eel is excellent cut in pieces and used with other fish as the basis for fish soup.

[*Moray eel* – French: *murène* Italian: *murena* Spanish: *morena*]

MOREL. This fungus, of which the most usual species in the kitchen are *Morchella esculenta* and *M. vulgaris*, does not have the parasol shape of most mushrooms and toadstools but has the cap covered with a honeycomb of pits which give a sponge-like appearance. Unlike most edible fungi, they appear in the spring, from March to May. They are usually cut up before washing in salted water to remove not just earth but also insects. Some fungus books suggest that morels should be blanched in boiling water before being prepared for the table or incorporated in sauces. They are not common in Britain but can be bought dried or canned. (*See* mushrooms.)

[*Morel* – French: *morille* German: *Morchel* Italian: *morchella* Spanish: *colmenilla*]

MORELLO. *See* cherry.

MORTADELLA is a large, often balloon-shaped sausage that originated in Bologna, which still produces the best examples, although mortadella is now also made in other towns and other countries. It is a finely textured sausage, usually containing large flecks of fat, and has been cooked by steaming so that it is ready to eat cold and finely sliced. The best mortadella is made with pure pork, but the possible ingredients listed by Elizabeth David in *Italian Food* (Penguin) for cheap mortadella include not just soya flour but also donkey meat. Mortadella is used in cooking in the stuffing for some sorts of pasta and in the croquettes called *suppli* together with mozzarella cheese.

MOTH BEAN (*Phaseolus aconitifolius*) grows wild in India and has been taken into cultivation fairly recently. It is useful because it is exceedingly drought resistant and so will grow where other pulses will not, even in the desert regions of

Rajastan. It is used whole or as a split *dal*, but is of small importance outside its locality. The seeds are green or black.

MOULDS are small fungi which can just be seen as downy, cottony or powdery plants, growing on stale bread, jam and rotten fruit. There are thousands of different kinds. Moulds reproduce and spread by means of minute spores which blow everywhere in the air (so keep windows closed and pots covered as far as possible when bottling jam). Some species of mould can be found to attack almost anything, even glass and chemicals.

Moulds need air to varying degrees. Some, like *Penicillium camembertii*, which grows on the rind of camembert and other similar *cheeses, need a lot. Others, like *Penicillium roquefortii*, which makes blue veins inside cheese, can manage with little air.

Moulds also require moisture. The spores need it to germinate, and the threads to grow. However, they do not need as much moisture as most other organisms and can often manage on what is condensed on surfaces from damp air. Although moulds will not grow on jams that contain plenty of sugar, the dilution at the surface produced by condensation may be enough to let them get hold. That is why dry, airy places are always advocated for storage.

Usually moulds prefer somewhat acid conditions (pH 3 to 6), but some are able to stand extremes (anything from pH 1 to pH 11), so pickles may be attacked on occasion. They also like warm but not hot surroundings and are slowed down by cold. Although poisonous moulds do exist, most merely spoil food with musty or bitter tastes. They are rarely harmful in any quantity that is likely to be eaten. An exception is the parasitic mould *Claviceps purpurea*, which affects cereals, especially rye. The black ears attacked by this parasite, which is called ergot, are virulently poisonous, causing delirium and often death. The illness was common in the Middle Ages; though it is rare today, its existence should be noted by grow-it-yourself survival enthusiasts.

[*Mould* – French: *moisissure* German: *Schimmel* Italian: *muffa* Spanish: *moho*]

MOUNTAIN ASH. *See* rowan.

MOWRA BUTTER. *See* fats.

MSG. *See* monosodium glutamate.

MULBERRY in Europe normally means the Common mulberry or Black mulberry (*Morus nigra*), a fruit which has been grown since ancient times, when it was probably introduced from western Asia. The tree has clusters of small flowers which together form one multiple fruit (unlike the blackberry which is formed from a single flower). Mulberries should not be picked until they are completely ripe (hence their non-appearance in greengrocer's shops); they are then purple, very juicy and will stain everything in sight. They can be eaten raw or made into jam or sorbet and can also be used in summer pudding (although Elizabeth David says that they should first be stewed).

In Asia, the leaves of the White mulberry or Silk mulberry (*M. alba*) are used as the food of the silkworm. The fruits are used dried as well as fresh in both sweet and savoury sauces.

[*Mulberry* – French: *mure* German: *Maulbeere* Italian: *mora* Spanish: *mora*]

MULLET. There are two sorts of mullet, grey and red, which belong to quite different groups of fish. Both are important as food.

Red mullet is actually two very similar species, *Mullus surmuletus* and *M. barbatus*, which respectively reach 40 cm (16 in) and 25 cm (10 in) in length. The family Mullidae, to which they belong, has some 50 species, including various goatfish. The Red mullet is found in the Mediterranean and from the Canary Islands to Norway, though it is rarely caught in northern waters. The red mullet is a great delicacy, and was much sought after by the Romans. The Emperor Claudius, it is recorded, once paid a sum of money computed to be equal to £50 for a single fish. The French sometimes call it *bécasse de mer* (sea woodcock) because it can be cooked without gutting, like woodcock; it is usually hung for 24 hours to increase the gamey flavour. If the fish is gutted, the liver, which is a great delicacy, should be left in it or incorporated in the sauce.

Because of its red colour, people sometimes confuse the Red mullet with the unrelated Red gurnard (*Trigla pini*), which has a more angular shape and does not have long barbels hanging from the underside of its mouth; the Red gurnard is not of the same quality.

The season for fresh Red mullet varies according to locality, but is generally during the summer months; fish imported from North Africa are available at other seasons and may be frozen.

Although prices are not what they were in Roman times, this is still not a cheap fish. Red mullet are very often sold already scaled. If they are to be gutted, this is best done through the gill opening. Recipes can be found in Alan Davidson's *Mediterranean Seafood* (Penguin), in any book on Mediterranean cookery and also in English cookery books, as *M. surmuletus* is caught off the south-western coasts of the British Isles. It does not reach North America.

Grey mullet. There are about a hundred species of Grey mullet (family Mugilidae), mainly in the warm seas. They are long, slender fish, usually in some shade of silver or grey and with large scales, but occasionally they are brightly coloured, like the Rainbow mullet from the Far East. They feed on weed, and some species, nicknamed *cochons de mer* (sea pigs) in France, swim far up estuaries with the tide. Species that frequent harbours are best avoided, as they can taste very nasty and at worst have their guts full of oil. Because of their vegetarian diet and ability to live in water of varying salinity, species of mullet are farmed in ponds and tanks; among them is the largest (up to 75 cm/30 in) and most widely distributed species, the common Grey mullet (*Mugil cephalus*),which in the US is called the Striped mullet (Black mullet in Florida). Particularly in the eastern Mediterranean area, mullets are plentiful and the female roes are salted and pressed to make *botargo.

Good species of Grey mullet, which are in general the ones that avoid ports, have firm, white flesh and a good taste. Among the best are the Grey mullet itself and the Golden grey mullet (*M. auratus*), which has golden spots on its gill covers. Most people will find difficulty in telling one species of Grey mullet from another, as the distinguishing features tend to be subtle. Mullets should be scaled carefully, as they bruise very easily, and gutted through the gills for preference, the roes being left inside. Some say that it is best to keep them for 24 hours before eating, but this service has usually been performed by the fishmonger. Others wash them in brine or vinegared water. This is a good fish, but not sensational.

[*Red mullet* – French: *rouget* German: *Meerbarbe* Italian: *triglia* Spanish: *salmonete*.

Grey mullet – French: *mulet gris* German: *grossköpfige Meeräsche* Italian: *cefalo* Spanish: *pardete*]

MUNG BEAN or **green gram** (*Phaseolus aureus*) is a tiny bean, which is usually green, but some varieties are yellow or black, and the latter can be confused from the outside with *black gram (which, to make matters worse, sometimes has green seeds).The difference is that the flesh of the seeds is yellow in mung and white in black gram.

Mung beans cook quickly without prior soaking. In total contrast to black gram, it is light, easily digested and 'cooling'. It has the reputation of not causing wind. In India, it is frequently given to invalids. It is eaten more as a whole grain or sprouted than split as a *dal. It is used particularly in recipes from Central and South India, although it is not a daily food. In China, too, it is often used as bean sprouts. The usual way to sprout these beans is to soak them overnight and then to hang them up loose in a wet sack which is occasionally dunked when it seems to be getting dry. The seed coats mostly come off when the sprouted gram is washed. Like all *sprouted legumes, mung sprouts should be very lightly cooked.

MUSCIAME. Dried dolphin meat, a speciality from the Ligurian and Tuscan coasts of Italy (Genoa, Camogli, Viareggio). Fishermen hate dolphins, which follow the fish and often break up the nets. The flesh of dolphins harpooned in the course of fishing (they are rarely deliberately hunted) is cut in strips, salted a few days, and hung in the rigging whenever the weather is sunny and there is a drying breeze. The finished product is hard as leather, black and usually covered in green mould. When this is wiped off with a cloth damped in vinegar, the *musciame* is finely sliced, marinated for half an hour in olive oil and often sprinkled with lemon juice like *bresaola. Slices are chewed with a slice of fresh garlic. It is an acceptable *zakouski* with vodka – the Polish painter Romain Bilinski used to serve it thus – but is perhaps only for the strong.

MUSHROOMS and other fungi provide some of the most delicious items in our diet, but most types, from *truffles downwards, are gathered in the wild. Continental Europeans are often fanatical about bringing in the yearly crop of wild fungi, which provides healthy exercise and the excitement of the chase. Pressure on some sorts of fungi is so great that they must be treated like game, with close seasons and laws to prevent them becoming extinct. As a friend wrote to me from Switzerland, 'Everyone knows his mushrooms to such an extent that if you come on one still standing after 4 a.m., you can be quite sure that it is no good, European countries have popular names for all the common or delicious sorts; to make sure that the boxes of wild fungi on sale in the markets are good, they

267

have professional fungus inspectors and regulations defining what may be sold (usually species that are not easily confused with poisonous ones).

Contrast this with the Anglo-Saxon approach, which is to regard all fungi except the Field mushroom (*Agaricus campestris*) as poisonous. The rule of thumb is also that it should grow in an open field and not in a wood or even near a tree. This is silly, because the best fungi grow in forests, and such prejudices deny people thousands of tons of free food every year. There are few popular names. Attempts to interest the British public in using 'toadstools' have so far failed. A brave and enterprising gentleman, William Delisle Hay, in 1887 wrote a book in which he gave hundreds of fungus recipes and invented many English names. He even gave the menu for a Fungus Feast, with ten courses and 32 dishes, starting with consommé of oak tongue and going on to puffball fritters with jam and savouries.

Most fungi are not poisonous. In Europe, a few people make themselves ill every year and perhaps one or two die from eating harmful species, but the casualty rate is minute when set against the total amount of fungus gathered, which reaches many thousand tons. Among European species, there are about half a dozen known killers, a number that will make the eater rather ill, and a lot that taste nasty; the majority are harmless, although they may not be worth gathering. It takes relatively little effort to learn how to recognize the really poisonous ones and to know the commonest and best edible sorts where you live. A feast will then await you when you scour the autumn woods.

Poisonous fungi. What complicates the fungus hunter's life is that the poisonous species are not restricted to a few easily recognizable groups but are scattered among the various sorts of fungi. Thus even the relatively safe and easily recognizable genus *Boletus* which includes the delicious *cèpe* (*B. edulis*) also embraces several unpleasantly bitter species and at least one poisonous but not deadly one, *B. satanas*. Anyone who wishes to eat wild fungi will not be content with the negative approach of merely recognizing the killers but will want to go after as many of the good ones as possible. For this, a good book on fungi, such as *Collins Guide to Mushrooms and Toadstools* by Morten Lange and F. Bayard Hora, is essential. The star performers among killer fungi belong to the genus *Amanita*, as do one or two quite delectable species such as the *oronge* (*A. caesarea*) and the tawny *grisette* (*A. fulva*). The species of *Amanita* have a ring round the stalk (but so do mushrooms) and a volva, an outer membrane that at first encloses the entire fungus but is ruptured as the cap expands. Usually it leaves a cup round the base of the stalk (so always dig doubtful specimens out of the ground) and often bits of broken volva on the cap. Unfortunately, the cup may have disintegrated or been eaten by snails and the bits washed off the cap by rain. A single specimen of anything may be misleading or atypical, which is why, at least to begin with, identification of fungi to eat should be made from several specimens.

Amanita muscaria, which has a red cap with white dots and is much favoured by gnomes and pixies, is far from being the most poisonous of the genus, although it used to be ground up in milk and used to kill flies – hence its name, fly agaric. It is hallucinogenic and seriously poisonous in quantity, especially when raw, but is eaten in small amounts by people who want to take a dangerous 'trip'. After treatment, it can be used as food, but it is not advisable to experiment with it. A similar but brown-capped species, *A. pantherina*, is more poisonous and causes serious nervous disorders; it can be confused with the blusher (*A. rubescens*) which is eaten in some places but is best avoided for risk of mistakes. It is advisable to reject all species of *Amanita* that, like these, have white gills, as they include the really deadly ones: the Death cap (*A. phalloides*) and its even more dangerous sisters, *A. vriosa*, *A. vema* and *A. bisporigera* – more dangerous because they are more easily confused with the Field mushroom (but edible mushrooms all have no volva and have gills that start pink or grey and get darker). In September 1918, 31 children died at a village near Poznan (which is now in Poland) when a few poisonous *Amanitas* got into the school stew. Even a taste can cause serious illness, and as little as 20 g (¾ oz) will kill.

Other deadly species include a tiny parasol mushroom, *Lepiota helveola*, and the small *Cortinarius orellanus* which is brownish red with a paler stem. This is so unlikely to be gathered that it has only recently been recognized as the runner-up to *Amanua phalloides* in the toxicity stakes; its symptoms are similar but may not develop for 15 days after eating. Various other species may cause vomiting or more serious digestive or nervous disorders, but are usually fatal only to the elderly or infirm. Many of them belong to genera that include edible species, such as *Corinarius* (again), *Clitocybe*, *Tricholoma*, *Ramaria*, *Russula* and *Agaricus*. As this last genus includes the mushrooms, it is worth mentioning here that the two species which can be poisonous, *A. xanthoderma* and *A. placomyces,* can be detected because the flesh at the base of the stalk (and sometimes other parts) in both species goes bright yellow immediately it is cut.

When you are about to take a new fungus into your repertoire, it is best to start by eating just one and to wait a few days to make sure that there are no ill effects. What you should not do is listen too much to local advice. Local people will teach you about the good kinds they know but will often say that perfectly good fungi are poisonous when they are not. In the Caspian area of Iran I once noticed a village green so covered with what looked like mushrooms that I stopped the Land-Rover and went to investigate. I thought I had better ask for permission before picking any, as they turned out to be a species of field mushroom and it looked as if the villagers were purposefully growing them. They warned me that the mushrooms were poisonous. It is always possible that what goes in one country is not the same in another. I therefore ate only one that night. Later we returned and picked baskets full, but the people of the village never believed us.

Many fungi which are excellent to eat when cooked, salted, dried or otherwise treated, are poisonous when raw. For this reason, never go into a market and buy unknown fungi without asking how they should be prepared. Other fungi may be good if fresh, but dangerous stale. Into this category comes *Gyromitra esculenta*, an odd-looking fungus that resembles a tangled coil of rope on a stem, rather than having the conventional toadstool shape. The knobbly cap is brownish, and the stem whitish. In spite of its name, *esculenta*, and the fact that it is sold in many Continental markets, it is poisonous when raw but safe when dried – and then only if the specimens were fresh and not rotted. As some people are allergic to it anyway, care is necessary.

I have only once been poisoned by fungus. I had eaten at a restaurant in Ulm in South Germany. Following dinner with a senior German businessman from Cologne, I woke at about two in the morning on the verge of vomiting and promptly made myself sick. After drinking several glasses of water, I repeated the process. I was trembling and in not very good shape, but eventually went back to bed. In the morning, I learned that the businessman had been taken back to Cologne by ambulance, following a heart attack. A call to the hospital revealed that the diagnosis had been incorrect – he had fungus poisoning. The wrong one from an inadequately checked batch had got into the dish. After prompt action, I was suffering no more than a slight headache.

The unpleasant effects of fungi are not always straightforward. There is the case of *Coprinus atramentarius*, a small species of ink cap, which grows commonly in clumps in grassy places, especially on manure. It is mentioned here not because it is very poisonous, but because it causes alarming symptoms to people who are drinking or are allergic to it. The substance that causes the symptoms is the same as a drug called Antabuse which is produced from another source and is used in the treatment of alcoholism.

First aid. Make yourself sick. Most people need only to press with a finger far back on the tongue; keep on doing this, then drink plenty of water and repeat the process. It is prudent, in cases of doubt, to keep the vomit in the hope that experts will be able to identify the fungus causing the trouble. Also, retrieve any trimmings from the dustbin. If the mushroom has been digested, castor oil (15 g or one tablespoon to a child and twice that amount to an adult) can be given. Drink plenty of water. If it is known that *Amanita phalloides* (or its friends) have been eaten, give a teaspoon of salt in a glass of water every 30 minutes and race the victim to hospital, although it may already be too late.

Cultivated fungi. Attempts to cultivate edible fungi have been made with some success from the earliest times. *Agrocybe aegerita* was grown by the ancient Greeks and Romans on discs of poplar, and goodness knows how long the Chinese and the Japanese have been growing other species on logs of oak, pine or chestnut – for instance, the *shiitake* (*Lentinus edodes*) and *matsutake* (*Tricholoma matsutake*), the cultivation of which is documented in Japan as far back as AD 199.The mushroom *Agaricus bisporus*, a species that grows on dung rather than among grass, was first cultivated in Paris at the turn of the 18th century, and for this reason is still called *champignon de Paris* in many countries. Mushrooms were grown on composted horse manure at first outdoors, but later in cellars. They vary from white to russet brown and may be scaly; some are very dense and hard, others soft and more like the Field mushroom. No cultivated mushrooms have the flavour of wild mushrooms, especially as buttons, and devices such as sweating them in vine leaves or cooking them with a fine sliver of garlic are attempts to improve matters. The inclusion of a few dried and soaked *Boletus* is another method. In the past, button mushrooms or larger ones with slightly open caps were sold; the stalks were separated for soups and flavouring. The stage at which mushrooms are picked depends on market preference and on growers' considerations. For one thing, once caps are open and the spores ripe (the gills have gone brown), it is easier for disease to spread round the production unit if it happens to be introduced. At one time, large open mushrooms were sold cheaply and were not grown intentionally, but they are now common as they have a better flavour.

In warmer countries, which have come under Chinese influence and where the temperature is not below 21°C (70°F), the Paddy Straw fungus (*Volvariella volvacea*) is commonly cultivated on rotting rice straw. It is best gathered as a button, with the volva still intact. These are excellent edible fungi, whether fresh or dried.

Other species can be cultivated, such as the Ink Cap (*Coprinus comatus*), which has too short a life to be a commercial proposition, and various wood fungi, such as Chinese Wood ears (*Auricularia polytricha*) and even Horns of Plenty (*Craterellus cornucopioides*). Unfortunately, most of the best will not thrive on dead wood or rotting vegetation alone, but need to be in a symbiotic relationship with the roots of growing plants or trees. Some success has attended the cultivation of morels and even truffles, but may be limited to planting the necessary trees and introducing the fungus into the place, rather than the intensive production used for mushrooms.

Dried fungi. Huge quantities of fungi are dried and can be bought in the shops. They vary from the sliced and dried *cèpes (Boletus edulis)*, which have a meaty flavour and are much used in Italian cooking (as *funghi porcini*), to the Chinese Wood ear. The Paddy Straw fungus from China is dried over charcoal for 12 hours. If these dried mushrooms get damp, they acquire a bad smell which goes when they are cooked.

The Japanese *shiitake* and *matsutake* are mainly dried in the sun or over charcoal fires, but they are also available canned or pickled. These fungi must be used or preserved when young and just beginning to produce white spore powder. After that, they become tough.

Dried fungi are very useful in the kitchen, and should be kept handy as a flavouring. *Funghi porcini*

need to be rinsed in warm water before use, and other species may have to be soaked for up to 24 hours. The easiest fungus to dry at home is the Fairy Ring mushroom (*Morasmium oreades*), which is common in fields and is easily recognized. It is necessary only to string the caps on cotton thread and to hang them in a warm, dry place. Once bone-dry, they can be put into jars, and they keep indefinitely.

Pickled fungi, salted fungi, and fungi under oil. Some countries with extensive forests, such as Russia, produce a glut of wild fungi, and pickling or salting are of great importance. Indeed, some of the species which are not so good when fresh (e.g. the Russian or Polish *gruzd, Lactarius scrobiculatus*) and are perhaps too acrid or even poisonous, become sought after and expensive once treated. In Britain, the only use made of the huge quantities of wild mushrooms that once grew (before pastures were ploughed up and stagged) was to extract the juices with salt and make mushroom *ketchup. Ordinary bottling must be done with care to avoid botulism, and a pressure cooker should be used. There are many methods of preserving fungi with salt, vinegar or oil.

Wild fungi are gathered all over the world. Some of them are large enough to make a meal for several people (I have a photograph of one from Zaire which is big enough to use as an umbrella); others are tiny. I would recommend particularly the *Boletus* species, which it is almost impossible to go wrong with, since the 'sponge' (where the gills are normally) keeps them entirely separate from any lethal species. Inedible species of *Boletus* either taste horrid or are only mildly poisonous.

When gathering fungi, it is best to take a flat basket or trug, and to lay the specimens down carefully, after inspecting them and cutting off the dirty stalk. Put the stalk downwards, so that grit cannot fall into the sponge or gills. Doubtful species should be kept quite separate until identified, as the spores from poisonous kinds can contaminate the others. Do not eat soft, old or maggoty specimens, as some species then become harmful.

In a peasant economy, people gather everything edible, and keen fungus amateurs may do the same just for fun. However, the cook, especially to begin with, had best limit the search to the very best fungi from a gastronomic viewpoint and to the sorts which are plentiful locally. There is a great divergence in opinion as to which fungi are best, and those most sought after in one country may be considered inferior in another. For instance, in Mediterranean countries, the Field mushroom is rated only second class. Culinary value varies sharply between species in the same genus. Thus, the Jew's ear (*Auricularia auricula*), which is closely related to the Chinese Wood ear, tastes of very little. Experts, too, differ in their opinions – Jane Grigson in *The Mushroom Feast* (Grub Street) writes off the St George's mushroom (*Tricholoma gambosum*),which fungus books rate very highly, in the last resort, you have to make up your own mind.

[*Mushroom* – French: *champignon* German: *Pilz* Italian: *fungo* Spanish: *hongo*]

MUSSELS. Familiar bivalves, mussels of various species are found in most seas and are usually dark blue to almost black, but may be yellowish brown, and one New Zealand species is bright green. The species found in Europe are the Edible mussel (*Mytilis edulis*) and the Mediterranean mussel (*M. galloprovincialis*), which are very similar and overlap in distribution. *M. edulis* and the similar *M. californianus* are found on the West Coast of the US and are sometimes sold in San Francisco. On the whole, though, Americans do not eat mussels, except locally on the coast or among particular ethnic groups. In Britain, the neglect of the mussel is not traditional: in the middle of the 19th century, mussels were 'farmed' in Britain to the extent that people complained of harbours being blocked. Today, there are mussel farms, *bouchots*, around the coasts of France and of many other European countries where mussels are keenly eaten. They will no doubt be cultivated even more in the future on account of the tremendous bulk of protein per acre that they make (4,535 kg or 10,000 lb of mussel meat per acre). Mussels take three years to grow to some 5 cm (2 in) long. They prefer slightly brackish water and tend to grow best near estuaries or in harbours, as the Victorians complained. In these days, such locations also offer sewage and pollution – if you gather your own, bear this in mind and make sure that your catch has come from a clean place.

Although other members of the mussel family lie buried upright in mud or bore into rocks, the mussels of the genus *Mytilus* attach themselves to rocks and harbour piles, or to the hurdles and ropes of the mussel farms, with a bunch of horny hairs called the byssus or beard. In the more civilized (and so usually more polluted) countries, mussels spend some time in purifying tanks before being sold. Even so, a few people are allergic to mussels, and even in the last century it had been observed that at certain seasons some suffered from rashes, asthma and other typically allergic reactions after eating them. Mussels, like oysters, can be poisonous, although the poison can be destroyed by cooking the mussels. Most people can eat mussels regularly all their lives without experiencing anything but benefit, since they are rich in *trace elements. Unless you are certain that mussels have been cleansed, place them in clean water with a little salt dissolved in it (some people put in a little flour or oatmeal) for a couple of hours, but no more or they will asphyxiate. Mussels must always be scraped to remove barnacles and weed, then scrubbed and well washed to get rid of sand.

The byssus should be gently pulled out. Any shells that gape should be thrown out, as should any that feel very heavy – they are likely to be full of mud. Use only fresh, live mussels, which pull their shells together strongly when disturbed. There are commercial methods of cleansing using recirculated water under ultraviolet light – the mussels are sick and thus their stomachs are emptied.

The clean mussels are opened by putting them wet into a pan – not a deep layer, and cooking on a high heat with the pan lid on tight. It may be necessary to add a few spoons of water or a dash of white wine (according to the recipe), but they should not be swamped with liquid. The moment the mussels are all open (it takes only a couple of minutes), they must be removed. Strain the juice through a cloth to remove any sand and use the liquid for sauce. To overcook mussels is to shrink and toughen them. Cold mussels can be served on the half-shell with mayonnaise. If sprinkled with lemon juice, covered with garlic butter and heated briefly in the oven, they make a delicious *hors d'oeuvre*. The recipes for mussels range from the relatively straightforward *moules marinière* (white wine and shallot) and *moules à la crème* (in cream) of Normandy to *mitili ripieni alla spezzina* (mussels stuffed with a mixture of spinach, minced meat, ham and Parmesan cheese, bound with egg and cooked in a light tomato sauce), a speciality of the Italian Riviera.

Smoked mussels can mainly be bought preserved in oil. They are made as follows: cooked mussels are removed from their shells and soaked for five minutes in a brine of 250 g salt per litre water (40 oz per gallon).They are then dipped in oil and smoked on mesh trays, in Britain for 30 minutes at 82°C (180°F) – elsewhere they are sometimes dried for 25 minutes, then smoked for a further 25 minutes at 71°C (160°F) – before being packed into jars, covered with oil and heat-processed in water at 121°C (250°F or 15 lb per sq in. pressure in a pressure cooker). A 225 g (8 oz) jar requires some 15 minutes. Smoked mussels are rather sweet. Though they are sometimes served as part of an *hors d'oeuvre* or as a cocktail snack, smoked mussels are perhaps better in combination than alone.

[*Mussel* – French: *moule* German: *Muschel* Italian: *mitilo, muscolo* Spanish: *mejillón*]

MUSTARD. The three species of mustard plant are all crucifers related to the cabbage, but they have quite different characteristics.

The exceedingly pungent Black mustard (*Brassica nigra*) is probably a native of Europe and grows wild as an escape in North America. The plant is very big – it can grow up to 2 m (6 ft) high – and as it drops its seeds very easily, it is not suitable for mechanical farming. It is thus grown less today than it was in the past, although it is the traditional seed to use in making condiment mustard.

White mustard (*Sinapis alba*) is also probably a native of Mediterranean Europe and is the mustard of mustard and cress (although rape seed is now often substituted).The seed is large, pale yellow and much milder in flavour than Black mustard. It has a characteristic taste which you can recognize quickly as being typical of American mustards. A little White mustard is used in English mustard, but it is forbidden in Dijon mustard.

Brown mustard, sometimes also called Indian mustard (*Brassica juncea*), has seed which looks rather like that of Black mustard but is a lighter brown or reddish. Although it is not as hot as Black mustard, Brown mustard has tended to replace it in condiment mustards in recent years because it can be harvested mechanically. Varieties of *Brassica juncea* from India have a rather rough taste if they are used for making European mustards, but their use is correct in Indian cooking, and after frying their taste is merely nutty. Mustard oil (*see* fats and oils) is important in Indian cooking.

The pungency of mustard comes from an essential oil which forms through enzyme action when ground mustard seed is mixed with water. (Hence if the enzymes are destroyed by heat no hotness is produced.)

When mustard powder is mixed, it must be left for 10-15 minutes before it develops its full strength. Mixing mustard powder with vinegar, salt or boiling water is inadvisable, since the treatment destroys part of the enzymes and may leave unconverted glucosides which are bitter, though vinegar and salt may be added after the taste has developed. White mustard seed, though not so well flavoured as black, can be useful because it contains enzymes that are less easily inactivated than those of black mustard. White mustard is also strongly preservative, which is why it is often included in the spices for pickle.

Mustard has been used as a spice for thousands of years. In Shakespeare's day, the mustard used in England was in the form of a thick sauce; it was later sold as a powder. A particularly fine quality was developed by Jeremiah Colman in Norwich during the 19th century, so much so that today English powdered mustard is virtually synonomous with the name of Colman. It contains wheat flour and turmeric as well as powdered huskless mustard seed. Mustard powder is the mustard to use in English recipes, for fish sauces, and sauces for vegetables – particularly vegetables of the cabbage family – for Welsh rarebit, and so on. A little powdered mustard in mayonnaise helps to stabilize the emulsion, as well as adding its flavour, but the practice is not universally approved of as it spoils the taste.

In recent years, mixed mustards have once more become popular in Britain as they have been for a long time on the Continent and in America. Of French mustards, the best known in England used to be the dark Bordeaux mustard (an imitation of it still seems to be every steak bar's idea of French mustard); Bordeaux was the port from which it was easily exported. Bordeaux mustard is mild and rather dark, because the whole seed, including the seed coat, is ground up to make it. It contains vinegar, sugar, tarragon and other herbs and spices and has a rather mild flavour. It is suitable for eating with foods that need a pickle-like complement, such as sliced sausages. It is not surprising, then, that German mustards, though quite distinctive, are generally of the Bordeaux type. Dijon mustard, on the other hand, is pale in colour (the seed coat is removed) much more pungent and with a cleaner taste of mustard. It is the mustard to eat with foods when it has to bring out and not mask their natural flavour (steaks, for instance, should never be eaten with Bordeaux mustard). It is also the type of mustard to be used in French recipes unless otherwise specified. American mustard (such as is eaten with hot-dogs) is very mild and consists mostly of ground white mustard and turmeric. An

English mixed mustard, Savora, developed at the turn of the century, is very popular in South America and France, but is too sweet and slimy for some tastes. More recently, dozens of other mustard types have been developed, some red, some bright green, mostly rather mild and very aromatic.

The most striking development in recent years, though, has been the vogue for grainy mustards. This has been traced to a mention in the back of Elizabeth David's *Spices, Salt and Aromatics in the English Kitchen* (Grub Street): 'If you ever see a French mustard in a grey stoneware jar, with a label bearing the name Pommery, buy it.' Inspired by these words, a fledgling entrepreneur brought a small truckload of this Moutarde de Meaux back from France and started a fashion for mustards made with whole crushed mustard seeds. Many other *moutardes à l'ancienne* have followed. Some are nice; others are beastly.

[*Mustard* – French: *moutarde* German: *Senf* Italian: *senape, mostarda* Spanish: *mostaza*]

MUSTARD GREENS. *See* Chinese cabbage.

MUTTON and **LAMB**. Sheep and *goats have been domesticated for many thousands of years. They are very closely related, and indeed, as travellers will know, it is not always easy to tell them apart. Sheep, however, are of very much greater importance as a source of meat and very much less important in Europe as a source of milk; the most celebrated use of ewe's milk is in Roquefort cheese. In Britain alone, there used to be 30 breeds of sheep, from the mature ewes weighing about 25 kg (55 lb) of sheep to the enormous Oxford Down with ewes weighing 110 kg (240 lb). In the Middle East there are the goat-like sheep of the deserts, the fat-tailed sheep, and even the fat-bottomed steatopygous sheep. The small sheep with orange spots in Islamic countries are not naturally spotted. The spots are painted on them with henna, and they are awaiting sacrifice for some feast.

Since the beginning of the last century, there has been a great change of opinion over the relative merits of mutton and lamb. Victorians considered young sheep tasteless and preferred mutton of 3-6 years old. 'Mutton of two years old is flabby, pale and savourless' is hardly an opinion one would read today. 'To suit the palate of an epicure, a sheep should never be killed earlier than its third or later than its fifth year, at which age the mutton will be firm and succulent, dark coloured and full of the richest gravy.' In these days, people are so afraid of

mutton being tough that in some places it cannot be sold as mutton but has inaccurately to be called lamb. Technically, a lamb is under a year – modern breeds put on weight very quickly. Indeed it is not economic for farmers to sell mutton any more because of the extra feed required, unless they can charge much more for it than for lamb. But the public expects to pay less for mutton than for lamb, and the mutton offered is mostly from old breeding ewes, which are killed at 3-4 years, before they need false teeth. Ewe mutton is likely to be too tough for roasting but is lovely boiled with herbs and eaten with onion, soubise or caper sauce, or pressure cooked and minced or curried. Fine mutton, reared to eat, is an expensive luxury and difficult to get. It is usually killed at 15-18 months.

Another speciality is milk-fed baby lamb, 3-4 weeks old and weighing 4-5 kg (9-11 lb), the ovine equivalent of sucking pig. This is technically known as 'house lamb' in Britain; it is a lamb born in winter, raised in shelter in a house or barn, and fed on milk. In France, such a lamb is the *agnelet* or Pauillac lamb. In Italy, roasted *abbacchio* or *agnello di latte* is a famous Roman dish, (some find kid, *capretto di latte*, even better).These very young animals may be rather tasteless and lacking in fat for some tastes.

Milk lamb should be eaten fresh, without hanging. Young lamb loses flavour after 3-4 days and is best after 2-3 days, depending on the weather. It used to be hung for three weeks. When a 'high' taste was generally liked, cooks went further and used mutton to imitate venison by making a gravy of woodcocks or other game birds that had gone too far to be roasted for table. Mutton is hung for a week.

Grass-fed lambs do not have much flavour at two months, when they weigh 7-8 kg (15-18 lb), and the ideal lamb is 3-4 months old and weighs at least 10 kg (22 lb). Big lambs can be 8-9 months old. The traditional season for lamb in Britain started at Easter and went on through the summer, with lambs coming from further and further north; by July and August, the lambs were coming from Scotland, and the season ended in November with lamb from the Hebrides. The top season was June and July. Nowadays, the old seasons do not have the same meaning, because of freezing and the evolution of breeds such as the Dorset Horn which lamb twice a year. However, autumn-born lambs do not have the flavour of spring-born ones as they have not been fed on fresh spring flowers and grass. Frozen lamb, which began to come from Australia and New Zealand during the 19th century, can now be so good as to be preferable to home-grown lamb during the off-season in winter.

Mountain breeds of sheep are in general rather active creatures and even the lambs can be tougher than those of lowland breeds, but they have a fine flavour. 'The mountain sheep are sweeter but the valley sheep are fatter.' Other famous mountain breeds are the Herdwick from Cumberland, the Cheviot and the Scottish black-face. On the other hand, yearlings raised on salt meadows near the sea have a very special flavour and are famous in gastronomy as *pré-salé*. The hardy little sheep from the Scottish islands, such as Soays, are also getting a reputation for excellence of flavour.

It is worth defining a few farming terms for sheep which will not trouble you in the butchers but might affect cooks who buy whole carcasses for the freezer. Hoggets and tegs are sheep that are over a year old – and therefore mutton – but less than two. Wethers are castrated male sheep, which have more meat compared to bone than young ewes but are not reckoned to be as sweet and moist.

There is disagreement over the best cuts, just as there is over the best age. In Victorian times, the front half of the sheep was regarded more highly than the rear, and many will agree that, though it is difficult to carve (and less meaty), the shoulder is nearly always better than the leg, while the often-despised breast is the tastiest part of all. Nowadays, lamb, like most other meat, is bred to have little fat – too little for the best taste. In Britain, the traditional accompaniment is mint sauce and in the US, mint jelly, but mutton and lamb combine well with many herbs and spices. Garlic and rosemary have been known even in Britain for many years, but another method is to rub the joint with powdered ginger before roasting it. Welsh mountain lamb – one of the best – is traditionally served with *laver. Another possibility is redcurrant jelly or alternatively rowan jelly. Boiled lamb would more likely be eaten with onion or caper sauce, but pickled samphire is also traditional and good. Other countries offer a whole gamut of lamb and mutton recipes, particularly in the Middle East, where they often contain cinnamon, which goes well with mutton. (*See* also *qawwrama*.)

Mutton hams are produced in many places. In Britain, they are traditionally made in the Border country between England and Scotland, and they are also made in several Muslim countries where eating pork is forbidden. There is even mutton bacon.

As always with meat, differences in cuts between countries can cause confusion. Thus, if both back legs are joined together and include the loin, then we have a joint for a grand occasion, a baron. Half the baron, i.e. one back leg with half the loin is a quarter. The shoulder can be whole, boned and rolled, or turned into fancy cuts, such as the American mock duck.

Essentially, the body apart from the limbs and their attachments can be divided into the back to the rear of the ribs and the back over the ribs, leading to the neck. The division is marked by the diaphragm, which separates the abdominal cavity from the chest. The back to the rear of the ribs is the loin. The back over the ribs is divided in Britain into best end of neck (the bit to the rear) and middle neck (leading to the scrag or neck). The whole part in the US is more simply called the ribs. As the middle neck chops lie under the shoulder blade, the chops from under the ribs are called 'uncovered' (*découvertes*). Each side of the back over the ribs is a *carre*, and two of them put together inside out in a circle make an American cut, the crown roast. In France, the long bony rib bit of the chops is removed as a flat, ribby piece, the *haute de côtelettes*. A not very attractive square of bone, periosteum and intercostal muscle, it nevertheless is excellent for a tasty *ragoût*.

Fat-tailed sheep and **fat-bottomed sheep**. The tails of most sheep are docked when they are lambs, because in long-wool breeds the tail gets clogged with manure and encourages flies. The shepherd fills his basket with lamb's tails and testicles as he goes through the flock; although this collection was the basis for a tasty shepherd's dish in times past, the tails were otherwise of no importance in Britain. However, fat-tailed sheep are bred for their enormously fat tails. Tails can weigh as much as 35 kg (80 lb). As the sheep have to drag their tails, the shepherds tie boards under them to protect them from the stoney ground; they sometimes even use wheels. Fat-tailed sheep are commonly reared in many countries of the Middle East, although usually not to the excessive state I have described. There was also a Cape breed of fat-tailed sheep. In the fat-bottomed sheep, the tail is reduced to a mere stump sticking out of an enlarged backside. In fact, both peculiarities are adaptations of nature to store food in hard, desert conditions and are equivalent to the camel's hump – bushmen living in the Kalahari desert also grew enormous fat bottoms at certain seasons. The meat of fat-tailed sheep usually has a strong but delicious taste, perhaps given it by the desert herbs.

[*Mutton* – French: *mouton* German: *Hammelfleisch* Italian: *montane* Spanish: *carnero*

Lamb – French: *agneau* German: *junges Hammelfleisch* Italian: *agnello* Spanish: *cordero*]

MYRTLE (*Myrtus communis*) is a plant with fragrant white flowers and leaves which grows wild in Mediterranean countries. Leaves are used for wrapping pork or stuffing small birds to impart its aroma after roasting and while the food is waiting to come to table. The black berries are edible, and can be eaten on a walk or dried and used in the same way as juniper, although they are milder. The Sardinians make oil from the ripe berries and, according to Elizabeth David, claim that it is superior to olive oil for frying fish.

[*Myrtle* – French: *myrte* German: *Myrte* Italian: *mirto, mortella* Spanish: *arrayán, mirto*]

MYRTLE PEPPER. *See* allspice.

MYSOST. *See* whey.

n

NAM PLA. The salty, matured fish sauce of Thailand, the equivalent of other 'rotten fish' sauces from South East Asian countries, such as *ngapi*. It is used both in cooking and as a condiment. The taste is much less fishy than the liquid from salted anchovies. In fact, if you didn't know what it was, you would probably think it was rather salty soy sauce.

NAPLES MEDLAR. *See* rowan.

NARA NUT. *See* butternut.

NASEBERRY. *See* sapodilla.

NASTOIKA. *See* galangal.

NASTURTIUM or **Indian cress** (*Tropaeolum majus*). This well-known garden plant, a native of Peru, has leaves with a cress-like flavour and can be used in salads. The flowers are also good to eat and for making nasturtium vinegar. The large fruits, when still green and tender, can be pickled by putting them in well-salted vinegar as they form, and they make a very nice, slightly pungent pickle, which can be used in a similar way to capers, although the taste is not identical.

[*Nasturtium* – French: *capucine, cresson d'Inde* German: *Kapuzinerkresse* Italian: *nasturzio* Spanish: *capuchina, nasturcia*]

NATIVE. *See* oyster.

NAVY BEAN. Variety of *kidney bean.

NECTARINE. *See* peach.

NEPAL PEPPER. *See* chilli.

NETTLE. There are many species of nettle (*Urtica*), some of which have a savage sting. Of the three European species, the Stinging nettle (*Urtica dioica*), which is distributed in temperate regions throughout the world, has been used since ancient times as a source of fibre – nettle cloth is excellent – and in spring the young tops are eaten before other vegetables come in. The stinging hairs are destroyed by boiling, but the nettle tops must be gathered with gloves. Cooked in the water that is left on them after washing, plus a little butter, they make a tasty green vegetable which was once considered to purify the blood (they even used to be forced under glass). Nettles were sometimes blanched by earthing them up, but that destroys part of their value, and they are sweet enough without. My grandmother, who came from Lancashire where nettle beer used to be sold on stalls, made it every year for the men working in the hayfield. At that season, great stone flagons frequently exploded in the larder during the night, or so it seemed to me as a child. Nettle beer is an excellent drink, more delicious and refreshing than ginger beer.

....

Nettle Beer

A bucket full of nettle tops and 4 good handfuls of dandelion leaves makes 9 lt (16 pt) of nettle beer. Some people also add a few handfuls of goose-grass (or cleavers – *Galium aparine* – a common plant that sticks to clothing) and other herbs. Boil the lot in the 9 lt (16 pt) of water with 50 g (2 oz) of bruised ginger. After 40 minutes' boiling, strain off the liquid and add to it about 2 cups of brown sugar plus the juice of a lemon for acidity. When the liquid is almost cool, float 25 g (1 oz) of yeast on top and leave it to ferment for 6-7 hours. Skim, stir in a tablespoon of cream of tartar and bottle, leaving room for expanding gas. The beer is ready as soon as it is judged gassy enough.

[*Nettles* – French: *ortie* German: *Nessel* Italian: *ortica* Spanish: *ortiga*]

....

NGAPI. From Burmese *nga* (fish) and *pi* (rotten, decayed), this is a dark grey paste of decomposed fish used in Burma as a relish and flavouring; without it Burmese food would be incomplete. The best quality is said to come from Moulmein, and the beauty of the local girls is attributed to its body-building qualities. The liquid drained from *ngapi* is similar to the Malaysian *balachan*, Vietnamese **nuoc nam*, the Thai **nam pla*, and is used in much the same manner. In Burma, the seed of the jungle tree (*Pithecolobium lobatum*) is also used, raw or cooked, under the name *ngapi* nut; it has a strong smell, reminiscent of *ngapi* itself.

NIACIN. *See* vitamins.

NICOTINIC ACID. *See* vitamins (niacin).

NIGELLA (*Nigella sativa*) is a plain-looking species of love-in-the-mist with creamy flowers; it is grown for its black seed which has a spicy taste and is sometimes known as *quatre épices* in France. It is a moderately important spice in Indian cooking and is often confused with onion seed and with black **cumin*. In Punjabi cooking, it is sometimes mixed with sesame seed and sprinkled on *nan* bread before baking.

[*Nigella* – French: *nigelle* German: *Schwarzkümmel* Italian: *nigella* Spanish: *neguilla, pasionara*]

NITRITES are formed from nitrates – potassium nitrate or **saltpetre* and sodium nitrate or **Chile saltpetre* – by heating or by the action of bacteria during the brining of meat. Nitrites turn meat pink and, even in small quantities, are lethal against many sorts of bacteria. Nitrites are also toxic to humans in any but very small amounts; the maximum amount permitted in food is officially laid down in most countries. Quantities used by commercial curers are of the order of 7-15 g (¼ to ½ oz) for 45 kg (100 lb) of meat, which in household quantities would require such accurate measurement that the use of nitrites as such in the home must be ruled out.

Fortunately, nitrite poisoning is rare. A well-documented outbreak did occur a few years ago in the US, when a waiter put sodium nitrite in restaurant salt-cellars by mistake. A number of citizens were admitted to hospital having turned blue – a symptom of nitrite poisoning. Good detective work was necessary to trace the offending restaurant, since only some of the salt cellars had been filled, and only those customers who had salted their breakfast lavishly were ill. Most of the poisoned also turned out to have hangovers, which cause an increased demand for salt. Nitrites (and so the nitrates from which they form) are currently under suspicion of combining with meat to form nitrosamines which are carcinogenic, but so far no safer substitute has been found to guard against botulism in preserved meats.

[*Nitrate* – French: *nitrate* German: *Nitrat* Italian: *nitrato, azotato* Spanish: *nitrato*]

NIXTAMAL. *See* masa.

NON-DAIRY CREAMER. *See* milk (milk substitutes).

NOODLES in oriental cooking may be made from wheat flour, with or without eggs, much in the manner of Italian **pasta*. However, many other types are called for in Chinese recipes and may be obtained from Chinese shops around the world. Noodles made of rice flour, which have a flavour of their own, are sometimes fried until they puff up, or soaked briefly and stir-fried, or used in dishes with anything from pork to lily buds. Noodles made with a basis of mung bean are as shiny as nylon and need soaking before they are cooked. They are mainly mixed with other ingredients; although they are rather tasteless, they have a special gelatinous texture when cooked. Noodles can be made from all manner of starchy substances, such as arrowroot.

Japanese noodles include *udon*, which is similar to macaroni, and *somen*, which is like vermicelli. *Soba* is thin buckwheat noodles, while *chasoba* (tea *soba*) is made of buckwheat and green tea. *Harusame* is made with soya bean. *Shirataki* is a very fine vermicelli which is made from a glutinous, yam-like tuber, devil's tongue (*Amorphophallus kanjac*).

[*Noodle* – French: *nouille* German: *Nudel* Italian: *pasta* Spanish: *pasta*]

NOPALES. *See* prickly pear.

NOYAU. To good peasants who do not like to waste anything, the kernels of apricots, peaches, plums and cherries present a challenge. Like bitter *almonds, they contain a glucoside which, when mixed with water (or the saliva in the mouth) is converted by enzymes into a mixture of benzaldehyde and deadly poisonous hydrocyanic acid. Noyau (from the French *noyau*, a fruit stone) is a *liqueur, cordial and useful flavouring, which consists essentially of a sugar syrup, usually with alcohol, flavoured with macerated kernels or sometimes with peach leaves or bitter almonds, which contain similar principles. Noyau had a reputation for being 'unwholesome' – naturally so, if there was cyanide in it. However, a quick boil will drive off the volatile poison, leaving only a delicate taste of benzaldehyde behind.

Noyau

Collect apricot stones, peach stones and plum stones. Wash them and dry them in the sun. When you have enough to produce a cup of kernels, crack them by hitting on the edge with a hammer, and extract the nuts. Put them through the liquidizer with water and leave them to macerate overnight. Strain the liquid, squeezing the last drops out with a cloth. Add enough sugar to make a syrup and boil for a minute. Cool. Add a little lemon juice gradually, tasting, adding more sugar (or honey if you like) until you get the balance to your liking. The acid lemon will have made a cloudy precipitate form. Let it settle, then decant the clear liquid and mix it with an equal quantity of brandy – the rather sweet Spanish 103 brand is excellent for this – or any grape or other spirits will do, provided the flavour is not too pronounced. The noyau can be drunk immediately and usually is.

NORI. *See* seaweed.

NORWAY LOBSTER. *See* scampi.

NUOC NAM is the best known of the salty, matured fish sauces and is very important in the cooking of Vietnam and adjacent Laos and Cambodia. It is available in specialist shops, and quite generally in France where the old colonial connection is still evident. Its simplest use is as a dipping sauce.

NUTMEG is the seed of a tree (*Myristica fragrans*) that is native to the Molucca Islands of Indonesia, but now grown in other tropical countries, notably in Grenada. Nutmegs should be bought whole (if they are white, they have been treated with lime), as ground nutmeg quickly loses its fragrance. A small grater kept in the jar with the nutmegs is a convenience. In quantity, nutmeg is a narcotic, but in ordinary amounts it is a most useful flavouring for meat, fish, vegetables (especially onions and spinach), sweets and cakes. The aril around the nutmeg seed is *mace.

[*Nutmeg* – French: *muscade* German: *Muskatnuss* Italian: *noce moscata* Spanish: *nuez moscada*]

NUT. Any large, dry fruit or seed with a hard shell and edible kernel is called a nut. There are hundreds of different kinds, most of them unknown outside the areas in which they grow, and the definition also covers sunflower seeds, melon seeds and other kernels which many people would perhaps not regard as nuts.

When thoroughly dry, most nuts may be stored in their shells for varying periods, depending on the kind, and can be held for longer periods in cold storage provided they are left in the shell.

Commercially, nuts are graded and, if they are for dessert use, the shells may be bleached or dyed to improve the appearance. However, the bulk of the nuts produced for sale are cracked and shelled in the factory, since the public prefers the convenience, even though nuts keep better in the shell, which protects them from the oxygen of the air and from micro-organisms. Many kinds go rancid rather easily once they have been shelled, unless they are packed in gas or in a vacuum. Rancid nuts are not only unpleasant but actually harmful.

Nuts are generally rich in oil. The very oily nuts like walnuts, pecans and Brazils have around 65% fats, and even the less oily peanut has 50%.The oils are released from the cells by pounding. Some nuts, however, like chestnuts and acorns, are mainly carbohydrate. As many nuts are also rich in calcium and iron (e.g. almonds and Brazils), as well as being high in potassium and low in sodium, they have important possibilities in the diet. A few (e.g. peanuts) are also high in protein.

Nut butters can be made from any of the oily nuts. The best known, of course, is peanut almonds, cashew nuts, Brazil nuts and even walnuts and pine nuts, although the product tends to be too oily. Nut butters can easily be made at home using the special nut butter attachment of a nut mill or even a meat mincer.

Details and techniques are given in the appropriate sections.

The most important nuts are *almonds, *peanuts, *Brazil nuts, *hazel nuts, *walnuts, *chestnuts, *coconuts, and *pistachio nuts. These are always generally available and are most used in cooking. A few other nuts, such as the *macadamia and the *cashew have recently become popular or, like *candlenuts, feature in important regional cooking styles. There are, however, many other nuts, especially from the tropics, which are of local importance and will be met with by travellers or as an occasional curiosity, but are not regularly exported.

[*Nut* – French: *noix* German: *Nuss* Italian: *noce* Spanish: *nuez*]

O

OATS and **OATMEAL**. Oats (*Avena sativa*) have been cultivated at least since the Bronze Age and in Britain since the Iron Age, but their origin is uncertain.

They are essentially a cereal of cold, wet places and so did not play a part in the economy of the early Mediterranean civilizations. Oats and rye grow further north than other cereals, and so are important in the less hospitable regions, such as Alaska and Norway. (Another species, the Black oat or Bristle oat, *A. strigosa*, is grown in hilly areas that are unsuitable even for *A. sativa*.). In Scotland, oats used to be a staple food, and part of a farm labourer's wages were paid in oatmeal.

However, oats are now mainly grown as an animal foodstuff. They do not contain a gluten that will stand up to make leavened bread, and the dominant flavour is slightly bitter and very characteristic. However, oatmeal is valuable from a nutritional viewpoint, as it has much the analysis of wheat but with more fat and biotin. Simple oatmeals are made by stone-grinding the grain, and fine, medium and coarse (or pin-meal) grades are available. Fine oatmeal is used for oatcakes; coarse oatmeal for porridge, haggis and white puddings. For many purposes, oat meal is better after being parched, that is, slightly roasted. Rolled oats, for breakfast porridge, are made from carefully dried, clean and graded oats, which have been pearled:

they have the husk ground off and are then steam-softened and rolled flat.

Rolled oats keep because heating destroys the enzymes which would act on the fats in the germ of crude meal to produce free fatty acids and thus cause the meal to go rancid; straight oatmeal is a bad keeper, which is why the Scots like pin-meal for porridge to be freshly ground. Oatmeal porridge (there are porridges made from other cereals, and during the Depression it was often made of stale bread, sugar and water) used to be the ubiquitous British breakfast starter. The technique of making porridge is similar to that used for *polenta* – grain is sprinkled into boiling water with the left hand while the right hand stirs it with a spoon or fork to prevent it going lumpy. Porridge can be made even from plain oatmeal by boiling for 20 minutes (most porridge oats are much quicker) but as half cooked – and often lumpy – nursery porridge was unpleasant, it became usual to leave it on the stove overnight in a double boiler (the stove would of course be a solid fuel one which provided a suitable heat), or to use an old-fashioned hay box – campers may boil the porridge up at night and roll the pan in a blanket to have ready-made hot breakfast. Porridge should always be sufficiently salted and may then be eaten with no more than the addition of fresh milk. With plenty of ice-cold thick cream, the combination of hot and cold is fabulous, but then even dry parched oatmeal and cream (crowdie) is splendid. Porridge lovers do not use the sugar, syrup or treacle that most people south of the border have on it. Porridge has regrettably been largely ousted by nastier breakfast cereals, even in Scotland.

Oatmeal, though, is more than a breakfast food; there are few things more delicious than small brown trout straight from the burn, rolled in salted oatmeal and fried over the camp fire; a similar treatment is excellent for herrings. Oatmeal has an affinity with onions, as in onion and oatmeal soup and in white puddings, all hearty food for the winter mountains, but for really heroic Scots winter fare, a *kale brose (bone stock, kale and oatmeal) would take some beating, though you could well prefer the famous Atholl Brose, which consists of oatmeal with Scotch whisky and heather honey.

White Pudding

Take 225 g (½ lb) of good coarse oatmeal parched to a light brown in a dry pan, 225 g (½ lb) or more finely chopped beef suet, a small onion, very finely chopped, and a good seasoning of salt and freshly ground black pepper or allspice.
Mix together – no water – and tie in a cloth into a sausage shape. Plunge the pudding under with a plate if necessary to begin with, and simmer it for 1½-2 hours. (More sophisticated versions are made by including minced pork or chicken and eggs in the mixture, and by cooking in sausage skin rather than cloth.) When the pudding is cool, remove the cloth. Slices of pudding can be fried or grilled.

Oatcakes

The simplest way of making oatcakes is to mix fine or medium oatmeal into a dough with salt and water, then to knead it for a couple of minutes. Sprinkle the top with a little oatmeal, and put the cake straight on to a hot, ungreased girdle or bakestone. Bake on both sides without allowing the cake to colour, and then put to dry by the fire or in a very cool oven. However, a little fat, butter or dripping is usually rubbed in before the water is added, and some people add a pinch of baking soda. Making neat oatcakes is not easy. It is best to knead enough for one cake at a time; as the dough must be slack. It gets very sticky. When the dough is rolled out, the edges crack (pinch them between thumb and finger). Round oatcakes are cut with a plate and then quartered to make the

shape in which they are sold in packets. Use plenty of oatmeal for dusting, but keep the girdle brushed clean.

[*Oat* – French: *avoine* German: *Hafer* Italian: *avena* Spanish: *avena*]

OCCA or **oca**. *See* yam (oka).

OCTOPUS is a creature that is widely regarded with revulsion (a local name for them is 'mansuckers'); a terrible fight with a giant octopus was described in Victor Hugo's *Toilers of the Sea*. It is true that octopuses are very strong and divers have occasionally been attacked by large specimens which they have disturbed, but skin divers usually find them to be rather shy and to have a certain nobility. The salivary glands of a few species, notably the little blue octopus of the Pacific and Indian Oceans, secrete a poison, and their bites can be rapidly fatal. European and American species, though, are harmless, and, unlike cuttlefish, octopuses rarely bite. Octopuses are highly regarded as food on most warm sea coasts, although in Britain and America no *cephalopods are traditionally eaten. An Aberdeen trawler skipper I once sailed with was horrified when I suggested that there were people who would be glad of the octopus he caught in his nets and threw away.

Octopuses are molluscs, so have no backbone and during evolution have lost the stiffening they once had. Unlike squids and cuttlefish they prefer to crawl rather than swim; they hide in holes. The lairs of octopuses are usually surrounded by the shells they have eaten and by stones, which they gather together and, when disturbed, pull over their door. There are hundreds of different species, of variable quality as food. Some are too big or too small, some very tough, and others have a strong and musky taste. The best have been compared to lobster.

Most European octopus recipes come from the Mediterranean and Portugal. The best known species is the Common octopus (*Octopus vulgaris*); the rather similar *O. macropus* has longer, thinner tentacles and is called *polpessa* by the Italians. They will be distinguished by shoppers in Mediterranean fishing ports, but most people elsewhere will not acquire that degree of expertise. Smaller octopuses of the genus *Eledone* can even be bought canned. There are two kinds. The Red (*E. moschata*) is the more tender, but has a strong musky flavour, while the White (*E. cirrosa*), which has a pale colour, lacks the musky taste but is tougher. The main problem with octopuses lies not in recognizing the kinds, but in cooking them so that they look presentable and are not tough.

In 1874, a gentleman named Sir John Burrows, gave an Octopus Luncheon in Brighton. His chefs were not versed in Mediterranean lore and neither were his guests. 'Its skin, which in process of boiling had become lividly purple, and had not been removed, was in places offensively broken, and its arms, shrivelled and shrunk, sprawled helplessly on the dish and somehow looked, as they proved to be, as tough and ropy as so many thongs of hunting whips. I shall never forget the utter loathing, ludicrously mingled with determination... which was depicted on the countenances of the guests.'

There are many ways of cooking octopus – it may be boiled or grilled – and the techniques for making it tender vary almost as much as those for cooking rice. The following method comes from Spain, where very good octopus is to be had.

When caught, the animal is quickly turned inside out, which kills it, then soundly beaten against the rocks. The red colour turns to grey. (Greeks say that the octopus should be beaten 40 times, but such exertion is hardly necessary.) Octopus bought fresh or frozen from the market must be beaten well with a bottle or a rolling pin. The insides are taken out (keep only the ink sac if the recipe calls for it) and the beak and eyes cut away. In the octopus, unlike cuttlefish and squid, the tentacles and not the body are the best part. Put a wine cork in the head (a Spanish trick to float the animal and ensure even cooking). Drop it into boiling water, no salt, with a potato – a big one for a big octopus and a small one for a small. Cook gently. When the potato is cooked the octopus is cooked. Take it out of the water, cool it, remove the skin and peel off the horny suckers. Cooked this way, octopus is white, tender and appetizing. Cut into convenient pieces, it may be simply dressed with chopped parsley, oil and lemon juice for a seafood salad. Other recipes cook octopus with wine, onion, garlic, tomato, peppers, herbs and oil. There are even recipes which include bitter chocolate. Dried octopus is good made into a soup, or it can be grilled. The Japanese are reputed to consider that the eyes are the best part.

[Octopus – French: poulpe, pieuvre German: Seepolyp, Krake, achtfüssiger Tintenfisch Italian: polpo Spanish: pulpo]

OFFAL in its general sense means garbage. In butchery, it is the bits of the carcass that are not straightforward meat, fat and bone. Thus it includes the head and all the main internal organs, notably *liver, *kidney, *sweetbreads (thymus), *tripe (stomach), *heart and *lights (lungs).

OILS. See fats.

OKA. See yam (oka).

OKRA, okro, ladies' fingers, or **gumbo** (Hibiscus esculentus) belongs to the mallow family. It has edible rocket-shaped pods, sometimes with 5-7 prominent ridges or with slight spines, coloured deep or light green, and of various lengths up to 20 cm (8 in). In buying, it is safer to choose small pods, as the long-podded varieties should be picked every 2-3 days; old ones are tough and fibrous – these plants belong to the same family as cotton, Deccan hemp and Cuba bast – all fibre plants – and are themselves used to make paper.

Okra has yellow flowers rather like cotton, grows 1-2 m (3-6 ft) high, and needs a frost-free warm climate. It is native to Africa and came via Egypt to Mediterranean Europe in the 13th century. It was probably taken by slaves to the Caribbean (where it is still very popular) and to the US, where it is an essential ingredient of Creole gumbo. Okra is grown in huge quantities in the southern states for the canning industry – it is very mucilaginous and therefore useful for thickening canned soups and sauces. It is used very differently in Greek, Balkan, Turkish, Middle Eastern and Indian cooking. Even the canned okra from the countries of the eastern Mediterranean is different to the canned okra of America.

Okra has a delicious flavour, but the mucilage gives it a slimy texture which many people dislike. In gumbo, this is necessary and is even added to with *filé powder, but in the Levant, where okra is a very important food, attempts are made to reduce the mucilaginous quality. The fresh pods are soaked for half an hour to an hour – even more – in vinegar, lemon juice or mixed vinegar and water before being cooked. Alternatively, they may be sprinkled with salt and left in the sun for an hour to dry. (Dried okras, small ones threaded on strings, are a common sight hanging in the shops in Turkey, and are kept in this way for use in winter. They are soaked before use and often stewed with mutton.)

In the US, okra is usually sliced, but in the Levant great care is taken to pare off the stalk without cutting into the pod. Cutting the pod lets the mucilage come out. Okra is usually fried before cooking it with meat, onion, tomato or whatever the recipe calls for. Frying also reduces the glutinosity. If you are using canned okras, American ones are best for American recipes and European ones (from Greece, Cyprus or Turkey) for Levantine recipes. Rinse canned okras before using them. As they are already cooked, they should be added late in the cooking and not treated as if fresh. However, fresh okras are usually available in Greek or Indian shops.

Bamieh bi zayt. This is a well-known *hors d'oeuvre* in the Lebanon. It seems to show off okra to perfection. Pare the tops of 3 cups of small okras, and, after washing, dry them well. Make a paste by pounding together a good handful of green coriander leaves, 8 cloves of garlic and ½ teaspoon salt. Also peel 10 small or pickling onions.

Fry the okras in plenty of olive oil until they are tender but still firm and green. Take them out, then fry the onions until they are golden. Pour off most of the oil and fry the pounded herb mixture a little. Slice 3 tomatoes into the bottom of a pressure cooker. Cover with okras neatly arranged on top. Put the onions on top of that, and sprinkle with about ½ cup of lemon juice. Add the fried herb mixture, and a little water, only just enough to stop the contents burning. Close the cooker. Cook for 12 minutes, open and simmer until the juice is almost all evaporated. Season with more salt if necessary, plus a pinch of sugar and pepper to taste. Place in a serving dish, arrange the vegetables, cool and chill.

OLALLIE. *See* raspberry.

OLIVE (*Olea europaea*) is almost certainly a Mediterranean native and may be descended from the oleaster, the wild olive which grows in many places around the Mediterranean. (The oleaster has tiny olives which are nearly all stone, and the bushes are very prickly.) Olive trees are very long lived and perhaps span a thousand years – some gnarled old relics are supposed to have been planted around the time of Christ. The very old trees still bear fruit. In the past, the olive was one of the mainstays for life in the Mediterranean basin, growing a little way inland around most of the coasts and penetrating a few miles into the mountain valleys. It also grows over a large area of Spain (the world's largest producer) and in a few inland places south of the Alps, where it has been planted. It was taken to America by the Spaniards. Today, it is also grown in California, South Africa, Australia and many other areas where there is a suitable climate. Some of the

many varieties are more suitable for pressing, others for preserving.

Olive oil. For oil the olives must be ripe. In the primitive method, the olives are crushed in a trough under a huge rolling stone like a millstone, and the liquid is squeezed out. This is purified by floating it on water – the streams run red in January with the washings. These old methods are still used in some mountain villages. The modern method is to squeeze the pulp under hydraulic presses and separate the oil with a centrifuge. Oil which is made by pressing, without any other treatment, is called virgin oil. However, there are considerable differences in the virgin oil from country to country. In Spain, for instance, virgin oil is often very rank – only Spaniards brought up on it would like it. In Italy, the *olii vergini* are divided into various grades: *olio extra vergine* with 1.0% acidity, *olio sopraffino vergine* with 1.0-1.5%, *olio fino vergine* with 1.5-3.0%, and *olio vergine* with 3- 4% acidity. Acidity, in fact, is the criterion by which oils are judged, but the buyer, visiting some village in the mountains to find an excellent salad oil, will pour a little into the palm of a hand, rub his hands together briskly to heat the oil and then cup them to smell it. Poor oil, with an acidity too high for eating, was in the past known as *lampante* (lamp oil, more or less), and it was used for burning. Even 25 years ago, olive oil was still being burned in lamps in remote places. The dross (*sansa*) left over from pressing still contains some oil, and this is extracted with solvents, which also extract other resinous substances. Poor olive oil, like seed oils, can be treated, first with an alkali to neutralize the acids, then by heating the filtration through earths or charcoal to remove the colour, and finally by steam-stripping in a vacuum to remove the flavour. *Lampante* oil which has been stripped is called *olio rettificato* in Italy; oil from the extracted residues is *olio di sansa rettificato*. Ordinary olive oil (*olio di oliva*) would consist of stripped oils with 5-15% virgin oil added for flavour, but if it is made by extraction from the *sansa*, it should be so labelled (*Olio di sansa e di oliva*).

Italy is usually associated with the production of the finest olive oils. But whether the finest comes from the Italian or the French Riviera is a matter of opinion and taste. Italy exports fine oils, but does not produce enough for her own requirements and has to import oil from elsewhere. Turkey, Tunisia and Morocco are other important producers. Some of the oil produced in Spain is excellent, but

olive

the Spanish themselves often have a love for very rank olive oil called *aruja* (which once upset the stomachs of tourists), which is at its worst if the olives have been allowed to get over-ripe and to lie on the ground, or if the trees were infested with insect pests. Georges Sand, in *Winter in Majorca* (which was written after her disastrous affair with Chopin in the Monastery of Valldemosa), said that you could always recognize a Mallorquine home by the stink of the oil. To this day, I have friends who find food quite tasteless without a good slosh of semi-rancid olive oil. All olive oil is costly, and good olive oil is very costly and hard to find – but it is worth looking for.

Because light affects oils adversely, the best you can buy – short of visiting the farm – will be in cans and not in clear glass bottles. Once the can is opened, what is not for immediate use should be kept in small, full bottles in the refrigerator. There is much to be said for the custom in many Italian households of using oilseed oils for cooking and olive oil always as a condiment which is always on the table for dressing vegetables and salads.

Pickled olives. To most of the world outside the olive-growing regions, there are three sorts of olives: green ones with stones, stuffed green ones (usually stuffed with pieces of sweet red pepper or anchovies but also with almonds, tunny, or even hot green chillies) and black ones. The counter in a market in Spain, Italy or Greece will confront the newcomer with a bewildering number of types for sale. So taste them before buying as you cannot tell their quality by eye alone.

Black olives are ripe olives. Commercially, they are usually black, but home cured ones may be brown or sometimes mottled, some may be wrinkled and others plump. The simplest way of preserving black olives is as follows. Select good, ripe olives, free of fly. Soak them for 24 hours in several changes of fresh water to remove some of the bitterness. Then put the drained olives into jars, fill the jars with cold 10% *brine – just strong enough to make a fresh egg almost float from the bottom. Put some carob leaves in the top of the jar to make sure that the olives remain under the brine. Leave the olives for 4-5 months before trying them. There is a belief that olives should be picked only when the moon is waxing.

Green olives are unripe. They are put down from September until the fruit ripens around Christmas. As soon as the olives are properly formed, in September, some are picked as broken or squashed

olives. They are split by hitting them gently with a mallet before putting them in pure water which is changed every day for up to two weeks. At the end of this time, most of the bitterness will have leached out (but some should remain).Then a brine should be prepared, again at about 10% strength (100 g per lt or 2 oz per pt), which can have fennel, bay, chilli, savoury or garlic boiled in it to taste. When it is cold, this pickle is poured over the olives. A slight lactic fermentation and the natural acidity of the olives makes them keep. After 2-3 months (by Christmas), these olives are ready to eat. Again, always ask to taste broken olives before buying – vendors in Mediterranean markets expect it; to ask is polite. Broken olives bought loose can be kept in a polythene bag in the refrigerator for a few days, but should be allowed to warm to room temperature before serving. Firm, bitter broken olives are excellent with bread as a simple opening to a meal.

After the September-October olives come the more familiar green olives. By this time, the olives are more oily. The original method of removing the bitterness was to soak the olives in *lye, but it is now more usual to employ caustic soda solution, in which the olives are soaked for six hours. You can observe the penetration of the caustic soda by cutting into an olive; when the colour change has reached almost the stone, the olives are ready. They have then to be soaked in frequent changes of water for three days to remove all the caustic soda. For pickling, the same 10% brine with flavourings is used as for black olives, which are ready to eat in a few days. In Spain, not everyone likes this quick method, and the bitterness of the olives is removed by soaking in changes of water over a 15-day period.

When the olives are just starting to colour, it is time to make what the French call the *olives d'été*, to be used the following summer. These olives are simply put straight into the 10% brine (perfumed as usual) and sealed in bottles. These olives are bitter (*olives amères* is an alternative name); the salt, the fermentation that takes place are perhaps substances in the olives, make them keep quite safely. When the olives are violet, just before they are quite ripe, they are also pickled in 10% herbed brine, usually after some knife cuts have been made in each one. These *olives taillées*, laid down around Christmas, are ready by April. They replace the early *piccolines*, which by this time have begun to soften or take on the taste of leather which is so characteristic of poor commercial olives. Shrivelled olives, which are to be pressed for oil, are also pricked, allowed to bleed, and treated for a day or so with the salt and herbs (they are *olives piquées* or pricked olives).

The nature of pickled olives depends not only on the method that has been used but also on the variety of olive. In Spain, for instance, many are named with simple, descriptive country names. There is the *aceituna zorzaleña*, a small round olive which gets its name from being a favourite food of certain birds (*zorzales*). Varieties named by their shape include the *picudilla* (pointed) and the *tetuda* (breast-shaped); a common type is known as *aceituna corval* (long). Olives may be called after a place (e.g. *Sevillanas*). A very small olive is the *manzanilla*, and the one reckoned to be the best of all is the *aceituna de la reina* (olive of the queen), which is very large. However, size is the last criterion by which to judge eating olives. Californian olives are often enormous but taste of nothing, while the tiny olives from Liguria taste excellent.

The olives used in cooking are usually black, but green olives are sometimes called for. It is a great mistake to add either indiscriminately to dishes as olives, especially green ones, do not marry well with all flavours. Because olives stuffed with red pepper look decorative when sliced across, they are often used to decorate snacks in which their taste or texture is unsuitable – caviar or scrambled eggs, for instance. And black olives will not do as imitation bits of truffle.

[*Olive* – French: *olive* German: *Olive* Italian: *oliva, uliva* Spanish: *olivo, oliva, aceituna*]

OLOROSO. *See* sherry.

OMUM. *See* ajowan.

ONION (*Allium cepa*) is certainly the most commonly used flavouring vegetable in the world and has been in cultivation for so long that the wild ancestors are unknown. In China and Japan, another onion species, *A. fistulosum*, has been cultivated since times immemorial. The onions are variously classified by botanists with daffodils in the family Amaryllidaceae, with the lilies in the Liliaceae, or in their own family, the Alliaceae. The genus *Allium* includes *garlic, *leeks, *chives and *shallots as well as onions. From the cook's point of view, onions are recognized by taste. There are dozens of species, of which some twenty grow wild in Europe. Tests carried out during World War II showed them all to be edible, although not necessarily nice. For instance, the wild garlic known as ramsons (*A. ursinum*), though used in a cheese, is fairly horrific in a camp stew, but an unknown species of onion I used in Kashmir was excellent. In Europe, most onions are cultivated varieties of *A. cepa*, which is the important species over most of the world. There are an enormous number of varieties with a wide variation in texture and flavour, as well as in season, size, flesh colour and keeping quality. Onions of a particular variety can be milder at the beginning of the season than they are at the end of it. Some Continental chefs say that you cannot make certain regional dishes properly without the correct variety of onion. For example, an authentic Flemish *carbonnade* cannot be made without strong Flemish onions (and the right beer), but they would be a disaster if used in a salad which calls for the mild, sweet Valencia onions.

Cooks who are well alerted to the quantity of garlic required in a dish are not always so sensitive about onion, perhaps because it is such a basic ingredient. Not only do onions vary in quality and intensity of flavour, but also in their usefulness for cooking. Some onions are naturally tough or remain tough when baked, boiled or fried. Others are watery and difficult to fry crisp.

For keeping, those with thick, dry outer skins and a neck dried off to a mere wisp are best. Often they are not the ones with the best flavour, and they may be hard and tough. Onions that have sprouted, have a woody core, feel soft when squeezed or are wet should be avoided, as should any that smell musty or are rotted around the neck. Even if part of a bad onion can be salvaged, it always has a bad flavour. Cut onion or chopped onion, if allowed to stand, soon gets a nasty smell (which is only tolerable in the kebabs of an Eastern bazaar where it is a part of the local colour). If chopped onion has to be kept handy, it should be lightly fried in butter (a chef's trick) and stored in the refrigerator. As onions are available all the year round, there is no need to preserve them. They are shipped from the Southern hemisphere in winter. Dried onion flakes can be useful in emergency, but some people use them too often.

Spring onions, green onions or scallions can be derived from several species, harvested young for use in salads. If the leaf in cross section is flattened (with a convex outer surface and concave inner one), then it is a *cepa* onion, and a real 'spring onion'. If the leaf is circular in section, then it will probably be what in Britain is known as a Welsh onion, a variety of *A. fistulosum*, which is also called the Japanese bunching onion and is much cultivated in the Orient. Both these species have hollow leaves.

Another oriental onion, the Chinese chive, Cuchay or Cantonese onion (*A. tuberosum*) grows wild in China. It is a bigger plant than the European chive and has flat, solid leaves. The flowers taste of a mixture of onion and honey and can be used in salads. The *chive proper (*A. schoenoprasum*) is very widely distributed around the world and has a thin, grass-like, round sectioned and hollow leaf, like the Welsh onion but much smaller. The sand leek *A. scorodoprasum*, grows wild in sandy soils from Scotland to the Caucasus and over most of Europe. The flavour is like mild garlic and it is cultivated occasionally. This species is sometimes called the rocambole, a name which is also used for some forms of garlic. The *shallot is now considered to be a variety of *A. cepa*, as are the Tree onion and the Egyptian onion, both of which produce clusters of small bulbs on the stems instead of (or as well as) flowers.

[Onion – French: *oignon* German: *Zwiebel* Italian: *cipolla* Spanish: *cebolla*]

ORACHE. *See* spinach.

ORANGE is a word derived from the Arabic *narañj*. Oranges came originally from the Orient, but their history has not been established with certainty. Bitter oranges, brought by the Arabs, may have been the first to be introduced to Europe. The first sweet oranges may have been those brought back by Vasco da Gama when he returned from his first voyage round the Cape of Good Hope in 1498. After that, they quickly spread to the West Indies and the warmer parts of America. Oranges were grown under glass in orangeries in more northern countries such as Britain, but could grow well in the ideal climate of the Mediterranean. The loose-skinned oranges, such as the tangerine, were not introduced to Europe until the early 19th century and to America until later still, although they had been popular in Japan and China for centuries.

Oranges belong to the *citrus group of the rue family (Rutaceae) and all require warmth. Oranges grown in the tropics often remain green when ripe, but the same varieties from climates like that of the Mediterranean normally go orange. Cold storage or treatment with gas will turn them orange. For sales purposes, oranges may be dyed to make them more orange (in the US this must be indicated with a colour-added stamp) when orangeness is

no criterion of excellence. The practices of dyeing oranges and waxing the skins are not a good thing if you want to use the peel for grating. Except in the tropics, oranges usually are ripe during the winter months. In Spain, which has a typical orange-producing climate, the orange season begins with the small loose-skinned oranges (mandarins, satsumas and clementines), which reach a peak at around Christmas – hence the association of tangerines with Christmas stockings. By January the big navel oranges are ripe, while the supply of loose-skinned oranges declines, and the bitter Seville oranges for marmalade are also coming in. The season ends with blood oranges. This pattern is more or less repeated in the US (which is now the world's largest producer of oranges) and the rest of the year is covered by imports.

Tight-skinned sweet oranges (*Citrus sinensis*) include the most popular oranges for eating and for juice. Among them is the Washington navel, a fine, usually seedless, dessert orange with the characteristic navel at the flower end. Navels were introduced to the US from Brazil in the 19th century, and get the name Washington because that is where they were first grown. (They are also called Riverside, where they became established in California, and Bahia, where they came from in Brazil.) The Shamouti variety, which is large and seedless, originally came from Israel (Jaffa oranges), but are now also grown in Cyprus and elsewhere. The other predominant sweet orange variety is the Valencia, a late one with a long season. Blood oranges usually have thin skins and are difficult to peel but have plenty of sweet reddish juice. In general, sweet oranges tend to be uninteresting if used in cooking. Perhaps these oranges should never be cooked as they usually acquire a taste like weak marmalade. Mixed into fruit salads, put with nuts and cheese, or into everything-but-the-kitchen-sink salads, orange sections are more often than not a mistake, as they tend to obtrude. They do not marry well with wine.

Loose-skinned oranges (*Citrus reticulata*) include mandarins, tangerines and satsumas, but perhaps not clementines which may be a tangerine X sweet orange cross. In any case the names have become confused. Mandarin denotes a Chinese origin, and tangerine should refer to a variety that was originally shipped from North Africa through Tangiers. The satsuma was originally Japanese, very small; it is hardy, standing quite a bit of cold compared to other citruses, and has very few, if any, seeds. Clementines, hybrid or not, are between a tangerine and an orange in character and are commonly grown in North Africa and Spain. King oranges may also be a cross. The variety was introduced into the US in 1882 as a heavy bearer, resistant to cold, but is not popular. The West Indian ortanique, with a thin, tough skin and flattened fruits, is probably a tangerine X orange cross; it is juicy and stores well. Tangerine X orange crosses are called tangors and include the Temple orange, which makes excellent eating. Tangelos, which are easily confused with tangors, are tangerine X grapefruit hybrids. Among them are the ugli, which is a bit like a sweet, loose-skinned grapefruit and may be very large, and the Minneola tangelo, which is a smooth, dark orange and has a nipple at the stem end. As in all citrus fruits, the skin of oranges is the packaging. You should reject fruit in which the skin is bruised – and loose-skinned oranges are more perishable than the tight-skinned kinds – but you should not allow yourself to be beguiled too much by nature's packaging. Thus, the Honey tangerine is very sweet but may not look so good from the outside. Tangerine peel is very different in scent from orange peel just as the fruit has a different taste); it is used dried as a flavouring in Chinese cooking. The peel can easily be dried by threading it on a cotton and hanging it in a warm place, but home-dried tangerine peel is likely to have a weaker flavour than that imported from China. The peel of fresh tangerines can be grated and used as a change in dishes that are normally flavoured with orange peel. As a child, I asked for it in icing for Christmas cakes because I detested the taste of bitter almond.

Bitter oranges, **Seville oranges** or **sour oranges** (*Citrus aurantium*) are the most important in cooking. A typical bitter orange has a rough, tough, dark orange skin; it is very aromatic, but the pulp is sour, astringent and full of seeds, indeed virtually inedible. Although the juice is excellent when properly sweetened and is used in drinks, the important part of a bitter orange is its skin. Some varieties provide the basic flavouring for Curacao and orange-flavoured liqueurs such as Aurum, Grand Marnier and Cointreau. Dried bitter orange peel is a standard ingredient in the *bouquet garni* used in the South of France. It is very easily dried, keeps up to two years and will be treasured as a flavouring by anyone who discovers it.

The passion for orange marmalade is particularly British; large quantities of bitter Seville oranges are imported every year for marmalade. Other, rather inferior bitter oranges come from Sicily (Malaga and Palermo). Given a good recipe, the goodness of marmalade depends entirely on the quality of the bitter oranges – something which cannot be judged by eye because as usual the best are often not the best looking. Oddly enough, it is difficult to buy Seville oranges in Spain, and our supply has often to be stolen from the park. Bitter orange trees, which are to be seen on roadsides in Mediterranean towns, may be recognized because they are large, thorny and have broadly-winged leaf stalks. They are also grown for the large flowers, which are used in the perfumery business. They are the basis of oil of neroli or *bigarde* oil (named after Anne Maria de la Tremoille, Princess of Nerole, who is supposed to have discovered it around 1670), which smells like *eau de cologne*. The flowers can also be made into a sweet aromatic jam by those who like shatteringly sweet things. Oil of petitgrain is produced by steam distillation of the leaves (other types come from the leaves of lemon and tangerine) and is used commercially as a flavouring in many foods, just as the leaves of oranges and lemons can be used as a flavouring in home cooking.

Bergamot (*Citrus bergamia*) is used mainly in perfumery as a source of an aromatic essential oil. It may be an orange cross, a smaller tree than the lemon or orange and grown particularly in Sicily and Calabria. The fruits are preserved and candied. In this respect its uses are similar to the *citron.

Calamondin may be a mandarin variety, a hybrid between a kumquat and a mandarin or a separate species (*Citrus mitis*); it originated in the Philippines. Calamondins are frequently grown for ornament and have small orange-like fruits which can be candied.

[*Orange* – French: *orange* German: *Apfelsine, Orange* Italian: *arancia* Spanish: *anaranjado*]

ORCHIL. *See* cudbear.

OREGANO or **wild marjoram** (*Origanum vulgare*) is a herb that is closely related to *sweet marjoram but is more pungent. It grows on calcareous soils in most countries in Europe, but there is a great difference between the flavours of leaves gathered in southern Italy, or those from, say, the South Downs of Britain, and of the *rigani* sold in Greece (where the name covers a number of *Origanum* species). In regional dishes, the authentic flavour can depend on obtaining the herb from the correct source.

Oregano is perhaps best known for its use in Italian cooking, but nowadays it is used all over the world in regions influenced by Mediterranean cooking. Fortunately it dries well, so fresh oregano is rarely necessary. Dried *rigani* from Greece includes flower buds as well as leaves.

[*Oregano* – French: *origan* German: *Oregano* Italian: *origano* Spanish: *oregano*]

ORRIS. The dried aromatic roots of a species of iris (*Iris pallida*) that is a native of Dalmatia. The smell is reminiscent of violets, but the taste is bitter. Though it was much used as a flavouring in the past, orris will rarely if ever be called for these days. It is still used commercially as the basis for 'violet' scents and flavours.

[*Orris* – French: *racine d'iris* German: *Veilchenwürzel* Italian: *radice di giaggiolo* Spanish: *raiz de iris florentina, raiz de lirio*]

ORSEILLE. *See* cudbear.

ORTANIQUE. *See* orange.

ORTOLAN. *See* birds.

OSMOSIS. I gained a rudimentary idea of osmosis at an early age from a French reader full of stories in which a know-all father imparted his encyclopaedic knowledge to his boys. In this case, he filled a bladder with sugar solution, and suspended it in fresh water. The sugar could not pass out of the bladder, but the water could pass in, and did so till the bladder burst – a case of nature trying, as usual, to iron out differences and make everything equal. The force that bursts the bladder is osmotic pressure, the bladder is a semi-permeable membrane (it lets the water through but not the sugar) and the whole phenomenon is known as osmosis. The walls of living cells are semi-permeable membranes. If cucumber slices are sprinkled with salt or put in brine, osmosis makes them wilt and water comes out of their cells. Osmosis in the other direction happens when wilted plants that are put into water regain their turgidity.

[*Osmosis* – French: *osmose* German: *Osmose* Italian: *osmosi* Spanish: *osmosis*]

OSTRICH (*Struthio camelus*) was originally domesticated, selected and farmed for its feathers,

mainly in South Africa. At one time, they were hunted almost to extinction, but huge fortunes were made by rearing them. The feathers are no longer fashionable for stoles or fans and are not even needed by nude dancers these days, but ostrich farms still exist. The skin makes a fashionable leather and the meat is dried to make *biltong. The eggs, which are equivalent to at least a dozen hens' eggs, are good, though strongly eggy in flavour.

[*Ostrich* – French: *autruche* German: *Strauss* Italian: *struzzo* Spanish: *avestruz*]

OXALIC ACID $(COOH)_2$ occurs in many plants, usually in the form of its potassium, sodium or calcium salts (oxalates). The acid and its salts are poisonous in any quantity. Some people are allergic or particularly susceptible to oxalic acid poisoning and should avoid spinach, sorrel, wood sorrel and rhubarb. Rhubarb leaves contain a much higher concentration of oxalic acid salts than the stems and, although they are sometimes eaten, have caused fatal poisonings. The poison is more active when the leaves are cooked in soft water. Herbalists contend that plants containing oxalic acid should be avoided by gout sufferers, probably not because of any casual connection, but because anything unwholesome is likely to act as a trigger, there is however, no medical evidence to confirm this. Oxalic acid inhibits absorption by the body of calcium and iron which have insoluble oxalates. For this reason, spinach, which contains 10 times as much iron and 20 times as much calcium as cabbage does, is not as good a source of these elements as it might appear to be.

[*Oxalic acid* – French: *acide oxalique* German: *Oxalsäure* Italian: *acido ossalico* Spanish: *ácido oxalico*]

OYSTER. Cut of *bacon.

OYSTER. Morsel of meat in the back of poultry.

OYSTER. The many species of oyster are distributed in all except polar seas: the museum at Arcachon, an oyster-growing centre in south-western France, exhibits a collection of over 300 types from around the world. They vary in form from the neat, flat oysters typical of Britain through the rough, misshapen oysters which have to be broken off rocks with chisel and hammer to strange oysters such as zig-zag shaped, purple shelled Cock's comb oyster (*Lopha cristagalli*) of the Indian and Pacific Oceans. The native British species is the Common European oyster or Flat oyster (*Osirea edulis*) which retains its eggs within the shell until fertilization. This makes them nasty to eat in the breeding season, which is in summer when there is not an R in the month. Other oysters, like the Portuguese oyster (*Crassostrea angulata*) and the American oyster (*Crassotrea virginica*) do not retain their eggs and can thus be eaten all the year round, although they are better at some times than at others, and may have an official season. Oysters vary considerably in flavour and texture, not only with the species but also with the place in which they are fattened. Because oysters are rather vulnerable to enemies, such as the Slipper limpets, and to severe winters, oyster beds get killed out from time to time, and have to be re-laid. Oysters introduced from elsewhere very often take on much of the flavour that is characteristic of their new home.

For commercial purposes oysters are cleaned by a sophisticated process which involves placing them in tanks of clean seawater under ultra-violet light for about a day and a half. Oysters, like other bivalves, feed on small organisms and other material that they filter out of the water, but they can equally pick up organisms of typhoid and salmonella from polluted water or the poisonous diatoms such as those that create the red tides. In clean water, they will gradually sweep harmful organisms out with the currents they create, and any such organisms will not infect the water but in treatment will be killed by the ultra-violet light.

You can eat oysters directly from the sea – this was the norm in the past and still is in many countries – but only with suitable care. They are safer in primitive countries where there are less sewers emptying into the sea. Oysters for eating raw should be alive and fresh. Opening oysters can be risky; even the skilled sometimes knife themselves in the hand. The usual method – but not the only one – is to hold the oyster in the left hand with the round side down (you do not want to lose the juices); it is best to use a cloth to protect the hand in case the knife slips. Wiggle the knife point between the two halves of the shell close to the hinge, and twist to crack it. (In species with beaks, the projections may have to be broken off with pliers first.) Push the knife in and sweep the blade carefully across, keeping the point tight against the upper shell – the object is to cut the muscle attachment as close to the upper shell as possible and not to damage any other part of the animal. Take off the flat shell, and either lay the oyster as it

is on the dish or (the usual British way) slip the knife under the oyster to cut it free from the bottom shell without spilling the juices and turn the oyster over, top side down and ready to eat. Some types with large beards need to have them cut off but usually this is hardly necessary. When oysters are eaten raw on the half shell, a squeeze of lemon, cayenne pepper, Tabasco sauce and brown bread and butter are some of the common accompaniments. Many oyster fanciers prefer them with no additions at all.

Cooking oysters is tricky as heat makes them tough. They should only just curl. Long cooking will make oysters disintegrate as they do in a steak, kidney and oyster pudding. For this, frozen oysters can well be used, but the slightly fishy taste they give can be a mistake. The adding of oysters to this dish stems from the days when oysters were cheap, not the luxury which they usually are now, and the oysters used may well have been pickled oysters.

The quality of oysters is reflected in their price. Names are locally important but the oysters will probably have been bought from somewhere else and laid in the fattening grounds from which they take their taste and their name, often in an estuary where the slightly brackish water makes the oysters fat (if it is too fresh, they get bloated and soft; they die if the salt concentration is under 3%). They are graded by size.

Oysters are also sold shucked – removed from their shells. In this form they can be packed in cardboard or plastic boxes and kept on ice (they last 7-9 days) for use mainly in cooking. Shucked oysters are also sold frozen, canned, or smoked. Frozen oysters will keep in the freezer for a month, but cannot be held in the freezer compartment of the refrigerator for more than a few days. Dried oysters are a Chinese ingredient.

Portuguese oysters or **Ports** (*Crassostrea angulata*) are much more irregular in shape than the flat oyster and much more like the American Virginia Oyster. Less prized than the flat oyster and best cooked, though mostly eaten raw, Ports are in season all the year. They prefer warmer waters but were introduced into the Bay of Arcachon on the Atlantic coast of France by accident when a ship with live oysters aboard sank there. They have recently been re-laid in British waters as well.

French oysters are usually known by their place of origin. Thus *Arcachonnaises* are very white Portuguese oysters (*Portugasies*) from the basin of Arcachon. *Belons* are rather pink oysters named after the Belon River in Finistère. *Bouziques* are *Portugaises* from near Sète, Herault – on the Mediterranean. *Marennes*, from the Vendée near Rochefort, may be green or white. The greens (*vertes*) are particularly famous for their colour and the special taste they develop (whether they are locally bred or brought in at 2-3 years from elsewhere) when they are fattened in deep pits or *claires* connected by channels to the sea. In these *claires* grows a particular type of green alga and the oysters become full of it. Brittany oysters or Bretons are flat oysters like the British natives and so are not in season in the summer. Bretons are excellent oysters, which are usually cultivated on limed tiles. They are often used for re-laying elsewhere, after which they cease to be Bretons and adopt the local flavour. The Cornish 'Helford River', Devon 'Yealm' and Essex 'Roach' have been re-laid with Bretons, as also the beds of Holland, which were restocked after disease had wiped out the existing stock.

Natives is the name given in Britain to oysters from the Essex and Kentish beds; correctly, they come from between the North Foreland and Orford Ness. This includes Colchester and Whitstable oysters but often other dud or illegitimate flat oysters steal into the act. Royal Whitstables or Royals are from the Whitstable Oyster Company (to which the word Royal – in the context of oysters – is exclusive) and are true natives although mostly re-laid from France. Pearly and with a small beard, they have a reputation for sweetness of taste (to some of us, any oyster is sweet). Colchester Pyefleets are from Pyefleet creek in the Caine estuary in Essex, one of the finest fattening grounds. Caine oysters have been famous since Roman times. The borough of Colchester has a charter from Richard I confirming its rights over Colchester Pyefleets, which are defined as coming from an area between North Bridge and West Ness. Duchy oysters are Helford River oysters from the Duchy of Cornwall.

Mediterranean oysters are more expensive and less good than those of the Atlantic. Off beat oysters, like the spiny oyster (*Spondylus gaderopus*, a member of another family), which skin divers can break off the rocks in many places, are considered good eating if they are taken from places (if they still exist) where pollution is not a problem. Their flavour is apt to be strongly of iodine and takes some getting used to. Still, I know people who greedily gobble up any shellfish.

American oysters. The Atlantic coast of North America is very rich in oysters. The main species is *Crassostrea virginica* which like the Portuguese oyster is not troubled by an R-in-the-month problem (although oysters are better outside the breeding season). Best known outside America are Bluepoints from the Atlantic coast of Long Island, but there are dozens of others with intriguing names and excellent flavours, such as Rappahannocks, Choptanks and Fire Island Salts. Some come from deep water, as much as 60 feet, others from shallow estuaries.

Pacific oysters. The Pacific coast of America is less fortunate in its oysters than the East Coast; the indigenous Olympia oyster is small. So as soon as the first railway to the Pacific coast was completed, the East Coast Virginia oyster was brought across and introduced. (There was no difficulty in doing so, as oysters live well for a number of days if they are packed in seaweed and kept moist.) The Japanese or Pacific oyster (*Ostrea laperoust*) is established in Puget Sound. The Japanese and Chinese have been eating and cultivating oysters for several thousand years.

Australian and New Zealand oysters. The rock oysters of New South Wales were re-laid from New Zealand and have taken on a local character from the waters in which they rest. The warm water oyster which lives on the northern part of North Island of New Zealand is *Ostrea crassostrea*, a rock oyster rather like the American and Portuguese ones. It lives high enough up to be exposed by the tides; as a result, it will keep fresh and alive for long periods. The oyster of colder Pacific water is *Ostrea sinuata*, a deep water oyster that is fished off the South Island of New Zealand.

[*Oyster* – French: *huître* German: *Auster* Italian: *ostrica* Spanish: *ostra*]

OYSTER PLANT. *See* salsify.

p

PAK CHOI. *See* Chinese cabbage.

PALM. A member of the family Palmae, and there are at least 4000 species, mostly in tropical and subtropical countries. Only one, the Dwarf fan palm (*Chamaerops humilis*), a very spiny denizen of Mediterranean hillsides, is a native of Europe, although many species are grown ornamentally in the warmer areas. Palms are typically tall, unbranched trees, with a crown of leaves at the top. Some smaller types are branched and there are even a few climbers, of which the most famous is the rattan palm (*Calamus rotang*), which has edible shoots and seeds but is important as the source of cane for making chair seats and baskets; local ropes made from it are used for tying wild elephants after capture. To palms we owe *dates, *coconuts, *betel nuts, palm oil (*see* fats) *sago and palm *sugar.

Toddy is the fermented juice of various palms, tapped by cutting off a flowering shoot and suspending a pot under it to catch the drips. After a day in the tropical heat, it is already fermented. Palm juice concentrated by boiling gives palm sugar.

The hearts, that is the terminal buds, of many species of palm are edible. Their flavour is usually mild and not very definite, but the texture is firm and delicious. One well-known species is the Cabbage palm, or Palmetto (*Sabal palmetto*), which grows, amongst other places, on the coast in the south-eastern parts of the US, and Mexico. This palm is used for brushes, especially those required to remain stiff in hot water, but the cabbages – i.e. hearts – are also eaten, hence the name. Palm hearts are usually boiled until they are just tender and eaten as a vegetable or cold as a salad with mayonnaise or vinaigrette. Some kinds are eaten raw and then only the tender centre is used.

Palm hearts of various kinds are eaten in the tropical countries where they grow. In the Caribbean, hearts of *palmito* or *chou palmiste* (depending on whether the place is Spanish or French speaking) are cooked in many ways, e.g. stuffed, fried in fritters or served in a cream sauce.

In India and Bangladesh, the men working in the mangrove forests cut the hearts out of the exceedingly prickly betel nut palm and eat its refreshing centre, raw or curried. Cutting out the terminal buds of palms in many cases destroys the plant – one reason why palm hearts are a luxury. People living outside the tropics have to be content with canned palm hearts, which are very satisfactory. Any hearts that are not for immediate use when the can is opened can be kept for about ten days in the refrigerator, providing they are in the canning liquid in a glass jar.

[*Palm* – French: *palme* German: *Palme* Italian: *palma* Spanish: *palma*]

PALO CORTADO. *See* sherry.

PAN or **betel**. Chewing betel is an ancient habit in the East. The red spit marks that greet the European traveller on street corners in India and Pakistan are symptomatic of betel chewing and not of tuberculosis.

Basic essentials for a *pan* are a *betel leaf (of which there are several varieties), which is filled and folded into a parcel, usually held together with a clove (which is not always eaten). The filling consists of *betel nut, *catechu (which gives the red colour) and *lime – the chemical, not the fruit – as a digestive. However, the contents are highly variable and street *pan* sellers make up the packet to the customer's requirements.

PANCHETTA. *See* bacon.

PANELA. *See* sugar.

PANIR and **CHANNA** are more or less the same: milk curds that hardly warrant the name of cheese. *Channa* is much used in India for making sweetmeats such as *rassgullas* and *sandesh*, and *panir* is for frying and currying; it is often mixed with peas (*matar panir*).

To make *panir* and *channa*, bring milk to the boil and then add respectively some lemon juice or sour yoghurt. As soon as the milk curdles, pour it into a clean cloth and hang it up to drain overnight. If you are in a hurry, take down the cloth after 10 minutes and immerse it in ice-water. When the curd is cold, squeeze out the water by pressing the bag. To ensure that the curd does not have an acid taste, use as little of the coagulating agent as possible – just enough to cause coagulation – and do not leave the mixture hanging long enough for the milk to go sour. After draining it, press the *panir* between boards or plates to consolidate it and to remove the last liquid. Leave it to dry, then cut it in squares or knead it according to the use to which it is to be put. Always use *panir* fresh.

PAO YÜ. *See* abalone.

PAPAIN is an enzyme, a vegetable *pepsin extracted from the *papaya. Although similar to pepsin in breaking down protein, it acts best in an alkaline or neutral medium, while pepsin prefers an acid one. It is presented in the form of a cream-coloured powder, often used as a meat tenderizer, and usually has a rather pungent smell. The best grade will tenderize (partly digest) up to 300 times its weight of lean meat, ordinary grades as little as 35 times. Papain is also used for clearing liquids which are hazy with protein – 80% of the beer made in the US is cleared with it.

Papain is obtained by making several cuts with a stainless steel knife or wooden spike, in the unripe fruit and collecting the latex which drips out in glass, porcelain or plastic containers. Tapping is usually limited to five times as the yield decreases each time. The juice is then dried either in the sun or in a dryer, but the temperature must remain below 50-60°C (122-140°F), above which the papain is damaged. The best drying temperature is 30-40°C (86-104°F). Commercial papain is often preserved with salt.

PAPAW (*Asimina triloba*) is a small tree of temperate North America (from New York to Florida and as far west as Nebraska), locally known as the Michigan banana or the custard apple. Indeed, it is the only member of the custard apple family, the Anonaceae, that grows outside the tropics. The fruit is kidney-shaped with a smooth yellowish skin; it contains large brown seeds surrounded by a sweet, yellowish pulp. Ripening papaws have a heavy, cloying scent and a taste that has been described as a mixture of bananas and pears. They are eaten by children and are often gathered after they have

fallen to the ground. Sometimes they are roasted or made into a purée and used in pies. *Papayas are also called pawpaws, which leads to unnecessary confusion.

PAPAYA or **pawpaw** (*Carica papaya*) is among the most important tropical fruits, and one that you miss when returning to colder climates. The papaya is a native of tropical America, but had already been introduced to India by 1600. It is now one of the commonest fruits in all tropical countries. The plant grows to 7½ m (25 ft) high, with the papayas clustered like giant Brussels sprouts around the main stem. There are separate male and female trees, as well as trees which are hermaphrodite or change sex from male to female.

As a crop, the papaya has a number of advantages: the tree begins bearing in a year, it gives both the highest production of fruit per acre and an income next only to the banana in tropical climates. It is very sensitive to frost. Papayas look, at first sight, like smooth, green melons with more pointed ends; the similarity continues when the fruit is cut, except that the seeds are black or grey, lying free in a hollow centre. They are semi-transparent, like caviar in appearance but like mustard and cress in taste, and are sometimes used as a condiment.

Unripe papayas are sometimes cooked as a vegetable or made into pickles. Ripe ones are much more important and are eaten raw as a fruit. The flesh is much finer in texture than that of a melon and ranges from orange to yellow in colour. The flavour is sweet, delicately perfumed and sometimes faintly sickly. The lack of acidity that is common in tropical fruits can be corrected with a squeeze of lime juice. At the beginning of a hot day, a papaya makes the best possible breakfast. The plant is also the source of the tenderizer *papain and so the juice and leaves are used locally for tenderizing in cookery.

[*Papaya* – French: *papaye* German: *Papaija, Melonenfrucht* Italian: *papaia* Spanish: *papaya*]

PAPRIKA is an orange-red powder made by drying and grinding special varieties of *sweet pepper that are said to have been taken to Hungary by the Turks. Although these peppers are pointed in shape, they do not have the pungency of chillies. The core and seeds of the peppers are usually removed before they are dried. Paprika is now produced in many countries apart from its native Hungary – Spanish *pimentón* is essentially the same spice, though the flavour is perceptibly different.

Many non-Hungarian paprikas are of poor quality, but at least they will not be adulterated with red lead, as they were said to have been on occasion in the past. Paprika is the essential flavouring of many Hungarian dishes including goulash and chicken *paprikás*; it is meant to be used in generous quantities rather than those that would usually be appropriate for black pepper or cayenne. It is a mild, sweet spice that in Hungary comes in varying grades – noble sweet, semi-sweet, rose, strong and commercial, in descending order of quality. Paprika, like most ground spices, does not keep for ever – if it is a dirty brown colour, it is probably stale.

PARAGUAY TEA. *See* maté.

PARA NUT and **PARADISE NUT**. *See* Brazil nut.

PARBOILING. A stage further than *blanching; half-cooking food in water before finishing in another way, usually by baking or frying. Food is parboiled either because the higher temperature of fat would dry it out or brown it too much before it was cooked through, or because it prepares the surface for the penetration of fat and flavour, as, for instance, when potatoes are roasted in meat juices.

[*Parboiling* – French: *faire bouillir, frire à demi* German: *halbkochen* Italian: *far bollire a metà* Spanish: *sancochar*]

PARFAIT AMOUR. *See* liqueurs and cordials.

PARMESAN. This name is used outside Italy for the group of cheeses the Italians call *grana*, of which the archetype is *parmigiano*. These cheeses, which are hard and old, have a special strong taste and are mainly grated for flavouring. *Grana* and other grated cheeses are indispensable in Italian cooking, in which they are one of the most common flavourings. Authentic cheeses from the region around Parma have PARMIGIANO-REGGIANO stamped on them.

The cheeses are very large – 25-35 kg (50-80 lb) is normal – and, being expensive, are bought in pieces. For cooking, the cheeses should be at least three years old, and get better up to four years. If kept longer than that, the cheese starts to go powdery. Today, a large amount of this cheese type is sold relatively fresh. It is cheaper, sweeter and softer, intended for eating, not cooking. The Bolognese find fresh *grana* goes particularly well with pears and have the saying 'Don't tell your wife how good cheese is with pears,' a fine example of Italian male chauvinist piggery. Parmesan is often sold grated in packets, but this does not compare with cheese that has been freshly grated.

PARSLEY (*Petroselinum crispum*) is an umbellifer of Mediterranean origin. It is the most commonly used herb in European and American cooking and second only to green coriander in the rest of the world. There are four main varieties of parsley, two of which are only locally common.

The least known is Neapolitan parsley, from southern Italy, which is grown for its leaf stalks rather in the same way as celery. The rather better known Hamburg parsley is grown for its root and is also called turnip-rooted or parsnip-rooted parsley. It was once popular in England, and is still grown in Germany and Switzerland as one of the root vegetables for flavouring soups.

The usual type grown in northern countries as a herb is Curly or Moss-curled parsley, which has dense, crinkly leaves. Mediterranean countries more often have the single leaved, plain or Italian parsley, which is not as decorative but stands sun, and indeed rain and snow, much better. I do not accept claims that the single-leaved type has a superior flavour, in fact, it is different, and ideally one would have both. The presence or absence of parsley in the local greengrocers can be taken as indicating the standard of local cooking, as a few fanatics are not enough to make them stock it. But parsley is not difficult to grow in window boxes of good compost (though it is slow to germinate). It can be kept going right through the winter with suitable protection and prevented from seeding by removal of the flowering stems.

Parsley can be frozen in bunches after being quickly dipped in boiling water to blanch it. Modern dried parsley is quite acceptable as an emergency substitute; it has been greatly improved in recent years. Home dried parsley usually has a hay-like flavour. A bunch of parsley and a means of chopping it quickly is a necessity in every kitchen.

Parsley oil, which is extracted by the steam distillation of parsley seed, is used as a flavouring in a variety of commercial products from ice cream to condiments.

[*Parsley* – French: *persil* German: *Petersilie* Italian: *prezzemolo* Spanish: *perejil*]

PARSNIP (*Pastinaca sativa*), like carrot, is an umbellifer. The thin, acrid roots of the wild parsnip, which are native to Europe, are inedible, but cultivated parsnips have been known for at least

2000 years – what unknown genius chose them for development or found the original mutation? Perhaps the roots were first used as a flavouring in soups, as they still are in Europe. They were an important ingredient of medieval English and European cookery, in which they were used as a sweetmeat (e.g. preserved in honey or made into fritters) and for medicinal purposes, for instance in syrups and as a cough remedy. Parsnips reached the West Indies in 1564 and Virginia in 1609. A century later, they were being grown by the North American Indians. The plant has now gone wild in the US and reverted to its original inedible state. Apparently though, these escapes, when given the benefit of horticulture, gradually resume the cultivated form.

Parsnips are winter vegetables – at one time, it was believed they had to be frosted to be edible. Up to a point, the later they are harvested the sweeter they are, but left too long, they may grow to a huge size and develop a woody core. Young parsnips need only be scraped; old ones have to be peeled and cut in pieces. When buying, look out for brown, rotten patches which may mean that most of the root is spoiled. Parsnips are usually boiled before they are dressed in a variety of ways (for example, roasted). They cook more quickly than carrots. Parsnips are sweet – they contain enough sugar to be used for wine-making – but have a peculiar taste that children in particular may not like. While parsnips are usually to be found among the winter roots in the shops, they are not very popular in Britain or the US. They are eaten in the countries of northern Europe to some extent, but hardly at all further south, or only as a flavouring in soups and occasionally as a garnish.

[*Parsnip* – French: *panais* German: *Pastinak, Pastinake, Pastinakwurzel* Italian: *pastinaca* Spanish: *chirivía*]

PARTRIDGE. There are no true partridges indigenous to North America, where the word is often applied to other birds like *quail or *grouse. However, European partridges were introduced into the US from Hungary, and so are often known as 'Huns'. They are naturalized in a number of states, as is the rather larger Chukar or Chukoor (*Alectoris chukar*), a bird of southern Asia, especially of India, which in Europe is found only in Thrace and southern Bulgaria. The common European partridge is the Grey partridge (*Perdix perdix*), which is distinguished by its grey legs. It is the most widespread species in Britain and is found from

Italy and Greece up to southern Scandinavia and eastwards into Persia and the Altai Mountains in Siberia. It is also the best of the European partridges and well entrenched in the gastronomy of every European country.

The Red-legged partridge (*Alectoris rufa*), known to sportsmen as the 'Frenchman' was introduced into Britain in the 17th century. It is not quite as good as the grey and is locally common southwards and eastwards from the Midlands. It is the main species in south-west France and in the Iberian Peninsula. Partridges are in season from 1st September to the beginning of February, after which they start to breed, the young being hatched (in Britain) in June. In young birds, the legs are yellowish, the beaks sharp and the under-feathers of the wings pointed. In older birds, the legs have turned grey. Young ones need hanging for not more than four days, but older ones can use a week, depending on the weather and personal preference. As the partridge is a small bird, one per person is needed.

[*Partridge* – French: *perdrix* German: *Rebhuhn* Italian: *pernice* Spanish: *perdiz*]

PASSION FRUIT or **Purple granadilla** (*Passiflora edulis*), a native of Brazil, is now grown in warm countries everywhere, including the Mediterranean region, where the fruits are rather inferior. The plant is a perennial climber that is often grown for its beautiful flowers. The fruit is about the size of an egg and is definitely purple when ripe, smooth to begin with and then becoming wrinkled. The pulp tastes delicious but is full of tiny black seeds, which discourage many people from eating it except rubbed through a sieve or made into a squash. In some countries, it is best to pick passion fruit with caution as the vines may harbour snakes. The Giant granadilla (*P. quadrangularis*) is purely tropical and has greenish yellow fruit. It does not have such a good taste as the passion fruit, and immature ones may sometimes be boiled and used as a vegetable. Also in the same genus is included the Water lemon or Yellow granadilla (*P. laurifolia*) and the curuba (*P. maliformis*) which are not seen much outside tropical America.

PASTA. The word comes from the Italian, and is the generic name for all forms of spaghetti, macaroni, vermicelli, ravioli, and so on; it is more appropriate than noodles, which comes from the German *Nudeln*, though Oriental forms of pasta are usually called *noodles. Italy is the undisputed world leader in pasta. Italians eat far more of it than anyone else.

Although the Chinese have eaten pasta for many centuries, it is not true that it was introduced into Europe when Marco Polo came back from his journeys in the Orient in 1293. Gadgets which look as if they were for making pasta have been found in Pompeii; in any case, macaroni is mentioned in writings from as early as 1200 – almost a century before Marco Polo returned. The Italians have developed the hundreds of different pasta forms and spread a liking for spaghetti around the world. However, Thomas Jefferson brought a spaghetti die back to the US from a trip to Italy in 1786 and used it to make quantities for himself and friends. No doubt other less famous people did so too, but it was not until the 19th century, with Italian immigration, that pasta was much eaten in the US. At the beginning of the last century, durum wheat was introduced as a crop into the US, and pasta manufacture began on a large scale when supplies from Italy were cut off in World War I. The Americans have their own names for several shapes. There is an old established tradition of pasta-making in Spain, and it is made in many other countries, including Greece and Israel.

Italian-type pasta is correctly made from high-protein, durum *wheat, which likes a hot, dry climate and is much grown in low rainfall areas around the Mediterranean, for instance in southern Italy and in Spain. In the US, it is grown in the arid lands of the Great Plains. The varieties grown are mostly Russian in origin. Much pasta is made from unsuitable wheat, but in Italy the best is labelled *pasta di semola di grana duro* (pasta of hard wheat flour), which is what you should aim to buy. Unlike pasta made from inferior materials, it will not cook to a gluey mass unless it is grossly overdone. The colour varies from translucent cream to pale brown. Good pasta (there are now excellent wholewheat pastas made in Italy and Britain) has a strong, delicious wheaty flavour. The simplest pasta, and the most popular, is made only from durum wheat flour and water, green pasta contains spinach (*con spinaci*), pink contains tomato (*Con pomodoro*) and others contain extra wheat germ, bran or gluten (*con glutine*), even malt (*con malto*). According to recent Italian law, pasta labelled *all'uovo* (with eggs) must contain at least four eggs per kilo (2¼ lb) of flour, a modest amount compared to the classic home-made pasta of Bologna, which uses ten eggs per kilo.

The simplicity of pasta made from flour and

water contrasts with the incredible variety of shapes that have been invented. The present score is around two hundred and more are continually being devised. Some of these forms are merely commercial or decorative fantasies, but many are functional, and the right pasta needs to be selected for each dish. Apart from tradition, which should be respected unless there is good reason to depart from it, considerations are as follows:

1) Pasta for broth should be small. Large pasta would be out of place and long strings would mean eating broth with a fork as well as a spoon, a ludicrous performance.

2) Pasta for soups like minestrone, which contain whole beans, pieces of vegetable, peas and so on, should be of a size comparable to the bits of vegetable. Tiny pasta would fill the spaces in between and make the soup stodgy.

3) Thin tubular pasta tends to get squashed flat, while thicker pasta stands up and keeps its shape. Tubes or shells are mechanically better able to resist squashing and so give a more open texture than leaves, strips or butterflies. So also does frilled pasta. Hollow pasta gets filled with sauce and holds it, and certain large tubular forms like *cannelloni* and *bombardoni* are designed for stuffing. Other stuffed pasta are packets, square, semi-circular, circular or twisted, of which *ravioli, anolini* or *tortellini* are examples.

Perhaps of even more importance is the surface-to-volume ratio, a stuffy way of stating the obvious fact that it takes less sauce to cover a piece of dough shaped into a ball than to cover the same piece rolled out into a large sheet, which has the same volume but a bigger surface area. Even more sauce would be necessary if the sheet were cut into strips. Ribbed forms of pasta (*rigati*) trap more sauce than smooth ones (*lisci*). Nevertheless, too much importance should not be given to the wonderful variety of shapes produced by the manufacturers in spite of the inventiveness that has gone into them. Most are named after the objects they resemble – butterflies, stars, seeds, wheels, clover leaves, elder flowers and so on. The list given below is mainly restricted to the more important and traditional shapes and some regional ones; there is little point in attempting an exhaustive catalogue of the silly ones. Some manufacturers grade their pasta by numbers in sizes like shoes and hats, but Italians also make free use of suffixes and diminutives which convey size, so that from *farfalle* come *farfallette* (small), *farfallini* (very small) and *farfalloni* (large). But there are other variations which confuse all but the most determined linguists.

The word *pasta* literally means 'dough'. *Pasta asciutta*, dry pasta, refers to dishes where the pasta is in a sauce as opposed to *pasta in brodo* – pasta in a broth. There is often confusion over the word *minestre*, which may just mean soups but may also include rice dishes and pasta in broth. Italians do not make fussily clear distinctions.

....

Cooking Spaghetti

Make sure that you have a good brand. The fact that it comes from Naples and is wrapped in blue paper with an old-fashioned label is no guarantee. If your spaghetti is turning out badly, either it is being overcooked or the brand is no good, more likely the latter. Allow 2½ lt (5 pt) of water for ½ kg (1 lb) of spaghetti, and salt it generously. When it is boiling briskly, put in the spaghetti, which should be stirred with a fork to prevent the strands sticking together (a little oil or butter added to the water also helps). Check frequently during cooking, because the pasta must not be overcooked but caught and drained immediately it is *al dente* – cooked but still springy rather than soft when bitten. The time cannot be given because it depends on how long the spaghetti has been dried, on its thickness, and even on such things as altitude and weather. Dried pasta might take about 15 minutes where similar freshly made pasta would take about five minutes. Half a kilo of spaghetti makes a substantial helping for four people. After draining the spaghetti, return it to the still-warm pan and mix it carefully with the other ingredients, according to the recipe. Serve it immediately from a hot dish on to hot plates. Spaghetti should always be freshly cooked and never be kept waiting or allowed to get lukewarm and glutinous. Most of these remarks also apply to other forms of pasta.

....

Classic Bolognese Pasta

This pasta is made fresh, contains eggs, and is for making any rich pasta dish, for stuffing as for *tortellini* or *ravioli*, or for cutting into strips (*tagliatelli*). It is made fresh every day in countless Bolognese restaurants and homes, and helped to earn the town the description 'Bologna the fat'. Use 1 kg (2½ lb) strong bread flour and 10 whole eggs. Nothing more – no water and no salt. Pile the flour on a large pastry board or spotless plastic table-top. Make a well in the flour and break the eggs into it. Mix and knead energetically for at least seven minutes (some say 15), pressing with all your weight on the dough with the ball of your hand. (As eggs vary in size it may be necessary to use a little extra flour.) At the end of kneading, small blisters should appear on the surface of the dough. Roll it out carefully into a sheet thin enough to see through. If it is required for *tagliatelli*, roll it loosely, cut it in strips, plump it up into nests and allow it to dry. If it is for *ravioli* or *tortellini*, stuff the pieces immediately. They may be laid out on a surface that has been sprinkled with semolina until you are ready to cook them.

If the quantity of eggs is reduced, an eggshell of water may be necessary, but this is frowned on by Bolognese chefs and is inclined to make the pasta sticky. Correctly made pasta can be rolled out without the board needing to be floured. In Italy, a long narrow rolling pin, rather like a broomstick, is used and the large sheets of pasta are handled dexterously by rolling them up around the pin.

When pasta is made in hot weather (like a Bolognese summer), it may be difficult to work before it dries out and starts cracking. The only solution is to work in a closed kitchen with no draught and the humidity pushed as high as possible. If the ball of pasta has to be kept before rolling out, the surface may be rubbed with a little oil, or the ball can be wrapped in plastic. These days, nearly everyone who makes pasta at home uses an electric pasta machine.

....

Some Forms of Pasta

Agnolini (Lombardy).Very like *tortellini*; stuffed.

Agnollotti, agnellotti or **agnolotti**, according to region, are from Piedmont, Tuscany and Liguria. Like *ravioli*, but may be round.

Anolini (Emilia-Romagna). Stuffed, usually semicircular.

Bavette and **bavettine**. Thin oval spaghetti.

Bigoli. Spaghetti from the Veneto.

Bows. American name for *farfalle* or *cravatte*.

Bucati and **bucatini**. From *bucare*, to pierce. Forms that resemble *macaroni*.

Calzone (Naples). Stuffed form like a folded pizza.

Cannelle – pipes. *Cannellini* and *cannolicchi* (small), *cannelloni*; *canneroni* (large).

Cappelletti – little hats. Reggio Emilia and Romagna have different forms.

Cavatieddi. Small dished pasta of Puglia.

Conchiglie – conch shells. Also *conchigliette*.

Cravatte – ties or bow ties. Also *cravattine*. Similar to *farfalle*.

Elbow macaroni (American). Many variations of short, curved tubes.

Farfalle – butterflies. Also *farfalloni*; *farfallini*, *farfalette*.

Fedelini. Very fine form of *vermicelli*.

Fettuccine. *Fettuccia* is a ribbon. The name used in Rome for strip pasta, like *tagliatelli* but usually a bit narrower. Also *fetucce*, which are wider, and *fetuccelle*, which are narrower.

Fiori di sambuco – elder flowers. Small stars for soup.

Fusilli. Squiggly or spiral form of spaghetti. *Fusilli bucati* are a squiggly form of *macaroni*. Used especially in Campania.

Gemelli – twins. Two short bits of spaghetti twisted together like cord. US name: twists Napolitani.

Giant shells. American equivalent of *conchiglie*.

Gnocchi. Small dumplings or lumps of pasta, usually shaped with a fork and ridged. They are often made at home from potato or semolina as well as from flour. Bought forms resemble the elongated rippled shells called *cavatelli* or rippled ribbon pasta in short bits. Any short form of pasta of roughly the size of small *gnocchi* is liable to be called *gnocchetti*.

Lasagne. Wide strips or squares of pasta, very often home made. *Lasagne verde*, green with spinach, are also common. Usually boiled and then baked with minced meat, cheese, sauce, etc. between the sheets of pasta.

Linguine – small tongues. Short lengths of oval-section spaghetti.

Lisci – smooth, as opposed to *rigati* (striated) or *trinati* (with frilled or lacy edges).

Macaroni. English and American spelling of *maccheroni*.

Maccheroni. Tubes of pasta in all sizes from something as thin as spaghetti to *cannelle*. There are variations such as *maccheroncelli* and many alternative names, even *spaghetti bucati* (pierced spaghetti).

Malfatti – badly made. Home made and shaped into balls.

Malfattini. Finely chopped. Romagna.

Maltagliati – badly cut. Rough, elongated diamonds.

Manicotti – muffs. Something like *cannelloni*. Large tubes, usually stuffed.

Nidi – nests. Tangles of pasta, a form in which it is made at home and sometimes sold.

*Noodles. The German name for pasta is *Nudeln*. In Germany, these would include *Makharoni* and *Spaghetti, Hausmachernudeln* (home-made), and the famous *Spätzle*. German noodles are not made with durum wheat flour.

Offelle. Like *ravioli*. Stuffed pasta from Trieste.

Orecchiette – little ears. Also called by other local names in the Bari, Brindisi and Taranto region. Home made by slicing a tiny roll of pasta and denting each slice with the point of a knife.

Pansotti. Local, usually triangular, stuffed pasta from Liguria.

Pappardelle. Broad ribbons cut in short pieces, one of the types that is often home made.

Pastina. Small pasta of any shape for broth.

Penne – quill or pen. *Macaroni* in shortish lengths

cut diagonally like a nib at the ends. Also *pennette* (tiny), *pennine* (small), *pennone* (large).Very common in Italy.

Perline – little pearls. *Microperline* or *perline microscopici* are even smaller. Used in soup.

Puntine – little points (the smallest). *Puntette* are larger and the same as *semini* (little seeds).

Ravioli. Very popular stuffed pasta, usually rectangular and cut with a crenellated edge. *Raviolini* are smaller. Usually freshly made but also available dried.

Riccio – curly, as in *fetucce riccie* (curly ribbons) or *lasagne riccie*.

Rigati – striped (from *rigare*, to rule). Many forms of pasta are made both smooth (*lisci*) and striated.

Rigatoni. Very large grooved tubes. A common and popular form.

Ruote – wheels. Also *ruotelline* (very small) and *ruotini* (small).

Sedani. Like celery (*sedona*) – ridged types of *macaroni*, usually in short bits for soup. *Sedani corti* (short) are the classic form to use in minestrone.

Spaghetti. Often sold in numbered thicknesses. Also *spaghettini* (thin) and *spaghettoni* (thick).

Stelle – stars. Also *microstelle* (smallest), *stellini*, *stellettine*, *stellette* (largest). Common types used in soup.

Tagliatelle. From *tagliare*, to cut. Ribbon pasta with eggs as made in Bologna, and a little wider than the Roman *fettucine*. Also *tagliarini, tagliolette, tagliolini*.

Tondo – round, e.g. *farfalle tonde*, round-winged butterflies as opposed to those which look more like bow ties.

Tortelli. Like *ravioli*, rectangular or triangular. Mainly from Italy.

Tortellini. Twists of stuffed egg pasta well described by an alternative name in Italian – Venus's navel. Those made in Bologna rank amongst the

world's greatest pasta dishes.

Tortelloni. Large versions of *tortellini*, but heavier and thus suffering by comparison.

Trenette. Like flattened spaghetti – the correct pasta with *pesto alla genovese*.

Trinati. A descriptive word meaning frilled as in *tripolini trinati*, a small member of the bow and butterfly family used in soup.

Trofie. Little twisted bits of pasta used in Liguria with *pesto*.

Vermicelli – little worms. Very fine spaghetti.

Zite. Large *macaroni* cut in lengths. *Zitoni* are the large version and *mezze zite* the average.

PASTEURIZATION is a process particularly applied to milk since *sterilization of milk by boiling produces a cooked flavour, decreases the vitamin content and causes undesirable changes in the proteins. Pasteurization – heating to a lower temperature – will kill the disease germs without these undesirable effects but also without complete sterilization. The method that is now usual consists of heating milk to 71°C (161°F) and holding it at that temperature for 15 seconds (after which it is cooled very rapidly). Milk being pasteurized must be continually stirred to prevent a skin forming. If the milk is already going sour, it will curdle when heated.

Pasteurization usually kills about 99% of the micro-organisms, including those of all the diseases which can be transmitted through milk: undulant or Malta fever, foot and mouth disease, typhoid, tuberculosis, scarlet fever, diphtheria, septic sore throat, polio, dysentery and summer diarrhoea.

Pasteurization is also used in wine-making to improve the keeping qualities of the wine (particularly wine with a low alcohol content) and as a remedy for various maladies that wine can develop.

[*Pasteurization* – French: *pasteuriser* German: *pasteurisieren* Italian: *pastorizzare* Spanish: *pasterizar*]

PASTIS. *See* liqueurs and cordials.

PÂTÉ, literally a pie; an apple pie in French is a *pâté de pommes*. The word has also come to mean what you might call a meat pie without a crust (although it is often enclosed in bards of bacon or pork fat), for which an alternative name is *terrine*. The French names have a certain refinement not possessed by the Anglo-Saxon equivalent, meat loaf. The borderline between *pâté* and some sausages, potted meats and meat pastes is ill defined. For instance, the Danish *leverpostej* or liver paste, used in *smørrebrød*, is a *pâté*. However, it is the French who produce by far the greatest range of *pâtés*.

There are many regional specialities and much variation from *charcutier* to *charcutier*, with products ranging from simple *pâté de foie de porc* or pig's liver, which is among the cheapest of meat dishes, through chicken, rabbit and duck to highly-truffled delicacies and the legendary *pâtés* of larks. The most renowned of all is *pâté de *foie gras*. I can only repeat Jane Grigson's advice: 'When you go into a strange *charcuterie* be brave. Take your time and buy small amounts of all the *pâtés*. Her book, *Charcuterie and French Pork Cookery* (Grub Street) is highly recommended for those who wish to make their own *pâtés*. Essentially, *pâtés* consist of minced, chopped or slivered meat with roughly an equal amount of fat, flavourings (onion, garlic, truffle, salt, pepper, nutmeg and or any spice mixture, wine or brandy) and often natural meat jelly. Eggs, flour, and white sauces are used as binders. Most *pâtés* need to be given one or two days to mature after making. If they are sealed while hot with a layer of fat, they will keep, like potted meat, for some weeks in the refrigerator.

Pâte without the final accent is a paste as in *pâte feuilletée* (puff paste), *pâte à crêpes* (pancake batter), and also *pâte d'amandes* (almond paste), *pâte de coignes* (quince paste), *pâte d'anchois* (anchovy paste), etc. *Les pâtes alimentaires* are pasta. But *pâtée* is a dog's dinner or a mash for cramming into geese or chickens.

PAUNCHING. The paunch is the belly, and paunching is removing the guts – usually of rabbit or hare. To paunch either, hold it with one hand by the back legs. Insert the point of a sharp knife in the underside between the back legs and slit forward as far as the rib-cage, cutting through skin and belly wall only. (Make sure you do not cut into the intestine or stomach by mistake.) Put a finger and thumb into the front end of the slit and grasp the pipe (oesophagus) that runs forward from the stomach. Pull it free, and the rest of the guts will fall out cleanly. After that the animal is usually hung in the skin (*see* hanging). Rabbits should be paunched as soon as possible after the animal is killed, but

hares are usually hung for up to a week (according to age) before being paunched (or skinned).

PAWPAW. *See* papaya.

PAYOUSNAYA. *See* caviar.

PEA. Probably native to the Near East, peas have been cultivated as food since at least the Bronze Age and occur in the excavations of Swiss lake dwellings. They were an important pulse and a good source of protein. The name of Garden peas is not an advertising gimmick, but distinguishes the modern sweet varieties (*Pisum sativum*) from the old Field peas (*P. arvense*, which is sometimes considered just a variety of *P. sativum*), which were commonly eaten up to the Middle Ages. These were not grown as a green vegetable, but were dried, perhaps split, and kept for winter. After soaking, they were lengthily cooked to make pease puddings or soups. They were a necessary staple.

Garden peas are eaten immature. There are now hundreds of varieties, and vast quantities are grown for freezing and canning. The gardeners' distinction between dwarf and climbing varieties does not affect the peas themselves or therefore the cook. Seed coats may be wrinkled or smooth; wrinkled ones are reckoned sweeter. Garden peas should be young and fresh – choose firm pods which rustle when scooped up. When a trial pod is opened (if the greengrocer refuses, suspect him), the peas should taste fresh and tender. The very best frozen peas, because they are picked at exactly the right moment, are often better than stale peas bought in the market. Nobody would claim, though, that they were as good as peas straight from the garden. Pea pods are edible when the fibrous part is removed, but a special type of pea, known variously as the sugar pea, snow pea or mange-tout (var. *saccaratum*) is grown in many countries; the pods are eaten whole when they are young and still flat. As these are popular with Chinese cooks, they are sometimes called Chinese peas.

Dried peas may be whole or split, bright green or yellow. They need to be soaked, usually overnight, before being cooked, although they can be reduced to a purée in a pressure cooker.

Other legumes to which the term pea is applied include *asparagus pea, *chickpea, *cowpea and *pigeon pea.

[*Pea* – French: *pois* German: *Erbse* Italian: *pisello* Spanish: *guisanto*]

PEA BEAN. A type of *kidney bean.

PEACH. Originally cultivated in China (where peach blossom symbolizes long life), the peach came to Europe thousands of years ago via Persia (hence the scientific name, *Prunus persica*) and was grown by the Romans. Trees from ancient stocks have often gone wild. There are many varieties, thousands it is reckoned, which may be simply classified into those with yellow and those with white flesh (of which the white-fleshed are usually the better for eating), into freestone, in which the flesh is separate from the stone, and clingstone in which it is attached. The semi-clingstones come in between. Finally, there are special varieties of peach such as nectarines (var. *nectarina*) which have a smooth, rather than downy, skin and a very rich flavour. Greengrocers are often not aware of the variety they are selling, and there is great variation in the quality of the same variety grown in different areas. In North America, where the peach is the third most important fruit, after the orange and the apple, peaches are put through a machine which removes their down at the same time as it washes them.

Among the best peaches I ever ate were in a peach orchard in Ontario during a strike of pickers. Told to help myself to the fruits which were already past the moment for commercial picking, I sat down on the grass in the drowsy, hot afternoon and listened to the plop, plop, plop of perfectly ripe peaches falling. Occasionally, I marked one that had just dropped and ate it while it was still warm from the sun. Such perfectly ripe peaches would not stand shipment; for that, they have to be picked when just mature but still firm. Bought peaches may benefit by keeping on a soft bed of cotton wool at home, but although they get softer, they do not get sweeter, and if they are greenish when bought they will never ripen at home. A peach with a pretty red blush may have an underlying green tinge and be unripe. You should look more for an underlying cream to yellow colour. When peaches are ripe, they may be put into the refrigerator, and if they are unwashed and perfect, they may keep for up to a fortnight. Many people like their peaches chilled (although that is not the best way to taste them), as a chilled peach is very refreshing. Some peaches peel easily, while others do not, depending partly on the variety. A knife rubbed gently along the skin helps to free it. For cooking, peaches can also be peeled like tomatoes, after a quick dunk into boiling water. (In commercial canneries, they may be peeled after immersion for a specified time in caustic soda solution.) Another way to deal with a peach skin is to dip the fruit into sugar boiling at hard crack, so you have a glazed peach, something equivalent to a super toffee-apple.

[*Peach* – French: *pêche* German: *Pfirsich* Italian: *pesca* Spanish: *melocotón*]

PEACOCK. In India, peacocks (*Pavo cristatus*) can be seen wild around the villages and are holy birds; they were once much prized for the table in Europe. The breast is as big as that of the turkey, to which the meat is really very similar. However, peacocks may have an unpleasant taste and smell if they have been feeding on certain buds. In India, when turkeys were unobtainable, I twice ate peacock for Christmas, and found it an excellent substitute.

[*Peacock* – French: *paon* German: *Pfau* Italian: *pavone* Spanish: *pavo real, pavón*]

PEANUT, groundnut, or monkey nut (*Arachis hypogaea*). The peanut is well named: it is a legume, and the nuts are the peas in the pod. It gets the name of groundnut because the plant pushes its pods into the earth, which must be loose enough for the 'peg' to push into it; otherwise there will be no nuts. Ripe peanuts have to be dug out like potatoes.

Peanuts are unknown in the wild, but are thought to have originated and first been cultivated in South America (from evidence in Inca tombs). Portuguese slave traders carried the nuts – a convenient ration for the voyage – from Brazil to West Africa in the early 16th century, and from there peanuts were introduced to the US. During the 18th century, they were grown in Carolina and other states. Today, peanuts are an important world crop, being rich both in oil (40-50%) and protein (about 30%).

The many varieties differ in size, number of nuts, pod, and colour (which can be anything from white or cream to brown, red or even variegated red and white).The small varieties usually go for oil and the larger, less oily ones for eating. Supplies come notably from China, Java, Nigeria and other African countries, Spain and the US.

Although India claims the largest production, which is mostly needed for home consumption, there are few Indian recipes based on peanuts, which are of greater importance in West African cooking – for instance, in the form of roasted meal they are a key ingredient of groundnut chop. The Egyptians make a soup, *foul sudani*, from peanuts. In Indonesian and Malay cooking, roasted peanuts, pounded to a paste, are the basis for *saté* (skewers of grilled cubes of meat in a peanut sauce), as well as for a salad dressing (*gado-gado*) and other dishes. In the US, there are dozens of recipes in which peanuts are used, mainly for sweet dishes, candy, cakes and cookies.

In virtually all recipes, peanuts are first roasted (although the green immature pods can also be eaten boiled, and in Java they are made into a fermented paste called *onchom* which is subsequently fried). Commercially, an oil is expressed from the nuts (peanut, groundnut or *arachide* oil). Peanuts are used as a basis for vegetarian nut meats, sauces, and even an artificial milk. They are suitable for adulterating coffee, cocoa and ground spices. Peanuts may be roasted in a very cool oven, only 115°C (240°F), until the nuts are dry, the flesh a pale brown colour and the skin brittle. A cruder way is to dry-fry the nuts in a pan over a very low heat. They must be stirred continuously. Over-roasting or burning spoils the flavour. On the other hand, roasting must be taken far enough to remove the raw flavour. Insufficiently roasted nuts do not keep.

When the roasted nuts have cooled enough to handle, rub them with your fingers to remove the brittle skins. They can then be winnowed off by dropping the nuts in front of an electric fan (or outdoors in the wind). Alternatively, the cook can use a hand fan or, less hygienically, blow away the chaff. Salt the nuts to taste.

Once the skins have been removed, it is simple to make peanut butter, using the special nut-butter plate of a nut mill. Salt, and a little vegetable oil, if necessary, are added to get the right flavour and consistency. Some varieties are oilier than others. In the absence of a nut mill, results can be obtained by quickly grinding the nuts in a whirling coffee mill, then pounding them in a mortar or even in a meat-mincing machine. Peanuts, like many other nuts, will 'oil' when pounded.

In theory, the most delicious results, for instance in Indonesian food, would be obtained from freshly shelled nuts, roasted and ground at home. This is a long job, especially if you have no children to husk the nuts and you do the roasting in a pan on the fire in the unsophisticated way. I do not think that the taste is worth the trouble – you can make delicious dishes with commercial peanut butter or crunchy peanut butter of a good brand – but in commercial peanut butter, the germ is removed to give better shelf life (otherwise it goes rancid), and that reduces the nutritional value.

Saté Sauce

The following tasty recipe was fabricated by the Indonesian wife of a Dutch friend, a restaurateur, who had been unable to get the correct type of *ketjap* in Europe. It is easy to make and is a close approximation to the real thing.

Melt 25 g (1 oz) butter in a saucepan, then add two tablespoons vinegar and four stock cubes, preferably French *poule-au-pot* cubes (or three chicken stock cubes and one beef bouillon cube). Mix well over a low heat until all is melted and then add up to one tablespoon of good dark brown sugar little by little, stirring and tasting until the sauce is no longer sour. But do not add so much sugar that the salty taste is destroyed. This is important: as sugar and salt tend to cancel each other, the operation requires some judgement in balancing the sweet-sour-salty taste. We have now made an artificial substitute for an Indonesian *ketjap* of a particular type.

Now add one finely minced large onion, two chopped cloves of garlic, a strip of lemon peel, a bay leaf, a small pinch of thyme and a good pinch each of ginger and chilli pepper. The thyme must on no account dominate. Continue to cook the mixture slowly until the onion is soft. Then remove the pan from the heat, add a small pot of peanut butter, blend well and pour in the juice (if any) from the meat. Heat gently, stirring all the time, and pour over grilled kebabs. Serve with boiled rice.

[Peanut – French: *cacahuètes, arachide* German: *Erdnuss* Italian: *arachide* Spanish: *cacahué, cacahuete*]

PEAR. The common pear (*Pyrus communis*) is a native of eastern Europe and the Middle East. Although there are about 20 species of pear in Europe and Asia – and some have been hybridized with the common pear – most of the good eating pears are derived from the one species. There are at least 5000 named varieties of which 20-30 are cultivated on a large scale. In Europe, France is generally regarded as the leading country for pears, but many are grown, for instance, in Belgium and Germany. Though pear trees do not stand quite the same range of climate as apples, they have deep roots and can endure stony, dry conditions which would not be tolerated by apples. Characteristic of pears, and unpleasant in some varieties, are the tiny hard grains (stone cells with woody cell walls) that make pears gritty. The best eating varieties are more or less grit-free.

Pears for sale are picked before they are quite ripe. They will ripen off the tree if they are kept in an even, nicely warm temperature, but then deteriorate very quickly. It is therefore best to buy them not quite ripe and keep them to the perfect moment which lasts at most a day. When they are ripe, they should be put in the refrigerator until eaten. Pears are ripe when pressing the neck gently shows they are just yielding. Some pears, Williams for instance, pass their peak within a matter of hours, and vigilance is necessary in obtaining perfect dessert pears. So is careful handling, as pears bruise easily. While bruised pears should not, of course, be bought, appearance, as with most fruit, is a poor guide to quality. There are some lovely looking pears (like Keiffers, imported from South Africa) which are dry and tasteless. Others, which look a bit rough, may taste wonderful. Some pears are only for cooking or bottling and not for eating. Others are for perry (the pear equivalent of cider). Many are multi-purpose. The pear for any particular use depends on season and the kinds that are available locally.

Of the many recipes for cooking pears, the best known are for poaching in syrups flavoured with red wine, vanilla, rum, almonds and so on. Cooked pears do not seem to stand up on their own but always seem to need other flavours to complement them. In general, they also lack acidity, are not even sour when unripe and tend to lose aroma on cooking.

Pears may be stored in the same way as *apples, although they need not be wrapped. As they ripen better at a higher temperature than apples, they could be kept in a cool spare room in the house before being brought into a warm room to finish ripening.

[Pear – French: *poire* German: *Birne* Italian: *pera* Spanish: *pera*]

PEARL BARLEY. *See* barley.

PEARL MOSS. *See* carrageen.

PECAN (*Carya illinoensis*) is the finest of the *hickory nuts, an American native indigenous to the Mississippi Valley and neighbouring states as far south as northern and central Mexico. It is much grown commercially in Oklahoma, Texas, Florida and Georgia. In general, it likes climates suitable for maize and cotton. In the US, the pecan does not thrive much north of the 40th parallel. Pecans have been introduced into other countries, such as South Africa, where the climate is suitable.

The pecan tree can grow to almost 61 m (200 ft) in height when conditions are favourable. The nut-producing varieties are propagated by grafting. Nuts of different types vary in size, quality and flavour.

Pecans are rather like walnuts, but have a smooth, elongated, usually rather thin shell. The flavour is also somewhat like a walnut but the pecan is oilier, in fact, it is the oiliest nut in common use, with 70% oil content being quite usual.

Nuts are harvested by knocking them off the tree with poles, and most of the crop is shelled by machinery after drying and treatment with ethylene gas to loosen the kernels. The proportion of meat to shell in the pecan is very high. The shells of nuts for dessert are frequently polished and dyed red-brown with a particularly hideous combination of dyestuffs that goes ill with the lovely natural colours of other nuts on the table.

Shelled pecans go rancid rather quickly unless they are sealed under gas or in a vacuum. The use of pecans in cakes, pies and candies is very much an American habit. Pecan pie, with loads of cream, will be part of the American-built heaven. Americans also use pecans in stuffing for turkey. The nut is now beginning to be used in Europe.

Maple Pecan Sauce

Gently heat 250 ml (½ pt) of maple syrup in a heavy saucepan until it begins to thicken, within 10 minutes. Cool slightly and add 200 g (7 oz) chopped pecans (or to taste). Use this sauce warm on ice cream for a totally American flavour.

PECTIN is the name of a class of jelling substances which occur naturally in many fruits, especially in cores, pips and skins, as well as in some vegetables such as split peas and lentils. The cell walls of unripe fruit contain pectose, an insoluble substance which changes to soluble pectin as the fruit ripens. However, when the fruit is fully ripe, the pectin in turn changes to pectic acid and methyl alcohol, which is why barely ripe fruit is generally the best for jelly. Pectins are chemically derived from carbohydrates, not, like gelatine, from protein, but likewise consist of the long-chain molecules, the typical structure for forming a jelly.

For a pectin jelly, it is necessary to have not only enough pectin but also enough acid and sugar in roughly the correct proportion. The effectiveness of the acid is related to the *pH (the sourness) of the juice; of the common fruit acids, tartaric is more effective than malic, which is more effective than citric.

The minimum acidity at which a pectin jelly will form at all is pH 3.46. A good quality home-made jelly forms at pH 3.3 (slightly more acid), and at 3.2 the jelly becomes stiffer. If the acidity is increased still further, to pH 3.1,the liquid begins to seep out of the jelly – it weeps. Boiling for long periods with acid tends to destroy pectin, as also does pressure cooking, and again the jelly becomes weak.

The third element in the balance is sugar. In fruit jellies, the necessary level will usually be somewhere near saturation (69-72%). If the percentage of sugar is more than this, a syrup may be formed and the jelly may not set at all, but the sugar may crystallize on cooling. Although setting can sometimes take place with as little as 40% sugar, such low-sugar jelly is stiff and, unless sterile, will not keep. A useful fact to know is that high acid content makes the exact sugar balance less critical, so that with the sourer fruit a larger quantity of sugar can be used.

Fruits that contain sufficient acid and pectin to set easily to jelly with the simple addition of sugar are: sour and crab apples, quinces, most plums but especially damsons, gooseberries, currants, cranberries, oranges, lemons and grapes. Blackberries, loganberries, raspberries and apricots are borderline cases. Sweet apples, pears, peaches, strawberries, cherries, huckleberries, guavas and figs – and non-fruit jam materials like vegetable marrows – lack either acid or pectin, or both. Recipes for making jams or jellies from these involve adding lemon juice, prepared pectin or other fruits rich in the missing components.

Pectin may be bought either as a liquid or a powder. It is usually made either from apple pulp or from the white part of citrus fruit skins (the albedo) and is a by-product of the juice industry. The pectin is extracted from the albedo with water acidified usually with a mineral acid. It can also be made at home.

Pectin

Shred 450 g (1 lb) of the white part of the peel of oranges or lemons, and let it stand in about 2 lt (3½ pt) of water with 125 ml (scant ¼ pt) of lemon juice, for 2-3 hours. Then add the same quantity of water again and bring the pan slowly to the boil. Boil 10 minutes with the lid on and stand it aside till next day. Then boil the mixture once more for some 15 minutes and bottle or use immediately.

Because the amount of pectin in fruits is so variable, as is also its quality, a simple test is necessary to find out whether there is enough of it in a fruit juice to form a jelly. The acidity can usually be guessed at by tasting. To test the pectin content, take a teaspoon of the juice, cool it, and drop it into a little methylated spirit (about three teaspoons). Shake the mixture very gently and then let it stand for a minute. If a jelly-like mass has formed, there is plenty of pectin. If there are a few blobs, and not very firm ones, then the pectin is probably just adequate. If there are only a number of small bits, then there is not enough pectin to make a jelly.

Jam is usually made with equal weights of sugar and fruit unless otherwise stated in a recipe. If there is plenty of pectin, then three-quarters the weight of the juice is a reasonable amount of sugar, but if the pectin is barely adequate this must be reduced to about 600 g (21 oz) of sugar per 1 lt (1¾ pt).

Once sugar has been added to juice with adequate pectin and acidity, boiling for no more than 10 minutes will produce a jelly that will set properly on cooling. The temperature of boiling is the most reliable test: it should be 104.5°C (220°F), but may have to reach 105.5°C (222°F).The usual tests for setting are:

1) The flake test. Dip the spoon into the hot jelly. Take it out and twirl it until the jelly on it has cooled a little. Let some of the cooled jelly drop off the edge of the spoon. If it forms a sheet and drops off cleanly as a flake, then the jelly will set when cold.

2) The cold plate test. Put a small blob of the juice on a cold plate and let it cool. Push the blob sideways with a fingernail. If it wrinkles, it will set when cold. A very few exotic fruits will not form a jelly, even though they have plenty of pectin, because they contain gummy substances which prevent setting.

[*Pectin* – French: *pectine* German: *Pektin* Italian: *pectina* Spanish: *pectina*]

PELARGONIUM. *See* geranium.

PEMMICAN. Originally hard rations for North American Indians when they were hunting, travelling or at war, it was made of dried meat – buffalo or deer – pounded with rendered fat, pressed into cakes and preserved in skins. Cranberries were also mixed in, and perhaps dried blueberries. The purpose of pemmican was to be sustaining rather than nice. Under 1 kg (2¼ lb) a day would suffice to keep a man doing hard manual work. This chewy food was adopted by explorers for rations on sledging trips. Sir John Richardson, an Arctic explorer in the 1820s, used a pemmican of lean meat dried in a malting kiln, ground in the malt mill and mixed with an equal quantity of melted suet, plus currants and sugar to taste. This was sealed in canisters instead of skins. Later versions of pemmican were more gourmet-orientated. The pemmican brought back from the 1922 Spitzbergen expedition was good (at least, I thought so as a child), and later versions even better. With modern freeze-dried meat and vegetables, vitamins and a better understanding of nutrition, there is no longer need for such heroic foods. If it is kept properly, pemmican will last indefinitely.

PENNYROYAL (*Mentha pulegium*) is a small creeping relative of mint with a strong and rather peculiar minty aroma. In Britain, dried pennyroyal is responsible for the special flavour of North Country black puddings.

[*Pennyroyal* – French: *pouliot* German: *Flohkraut*, *Poleiminze* Italian: *puleggio* Spanish: *poleo*]

PEPINELLO. *See* chayote.

PEPPER originally meant vine pepper from a plant of the genus *Piper*. The *chilli peppers and *sweet peppers, which came in later from tropical America, stole the same name because they are more or less pungent.

Black pepper and white pepper both come from the same plant, *Piper nigrum*, a climbing vine native to the tropical forests of monsoon Asia. The vine produces hanging strings of dark green berries, which turn bright red when ripe. If the green berries are picked and dried, they darken to form black pepper. Ripe berries are made into white pepper by the removal of the red skin and pulp. The ripe berries are stacked in piles to promote fermentation, which softens the outside. When this is washed off, the white inner seeds are left and are dried in the sun. Although there is some difference in the flavour between the black and white pepper, it is better experienced than described. White pepper is more expensive and less aromatic; it is used in white sauces or in any dish where black pepper would give a speckled appearance. Pepper should always be freshly ground in a mill, partly because its flavour is volatile and lost very quickly, and partly because you can then be sure that it has not

been adulterated. *Mignonette* pepper (also called shot pepper), which is used in French cookery, is coarsely-ground pepper made by roughly grinding and sifting peppercorns. A coarsely-set pepper mill produces an approximate equivalent.

Green peppercorns are the berries of *P. nigrum* which have been canned rather than dried. Their flavour is fresh and pungent, without being excessively hot; it particularly suits meats, poultry and fish. Once the can has been opened, green peppercorns will keep for up to six weeks in a well stoppered glass or stoneware jar in the coldest part of the refrigerator.

Long pepper – *P. longum* from India and *P. retrofractum* from Java – is occasionally called for in Oriental recipes. Their flavour is rather similar to that of black pepper but slightly sweeter, and black pepper will usually do as a substitute. *Betel leaves come from a species of pepper (*P. betel*). Other plants which are popularly known as pepper are listed below.

Cubeb pepper (*Piper cubeb*) is an aromatic, pungent and acrid spice. Originally from the East Indian 'Spice Islands', it is now also grown in the West Indies and Ceylon. A collector's piece today, used mostly as a source of medicinal Cubeb camphor, cubeb pepper was important in the past and was one of the spices used in preparing the spiced aperitif wine called hippocras.

Jamaica pepper or **myrtle pepper**. Although the aromatic berries of the myrtle were used once as a substitute for pepper, myrtle pepper (*Pimenta dioica*) is not from myrtle but is *allspice, which is a member of the myrtle family.

Kava pepper (*Piper methysticum*), although related to black pepper, is not a spice, but is the basis of *kava* or *kava-kava*, a drink from Samoa and other South Pacific islands. The women chew the fibre of the plant, mixing it well with their saliva and spitting the mush into a pot. The intoxicating nature of this drink is not due to alcohol, nor to the women's spit, but to alkaloids released by the salivary enzymes.

Pepper-grass describes various plants with pungent fruits that are sometimes used as spices and are gathered wild in rural areas. They belong to the cabbage family (Cruciferae) and are close relatives of garden *cress (*Lepidium sativum*). The Wild pepper grass (*Lepidium virginicum*) of North

America is naturalized in Europe, and Roadside pepper-grass (*Lepidium ruderale*), a native of Europe, is naturalized in North America and Australia.

Pepper-root. Pungent roots of *Dentaria*.

Pepper-tree. Name given to various trees, notably the common ornamental *Schinus molle*, oil from which is used commercially as a food flavouring.
   [*Pepper* – French: *poivre* German: *Pfeffer* Italian: *pepe* Spanish: *pimienta*]

PEPPER DULSE. *See* seaweed.

PEPSIN is an enzyme that digests protein. It is usually prepared from fresh pig's stomachs and presented as a creamy-white, slightly acid powder. In contrast to *papain (which is often called vegetable pepsin), pepsin performs best in an acid mixture containing hydrochloric acid, which is not surprising as those are the conditions which exist in the animal's stomach. It works best at 52°C (125°F), which is a bit hotter than it is asked to perform at in nature. In solution, it is destroyed by temperatures over 70°C (158°F).
   Pepsin works like *rennet in coagulating milk and is used in cheese-making.

PERCEBE. *See* barnacle.

PERI-PERI. *See* piri-piri.

PERIWINKLE. *See* winkle.

PERMANGANATE OF POTASH. *See* disinfectants.

PERRIER. See water.

PERSIMMON or **kaki** (*Diospyros kaki*) is a tree of the same family as ebony; it is a native of China. It has been introduced all over the world and is grown in suitably warm parts of North America as well as in Mediterranean Europe. It is easily noticed, as the fruit does not ripen until well into winter when the leaves have fallen and the orange or scarlet fruit stand out against the winter landscape like lights on the tree.
   There are many varieties, especially in China and Japan, some with yellow fruits. The persimmon is very astringent and full of tannin until thoroughly ripe – and in appearance over-ripe – yet the fruits have to be marketed early as they do not keep

well. In China and Japan, the tannin is sometimes removed by soaking in *limewater, and they may be ripened with ethylene gas. Sometimes the Chinese allow them to freeze on the tree, and they are also dried. Persimmons, though usually eaten raw, can be puréed and made into ice cream or used in cakes.
   The Mabolo or velvet apple (*Diospyros discolor*) is a tropical fruit of fair quality which is closely related to the persimmon. It is grown in the Philippines, Malaya and Ceylon.

PE-TSAI. *See* Chinese cabbage.

PEWTER is one part lead to four to six parts tin, although sometimes brass or copper replaces lead in the alloy. Pewter was known in ancient China and used by the Romans. Today it is not much made, as anything containing lead is out of fashion when it comes into contact with food and drink, but many people like drinking beer from pewter mugs. It should be kept clean by rubbing with fine sand.
   [*Pewter* – French: *étain* German: *Hartzinn* Italian: *peltro* Spanish: *peltre*]

pH is a measure of acidity or alkalinity which was devised by the Norwegian biochemist Srensen in 1909. Its basis need not greatly concern us here; in fact, the pH is the logarithm of the reciprocal of the hydrogen ion concentration. What matters is that the pH scale provides a measure of the effective acidity or alkalinity of a solution which works irrespective of the actual acids or alkalis present and uncomplicated by the fact that weight for weight, some acids and alkalis are stronger than others. In short, a solution of sulphuric acid and a solution of citric acid of the same pH taste equally sour.
   The pH scale runs from 0 (the most acid) to 14 (the most alkaline), with a neutral point at pH 7.0. Examples measured on this scale are: lemon juice pH 2.3, orange juice pH 3.3, sour milk pH 4.4, fresh milk pH 6.6, distilled water pH 7.0, limewater pH 8.0, 1% bicarbonate of soda solution pH 8.0, 1% washing soda pH 11.0, 1% caustic soda solution pH 13.0.
   pH is easily measured with indicator papers which change colour according to the acidity or alkalinity of the liquid into which they are dipped. The litmus paper of school chemistry is a crude indicator. it goes red for acid and blue for alkali – but the distinction is not sharp. More sophisticated papers can be bought from the chemist and allow the pH to be read with certainty.

PHEASANT (*Phasianus colchicus*). The most widespread of all gamebirds, the pheasant was introduced into Europe from further east many centuries ago and is now completely naturalized and resident over most of Europe. In North America, pheasants were introduced at various times during the 18th and 19th centuries, and are now acclimatized in many areas, though less so in the southern parts of the US, which are almost outside their favoured climate. Everywhere in their distribution, pheasants are shot for sport and also bred for the table. The season varies slightly from country to country; in Britain it is from October through the winter to February and in the US roughly from 1st November to 14th February; in some other countries, the season is more restricted. There are markets where pheasants, like other gamebirds, must carry an official tag, and it would be unwise to show an out-of-season bird even if it had been obtained lawfully from the freezer. Other species of pheasant come mostly from the Himalayas and south-west China; among them are some of the most beautiful of all birds. A few exotic species have become naturalized in parts of Europe.

A brace of pheasants traditionally consists of a hen and a cock; the hen, which lacks the enormous tail and bright colours of the cock, is regarded as the better eating. In a young cock, the spurs are short and rounded, the beak more pliable than in older birds, and the feet are soft and smooth, while in old birds they are rough and scaly.

The birds should never be plucked before being hung. How long pheasants should be hung must obviously depend in part on the weather, a bird badly holed with shot cannot be hung for as long as a well-shot bird or a bird reared specially for table.

The recommended time can vary between four days in warm weather to three weeks in frosty weather. The degree of highness is a matter of taste, although there is general agreement that fresh pheasant is uninteresting. Pheasants can be said to be ready when they get a slightly 'off' smell. Pheasants are sometimes hung by the neck, but usually by the feet, in which case some blood beginning to drip from the beak is a sign that the birds are just about ready. The bird is also said to be ready when the long tail feathers can be easily pulled out. As the meat is inclined to be dry, pheasants are best barded but never larded. In France, a couple of Petit Suisse cream cheeses are sometimes put inside pheasants before roasting to provide the necessary moistening.

[*Pheasant* – French: *faisan* German: *Fasan* Italian: *fagiano* Spanish: *faisán*]

PHOSPHORIC ACID (H_3PO_4) is colourless, syrupy and odourless. It is used by industry to provide acidity in soft drinks and is regarded as harmless in the very small concentrations used for this.

[*Phosphoric acid* – French: *acide phosphorique* German: *Phosphorsäure* Italian: *acido fosforico* Spanish: *ácido fosfórico*]

PHYSALIS FRUIT. The genus *Physalis*, with about one hundred species, belongs to the tomato family, and some half a dozen are cultivated, mainly in warm countries, as they are sensitive to frost.

Chinese lantern plant or **bladder cherry** (*P. alkengii*) is the best known, and is grown for the decorative effect of its red papery calyx, the husk which looks, as the name suggests, rather like a papery lantern. This lantern surrounds a berry which is edible when ripe.

The members of the genus that are cultivated for their fruit have the same general appearance, but the lantern is light brown and not decorative.

Cape gooseberry (*P. peruviana*), in spite of its name, is a native of South America, but early in the last century had become an important crop in South Africa. The plant is also produced to some extent in southern Europe. The flavour is rather like a gooseberry, though with less character. They can be bought, canned, as Goldenberries. Cape gooseberries make good jam. Allow equal weights of sugar and fruit, and bottle the jam the moment it will set.

Ground cherry, **strawberry tomato**, or **dwarf Cape gooseberry** (*P. pruinosa*) is native to parts of central and eastern North America, from New York to Florida and west to Iowa and Minnesota, but is local in occurrence. Used for jam and pies, the fruits may be stored for a month or more, during which time they become sweeter. Ground cherries are also a popular wild fruit in Hawaii, where they are called *poha* and are used particularly to make a syrupy preserve.

....

Poha Preserve

Make a thick syrup by boiling together 675 g (1½ lb) of sugar and 225 ml (8 fl oz) of water, a stick of cinnamon and a sliced lemon for about 10 minutes.

Add 1 lt (1¾ pt) of ground cherries and boil until they become clear. Leave to cool overnight. Next day bring to the boil and bottle.

....

Tomatillo, jamberry or tomate verde. Native to Mexico, the tomatillo (*P. ixocarpa*) was used by the Aztecs. The berry is larger than the other *Physalis* fruits and completely fills the lantern, so that it seems to be in a husk. When ripe, the fruits are variously coloured, depending on the variety, but they generally look like small green tomatoes. In fact, *tomatillo* means small tomato in Spanish. The tomatillo is rather flavourless unless boiled for a few minutes. Its particular culinary importance – though it is used for jams, and for chutneys in India – lies in its being an essential ingredient in *guacamole* (a purée of avocado pear with chilli and other seasonings), as made in the north of Mexico where the fruit is often called *tomate con cascar* (with husk). Canned tomatillos are available as well as the canned *salsa de tomatillo*. The canned fruits, when used in *guacamole*, require no further cooking.

....

PICCALILLI. *See* pickles.

PICKLED FISH. *See* caveach.

PICKEREL. *See* pike.

PICKLES and PICKLING. Pickling is an old method of preserving food by immersing it in brine or vinegar. Pickle is a word with wonderful spelling variations in Middle English, and it will only take a marketing man to notice this for us to be faced with jars of 'Ye Olde Pekille, Pykyl, Pekkyll or Pykulle.' Preservation depends on the sensitivity of putrefactive organisms to salt and acetic acid, and occasionally to other acids and spices. Although meat curers call the brines they use 'pickle', popular usage restricts pickles to foods, usually vegetables and fruit (but sometimes meat and fish) preserved in various ways and used as a relish. Pickles are made by traditional methods all over the world, from Korean and Chinese pickled cabbage to British pickled walnuts. Pickles also include what the Americans call relishes and the English call *chutneys. The word covers a vast number of preparations and different techniques for making them, but there are some basic varieties and considerations which are dealt with below. In general, vegetables to be pickled must be firm and as fresh as possible. Acid or salt must be sufficiently concentrated to ensure that the pickle keeps. Pickles may or may not need the addition of garlic, herbs and spices, but of over-riding importance to their flavour is the critical balance between sourness, saltiness and sweetness.

Air, since it contains oxygen, is the enemy of pickles. It causes discolouration, encourages the growth of moulds and the degrading of vinegar by bacteria. It should be kept at bay by filling jars to the brim, dislodging bubbles and covering carefully. Pickle should always be held under the surface of the pickling liquid; vegetables being pickled in bulk should be weighed down with stones or boards.

*Alum is sometimes used in pickles to harden the vegetables. A piece the size of a bean will do for 4½ lt (4 qt) of vinegar, the amount is not critical and is usually given in the recipe. Although alum is harmful in large doses and is not favoured by the authorities, it has a low toxicity, so is all right in the small quantities needed in pickles. It has been used in food for hundreds of years.

*Brine. A 10% brine strength is commonly used for discouraging unwanted bacteria and for holding vegetables before pickling. This is particularly necessary when vegetables that crop at different seasons are eventually to be put together in a mixed pickle, such as piccalilli.

Colour. Pickles should look attractive, so colour is important. Reasons why pickles discolour include: a) leaving cut surfaces exposed to the air instead of dropping the vegetables into water and lemon juice as soon as they are cut; b) using hard water for brine; c) using brown vinegar, d) using ground spices and leaving spices in bottles. But it is more important that pickles should taste good than look good, and if you find it hard to make white pickles, the alternative is to colour them red with a slice of beetroot, as is often done in the Middle East. Turmeric turns pickles yellow, but adds its flavour.

Covering. Pickles must always be covered with liquid and the jar sealed to prevent evaporation. Pickles containing oil should remain under it, and a layer of oil can sometimes be used on top of pickles to help seal them. Jars with bare metal lids should be avoided, as a vinegar-salt mixture is very corrosive to metal.

Drying. Some ingredients are very watery; others, like capers, can gain in strength of flavour by being wilted in the sun before being pickled. When there is no sun, water may have to be removed by salting and squeezing. Watery pickles do not keep well, as the vinegar may become diluted by the juices below the critical level of acidity. Failing all else, it may be necessary to use extra salt or strong, distilled vinegar.

Dill pickles. Cucumbers preserved by a lactic-acid fermentation and flavoured with dill (or its oil) and usually some garlic are called dill pickles. This is one of the most popular types of pickle especially (with ethnic variations) in the US and Central and Eastern Europe.

Fermentation. Alcoholic fermentation can occasionally occur in sweet pickles or chutneys left open in hot weather, but is unimportant in this context compared to *lactic acid fermentation, which occurs in the making of dill pickles and *sauerkraut*. It is the reaction that takes place in silage, and is analogous to the souring of milk. The lactic acid acts as a preservative. Most of these pickles were originally devised in cool countries for keeping during cold winters, and they will not stand safely in hot climates, where they need to be packed in jars and sterilized. They should, in any case, always be kept in a cool place, such as a cellar.

*Garlic is pickled whole in Middle Eastern countries and has a rather startling flavour, but a clove or two is quite a normal part of pickling spices, and often improves the pickle.

*Gherkins. Tiny relatives of the cucumber.

Hardening. Vinegar tends to harden vegetables, and will delay softening when fruits, such as apples, are cooked in it when making chutney. If a pickle seems to be too soft, the next year try adding alum (*see above*). Tannin is another hardener, which is one reason why oak leaves or black-currant leaves are used in dill pickles in Poland and elsewhere.

Herbs and **spices**. The flavouring of many pickles may be traditional, but it is also often an individual matter. In commercial pickle-making, this is an area of closely-guarded secrets, and mixtures of extracts and essential oils are used for greater control and a standard product. At home, you use the raw ingredients, which should (unless otherwise instructed) be put into a muslin bag and boiled or infused in the vinegar and removed before pickling. Whole spices are also put into the jar, for slow diffusion. Common flavourings are black or white peppercorns, garlic, shallots, onion, whole bruised ginger, tamarind, bay, cloves, cinnamon or cassia sticks, chillies, cumin, coriander, fenugreek, turmeric, white mustard seeds, horseradish, dill, fennel, sage, savory and other items like rue and asafoetida in tiny quantities. Although pickle-spice mixtures can be bought, the more interested cooks (such as the readers of this book) will make their own formulae to suit individual pickles. A standard mixture might be six black peppercorns, two allspice, a large blade of mace, a clove or a chilli, with a pinch of coriander and white mustard seeds, and a few white peppercorns. Too much clove is overwhelming.

Maturation. Pickles and chutneys vary in the time they need to be kept before they can be eaten. Some are designed to be ready very quickly, even the same day, while others need six months. With highly-spiced, thick chutneys, the longer the better, up to a year. A few pickles improve up to 20 years, but most reach a climax and then deteriorate.

Moulds are likely to grow on anything, including the top of pickles, and are not too discouraged by acidity, especially if there is air around. The white scum which forms on vats of fermenting cucumbers and *sauerkraut* should be skimmed off every ten days. It is a natural growth and quite harmless, but invites secondary organisms which will turn the pickle musty.

Lemon and **lime juice**, being very acid, are preservative and in some cases replace vinegar in pickles. As the citric acid in them is not as good a preservative as acetic acid, it is necessary to follow recipes and not simply to swap lemon juice for vinegar on grounds of health or availability.

Oils are preservative only because they coat the ingredients and tend to exclude air. Mustard oil may also have some special preservative action. There are many oily pickles of Asian inspiration, including pickled fish and pickled chicken and pork. These are all cooked pickles. If I use other oils instead of mustard oil, I always include white mustard seed with it.

Onions. Pickled onions are so popular in Britain that they deserve special mention. Although many are grown locally, they also come into the country from places as far apart as Holland, Poland, Bulgaria, Hungary and Egypt. In the trade, they are classified into three types: the large Ware onions, which are used sliced; the Baby Ware onions which are small specimens of large onions; and the Silver-skins, which come from Holland and are a different type altogether. The smallest are used as cocktail onions.

Commercially, onions are peeled by machine. After the onions have been topped and tailed, either the skin is burned off (the 'flash' method), or the onions are put into a machine which slits the outside skin lightly, and blows it off with a high pressure blast of air. For ease of peeling at home, dunk them, a few at a time, into boiling water for 30 seconds (or even up to two minutes) and refresh them in cold water. The skins then come off easily. Onions are always brined for 24 hours before being pickled in vinegar. In some quarters, shallots are thought to make better pickled onions than onions do.

*pH. The degree of acidity needed to make a pickle keep depends on storage temperature, type of pickle and the spices present. A pH below 4 is safe; if a pickle tastes nicely sharp, it is pretty sure to keep.

Piccalilli. A pickle of unknown origin, and a very different commodity in Britain and America. In Britain, it is a mixed pickle in a thick, opaque vinegary sauce full of ground white mustard and turmeric – in the US, it would probably be called mustard pickle. American piccalilli would in Britain be called a sweet mustard pickle.

Salt used for pickling must be pure (not table salt, which is doctored to make it free-running). Special salts are sold for pickling, but any good kitchen salt will serve the purpose.

Scum. See above, moulds.

Sun. Sunlight is antiseptic. It kills micro-organisms, bleaches, and encourages various chemical changes, some of which (see fats and oils) are not beneficial, while others may be. In India, a country with plenty of hot sun and a love of pickles, jars of pickles are very often stood in the sun to mature. The heat speeds the reactions, but the light keeps fermentation in check. Sun is also used to wilt and dry vegetables to reduce their moisture content before pickling. Pickles exposed to sunlight out of doors should be only lightly covered and brought in every night.

Vessels. Since vinegar and salt together are corrosive (the mixture is recommended for cleaning copper), metal vessels should preferably not be used. However, stainless steel is an exception and, at a pinch, aluminium pans can be used just for boiling, but brass or copper preserving pans never. Enamel pans are better, and glass is good. For the jars, glass is usual, but good stoneware is all right. Beware of lead glazed *earthenware jars which could be lethal.

*Vinegar. For good colour, many people use either white wine vinegar or white (uncoloured) malt vinegar. But otherwise, the colour of the vinegar used is immaterial. It is important to use genuine vinegar and not the synthetic stuff that so often spoils commercial pickles. Living in a wine-vinegar country, I often think that English pickles are best made with malt vinegar, but the choice is of little consequence since in nearly every case the vinegar containing the spices and herbs is brought to the boil. The congenerics of a fine vinegar and even the distinction between wine and malt vinegar, therefore tend to be lost; the basic tastes are also overlaid by the spices. Strong spirit vinegar may be necessary for pickling very watery materials, like plums and tomatoes, unless they are slightly dried out before pickling.

*Walnuts. Pickled unripe walnuts are a great British institution (perhaps because walnuts often refuse to ripen in Britain). Most of the walnuts for the pickle industry, though, come in barrels of brine from Italy Sunning is an important part of the pickling process as it helps to blacken the walnuts properly.

*Water. If hard water is used for the brining of vegetables, they are liable to have a bad colour. Indeed Leonard Levinson, in his *A Complete Book of Pickles and Relishes* (Hawthorn) even gives a pecking order of places in the US, based on the suitability of their water for making good pickles. If there are problems with the water use rain-water or even distilled water.

Indian Onion Pickle

Peel 2.5 kg (5½ lb) of onions and cut them almost through in the form of a cross but without separating the parts. Add 100 g (4 oz) salt, 50 g (2 oz) powdered mustard, ½ teaspoon turmeric, and up to 15 g (½ oz) chilli powder (depending on the strength of the chilli and the toughness of your mouth). Mix all together in a basin with ¼ cup of oil and a little water to moisten the spices and salt and get the onion coated. Then put the whole lot into a jar and just cover them with water. Keep the jar loosely covered in the sun for 4-5 days to ferment. Cool overnight and the pickle is ready to eat.

Indian Mango Pickle

Wash plump but under-ripe mangoes and slice them into brine to prevent discolouration. Mix the mango with salt (four parts by weight of mango to one of salt) and leave in a jar in the sun for five days. Then mix the salted mango with spices. 125 g (4½ oz) fenugreek, 25 g (1 oz) nigella, 25 g (1 oz) turmeric, 25 g (1 oz) black pepper and 25 g (1 oz) anise – all ground – per 1 kg (2 lb) of mango. Add a little rape seed oil to get the mango and spices mixed evenly. Put the mixture into a jar and cover it with more rape seed oil. In 2-3 weeks it is ready to be bottled.

Middle Eastern Pickled Turnip

These pickles are often eaten as part of the *meze*, with drinks, and can be seen in shops everywhere from Lebanon to Persia. Take turnips the size of tennis balls, wash them and slice off the tops and bottoms. Then cut them into slices some ½ cm (¼ in) or so thick, but the slicing stops short of cutting right through so that the result is like a book held together by 1 cm (½ in) of unsliced turnip at the bottom. These 'books' are put to soak for 12 hours in fresh water, after which they are put into glass jars with a slice or two of beetroot to give colour, and several cloves of garlic. The jars are filled with a pickling liquid made of one cup vinegar and two teaspoons salt to two cups water. The pickle is ready to eat in about three days in normal weather.

Quick Pickle

Thinly slice equal quantities of sour apples, cucumbers or celery, and young onions – sufficient to fill a 1 lt (2 pt) jar. Put them into a basin and mix in two teaspoons salt, one teaspoon chilli (or more to taste), and four tablespoons each soy sauce and sherry, pack into the jar and cover with vinegar. This pickle can be used the same day.

[*Pickles* – French: *conserves au vinaigre* German:

Eingepökelte Italian: *sottaceti* Spanish: *encurtidos*]

PIECES. *See* sugar.

PIG. *See* pork, ham, bacon.

PIGEON was once a popular food in Europe, and many a house had a dovecote or pigeon loft. Pigeons, with the minimum of care, would range far and wide, gleaning and finding most of their own food. They are supposedly best from mid-summer to Michaelmas (29th September), when many of the birds would be young. The squabs of wild pigeons were also taken from the nest just before they flew; to ensure they remained to become fat, country boys used to climb to Wood pigeons' nests and tie a string to each young pigeon's leg. The string was threaded down through the sticks of the nest, and a piece of stick tied close on the other end. Thus, the birds could move but not fly away, and were in due course collected for the table.

Today, pigeons are not favoured in Britain because many people see the scavenging flocks in towns, and suspect that the birds seen in the poulterer's shop may be these dirty town pigeons or, worse still, country birds which have been eating seed poisoned with insecticides. However, squabs are commonly on sale in markets in many European towns, and properly fattened little birds of table breeds are available almost everywhere. Squabs should be about four weeks old, and the best have never eaten whole grain; they are a delicacy. Young pigeons are also excellent for any cooking method but older ones are fit only for stewing, game stock or pies.

Pigeons are best starved for 24 hours before being killed (or so the experts say) and, when dead, should be hung up by the legs and bled. If not, the meat will be dark. They should also be plucked when still warm – never scalded to loosen the feathers – and drawn while fresh. Domestic pigeons are best eaten fresh; the longer they are kept the less flavour they have. Wild pigeons may need hanging for a day or two. The Wood pigeon (*Glumba palumbus*) and the Rock dove (*Glumba livia*), which is claimed to be the ancestor of the domestic breeds and feral town pigeons, both have their supporters as the best British wild pigeon. Among US species, Mourning doves are eaten in some states, while White-winged doves occur in the south and south-east, and the Western band-tailed pigeon is eaten in the West. Among my old records, there is a wild account of a feast on Passenger pigeons (now extinct) which flocked in incredible numbers to Kentucky.

There are some 475 different species of pigeon and dove in the world, many of which provide very good eating, such as the Australian Wonga-wonga, which has white and delicate flesh. Others have way-out habits, such as the pigeons which feed on nutmegs. All are edible to a greater or lesser degree, but some are best skinned rather than plucked. In China, hardboiled pigeon eggs are a delicacy; if they are taken carefully from the nest, one at a time, the birds will continue to lay.

[*Pigeon* – French: *pigeon* German: *Taube* Italian: *piccione* Spanish: *paloma*]

PIGEON PEA or **red gram**. An important pulse (*Cajanus cajan*) which originated in Africa and are a crop of warm countries – they stand no frost. They are important for food in the Caribbean (as gunga peas or gungo peas), tropical America, Africa and the Orient – they had already reached Asia in prehistoric times. In India (where they are *arhar*, *tur* or *toor*, or *tuvaram*), they are second only to chickpeas in importance. The colour of pigeon peas ranges from red to white, brown, mottled or black. It is split and husked as **dal*. The green pods can be used as a vegetable. Pigeon peas are said to be slightly narcotic and can be blamed for the nap after a large curry tiffin.

PIGNUT. Alternative name for **chufa nut*.

PIGWEED. *See* purslane.

PIKE might well be described as the barracuda of fresh water, it is a long, fast, very savage fish which will not only clear a pond of other fish but also grab young water birds swimming on the surface. The European pike (*Esox lucius*) is also found in Asia and is fished commercially in the Caspian Sea. Parallel species in North America include the pickerel (*Esox niger*) – in Britain the name pickerel retains its original meaning: a small pike. The French count the pike among the finest of food fishes, but in Britain it is not highly regarded. I have known people in Ireland treat the pike with nothing short of revulsion because of the peculiar smell it has when caught and the slime it exudes, not to mention its murderous habits. The temptation to wash off the slime as soon as the fish is caught should be resisted, as the slime contributes to the quality and tenderness. Pike are also improved by hanging overnight; the mouth and throat should be stuffed with salt. Alternatively, the fish may be

rubbed with salt and left for eight hours or so. A good pike for the fisherman weighs around 4 kg (9 lb), although they can be much bigger. For the cook, 2-2.5 kg (4½-5½ lb) is a better size, unless the flesh is intended for *quenelles*, as large pike are tough.

Pike may be scaled with a grater, but if the fish is to be skinned after cooking, this will be easier if the scales are left intact. The roes are considered slightly poisonous and are sometimes but not always rejected. The liver, though, is a delicacy and can be used in the sauce. The season for pike runs from May to January, as spawning goes on from the end of February to the end of April in most places. Pike taken from good, clean waters should not taste muddy; others may benefit from a soak in vinegared water. The fish may be cooked in a number of ways – *quenelles de brochet* are a famous French creation. A small pike of 1.5 kg (3¼ lb) will take about 25 minutes to poach in a *court-bouillon*.

[*Pike* – French: *brochet* German: *Hecht* Italian: *luccio* Spanish: *lucio*]

PILCHARD. The name given to the adult **sardine* when it is fished around British coasts.

PILLI-PILLI. *See* piri-piri.

PILONCILLO. *See* sugar.

PIMENTO or **pimiento**. *See* sweet pepper.

PIMENTÓN. The Spanish equivalent of **paprika*, powdered, red sweet pepper, a very important spice in Spain. It is used in many dishes and is characteristic of several sausages such as *chorizo* and *sobresada*. In *escabeche* of fish, it has, in addition to its role as a flavour, some preservative action. *Pimentón*, as sold loose in Spanish markets, is a brilliant, dark-vermilion or tomato-red. Although inexpensive, it is said to be frequently adulterated with other substances ranging from dried tomato residues to ground almond shells. In buying it, make sure that it has a good, strong aroma. It is best not to keep *pimentón* too long, as it tends to lose its taste. When cooking with it, mix it into the hot fat of fried dishes, as this amalgamates it and gives the best colour.

PIMIENTA. Spanish for **pepper*.

PINEAPPLE (*Ananas comosus*), on a world basis, is the most important tropical fruit. It originated in

South America – varieties still grow wild in Brazil – and it was cultivated in the West Indies before the arrival of Columbus, whose men relished it. Very soon it spread to tropical areas around the world, although its cultivation was at first haphazard. Because of its appearance, the Spanish called it *piña* (pine cone). Today, the Hawaiian Islands are the largest pineapple producers. The plant was introduced there by a Spaniard, Don Francisco de Paula y Marin in 1790, and scientific growing was started by an English captain, John Kidwell, towards the end of the 19th century. The canning of pineapple began in 1900; today the tonnage canned is immense.

Pineapple plants are perennial and continue bearing for a long time if allowed to, but commercial growers renew the plants every few years. The fruit is the result of the fruits of the whole inflorescence fusing into one. Most varieties are seedless.

To be really good, a pineapple must ripen on the plant, because the stern is full of starch, which is converted to sugar and rushes up into the fruit at the last minute. In the moment of ripening, the pineapple receives enough sugar to double its content almost overnight, but this sugar never reaches the fruit if it is cut immature. Thus, fruit imported into temperate regions by ship never ripen properly in spite of being kept, and people who have eaten pineapples in the tropics rarely buy them back home. Pineapples that have been shipped by air are another matter.

Pineapples should always be bought ripe. Unripe ones are tasteless – don't believe the greengrocer who says, 'it'll ripen in a warm place.' It won't. Over-ripe pineapple is also nasty. Avoid fruits with discoloured patches or bruises, dried-up or shrivelled ones, and any with wilting leaves. There should be a nice pineapple smell, and you should be able to pull out a leaf of the crown. Pineapples will keep for 2-3 days in a plastic bag in the refrigerator.

Europe gets pineapples from a number of places, including Africa, the West Indies, the Azores and the Canary Islands. In the US, pineapples are grown in Florida, and some come from Mexico and Puerto Rico. But the classic is the Smooth Cayenne from Hawaii, weighing up to 3-4 kg (7-9 lb) and used for both canning and eating fresh.

Apart from sugar, acid and the lovely taste, pineapple contains a digestive enzyme, bromelin, which digests proteins such as egg white, gelatine and the protein in meat. Hence, raw pineapple cannot be made into a gelatine jelly, though *agar-agar will do the trick. Recipes calling for pineapple and gelatine specify canned or cooked pineapple, as heat puts the bromelin out of action. Pineapple is used in many sweets and in fruit salads, as well as for preserves. It is cooked with ham and pork. Savoury dishes containing it often incorporate Hawaii in their name. In the US, pineapple often is flavoured with a dash of vodka or white wine; in Europe, with kirsch.

Pineapples were already common in Europe in the 19th century, when they were grown in heated glasshouses; there are dozens of recipes in Victorian cookery books. The skin and parings were boiled with sugar to make flavourings for creams. In canning factories now, the parings are used for juice – nothing is wasted.

[*Pineapple* – French: *ananas* German: *Ananas* Italian: *ananas* Spanish: *piña*]

PINE NUT. Although the seeds of pine trees are in general edible, many are too small to be of value, and others have a strong taste of turpentine which cannot be sufficiently reduced by roasting. There remain a good number of species producing excellent nuts, which have been used as food from time immemorial. Some kinds were of more than local importance; husks have been found in the rubbish tips from Roman camps in Britain. In North America, the nuts were a favourite food of the Indians, and even today it is the Indians who collect the cones of the Two-Leaved nut pine commercially in Colorado, Arizona and New Mexico.

The Mediterranean Stone pine (*Pinus pinea*) provided the original nut used in European and Mid-Eastern cooking. The Stone pine is the romantic umbrella-shaped tree of Italian landscape paintings. It grows wild in coastal districts from Portugal to the Black Sea, and has been planted on the North African coast. In places, the forests of Stone pine are beautiful and extensive. Particularly famous is that at Ravenna on the Adriatic coast of Italy, but other notable Italian localities are Viareggio, San Rossore, Fallonica and Castelfusano. In Spain, the best nuts come from Huelva, and the second best are from Tarragona.

The large, shiny cones of the Stone pine are gathered between November and March and are stored until the summer, when they are spread out in the hot sun to open. The nuts can be then shaken out of the cones. Cracking and extraction of the kernels is nowadays done by machinery. The kernels keep well in cool, dry places (or, if necessary, in a jar in the refrigerator), but are always expensive.

Pine nuts are white or cream, soft in texture, with a slight 'pine' flavour. They may be eaten raw, but are better fried or roasted (they burn very easily) when they taste more nutty. They are to be had chocolate coated or made into a nut butter, but their main interest lies in their use in Mediterranean cooking.

In France, Stone pines grow in Provence and to some extent in the pine forests of the Landes (in *omelette landaise*, pine nuts are fried gently in butter before turning in the eggs in the usual way), but you could not say that *pignons* were an important ingredient in French cooking. In Spain it is another matter. One finds *piñones* in every shop, and uses range from sweet preparations such as *pinonate* (a paste of pine nuts and sugar) or *bandullo gallego* (a type of pudding or cake with pine nuts on top) to *bacalao* with raisins and pine nuts, and *escaldums* (a chicken dish from Majorca with onion and tomato, butter and marjoram).

At the other end of the Mediterranean, in Turkey, Greece and the Lebanon (where there are some fine Stone pines to be seen from the airplane as you land in Beirut), pine nuts come in a variety of sweetmeats, in jam, pilau, rice pudding, and stuffings for chicken, turkey, vine leaves and vegetables. In Italy, sweet things containing pine nuts include *zelten* and *strudel* from the Trentino Alto Adige (with a strong Austrian influence) or *pan giallo* or *pizza di polenta* from Lazio, even the *fave dei morti* or *charlotte alla milanese* of Lombardy and the *pinoccate* of Umbria. Pine nuts are also a usual ingredient in the extraordinary *sangumacclo*, which, with many regional variations, consists of pig's blood with candied citron peel, sometimes sultanas, sugar and even chocolate. They are used with spinach (*spinaci alla romano*), pasta and cauliflower (*pasta coi cavolfiori*) peppers or aubergines (*capunatina di melanzane*), and *sardele in saar* from Venice (in which sardines are marinated in vinegar), sardines (*pasta con le sarde*), and with swordfish (*agghiotta di pesce spada*) from Sicily. Also, as in Spain, there are pine nut and dried grape combinations in regional recipes for *bacalao* and stock-fish (as in *stoccafisso in agro dolce*), and for hare (*lepre alla trentina*). These combinations are a survival from an ancient style of cooking.

But the most sophisticated recipes using pine nuts come from around Genoa, where pine nuts go whole into a variety of dishes, and are pounded to form the basic thickener of sauces. Best known of these is the famous *pesto alla genovese*, a superlative sauce for pasta made from pounded pine nuts, garlic, cheese and basil. From the region come such specialities as *salsa al funghi* (soaked dried Italian fungi pounded with garlic, anchovy, pine nuts and tomato), *salsa alla genovese* in which pine nuts are pounded with capers, anchovy, parsley and olives with a dash of garlic and vinegar, and *salsa verde alla genovese* (pine nuts pounded with basil, garlic, anchovy, salt and oil) to go with the boiled meats known as *bollito misto*, and *salsa piccante* (*see below*). From the US come *piñon* cookies.

It is rarely necessary to peel pine nuts, as you buy them ready to use, but the Spanish soak the nuts in tepid water for half an hour as a preliminary.
The most important edible-seeded pines are:
P. pinea. The Mediterranean Stone pine. Portugal to the Black Sea.
P. cembra. The Swiss Stone pine or Arolla pine. (German: *Zirbel*) from the Alps, Central Europe and Russia. 'Russian nuts' in Norway.
P. roxburghii. The Chir pine of West Himalayas and Afghanistan.
P. gerardiana. The Nepal Nut pine of Himalayas which gives 'Neoza nuts'.
Pinus cembroides. The Two-Leaved nut pine. Colorado to Mexico.
Araucaria araucana. Chile pine or Monkey-Puzzle tree. In Chile, it produces enormous cones. The seeds are eaten roasted.
A. augustifolia. The Para pine from Brazil.
A. bidwillii. The Bunya-bunya pine from Queensland.

Salsa piccante

Pound together a handful each of chopped parsley and capers with two anchovies and some white breadcrumbs soaked in olive oil. Rub through a sieve and stir in more oil, a little vinegar, salt (if necessary) and black pepper. Use as a sauce for fish or vegetables – cauliflower, green beans, scorzonera – at your choice.

[*Pine nut* – French: *pignon* German: *Piniennuss* Italian: *pignolo* Spanish: *piñon*]

PINTO. Variety of *kidney bean.

PIRI-PIRI, peri-peri, or **pilli-pilli** dishes are meat or fish served with a special hot-pepper sauce. Piri-piri dishes are Portuguese African, particularly from Mozambique, but the hot sauce has been taken into Portuguese and South African cooking generally and has its addicts. Laurens van der Post reminisces about its preparation in *First Catch Your Eland* (The Hogarth Press). 'Of course, every cook in Mozambique has his own particular way of preparing piri-piri. I have chosen one provided by a Portuguese housewife of Mozambique. According to her instructions, one begins by squeezing out some lemons, passing the juice through a sieve, warming it in a pan, inserting peppers and chillies that must be red (and freshly picked, she emphasised). They are simmered on a low heat for just five minutes. The mixture is then taken from the stove, separated from its juice and the peppers pressed into a fine paste. A pinch of salt is added and the pounding continues until there are no lumps left in the pulp. This pulp is returned to the pan with the original lemon juice and further simmered while being constantly stirred. This then is the piri-piri sauce which can be eaten with steak, mutton, fowl, fish and crustacea and always best I would say with rice of some kind to provide the exact civilising corrective to the pagan incitement of the sauce.'

As for other ways, in some cases, the stem ends of small red chillies are put in olive oil and stored for a couple of months before being used. Other cooks let the peppers and any spices infuse in the oil in a slow oven or on top of the stove, while the flavours can also be blended by standing the seasoned oil in the hot noon sun. Piri-piri is also available in a powdered form.

PISANG STARCH. *See* banana.

PISCO. *See* brandy.

PISTACHIO NUT or **green almond**. The nuts are borne on a small deciduous tree (*Pistacia vera*), native to Asia and still found growing wild in the mysterious ranges around the head-waters of the Oxus. It was brought into the Mediterranean many thousands of years ago and reached Italy from Syria during the reign of the Emperor Tiberius. The tree can withstand very poor conditions. It will grow on dry, rocky hill-sides, as long as it gets hot summers. In Europe, it is grown in southern Italy and Sicily as well as in Greece and to a small extent in France and Spain. In the US, it has of late been grown in California, Texas and Arizona. However, most travellers would associate pistachio nuts with Islamic countries of the Middle East and North Africa, Persia and Afghanistan, Tunisia and Algeria. They go with the salted melon and sunflower seeds sold on street corners; the salted nuts are sold in the bazaars in their horny shells, open-lipped like biscuit-coloured bivalves.

The growing nuts look like clusters of small olives. The flesh may be an intense green or sometimes paler, according to variety. The skin adhering to the nut is papery and red-brown to creamy. The nuts are gathered when the outside begins to shrivel and to turn yellow. They are spread out in the shade to dry for a week or more. Since the shell gapes to expose the kernel, there is no need for cracking. Once dried, pistachios keep well.

The flavour of the pistachio is mild, but in some varieties there is a resinous taste which is a reminder of the mastic and terebinth bushes to which the pistachio is closely related (both of them can be used as root stocks for grafting). The resinous taste is particularly strong in wild nuts and is said to be preferred by the inhabitants of Turkestan. The cultivated varieties vary considerably. They are propagated by grafting, although nuts are often planted. As there are male and female trees, a single pistachio tree is useless; and male trees have to be included in every orchard for pollination. It takes 15-20 years for the trees to come into anything like full production, but some nuts are produced four years after grafting. Trees yield between 9 kg (20 lb) and 27 kg (60 lb) of nuts, which are always expensive, usually three or four times the price of other nuts.

Apart from being salted to eat by the handful, they are mainly used in cooking for their decorative effect. They appear in various sweetmeats, and are also included in stuffings, *pâtés* and stuffed meats (like the Genovese *cima* and the *coppa romano*), where they look like green islands in the slices. There is also the famous pistachio ice cream, particularly of Italy and the US. If this is not expensive, it is certain to be faked with other nuts and green colouring. Other uses of the nuts as a main ingredient are limited, but include the cake-like *mazaresi al pistacchio* of Sicily. Pistachio nuts are sometimes added to expensive Indian pilau dishes. They are grown to some extent in Kashmir, but are mostly imported from Afghanistan.

To remove the skins from pistachio nuts and leave the nuts with a fine green colour, blanch them in salted water, then treat them as you would *almonds. A beautiful green oil can be pressed from pistachio nuts, but it is too expensive for use in the kitchen (although it is used in perfumery), and it also goes rancid very quickly. The nuts contain about 54% oil and 22% protein, so they have good food value.

[*Pistachio nut* – French: *pistache* German: *Pistazie* Italian: *pistachio* Spanish: *pistacho, alfóncigo*]

PI-TSI. *See* water chestnut.

PLAICE. *See* flatfish.

PLANTAIN. *See* banana.

PLOVER. Plovers are small waders. Most of these birds, including the rare dotterel, were formerly shot and netted for food in Britain and elsewhere in northern Europe. Now the British plovers are sadly reduced in numbers, and, as with any wild bird, it is important to check the status of a species before using it as food. Gastronomically, the Golden plover (*Pluvialis apricaria*) is reckoned the best, followed by the Grey plover (*P. squatarola*) and finally the lapwing or Green plover (*Vanellus vanellus*), which is less nice to eat but whose *eggs were once collected. Plovers are usually hung for a day or so before cooking, and they should be eaten only in winter.

[*Plover* – French: *pluvier* German: *Regenpfeifer* Italian: *piviere* Spanish: *chorlito*]

PLUCK. The heart, liver and lungs of animals, often hung up and offered for sale as one unit in less sophisticated countries.

PLUCKING. Pulling out the feathers of birds. Commercial plucking of chickens is done by machines, the simplest of which is a revolving drum with rubber spikes or pieces of hose pipe sticking out, against which the birds are held. Before plucking, the birds are immersed in hot water at about 50°C (122°F) to loosen the feathers. Plucking by hand is a tiresome business and must be done with patience, as it is easy to tear the skin of the bird. The large wing feathers may have to be pulled out with pincers. After plucking, the fine under-feathers need to be singed off with a taper. In the Orient, chickens are very often skinned, a much simpler operation which also allows spices to enter and is correct for curries.

PLUM (*Prunus domestica*) is a hybrid between the sloe (*P. spinosa*) and the Cherry plum (*P. cerasifera*), which originated naturally in western Asia where the two species grow wild together and hybridize freely. The *sloe looks like a tiny blue-bloomed plum and the Cherry plum resembles a red or yellow cherry.

The gage or greengage, which grows wild in Asia Minor, is sometimes treated as a separate species (*P. italica*) but is usually held to be a subspecies of *P. domestica*. Another plum species, the Japanese plum (*P. triflora*),which is actually a native of China, is the ancestor of some warm-country plums such as the Abundance and Burbank varieties. Now of lesser importance are the *bullace (*P. domestica* ssp. *insititia*), which is sometimes considered to be a separate species, and the *damson (*P. damascena*).There are also numerous indigenous American wild plums such as the Chickasaw (*P. angustifolia*), Oregon plum (*P. subcordata*), Texan plum (*P. orthosepala*) and others, including the *P. americana*, *P. nigra* and *P. hortulana*, which have been domesticated. The fruit of the last two is small and used for jam. The peach plum (*P. maritima*) of the East coast is also a jam plum. Plums have been cultivated seriously since classical times. Many of the best plums have been first found growing in woods and from there taken into cultivation. Plums show enormous variation in colour, size, taste and fruiting season. Of the plums proper, as opposed to greengages, some are red, some yellow and some purple or almost black. The flesh may be greenish, yellow, red or purple. There are clingstone and freestone varieties, cookers and dessert plums. Some varieties always remain sour even when ripe and some become exceedingly sweet. And the number of varieties is huge – over 1000 in Europe. In California, where 90% of American plums are produced, about 40 varieties are under commercial cultivation, although no more than a dozen are grown in great quantity. As with other fruit, the number of important commercial types is gradually becoming less.

Plums will grow in any warmish temperate climate, but do best with a hot summer and cold winter. However, some can even be grown at elevations in the tropics, especially those derived from Japanese plums. Out-of-season plums for the Northern hemisphere come from South Africa or South America, but plums are best when picked only just before they are ripe. In buying, you should naturally avoid over-ripe or damaged fruit, but slightly under-ripe fruit will ripen in any warm room. Plums need to be put into the refrigerator when ripe and can be held there for a day or so.

In the US, the Santa Rosa makes up 35% of the California crop and is of Japanese descent, having been bred by Luther Burbank (who brought Japanese plums to the US a century ago) and named after the town in northern California where he lived. In Britain, the Victoria, with red-over-yellow rather translucent skin and nice, but not outstanding, taste is well known. The variety was found in a Sussex wood in about 1840. The greengage is named after Sir Thomas Gage who reintroduced the fruit from France (where it is called Reine Claude) into Britain in about 1725. English greengages are often not good to look at but have a superb flavour. French varieties, grown in a climate that suits them better, are twice the size and perhaps the most delicious of all the plums to eat for dessert.

Of the other greenish-yellow plums, one ought to notice the Pershore Egg, grown in huge amounts for jam in western England and the Mirabelle, a small yellow-green gage much grown in Alsace (England is too cold). Mirabelles are sweet and are used both for preserves and for the *eau-de-vie* called after it – mirabelle. The other famous plum *eau-de-vie* is called quetsch, after the quetsch plum which is ripe in August and is also excellent for cooking. Quetsch plums, stoned and baked flat on dough, make the well-known *Quetschenkuchen*. A cut made inside the halves of each plum prevents them curling up in the heat of the oven and is one of the secrets of these neat confections and of tarts containing tidy rows of halved plums.

Prunes. Although any plum can be dried, varieties specially suitable for the purpose have been developed. Of these the *prune d'Agen* and *Fellemberg* are two of the best known. Prunes used to be produced mainly in southern France where the weather makes it possible to dry fruit out of doors. Some sorts of prune (*pistoles*) are peeled, stoned and flattened, other are pricked or blanched, and some are dried in ovens. In the old days, French prunes were sent from Agen down the Garonne and shipped from Bordeaux, usually packed in osier baskets. Today prunes are produced on a large scale in California and elsewhere. Modern commercial prunes have sometimes been treated with lye to soften the skins; they are big, black and beautiful after being glossed by heating in steam or boiling brine and perhaps coated with glycerine or liquid paraffin. Carlsbad prunes, known also as Carlsbad plums, are large dessert prunes meant to be eaten with dried fruits at the end of a meal. If prunes are soaked, cooked and puréed, then mixed with cream, they make the most wonderful ices – a far cry from the nursery stewed prunes once favoured for inducing regular bowel movements. Prunes stoned and stuffed, or wrapped in bacon and grilled

make well known savouries. They can be included in meat dishes and also figure in some stuffings for turkey and goose, and they go especially well with pork. In Germany, plums go with potato, beans, and smoked sausage (*Mett-wurst*) into a stew or *Eintopf*. The Chinese make hot sauces containing plums as well as chilli and garlic.

[*Plum* – French: *prune* German: *Pflaume* Italian: *susina, prugna* Spanish: *ciruela*]

POACHING comes from the same source as the French word for pocket, and was originally applied only to eggs. If they are put into almost boiling water, they soon become surrounded by a coating of coagulated white and so are in a pocket. But the word now covers cooking almost anything gently in hot, but by no means boiling, liquid. The word 'simmer', at least by its sound, denotes some slight movement of the liquid and a slightly higher temperature.

POI. *See* yam (dasheen).

POISONING. We are talking here about accidents rather than felonies. Food poisoning is usually understood to mean food contaminated by harmful organisms (or the poisons they generate) rather than poisoning from eating poisonous animals or plants or poisoning from chemical poisons which somehow have got into the food. Even poisonings from the long-term effects of additives and colourings are excluded, as are personal allergies. However, from the point of view of the sufferer (and the poisoner), the definition may be academic.

At one time food poisoning was thought to be due to ptomaines (from *ptoma*, the Greek for a corpse), protein breakdown substances with delightfully evocative names like putrecine and cadaverine formed in decomposing food. The ptomaine theory of food poisoning has long since been abandoned and so the word becomes meaningless, but in popular parlance ptomaine poisoning persists. It usually describes poisoning caused by *Staphylococcus*, the least serious of the three main categories of food poisoning, which are dealt with below in descending order of nastiness.

Botulism. A type of food poisoning (fortunately rare), from which more people die than recover – the mortality is 65%. It is caused by a deadly poison (of the 'test tube in a reservoir will kill a whole city' category), made by a soil organism, *Clostridium botulinum*. This is entirely anaerobic and will not grow when any oxygen is present, so it finds ideal conditions in canned foods. Beans, spinach, sweet corn, meat, fish, milk and cheese have all been culprits, as well as canned salmon. Occasionally the organism can find a place to grow even in the depths of hams, sausages and salted, dried or smoked fish.

The problem is that *Clostridium botulinum* is a spore-forming organism and, except in acid conditions, its spores are almost impossible to kill by boiling. They can stand several hours at 100°C (212°F). Only when the temperature is pushed up higher in a pressure cooker or an autoclave (as it is commercially) can we make canned or bottled vegetables, meat or fish really safe. Though the spores of the botulism organism can stand so much heat, the poison it produces can be made harmless even by boiling for as little as one minute. This means, of course, that you cannot get botulism from thoroughly cooked, hot food. Botulism poisoning has features in common with another killer, the toadstool *Amanita phalloides*, in that there are no immediate symptoms after eating, and no warning before the poison has been thoroughly ingested into the system. With botulism, there are rarely signs for at least hours, and often a day or more goes by before there are even stomach upsets. The real damage, however, is done to the nervous system, and early symptoms are double vision, difficulty in swallowing and speaking, giddiness and laboured breathing, finally leading to respiratory paralysis and death. As with the *Amanita phalloides*, the merest taste can be fatal. Cans of food – it is cans of vegetables, especially home-canned ones, that are most likely to cause trouble – may sometimes have an off smell and taste, but blown cans should always be discarded without tasting. Home bottlers and canners of anything other than acid fruits should follow instructions scrupulously. Botulism organisms will not develop in conditions of high acidity or where there are plenty of spices and salt. They also dislike saltpetre or nitrites.

Salmonella. There are some two hundred organisms in this genus of bacteria and some cause the typhoid-like illness paratyphoid (though not typhoid itself), while others bring about severe or mild gastroenteritis. They get into the system through contaminated food and water. There is no unusual smell or taste by which contaminated food can be recognized. Symptoms begin possibly the same day (within seven hours), but that is a minimum and they may not start for up to three days. They are stomach pains, diarrhoea, bad smelling liquid stools, thirst and perhaps vomiting (which you might expect from any digestive upset), but also high temperature, chills and headaches. This is an infection and can be cured with antibiotics. The bacteria in the contaminated food and drink can be destroyed by boiling.

Staphylococcus belong to a genus of organisms including those that cause boils, pimples, and suppurating cuts and abrasions. The genus also contains organisms that commonly cause food poisoning. These can stand concentrations of sugar and salt that would kill other micro-organisms (like those of typhoid, for instance). They find suitable nutrients in sausages and meat pies, milk, cheese, cream cakes and sandwiches. Unlike *Salmonella* poisoning (but like botulism), staphylococcal poisoning is due to the accumulation of toxins which the organisms have made (though the upsets may, to the layman at least, be rather similar) and there is neither infection nor fever. In *Staphylococcus* toxin poisoning, the symptoms come on almost immediately after the food has been eaten – in an hour or so – depending on susceptibility, circumstances, and how much poison was taken. Antibiotics will not fix this illness (as there is no infection), but recovery is usual after a few days on a light diet. The symptoms can be severe while they last. Food containing *Staphylococcus* toxins cannot be detected by taste or smell. The toxins cannot be destroyed by ordinary cooking; they can stand up to 30 minutes boiling without being made harmless.

However, *Staphylococcus* poisoning is usually the result of carelessness. If foods which might be contaminated and might provide favourable conditions for the organisms are kept in the fridge then there are unlikely to be any problems. But if the foods are kept lying about in the kitchen (which, even in winter, will be of a sufficiently high temperature), then poisoning is always possible. And it happens quickly. On hot summer days, with temperatures around 30°C (86°F), sufficient toxin can develop in food in as little as five hours – between lunch and dinner – to cause illness.

Chemical contamination. One source of chemical contamination which is easily avoided is the action of the food on the surface of the container. This can be obviated by never leaving acid foods or drinks in lead-glazed earthenware containers, or metal ones.

Poisonous chemicals are likely to get into food only as a result of carelessness. Medicines, weed-killers, slug-death and sprays for the garden, ant and cockroach powder, and other toxic substances should be kept out of the kitchen and, where there are children about, locked up. Cleaning solutions – which may include strong bleach, ammonia, caustic soda and hydrochloric acid – should be treated with respect and rinsed away thoroughly with water after use. Substances such as saltpetre which can be poisonous if used in quantity instead of common salt, should be clearly labelled. If poisoning occurs, send immediately for a doctor, but begin first aid – don't wait for him to arrive.

Corrosive poisons, such as acids or caustic soda which burn the mouth and lips demand special treatment. If the poison is acid, give bicarbonate of soda, magnesia or chalk mixed with water. If it is carbolic acid, give 1-2 tablespoons of Epsom salts or Glauber salts in water. If the poison is an alkali, give vinegar and water, or lemon or even orange juice diluted with water. If the caustic poison is unknown, give large quantities of water or some milk. *With corrosive poisoning of any kind, never try to make the patient sick.*

However, irritant poisons, which do not cause burning of the tissues, can be treated with an emetic and plenty of water to drink. Poisoning by alkaloids and narcotics (which affect the nervous system) should also be treated by making the patient sick, unless he is unconscious. Strong black coffee combats drowsiness.

Good emetics are two tablespoons salt in a glass of warm water, or one dessertspoon of mustard in a glass of warm water. Best of all, as it does not irritate, let the patient drink large quantities of tepid water, and then press down at the far back of his tongue (or tickle his throat) until you find the place which makes him gag. Continuing to press or tickle will make him sick. The patient should then take more water and repeat the process until his stomach is washed out.

Poisonous animals. Some fish are poisonous, occasionally just in certain seasons, and it is better to follow local advice unless you are absolutely certain the locals are wrong. Also remember that it is possible for a fish to be edible in one place and harmful in another because of its food. Sometimes fish are claimed to be good when small but harmful when large. Some barracudas come into this class. In fact, in Malaysia they say that barracudas become poisonous at certain times of the year because they eat poisonous sea snakes (a rather unlikely explanation), and it is commonly agreed in the

Caribbean that the large barracudas there (around 1 m/3 ft and over) have poisonous flesh which, when eaten, causes pain in the joints, trembling and vomiting. Perhaps the most famous poisonous fish is the pufferfish which is eaten under the name of *fugu* in Japan, but only after preparation by experts officially licensed in the art. The blood and liver of this fish is very poisonous indeed and even eating the prepared flesh causes numb mouth and lips. Another dangerously poisonous fish is the Oil fish (*Ruvettus pretiosus*) which also causes numbness of the tongue, hands and feet as well as pains in the chest and stomach. Unfortunately, there are no rule-of-thumb methods of telling the good from the poisonous fish; indeed some excellent fish such as the garfishes with their green bones, look as if they might be poisonous when they are not. However, the US Air Force's survival instructions advise against eating the fish of shallow waters and reefs which are round or box-like and have hard skins and bony plates or spines, small parrot-like mouths, small gill openings, or belly fins small or absent. These are the pufferfish, file fish, globe fish, trigger fish and trunk fish of tropical seas. In particular, never eat the livers or roes of any tropical fish without knowing that they are safe. Some northern fish have livers overloaded with vitamin A which, like Polar bear liver, can also be poisonous. Cooking does not destroy the poison of such fish. (It is worth mentioning that many fish have poisonous spines, some lethal – the stonefish has thirteen unlucky spines causing agony and death.)

In general, fresh molluscs and crustaceans whether from land (like snails) or water, are not poisonous. However, bivalves, which feed by sieving small organisms and other food particles out of the water, are easily contaminated, possibly by pathogenic bacteria (including those causing typhoid, paratyphoid and *Salmonella* poisoning in general, cholera and hepatitis) from untreated sewage that has been spewed into the sea or rivers. Snails may have eaten poisonous plants (which is why they are starved or fed on lettuce for several days before being cooked). Once they are dead, molluscs and crustaceans provide excellent conditions in which bacteria can multiply, especially as we are in most cases dealing with the whole organism, including the gut. Shell fish should therefore always be fresh, and damaged or dead specimens thrown away; it is best to buy live crabs and scallops in preference to one the fishmonger may have had on ice for several days. In certain areas of the eastern Pacific, for instance around the coasts of California, there are occasional plagues of a highly lethal form of plankton, the dinoflagellate *Goniaulax catenella*, which causes red tides. In huge numbers, this tiny animal, with its red dot, makes the sea look red. It secretes a virulent poison that attacks the central nervous system and causes death to anyone eating contaminated shellfish. Anyone gathering shell fish on tropical rocks or reefs should handle cone shells with great care, as some of them can shoot out a poisonous, even lethal, dart from the narrow end.

Poisonous plants. Contrary to popular belief most fungi are not poisonous. However one or two are often fatal, even if taken in the least amount (*see* mushrooms). The *moulds, which are also fungi, are usually not harmful in the quantity that is likely to be eaten, but a few can be – the mould on peanuts is carcinogenic and the black fungus, ergot, that attacks cereal heads, especially rye, is very poisonous. It is not at all common these days.

Apart from the poisonous plants which tempt children with their berries, there are a few plants which cooks should be alert to. Sometimes people have been poisoned by oleander, which is highly poisonous, when they have used the wood to make meat skewers. Anything smelling strongly of bitter *almonds should be avoided, as this often indicates the presence of cyanide (prussic acid). Everyone in Britain knows that you should avoid Deadly nightshade, a plant, incidentally, that is much over-rated in its poisonous effect probably because of the dire warnings given to children. For something really poisonous, we have to go to the legendary Ordeal tree of Madagascar (*Taughinia venenifera*) a seed of which, no larger than an almond, will reputedly kill twenty people. More dangerous in practice are plants which contain a lot of oxalic acid (such as rhubarb leaves) and are poisonous in quantity, but which might be eaten, and have been eaten, in emergency.

Allergies. It is possible to have an allergy, either inherited or developed, to certain foods, and to react to them as if they were poison. An example of an inherited allergy is favism, sufferers from which get headaches, vertigo, vomiting, fever, and enlargement of the spleen and liver as a result of eating broad beans. This allergy is common in people who have Levantine blood, with ancestors who came from Greece or Armenia. It is relatively common in Sardinia, Sicily and southern Italy, as well as in certain ethnic groups in North America.

Some sufferers from favism will be made ill by just the pollen of the broad bean plant. Many people, perhaps more than suspect it, are adversely affected by wheat *gluten, others by cheese, and so on. An example of a developed allergy: some of those who have been made ill by shell fish seem to have to give them up permanently. In this context, I remember being told many years ago by a Spanish fisherman, that if I ate the flying fish I had caught I would become allergic to shell fish, at least for several years. I did not risk putting this piece of local folklore to the test. Allergies to components of the diet are only beginning to be understood; they are an aspect of eating that should not be forgotten.

POITRINE FUMÉE. French for *bacon.

POLE BEAN. *See* kidney bean (green bean).

POLENTA. *See* maize.

POLLACK. *See* cod.

POLLOCK. US name for coal fish (*see* cod).

POLONY may come from Polonia, the medieval Latin for Poland, or from Bologna. Either way, it now means a sausage of partly cooked, finely ground pork which has been coloured with dye. It may contain a proportion of beef and is likely to have been hot smoked. Polonies can be fried or grilled.

POLYSACCHARIDES. *See* sugar.

POLYUNSATURATES. *See* fats.

POMEGRANATE (*Punica granatum*) is neglected in most of Europe. The fruit is a large, thick-skinned berry with a mass of seeds each surrounded by juicy jewel-like pulp; the whole fruit is divided internally by tough membranes into irregular compartments. A good pomegranate is large, very juicy and has a good balance of sugar and acids. The colour of the inside varies from colourless to dark purple-red, which looks prettier but does not necessarily have a better taste. Poor pomegranates range through sour, astringent types with a high proportion of membranes, to those that are completely inedible.

Pomegranates originated in southern or western Asia. They were spread by the Phoenicians and the Romans got theirs from Carthage – hence the name *Punica*. Pomegranates require a very hot, dry summer to reach perfection – they resist drought, but need irrigation – and they will stand considerable frost in winter, so they are a typical fruit of Middle Eastern gardens. They are grown in California and in all Mediterranean countries; Puglia in Italy, Spain and Cyprus export the fruit.

The tree is small – evergreen or deciduous according to climate – and is covered with sharp spines. The fruits are painful to pick. The typical flower is vivid vermilion, but there are white-flowered kinds (usually with poor fruit) and even double-flowered varieties which are purely for decoration. The wild pomegranate or *daru*, which grows profusely in parts of the lower Himalayas, is not edible but the seeds are dried and become an important condiment, the *anar dana* of Indian cooking. Dried pomegranate seeds of sour varieties are sprinkled on meat dishes in Middle Eastern cooking.

Good eating varieties have a superb flavour and make a fine dessert fruit if time is taken to remove the masses of glassy red or pink seeds and to separate them out from the yellowish membranes. The whole mass, ice-cold and rather like a pile of red crystals, looks wonderful served in a silver dish. The juice of pomegranates is used in meat and chicken dishes in Persian cooking, for instance in the magnificent dish called *fesenjan* or *faisinjan*, which is duck or chicken with walnuts and pomegranate juice. The juice is the basis of the sweet syrup *granatine* or *grenadine*, which is used in drinks. A long drink made of freshly-squeezed pomegranate juice, chilled and mixed with Dutch gin (a 'Stobart Special') is fantastic for anyone looking for something bracing and new, but the problem with squeezing the juice from pomegranates is that too much tannin exudes from the membranes and makes the juice astringent. To remove some tannin, a little dissolved gelatine can be stirred in. The gelatine reacts with the tannin to form an insoluble compound – a cloud which can be settled, filtered or removed by fining. If the fruit is allowed to shrivel before being crushed, the tannin is less. The pomegranate season is from the end of summer, reaching a peak in October and going on to Christmas. Pomegranates are sometimes associated with Halloween. In a polythene bag in the refrigerator, pomegranates will keep for several weeks.

[*Pomegranate* – French: *grenade* German: *Granatapfel* Italian: *melagrana* Spanish: *granada*]

POMELO. See Shaddock.

POPCORN. *See* maize.

POPPY SEED used in cooking comes from the opium poppy (*Papaver somniferum*) which is probably a native of Central Europe. Used as a drug in classical times, poppy seeds were already being cultivated in India and China by AD 800. The drug is obtained from the latex which oozes out if the green seed pod is slashed, but when the seeds are ripe all traces of the opium alkaloids, such as morphine and codeine, are gone, and poppy seeds become a good food – an edible oil can be expressed from them. Poppy seed varies enormously from the relatively large, grey-blue type commonly seen sprinkled on German and Jewish breads and cakes to the much smaller, pale cream seed used in India to thicken curries. Botanists insist that the two come from the same species. The taste of baked poppy seed is pleasantly nutty, a little like sesame seed, and perhaps rather nicer. It is a frequent constituent in curry powders and in the masala to be ground for curries, but unless it is roasted it has little flavour. Indians never use flour to thicken curries, and poppy seed makes a nice sauce, but in many recipes the quantities used are insignificant and the poppy seed may only have been included from tradition or perhaps for medicinal reasons.

PORK, from the French, refers to the meat and pig, from Middle English, refers to the animal. Swine comes from the Old English *swin* (Latin *suinus*). Hog (a usual word for a pig in the US) in Britain usually implies a castrated male reared for slaughter. A boar is an uncastrated male pig; a sow, a female; a gilt (from the old Norse), a young sow.

Perhaps no other animal has been as important as the pig to man's survival in Europe as well as in China and South East Asia. The highly evolved and custom-built pigs of today are the result of crossing the European pig, which was a ridge-backed animal, not far removed from the wild pig (*Sus scrofa*), and the plumper Chinese pig. This cross is attributed to Robert Bakewell who bred stock in the English Midlands in the middle of the 18th century. Today, very intensive upgrading and inbreeding helped by artificial insemination (which has come in generally since World War II), has produced pigs tailor-made for the bacon industry, with long bodies and a small amount of fat, and the old fat pigs (going under such delightful names as Birmingham Cutter) are either hard or impossible to get, even if you should want them. Pigs are a lot leaner than they used to be and European butchers tend to trim off most of the fat to make the meat leaner still.

The flavour of pork and the hardness of the fat depends on the food with which the animal has been fed, so that pork for special purposes may come from animals that have been fed, for example, on peaches or acorns. Pigs are fastidious and have a very lively gastronomic sense, in spite of their greed. Following the tastes of man, they will readily eat truffles (and would no doubt get stoned on a good château-bottled wine if their masters could spare it). Pigs are clean by nature, and the mud on a wild pig is more correctly regarded as a mud-pack for beauty treatment than a sign of slovenliness. In peasant societies, pigs are kept in atrocious conditions, but that is not the fault of the pigs. Neither are they to blame for the long and close association with man, which has meant that they share with humans a number of unpleasant parasites and diseases. Both Jews and Muslims regard pigs as unclean from a religious point of view, and it is said that this shows a practical approach to hygiene. But why? It was only necessary to cook the meat thoroughly to be safe. However, religious food laws have meant that a large area of the world, stretching from Turkey to Pakistan and southwards over northern Africa, has been denied the pig's many advantages. Here man must depend on the goat and sheep, animals which may be more suited to the arid regions that make up much of this part of the world, but do not have the pig's versatility. As for the diseases, which undoubtedly exist, the danger is greatly reduced with animals kept under clean modern conditions, though it is still inadvisable to eat pork which has not been cooked to a high enough temperature throughout or which alternatively has not been salted for long enough to kill harmful parasites. A veterinary inspection stamp is not an absolute guarantee of safety.

Most of the important culinary products of the pig have been covered elsewhere in this book, e.g. *ham, *bacon, *sausages, *lard – more food products are derived from the pig than from any other animal. The pig is, for instance, the only mammal whose skin we eat. We tend to take this for granted, or perhaps think we do so because of its relative hairlessness compared with the cow or the sheep. However, pigs in cold countries, such as northern China, may have quite hairy coats; in any case, even the baldest pig has to be scalded and have its bristles scraped off during preparation by the butcher. In peasant economies, the family pig (which is like a good dustbin that converts kitchen waste to more food) is still killed in the autumn, usually in November, at well under a year old. The occasion is one for both work and feasting. In the Spanish *matanza*, the pig is caught and dragged squealing to a wooden table on which it is held while a knife is plunged into one of its arteries. This, it is claimed, with dubious justification, makes the animal instantly unconscious. It is necessary for the heart to go on beating for a while so that the blood is pumped out. (Modern methods are more humane because the pig is first knocked out with an electric shock to the head.) After the killing, the carcass is scalded and scraped free of bristles, the entrails are removed and the carcass hung up to cool. The insides are sorted out, but the gall bladder is almost the only part of the pig that is thrown away. The intestines are opened out, washed in a stream, turned inside out, scraped, salted and soaked to cleanse them for use as sausage skins. It is a day's work for most families to turn a pig into the hams, bacon and sausages that will subsequently be cured, dried and smoked to provide food over the winter. The variety of products made from the pig is a wonderful tribute to man's invention, since virtually nothing is wasted. Cooks who have not experimented are recommended to try trotters, head, ears and all the other parts that are neglected in countries where people can afford to live on gammon and pork chops.

In most European countries, the skin is usually cut off the joints and used separately It is very gelatinous and a most useful addition to the consistency of an assortment of dishes. In Britain, Denmark and other northern countries, the skin is usually scored and crackled when pork is roasted. For good crackling the skin should never be basted with fat, which turns it to leather, but may be brushed or basted with water which produces bubbly-looking crackling. If skin is roasted without scoring, it is inclined to turn into a hard sheet (where I live in Spain, suckling pigs are not properly scored for roasting) and scoring needs to be done neatly and carefully. It is something that butchers rarely have time to do properly and you should do it yourself. As with other meats, the way pork is cut up is subject to great local variation. In some countries a leg of pork is very difficult to obtain as legs all go for ham. On the other hand, the fillet, which does not cure well and is removed from bacon ribs, much in demand in America and China, may be inexpensive if there is not the specialist demand for them. Pig's liver is always cheap, often ridiculously so; though inferior for cooking in its own right, it is the best liver for *pâté maison*.

Salt pork. A light brining often improves pork. The heavily-salted pork used on ships in the past and known to sailors as salt junk was nothing like the salt meat we are used to, which is pinkish and served with fresh vegetables. It is said to have had something of the appearance and hardness of old mahogany, and was so salty that it could blister the tongue. Of course, at sea in sailing ships, with limited fresh water, it was not even soaked properly before being used. This unappetizing stuff was commonly believed to be the cause of scurvy, and so any fresh meat or fish, even of unpalatable sorts was eaten by sailors, but in vain, as it was fresh fruit and vegetables, even sprouted beans and grains, that contained the vitamin C they needed. Nowadays there are better things to eat during the winter or on long sea voyages. When we complain about the additives introduced by the food technologists, as indeed we should, we ought also to remember salt junk as an example of the crude expedients once used in preserving food.

[*Pork* – French: *porc* German: *Schweinefleisch* Italian: *carne di maiale* Spanish: *carne de cerdo*]

PORT. Portuguese *oyster.

PORT, by legal definition in Britain but not necessarily elsewhere, is a wine from a particular region in the valley of the Douro river some 80 km (50 miles) inland from Oporto in northern Portugal. The hillsides where the vines grow are very steep, and holes for vines often have to be blasted in the rock.

The port that was originally shipped to Britain was just a full bodied red wine, often fortified with brandy to make it travel better. It was this, not modern port, which was said to have given the 18th century Englishman his gout. From about 1830, however, the brandy began to be added before fermentation was complete. At an alcohol concentration of 20% the yeasts die, and further fermentation cannot take place. It is the remaining unfermented grape sugar that makes port sweet.

Until fairly recently, port was made by old methods in very picturesque surroundings, and the grape crushing was done by foot. There are now destalking machines, and cleverly devised methods which remove much of the hand work without altering the quality of the wine. Crushed pips and stalks would ruin the taste, as port, unlike sherry, is fermented with the skins. When the moment is judged right, the fermenting juice is run off straight into huge casks which already contain brandy. Fermentation then stops. The proportion is about 22 lt (about 40 pt) of brandy to 100 lt (176 pt) of half-fermented must. This brings the alcohol strength to about 20%. Some two months later, the new wine is run off the lees and shipped down to Oporto. There, in the shippers' lodges (which are like cellars except that they are not underground), the various wines are blended in the shippers' various styles.

Ruby port is a youngish wine which has not lost its colour, and is blended sometimes with tawny. Tawny is older, and has mellowed and become orange-red. White port is made from white grapes. Vintage port is made only in years when the shippers consider the vintage to be exceptional, and it gets special treatment. After the best blend has been determined, the chosen wines are mixed in huge wooden vats and left there for two years before they are shipped to the wine merchants. There the port is rested for a couple of months and then bottled. (In my grandmother's house, a pipe – 56 dozen bottles – was bought and bottled for each son and put in bins in the cellars.) Bottles are ideally black, but usually they are just dark. Very good, long corks must be used to make a tight seal against the air while the port matures. After the bottles have been filled and corked, they are stood for several days before the corks are sealed by dipping the neck of each bottle in a mixture of paraffin wax and tallow. They are then laid on their sides in bins, where they should remain undisturbed for at least 15 years. Certainly vintage port must never be moved before it has lain for 7 years or before the deposited crust has hardened. As the bottles are put down, they are marked with a streak of whitewash to indicate the upper side. Vintage port should not be drunk before it is 15 and preferably 20 years old. It usually goes on improving for up to 40 years, but after that may deteriorate.

Old port must be decanted with great care. The whitewash mark must be kept uppermost and the bottle kept steady when the cork is removed. With exceedingly old vintages – 40-50 years old – the cork may have started to crumble; the neck of the bottle then has to be removed. Before tackling this tricky job, stand the bottle upright for a day or so. Then heat the claws of a bottle tong until they are red and clamp them around the bottle neck beneath the flange. Hold them there until the redness has disappeared, then remove them. Place a cold wet cloth against the neck which, because of the contrast in temperature, will break off.

At table it is traditional to pass the port decanter to the left, but this is only a matter of convenience. It is an old custom, and practical because each person fills his glass and then places the decanter next to his neighbour's glass on the latter's right. Port is not very popular in the hotter countries. It is a drink for the winter or for damp days, which is why it is still popular in Britain, though it is drunk to some extent in other countries of the Commonwealth, particularly Canada, as well as in Scandinavia and Switzerland. Perhaps surprisingly, France is the largest importer of port, which is drunk there as an aperitif. In cooking, its use is virtually limited to English dishes – jugged hare, Cumberland sauce and a few sweet dishes. Port-type wines are made in South Africa, Australia, California and elsewhere, with varying success, but as yet without great distinction.

[Port – French: *porto* German: *Portowein* Italian: *vino di Oporto* Spanish: *vino de Oporto*]

PORTULACA. *See* purslane.

POTASSIUM PERMANGANATE. *See* disinfectants.

POTATO. The potato crop of the world exceeds even the wheat crop in volume and value. Some 90% of potatoes are grown in Europe, but there is hardly anywhere except the lowland tropics and the polar ice regions (excluding part of Greenland) where they are not grown. They are the world's best-known vegetable.

The potato (*Solanum tuberosum*) belongs to the nightshade family and is a native of the Andes, particularly of the region around Lake Titicaca. It was an important staple for the Incas. First mentioned in Pedro de Leon's *Chronica del Peru* in 1553, potatoes were brought back to Spain by the *conquistadores* without arousing much interest there. Since potato, from the native word *batata*, originally referred to the *Sweet potato (a hot-country plant of quite a different family), early references were confused. Even today, in Spanish, *patatas* are potatoes and *batatas* are Sweet potatoes.

Tubers brought to Britain by Sir John Hawkins in 1563 were probably Sweet potatoes, which do not thrive in the British climate. It is possible that the forerunner of today's potato was brought back from Chile by Thomas Heriot, a botanist, when he returned on one of Sir Francis Drake's ships in 1586. Either they were given to Sir Walter Raleigh or he brought them back himself. What is certain is that he got tubers from somewhere and had them planted on his Irish estate at Youghal, County Cork. They were not a very choice kind, long and knobbly, with deep eyes (these were not bred out until the late 18th century). However, by 1633, when the first illustration appears of a potato in the second edition of Gerard's *Herbal*, we find it listed there as the 'potato of Virginia': 'The Indians do call this plant pappus, meaning roots: by which name also the common potato [did he mean Sweet potato?] are called in most Indian countries. The temperature and virtues be referred unto the common potatoes, being likewise food, as also a meat for pleasure, equal in goodness and wholesomeness unto the same, being either roasted in embers or boiled and eaten with oil, vinegar and pepper, or dressed any other way by the hand of some cunning in cookery.'

But parsons and politicians showed less enthusiasm. 'Baulion saith that he heard that the use of these roots was forbidden in Burgundy (where they call them Indian artichokes) for that they were persuaded the too frequent use of them caused the leprosy.' Gaspar Baulion had encouraged farmers near Lyons to start growing potatoes in 1593, but they were stopped by the authorities in Besancon because of that superstition. Scottish preachers considered potatoes unfit food because they were not mentioned in the Bible.

Potatoes were accepted gradually in Ireland, and by 1739 they were being extensively grown in Scotland and were becoming known in Holland, Germany and Italy. In France, the potato was popularized in the eighteenth century by the enthusiasm of Antoine Auguste Parmentier, with the help of Louis XVI, who even used a potato flower as a buttonhole on one occasion. Hence, in culinary French, *parmentier* signifies that a dish contains potato.

Potatoes returned to America in 1719, with Irish immigrants to New England; in Ireland, the population had begun to depend on them. Potatoes were a crop that gave a heavy yield and suited the climate of Ireland. But first a leaf-curl virus spoiled the breeder's efforts; then, in 1845, came the potato blight after a warm, damp summer. Blight is caused by a fungus; potatoes go black and turn to a mass of rotten slime. The result of the potato blight was famine, with far-reaching political and human consequences. Today, with seed potatoes grown in cold, blight-free areas, such as Scotland, blight is less of a problem. Scientific breeding has produced disease-resistant varieties, but the dangers which would go with dependence on one crop are still sometimes demonstrated.

Potatoes have excellent nutritive value when fresh, being rich in vitamin C and potassium (0.6%), when these are not allowed to leach out into cooking water. Frying, steaming or pressure cooking are good from this point of view, but when potatoes are peeled, left to soak in cold water and boiled, most of the soluble nutrients are removed. Although potatoes contain 18% carbohydrate, mainly as starch, they also have 2% of good protein, and since the rest is almost all water, they are not very high in calories – unless, of course, they are fried or eaten with tons of butter, but that is hardly the fault of the potato.

It is often said that the best part of the potato is in the skin. If you hold a thin slice of potato up to the light, you will see that just inside the skin there are several denser layers, and that the middle part of the potato is more transparent. This middle part contains less starch and nutrients, and more water than the outer layers. Since peeling removes a good part of the outer layers, peeling is a wasteful practice. Cooking potatoes in their skins gives them a special taste which is not universally liked. It also restricts the use of potatoes as a 'neutral' vegetable. If potatoes are young and freshly dug (depending to some extent on variety), the skins can be scraped off easily or rubbed off with a coarse pan cleaner. The skins are not loosened by dunking them in boiling water. While some potatoes can be scraped after being in boiling water for 2 minutes, there is no certainty that one variety will behave like another. It is important at least to use a peeler that removes only the finest sliver of skin, and to cook potatoes immediately after they have been peeled.

Only a few of the many potato varieties are grown commercially. Recognizing even these few is difficult; most cooks do little more than distinguish between the white and the red ones (though varieties sold in Britain should now be named). Greengrocers are rarely much help; they often do not know whether a potato is waxy or floury, which to the cook is fundamental. Floury ones have more starch in their surface layers; this swells when they are heated and bursts the skin. Waxy potatoes are best for potato salad, but make a gummy mess when mashed. Other differences are less fundamental. For instance, some potatoes have white flesh (which is preferred in the US) and others have the yellower flesh opted for in parts of Europe. Sizes and shapes also vary greatly. There are kidney-shaped ones, such as the very special Jersey Royal Kidney, and enormous ones, like the Idahos, which are best for baking.

Varieties are chosen by farmers to be disease free and give heavy crops in the potato-growing localities. Some may be grown because they are good keepers, and market preferences are also considered. The British particularly like the floury, red-skinned potatoes, such as King Edward (Redskin or Kerr's Pink in Scotland). But what is valued in one place is not in another, and although reds tend to be more in demand and therefore more expensive in Britain, this is not the case elsewhere.

It is rare for potato varieties to be chosen and grown for their outstanding flavour, but early varieties are grown for use as new potatoes. Main-crop potatoes lifted too soon and sold as new potatoes are inclined to be soapy and to blacken after they are cooked. New potatoes of quality come only from earlies grown for the purpose. In spite of the 'new potatoes' that are now imported, it is still common in Britain for people with small vegetable gardens to grow a few earlies for the incomparable pleasure of eating them freshly dug in early summer. This passion is not pursued to the same extent elsewhere. In the US, many seedsmen's catalogues do not even give potatoes a mention or do not offer more than a couple of well-known varieties, like Red Russet or Idaho.

Potatoes are usually bought in larger quantities than other vegetables, and it is worth knowing a little about storage and the blemishes from which they are likely to suffer. Potatoes with rotten patches, holes or cuts made during lifting should clearly be rejected. Scabs, caused by limey soil, are not of great consequence, but dark patches may indicate blight or may result from the improper use of chemical fertilizers, a condition whose causes are not yet fully understood. Green potatoes have been exposed to the light; they taste bitter and contain mildly poisonous alkaloids called solanines, which can cause an upset stomach. Withered potatoes are old and have lost their vitamins. Potatoes that have been allowed to get too cold taste sweet (which is why potatoes should never be stored in the refrigerator). Sometimes but by no means always, the sweetness goes off if the potatoes are kept for a week in a very warm kitchen.

Potatoes that are very irregular in shape or have big eyes are wasteful. Good-sized, regular and smooth-skinned potatoes are easier to peel. (Buying cheap potatoes may not be economical.) The washed potatoes, which are sold in bags in many supermarkets, go green quickly and will not keep well because the skins have been damaged by the high-pressure hoses used to clean them. When potatoes are mature and have been lifted at the right moment, they keep well in cool, dry, dark conditions. Eventually, they will start to sprout, though, and anti-sprouting agents are often used to inhibit sprouting. In sprouted potatoes, the starch has been partly converted to dextrin and the food value is reduced. In some countries, ready-peeled and chipped potatoes are sold in bags. As they have to be treated chemically with antioxidants and preservatives to keep them white, they are not allowed everywhere. Hollow potatoes can usually be blamed on a drought followed by a very wet spell.

Potato flour, **potato starch** and **instant potato**. Potatoes are steamed, dried and ground, or the starch is extracted by pulverizing and washing, to make various products for use in the kitchen. Potato starch or flour is of special importance to people on a gluten-free diet. It can be used for thickening, but tends to have a taste of its own. Also, it is called for in various cakes and biscuits where a tender starch is needed. Instant potato or powdered potato is typical of the cooked and dried product. Some brands are a good substitute if you are in a hurry; others are nasty.

[Potato – French: *pomme de terre* German: *Kartoffel* Italian: *patata* Spanish: *patata*]

POTTING. 'By potting is generally meant the operation of preserving edible substances in a state for immediate use in small pots or jars', says *Cassell's New Dictionary of Cookery*, published at the turn of the last century. 'Potted meats, fish etc., are commonly sold in shops. They are all intended for relishes, and are spread on bread like butter.'

The method of preserving perishable foods in pots is far, far older than preservation in sealed, sterile glass jars. As a means of preserving meat, fish and shell fish, it depends essentially on sealing with fat. The contents of a pot, unlike the contents of a *terrine*, for instance, offers a small surface to the air in relation to its bulk (unless the pot is very shallow). When things are cooked with plenty of fat and little water, the temperatures are high enough to kill most organisms, and what few might be left are sealed in, unable to spread or infect their surroundings because they are isolated by solidified fat. The hard fatty surface prevents contamination from the air, especially if it is covered with a bladder as used to be the practice in the

past. When refrigeration came along, such methods of preservation became unnecessary, but the tradition of tasty potted meats remained. Potted food – as opposed to food in a pot – implies some degree of preservation combined with readiness for immediate use. In this category come the French *confits* of goose, duck, turkey, rabbit and pork, as well as *rillettes*, *rillons*, *rillots* and *rillauds*, because spreading like butter is not a necessary part of the scenario, although potted products in England were nearly always pounded to a paste. I would also include the Arab *qawwrama, as this is a *confit* of fat-tailed sheep preserved in fat and designed to keep all through the winter.

The extent to which potting was done in the past is not realized today, and as the deep freeze makes the long-term conservation of potted foods easy, we might pay them more attention and revive old recipes. In the *Cassell's*, which is typical of its period, there are dozens of recipes for potting, which mention among fish – herring, char, trout, salmon, eel, lamprey and sprats; among shell fish – lobster, crab, crayfish, shrimps and prawns; among game – hare, rabbit, pheasant, partridge, larks; among meats – beef, mutton, veal, fowl, ham, tongue, and mixtures such as ham and fowl, veal and tongue. In general, all were made the same way, by cooking the meat or fish, pounding it with salt, cayenne, mace or nutmeg, and butter, baking in a moderate oven, and pouring an extra layer of clarified butter on top.

From a safety point of view, there are objections to some of the old recipes for pounding or repotting the pastes when they are cold, then sealing them without re-sterilizing by heat. Some of these recipes could have caused botulism. However, there will be no problem if potted meats are eaten within a few days or kept in the freezer.

Potted cheese is in a different category because the cheese was not cooked, merely pounded to a paste with butter and flavourings before being put into pots. It was then covered with a layer of clarified butter to prevent it drying out (though it would have continued to mature like any other cheese). No doubt potting cheese was often regarded as a way of using up the bits and keeping them for a day or so, but there are some distinguished recipes, such as Boulestin's for Roquefort pounded with butter and a dash of armagnac, which Elizabeth David recommends in her *Spices, Salt and Aromatics in the English Kitchen* (Grub Street). As she remarks 'the old recipes are coming back into use as methods of giving flavour, character and improved texture to factory cheeses which have so little personality of their own.' Recently, a number of commercially-made potted cheeses have also come on the market. In them, cheese is mixed with wine, beer, garlic, and herbs in various ways. Many are nice, but their claim to be potted would rest only on their being sold in pots (and many of them are sold by weight in cut pieces) as they are not sealed with clarified butter or sterilized and are not meant to be kept.

POURGOURI. *See* burghul.

POUTARG. *See* botargo.

PRALINE. A mixture of caramelized sugar and roasted nuts used in confectionery and on ice cream. The simplest way to make it is to put nuts and sugar (in equal quantities or more nuts than sugar) in a copper pan and to stir the mixture over heat until the sugar starts to caramelize, by which time, if the heating is done slowly, the nuts should also be sufficiently roasted. Turn the praline out (correctly, on a marble slab) and let it cool. Grind it in a mill or crush it in a mortar, and store it in an airtight tin. Some recipes involve roasting the nuts and caramelizing the sugar separately.

[*Praline* – French: *praline* German: *gebrannte Mandel* Italian: *mandorla tosta* Spanish: *almendra garapiñada*]

PRAWN. *See* shrimp.

PRÉ SALÉ. *See* mutton.

PRESERVATION. All foods deteriorate when kept beyond their natural life, which may be anything from a few hours to a year or more. Storing food is not a human innovation – various mammals store the food which is necessary for their survival over the winter, using things which have dried naturally, or nuts, grains and pulses, which are dormant but alive. Insects also store food – bees were making a good job of refining and sealing up honey long before the appearance of man.

Foods are open to attack by *micro-organisms and even by their own enzymes. Storage methods are all designed to minimize spoilage, if not to remove it entirely. Until the middle of the 19th century, the methods in use had all been discovered by chance, and the reason that they worked was not understood; it was not until Pasteur showed the causal role played by micro-organisms in fermentation and decomposition that progress could become systematic and rapid. Today, many of the old methods, like smoking, are now retained only for the flavour they impart to the food, and a revolution has taken place in our eating habits.

Not all methods of preservation actually kill the micro-organisms – the low temperatures of *freezing immobilize them, as does the absence of water produced by *drying. Other methods, though, do involve killing all the micro-organisms in the food – *sterilization – and preventing other organisms getting in. The most important method of sterilization is heating, but there are others, mainly involving chemical *preservatives. Micro-organisms are also killed by ultra-violet light (even that in sunlight) but much more effective are other rays and radiation, which kill all living tissue. It is even possible to sterilize food in the can by radiation which will go through the metal. However, this treatment, promising though it may be at first sight, appears to cause changes in the food which lead to bad flavour, and work on the irradiation of food is still largely experimental.

Unless the sterilized food can be sealed (or unless preservatives are added), it is open to immediate reinfection. Early methods depended on a capping of fat or clarified butter. *Potting is not suitable for very long-term preserving as fats eventually go rancid. So do oils, which are used similarly: *mushrooms, *basil, *sardines and *anchovies are commonly preserved under olive oil in Mediterranean countries, and mustard oil preserves pickles in India. The main methods of scaling, though, are *bottling and *canning.

The other traditional method of preserving was salting, which involved applying common salt, often mixed with saltpetre, either as a *brine or by *dry-salting. Salt works mainly by osmosis – preventing the organisms from getting water, it is toxic to some organisms but tolerated by others. In sufficient strength, it will stop virtually all organisms as well as inhibiting the action of enzymes. Sugar in sufficient concentrations also stops micro-organisms from getting water, it is a preservative, for example, in jams.

*Smoking is usually an adjunct to salting and drying. It covers the surface of meat or fish with a layer of chemicals that have antiseptic properties. Today, its importance as a method of preservation is minimal.

A few modern methods are important industrially but not possible in the home – for example, the removal of micro-organisms from liquids by filtration which, if done effectively, will make them keep. The shelf life of *flour is much increased by the removal of the germ from the grain – nutritionally a harmful practice. In some cases, the enzymes in the germ are inactivated by heating before it is returned 'dead' to the flour.

PRESERVATIVES are substances that are added to foods to make them keep; they destroy or at least discourage micro-organisms or slow down natural processes that cause spoilage. Into the last category come anti-sprouting agents, which are sprayed over vegetables, mainly potatoes, to prevent them sprouting in store. For their safeness, we can only trust to the vigilance of the governmental agencies which monitor our food.

Although the term preservatives conjures up thoughts of sinister additives produced by the petrochemical industry, the description covers many things that food manufacturers would consider old fashioned or downright folksy. Herbs and spices contain essential oils which can be antiseptic, often quite strongly so; thymol, which is found in thyme, is used in mouthwashes.

Cloves, cinnamon, white mustard and even pepper have similar properties. The preservative action of spices is important in sausages and pickles, while curries will keep sweet for several days in the hot Indian summer. White mustard seed is particularly effective in chutneys. A clove in stock will help keep it sweet as well as adding background flavour.

The most important traditional preservatives are salt (in *brines and *dry-salting), sugar (in *jams), vinegar (in *pickles) and *lactic acid (which is produced in *sauerkraut* and fermented pickles). Various nasty substances, including *disinfectants such as formaldehyde, which were used in the past as preservatives, are now generally forbidden. Some preservatives which are purely industrial in application are outside the scope of this book. For example, carbon dioxide under great pressure stops yeasts from growing and is used to hold fruit juices, such as crude apple juice, in bulk before filtration, sterilization and bottling.

Most preservatives are acids – in sufficient strength, and given sufficient time to operate, any acid will prevent putrefactive bacteria from growing and will kill disease organisms. The hydrochloric acid in the stomach kills most of the bacteria that we eat. Certain acids, though, have antiseptic properties over and above those that result from their acidity. They thus come into the category of chemical preservatives.

Apart from germ killing, the other important preservative function is preventing oxidation. The effect that oxygen can have on food is demonstrated by the way that cut surfaces of apples or potatoes turn brown when exposed to the air. Oxygen is a prime destroyer, which attacks many foods, helped by enzymes and the ultra-violet rays in sunlight. Oxidation destroys such vitamins as vitamin E very quickly and turns fats rancid. In the kitchen, discolouration of vegetables and fruit is prevented by using lemon juice. Commercial anti-oxidants include sulphurous acid and its derivatives.

*Acetic acid is the acid of vinegar, for which it is used as a substitute in some cheap pickles.

Benzoic acid and **sodium benzoate**. Benzoic acid was discovered in gum benzoin in 1608 and prepared from urine by Scheele towards the end of the 18th century. It can be bought from pharmacists in the form of white, shiny needles. More commonly used as a preservative is the sodium salt, a crystalline powder with a sweetish, astringent taste. Sodium benzoate is slightly alkaline (pH 8), but must be used in slightly acid conditions if it is to be effective as a preservative (in an alkaline medium, such as milk, it has almost no preservative effect). In the countries – including the UK and US – where sodium benzoate is allowed, 1 part per 1000 is considered safe. It is used particularly in fruit juices and tomato sauces (which are acid) to prevent spoilage after opening. Cranberries, which have remarkable keeping qualities, contain natural benzoic acid.

Boric acid is a mild antiseptic, which used to be a standard item in medicine cupboards. It was once a common preservative for margarine, butter, cream, caviar, ham, etc. Most foods are preserved by 0.5% of boric acid, but it is now banned for commercial products in the UK and US, though many other countries allow it. There is probably no harm in its occasional home use, provided the dosage is properly measured, but few recipes specify it.

*Citric acid is an anti-oxidant and a weak preservative. However, bottled lemon juice has to be treated with sulphur dioxide, which has the same properties much more strongly.

*Lactic acid is unusual in being a preservative that is normally formed in foods by fermentation rather than added to them.

Salicylic acid and its sodium salt sodium salicylate have been used as commercial food preservatives in some countries but are forbidden in others. Salicylic acid is chemically related to aspirin – acetylsalicylic acid – and is medically used in rheumatic liniments and for treating corns (it loosens, swells and softens the surface cells of the skin). It is poisonous if used too freely over a long period, and some people are allergic to it, as others are to aspirin. However, recipes from Italy use salicylic acid as a preservative in home-made tomato concentrates at the rate of 1 gram per kg (2¼ lb) *and no more*. At this rate, and for home use, when you know how much you are using the preserved food, it must be relatively harmless, but like any chemical it is not something to throw in by the handful. The advantage of such chemical preservatives over complete sterilization by heat, is that they do not alter the flavour.

Sorbic acid is used to stop the growth of moulds on cheese and bread.

Sulphur dioxide (SO_2), **sulphurous acid** (H_2SO_3), and **sulphites**. Sulphurous acid is not known in a pure state, but, at least in theory, is formed when sulphur dioxide (for instance, from burning sulphur) is dissolved in water. Sulphurous acid and sulphites are toxic to all micro-organisms, but especially so to wild yeasts. Metabisulphites, particularly in the form of *Campden tablets, are the most convenient source of sulphur dioxide on a domestic scale. In this form, they are invaluable to home makers of wine, beer and cider. Sulphur dioxide is also used in fruit juices and in the drying of fruit. There are limits in most countries on the concentration of sulphur dioxide and its derivatives permitted in foods. Sulphurous acid is also an anti-oxident and a bleach.

[*Preservative* – French: *préservatif* German: *Schutzmittel* Italian: *preservativo* Spanish: *preservativo*]

PRESERVED FRUIT. *See* candied fruit.

PRESSURE sometimes has to be applied with a weight – for example, to cheese, *gravlax*, tongue and *terrine* – or even with a special press, as used with duck to squeeze out the juices. Most serious cooks have their own favourite weights – old kitchen weights, stones, bricks wrapped in polythene bags and so on. The use of weights bears

thinking about since the right pressure for any job has some importance. Pressure of this type is used to squeeze out juices, to firm, to remove air pockets, to shape, or to make food stay in contact with the heat, as in frying a spatchcocked chicken for recipes such as *polio alla diavola*.

The main significance of pressure to the cook, though, is its effect on the boiling point of water, both with variations of *altitude and in *pressure cooking.

[*Pressure* – French: *pression* German: *Druck* Italian: *pressione* Spanish: *presión*]

PRESSURE COOKING. The higher the pressure, the higher is the temperature at which water boils. Thus, increasing the pressure allows a vessel containing water to reach a higher temperature than the 100°C (212°F) at which it would otherwise stay until all the water had boiled away.

The principle is used in the pressure cooker and autoclave (the large scale equivalent of the pressure cooker used in commercial canning and for sterilizing in the operating theatre).

The first pressure cooker, known as the *digesteur d'aliments*, was invented in 1675 by a Frenchman, Denis Papin. In this, the top of the vessel was held down by a huge clamp, and the valve – where the steam escaped when the set pressure was reached – was held down and adjusted by a long arm with a weight sliding on it (Papin subsequently settled in England and worked with Robert Boyle on the steam engine.)

The modern pressure cooker is much simpler but the principle is the same: sealing in the steam to cause an increase in the pressure and therefore in the temperature. The higher temperature results in more rapid cooking; it can cut times by at least two thirds.

Household pressure cookers are made of aluminium or stainless steel; they should last for many years if looked after carefully. The basic components of a pressure cooker are: a body and cover made of a gauge of metal that will withstand at least six times the maximum cooking pressure, a pressure control, a safety plug, a gasket or sealing ring, and a locking device to keep the cover firmly pressed down.

Separators allow more than one food to be cooked at a time – perforated separators are for small or cut fruit and vegetables; solid ones are for rice and for tinned and frozen foods. A trivet may be used to keep the contents away from the bottom of the pan. Many versions have more than one level of pressure.

High pressure (15 lb/sq. in. or 1.05 kg/sq. cm.) is for everyday boiling, stewing, braising and pot-roasting meat, poultry, fish, vegetables and milk puddings.

Medium pressure (10 lb/sq. in. or 0.7 kg/sq. cm.) is for softening fruit for jams, jellies and marmalade, cooking vegetables for chutneys and sauces and for blanching vegetables for freezing.

Low pressure (5 lb/sq. in. or 0.35 kg/sq. cm.) is for steaming puddings and preparing fruit for *bottling. The liquid used for pressure cooking should never be less than 250 ml (½ pt) – don't forget it. A pressure cooker can work only if it has liquid inside to produce steam. The amount of liquid used depends on the type of dish and the length of cooking time, but not on the quantity of food being cooked. The liquid itself must be one that produces steam when it boils – such as water, stock, soup, gravy, wine, beer, milk – and not fat or oil alone. However, watery foods like meat can produce a lot of their own liquid. Don't fill a pressure cooker more than two-thirds full with solid foods, as the steam must circulate freely. With liquids such as soup, milk puddings or fruit, do not fill the cooker more than half full, to allow room for them to rise when they come to the boil. The manufacturer will supply a book of instructions with the pressure cooker, to start with, you should accurately follow the timings quoted for cooking.

Pressure cookers are excellent for many foods. They enable vegetables such as beetroot and potatoes to be quickly steamed with little loss of nutrients, and they save time and fuel. They are not ideal for dishes in which flavours must amalgamate and temper over a period of time. Their drawback is also that as the container is sealed one cannot test, taste or stir without removing the lid; to do that, pressure must first be reduced by cooling in a basin of cold water under a running tap. The sudden reduction of pressure can sometimes destroy the texture of what is being cooked.

PRICKLY PEAR, **Cactus pear**, **Indian fig**, **Indian pear**, **Barbary pear** or **tuna fig** is not related to the pear or the fig but is the fruit of *Opuntia*, the familiar cactus which has large plate-like pads. The best fruit are said to come from *O. magacantha*, a native of Mexico, but the prickly pear that grows in Europe is *O. fiscus-Indica*, which is well established in the Mediterranean and North African areas, but also came from Mexico.

The fruits, which have very nasty spines, are borne along the edges of the green pads and, when ripe, are yellow-green, rosy-red, purple or almost black. Although some sorts are small, the largest reach 12 cm (5 in) long. Some plants produce two sets of fruit; the second crop – ripe in October and going on to December – are larger and better to eat. Prickly pears can be fairly tasteless, like slightly sweet, over-ripe cucumbers, with lots of small seeds embedded in the flesh, but some varieties can be good. In the US, the best are large and rose coloured, but in Europe – especially in Sicily – the nicest ones have whitish or yellowish fruits. In Sicily, these are called *bastardi* or *bastardom*. They keep through to January and are often cut with a small piece of the pad attached to keep them fresh.

To gather the fruits, you need to have your hands well protected, as the spines are tiny, irritating and difficult to get out of your skin. When the fruits have been cut off, the spines must be rubbed off them and rinsed away. Even so, it is safest to extract the pulp while holding the fruit with a thick cloth, tongs or leather gloves. Cut off both ends of the fruit, and slit the skin from end to end, so that the pulp can be loosened and removed. This can be chilled and eaten raw, but may need a squeeze of lime or lemon, as it tends to lack acidity.

The pads of the prickly pear are eaten in Mexico, where they are called *nopales* (the fruits are called *nopalilas* or *tunas*). Very young pads are best and should have the spines but not the skin removed before cooking. They are then cut into small pieces (about 1 cm or ½ in thick) and cooked in well salted water until they are tender. They are then drained and washed under the cold water tap until they are no longer slimy. They are used in soups, cooked as a vegetable, or added to the vegetables for a Spanish-type omelette. They may also be slivered and eaten raw with scrambled eggs.

Nopales are available canned *en *escabeche*, in vinegar, in brine, and in water (*nopalitos tiernos al natural*, the best to use). Fresh ones appear in US markets that sell Mexican ingredients, but they are not used in Europe, although they could well be in the Mediterranean countries.

[*Prickly pear* – French: *figue de Barbarie* Italian: *fico d'India* Spanish: *higo chumbo*]

PRIMOST. *See* whey.

PROOF SPIRIT. This is not pure *alcohol but an antiquated concept fortunately becoming obsolete as it caused confusion. An old description is as follows: 'Formerly a very rude mode of ascertaining the strength of spirits was practised called "The Proof". The spirit was poured upon gun-powder and inflamed. If at the end of the combustion the powder took fire the spirit was said to be "over proof". If the spirit contained much water the powder was rendered so moist that it did not take fire, in which case the spirit was said to be "under proof".'

Proof spirit became defined by act of Parliament in the reign of George III as 'such as shall, at the temperature of 51 degrees of Fahrenheit's thermometer weigh exactly twelve thirteenth parts of an equal measure of distilled water.' In more modern terms, British Proof is roughly 57% per cent alcohol by volume at 15°C (60°F), or virtually 50% by weight (a measure which is of course independent of temperature). Its specific gravity is close to 0.8 at 60 °F. The US, in an attempt to rationalize the system, redefined proof spirit as to 50% alcohol by volume.

Many labels still express alcohol content as a percentage of proof strength. To convert British proof to degrees Gay Lussac (effectively the percentage of pure alcohol) multiply by 4 and divide by 7. Gay Lussac to proof, multiply by 7 and divide by 4. US proof to Gay Lussac, divide by 2. Gay Lussac to US, multiply by 2. US proof to UK proof, multiply by 7 and divide by 8. UK proof to US proof multiply by 8 and divide by 7.

PROSCIUTTO. *See* ham (Italian).

PROSO. *See* millet.

PROTEINS are exceedingly complex, organic nitrogen compounds which form part of all living cells and are in a sense the basic stuff of life itself. Enzymes, for instance, are proteins. They are particularly concentrated in meat and fish, in cheese and eggs, in nuts and in legumes – especially soya beans. Proteins differ widely in their characteristics. Some are soluble or easily mixed with water (such as egg white) while others (such as the casein from milk) are insoluble. Proteins start to coagulate at 50-60°C (122-140°F) and are completely coagulated at around 65-70°C (149-158°F) but some need higher temperatures (e.g., milk protein 100°C or 212°F). Proteins may harden to horny substances when strongly heated. Thus, egg white, when heated, at first becomes solid and insoluble, but, when fried in very hot fat, it becomes downright hard and brittle. However, coagulated proteins can be hydrolysed by acids and enzymes into their constituent building bricks, the *amino acids, and most are broken down by the digestive enzymes in our bodies. The

breaking down can also be achieved by long, slow cooking, but dry heat can destroy amino acids, particularly lysine.

The daily requirement of protein for an adult would be satisfied by about 225 g (½ lb) of meat or chicken per day with no protein coming from any other source, but most people in Europe and America get their requirements from a mixed diet, and 100-150 g (4-5 oz) of meat a day is enough.

[*Protein* – French: *protéine* German: *Protein* Italian: *proteina* Spanish: *proteina*]

PROTOZOA are microscopic, single-celled (or non-cellular) animals. The parasitic forms have complicated life cycles and cause many nasty tropical diseases, such as malaria, sleeping sickness, amoebic dysentery and bilharzia. The most effective precaution against waterborne protozoans in the tropics is boiling; covering food and water helps protect against protozoans carried on flies. Marine protozoans are an important element in plankton and form part of the food of many shell fish. Some are poisonous, and may be dangerous when they are present in exceptionally large numbers, as in the notorious 'red tides' (*see* poisoning).

PRUNE. *See* plum.

P'SST. *See* monosodium glutamate.

PTARMIGAN. *See* grouse.

PTOMAINE. *See* poisoning.

PULASAN. *See* lychee.

PULSES. The general term for all ripe, dried, edible seeds of *legumes: peas, beans, grams and lentils. They are the main source of protein for poor people, but their use is particularly developed in vegetarian India.

Pulses are generally soaked before cooking; the drier they are, the longer the soaking needed. However, in warm weather, an unpleasant fermented taste may result from the activity of micro-organisms or from the onset of changes leading up to germination. It is probably better to cook pulses without soaking whenever possible. Exceptions are very old, dry beans or very large beans which have to be kept looking nice, with their skins on, to be used, for example, in an *hors d'oeuvre*. For such purposes, large beans are best given a very full soaking in the refrigerator, so they look thoroughly plump, not wrinkled, before they are cooked. Bicarbonate of soda in the water helps to soften the skins.

Pulses should be very well cooked – pressure cookers are useful for this. Pulses may be found indigestible and windy but these effects may be lessened by a preliminary short cooking (with a pinch of bicarbonate of soda) and a thorough rinsing, followed by a new start with fresh water. Salt should never be added until the beans are cooked. Whether they are can usually be determined by blowing on a few of them; if they are cooked, the skins wrinkle. Certain spices, notably cumin, may be used in pulse dishes to counteract indigestibility. Peeled lentils and *dals* are more digestible than unpeeled ones.

Haricot Beans. Cook the beans without prior soaking for 6 minutes in a pressure cooker, start them in cold water with 1 teaspoon bicarbonate of soda to 450 g (1 lb) beans. Open the cooker, drain the beans and rinse them well under the tap. Start again with fresh water (and any flavourings called for in the recipe). Cook for 40 minutes or more (depending on the age of the beans).

[*Pulses* – French: *plantes légumineuses* German: *Gemüsepflanzen, Hülsenfrucht* Italian: *plante leguminose* Spanish: *legumbres*]

PUMMELO. *See* shaddock.

PUMPKIN. *See* marrow.

PURPLE GRANADILLA. *See* passion fruit.

PURSLANE, pussley, pigweed, or **portulaca** (*Portulaca oleracea*) is a spreading annual with fleshy leaves. It grows wild over most of southern Europe and in Asia, and is a common weed in the US, although it is said to have originated in India, where it is known as *kulfa*. It is also popular in Arab countries, as *bagli*.

Wash it thoroughly, as it can be gritty. Tender shoots can be dressed with oil and vinegar to be eaten raw as a salad, as purslane was hundreds of years ago. The taste is mild, slightly sour, and the texture is mucilaginous, something like okra but less so. Although it also makes an excellent vegetable, it is now neglected, and most people would not even recognize it growing. With its fleshy leaves and stems, it superficially resembles samphire (although the taste is quite different); perhaps that is why it was often pickled. Purslane is easy to grow and

freezes well. It would be worth another look.

....

Fattoush – an Arab salad

Put ½ cup of Arab (or other) bread, broken in pieces, into a bowl. Sprinkle it with sumac water (made by infusing some sumac seeds in water for a quarter of an hour or so and squeezing out the red juice) or some lemon juice. Add 3 chopped small (ridge) cucumbers, or a Cos lettuce torn to bits, a chopped green pepper, a chopped tomato, a small handful each of chopped parsley and mint, and purslane leaves. Add some chopped onion, a good sprinkling of salt, and season with ½ cup of good olive oil before mixing. Also add 2 cloves crushed garlic – the lazy way is to liquidize these in the oil before adding it. Adjust the seasoning with more salt and lemon juice as necessary.

[*Purslane* – French: *pourpier* German: *Portulak* Italian: *portulaca parcellana* Spanish: *verdolagas*]
....

PYROLIGNEOUS ACID, sometimes called liquid smoke, is made by the destructive distillation of wood. Sawdust is heated in an iron retort, and the vapours are caught and condensed. It consists of 6% acetic acid and small amounts of creosote, methyl alcohol and acetone (a solvent which is used in nail-polish remover and film cement).The yellowish liquid was used at one time as a pickling liquid, but today it appears mainly as an artificial smoke flavouring and also, in tiny amounts, in a wide range of unlikely products from butter and caramels to rum and ice cream. It is corrosive and poisonous except in dilute form.

q

QAWWRAMA. This is mutton preserved in its fat, much used in Lebanese cooking and interesting because it echoes products made in France with pig and goose. For *qawwrama*, sheep are fattened for killing at the end of November, in the last weeks, the women stuff food individually and by hand into the mouth of each sheep. The animals become so fat that they can scarcely move. After slaughter, the fat is cut from the carcass and rendered down in a large brass pan. Meanwhile, the lean meat is cut in pieces, pressed to remove much of the liquid (it would not keep with too much water in it), and finally fried in the mutton fat. It is seasoned with pepper and salt. Meat and fat are packed, scalding, into earthenware crocks and are sealed in with clay. These jars of *qawwrama* keep all winter. *Qawwrama* is used in stews, for stuffing vegetables, for frying eggs and for many other purposes. A Lebanese idea of a good breakfast is *kishk* (a soured mixture of wheat and milk which has been dried to a powder for storage – another local staple) mixed into a porridge with water and laced with onions and garlic fried in *qawwrama*. A good healthy dish to start the day.

QUAHAUG or **QUAHOG**. Hard-shell *clam.

QUAIL (*Coturnix coturnix*) is the smallest European game bird, like a tiny partridge, and the only one that is migratory. Quails breed in much of Europe and into Asia as far as China, but migrate southwards in winter. The quail is now a protected species in Britain. Quail are eaten fresh. Sometimes, in the past, cooks left the *trail in, as with woodcock, but it was more usual to draw them. Head and neck were also removed, and the wing ends and feet; then the birds were trussed and wrapped in a slice of bacon and a vine leaf for roasting.

Enormous numbers of quail were netted on migration as they crossed Italy, and the London market was supplied from there, but today they are diminished in numbers and quails are reared specially for the table. The Japanese have been doing this with their local species for a very long time, as well as keeping them for laying, as hard-boiled quails' eggs are a delicacy. The Japanese quail is the species that is normally reared as it can be bred in small cages. The birds start to lay eggs when they are a mere 6 weeks old. As they can lay up to an egg a day all year and make very efficient use of their food, they are becoming increasingly important. There are native species of quail in most countries. US species include the bobwhite (*Colinus virgintanus*), which is easy to rear, although it does not thrive in the British climate, it has been introduced in a few places in England as well as in Germany, where another, larger US species, the California quail (*Lophortyx californicus*) has also been introduced.

[*Quail* – French: *caille* German: *Wachtel* Italian: *quaglia* Spanish: *codorniz*]

QUASSIA is a bitter tasting wood, originally from a small tropical South American tree (*Quassia amara*) but since the early 19th century more usually from a larger Caribbean tree, the Bitter ash (*Pacrasma excelsa*). Both are used as a source of bitters for tonic wines and aperitifs.

[*Quassia* – French: *quassia* German: *Quassia* Italian: *quassia* Spanish: *cuasia*]

QUATRE ÉPICES. A mixture of four spices used as a flavouring, particularly in French *charcuterie*. There is no standard mixture and the name is sometimes applied to *allspice, as well as to *nigella. *Quatre épices* can even be a mixture of more than four spices. There are many formulae for such mixtures, a few of which follow.

Percentages by weight

Pepper	51.5 (white)	70 (black)	62.5 (white)
Nutmeg	29	10	17.5
Ginger	13	–	15
Cinnamon	–	10	–
Cloves	6.5	10	5
	100	100	100

QUETSCH. *See* fruit brandy, plum.

QUIN. *See* scallop.

QUINCE (*Cydonia vulgaris*) is related to pear and apple. The fruit may be pear-shaped or apple-shaped, according to variety, and their colour is golden when ripe – possibly this is the original 'golden apple' of classical legend. If so, when Paris judged the beauty contest between Aphrodite, Athena and Hera, the prize must have been presented as a joke because a bite of a raw quince would surely have given even Aphrodite a sour expression. Or was she expected only to smell it? A ripe quince has a wonderful perfume. The quince comes from western Asia, from that exciting corner between the Black and Caspian seas where until recently there were virgin tracts of primeval forest. Wild quinces in Europe have probably escaped from cultivation, and there are a number of cultivated varieties – though comparatively few beside pears and apples. Aroma and quality depend upon the type, and this is reflected in the quince jams made in different places. Quince jam is reckoned a luxury in Britain, but it is not easy to get, and is not generally popular, especially with children. The fruit contains plenty of pectin and sets to a good jelly; the astringency is destroyed by cooking. A thick paste of quince purée boiled down with sugar until it can be set into a tough slab is a confection made in many places from the Middle East through Spain and Portugal to France, which has a famous version called *cotignac*. Quince paste may be good, but is often over-sweet and insipid, especially when filled out with cheaper apple pulp. In Spain, it is called *carne de membrillo* (quince meat) and is generally eaten with cheese, a habit that has spread to Latin America, where the quince forests of Uruguay are famous. The word marmalade comes from the Portuguese for quince – *marmelo*. Quinces may have been introduced to Britain in the mid 10th century by the English king, Edgar, during the 16th and 17th centuries hundreds of recipes for quince marmalade appeared in cook books. Most of these were for pastes and jellies which were equivalents of the Italian *cotognata*.

Quinces are cooked with meat in many countries; the custom possibly originated in Persia. There are even Persian dishes in which quinces are stuffed with meat mixtures. In Romania, quinces are cooked with beef, veal or chicken and onion – the meat and quinces are usually first fried and then combined in a sort of stew, thickened a little with flour and made slightly sweet-sour with brown sugar or caramel and a dash of vinegar. In North Africa, especially in Morocco, stews (*tagine*) of lamb or chicken often contain quinces. Even in Britain, quince sauce was often served with partridge, although this custom has largely died out. Recipes for stuffed quinces, *tagine* and quince paste will be found in Claudia Roden's *A Book of Middle Eastern Food* (Penguin) which includes also a fabulous way of preparing compote of quinces.

Quince Compote

Peel and core 1 kg (2 lb) of quinces. Cook the peel and cores with the juice of half a lemon, 250 g (9 oz) sugar and 400 ml (¾ pt) of water for half an hour. Meanwhile, slice the quinces and put them into a bowl (if you want them pale, cover them temporarily with lemon juice and water as they quickly discolour in air). Strain the syrup from the pan, squeezing out all the juices over the quinces and cook the quince slices in this flavoured syrup until they are tender. Check for sweetness and acidity. Chill and eat with thick cream.

[*Quince* – French: *coing* German: *Quitte* Italian: *cotogna* Spanish: *membrillo*]

QUININE. Most famous as an early anti-malarial drug, this exceedingly bitter *alkaloid is extracted from various species of the South American *Cinchona* bush. It is used, very dilute, in Indian tonic water. Liquids containing quinine, as opposed to other bitter substances, may be recognized by their pale blue fluorescence.

[*Quinine* – French: *quinine* German: *Chinin* Italian: *china, chinina, chinino* Spanish: *quinina*]

r

RABBIT and HARE belong to the same family, Leporidae. A strong distinction is made between hares and rabbits in Britain: hares have red meat and rabbits have white. But when the English names are used in other countries, the original distinction becomes blurred. Are American jack rabbits and Snowshoe rabbits really hares, when they belong to the hare and not the rabbit genus? The important point is whether the flesh is dark or light, and hares and rabbits anywhere can be judged by this criterion and recipes selected accordingly.

Hares are easily distinguished from rabbits by their darker colour and longer, more powerful back legs. There are two, possibly three, species of hare in Europe. The Common or Brown hare (*Lepus europaeus*) is distributed right across Europe and through to eastern Asia. The Varying, Blue, Scottish or Alpine hare (*Lepus timidus*) – not the same species as the Varying hare of North America – is found in the Alps, Scotland, Ireland and Scandinavia; in snowy places, it turns white in winter. Compared to the Brown hare, it has a smaller body and shorter ears, but a larger head and longer legs. The Mediterranean hare (*Lepus capensis*) which is found in Spain, the Balearic Islands, Sardinia and Crete, is strongly coloured and a little smaller than the Brown hare, of which it might be a variety.

Young hares can be told from old ones because they do not have a widely spread cleft in their hare-lip and they have sharp claws and tender ears. Up to a year old, they are called leverets. Old hares can never be roasted, but must be jugged or stewed. Unless hares have been badly shot and therefore have to be eaten immediately before they stiffen, they need hanging by the hind legs for at least 3 days – 5 days is better, or 7-8 days if the hare is large and the weather is cool (older books say from 10 days to a fortnight) – *without drawing*. When the hare is drawn just before cooking, the blood, especially that trapped in the chest cavity, should be saved if it is to be used for thickening the sauce (this may give rather too strong a flavour for some tastes).The best part of a hare is the back; the hind legs come second. Shoulders and forelegs are usually stewed or used for soup. Hare is very often marinated in a mixture of olive oil and wine, flavoured with crushed juniper berries, thyme or mixed herbs. If it is to be roasted, it is usually *larded to prevent the flesh going dry.

In Britain, hare is a cheap meat, but in Europe it is expensive and likely to figure in rather grand recipes. In French regional cooking, there are many marvellous hare dishes ranging from the simple *civet de lièvre landais* to the more luxurious creations such as *râble de lièvre à la crème* (saddle of hare baked in cream). Germany has a version of jugged hare (*Tippenhaas*) and saddle of hare sauced with horseradish and red currant jelly (*Hasenrücken mit Meerettich*) or with cream (*mit Sahne*); the liver is sometimes cooked as a separate dish. Italy has many excellent hare dishes, including several way-out ones such as the fantastic *lepre in dolce e forte* from Tuscany. This contains among its ingredients pine nuts, the candied peel of orange and citron, sultanas, chocolate, *cavallucci* (a sweetmeat from Siena which includes walnuts and aniseed), wine, sugar, garlic, rosemary, basil, celery, tomato, parsley, onion, carrot, sage, bay leaves, oil and vinegar. It is one of the Italian sweet-sour (*agrodolce*) dishes of ancient origin.

The most famous British hare dish is jugged hare, which is traditionally cooked in a pot that stands in water (but today more usually in the oven) and is lengthily simmered with port or burgundy and gravy.

Jugged Hare

Cut the hare into pieces and brown them lightly in butter or bacon fat. Put them into a stoneware jar and pour in a large glass of red wine – port or burgundy. Turn the pieces and leave it while making a forcemeat. This consists of 6 heaped tablespoons of fresh breadcrumbs, the grated rind of a lemon, a small handful of parsley finely chopped, ½ teaspoon mixed thyme and marjoram, plus seasoning of salt, pepper and nutmeg. To this, add a tablespoon of butter or some suet, and the yolk of 1-2 eggs for binding.

When the forcemeat has been made, cut 450 g (1 lb) of steak into thin slices, and spread each with a little of the forcemeat. Roll and tie these steak olives, brown them in butter and add to the pot with a very finely-chopped onion and some gravy. Cover the jar closely and stand it up to the neck in boiling water. Keep the water boiling for 1½-2 hours, depending on the age of the hare. Ten minutes before serving, make the rest of the forcemeat into balls, fry them and add them to the pot. Adjust the seasoning, remove the string from the steak olives and serve the dish garnished with triangles of bread fried in butter and accompanied by red currant jelly. The gravy should be naturally thick, but if it needs thickening, do so with the blood (mixed with a teaspoon of vinegar to prevent curdling) or a little arrowroot mixed with butter. The steak can be omitted, but is a usual part of jugged hare, at least in the north of England.

....

Rabbits. The European rabbit (*Oryctolagus caniculus*) is a native of south-west Europe which has been introduced into many parts of the world, including Britain. Before myxomatosis was let loose, rabbits were so plentiful that they could hardly be given away; they kept many unemployed miners alive during the hungry 'thirties, when it was not difficult for a good shot to kill thirty or more rabbits in an hour, in places they swarmed like vermin. Now rabbit has become more costly than chicken and frozen rabbit is imported into Britain from China. Wild rabbits, if they were young and particularly if they had fed on bark, were regarded as superior in flavour to domestic rabbits; a nest of really young ones made a fine brawn.

Wild rabbits are not found in the coldest parts of Europe – in the north or on high mountains – but are regularly eaten everywhere else. The weight of a fully grown rabbit undressed may reach 2 kg (4½ lb), but is normally less. Rabbits can live up to 13 years, though 5-6 is more usual. In young rabbits, the claws are sharp and smooth, the coat soft, and the ears easily torn. In old rabbits, the claws are long and rough, the ears are tough and the coat may be turning grey. Unlike hares, rabbits are not hung – they ought not to have been killed more than a couple of days, and are best when still stiff. If kept too long, rabbit meat smells, and the flesh goes slimy and slightly blue.

To skin a rabbit, cut round the first joint of each hind leg (or chop off). If the rabbit has not been already paunched, make an incision in the skin of each hind leg and slit back as far as the tail, then insert the hand between the skin and flesh and free the skin right over the back. (If the rabbit has been paunched, the belly wall and skin must be separated by pulling them apart, and then the procedure is the same.) The skin can be pulled off each leg, like turning a glove inside-out, the skin pulled forward and the front legs freed in the same way. With a little help from a knife, the skin can be pulled forward over the head, but some lazy people just chop the head off as it contains little meat. The rabbit now is ready to be gutted (leaving only the kidneys). The green gall bladder must be carefully cut from the liver, and the liver and heart saved. Wash the rabbit and giblets well and dry them. Rabbit is sometimes soaked for an hour in slightly salted water before cooking. Table breeds of domestic rabbit can grow to a huge size, but remain tender and white. Young rabbits of the giant breeds weigh 2 kg (4½ lb) – as much as a large wild rabbit – when only 8 weeks old, and reach 4 kg (9 lb) at 6 months. A dressed rabbit is not much over 60% of its live weight (a hare 75%).

As rabbits used to be so cheap and common, there are innumerable simple recipes for cooking them, but they seem not to have merited very royal treatment. Rabbits with champagne, truffles and cream will no doubt come now that they are expensive. Meanwhile there are fine recipes of peasant origin including the Italian *coniglio alla sanremese* (rabbit 'roasted' brown in an earthenware pan with wine, onion, thyme, rosemary, bay, pounded walnuts and tiny Ligurian black olives) or the Spanish *conejo a la ampurdanesa*.

....

Conejo a la ampurdanesa

Fry a rabbit cut in pieces to a golden brown colour. Take it out of the pan and fry one sliced onion and two cloves garlic. Add a skinned, de-seeded and chopped tomato, fry it a little, then put back the rabbit. Then add one glass wine (which should be *rancio* – the word is the same as rancid – an aged Spanish wine which is almost amber in colour, it is off but not vinegary) and a *bouquet garni* of bay, thyme and parsley. Cook gently for 15 minutes, then add several mushrooms (which should correctly be the orange *Lactarius*, in Catalan country known as *robellones*) in pieces and a good handful of chopped mixed pine nuts, hazel nuts and almonds. Cook on gently for 30 to 40 minutes until the meat is tender.

[*Rabbit* – French: *lapin* German: *Kaninchen* Italian: *coniglio* Spanish: *conejo*

Hare – French: *lièvre* German: *Hase* Italian: *lepre* Spanish: *liebre*]

RADISH (*Raphanus sativus*) is eaten for its roots, although the top is also edible. The plant has been cultivated for so long that its wild ancestor is unknown, but occasionally a radish that has gone woody suggests what the original radish might have been like once. Radishes are annual or biennial. They are unfamiliar as adult plants because the small varieties are in the ground for no more than a month before being pulled and eaten. The enormous number of varieties differ in pungency; in colour from white, through pink to red, to two-coloured – red on top and white below – and even black; in size, from marbles to huge winter radishes a foot and more long; in shape from ball to cylinder and spinning-top. The small varieties must be lifted young, as they tend to become hollow when left in the soil for even a few days too long. Commercially grown radishes are now lifted and topped by machines which handle six rows at a time; by big American producers, they are also sorted, washed, cooled in ice-cold chlorinated water, bagged, weighed and sealed, all by machinery, before being delivered to the supermarkets in refrigerated trucks. Peering through the bag, you have to decide if the green bit looks fresh, because if it is not, the radish will also be hardly fresh; a surreptitious squeeze will show if the larger ones are hollow. If they are sold in bunches without wrapping, radishes should look bright and fresh (not just doused with water). Radishes can be kept for a couple of days if they are stood root-end down in a soup-plate of water, they can even be revived a little if wilted, but they will never taste as they do when pulled fresh from the garden.

For keeping, there are the huge winter radishes, such as China Rose, which are as big as a slicing sausage. A black-rooted type, shaped like a beetroot, is known as Black Spanish, but is rarely seen in Spain. These large winter radishes are peeled and cut into pieces – chips, slices or grated – and are excellent. A large white variety is the Japanese *daikon*.

The *daikon*-type (or China Rose) will keep for two weeks in the bottom of the refrigerator. *Daikon* is used in many ways peculiar to Japan – for example, grated with red caviar, or shredded and used in garnish for soups. *Daikon* is also the basis for pickles – *takuan* for instance.

The small radishes belonging to varieties with names like Cherry Belle and French Breakfast are usually eaten fresh in salads, whole, sliced or sometimes used for decoration, cut nearly through to the top in segments and dropped into ice-water, so that they open like flowers. In France and Italy, radishes are eaten as part of an *hors d'oeuvre* with butter (the four *hors d'oeuvre* of Rossini were radishes, butter, anchovies and pickled gherkins), although I prefer them with salty sheep's-milk cheese as eaten in south-eastern Europe. It is a pity that so many radishes now seem to taste of little more than stagnant water – perhaps they are grown by hydroponics. Radishes are sometimes cooked like turnips, but are not very interesting.

[*Radish* – French: *radis* German: *Radeschen* Italian: *rafano* Spanish: *rábano*]

RAGI. *See* millet.

RAISINS are traditionally muscatel grape varieties dried in the sun. Some of the best come from Malaga in Spain, and the very finest dessert raisins are at least partially dried on the vine, still attached to the stalk in a bunch. The stalk is almost, but not quite, cut through to stop the sap getting to the bunch, and the leaves are removed to let the hot sun bathe it. Slightly less expensive bunches are dried by laying the grapes out on mats. Seedless raisins may be raisins stoned by machine – the best – or dried seedless grapes, which lack the full muscat flavour. Other dried grapes are *currants and *sultanas.

[*Raisin* – French: *raisin sec* German: *Rosine* Italian: *uva secca* Spanish: *paso de uva*]

RAMBUTAN. *See* lychee.

RAMPHAL. *See* custard apple.

RAM'S-HEAD PEA. *See* chickpea.

RANCIDITY. Rancid butter has a characteristic taste caused by the formation of butyric acid through a process of hydrolysis. Most rancid tastes, however, are produced by the oxidation of fats and oils exposed to the air. Commercially, this is prevented in freeze-dried meat products and in sausages by the addition of anti-oxidants; at home, rancidity can be very much delayed by storing fats and oils in full containers in the refrigerator. As cold very much slows down the chemical process, keeping salad dressings, mayonnaise, margarine, drippings and butter in the refrigerator is also sound practice, while the pan of oil or pot of old dripping kept for deep frying is not good sense for either the flavour of the food or good health in the family. Rancid flavours which develop in crude vegetable oils, particularly in olive oil made from olives that have been damaged by fly or that were half-rotted on the ground, are removed by 'stripping' (extracting the flavour), although some Spaniards, who have been used to semi-rancid oil since childhood, actually come to like it. The yak butter that Tibetans put in tea is also usually rancid.

RAPE (*Brassica napus*) is an outstandingly versatile and valuable species of food plant. It probably originated by hybridization between cabbage (*B. oleracea*) and turnip (*B. rapa*), but its history is uncertain; some varieties are of relatively recent origin, while others have been in cultivation since ancient times. Rape may be annual or biennial and may or may not have a tuberous root. The varieties grown for their roots are the *swede (var. *napobrassica*) and the rutabaga (var. *rutabaga*).

The non-tuberous varieties, such as the biennial var. *arvensis*, are known as rape, cole or coleseed. These are grown very widely as feed for cattle (to the distress of beekeepers who find that honey produced from the yellow rape flowers has an unpleasing crystalline texture).The seeds are the source of rape-seed or colza oil (*see* oils and fats); after this has been expressed, the residue is still oily enough to be worth making into rape-seed cake for feeding to cattle.

It is only in these days of the Trade Descriptions Act that rape has entered the culinary vocabulary of the urban British public. Greengrocers now distinguish rape from turnip tops as a spring green vegetable, and supermarkets even offer punnets of rape and cress, thus acknowledging a practice that has been common for years – rape seed tends to be cheaper than mustard seed and the seedlings keep better in warm weather (they differ from mustard seedlings in having leaves that are more intensely green). *Chinese cabbage may also be a variety of rape.

[Rape – French: *colza* German: *Raps* Italian: *colza* Spanish: *colza*]

RASPBERRY and loganberry. The many species of raspberry belong to the same genus (*Rubus*) as the blackberry and the dewberry in the cooler parts of the Northern hemisphere. However, there is a vast difference in taste between a raspberry and a blackberry (though not between a blackberry and a dewberry).

Raspberries occur in the cooler parts of the Northern hemisphere. The species that is native to Britain (*R. idaeus*) also grows wild all over Europe, except Portugal, Iceland and Turkey. Its natural habitat is damp woods, and it likes a brisk climate – and it is in Scotland, notably around Blairgowrie in Perthshire, that the best raspberries are grown commercially in Britain. From there, they are exported frozen even to the US. Raspberries are less known in Mediterranean countries, except near rainy mountains.

In the horticultural varieties of raspberry, flavour has to be balanced against disease-resistance and cropping. Although red is the usual colour, there are white, yellow and golden raspberries (which are soft and richly flavoured), as well as black-fruited raspberries developed from the American species, *R. occidentalis*. A small proportion of wild raspberries, particularly in Scotland, are pale yellow.

Since raspberries, like most fruit, are best when fully ripened on the cane and are highly perishable, those bought in shops are often suspect, doubly so if they are cheap. Damp stains on the bottom of the punnet will indicate that the fruit underneath is rotting, but however careful you are, it is still likely that a few raspberries will be mildewed when the punnet is tipped out, and they may have already given a musty taste to the rest. The bad ones should be picked out with a toothpick to avoid more squashing and further contamination. Frozen raspberries are in perfect condition and may be a better buy than dubiously fresh ones.

Good raspberries have a very delicate taste which is easily destroyed by cooking. To get the most of their flavour, it is better to squash them against the roof of the mouth with the tongue than to bite them. They are best eaten raw or 'cooked' by pouring boiling sugar syrup over them. Sweet, beautifully-flavoured raspberries may be seedy (their only fault), and are then best put through a fine hair sieve, never a metal one. Raspberry sorbet and the figs in raspberry syrup of French *haute cuisine* are delectable but expensive; most of us, though, can manage very nicely with fruit from the garden eaten with properly-aged Jersey cream and a sprinkle of fine sugar. The best raspberries I ever tasted came from a single wild bush in a gorge in the South Tirol. I wish I had marked it.

Raspberries contain 1.75-2% pectin, plus sufficient citric and malic acids to set into a jelly or jam. When in good condition, raspberries will keep for a couple of days in the refrigerator, but washing, if needed, should never be done until the last minute.

Although the European raspberry varieties come mainly from *R. idaeus*, there are also cultivated varieties of the American *R. strigosa*. Other 'raspberries', such as the hinsar and the dark, pointed *kailka*, are so refreshing in spring to the thirsty Himalayan traveller that they might one day be cultivated, as is the golden-orange wineberry (*R. phoenicolasius*) of northern China and Japan.

The loganberry (*R. loganobaccus* in older works) is a species that originated as a natural hybrid between a raspberry and a blackberry, the marriage having been consummated in the garden of Judge J. H. Logan at Santa Cruz, California. He gave his name to the offspring. Loganberries are now less popular than they used to be, but are still canned in quantity. A similar hybrid of more recent origin is the boysenberry, which is grown quite widely. This berry is long and dark red, but is rather acid and lacks the raspberry's delicate flavour. There are various other curiously named berries derived from species of *Rubus*. The youngberry was bred by Mr B. M. Young in Louisiana; it is large, wine-red and sweet. The olallie is a cross between a youngberry and a loganberry; it is medium sized, black and extensively grown in California. However, the bingleberry, no doubt named by Pickwick, is a variety of the dewberry. These curiosities are all of more than academic interest, as they turn up in cans and in garden catalogues; none of them beats the raspberry for flavour.

[Raspberry – French: *framboise* German: *Himbeere* Italian: *lampone* Spanish: *frambuesa*]

RATAFIA. Victorian cookery books are full of recipes for ratafias, now largely forgotten. There were apricot, blackberry, black currant, cherry, angelica, gooseberry, orange-flower, quince, raspberry and rose ratafias, as well as cakes, creams, cheesecakes, ice creams, puddings and biscuits flavoured with common ratafia. The common factor, regardless of what else ratafias contained (mainly the juice of the fruit concerned and strong brandy), was bitter *almonds, or the flavour of bitter almonds derived from the kernels of apricots, peaches, plums and cherries, or from the leaves of peaches and apricots gathered in spring. *Noyau is a ratafia. Books generally advise that ratafias be both taken with and used with moderation as flavourings, not only because too much bitter almond taste is unpleasant but because it is poisonous in quantity, although heating will drive off the very poisonous hydrocyanic acid and leave only the benzaldehyde,

which is lethal in large doses.

Ratafia today usually refers to ratafia biscuits or macaroons with a strong bitter almond flavour, which in Italy are called *amaretti*. These are sometimes used as a flavouring.

RAVIOLI. *See* pasta.

RAY. *See* shark.

RAZOR SHELLS are bivalve molluscs which belong to the genera *Solen* and *Ensis*. They have shells shaped like an old-fashioned cut-throat razor, either straight or slightly curved. They are distributed throughout the world. These shellfish lie buried in sand in a vertical position with their siphons – inhalant and exhalant – at the top. They may be at the surface or down in a burrow. In many cases, they live just at or below low tide mark and are best fished at low springtides. An indication is a keyhole shaped hole in the sand, from which occasional squirts of water are ejected. The traditional way of catching a razor shell is to put a teaspoon of salt into its burrow and grab it as it pops out. This has to be done neatly and without hesitation; if the animal is missed, there will be no second chance to grab it. A more modern method, and one which can be used under water, is to fill an old plastic squirt bottle, of the sort used for washing-up liquid, with saturated brine, and to squirt that into the holes. Razor shells are regarded as good eating, although I find them rather strong tasting. Some people eat them raw like oysters – there is no problem in opening them as they cannot close tightly – and they are also made into soup or included with other shellfish. Intrepid Italians can be observed catching and eating them raw on Adriatic beaches, notably the Lido in Venice. It is in Mediterranean countries that you will mostly find them in markets, but they are too tedious to catch for there to be much commercial exploitation, although they are canned in Spain.

RED GRAM. *See* pigeon pea.

RED SORREL. *See* mallow.

REDUCING is concentrating a liquid by boiling to evaporate some of the water. Reducing increases flavour of non-volatile constituents but may reduce the flavour of the volatile ones, such as essential oils of herbs and spices or the acetic acid in vinegar. It may also concentrate salt to unpleasant proportion;

final salting is done after and not before reduction.

REFRESHING is cooling hot food quickly by putting it under a running tap or by plunging it into ice-water. This stops further cooking by residual heat and firms up the tissues. Refreshing is part of the usual French method of cooking vegetables which are boiled, drained when not quite done, refreshed, and later heated and finished in cream or butter. Other foods that would suffer from over-cooking, like shellfish, may be refreshed when they are removed from the cooking water.

REFRIGERATION. Since earliest times, food has been kept cool in ice-boxes or ice-chambers wherever there was winter snow. The snow or ice was stored in deep pits or special ice-houses and was usually covered with straw to provide insulation. A large body of snow, if well protected, would last all through the hottest summer. In Tabas, a most remote town in the middle of the Dasht-i-lut, one of the great deserts of eastern Persia, I saw a huge domed pavilion, which I was told was an ice-house that had fallen into disuse. Even such a hot area would have had enough snow in winter to justify the building of such a structure.

It was known by observation, of course, that food kept longer in cold weather. It had also long been understood that when salt was mixed with ice it lowered the temperature, so that other things in contact with the mixture could be frozen. In 1876, meat was shipped across the Atlantic from America to Britain using ice and salt as the freezer, and before the turn of the century meat was regularly being shipped in refrigerator ships through the tropics from Australia and New Zealand. It was not, however, until after World War I that household refrigerators began to be common and to replace the cool cellars and larders which were once as essential in a house as a kitchen or a bedroom. Today, when houses are built without cool larders, we are compelled to keep many foods colder than they should be because we have nowhere else but the refrigerator.

This invention depends on the fact that when liquids boil they absorb heat, but that if the vapour is compressed, it gives off the heat it has absorbed and returns to a liquid. A refrigerator uses a substance such as ammonia or freon, which is a gas even at the low temperature inside a refrigerator, but will become a liquid under pressure. This substance circulates continually, vaporizing and extracting heat as it passes in pipes inside the refrigerator and being compressed back to a liquid –

giving off the heat it has absorbed – outside, at the back of the refrigerator.

You could say it was pumping the heat out. By this means the modern refrigerator will freeze water and ice cream in the freezing compartment or will keep frozen food frozen. Cold air, being denser than warm air, falls, but the proximity of the freezing compartment means that in practice the top part of the refrigerator is cooler than the bottom.

[*Refrigeration* – French: *réfrigération* German: *Ahkühlung* Italian: *refrigerazione* Spanish: *refrigeración*]

REGULO or gas mark. A system of numbers used on gas cooker ovens and representing approximate temperatures inside the oven as follows:

Regulo	°C	°F
½	120	250
1	135	275
2	150	300
3	160	325
4	180	350
5	190	375
6	200	400
7	220	425
8	230	450
9	240	475

Regulo devices originally set the flow of gas and not the temperature, which varied according to the type of gas and pressure. In modern ovens, the gas regulator is linked to a thermostat and the regulo mark does indicate a particular temperature.

RELIGIOUS FOOD LAWS. Christians are not subjected to religious dietary laws or expressly forbidden to eat certain foods or instructed to have their meat killed in specified ways. Even 'fish on Fridays' is no longer observed by most denominations, although in Catholic countries, in spite of official abolition by the Vatican Council in the mid-1960s, the old custom is still widely observed through force of habit. Muslims, Jews, Hindus, Jains and other religious groups do however have dietary rules. Very orthodox followers of these religions are unlikely to accept an invitation to eat in the homes of people of different faiths. However, cooks ought to know in broad outline what the religious food laws specify, if only because it may sometimes prevent social embarrassment to be able to provide a meal which is acceptable to people with another religion. These laws also explain many of the characteristics of ethnic cooking – why, for instance, the Middle East is not full of delectable pork recipes and why Arabs may, but Jews may not, cook meat with yogurt. The popularity in Jewish cooking of stuffed dishes in which a little meat can be made to stretch a long way goes back to the days of the ghettos, where kosher meat was a scarce commodity. This scarcity and the large number of ingredients that were forbidden led to a cuisine which produced the maximum variety from a rather limited range of raw materials. Hindus, who were to a large extent vegetarian, developed varied and elaborate vegetable dishes. A humble ingredient such as *dal can be turned into literally hundreds of very different dishes.

Dietary laws can be seen as a way of transforming the preparation and consumption of food into an act of worship or merely as the expression of principles of health and hygiene that were once essential in the hot countries of the Orient. Either way, the laws were used both to protect and to proclaim the identity of the religious group. For Jews and Hindus, who until quite recently neither encouraged nor recognized converts, the laws created a barrier between their communities and an impure world, breeding a sense of exclusiveness, of a special relation with the deity, which helped them survive in the face of hostility or persecution.

Islam, on the other hand, was fiercely proselytic and saw in the convert's abstinence from pork and alcohol a tangible sign of allegiance to his new religion. The food laws and customs bind all Muslims together, irrespective of origins or social position. In a traditional Muslim household, the sexes do not mix at meals and all the men sit around a large communal dish of food and eat from it. Any newcomer, provided he is a Muslim, will also be invited to partake of the meal, a practice that may not be particularly hygienic but that indicates a sense of equality in the eyes of God.

Christianity and Buddhism, which started as movements of reform or revolt among, respectively, Jews and Hindus, reacted against the rigid concept of food laws. These were relaxed by the Buddhists and largely abandoned by the Christians, and both religions substituted simple, plain diets which they sought to combine with a rather austere way of living. Christianity has no religious food laws in the sense that no food is forbidden or considered impure. However, abstinence from meat and rich foods during Lent is a tradition of the older denominations, and in many countries there are special dishes associated with Lent. Shrove Tuesday

or *mardi gras*, before Lent, also has its own dishes, of which pancakes are the most famous, many of them designed to empty the larder of rich ingredients in a final pre-Lenten eating binge.

Jews. The Jewish dietary laws (*kashrut*) are very ancient, many of them from the Bible. To be fit for eating, animals must have cloven hooves and chew the cud. This allows beef, mutton, goat, and venison, but rules out horse (which doesn't have a cloven hoof or chew the cud) and pork (because the pig, though it has a cloven hoof, does not chew the cud and is also regarded as unclean). Most birds are allowed (except birds of prey), but seafood must have obvious fins and scales (which rules out eels and shellfish, both crustaceans and molluscs). The eggs and milk of prohibited animals are also not allowed, which rules out mare's milk and the roe of some fish. Hen eggs must be perfect, and a blood spot means that the egg should be discarded.

To be kosher, which is to say suitable for consumption by orthodox Jews, meat must be slaughtered in the prescribed way by the *shochet* who is licensed by the rabbi. The Jewish butcher must not only be able to slaughter by cutting the throat of the animal so that trachea, oesophagus, jugular vein and carotid artery are quickly severed (the animal almost instantly loses consciousness), but must also be fully conversant with the law of *shechitah* and be able to examine the animal outside and inside for any disease, malformation or impurity (such as a foreign body embedded in the gizzard of a chicken) which would make the animal *trefah* – unfit to eat. The care taken over the slaughtering of animals is to ensure the ritual purity of Jewish food and to avoid unnecessary suffering to the animal, but is also a sign of respect for the life that is being taken. In fact, the consumption of meat has constantly posed a problem to Judaism. The Torah says: 'I would prefer that you abstain from eating meat altogether'. But it goes on to say that: 'since your desires cannot be stopped nor your nutritional requirements altered... since you will eat meat and perhaps need to eat meat, you may ... but with one restriction – that you have reverence for the life you take.' Meat must be eaten within a day or so of slaughter, and it must be soaked in a vessel kept for the purpose and salted for an hour in a perforated container which will allow the blood to flow away. Then, after rinsing, it is pure or 'kosher'. It is worth noting that kosher meat is acceptable to Muslims in places where true *halal* meat is unavailable.

The sharpest distinction between Jewish and Muslim food law is the question of eating meat and dairy products together. The Bible says: 'Thou shalt not seethe a kid in his mother's milk' (Deuteronomy 14.21). Orthodox Jews go to excessive lengths to avoid any possible mixing of dairy products and meat at the same meal. Tea or coffee with milk cannot be taken until six hours after meat has been eaten. Separate pots and dishes have to be kept for dairy products and meat; even table cloths and bread that have been on the table when meat has been served must be set aside before a meal containing milk products may follow. This law makes it impossible to cook meat dishes with butter (the basis of so much French cooking) and is the reason why Jews use chicken fat, the nearest animal fat to butter in texture and character. While there are plenty of Jews who eat ham and enjoy French cooking, it should not be taken for granted that all Jewish acquaintances will do so.

Muslims, like Jews, may not eat pork. The meat they do eat must have been killed deliberately and in the correct way; in practice, Muslim butchers (even those in meat factories) are licensed by a mullah and the meat is known as *halal* meat. The animal must have been killed by having its throat cut while the slaughterer says 'In the name of Allah, Allah is most great.' Muslims are not allowed to eat blood, and may not eat the meat of animals which have died by accident, except in dire necessity. Muslims may not, of course, eat bacon or ham or pork – the hams of the Middle East are mutton hams. Muslims are also forbidden to drink alcohol (though many do) or even to put wine or spirits in their food. The use of gold or silver plates is also forbidden, so put them away when entertaining the local oil sheik. In general, the laws governing Muslim food are very like those governing Jewish food but with one major difference – lamb cooked in milk or yogurt is one of the great Arab dishes.

Hindus have complex religious food laws that vary according to caste and region. Many high caste Hindus, particularly women, are vegetarians. Some eat eggs, some not; some fish but not meat, and so on. Prohibitions even extend into the vegetable world. Very orthodox Brahmins (the priestly caste) abstain from onion and garlic. The really strict Brahmin will eat only food cooked by himself or someone of his own caste in his own kitchen, and there are rituals to be observed (such as the cook taking a bath before preparing the dishes) which are hardly followed outside India. Hindus who are willing to visit European households for dinner will evidently accept food prepared in a European manner, but it is necessary to ask if they are vegetarians or if they eat meat. Never serve beef when you have Hindu visitors; the cow has for long been considered sacred, though a thousand or more years ago, even the Brahmins ate beef. Many Hindus regard alcoholic drinks with horror. However, *bhang*, a paste prepared from the cannabis plant, is legally available in India and is frequently added to drinks and sweetmeats at festival time.

Buddhists base their religion on the teachings of Prince Siddhartha Gautama, the Buddha, who was born in Northern India in the 6th century BC. Although the Buddha did not forbid his disciples to eat animals, he advised them not to kill for food, nor to allow anyone else to kill for their special benefit. The Buddha himself died as a result of eating bad pork (which had been offered by a poor man whose feelings would have been hurt if he had refused it), but today many Buddhists are vegetarians (particularly in Japan), so some vegetarian dishes should be offered as well as meat when Buddhists come to dinner.

Jains have a religion that is a branch of Buddhism characterized by an extreme respect for life. So Jain priests brush the ground where they walk, and wear a pad over their mouths to prevent not only the accidental inhalation of small creatures but even their hot breath distressing the very air. Naturally Jains will not eat meat, fish or eggs but will usually take butter and milk. Some will not eat onions, garlic or red-coloured vegetables. A Jain priest is not even allowed to beg for his food, since that might cause someone to kill the vegetable on his behalf. He may only eat food if it is unsolicited and offered freely to him. In that case, it is already dead.

Parsees are followers of the prophet Zoroaster who first came to India to escape persecution by the Muslims in Iran around AD 750. Parsees eat meat and drink alcoholic drinks freely, but many do not approve of smoking because fire is sacred to them.

Sikhs. The Sikh religion was founded by Guru Nanak in the late 15th century. Sikhs eat meat, even beef, but will not eat meat killed in the Muslim manner (by cutting the throat of the animal) as they regard this as a cruel practice. Sikhs in India tend to avoid beef but only out of respect for the Hindus among whom they live.

RENDERING is melting chunks of animal fat down to a liquid. Put the fat in a pan on top of the stove or in the oven at low heat and cook it gently until the fat is liquid and the remaining solids are crisp. These bits, drained and cooled, are delicious, and the fat, transferred to a covered container and kept in the refrigerator, is an excellent frying medium.

RENNET is an extract from the stomach lining (abomasum) of an unweaned calf or any similar substance for curdling milk. Rennet is mainly used to set the curd for cheese, but also for making curds and whey, junket and similar preparations. The action is produced by rennin, an enzyme which coagulates milk proteins and is present in quantity in the stomachs of unweaned baby mammals, as well as in other animal's digestive tracts. Calves' stomachs are the classic source of rennet, but the stomach linings of young pigs, kids, lambs and even hares and rabbits were sometimes used. The gizzard lining of chickens or turkeys makes gallina rennet, which produces a more delicate curd.

In the past, pieces of salted and dried calf's stomach were sold by butchers. There were many recipes for preparing rennet from scratch; the simplest was to wash the abomasum carefully, rub it well with salt and pack it, with plenty more salt, in a jar. After a month, it was taken out, drained and stretched on sticks to dry. Once dry, it would keep for weeks. A piece about 5 cm (2 in) square, soaked in half a cup of hot water for 4-5 hours would yield a liquid, 2 tablespoons of which would curdle 4.5 lt (8 pt) of warmed milk. However, the strength of action was very variable. Today, it is more usual to buy rennet essence. In emergency, though, the cook can easily make gallina rennet by washing the lining of a chicken or turkey gizzard well, rubbing it with salt, stretching it and drying it. For a start try using the same quantity as for calf rennet. Vegetarians must use plant rennet. One type can be made by infusing the flowers of *lady's bedstraw in water. According to an old recipe, you will need about a cup of a strong infusion (made by pouring boiling water over the flowers and leaving them overnight) to curdle about 32 lt (56 pt) of milk; excellent cheese results. The juices from the fig tree and certain thistles have the same curdling effect.

[Rennet – French: présure, caillette German: Renette Italian: caglio, presame Spanish: cuajo]

REPTILES represent an evolutionary stage between amphibians such as frogs – whose young have gills and live in water – and the birds and mammals. They are cold-blooded, lay eggs and have a general structure similar to our own, but much more primitive. Most Europeans treat the thought of reptilian food, apart from *turtle, with horror. Less so Americans, who have a large number of small turtles in their lakes, rivers and marshes, as well as on the coast, and who, on occasion, will eat alligator and rattle-snake. Having tried grilled snake with the Australian aborigines and boiled gorpad lizard with some Indian aborigines, I must confess to a certain revulsion which prevents me from giving an unbiased judgement, just as I would find difficulty in judging rat, dog or boiled scorpion, all of which get eaten by someone. Some of these foods, like the gorpad I ate by the roadside in South India, are supposed to have magical or medicinal significance. The gorpad is said to make a man impotent if it happens to hit him with its tail while being captured, but it confers exceptional sexual stamina on those who eat it. However, this is a book on gastronomy. Reptile eggs are also eaten, and turtle eggs are regarded as a delicacy, but the eating of wild crocodile and turtle eggs is to be avoided where, as in most places, they are endangered species.

RESIN. Various resins and gums are used for flavouring. Particularly worthy of notice is the Greek wine retsina, which is often made with no more effort than putting a few bruised pine cones into a barrel of white wine. Resin is a preservative, but an acquired taste.

[Resin – French: résine German: Hartz Italian: resina Spanish: resina]

RETINOL See vitamin A.

RHUBARB (Rheum raponticum) has been judged to be legally a fruit (at least in the US), although it is actually a leaf stem. The word 'rhubarb' is possibly coined from rha (Greek for Volga) and barbarium (Latin for barbarian), the plant having first, it seems, been introduced from Russia to Britain in 1578 (not long before Gerard's Herbal was written). It could also come from the Greek rheo (to flow), for reasons which will be obvious to those who remember the revolting Gregory's Powder, of which medicinal rhubarb is a main constituent. At any rate, it was, to begin with, used for decoration in gardens and no doubt as a purge.

It was not until the beginning of the 19th century that rhubarb began to be prepared as a fruit. Its popularity rested on its being the first fruit of spring, and it was commonly forced (with straw and bottomless buckets) to produce tender pink stems. It does not seem to have caught on in Mediterranean climates because it needs a cold spell in winter to grow properly and because oranges and other spring and winter fruit are available when rhubarb would come in. In Britain, after a great vogue in Victorian times, the popularity of rhubarb has declined. Best flavoured is the early spring or Champagne rhubarb also called Dresden rhubarb, which has been forced. A great deal is produced in darkened greenhouses in Yorkshire. Older outdoor rhubarb, which has bright red stems and large dark green leaves, has usually to be peeled. In the US, both field and hothouse varieties are grown, the latter being available throughout the year. It is grown in the more northern states. Recipes come almost entirely from northern Europe; in Italy and Spain, rhubarb is virtually unknown. Rhubarb when young and pink, is excellent. It mixes well with other fruits and take flavours such as ginger. Angelica has also been much praised as a partner for rhubarb.

The acidity of the stalks, which is greater in plants grown in the open than in forced ones, is due to malic and oxalic acids. Oxalic acid is poisonous in quantity, but for ill effects you would have to eat a lot. The leaves, however, can apparently be poisonous and, although they have sometimes been eaten without ill effect there have been poisonings and deaths. Boiling rhubarb leaves is an excellent way of cleaning pans (even stewing the stalks make the pan shine).

[*Rhubarb* – French: *rhubarbe* German: *Rhabarber* Italian: *rabarbaro* Spanish *ruibarbo*]

RHUBARB CHARD. *See* beets.

RIBOFLAVINE. *See* vitamin B$_2$.

RICE (*Oryza sativa*) is the staple grain of over half the world's population, although the tonnage of wheat produced each year is actually greater. Another species, Red rice (*O. glaberrima*) which has a red bran layer, is grown in parts of West Africa. *Wild rice, however, is not closely related to rice.

Rice was taken into cultivation somewhere in southern Asia a very long time ago; it has certainly been in use in India and China for over 5000 years. However, it is a comparative newcomer to Mediterranean civilizations; it got to Egypt between 400 and 300 BC. It gradually became established in the Middle East, and the Arabs took it with them to their colonies in Sicily, southern Italy and Spain, but not until about AD 1000. Half a millennium later, in Elizabethan times, rice was being imported into England from Spain. It was made into porridges, puddings and, as Gerard wrote in his *Herbal*, 'many other kindes of food is made with this graine as those that are skillfull in cookerie can tell.' In fact, he tried growing rice in his own garden in the year 1596 but not surprisingly it did not set seed 'in that unseasonable year' (it was one of the worst in the 16th century), which suggested both that rice cannot be cultivated so far north and that the British climate has not altered much.

Today, Europe's most important rice-growing area is the Po Valley in northern Italy, where rice was first introduced in the mid-15th century by the Venetians, who were then powerful and wealthy from trading with the East. Rice is also grown in Portugal and Spain. More recently, cultivation has been pushed north into Hungary and to the Camargue in France. This, at present, is its limit; no variety can profitably be grown nearer the pole than 45°N.

In the US, rice was first successfully cultivated near Charleston, South Carolina, in 1694. American rice is still known as Carolina rice, although it now comes mainly from Texas, Louisiana, California and Arkansas. The US has a large export surplus and over half the rice eaten in Britain is Carolina rice – an all-purpose rice distinguished for nothing. Some 90% of the world's rice is still grown and consumed in the monsoon regions of Asia. In a year, the average Englishman eats only a little over 1 kg (2¼ lb) of rice, an amount which would keep a hardworking farmer in South China going for a bare two days. (In the north of China, as in the north of India, the staple cereal is wheat.)

It is not surprising that the natives of northern Europe and North America are comparatively ignorant about rice. Cookery writers often fail to specify the kind of rice for a dish and the result is likely to be pilau coming out like pudding. In India alone, there are between three and four hundred major rice varieties in cultivation, and over a thousand all told are grown there. The world total is said by some experts to be over ten thousand varieties. Anyone from the south of India should be able to recognize at least twenty sorts in the bazaar, rices which differ not only in such obvious characters as whether they are long or short grain, polished or unpolished, raw or parboiled, but also in colour, translucency, smell, age, cooking quality and, of course, price. If the shopper in India does not know a particular type and quality, then the stall-keeper certainly will. The same rice expertise exists in South East Asia, China and Japan, and to some extent extends into the Middle East – especially into Iran – and even to Italy, where rice is preferred to pasta in the parts north of the Po. Selection of rice elsewhere is a hit or miss business when neither the buyer nor the seller is expert. In general all one can say is that what the shops call 'long-grained rice' is intended to cook with grains separate, although length of grain is not an infallible criterion. Some very long-grained varieties cook mushy and some of the finest pilau rices have small round grains.

Varieties. Rice in its natural state, after the husks have been removed, has a brown or reddish-brown skin and is usually known as unpolished, unpearled or brown rice. It has a stronger taste and is more easily digested than white, pearled rice, but it also takes longer to cook and may require some preliminary soaking. Unpolished rice can be nice, at least as a change.

However, most people prefer their rice white, although brown rice is greatly superior in food value. Even Confucius liked his rice white. In his time, as it still is in many places, this was produced by hand pounding until most but not quite all the skin was removed from the grain. When machines took over to 'pearl' rice, they did a much more thorough job, and rice eaters began to suffer from beri-beri. This disease was subsequently shown to be due to a deficiency of thiamine (vitamin B_1), which had been lost with the rice skin. Pearled rice also loses protein and oil; it is usually known as polished rice, although real polished rice is actually polished with talc or chalk and glucose after pearling. This makes the grains shine but reduces the nutritional value even more.

Parboiled rice is a newer development designed to improve nutritional quality and yet give a product less coarse than brown rice. It will be met with in countries where rice is the staple food and FAO nutrition experts abound. Parboiled rice has been steamed in the husk to impregnate the grain with some of the nutrients. This makes the taste rather peculiar, and parboiled rice is likely to have a characteristic smell which many people do not like. It is important only to those who subsist mainly on rice. Genetic variation, breeding and selection have produced thousands of varieties, but plant-breeders are mainly concerned with heavy-cropping

varieties geared to particular soils and conditions. Unfortunately, high yield does not often go with fine quality. In any case, opinions vary in different parts of the world as to what is good rice and dishes may need a certain rice with special qualities. Most people, though, want a rice which, with a modicum of care, cooks so that the grains do not stick together. However, a few dishes need a rice where an absorbent, tender or even sticky grain is necessary for success.

The way a rice cooks depends on the relative amounts of various forms of starch in the grain and especially on the percentage of amylose. A rice with at least 25% amylose is preferred in most countries, though not in Indonesia or in the Philippines. If there is less than 20% amylose, the rice cooks sticky – some of the best flinty pilau rices have 30% amylose or more.

Rices vary in temperature at which the starch grains swell irreversibly; it will be somewhere between 69°C (156°F) and 75°C (167°F) – well below boiling. They also vary in the quantity of water they absorb. Dogmatic recipes are misleading, as no two rices cook in an identical way. In general, rice absorbs between its own volume – cup for cup – and twice its volume of water, but I once bought a very costly Saudi Arabian variety of rice from a Bedouin trader and found to my amazement that it absorbed no less than nine times its volume of water and would not cook properly with any less.

Not only the variety but the age of a rice has much influence on the way it cooks. The grains of freshly harvested rice cook more quickly, absorb less water and stick rather more easily than those of older rice of the same variety. In India, it is claimed that new rice is not easily digested and fine pilau rice is sometimes matured for many years. On the other hand, in Japan new rice is eagerly sought for special dishes. There, November rice, freshly harvested, tastes best. Country people living in towns send home for sacks of early rice from their district. Their very word for a meal is *gohan*, meaning rice, and Japanese don't feel they have eaten without a bowl of rice. Moist new rice – *shinmai* – needs less water, and as the year goes on, more water is required in cooking.

Washing. It is sometimes said that rice should not be washed before cooking unless it is very dirty and that even then it should only be washed with a damp cloth. True, washing has been proved to result in a slight loss of nutrients. Even so, logic and the consensus of opinion say that rice should be washed to remove milling and polishing dust, which tends to cook to a glue and sticks the grains together. This is disastrous when cooking is by the total absorption method (*see below*).

Soaking. Some authorities advocate soaking rice in water for from 30 minutes to several hours; others are equally adamant that soaking spoils the flavour. I hesitate to be dogmatic here – some varieties possibly need soaking, but it is not generally advised except for pilau. Soaked rice cooks more quickly, which helps keep the grains separate. Naturally, soaked rice absorbs less water in cooking.

Oiling. Some cooks rub rice with oil to coat the grains in the hope that this will prevent them from sticking together. Others put butter in the cooking water. Oiling may make a marginal difference to poor rice but it is surely better to buy one of good quality; such tricks then become unnecessary.

Frying. For pilau, *paella* and similar dishes, dry rice is fried in oil or butter until it becomes translucent before liquid is added. The oil impregnates the outer layers of the grains and helps keep them separate. There are also dishes in which the rice is fried brown.

Steaming and **fluffing**. In many countries, when cooking is completed (or almost completed), the rice is left on a low heat to 'steam' or 'fluff' until it looks like blossom. Not all varieties of rice will blossom in this way.

Drying. Allied to steaming is the drying and resting of rice, which is especially necessary after cooking by the 'excess' water method (*see below*). This is done, with the lid on, over a very low heat. A cloth tied around the lid, or a special cushion to act as a lid (as is used in Turkey) will absorb steam and avoid wet drips from condensation. Or turn the lid upside down and put a few glowing pieces of charcoal in the top as they do in India. The pan may also be put in a low oven.

General principles. Arguments over the best way to cook rice can be vitriolic, as over half the cooks in the world are cooking it daily in their own kitchens. For instance, south Indians put no salt in the water – they say it ruins the rice – but elsewhere rice cooked with no salt is considered insipid. One school of thought says that once the pan boils, it is ruinous to

lift the lid even to see if the rice is done, but rice is often cooked with no lid on. Some cooks start rice in cold water, others say the water must be boiling. Many, but not all, agree that once the water comes to the boil the heat must be lowered. Cooked rice may be rinsed with cold water, hot water or not at all. How are we to judge who is right when even the hardness or softness of the water affects the outcome? For beginners, the following practical advice is based on a consensus of opinion:

Buy the correct rice for the dish you wish to prepare, although you may have to locate a shop of the right ethnic variety in order to find it.

1) For pilau, a Basmati, Delhi or Dehra Dun. Such rice also does well for Persian '*polo*' and rice stuffing for chicken; it is excellent for boiled rice with curries and other such dishes.

2) For puddings, a good pudding rice. There is no point in using an expensive pilau rice for this purpose as it neither absorbs well nor goes creamy, and the strong 'mousey' flavour is inappropriate.

3) For risotto, try to get Italian rice with large fat grains, such as *arborio* or *vialone*, which are grown specially for this purpose.

Always measure rice by the cup (not by weight) before washing it if you are going to cook it by the total absorption method. Allow ½-1 cup per person (1 cup is safer if you are making curry).

Wash the rice in several changes of water until it is almost clear of milkiness. Drain it well and spread out in the sun to dry if you are not going to use it immediately. Allow for any water trapped in the grains of wet rice if you are using the absorption method.

Do not soak the rice unless you are quite sure that it is an exceptional variety or the recipe needs it, as does a pilau made in the classical manner.

Whichever the method of cooking, always use a big pan to allow the rice to expand and to lie as shallow as possible. Otherwise the bottom layers will be compacted by the weight of rice on top; the lower layers will also cook faster than the top ones and will become soggy.

Excess Water Method (for poor varieties)

Put the washed rice into plenty of boiling water, salted for most dishes, but not if it is intended to accompany curry. Turn down the heat when the pan comes to the boil and watch carefully, squeezing a grain between the fingers – or tasting it – every few minutes to begin with, but almost continuously as soon as it seems to be nearly ready. Poor rice is particularly prone to going from just right to a sticky mass in a few seconds. The moment the last trace of hard centre has gone – too soon is better than too late – drain quickly, preferably in a wide, flat sieve and using a light hand. To dump it heavily in a conical strainer would lump it together. Immediately run it for a few seconds under the cold tap (hot water is sometimes used for rinsing cooked rice, but cold water immediately stops it cooking). While the rice is draining, rinse and dry the pan, put some butter or oil in the bottom and put the pan on the heat. Return the rice gently to the pan. Wrap a clean cloth around the lid and cover. Turn down the heat to the lowest possible level (put an asbestos mat under the pan) and let the rice steam and dry for ten minutes. Alternatively put the pan in a slow oven. When serving, turn the rice out and fluff it gently with a fork

Total Absorption Method

If the rice is wet from washing, allow a cup of cold water for each cup of rice, although the precise quantity required depends on the variety and age of the rice. Put the pan on a high heat. The moment the water comes to the boil, turn the flame down to a gentle boil and, as the water is absorbed, turn it even lower. You can transfer it to a low oven. Leave it until all the water has been absorbed and the rice has expanded. Then fluff the rice up with a fork and serve. This is by far the better method to use with good rice, but it is risky with sticky, poor rice – after the first minute of boiling, the grains are always in contact with each other and have a good chance of sticking together.

India. Unpolished village rice is *ukad*, which is reddish, dusty and with a thick grain. It has a peculiar smell while cooking. For soaking and grinding to make batter for *dosas*, *idlis* or for making puddings or *conjee* (any dish in which the rice does not have to be kept in separate grains), any ordinary grade of rice will do. When it comes to rice to eat with curry, the requirement is a rice which can be cooked so that the grains remain separate. In South India, where large quantities of rice are eaten, people prefer a rice which will absorb the rather liquidy curries and *sambar* which are the normal fare. In Northern India, where *roti* (*chapatti*, *puri*, *parata* and other kinds of bread) are the staple food, fine varieties of rice are favoured by

those who can afford them. For pilaus and *birianis* the best, long-grained rice is a must – the delicate crescent-shaped *jeera-sali* (with grains shaped like *jeera*, cumin seed). Rices of this type are sold as Basmati rice, Dehra Dun rice or pilau rice. They have a strong perfume (they say you can smell some varieties when they are growing in the field) and are always cooked by the absorption method, not in excess water. Such high quality rice is expensive but it is impossible to make *biriani* or good pilau without it. Patna rice of good quality will remain separate but does not have the lovely aroma of Basmati varieties.

Middle East. Iran grows some of the finest rice in the world, if fine is taken to mean varieties which keep separate through any maltreatment and do not cook to a mush. This part of the world is the original home of the pilau. In Iran, rice is called *chilau* (or *polo* when cooked) and is cooked by the absorption method. Often butter is added, which fries a layer next to the pan so that skilful cooks can turn out rice cooked in this way to form a moulded pile, golden brown on the outside where the rice has fried, but with the rice inside so perfect that it drops to pieces in snow-white grains the moment the golden skin is broken. Qualities of rice in ascending order are: *champa*, *sadri*, *darbori*, and the most costly, *domsiah* or royal rice.

Other countries of the Middle East and Levant eat a great deal of rice (it gradually gives way to *couscous towards the west of the North African coast), but nowhere does it approach the perfection of Iran. However, there is a useful Egyptian method of cooking rice which I learned from a German friend in Togo, West Africa. It is one I now always use in camp and often at home for large outdoor parties when my stove cannot cope. Scaled down, it will work for smaller quantities.

Egyptian Rice (Blanket method)

This is the method par excellence for those who like to drink with their guests. Measure out the rice. If you wash it, dry it well in the sun; otherwise use it unwashed, depending on the rice. Heat oil in a pan with a well-fitting lid (it is usual to fry a sliced onion in this before adding the rice). Put in the rice and fry gently until it becomes translucent (or, if you like, you may continue until it begins to brown). Add water at the rate of, say, 1½ times the volume of rice (whatever your rice takes for complete absorption). Bring to the boil and continue cooking until the rice has risen above the water and the surface is pitted with little holes like mud geysers blowing steam. Clap on the lid. Quickly wrap the pan in newspaper and enfold completely in a blanket. In half an hour the rice is cooked, but it can be left several hours if necessary. Fork the rice loose as you turn it out.

Italy. The cheapest rice is usually labelled *commune*, meaning common ordinary (well-known varieties are *originario*, the oldest, and *balilla*).These have a small, tender, round grain, and cook in about 14 minutes. They go easily to a mush and are used for soups and puddings.

Semi-fino or semi-fine varieties include *ardiz-zone* and *maratello*. The grains are oval, the price is up a little, and the cooking time has also gone up to about 15 minutes. This is the rice which is best used for *minestrone*. It is also sticky enough to hold together in a mould or timbale.

Fino (fine quality) varieties are R B 265, *razza 77*, and the most famous of all, *vialone*. *Fino* is long and tapering. The cooking time has gone up to 16 minutes. *Fino* is particularly used for risotto – especially the *vialone* which is able to absorb a lot of liquid and flavour while retaining its structure during relatively long, slow cooking. *Fino* is also used in the many Italian dishes of rice mixed with seafood or vegetables.

Superfino (superfine), with even longer, bigger grains includes *arborio* and *carnaroli*. The cooking time is 18 minutes. *Arborio* is very absorbent and makes top-quality risotto.

Commercially, Italian rice is graded for the convenience of the shopper. For example, one firm, Curtiriso, pack their soup rice in yellow boxes, the rice for risotto in green, and the pilau-type rice in blue.

Spain. Rice in Spanish is *arroz* from the Arabic *roz*; it has been grown in Spain for 900 years. For a country that has been growing rice so long, Spain is remarkably indifferent to quality. It is only quite recently that fairly good *arroz de grano largo* (long-grain rice) has been in the shops. Spanish rice is generally poor quality, short-grained, pudding rice. *Arroz blanco* (white rice) is rarely cooked in Spain; rice is usually flavoured and coloured with saffron or cooked with fried onions and tomato (*sofrito*); often it is fried and cooked with other ingredients as in that most Spanish dish, the *paella*. Many Spaniards still call this dish *arroz*; it has only been called *paella* since the beginning of the last century.

It must be cooked in a very shallow pan 2.5-4 cm (1-1½ in) deep. In a saucepan, Spanish rice goes to a mush. *Paella* must thus be cooked in a pan of a size to fit the number of servings to be made. That is why you see so many varying sizes of *paellera* in Spain, ranging from small home versions, to giant pans serving 30 or 40 people. A *paella* can only be cooked properly over a burner with a flame wide enough to cover the bottom (special gas burners are sold in Spain for this purpose) or, as originally intended, over an open wood fire, which also contributes to the flavour. The heat must be spread evenly. *Paella* is best eaten on a picnic beside the sea or river, as it is by nature messy. Many books say that anything can go into a *paella* but – God help us! – this is only true if you know what 'anything' means because you have learned to cook properly in the Spanish idiom.

Paella

Ingredients for 4-5 people: Rice of average quality, say 3 cups. Peas, 2 handfuls of pods. ¼ lb of mussels in their shells. ¼ lb of large prawns or scampi.¼ lb of lobster or crayfish (you could use freshwater crayfish, mantis shrimps, even small crabs to obtain the necessary flavour). A small squid. Fish can go in – though it is less usual – provided you put it in late enough not to cook to pieces – and bone it. A small chicken. A bit of lamb or even pork, if you have some. 1 or 2 globe artichokes. 1 large onion. 2 tomatoes. 8 cloves of garlic. A small bunch of parsley. A good pinch of saffron (or 1½ packets of fake saffron, which they usually use in Spain these days, real saffron being so expensive). A handful of mushrooms. Salt, pepper and cayenne.½ cup of cooking oil. A small tin of sweet red peppers (pimentos).

Method: Shell the peas. Scrape and clean the mussels and open by heating them in a pan with the lid on for a minute or two. (Throw away any that fail to open.) Remove half the shell but keep the flavourful liquid for adding (strained of any sand) later. Remove the more annoying legs from the crustaceans, or, if it is for an elegant party, it is best to fry the crustaceans in the oil until they are just firm and then shell them. Put the legs and shells with the mussel water, (and fish bones if any), into say 8 cups of water and make a stock to further concentrate the flavour. Take out the guts and ink sac from the squid and cut it in bite-sized pieces. If fish is used (usually for economy), bone it and also cut it into bite-sized bits. Clean and joint the chicken into smallish bits, and do the same for any lamb or pork you intend adding. Carefully and thoroughly slice off the tough parts of the artichoke with a sharp knife and remove the choke. Peel any stalk – that is one of the best parts. Cut into finger-nail-sized pieces and put in water with a good squeeze of lemon to stop blackening. Roughly chop the onion. The rest you can do during the cooking.

The object in making a *paella* is to add all the different ingredients, timing them in order, so that you finish with all of them cooked to perfection at exactly the same moment.

Put the oil in the *paellera* and see that the heat covers the bottom of the pan evenly. When the oil is hot put in the pieces of chicken and meat to fry, moving them about with a long stick or spoon until they are starting to brown. Then add the pieces of squid and move everything round for a further 5 minutes. Next put in the artichoke bits and the shelled peas, scraping the pan to prevent sticking. After a moment or two, you can add the chopped onion. Fry on, still scraping the bottom of the pan if anything seems to be sticking. Now add the mushrooms in bite-sized pieces and the tomatoes. Fry on for another few minutes, then put in half the garlic cloves, crushed, and a cup of rice for each person. (I have said three cups of rice – which makes this *paella* do for 4 to 5 persons, but of course you can vary the proportion of rice to goodies according to the circumstances. I am describing a good *paella* for hungry people.) Turn the rice in the hot fat until it is well coated and becomes translucent. Then pour in sufficient boiling water (or stock, if you are doing an elegant version) to cover all the ingredients. Add a pinch of cayenne pepper and a pinch of cinnamon if you like it. Give the pan a stir. Add salt, the soaked saffron or the half packet of fake saffron colour. Stir again and do not (as I do) tip the whole goddam pan into the fire in your excitement.

After 5 minutes, when the liquid begins to be absorbed, you can push the prawns, lobster, mussels and so on into the surface, preferably into a radiating pattern. This way, the shellfish is not overcooked, as it is in so many versions when the mussels are fried and shrink to leather.

You should, when making a *paella*, always have a kettle of water boiling and a spatula or flat paddle (a *paella* for 40 needs an oar). If the *paella* is getting too dry, you can add a little boiling water, not too much, and with the spatula you can help guard against sticking without disturbing the rice.

Meanwhile take the other 4 cloves of garlic and the parsley. With a little salt, pound them to a paste

in a mortar (or liquidize) and pour on a little boiling water (2-3 tablespoons) to make a green liquid. Open the can of red pimentos, drain and cut the pimentos into strips.

Taste the *paella*. If it is cooked, sprinkle the green liquid all over. Cook a minute longer while you decorate the surface with the strips of red sweet peppers. Garnish with quarters of lemon placed round the edges, carry to table and serve directly from the *paellera*.

The perfect *paella* is neither too dry nor too wet, the rice is not overcooked – rather the contrary – and it should be served and eaten at once. Restaurant *paellas* are usually assembled from precooked ingredients and oven-heated.

[*Rice* – French: *riz* German: *Reis* Italian: *riso* Spanish: *arroz*]

RICE BEAN (*Phaseolus calceratus*) A small bean of Indian origin, rather similar to the *mung but distinguished from it by prominent white hilum (scar) raised above the surface and crinkled at the edges. The beans may be yellow, brown, maroon and black, or mottled. This bean is particularly grown in Nepal and Assam. The Indian name is *sutari* or *meth* (*shiltong* in Nepal). It is regarded as inferior to mung, but contains more calcium than any other bean.

RICE PAPER is made not of rice but of various plants – the rice paper plant (*Tetrapana papyriferum*), the *nakai* (*Edgeworthia tomentosa*) and the *maisin* (*Wickstroemia canescens*). Although rice paper is used in China and Japan for other purposes such as painting, it has a traditional use in cooking to provide edible bases for macaroons and biscuits.

[*Rice paper* – French: *papier de riz* German: *Reispapier* Italian: *carta cinese* Spanish: *papel de paja le arroz*]

RICING is forcing starchy and mealy foods, such as potatoes and chestnuts, through a perforated device, from which the food falls in a light mound slightly resembling a heap of rice.

RIGATONI. *See* pasta.

ROASTING. Meat was originally roasted by turning it in front of a glowing fire. In other words, it was cooked by radiant heat in free air. The meat was either turned on a spit or suspended, and there was a drip pan underneath so that the juices were caught and used for basting. Grilled or broiled meat was cooked on a grid iron over glowing coals. There could be charring, some of the drippings were wasted, and the meat took the smell of fire (and in most cases of burning fat). Meat cooked in an oven was baked meat. Meat baked in an old-fashioned oven was not subjected to intense radiant heat, and since the ovens were not ventilated, the meat was cooked by hot, moist heat. This moister heat means that oven-cooked meat requires very little basting, while truly roasted meat must be basted almost continuously to prevent it drying up.

Roasted joints now have to be divided into two classes – those cooked before an open fire and those cooked in an oven. There are not many kitchens, except in country places, where the old-fashioned open fire and bottle jack are now in use. Nor can we wonder at this, for the disadvantages of this way of cooking are many: the great cost of fuel due to the large fire that is necessary; the discomfort of those in charge, as incessant basting is required; and the loss of weight caused by the melting of the fat and the evaporation of the juices. Yet it must be said that there is no other way of cooking a joint quite equal to roasting it before the fire. Surrounded by air and exposed to the direct heat of the fire, it has a flavour distinctly its own, which can only be described as 'tasting of the fire'.

Much that is called roast meat today is in fact baked. Anyone who still has a fire, preferably wood, in the grate and a greater love of good food than elegance might like to try a cottage method I learned in Sardinia. Hammer a strong nail or hook into the wall below the mantelpiece and in the centre. Tie a string to a leg of lamb and hang it just in front of the fire. Put a baking tin under it to catch the drips, and to provide a receptacle for the basting fluid which consists of water, salt, garlic. Baste continuously using a bundle of rosemary as a brush. The water in the pan should gradually dry up. Don't baste at all for the last 10 minutes. Some ingenuity – but not much – is needed to turn the meat so that all sides get the fire.

The electric roasting spits which are now becoming common do a good job of roasting our modern small joints in the correct manner.

[*Roasting* – French: *rôtir* German: *braten* Italian: *arrostire* Spanish: *asarse*]

ROBALO. *See* snook.

ROCAMBOLE. *See* onion.

ROCK CANDY. *See* sugar.

ROCKET (*Eruca sativa*) is a salad plant that is sometimes neglected but is commonly used in Italy. It grows wild in much of Europe, but cultivated varieties are less violently flavoured, with larger, tenderer leaves and excellent potential. Rocket has a peculiar, pungent flavour, unmistakably a crucifer – a member of the cabbage family – but very original. It grows easily from seed and is an excellent addition to green salads. A recommended plant.

[*Rocket* – French: *roquette* German: *Rauke, Raukenkohl, Senfkohl* Italian: *ruchetta* Spanish: *oruga*]

ROCK LOBSTER. *See langouste.*

ROCK SALMON or **rock eel**. *See* shark.

ROE is the ovary (hard roe) or testis (soft roe or milt) of a fish. Roes are very often a delicacy, as for instance are those of herrings. Some expensive products are made with roes, including *caviar, *tarama, *botargo and *smoked cod roe. Milt herring is preserved in a sauce containing the soft roe. However, roes from unknown fish are to be avoided, as a few from Arctic and tropical waters are poisonous (e.g. some sharks and globe fish).

In Britain, roes from cod, haddock, coley and other white fish are boiled in highly salted water, allowed to cool in the water and then eaten as they are or sliced, fried and served hot. The soft roe or milt of herring can be bought separately; it is usually fried and served on toast, and is reputedly an aphrodisiac.

[*Roe* – French: *oeufs de poisson, laitance* German: *Rogen, Fischlaich* Italian: *uova, latte di pesce* Spanish: *hueva, lechas*]

ROLLMOP. *See* herring.

ROSE (species of *Rosa*) is not of great culinary importance, except in the Middle East, where rose water as a flavouring appears in many sweet dishes and rose petals are made into rose-petal jam (which is scented and sickly sweet). All rose petals are edible so long as no poison sprays have been used on them, but they are not always very aromatic. Rose-flavoured liqueurs are made, notably in Bulgaria, but most of these concoctions are too sweet for Western palates. However, the list of uses goes all the way from rose vinegar (flavoured by having the petals macerated in it), through crystallized rose petals for decoration, and rose-flavoured candy, to rose-flavoured butter.

The method of making the latter is a good example of *enfleurage*, a process used in the perfume industry for capturing delicate scents. A pat of butter, loosely wrapped in paper is embedded in a pot of fragrant fresh rose petals and kept in a cool place overnight. The butter traps the rose scent just as surely as it would trap the scent of kippers if it were left uncovered near them in the refrigerator. Rose petals are also put into cherry pie, and rose brandy is made by infusing them.

Rose hips, especially those of the wild rose (*R. canina*) were in the past used to make preserves and even as a cooked fruit. As Gerard says, the 'fruit when it is ripe maketh the most pleasant meats, and banketting dishes as tarts and such-like.' A wine can also be made by fermenting rose hips. The hairs surrounding the seeds inside the fruit are very irritating to the gut and should be carefully washed or strained away. Hip jelly is good and so is rose-hip syrup. The latter came into prominence during World War II, when it was realized that hips were a valuable and neglected source of vitamin C. Rosehip syrup is very rich in this, and schoolchildren were officially asked to collect hips so that the syrup could be made.

[*Rose* – French: *rose* German: *Rose* Italian: *rosa* Spanish: *rosa*]

ROSE FAMILY.

The family Rosaceae, which includes more than 2000 species, is of enormous gastronomic importance. Apart from the *rose itself, which contributes its petals as well as its hips, and the *burnet, of which the leaves are used, the family is notable for its fruit – it is incomparably the most important group in this respect, at least in temperate zones. Some of the fruit are drupes, with a single hard-cased seed (the stone) and a fleshy outer layer, they may be valued for their stones, as in the *almond, or for their flesh as in the *apricot, *peach, *cherry and *plum. Others are pomes with a group of small seeds, as in the *apple, *pear, *quince, *medlar and the smaller but similar fruit of the *rowan. The genus *Rubus*, which includes the *blackberry and *raspberry, has compound fruits made of a cluster of small drupes or druplets. The *strawberry is very different in structure as it is not the outer layer that swells, but the inside or receptacle to which the seeds are attached – hence the position of the seeds studding the outside of the fruit.

ROSELLE. *See* Jamaica flower.

ROSEMARY.

One of the commonest wild plants of dry Mediterranean hillsides, rosemary (*Rosmannus officinalis*) is very strongly aromatic with a camphor overtone. It grows well enough as far north as southern Britain, where it was introduced by the Romans. As a culinary herb, it is much used in Italy (less so in other Mediterranean countries), and has in recent years become fashionable for flavouring lamb (an Italian custom), but it can be used with discretion in many dishes. It is sold dried or powdered, but a fresh sprig is best.

[*Rosemary* – French: *romarin* German: *Rosmarin, Rosmarein* Italian: *rosmarino, ramerino* Spanish: *romero, romario*]

ROWAN and SORB.

The rowan or Mountain ash (*Sorbus acuparia*) is a common tree all over Europe except in dry, limy soils, and in North America two related species, *S. americana* and *S. scopulina* (which has larger fruit), are known as Mountain ash. The red berries begin to be ripe in August, and as a number of garden varieties are grown for decoration, the berries are available both in town and country. Although too tart and bitter to eat, they make a fine jelly – either alone or with an equal quantity of apples, and rowan jelly is a splendid and traditional accompaniment to venison.

Rowan Jelly

Wash the berries and put them in a pan with enough water to cover them. Simmer gently until the water is red and bitter. Strain the juice through a jelly bag without squeezing (squeezing, which is sometimes recommended, makes a cloudy jelly). For every 600 ml (1 pt) juice add 450 g (1 lb) sugar and boil until it jells. Put in jars. This is sometimes left to mature for 2 years before use.

Rowan berries were also a popular ingredient in country wines, and Samuel Pepys mentions in his diary that he had found ale brewed with rowan berries the best he had ever tasted. Today, with the new vogue for home wine-making, rowan berries are even being dried for use by wine makers and home brewers who are not able to pick their own.

The Sorb apple or Service tree (*Sorbus domestica*) is a close relative. The sorb is a native of southern Europe, but is naturalized further north and, unlike the rowan, is cultivated for its fruit, which look like small green apples or pears. When unripe, they are exceptionally acid. There are a number of named varieties with either round and pear-shaped fruit which are grown especially in Liguria and Sicily. Good varieties can be eaten as fruit, but they are also used for making a drink, which is not very alcoholic and is similar to cider. They are also dried in the sun and threaded on to strings. In countries further north they are 'bletted' like *medlars.

In North America, what are called Service berries (*Amelanchier florida*) belong to another related genus of the same family, *Amelanchier* which has some twenty species including june-berry (*A. canadensis*), Swamp sugar pear (*A. intermedia*), shadberry and the Snowy mespilus (*A. ovalis*) of southern Europe. Some of these are cultivated for ornament, and the Service berry has gone wild in Europe. Many of them have excellent fruit, which was once much used in North America by the Indians and is still gathered and made into pies by knowledgeable country people. Another cultivated small, almost berry-like rose family fruit of Europe, is the *azerole* or Naples medlar (*Crataegus azarolus*), a native of the Mediterranean and western Asia, which has also been introduced into North America. It is, in almost all respects, just like a large version of hawthorn (*C. monogyna*), with fruit about the size of a crab apple and yellow, white or red fruit according to the cultivated variety. The flesh is crisp, yellowish, tasty and perfumed, with three or four hard seeds. The Naples medlar is eaten as a fresh fruit or is made into jam. The hawthorn itself is not much good as a fruit, though harmless. The young buds are often eaten in spring by children as 'bread and cheese', and are no doubt healthy or worth a try in salads.

[*Rowan* – French: *sorbier des oiseaux* German: *Eberesche* Italian: *frassino di montagna* Spanish: *serbal*]

RUE. This famous old medicinal herb, a member of the same botanical family as oranges and lemons, is rarely found wild in Britain, but is common over most of southern Europe. There are three species – Common rue (*Ruta graveolens*), Fringed rue (*R. chalepensis*), and Mountain rue (*R. montana*) – with slight flower differences and varying degrees of woodiness. There are also a number of garden varieties. All have the rather nasty rue smell, but wild plants from dry Mediterranean hillsides are particularly strong and repulsive. Rue is sometimes used in very discrete amounts as a culinary herb. It has been recommended for use with eggs and cream cheese, and in vegetable juice cocktails. It is also put as a flavouring into *grappa* and is the herb you see in the bottles labelled *con ruta* (with rue).

Medicinal effects are varied and stimulating, but it is poisonous in any quantity.

[*Rue* – French: *rue odorante* German: *Route, Gartenraute, Weinkraut* Italian: *ruta* Spanish: *ruda*]

RUM is a spirit distilled from the fermented leavings of the cane sugar industry; the molasses, the scum which rises after liming, and other residues. The product varies between white cane spirit – a fire water that does not merit the description 'rum' – to the rich, dark, flavourful rums containing large amounts of fruity esters. All the best rum starts as a West Indian product, although it is made in many other places, in fact, anywhere that sugar cane grows. Many of the rums, such as that of Mexico, are light and without character. Others, like that distilled in Madeira, are used to fortify wine. The rums of importance are as follows:

Jamaica produces the most highly flavoured rums, with the exception of those from Martinique, though they are lighter than they were in the last century. Jamaican rums are made to high standards under very strict control and are probably the best to use in sweet dishes.

Martinique makes excellent, highly-flavoured rums much used in France.

The US produces more rum than any other country. New England rum was made in Colonial days from molasses shipped up from the West Indies, and taxes on it were resented in Boston just as much as the tax on tea. Though excellent, the flavour of American rum is less refined than that of good Jamaican.

Barbados makes a medium rum with many additions other than those natural to a cane-sugar product. They may include wine, raisins and bitter almond.

Demerara. Named, like the sugar, from a district near Georgetown, Guyana, this is very fruity rum with many additions, such as plums, raisins, caramel and spices. It is very popular in Britain.

Cuba is famous particularly for *daiquiri*, and produces light-coloured rums, with natural 'rum' flavours removed by filtration and a light new flavouring of fruit, bay, sugar and secret ingredients added. The colourless Bacardi rum, the sort usually made into *daiquiris*, originated in Cuba but is now made in Brazil.

Rum was a common kitchen ingredient in the last century, when fruity rums were particularly in fashion. It is still used in confectionery all over Europe and is a better flavouring than brandy in most cases. Less commonly, rum is used in savoury dishes, with meat, fowl and fish. It goes excellently with shell fish, as fishermen in Spain have discovered, and it is used in one of the six courses of the famous *langostinara* of giant prawns (or *shrimps) from San Carlos de la Rapita at the mouth of the Ebro river.

Langostinos al Ron

Cook the *langostinos* on the *plancha* (i.e. the hot top of the stove or in a dry frying pan) until they are just dry. Then fry in olive oil, salt to taste and flame in rum.
   [*Rum* – French: *rhum* German: *Rum* Italian: *rum* Spanish: *ron*]

RUNNER BEAN (*Phaseolus coccineus*) originated in South America and was brought to Europe as a decorative plant – there are varieties with vermilion, scarlet, and white flowers – but it has for long been the most popular green bean grown in British vegetable gardens. Runners are perennials, which are grown as annuals as in cold climates where they are killed by the winter frosts. They are nearly always eaten as green beans, and British gardeners have a tendency to pick them when they are so old and tough that they have to be sliced. Slicing beans is known as 'Frenching' in the US, although it is certainly not the practice in France. Runners are climbers (pole beans) and so are not usually grown commercially for dried seed (being difficult to harvest by mechanical means), but if left on the plant until they are ripe, the beans are excellent. The flavour of runners is somewhat stronger than that of French beans.

RUSH NUT. *See* chufa nut.

RUSKS. Dry, airy slices of a bread, cake or scone basis are called rusks, and some are only one degree removed from toasts. When rusks are called for in a dish (usually as a base on which something is spread) it is important to consider which of the many kinds should be used. A double baking is involved in making rusks as in *Zwieback* and *biscuits* in their original form. The word rusk is said to come from the Spanish *rosca*, but those – at least today – are ring shaped. There are large ones called *roscónes* and small ones called *rosquillas*, and they may sometimes be fried as well as baked, so have very little to do with rusks as we know them. Their rusks, sold in packets, are called *biscottes* or *toastada*.

[*Rusk* – French: *biscotte* German: *Zwieback* Italian: *biscotti* Spanish: *biscotte, tostada*]

RUTABAGA. *See* swede.

RYE (*Secale cereale*) is a recent cereal compared to wheat or barley. It is thought to have been first noticed as a weed in cornfields in the arid areas around Mount Ararat, that snowy cone you pass on the road going east from Erzerum into Iran, where Noah's Ark is supposed to have been grounded after the flood. The usefulness of rye rests on its ability to tolerate cold conditions, in which wheat would be uncertain. It also has a better bread-making quality than barley, as it contains a sufficiency of gluten. Up to the mid-19th century, it was the staple bread grain in much of northern Europe – in Germany, Poland and particularly Russia – and was much used by the early settlers in North America. In those days, people considered rye bread inferior to any made of wheat, and it is only in recent years that it has come to be valued. Perhaps one reason why it was denigrated in the past was that with rye there was always danger of poisoning from the *mould, ergot, which is now very unlikely.

Rye flour is a dirty grey colour, though it is frequently lightened by mixing with wheat flour, sometimes with barley flour and with maize flour in America. It is the flour of black bread (*schwartzbrod*), pumpernickel and some crispbread. The texture of rye bread is close and the taste is characteristic and usually slightly sour, partly because of sourdough methods of rising it, which take longer than is necessary with wheat bread. Unfortunately, good rye bread is now difficult to find, as tastes have changed. The market in Innsbruck, where I used to buy beautiful, round polished rye loaves to take to the mountains (rye bread keeps better than wheat bread), now sells a very inferior product. Rye bread is an essential in making Scandinavian open sandwiches, and goes best with German and eastern European sausage. The grain is the basis for rye *whisky (although it is cut with other grain) and is used for making beer in Russia as well as gin in Holland and some sorts of vodka.
   [*Rye* – French: *seigle* German: *Roggen* Italian: *segala* Spanish: *centeno*]

S

SABRE BEAN. *See* Jack bean.

SACCHARIN is now the only non-carbohydrate sweetener that is permitted in Britain. It was discovered by accident in 1879 by chemists at Johns Hopkins University who were doing research on the derivatives of toluene, which is a constituent of coal tar. One of them found that his food tasted sweet and also found the sweetness on his hands, although he had washed them before eating. Tracing the cause back to the experiments led the scientists to identity saccharin, which has a chemical name that can be given as orthosulphobenzimide. It is insoluble in water, and saccharin tablets are made either of its soluble sodium salt or of a mixture of saccharin and bicarbonate of soda which react together when moistened. Either way, it is sodium saccharin that sweetens your cup of tea. Although estimates of its sweetness vary, it is around 400 times as sweet as cane sugar and more than ten times as sweet as *cyclamates.

It has been used as a sweetener since 1894, when a method of making it commercially was first patented. The food manufacturers' main reason for using saccharin is its cheapness – as one food science textbook puts it, 'one shilling's worth of saccharin is equivalent in sweetening power to one pound's worth of sugar.' In Britain, the only restrictions on the amount of saccharin in food are in soft drinks where there are legal maxima and in ice cream where it is not permitted at all.

Although saccharin was suspected along with cyclamates of being linked with bladder cancer and was banned in some countries, it seems to be the safest artificial sweetener that we have, presenting no health problems if it is used in moderate quantities. However, although there are no legal limits on the use of saccharin in many foods, manufacturers do take account of the 'Acceptable Daily Intakes' recommended by the WHO: 0.5 mg per kg of body weight or 0.15 mg per kg of body weight for dietetic use. The main disadvantage of saccharin is its unpleasant lingering aftertaste, which is said to be caused largely by impurities that can be avoided in newer methods of synthesis.

Saccharin is a substitute only for the sweetness of sugar and has none of its nutritional or preservative qualities. It passes unchanged through the body, being excreted in the urine. Because it is not metabolized by the body, saccharin is valuable in diets for diabetics and slimmers.

[*Saccharin* – French: *saccharine* German: *Saccharin* Italian: *saccarina* Spanish: *sacarino*]

SACCHAROSE. Sucrose. *See* sugar.

SACCHAROMETER. *See* hydrometer.

SAFFLOWER or saffron thistle (*Carthamus tinctorius*) comes from India but is unknown as a wild plant. It can be grown quite well even in Britain and similar temperate areas. The orange-red flowers contain a dye (carthamin) which may be used to colour food and as a substitute for saffron, although false saffron does not have the proper flavour. The seeds have greater commercial importance as a source of safflower oil, which is a good kitchen oil that is also held to be safe for people with a tendency to atherosclerosis. It is often mixed with other oils in proprietary brands but can also be bought separately. The seeds and even the leaves of the plant are edible.

[*Safflower* – French: *carthame* German: *Saflor* Italian: *cartamo* Spanish: *cartamo*]

SAFFRON consists of the stigmas of the saffron crocus (*Crocus sativus*). It is an ancient spice, with a peculiar, unique flavour and a strong yellow colour. Nowadays, it is enormously expensive, because of the hard work involved in extracting it from the flowers. Luckily, only a pinch is needed to flavour any dish; the dried stigmas are first soaked in a little milk or water for 15 minutes or so to loosen the dye.

Powdered saffron is almost always a dye (such as carthamin from *safflower), a cosmetic with no flavour that is best avoided. Cheap saffron does not exist and anything masquerading as such is almost certainly the stamens of some other yellow flower, such as marigold. Where saffron is needed, as in

Mediterranean fish soups and some Kashmiri dishes, there is no substitute for it. There are versions of Spanish *paella* which use no saffron; Spanish restaurant *paellas* are likely to be made with dye.

[*Saffron* – French: *safran* German: *Safrangewürz* Italian: *zafferano* Spanish: *azafrán*]

SAFFRON THISTLE. *See* safflower.

SAGE. Garden sage (*Salvia officinalis*) is a perennial that is a native of southern Europe; it is plentiful, for instance, on the Adriatic coast of Yugoslavia. There are many culinary varieties; since sage is usually grown from cuttings passed from one person to another, it is as well to look for a good, aromatic plant to use for cuttings. Sage dries well and is one of the few herbs still regularly used in Britain. It is used particularly in Germany and Italy, less so in France and Spain. The flavour is powerful and with overtones of camphor.

[*Sage* – French: *sauge* German: *Salbei* Italian: *salvia* Spanish: *salvia*]

SAGO is virtually pure starch extracted from the sago palm (*Metroxylon sagu*) and to a lesser extent from other plants (palms and cycads) which develop a similar starchy pith. The sago palm grows in swampy places in southern Asia. It looks like a typical palm, but has the peculiarity that just before it flowers (when it is about 15 years old) it builds up a large reserve of starch to be drawn on for the reproductive effort. At this point, man intervenes, cuts down the palm, extracts the pith from the stem, grinds it up, washes out the starch with water and allows it to settle. After the clear top water has been poured off, the wet starchy paste can be dried into a flour or granulated through a sieve to give the well known pearl sago. It is this latter which provides the much-feared nursery pudding known for generations as 'frog-spawn'. Few, if any, important European dishes are based on sago, although it is sometimes used in place of pasta in broths and there are various sweets made from it. In parts of the Orient, it has more uses, although mainly in its floury form, which root. In South India, it is used in various sun-dried wafers and deep-fried vegetarian patties, such as *vattala, pakoras, vadas,* and *chakli:* Sago is also used throughout South East Asia. Rosemary Brissenden's *South East Asian Food* (Penguin) gives a recipe for the Thai *saku sai mooh,* which consists of envelopes of sago paste steamed with a stuffing of pork, roasted peanuts and onion.

Sago Vadas (Indian)

Make 450 g (1 lb) plain mashed potato. Soak a cup of sago in water for 20 minutes, drain it and mix it with the potato. Add 100 g (4 oz) coarsely pounded peanuts, a finely chopped mixture of 4 green chillies and a small handful of green coriander leaves, some lemon juice and salt to taste. Knead all this together into a dough. Roll bits of the dough into table-tennis ball size, flatten them and fry them until brown. Serve with green chutney as a snack

[*Sago* – French: *sagou* German: *Sago* Italian: *sagù* Spanish: *sagú*]

SAITHE. *See* cod (coal fish).

SAKE is Japanese rice wine. It usually has an alcoholic content of about 15% (like a very strong European wine) and is served warm. *Sake* is a necessary ingredient in Japanese cooking. A sweet, less strong rice wine known as *mirin* is used only for cooking and is often required to be mixed in equal quantity with soy sauce. A substitute for sake in cooking is a dry sherry.

SALAD. By far the most popular of the salad vegetables is *lettuce, but there are many others, notably the various types of *chicory and *cress. One of the most useful, and a popular winter salad in European countries, is Lamb's lettuce or Corn salad (*Valerianella locusta*), an annual member of the valerian family that is a native of Britain, most of Europe, the Middle East and North Africa. It was introduced into the US at the beginning of the 19th century. When young, not far beyond the seedling stage, the small roundish leaves make an excellent salad, with a pleasant, sometimes almost primrose-like taste. If the plants are too large or grown in the wrong conditions, they are inclined to be tough.

A plant I particularly like in salads is *rocket, and others are fond of tender leaves of raw *spinach, of acid-tasting *sorrel and of *dandelion leaves (which are best if the plant has been blanched under a tile). A garden flower with peppery-tasting leaves that can be good in salad is *nasturtium.

Dozens of wild herbs with pungent, peppery flavours can be used in salads, especially crucifers such as the cresses and the leaves of *Lady's smock or Cuckoo flower (*Cardamine pratensis*). Milder flavours come from the Salad burnet (*Poterium sanguisorba*) and the small new buds of hawthorn in spring.

Some people like to mix their lettuce with wet

tomato or purple-staining beetroot, but neither is very aesthetic. A careful admixture of other leaves and herbs will make something beautiful as well as refreshing and interesting – salads repay a little experiment.

[*Green salad* – French: *salade verte* German: *grüner Salat* Italian: *insalata verde* Spanish: *ensalada*.

Cuckoo flower – French: *cardamine des prés* German: *Wiesenschaumkraut* Italian: *billeri* Spanish: *cardamina*.

Burnet – French: *pimprenelle* German: *Pimpinelle* Italian: *pimpinella* Spanish: *pimpinela*.

Lamb's lettuce – French: *mâche, valérianelle* German: *Acker Salat* Italian: *erba riccia* Spanish: *canonigo, valeriana cultivada*]

SALAD DRESSING. The most primitive salads are not dressed at all, but rely only on the flavours of the salad materials. A meal in an Iranian village stands out in my mind. Rice and kebabs were served with a bowl of onion tops and branches of Russian tarragon.

The word salad is derived from the Latin *sal* (salt), and the simplest salad dressing is salt. A dressing of olive oil, salt and vinegar is also an ancient one. Lemon juice, which some prefer as the souring agent, is much used in the Middle East, especially where wine, the forerunner of vinegar, is frowned on for religious reasons.

From simple beginnings, both salads and the dressings have increased in complexity, and by the beginning of this century cookery writers were mildly deploring the growing use of ready-made dressings bought from the grocer. Some of these dressings are quite good, but most dedicated cooks will want to make their own. The dressing of the salad at table can be part of the gastronomic ceremonial. The type of dressing to be used must depend on the ingredients in the salad. It is a subject that gives rise to strong prejudices. For instance, I dislike salads that are a bewildering *mélange* of ingredients dressed with a thick heavy dressing and I cannot understand anyone finding such creamy treasure hunts stimulating.

Oil and Vinegar, Vinaigrette or French Dressing
The classic directions are to use 1 part wine vinegar to 3 parts olive oil. Salt is left to the salad mixer's discretion. The amount – according to the old Spanish saying – needs a wise man to determine. The oil should preferably be a good, light olive oil with a delicate flavour. Strong-tasting olive oils, such as the Spanish oil which has the very respectable label *virgin*, are overwhelming. If you can't get

good olive oil, it is best to turn to light seed or nut oils, which have little flavour (most of it has been stripped out in refining). Avoid the thick oils like maize oil, which tend to make salads greasy. The vinegar should preferably be a good wine vinegar, and should be chosen with some thought. Tarragon or other flavoured vinegars are sometimes used. Cider vinegar seems mainly to be a modern health fad, but it has a distinctive taste which some people like better than that of wine vinegar. There are even said to be those who prefer malt vinegar, which in general is frowned upon.

For a simple lettuce salad, using a good olive oil, the proportion of 3 oil to 1 vinegar seems wrong, and something like 4 to 1 is better. Those who mix a salad with a flourish, by eye, with lots of splashing about, will usually find this is what they arrive at by instinct if they pour the oil with some generosity. Mixing the salad with the dressing may need to be done some time before the meal for vegetables which need to absorb the dressing – beetroot, celery and celeriac, for instance – but a green salad should always be mixed at the last minute, very thoroughly. This can be done with the hands, which is best for a large party, but then the process has to be done in the kitchen. Salad bowls are often too small and badly designed for mixing at the table. Sloping sides tend to make the leaves slide up over the edge. They discourage efficient mixing and encourage the spread of salad over the table. A fairly deep, straight-sided container is better. You can mix any salad thoroughly in it. Garlic is best introduced by rubbing it on a slice of bread and laying it on the bottom of the bowl under the salad, but you will then need a little more dressing – the bread absorbs some of it.

Soulie

One of the simplest dressings I know was always made by an old Irish friend who did not know where the name came from, but said it was traditional in his family. It is useful for anyone who does not like oil. My friend heated vinegar in a large spoon with some sugar, and when the sugar had dissolved poured the hot sweet-sour soulie over the salad.

Bacon Fat Dressing

Dice about 100 g (4 oz) of streaky bacon (according

to the size of the salad) and fry it gently until it browns and the fat runs out of it. Then deglaze the pan with a tablespoon of vinegar, pour the mixture hot over the salad and mix. This is particularly good for salads of slightly bitter ingredients, like spinach, chicory and dandelion.

There are dozens of salad creams on the market, mostly based on oil-water-vinegar emulsions with flavourings and stabilizers, and sometimes with starch and thickeners. Home-made creamy dressings can be based on *mayonnaise, fresh (or sour) cream, yoghurt or, as with boiled dressings, a cooked 'custard' of egg, flour and milk. With a modern blender, it is also easy to make creamy dressings (which will hold for a day) by emulsifying oil, water and vinegar, using no more than mustard or garlic or both as a stabilizer, in the same way that egg yolk is used as a stabilizer in mayonnaise. For example, mix a heaped teaspoon of mustard with water and leave it to brew for 10 minutes. Meanwhile, temper some vinegar with sugar to taste, add salt and put with the mustard in a liquidizer. Blend in the oil, beginning with a few drops at a time, with the liquidizer at full speed. Flavour with herbs if desired.

Thousand Island Dressing

Into 250 ml (½ pt) of mayonnaise, mix 2 teaspoons tomato purée, 1 teaspoon French mustard, a pinch of cayenne pepper and 1-2 teaspoons Worcestershire sauce. Then gently stir in 2 dessertspoons each finely-chopped celery and sweet pickle, 1 teaspoon chopped capers and 1 chopped hard-boiled egg. Adjust the seasoning and serve on Iceberg lettuce.

[*Salad dressing* – French: *assaisonement pour la salade* German: *Salatsosse* Italian: *condimento per l'insalata* Spanish: *aliño*]

SALAME (plural salami). To many people, salame is one thing – a toughish, dry sausage which, when sliced, is dark red speckled with bits of white – but in Italy there are dozens of different types. Salame is made all over the world – fine types come from Hungary, Germany and Denmark. Plenty of bad salami is also made, even in Italy, where there are scandals over plastic salami from time to time. However, when salame is good, it is very good.

First of all, it is worth mentioning cooked salame (*salame cotto*) which is an inferior product made from pork, or a mixture of meats not suitable for making raw salame. *Salame cotto* is relatively cheap and depends almost entirely on spices for its flavour.

It is often dyed red to improve the colour. The more familiar raw salame (*salame crudo*) is made generally of lean and fat pork, in which case the Italians indicate this with a metal tag bearing the letter S, but sometimes with the addition of beef or other meats (marked SB on the tag). As salame is eaten raw, its safety depends on the action of the salt and on long enough maturation to kill undesirable micro-organisms.

Almost every district in Italy has its own variety, and there is great variation in flavour and quality – in the toughness of the meat, the size of grain, the texture, colour and flavour. Even within a local idiom, there is variation. For instance, salame labelled *nostrani* (meaning locally made) is often coarser in texture than the usual type for the district. In general, the salame of southern Italy is likely to be more highly spiced than that from northern parts of the country and to contain red pepper. Some sort of classification is possible into lightly and strongly flavoured types:

The lightly flavoured types are those that most of us are familiar with: the Milanese salami (*crespone* and *bindone*), and the Hungarian, Tuscan and Alpine varieties. The expensive salame from Felino near Parma, is made from the same quality meat as Parma hams, and contains no spices except a very little pepper. It is not even matured for very long (2-3 months) and has a beautiful sweet taste. Another famous salame in this category comes from around Varzi, a town in the province of Pavia.

Strongly flavoured types of salame include the Genoese (of pork, veal and pork fat), Piedmontese, Neapolitan, Sicilian and Sardinian, as well as *salame d'aglio* (garlic salame) and *salametto*. There are also excellent strong types from Yugoslavia, which also produces mild types similar to those from Hungary. Among the more off-beat salamis are the *finocchiona* and its smaller cousin, the *finocchietto*, of Florence which are flavoured with wild fennel seed. The *salame di cinghiale* (of wild boar) is very finely minced and usually contains sugar as well as salt and spices.

Salame di fegato is made of liver with salt, spices and white wine. There are many other flavourings for salame used in Italy and elsewhere. Some of these, such as crushed black peppercorns, are applied externally, while others are added to the contents (as in the orange-coloured Hungarian paprika salame).

American salame comes in German and Kosher

as well as Italian varieties. Milano has a fine texture, while Genoa, which is characteristically corded for hanging, is coarser.

Salame should be sliced fine for an *hors d'oeuvre*, and it is thoughtful to remove the threads of skin, especially if the slices are being put into buttered rolls to make a sandwich.

SALAMELLA. *See salsiccia.*

SALICYLIC ACID occurs naturally in some plants, notably in birch bark and in the leaves of wintergreen where it is in the form of methyl salicylate, which is the main component of oil of wintergreen. However, it is normally synthesized. It is used as a *preservative, but is illegal in food in many countries, including the US.

[*Salicylic acid* – French: *acide salicylique* German: *Salizylsauer* Italian: *acido salicilico* Spanish: *salicilico*]

SALMON originally meant only *Salmo solar*, a species which spawns and is caught in the rivers of Europe – from Norway to Spain, in Iceland, in one river in Greenland, in Canada and on the East Coast of the US. The name is also given to many closely related fish from other parts of the world, some of which are commonly frozen or canned, and to a few that are unrelated, such as the Indian salmon, the *rawas* (*Eleutheronema tetradactylus*).These, like the salmon, are oily fish.

The true salmon is a splendid fish that normally weighs 4-12 kg (9-26 lb) or more. North American and western European salmon live their sea lives somewhere off the coast of Greenland but ascend the rivers to spawn, each salmon returning to the river where it was born. Some salmon come up river in the spring (spring fish) and may be caught in January (for example, rod fishing on the River Tay in Scotland opens on 15th January and netting some three weeks later), but other salmon do not run up river until the summer or early autumn. None, however, spawn until the autumn. The close season varies from river to river. Though regulations vary, salmon may not usually be sold (even if it has been caught legally on rod and line) during the season when commercial netting is not permitted. At such times only frozen or imported salmon will be available. Some salmon migrate to the sea at the end of their first year, but others remain for two or even three years. Before going to sea, the young salmon become silvery and are then known as smolts. Some fish remain in the sea for only a year before returning to their river to spawn; these are excellent small salmon of 1.5-3 kg (3¼-6½

lb), known as grilse. Only when a fish has lived for 2-3 years in the sea does it return as a fully grown salmon. After salmon have spawned they are known as kelts. They are thin and useless, as they have starved themselves during their time breeding in the river. Some kelts make it back to the sea in December and return for a second, and more rarely, a third time, to breed, but many die after only one spawning.

If you can afford it, you may eat fresh salmon happily from February through the summer to the end of August, the best fish being by repute the first spring fish. For the rest of the year, though, salmon will come chilled or deep-frozen from Canada, Norway or Japan. Fresh salmon should indeed be as fresh as possible, because after a few hours the creamy 'curd' disappears and the delicate flavour begins to go. Like other fresh fish, it is stiff, shiny and bright. The best fish are said to have large 'shoulders' and a small head. Most buyers, though, will be thinking of just a cut from a fish, in which case the middle part is the best.

Salmon is scaled and cleaned in the normal manner before cooking. It may be poached for roughly 20 minutes per kg (10 minutes per lb) plus 20 minutes extra in a *court-bouillon*, but the water must never boil – a trick to make certain of this is to take out some of the hot liquid and substitute cold, thus lowering the temperature. An adaptation of the Chinese method of crystal cooking, used for chicken, also works well for salmon. The *court-bouillon* in which the salmon rests is kept just on the boil for 3 minutes, then the heat is turned off and the lid is kept on tight. The salmon will be cooked when the liquid is cold. Salmon is excellent grilled, steamed, or cooked in many other ways (see, for example Alan Davidson's *North Atlantic Seafood*, Penguin). *Smoked salmon is a delicacy in its own right.

In the past, salmon was abundant in European rivers – there is a much-quoted servant's contract which stipulated that salmon should not be served more than twice a week. By the beginning of the 19th century, however, the pollution of rivers was well under way, and over-efficient netting depleted the fish population still further. In North America, salmon was also super-abundant, and the Indians once made pemmican from dried salmon. Later, salmon was canned in huge amounts, and in this form it could be called a poor man's food up to World War II.

Pacific and North American salmon. In North American rivers, *Salmo solar* averages only 4.5

kg (10 lb) in weight. It is much less important commercially than the Pacific species of salmon, which belong to the related genus *Onchorhynchus*. These are the basis of a huge canning and fishing industry that deals with a million tons of salmon a year.

Of the Pacific salmon, one, the Cherry Salmon (*O. masu*) is found in the sea off Japan. The other five are found in North American rivers that feed into the Pacific (and in some cases on the Asian side of the ocean as well). In ascending order of size, these salmon are the Pink or Humpback (*O. gorbuscha*), the Sockeye or Red (*O. nerka*), the Coho or Silver (*O. kisutch*), the Chum or Dog (*O. keta*) and the Chinook, King or Spring (*O. tschawytscha*) which averages 10.5 kg (23 lb) but not uncommonly reaches 23-36 kg (50-80 lb). The Pink salmon and the Coho salmon are also found in the Atlantic. In general, the life cycle of Pacific salmon is similar to that of *Salmo salar*, although the time spans vary according to species; the salmon may be anything from two to eight years old when it makes its spawning run up river. Pacific salmon normally die after spawning, which takes King salmon and Chum salmon as much as 2000 miles from the sea to the headwaters of the Yukon River.

In commercial terms, the Pink salmon is the most important, making up half the catch, with the Chum salmon accounting for a third and the Sockeye salmon for almost all the rest. The Chinook salmon and the Coho salmon are much sought by the sporting fisherman. In Russia, the roe of the Chum salmon is made into red *caviar.

[*Salmon* – French: *saumon* German: *Lachs* Italian: *salmone* Spanish: *salmón*]

SALMONELLA. *See* poisoning.

SAL PRUNELLA or **sal prunelle**. Sal prunella is old-fashioned, crude *saltpetre in the form of cakes, and is often mentioned in farm cures for ham and bacon. Being impure, and having been heated, it contains potassium nitrite as well as nitrate and so gets off the mark quickly. It is safer to use formulae which do not include it.

SALSICCIA is a general term in Italy for any smallish sausage, whether fresh or dried. Such sausages are made in many regional types all over Italy. The ordinary *salsiccia fresca* (fresh) or *luganega* is usually thin and continuous, not pinched or twisted into individual sausages. The *salsiccia salamella* is thicker more the size of the British

banger – and is divided into sausages with looped string. Its varieties include the *salamella milanese* (from Milan) and the *salamella vaniglia* (flavoured with vanilla). Then there are the *salsiccia toscana* (with garlic, pepper and anis), *salamella di cinghiale* (wild boar), *salsiccia da riso* and *salsiccia da potata* (containing rice and potato), *salsiccia bolognese* (from Bologna, containing minced heart and lungs), *salsiccia napoletana* (from Naples, a pork and beef sausage strongly spiced with red pepper), *salsiccia matta* (made of giblets and spleen), and *salsiccia di fegato* (liver flavoured with pepper and fennel seeds). These sausages are usually to be eaten cooked, but some of them are smoked, including *salsiccia di Palermo* and *salsiccia milanese affumicata* (smoked sausages from Milan), and some are hung to dry for a couple of months before eating – *salsiccia secca* or *salsiccia asciutta*.

SALSIFY, oyster plant or **vegetable oyster** (*Tragopogon porrifolium*) is a purple-flowered composite related to lettuce. Its long, white tap-roots, which look something like very slender parsnips, make an excellent winter vegetable. Salsify is popular in France and Italy but is out of fashion in Britain and the US, being more likely to turn up in cans in the supermarket than fresh at the greengrocers's. Often confused with salsify, and often preferred to it by those who know the difference, is the closely related scorzonera or Black salsify (*Scorzonera hispanica*), which has black-skinned roots and yellow flowers. Like salsify, it is a native of southern Europe. In the Middle Ages, scorzonera was valued as a medicine rather than as a vegetable; later, it was strongly recommended as a vegetable by the head of Louis XIV's kitchen. In Britain, the roots were not just eaten as a vegetable but were also candied.

The eclipse of scorzonera as a vegetable has been attributed by Eleanour Sinclair Rohde to the custom of peeling root vegetables, which appears to have become prevalent in the Victorian period. Scorzonera suffers more than other roots from peeling as it bleeds profusely. Both salsify and scorzonera are best dealt with by washing off the earth and cooking them whole in boiling salted water for 30-45 minutes or by steaming for perhaps an hour until they are tender. The skins will then rub or scrape off quite easily, and the roots can be cut into short lengths ready for further treatment (it is in this form that salsify is canned). Salsify and scorzonera may be served cold with *sauce vinaigrette* and hot *au gratin* or fried in butter. The young leaves of both plants can be used in salad, and Boulestin recommends putting the young flowers of scorzonera in omelettes.

Another member of the same genus as salsify is goat's beard or Jack-go-to-bed-at-noon (*Tragopogon pratensis*). It is a common roadside plant in Europe and is cultivated in Italy under the name *barba di frate* or *barba di prete* (monk's or priest's beard). Its tuft of grass-like leaves is eaten, cooked like spinach, but it does not break up and is considered a delicacy. In Britain, where a small form is found, the tap-roots of goat's beard were once eaten like those of salsify.

[*Salsify* – French: *salsifis* German: *Bocksbart* Italian: *sassefrica* Spanish: *salsifi*]

SALT or, more precisely, common salt is sodium chloride (NaCl). An essential item in the diet of humans and other animals, it is also a basic taste which is detected on the tongue; food without it tastes insipid. Salt has been extracted and used since Neolithic times. It became an important article of trade in the Bronze Age.

Most of us today get too much salt in our diet – we like it, partly as a result of becoming accustomed to it at a very early age, and so we wolf such things as salted peanuts, salt meat and olives. Too much salt is a contributory factor in heart disease and perhaps also in other diseases as well. The only time we are likely to need supplementary salt is when we are sweating profusely, whether crossing a desert or labouring in a steelworks. The natural reaction then is to drink large amounts of fluid, but sweat contains salt as well as water, and both need to be replaced – lack of salt can cause heat exhaustion.

The global reservoir of salt is the sea – it has been calculated that there is enough salt in the sea to cover the world's land masses to a depth of 35 m (115 ft). The average concentration of salt in seawater is about 35 g per lt (¾ oz per pt), but the Red Sea is about 15% saltier, while the Dead Sea contains a staggering 200 g per lt (4 oz per pt). On the other hand, the Black Sea is less than averagely salty and the Caspian Sea is only brackish – cows come down to it to drink.

Sodium chloride is only the most important of many salts in seawater. The next, in descending order of concentration, are magnesium chloride, magnesium sulphate (Epsom salts), potassium sulphate, calcium carbonate, and potassium and sodium bromides. Salts of many other elements are also found, some of them in infinitesimally small quantities. Sea salt does not contain all these things

in the same proportions unless it is completely unpurified, made by drying out seawater completely. Often, only part of the mineral content is crystallized out from seawater, and sea salt may also have been partially purified by recrystallization.

Sea salt is evaporated naturally in bays or enclosures and is also called bay salt in older books or *gros sel*. Salt may be produced in a similar way from salt marshes. The bays may be dried out completely or the salt crystals raked out of a saturated solution. Sea salt may also be made by evaporating the water over a fire, and was once made in quantity by this means, in wide earthenware pans – a method that dates back to the Iron Age, if not earlier.

Rock salt is found in deposits derived from the drying of ancient seas. It may be mined as a crystalline mineral, but a more modern and prosaic method is to pump water down into the salt, remove the brine which is formed, and evaporate it. The flavour of rock salt depends on the impurities present – ancient seas did not necessarily have the same composition as those of today – and some deposits may contain poisonous substances, such as arsenic. They may be stained red with iron or grey with other minerals. Edible rock salts in a roughly crushed form are sold for use in the wooden salt mills that some people use at table.

The old-fashioned block salt was made with crystalline salt poured into moulds when it was still hot from the evaporating pans. It contained just enough dampness to stick the crystals loosely together in the block. In the kitchen, it had to be grated. Dairy salt and cheese salt were varieties of block salt that had been crushed mechanically and were sold in sacks. This crushed salt is basically the ordinary type of kitchen salt used today. Block salt itself is no longer common but is still produced in England by Ingram Thompson's Lion Salt Works at Nantwich. Salt produced by the open pan method is 98.5% pure sodium chloride, the rest being mainly gypsum (calcium sulphate). When open pan salt is used in *brine for meat, the calcium sulphate reacts with the phosphates in the meat to form insoluble calcium phosphate, which makes the brine cloudy. Vacuum salt, evaporated and purified in vacuum pans, does not cause this problem as it is 99.9% pure and contains virtually no gypsum. It is free running and is the basis of table salt, which is very finely ground and has had magnesium carbonate added to prevent caking. Sometimes starch and other carbonates and bicarbonates are also included. Dendritic salt, a new form of salt with star-shaped crystals, has a fine, soft and floury texture. It is particularly used in manufactured seasonings and for mixing with spices. It is made from purified brine in vacuum pans and is 99.64% pure. Pickling salt is a very pure salt, since impurities can darken pickles.

Iodized salt, with iodine salts added, supplies dietary iodine, a health precaution that is essential in areas with a natural iodine deficiency (sea salt will not supply an adequate quantity).There are also salt substitutes for use in low-salt diets – usually depending on potassium salts which may be beneficial in many heart cases but should be used only after medical consultation. Other salt mixtures such as bio-salt are compounded for health purposes. It will almost certainly be found that the mineral intake is of more importance to health than most medical opinion believes at present.

Meanwhile, cooks use salt freely for flavour and preservation. Salt seems to sharpen our awareness of other flavours. A normally salted food will contain about 0.9% salt, about the same content as that of the body. Water for cooking potatoes and greens should obviously be much more highly salted, as we are not usually going to drink it. 355 g salt per lt. (35.5% or 7 oz per pt) is a saturated solution at 0°C, and salt is only slightly more soluble in hot water – only 396 g per lt (just under 8 oz per pt) will be dissolved when the water is boiling. Ordinary impure salt will absorb water from the atmosphere unless it is stored at a relative humidity of under 75 per cent. Damp salt may be dried in a slightly warm oven with the door ajar, but it will cake and will need to be crushed and sifted. Spiced and herbed salts are made by mixing dried salt with ground aromatic seeds, spices or herbs. Garlic or onion can be pounded into bone dry salt, the moisture being absorbed and the substance preserved by the salt, but the mixture should be kept sealed, as the flavour is destroyed by oxygen.

The selection of the right salt is important in cooking. Good sea salt (such as Maldon salt from Essex) is the best – I take my own bag down to the pile at the local salinas in Majorca, where the salt is pink and slightly dirty but has a superlative flavour. By the time it is put into a packet and sold in a 'gourmet' shop, it is several thousand per cent more expensive. Also the crystal size of salt matters. Fine salt dissolves quickly, but is not recommended for *dry-salting. Of course, most people will continue to use free running table salt for everything because of its convenience, but perhaps it will eventually become gastronomically or even socially unacceptable, like factory-ground pepper.

[Salt – French: sel German: Salz Italian: sale Spanish: sal]

SALT COD or bacalao. Cod live in huge numbers in the North Atlantic and have always been an important food for the maritime countries of Northern Europe. Fishing boats ranged far into stormy seas – the Shetlands, Lofotens, Bear Island and the White Sea were familiar names to cod-fishers, who were always finding new grounds. In the middle of the 19th century, Rockall was where the cod were 'as big as donkeys and as common as blackberries'. Much earlier, the boats had favoured the Newfoundland Grand Banks on the other side of the Atlantic. With enormous numbers of fish being caught at certain seasons, it was fortunate that cod did not have oily flesh and so could be salted and dried without difficulty. The fish were gutted, salted and packed in flats at sea, later washed and put out on the rocks to dry, which was why they were called klip-fish or simply rock-fish (not to be confused with dried, unsalted *stockfish).This simple process justified voyages to productive fishing grounds far from the markets. There was a ready sale for dried fish in southern Europe. As long ago as the 15th century, British merchants began shipping bacalhau into the Minho in Portugal and bringing back wine. Soon the whole of Catholic Europe came to depend on salt cod for Friday and Lenten dishes. It was inexpensive and easy to transport. America too, began producing it in quantity. Thoreau (writing in the first half of the 19th century, when cod was still caught on long sea-lines) described it as 'stacked up like cord-wood' around the wharves of Provincetown on Cape Cod. Less than 40 years after the discovery of that arm-shaped peninsula by the English explorer Bartholomew Gosnold in 1602, New Englanders were drying well over a quarter of a million codfish annually. Cod, which has always been associated with Boston, had quickly become a New England staple. Today, with large trawlers and refrigeration, dried salt cod is of less importance. In any case, northern countries never made a virtue of necessity nor did anything very much with salt cod gastronomically. 'Salt cod,' says the Revd J.G. Wood in his famous Natural History (1863) 'is to many persons a great dainty, but to others, among whom I must be reckoned, it is insufferably offensive, and even with all the additions of sauce and condiment is barely eatable.'

Certainly few people could be sinful on salt cod and parsnips which have been boiled and served with an egg sauce. On the other hand, in the Mediterranean regions, from Spain through Provence, Italy and Greece to Yugoslavia and the Middle East, methods were devised for making this unpromising material as palatable as possible. As a result, Lent could no doubt be endured on a diet of *brandade de morue* with cream and truffles. Now there are at least two hundred delicious ways of preparing what was originally just a very basic fodder. Because salt cod has become a part of traditional cooking, it can be obtained easily anywhere in southern Europe, though it is no longer very cheap. It is hung or stacked up in grocers or in markets, or on sale ready-soaked every Friday. It is even available in plastic packets.

Buying and Choosing. *Bacalao* (which may be ling as well as cod) should have white flesh and black skin. Yellowish-looking pieces are supposed to be old. In Mediterranean countries, you can usually judge the quality by the price, unless a dishonest merchant has seen you coming. Experts distinguish the thin sides and belly from the thick back and tail. For many dishes, the sides and belly part, which is not so good looking, is better, being more gelatinous and of finer texture. Some cooks go so far as to say that the two parts should be soaked and cooked separately.

Soaking in running water, or in water changed frequently (every 3 hours) is necessary before cooking. Depending on the quality of the fish, 24-48 hours of soaking at room temperature is needed. A modern method from Spain leaves the salt cod soaking undisturbed in a bowl (on a rack so the water can reach underneath) in the refrigerator for 2 days. The water is not even skimmed. After that, a final soaking for 6 hours, with a couple of changes of water, will make the fish ready to cook.

Scalding. Some people, notably the Basques, scald the salt cod after it has been soaked. They put it in a pot of cold water, skin-side up, and put it on the heat until the water is not quite boiling. After this, the fish is taken out or left to cool in the liquid, according to the requirements of the subsequent preparation. After scalding, the fish can be boned.

Poaching is the more usual preliminary to cooking. Use an earthenware or enamel pan, as metal can cause discoloration. It is also best to use rainwater. Poaching time is 16-18 minutes. As salt cod must never boil (as it will then become stringy), bring it almost to boiling, then throw in a glass of cold

water, and finish the poaching on the lowest possible heat. Allow 150-200 g (5-7 oz) per person.

Bacalao a la vizcaina

One of the great classical dishes of northern Spain. The fish is cooked in a spicy, but not too spicy, red pepper sauce made with *ñoras* – globular red *sweet peppers which visitors to Spain have certainly seen dried and hanging in chains in the shops.

Soak 1 kg (2¼ lb) *bacalao* and 12 *ñoras* (de-seeded, skinned if possible and chopped) for 24 hours. Cut the fish into matchbox-sized bits and scald (as described above), leaving it to cool in the broth. Reserve about 250 ml (½ pt) of broth. Bone the fish. Flour it lightly and fry without browning it in a little oil. Arrange in a casserole, skin side down. Add the rest of the 250 ml (½ pt) oil to the frying pan. Fry 50 g (2 oz) cubed bread until it is brown, then add 50 g (2 oz) scraps of raw ham or unsmoked bacon, 2 cloves garlic, 450 g (1 lb) chopped onions, a bay leaf and the *ñoras*. When the onion is cooked, add 1 heaped teaspoon *pimentón* and moisten with some of the reserved stock in which the *bacalao* was scalded. Cook the flavourings for a further 10 minutes, then put them through a Mouli to make a sauce. Adjust the salt and sugar. Add more broth if necessary. Cover the *bacalao* with the sauce and cook in the oven, shaking the casserole from time to time for 15 minutes or until everything is hot.

SALTPETRE takes its name from the Latin *sal petrae* (salt of stone); chemically it is potassium *nitrite (KNO_2) formed by denitrifying bacteria. Although a pure nitrate will not redden meat, it does have a preservative effect, as it is particularly active against the lethal anaerobic *Clostridium botulinus* (*see* poisoning). When nitrites are put directly (in tiny amounts) into commercial cures, some saltpetre is also added. As saltpetre hardens meat, it should not be used to excess. Saltpetre is a powerful oxidizing agent (which is why it is used in gunpowder and fuses), so butchers often mix a proportion of it with the sawdust used in smokehouses. It starts the sawdust burning and ensures that it smoulders steadily.

[*Saltpetre* – French: *salpêtre* German: *Salpeter* Italian: *salnitro* Spanish: *salitre*]

SAMBAL. South East Asian term covering both dishes of meat or fish fried with chillies and condiments in which chillies are an important constituent. The latter are equivalent to the Middle Eastern *harissa but contain a wider variety of ingredients, such as *trasi. A number of these sambals are sold in jars and should be used with great caution as they can be extremely fiery. Recipes for both sorts of sambal are in Rosemary Brissenden's South East Asian Food (Penguin).

SAMBUCA. See liqueurs and cordials.

SAMPHIRE or **Rock samphire** (Crithmum maritimum) is an umbelliferous plant with thick fleshy leaves which grows wild on cliffs over much of Europe and locally in Britain. It has a very strong, pungently aromatic smell and taste. Pickled samphire, though nowadays almost unknown commercially in Britain, is still commonly sold in Spanish markets. It may also be eaten as a vegetable (cooked in butter) or put into salads, though it is rather strong for that purpose.

In the US, the plants that are often described just as samphire are not Rock samphire but Marsh samphire, usually known in Britain as glasswort. These peculiar plants, members of the genus Salicornia, belong to the same family as beets and spinach, but have fleshy leaves surrounding the stem, so that the plants look as if they have fleshy stems and no leaves. They are very common in salt marshes.

[Samphire – French: fenouil de mer, bacile German: Meerfenchel Italian: critmo, finocchio marino Spanish: hinojo marino]

SAND-EEL or **sand-lance** is any North Atlantic fish of the genus Ammodytes, as well as a Mediterranean relative, Gymnammodytes cicerellus. All are very elongated and none exceeds 20 cm (8 in) in length; they escape from predators by burrowing into the sand, which they can do with great speed. According to Alan Davidson, sand-eel is often referred to (and used as) *whitebait in the US.

[Sand-eel – French: lançon, equille, cicerelle German: Sandaal, Sandspierling Italian: cicerello Spanish: barrinaire]

SAN PELLEGRINO. See water (mineral water).

SANWA. See millet.

SAPSAGO. See Schabzieger.

SAPODILLA, **sapodilla plum**, **tree potato**, **sapota**, **zapote**, **naseberry** or **chiku** (and various spellings of the last two). The sapodilla (Achras sapota) grows wild in the forests of southern Mexico and the northern part of Central America. As a cultivated fruit, it has now spread all over the tropics and is commonly seen in the markets of India, South East Asia, the West Indies and tropical America. It is also grown in Florida and in Israel. However, it is at its best when grown in a strictly tropical climate. Since it will keep at least 5-6 weeks if picked immature and shipped in cold storage, it could easily be exported to the colder countries, where it has not yet become popular.

The tree is small, slow growing and evergreen, with glossy light green leaves and a wood that is famous for its durability – carvings over 1000 years old have withstood the tropical climate in Mayan ruins. It therefore seems likely that the fruit was eaten in the days of this ancient civilization.

The sapodilla looks like a regular, rounded or oval potato with a rough brown skin covered in scurf which begins to be lost as the fruit ripens. At the same time, it becomes more orange and less brown. Since the fruit is quite uneatable before it is ripe and is usually picked immature, it is as well to know that an unripe fruit shows green when it is scratched with the thumb nail; in ripe fruit, the scratch shows yellow. Since unripe fruit will ripen if left in a basket in a warm room, it is not necessary to anger the fruiterer by scratching his fruit. Ripening can be held back or the ripe fruit can be stored for some time in the refrigerator.

The fruit is usually eaten as an uncooked dessert fruit. It must be peeled. Inside there is an orange-brown or yellow-brown, slightly grainy translucent flesh. There is a core with a few large shiny black seeds which are easily removed. Poor varieties have a hard flesh and a gritty texture; good ones are soft and smooth. The taste may best be described as 'vegetable brown sugar'. You may find sapodillas delicious, but equally you may think them oversweet and lacking in acidity. They are liked by children and may be an interesting addition to a fruit bowl which is intended to be a decorative feature of the table.

They may be made into a jam, preferably with citrus or other more tasty fruits. They contain 8-12% sugar and, in the West Indies, are boiled down into a fine syrup.

The names of this fruit are exceedingly confused. Sapodilla is the name used in Florida, derived from the Spanish zapotillo, meaning little zapote.

The name sapota or sapote really belongs to the unrelated Marmalade plum (*Calocarpum sapota*) and the Green sapote (*C. viride*), so is better avoided. All these names come from the native *tzicozapotl* or *tzapotl*, as does also chiku, which is a good name to use. The name naseberry is a corruption of the Spanish for *medlar, a fruit from the quite unrelated rose family. The French also use the term *nèfle d'Amérique* which also means American medlar. The White sapote (*Casimiroa edulis*) is not a relative and belongs to the same family as rue and citrus fruits. The most important use of the sapodilla is as a source of chicle, which is the white latex from the tree. It is the correct basis for chewing gum and exported in quantity from Central America.

[*Sapodilla* – French: *sapotille, nèfle d'Amérique* German: *Sapotiglis* Italian: *sapota, sapotiglia* Spanish: *chicozapote*]

SAPUCAYA NUT. *See* brazil nut.

SARACEN CORN. *See* buckwheat.

SARDINE (*Sardina pilchardus*) is a young pilchard, a fact that was not known a hundred years ago when they were thought to be different fish. Since ancient times the sardine has been fished in the Mediterranean with lights on calm, moonless nights, at first with torches, then with acetylene lamps and today with bigger boats and electricity. Sardines swim in shoals and are caught in huge quantities, far exceeding immediate demand. In the past, they were salted and dried. They are used today in this form mainly in Mediterranean countries. In Spain, these sardines are often used to garnish local types of *coca* or pizza.

Sardines were the first fish to be canned (in 1834). The canning business is now enormous, particularly in Portugal. The method was evolved of canning sardines in olive oil (which in the early days took care of any imperfect sterilization), but since olive oil has gradually become expensive, the cheaper grades are now more usually canned in other edible oils. There are also sardines canned, for example in tomato sauce, in *escabeche* or with chillies, and quality has suffered as a result. In Edwardian times, the best grocers sold only sardines they had matured and turned regularly for several years, but French sardine canners consider that such practices are foolish and that two years is the maximum time that sardines should be kept – and French sardines are reputedly the best. Famous names are Phillippe et Canaud, Saupiquet,

Cassegrain and Amieux, but the Rolls-Royce of the sardine world is canned in Bordeaux by Rodel whose sardines are grilled and then matured for a year in vats of olive oil before canning. They are expensive and scarce. Connoisseurs claim that fine sardines should be served without seasoning on slices of hot buttered toast (although the French opt simply for bread and butter), but cheap sardines are improved by black pepper and lemon juice.

Fully grown sardines are fished off the coast of Cornwall as pilchards or gipsy herrings. The catch was originally just salted, or salted and smoked for export; smoked pilchards were known as 'fair maids', which was said to be a corruption from the Spanish. Pilchards today are canned, but those in tomato sauce are often small herrings. As fresh fish, pilchards can be distinguished from small herrings by raised lines that run backwards from the eyes. On the other hand, sprats have a line of spiny scales which form a keel to the belly. Their young, canned in oil like sardines, are sold as brisling.

Fresh sardines are popular near coasts where they are caught. They were not thought to travel well, but are now exported frozen in some quantity. On their native shores, they are cheap, oily, and delicious. Completely fresh sardines are possibly at their best cooked in the simple Spanish style, *a la plancha* – just thrown on top of a hot stove, cooked on both sides and served with parsley and lemon juice. However a Marseilles chef, Monsieur Caillat, collected a hundred and fifty sardine recipes for his book, and there are certainly more.

In the US, all real sardines are imported, as there are no true sardines in America; for local canning, young herrings are used in their place. Similar species of fish are found all over the world. Examples include the Oil sardine (*Sardinella longiceps*) and the Rainbow sardine (*Dussumieria acuta*), which is fished and canned off the south-west coast of Kerala in India.

[*Sardine* – French: *sardine* German: *Sardine* Italian: *sardina* Spanish: *sardine*]

SASSAFRAS (*Sassafras albidum*) is a North American tree of the laurel family; it yields an essential oil that is present throughout the plant but is most concentrated in the root bark. It lends its flavour to root beer and to sassafras tea, an infusion of the bark, leaves or buds that was popular in parts of the US as a tea substitute in the early 19th century. The dried leaves are used to make *filé powder.

[*Sassafras* – French: *sassafras* German: *Sassafras* Italian: *sassafrasso* Spanish: *sasafrás*]

SATÉ. *See* peanut.

SATSUMA. *See* orange.

SATURATED SOLUTION. A solution containing the maximum amount of salt, sugar, soda or any other substance that can be dissolved in a volume of water. If more of the substance is added, it will lie undissolved on the bottom of the vessel. However, the quantity that will dissolve increases with temperature. Sometimes there is only a small rise in solubility as with salt, but at other times the increase is spectacular, as with saltpetre.

SAUCISSE. A small French or Swiss sausage (as opposed to the large *saucisson*). *Saucisses* are usually 2.5-4 cm (1-1½ in) in diameter and fresh rather than cured, so that they are for cooking and eating hot. They include French equivalents of *chorizos* (*saucisses d'Espagne*) and Frankfurters (*saucisses de Francfort* and *saucisses de Strasbourg*). *Saucisses de campagne*, country sausages, are made of mixed lean pork and fat bacon. They are dried for up to a week and contain seasonings that vary widely according to charcutier and locality. Poached gently for 20 minutes rather than fried, they are used in heavy soups and stews for the winter. Sausages of greater refinement include *saucisses de Périgord*, with black truffles and white wine, and *saucisses au champagne*, lightly spiced and flavoured with champagne and black truffles. *Saucisses de Toulon*, which contain meat that is coarsely chopped rather than minced, are the correct sausages to use in the regional *cassoulet*. *Saucisse en brioche* is sausage baked in a *brioche* paste, something like a very large and delicate sausage roll, which is sold by the slice. It is warmed and eaten as a first course.

SAUCISSON. Large or very large sausage from France or Switzerland. *Saucissons* are often supported in nets or bound. They are salted, dried and usually smoked but not cooked. Before they are ready to eat, they are kept for four or, better still, six months. Like cheese, they are now mainly a factory product and are matured, sometimes with the help of moulds growing on the skin. They are sliced and sold by weight usually for eating cold as an *hors d'oeuvre* or in sandwiches. The many types have minor variations in texture and content. Many are named after their places of origin. The odd one out is *cervelas, which is a boiling sausage and intermediate between *saucisses* and *saucissons* in size.

SAUERKRAUT is shredded, lightly salted cabbage which has fermented and is preserved by the *lactic acid from the fermentation. It seems probable that it was discovered by the Gauls, who were in the habit of salting food for winter, but the Romans knew the rudiments of making silage (which is animal fodder preserved for the winter by lactic acid fermentation). At any rate, *Sauerkraut* was in use in the Middle Ages. Cabbages and pigs were staples that allowed survival in a hard winter. '*Chi semena le verze e un porco ingrassa par l'inverno al se la passa...*' (roughly: he who sows cabbages and fattens a pig will get through the winter) is the Italian version of a proverb that was relevant for much of Europe. *Sauerkraut* was important, though, in central and eastern Europe, where the ground was often snowed under. Until the arrival of the potato in the 18th century, the other main standby was the beetroot. *Sauerkraut* had the then unrecognized virtue of containing adequate vitamin C. Captain Cook credited the good health of his crews to it long before vitamins were ever heard of.

Western European languages all derive their names for this food from the German (e.g. the French *choucroute*), and Germany and Austria are the centre of the *Sauerkraut* tradition, although it goes west into Alsace and Lorraine, east into Poland and Russia, and south into Hungary, Italy and the Balkans. As a dish of any refinement, *Sauerkraut* doubtless had to wait for the development of fine and suitable cabbage varieties. In the past, it was widely made on farms, but some areas and villages were specially famous for the high quality which they produced. *Sauerkraut* needs space and cool cellars; making it at home can be rather smelly. It can be bought in cans (which mostly come from Holland) or loose from the tub in delicatessens. There are many variations; most commonly, it is flavoured with juniper berries or caraway seed, but some *Sauerkraut* may contain fennel seed and other ingredients like grated quince or beetroot, which colour it respectively yellow and red. (In Russia, it is also quite common to salt and ferment grated beetroot in its own right.)

Sauerkraut is made in a straight-sided tub with a loose top and a false lid that fits down inside it. The cabbages are first weighed and 1½% of their weight of salt is measured out. Some recipes advocate up to 4% salt, but 1½% is more usual. The cabbages are cleaned, washed and finely shredded. The barrel and its lids are scalded, and a white cotton cloth large enough to cover the false lid is sterilized, together with a large, non-porous stone to act as a weight.

The bottom of the tub is usually first covered with a few whole cabbage leaves and then the shredded cabbage is firmly packed down in layers, each sprinkled with salt and with salt on top. The tub ought to be about two-thirds full. It is covered with the cloth, topped with the wooden false lid, weighted down with the stone. In a day, the false lid should be immersed in liquid extracted from the cabbage. Fermentation will begin in which the sugars in the cabbage are turned to lactic acid. Depending on the temperature, the *Sauerkraut* should be ready in about 3 weeks or a little more. The surface of the liquid will become covered with a scum of yeasts or fungi which should be skimmed off. A sample of the *Sauerkraut* may be taken with a wooden fork for testing. When the cabbage is ready to eat, the liquid on top is taken off with a wooden bowl (and makes a good soup), the required amount of *Sauerkraut* is taken, and the cloth, which has first to be rinsed in boiling water is put back with the false lid and weight on top.

The liquid may be topped up with plain cold water, salt water or white wine. The latter, of course, adds to the flavour. Once fermented, the tub of *Sauerkraut* has to be kept in a cool cellar.

There are many ways of cooking *Sauerkraut*. First, it should be tasted and washed briefly in a strainer held under the cold tap if it seems too acid. (In Austria they like it sour, in Germany less so.) It should then be teased out until it is free of lumps.

Flavourings which can be added include apple, garlic, onion, bay, juniper berries, caraway seed, white wine, fried bacon and bacon rind. A typical way is to fry diced bacon crisp with a little chopped onion, then to add about half the weight of water that you have *Sauerkraut*, a large piece of smoked bacon rind, a small clove of garlic (unpeeled but crushed), a bay leaf, a few juniper berries, a pinch of caraway seeds, a few peppercorns, and salt if needed. Cook slowly for 30-60 minutes, in which time the water should be absorbed – how long it takes depends on the *Sauerkraut*: do not cook it to a mush. If a lot of liquid is left, thicken it with a little cornflour or potato, but not too much. Water in which bacon has been boiled can be used if it is handy, as it often is in restaurants. Serve *Sauerkraut* with boiled bacon, frankfurters or other smoked sausage, bread dumplings and potatoes. The Chinese also make forms of pickled cabbage, as do the Koreans with *kimchi.

[*Sauerkraut* – French: *choucroute* German: *Sauerkraut* Italian: *salcrautte* Spanish: *chucruta*]

SAUSAGE. The word comes from the Latin *salsus*

– salted. Originally, sausages were a means of organizing and preserving the blood and the odd bits of the pig that were left over after the hams and bacon sides had been taken. These bits were mixed with salt, saltpetre, herbs and spices, enclosed in sections of carefully cleaned gut, dried, smoked and hung in a cool place. As sausages, the scraps would keep good for months. Otherwise they had to be eaten immediately, an unnecessary luxury in a hard pressed community. An added bonus was that the sausages would age and mature like cheese; they actually improved in flavour with keeping. Sausages inevitably came to be made not just for survival but also purely for gastronomic delight (apparently becoming so popular in ancient Rome that at one point they were banned). Over the ages, they have attracted much culinary attention, with the finest spices and the best cuts of meat being put into them. However, they were also a godsend for the less scrupulous butchers. As one early 20th century cookery book advises, 'the great advantage of home-made sausages over bought ones is that in the former case one knows what is in them.'

Many sausages have long since lost their original peasant functions: they are often for eating fresh and some are even skinless. In Britain, fresh sausages are usual, but then the British culinary heritage lacks variety in its sausages. There are the university variations on the standard British sausage or banger – the Oxford and Cambridge sausages – as well as sausages of beef, veal, mutton and even turkey but they all have to be eaten fresh and cooked, never raw. The British have no tradition of matured, well hung sausages. Rare recipes for dried sausages prove the rule, because they are clearly foreign in origin (e.g. Yorkshire polony). Some British sausages are called 'puddings' – the black puddings and the white puddings, not to mention the 'great chieftain o' the pudding race,' the *haggis, which can certainly be claimed as a sausage.

Sausages intended to be eaten fresh should not be kept for more than a few days in the refrigerator (although they may be frozen). Commercial sausages often contain preservatives, because their contents offer ideal growing conditions for micro-organisms, including nasty ones like botulism bacteria. Sausages made of raw and uncured pork should always be thoroughly cooked. On the other hand, sausages that are bought already cooked, even if they are intended to be eaten fresh (like frankfurters and black puddings), can be eaten safely cold. A few cooked sausages (e.g. mortadella), will keep for a time if they remain uncut. Rather strangely, in the really long keepers (e.g. salame, chorizo) the meat is uncooked. Sausages made of raw pork are perfectly safe (like raw ham) if they have been properly hung to mature. Any harmful organisms, such as those of *trichinosis, have had time to be destroyed by the salt. One might say the meat has been 'cooked' by the salt and saltpetre content.

Types of sausage for keeping are meant to be hung in a cool, dry place, so that air can circulate all round them – never against a wall. Any cut surface is best protected by a piece of oiled paper. Once sliced, the sausage has to be kept in the least cold part of the refrigerator and must be well wrapped to stop it drying out. The flavour does not improve in these conditions – it is best to buy only what you need for immediate use. Sliced sausage, such as mortadella, bought shrink-wrapped in packets from the supermarket cold cabinet, is usually a convenience food for those who value convenience more than food.

Every European country can offer a range of sausages, some of which are national and local specialities, while others are home-produced versions of sausages which originated abroad (a large number of Scandinavian sausages fall into this category). Some types like frankfurters and salami seem to be made in some form almost everywhere in Europe; less international sausages may spread from their homeland to neighbouring countries and change a little on the way, as in the case of the Spanish *chorizo which becomes the chorizo Basquais and the saucisse d'Espagne in France and the chourico in Portugal. America has adopted the sausage varieties brought in by immigrants from Europe and in some cases has changed them – the Italian Bologna sausage has given birth to a whole range of American descendants. There are also Chinese sausages, which are made of cured pork and tend to contain sugar as well as salt and spices.

Sausages are an important part of French charcuterie. Although the basic number of types is not great, there are hosts of local varieties, often distinguished by the name of the town or locality where they originated, and some with names that are quite unknown except where they are made. The differences between local types are usually small; the excellence of a sausage will depend mainly on the charcutier who makes it. French sausages that need cooking are two made with intestines,*andouilles and *andouillettes, the chubby *boudin blanc and boudin noir (the equivalent of *black pudding),*crépinettes and gayettes (which could be said to approximate to the English

faggots), merguez (a short, spicy sausage for grilling that is Algerian in origin), *cervelas and a variety of *saucisses. Matured and usually large sausages are *saucissons.

The most famous matured sausages of all come from Italy and are plurally known as *salami; they vary from the slick, factory produced versions from Milan to rough, gnarled-looking peasant varieties. Also for eating cold and finely sliced, often as part of a mixed antipasto are sausages in which the ingredients are not chopped or minced but which are made with pieces of cured meat – notable examples are bresaola, coppa and culatello. The most famous cooked sausage for eating as a cold cut is *mortadella from Bologna. Small fresh sausages for cooking and eating hot are mainly known as *salsiccie. There is also the Italian equivalent of *black pudding, sanguinaccio. Two specialities of Modena and the surrounding area are boiling sausages with a filling that includes pork skin from the head and snout to produce a gelatinous texture. They are *cotechino, which comes in a sausage skin and *zampone, which is a boned and stuffed pig's foot. Italian sausages may bear official tags made of metal to indicate the meat content: S for pork (darne suino) only, SB for pork and beef (suino and bovina), O for mutton (ovino) and E for horse meat (equino).

Although Italy is credited with having the finest sausages, Germany can claim to be the sausage-eating centre of the world, and neighbouring countries in all directions share much of the German passion for sausages. There is no good meal that is more easily prepared than a selection of sliced German sausages with black bread, German mustard, pickled cucumbers and German beer. Sausages for eating cold (either sliced or, in the case of the softer varieties, spread) include *Bierwurst, Blutwurst (*black pudding) and its Thuringian variant Rotwurst (which contains black pepper and large lumps of meat), *cervelat, and finely ground Extrawurst; Leberwurst (*liver sausage), Mettwurst and Teewurst are often soft and spreadable. Landjäger are unusual in being pressed into a square shape; they are cured, smoked and dried sausages for eating raw. Raw sausages for grilling are *Bratwurst, but the hot sausages most foreigners associate with Germany are smoked, poached sausages eaten with Sauerkraut, although this is equally a dish from eastern France – surprisingly, more Sauerkraut is consumed in France than in Germany. The internationally famous names are the *frankfurter and the Austrian *Wienerwurst. German sausages, like those from France and Italy, have a plethora of regional and local names. Many are described in Antony and Araminta Hippisley Coxe's *The Book of the Sausage* (Pan).

In any type of sausage, there is always great variation from maker to maker. Governments may define sausage types and may legislate to specify the permitted constituents (how much horse can go into a beef sausage before it becomes a horse sausage), but wide differences in texture and taste are allowed. You can learn about sausages, as about any food, only by trying and tasting boldly.

[*Sausage* – French: *saucisse* German: *Wurst* Italian: *salsiccia* Spanish: *salchicha*]

SAUSAGE SKIN is traditionally made from the cleaned guts of pigs, sheep or cattle, but because of the continual battle for standardization and mechanization fought by the big manufacturers, there are now skins which do not vary in size and are made of reconstituted collagen (a sort of dried jelly), cellulose, and even plastic. Small quantities of skins suitable for home use can usually be ordered through the local butcher. They range in diameter from narrow sheep casings for little chipolatas, to wide beef bungs for mortadella or other large sausages. Real skins are preserved in salt – usually dry but sometimes in brine – and will keep indefinitely. When needed, skins should be soaked in fresh water for twelve hours or so, and washed out with running water (using the sausage skins like a hosepipe on the tap).

Preparing your own sausage skins is a fiddly job (commercially, they are cleaned by machine), and is hardly something to tackle except on the farm, as it involves washing out the intestines, cutting them in suitable lengths, dissecting away the mesentery and fat, turning the guts inside out over a stick, and scraping off the slimy inner lining. This comes away more easily if the skins are first soaked in frequent changes of clean water for a couple of days, as this allows the glandular lining to soften. However, in Spain, where the annual *matanza* (pig killing) is still a lingering custom, the cleaning is done with salt and lemon juice, all on the same day, as meat from a pig killed in the morning has to be minced, salted, spiced and packed into sausages before night. Indeed, in primitive conditions the job had always to be done without delay. However, skins made in the old way look somewhat heavy and opaque. The commercial skins of today are more elegant and are often bleached for the sake of appearance.

[*Sausage skin* – French: *peau à saucisse* German:

Wursthaut Italian: *pelle di salsiccia*]

SAUTÉEING. From the French *sauter* (to jump), this is cooking food in hot fat while shaking or tossing the ingredients. The correct pan is a *sautoir*, which looks like a frying pan with upright, slightly higher than normal sides, to prevent the food falling out when it is being shaken.

SAVELOY is etymologically the English equivalent of *cervelas. It is made commercially with finely minced cured pork plus cereal and is smoked. Heated in the deep fryer, saveloys are one of the less delicious sidelines of some fish and chip shops. The home-made saveloy, however, is doubtless a far, far better thing.

SAVORY. A labiate herb that is little used in English cooking, but is of some importance in France, Switzerland and Germany, where it is traditionally used for flavouring beans. There are two species commonly grown, both Mediterranean plants – summer savory (*Satureja hortensis*) and winter savory (*S. montana*),which is generally regarded as the less good of the two.The taste is vaguely like thyme, but much more bitter and biting; savory is a distinctive herb, to be used with discretion, as you can easily have too much of it. In Provence (as *poivre d'âne*) and in the Basses Alpes in France, savory is the traditional covering for the small white Saint Marcellin cheeses (although some are now covered in rosemary).

[*Savory* – French: *sarriette* German: *Bohnenkraut, Kölle, Winter Bergminze* Italian: *savore, santoreggia* Spanish: *sabroso*]

SAVOY. *See* cabbage.

SAWFISH. *See* shark.

SCALD. *See* flatfish (lemon sole).

SCALDING is in most cases the same as *blanching. It also refers to pouring boiling water over a freshly killed pig to loosen the bristles, which can then be scraped off with a knife.

[*Scalding* – French: *blanchir* German: *abkochen, abbrühen* Italian: *scottare* Spanish: *limpiar con agua muy caliente*]

SCALLION. *See* onion.

SCALLOP or **scollop** is the fan-shaped shell on

which the Shell Oil trade mark is based. There are many species in all seas. Unlike the majority of bivalves, scallops can swim by flapping their shells together, though many can also attach themselves like mussels to weeds, or rocks by a byssus of threads. They are usually obtained by dredging or trawling. Scallops are often opened and cleaned by the fishmonger (or processed at sea, with only the muscle being brought ashore, usually frozen); otherwise they should be well scrubbed and then opened with a knife, as are other bivalves. The white muscle, which is eaten, is most easily cut out with scissors. In Europe – but not in America – the red 'tongue' or 'coral' is included with the white muscle. The rest is discarded, although the beard can go into soup.

Scallops are most often cooked in a sauce and served in the shell – there are many fine recipes, particularly from France. A typically Norman example is *coquilles Saint-Jacques havraise* – scallops sautéed in a shallot butter, mixed with prawns, and heated in the shell with a sauce made of thick cream, flavoured with white wine, Noilly Prat vermouth and black pepper.

The species that is found around the coasts of northern and western (Atlantic) Europe is the Great scallop (*Pecten maximus*).The usual Mediterranean species, the Pilgrim scallop (*P. jacobaeus*), is a little smaller but is also prized; it is best in autumn and winter. Another large North Atlantic species that is commercially fished from America is the Atlantic deep-sea scallop (*Placopecten magellanicus*).A smaller, northern species is the Iceland scallop (*Chlamys Islandica*). Other small species may be eaten raw as well as cooked; among them are the Queen scallop or quin (*C. opercularis*) and the Variegated scallop (*C. varta*), known in France respectively as *vanneau* and *pétoncle*, and the Bay scallop (*C. irradians*), which is the best scallop of eastern North America. All species can be cooked in the same ways.

The white muscle meat of the fan shell (*Pinna nobilis*) is eaten like the scallop, either cooked or raw, in Mediterranean countries. The shell has a narrow wedge shape and is commonly 50 cm (20 in) long, where the scallops mentioned above are not usually more than 16 cm (6 in) long in the case of the Great scallop, and the small species normally reach only about 8 cm (3 in).

[*Scallop* – French: *coquille Saint-Jacques* German: *Kammuschel* Italian: *pettine, ventaglio* Spanish: *concha de peregrino*]

SCAMPI is the plural of the Italian name (*scampo* is the singular) for the Norway lobster or Dublin Bay prawn (*Nephrops norvegicus*). Because the demand for scampi is so great, other imported crustaceans are often substituted (when the tails alone are sold, only experts can tell) and the name has rather lost its original meaning. Even the Dublin Bay prawns fished around Britain are not as tasty as scampi from the muddy sand bottom of the Adriatic, and the substitutes are often very inferior. The *scampo* is a fairly close relative of the lobster, with claws and the same general anatomy, but is much smaller – no more than 25 cm (10 in) long at the very most. The meat is in the abdomen or tail. While perfectly fresh scampi tails may be poached for around 10 minutes in salted water and served with no more than melted butter, the average Italian recipe is much fiercer. For instance, the tails might be threaded on skewers alternately with sage leaves, marinated for an hour in oil and cognac, then grilled briefly (basted with the marinade) over a clear fire. Although they are such a popular commodity today, scampi were almost unheard of outside Italy until after World War II. Indeed the very name Dublin Bay Prawn was almost a term of contempt describing the part of the catch that could be sold only by being hawked through the streets of the city. In the US, scampi can be the tails of any large shrimps.

[*Scampi* – French: *langoustines* German: *kaisergronate* Spanish: *cigalas*]

SCARLET RUNNER. *See* runner bean.

SCHABZIEGER or **sapsago** (US). Hard Swiss cheese containing *melilot from the Glarus region near Zurich. An important flavouring.

SCOLLOP. *See* scallop.

SCORZONERA. *See* salsify.

SCOTCH PIECES or **SCOTCH**. *See* sugar.

SCREWPINE. *See* kewra.

SCROD or **schrod** is baby cod or halibut, and is highly regarded along the New England coast. The flavour is delicate, and it is best cooked simply.

SEA ANEMONE is a polyp, a primitive animal related to corals and jellyfish. It consists essentially of a digestive sac, and a ring of tentacles surrounding the mouth (which doubles as the anus).The tentacles are armed with special cells which shoot out poison darts to paralyse their prey.

These often beautiful, flower-like creatures are not commonly used as food, but two European species are eaten in France. They are the Beadlet (*Actimia equina*) and the Oplet or Snakelocks anemone (*Anemonia sulcata*), a species with longer tentacles. Both vary in colour from brown to green, but the Beadlet, as its French name *tomate de mer* (sea tomato) suggests, may also be red. Both are common in British waters. To prepare them, remove the tentacles, turn the rest inside-out and wash the body cavity clean. Remove any sand and rock adhering to the foot. Use them in soup or fry them in batter. Alan Davidson's *Mediterranean Seafood* (Penguin) gives recipes for this little known esculent.

[*Sea Anemone* – French: *anémone de mer, ortie de mer* German: *Seeanemone* Italian: *anemone di mare* Spanish: *anémona de mar*]

SEA CUCUMBER is a holothurian, a roughly sausage-shaped relative of sea anemones and sea urchins. Dried holothurian, known as *bêche de mer* or *trepang*, is used in Chinese cooking. To prepare these unpromising objects, which are bought whole, first wash and clean them, then soak them overnight. Next day, blanch them for 5 minutes in boiling water, cut them open and gut them. Simmer them for 4 hours and they will swell and become gelatinous.

[*Sea Cucumber* – French: *cornichon de mer, concombre de mer* German: *Seewalze, Seegurke, Meergurke* Italian: *cetriolo di mare, cocomero di mare* Spanish: *cohombro de mar*]

SEA DATE or **date mussel** (*Lithophaga lithophaga*). A bivalve, the size, shape and colour of a date, which lives in holes which it bores in marine rocks. Sea dates are much appreciated in Mediterranean countries for their delicately sweet taste. Though usually eaten raw, they are also excellent when cooked.

[*Sea date* – French: *datte de mer* Italian: *cetriolo di mare, cocomero di mare*]

SEA EAR. *See* abalone.

SEAKALE (*Crambe maritima*) is a cruciferous plant with tough, thick leaves. It grows wild in many places on sea coasts in northern Europe. In the past, it was much cultivated for its blanched shoots which, when cooked like asparagus, were considered a delicacy. Today, it has to be classed as

a rare vegetable. The vogue for seakale in fact lasted for only about 150 years, since its cultivation dates from the end of the 18th century though from time immemorial the inhabitants of various parts of the coast have been in the habit of searching for it when blanched by the drifted sand, and cutting off the white shoots close to the crown of the plant. It is the blanching process which makes seakale so delicate. Unblanched it is worthless. Wild seakale may be blanched intentionally by piling up shingle to cover the crowns. The action of light gives seakale a bitter taste; it must always be kept in the dark until it is cooked and should never be bought if it has the slightest colour. In Britain, it is one of the earliest vegetables and has a season from January to June. In the US, it is virtually unknown.

To prepare seakale, wash it carefully, brushing it, if necessary, to remove grit. Cut out the black parts of the roots and tie the rest in bundles, as for asparagus. Put it into rapidly boiling, salted water and fast-boil it until it is tender. Drain and serve it with melted butter. Tender young seakale will take 20-30 minutes but older plants can take up to 50. The water should be changed half-way through cooking if it has become bitter.

[*Seakale* – French: *chou marin, chou de mer* German: *Strandkohl* Italian: *cavolo marino* Spanish: *berza marina*]

SEA LETTUCE. *See* seaweed.

SEA-MOSS. *See* carrageen.

SEA SPINACH. *See* beets.

SEARING is sealing the surface of meat at the start of cooking by briefly exposing it to very strong heat.

SEA URCHIN. A spiny, more or less spherical creature related to starfish and sea cucumbers. Many species are eaten around the world. In Europe, the species known as the Edible sea urchin is *Echinus esculentus*, which is 12 cm (5 in) across and occurs from Scandinavia to Portugal, but this is less delicate in flavour than two smaller species of 7-8 cm (3 in) across. These are the northerly Green sea urchin (*Strongylocentrus droebachiensis*), which occurs on both sides of the Atlantic down to the English Channel and New Jersey, and the more southerly *Paracentrotus lividus*, which is dark purplish-brown, almost black in fact. The latter is the sea urchin commonly eaten in Mediterranean regions (it is found as far north in the Atlantic as

Gulf Stream-warmed southern Ireland). In the past, sea urchins were sometimes called sea-eggs, because they were dipped for a very short time in boiling seawater, opened and eaten like eggs. All the contents except the gut are edible, but more often only the roes (five equally spaced vertical strips of orange stuff) are scooped up with a soldier of bread and eaten raw with at most a squeeze of lemon. Sea urchins can be opened simply with a pair of scissors: poke a blade through the shell and cut round the equator (there are fancier ways and a special cutter called a *coupeoursin*). Be careful not to get spines in your fingers. Remove the digestive tract and wash the rest in seawater. Sea urchins are at their best when the roes are ripe, just before breeding. They may be gathered easily by skin divers, but it is a job that requires gloves. The urchins must be alive until you are ready to eat them; once they are dead, they do not keep. There are recipes for cooking the roe with scrambled egg, and it makes a wonderful sauce if it is scooped out with a spoon and mixed with a little mayonnaise in the liquidizer. The flavour is vaguely like crab. A paste of sea urchins (*uni*) can be bought in shops that specialize in Japanese food.

[*Sea urchin* – French: *oursin* German: *Seeigel* Italian: *riccio di mare* Spanish: *erizo de mar*]

SEAWATER is used sometimes as a cooking liquid for fish or shellfish, especially in fishermen's recipes. Because of the many substances dissolved in it, seawater has a certain bitterness which is not found in a brine of pure *salt.

[*Seawater* – French: *eau de mer* German: *Seewasser, Meerwasser* Italian: *acqua di mare* Spanish: *agua de mar*]

SEAWEED belongs to the group of primitive plants called algae. These can be divided into three main groups – green, red and brown – of which the brown are the most plentiful, especially in northern seas, but the least interesting to the cook. Commercially, however, they have become very important in recent years as a source of alginates, the jelly-like, mucilaginous substances which are used as stabilizers and general goo-producers in the food industry. For example, in commercial ice cream, they keep the emulsified pig's fat in suspension and prevent the growth of ice crystals.

Of the green algae, the only one of any importance in Europe is the Sea lettuce (*Ulva lactuca*),which actually looks rather like lettuce leaves that have become wilted and transparent

with age. It is also known as Green laver, Lettuce laver or ulva; it is cooked like true laver, but is less interesting. True *laver which has gastronomic importance and an entry to itself, belongs to the red algae along with dulse, *carrageen, and the seaweeds from which *agar-agar is obtained.

Dulse (*Rhodymenia palmata*), in theory, is supposed to be used raw in salads – and must have its devotees. There are also mentions of dramatic Scottish recipes, which include wrapping it around red-hot tongs, but it is also referred to as a masticatory, and they can say that again. I chewed some long ago, when on a marine biological course at Port Erin, Isle of Man, and it seemed like rubber sheeting laced with iodized salt. However, André Simon says that the great Alexis Soyer included it in his St. Patrick's Day Soup. Dried dulse remains pliable, and the Irish used to chew it like tobacco, just as Icelanders today chew another red alga, Pepper dulse (*Laurencia pinnatifida*),which has a pungent flavour and, according to Alan Davidson in *North Atlantic Seafood* (Penguin), was used in Scotland as a condiment rather than a food.

The subject of edible seaweeds is a happy hunting ground for those interested in what the half-starving Irish or Hebridean crofters managed to live on in the past (they were hard and healthy people when they survived), but is worthy of only a brief mention here.

Kelp,the general name for any of the brown seaweeds, is a source of iodine (as extracts or tablets) in health diets. Murlins (also called dabberlochs, henware or honeyware) is *Alaria esculenta*, a brown alga, but, as its specific name suggests, it is edible, if less palatable than the red algae. Tangle and redware (*ware* and *ore* mean seaweed) are words used in Scotland and New England but do not have exact meanings except locally – in Orkney, redware is Pink laver (*Porphyra lacinata*).

Seaweeds are eaten in many other parts of the world. For instance, there is the *Durvillea antarctica*, the *alga mar* (seaweed) of Chile, which is exported to the US. However, it is in Japan that the use of seaweed is of vital gastronomic importance, so much so that many species are cultivated. (Seaweeds are also cultivated in other parts of the Pacific, for instance in Hawaii, where seventy varieties are eaten.) *Kombull is the seaweed ingredient of the ubiquitous Japanese stock, *dashi*, for which black sheets of the dried weed are cut into small bits; it can also be made into a tea, or soaked and cut in strips for wrapping up pieces of raw fish to make *sushi*. *Nori*, from a red seaweed related to laver, is also dried in black sheets and is also used for wrapping *sushi*; after crisping over heat, which makes it go purplish, it can be crumbled over foods as a flavouring and garnish. *Wakame*, which comes in long curly strands, is soaked, the leaves are opened out and the midrib is removed; this seaweed may be used as a decoration.

Less use is made of seaweed in China than in Japan, but various kinds can be bought in Chinese markets. Purple laver is dried for use in vegetable soups. There is also a hair-like seaweed used in savouries and vegetable dishes. All dried seaweeds need to be soaked before use.

[*Seaweed* – French: *algue* German: *Alge* Italian: *alga* Spanish: *alga*]

SEMOLINA. The word comes from the Italian and refers to the larger particles of endosperm which are sifted out in the milling of cereals. Although it was originally applied to durum wheat, it may now mean any very coarse flour (e.g. rice semolina, maize semolina). Unqualified, though, it always means semolina from wheat.

Semolina differs from flour, which is much finer, in that when cooked it has a texture more like a porridge than a paste. This makes for lightness in many dishes. For instance, *gnocchi* made with fine flour are stodgy unless they are lightened by the addition of other substances such as semolina or mashed potato. Cooked semolina is an excellent binding agent for *croquettes*.

Nursery semolina puddings give no indication of the wonderful sweets in which semolina is used in the Middle East and in India. When fried in butter to a pale golden colour and then sweetened, the taste of semolina is delicious. Some of these confections are dry, with the semolina grains remaining separate – almost like a *couscous.

[*Semolina* – French: *semoule* German: *Griessmehl* Italian: *semolino* Spanish: *semolino*]

SELSCHCAREE. *See* bacon.

SELTZER. *See* water (mineral water).

SERCIAL. *See* madeira.

SEREH or **serei**. *See* lemon grass.

SERVICE TREE and **SERVICE BERRY**. *See* rowan.

SESAME. A few years ago, the word sesame had only one association for people in Britain and the US; Ali Baba and the Forty Thieves. Now people know about **tahina* and even about the use of sesame oil in oriental cooking. Sesame seed is popular in vegetarian diets for its high content of protein and polyunsaturates. The sesame plant (*Sesamum indicum*) probably originated in Africa but has been cultivated in India and China since ancient times. Today it is grown all over the world in tropical and subtropical climates, even in Mediterranean countries, but it will stand no frost. The plant is a strong, erect annual which reaches 2 m (6½ ft) high. When the seeds are ripe, the plants are cut, bundled and stacked upright to dry; they can then be turned upside-down and the seeds shaken out.

Sesame seeds are small, usually white and of a flat pear-shape, but they can be cream to brown, red or black. They contain around 50% oil, which can be extracted by cold pressing. Good sesame oil is almost tasteless and colourless. It can be used for salads and cooking. Under the name of gingelly oil, it is one of the most important cooking oils in South India and in Mexico, although the sesame plant does not give such a high yield of oil per acre as some other oil seeds. When raw, the seed itself is rather tasteless but gentle roasting makes it take on a most delicious nutty flavour. It is used sprinkled like poppyseed over bread and cakes in baking. Mixed with a pinch of *kalonji* (**nigella*) seed, it is often sprinkled on *nan*, the North Indian leavened bread, or simply fried and mixed with sugar. Added to rice, it is used in Indian versions of stuffed peppers. In sweet dishes, sesame seed makes one of the finest *halvas* (which can be bought ready-made in shops selling Turkish specialities).

[*Sesame* – French: *sésame* German: *Sesam* Italian: *sesamo* Spanish: *sésamo*]

SEVICHE. *See* ceviche.

SEVRUGA. *See* caviar.

SHAD are members of the herring family which reach 60 cm (2 ft) in length. They are normally marine fish but swim up rivers to spawn (and this is when they are best for eating). Their big disadvantage is that they are very bony. The European species are the Allis shad (*Alosa alosa*) and the slightly smaller Twaite shad (*A. fallax*). The American shad (*A. sapidissima*) is more popular than its Old World equivalents.

[*Allis shad* – French: *alose* German: *Alse, Maifisch* Spanish: *sábalo*

Twaite shad – French: *alose feinte* German: *Finte,*

Maifisch Italian: *cheppia* Spanish: *saboga*]

SHADBERRY. *See* rowan.

SHADDOCK (*Citrus grandis*) originated in South East Asia, where it is still planted commercially and is called the shaddock in the Caribbean because it was first brought there by a Captain Shaddock; *pomelo* or *pummelo* is the usual name in Asia. It is the largest of the citrus fruits, sometimes weighing as much as 10 kg (22 lb), and looks something like a huge grapefruit with a coarse, thick rind. Inside, shaddocks are often rather dry, with a hollow core, and segments enclosed in thick, tough and leathery membranes, which easily peel away from the flesh beneath. The juice capsules of the flesh are enormous and usually pink. The taste is described as 'aromatic, spicy and bitter' – to me, it is vaguely like the taste of grapefruit with a dash of Angostura. Although the whole fruit is coarse and dry, it can be a very welcome thirst quencher to the traveller who finds it on a hot day. However, the chief distinction of the shaddock is that it is probably the ancestor of the *grapefruit.

[*Shaddock* – French: *pamplemousse* German: *Pampelmuse* Italian: *pampelimosa* Spanish: *pamplemusa, citrus decumana*]

SHALLOT. Although older books give the shallot as a separate species, *Allium ascalonium*, it is now regarded as a variety of onion (*Allium cepa* var. *ascalonium*). Shallots and types known as potato onions and multiplier onions have bulbs that multiply to produce clusters joined at the root end. Shallots may be round and with red-brown skins, like onions, or elongated and with skins tending towards grey blue (in forms which are usually grown further south and have a slight garlic overtone in their flavour). Shallots are much favoured in French cooking and make the best pickled onions. They are more expensive to buy than ordinary onions and are small to peel, but in addition to their special flavour, they also are excellent keepers.

[*Shallot* – French: *échalote* German: *Schalotte* Italian: *scalogno* Spanish: *chalote, cebolleta*]

SHAMA. *See* millet.

SHANK. The lower part of the front leg in mutton and lamb.

SHARK, dogfish, ray and skate are grouped

together, because they have skeletons of hard cartilage and not of true bone. In some ways they are a rather primitive group – the first sharks appeared on earth some 300 million years ago, since when they seem to have changed little. Their skin is covered with tooth-like scales (which may be large on some rays), and is rough, like sandpaper. All the cartilaginous fish are carnivorous (although some, such as the whale sharks, feed by straining small crustaceans out of the water).They are entirely marine, despite the fact that some sharks may venture some distance up large rivers, such as the Amazon and the Ganges.

I think that no cartilaginous fish reaches the highest gastronomic pinnacle (except in *shark's fin soup), but many make good food. In general, they can stand a little over-cooking – one reason for the popularity of dogfish and skate in fish-and-chip shops – and there is no problem with bones. All cartilaginous fish are likely to smell of ammonia, because of the presence of urea in the tissues, as they have a somewhat different physiology to other fish – the concentration of urea counteracts the osmotic effect of seawater, which would otherwise be constantly taking water out of their bodies; bony fish cope with the problem by having large and efficient kidneys.

This smell is neutralized by cooking them in black butter or by deep-fat frying, or, if the smell is not strong, by poaching them in acidulated water.

Sharks are not generally thought of as good food in Britain and the US. However, the flesh of many sharks is commonly eaten, and some is quite good. Sharks have the distinction of being the world's largest fish. Whale sharks, which fortunately are inoffensive, grow up to 20 tonnes or more and are sometimes 21 m (70 ft) in length. On the other hand, the smallest shark is only 17 cm (7 in) when fully grown and weighs no more than 70 g (about 3 oz). In general, sharks are not benign creatures, and some are famed for their ferocity, among them the Great White shark (*Carcharodon carcharias*), which can grow to a maximum of 11 m (36 ft).

The Porbeagle shark or Mackerel shark (*Lamna nasus*) is found throughout the world and is seasonally common in British and American waters. It has a stout appearance and gets its name from a fancied likeness to a porpoise. Porbeagles grow to up to 4 m (13 ft) long; although voracious eaters of fish, they are regarded as harmless to man. I have heard of one springing at a fisherman and tearing his clothes, but it is more usual for them to rip the nets. In the past, they were considered inedible by the British, but the French value them as *veau de mer* – the flesh is said to be rather like veal and is dry unless larded. It can be grilled in steaks, like swordfish, and the flavour is delicate and good.

The Blue shark (*Prionace glauca*), also common in European waters, is sometimes passed off as tunny. The Hammerhead shark (*Sphyrna zygaena*), which can be found in the Mediterranean and is common on the Atlantic coast of North America, is quite palatable when young. However, the 3.5m (12 ft) monsters we used to catch on a rope in the Gulf of Carpentaria were not worth eating.

The tope (*Galeorhinus galeus*), a small shark which visits British waters in spring and summer, has become a popular sporting fish in recent years. Large topes run to over 30 kg (67 lb) and can be 3m (10 ft) long. They are liable to smell strongly of ammonia, which has given rise to the nick-name Sweet William, but as with other sharks, the smell will tend to vanish on cooking.

Dogfish are small species of shark, so-called, perhaps, because they sometimes hunt in packs. There are many kinds, varying in size, appearance and the quality of their flesh (which is marketed in Britain as rock salmon or rock eel).They are found in seas almost everywhere. Of the well-known European species, the best may be the Spiny dogfish or Spur dog (*Squalus acanthias*), which has a spine in front of its dorsal fin and reaches a maximum length of 115 cm (45 in).The Smooth hound (*Mustelus mustelus*) is slightly bigger at 160 cm (63 in) and is also considered fairly good eating. The most common British dogfish, though, is the Larger Spotted dogfish or Nurse hound (*Scyliorhinus stellaris*); it can reach 120 cm (47 in) and is a bit coarse and tasteless. The Lesser Spotted dogfish (*Scyliorhinus caniculus*), 75 cm (29 in) long, is also common in British waters and is slightly better.

The US has the same or similar species of dogfish, which may be used for all European recipes. There are few serious recipes for dogfish, although the Italians will take trouble to get the belly of the Spiny dogfish, rather than the back. In Germany, the belly flaps of the dogfish, hot-smoked, are a delicacy.

The Angel fish, Angel shark or monkfish (*Squatina squatina* and other species) is a flattened, bottom-dwelling shark which has its pectoral fins forming 'wings'. It is in many ways intermediate between sharks and rays. Some Angel fish grow up to 3 m (10 ft) long. Although they were once despised as food, their flesh is good and there are few bones.

Rays and skates cannot be distinguished scientifically as both names are given to members of the same group of flattened cartilaginous fish. However, the name skate is very often given to the members of the group that are eaten, while ray describes the vast creatures like the Manta ray or Devil fish, which are caught for sport, the Sting rays, which have a spike and associated poison glands in the tail and can inflict a terrible wound (they are quite good to eat), and the Torpedo ray or Electric ray, of which there are some 35 species, all capable of delivering a powerful electric shock.

Rays and skates are kite-shaped fish with pectoral fins that have been modified into 'wings' in the course of evolution. They swim with undulating, wave-like motions of the wings, and the tail is used mainly as a rudder, although it can also be a weapon. Skates are lazy and slow-swimming, in spite of their supersonic shape. They spend a great deal of their time lying on the bottom, usually on sand or mud, waiting for their prey, which they surprise rather than chase. Species of skate range from less than 1 m (39 in) long to good-sized fish like the Common skate, which can grow to 2.5 m (8 ft). Skates are found in all oceans, but not all the many species are equally excellent. They are often sold skinned and jointed – the wings are the most valuable part. Years ago, it was forbidden to carry whole skate openly through the streets in some parts of Britain, because they were considered indecent.

The Common skate or tinker of Europe (*Raja batis*) has a long, pointed snout and smooth skin. It is considered good eating, as is the Thornback ray (*R. clavata*), another species common in British waters – it also occurs in the Mediterranean, but not on the west side of the Atlantic. Although it grows to only 1 m (39 in) long, it can give a nasty wound with its thorny tail. Common skates on the American East Coast are *R. laevis* and *R. erinacea*, while on the West Coast, *R. binoculata* is found. Skates are not easy to identify, especially the young, which are called 'maids'.

The taste of skate improves with a couple of days' hanging – no more, or the ammonia smell will become too strong. The liver is esteemed; it is poached, pounded and made into a sauce, or slivers of it are put inside skate fillets, which are then rolled up, tied with thread and poached. As the bones are very gelatinous, they give an unctuousness to the flesh when the wings are fried and make a jelly which sets when poached skate cools. In large skates, the thick part of the wing is the best buy, as there is more meat in proportion to skeleton. After hanging, skates are always skinned on both sides.

The Guitar fish (*Rhinobatus rhinobatus*), from the southern Mediterranean, looks a little like the Angel shark but is a true ray. It grows to 1 m (39 in) in length and is moderately good to eat. Similar species from warm seas grow to 2.5 m (8 ft) and are used for liver oil as well as for eating. Also fished as a source of liver oil are the sawfish (species of *Pristis*), large tropical relations of the rays which have a long, toothed 'saw' on the front of the head; they are not usually eaten, as far as I know, although doubtless someone loves them.

[*Porbeagle shark* – French: *taupe, laurie, latour* German: *Heringshai* Italian: *smeriglio* Spanish: *marrajo*.

Hammerhead shark – French: *requin marteau* Italian: *pesce martello* Spanish: *pez martillo*.

Spiny dogfish – French: *aiguillat* German: *gememer Dornhai* Italian: *spinarolo* Spanish: *agulat*.

Smooth hound – French: *emissole* German: *Glatthai* Italian: *palombo* Spanish: *musola, cazón*.

Nurse hound – French: *grande roussette* German: *Hundshai* Italian: *gattopardo* Spanish: *alitán*.

Lesser-spotted dogfish – French: *petite roussette* German: *kleingefleckter Kaltenhai* Italian: *gattuccio* Spanish: *gato*.

Angel fish – French: *ange de mer* German: *Meerengel* Italian: *squadro* Spanish: *angelotte*.

Common skate – French: *pocheteau (blanc)* German: *Glatttroche* Italian: *razza* Spanish: *noriega*.

Thornback ray – French: *raie bouclée* German: *Keulenrochen, Nagelrochen* Italian: *razza chiodata* Spanish: *raya de clavos*.

Guitar fish – French: *guitare de mer* Italian: *pesce violino* Spanish: *peces guitarra*]

SHARK'S FIN and **SHARK'S STOMACH** are much prized in Chinese cooking and are available dried from Chinese provision shops. The dried stomachs, after soaking, are sautéed or made into soup; the fins are made into soup or cooked in other ways. Both are expensive. Top quality fin is in long filament, the lowest quality in odd pieces.

Shark's fin threads, which have been bought ready prepared, should be soaked in water for about 20 minutes before use. Of the cruder dried fins, yellow ones need boiling for about an hour and black ones for considerably longer (boil it for 2 hours, take off the black skin, and boil the flesh again for 1-2 hours in new water, then drain and shred it).The prepared shark's fins (sold in packets) are equivalent to double their weight of yellow

and treble their weight of black. Fresh shark's fins need to be cleaned of all skin, meat and cartilage other than the fin. They can be trimmed, boiled for 5 minutes and left to soak for 4 hours, after which the skin and bones can be separated from the fins. These are then boiled for 6-7 hours, with the water being changed every 2 hours, before they are dried in the sun. Most people will prefer to use a packet of prepared fins.

Soupe aux estomacs de requin (*Canh bong cá*) Soak 100 g (4 oz) dried shark's stomach (*bong cá*) for 1 hour, then drain and cook in hot oil. The stomach softens and swells; after some 20 minutes, it becomes crisp. Put it into 1 lt (1¾ pt) of stock made with chicken and lean pork and add 25 g (1 oz) each of Chinese mushrooms and dried lily flowers (soaked). Season the soup with salt, pepper, monosodium glutamate and powdered ginger, then cover and simmer it for 30 minutes. Make an omelette with 2 eggs, slice it and add it to the soup before serving. Sprinkle with some chopped chervil, chives and tarragon.

SHELL BEAN. *See* kidney bean. US term for a bean that is ripe but not dried.

SHELL FISH is a collective term for aquatic, usually marine, animals that are not fish. The main components in this delicious ragbag of biologically diverse types are *crustaceans and *molluscs.

SHERRY comes from the province of Cadiz in the south-western corner of Spain. The main variety of grape is the white Palomino, which makes the finest wine when it has been grown on the white *albariza* soil. Other grape varieties, notably Pedro Ximenez and Moscatel, are used to make sweetening wines. When the bunches are picked, they are first spread out on esparto grass mats for a day or more to dry, which increases the percentage of sugar in them. Until after World War II, the grapes were, whenever possible, trodden in wooden troughs by men wearing specially nailed boots. (French wine presses were found to give an inferior sherry.) More recently, German presses, which squeeze the grapes more kindly, have been installed. These have replaced the old methods without loss of quality.

Sherry comes from three towns and their areas. Jerez de la Frontera and Puerto de Santa Maria produce very similar wines but Sanlúcar de Barrameda has very different wines and is the source of all the *manzanilla* – the main types of sherry are listed below. A special characteristic of sherry making is the *flor*, a white mat of micro-organisms which forms on the top of some butts several months after the vintage and causes the wine in the butt to develop into *afino*. Another characteristic is the *solera* system, which was introduced around 1800, in which any wine drawn off from the oldest butt is replaced by an equal quantity from the next oldest, which in turn is replaced from the third oldest and so on until finally the youngest wine enters the chain. Sherries are fortified by adding pure alcohol, not necessarily produced from grapes, which prevents unsuitable organisms developing. Sherry is usually also blended and sweetened. There are a few straight sherries, but these entirely natural *finos* and *olorosos* are bone dry, as the sugar has been fermented out, and would not please the majority of drinkers.

When a bottle of sherry is opened, it should not be kept hanging about until the next anniversary. In spite of its high alcohol content, most sherry will deteriorate. Indeed a *fino*, even when unopened, will deteriorate in the bottle and will be noticeably less good in three months. True sweet sherries deteriorate more slowly – some even improve with keeping, but it takes ten years for the difference to show, and then it may not happen. The general rule is to buy sherry as you want it. Dry sherries should be served cold, down to 3-4°C (38°F) for a dry *fino*; 5-10°C (40-50°F) is more usual. A sweeter sherry can be a little warmer and a sweet dessert sherry can be at room temperature. There is no law about this – it depends on personal preference. Since cold interferes with the sensation of sweetness the colder a sherry is served the drier it tastes. Sherry should be served in appropriate glasses, either the special 'dock' glasses or tulip wine glasses, and only filled half way up to allow room for the bouquet to fill the space. Sherry is one of the wines most used in cooking, and a dry sherry is most adaptable for this purpose; sweetness can always be added. Because a sherry is to be used for cooking, it does not mean that any old cooking sherry will do; indeed, the very idea of cooking sherry is an abomination. Equally, however, the special qualities of very rare sherry would get lost in cooking.

Amontillado is considered to have something of the taste of a *montilla* – hence the name. A certain number of *finos* will develop into *amontillados* if they are kept in the butt for eight years or more, but as it will not always happen, and the result is unpredictable, real *amontillados* are rare and costly. What is sold as *amontillado* is a blend which tries to imitate the flavour and is more correctly an *amontillado*-type sherry.

Bristol milk and **Bristol cream**. Bristol milk, the older type, is a sweetened *oloroso*. Bristol Cream is mentioned because it is the most popular sherry in the US. It is a sweetened blend of *oloroso* and *amontillado* sherries made to a secret recipe that belongs to Harvey's of Bristol. Though it is formulated there, the sherries are from Spain.

Cream sherry is sweetened and blended; it is for the end of a meal, to be drunk with sweet dishes, but is better perhaps with strong cheeses such as Gorgonzola, *cabrales* or Roquefort.

Fino. When a *flor* develops on a young sherry (except in Sanlúcar), it turns into a *fino*. This is the lightest type of sherry (except for *manzanilla*) and is pale in colour. A *fino* that is aged in the butt may perhaps turn into an *amontillado* or remain as an aged *fino*; if kept in bottle, it will deteriorate. *Fino* is the most popular type of dry sherry and a good one to steal for use in the kitchen. It can be used in Japanese and Chinese cooking when genuine rice wines are not handy. If a bottle of *fino* is kept handy in the kitchen cupboard, there is, of course, every chance it will go off – a good excuse for drinking it. *Fino* is served cold with prawns, olives and other *tapas*, *meze* or *hors d'oeuvre*.

Manzanilla. Wine from Jerez de la Frontera must be taken to Sanlúcar to become *manzanilla* and Sanlúcar wine to Jerez to turn into *fino*. This is because a rather different *flor* develops in each microclimate, one of the subtleties of wine-making. *Manzanilla* is usually very dry, too dry and severe for most people, and has a slightly medicinal taste. It is normally served cold with seafood and is often drunk with *tapas* at bars in Spain. It is good in cooking, especially in sauces, less so for sweet dishes.

Montilla is not strictly a sherry, for legal reasons, but it is a very similar wine grown on similar white soil a little north of the sherry districts, towards Córdoba. Because the wines of Montilla are naturally rather stronger than sherry, they are not fortified. They have very much the same sherry flavour and a taster will know immediately that they are from the same stable. *Montillas* are fine aperitif wines, less known and often a little cheaper than real sherries. They are excellent for cooking and as an aperitif are served cold like a *manzanilla*.

Oloroso means odorous in the nicest sense. It is the basic wine of the sherry district which has not been changed by a *flor*. It may be sweetened, and fortified with alcohol. An *oloroso* in Spain is dry, but elsewhere it will almost always be sweetened to make it medium. It is the archetypal sherry, the one that people borrow to use in a trifle. With a more expensive *fino* for those who like it dry, an *oloroso* is the basic fuel for a sherry party.

Palo cortado. A rare type of sherry for connoisseurs. It is a separate type, rather dark, but dryish and unusual. It would only be for a special occasion.

Sherry type wines come from South Africa, Australia, California, Cyprus. There is even British sherry, which has been made from dried fruit since the beginning of the century. South African sherries will not be distinguished from run-of-the-mill Spanish sherries except by experts, and even then not in blindfold tests. Others vary in quality from good to awful. You have to rely on your own palate and judgement.
[*Sherry* – French: *vin de Xérès* German: *Sherry, Jerezwein* Italian: *vino di Xeres* Spanish: *jerez*]

SHIITAKE. *See* mushrooms.

SHIN. In beef butchery, the shin is the lower part of the front leg and is equivalent to the shank in mutton or lamb and part of the hand in pork.

SHIRATAKI. *See* noodles.

SHORTENING. Any kind of fat or oil used to make pastry brittle and crisp – i.e. short, an adjective that also crops up in shortbread and shortcake. Shortening is the normal US term for fat, especially that used in baking.

SHRIMP and **PRAWN**. Both names indicate small crustaceans related to lobsters, though much smaller, except for a few giant forms. Most live in the sea or in brackish water, but some are found in rivers and lakes. Great confusion is caused because the English names prawn and shrimp, which originally described two sorts that were fished off British coasts, have now acquired general meanings, and these differ in Britain and the US. In Britain, a shrimp is small – at least in common parlance – and

a prawn is large, but in the US all sizes are now called shrimp. So to Americans, jumbo shrimp is a perfectly logical description. Further confusion is caused by the use, particularly in Scotland, of the word prawn to describe the Norway lobster, alias *scampi.

There are thousands of species of prawn and shrimp in the world and the high prices they fetch have made it commercially worthwhile for them to be flown refrigerated from the most remote places. In the jungle waterways of Asia, you can nowadays find fishermen netting with primitive gear and filling bamboo cages with huge live prawns for eventual shipment half way round the world. Prawns and shrimps are not easy even for a zoologist to identify, and the scientific nomenclature is littered with confusing synonyms. The best that the layman can hope to do is to recognize the types that are in the local market by their appearance and popular name, and, by experience, to get some idea of their quality.

In Europe, small shrimps are usually sold cooked because they are very perishable when fresh – in Britain, they are traditionally cooked in sea water by the fishermen on board the catching boats. They are no longer caught by hand in shrimp nets, but by boats dragging a fine meshed net along the sea-bed. They may also be caught in nets drawn over estuary flats at low tide by horses, or now more often by tractors. In Britain, most shrimps are still hand-peeled; a good peeler can deal with 2.5-3 kg (5½-7 lb) per hour. About 300 shelled shrimps make 500 ml (1 pt).The pint is the measure by which they were traditionally sold. A pint is some 275 g (10 oz) of unpeeled and 340 g (12 oz) of peeled shrimps.

Live shrimps, which you will probably have netted yourself on the shore, should be thrown into boiling seawater as soon as you get home, and cooked for a minute or so. They become opaque when cooked. Depending on the quantity you have in relation to the amount of water and heat, they may be done almost as soon as the pan comes back to the boil, so keep tasting. Shrimps cooked too little are soft; cooked too long and too fast, they go tough, but gross overcooking will turn them into a mush. Shrimps and prawns should be simmered and not violently boiled.

There are machines for peeling the larger deep water shrimps which can handle the work done by as many as 16 hand peelers. To do the job by hand, take the cooked shrimp by whiskers and tail, straighten it out, telescope it a little by pushing the tail towards the head until the shell bulges out and then pull gently apart. The flesh of the tail – the only part that is eaten – should then come free.

The two commonest shallow-water species of the English Channel, North Sea and British coasts are the Brown shrimp (*Crangon crangon*) and the Pink shrimp or Aesop prawn (*Pandalus montagui*),which are respectively 6 cm and 5 cm in length. The Pink shrimp looks prettier, but the Brown tastes better. Famous places for shrimps in Britain are the Lancashire coast, especially Morecambe Bay, the Wash and the Thames estuary. They are much fished in shallow water off Holland and the French coast, as well as in Denmark, where tiny pink shrimps are used to cover an expensive but delicious open sandwich (*rejemad*). In Britain, shrimps potted in butter and flavoured with mace are a famous delicacy which can be bought ready prepared. Frozen shrimps are a poor second; although frozen when fresh, they seem to lose flavour.

Prawn is a word that might beneficially disappear from the English cook's vocabulary. The creature to which it properly refers is the Common prawn (*Palaemon serratus*), a coastal species about 10 cm (4 in) long that is actually not at all common around the coasts of Britain; it is scarcely fished on a commercial basis. Its place in the fish shops is usually taken by the species that the Department of Trade thinks should be called the Deepwater shrimp (*Pandalus borealis*); a second, as yet unexploited, species, *Pandalus bonnieri*, is found off the west coast of Scotland. Both are 10-12 cm (4-5 in) long. The Deepwater shrimp, which is unofficially referred to as the Deepwater prawn or Northern prawn, has been fished for some years by the Danes and Norwegians, but not with any success by the British until 1970.

Cooking is the same as for shrimps, but they will take about 5-7 minutes to cook, and large ones may be peeled before cooking, split down the back, deveined and opened flat. (The fan is left on to serve as a handle.) At least since Victorian times, prawns prepared in this way have been fried as prawn cutlets (butterfly shrimp in the US). King prawns, which usually make this dish today, are imported (e.g. from Malaya). Other old British prawn dishes include prawn and lobster soup, prawn pie and curried prawns in the Anglo-Indian manner.

A pint contains about 40 unshelled and 120 shelled prawns or Deepwater shrimps; the weights would be roughly the same as for shrimps.

A few of the many other prawns found in

European Atlantic and Mediterranean waters need special mention. There are, for instance, the very large and striking blood-red species, *Aristeomorpha foliacea* and Edwards's Red shrimp (*Plesiopenaeus edwardsianus*), which can go up to 30 cm (1 ft) long, although 20 cm (8 in) is more usual; they live at a depth of some 250 m (822 ft).The Red prawn (*Parapenaeus longirostris*) is not quite so large, rarely exceeding 16 cm (6 in) and usually only 12 cm (5 in) long. It lives at great depths and frequently gets squashed when it is hauled up with the other creatures in the trawl. Perhaps this is why it is usually sold cooked in Italian markets, where it is called not only *gambero rosa* (pink prawn) but also *gambero bianco* (white prawn).This and another species, *Aristeus antennatus* (which is red), are known as *gamba* in Spanish restaurants.

In Spain, both species are commonly sold raw in the markets. They are frequently rather soft, with an off smell, but many people acquire a liking for a 'bad prawn' taste (*see trasi*), which blends well with garlic. The aristocrat of the European prawns, and possibly a claimant to the title of best crustacean in the world (its perfumed and delicate flesh is superior to that of any crayfish or lobster) is *Penaeus kerathurus*, which the Spanish call *langostino* and the Italians *mazzancolla* or *gambero imperiale*. Large – around 20 cm (8 in) long – and pale garnet-red striped with dark garnet on the tail, it lives on the muddy bottom off the estuaries of rivers, usually buried with just its head sticking out and at only about 30-40 m (100-130 ft) deep. To eat this fabulous prawn to perfection, you have to go to the Mediterranean, best of all to San Carlos de la Rapita at the mouth of the Ebro river in Spain, where they make a feature of serving them absolutely fresh. The town's badge is a golden prawn. A *langostinara* (prawn feast), which is costly but worth every penny as a gastronomic experience of almost Chinese sophistication, is a meal composed entirely of *langostinos* cooked in different ways. First come plainly-poached *langostinos* with sweet cos lettuce, then *sopa*, a vegetable stock made by boiling onion, garlic, tomato, parsley, oil and salt for a quarter of an hour, in which the *langostinos* are cooked for 3 minutes. After that, they are taken out and peeled. The stock is put through a sieve and thickened with *beurre manié*. The *langostinos* are peeled and served in a soup bowl with the soup poured on top. Next are *langostinos a la plancha*, cooked by sprinkling the top of the stove with salt and laying whole *langostinos* on top. *Langostinos al ron*, a traditional dish in San Carlos de la Rapita, is made by first drying the *langostinos* on top of the stove for a moment and then frying them in fine olive oil. When done, they are flamed in *rum and salted to taste. The fifth dish is *langostinos marinera*. A basic sauce is made by pounding together garlic, parsley, toasted almonds and fried bread. A drop of brandy is added and some tomato purée. The *langostinos* are fried for a moment in olive oil and taken out; into the pan is put the sauce. It is seasoned with a little white pepper and salt, and coloured with a little *pimentón*. Then whole clams (*almejas*) are added, and when they open, the *langostinos* are returned to the pan, fried for 2-3 minutes at most and served. (I am indebted to the kitchen of the Hostal Miami in San Carlos for the skeleton recipes; the proportions are, of course, their secret.)

In the US, which eats more shrimp than any other seafood, there are three important species. The Northern shrimp, the American name for *Pandalus borealis*, is found in northern off-shore waters of both the Atlantic and the Pacific. The Southern shrimp, from south-eastern and Gulf state waters, is of roughly the same size as the Northern shrimp. The North Pacific shrimp which is caught from California to Alaska, is much smaller. However, huge quantities of shrimp are imported from all over the world. The largest come from Pakistan and Ecuador, some of them 60 g (over 2 oz) each, and there are small shrimps from Denmark and Holland. Newer methods of flash-freezing shrimps individually have greatly improved quality, but the best seafood in America, as elsewhere, is found on the coasts, where local shrimps with local names, are cooked in traditional ways.

Shrimps and their relatives are very popular in most regions of the world. For example, in Japan, prawns are eaten in dozens of ways, as you might expect in a country that makes so much use of food from the sea. Famous species are the large *Penaeus japonicus* (20 cm or 8 in long), the common Japanese prawn, and equally large *Penaeus nipponensis*, the Japanese Red prawn. The strangest way the Japanese eat prawns is alive – as Europeans and Americans do oysters. In a ritual called *odori* (dance), the living prawn is beheaded, shelled and gutted so rapidly that the diner can pop it still moving into his mouth. At the other end of the freshness scale, there are preparations of pounded and dried rotten prawns and shrimps used particularly in the cooking of South East Asia. The best known is *trasi, from Indonesia.

[Brown shrimp – French: *crevette grise* German: *Garnele, Krabbe* Italian: *gamberetto grigio* Spanish: *quisquilla gris*.

Common prawn – French: *crevette rose, bouquet* German: *Sägegarnele* Italian: *gamberello* Spanish: *camarón, gamba*.

Deepwater shrimp – French: *crevette nordique* German: *Tiefseegarnele*.

Aristeomorpha foliacea – French: *crevette rouge* Italian: *gambero rosso* Spanish: *langostino moruno*.

Parapenaeus longirostris – French: *crevette rose du large* Italian: *gambero rosa* Spanish: *gamba*.

Penaeus kerathurus – French: *caramote, grosse crevette* Italian: *mazzacolla, gambero imperiale* Spanish: *langostino*]

SHUNGIKU. *See* chrysanthemum greens.

SIERRA. *See* snoek.

SIEVA BEAN. *See* butter bean.

SIFTING. Putting through a sieve to take out lumps or coarse particles, but also a method of mixing (sifting together) and of getting air into flour for lightness.

[*Sifting* – French: *tamiser, passer au crible, sasser* German: *durchsieben* Italian: *stacciare* Spanish: *cerner*]

SILVER (Ag) does not appear to be regarded by anyone as an essential trace metal in the diet. Like most metallic salts, those of silver are poisonous in any quantity. Silver is also very poisonous to micro-organisms; drinking water used to be kept for preference in silver jugs (which helped to purify it, although the reason was unknown). Modern filters of porous material used for purifying water are often impregnated with colloidal silver, which eliminates the need for periodic heat sterilization – otherwise the bacteria live in the pores of the filter and gradually get pushed through like fat men through a maze, but the silver kills them.

Silver is the best of all conductors of electricity – better than copper – and is a good conductor of heat, but it is soft unless mixed in alloy with other metals. It stands up well to ordinary kitchen acids but is easily tarnished by anything containing sulphur, silver spoons go brown if they touch egg, and silver-lined pans should not be used for omelettes. However, silver looks beautiful on an elegant table, and silver-covered copper (Sheffield plate) serving dishes and chafing dishes are the best of all, combining beauty with conductivity. Silver-lined copper pans for making *crêpes* and for *flambés* can be bought in specialist shops. Tinners will sometimes line pans with silver. The result is not much more expensive but is a lot longer lasting than tin.

[*Silver* – French: *argent* German: *Silber* Italian: *argento* Spanish: *plata*]

SIMMERING is cooking just below boiling point, with the liquid just trembling. In the old days, this meant pushing the pan to the side of the stove; with gas and electricity, it is often more difficult. The usual simmering temperature is 96-98°C (205-209°F), but for meat a somewhat lower temperature of 82-87°C (180-189°F) is often recommended. However, the temperatures used in simmering are not precise – that of boiling water is easily recognizable and simmering is just below it. The temperatures are not directly related to those needed to coagulate proteins, kill harmful organisms, or soften tissues. It is likely that cooks who use thermometers can make considerable improvements in their cooking by using lower simmering temperatures than they would otherwise do.

[*Simmering* – French: *boullir lentement* German: *langsam kochen* Italian: *sobbollire* Spanish: *hervir a fuego lento*]

SINGEING quickly with a flame such as that from a spirit lamp is used after plucking to remove the last traces of feathers from poultry.

SKATE. *See* shark.

SKIM MILK or **skimmed milk** is *milk after the cream has been skimmed off, but today is more often milk in which the cream has been removed in a separator. It can be bought in most countries and is much used by people on a low calorie diet.

[*Skim milk* – French: *lait écrémé* German: *entrahmte Milch* Italian: *latte scremato* Spanish: *leche desnatada*]

SKIMMING is removing scum, fat or froth from the surface of a liquid. Scum is usually most easily removed with a perforated spoon; solid fat can be taken off when the liquid is cold (but there are also gadgets – separating spoons – to help separate liquid fat and water).The last vestiges of fat may be removed by applying kitchen paper or blotting paper to the surface.

[*Skimming* – French: *écumer, écrémer* German: *abschäumen* Italian: *schiumare* Spanish: *desnatar*]

SKINNING. *See* drawing.

SKIPJACK. *See* bonito.

SLIVOVITZ. *See* fruit brandy.

SLOE is the fruit of the blackthorn (*Prunus spinosa*), a relative of the plum that grows wild all over Europe. Its equivalent in the US is the wild plum (*Prunus americana*). Sloes look like tiny, spherical plums and have a heavy bloom, which makes them appear blue, although the skin is purple to black when this is rubbed off. The pulp of the fruit is greenish. Even if the sloes are left on the tree until late in the autumn, they never get sweet and are always astringent. Sloes are sometimes used in apple jelly and in dishes with apples to which the sloes add a punch, but their most important use is in sloe gin.

For this, sloes should be gathered in late autumn, pricked or crushed (together with a few of the stones) and put into bottles, which are then filled up with gin. After corking and leaving for a few months, decant the liquid and sweeten it to taste. Sloe gin is a particularly English drink, which was very popular in Victorian times. Recipes abound – several of my aunts kept recipe books which seemed to have contained recipes for little else – but all are essentially the same. Made with 95% pure grape spirit (a method used in Italy), it is even better and becomes very bracing indeed – it might perhaps be called sloe vodka. The lovely dark red colour comes from the skins of the sloes. The French liqueur *prunelle* is also flavoured with sloes.

[*Sloe* – French: *prunelle* German: *Schlehe* Italian: *prugnola, pruna selvatica* Spanish: *endrino*]

SMETANA. A thick, rich sour-cream product, which is basically made by adding a quantity of sweet double cream to sour cream. It is altogether a different product in its native Russia to the *smetana* sold in British supermarkets, which is more like a thick buttermilk.

SMOKED SALMON. The word 'kipper' probably comes from the Dutch *küppen*, meaning to spawn, and was first applied to out-of-season salmon, emaciated objects that were usually split and smoked to make them more palatable. From as early as the 14th century, there are references to the 'kipper times' in the Thames salmon fishery.

Smoked salmon is now an expensive delicacy. To ensure a continuity of supply, it is prepared mainly with frozen salmon from Canada, Norway, Ireland and Britain. The colour of the flesh can vary from the very pale Polish Delta to the rich red of Canadian. The fat content can also vary from 3% to 20%.

To prepare a whole salmon for smoking, gut it and clean the belly cavity; the thick core of blood next to the backbone should be scooped out with a teaspoon. The head is cut off, and the fish is split into two filleted sides, leaving the lug bones on the fish. As a filleted side is rather soft to handle, a loop of string is passed through the lug flaps under the fin on the lug bone. This facilitates handling and is also used to hang up the side, which is then ready to be brined or dry-salted.

Brining gives a much better appearance to the finished side but makes the drying take much longer. More often, vacuum-dried salt is used. The fillets are laid, skin down, on a 1 cm (½ in) thick bed of salt. The cut surface is sprinkled with salt thickly on the thickest part of the fish, tapering to very little on the thin tail. After salting, which can take 4-5 hours for grilse (young salmon) and up to 24 hours for larger sides, the surface salt is washed off and the fillets are hung to drain. In traditional kilns, the fish can be left to drain overnight before being smoked in a dense smoke for several hours. The smoke is produced from smouldering white wood sawdust, but hardwoods, peat or juniper can be used to impart different flavours.

The finished side should have a pleasant smoky aroma and feel firm when pressed with the finger tips at the thickest part. In a good cure, the weight loss is about one-third from the whole fish.

The sides can be vacuum-packed in plastic sleeves, or sliced, interleaved with cellophane and laid back on the skin before vacuum-packing (this has the appearance of a whole side). Any such smoked salmon products should be kept chilled and can be frozen for longer-term storage.

SMOKIES, normally referred to as Arbroath smokies, are prepared from either small haddocks or small whiting. The fish are gutted, decapitated and cleaned. They are then brined in a strong brine for 30-45 minutes, according to size, and tied in pairs by the tails. The pairs are hung over wooden bars and smoked in pits over billets of wood and wet sawdust until they are cooked and brown coloured. Smoking time is about 2 hours at 71°C (160°F), which is to say that they are hot smoked and the flesh is cooked. Smokies need to be very fresh (when they feel tacky or oily), as they do not keep for more than 4 days even if they are chilled.

For cooking, Arbroath smokies should be skinned, opened to remove the bone, buttered inside and refolded, before being grilled lightly or baked in the oven. They may also be eaten cold, like their *herring equivalent, buckling, or they may be heated by placing them whole in near-boiling water for a few minutes.

SMOKING was originally used, in conjunction with salting and drying, to preserve fish and meat. It may possibly have been done by prehistoric man; certainly it was by the Egyptians and the Chinese, and primitive methods are still used in many parts of the world. For example, East African *bonga* is made on large oil drums covered at the open end with wire mesh. The fish are laid on the mesh and cooked over a charcoal fire, and then wet wood shavings (or sawdust) are scattered over the embers to produce a dense smoke.

Traditionally, smoked foods were preserved by the combined effects of drying, of bacteria-killing chemicals in the smoke and of the high salt concentrations. Present-day smoke-cured foods, both fish and meat, contain much less smoke and salt, and are thus more dependent on refrigeration to keep them in an edible condition. That is to say, smoking as a method of preservation has been made redundant by the modern technologies of canning, freezing and drying, but it is now valued for the flavour it gives, and for that reason is handled with more subtlety.

Smoking fish, meat, poultry and game is preceded by treatment with salt – either *dry-salting or immersion in *brine, which may contain spices and flavourings and perhaps sugar to help tenderize the tougher lumps of meat. Books on smoking may well quote brine strengths as a percentage of the strength of a saturated solution – the usual strength is about 80% of saturation 270 g per lt (5½ oz per pt) – and the brining time is often much less than it would be if the brining were the only method of preservation: a matter of hours or even minutes rather than days. For large pieces of meat such as hams and haunches of venison, brine can be introduced into the middle, where it might not otherwise penetrate, by means of a brine pump, which is something like a large hypodermic syringe and requires much the same degree of cleanliness to avoid introducing bacteria along with the brine. After brining, most products are hung up to dry before they are smoked.

Books on smoking, such as Keith Erlandson's

Home Smoking and Curing (Barrie & Jenkins), offer all manner of designs for smokers, ranging from sophisticated constructions down to improvisations around such items as empty oil drums and dustbins, dead refrigerators and disused outdoor privies. What all these things have in common is a smoke chamber with ventilation holes at the top and a device to feed the smoke in evenly at the bottom – the simplest is a smoke spreader made of a perforated metal sheet covering the bottom of the chamber. The chamber is fitted with bars from which the food can be suspended in the smoke. Beneath the chamber (or away from it if a smoke duct is built between) is the source of the smoke, a heap of smouldering sawdust. Sometimes there is also a source of additional heat such as a gas ring.

The sawdust used for smoking must not be wet, or it may give a mouldy flavour to the food. That apart, there is no absolute consensus of opinion about the sawdust that should be used. The most favoured are hardwoods such as oak, beech, birch or hickory, which burn slowly and steadily. Softwoods, such as deal, are resinous and are said to produce a bitter taste in the smoked food. Because they also give a good colour, a proportion is sometimes added to the hardwood sawdust. Aromatic woods such as juniper and rosemary may also be burned in the final stages of smoking to add their own special flavour.

The basic smoke-curing process is cold smoking, in which the food is smoked at 10-29°C (50-85°F), and ideally at 24-27°C (75-80°F).This means that the food is smoked without being cooked, although it is partly dried – the weight loss that results can be used as an indication of how the smoking is progressing (smoking is completed when the weight loss compared with the untreated product is 17-18% for salmon, 25% for cod roe and 12-14% for Finnan haddock). A few cold-smoked foods are eaten raw, among them *smoked salmon, smoked cod roe and smoked fillet of beef, but the majority, including *Finnan haddock, kippers and smoked *bacon, are cooked before they are eaten.

Cold smoking is also a stage in the preparation of hot smoked foods. After the product has been given its smoky flavour and slightly dried by cold smoking, the temperature is raised to about 82°C (180°F) for fish, which is likely to disintegrate at higher temperatures, but anything up to 150°C (240°F) for meat, game and poultry. From its cooking in hot smoke, as long as this has not been too long or at too high a temperature, the result will be delicately flavoured and ready to be eaten cold after it has been left to mature in a cool place

for 24 hours. Hot smoked products include smoked mackerel and trout, buckling, *smokies and a variety of smoked game and poultry.

The small smokers, such as the Abu Smokebox, that are sold in kitchen shops produce hot smoked trout and other small items by a rather different method. These smokers are closed boxes heated from below to ignite the sawdust on the floor of the box; the food rests on a rack with a drip tray to prevent the juices from falling on the sawdust. The whole apparatus gets rather hot – hotter than in other hot smoking processes – and the food is cooked in about 20 minutes to give a product that is probably acceptable rather than exquisite.

The success of smoked foods is almost as dependent on the quality of the raw materials as it is on the expertise of the smoker. Fish must be very fresh (or it can be frozen and freshly thawed) and the blood that lies along the backbone must be scooped out. Game birds should not be hung for more than 3 days before they are brined, while beef and venison need to be aged for at least a week. Brine should be made up freshly for each batch of food to be smoked, and vacuum-dried salt, which does not have added magnesium carbonate, should be used in making it (or for dry salting).

Cold smoking without prior salting can be applied to a small variety of other foods – a curious assortment, including nuts, bilberries, hard-boiled eggs and cheese. Mild hard or semi-hard cheeses are suitable for smoking. For Austrian smoked cheese, though, it is not the cheese itself but the milk that goes into it that is smoked.

Smoke roasting, a process that is less known in Europe than in America, is cooking meat such as steak or spareribs in hot smoke at 93-107°C (200-225°F) without salting or cool smoking – the meat is simply seasoned and given a coating of oil. Unlike hot-smoked meat, it needs to be cooked.

In the main, smoke-curing is now in the hands of large food manufacturing companies which use modern technology to give a standardized product. Various lines of research have evolved processes for applying smoke in liquid form. The first such technique emerged some 40 years ago, when the Japanese used pure *pyroligneous acid from the destructive distillation of wood. This tasted and smelled like strong vinegar. More modern liquid smokes, some from natural sources and others produced chemically are still in the experimental stage. Applying the theory of electrostatic precipitation, which is used for painting cars, smoke can be deposited on fish and colours it in a matter of minutes. However, it fails to penetrate the surface and is not always pleasant to taste. But sooner or later the scientists will conquer these little problems and come up with a product sufficiently standardized – and characterless – to suit the food industry.

[*Smoking* – French: *fumer* German: *räuchern* Italian: *affumicare* Spanish: *ahumar*]

SNAIL. Many kinds of snail are eaten. Even in Britain, snails were traditionally eaten in a few districts; they were thought to be good for the lungs. Glass blowers, for instance, thought that eating snails gave them plenty of breath, and recipes for snail water and snail broth appear in 17th century and earlier recipe books as a remedy for consumption. However, snails were not regarded as a delicious food, but were usually looked on with some disgust, perhaps because of the slime which the snail pours out as a carpet to walk on. 'I once knew an old woman,' said the Revd J.G. Wood (1863), 'one of the few wearers of scarlet cloaks, who used daily to search the hedges for snails, for the purpose of converting her milk into cream. This cheap luxury was obtained by crushing the snails in a piece of linen, and squeezing their juice into the milk. She showed me the whole process which I afterwards imitated as far as the mixture with the milk, but could not bring myself to test the result by taste.'

The Romans had no such squeamishness and regarded the snail as a luxury. They went in for snail culture, building special houses called *cochlearia*, in which snails were fattened on a mixture of meal and wine. The scholar Marcus Terentius Varro (116-28 BC) even wrote on the subject in his *De re rustica*, and the tradition of snail-farming continued in Europe. Today, once more, snaileries are on the increase, although wild snails gathered after rain still form the majority of those eaten. Indeed, so avidly are snails gathered that laws have had to be passed in some countries making close seasons for snails in order to prevent their near extinction. Snails are becoming expensive. In France, where the annual consumption of snails is reckoned in hundreds of millions, you will have trouble finding even a single snail in the Burgundy vineyards – I know, as I have hunted them there. To satisfy demand, snails have to be imported from Yugoslavia and elsewhere.

The snails are alive; canned snails sold with a bag of shells attached are a fairly recent innovation. The best known species of snail for eating is the large Roman snail (*Helix pomata*), which is called the Burgundy snail by gourmets and is found over

much of Europe. It has been introduced into Britain (some say by the Romans but that is doubtful) and it can sometimes be found, but only in chalk or limestone country, as it needs a lot of lime to make its shell. Contrary to popular belief, the common Garden snail (*H. aspera*) is excellent to eat and, with two other species (*H. vermiculata* and *H. nemoralis*) is regarded, for instance by the people of Liguria, as better than the large 'Burgundy'. Comeford Casey, writing at the turn of the last century in his *Riviera Nature Notes*, says that 'Labouring men eat *Helix pisena* and *Helix variabilis* boiled with beans' and that '*Helix operta*, the glass snail, is considered a great delicacy by the Niçois, especially when it is found closed by its operculum.' *En passant*, we learn that 'In the "Eight Communes" of the Ventimiglia district a law was passed imposing a fine of four lire on persons caught stealing snails from their neighbours' ground. If the thief was mean enough to pilfer them by night, the fine was doubled.' The Italians, however, are not usually such dedicated snail eaters as the French, although they have at least one festival – the *Sagra delle lumaca* at Molini di Triora which takes place on a Sunday at the end of September – and dozens of regional snail recipes, to set against the better-known French ones.

Small snails are fried with onions, cooked with garlic, rosemary, parsley, tomato, dried fungi, olive oil and white wine; they are also cooked with oil, butter, raisins and pine nuts – even with mint. The Spanish offer snails roasted on rocks and seasoned with salt and oil, snails in *paella*, and particularly snails poached in a *court-bouillon* containing wild fennel and eaten with the strong garlic mayonnaise which the Catalans call *alioli*.

Snails are most easily gathered after rain; a good strategy is to go out at night with a torch. You will need to get a dozen large Roman snails or about twenty of the smaller species (*petits gris*) per person. When the catch is brought home, put the snails in a box – a tin with holes punched in it for air is good – and keep them for a week while they clean themselves of any plants they may have eaten that are poisonous to humans. (If the snails have been taken from a garden, they may have been contaminated with poison sprays and may die.) During this period, some people starve them completely; others fatten them on lettuce leaves, herbs (like fennel), bran or flour. At the end of the week, the snails should be washed and inspected. Any dead ones must be thrown away.

The next step is to remove the slime. Put the snails in a basin, and mix them with salt – preferably coarse salt – and stir them about gently for 10-15 minutes, until they foam. Some cooks add a little vinegar. Then wash the snails in cold water and repeat the de-sliming process if necessary until all the snails' slime glands are emptied. (It is not a critical process, as the slime is not harmful – peasants preparing small snails often do not bother.) After giving them a final wash, plunge the snails into boiling water for from 3-5 minutes, until it is possible to extract the animals with a fork. Screw each snail out of its shell (this is not done for small species in the snail-eating countries, but I always do it even for large garden snails) and pull off and discard the black 'visceral spiral' – which is in the top of the shell. It is not poisonous, but it contains the liver and, in large snails, is bitter. Now wash the snails, put them into boiling water again for 10 minutes and drain them. Finally, cook them until they are tender (which will take 3 hours for Roman snails, but less for garden snails) in a *court-bouillon* of salted water flavoured with an onion stuck with a clove, salt and pepper, bay, thyme and parsley. A glass of white wine or a dash of vinegar is usually added. Meanwhile, clean the shells by boiling them for 30 minutes in water with added bicarbonate of soda; rinse them well and dry them.

When the snails are cooked, let them cool in the *court-bouillon*, and then put them back into their shells with garlic butter. When the snails are required, put them into a hot oven (you can keep the shells upright by pressing them into a bed of salt) for 5 minutes to heat and to melt the butter.

Garlic Butter

This is the standard formula given me by Chef Roy of the Hotel du Nord in Dijon (who also gave me a one-in-a-million Burgundy snail shell with a left-handed spiral), whom I once filmed for television as he prepared snails. The quantities need scaling down for home kitchens. Pound together 200 g (1 oz) garlic, 25 g (1 oz) shallot, 125 g (5 oz) parsley, 1½ teaspoons pepper, 25 g (1 oz) salt and 1 kg (2 lb) good unsalted butter.

Such sophistication would be regarded as very sissy by the peasants who live around me in Majorca. They take their snails, the smaller local species, keep them a few days (while they collect enough) or buy them from the sack in the market, and simply dump them into a pan of cold water and cook them. (They say that the snails draw back into their shells if they are put straight into boiling water.) Salting to

remove the slime is said to be necessary only when a tray of live snails are to be put into a hot oven and baked. Snails which have sealed themselves up with a chalky operculum in order to hibernate need to have this seal scraped away before cooking. As they have already been starving, they are the safest of all snails to eat.

[*Snail* – French: *escargot* German: *Schnecke* Italian: *chiocciola, lumaca* Spanish: *caracol*]

SNAP BEAN. *See* kidney bean. US term for green bean.

SNIPE. *See* woodcock.

SNOEK or **Australian barracuda** (*Thyrsites atun*) is a relative of the tunny and the mackerel. It is found in the Southern hemisphere only, and is eaten in south-western Australia, New Zealand, and in parts of South Africa and South America (in Chile, it is known as *sierra*). Fresh or smoked, snoek is delicate and delicious, and its flavour would be a revelation to those who remember canned snoek as an element in Britain's post-war austerity diet.

SNOOK or **robalo** is the name of several pike-like fish from the tropical Atlantic and Pacific Oceans. The Common snook (*Centropomus undecimales*) may weigh 14 kg (30 lb), though 1.5-2 kg (3-5 lb) is the average. The flesh has a fine flavour and is found in local markets where the fish is caught (it is a popular game fish in Florida).

SNOWY MESPILUS. *See* rowan.

SOAKING. In cooking, foods are often soaked to remove salt, to soften them, or to reconstitute dried products. Important considerations are to make sure that the soaking liquid gets to all parts, and to maintain the correct temperature, remembering that chemical and physical actions are in general speeded up by warmth, but the same warmth also increases the activity of micro-organisms that cause spoilage. Soaking does not necessarily imply the softening of tissues; that is *maceration.

SOBA. *See* noodles.

SODA may mean *caustic soda, *washing soda or *bicarbonate of soda (baking soda).

SODA WATER was originally a medicinal alkaline water made by dissolving small amounts of *bicarbonate of soda in water. Today, it is water containing dissolved *carbon dioxide, which has been forced in under pressure and consequently comes out again in bubbles when the pressure is released. Some brands are made slightly alkaline with soda. Soda water can also be made at home with one of the various gadgets on the market that use small capsules or cylinders of compressed carbon dioxide.

Producing soda water at home used to be rather more laborious, as is shown by the instructions offered by *Cassell's New Dictionary of Cookery* (1904). 'Sodiac powders: Take 5 drachms of citric or tartaric acid, pound it fine and divide it into twelve parts, folding each in a *white* paper. Take 6 drachms of carbonate of soda, pound it fine and fold it in [twelve] *blue* papers. Half fill two half-pint tumblers with water, stir into one a powder from the white paper, in the other one from the blue; when the powders are quite dissolved pour one to the other, and perfect soda water will be instantaneously produced in its utmost perfection.' The same article describes the gazogene, 'a portable apparatus for aerating water', in which the chemical process took place in one compartment and the liquid to be aerated went into another joined to the first by a tube. 'By means of the gazogene, water, wine, ale etc. may in a few minutes be rendered brisk and piquant by means of carbonic acid.'
[*Soda Water* – French: *eau de Seltz, soda* German: *Sodawasser, Selterswasser* Italian: *acqua di seltz, acqua gassosa* Spanish: *agua de seltz, agua de soda*]

SODIUM BICARBONATE. *See* bicarbonate of soda.

SODIUM CARBONATE. *See* washing soda.

SODIUM HYDROXIDE. *See* caustic soda.

SODIUM NITRATE. *See* saltpetre.

SOFT WATER. *Water with little dissolved mineral content, which in hard water is made up of calcium salts; it is sometimes slightly acid. Water from moorland and boggy mountain areas is usually soft.

SOJA. *See* soya bean.

SOLE. *See* flatfish.

SOLUBILITY. *See* saturated solution.

SOMEN. *See* noodles.

SONCOYA. *See* custard apple.

SORB. *See* rowan.

SORBIC ACID. *See* preservatives.

SORGHUM. *See* millet and sorghum.

SORREL. There are several species of sorrel, which belong to the same genus as dock plants. When cultivated, they look something like spinach. The three native European species are sorrel (*Rumex acetosa*), Round-leaved sorrel (*R. scutatus*) and sheep sorrel (*R. acetosella*). *R. scutatus* has been introduced in a few places in Britain; the other two species are common natives in Britain and North America. The cultivated forms are derived mainly from *R. acetosa*. As its acid-tasting leaves contain oxalic acid, it is not advisable to eat it in large quantities, particularly in salads, to which it can nevertheless be a delicious addition. As a sour and refreshing basis for soups, purées and sauces, as a flavouring herb in omelettes and as a stuffing ingredient for fish, sorrel is unbeatable. It is surprising that it is now relatively little known in Britain and America. However, this was not always so. Green sauce, made with pounded sorrel, vinegar (or lemon juice) and sugar, was a popular accompaniment to meat and poultry until the 18th century, and the practice still survives, at least in parts of Yorkshire. Indeed, green sauce was the dialect name for sorrel in many parts of England; other names were sour dock and sour grass. An allied plant, Herb Patience (*R. patientia*), is eaten like spinach.
[*Sorrel* – French: *oseille* German: *Sauerampfer* Italian: *sauro* Spanish: *acedera*]

SOUR CREAM is a delicious ingredient of Russian, Polish, Hungarian, Romanian and German cooking, and is becoming popular in Britain and the US, where it can now be bought easily. Yoghurt cannot be used in place of sour cream, as it is less rich in fat and different in taste. If sour cream is not available, it can be made from fresh cream kept at 30°C (86°F) or thereabouts, but only if a starter such as cottage cheese is added. Pasteurized cream may merely go bad and taste very nasty. A little yoghurt or some sour milk may also be used as a starter. Otherwise, it is better to make imitation sour cream by adding lemon juice or a drop or two of vinegar (not enough to recognize) and then stirring. It will thicken rapidly. The sourness will, of course, be due to citric and not lactic acid. The drop of vinegar (and it must really be very little) is not essential, but soured cream does naturally contain a tiny amount of acetic acid.

*Smetana in Russia is a mixture of sour and sweet cream.

[Sour cream – French: crème aigre German: sauere Sahne Italian: panna fermentata Spanish: jocoque]

SOURDOUGH is a natural leavener used as a 'starter' for bread – the result is sourdough bread. To make sourdough starter mix 1 cup each of flour and water with a dessertspoonful of sugar, and leave it in a warm place for 3 days to ferment. The bread is subsequently made by using a mixture of this sourdough starter and yeast.

That is a sophisticated modern version. Originally, sourdough was indeed just sour dough. A piece of a previous batch of bread dough was kept moistened with water as a starter – it contained yeasts as well as acid-producing bacteria acids that stopped the dough from going bad. It could also be mixed with water and fed with sugar and more flour to keep it going. Prospectors in the Alaska Gold Rush got the name sourdoughs because they kept a pot of the starter going and took it with them up country. Exactly the same thing happens today in Australia where the cattle drovers and remote farms use 'hops'. Sourdough is an old country technique of bread-making that was very widely used in the days when yeast could not be so easily bought. Today, with dried yeasts, it is not necessary to use sourdough any more, but many people like the taste, especially in rye breads. In the US, it is possible to buy ready made sourdough starters, which make quite good sourdough bread. San Francisco is renowned for its sourdough French bread, which owes its particular taste to a particular strain of bacterium that is unique to the city. The bread is at its best when made just with sourdough starter and no added yeast.

[Sourdough – French: levain German: Sauerteig Italian: lievito naturale Spanish: levadura]

SOURING AGENTS are acid substances and are very important in cooking. Today, the usual ones used in Europe and America are lemon juice and vinegar, both of which are easily added and usually ready to hand. Yoghurt, sour milk, and butter milk are other useful sour products. Sour and unripe fruits (such as sour apples or sour grapes), and the *verjuice which can be squeezed from them, are other possibilities. So also are sour *pomegranate seeds, dried *mango powder (amchur), *tamarind,

roselle (which is a *mallow), *sorrel, wood sorrel and *rhubarb. The use of different souring agents, because of their flavour overtones, can make very interesting and subtle changes in salads and other dishes.

SOUR MILK has many uses, provided it has gone properly sour and is not evil-tasting or bitter, as will be the case if the milk has been pasteurized, which prevents the preservative lactic acid from developing. As virtually all milk is now pasteurized, it is safer to use cultured buttermilk whenever sour milk is called for in recipes. In British cooking, sour milk is typically used in scones, but it can with advantage be used in mashed potatoes, soups and gravies or be allowed to curdle thoroughly for making cottage cheese. Unpasteurized milk and cream can be soured by the addition of yoghurt, cottage cheese or any other soft cheese and holding them at 25-30°C (77-86°F).

[Sour milk – French: lait caillé, lait aigre German: Sauermilch Italian: latte acido Spanish: angola]

SOUR MILK PRODUCTS. Milk of all kinds contains *lactose which can be fermented by many species of bacteria with the formation of lactic acid (sometimes yeasts also ferment it to alcohol). During the souring, other substances are produced in the milk – creamy flavours, buttery flavours, fruity and vinegary flavours (acetic acid) – and these are important. They dictate the type and quality of the finished product. The bacterial activity also causes the coagulation of the milk – the formation of curd. This may be firm or watery, ropy or slimy. Some bacteria attack fats and proteins; they may result in bitter, rancid, fishy and putrid flavours. (Prolonged action of micro-organisms has other effects, which lie more in the sphere of *cheese-making.)

In making sour milk products, it is important to keep a few general principles in mind. Everything should be clean – preferably sterilized by boiling and nothing should be left uncovered for long; you do not want the milk to be contaminated with lots of the extraneous organisms which are always in the air. The culture you use to start your sour milk product may be bought specially, or it may be a pot of yoghurt, sour cream or buttermilk from the supermarket (as long as it is not sterilized), or it may be part of the last brew kept back specially as a starter. Remember that in all cases it will be a mixture of organisms, not a pure culture, and that the control you have over it is exercised via the temperature at which you incubate it, which is critical. It is best to buy a thermometer reading from 0-100°C.The quantity of starter you use is important. For several reasons it affects the relative numbers of organisms, and so the end product. Too much starter often causes over-sourness. Electric yoghurt makers are not necessary, though they can be convenient; people made sour milk products long before electricity was heard of. A saucepan, a suitably-sized stoneware jar and a means of keeping the jar warm (an expanded polystyrene box, keep cool picnic bag, tea cosy, muff, lined box or even blanket) are all that you really need.

Milk can be from cow, goat, sheep, buffalo, reindeer, camel or mare. Some milks, like mare's, contain more sugar than others and are suitable for alcoholic fermentation. There are dozens of different variants on the theme of sour milk or cream, but they seem all to have originated with the ancient tribes of Central Asia. Yoghurt, for instance, reached the Middle East via Persia. It was known as 'Persian milk' in 13th-century Arabia. Sour milk products are now well known in northern Europe (the Lapps use reindeer milk): there are local sour milks such as the Finnish *piima* or *viili* and Scandinavian ropy sour milk, called *rangmjolk* or *täte*, which is slightly alcoholic and may be clabbered and flavoured with butterwort (*Pinguicula vulgaris*),that insectivorous plant of northern bogs. North Russian sour milk is *prostokvash*, which is soured at 30°C (85°F). A very hot day will do it, and the same temperature is used to make *sour cream in Russia, Hungary and Central Europe generally.

*Yoghurt (variously spelled) is by repute the sour milk product of Bulgaria and Turkey, but is made in local ways in the Middle East and through Iran to India. In Persian, it is called *mast* and from it comes *mazoon* in Armenia and *matsoni* in Georgia, as well as *masturad* in Sicily. It is *leben* in Egypt and the rest of North Africa, and *laban* in Syria and Lebanon. Almost the same product is called *dahi* in India, where the best is made from buffalo milk. In the Balkans, the most delicious yoghurt is made from sheep's milk, sometimes from goat's milk; cow's milk yoghurt, which is the commonest further west, is considered as inferior. Yoghurt is a hot-country product and uses thermophilic (heat-loving) bacteria which grow best at 40-45°C (104-113°F). It plays an important role in the cooking of the Middle East and India, and is mixed with sweetened or well-salted cold water and flavourings to make wonderful hot-weather drinks (*doogh, ayran* or *lassi*).

Of the more exotic products, acidophilous milk has become a new health fad and is readily available. This is a culture of *Lactobacillus acidophilus*, a common inhabitant of the human gut, which, unlike the yoghurt bacterium (*Lactobacillus bulgaricus*), can survive inside the human digestive tract but will continue to grow only if it is given milk or milk sugar to feed on. Acidophilous milk is much used in Russian sanitoria, but its flavour is not as good as that of yoghurt. The Russians also have *kéfir* made from cow's milk and *koumiss* from mare's milk, which are both alcoholic, as is *kyrynga*, which is made in Central Asia. Another Asian sour milk product, *chal*, is made from camel's milk.

SOUR SOP. *See* custard apple.

SOUTHERN LOBSTER. *See langouste.*

SOYA BEAN, **soybean**, or **soja bean**. Surely one of the most depressing statements ever made is that the world could support a population of sixteen thousand million people if everyone ate soya beans instead of meat. An acre of these beans can keep a moderately active man alive (but not necessarily contented) for 2200 days, while the same acre could keep him for only 75 days if he lived on beef. The soya bean is the richest natural vegetable food known to man – and one of the dullest, a typical example of the perverse sense of humour of the Creator, who never seems to make anything without snags. Why should the soya bean not have been delicious as well as full of oil (18-22% in the dried beans) and protein (35%), not to mention carbohydrate? We read of special varieties of soya with a delectable taste – there are over a thousand known varieties – and seeds that are black, chocolate, brown, reddish, greenish or yellow, but they never seem to reach the shops. No wonder, then, that they were not taken seriously outside the Orient until research was able to show their outstanding food value.

The plant (*Glycine max*) is a legume from eastern Asia and has been in cultivation in China for thousands of years, the first written mention being in *The Heavenly Farmer* by Emperor Sheng-Nung in 2838 BC. Confucius fans will like to know that he called it *shu*. The first news of the soya came to Europe when the German botanist, Engelbert Kaenfer, came back from a visit to Japan in 1692. The beans were grown in Kew in 1790. Later still, the American expedition to Japan led by Commodore N.C. Perry in 1854 brought back two varieties (Japan pea and Japan bean), but still nobody, it seems, liked them.

It was not until the 20th century that scientific research revealed the great nutritive wealth hidden in the seed. Today, the US produces more even than China, indeed a third of the total world soya output – one of the most important changes in agricultural economy that have occurred to date. It is not grown in more northern latitudes as the climate is too cold for it. It looks like a typical bean, but it has not been much eaten in Europe and America because it can have a peculiarly gelatinous texture which some people do not like. It is also very inferior in flavour when compared, for instance, to Lima or kidney beans. Perhaps it is its oiliness which prevents it marrying well with other flavours, such as tomato sauce. More often it is used in the form of a flour (sometimes treated to remove any bitterness) to pad other foods; most people who were around in Britain during World War II will remember with as much horror as gratitude those traumatic 'pork soya links'. Unlike most other flours, soya flour is high in protein and low in carbohydrate. It is often used by bread bakers as a dough improver. Soya beans can be *sprouted and used in the same way as mung bean sprouts, but they have a much more beany flavour and are not nice raw – they need steaming to make them palatable.

Soya oil, possibly the world's most important vegetable oil and the basis for margarine, is used as a cooking oil and is cheap, but it is one of the least attractive of all the vegetable oils. However, from soya beans come a whole range of other products. The beans can be mixed with cereal and fermented to make *soy sauce. They can be made into a milk which, with certain additives, can be used to feed babies, and the milk can be used to make approximations to vegetable yoghurt and vegetable cheese, as well as the soya bean curd that is known as *tofu* in Japan, but is of Chinese origin. The Chinese even dry the curd skin, and it is commonly sold in Chinese shops. Finally, of the Oriental products there is *miso* from Japan, an ingredient made of soya beans and cereal grains fermented with water and salt for use in soups and sauces; its residue, *tamari*, the liquid that rises to the top during fermentation is probably the inspiration for *soy sauce. There are various types of *miso*, which will be specified in Japanese recipes. *Miso* dissolves in water, if it is used in soups, they should boil after it has been added.

With modern Western technology, we enter a new field, the field of the soya-protein isolate. The simple form is sold in the form of granules or grits,

and is used – as was the earlier soya flour – for adding to manufactured foods, sausages, mince, savoury pies, etc. (In most countries, it has to be mentioned on the label.) More sophisticated food technology has produced Textured Vegetable Protein – *TVP – a fibrous substance which can be formed into fake chicken, steak, ham, and bacon. It has been forecast that TVP will become to meat what margarine has become to butter. Textured and flavoured soya is also used in sweets, where it stands in for coconut.

Tofu

Mix 1 cup of soya bean powder with 4 cups of water and let it soak for half an hour, giving it an occasional stir. Then put the mixture on the heat and bring it to the boil, stirring all the time. As soon as it boils, lower the heat to simmer for 5 minutes. Then turn off the heat and add 4 tablespoons of lemon juice. Stir until the protein begins to curdle. Finally, after giving it time to curdle properly, tip the curd into a clean cloth and hang it up to drain, as if you were making cottage cheese. When it has drained, the *tofu* should be a compact curd, white and with very little taste. It can be preserved under water in the refrigerator for several days.

Recipes for using *tofu* will be found in Japanese cookery books, and sometimes in health food or vegetarian books. Like the Indian *panir*, which is made from milk, it has almost no taste of its own, but is nice cubed, fried golden and mixed with other things. It makes a very good curry treated in the Indian way, as for curried *panir* and peas.

[*Soya* – French: *soja* German: *Sojabohne* Italian: *soia* Spanish: *soja*]

SOY SAUCE or **shoyu**. This condiment, with its slightly sweet, salty and meaty taste, is an ancient and important ingredient in the cooking of China and Japan, but it has also been popular in Britain for over 300 years and is said to be one of the ingredients of Worcestershire sauce. There were even silver soy labels to hang on bottles long before the bean itself had registered as more than a curiosity in the West. Since soy sauce is used as much (and probably more) in China and Japan as we use vinegar, its making is a huge commercial undertaking today, but the basis of the sauce – although there are many ways of making it and many different types of it – is best understood by reference to an old description for the Japanese version.

Soya beans are first boiled until tender, then they are pounded in a mortar with an equal weight of coarsely-ground barley or roasted and cracked wheat. The mixture is then covered and left in a warm place to ferment. When the mass is sufficiently fermented, a weight of salt equal to the original weight of beans is added and well mixed in. It is all covered again and left to do its worst for up to three years, during which time it is well stirred or beaten every day. At the end of this time, the brown juice is pressed out through cloth, put into a tub and left to settle. When it is clear, the sauce is racked off and is ready for use.

There was a time when soy sauce was difficult to get, but now it is easy to buy the dark, light and other varieties that are necessary in Chinese, Japanese and South East Asian recipes. The very heavy Indonesian ketjap (ketjap manis or ketjap benteng), which is a type of soy sauce, can be made, if it is not available, from any dark soy sauce by adding half its volume of molasses and sweetening with brown sugar (about 3 parts to every 8 of molasses) – this solution is suggested by Rosemary Brissenden in her excellent South East Asian Food (Penguin). Friends from Java, unable to get ketjap in Europe (it is available in Holland), experimented and found a superior French stock cube called Poule au pot. They claimed that this, mixed with brown sugar, gave results at least as good as the real thing. Another ketjap substitute is saté sauce, which is made with *peanuts.

[Soy sauce – French: sauce piquante (de soja) German: Sosse von Soja Italian: salsa di soia]

SPAGHETTI is the most popular of all forms of *pasta. It can be bought in an assortment of grades of different diameters and lengths. It should not be broken into short lengths, as this makes it difficult for the eater to twist it around the fork. Many people eat spaghetti with a fork and spoon, using the spoon as a hollow in which to twist the fork, but purists eat with a fork alone, twisting the forkful against the plate. The latter is more refined, and demonstrates your expertise, but is slower.

[Spaghetti – French: spaghetti German: Spaghetti Italian: spaghetti Spanish: espaguetis]

SPATCHCOCK, according to The Concise Oxford Dictionary, is a fowl killed and cooked in a hurry, i.e. with dispatch. In cooking, a spatchcocked chicken has been split along the middle of the breast bone, opened and flattened out for grilling.

SPECIFIC HEAT. It takes more heat, and therefore longer, to heat up some substances than others, and these also hold more heat than others. They therefore cool down more slowly. Specific heat is the scientific measurement of this: it compares the amount of heat necessary to raise the temperature of a substance one degree with that necessary to raise the same mass of water by one degree. Copper has a very low specific heat; a copper pan heats and cools quickly. As it is also a good conductor, it responds rapidly to the cook's adjustment of the flame and is therefore ideal for pans. Earthenware has a very high specific heat; it heats slowly, but retains its heat and cools slowly. Its temperature cannot be made to fluctuate quickly; it is ideal for containers for hot food on the table, which copper is not. Other types of kitchen ware fall somewhere in between.

SPECK. See bacon.

SPICE. The word comes from the same root as species and meant a kind of merchandise. It originally applied to aromatics shipped in from the Orient and, therefore, excluded herbs (and their seeds) grown in Europe. Today, it is more conveniently used to include all dried aromatic seeds as well as the original oriental spices, and it can also cover dried chillies and allspice from America.

[Spice – French: épice German: Gewürz Italian: spezie Spanish: especia]

SPINACH. The common spinach (Spinacea oleracea) is thought to be of Persian origin; it was not known to the Romans, but was probably introduced to Europe by the Arabs and was being grown in Britain by the middle of the 16th century. Like most unusual foods at that time, it was regarded as medicinal – it is mildly laxative. Spinach might also seem to be a valuable source of minerals, as it contains a lot of iron and more calcium than any other common vegetable. However, its oxalic acid content is high and combines with the calcium and iron to form insoluble oxalates, making the minerals effectively unavailable. So spinach is valuable mainly because it is delicious, both cooked and, when young and tender, raw in salads. It is best cooked by the conservation method in the moisture it retains from washing. Spinach can sometimes be awkwardly gritty. It should ideally be soaked in cold water for an hour or so to loosen the grit, and then rinsed in several changes of water. Always take the spinach out of the water (rather than pour the water off it) so that the dirt is left behind. The process is speeded up and initial soaking rendered unnecessary if you use very hot water for the rinsing.

Good King Henry (*Chenopodium bonus-henricus*), also known as all-good or mercury, is called *bon-Henri* in France and is a perennial relative of spinach. Its flavour is good, but it needs to have the water changed during cooking. The tender young flower buds are the best part to eat. Nowadays it is an unusual vegetable.

New Zealand spinach (*Tetragonia expansa*) belongs to another family (Aizoaceae, which also includes the garden *Mesembryanthemum*). It is frost tender but thrives in dry regions and so it is the spinach grown in the warm, drier countries. The plant, which has characteristic fleshy, triangular leaves, was first introduced to Europe by Sir Joseph Banks in 1770 and was grown in Kew Gardens in 1772. As it is inclined to be bitter, the water may be changed during cooking. It is best eaten young.

Orache or **Mountain spinach** (*Atriplex hortensis*) is a member of the same family as spinach and is called *bonne-dame* in France. It is an annual which grows up to about 2 m (6½ ft) high. It has large, arrow-shaped leaves, often with toothed or crinkly edges, and is a good spinach substitute. Varieties with red or yellow leaves are sometimes grown for ornamental rather than culinary reasons, but are no less edible than green varieties.

Spinach beet or **Swiss chard** is a form of *beet that is grown for its leaves and its thickened leaf stalks. Sea spinach is the wild form of the same species.

Among other leaf vegetables, young stinging *nettle tops make an excellent 'spinach', with a very good flavour but a slightly dry texture. They are useful to mix with other foods and in stuffings. The other members of the goosefoot genus, even Stinking goosefoot (*Chenopodium olidum*), which has an unpleasant smell, that is said to be like stale salt fish and is caused by a substance called trimethylamine, is perfectly good to eat when boiled. Another family with green leaves that are eaten like spinach is the *mallow family, various species of which are quite good. Dead-nettles, which are not nettles but labiates related to sage, also have leaves which can be boiled, notably those

of the White dead-nettle (*Lamium album*),which is also good in soups and stuffings. Then there is the amaranth (*Amaranthus*), of which there are some fifty species, mainly from warm climates; several are used as greens in countries from Italy to India. These are mostly annuals. *Fenugreek (*methi*) is much used as a green in Indian cooking, but it can be excruciatingly bitter. Indian spinach is also called Malabar nightshade. There are two species: *Basella alba*, from India, and *B. rubra*, from China. They are sometimes grown in France and can be treated just like spinach.

[*Spinach* – French: *épinard* German: *Spinat* Italian: *spinaclo* Spanish: *espinaca*]

SPINY LOBSTER. *See langouste.*

SPORES of moulds and other fungi are analogous to seeds of higher plants – they are a means by which the plants multiply and spread. Spores form the powdery cloud given out when moulds are disturbed and the smoky-looking dust that comes out of ripe puffballs. Mould spores are a nuisance to the cook, because they are usually in the air and will settle on the surface of jam, indeed on any food, that is left uncovered even for a few moments. Mould spores are killed by a short boiling.

The spores of bacteria are very different. They are formed by relatively few rod-shaped species (about 150) and their purpose is not to multiply the numbers but to enable the organism to survive conditions which would kill it in its normal, actively proliferating state. Bacterial spores cause problems, as they survive a long time (up to ten years on occasion) and are exceedingly hard to kill.

Spores, however, can be regarded as only potentially troublesome, because they will not cause food spoilage or poisoning so long as they do not germinate. To germinate, the food, temperature and *pH must be right as well as the amount of air (or lack of it) and other critical conditions. Making sure that these conditions do not occur in food is one of the crucial factors in *preservation.

[*Spore* – French: *spore* German: *Spore* Italian: *spora* Spanish: *espora*]

SPRAT (*Sprattus sprattus*) is a small fish, about 15 cm (6 in) long, found around the coasts of Europe from the Black Sea to Norway. In Britain, it is in season from November to March, in the Adriatic in spring and autumn. It is an oily fish, closely related to the sardine and the herring; it can be distinguished from both by its characteristically serrated belly (it has a row of spiny scales running along it). Also, the front of its ventral fin lies directly below the front, rather than the middle, of the dorsal fin. Fresh sprats are best grilled, as they are very oily, and served sprinkled with lemon juice. They are also salted, smoked and potted. Small ones are canned in oil or tomato sauce under their Norwegian name, brisling, but are less good than sardines.

Salting Sprats

The sprats should be firm, silvery and completely fresh. After cleaning and decapitating them, put them into strong, cold brine for an hour. Then drain them well, dry them and pack them in layers in a salting jar. Each layer should be well sprinkled with a salting mixture in the proportion of 450 g (1 lb) salt to 25 g (1 oz) saltpetre and 1 tablespoon sugar. When the jar is almost full, give a final sprinkle of the salting mixture and press down the mass as for *anchovies. They will form a brine, and the sprats must be kept totally immersed in it; otherwise, they will go rancid. They will be ready in 3-4 months. Prepare them by pouring a kettle of boiling water over them in a basin, skinning them, and serving them hot. Dried and smoked sprats are best skinned and eaten raw.

[Sprat – French: esprot, sprat German: Sprotte Italian: spratto Spanish: sardineta]

SPROUTED SEEDS. When seeds sprout, many enzymes concerned with mobilizing the food reserves become active (an important stage in the production of *malt). At the same time, vitamins, particularly vitamin C, which were not present in significant amounts in the dormant seed are produced. Sprouted beans would have protected sailors from scurvy had the reason for the disease been known and not ascribed to 'salt junk', the mahogany-coloured dried salt pork. Today, sprouted seeds enjoy increasing popularity, particularly among health food enthusiasts, as they are quickly and easily grown at home.

The most widely known sprouted seeds are bean sprouts, which have been used in China for some 3000 years. The most usually and easily sprouted bean is the *mung bean. After sprouting, which takes 3-4 days or until the sprouts are 5 cm (2 in) long, the taste is mild. Mung bean sprouts can be eaten steamed or raw as a salad. However, bean or pea sprouts which are to be eaten in any quantity

should be cooked (though they need only be simmered or steamed for 3 minutes). Raw legume sprouts and seeds contain a substance that inhibits trypsin, one of the enzymes with which we digest protein. The trypsin inhibitor is quickly destroyed by heat.

Mustard and cress may be sprouted in soil and are commercially grown in peat. Other seeds may be grown on flannel, tied in a cloth or put in a commercial sprouter, but a fairly foolproof and very popular way is the jam jar method. As beans and seeds increase in volume up to ten times the original size as they sprout, use a jar large enough to allow for this expansion. Put the seeds into a clean jar. Cover the opening with a piece of loosely-woven cloth, such as muslin, or, better still, nylon net, and fasten the cloth securely around the jar neck with string or a strong rubber band. Fill the jar with tepid water, shake the water around, then let it drain out through the cloth, and lay the jar on its side. Repeat this two to four times a day, or often enough to keep the seeds moist. If they are too wet, the seeds will rot; if they are too dry, they will die. Remove any seeds that do not sprout when the others have, and continue wetting and draining the sprouts until they are ready to eat. Nylon net should be rinsed between uses; muslin needs to be sterilized. Sprouts can be kept for a month in a sealed, partly inflated plastic bag in the vegetable tray of the refrigerator.

Buy untreated seeds that are specifically for sprouting, rather than seeds intended for planting, which may have been treated with retardants, fungicides or insecticides. Some instructions suggest soaking the seeds for several hours before putting them into the jar.

Mung beans should be put in plenty of water and soaked for 12-24 hours, until they just start to burst their skins. Drain off the water and follow the instructions above for the jam jar method. When the sprouts are ready, they will taste of freshly-shelled peas. Tip them into a large basin of water and swish them around gently to loosen the husks. With a bit of jugglery, the husks can be tipped away, leaving unbroken, mostly husk-free, shoots. Remove any lingering husks by hand if you object to them. If the beans go mouldy before they sprout, try next time using boiled and cooled water, as the water could be the source of the mould spores.

Soya beans are the most nourishing of all but not very easy to sprout. They need to be soaked for 8-10 hours and then put into the sprouting container and kept in the dark. The best temperature for sprouting soya beans is 20-25°C (68-77°F), and they should be dunked in tepid water several times a day, as they will otherwise go mouldy. It is best to tip the beans out on a tray, very gently, every day and look for any that seem to be going bad or refusing to sprout, as bad beans can give a rank flavour to the entire batch. In 3-4 days, the sprouts will be up to 5 cm (2 in) long and ready to eat. Rinse them well in cold water and steam them quickly in very little water. Their raw taste is more 'beany' than that of mung sprouts.

Lentils are delicious sprouted and are ready when the sprout is about 2 cm (1 in) long. Their flavour is sweet and delicate.

Peas. Whole dried peas produce sprouts with a fresh pea flavour and are ready when the sprout is about 5 cm (2 in) long.

Wheat sprouts taste of newly-picked maize, and are best at about 1 cm (½ in) long, while they are tender and before they become thready.

Alfalfa gives very fine shoots of about 2 cm (1 in) in 3-4 days, with a delicate, pea-like flavour. It is easy to sprout and keeps green if grown in the light.

Most sprouts are eaten at an early stage of development, but it is also common to grow seeds on to the cotyledon stage, when they are a stalk with the two first false leaves – as in mustard and cress. Other commonly sprouted seeds include adzuki beans, fenugreek, and chickpeas.

SPRUCE is a coniferous tree of the genus *Picea*. Essence of spruce is used to flavour spruce beer. It is made by boiling the green tips of Black spruce (*B. mariana*) in water, and then concentrating the liquor, without the spruce tops, by boiling it down. Other species of spruce are also used. For instance, the Norway spruce (*P. abies*) was traditionally used in northern Europe to make 'black beer', the most famous variety of which came from Danzig. The antiscorbutic beer of the Tsarist Russian army was made of spruce tops, horseradish and beer flavoured with ginger and calamus. After fermentation, a little cream of tartar was added for acidity, plus tincture of mustard and strong spirit for a kick, as if it did not have enough already. In the more prosaic modern world, spruce oil – also called

hemlock oil – is used as a flavouring in root beer, ice cream and chewing gum. The hemlock from which it is extracted is an American conifer of the genus *Tsuga* and not the poisonous umbellifer (as taken by Socrates) to which the name is given in Britain. As a flavouring, it is more popular in North America than in Europe.

[*Spruce* – French: *sapin* German: *Fichte* Italian: *abete rosso* Spanish: *pinabete*]

SPRUE. Thin, green spears of *asparagus.

SQUAB. *See* pigeon.

SQUASH. *See* marrow.

SQUID are the most numerous of the *cephalopods and the most important as a food, particularly in Japan. There are about 350 different species, ranging from tiny creatures a few centimetres long to giant squids which reach over 18 m (60 ft) in length and are among the most formidable marine predators. Octopuses are bulbous, and cuttlefish are shield shaped, but squids are more like torpedoes, with a fin on either side. They have eight arms and two tentacles, like cuttlefish; the tentacles are normally kept retracted, ready to be shot out to grab the prey. The common inshore species of the North Atlantic and Mediterranean are members of the genus *Loligo*, but various oceanic species can also be eaten.

Freshly caught squids are amongst the most beautiful of marine animals, firm and with iridescent colours, looking as if they were embedded in crystal glass. Within minutes of being landed, they assume the unappetizing, flabby appearance they have on the market slab. Squid is available frozen, dried (a staple food in China) or canned. Because of pollution and overfishing in the Mediterranean, the use of frozen squid has greatly increased in Europe over the last two decades; fortunately, they keep their flavour and are even tenderized by freezing.

Squid are fished commercially at night with lights; the hope is to attract a shoal to the surface. In Majorca, they are fished by 'jigging', which demands some skill and is one of my favourite sports. A lure, which loosely resembles a small squid, is made from a spindle-shaped lead weight, bound with white and coloured cotton string. It has a crown of fine, unbarbed hooks at its base. To fish, the lure is lowered until it touches bottom and is then raised about a metre, after which the fisherman has to make it imitate the movements of a small squid jetting upwards in an attempt to reach the surface. That is, the lure is jerked upwards and then allowed to sink back slowly almost to the point it started from before being jerked up again. A sudden heavy drag on the line indicates that the bait has been seized by a squid, which must then be pulled in steadily, in a continuous movement, right into the boat. The hooks are unbarbed, and if the pull is slackened (as it is in the boat) the squid drops off – it is rather easy to lose the catch, especially if there is any hesitation when the creature breaks surface. Jigging is best done in the late afternoon and evening. When it gets dark, the jigger must abandon his sport, unless he has lights, and go home for a well-earned drink.

To prepare a squid, take hold of the head and pull it out with the contents of the mantle cavity (mostly attached). Clean out all the remaining guts, reserving the ink if it is needed. Make a slit and pull out the transparent 'pen'. Remove the slimy skin and wash the body, which is the best part. Cut off and skin the arms and tentacles, removing any horny suckers. If you want to use the head, remove the eyes and the beak.

There are dozens of recipes for squid in Mediterranean cooking, and the body is often stuffed. Almost everyone seems to like the fried rings of squid called *calamares a la romana* in Spain.

....

Calamares a la romana

Clean the squid and cut the body across into ½ cm (¼ in) rings. Dry them and salt them lightly; dip the rings in flour and then in beaten egg. Alternatively, use a batter made with 2 eggs, 4 dessertspoons of flour and enough water to make it fairly thin. Fry the rings until they are golden, but be warned that they may explode with some violence in the early stages of frying. Eat the rings as they are with a squeeze of lemon, with mayonnaise or with the Romesco sauce which the Spanish make with *sweet peppers.

[*Squid* – French: *encornet* German: *Kalmar* Italian: *calamaro* Spanish: *calamar*]

....

SQUIRREL. There are many different species in the US, where they are commonly eaten in country districts. Among them is the Grey squirrel (*Sciurus carolinensis*), which is common from Maine to Dakota and south to Texas and the Gulf states. It has been introduced into Britain where it is now a pest. Although some sorts of squirrel are locally protected, most are hunted. The meat of young squirrels may be white or pink; it is tender and can be grilled. The meat of older squirrels needs to be stewed for 1½-2 hours, and there are classic regional dishes incorporating corn and various vegetables. As Grey squirrels strip bark from trees and are classed as vermin in Britain, it might be sensible for the British, too, to eat them.

[*Squirrel* – French: *écureuil* German: *Eichhörnchen* Italian: *scoiattolo* Spanish: *ardilla*]

STAPHYLOCOCCUS. *See* poisoning.

STAR ANISE is a component of *Chinese five spices and of some sorts of mixed spice. Its flavour, which is rather more bitter than that of European *anise, depends on the same essential oil, anethole. It is star anise from which this is mainly extracted for use as a flavouring in drinks and confectionery. In its own right, star anise is important as a spice in Chinese cooking. The star-shaped fruits, which are dried before they have ripened, grow on a small evergreen tree (*Illicium verum*), a member of the magnolia family native to China. It is said that an English sailor first brought the spice to Europe at the end of the 16th century.

STARCH is built up in plants as an end product of photosynthesis. Starch molecules are formed by the linking together of many molecules of *glucose. In the form of granules that are virtually insoluble in water, starch constitutes a plant's reserve energy store. Although there is some starch in many plant tissues, it tends to be deposited in seeds and in special storage organs such as tubers – hence the importance of potatoes, cassavas and cereals in the human diet. Rice contains about 80% by weight of starch, wheat 70% and potatoes 20%.

When starch grains are heated in water, they swell up and form a paste, which is the basis of thickening. (When starch is heated dry, but not burned, it is converted to *dextrin.) Fairly pure forms of starch such as *cornflour, *tapioca and *arrowroot and potato flour are used in the kitchen mainly as thickeners and stabilizers for sauces, gravies and sweet dishes. A less usual starch is rice starch, which is called *crème de riz* in France (and marketed in Britain under the misleading name of ground rice). Both this and the *fécule* (potato starch) packed by the firm of Groult are recommended by Elizabeth David for binding and stabilizing soups.

Because the choice of starch greatly affects the way food looks and behaves, the food industry has brought all its scientific might to bear on the subject. Some of the resulting knowledge is useful at home as well as in the factory. The two significant factors in the behaviour of starches are the size of the starch grains and the balance in them between the two main forms of starch, amylose and amylopectin. Grain sizes in thousandths of a millimetre run from 5 for rice starch and 15 for corn starch to 100 for potato starch. The larger the grains, the more easily they absorb water and the lower the temperature at which thickening takes place – the temperature needed is always higher than that for coagulating protein. Maximum thickening takes place at around 93°C (200°F). Stirring is essential to disperse the grains and prevent lumps until that temperature is reached. A few minutes' more cooking is required to remove the starchy taste, but stirring during this time is to be avoided as it may break open the swollen starch cells and actually decrease the thickness.

Root starches such as arrowroot and tapioca have large grains that are low in amylose. They thicken at lower temperatures than cereal starches and remain fluid, though gooey, when cooled. Cereal starches from corn (maize), wheat and rice, on the other hand, have small grains that are high in amylose. They make a cloudy paste which sets to a solid gel when it is cooled. Cornflour, which is a popular thickener, is also an example of the pitfalls that can await the unwary food manufacturer. First of all, it is attacked by acids like those in some fruit which cause hydrolysis and hence thinning. When it cools, a cornflour paste sets to an opaque rubbery gel, which could be a disaster in fruit pies. It is also unsuitable for anything that is to be frozen, as freezing and thawing make water separate out from the gel. The food industry, however, has the answer to all these problems in the form of waxy starches made up almost entirely of amylopectin which produce thick, clear pastes that do not gel when they cool or break when they are frozen. The same desirable characteristics are to be found in modified starches which have been altered chemically to form cross-linking between the molecules, a treatment that increases resistance to acids. Special high-amylose starches, which set very firmly, are used to make deep-frying batter that sticks very tightly to the food that it covers. Finally among the wonders of food science, we have instant (or pre-cooked) starches. These have been cooked and dried so that they will absorb water without needing to be cooked again. They are the basis of instant desserts as well as being used to stabilize whipped cream so that it will last for several days without separating.

Instant starch opens up all manner of labour-saving possibilities to tempt the caterer. 'Suppose,' says a catering textbook, 'you wanted to make a cherry pie using canned cherries and a pre-baked pie shell, could you finish the pie without further cooking?' 'Yes,' it replies, 'by thickening the cherries with pre-cooked starch and using a whipped cream topping instead of a pastry top.' (Ceserani, Lundberg and Kotschevar. *Understanding Cooking*, Edward Arnold).

Instant starch has to be mixed dry with a lot of sugar to separate the grains, as they absorb water so eagerly that they need to be kept apart to prevent them forming lumps. Something of the same principle is involved in the essential process of dividing starchy thickeners with other substances before adding them to hot foods so that they do not go lumpy – examples are flour and butter blended in *beurre manié*, flour and hot fat (which contains no water) in *roux*, or simply a smooth mixture with cold water. Those besotted with the romance of cooking might like to know that this latter is known variously in the trade as slurry, whitewash or jayzee.

[*Starch* – French: *fécule* German: *Kohlehydrate* Italian: *amido* Spanish: *fécula*]

STARCH SUGAR and **starch syrup**. *See* glucose.

STEAMING. At normal atmospheric pressure, a pan of water produces steam when it boils at 100°C (212°F); although the pan is still being heated, the steam is also at that temperature. It is no hotter than the water is but it contains the extra heat that it absorbs when it vaporizes. It will give up this extra heat when it condenses back to water. Vegetables should be steamed over rapidly boiling water. They receive their heat from the steam that condenses on them and hardly reach boiling point themselves. However, the water that condenses and drips back dissolves out less of their soluble salts, vitamins and natural flavours than they would lose in boiling water. Steaming above the liquid in a *pressure cooker, thus at above 100°C (212°F), is a particularly good method for vegetables such as potatoes and beetroot. Steaming covers a wide range of techniques from the heating of *couscous over the stew in a *couscousière* to cooking steamed puddings in basins and steaming bean shoots in a very little water in the bottom of the pan.

[*Steaming* – French: *cuire à la vapeur* German: *dünsten* Italian: *cuocere a vapour* Spanish: *cocer al vapor*]

STEEL. *See* iron.

STEEPING is the soaking, usually prolonged, of a solid food in a liquid. It therefore includes processes for introducing preservatives or flavourings, such as brining and marinating, but also soaking for the reverse effect: making extracts of soluble substances like essential oils and colourings.

STERILIZATION means the total destruction of all living organisms, including their spores. Most micro-organisms in their vegetative stages are killed in 5 minutes at 80°C (176°F) or in half an hour at only 62°C (144°F), as in pasteurization, but heat-loving bacteria, like those of the compost heap can stand 80-90°C (176-194°F) for 10 minutes. A few minutes fast boiling will kill even these, but it will not kill spores. This is why temperatures above 100°C (212°F) generated in a pressure cooker or autoclave are used in *preservation in the canning or bottling of foods in which dangerous spores can germinate. A temperature of 122°C (252°F) for 30 minutes will kill all spores and give complete sterilization. This is the temperature of a pressure cooker at 15 lb/sq in (1.05 kg/sq cm), but most pressure cookers work at 5-10 lb/sq in (0.35-0.7 kg/sq cm) – with temperatures around 112°C (234°F) and in that case sterilization takes longer. Instructions are given by the makers of pressure cookers and should be followed exactly. Proteinous and albuminous substances take longer to sterilize than do fruits and vegetables.

Dry sterilization in the oven needs a higher temperature for a longer time, as organisms are more susceptible to wet heat than to dry. It takes baking at 180°C (356°F) for 1½ hours to sterilize glass jars.

Finally, there is the method known as discontinuous heating. This consists of killing the vegetative bacteria by boiling, and waiting (preferably incubating) for long enough to allow the spores to germinate, then heating again to kill them. The process will need to be repeated several times to insure complete sterilization. Discontinuous heating is not a method usually used in the kitchen.

[*Sterilization* – French: *stérilisation* German: *Sterilisation* Italian: *sterilizzazione* Spanish: *esterilización*]

STERLET. *See* sturgeon.

STEWING is defined by Webster as 'boiling slowly or simmering,' but it should not be *boiling*, slowly, or at any other speed. Stewing is done in a pot with a firmly-fitting lid and at a temperature below boiling point – it is in effect the same as *simmering. The proteins in meat are coagulated at a temperature considerably below the 90°C (194°F) of simmering, while the mechanical effects of rapid boiling will spoil the texture of any stew. In most cases, as little liquid as possible should be used so that the gravy becomes thick

[*Stewing* – French: *cuire à l'étuvée* German: *schmoren* Italian: *cuocere in umido* Spanish: *estofar*]

STOCK CUBES are marketed as a short cut in making a variety of stocks. The usual flavours are chicken and beef, but there are also mushroom, onion and other stock cubes for particular purpose (such as *pot au feu* cubes).They are made according to each manufacturer's secret formulae and mainly consist of salt, monosodium glutamate and chicken or beef flavour (which may or may not have involved poultry or cattle), plus a binder. They vary enormously, according to price and manufacturer. Some stock cubes are awful, and it is easy to dismiss them all, but good ones are very useful for reinforcing flavour or to cover an emergency. They are, however, only a source of flavour, not of nourishment.

STOCK or **fumet**. Extract of meat, bones, fish, fowl, game or vegetables, usually made by simmering the ingredients for a long time in water to extract their essence. Stocks are not served in their own right, but are the basis for other things, not only for soups, but most important of all, for sauces. Ideally, a good stock should always be available, and 'if there is fresh stock made every week a reputation as a good cook will almost inevitably follow.' (Len Deighton's *Action Cook Book*, Penguin). Fortunately, it is not really necessary to make stock every week, because it can be concentrated and kept in the freezer or the ice compartment of the refrigerator. In Victorian Britain, the accepted rule of thumb for making stock was a pound of meat to a pint of water (almost 800 g per lt). But even before World War I such proportions began to be considered extravagant, and now most of the classic recipes are strictly for millionaires. For instance Urbain-Dubois, writing in 1869, indicates taking a whole shoulder of veal to make stock. Chefs these days make their stock from bones, and even beef bones do well, though not, of course, for delicate white sauces. One thing is sure: while excellent stocks can be made from beef bones, veal bones, chicken carcasses and feet, tough old hares and fish heads, the stock-pot should never be treated as a rubbish bin.

A Basic Stock

Take a pile of veal bones or beef bones, wash them, break them into bits, and put them in a hot oven until they are dark, almost black. Cover them with cold water and bring them slowly to simmering point, but never boil them. Skim the stock frequently, especially at the start. Keep it simmering for 6-8 hours. Strain it and remove as much fat as possible from the surface. Now mix together some raw, completely lean mince with finely-chopped carrot and celery and some white of egg. Stir this mixture into the stock. Bring it back to simmering point and simmer for 15 minutes. A thick scum will form on top. Strain the stock through a cloth. The purpose of the meat and vegetables is not only to help the egg white in the clearing process, but to give extra fresh flavour. Fat can be removed by cooling the stock and then picking it off when it has solidified, or by skimming and blotting with paper.

For a very white stock, use veal bones and blanch them. Stock should be salted very lightly, if at all, or it will get too salty when reduced. If stock is to be used for opaque sauces, such as *demi-glace* or *sauce espagnole*, then it is not necessary to clear it at all. Once made, the stock may be reduced by boiling to a brown jelly which sets on the bottom of the pan when cold. This jelly can be cut into squares and put into the freezer. It will keep for a year and is always ready as a basis for French sauces, such as the foundation sauces, *demi-glace* and *sauce espagnole* (which lead to Bordelaise, Bourguignonne, Châteaubriand, Financière, Lyonnaise, Poivrade and Périgueux sauces), or the white foundation sauces, such as *velouté* and *allemande*, which open up other culinary vistas.

There is little point in making fish stock in advance because it must cook for only half an hour at most – it will acquire a nasty taste if it is much overcooked. Game stock can be made by anyone with access to tough old hares and old birds. *Larousse Gastronomique*, which is authoritative on sauces, says that to cook 'in the grand manner', you should have at hand: clear soup, veal stock, brown thin stock, brown thick stock, juice of braised meat, poultry stock, game stock, fish stock, and various jellies. Those who cook Chinese food might well add 'High broth' (chicken and pork) and maybe beef and shrimp broth; a mutton broth flavoured with onion, cinnamon and cloves is useful for Indian cooking, though not traditional, as it would go bad without refrigeration. The trick is not to have every sort of stock in the freezer, but to have a few to suit the dishes you are likely to cook.

[*Stock* – French: *consommé* German: *Suppenbrühe* Italian: *brodo* Spanish: *caldo*]

STOCKFISH is cod, hake, ling or similar white fish, gutted, beheaded and split, then washed and dried in the air without salt. It is often confused with *bacalao*, which is dried, salted cod and has a somewhat different flavour. Stockfish has to be very dry to keep in warm climates. It is popular, for instance, in parts of northern and central Italy, where it may be cooked with white wine, onions, herbs, black olives and potatoes, or eaten with polenta. Basic preparation in Italy is to beat the fish to break the fibres and then to soak it for a week in many changes of water. However, in other parts of Europe, the treatment done is very different, though it may be equally heroic. In Holland, Belgium and Germany, where stockfish is also popular, it is soaked in limewater. In Norway, for *lutefisk* (lye fish), a traditional Christmas dish, the stockfish is soaked in fresh water with frequent changes for 2-3 days, then in *lye for another 2-3 days and finally returned for 2-3 days to many more changes of fresh water. After its chemical battering, the fish is cut in large pieces and simmered for a minute in unsalted water. Then salt is added at the rate of 50 g (2 oz) to 1 lt (1¾ pt) of water and the fish is simmered for a further 5 minutes. After that, it is ready to be drained, and served with boiled potatoes, yellow split peas and melted pork dripping or butter. *God yul.*

[*Stockfish* – French: *stockfisch* German: *Stockfisch* Italian: *baccalà, stoccafisso* Spanish: *bacalao seco*]

STONEWARE is hard and mechanically strong pottery which has been fired at temperatures in excess of 1200°C (2200°F) and, unlike *earthware, is not usually porous nor particularly resistant to thermal shock. Modern glazes used on stoneware have low lead solubility and salt-glazed stoneware is especially good for storing acid substances.

Much ovenware is stoneware with a greater porosity and higher resistance to thermal shock than average. Although it is not easily broken, ovenware can rarely be put on top of the naked flame of a gas stove.

[*Stoneware* – French: *grès, potérie de grés* German: *Steingut* Italian: *lareggio* Spanish: *gres*]

STRAWBERRY is unique among fruit in having the seeds dotted around on the outside rather than embedded within. Although strawberries are canned and frozen (neither with any great success) and are made into jam, they are above all a fruit for eating fresh: strawberries and cream has always been one of the great treats of the English summer. Because they are both easily damaged and highly perishable, strawberries used not to be sent great distances to market. Nowadays, however, British greengrocers sell strawberries not just from southern Europe, which arrive some weeks before the home-grown ones, but from California and South Africa which supply out-of-season strawberries for the luxury market (which too often has to be satisfied by the visual experience rather than the flavour, which can be anything but luxurious).

To avoid damage in picking and to ensure that the fruit appears in perfect condition when it gets to market, the fruit farmers gather their strawberries before they are perfectly ripe, even if they have only to travel for a matter of hours. As always, though, fruit ripened on the plant has incomparably the best flavour. Now that increasing labour costs have persuaded farmers increasingly to invite people to pick their own fruit, strawberries are the ones that most repay the effort, as the farmers let the public go to work on fields of fully ripe fruit which may have gone too far to survive commercial distribution but are at their best for immediate consumption. It makes a fantastic difference if every strawberry in a bowl has been picked at its peak.
Strawberries are members of the rose family, low plants that spread by sending out runners which root at the end and thus form new plants – this makes them very easy to propagate vegetatively. The Wild strawberry of Britain and Europe, *Fragaria vesca*, has small fruit with a fine flavour that is also found in the rather larger cultivated varieties which are known as Alpine strawberries or *fraises de bois* (at least one sort of which is white rather than red). A second species, the Hautboy or Hautbois strawberry (*F. moschata*) from central and eastern Europe, is now rarely grown; it has fruit with a musky flavour and without seeds at the stalk end. Both the European species went out of favour because they were not susceptible to much 'improvement' by the plant breeders, which meant above all that they could not be persuaded to produce large fruit. Alpine strawberries are still grown commercially in Europe, for example in France, where flavour can still be as important as size. The two species have the advantage that they can be raised from seed and that for some reason their fruit is not taken by birds.

Modern strawberry varieties are all derived from North and South American species with seeds sunk in the surface of the fruit rather than sticking out from it. The first American species to arrive in Europe, in the early 17th century, was the Scarlet woodland strawberry (*F. virginiana*) from the eastern US. A variety of it, Little Scarlet, is still grown for jam-making. The Pine Strawberry (*F. chiloensis*) from the West Coast of South and North America was brought to Europe in the 18th century; its fruit, which is pink or whitish, is said to taste distinctly of pineapple. The Garden strawberry (*F. X ananassa*) is a hybrid of these two species, which in nature were separated geographically; it first appeared in France in the early 19th century but was quickly taken up elsewhere. There is now a plethora of varieties in all sizes from medium to gigantic to fit particular local conditions. How good any of them are can be determined only by tasting; appearance seems even less of a guide with strawberries than with any other fruit.

[*Strawberry* – French: *fraise* German: *Erdbeere* Italian: *fragola* Spanish: *fresa, fresón*]

STRAWBERRY TOMATO. *See* physalis fruit.

STRAWBERRY TREE. *See* cranberry.

STRING BEAN. *See* kidney bean. US term for green bean or French bean.

STUFFING, **FORCEMEAT** and **FILLING**. It is unnecessary to try distinguishing exactly between these inexact words. They are all preparations that are put inside something, although forcemeats are occasionally rolled into balls and fried or cooked alongside the main ingredient. Stuffings must be suitable; you should not stuff something that has a delicate flavour with a strong stuffing that would overwhelm it, and it is sensible to stuff a fat goose with something absorbent and a dry guinea fowl with something juicy. Some stuffings are intended to flavour and are not expected to be eaten, like the handful of tarragon in the chicken, or an orange in a duck. When foods are stuffed, especially with a raw stuffing, they take longer to cook, which can sometimes be a disadvantage. Stuffings absorb flavour and juices from whatever they are inside, which they do not if they are cooked separately. Some dishes – *ravioli, cannelloni* or *crépinettes*, for instance – are stuffing done up in parcels. Other stuffings are there because the article concerned was clearly created to be stuffed – squid and sweet peppers are examples. Some made-up stuffed dishes, like cucumbers stuffed with mince and sauced with sour cream, make an economical dish from ingredients which would otherwise be formless, but there are also stuffed foods which are no more than a fantasy or a gimmick. Stuffings are worth some thought and trouble. They are not leftovers or things to be bought ready-made in a packet.

The general rule for the quantity of stuffing is 1 cup per 450 g (1 lb) for birds and about half that amount for fish. A simple stuffing for birds is made from 150 g (6 oz) of fresh breadcrumbs, 100 g (4 oz) of butter and an egg, if binding is necessary. Flavourings to be included are onion (parboiled), thyme and grated lemon zest, or sage, fruit, nuts, herbs of many kinds, and celery, but not all together. Always adjust the salt and sourness (with lemon juice) and check carefully by tasting.

Stuffing for Tortelloni

Mix together 250 g (9 oz) ricotta cheese, 50 g (2 oz) cooked spinach, a good grate of nutmeg, 2 eggs, 150 g (5 oz) Parmesan cheese, salt, and a finely-pounded clove of garlic, at your discretion. Taste and adjust the seasoning if necessary. Roll *pasta out to rather over 1 mm (say about $1/16$ in) thick, cut it in 5-6 cm (2-2½ in) diameter circles or squares, put filling on each piece, fold it over, seal the edge and press the ends together. Boil it for 4-5 minutes in salted water and serve with butter, tomato sauce and grated Parmesan cheese.

Rice Stuffing for Tomatoes

Take 4 beautiful large ripe tomatoes. Cut off a lid, scoop out the middle (keeping the flesh and juice) and sprinkle the insides with salt, pepper and a little olive oil. Put 4 dessertspoons of cooked rice in a bowl and add some chopped parsley and chopped basil, a crushed clove of garlic, a pinch of oregano, several spoons of olive oil and the juice and flesh of the tomato. Mix well and then remove the garlic, which is there to give only a taste. Divide the stuffing among the tomatoes, and replace their tops. Put them in a fireproof dish, standing each tomato on a slice of cooked or raw potato. Sprinkle with oil and cook in a hot oven for 45 minutes. Serve hot or cold as an hors d'oeuvre.

Stuffings for Fish

1) a ½ cup of chopped parsley, a pinch of chopped fresh thyme and 2 or 3 crushed juniper berries mixed with 3 tablespoons olive oil.

Alternatively 2) a cup of chopped sorrel and ½ cup chopped spinach, both raw, a little garlic, ¼ cup breadcrumbs, 4 finely-chopped mushrooms, salt and pepper, mix together and bind with an egg and a couple of tablespoons of cream.

[Stuffing – French: farce German: Füllsel, Füllung Italian: ripieno Spanish: relleno]

STURGEON. There are over two dozen species of sturgeon, all found in the Northern hemisphere. They live in the sea or in very large lakes, but, like salmon, they swim up the rivers to spawn. Many species are armoured with plates and have a shark-like tail. Their weird, pre-historic appearance is not entirely misleading – they have many ancient characteristics and zoologically are classified somewhere between cartilaginous fishes and bony fishes. They are bottom-feeders, with no teeth, and are quite harmless.

Sturgeon are known mainly for the *caviar they provide, but their swim bladders make the finest *isinglass, and dried sturgeon spine is viziga, which is used in the legendary Russian fish pie, coulibiac. The head of the sturgeon is especially valued in some countries because of the variety of different types of flesh in it, but most species are not much prized for their flesh in the countries where they are common. Sturgeon is a meaty, pink-fleshed fish, very suitable for grilling, but the ones I have eaten have a peculiar taste, perhaps because they have been slurping mud at the bottom of the Caspian. The exception is the small sterlet (Acipenser ruthenus) of the Black and Caspian Seas which goes up the Danube to spawn (or did) and which I have eaten in Budapest and Belgrade. Other species are better after heavy marinating in vinegar or wine to kill the taste of sturgeon.

The Atlantic sturgeon (A. sturio), which reaches fish shops on occasion, is found in the North Atlantic and the Mediterranean, but not in the Black Sea. The sevruga (A. stellatus), the osciotre (A. guldenstädtii), and the giant belgua (Huso huso) are found from the Black Sea through the Caspian to the Sea of Azov – the osciotre as far as Lake Baikal. The North American species A. rubicundus of the Great Lakes is (or was) important. Smoked sturgeon, as made in Turkey, is considered a great delicacy which, with smoked sword fish, is sometimes held to be the equal of smoked salmon (but I feel that no-one understands smoking as do northern Europeans). Like smoked salmon, it must be cut thin and along the side.

[*Sturgeon* – French: *esturgeon* German: *Stör* Italian: *storione* Spanish: *esturión*]

SUCCORY. *See* chicory.

SUCROSE. *See* sugar.

SUET is the hard fat from around the kidneys of beef or mutton, beef being better flavoured and more usually used in cooking. Suet was formerly more important as an ingredient than it is today, especially in Britain and the US. Such famous old fare as suet pudding, steak and kidney pudding, suet dumplings, spotted dick and jam roll all depend on it. Today, most people buy ready-prepared suet in packets and would not know how to start from scratch if they suddenly needed it in a country where the packets are not available (which, in fact, is most countries), but fresh suet has the best taste.

Take the fat from around beef kidneys, and with the fingers free it from as much connective tissue as possible. Dust the suet liberally with part of the flour that has been weighed to be used in the pastry and chop it with a sharp knife, dusting on more flour to prevent the knife sticking to the suet when it seems necessary. Continue chopping until you judge it fine enough to make pastry. Once freed from the membranes, suet will keep for weeks in the refrigerator.

[*Suet* – French: *graisse de rognon* German: *Nierenfett* Italian: *grasso di bue* Spanish: *sebo, sain*]

SUGAR normally means sucrose ($C_{12}H_{22}O_{11}$), the sugar of sugar cane and sugar beet. More generally, sugars are carbohydrates made by green plants from carbon dioxide and water, using the energy of sunlight. In the process, carbon dioxide is removed from the air and oxygen returned to it. When we use sugars in our bodies, we reverse the process, turning carbohydrate to carbon dioxide and water, and using the energy that is released. We take in oxygen and put out carbon dioxide. There are three main grades of carbohydrate – in ascending order of complexity:

1) the simple sugars, the monosaccharides, such as *glucose, *fructose and *galactose.

2) the more complex sugars, the disaccharides, like sucrose (cane or beet sugar), *maltose (malt sugar) and *lactose (milk sugar), with molecules that are two molecules of simple sugars joined together.

3) the most complex carbohydrates, the polysaccharides, like *starch, cellulose (of plant cell walls) and glycogen (animal starch as stored in the liver), which are many molecules of simpler sugars joined together.

Plants commonly store food in the form of starch grains, which are virtually insoluble in the watery cell fluid, but some store it as sugar. They also produce quantities of sugars (but not of starch) in ripe fruits, and sugar flavours the nectar of flowers. Both nectar in flowers and the sweetness of ripe fruits are means by which plants bribe animals to assist them, respectively in reproducing and spreading their seeds.

Sugars are all sweet but not equally so. They may be compared by giving sucrose a mark of 100, when others on the scale are as follows:

fructose 173
sucrose 100
glucose 74
maltose 32
lactose 16

Looking at these, one may well wonder if the making up of babies' bottle milk formulae from dried cow's milk with the sugar content increased with sucrose instead of lactose is not training modern man to a fattening sweet tooth.

The earliest sweeteners were honey, sweet fruit and syrups concentrated from fruit – an example is the *dibs made in the Lebanon. *Maple syrup and maple sugar were being made by the American Indians long before settlers arrived from Europe, and probably palm sugar, which is also made by boiling down sap, was made before cane sugar, as this involved squeezing out the juice, a slightly more advanced technology. Today, highly purified sucrose extracted from either sugar cane or sugar beet is the almost universal sweetener.

Sugar cane (*Saccharum officinarum*) is a huge grass which grows higher than a man's head and has a thick, solid stem that contains as much as 10-15% of sugar. There are varieties for chewing, but their taste is a flat sweetness that is not relieved by any balancing acidity. The plant is a native of tropical Asia and needs a hot climate. Legend suggests that the Polynesians were the first to use sugar cane as a source of sweetness. However, it was certainly known in India at a very early date, as the word sugar derives from Sanskrit. In 510 BC, the

Persians noted sugar in use in the Indus Valley, and during Alexander the Great's invasion, the Greeks also learned about it. It was still crude brown sugar, of the type of *jaggery, and nothing at all like the refined white sugar of today. Later, sugar cane was taken to Persia, where the first refineries were set up in the 7th century AD by the Arabs who, being chemists, made technological improvements, such as the addition of alkali. Sugar was by then used in medicine to preserve it and to disguise the taste of drugs. It was also the Arabs who first introduced sugar to Europe, and sugar cane was grown in some warm areas including Cyprus, Sicily and Andalusia, although it does not really thrive in a Mediterranean climate. It was taken to Madeira around 1420. However, by the end of the 15th century Venice had become the sugar-trading centre of Europe; most of the sugar was brought from the Orient, and it was vastly expensive. One of the first references to it in Britain is to a cargo of 100,000 lb which arrived in London in 1519, and which the Venetians exchanged for wool.

Columbus took canes to America from the Canary Islands during his second voyage in 1493.They were first planted at his headquarters on the island of San Domingo in the Caribbean, where he reported the canes grew faster than anywhere else in the world. Soon they were taken to other Caribbean islands and to the mainland, for example to Brazil. The planters who grew the 'white gold' became vastly rich. By the early 18th century, the West Indies was the main source of supply and it was a prime reason for the slave trade. The first refinery in England had been built in 1544, but sugar was still very costly. In the 18th century, when coffee and tea drinking became the vogue, the demand for sugar increased sharply. In 1700, the whole of Britain used a mere 10,000 tons, but by the end of the century consumption had grown to 150,000 tons per annum. An even more spectacular increase came after 1874, when Gladstone removed the tax which had previously kept sugar in the luxury class. By 1885, the yearly consumption had grown to over 1,000,000 tons. Today, Britain uses 2,300,000 tons a year. Of course, there has been an increase in population in the interim, but the quantity consumed shows that refined sugar is a major element in many people's diets, to the tune of roughly 1 kg (about 2 lb) per person per week.

Sugar from sugar beet (Beta vulgaris var. cicla) came as a direct result of the British blockade of Europe during the Napoleonic wars. In 1747, a German chemist, Andreas Marggraf found up to 6.2% of sugar in certain varieties of beet, but early efforts to exploit the discovery were a commercial failure. It was not until 1811, when Napoleon ordered an investment to be made in the process, that much progress was made. Later, the new crop was officially encouraged in Europe and North America. By 1880, beet had replaced cane as a source of sugar in a number of countries. Britain, however, still obtained most of its sugar from the West Indian colonies. Two World Wars, though, encouraged even the British to be as self-sufficient in sugar as possible. Today, the growing of beet, which has been improved to contain 15 to 20% of sugar, is still spreading; beet is even being grown in the north of India, a country associated with the origins of sugar cane production. At the moment, 40% of the world's sugar comes from beet. Refined sugar is 99% sucrose; it is not possible to tell by taste whether it is from beet or cane, but sugar beet molasses is not nice and edible like cane molasses. It is a raw material for industry (e.g. in the making of *monosodium glutamate) and an animal food-stuff. There is thus no brown sugar from beet, unless it has been made artificially.

Primitive methods of sugar production are still to be seen in sugar-producing countries. In India, for instance, the lovely smell of sugar in the making still pervades villages in the cold weather. The cane is passed between two large cog wheels turned by oxen, and the juice is boiled down in wide, open pans over a fire composed of the dross from the cane crushing. Lime is thrown in to neutralize the acids, and the surface is skimmed. Later, the dark brown, richly smelling, sticky jaggery is scraped from the pans. (Boiled with butter, jaggery makes just about the best toffee in the world.)

In the large factories, the extraction process, though sophisticated, is similar. A boiled mass of sugar crystals and sticky molasses is obtained which is called massecuite and is essentially the same as jaggery. But then the mixture is put into a centrifuge and the molasses is spun out. The residue is crude brown sugar, which is sticky, but less so than jaggery. Raw sugar sounds delicious, but, as imported in bulk, it is likely to be full of trash, soil, dirt, bacteria and moulds and even creatures called sugar lice (Carpoglyphus anonymus or Acarus sacchari). In the refineries, it is softened with warm syrup, centrifuged, strained, treated with lime and carbon dioxide, and decolourized with bone charcoal. Finally, the clear syrup is boiled under reduced pressure until the introduction of a small number of 'seed' crystals causes crystallization.

Though refined, it is still a mixture of crystals and syrup and has to be centrifuged again and dried in granulators before it is ready to be graded by sieving.

Beets have to be shredded and the sugar dissolved out with warm water to produce a sugary solution which is treated with lime, carbon dioxide, sulphur dioxide, and so on in successive processes until it can be evaporated, crystallized and centrifuged in the same way as cane sugar. The largest producers of cane sugar are Cuba, Brazil and India; the USSR, Europe and the US are the big beet sugar areas.

Caster sugar is drawn from the evaporating pan at the correct crystal size. Icing sugar is made by powdering the crystals in a mill. Lump or cube sugar is made by compressing moist sugar in moulds and then drying it. In the old days, the moist refined sugar was poured into a mould shaped like a volcano (a Venetian innovation) to produce loaf sugar, which had to be broken up with special tongs. Real loaf sugar is still used in some parts of the Middle East, but the name is applied to any lump sugar in the US.

Sucrose from cane or beet will dissolve completely in about a third of its weight of water at room temperature. More will dissolve in hot water but will crystallize out again on cooling. Sucrose syrups boil at a higher temperature than pure water, but if the sugar is heated dry, it will melt at about 160°C (320°F) and will then cool to a straw-coloured, glassy substance called barley sugar.

Confectioners make good use of the different physical states in which sugar can exist when it is heated to various temperatures. It is tricky to melt sugar by itself, as it is apt to overheat in spots and then caramelize. Thus it is usual to add a little water to the sugar. Even so, heat must be applied gently until the sugar has completely melted, after which the temperature is best raised as fast as possible without causing it to burn – in general, the longer sugar is heated, the greater the degree of caramelization or darkening. (Once the added water has boiled away, the sugar begins to lose the water of crystallization, which is an integral part of the sugar crystal.)To prevent unwanted caramelization, never let the sides of the pan overheat, and keep them free of sugar by brushing or sponging them down with cold water. Professional confectioners may boil the sugar with the lid on the pan – called 'steaming down' – so that the sugar on the sides gets wet with steam.

Sugar heated above 120°C (250°F) will almost certainly grain or candy unless steps are taken to stop it. With graining, the sugar goes into an opaque hard lump when it cools. To prevent this, a lowering agent must be added. For home-made toffees, this is often a dash of vinegar or lemon juice, but serious sweet-makers mostly use thick glucose syrup at the rate of 1 kg (2¼ lb) glucose to 4 kg (9 lb) of sugar.

However, in hot countries it is better to use cream of tartar – 10 g (1½ level tablespoons) of cream of tartar to 4 kg (9 lb) of sugar. Dirty pans also cause graining, as does inadequate skimming when the sugar boils. To test the various stages of sugar boiling, professionals will dip their fingers into cold water, then quickly into the sugar and back again into the cold water. Anyone lacking speed or confidence (which means almost everyone) should use the handle of a spoon or a short iron rod instead of fingers. For large quantities, it is best to use a sugar thermometer, which will be graduated up to about 200°C or 400°F. Keep it handy in a jug of very hot water, as clipping it to the side of the pan (which the design suggests) will get in the way of the brushing down.

Sugar Boiling

As sugar is heated, it changes constantly, and the stage it has reached is related to the temperature. The stages have been given names by the confectioners, but there is much variation (at least from five to thirteen) in the number of stages identified by different authorities, and there is no absolute agreement on the temperatures at which the stages are reached, not surprisingly, as there is another factor which affects the state of sugar – the speed of heating. The following list represents the stages that might be recognized by cooks in old-fashioned kitchens.

1)Thread – 102°C (215°F). If a little of the liquid sugar is taken out, it can be pulled into brittle threads between the thumb and the forefinger. This and the next stage are used for candying fruit, for liqueur making and for icing.

2) Pearl – 106°C (222°F).The thread formed between thumb and finger can be stretched. The name of the stage comes from the fact that the sugar is boiling and forms small pearl-like balls.

3) Blow or soufflé – 110°C (230°F).The bubbles in the boiling sugar look like snowflakes, and if you dip in a perforated skimmer and then blow through the holes, bubbles or flakes will form. This is the

temperature for making sugar candy.

4) Soft ball – 116°C (240°F).The sugar clinging to the skimmer will now, when shaken, produce a feathery, downy effect. The syrup is now beginning to thicken and will form a soft ball if a little of it is dropped into cold water. This is the temperature for fondants, fudges, peppermint creams and the final stages of fruit candying.

5) Hard ball – 121°C (250°F).If some of the syrup is dropped into cold water, it will make a hard ball. This is the temperature for caramels, nougats and soft toffees.

6) Light crack (or crackling) – 129°C (264°F). If a rod is dipped in the sugar, then quickly plunged into cold water, the sugar forms a hard layer. Alternatively, you can use a wetted finger, a rather risky business unless you have the lightning fingers (and hardened) of a professional cook. If you put the cooled sugar in your mouth, it will stick to your teeth. It is used for toffee icings: slightly higher temperatures are used for most toffees. At the light crack stage, sugar begins to turn pale yellow in colour.

7) Hard crack – 143°C (289°F).The cooked sugar becomes harder and more glassy. A coating on a rod (or a daring wetted finger) will, when plunged into cold water, come off in thin films that crack like glass. At somewhat higher temperatures, around 150°C (302°F), the sugar reaches a suitable state for making barley sugar, butterscotch, boiled sweets, fruit drops and brittles. Slightly higher still and caramel is just starting to form – this is the temperature for spun sugar and for dipping fresh fruit such as peaches, apricots and grapes to give them a crackle covering.

8) *Caramel – 180°C (356°F).There is now very little water left in the sugar. It darkens and progressively loses its sweetness, eventually forming *browning. At higher temperatures still, it finally burns to carbon. Sucrose warmed with a dilute acid, such as sulphuric acid, is split by *hydrolysis into two simpler monosaccharide sugars – glucose and fructose. Enzymes in our insides and in the saliva of bees also break down sucrose into these two simpler sugars.

Sugar has other important effects, apart from sweetening in cookery. In high concentrations it acts as a *preservative; in bottling and canning, it helps to maintain both texture and flavour in fruit; in *freezing, fruit is best if it is first coated with sugar or frozen in a 40% sugar syrup; in baking, the effect of sugar is to maintain the elasticity of the gluten so that it stays flexible for longer and so allows the cake to rise better – it does not set rigid too soon;

it has a similar effect on the protein of egg in cakes and custards; it combines with the pectin in fruit (in the presence of fruit acids) to form a jelly; it forms both bulk and texture in cakes and ice creams; by encouraging peptization in marinades, it helps meat to become more tender, and it counteracts the hardening effect of saltpetre in cures for ham and bacon. On the debit side, sugar undoubtedly contributes to dental worries by encouraging decay bacteria in the mouth, and overconsumption has been blamed for a number of modern illnesses, but evidence here is so far inconclusive. Too much of most things is harmful; exactly how much is too much is difficult to decide.

Types of sugar

Barbados sugar. Sugar-cane cultivation was introduced into Barbados in the 17th century, and the sugar from there had a high reputation. Many sugars were once labelled with the name of the place of origin and some names have stuck. Barbados is a dark brown, moist sugar with a fine 'rummy' taste and not too coarse a grain for cakes. It is also known as moist sugar in the US.

Bee sugar. Rough sugar used by bee-keepers to maintain hives over winter, or at any time when there is no honey flow, which may be the hot dry season, in some countries. If they were not fed sugar, the bees would eat the honey that the bee-keeper wants from them, or would starve if it were taken. The saliva of bees converts sucrose to glucose and fructose, and the result is stored in the comb. The cells look white and are easily recognized; they should not be sold as honey. (In wartime Britain, some kept bees to get an extra ration of sugar).

Brown sugar. In the past, brown sugar was sugar partly purified and containing residual molasses which gave it flavour. Today, most brown sugar is a reconstituted product made by adding calculated amounts of suitable cane molasses to purified white sugar. People used to old-fashioned Barbados or Demerara will find the result rather insipid. Examples of reconstituted brown sugars are Tate & Lyle's light brown soft, a fine-grained, creamy-golden sugar for use when a slight, but not too pronounced, brown-sugar taste is needed, and their rich brown soft sugar, which is darker and has a stronger, but still mild, flavour. Many cooks prefer the traditional brown sugars which are less widely available and more costly.

Caster sugar or **castor sugar** – Both spellings are correct – is a very fine but crystalline sugar (called superfine in the US) the best for many purposes. It blends beautifully in cake mixtures, gives a sparkle finish when sifted over anything for decoration and is the one to use in meringues. As it dissolves quickly and is therefore seemingly sweeter than coarser-grained sugar, it is the ideal to have in the sugar caster on the table.

Coffee sugar. A form of sugar candy.

Coloured sugar. Some sugar is dyed brown to simulate brown sugars. Coarsely crystalline sugar candy (*see below*), is sometimes dyed for decoration. Sometimes mixed colours turn up on the coffee table. Coloured crystals are also used in cake decoration. They may be made by putting colours on the palms of the hands, rubbing the crystals between them and then drying the coloured sugar. Traditionally, colours used were cochineal for pink sugar, spinach juice for green, saffron solution for yellow, chocolate syrup for brown and indigo for blue. Nowadays the colours would probably be synthetic.

Confectioner's sugar. US name for icing sugar.

Crystal sugar. Sugar candy.

Cube sugar. Hard, small grained crystalline sugar pressed moist into blocks, dried and cut into cubes of various sizes; some are wrapped in paper. Cube sugar, though more expensive than loose sugar, is preferred by cafes and restaurants where portion control is important. On the tea table it is less easily spilled and looks more elegant. It is also more elegant in champagne cocktails. In the kitchen, it is sometimes useful. It can be rubbed on lemons or oranges to remove flavouring oils without the bits of zest you would get if the peel were grated. Lump sugar tends to vanish in households where there are children (who like to stuff a lump into a hole in an orange, and suck it).

Demerara sugar. A brown sugar with large crystals and fine flavour named after the Demerara district in Guyana. It is less moist than Barbados sugar, varies considerably in quality, and is less widely available than it used to be. A modern equivalent, made from refined white sugar with added molasses is Tate & Lyle's 'London Demerara',

but many prefer the original even though it is more expensive. 'London Demerara' is described as having a pleasing golden colour with a delicate syrup flavour. There is a 'Demerara' sugar from Barbados, which is said to be pure cane sugar, and has more flavour than the London variety. The large crystals make demerara-type sugars ideal for use on cereals and porridge. They are traditional sweeteners for coffee and are also used in meat dishes, for example on ham.

Dark brown sugar. US name for Barbados sugar or for a dark form of brown sugar (*see above*).

Foots. Crude, unrefined sugar, containing molasses and uncrystallizable sugars, is called foot sugar because it was originally the sugar which crystallized and sank to the foot or bottom of the barrel. It has a high proportion of molasses and is the crudest of all the brown sugars.

*Golden syrup is a uniquely British product which is pale yellow and has a thick, honey-like consistency. Its taste is unique, delicate and quite unlike molasses.

Granulated sugar. Ordinary, refined crystalline sugar as used in the kitchen.

Icing sugar, called powdered sugar or confectioner's sugar in the US, is a fine, very white powdered sugar made by grinding it in a mill to the required consistency. It is likely to contain a harmless anti-caking agent like starch or calcium phosphate, and is used for decorating cakes and for dusting, as on Turkish delight and other sweets. It dissolves instantly, is very sweet to the taste, and is used in whipped cream and in uncooked sweets (such as chocolate truffles and fondants), where there should not be a grainy texture. It is also used in meringues, but less so than caster sugar.

*Jaggery. Indian crude sugar or *gur*.

Light brown soft sugar. A form of brown sugar.

Loaf sugar. US name for cube sugar.

London Demerara. A Tate & Lyle imitation of Demerara sugar.

Lump sugar. Cube sugar.

Maple sugar is made by reduction of *maple syrup.

Moist sugar. US name for Barbados sugar.

*Molasses. A dark, treacly mass of sugars and other substances left over from sugar refining.

Palm sugar. Sugar made by boiling down the sap of various *palms.

Panela. Hard, dark Colombian sugar formed into loaves.

Penang sugar. So called after its port of shipment, a type of foots.

Pieces or yellows. Soft brown sugar produced by crystallizing the syrup from which the crystals of refined sugar have been separated out. It is slightly sticky because the crystals have a coating of the mother liquor.

Piloncillo. Crude brown sugar from Mexico. Very dark and shaped in the form of small corks, sometimes wrapped in raffia and also called *panocha*. Very dark Barbados sugar is the best substitute.

Powdered sugar. US name for icing sugar.

Preserving sugar. Pure refined sugar in large white crystals or irregular small lumps used for making jams, jellies and marmalades. Although ordinary granulated sugar can be used for this purpose, preserving sugar is more convenient, as it does not form a compact mass and thus needs less stirring. In the initial stages of jam-making, there is less likelihood of the pan catching, or of caramelization and burning.

Raw sugar. Crude brown sugar as it is shipped to the refinery.

Rich brown soft. A form of brown sugar.

Rock candy. US name for sugar candy.

Sand sugar. Light brown sugar looking like damp sand, the same as soft sugar, i.e. pieces.

Scotch pieces or scotch. Highly-refined, moist sugar pieces (see above).

Soft sugar. The light brown sugar of the US, a refined, paler type of brown sugar also known as sand sugar or pieces.

Sugar candy, called rock candy in the US. Large sugar crystals are sometimes attached to strings or twigs in bottles of liqueurs (*fior d'Alpi*).They have to be grown by putting crystals into a saturated sugar solution and allowing the water to evaporate slowly. Smaller sugar candy crystals are used as coffee sugar.

Sorghum. Syrup or sugar from sweet sorghum (*see* millet).

Superfine sugar. US name for caster sugar.

Syrup. *Golden syrup.

*Treacle is a rather vague term that has been used to cover everything from Golden syrup to molasses.

Unrefined sugar is raw sugar, *jaggery or *gur*.

White sugar includes all the highly refined sugars that are 99% sucrose.

Yellows. Pieces (*see above*).

[*Sugar* – French: *sucre* German: *Zucker* Italian: *zucchero* Spanish: *azúcar*]

SUGAR APPLE. *See* custard apple.

SULPHUR DIOXIDE, sulphurous acid, and sulphites. *See* preservatives.

SULPHURIC ACID (H_2SO_4), when concentrated, is known as 'oil of vitriol' and is a most dangerous corrosive substance. As the murderer Haig demonstrated on a number of old ladies, it will completely dissolve a human body. Sulphuric acid in a dilute form is used in car batteries, but even at that strength it is very corrosive. It is much used in the chemical industry, sometimes in processes that relate to food (e.g. the synthesis of saccharin). In a very dilute form, it has been used in soft drinks and at such extremely low strengths is probably harmless.

[*Sulphuric acid* – French: *acide sulfurique* German: *Schwefelsäure* Italian: *acido solforico* Spanish: *ácido sulfúrico*]

SULTANA. Dried, seedless grape, golden brown

and very sweet, with a mild and characteristic taste. They originally came as an export from Turkey, mostly through Izmir (then Smyrna), and were known as Smyrna or Sultana raisins to distinguish them from currants from Corinth. True, sultanas still come from Turkey and Greece, but the bulk of the world's production now comes from California and Australia, where the seedless grape varieties that are used lack the sultana flavour and are mainly sweet. In the US, they are called golden seedless raisins. There are other seedless raisins which come somewhere between sultanas and the dried or Valencia raisins but lack the raisin flavour.

In some countries, sultanas are allowed to be dressed with mineral oil to prevent them over-drying and to give them a gloss. In Britain, for instance, 1 g is allowed in 200 g of fruit, and it is assumed that this will be much reduced by washing before the fruit is used. Mineral oils interfere with the absorption of the fat soluble vitamins, and they, or the impurities they contain, have other possible ill effects, so you should look for sultanas that are less beautiful and glossy, but may be more wholesome.

Although sultanas have usually been cleaned of grit, it is still best to wash them. Pour boiling water on them, leave it a moment, and then take the sultanas out with a perforated spoon to avoid disturbing any sand, which will have fallen to the bottom. Washing sultanas also plumps them a little, but may slightly reduce the flavour.

[*Sultana* – French: *raisin de Smyrne* German: *Sultanine* Italian: *sultanina* Spanish: *paso de Corinto*]

SUMAC is a shrub or tree which belongs to the genus *Rhus*. This includes poison ivy (*R. toxicodendron*) and other poisonous plants, some decorative species well known to gardeners, and a number of useful plants that provide Japanese lacquer, Copal varnish and tannin for leather. The sumac of Mediterranean Europe (*R. coriaria*), also known as the Elm-leaved sumac or Sicilian sumac, has hairy fruits, which are dark red to purple when ripe. The hairs are rich in *malic acid, and the berries have a sour and pleasantly astringent taste. They are an important souring agent in the cooking of some areas of the Middle East, notably Lebanon, and are also used to make a sour drink: the dried berries are infused in cold water for 20 minutes and then the juice is squeezed out. This is both refreshing and a useful medicine, recommended for 'Beirut belly'. Lebanese homes traditionally kept a supply of the dried berries, which had

preferably been gathered in the mountains where the quality is best. I have only once managed to buy dried sumac berries in London and the quality was disappointing. However, as sumac grows in gardens, there is nothing to prevent experiment. The berries should be ripe and of the correct species.

In North America, there are a number of sumacs, but the Scarlet sumac (*R. glabra*), a familiar wayside tree, has large, dense clusters of red berries that are covered in acid hairs like the European equivalent; they are wholesome and can be used to make a refreshing drink, as well as probably being a satisfactory substitute in Lebanese cooking. One poisonous sumac, which could possibly confuse, has white berries in strings. Sumacs with smooth, hairless fruits should be avoided, as they are likely to be poisonous.

[*Sumac* – French: *sumac* German: *Färberbaum, Sumach* Italian: *sommacco* Spanish: *zumaque*]

SUNFLOWER. The Annual sunflower (*Helianthus annuus*) has long been grown as a crop, particularly in Russia, Romania, Hungary and Bulgaria, but increasingly so in other countries, and today sunflowers can be seen in fields almost anywhere that there are suitably warm summers – even sometimes in southern England. In countries where people are in the habit of nibbling to pass the time, salted sunflower seeds are popular. (In Spain, my children are always nibbling *pipas*, salted sunflower seeds that are sold in packets.)

However, the main use of sunflower seeds is as a source of oil which makes up about half of their weight. Sunflower oil is light and has a high percentage of polyunsaturated fatty acids and a low percentage of saturated fatty acids. With safflower oil, it is one of the best oils for use in cholesterol lowering diets. Because of these qualities, it has become quite widely available, but the product sold in supermarkets is apparently stripped because it is very nondescript in flavour. The cold-pressed oil, which is taken off without heat, is inclined to be expensive, but is an excellent oil for salads. The second pressings, made after heating the residues, are good for most other cooking purposes.

Sunflowers probably originated in the Americas, but exactly where is in some doubt. They have been cultivated in Europe since the mid-16th century. Young buds of sunflowers are edible and can at a pinch be used in salads; they are best boiled. Recently, machine-shelled sunflower seeds have come on to the market and open up new possibilities for those who like to experiment, as they are a healthy and nutritious food.

[*Sunflower* – French: *girasol, tournesol* German: *Sonnenblume* Italian: *girasole* Spanish: *girasol, mirasol*]

SURAM. *See* yam (elephant's foot).

SWAMP SUGAR PEAR. *See* rowan.

SWEATING in cookery means heating gently for a short time in butter (or other oil or fat) without any liquid so that the substance being cooked does not fry or brown. It is a process generally applied to green vegetables or to onions, and is usually maintained until the vegetable becomes soft.

SWEDE and **RUTABAGA** are members of the same species as *rape (*Brassica napus*) and are grown for their roots. In Scotland and the US, swedes are called turnips. In general, Swedes (var. *napobrassica*) are larger than turnips and have yellow flesh, although there are sorts in which the flesh is white (called French turnips in the US). The skins may be purple, white or, in the rutabaga (var. *rutabaga*), yellow. Whatever its colour, a swede or rutabaga can always be distinguished from a turnip, which is smooth right up to the base of the leaves, instead of having a number of concentric ridges or scars at the top.

Swedes are more recent in origin than turnips, and in spite of their name (which is shortened from Swedish turnip), probably originated in Bohemia in the 17th century. Although they are similar to turnips in flavour, opinions as to their culinary merit are sharply divided between those who claim that swedes are best as food for cattle and those who find them delicious and indeed superior to turnips because sweeter and with a dryer texture.

[*Swede* – French: *rutabaga, chou navet* German: *Streckrübe* Italian: *rapa svedese* Spanish: *rabo sueco*]

SWEETBREADS are soft, white, and in themselves rather flavourless, but are regarded as a delicacy. They are, or should be, the thymus glands of young animals – usually calves or lambs. The thymus is large in young animals, but in older animals it virtually disappears. The glands are situated in the chest, and their function is concerned with the immunity of the young animal and the production of white blood cells. Sweetbreads are also taken from the pancreas, and other glands, including the testes, are sometimes passed off as thymus. These are all good, but are not true sweetbreads.

To prepare sweetbreads, soak them for an hour or so in cold water to remove any blood. Then trim them and poach them in stock or *court-bouillon* for about 10 minutes. After that, cook them in one of the many ways that are particularly to be found in books on French cooking.

[*Sweetbreads* – French: *ris de veau, ris d'agneau* German: *Bröschen, Kalbsbries, Kalbsmilch* Italian: *animella* Spanish: *lechecillas, mollejas*]

SWEET CICELY (*Myrrhis odorata*).This old-fashioned herb is a stout umbelliferous plant with white flowers, hollow stems and a taste which is supposed to be myrrh-like, but is something between anise and lovage. It is little used these days, but the leaves and seeds can be used as a flavouring, and the roots can be boiled for eating as a vegetable or cold as a salad. It can be found wild over most of Western Europe; in Britain it is mainly found in northern England and southern Scotland.

[*Sweet Cicely* – French: *cerfeuil musque* German: *wohlriechende Süssdolde* Italian: *mirride odoroso* Spanish: *perifollo oloroso*]

SWEETCORN. *See* maize.

SWEET FLAG. *See* calamus.

SWEET GALE. *See* bog myrtle.

SWEET LAUREL. *See* bay.

SWEET MARJORAM or **knotted marjoram** (*Origanum majorana*) is a perennial labiate herb, a native of Africa that is cultivated in Southern Europe. Further north, it is grown as an annual. It is beautifully sweet smelling and one of the most important culinary herbs in European cooking. As the delicate flavour is destroyed by prolonged cooking, marjoram is best added shortly before the dish is ready or used in dishes such as omelettes which are cooked rather little. A closely related herb is *oregano, which does not have the same sweetness. Nor does Pot marjoram (*O. onites*), which is much more hardy. It is useful in strongly flavoured dishes in which the delicate taste of sweet marjoram would be wasted.

[*Sweet marjoram* – French: *marjolaine, origan* German: *Marienkraut, Marjoran* Italian: *maggiorana* Spanish: *majorana*]

SWEET PEPPER, bell pepper or pimento. Both sweet peppers (*Capsicum annuum*) and *chilli peppers came from tropical America and have been cultivated for so long that their origins are muddled. Opinions differ as to whether they should be regarded as one or more species, and the travelling cook will be further confused to come on large horn-shaped peppers which are mild and sweet as well as others, identical in shape, that almost blister your fingers when you touch them. Some long, chilli-shaped varieties (like the American Cubanelle and Sweet Banana) are actually sweet peppers. The squarish and tomato-shaped varieties, commonly called bell peppers, are usually sweet, but some have quite a nip to them. The colour range is from green (there are pale and dark green types) ripening through yellow and orange streaks to red; there are also varieties which are yellow when ripe, or variegated, or even almost black, and there are parchment-coloured varieties used for pickling, which might be called either hot-sweet or cool-chilli. Sweet peppers also vary in flavour – some modern greenhouse varieties are almost tasteless while others have a superb capsicum flavour which develops especially when they are roasted. Thickness of flesh is another factor to be noticed – some are thin-fleshed and others juicy – and the skin of some (especially commercial varieties for export) is often thick and leathery.

Although sweet peppers have been established in the cooking of the countries around the Mediterranean, in Portugal, the Balkans and Romania (where I first ate them) for some time, they are late comers to most European cooking because the first varieties of sweet pepper to be introduced were rather fiery and unreliable. In any case, they were grown only where there was a very hot climate. It was only with the development of new varieties that they could spread further north. Today they are grown under glass even in Britain. In the 19th century, British and even French cookery books scarcely mention sweet peppers. A similar evolution has been going on in the US. On the other hand, in very hot countries like India there tends to be a greater love of very hot chillies (sweet peppers are called *Kashmire mirch* – Kashmir peppers in Hindi), leaving the sweet peppers for areas that like less spicy food.

Both sweet and hot peppers have very little food value and, although they have a notable content of vitamin C, their main gastronomic role is to provide flavour. They are also conveniently hollow and make splendid containers for stuffings. So widely used are peppers these days that it is difficult to think what Spanish, Italian, Chinese and many other national cuisines could have been like without them. Dried sweet peppers, *paprika from Hungary and *pimentón* from Spain, are crucial to their respective national cuisines.

Before World War II, it would have been possible to find many people in Britain, even those claiming to be gastronomically sophisticated, who had never eaten a sweet pepper and did not know how they should be prepared. Now peppers are a routine food, at least raw in salads. It is unfortunate that so many of the varieties sold commercially taste more of pea-pods than of fine sweet peppers; others are bitter and overwhelming unless used only in small quantity. Finding a good – and suitable – variety, makes an enormous difference to the dishes in which peppers are used. For stuffing, cooks often like flat-bottomed, boxy peppers which will stand upright; the stem end is cut off and the seeds and septa removed before stuffing. Peppers that have to lie on their sides are best slit down the side, cleaned, stuffed and left with the stalk end intact. Peppers to be marinated in *vinaigrette* or olive oil should be grilled, preferably by throwing them on to hot charcoal, peeled and put to marinate whole, with the seeds intact as this gives them the very best flavour. If they are to be preserved under oil, the seeds can be removed later.

Some dishes require particular types of sweet pepper. In Spain, for example, Romesco sauce is only authentic if it is made with the elongated, top-shaped Romesco peppers that are grown around Tarragona. Among other Spanish peppers, *ñoras*, which are round and (like Romescos) only slightly piquant, may be found in their dried form in every Spanish market; they are the flavouring of dishes *a la vizcaina* and are also called *pimientos choiceros* – the peppers in *chorizo sausages (in which *pimentón* is also used).

Stuffed Sweet Peppers (India)

Boil and mash 4 potatoes. Slice and fry an onion in a dessertspoon of fat – ideally Indian clarified butter (*ghee*) – until it is soft. Add the potato, and 1 teaspoon *garam masala, ½ teaspoon turmeric, 1 tablespoon mango powder (*amchur*) plus salt to taste. Slit 6 smallish sweet peppers and remove the seeds, preferably through the sides. Stuff them with the potato mixture. Heat another tablespoon of fat in a frying pan. Put in the stuffed peppers with a little water. Sprinkle with salt and cover with a lid.

Cook slowly until the peppers are soft.

If *amchur* is not available, use lemon juice to sour the stuffing, but the flavour will not be the same. *Amchur* is used in many other Indian dishes as a souring and flavouring agent.

[*Sweet Pepper* – French: *poivron* German: *Ziegenpfeffer* Italian: *peperone* Spanish: *pimiento*]

....

SWEET POTATO (*Ipomoea batatas*) is a tuber formed on a plant of the convolvulus family. It is native to tropical America but has spread all over the tropics, where, with yam, cassava and taro, it forms the basic starchy staple of many poor people. Sweet potatoes also have some importance in the Mediterranean countries, and now, due mainly to the influx of immigrants, they are available as imports in most places in Britain. There are two main types, the dry, yellow-fleshed and mealy varieties, and the softer, more watery and generally sweeter white-fleshed varieties, which are more favoured in the tropics. The skin may be white, red or purple.

Sweet potatoes are grown in the US, mainly in Louisiana, North Carolina and Georgia. There are many ways in which they are prepared, and sometimes they are even used mashed in cakes and sweet dishes. Perhaps the simplest and best way to treat them is to peel them and cook them (for about an hour) in the pan with roasting meat, having first sprinkled them well with brown sugar, butter and a pinch of cinnamon – the sweet potato is not quite sweet enough without added sugar. They are also delicious baked in their jackets. They do not store as well as ordinary potatoes, but can be kept for a week or more in the larder. They must not be stored where frost can reach them.

[*Sweet Potato* – French: *patate douce* German: *Batate* Italian: *patata* Spanish: *batata*]

SWEET SOP. *See* custard apple.

SWEET WOODRUFF (*Galium odoratum*) is a woodland herb, with white flowers, which grows on chalky soil over most of Europe and in Britain. When crushed, the plant gives off an aromatic smell of new mown hay (caused by a substance called coumarin) which is intensified when it is dried. Sweet woodruff is an essential ingredient in the German *Maitrank* (May drink), which is made by infusing the herb in Rhine wine, and it is used for similar purposes in other countries, including the US (where it goes into May-wine punch).

[*Sweet Woodruff* – French: *glycérie* German: *Waldmeister* Italian: *asperula, stellina odorosa*

Spanish: *aspérula olorosa*]

SWISS CHARD. *See* beets.

SWORD BEAN. *See* jack bean.

SWORDFISH (*Xiphias gladius*) is among the largest of the bony fishes and is found in all oceans. It may weigh 70-100 kg (155-225 lb), and it is possibly the fastest of all fish, being able to do over 100 km (60 miles) per hour. Its head is extended forward into a long point, or sword. When angered, it is formidable because it uses its sword as a ram, although normally the sword is used sideways to stun or maim the fish or cephalopods which are its prey. The swordfish has excellent, rather firm white flesh, and is eaten everywhere it is caught, often grilled in steaks or *en brochette*. However, there is a much greater variety of recipes from Sicily and Calabria because the swordfish migrate along those coasts in the breeding season and have been caught there since ancient times. (Normally this fish is a loner, not tolerating the presence of other fish, and keeping to itself in deep water.) As with the tunny, Mediterranean people regard the belly as the best part. Swordfish are also caught in Turkey, netted in season in the Bosphorus, and it is from here that the delicacy of smoked *kilic* (swordfish) has become known; it has been claimed as the equal of smoked salmon when at its best, although the ordinary smoked swordfish packaged in oil that is found in European supermarkets is not more than very nice. It has also been likened to smoked *sturgeon. Before smoking, the pieces of boned swordfish are first salted in barrels, pressed down under a wooden disc and weighted with a stone. The salting is short –12-18 hours – after which the pieces are washed in strong brine and hung in a current of air in a shady place to dry for 2-3 days. Finally, the pieces are smoked for 10-12 hours and are then ready for use.

The product may be known as *mersine*. Blue marlin (*Makaira nigricans*) and White marlin (*M. albida*) are similar large fish that are found in the Caribbean and off the East Coast of the US; they are less good to eat than the swordfish.

[*Swordfish* – French: *espadon* German: *Schwertfisch* Italian: *pesce spada* Spanish: *pez espada*]

SYRUP. *See* corn syrup, golden syrup, maple syrup.

SZECHUAN PEPPER. *See* Chinese pepper.

t

TABASCO SAUCE. A hot chilli sauce, with a very characteristic flavour, made from the tabasco variety of chilli pepper, which is said to have been brought to Louisiana from Mexico in 1868. Tabasco, which contains chillies, spirit vinegar and salt, is one of the world's most famous bottled sauces. It is found on every cocktail bar for use in a Bloody Mary, and many like it on shellfish, particularly oysters. Imitations are inferior.

TAGLIATELLE. *See* pasta.

TAHINA has emerged from its ethnic origins and become internationally known in recent years. It is an oily paste made of *sesame seeds, which have usually been roasted first to give a strong nutty taste, and is a staple in most of the countries around the eastern end of the Mediterranean. Sesame is difficult to grind or pound at home to the required fine oily state, but *tahina* is generally available anywhere where there are Greek or Lebanese shops. Typical uses for *tahina* are to be found in Mrs Khayat's lovely book *Food from the Arab World* (Khayats, Beirut, 1959) in which, for instance, she gives recipes for *homous bi tahina*, a dip to use with Arab bread; and for *taratour bi taheeni*, a mayonnaise-like sauce in which lemon juice and *tahina* are emulsified and flavoured with salt and garlic – a sort of Middle East *aïoli*, which is excellent for salads and fish. There is even a variant on the *aubergine purée that is sometimes called poor man's caviar, in which *tahina* plays a role. I may say that my copy of Mrs. Khayat's book was heavily annotated and exclamation marked by the famous Lebanese belly dancer Leila (whose navel appeared in *From Russia With Love*), a fiery lady, who did not approve of the amount of garlic suggested by Mrs Khayat. I like the full amount of garlic myself, but in this type of dish the quantities are very much 'to taste', though never 'if liked'.

A point to notice is that when lemon juice is added, *tahina* first goes to a sticky, crumbly paste, but if you continue to stir in drops of lemon juice (or water if it gets too sour), it gradually turns to a beautifully smooth cream. *Tahina* is something with which to experiment. It keeps almost indefinitely in a glass jar in the refrigerator.

Homous bi tahina

Soak and cook chickpeas or used canned ones. Put the juice of a lemon into the blender, and a little water if necessary to cover the blades, and add 2 tablespoons of *tahina*, a little at a time. Now add 1-2 cloves of chopped garlic, and blend. Finally add some 5-6 tablespoons of chickpeas and some salt. Blend again and adjust the taste by adding more *tahina*, garlic, salt or lemon. When the *homous* is to your liking, pour it into a serving bowl and sprinkle it with a little chopped parsley or decorate with a sprig of mint. Dribble good olive oil on top in a circle for an authentic decoration. Authentic, too, would be to dip in bits of pitta bread, but snippets of any bread will do.

TALLOW. *See* fats.

TAMALE FLOUR. *See* masa.

TAMARI. *See* soya bean.

TAMARIND or **Indian date**. The beautiful tamarind tree (*Tamarindus indica*) is probably a native of tropical East Africa, but it has been cultivated in India since time immemorial and today is grown throughout the world in suitably warm climates, even to some extent in the Mediterranean countries. It is the pulp around the seeds that is used. It has a fruity sour taste, as it contains a lot of tartaric acid, and can be made into refreshing drinks. Tamarind sold in shops is a brown sticky mass of pods, containing fibre and a number of seeds. It is an excellent souring agent and is much used in Indian cooking.

To prepare it, pour a small amount of boiling water on a knob of tamarind, wait for it to cool, then rub and squash it with the fingers until a purée is formed. Fibre and seed can now be sieved out. Tamarind purée is mildly laxative. Sometimes recipes say that it can be replaced by lemon juice, but the result is never quite the same. Sweetened tamarind syrup can also be bought and is used as a basic for fruit drinks.

Tamarind Sauce

Soak 450 g (1 lb) tamarind in enough vinegar to cover it. When it is soft, rub it to a purée with the fingers. Pass the purée through a sieve and throw away the seeds and fibre. Now scrape 100 g (4 oz) fresh ginger and cut it into small pieces. Peel the same weight of garlic and clean the same weight of hot red chillies. Put all in the liquidizer (adding more vinegar to cover if necessary) and churn to a pulp. Add 100 g (4 oz) kitchen salt and 225 g (½ lb) sugar. Boil the mixture. To balance the sweet-sour-salt relationship, add more sugar or more vinegar. (Usually about ½ lt or 1 pt of vinegar in all is required but the quantity depends on the sourness of the tamarind.) The sauce can be bottled and is used in the same way as a chutney or wherever a hot, pungent sauce is needed with meat or vegetable dishes.

[*Tamarind* – French: *tamarin* German: *Tamarinde* Italian: *tamarindo* Spanish: *tamarindo*]

TANDOOR. *See* baking.

TANGERINE, **TANGELO**, and **TANGOR**. *See* orange.

TANNIA. *See* yam (yautia).

TANNIN. The tannins, which include tannic acid, are strongly astringent substances that occur in many plants. Their original use was in tanning leather, as they have the ability to coagulate and toughen proteins, especially those in skin. Similar effects can be produced in our insides if we consume many bitter acorns, horse chestnuts or oak leaves or even drink too much old, stewed tea. 'Tea drinker's dyspepsia' is not unknown in Britain among habitual drinkers of strong tea. Milk helps to counteract the tannins by reacting with some of them before they hit the stomach. In cooking, substances which contain tannin may be used in pickling (e.g. in dill pickles) to help firm up the vegetables – oak leaves are commonly used for this in Poland. Soaking salted fish in tea rather than water to remove the salt – a method that is sometimes used in France – perhaps has a firming action. Tannin is also mentioned in wine literature, because it occurs in the skins, pips and stalks of grapes (and also comes from oak casks); it is an important element in red wines, particularly in clarification. Young wines with prospects are rough with tannin, but with maturation the tannin gets

less and is involved in the formation of crust inside the bottles.

[*Tannin* – French: *tanin, tannin* German: *Gerbsäure* Italian: *tannino* Spanish: *tanino*]

TANSY (*Chrysanthemum vulgare*) is a herb of the composite family, a common wayside plant over almost all of Europe. It has button-like yellow flowers and was once an important medicinal herb, perhaps because of the belief that what tastes nasty must do you good. Nevertheless, tansy is much referred to as a flavouring in 16th and 17th century recipes. Today few people will bother with it, and most dislike it.

[*Tansy* – French: *tanaisie, barbotine* German: *Rainfarn, Wurmkraut* Italian: *tanaceto* Spanish: *tanaceto*]

TAPIOCA is a starchy food made by peeling and grating *cassava root, expressing the juice, and soaking the residue in water. The pulp is then kneaded to release the starch grains, strained to remove the fibre, and dried to a paste. Finally the paste is heated on an iron plate until it forms into the typical balls, flakes or pearls of tapioca. It may also be ground into a flour. Tapioca has an international reputation for digestibility and so, as one Spanish book says, '*es aconsejable para los niños*'. Children do not always find it so advisable, and many adults will remember tapioca pudding with horror (although two of this book's editors loved it). It can be used in soups in the same way as pasta or pearl barley. A classic Brazilian pudding is made in the same way as English tapioca pudding but with red wine or grape juice substituted for milk. The result is served cold with a vanilla-flavoured cream.

[*Tapioca* – French: *tapioca* German: *Tapioka* Italian: *tapioca* Spanish: *tapioca*]

TARAMÁ. Dried and cured female roes of grey mullet, pressed and sold from the barrel in Greece. Virtually the same as *botargo. As Elizabeth David said as far back as 1950 in her *Mediterranean Food* (Penguin), the taste is not unlike that of English smoked cod's roe. In fact in Greece, where *taramasalata* is a popular part of the *meze*, cod's roe, imported in barrels, is commonly used as a substitute for the roe of mullet.

Taramasalata

Put *taramá* in water and soak it for 5 minutes or so, as necessary, to remove part of the salt. Squeeze to remove some of the water. Pound the roe in a mortar, adding olive oil and lemon juice alternately, as if making mayonnaise, and tasting as you go. Finally mix in a little finely chopped onion and a little chopped dill. Serve with good bread, toast, brown bread or *pitta*, spread or as a dip.

TARO. *See* yam (dasheen).

TARTAR. *See* argol.

TARRAGON is one of the great culinary herbs. It is a perennial with narrow leaves and a very distinctive smell when crushed. There are two kinds, French tarragon (*Artemisia dracunculus*),which is the finest but rarely if ever sets seeds, and Russian tarragon (*A. dracunculoides*), which can be grown from seed but has a rather different flavour. Unless you know the smell, it is very difficult to tell the difference, but if the plant sets viable seed, it will be the Russian. The safest way to start your own tarragon is to find someone with a good, fine-tasting plant and to steal a cutting. Once established, tarragon seems to stand any amount of butchery and goes on for ever, although it is choosy about where it likes to grow and needs good drainage, sun and shelter. It has a strong but subtle flavour, quite unlike any other herb, and is particularly famous for its use with chicken, although it can be used in many other ways – in butters, sauces and salads, and with eggs and fish. It is essential in many French dishes and also, of course, as the flavouring herb for tarragon vinegar (which is labelled *à l'estragon*) – you can make this for yourself simply by picking tarragon just before it flowers and pushing the sprigs into a bottle, which is then filled with white wine vinegar, stoppered and left for two months before use.

[*Tarragon* – French: *estragon* German: *Estragon* Italian: *targone* Spanish: *estragón*]

TARTARIC ACID is an organic acid common in plants, especially in sour fruits, such as tamarind. It is the main source of acidity in wine, in which 0.2-0.6% is present. The acid can be made by treating *argol with sulphuric acid and is available as a white crystalline substance from chemists. It is very sour – much sourer, weight for weight, than *cream of tartar. It can be used in home-made soft drinks and makes a passable substitute for lemon juice.

[*Tartaric acid* – French: *acide tartrique* German: *Weinsteinsäure* Italian: *acido tartarico* Spanish: *ácido tartárico*]

TASTE POWDER. *See* monosodium glutamate.

TEA. The word probably comes from *tay* in the Cantonese Amoy dialect, and that is how it was pronounced by our ancestors. Tea is native to south-west China (and Assam), and has been drunk by the Chinese for many centuries, but was not really known in Europe until after Dutch ships brought some back in 1610.The first authenticated British reference is by a Mr Wickman of the East India Company agency in Firando, Japan, in 1615. It was not until the 1640s that tea began to come into Britain and France in any noticeable amount. During the years of Cromwell's power, there were great advances in the use of tea, at first mainly as a medicinal brew. In 1660, Samuel Pepys recorded tasting his first sup. By the time that Charles II returned from exile two years later, tea had become a meal. Fine cups and saucers, bowls, teapots, spoons, trays and caddies for keeping the precious tea were soon introduced, and the presiding host or hostess brewed and poured the tea – an echo of the Japanese tea ceremony, perhaps. The social history of tea had begun. Colonists in America had begun to drink tea, too, and the British government's refusal to remove the hated tax on it, along with the grant of a monopoly to the British East India Company for supplying tea to the colonies, led to the colonists burning tea-laden vessels in Annapolis, Maryland and tipping tea cargoes into Boston Harbour in the famous Boston Tea Party in late 1773.

During the 18th century the imports of tea to Britain had increased over 45-fold, but it was still highly taxed and thus expensive. At the end of the century, Sir Joseph Banks suggested growing tea in India and even visited China to collect seed, so that some 50 years later, when Major Robert Bruce found tea growing wild in Assam, there were also tea plants from China in the botanical gardens in Calcutta. With the spread of plantations in India, tea gradually became the drink not only of every Briton, but indeed of every Indian. Tea is best when fresh, and in the reign of Queen Victoria it came by fast sailing ships. In the great race from Foochow to London in 1866, the tea clippers took only 99 days to complete the 16,000-mile voyage, and the first two arrived within 10 minutes of each other. By 1880, Britain was importing 160,000,000 lb of tea a year, most of it from India, which is still the largest producer of tea in the world. The British still drink some five times as much tea as coffee, unlike the Americans, who drink twenty-five times as much coffee as tea.

At first, tea was never drunk with milk. It was China tea, of course, to which the Dutch ladies added sugar and even the leaves of peaches and plums to give it a bitter almond kick. Tea taken to the accompaniment of cakes and sandwiches (an idea that hardly originated in China) is said to have been the invention of Anna, Duchess of Bedford, at a house party in 1840. In the north of England, high tea is a substantial meal eaten at around 5.30-6 p.m., when the breadwinners return home from work. It consists of meat or fish as well as bread, pies and cake, all washed down with tea. Until recently, there was some social distinction according to whether tea was a proper meal or just a way of tiding over until dinner, the main evening meal.

Tea is much drunk in Russia and Iran (where the samovars keep the water, not the tea, hot). In Syria you may get a cup of cardamom-flavoured coffee from the police at some remote border (if you are not there under arrest), but, in Iran, it will be a glass of hot, sweet, milkless tea. In India, except in the south, where the preference tends to be for coffee, tea will be thick with milk and sugar, and sometimes strongly flavoured with mint as well. It is made by boiling milk, sugar and sugar and water with tea for 2-3 minutes, and then straining it.

Tea is the leaf of a tree, *Camellia sinensis*. Left alone, it will grow 7.5 m (25 ft) high, but it is pruned to form a low bush for ease of gathering. The leaves look something like bay leaves, and the flowers are beautiful, white and sweet smelling. Because the plant likes heavy rainfall, the typical tea garden is as often as not seen as terraces of neat bushes on mist-shrouded hills. Most beautiful are the tea gardens in Ceylon, with waterfalls, swirling clouds, and orchids in the trees. Most dramatic, though, are the gardens in northern Iran which you come on when you cross the Elburz Mountains, leaving the desert and, within the space of a few miles, plunging into dense rain forest along the Caspian Sea.

The flavour and quality of tea depends on the variety and on the soil and climate where it is grown. Fresh tea leaves are mildly astringent and stimulating to chew. They are processed in three ways. For green tea, the fresh leaves are dried immediately after picking to inactivate enzymes and prevent oxidation. For Oolong tea, the leaves are half-fermented, producing tea a stage between green and black. For black tea, the leaves are wilted, bruised by rolling and allowed to ferment in contact with air, so that they are oxidized (like a browning apple) before they are dried. For all types, the leaves are still picked by hand, usually every 7-10 days, in part because the grade of tea depends on the size of leaf – it is the labour-intensive nature of the crop that prevented tea being grown on any scale in the US.

For ordinary black tea, the plucked leaves are taken to the factory and spread on racks at a temperature of 25-30°C (77-86°F) to wilt. By gentle drying, the moisture content is reduced somewhat, and the leaves become flexible. At this stage, they are rolled in machines that break up the cells (this was once done by hand) and expose the juices to the air. The rolled leaves are once more spread on trays and allowed to ferment. As the juices are oxidized, the leaves turn red-brown, after which hot air is blown through the trays until the rolled leaves are dry and the enzymes have been killed. In the case of smoky China teas, such as Lapsang Souchong, the rolled leaves are dried over a wood fire to give the characteristic tarry taste.

Teas are named after their type and leaf size, and the place of origin. Some teas are flavoured with flowers or with essential oils, and many are blended, a practice that began at the tea table when hostesses, realizing that mixtures were often better than single teas, made their own combinations. Today, this is done by expert blenders who have access to a huge range of teas. Blending allows the deficiencies of particular teas to be balanced out. Teas may also need to be matched to the water used to brew them. Price is another factor in blending – a mixture of the best teas with cheaper ones will offer some of the fine flavour without being too costly. Tea caddies of the early 18th century had compartments for six or eight different teas to be blended at home, but by 1800 the blending was beginning to be done at the grocers, often to formulae provided by their clients. Earl Grey tea is probably the earliest of such blends that is still available in the shops.

Hard water makes poor tea, and if naturally soft water or rain water is not available, distilled water might be used. Water from a softener is often better than hard water, but not ideal. Tea is best made by putting the leaves into a hot teapot of suitable size at the rate of 1 heaped teaspoon per person, with an extra one for the pot. The water must be fresh and have only recently come to the boil, and the pot must be taken to the kettle – not the kettle to the pot. Pour the boiling water over the leaves and let it brew for 3-5 minutes, according to the type of tea, stirring it after 2 minutes to open the leaves. If tea is to be kept hot for long, reheated or used cold, it should be strained off the leaves after 5 minutes so that excess tannin is not infused.

A cup of tea contains something under 1 grain of caffeine and 2 grains of tannin. Several cups are stimulating, yet not harmful, but 'stewed tea' may contain enough tannin to tan the stomach lining, and people swigging cuppas from dawn to dusk may suffer from tea-drinker's dyspepsia, especially if they eat quantities of cakes and biscuits as well. (China tea is unlikely to cause such problems, as it is taken weak without milk, and not very hot.)

Assam. The extreme north-eastern corner of India, stretching between Darjeeling and Kohima, is an area with some of the highest rainfall in the world. Assam teas are usually full-bodied and provide the strength in many blends. For quantity, this is the most important tea area in the world.

Black teas are fully fermented teas that are used in all the standard English blends. Most of the teas from India, Ceylon and Africa are black, and there are also black teas from China.

Brick. Coarse leaves, stalk and dust, steamed and pressed into bricks. Rich paste is often added to hold the leaves together. Exported from China to Russia and also used in Tibet, it is easily transported and is the type that is brewed up with yak butter and salt. At one time tea bricks were used as a form of currency.

Broken grades, such as broken Orange Pekoe, are generally of good quality. Better grades contain tip. Flowery broken Orange Pekoe is fine quality tea with tip and is much sought after by connoisseurs.

Ceylon (now Sri Lanka) started to produce tea in 1868 and gave its name to teas of a totally different type from the original China teas. The tea grown at 1800 m (6000 ft) or above is of great quality, with teas being less good. Political and economic upheavals in Sri Lanka meant for a time that the quality of the tea was not of its previous high standards, but the quality is now returning. The teas from Indonesia are very similar in character. Many of the planters in Sri Lanka (mostly Scottish by birth), who were forced out for political reasons, moved to Africa, where there is a thriving and expanding tea industry that produces excellent quality teas.

Ching Wo from Fukien province in China has a rather pungent taste which is liked in some European countries, but is little used in Britain.

Congou. The largest leafed of the China black teas, usually made with the third or fourth leaf on the plant.

Darjeeling teas from the Himalayan foothills in northern India are noted for their fine flavour and are very expensive. They are grown up to 2100 m (7000 ft) and production is limited. The best Darjeelings are usually blended with teas of similar character but lesser quality from the lower slopes in order to make them commercially attractive.

Dragon's Well. The alternative name for Lung Ching tea.

Earl Grey is the name given to a blend originally formulated by the second Earl Grey. It was given to his grocer, who was a partner in the firm of Robert Jackson. The name was never registered, and the blend has been copied by other tea companies. Earl Grey has become a generic term for tea scented with oil of bergamot.

Flowery Orange Pekoe. A large-leaf tea with a lot of tip; as the season progresses, however, there is less and less tip.

Golden tips. The first young leaf of the tea bush.

Green teas are much used in China and Japan, but little today in Britain, although in the 18th century, before Indian tea became predominant, Singlo, Turankay, Hyson and Gunpowder would have been known to most hostesses.

Gunpowder is one of the Chinese green teas. In appearance it is grainy, rolled into balls, as suggested by its alternative names of pearl or pinhead tea. The liquor is pale, with a sharp, distinctive taste. This tea is popular in North Africa, especially in Morocco, where it is frequently flavoured with mint.

Hyson. A Chinese green tea, as is Young Hyson. It is of very good quality, expensive and full of flavour.

Ichang. A China tea from Hupeh, grown high in the

mountains. It is rare and costly, with an exquisite and mellow flavour.

Jasmine. A China green tea that is mixed with jasmine flowers and then steam heated for 5 minutes before being dried in a spin dryer.

Keemun. A black China tea from Keemun county in the beautiful Huangshan Mountains in southern Anhwei province, south of the Yangtse. The best have a delicate flavour and scent.

Kenyan teas have a quality of their own, between the thick heavy teas from North India and the light flavoury teas of Sri Lanka.

Lapsang souchong. A large-leafed black China tea with a distinctive tarry taste and smell derived from the smoke of the fires over which it is dried. It comes from Fukien on the Chinese mainland and from Formosa. The tarry flavour is so strong that is has to be stored separately in tea warehouses to avoid the standard teas picking it up.

Lung Ching or **Dragon's Well**. An exotic China tea with a flat, green leaf and a distinctive taste. It is produced only in small quantities.

Oolong. The leaves are allowed to ferment, but fermentation is then stopped by heat. These teas are produced in China and Formosa. The best early crop tea has a peach-like flavour, with a large bold ragged leaf. The finest have a very good show of white tip.

Orange pekoe is a large-leaf tea of orthodox manufacture. It is not now used extensively in Britain, but continues to be popular in Continental Europe.

Panyong. Rather like Keemun, but with a slightly different flavour and usually of better quality, this tea is from Fukien province in China.

Pekoe. A grade of whole-leaf tea of orthodox manufacture.

Pekoe suchong. A rolled bally type of leaf.

Russian tea comes from the wet strip along the foothills of the Caucasus mountains in Georgia. The Russians produce all sizes of tea, but they do not generally have the quality of the best China teas.

Souchong (from the Chinese "*siao-chung*", meaning larger leaves). Very large leaf size from China; it is larger in size than Pekoe suchong.

Twankey. A green tea, popular in the 18th century.

Yunan. Teas from this province of China have a distinctive flavour and are frequently used in blends.

TEA SUBSTITUTES and **TISANES**. There are dozens of these, of which the most important is *maté. Some of the infusions, such as the Cape or Boer Bush tea (*Cyclopia vogeli*) of South Africa were serious tea substitutes, as also was New Jersey tea (*Ceanothus americanus*), a member of the heather family which, like orange tea, was used by the early American colonists as a protest at the time of the Boston Tea Party.

Many of these teas have a medicinal purpose, although some, like *lime tea from the flowers of the linden, are very nice as a drink. Strawberry tea from Germany is made from the dried young leaves of wild strawberry plants; Algerian tea or *thé Arabe* (*Paronychia nivea*) is used medicinally in France; Swiss tea is made with relatives of yarrow, such as *Achillea mosdiata* and *A. nobilis*; Japanese tea (*ama tsja*, tea of heaven) is the leaves of species of Hydrangea such as *H. serrata*. Others are Mexican tea (*Chenopodium ambrosioides*), Réunion or Faham tea (*Angrecum fragrans* and other species), and a tea made from the garden bush, *Chimonanthus fragrans*, which is claimed to be so good that it may be cultivated for the purpose, *camomile tea (*Matricaria recutita*), Oswego tea, from Red bergamot (*Monarda didyma*), Malay tea (*Eugenia variabilis*), Long Life or Bencoolen tea (*Glaphyria nitida*), Mountain tea (*Gaultheria procumbens*), Barbary tea (*Lycium barbarum*), Steckel tea (*Borbonia parviflora*), and even tea from the dried leaves of the *sloe – the list goes on for ever. In Europe, aromatic teas were also made of the flowers of rosemary and lavender, from gorse, dittany, ground ivy (Gill tea) and willow herb (*Kaporie* tea in Russia). Speedwell is said to have been an almost universal adulterant of tea in Europe. With a wide range of aromatic herbs also available to try, there are exciting possibilities for experiment here.

[*Tea* – French: *thé* German: *Tee* Italian: *tè* Spanish: *té*]

TEFF. See millet.

TEMPERATURES are given in this book in

*Celsius (Centigrade) and *Fahrenheit. For the kitchen, thermometers are much to be recommended as they take the guess-work out of many operations, such as frying, jam-making, sugar-boiling, yoghurt and cheese-making, and roasting. Perhaps, if you are doing something very frequently, perhaps professionally, you can learn to judge by eye and experience, but most of us are not in that position. Tests like the time taken for paper to go yellow or bread cubes to go brown in the oven are a nuisance. A thermometer gives certain and accurate results and materially helps towards better cooking. Thermometers reading 4-225°C (40-440°F) will handle all normal kitchen requirements. They are filled with mercury. For sub zero temperatures, thermometers are usually filled with coloured alcohol which, unlike mercury, will not freeze in any temperature the cook is likely to deal with, but cannot be used for hot things. When taking the temperature of a liquid, first stir it to make sure that it is evenly heated and, if possible, leave the bulb in the liquid while taking the reading.

An oven thermometer may sometimes be necessary if you have an old-fashioned stove, and a roasting thermometer – one that you push into the centre of the meat – can be exceedingly useful.

Some temperatures

Conversions in this list are approximate and are as accurate as the various circumstances demand.

0°C 32°F	Ice melts or water freezes, depending on whether heat is being added or taken away.
49°C 120°F	Add starter and put yoghurt to bed.
60°C 140°F	Internal temperature for rare beef.
63°C 145 F	Internal temperature of under-done beef and mutton.
65°F 150°F	Egg begins to thicken and coagulate.
70°C 160°F	Pasteurization temperature.
71°C 160°F	Internal temperature of medium roast beef.
74°C 165°F	Internal temperature of roast lamb.
80°C 175°F	Internal temperature of well-done beef. Proteins have curdled. Mutton is well done. The correct internal temperature for veal.
85°C 185°F	Internal temperature for roast pork.
90°C 195°F	Simmer.
93°C 200°F	Low oven. Temperature for meringues, baked custards, etc.
102°C 215°F	Thread stage for sugar.
110°C 230°F	Blow stage for sugar. Gas oven (*Regula) ¼.
116°C 240°F	About right for fondant icing.
120°C 250°F	Hard ball for sugar. Gas oven ½.
135°C 275°F	Gas oven 1
137°C 278°F	Temperature for shallow frying in butter.
143°C 289°F	Hard crack stage for sugar.
150°C 300°F	Gas oven 2. Madeira and fruit cake.
160°C 320°F	Gas oven 3. Slow roast for most meats. Start of frying range for choux paste, etc.
180°C 350°F	Gas oven 4. Medium. Slow roast for pork. Middle of frying range and usual for doughnuts, fish, chips, meat etc. Caramelization sugar.
190°C 375°F	Gas oven 5. Usual roasting temperature for meats. Top of frying range for finishing.
200°C 400°F	Gas oven 6. Hot oven. Pastry, sponge, Swiss roll, muffins, browning meats.
220°C 425°F	Gas oven 7.
230°C 450°F	Gas oven 9. For puff pastry. soufflés, baked Alaska, some bread, croissants.
240°C 475°F	Gas oven 9.Very hot. Bread batons.
260°C 500°F	Gas oven 10 – Maximum heat – too hot for baking at home, but used by bakers for bread rolls.

[Temperature – French: température German: Temperatur Italian: temperatura Spanish: temperatura]

TENDERIZING. Simple, old-fashioned methods of tenderizing are mechanical – heating or pounding to break up the fibres. The Greeks batter an octopus on the rocks at least 40 times to make it tender, Italians beat stock-fish and some optimists beat tough steaks in the hope it will improve them. Another simple method of tenderizing is hanging and aging. We do that to game as a matter of course, but often forget that meat also needs hanging, which only the best butchers do properly.

In hanging, the tenderizing process is done by enzymes in the meat which break down the protein. If hanging is done in the right cold conditions, it will not be accompanied by bacterial putrefaction. Tenderizing is also achieved by heat, if it is properly applied over the correct period, but equally heat can toughen. The first reaction of protein to heat is to coagulate – as is well illustrated by the white of a boiled egg. Overcook the white and it goes like rubber, taking an hour or more of boiling to become soft again, a lesson anyone cooking meat should remember. On the other hand, if an egg is lightly poached or coddled at below boiling point, the white is very tender. Sugar on meat is a tenderizer because it encourages the enzyme processes. Acids, such as vinegar and lemon juice, in marinades slowly tenderize by hydrolyzing proteins to amino acids, although their immediate action is to coagulate and harden, especially if heated. Commercial tenderizers rely on *papain, an enzyme which digests protein. Usual food grade tenderizer will digest about 35 times its weight of protein, but will of course tenderize only the tissues with which it comes in contact, which is why treating meat (except minced meat) with tenderizer is a poor substitute for proper hanging. Papain is deactivated by the heat of cooking. A few people are allergic to it.

TEPARY BEAN (*Phaseolus acutifolius*), is a drought-resistant species grown in arid country such as that of Arizona and Mexico, but is only of local significance.

TERRAPIN. *See* turtle.

TEXTURED VEGETABLE PROTEIN. *See* TVP.

THERMOMETER. *See* temperature.

THIAMINE. *See* vitamin B_1.

THICKENING is closely related to *binding. Liquids may be thickened naturally, without addition, by reduction by boiling, but it is usually necessary to add something, and whatever is added has to be right for the dish, not only in flavour and texture, but also in colour. Satisfying all these demands makes it difficult to substitute one thickener for another. Dishes do not retain the same character. If a *coq au vin* is thickened with *beurre manié*, it will not have the same dark, rich colour of one thickened in the traditional way with the bird's

blood. Equally, if you do as French chefs often do in India and thicken a curry with cream, then you completely alter the character of the dish (although it will still be delicious).

Some of the thickeners used by food manufacturers, such as alginates and carob-bean gum, are not generally available in the shops. Others, such as the gums, are little used except for specialized purposes, partly because they are not much known in these days, although some, like *gum Arabic, were much used in the past. Thickeners are also often stabilizers, helping to prevent emulsions from breaking, suspensions from settling and mixtures from separating into layers.

Starchy thickeners. Flour is the most commonly used of all thickeners, and is easily incorporated into liquids in the form of *beurre manié*, flour worked to an intimate paste with an equal weight of butter, which prevents the formation of lumps. *Beurre manié* is especially convenient because it can be added bit by bit until the required thickness is reached. Starchy thickeners depend on the capacity of starch grains to burst and form a soluble starch jelly when heated to around 75°C (167°F). Another is *cornflour, which forms a more glassy jelly. It can also be mixed with butter or made into a cream with cold water before being stirred into the hot dish to be thickened. *Arrowroot is even purer starch and gives an almost transparent jelly. Tapioca flour and potato flour are among other forms of *starch that can be used. Starchy thickeners must in most cases be properly cooked or they may retain a starchy taste.

Egg yolk is an excellent thickener, as it gives a rich, smooth texture. It should be added when the sauce is cool enough for you to dip a finger in without screaming, and the yolks are best smoothed with a very little water as a preliminary. After they have been stirred in, the sauce should be heated over water in a *bain-marie* or double boiler – not on a direct flame unless you have a fine, thick copper pan and some skill. If the egg gets too hot anywhere on the bottom of the pan, it will form lumps of scrambled egg. Stirring with a wooden spoon should be continuous until the sauce thickens correctly, and then it must not be allowed to get any hotter. A sauce thickened with egg will curdle if it becomes too hot and must never be boiled.

Blood is a good thickener and can even be simmered in certain conditions, although it is better not to try it. Otherwise, blood behaves rather like egg yolk. It is used particularly in thickening jugged hare and the classic Burgundian *coq au vin*, for which the bird's blood is collected when it is killed and immediately stirred with a little vinegar and brandy just enough to prevent coagulation. Solid coagulated and cooked blood of various kinds is sold in my local market in Spain. I know of people who have tried blending this with water – a sort of reconstituted blood, but as the brew is merely watered down coagulated blood, it cannot be expected to coagulate again and work as a thickening.

Creamy thickeners. Stirring thick or sour creams into juices at the last minute and off the fire is a delicious and simple way of giving body to many sauces. Creamy mixtures of nuts, coconut cream, *tahina*, ground poppy seed and even peanut butter can also be used to give body in appropriate dishes. The important thing is always to avoid breaking the emulsion or to allow curdling. To lessen the shock on incorporating the mixtures, some of the liquid to be thickened should be stirred into the creamy thickener before it is added. A German chef, famous for his soups, advised me to think of adding mayonnaise to appropriate soups, and of course *aioli* is essential in the Provençal *bourride* and in several other French fish soups, where its function is also to add a strong flavour of garlic.

Jelly-like substances. A thick consistency, something like bird's-nest soup, can be obtained by thickening with gelatine, or, as would be preferred in some dishes, with a strong meat jelly or aspic. Another variation on the same theme comes from using *agar-agar (from which fake bird's-nest soup is made in France) and even *seaweeds such as carrageen moss. In the food trade, *pectin is sometimes used; it sets when fruit acids and sugars are present.

[*Thickening* – French: *épaississant* German: *Eindickmittel* Italian: *sostanze usata per condensare* Spanish: *espesativo*]

THRUSH. *See* birds.

THYME is one of the great herbs of the European kitchen and belongs to the family of the labiates, which contains so many of our best culinary herbs – notably mint, sage, oregano and basil. The species most often used in cooking is the Garden thyme (*Thymus vulgaris*); there are many other species of thyme, both garden and wild, mostly plants that like dry, stony limestone soil. Although they all have a basic taste pattern, in which thymol predominates, there are many variations, which may be better or worse from the culinary point of view. As I write I have before me a beautifully flowering wild thyme, which has a strongly acid smell and is quite unsuitable for cooking. Thyme needs to be chosen very carefully, though I have no doubt that the best thyme comes wild on the hillsides of Provence and Liguria; even there, you have to know from experience what to gather. (The worst to look at, as usual, tastes the best.)

Thyme, bay and parsley are the brothers in the *bouquet garni*. A very small amount can make all the difference to a dish. There is no herb to equal it in dishes that involve long, slow cooking in a casserole. Most people must be content with dried thyme, which is as good as fresh thyme, but should be bought in small quantities and continually renewed. Thyme goes with beef (though rarely with veal), with lamb, pork, with all sorts of birds and game, but especially chicken, with fish, eggs – almost anything that can benefit from an aromatic flavouring.

[*Thyme* – French: *thym* German: *Thymian* Italian: *timo* Spanish: *tomillo*]

TIA MARIA. *See* liqueurs and cordials.

TIGER NUT. *See* chufa nut.

TIN (Sn) is a metallic element, which forms the coating of tin cans and copper pans. It is probably, but not certainly, a trace element needed by man, as it is for animals. Tin has been very much used since the middle of the 19th century for coating iron, primarily to stop it rusting in what we know as tin plate – or simply tin. In this form it is used to manufacture tin cans for food. With some cans, small quantities of tin dissolve into the contents and have a bleaching effect on fruit like pears, peaches and golden plums. In fact, a tin compound, stannous chloride, is an anti-oxidant, which is used in some countries for whitening canned asparagus. Lacquered cans are used for fruit such as strawberries in which the colour content is important. Tests so far made seem to indicate that tin has a low toxicity and in the amount that usually gets into food is quite safe. However, if food is kept in opened cans, the presence of the oxygen in the air means that the tin will be rapidly dissolved. That is why food should not be left in cans that have been opened.

[*Tin* – French: *etain* German: *Zinn* Italian: *latta, stagno* Spanish: *estaño, lata*]

TISANE. *See* tea substitutes.

TOADSTOOL *See* mushrooms.

TOCINO. *See* bacon.

TOFU. *See* soya bean.

TOHEROA (Maori for long-tongue) is a large bivalve (*Amphidesma ventricosum*) found in the sand of certain beaches in the North Island of New Zealand. It is the basis for the fabled toheroa soup. Mechanical means of collecting the shellfish almost resulted in its extermination and now its taking is strictly regulated and, although it is canned, it is a luxury that is not easily found, even in New Zealand.

TOMATE DE MER. *See* sea anemone.

TOMATE VERDE. *See* physalis fruit.

TOMATILLO. *See* physalis fruit.

TOMATO. As tomatoes are now one of the world's most important foods, it is amazing that they were for so long regarded with suspicion and grown only for decoration. 'Gold and unhealthy' was how one Elizabethan herbalist described them. Perhaps it was because, like potatoes, they were rather obviously related to the deadly nightshade. Tomatoes (*Lycopersicon esculentum*) may have originated in Peru and Ecuador, but they had been domesticated and had moved up into Mexico long before the Spanish arrived in America. The name tomato, in fact, is derived (through the Spanish *tomate*) from the Aztec *tomatl*. The Spanish brought the plant to Europe in the 16th century, and Gerard's *Herbal* says that they ate it with oil and vinegar as a salad, but it did not become popular. In Britain and France, it was known as the 'love apple' (*pomme d'amour*), which perhaps came from the Italian *pomodoro* – golden apple – because the first varieties in Europe were yellow. It was not until the 18th century, after two Italian Jesuit priests had brought a red variety back with them, that tomatoes began to be taken seriously for eating. It was in southern Italy that tomatoes first became popular, and for some time they remained a food of the poor. In his *Cuoco galante*, published in 1778, the Neapolitan abbot, Vincenzo Corrado, gives a recipe for a tomato sauce

– but he recommends it for fish and meat, not for pasta or rice. He also offers recipes for stuffed tomatoes of various kinds. A chef to Catherine II of Russia, a Roman named Francesco Leonardi, author of *Apicio moderno* (1790) seems to have been the first to write about tomato sauce with spaghetti, but such a dish was a poor man's, not a court chef's invention. It was not until 1835 that tomatoes began to be adopted in the US, where millions of tons are grown today

Among the bewildering number of tomato varieties are the gigantic ones with evocative names like Beef-master that run to almost 1 kg (21b) per fruit, down to cherry and cocktail tomatoes (with names like Sugar-lump) which are no bigger than marbles. However, apart from such fancy tomatoes, which also include the yellow, orange and pink varieties, there are numerous more normal types, each with its own purpose.

Salad tomatoes are for slicing raw, for use in mixed salad and *hors d'oeuvre*. A salad variety should have a good acid-sweet balance and certainly, when fresh off the vine, the proper tomato taste. This is so often lacking in bought tomatoes, especially those produced out of season or with too little sunshine.

Cooking tomatoes are not just salad tomatoes that are past their prime. For stuffing, tomatoes must be of the right size, and it is noticeable that some varieties cook particularly well, while others are better bottled. For example, the very old Italian variety, San Marzano, one that is often peeled and canned, lends a special quality to Italian canned tomatoes.

Sauce tomatoes are usually the plum tomatoes, which make the best concentrates and sauces. Varieties include Roma, which, despite its name, is an American tomato. Plum tomatoes have more meat than juice and are often rather tasteless raw, and almost without seeds.

Juice tomatoes are different again. For salads, too much juice in a tomato is bad – people even let tomatoes drain. For cooking and making a dry paste, it is a nuisance, but for tomato juice, the really juicy varieties perform best in the home juicer.

Growers tend to select mainly for commercial considerations, suitability to climatic conditions, soil, disease resistance, yield, storage and shipping qualities (which means a good thick skin – American varieties have lately been developed with thick enough skins to survive picking by machine). Regular form and attractive colour are commercially more important than taste, because most people buy by appearance. However, in farmers' markets, you will often do best by looking for the smallest, roughest tomatoes because these usually have the finest taste, and they are likely to be cheaper. The canning companies organize the cultivation of huge areas of tomatoes under contract with the varieties they find best for their purpose. In general, canned tomato products are excellent and a great help to the cook. Sometimes tomatoes acquire tastes in canning which may even be preferred for certain dishes. However, brands vary in flavour, so look around and experiment before making a recipe standard. Tomatoes mix particularly well not only with basil and garlic, as has long been known, but with bay, thyme and oregano. They also go well with cheese, with peppers and with meaty flavours. Ripe and well-flavoured tomatoes can even be eaten as a fruit with sugar and cream. (For this, they should be dunked in boiling water for a moment to loosen the skin, peeled, cut in quarters and de-seeded.)

Tomatoes have a range of tastes depending on the length of time they are cooked. For instance, chopped and very lightly cooked, as in the sauce for *spaghetti all'amatriciana* (*see below*), they have a delicious, fresh flavour – this dish should never be overcooked or contain onion or chilli peppers, as it is the unalloyed taste of fine tomatoes that is important. Tomatoes baked soft have yet another taste. They are best done in an old-fashioned, wood-fired, baker's brick oven so that they get a slightly smoky taste from the ashes.

Pa amb olli – Bread and oil (Catalan Spain)

This is a popular snack everywhere and loved even by children who do not usually like tomatoes. Take a thick slice of good bread, cut a juicy tomato in two and press the cut face on to the bread to impregnate the surface with juice. Dribble good oil (preferably olive) all over it and salt generously. As with every simple dish, the quality of each of the ingredients is of the utmost importance. The bread might be from a large round Majorcan loaf, the salt a crude one from the Salinas, while the oil should be light and pleasant.

Panzanella (Tuscany)

Soak 8 slices of stale, good bread in spring water until they are soft, squeeze them out gently and crumble them roughly into a bowl. Thinly slice a cucumber, a large mild onion and 4 ripe tomatoes into the bowl. Add some chopped basil leaves, good olive oil, a little wine vinegar, and salt and pepper. Mix and put in a cool place until lunchtime.

Spaghetti all'Amatriciana

This dish is named after Amatrice, a small town between Rome and the Abruzzi. For 400 g (14 oz) of spaghetti, to be boiled in the usual way, take 300 g (11 oz) of ripe tomatoes of a sweet, fleshy variety suitable for sauce, dip them in boiling water, peel and de-seed them and break them into small pieces. Fry 100 g (4 oz) of diced, fat *bacon (it should be *guanciale*) gently in some good olive oil and, when it starts to colour, add the tomato and turn up the heat. When the tomato has become soft, but not overcooked, add salt and pepper to taste, mix it with the cooked spaghetti and sprinkle with 50 g (2 oz) of grated Pecorino cheese.

Passato – Bottled Tomato Purée

Peel the tomatoes and remove the seeds. Simmer with chopped onion at the rate of 1 kg (2 lb) onion to 10 kg (22 lb) de-seeded tomato, plus 3 cloves garlic, 2 handfuls basil leaves, 2 bay leaves and a bunch of celery. Simmer until the mixture has reduced by half, then salt to taste and put it through a Mouli. When the purée has cooled somewhat, put it in bottles of a suitable size for household needs, close and sterilize by heat. Alternatively, add *salicylic acid as a *preservative at a maximum rate of 1 g acid per 1 kg (2¼ lb) of sauce – tomatoes already contain salts of salicylic acid. Cover the contents of each bottle with a little olive oil and close with a sterilized cork. The *passato* will now keep without heat treatment. A third method is simply to deep-freeze the *passato* in cartons.

Dried Tomatoes in Oil

Halve the tomatoes and spread them on trays in the hot sun to dry. When they are almost leathery, sprinkle them with salt, put them in jars and cover them with olive oil.

[*Tomato* – French: *tomate* German: *Tomate* Italian: *pomodoro* Spanish: *tomate*]

TOMATO SAUCE. Commercially-bottled tomato sauces are intended for table use and are more or less synonymous with tomato ketchup. Tomato sauce for spaghetti is not the same thing.

....

Tomato Sauce for Spaghetti

Peel and remove seeds from 1 kg (2 lb) plum tomatoes (or canned, peeled tomatoes). Put a small, finely chopped onion, 1 crushed clove garlic, 5 dessertspoons olive oil and 25 g (1 oz) butter in a pan and fry gently. When the onion is soft, add the tomato, several leaves of basil, salt and pepper. Cover and simmer slowly for about an hour, stirring occasionally to prevent the tomato from sticking. Put the sauce through a sieve or Mouli, add a pinch of sugar and another 25 g (1 oz) butter. Adjust the seasoning. Serve with spaghetti. This quantity of sauce will do for 400 g (14 oz) pasta. Grated Parmesan cheese should be sprinkled generously on each serving.

....

TOPE. *See* shark.

TORTELLINI. *See* pasta.

TORTILLA FLOUR. *See* masa.

TRACE ELEMENTS are essential for health but required in such small amounts that it is only in recent years that the quantities have begun to be measured, although the presence of such elements has long been known. Many of the trace elements are harmful in larger amounts, even if these are still microscopically small, so ill-health could result from too much as well as too little. Trace elements known to be essential are chromium, cobalt, copper, iodine, manganese, molybdenum, selenium and vanadium. Those probably essential, and essential to animals are flourine, nickel, silicon and tin.

TRAIL is the collective term for the entrails of such animals as snipe, woodcock, plover and red mullet. In these cases, the trail is not removed before cooking and is considered a delicacy.

TRASI. *See* balachan.

TREACLE. Originally medicines were often mixed with honey, but later, thick, sticky sugar syrup was used. This original function remained in that devilish school medicine 'brimstone and treacle' (flowers of sulphur and molasses) with which, I remember,

our German matron tried to purify the blood of the school. (Spoonfuls dotted by 'accident' into her hair were an effective counter.) But treacle pudding, treacle tart, treacle parkin and treacle toffee were all another matter.

Treacle is a variable substance. Black treacle is molasses; a slightly lighter version is West Indian treacle, which still has the authentic molasses taste. A much lighter, medium brown syrup made by refining molasses is also known as treacle but has a much less strong molasses taste. Finally *golden syrup is often loosely called treacle.

The expression 'treacle' is not normally used in the US, where the niche is filled by corn syrups (light or dark), molasses (light or dark), caramel or brown sugar syrups made at home and maple syrup. Indeed, the world of treacles and syrups is one where there is almost total confusion in older books, although writers of recipes are now becoming more specific.

[*Treacle* – French: *mélasse* German: *Sirup, Melasse* Italian: *melassa, sciroppo di zucchero* Spanish: *melaza*]

TREE POTATO. *See* sapodilla.

TREPANG. *See* sea cucumber.

TRESTERBRANTWEIN. *See* marc.

TRICHINOSIS. One of the most terrible parasites to infect man is a tiny nematode worm, *Trichinella spiralis*, which also lives in pigs, rats and other animals; humans can get this from eating measly pork. The spotted measly appearance is produced by the millions of tiny worms encysted in the muscle, which could contain as many as 80,000 worms in 25-30 g (1 oz).

When measly meat is eaten and digested, the *Trichinella* worms are released to mate. The females bore into the wall of the gut and deposit their offspring in the lymph system.

Prevalence of trichinosis varies from country to country. It is more common in the US than in Europe. Although meat which is sold today has been subjected to rigid inspection, risk of this disease is the main reason why sensible people avoid rare pork and fry samples of *pâté* and sausage meat before tasting them for seasoning. Cooked or smoke-cooked sausages such as mortadella and frankfurters are safe because worms are killed at temperatures as low as 70°C (140°F) maintained for a specific length of time. They are also killed in meat that is kept frozen at -15°C (5°F) for three weeks.

417

Raw pork products such as raw ham, bacon, salame and *chorizo* sold in shops are safe as they have been hung long enough for any trichinella worms to have been killed by the salt, saltpetre and spices.

[*Trichinosis* – French: *trichinose* German: *Trichinose* Italian: *trichinosi* Spanish: *triquinosis*]

TRIPE is usually the stomach of the ox, but the stomachs of sheep and pigs are also used, especially in peasant communities. There are several varieties of tripe. Most people will have seen cows or bullocks lying in the fields and chewing the cud. These ruminants stuff themselves with grass, without chewing it until they have filled the bag of the first stomach, the rumen. The lining of this is of warty villi. When it settles down to chew the cud, the animal regurgitates the grass, now in the form of rough balls, which it chews at leisure into a purée. This well chewed grass, when swallowed a second time, goes, via the reticulum, a smaller bag lined with a honeycomb structure, to the psalterium, which has a lining with folds or leaves, and finally into the abomasum, which is ridged. There are thus four parts to the ruminant stomach, each recognizable by the form of the lining.

If you are starting from scratch, the stomachs have to be cut open, separated into manageable pieces and cleaned carefully. After washing in several changes of water and cutting away any bits and pieces, the tripe is scalded and scraped inside to remove any slime. Kettles of boiling water are poured liberally over it. The tripe must then be soaked for 3-4 hours in water which contains a little salt and vinegar. After a final scrape and wash, the tripe is dropped into boiling, salted water, cooked for about 30 minutes and then drained. It is now ready for basic cooking. This may be done in a pan or pressure cooker with flavouring herbs and vegetables. Ordinarily, tripe needs many hours of cooking – 16 hours simmering was recommended in the past, but then it was easy to leave a pan at the back of the kitchen range. Today, in Western countries, tripe is usually sold only after it has been cleaned and cooked, i.e. dressed. (This is the only way in which tripe is allowed to be sold in some countries.) Even so, it may need some hours of further cooking to become tender.

The most delicious tripe is veal tripe, and the best part is the honeycomb; thick and white is better than thin and brownish. The British method of cooking tripe, tripe and onions (a famous dish in the north of England), is for tripe addicts only, as it has a strong visceral flavour. The most famous tripe

dish is *tripes à la mode de Caen*, from Normandy, in which tripe is cooked in a sealed pot for at least 10 hours with calf's foot, onions, vegetables (carrot and leek), a *bouquet garni* and cider. For good measure, it gets a lacing of Calvados. Best of all for those who do not relish tripe, is the spicy Spanish *callos a la madrileña*, in which tripe is cooked with calf's foot, *chorizo* and *morcilla*, onion, garlic, white wine, brandy, sweet and chilli peppers, *bouquet garni*, the usual seasonings and a squeeze of lemon juice. Both this and *tripes à la mode de Caen* can be bought canned or frozen and can be nearly as good as the freshly-made article. In Italy, tripe is cooked with white beans, with tomatoes and with cheese; these dishes are also delicious. In general, tripe is not as popular as it used to be. Most of it is reduced to an unrecognizable state and used by the food industry.

[*Tripe* – French: *tripes* German: *Kaldaunen, Flecke, Kutteln* Italian: *trippa* Spanish: *callos*]

TRIPLE SEC. *See* liqueurs and cordials.

TRITICALE is a new cereal, a cross between wheat and rye. It has a higher protein content than wheat and a much higher amount of the essential amino acid, lysine, which is already used to fortify some breads. In America, bread made from this cereal is known as triti bread, but it is not yet in general use on a wide scale. Triticale (a hybrid word derived from *Triticum*, wheat, and *Secale*, rye) is also used as a *sprouted seed.

TROUT and **CHAR** belong to the same family as the salmon. They were always important freshwater fish to people who lived within reach of lakes and fast-flowing streams, but now they are extensively farmed, even in places where there is no permanently running water.

There is much argument over which is the best trout. The answer depends on the water in which the trout has lived, the food it has eaten and, perhaps equally, on its birthplace; local loyalties play a major part in any gastronomic argument, but it is generally conceded that the Sea trout (also called the Salmon trout because the flesh is pink) is the finest of all and one of the most delicious fish in the world. The Sea trout is merely a variety of the Common trout (*Salmo trutta*) of Europe and (like the Rainbow trout) it sometimes goes to sea, where it gets its pink colour and delicious flavour, perhaps from the crustaceans it eats there. The same fish is called the Brown trout when it occurs in streams and burns, and those who as children caught them in the mountains and cooked them rolled in oatmeal over the campfire within minutes of landing them will no doubt think these the best they have ever tasted. Sportsmen the world over will find their local trout best. All agree that the same trout living in lakes, though they grow large, are less tasty, and that goes for trout raised on trout farms (*truites d'élevage*), although their flavour depends on their food in the last weeks before they are killed.

Trout of various species have been moved about and introduced from one country to another. For instance, the Brook trout (*Salvelinus fontinalis*) is a native of cold East Coast streams in North America, but is now well established in Europe, after its introduction in 1882.The Rainbow trout (*Salmo gairdneri*), a native of California, has gone all over the world, even (with other species) to the Southern Hemisphere, where there were no trout before. So trout now abound in streams from New Zealand to the Andes, and you may eat them from the Arctic Circle to the Equator (they are fished in the streams of Mount Kenya).

The Rainbow trout is the species often cultivated in trout farms, as it will stand much more stagnant water than the Brown trout. It is inferior in flavour, but good enough, and is available all year, which the Common Brown trout is not.

As trout are so delicious and Sea trout reckoned by some to be better than sole (and certainly better than salmon), there are hundreds of trout recipes. It is best to kill large trout by stunning them, or to insert a finger in the fish's mouth and quickly snap its head back to break the neck if it is small. The fish may be gutted neatly through the gill opening or by a small ventral incision or (if for stuffing) by cutting down the back, removing the backbone and guts, but leaving the ventral skin intact. To be cooked *au bleu*, trout must be taken alive from the water and cooked within minutes of killing, as otherwise the blue colour will not develop.

The chars are very similar to trout, belonging to the same genera, and for all practical purposes are the same. They tend to be marine but also to have populations in very chilly mountain streams and lakes. The Arctic char or *omble chevalier* (*Salvelinus alpinus*) is found in Arctic seas but also has landlocked populations, for example in Lake Windermere in England and Lac Leman in Switzerland. One of the finest fishes, it is best baked and eaten with butter as the only sauce.

Smoked trout is a well-known delicacy, but potted char less so. The former may be made at home by lightly brining the fish and then hot smoking it in a home smoker. Potted char is easily made according to the following recipe.

Potted Char

Gut, behead and bone the char but do not wash it; merely wipe it clean. Rub it well with mixed spices. The proportions of spice will depend on the strength of the ingredients used, but start by grinding spices together in the proportion of 2 teaspoons pepper, 1 teaspoon allspice, 4 teaspoons mace, 1 teaspoon of cloves (or less) and 2 teaspoons of nutmeg – these quantities would be sufficient for 14 kg (31 lb) of fish and can be scaled down as required. Bake the fish, covered with butter, in a slow oven for 5 hours or until the bones have melted away. Drain off the butter and press the fish firmly into pots, then cover it with some of the melted butter. This method is for trout, eels, sprats, shrimps or prawns.

[*Trout* – French: *truite* German: *Forelle* Italian: *trota* Spanish: *trucha*]

[*Char* – French: *omble chevalier* German: *Rotforelle, Siebling* Italian: *ombrina* Spanish: *umbra*]

TRUFFLES are very important in *haute cuisine*. They are fungi which most people know only as something expensive bought in a tin (even the peelings are canned, though canned truffles are not, on the whole, worth bothering with) or as the black specks in the *pâté*. There are a number of species of truffle which are something like underground puff balls, although they are not closely related. Some, like the *terfezias* of the Middle East and North Africa, are good, but not sensational. Two – the Black or Périgord truffle (*Tuber melanosporum*) and the White or Italian truffle (*T. magnatum*) – are outstanding delicacies.

Best known is the Black truffle, which is irrevocably associated with French cooking. The best are found locally in hilly country around the edge of the Massif Central. In the west, they go southwards from Périgord. In the east, they can be found on either side of the Rhône valley as far north as Burgundy. Their season is from November to March. As Black truffles are so expensive and so much in demand, inferior species which look something like them are often substituted. With peeled truffles, a microscopic examination is needed for the fraud to be detected. Truffle bargains must always be suspected. Black truffles are very black and are covered with warts which trap the earth between them and make them difficult to clean. They have a strong perfume and are usually eaten cooked or chopped up and put into dishes as a flavouring.

The White truffle is found particularly in the foothills of the Appenines on the south side of the Lombardy plain in North Italy. It is smooth, irregularly shaped and of a creamy colour outside. It can be found in all sizes, occasionally almost as large as a football. White truffles are even more expensive than black truffles and have an even stronger smell. However, they have very little taste and are mostly eaten raw, sliced very fine over the food with a special cutter (which includes razor blades) to give a mouth-watering, though indescribable perfume. The centre for white truffles is the Italian gastronomic mecca of Alba, 64 kilometres (40 miles) south-east of Turin. The season is from October until snow stops play before Christmas. Truffles of both kinds grow only in association with certain plants and trees. As yet they cannot be cultivated like mushrooms, and several fortunes await anyone who can learn how to do it. Truffles of the kind we are talking about usually grow about 30 cm (1 ft) underground, and their presence is detected by dogs or by pigs (but they try to eat the truffles). Fresh truffles can be kept for some days in the refrigerator and can be sent by mail from centres like Alba.

[*Truffle* – French: *truffe* German *Trüffel* Italian: *tartufo* Spanish: *trufa, criadilla de tierra*]

TRUSSING is tying up meat into a tidy form for cooking. The term is usually applied to birds. There are many opinions as to the 'correct' way to truss this or that, but at best these ways are only traditions or means which have been found most practical or convenient. Trussing was more important when birds and joints were roasted on spits and turned before the fire. Trussing is also important to butchers and poulterers, who wish to make a bird look fatter (by pushing legs up under the skin of the breast) and a joint neater. In fact, it is a form of presentation.

For trussing which looks professional, you can use a trussing needle to pass the string right through the body of the bird. Alternatively, you can stick a skewer through for anchorage. Both methods puncture the skin and let out some of the juices. The easiest method is to put a hitch in the middle of the trussing string and tie this round the parson's nose, which gives the necessary anchorage. The ends of the legs can then be tied down to this, and the string passed forward to encircle the body around the wings, thus holding them in the position required. Soft, plain white cotton string is the best to use for trussing, being wholesome and tasteless.

Sewing up after stuffing should be done with cotton button-hole thread.

[*Trussing* – French: *trousser, brider* German: *dressieren* Italian: *preparare un pollo* Spanish: *espétar*]

TUNA or **tunny**. There are a number of species, the best known being the Blue-fin tuna (*T. thynnus*), the Yellow-fin tuna (*T. albacares*) and the Long-fin tuna or albacore (*T. alalunga*). They are related to mackerel and sometimes included in the same family. The classic tuna of the Mediterranean is the Blue-fin, which also occurs in the Black Sea, and off the Atlantic coasts of Europe and America. This fish is usually up to 2 m (over 6 ft) long and averages about 150 kg (330 lb), though it may be considerably larger. The Mediterranean tuna fisheries have been declining as the sea has become polluted, but it is there, and particularly in Italy, that the gastronomic treatment of tuna is centred. Tuna gather in shoals and migrate inshore to their breeding quarters, at which time they have always been caught in enormous numbers. The traditional method, still used in places, is the *madrague*, the Sicilian tuna trap, which consists of nets which conduct the tuna into a series of netted enclosures. The last one, called the *camera della morte*, has a net floor which can be raised by ropes to bring the fish to the surface and within reach of gaff and club; the killing is a wild and bloody ritual. Fresh tuna has been likened to veal and is perhaps the only fish to have had 'cuts' like cuts of meat. The glut of fish each year meant that it had to be preserved. In early times, tuna was salted and preserved in oil in the local manner, but for a long time canning it has been an important industry, and canned tuna is used in important Mediterranean specialities such as *salade niçoise* and *vitello tonnato*.

During the first run, which in Sicily is in May and June, the fish are in prime condition and ready for spawning, and *botargo is made from the female roes. Later in the summer, when the fish are spent, they return thin and empty. At that time – up to the end of September – the flesh is inferior and blackish in colour. Before canning, tuna are beheaded and hung from the tail to drain out the blood. The flesh is then washed and soaked to make it as white as possible. It is then cooked in a herbed brine and finally canned under oil or water. Good canned tuna, which still retains its firm, meaty texture, is a relatively expensive item. The best part is the *ventresca*, the lower part and belly wall. A relation of the tunas, the Pacific *bonito or skipjack is canned as skipjack tuna.

[*Tunny* – French: *thon* German: *Thunfisch* Italian *tonno* Spanish: *atún*]

TUNA PEAR. *See* prickly pear.

TUNNY. *See* tuna.

TUR. *See* pigeon pea.

TURBO. *See* abalone.

TURBOT. *See* flatfish.

TURKEY (*Meleagris gallopavo*) is a bird that is indigenous to America. It had already to an extent been domesticated in Mexico by the Aztecs before the arrival of the Spanish. Turkeys were established in Spain by 1530 and in England by 1540.The Mexican stock was then taken back to America, to New England, by the colonists, and these turkeys are probably the ancestors of present-day domestic breeds.

Wild turkeys can still be found from Pennsylvania to Florida and westwards to Colorado and Arizona, as well as in Mexico. They are smaller birds than the huge modern table breeds which are scarcely capable of getting off the ground, and they are lean, not fat. Even so, a big tom can weigh up to 9 kg (20 lb), although they are more usually 6 kg (over 13 lb), with the females up to 4½ kg (10 lb) and less. As the birds have been shot, their meat will be dark; they need a lot of basting or they will be dry, but they are very meaty.

The many attempts to naturalize turkeys as game birds in Britain and elsewhere in Europe have been unsuccessful. There are now a great number of breeds in assorted colours and offering a range of sizes at maturity; they have also been bred for commercial considerations such as hardiness, disease resistance and efficient utilization of foodstuffs. In Britain, the favoured commercial breeds are the Broad-breasted Bronze turkey and the Beltsville Small White, which give birds of top weight. The breeding of huge-breasted, ungainly turkeys can be managed only by artificial insemination. In a year, hen turkeys will lay 70-80 eggs, which are very large and have an excellent flavour and a nice speckled brown colour, but the low rate of production is not interesting to egg producers. The eggs hatch in 28 days. It takes about 9 months to produce top-weight birds, but they may be killed at anything over 4 months;

old turkeys are tough and useless. Modern turkey production is highly organized – turkeys are no longer generally driven into town in flocks for Christmas, as they once were (and still are in some towns in Europe). They were even equipped with boots to keep their feet in condition. Although mainly eaten at Christmas – and in the US also for Thanksgiving – turkeys are now becoming a popular year-round food, thanks to small breeds and deep freezing.

When buying fresh turkeys, look for the maximum amount of breast and small legs. Hens are reckoned a better buy than toms; although the tom may be bigger, his bones weigh heavier, and hens are generally more tender. However, with modern commercially-raised birds, there is not all that difference. After killing, turkeys are normally hung for 5-7 days, depending on the weather. An old method was to hang the bird suspended by a cord tied round four large fail feathers. As soon as the bird dropped (on to a cloth hung below to receive it), it was ready to be cooked immediately. (This probably works only with an average-sized turkey.)

Turkeys are stuffed in various ways and, being so large, can accommodate two stuffings, one mild and the other stronger. Commonly used are sausage meat, veal forcemeat, chestnut, celery, celery and dried apricot, apple and prune, and oyster stuffings. A practical one (where veal is not available) is made from minced cooked chicken mixed with breadcrumbs and butter, flavoured with lemon rind and juice, or mixed with smoky ham. It is better to serve sausages with the bird than to use sausage meat as stuffing.

When buying turkey, allow at least 450 g (1 lb) per person and preferably more to allow for eating cold later. Cordon Bleu today advises about a 6 kg (13-14 lb) bird, weighed, plucked but not dressed, for 8-10 people, but in my grandmother's family it was ten aunts to an 11 kg (25 lb) turkey at Christmas, which allowed for friends, cold turkey and the kitchen. If calculating for a frozen bird (which has lost head, neck and feet), you can drop the weight requirement by about a quarter – and do not forget that the bird takes 2 days to thaw out. With slow roasting at 160°C (325°F), 22 minutes per pound (total weight including stuffing) is about right. A turkey that is ready early can rest for half an hour outside the oven; if it is late, you will have to go on drinking. In recent years, turkey has replaced chicken in many preparations of fine quality, such as in the classic stuffing for *tortellini*, into which it goes with raw ham and parmesan cheese.

[*Turkey* – French: *dinde, dindon* German: *Puter, Truthahn* Italian: *tacchino* Spanish: *pavo, pava*]

TURMERIC (*Curcuma longa*) is a spice of the same family as ginger, but without any of ginger's hot flavour. It is the rhizome of a plant indigenous to humid, hilly districts of South and South East Asia. The spice is prepared by boiling the rhizomes, peeling them and drying them in the hot sun for several weeks. As whole pieces of turmeric are very hard, it is one of the few spices it is better to buy ground, as it will certainly break the blades of an ordinary coffee grinder. The taste is slightly bitter and musty. The colour is bright yellow; alcoholic extracts of turmeric are used as a food colouring. Turmeric is the spice that colours curry yellow, and it is used in quantity in piccalilli and to give colour to mustards – it is usually detectable as a taste in American mustards. It has been known to be mistranslated as 'saffron' in Indian cookery books.

[*Turmeric* – French: *curcuma, safran d'Inde* German: *Gelbwurz, Turmerikwurzel* Italian: *curcuma* Spanish: *cúrcuma*]

TURNIP (*Brassica rapa*) has been cultivated and used as food in Europe since very early times. Turnips are grown for both their roots and their green tops. Some varieties are large and grown for animal feed on farms; others are small and grown in market gardens as human food. Both are good to eat. Turnips may be globular or long, and white, green or purplish according to type. They usually have white flesh. Varieties such as the Tokyo hybrid grow very fast and will produce succulent white turnips, a little bigger than a radish, in not much over a month from planting. Such small turnips have a delicate taste, but some stalwart fanciers prefer the stronger taste of a large farm turnip. Children usually like the taste of raw turnip and will eat a slice of one from a field, but often hate it when cooked. (Field turnips should not be confused with other root crops such as *swedes and mangolds – another variety of beet, which taste horrible, though they are harmless.) There are many delicate French ways of cooking small turnips, a vegetable more popular in France than elsewhere. Turnip plays a part as a flavouring vegetable in stews and soups. Grated raw turnip is an excellent salad flavouring ingredient and is often included in coleslaw.

Turnip tops or turnip greens, which will sprout in March if turnips are left in the ground, are excellent and make a very nice, sweet-tasting green when boiled as cabbage or broccoli would be and served with butter.

[*Turnip* – French: *navet* German: *Rübe* Italian: *rapa* Spanish: *nabo*]

TURTLE and **TERRAPIN**. In common usage, a turtle is a tortoise that lives in water. Many are eaten (although not the Ganges turtles, which live on dead bodies), and in particular the huge marine Green turtle (*Chelonia mydas*), the species most used for turtle soup. Also famous are certain terrapins of North America, small turtles which live in salt marshes, lakes and rivers, especially in the Gulf States and East coastal swamps of the US. Books from the 19th century are full of Chicken tortoises, Salt-water terrapins, Alligator terrapins and so on, as these were sold in thousands in the markets. Today the most usual is the Diamond-back (the best are claimed to come from Chesapeake Bay), which is also available canned.

Terrapins are killed either by chopping off their heads or by plunging them alive into boiling water. After scalding for about 5 minutes, the outer skin can be removed by rubbing with a rough cloth. There are many ways of cooking them, but a usual one is to simmer the whole animal in salted water for 1-1½ hours, until the shell begins to crack and the feet to fall off. The shell can now be cut open around the under edge, the two halves separated and the stomach, gall bladder and large intestine removed. The small intestine is often left in (like the trail of a woodcock) and, with liver and eggs, is served with the rest of the meat. The claws are pulled out and discarded before serving. Terrapin is often seasoned with sherry or madeira, and an average terrapin serves two people. American cookery books have many recipes, but although live terrapins used to be imported occasionally into Britain, people in Europe, where there are no suitable small turtles, must usually be content with canned terrapin.

Green turtles are taken sometimes in the Mediterranean and on the warmer Atlantic coasts of Europe, but they are becoming rare. Beaches are occupied by sunbathing humans, and too many eggs have been taken. The famous soup served at the banquets given by the Lord Mayor of London used to be made from Jamaican turtle which came over on sailing ships to the Port of London, alive and nailed to the decks. Turtles in those days were so plentiful that many ships captured them and carried them for fresh meat. Today, most of the turtles come over frozen. If ever faced with a live turtle, you would have to chop off its head and hang it up by the hind flippers overnight to drain off blood. Next day, the flippers would be cut off at the joints, and the two halves of the shell separated by cutting round about 5 cm (2 in) from the edge. (The upper shell is known as the calipash and the lower the calipee.) After any water had been drained out and the stomach and intestines and, above all, the gall bladder removed with care, the meat could be treated as veal (which it resembles), or the creature could be made into soup. For this, the flesh and green fat are reserved, and the two halves of the shell with the flippers put into boiling water. After a few minutes' boiling, the flippers can be taken out and skinned, but the shells need somewhat longer cooking until the bones can be easily removed. A stock is made from the liver, heart, kidneys and bones; in it are then boiled the meat, flippers, and head. Also needed, though, are ham and veal plus thyme, marjoram and basil (the turtle-soup herbs), parsley, bay, cloves, mace, etc. Soup can also be made from dried turtle meat, which requires soaking for 3 days before cooking. (It is easier to buy a can.)

Turtle soup for the Lord Mayor's banquet in London is a massive operation. Only female (cow) turtles are used. About 200 kg (440 lb) of veal bones are boiled for 2 days and nights to make some 450 lt (800 pt) of stock. This is strained and seasoned with thyme, marjoram, basil and parsley, 9 lt (16 pt) of sherry and 4½ lt (8 pt) of sweet white wine. In this, 3 turtles of 70-80 kg (170 lb) total after cleaning are boiled day and night for another 2 days (or more) until the lower shells have been reduced to a yellowish gelatinous consistency and can be cut in cubes, while at least part of the upper shell has gone soft and green. After standing a week to settle, the soup is cleared with egg white and reduced to 225 lt (400 pt) which, when cold, sets to a stiff clear jelly. The soup is readied for the banquet by being boiled up with more sherry, and some diced, gelatinous meat is added. It is served with Birches Punch (a secret mixture which is mostly brandy and Jamaica rum).

Since an outcry by conservationists several years ago against the excessive killing of turtles for food, efforts have been made to breed turtles specially to fill the demands of the kitchen. Such projects are still very much in the developmental stage; while some turtle farms are having success, the supply of farmed turtles has not yet begun to fill the manufacturers' needs.

[*Terrapin* – French: *terrapène* German: *Desenschildkröte* Italian: *tarataruga aquatic* Spanish: *tortuga de agua dolce*]

[*Turtle* – French: *tortue de mer* German: *Meerschildkröte* Italian: *tartaruga, testugine di mare* Spanish: *tortuga (de mar)*]

TUSCARORA RICE. *See* wild rice.

TVP or **textured vegetable protein** is a high-protein foodstuff manufactured from plant protein (often from *soya beans, but in Britain also from field beans) which, when processed resembles meat in texture and is intended as a meat substitute. Originally, it was aimed at the vegetarian market, but in recent years it has found its way into an assortment of processed foods.

Three basic methods produce different textures of TVP. The simplest is merely a matter of flavouring and colouring the concentrated protein, which is marketed and used in the form of granules. When they are reconstituted, these look like ground meat. The second method uses mainly soy proteins, which are dissolved in alkali to form a gel and then coagulated in acid. The protein is then extruded like synthetic fibres and emerges in a variety of textures, from tough to tender. The result can be used in stews and casseroles. The most expensive method involves spinning high-protein soy preparations into fibres. These are stretched on reels, and excess salt and acids are washed away. The fibres, blended with flavours, colours, extra nutrients and binders, are heat-processed and formed into steaks or cubes. A proportion of meat may be added for flavour and colour, particularly in canned TVP 'meat' products; dried TVP products are also likely to be flavoured.

u

UDDER has somewhat fatty white meat, which is not generally valued. It can be cooked in a number of ways – braised, stewed and served with onion sauce, or lightly salted, boiled and served cold with *vinaigrette* sauce. Udder is rarely seen in butchers' shops or even in European markets, but seems to have been popular enough in the past. André Simon's *Guide to Good Food and Wine* quotes two recipes from La Varenne (1654), and from Pepys: 'Mr Creed and I to the "Leg" in King Street, to dinner, where he and I and my Wife had a good udder to dinner' (11th October 1660). It is (or was) much used in Italian cooking in the contents of stuffed pasta such as ravioli.

[*Udder* – French: *tétine, mamelle* German: *Euter* Italian: *poppa, mammella* Spanish: *ubre*]

UDON. *See* noodles.

UGLI. *See* orange.

UHT MILK. UHT stands for ultra high temperature. A recent method of sterilizing milk by a treatment midway between *pasteurization (which does not produce sterility) and conventional sterilization by autoclave. UHT treatment kills all organisms without greatly altering the taste, but it does not inactivate all the enzymes the micro-organisms have produced. Thus, although UHT milk will keep without souring for up to six months even at ordinary room temperature (providing it has been bottled or packaged in perfectly aseptic conditions), it will eventually gel because of the enzymes.

UHT milk is useful in countries with an inadequate dairy industry – such as those in the Middle East – or where there is an overwhelming tourist influx at certain seasons. It is more expensive than pasteurized milk and so, for ordinary purposes, would not replace it. However, it is increasingly taking over as the only milk to be had in small shops and supermarkets, which can thus avoid the problems of dealing with fresh, perishable milk. A bottle of UHT is a useful reserve to keep at home as a standby, and it does not even have to occupy

space in the refrigerator until it is opened.

ULLUCO. *See* yam (ulluco).

UMBELLIFER. Plant belonging to the family Umbelliferae, which has small white, yellow or pink flowers usually arranged in large, flat-topped bunches called umbels. Among the 2700 species mainly from temperate areas of the northern hemisphere are quite a number of culinary importance either as vegetables or as flavourings. *Carrot, *parsnip, celeriac (*see* celery) and *Hamburg parsley are all umbellifer tap-roots. The family is second only to the labiates for its herbs: *alexanders, *chervil, and *parsley are used for their leaves, while the seeds of other species are important as flavourings – *ajowan, *anise, *caraway and *cumin. Some are valued for both leaves and seeds: *coriander, *dill and *lovage; so are *celery and *fennel, which are best known for varieties with leaf stalks that are used as vegetables.*Asafoetida is solidified from the juice of an umbellifer. Another umbelliferous herb, *angelica, appears in the kitchen mainly as candied stems.

V

VACUUM. Space without anything in it, not even air, is a vacuum. However, we talk loosely of a vacuum when we mean a partial vacuum, with most of the air removed from a container. Cooks come across vacuum flasks, which have double walls; the air between has been pumped out so that heat cannot pass either way between the two walls by ordinary conduction or convection (air currents). Radiant heat is stopped by silvering the glass so that the heat rays are reflected back from where they came, and the flask thus insulates its contents against changes in temperature.

Reduced pressure lowers the temperature at which liquids boil, as it does at a high *altitude. In a partial vacuum, water will boil even at room temperature (and astronauts' blood would boil in space if they were not in pressure suits).This is made use of commercially in drying foodstuffs that are easily spoiled by heat. You can think of it as reduction boiling at low temperatures. Even ice will evaporate straight into water vapour at reduced pressure, and freezing in a partial vacuum is the modern technique of freeze-drying.

[*Vacuum* – French: *vide* German: *leerer Raum, Vakuum* Italian: *vuoto* Spanish: *vacio*]

VAN DER HUM. *See* liqueurs and cordials.

VANILLA. Real vanilla comes from the pod of a climbing orchid (*Vanilla planifolia*), which is native to tropical American forests. Before the Spanish arrived in America, it was already being used by the Aztecs as a flavouring for chocolate. The pods are picked unripe – they are yellow, with no vanilla taste. Flavour develops through the activity of enzymes when the pods are packed tight and allowed to sweat in boxes. They go black and acquire a white frosting of strongly aromatic vanillin crystals, which are what to look for when buying (although they can be faked).

Good vanilla pods are expensive but last a long time. Pods kept in a jar of sugar will impregnate the sugar with their flavour. For stronger vanilla flavour, the pod can be heated in the liquid to be flavoured,

then rinsed and dried so that it can be used again.

The best vanilla essence is made by extracting the flavour from real vanilla pods with alcohol, but a vanilla flavour may also come from synthetic vanillin made from eugenol, which occurs naturally in clove oil. Being much cheaper, vanillin is much used as a flavouring in butter, margarine, ice cream, chocolate, drinks and liqueurs. In large doses, it is poisonous but it is such a powerfully aromatic substance that only a minute amount is necessary for effect. As usual with virtually pure synthetic flavours, it lacks the complementary aromas of natural vanilla and is crude by comparison.

Vanilla needs to be used with great discretion, but is then a most useful flavour both in a dominant role and below the level of recognition. The violent vanilla flavour of many commercial products can be duplicated in the kitchen by anyone with a heavy hand.

[*Vanilla* – French: *vanille* German: *Vanille* Italian: *vaniglia* Spanish: *vainilla*]

VEAL. *See* beef.

VEGETABLE GELATIN. *See* agar-agar.

VEGETABLE OYSTER. *See* salsify.

VEGETABLE PEAR. *See* chayote.

VEGETABLE SPAGHETTI. *See* marrow (*Cucurbita pepo*).

VELVET APPLE or **mabolo**. A close relative of the *persimmon.

VENISON is the meat of deer. In Europe, the smallest species, the Roe deer (*Capreolus capreolus*) is thought to make the finest venison, followed by the Fallow deer (*Dama dama*), the species which is partly domesticated in deer parks. The flesh of the Red deer (*Cervus elaphus*), which is hunted in the wilder parts of Scotland, is less choice. However, attempts are being made in Scotland to farm Red deer for venison on a commercial scale. The reindeer (*Rangifer tarandus*) is domesticated and kept in large herds in Arctic Scandinavia (and experimentally in Scotland); it is considered inferior to the other European deer for eating, although smoked reindeer tongue is a delicacy.

Very young deer are considered to lack taste, and older animals must be well hung and marinated to make the meat flavourful and tender. Dozens of marinades are used, of which the following is typical, and gives the meat a slightly sour taste. A haunch of venison should remain in it for 4-5 days, depending on the weather. As it is inclined to be dry, venison is best when larded with strips of fat.

Marinade for Venison

Chop 10 carrots and 12 onions. Cook them gently until they are soft but not brown in 50 g (2 oz) butter, with 3 cloves, 2 allspice berries, 10 bay leaves, a large pinch of thyme, 10 juniper berries, salt and peppercorns. Then add ½ lt (1 pt) each of wine vinegar and stock. Boil for 2 minutes, then cool and strain the marinade over the haunch. Turn the haunch in the marinade from time to time. The mixture can also be used for *boar.

[*Venison* – French: *venaison* German: *Wildbret* Italian: *selvaggina, carne di cervo o capriolo cacciaggione* Spanish: *carne de venado*]

VERBENA or **lemon-scented verbena** (*Verbena tryphilla*) has a place in many gardens. It is a native of South America and requires a warmer corner or sunny window. The flavour is rather rankly lemon, such as the Spanish *hierbas*, which are often home made and digestive. It is also a passable substitute for *lemon grass in South East Asian dishes. Although it is inclined to be reminiscent of old-fashioned soaps, it can be used with caution in sweet dishes, fruit salads and cups to give a lemon-peel touch, but the peel of a fresh lemon is usually nicer.

[*Verbena* – French: *verveine* German: *Verbena, Zitronenstrauch* Italian: *verbena* Spanish: *verbena*]

VERDELHO. *See* madeira.

VERJUICE, from the French *vert* (green) *jus* (juice), is the sour juice of unripe fruit and was more used in the past as a souring agent than it is today. In France, it was the juice of unripe grapes and, in Britain, the juice of unripe apples or crab apples

fermented for a day or so to remove any small amounts of sugar. After skimming and salting, the verjuice would keep well. It was sometimes concentrated by boiling. The main use for verjuice today is in prepared mustards. In recipes, the usual modern substitute is lemon juice. However, with a modern centrifugal juice extractor, the way is wide open for experiment.

[*Verjuice* – French: *verjus* German: *Obst-Traubensaft (bes. von unreifen Früchten)* Italian: *agresto* Spanish: *argraz, agrazada*]

VERMICELLI. *See* pasta.

VERMOUTH is named after the German for wormwood (*Wernut*).Wine has been aromatized with herbs and spices since ancient times, and such brews became particularly popular in northern Italy during the Middle Ages, where home-made versions were used as aperitifs. In 1786, a Turin cellar owner called A. B. Carpano started making vermouth on a large scale and thus founded not only the house of Carpano but also began a business which has been centred in Turin ever since. Vermouth is essentially a mixture of wines from various parts of Italy, blended with infusions of many herbs, flowers, barks and spices, and slightly fortified with alcohol to bring it up to a strength of 16-18°. It may be sweet or dry, white or coloured brownish-red with added caramel.

Vermouth is now made all over the world in the wine-producing countries. Recipes for vermouths are the manufacturers' secrets and are occasionally changed to suit changes in taste. Vermouths were originally intended to be taken neat before a meal (and can be drunk with the first course), but today huge quantities go into cocktails. Indeed, it was cocktails such as Martinis that made vermouths internationally famous. Because vermouths are fortified, they keep fairly well once opened, particularly the heavy, sweet ones; the lighter, white vermouths begin to deteriorate after 3 weeks, even when the bottle is closed, though they go off less rapidly in the refrigerator, which for other reasons is the best place to keep the bottle.

Flavouring ingredients known to go into vermouths include angelica root, anise, calamus, cinnamon, cloves, coriander, camomile, bitter orange peel, peppermint, orris, quassia, quinine, gentian, nutmeg and, of course, wormwood. With so much variation, the instruction to use vermouth in a sauce for fish, for instance, is not very meaningful, but specific vermouths are used as flavourings in sauces and can be excellent.

[Vermouth – French: vermouth, vermout German: Wermut Italian: vermut Spanish: vermut]

VESIGA or **viziga**. *See* sturgeon.

VETIVER. *See* khas-khas.

VE-TSIN. *See* monosodium glutamate.

VICHY. *See* water (mineral water).

VINEGAR was originally sour wine (*vin aigre*),as opposed to alegar (sour ale), but today only the one word is used. Any alcoholic liquid which does not contain more than about 18% alcohol will sour if exposed to the air. Souring is caused by bacteria that attack alcohol and oxidize it to acetic acid. As they require oxygen, the bacteria grow on the surface and stick together to form a skin, usually known as vinegar plant or mother of vinegar. It may be used as a starter.

Since vinegar comes from natural processes, it has been known for as long as wine or ale. In fact, vinegar is one of the oldest ingredients in cooking and was used in Europe for thousands of years before lemon juice was even heard of. Vinegars normally contain 4-6% of *acetic acid, but the strength can be increased by distillation, and 'essence of vinegar' can be up to about 14%. Vinegar is commonly made by souring wine, ale (malt vinegar) or cider (cider vinegar), but vinegars are produced locally from perry, mead, rice wine, and from fruit wines brewed with anything from currants to cashew apples.

Wine vinegar is usual in countries like France, Spain and Italy where wine is produced in quantity, but it is not necessarily very good because it happens to be made of wine. It may be made of wine that is scarcely fit to drink, and it will be made by the quick process, in which wine is sprinkled over a container full of wood shavings (to provide a large surface) with a revolving 'sparger', a miniature version of a sewage works sprinkler. As the wine dribbles down over the shavings, it is violently attacked by the organisms that cover them, and everything is kept well oxygenated by air blown in at the bottom. In the process, quite a lot of heat is generated – the tank is maintained at 35-38°C (95-100°F), which is hot enough to drive off any of the finer and more volatile flavours.

This is why the best vinegar is still made by the old Orléans process, in which barrels are filled with a mixture of 3 parts wine to 2 parts vinegar and innoculated with mother of vinegar and left open to allow air to enter. Establishing the vat with vinegar prevents the growth of unwanted organisms and encourages vinegar organisms, which grow best in acid conditions. In the Orléans process, the organisms slowly turn the alcohol in the wine to acid without getting hot and without losing the finer flavours of the wine. At intervals, vinegar is drawn off and more wine is added. Since this is a slow process, Orléans process vinegar is expensive, especially as the finest vinegar starts with good wine. However, the amount of vinegar used in dressing a salad ought to be small, and it is worth finding a fine wine vinegar to keep just for this purpose. The difference it makes to a salad is enormous.

The town of Modena in northern Italy produces fine wine vinegar, *acelo balsamico*, which is matured for years – it is said that it is usable after ten years, better after thirty, better still after fifty, and at its best after a hundred or more. It is too good to use for anything except salads.

Special types of vinegar come from particular wines, for example sherry vinegar. Malt vinegar is essentially beer vinegar (except that the beer is not hopped) and is usually coloured brown with caramel. It is less sour than the run-of-the-mill wine vinegar, but nice flavours do not come from the fermented malt, although some aromatics may be generated by bacteria. Cider vinegar has long been popular in the north-eastern US and in recent years has also become better known in Britain. It is supposed to be more healthy and is a basis for a few American folk medicines. However, cider vinegar has an apple juice taste which a few people, including myself, do not find particularly attractive. White vinegar is as colourless as water (white-wine vinegar has some colour) and is used in pickles for cosmetic reasons. It can be made by decolourizing ordinary vinegar with animal charcoal or can be faked with acetic acid and water.

Very strong vinegars, such as essence of vinegar, spirit vinegar and distilled vinegar, are used to preserve very watery vegetables or in any other situation in which ordinary vinegar will become overdiluted. They are made by concentrating vinegars by distillation or by diluting strong synthetic acetic acid with water.

Vinegar is very easily made at home by putting wine (including home-made wine) or any other alcoholic liquid into a container preferably one with a tap at the bottom, and adding a piece of mother of vinegar to act as a starter – or at least putting some vinegar in to increase acidity. Without this, the wine may go off before it has developed its own acid. The container should be kept in a warm kitchen. A skin of mother of vinegar will shortly form over the wine. If this later becomes too white and thick, the top layer should be removed as it may block air getting to the underlying bacteria; the underlying pink skin, should be left. When it is ready, some of the vinegar can be run off (or siphoned off from the bottom if it is in a vessel with no tap) and more wine added. Vinegar exposed to the air will lose strength, because of bacteria which attack the acetic acid, so vinegar bottles should be well filled and corked.

In the past, it was quite usual for cooks to make sugar vinegar, something which can be done quite simply as follows: boil a suitable volume of water and add sugar at the rate of 150 g (5 oz) per 1 lt (1¾ pt); within reason, quantity is not critical. You can use brown sugar or add molasses for flavour. Traditionally, the liquid, when cool, was put in a not quite full cask and a piece of toast covered in yeast was floated on top. A piece of brown paper was pasted over the bung hole and well pricked with a skewer to let in air. A barrel of sugar and water, if put down in April, would be vinegar ready for bottling by September. It would go more quickly if mother of vinegar was added.

Old directions for making mother of vinegar are to put 100 g (4 oz) sugar and 225 g (8 oz) treacle in 3½ lt (6 pt) water, bring to the boil, then cool, cover and leave in a warm place for 6 weeks; if all goes well, mother of vinegar will form on top and can be used as a starter. Home-made vinegar is best pasteurized or brought almost to the boil before bottling.

Vinegar is often flavoured with various herbs and aromatics, the best known varieties being tarragon, chilli and garlic vinegars, but cucumber, basil, rose, violet, celery (with celery seed), cress or mustard (also with seed) and shallot vinegars are also made. To make any of these, it is necessary only to infuse the flavourings in a bottle of vinegar for some days. Some vinegars were made with quite complicated mixtures of herbs, garlic, onion and spices. They then verged on bottled sauces. Sweet fruit vinegars (such as raspberry, currant and gooseberry) were made to be diluted and used as refreshing summer drinks, but these have gone out of fashion.

Vinegar is preservative, because of its acetic acid content, which is why it is used in pickles and chutneys. As vinegars vary, it may be best to dilute them with a little water and not to slavishly follow recipes with full strength products. Tiny amounts of vinegar can improve some surprising things (yoghurt and strawberries are examples).

A Japanese sweet vinegar, which is used for seasoning rice, is called *yamabukusu;* a substitute can be made by adding 3 tablespoons sugar, 3 teaspoons, salt and a pinch of monosodium glutamate to a cup of vinegar.

[*Vinegar* – French: *vinaigre* German: *Essig* Italian: *aceto* Spanish: *vinagre*]

VINE LEAVES. The principal use for vine leaves is for stuffing to make the Levantine specialities known loosely as *dolmades* (Greek), *dolmas* (Turkey) or *mashi* (Lebanon). Young vine leaves are used – the third and fourth from the tip are said to be best – as older ones are tough. (If gathering them yourself, be careful that the leaves have not been sprayed with chemicals.) Some vine leaves have a ragged, heart shape, but others are deeply indented and do not therefore make a good wrapping. The leaves of wild grapes can be used in the US. Vine leaves can be bought fresh throughout the summer in the markets of eastern Mediterranean countries. For winter, they are salted in barrels and sold loose. They may also be bought shrink-wrapped or canned – a 425 g (15 oz) can holds 40-50 leaves.

Before vine leaves can be stuffed, they must have the stalks removed and be blanched for a few minutes in boiling water until they are pliable. It is best to blanch a few at a time, as a large number of leaves dumped into the pot will stick together and the outer ones will be done before the heat reaches the inner ones. However, since vine leaves take 45-60 minutes to cook, over-blanching is merely an inconvenience. Canned vine leaves and salted leaves from the barrel need to be rinsed in warm water to remove salt before they are used.

There are many stuffings for *dolmas* – mixtures of meat, rice and vegetables, which often contain pine nuts. They may be flavoured with herbs such as parsley and mint. Some recipes are intended for eating hot; others cold. They are stuffed by laying them out with the veiny underside upwards, placing a small amount of stuffing near the stalk end, which is then folded over the stuffing. The side lobes of the leaf are folded inwards and the package is then rolled up so that the tip of the leaf is on the outside. Recipes for stuffed vine leaves, both hot and cold appear in Claudia Roden's *A Book of Middle Eastern Food* (Penguin).

Vine leaves have a characteristic though mild taste and cannot be properly replaced by other leaves. Apart from being stuffed, they are sometimes fried in batter, cut up in salads, or used for wrapping small birds and lining pans in which other foods (such as mushrooms) are gently cooked. Many outdoor vines in Britain do not produce worthwhile grapes, and it would be better to use them to provide vine leaves. Once you become hooked on *dolmas*, especially for parties, it is difficult to do without them.

[*Vine leaf* – French: *feuille de vigne* German: *Rebenblatt* Italian: *foglia di vite* Spanish: *pámpano*]

VIOLET. The French name for a grey-brown sac-like tunicate (*Microcosmus sulcatus*), an animal that lives fastened to rocks at a depth of 30-100 m (100-300 ft) in the Mediterranean. The soft, yellow insides are eagerly eaten raw by *aficionados* in France, Spain and Italy. The taste is strong, sour, marine and iodine-like. I spat mine out.

[*Violet* – French: *violet, figue de mer* Italian: *limone di mare, uovo di mare* Spanish: *probecho*]

VIOLET. The Sweet violet (*Viola odorata*) is edible, as presumably, are other species, and the flowers may be bought preserved in sugar. They are mostly used as cake decorations. Violet is the main flavouring in the very sweet, violet-coloured liqueur known as *parfait amour*. The leaves and flowers are harmless and may be used for fun in salads. They are slightly laxative. Violets were used a lot in the 17th century, and recipes for violet syrups and sweetmeats abound in cookery books of the period.

*Orris may be used to provide imitation violet flavourings, for example in chocolate creams.

[*Violet* – French: *violette* German: *Veilchen* Italian: *viola mammola* Spanish: *buglosa*]

VIPER'S BUGLOSS (*Echium vulgare*) is a common European flower of the borage family. It is hairy, with blue flowers and pink buds. Like borage, it has a cucumber flavour and may be used for the same purpose – to decorate iced cups.

[*Viper's Bugloss* – French: *vipérine* German: *Natterkopf* Italian: *vipérino* Spanish: *bugloss*]

VITAMINS are not ingredients we buy and stuff into the food – as yet – but they need to be watched, because cooks are responsible for the health of the people they feed and because, in cooking, vitamins can easily be destroyed, thrown away or lost. It was discovered long ago that scurvy on long voyages could be prevented by taking lime juice, and housewives accumulated a lot of know-how about keeping their families healthy on fresh food, but it was not until 1912 that the biochemist Sir Frederick Gowland Hopkins put vitamins firmly on the map.

Vitamins are organic substances of various sorts that the body cannot manufacture for itself but needs in small amounts in order to function properly. Originally, vitamins could not be identified by chemical names (although one, niacin, had actually been synthesized in the 19th century), and so they were known by the letters of the alphabet. Later, some were found not to be one vitamin but several – in particular, vitamin B was split into B_1, B_2, B_3, and B_{12}. The whole series was called the B vitamin complex, because the vitamins did not work in isolation from each other, but were inter-related. As techniques improved, the chemical structure of the vitamins began to be worked out and, during the 1930s, many were synthesized (vitamin C, 1933; vitamin B_2, 1934; vitamin D_2, 1935; vitamin B_1, 1936). All the vitamins were eventually given chemical names, and some that had earlier been called vitamins were found to be inessential and so dropped. This accounts for the untidiness of the list today. Vitamins are now big business for pharmaceutical companies, which like us to swallow a lot of pills. Although a few people with inherited peculiarities may need more than average amounts of certain vitamins, a balanced diet generally provides enough to maintain good health without vitamin supplements. Any extra is usually just eliminated from the body and is a waste of cash. Cooks should be concerned to retain the vitamins in everyday dishes, but it is not always easy to know if cooking is damaging the vitamins. Only a few of the more important vitamins are dealt with below.

Vitamin A or **retinol**. Deficiency causes night blindness and later flaky 'toad skin', even wrinkles on the cornea of the eye, but risk of deficiency is slight in Europe or America. In cooking, retinol is fairly resistant to heat and, being fat soluble, is not dissolved out into the cooking water. It is, however, easily destroyed by light and by rancid fats.

The normal daily requirement for normal people is satisfied by as little as 10 g (⅓ oz) of liver, 40 g (1½ oz) old carrots or 75 g (3 oz) new carrots, 75 g (3 oz) spinach, margarine or butter, or 4 eggs. Cheese, milk, cream and apricots are also useful sources. Fish liver oils contain a lot of vitamins, particularly halibut liver oil, which contains 150 times as much as cod liver oil.

As vitamin A is stored in the body, one serving of liver, 100 g (4 oz), would cover a week's requirement. Retinol is not excreted in the urine, and too much is toxic. The liver of sharks, whales and polar bears are reckoned to be dangerous because of their retinol content. Polar-bear liver is fantastically rich in retinol – but is nevertheless the first part eaten by Eskimos, who take it raw, and warm, from the kill. Carrots are not rich in retinol itself, but contain its precursor, carotene.

Vitamin B$_1$ or thiamine. Deficiency causes beriberi and nervous disorders; the risk is slight in those who eat a reasonable diet, as it occurs in most fresh foods, but alcoholics can suffer. They tend to eat badly and have an increased demand for this vitamin. Mild deficiency sometimes contributes to mental confusion in old people.

The normal daily requirement varies with the individual's carbohydrate metabolism, because thiamine is concerned with the release of energy from glucose. Men usually require more than women, and the physically active more than those who lead sedentary lives. Thiamine requirements cannot be supplied by a single serving of any one food (except perhaps a massive amount of cod's roe), but must come from a variety. Rich ones are wheat germ, Brazil nuts, unroasted peanuts and roasted pork, while oatmeal, bacon and eggs, kidney, liver and bread (both brown and white) would all make their contribution. Synthetic thiamine hydrochloride is often added to breakfast cereals, peanut butter and breads to replace that lost in the manufacture. It may sometimes be added to such items as skimmed milk and bottled drinks. Thiamine is not stored (although there is some reserve in the body cells); as any excess of immediate requirements is lost in the urine, it is not toxic in excess. Thiamine is easily destroyed by heat in cooking, especially in the presence of an alkali, such as bicarbonate of soda. Also, being water soluble, it is easily dissolved out by cooking water. Even toasting a slice of bread destroys up to a third of the vitamin, and reheating or keeping food warm is exceedingly destructive.

Vitamin B$_2$ of which riboflavin is an important component. Deficiency in adults is not marked by an obvious disease, but causes vague symptoms like sore tongue, cracks at the corners of the mouth and itching eyes. It stunts growth in children. Riboflavin is necessary for proper functioning of the muscles, so people doing hard physical work need it, athletes need it, and men usually need it more than women (they usually have bigger muscles), but as with all vitamins – B complex ones in particular – it is little use on its own without the others. The risk of deficiency is negligible in an averagely good diet. The normal daily requirement could come from one

large serving of liver or kidneys, but cheese, milk, eggs and yeast extracts are also good sources.

In cooking, riboflavin is relatively stable to heat, but will be destroyed by an alkali like bicarbonate of soda. It is also soluble in water and will be leached out when food is boiled, so use the cooking water to make gravy and stock. Ultra-violet light rapidly destroys riboflavin, and milk in a bottle left in the sun or even under fluorescent light will lose its riboflavin content in a few hours.

Niacin or nicotinic acid has for long had no B number, but is an important member of the B-vitamin complex. Deficiency causes pellagra; the risk is small in people living on normally adequate diets, but may occur in alcoholics. Our normal daily requirement would be contained in one helping of liver or be made up from other meals. Good sources are liver, kidneys, sardines and other oily fish, peanuts, cheese, eggs, mushrooms, milk and pulses. Best of all are meat extracts, yeast extracts and wheat bran. Niacin is supplied to a significant extent by coffee and beer. Niacin is little affected by the heat of cooking, but is water soluble and some 40% may be lost from vegetables that are boiled in a lot of water. People got pellagra from a maize diet because they were poor and unable to afford meat, eggs or milk. Maize, unlike other cereals, lacks the amino acid, trytophan, which can be turned into niacin by the liver if vitamins B$_1$, B$_2$, and B$_6$ are present.

Vitamin B$_{12}$ or cyanocobalamin is used as a cure for pernicious anaemia, because the vitamin is concerned in the formation of red cells in the blood, although the disease is not caused by vitamin deficiency. The risk of a deficiency in the diet is more or less zero, except among vegans – vegetarians who eat no food of animal origin, no milk, cheese or eggs.

Vitamin C or ascorbic acid. Serious deficiency causes scurvy; the breakdown of connective tissue proteins. First symptoms are easy bruising, bleeding and spongy gums, followed by loss of teeth, weak bones and internal haemorrhages. It is still uncertain what harm a slight deficiency might do. As early as 1601 it was discovered that lime juice prevented scurvy, although it took almost 200 years, until 1795, for lime juice to become a compulsory issue in the British navy, which as everyone knows caused Americans to give the British the name 'lime juicers' and then 'limeys' (though it seems to have been lemon juice rather than lime juice that was actually issued.)

The normal daily requirement is uncertain, but most people eating plenty of fresh fruit and vegetables get enough. Common foods particularly rich in vitamin C are black currants and strawberries, watercress and green peppers, cabbage, cauliflower and Brussels sprouts. Oranges and lemons are all right but not sensational, but apples, carrots, pears, bananas, plums, celery and beetroot are less good. The risk of deficiency is small, except among those who perhaps for dietary reasons (e.g. the Atkins diet) eat almost exclusively fish, fats, eggs and meat – they will need supplementary vitamin C.

Vitamin C is very easily destroyed in cooking. Before you even start to cook them, vegetables that are not fresh, are wilted or have been stored for long in the refrigerator will have lost much of their C vitamin content. Air also destroys vitamin C and so do enzymes in cut-up fruit and vegetables that are exposed to the air. Heat destroys the vitamin – the longer food is kept hot, the more is lost. Vitamin C is dissolved out by water and destroyed by alkalis like bicarbonate of soda. Effectively, then, we have to rely on fresh uncooked fruit and vegetables for our main supply.

Vitamin C is not stored in the body beyond a certain saturation point, and excess is then excreted. Its use in a large dose (1 teaspoon of ascorbic acid) taken at the start of a cold has almost gone into folk medicine in the last few years, but the case for it is still very much in doubt. So is the value of saturating the body with it to ward off colds. Synthetic ascorbic acid is used in manufactured food as an antioxidant, and by the bread industry to accelerate the proving and maturing of bread dough – this does not increase the vitamin content of the bread as baking does away with the vitamin C.

Vitamin D is a complex of substances including calciferol (D_2) and cholecalciferol (D_3). It is found mainly in oily fish, margarine (into which it is put) and eggs. It also forms when the skin is exposed to the sun. Deficiency prevents calcium from being properly absorbed and so leads to rickets. The risk of deficiency is greater in winter and people who spend their lives indoors, especially young children in cloudy climates. Most adults get enough to supply their needs.

The normal daily requirement would be easily supplied by a serving of herrings, kippers, mackerel, or eels, but most people probably get their supply

from the sun, and from margarine and eggs. Cod liver oil is exceedingly rich in vitamin D, and 1 teaspoon of it a day will provide all anyone could wish for. In cooking, vitamin D is not destroyed by heat (except in frying) and, being fat soluble, does not dissolve out in cooking water.

Too much vitamin D is toxic and may cause calcium to be deposited in the circulatory system. (It can also harm the unborn child if an expectant mother goes on a cod liver spree.) The worry at the moment is that because manufacturers enrich milk, flour, cereals and baby foods, some people may be getting too much vitamin D in their diets.

[*Vitamin* – French: *vitamine* German: *Vitamin* Italian: *vitamina* Spanish: *vitamina*]

VIZIGA, **vesiga** or **vyaziga**. *See* sturgeon.

VODKA means 'little water' and is derived from the early Russian *shizenennya voda* meaning 'water of life'. In fact, it has the same sort of origin as whisky and *aquavit* in monkish medicine. It is not sure whether vodka was first produced in Poland or Russia. Unlike the other great spirits, it does not aim to be flavoured by *congenerics coming over in the still. It is the purest of all spirits and consequently may be distilled equally from grain, potatoes, wine or any fermentable mash. Colour and lingering flavour may be removed by animal charcoal or by distillation to a high degree of purity. Flavourings can be added afterwards by both the maker and the cook. Before World War II, vodka was little drunk outside eastern Europe, but now its popularity rivals gin, and it is distilled in Britain, the US, and almost everywhere else where people like to drink. One of its attractions is that since it contains virtually no congenerics, you can sober up quicker and with less hangover from it than from any other drink.

A Polish friend of mine let me into the secret of his own home-made vodka. He took the best pure grape spirit distilled in Italy – some 95% pure – and cut it with an equal volume of water, adding to each bottle a level teaspoon of sugar, which soon dissolved in the water. He told me with some glee how some Polish visitors, vodka connoisseurs, had complained that the vodka he offered, the best brand obtainable and bought specially for them, was not fit to drink. Rather upset, he had gone into the kitchen, unearthed a very old empty bottle of some pre-war brand from a cupboard, rinsed it and filled it with his home-made brew. 'Fabulous,' they said. 'That's the real stuff.' I don't think anyone could have pulled the trick with whisky, brandy, rum or even gin. Vodka can be flavoured. A coil of lemon zest or a sprig of wormword put into the bottle and left a few days will give it taste and a most potent effect. Flavoured and fruit vodkas are sold. Vodka is much used instead of gin in cocktails and is used for its own sake in a Bloody Mary. As vodka is more or less flavourless, it is rarely used for flaming, but is the best thing to use when an alcoholic solvent is required (unless you are in a country where you can buy strong potable alcohol).With it, you can make your own essences by infusion, and you can use it as a spirit for preserving fruit provided that the vodka is strong and the fruit not too watery.

[*Vodka* – French: *vodka* German: *Wodka* Italian: *vodka* Spanish: *vodka*]

VYAZIGA, **Viziga.** *see* sturgeon.

W

WAFER. A thin, crisp biscuit, in many respects similar to a waffle (which comes essentially from the same word via the Dutch) but thinner and crisper. They really need to be baked in wafer-irons which are made especially for the purpose. The irons are heated on both sides, rubbed with a little butter, and then filled with a teaspoon of batter. They are then closed almost immediately and put back on the heat. When it is cooked on both sides, the wafer is immediately removed, sometimes curled round a wooden spoon handle while it is still flexible but often left flat. After being trimmed and allowed to cool and dry, wafers must be stored in a dry tin. The simplest wafer batter consists of only flour and water, but most contain sugar, egg and cream. Nowadays, most people buy wafers that have been made by machinery. There are recipes for making wafers in the oven, but these are more like biscuits or cookies.

[*Wafer* – French: *pain à cacheter* German: *Waffel* Italian: *cialda* Spanish: *barquillo*]

WAKAME. *See* seaweed.

WALNUT (*Fuglans regia*) is misleadingly named the English walnut in the US to distinguish it from the native American species. The walnut tree is a native of south-eastern Europe and its range extends across west and central Asia into China. Although walnuts were important to the ancient Greeks and Romans, they are said not to have been established in Britain until the 15th century. The early colonists took them to plant in North America. Walnuts have also been introduced into Australia, New Zealand, South Africa and South America. They are an important crop in China, where the papershell varieties are mainly grown. The leading walnut country, however, is France, although it is fast being overtaken by the US. Nuts are produced particularly in the departments of Dordogne and Lot as well as in the valley of the Isère near Grenoble. In the past, walnuts were an essential food in some districts, not only as nuts but also for their oil, which was once as important as olive oil in French kitchens, but today it is too expensive for general use. Italy is another important producer, with nuts grown in small areas over the whole country. The bulk for export come from the south – around Naples, Sorrento and Benevento. Strangely, in Italian cooking, walnuts are more used in the north. In the US, there are huge orchards in California and Oregon.

Every country has its favoured varieties, which are propagated by grafting and have been selected for such qualities as size, ratio of meat to shell, texture, flavour and absence of astringency. Some varieties are very hard and difficult to crack, while others have thin, papery shells, but all need to have a tight seal between the halves for good keeping. There are also freaks such as the French *noix noisette*, with nuts no bigger than a hazel, delicately flavoured and full of oil, and the gigantic *bijou*, which was once polished and mounted in metal to make elegant cases for jewels or, more humbly, cradles for little dolls.

Walnut trees are self fertile, and the fruit are

borne on the outer branches. Towards the end of September, or in early October, the husks split open and the fresh, ripe nuts fall to the ground. Help can be given by shaking the tree or beating it, and the nuts must be picked up almost daily as any left lying on the ground quickly become discoloured and mouldy. In some unfavourable years there are many 'stick-tight' nuts which cause problems by being separable from the husk only with difficulty. Walnuts are usually washed and then dried outdoors, but they must not be left in the hot sun for more than two hours at a time, as the heat may make them split open, and they will then not keep. Commercially produced walnuts are often bleached and dried artificially in a stream of warm air at a maximum of 43°C (110°F).

Green walnuts are made use of at all stages of ripeness. For pickling, the fruit is taken green and the shells not yet formed. They usually reach this stage in late June, and the fruit are tested by pushing a skewer right through them in several directions (the shell begins to form near the end away from the stalk). Nuts for pickle should not be too young, as they tend to disintegrate or go mushy, but of course they are no use once the shell has gone hard. In between, there is a short period when the walnuts are just right. Where the recipe calls for the husk to be skinned this may be done by scalding and rubbing the skin off with a rough cloth. Products made from the green nuts in Britain are walnut pickle, walnut ketchup, and walnut jam – in fact, the bulk of home-grown walnuts go for pickle and are not allowed to mature. In France, a cordial, *brou de noix*, is made from green walnuts. In Italy the equivalent is *nocino*, a stomachic that is especially popular in Lombardy and is also used to flavour ice creams. When the husk is still green, but the kernels are properly formed, the nut can be extracted, peeled and preserved in syrup – as they are in the Middle East – or used to make *cerneaux au verjus*, the skinned immature kernel marinaded in *verjuice for an hour or so, then seasoned with pepper, chopped shallot and sometimes vinegar – Elizabeth David's *French Country Cooking* (Grub Street) gives recipes.

Nocino

Cut about 30 green walnuts into quarters and put them in a large screw-top jar with a good sliver of lemon peel, a couple of small bits of cinnamon stick and half a dozen cloves. Cover with 1 lt of 90% alcohol (or as strong as you can get it), put the lid on and leave the jar in the sun for a month, shaking it every day. At the end of this time, add 500 g (1 lb) sugar and leave for another two weeks in the sun, shaking the jar every day as before. Filter and bottle the *nocino*, which should be left for a year before using.

Pickled walnuts. Pickled, unripe walnuts are well known in England but not at all, or rarely, in the countries further south where the nuts are mainly produced. The fruit are often prepared for pickling by scalding and skinning, but Mrs Beeton suggests pricking the skins well with a silver fork. Such treatment allows the vinegar to penetrate and accelerates pickling. The walnuts must now be put in brine strong enough to float a fresh egg, which means 100-150 g per lt (2-3 oz per pt) of salt. They are left submerged, weighted down under a board, for 6 days and are stirred at least once a day; then the brine is changed and the walnuts are left for a further week. A total of 12-13 days salting is usual. After this, the fruit are drained, spread out in a single layer, and put in the sun (if there is any). They are left exposed and turned occasionally until they go black all over, a process which may take up to two days, depending on the conditions. Now the black fruits are packed into jars, covered with spiced vinegar, sealed and left for at least a month, but preferably several months, before using.

There are many formulae for making the vinegar, one of which is as follows. For each litre (2 pt) of vinegar add 1 small onion, 1 crushed clove of garlic, and 20 grams (¾ oz) each of bruised ginger, black pepper corns, cloves, allspice, cinnamon stick and mustard seed, plus a large blade of mace and 2 bay leaves. Bring to the boil, simmer for five minutes and allow to cool, preferably overnight. Strain the vinegar and cover walnuts with it. If hot vinegar is poured over the walnuts, they will take less time to mature but the results are marginally less good.

Ripe walnuts are sold whole or shelled and as ground or broken nut meat. When buying walnuts in the shell, look carefully to make sure that the seal between the halves of the shell is good – you should certainly not be able to pull the two halves of the shell apart. Without actually opening some nuts, it is impossible to tell if kernels have been over-dried. New walnuts, on the other hand, have sometimes been soaked in water to make them heavy and moist. They are good for immediate use but will not keep. Shelled nuts quickly go rancid – dark, bitter, stale kernels are an abomination and will spoil any dish they are put in.

New walnuts are very digestible, but the skin of the kernels is bitter and should be removed. In some varieties, it will easily peel off after a short soaking in cold water, but others may have first to be scalded for a few seconds in boiling water and then dropped into ice-water. Skinned, fresh walnuts are a great delicacy in the Middle East.

With time, after drying and maturing, walnuts become more oily and less easily digested, but the skin loses much of its bitterness. Even so, the skins should be removed for any delicate walnut dish. You can pour a kettle of boiling water over the kernels and take off the skins with your fingers as soon as the nuts are cool enough to handle. Alternatively, they may be put into a gentle oven until the skin becomes brittle and can be rubbed off with a cloth.

The best known use of walnuts is in sweets, cakes and ice creams. Whole or chopped walnuts are now also commonly used in salads, as part of a garnish for stews and even as the main ingredient in walnut soup. They are excellent both for their flavour and to give texture when they are pounded or minced. From France there is *sauce raifort aux noix, l'aillade toulousaine* (walnuts pounded with garlic and stirred into an emulsion with olive oil), and sometimes they are used to make the traditional *raïto* of Provence. In Italy, walnuts are pounded with the pine nuts for *pesto alla genovese* and form the nut base of a pesto variant, the *pasta alla fornala* of Tuscany. Skinned walnuts pounded with soaked bread, a lot of parsley, salt, oil and a trace of garlic (½ clove to ½ kilo of nuts), diluted with cream or curdled milk, form the *salsa di noci* of Liguria. It is used on a local type of ravioli, which is stuffed with a cooked mixture of herbs such as Swiss chard, borage and wild chicory. A sauce from Piedmont uses pounded walnuts moistened with broth and mixed with mustard and honey as an accompaniment for a *bollito misto* (mixed boiled meats). In all cases, the walnuts are first peeled after blanching in boiling water.

Walnuts are grown in the Balkans, especially in Albania and Romania. Bulgaria has a sauce very similar to the Italian *salsa di noci*. Greece has a walnut sauce to use with hare. From Iran comes the superlative *fesenjan* in which lamb, duck or chicken has a sauce of pounded walnuts and sour fruit juice. Rather similar combinations are found in Kashmir.

Khoresh Fesenjan or Faisinjan

Koreshtha (the plural of **khoresh**) are Iranian dishes that are eaten with rice. They are something between a stew and a sauce and usually combine meat, nuts and fruit.

Chop a large onion and fry it gently in 1 tablespoon of butter till just soft, then add 500 g (1 lb) walnuts, skinned and ground fine. Mix them in, continue frying gently for 2 minutes, then add 500 ml (1 pt) of water and simmer gently for about 30 minutes.

Meanwhile finely chop a small onion and add it to 500 g (1 lb) finely minced lamb. Fry the mixture in as little fat as possible until the meat browns. Add it to the simmering walnut mixture, adding more water if necessary. Season with salt and pepper, and continue simmering for an hour. Now add 250 ml (½ pt) pomegranate juice and 200-250 g sugar (depending on the sourness of the juice) and continue to cook gently until the oil separates and comes to the surface. Make a final adjustment of seasoning with sugar or lemon juice, and serve with rice. As a substitute for pomegranate, the juice of sour cherries or even plums could be used, but the taste would not be quite the same.

Çerkes Tavugu (Circassian chicken)

There are many variations on this famous dish. It may be served hot or more usually cold, and is highly recommended for a cold buffet. The quantity of sauce in the following recipe is sufficient to go with 2 kg (4½ lb) chicken, which has been cooked by being carefully simmered with flavouring vegetables in its stock and cut in suitable pieces, or boned and diced for a fork supper. Finely grind 150 g (5 oz) peeled walnuts and mix with 1 tablespoon paprika or *pimentón*. Pound or press a little to bring out some of the oil from the nuts. Use a cloth to squeeze out some of the red oil, which is kept aside for decoration. (Additional oil can be used for this, but it makes the dish a little too oily.) To the walnuts add about 150 g (5 oz) bread soaked in chicken stock. Pound together (or liquidize), adding more chicken stock to make a thick sauce. Season to taste. Mix half the sauce with the chicken, and spread the other half on top. Dribble red oil over the dish in a decorative pattern.

Walnut oil, which was once important in France, Switzerland and North Italy (Piedmont) for salads and cooking, is now becoming scarce as it is even more expensive than olive oil. It has a very individual taste and goes rancid rather easily.

American walnuts. There are a number of species of walnut found growing wild in North American forests, two of which have some gastronomic and commercial importance, and are also cultivated. Members of the walnut family and similar in many respects are the *hickories, including *pecan. The Black walnut (*Fuglans nigra*) has a large nut, but the shell is very hard and special crackers are necessary. The flavour is strong and is not lost in cooking. The White walnut or butternut (*Fuglans cinerea*) has a shell that cracks without difficulty, and the flavour is excellent.

[*Walnut* – French: *noix* German: *Walnuss* Italian: *noce* Spanish: *nuez negal*]

WARBLER. *See* birds.

WASHING SODA ($N_2CO_3.10\ H_2O$) is crystalline sodium carbonate. In the past, it was used in every home as a cleaner, but its place has largely been taken by modern detergents. In Kashmir, my cook liked to put it in his tea (which it turned blood red), a local custom that I cannot recommend. Washing soda dissolved in water would produce the nearest thing to old-fashioned *lye, which was mainly potassium carbonate, but it is more usual to use caustic soda as a substitute.

[*Washing Soda* – French: *soude de commerce* German: *Bleichsoda* Italian: *soda per lavare* Spanish: *sosa para blanquear*]

WATER (H_2O). From the point of view of the hydrologist, there are various sources of water. Surface water, which runs off without sinking down into the ground, is unlikely to contain much in the way of minerals, but is likely to contain silt. It comes from lakes and rivers. Mountain water can be very pure but can also contain powdered rock, especially if it comes from melting glaciers. Such water looks milky and should be stood to allow the particles to settle, as drinking it can irritate the intestine. Bog water, a practical rather than a scientific classification, usually comes from moorland areas where the rocks are impervious. It is sometimes brown with peat and may tend to be acid but contains very little dissolved mineral – it is very soft.

Water from underground has soaked down through porous rocks and become part of the water table. It comes from wells, artesian wells and springs. Unless it has come from a limestone cave (when it may be a river that has flowed through tunnels from a pot hole in the hills above) or has flowed through fissures, it is likely to be bacteriologically pure but will contain dissolved minerals. The nature and quantity of these minerals depends on the rocks through which the water has passed. Soft water is very good for washing and cooking, for making tea and whisky – it is good in whisky too – but may not be quite as healthy as hard water, which contains dissolved minerals. Statistical studies have shown heart disease to be more prevalent in areas with soft water than in those with hard water. The reason is not understood at the moment and may have no direct causal connection with the water itself but might, for instance, possibly be due to the fact that soft water dissolves lead from lead pipes, which should not be used for it.

Distilled water is the ultimate in soft water, as it has nothing at all dissolved in it. Apart from its flat taste, one Italian *professoressa* has written that it is damaging, a 'true poison', because in the long term it dissolves and removes essential minerals from the body. The point is purely academic, because most people meet distilled water only as something to put into car batteries and steam irons. (For such purposes, the water distilled in the refrigerator when moisture condenses to ice around the freezer compartment can be saved when the refrigerator is defrosted.) Distilled water makes very good tea, especially cold tea which never goes cloudy on standing; there is no harm in using it for this.

Hard water is particularly found in chalk, limestone or dolomite areas, and the chemicals responsible for hardness are mainly bicarbonates, sulphates and chlorides of calcium, magnesium, sodium and potassium. (There may also be small amounts of nitrate from mineral sources, but more than 30 parts per million is almost certainly a sign of contamination.) When water containing bicarbonates of calcium and magnesium is boiled, the bicarbonates are changed to insoluble carbonates. This produces deposits on pans and furring on kettles. The bicarbonates that can be removed by heating are a source of temporary hardness, as opposed to the permanent hardness caused by the sulphates and chlorides of calcium and magnesium, most commonly by gypsum (calcium sulphate), that stay in solution when the water is boiled. Hard water is not good for making tea or for cooking. Good drinking water should not have more than 500 parts per million of dissolved solids. However, the calcium bicarbonate in hard water is thought to be a source of calcium used by the body.

Safety. It is possible to have water so rich in poisonous elements that it is not safe to drink. You would not happily drink water in old lead or copper mines. Some natural waters contain arsenic and other poisons, are radio-active or are just downright nasty because they contain salt or alkali. Usually, however, the possible problem is sewage contamination. Rivers usually have water that is contaminated with sewage, but may be used to feed reservoirs; even in the 19th century London water was described as 'very dilute sewage'. Today at least it is purified and chlorinated sewage, but the ingredients can be detected in the taste. In the countries where the banks of streams are used as lavatories or the separation between water mains and sewers is not impeccable, the result can be epidemics of cholera, typhoid and dysentery. Water containing ammonia, nitrites, phosphates or hydrogen sulphide (which gives a smell of rotten eggs) is probably contaminated with organic waste but is not necessarily harmful. Most bacteria in water are harmless saprophytes that live on the organic matter it contains. It is only when a carrier has added pathogenic organisms (not only bacteria but amoeba and bilharzia as in parts of Africa) that there is trouble. Boiled water is safe (and so therefore is tea); and any tap water that smells of chlorine is drinkable, though it may taste unpleasant. The taste of chlorine can be removed by adding a small pinch of powdered sodium thiosulphate, which is well known to photographers as 'hypo' and is easily bought at the chemist. Water-sterilizing tablets containing a chlorine-releasing compound, such as sodium hypochlorite, can also be bought at chemists; they work well so long as instructions are followed to the letter, which is mostly a question of waiting half an hour before drinking the water. If all else fails, water from the hot tap (if it is really hot) can be used, as most pathogenic organisms are fragile and cannot withstand water at temperatures that are too hot to dip your hand in. The best solution of all for travellers who don't want to go to the American Embassy whenever they would like a drink of water is to buy a water sterilizing filter pump that makes use of a filter candle. The pores of the filter candle are too small to let bacteria pass, but water can be forced through. In old models, the candles had to be boiled regularly because bacteria were eventually forced through like fat men pushed down a narrow passage, but modern filter candles are impregnated with colloidal silver which kills trapped bacteria. Parasites which might be in water are even larger. Only viruses can get through a filter candle.

Drinking water. Water makes up 60-70% of the human body, mostly in the cells; there is far less in the blood and other body fluids. Under average conditions, we lose some 2 lt (3½ pt) a day mainly in urine, in sweat and through the lungs in breathing. This has to be made good by eating moist foods and by drinking liquids. Although it is possible to fast for weeks and still recover, someone from whom all sources of water have been withdrawn will last 60-70 hours (more in cool moist conditions, less in a dry, hot, windy desert) and will die after the loss of some 20% of body water. And thirst is awful. Anyone who has travelled in deserts knows that there does not seem to be enough water in the whole wide world to stop the craving.

Good table water is clear, colourless and almost tasteless. Unlike boiled water or distilled water, it is not flat because it contains some dissolved air, as can be seen by the bubbles that come out when water is stood for long in a glass. Water should always be on the table at meal-times, especially for weight watchers, as it helps to fill the stomach. It might be served in a glass jug, which looks clean and attractive, in a silver jug (silver helps to destroy bacteria and is traditional in some places), or in an unglazed earthenware pitcher, which keeps the water cool by evaporation. How many people who bother greatly over the wine bother equally over the water? (The Turks, though, are great connoisseurs of water.) The temperature should be ideally 9-12°C (48-54°F) for European tastes, with an outside range of 7-14°C (45-57°F). Americans prefer water below the 7°C (45°F) which is regarded as the lowest comfortable temperature in Europe, at 5.5°C (42°F), which seems very cold indeed, or even lower. This might be called ice-water, swigged in long draughts, it is not very good for the stomach. However, whatever you do, bad-tasting tap water is not going to taste good just because it is served in a nice jug at the right temperature. The alternative is mineral water.

Mineral water and **bottled water.** My grandmother was as keen as any European on visiting spas and hydras to have baths and drink the waters everywhere from Harrogate to Bad Homburg. She believed that the French drank mineral water simply because French tap water was full of typhoid. It did not occur to her, or to others of her generation, that they also drank it because it was nice. The mineral waters she drank were medicinal and nasty, while her tap water from the millstone grit of the Peak District in Derbyshire was excellent (water from there is now carbonated and bottled).

The French have 1200 registered springs, of which fifty produce water that is bottled for general consumption. A bottle of mineral water is also a normal part of a meal for many people in Italy, Spain, Germany and other European countries. And now the British are beginning to realise that good water, whether still or gassed, can be delicious. The bottle of San Pellegrino water with dinner on a hot evening in Rome is something to look forward to.

Bottled waters are often divided into table waters, mineral waters (which are slightly medicinal) and medicinal waters, but it will be a matter of opinion where the line will be drawn. Some, such as the waters containing arsenic (La Bourboule and Royat), will never be drunk except on doctor's advice, and nobody drinks the sulphurous waters of Harrogate and Bath for fun.

At the opposite end of the scale are the very pure waters, such as Evian, the largest-selling water in France, which is still and comes from springs in the French Alps (Haute Savoie), and Perrier, full of natural gas, from Vergèze in the South of France. Malvern water, from Worcestershire in the West of England, is still, pure and very slightly alkaline. San Pellegrino, which comes from springs near Milan, is artificially gassed but is an excellent table water with a very refreshing taste. Solares from near Madrid is a good table water from Spain.

Slightly more mineralized waters are drunk because people like the taste or because of a diet, but are scarcely medicinal in the usual sense. Among them is Vichy Célestins (Célestins, because there are other, openly medicinal Vichy springs) from the Allier valley near Vichy, Central France; it contains a relatively large amount of bicarbonate of soda and enough common salt to give it a salty taste. Others from France are Badoit, which is moderately alkaline and lightly gassed and Contrexéville (Centrex), which is still and also slightly alkaline; it is mildly laxative as it contains some magnesium sulphate (Epsom salts) and is popular with French girls as a diet drink. In Germany, the most famous table water is Apollinaris, a strongly effervescent, very slightly alkaline water, from a spring in the valley of the Ahr

in the Rhineland. Seltzer water from Oberselters in Westerwald, also in the Rhineland, is much imitated artificially all over the world, as is Vichy water. Other alkaline German waters are Johannis and Krontal, and optimists take them for hangovers. Dozens of varieties are reputedly good for 'flushing out the kidneys', while others are purgative. Homburg, Marienbad and Vittel contain iron.

Undoubtedly the water you drink has a bearing on your health and may account for variations in medical statistics from area to area. The value of bottled table waters tends to be overstated by the advertising copy that goes with them – the good effect of taking the waters at spas was probably as much due to drinking some water instead of just wine as to anything else.

Water in cooking. Soft water is best for cooking, for making tea, for brines to make pickles, for boiling vegetables and so on. Hard or alkaline water may make cabbage greener, but it destroys vitamins. The cloudiness, due to chalk thrown out on boiling, is unsightly in cold tea, but may be dispelled by acidifying with lemon juice. Certain fountains in Rome have reputations for producing good cooking water, and several chefs I know regard the use of mineral water as one of their 'secrets', especially in pastry and pasta. A water softener is helpful in kitchens where there is very hard water.

[*Water* – French: *eau* German: *Wasser* Italian: *acqua* Spanish: *agua*]

WATERCRESS. *See* cress.

WATER CHESTNUT. The common water chestnut (*Trapa natans*) is a floating water plant with sharply-angled, diamond-shaped, serrated leaves that can be seen in ponds and lakes in southern Europe. The fruits have four woody horns. The meat of the nut inside is floury, and has a pleasant taste. It is sometimes eaten, usually after the nut has been boiled or roasted. Alternative names are Water caltrops or Jesuits' bread. A closely allied species, Singhara nut (*T. bispinosa*), is an important local food in Kashmir, where it is grown in the lakes, while the other species of the genus, the Chinese ling (*T. bicornis*) has horns like a water buffalo and a similar chestnut-like kernel. It is much eaten in China and a flour is made from it. In European cooking, water chestnuts are sliced and added to meats and stews; they are the main ingredient of a risotto made in the Loire region of

France.

Gastronomically more important is Chinese water chestnut, or *pi-tsi* which is quite another thing, the tuber of a sedge (*Eleocharis tuberosa*), and not a nut at all. It is comparable to the *chufa nut (which also is not a nut but the tuber of a sedge). These water chestnuts are a common ingredient in Chinese food, and can be bought canned in water. Like bamboo shoots, they retain their crispness when cooked. Their name comes from the appearance of the fresh tuber, which is chestnut coloured though otherwise only vaguely like a chestnut in appearance. The South American tuber *jicana* is sometimes substituted, and is available in the US.

[*Water Chestnut* – French: *saligot, macre, chataigne d'eau, corniolle* German: *Wassernuss* Italian: *frutto della castagno d'acqua*]

WATER LEMON. *See* passion fruit.

WATERMELON. *See* melon.

WAX BEAN. Waxy-looking variety of green bean (*see* kidney bean).

WEATHER. Daily changes in barometric pressure make slight differences to the boiling point of water, but not large enough to cause trouble in the way that *altitude can. Temperature is of much greater importance (unless the kitchen is air-conditioned). For instance, a humid hot atmosphere is bad for pastry-making, and good puff pastry is almost impossible to make and work with in a hot kitchen. In summer in Italy, when the weather is hot and dry, cooks have great difficulty in making shaped pasta like *tortellini*, because the pasta dries and cracks before the dozens of little squares can be filled and twisted. In hot weather, you may have to make use of the refrigerator, even in such normally simple operations as making butter icing, but with operations too large for the household refrigerator to handle, you may well face disaster unless you do the work at night or very early in the morning. On the other hand, some preparations do better in warm weather, it is marginally more trouble to make mayonnaise and yoghurt in winter than in summer.

[*Weather* – French: *temps* German: *Wetter* Italian: *tempo* Spanish: *tiempo*]

WEIGHTS and **MEASURES**. Ingredients are most easily measured out by volume, as this can be done with the simplest and least expensive equipment.

The disadvantage is that it is inaccurate, particularly for measuring powdered or granular solids, as it does not take into account the size, shape and evenness of the particles, or of the way they are packed into the measure.

However, accurate measurement is mainly unnecessary in cooking (the exception is some baking). It is anyway silly to bother with fine fractions, when the substances being measured are so variable in themselves. A rough measure is also good enough if it takes a fairly large variation to give a different result. We are not manufacturers called on to produce a standard article. People who painstakingly level off a quarter teaspoon are rarely good cooks. They are usually trying to dodge the responsibility of making a judgement on the evidence provided by the eyes, tongue and nose. But it can be equally disastrous to abandon measuring altogether. I am impressed by professional chefs who can usually recite the quantities of a recipe by heart, but who, when cooking, are continually making slight adjustments. They are using both the measures and their senses in the very best way.

We have now entered an era of increasing standardization to metric measures, but this does not mean that we should throw away our old cookery books. To do *conversions of weights from the British and American measures to metric is only a matter of multiplying or using tables. It is also very simple to make old spring-balance scales with the metric weights so that you have both (printed metric scales are sold for some old scales of standard makes). For volumes, it is best to keep sets of metric, British and American standard cups and spoons, and to work the recipe from the original. The cost of plastic measures is small, and the time saved soon pays for them. To avoid mistakes, have each set in a different colour.

All systems of weights and measures start with something arbitrary. The grain was an average grain of wheat, the carat was a carob bean, and the Indian *masha* was the seed of the black gram. The innovation in the metric system was not in its basic unit, which in its way was as arbitrary as any, but because the various units were linked and made dependent one on the other. The other difference, of course, was the division of units into 10 parts. Very shortly, the old measures may be a matter of history, but we will still have our old cookery books and it is another matter whether the old habits will completely die.

British & American volumes | Metric equivalents

	British	American
l gill (gl)		
4 gills = 1 pint (pt)	142 ml	118 ml
2 pints = 1 quart (qt)	568 ml	473 ml
4 qrts = 1 gallon (gl)	4.54 lt	3.79 lt

From the conversion table you will see that while the Imperial pint is more than half a litre the US pint is less. Up to the mid-19th century the British and American measures were the same, but on the other hand, a gallon of wine was 231 cubic inches and there was another gallon of 282 cubic inches for beer. On this basis, a gallon of water weighed roughly 8 ⅓ pounds; a pint did not weigh exactly a pound nor did a fluid ounce, of which there were 16 to the pint, weigh exactly one ounce. In other words, the system was a mess. (You must remember in all this that a fluid ounce is a measure of volume, not of weight, and that the weight of a fluid ounce will vary according to the density of the substance being measured.)

In the 19th century, the British made an attempt to rationalize things by introducing a new gallon, an Imperial gallon, which was a measure of water weighing 10 lb (instead of 8 ⅓ as previously) and, equalling 277 cubic inches. In 1864, the apothecaries' fluid ounce was changed to be exactly an ounce of water, which gave 20 instead of 16 fluid ounces to the pint. The American measures stayed put. This has had British and American cooks, publishers and food manufacturers swearing ever since.

For small quantities in the kitchen, the difference between American and British fluid ounces can be ignored. In fact, the British fluid ounce is 28.4 ml and the American is 29.6 ml. This means that the conversion rate between British 20 fl oz pints and American 16 fl oz is not, as you might expect, 20:16, but 6:5.

With weights, the situation is a little simpler, as the smaller measures are the same on both sides of the Atlantic.

Avoirdupois (British)

	.	1 dram or drachm (dr) (1.77 g)
16 drams	=	1 ounce (oz) (28.34 g)
16 ounces	=	1 pound (lb) (453.6 g)
14 pounds	=	1 stone (st) (6.34 Kg)
28 pounds	=	1 quarter
4 quarters or 112 pounds		
	=	1 hundredweight (cwt) (50.8 Kg)
20 hundredweights		
	=	1 ton (1016 Kg)

The American avoirdupois system is basically the same except that the stone has been dropped and the large commercial weights have been rounded off.

100 pounds	= 1 hundredweight (45.4 Kg)
20 hundredweights	= 1 ton (907 Kg)

The British ton of 2240 lbs is known as a long ton and the American ton of 2000 lbs is called a short ton. The British ton is closer to the metric ton or tonne, which is 1000 Kg (2205 lb).

Kitchen measures. In Britain and Europe, most kitchens have scales, but in the US, standard cups and spoons are used to measure both liquids and solids. This system is both less accurate and sometimes means that the textures of solids must be specified – for example, a cup of coarse salt does not weigh the same as a cup of fine salt. There is actually a British standard measuring cup, but it has never been very popular and British households tend to rely on ordinary cups and spoons or to use a graduated measure. Although crockery is not standardized, the approximate sizes of cups are as follows: breakfast cup 7-8 fl oz (200-225 ml), teacup 5 fl oz (140-145 ml), coffee cup 3 fl oz (80-85 ml).The British standard cup in Imperial measures is ½ pt or 10 fl oz, and 4 British cups are thus roughly the same as 5 US cups (which are 8 US fl oz each).The British but not the Americans use the dessertspoon, which is 2 teaspoons (10 ml), but the teaspoon and tablespoon are the same on both sides of the Atlantic. For measuring solid ingredients, all spoons are level ones unless otherwise stated in the recipe.

American cups and spoons

1 teaspoon =			5ml
3 teaspoons	= 1 tablespoon =	½ US fl oz	15ml
2 tablespoons =		1 US fl oz	30ml
16 tablespoons=	1 cup	8 US fl oz	236ml
2 cups	= 1 US pint	16 US fl oz	473ml

Can sizes. Most cans these days are well labelled to show how much they contain. However, American recipes may confuse non-American readers by specifying quantities of canned ingredients in US can sizes, which are as follows:

8 oz	= 1 cup (US)
Buffet	= 1 cup
Picnic	= 1¼ cups
No 300	= 1¾ cups
No 1 tall	= 2 cups
No 303	= 2 cups
No 2	= 2½ cups
No 2½	= 3½ cups
No 3 cylinder	= 5¾ cups
No 10	= 12-13 cups

Shop and market measures. In the past, many solid foods were sold by volume measure.

The measure itself is cheap and portable, while the measuring itself is easy and quick. Things bought by the measure included not only seeds like grains of wheat, which will pour, but less manageable things like mussels and shrimps. As long as the commodity was reasonably cheap, the inaccuracies inherent in the system did not matter and were more than offset by the pleasure of being able to buy a measure of absolutely fresh shrimps straight from the boat. The larger measures on both sides of the Atlantic are:

4 quarts	= 1 gallon
2 gallons	= 1 peck
4 pecks	= 1 bushel
8 bushels	= 1 quarter
36 bushels	= 1 chaldron

However, it is easy to cheat in filling a measure, and therefore many of the traditional volumes were defined legally in terms of weights of particular commodities. The following list contains some of these and some other old measures.

Bushel	Wheat	60 lb(UK and US)
	Barley	56 lb (UK)
		48 lb (US, but 32-50 lb in various states)
	Oats	39 lb (UK)
		32 lb (US)
	Rye	60 lb (UK)
		56 lb (US)
	Corn (maize)	56 lb (US, but 52-56 lb in various states)
	Potatoes	60 lb (US, but 56 lb in North Carolina & West Virginia)
Quarter	Wheat	480 lb (UK)
Peck	Flour	14 lb
Bag	Cocoa	112 lb
	Coffee	140-148 lb
	Sugar	112-196 lb
	Rice	168 lb
	Black pepper	316 lb
	White pepper	168 lb
	Hops	280 lb
	Sago	112 lb
Sack	Flour	280 lb
	Potatoes	168 lb
Chest	Tea	84 lb
	Cloves	200 lb
Matt	Cloves	80 lb
Pocket	Hops	168-224 lb
Hogshead	Sugar	13-16 cwt
Barrel	Anchovies	30 lb
	Butter	224 lb (or 4 firkins)
	Raisins	256 lb
	Beef	200 lb
	Flour	196 lb (US)

Some commodities had their own elaborate vocabulary of measures. For example, a cran of herrings in Scotland was 37½ gallons; a maze of herrings in Ireland and the Isle of Man was 615 fish; a warp was 4 herrings; a long hundred was 33 warps or 132 herrings; ten hundred was 1320 herrings.

Other weights and measures. European cookery books rarely devote space to defining exactly what they mean by a glass, a cup or a spoon. On the occasions when greater accuracy is needed, a measure is qualified by an exact metric weight. More often, spoons are used, as a measure and the pinch, the knife point and the drop seem adequate to convey small amounts. European women seem on the whole to be more confident and more familiar with their own cooking traditions than their English-speaking counterparts. They do not feel the need for hair-splitting measures. As one Italian chef put it, 'cooking is a living art and so recipes should not become fixed.' After all, different conductors give markedly different renderings of Beethoven even though they may be using the same score. In cooking, we must avoid the soulless metro-nome beat of fussy weighing.

There are a few terms that may require explanation. In France, a *bonne livre* (i.e. a good pound) means 500 g (the *livre* was one of the old measures in use up to the French Revolution; it weighed 489.5 g and was 16 *onces*, so that an *once* was 30.6 g – the system was like avoirdupois although the quantities were not identical). A *cuillerée* is a spoonful, and a *cuiller* or *cuillère* (spoon) can be taken to be a tablespoon but may be more accurately defined as *une cuillière à bouche* (a tablespoon), as opposed to *une cuilliere à café* (a teaspoon). Other rough measures are *une tasse* (a cup), *une tasse à thé* (a teacup), *un verre* (a glass) and *un verre à liqueur* (a liqueur glass).

Italians use the metric system and recipes are in *grammi, kilogrammi, litri* and *decilitri*. An *etto* or *ettogrammo* is a hectogram (100 g), a common measure as are half (*mezzo*) and quarter (*quarto*) of the metric measures (e.g. *un quarto di litro di vino bianco* – a quarter of a litre of white wine). *Una cucchiaiata* is a spoonful, *un cucchiaio* being a spoon, again normally a tablespoon (*cucchiaio de tavola*). A *cucchiaino* is a teaspoon. Equally, Italian recipes use glasses (*un bicchiere di vino blanco* – a glass of white wine); you are expected to have some idea of how much wine to use in spite of the fact that this varies with the acidity of the wine, but as a basis you can take a wine glass as being a bit less than an American cup (8 fl oz). Problems come with the many Italian variants. *Un bicchierino di cognac* (a little glass), *un pizzico* or *una pizzicato* (a pinch) and *un pezzetto* (a small piece) are straightforward, but then there are *una manciata* (a handful) and *una manciatona* (a big handful). Herbs, which are much used fresh in Italian cooking, are usually given in terms such as *una foglia di lauro* (a leaf of bay), *un gambo di sedona* (a stalk of celery), *un spicchio d'aglio* (a clove of garlic), *un rametto di rosmarina* (a sprig of rosemary). Other useful Italian quantity words are *una puntina* (a point – very small amount), *un noce* (a walnut), *una scatola* (a tin), *una bustina* (a small envelope, for example of yeast), or

una fetta (a slice).

The Spanish also give their recipes in metric weights and measures, *kilos, grammos, litros* and *decilitros* but also in *cucharadas* (spoonfuls) and *cucharaditas* (teaspoonfuls) as well as *vasos* (glasses), *tazas* (cups), *tacitas* (little cups) and *copas* (small glasses). Spoons may be *colmada* (heaped), or *escasa* (scant), even *muy colmada* (very heaped). *Hojas* are leaves (*un hoja de laurel* is a bay leaf). For garlic, a *cabeza* is a head and a *diente* is a clove. *Un trozo de cebolla* is a slice of onion. *Un rodaja de chorizo* is a round of *chorizo* (sausage). A *ramita* is a sprig, as in a *ramita de perejil* (a sprig of parsley). A *papelillo* is a little paper or envelope, as in *papelillo de azafrán* (a small packet of saffron). Spanish recipes often go in for fractions of a litre as in ⅛ *litro de lece* (⅛ litre of milk).Who would say 12.5 decilitres outside a laboratory?

As acceptance of the metric system spread across the globe, national systems of weights and measures were progressively eliminated. The Greeks, for example, had the *oke*, which was 1.27 kg (2.8 lb); the Arabs had the *okieh*, which was 213 g (7½ oz), and the *rotl* of 2.5 kg (5½ lb). In Malaysia, the basic measure of weight was the *tahil* of 38 g (1⅓ oz); volumes were the *chupak* and the *quantang*, respectively about a quart and about a gallon (Imperial). In India, the *tola* was 11 g (0.4 oz), the weight of a rupee coin, and was divided into 12 *mashas*. Larger units were the *chattak* or *chitak* (5 *tolas*), the *powa, pau* or *pav* (4 *chattaks*), the *seer* (4 *powas*, 2 lb or 930 g) and the *maund* (40 *seers*). Perhaps the most amazing of all measures was an Indian measure of volume, the *tin*, based on the cylindrical tin which was the export pack of 50 Players Navy Cut cigarettes; it held 8 fl oz and was thus the same as an American cup.

Compared to all this confusion, the delight of the metric system lies in its simplicity. Although there are a plethora of metric units, the kitchen basics of weight and volume are taken care of by just four. Volume need be thought of only in cubic centimetres (cc) or millilitres (ml) – same thing – and in litres, which are 1000 ml. Weights will be expressed in grams or Kilograms, which are 1000 g. For all practical purposes, the gram and Kilogram are the weights of respectively a millilitre and a litre of water. Life will be much simpler when we are all thinking metric, but for the moment it is useful to have simple formulae for rough *conversions.

WHALE. In the first edition of Thomas Pennant's *Natural History*, published in the 18th century, whales are classified with fishes. We now know that they are not only mammals but highly-evolved and sensitive ones that suffer greatly from the explosive harpoons fired into their bellies. As many of the species of whale have been almost hunted to extinction, where previously they were found by the thousand, the commercial hunting of whales has been banned by most, but unfortunately not all, countries.

Whale oil, which is obtained by rendering the blubber, was until recently an important ingredient in margarine (it is still used in Japan and Russia). After refining, it is a clear, flavourless oil, and suitable for cooking. Whale meat at its best is good – like rather coarse and porous beef. On the *Norsel* in the Antarctic, we used to eat steaks cut from the back of a young cachalot (reputedly one of the best), but it had first been hung up for several weeks to drain, as fresh whale meat is watery. The taste was good, provided that every bit of the brown outside – where the air had caused oxidation – was removed. If any of this was left, even a tiny amount, the taste became fishy or tinny. Just after World War II, whale meat was often sold in Britain, but it was cut into square steaks and exposed to the air, the surest way to give it that nasty overtone. It was, I am sure, this ignorant handling that got whale meat its bad reputation. So if for any reason you are faced with eating whale, keep the meat in large chunks – 20 kg (44 lb) is not too much – hang them in cold conditions to drain, and cut steaks only as you need them. Be very careful to trim off all brown or discoloured meat (for the dog) right down to the red meat inside, then cook immediately. Whale meat is good treated as steak and onions, and I have no doubt that some burgundy would help

[*Whale* – French: *baleine* German: *Wal* Italian: *balena* Spanish: *ballena*]

WHEAT has been cultivated in Eurasia for at least 6000 years, but was unknown in America until after 1529, when it was taken to Mexico by the Spaniards. It is a staple grain of most of the world – wheat, rather than rice, is eaten in northern India and northern China. As is usual with plants that have been cultivated for thousands of years, the exact origin of wheat is uncertain. There are several species involved and many hybrids. Some ancient wheats, with romantic names like spelt and einkorn, are mainly of interest to the plant breeder, although they are still occasionally cultivated in primitive conditions or used as fodder mixed with other grasses as are emmer (*Trincum dicoccum*)

and English wheat (*T. turgidum*). By far the most important wheat is the Common wheat or Bread wheat (*T. aestivum*), which may be red or white in colour, hard or soft in texture, winter or spring grown. Also of importance are the amber or *durum* wheats (*T. durum*), which have long flinty grains and high protein; they are of little use for cakes or bread, but make the finest pasta. They are grown around the Mediterranean and in other parts of the world where there are similar dry conditions.

A farmer has to choose wheats which are suitable for his land and climate. He may choose winter wheat (which will stand over winter) or spring wheat (which is sown in the spring and is harvested later the same year), but from the cook's point of view the difference is not very significant. In cooking it is the distinctions between hard and soft wheat that are important. Hard wheat consists of flinty, rather translucent grains which are relatively rich in protein and usually have good milling characteristics, whereas soft wheat grains are opaque and rather starchy; they produce fluffy, amorphous particles when milled. Although there are exceptions, flours from hard wheats tend to be strong, which is to say that they make loaves of good volume and texture. By contrast, soft wheats yield flours which are usually weak and of poorer bread-making quality, although they are best for making biscuits, cakes and pastries.

Wheat, like most other cereals, is a grass, and the grains are arranged in a tightly packed inflorescence called the ear from which they are separated during threshing, which nowadays is usually one of the processes that is done in a combine harvester. The outside of the grain consists of several different layers, which are removed as *bran during *milling. At one end of the grain there is a tuft of fine hairs known as the beard and at the other end, somewhat to the side, is the germ or embryo. The inside of the wheat grain is known as the endosperm and is the food reserve, to be used by the seed when it first sprouts. The endosperm makes up about 85% of the grain, the bran 13% and the germ only 2%. There is a crease in the wheat grain which is a nuisance to millers because it interferes with the clean removal of the bran.

Although wheat is mainly ground to a flour, it may also be boiled whole (but hulled) in milk when fresh to make into frumenty, a pudding flavoured with cinnamon, or it may be boiled and crushed to make *burgul or even sprouted to make a type of malt for brewing.

[*Wheat* – French: *blé* German: *Weizen* Italian:

frumento, grano Spanish: *trigo*]

WHEAT GERM is the embryo plant, which is removed and separated from the wheat grain during the milling of white flour and is sold as a separate product. Wheat germ is rich in proteins, fats, minerals and vitamins B_1, B_2, B_6 and E. However, health considerations apart, fresh wheat germ has a delicious flavour. It may be mixed with white flour to give its taste to bread and scones. I like to eat it raw with fresh cream or yoghurt and honey.

Once a packet of wheat germ has been opened, it should be kept in the refrigerator, as the oil it contains quickly goes rancid – the reason why wholemeal flour does not keep well. Wheat-germ oil, extracted by pressing, has a powerful flavour. It is too costly to use in the kitchen, but may be beneficial as a diet supplement. It rapidly deteriorates on exposure to air, and, once opened, a bottle should be kept in the refrigerator, well closed and quickly used.

WHELK (*Buccinum undatum*) is a gastropod, a large marine snail, which, in rugger club folklore, was credited with gargantuan aphrodisiac powers. It is locally popular today, but for its past it will suffice to quote my grandfather's copy of Wood's *Illustrated Natural History* (1863), typical of the enthusiastic but snobbish natural history of Victorian days. The whelk 'is one of the most carnivorous of our molluscs, and among the creatures of its own class is as destructive as the lion among the herds of antelopes ....Vast quantities of whelks are taken annually for the markets, and are consumed almost wholly by the poorer classes, who consider them in the light of a delicacy. They are however decidedly tough and stringy in texture, and, like the periwinkle, which is also largely eaten, not very digestible. The mode of taking these molluscs is very simple: large wicker baskets are baited with the refuse portions of fish, and lowered to the bottom of the sea by ropes. The ever-hungry whelks instinctively discover the feast, crowd into the basket by thousands, and are taken by merely raising the laden basket to the surface, and emptying into a tub.'

Whelks are best when they are small. An old English method for small ones is to allow them to cleanse themselves for an hour or so in water and to boil them for 45 minutes in salt water or seawater before eating with vinegar, like winkles. Large ones, according to this method, are boiled for as long as an hour and a half, taken from their shells,

coated with breadcrumbs and fried. The French, on the other hand, realize that boiling any shellfish, except for a long period, makes them tough, and poach whelks for only 15 minutes. Other species apart from *Buccinum undatum* are sometimes sold as whelks. All these gastropods vary in toughness, but none of them is exactly tender and none can be described as a delicacy.

[*Whelk* – French: *buccin* German: *Wellhornschnecke* Italian: *buccino, bollicina* Spanish: *buccino*]

WHEY. When milk is curdled, either by rennet or by souring, the liquid that runs from the curd is called whey. It is regarded as healthy, as in the following example of pompous old-fashioned wisdom: 'Whey decanted from the curds and sweetened affords a favourite sudorific draught, which may be advantageously partaken of at bedtime whenever there is a threatening of cold in the head.' Whey contains all the ingredients of milk, except the casein and fat, but is sometimes thrown away. It can form the basis of soup – I often make *gazpacho* with the sour whey drained from yoghurt cheese. In Scandinavian countries, the whey drained off when other cheeses are made is turned into the popular whey cheese, *mysost*. To make this, the slightly sour whey is boiled until it is reduced to a brown, sticky mass consisting mainly of partly caramelized lactose. During the boiling, any coagulated albuminous material that forms a scum is skimmed off and kept aside to be fixed back into the cheese later. Sometimes brown sugar is added, or spices, such as caraway, cumin, even cloves, are used as flavouring. When the boiling is finished, after 5-6 hours, the volume is reduced to about a quarter of the original. Now the skimmings are returned and stirred in well; stirring continues throughout the time that the mass is cooling to prevent the formation of sugar crystals which would make the cheese grainy. When it is set, the *mysost* is cut in blocks, waxed and wrapped.

There are many variants of this cheese. *Gjetost* is made from the whey of goat's milk, *primost* or *fløtst* is softer and contains more fat, and *gomost* is made by the same technique but from whole milk. The flavour of whey cheese is sweet and, to most people not brought up on it, is an acquired taste. (For instance, it was endlessly on the table during the voyage south with the Norwegian-British-Swedish Antarctic expedition of which I was once a member, but I always disliked the sweetness and longed for a piece of really cheesy cheese.)

Whey

Dilute 1 tablespoon of white wine vinegar with an equal amount of water and pour it into a saucepan of boiling milk. The milk will curdle. Clear it with an egg white (whisked up with the crushed shell), strain the mixture through muslin and sweeten it to taste. Lemon juice can be used instead of vinegar to make lemon whey. If the egg is omitted, the curd can be used for tarts and so on, but the whey will not be clear. Whey can also be prepared with a dry white wine or dry sherry, both of which will curdle milk. Old-fashioned curds and whey are made by adding rennet to milk and then warming it until the curds and whey separate. (If the curds set peacefully, they make junket.) Curds and whey are tolerable if eaten with cream and honey or sugar, but most people find them rather tasteless.

[Whey – French: petit lait German: molke Italian: siero di latta Spanish: suero (de la leche)]

WHIFF. See flatfish (lemon sole).

WHIPPING is also called whisking (which usually applies only to egg white) and beating (which may apply to many things and implies heavier work). It is a texture-producing operation and involves frothing up and the introduction of air bubbles into whatever is being whipped – nearly always either cream or egg white. Although it seems to be a very simple operation, there are a number of points to be considered. For instance, the size of the air bubbles. With a given amount of egg white, we can obviously get a greater bulk of beaten egg if the bubbles are large than if they are small, but the froth will not be so strong mechanically and will collapse more easily. This means that we are not only concerned with the length of time and degree of whipping (because the longer the whipping, the smaller are the bubbles), but also with the implements we use.

Implements and utensils. Chefs use balloon whisks and copper bowls – one of the few places where unlined copper is normal – but such apparatus, though it is undoubtedly the best, is expensive. The smaller wire whisks and any glass or china bowl will do almost as good a job, and the wire coil whisks are as good or better for whisking egg white. With electric beaters, it is easy to overdo the whipping, as they are so quick that things can be spoiled in a moment. Hand-held electric whisks are better than the fixed models, as they can be used more flexibly. (The old hand-turned type of whisk is – or should be – obsolete. It needs two hands, is hard work and does not do as good a job as a simple, inexpensive coil whisk.)

Whipping cream. In some places, whipping *cream is sold. It is a grade in between single and double cream, or a mixture of the two. Double cream but not single cream can also be whipped. Canned cream and bottled cream will whip, and unsweetened evaporated milk can also be whipped if the unopened tin is boiled for 20 minutes and then cooled. It does not, however, taste like fresh cream. Sour cream very rapidly thickens but will not whip properly as it turns too easily to butter. Reconstituted cream will not whip. Cream should be whipped only to the point where it will hold a peak. If whipping is carried on after that, the cream will turn to butter.

Whipping egg white. Egg white has a special capacity for holding air bubbles when it is beaten. The white contains several proteins, but the most important from the point of view of beating are the *albumins, particularly oval-bumin, which foams best in acid conditions. Acid also tenderizes protein and makes it stretch more easily. Therefore a pinch of cream of tartar is often added to egg white to be beaten (but for meringues is likely to make the result rather sticky). Salt also helps foaming, and sugar helps in two ways – it gives the foam stability and helps mechanically to get air into the mass. Fat, on the other hand, is the enemy of foaming – not even a speck of egg yolk must be allowed to get into the white when eggs are separated, and the bowl must be free from grease and from any traces of detergent.

In practice, chefs add the acid and salt at the beginning and the sugar when the eggs are nearly whipped. However, fresh eggs at room temperature in a clean bowl should whisk up without difficulty.

The degree to which egg white is beaten is very important in cooking. The more the eggs are beaten, the more the egg white is stretched, and it can be beaten (overbeaten) to the point where it can stretch no more. The bubbles cannot then be inflated further when the air inside expands in baking. The stages are as follows:
1) Large bubbles. The white is still runny and it is little more than mixed well. It is used for blending with liquids, for coating and for clearing stock.
2) Smaller, but still fair sized bubbles. The peaks are

rounded and will not stand up. Used for sponge cakes, soufflés and foamy omelettes.

3) Small air bubbles. The stiff foam stands in peaks; it is smooth, with no fluidity. For meringues, cake icing and some cakes.

4) Dry and brittle. It can be cut or pulled into bits. The proteins will not stretch any more and so no good for most purposes.

[Whipping – French: battre (eggs), fouetter (cream) German: schlagen Italian: sbattere Spanish: batidor]

WHISKING. See whipping.

WHISKY or whiskey. The spelling is whisky for Scotch and Canadian, whiskey for Irish and American. The word is a corruption of the Gaelic uisage (water) beatha (life) – usquebaugh in Ireland – a translation of the Latin aqua vitae (water of life), as spirits were originally medicinal. The art of *distillation was brought over from the Continent by monks. Although the first known written reference to the drink is as late as 1494, whisky must have been made long before that. Distilling whisky soon became usual kitchen work on many Scottish farms. Since it was distilled only twice, there was no danger of explosion, and the work was well within the capability of even the humblest servant. In those halcyon days, there was no excise duty – Parliament borrowed that idea from the Dutch to raise money to fight Charles I and it has stayed ever since.

Barley grown on the farm was wetted and sprouted, dried over a peat fire (which gave a smoky taste), ground to a grist, mixed with water, and stood in a warm place for the enzymes to work. The sugary result was mashed with yeast and left to ferment (very much as in *brewing).The alcoholic result was distilled, always in pot stills of much the same sort as are used to make malt whisky to this day. Blended Scotch, which we know best (the world now drinks over one hundred million gallons of it every year) was then unknown.

By law, all whisky must be at least 3 years old before it may be sold for consumption in Britain, and similar laws apply in other countries, although the minimum time may be up to 5 years. In practice, however, whisky is usually matured for much longer than is required by law.

The newly distilled spirit is placed for maturing in casks made of oak, which is permeable and allows the air to pass into the whisky and evaporation to occur. During this process, certain undesirable secondary constituents are removed, producing a mellow and mature whisky. The period of maturation is affected by the size of the casks, the strength at which the spirit is stored and the temperature and humidity of the warehouse. The lighter grain whiskies require less time to mature than the fuller, more mellow malt whiskies, which are often left in the casks for 15 years or more.

Malt whisky is made from malted barley and is distilled in pot stills. There are 117 distilleries making malt whisky in Scotland. The whisky from each has its own characteristic aroma and flavour, just as wines from different vineyards have theirs. Exactly why this should be so is not fully understood, in spite of enormous efforts to find out. Some of the difference comes from the water and some from the peat used to dry the malt – the air and climate may even play a part. However, if peat and water, with Scottish distillers, are taken from Scotland to other parts of the world, the whisky never turns out as well as it does in Scotland.

Even the lowliest malt whiskies are more expensive than the everyday brands of blended whisky, which contain grain spirit. Some are in limited supply and are mostly exported, while others are used mainly by the blenders. In addition to straight malts, from single distilleries, there are also blended ones in which malt whiskies only are mixed. If the age of blended whisky is specified, it must by law be the age of the youngest used in the mixture and not an average. Malts should be drunk neat or with a little good cool water. Ice and soda water both destroy the flavour.

Grain whisky is made largely from unmalted grain. The starch in the grist is converted to sugars by mixing it with malt which has an excess enzyme capacity. The sugary liquid can now be fermented. Distillation is carried out in continuous patent stills, the first of which was the coffey still, introduced in 1831. Grain whisky is very light, with almost no taste of its own, and the only straight grain whisky on the market is Choice Old Cameron Brig, which is made by John Hay & Co. Most of the huge output from modern plants goes for blending with malts.

Blended whisky has been made since about 1860. It uses the highly rectified spirit that is produced by the patent stills. Such spirit contains little of the congenerics which give malt whisky its taste, and incidentally its power to produce hangovers, but blending with tasty malts results in a light product with good flavour. It is also more consistent, a great commercial asset, as the expert blender could add varying quantities of different malts to the basic grain whisky and obtain an almost constant result. Colouring could be done with caramel. The ever growing popularity of blended Scotch as a drink, has led many people to try to make it elsewhere, notably in Japan, but it has never been reproduced exactly.

Irish whiskey is made in much smaller quantity than Scotch. It is made only in pot stills – but in very large ones – and from a mixture of malt and unmalted grain, the excess diastase in the malt being able to convert the starch in the grain to sugars. Irish whiskey is distilled three times (not twice like Scotch) and thus is relatively tasteless to begin with. It acquires its flavour during maturation in casks. Casks are vital to Irish whiskey and one of the main skills in its making lies in deciding the proportions of whisky to be mixed from different sorts of cask. Sherry casks (for a full flavour), new casks, American casks, and sometimes rum and brandy casks are used.

American whiskey. Corn whiskeys, as made in the early days, were often pretty rough, as names like Old Tomahawk, Busthead and Red Eye attest. The tradition of fearsome home brews in the US continued when their evolution was temporarily slowed down by the Volstead Act. During prohibition, people drank what they could get. Apart from that lapse, a tradition of freedom exists in many states, where the citizens can, if they want, distil a certain generous quantity for their own home use. Commercial distillation is now carried out almost exclusively in huge continuous stills; the old pot stills have long since been replaced. Most famous American corn whiskey is bourbon, named after Bourbon County in Kentucky. It is said to have been discovered accidentally in 1789, when a Rev Elijah Craig, who was a farmer as well as a preacher, put his whiskey (already good because of the local water) into charred barrels of white oak to mature. The resulting whiskey was exceptional, and to this day Kentucky bourbon is famous. The law, however, recognizes bourbon as whiskey made with a particular technique, and so bourbons are produced in other States and even in Canada. They are still legally bourbons if they are distilled from a mash of at least 55% corn (maize) and matured for at least 2 years in new, charred white oak casks in unheated warehouses. Bourbon must also be not less than

80 US proof (40° spirit). Unblended bourbons are called 'straight' in the US, and those 'bottled in bond' have been stored under government supervision for 4-8 years as well as being 'straight' and 100 proof. The more ordinary blended bourbons are usually around 87 proof. They have less taste and less congenerics. Other corn whiskies abound and one of the great pleasures of a visit to the US is organizing a tasting session; this can be arranged in any bar with the help of the natives, who will be eager to co-operate. The term 'sour mash' – as opposed to 'sweet mash' – means that the wort (called beer in America) is fermented with sour residues, while sweet mash is fermented only with fresh yeast. There is a considerable difference in taste.

Rye whiskey, as the name suggests, is made with a high proportion of rye (which is sometimes also used in other whiskies) as well as barley. The method of making rye is not much different, but it is matured in heated warehouses to achieve its individual flavour. Rice spirit is in essence a whisky.

*Liqueurs based on whisky include Drambuie and Glayva. In recent years, following the world-wide upsurge of the popularity of whisky as a drink, it has also come to be used as an ingredient in cooking. Dishes such as *fagiano* (pheasant), *al whisky, scampi al whisky* and *langouste au whisky* now appear in Mediterranean restaurants, where whisky hardly penetrated before. In fact, whisky is a good spirit for flaming and, according to Elizabeth David in *French Provincial Cooking* (Grub Street), is the best substitute for Calvados in Norman cooking if the real thing is not to hand.

[*Whisky* – French: *whisky* German: *Whisky* Italian: *whisky* Spanish: *whisky*]

WHITEBAIT are small fish, no more than 5 cm (2 in) long, which are caught in quantity in shoals in the estuaries of some British rivers, notably the Thames. They used to be caught in summer and eaten locally, but today they are usually fished in late September and frozen immediately. Fresh whitebait is a rarity, but as the fish freeze well, the delicacy is now available all the year round. In Victorian times, whitebait were given a specific scientific name, *Clupea alba*, but they are now known to be the fry of sprats and herrings in Britain. In the 18th century, it was the custom for the Cabinet to hold a Whitebait Dinner in early June, towards the end of the parliamentary session, either at The Ship at Greenwich or the West India Dock Tavern. The function was considered too frivolous by Mr. Gladstone; he cancelled it, and the custom was never re-established. Now, whitebait is to be found on the menu of expensive restaurants.

In other parts of the world, young fish of different species are highly regarded and are eaten in season. Even in Britain at one time, freshwater fish, such as stickleback and minnows, were netted and passed off as whitebait. (They were said to be excellent and, to most people, not easily distinguishable.) The French *blanchaille* is not quite identical to whitebait, and in most Mediterranean countries baby sardines, with a few anchovies among them, are eaten. These small fish are not gutted, but merely coated with flour and fried in hot oil. Flouring needs to be done with some care – if freshly rinsed, wet fish are dumped into a bag of flour, the result is heavy lumps of dough with fish tails sticking out of it. The fish must be almost dry before they are shaken in seasoned flour.

Notably in Liguria and in Mediterranean Spain, very tiny fry are also sold. They are so small that they look like a mass of jelly with thousands of pinpoint eyes in it. This mass, known as *gianchetti* or *bianchetti* in Italy (and *poutine* in France) is mixed with egg and made into omelettes or can form the basis for a fish soup. It is rather expensive and very nutritious. Any other such small fish can be treated in the same manner.

....

Frittata di gianchetti

For 450 g (1 lb) of tiny fish, beat up 6 eggs and mix in 3 dessertspoons of grated Parmesan cheese and a mixture of ½ oz of parsley, I clove of garlic and a few leaves of marjoram, finely chopped together. Add salt and pepper to taste and fry as omelettes.

[*Whitebait* – French: *blanchaille* German: *Sprotte* Italian: *pesciolini* Spanish: *chanquetes*]

....

WHITING. *See* cod.

WHORTLEBERRY. *See* cranberry.

WIENERWURST is the rival to the *frankfurter for the honour of having been the original hot dog sausage. It contains pork plus beef or veal, lightly cured and chopped. The sausages are smoked, poached in water and hung up to dry. How far wienies differ from franks is another matter. In some cases, the meat may be less finely ground; in others, the only difference is in the name and hence the city to which their origin is ascribed.

WILD MARJORAM. *See* oregano.

WILD RICE, Indian rice or **Tuscarora rice** is a large, handsome grass (*Zizania aquatica*) native to the eastern and central parts of North America; it also grows in Formosa, China and Japan. Wild rice, which is not in any way a variety of rice, grows in shallow lakes and ponds; at a distance, the plants look like any other reed-bed. The species has spread outside its original area and over much of the US, as it has been planted as food for waterfowl. Originally, it was an important wild food used by American Indians – Sioux and Chippewas often fought over it – and now the Indians are the only people allowed to harvest it for sale, although it can, of course, be gathered for home use by anyone who finds it. The ripe grain is harvested by shaking the plume-like heads of the grass directly over a boat. The grain, which is purplish-black, is spread out to dry, and must then be husked. This is done by first parching it (stirring it over a low fire for an hour in an iron or earthenware pot), then lightly pounding it to loosen the husks and finally rubbing it between the hands. The young Indian men trod it in a half-sunken tub, taking some of their weight on a pole, and wearing new mocassins. When the husk is loosened, the grain is tossed in a light breeze to winnow off the chaff, and stored. Before being used, wild rice must be washed to take away the smoky taste. It can then be boiled, like rice, in lightly salted water. It takes about half an hour, maybe more, to cook, but should not become mushy. Then it should be drained and left to steam over boiling water for 10 minutes. Finally plenty of butter is added and mixed in before serving. Wild rice is nowadays an expensive delicacy, which is sold in packets ready to cook. It goes well with chicken and turkey, with pheasant and quail, and with any delicately flavoured food, such as oysters. Turkey stuffed with it is a traditional Thanksgiving dish in Minnesota. Wild rice can also be ground to a flour and mixed (25%) into ordinary flour to make batter for pancakes and muffins.

WINDSOR BEAN. *See* broad bean.

WINE. Wine is the natural partner of most great European cooking – only a few dishes call for beer or spirits. It is not chance that 80% of the world's wine is produced in Europe and that most of the rest comes from places that have been colonized by Europeans and where food is cooked in the European tradition. In fact, so close is the partnership between wine and food that many dishes are considerably diminished without the wine to go with them.

A small number of rich connoisseurs can buy wines so good that it becomes legitimate for them to choose the food to go with their wines and not vice versa. Anything which might spoil their delicate appreciation by an intrusive food flavour must be avoided. Vinegar or orange juice will drive them crazy – in spite of the tourists' depraved love of Sangria, orange and wine do not go well together. Tons of garlic, handfuls of herbs, or Indian spicing will not be welcomed either, though they will not spoil the wine.

The occasions when food must give way to wine are rare. Usually wine is chosen to complement the food, to make it taste better, and for this reason (if for no other), cooks must take an interest in it. In a sense, wine is as much a cook's business as the sauces or the garnish. Every cook should therefore possess at least one of the many books on wine and know something about it – as there are many excellent paperbacks available, no-one can plead poverty. On the other hand, avoid becoming a wine snob. Wines are like paintings – it is easy to recognize the great masters but few can afford to buy them. As for the rest, your opinion is as good as anyone else. It is best to buy what you like, can afford and can live with. It is significant that people in wine-drinking countries like to drink their wine, not sniff it. Any real wine lover who is invited to dinner will not swirl the wine in his glass, hold it up to the light, or take a large slurp and chew it. Neither will he groan audibly. He will only ask that the wine is properly married to the food, however humble. Some dishes indeed need rough wine (but it is a mistake to think that any dish, even a curry, can be so highly spiced that you cannot distinguish good wine from bad through it).To buy wines of better quality than are suitable for the food is extravagant and silly.

Cooking with wine. In wine-drinking countries – which means the Mediterranean countries, Portugal and parts of Spanish America – wine, like Everest, is simply there. In some drier places, it may be easier to get than water and is always at hand to slosh into the food without a second thought. For this reason, wine in food was seized upon by more northern people as a symbol of nostalgic Mediterranean sunshine. The error in this is that you can have too much of it, as of all good things. Whole books

are devoted to cooking with wine as if it were some magic ingredient synonymous with French cooking or gastronomic ecstasy, not just another ingredient like, say, water. Wine is supposed to be great, a big deal – a dash of wine will 'gourmetize' anything from Irish stew to hamburgers. It will not. Wine is something to be used and is no more the hallmark of great cooking than are lashings of cream or butter. It is true that in some parts of the continent up to a third of the meat dishes, particularly chicken or game, contain wine, and wine may also be in a number of fish dishes. (It is rare to find wine in vegetable dishes.) But they are not necessarily the best dishes. And what wine! A number of books seem to suggest that food can be improved by using wine dregs collected and bulked from a number of bottles. Recipe books are not discriminating about the wine to be used. Nobody would suggest saving ends of bottles for cooking except in countries blighted by a Protestant tax ideology (or in lucky houses where the supply is so liberal that ends of bottles are left over). Apart from the fact that anyone who does much Italian cooking will need a bottle of Marsala in the cupboard (as well as the more usual bottles of dry sherry and port), there are a certain number of rules about wine in food to be formulated:

1) Be selective about the dishes to which you add wine. A serious cook, who is not too impoverished does not save dregs, or use vinegar. (If you are too impoverished, it is better to be in a Mediterranean country.)

2) Cooks should be conscious of the effects of different wines and register that any old bottle will not improve a dish simply because it has wine on the label. The wine used in a dish is critical. It should ideally be a wine from the district where the dish comes from (until you have learned to improve on it) and should be something you would drink. In a wine-producing country who would keep bad wine in the house just to use in the cooking?

3) It is perfectly easy for any cook to choose wines for the kitchen. It needs only some experimentation (and drinking the balance), a pleasurable enterprise. Then the wines selected on price and quality should be rebottled in *small* bottles. The best way is to use small, wine-glass-sized plastic bottles, fill them, squeeze them so that the wine just reaches the top, and seal them with no air inside. The wine will keep good for months. An alternative is to use one of those modern devices with a plastic bag and a spiggot, which means that the wine never gets exposed to air.

Anyone should be able to keep a supply of good wine on tap in the kitchen. As for choosing the wine, even at the lowest level, be careful to avoid wine that is 'chemical'. Frankly, what is 'chemical' is difficult to discover. Everyone in the wine countries talks about it, but nobody will answer honest questions. For many years I bought my house wine from a small winery. It was cheap and good. Later it became less good, and my neighbour, a local man, told me it was now chemical. It seemed to me unlikely, but when I try to cook with this wine, it breaks – becomes thin and acid. Experienced cooks will know immediately what I mean. Bad wine does break when used in cooking. Wine merchants might take the trouble to study and advise on the inexpensive but good wines for cooking. Cookery writers in English do not often state (as some European writers do) that you should use, for instance, a Burgundy or a rough Barbera or even, less specifically, a full bodied red wine or a dry white wine.

[Wine – French: vin German: Wein Italian: vino Spanish: vino]

WINESTONE. See argol.

WINEBERRY. See raspberry.

WINKLE or periwinkle (Lutorina littorea) is a small, blackish brown or olive sea snail, rounded in shape and with a circular opening. It is found on rocky coasts around Britain and elsewhere in Europe. The true periwinkle is found at about low tide mark, where it can be easily gathered in quantity. Unlike the much larger *whelks, they are herbivores. To prepare them, wash them well in several changes of water, then leave them in plenty of fresh water for half an hour before washing them again. This helps to get rid of the sand. Meanwhile, let some seawater stand to drop its sediment. Decant it into a pan and bring it to the boil. Alternatively use salted water, but seawater is traditional. Now, strain the winkles, shake them to make them withdraw into their shells and drop them into the boiling water, boil them for 15 minutes. Extract them with a pin (they can be eaten hot or cold) and sprinkle them with malt vinegar. Winkles are not for gourmets but are, as the old books always say, the food of the poorer classes. (So, once, were salmon, eels and oysters.) A visit to Southend with a pretty girl, a turn on the pier and a feed of winkles sprinkled with vinegar (preferably with buttered brown bread) used to be something to remember. But a saucer of commercially shelled winkles full of sand and grit is not to be recommended.

[Winkle – French: bigorneau German: Uferschnecke Italian: chiocciole Spanish: bigaro]

WITCH. See flatfish.

WONG BOK. See Chinese cabbage.

WOOD comes into contact with food as spoons, pestles, bowls, boards, planks, skewers and assorted utensils and containers. It is always to some extent porous and will pick up flavours even if it is itself tasteless. Oils and fats, like bacon fat, will impregnate wood. It is best to keep wooden articles, particularly bowls and spoons, for certain specific purposes; otherwise wrong flavours can be introduced. It is possible for a wood bowl to make chocolate cream taste of bacon fat or garlic.

On picnics and when camping, be careful that sticks used as spits for meat or for stirring are not poisonous. People have died from using woods like oleander. Wood from oak, beech, hazel, blackthorn, cherry and olive – from any tree with fruit you would eat – is safe.

Wood is a very good heat insulator. In the Himalayas, I always carried a wooden bowl for my cocoa. A deep wooden plate – the sort they make in the Czech Republic with a burned pattern is nice – makes a wonderful dish for the morning bacon. Wooden platters for steak are kind to knives and also help keep the steak warm.

Wooden moulds and shapers for butter should be made of box. The very best salad bowls are made from olive wood, which has the right taste and a beautiful pattern. Tubs and barrels are most usually of oak, which is good for sauerkraut and pickles. Birch is often used for culinary objects from Scandinavia. Utensils from tropical countries are likely to be made of unknown hardwoods, and sometimes have a taste which – as with most woods – will disappear with usage. Most wooden spoons are made of beech, as are chopping boards, but hornbeam is favoured for butcher's blocks.

Wooden salad bowls and salad spoons should never be washed with soap and water. If necessary, they may be rinsed in water, but otherwise should simply be wiped dry with kitchen paper.

[Wood – French: bois German: Holz Italian: legno Spanish: leña]

WOODCOCK and **SNIPE** belong to the same family of waders. The woodcock (Scolopax rusticola), which is rather a fat, squat bird, is common in damp woods and on boggy ground, although it is not exactly a marsh bird like the snipe. It occurs at some time of the year over nearly all Europe, but moves southwards in winter, being partially migrant. It is very widely distributed and occurs right through Asia to Japan. The woodcock of North America (*Philobela minor*) is a close relative, but slightly smaller. The season in Britain is from 1st August to 15th March, but woodcock are at their best 2-3 weeks after they have arrived from migration, usually in October and November. They should be fat.

They are usually hung only for a day or so before being plucked completely (including head and neck), very carefully as the skin is tender. After that, the body is singed and the nails are cut off the claws, but the birds are not drawn in Europe, although they may be in the US. They are trussed by folding the legs up and tucking the head under one wing before these and the legs are tied close to the body. Another way is to twist the neck over the legs and hold them in place by pushing the beak into a leg like a skewer. Cooking should be short (7 minutes each side on the grill is recommended). Woodcock are served on a piece of toast to catch the trail, which comes out during cooking and is considered a great delicacy.

The snipe, of which there are many kinds (the Common snipe is *Gallinago gallinago*) is a slightly smaller bird than the woodcock. Though delicious, it is inferior by comparison. Snipe are best when fat in winter. They are eaten fresh, not hung and are sometimes skinned if they smell fishy, as this removes the strong flavour, which the snipe can acquire from the marshes where they live. Young snipe are best and can be told by their feet (which are soft and tender), by their pointed flight feathers and the downy ones under the wings. Snipe roast in 15 minutes; the trail is left in them, but the gizzard is often removed before roasting.

[*Woodcock* – French: *bécasse* German: *Waldschnepfe* Italian: *beccacia* Spanish: *becado*

Snipe – French: *bécassin* German: *Bekassine* Italian: *beccacino* Spanish: *agachadiza*]

WOOD EAR. *See* mushrooms.

WORCESTERBERRY. *See* gooseberry.

WORCESTERSHIRE SAUCE came into existence at the beginning of the reign of Queen Victoria, when a barrel of vinegar and spices made up for a customer to an Indian recipe was left forgotten for some years in a chemist's cellar in Worcester. The shop's name was Lea & Perrins. During a subsequent spring-cleaning, it was about to be thrown out when prudence suggested that it should first be tasted. Thus was born what is probably the world's best known and most ubiquitous bottled sauce, one which has become a standard ingredient. It is used in many dishes ranging from soups and sauces to salad dressings, and small quantities are a 'chef's secret' in many recipes. Worcestershire sauce is made by a maturation process; the exact formula is secret. Although it is much imitated, nobody seems to be able to get quite the taste of the original.

WORMSEED. *See* epazote.

WORMWOOD (*Artemisia absinthium*) is a relative of *tarragon that is a native of Britain and most of Europe. It was used in the past for medicinal purposes as well as to flavour herb wines and aperitifs – its name comes from the same root as that of vermouth. In such drinks it is usually only one of a number of flavourings. The essential oil that can be extracted from wormwood is a narcotic poison, and readers of Emile Zola will know about the appalling results that came from the use of wormwood in absinthe.

[*Wormwood* – French: *absinthe, armoise amère, génépi* German: *Absinth, Hilligbitter, Wermut, Wurmkraut* Italian: *assenzio* Spanish: *ajenjo*]

WORT is the sweet, watery solution which is fermented to make ale or beer. It can be made naturally from *malt by mashing or produced with malt extracts and sugars. In commercial brewing, the wort may contain, among other additives, malt extracts, partly caramelized or burnt malt and substances to give a frothy head. (Some countries, such as Germany, have strict laws which forbid the use of additives in beer.) The solid residue from mashing in breweries is washed with a spray of water – a process called sparging – at 77°C (170°F), a temperature which destroys the enzymes but dissolves out any remaining sugars. The wort is in any case boiled to kill all the enzymes before fermentation.

For making beer, the wort is boiled with *hops to give it a bitter flavour. The stronger and heavier the beer is to be, the more bitterness it normally needs. As a rough guide, the following quantities have been recommended as giving an average taste. For 20 lt (36 pt) of wort: light beer (3-4% alcohol)

60-65 g (2-3 oz) hops; medium beer (4-6% alcohol) 85-170 g (3-4 oz) hops; strong beer (6-8% alcohol) 170-227 g (4-6 oz) hops. In made-up worts, reduce the amount of hops if the sugar exceeds the malt extract; increase it if malt extract exceeds sugar. The hops should be boiled in the wort for 1-2 hours to extract the flavour. In home brewing, the acidity of the wort may be adjusted with citric acid or lemon juice.

[*Wort* – French: *moût* German: *Bierwurze* Italian: *mosto* Spanish: *jugo de lupolo*]

WURST. German for *sausage.

y

YAM and lesser-known tubers. Faced with a variety of yams, *cassava roots, *sweet potatoes and other tubers in an unfamiliar tropical market, even moderately expert people are likely to become confused. The only solution is to try them. Further confusion is caused because almost any starchy root, from sweet potato to yautia is likely to be called a yam. Strictly speaking, yams are only species of *Dioscorea*, but such a succinct definition has reached neither the market nor the kitchen. With few exceptions, yams in the widest sense are tropical or sub-tropical plants, some of which are exceedingly important staples, mainly in the poorer areas of the world. Some are grown, often as animal feed, in the southern parts of the US, while in Britain a whole range appears in shops patronized by Caribbean, Pakistani or Indian immigrants. Virtually all these tubers are starchy, tasteless, and without personality, but anyone who is exploring particular areas of ethnic cooking may need them for authentic dishes. Other yams will be met with only on distant travels. Most are usually boiled and mashed, roasted or fried. Never eat an unknown yam raw, as some kinds are acrid, even poisonous, until cooked.

True yams belong to the genus *Dioscorea*, which has some 250 species, all climbing vines with large storage roots, mainly with one large tuber, although a few produce a number of small ones. Yams are mostly tropical and subtropical plants originating in the Old World – the cush-cush yam or yampee (*D. trifida*) is the only one from America. Yams from Japan and northern China (*D. apposita* and *D. japonica*) have been tried in Europe and might have caught on if people had liked them. The yam *par excellence*, however, is tropical. It is the Greater or Asiatic yam (*D. alata*), which can grow to an enormous size, perhaps to 40 kg (90 lb), but that would be unusual. In any case, the smaller specimens are best to eat. This yam is grown in southern India, South East Asia and the Caribbean. The White yam (*D. rotundata*) (*ratalu* in India) and the Yellow yam (*D. cayenensis*) are also important, particularly in West Africa. There are very many others.

Elephant's foot or **suram** (*Amorphophallus campanulatus*) is a member of the arum family which is a native of India, where it is called *zemikand* and is very commonly grown there. It is important because the tubers keep for a long time and so may be seen as an import in other countries. There are two types, one smooth-skinned, high yielding but very acrid (although this can be somewhat reduced by boiling) and the other much better to eat and free from acridity. The flesh is white or pale pink.

Dasheen, taro, eddo, colocasia, old coco-yam, elephant's ear, or **arvi** (*Colocasia antiquorum*) has been cultivated for so long and propagated vegetatively that it very rarely flowers. It is grown in damp places in the tropics and has leaves like those of the related arum lily but much larger. The leaves, as well as the corms, are much eaten in parts of India and are suitable for stuffing. Before they can be eaten, the corms (swollen underground stems) must be baked or boiled to destroy the acrid crystals of calcium oxalate which they may contain. From them is made the starchy paste called *poi*, a staple in the Pacific. To make this, the corms are boiled until they are soft and pounded in a mortar. Then water is added and the mass is allowed to ferment. Opinions of *poi* vary. It has been described as faintly acid and very palatable, but also as being like sour library paste. Dasheen or eddo are the Caribbean names; taro is the Pacific name. It is grown to some extent in the southern US.

Yautia, **tannia** or **new cocoyam** (*Xanthosoma sagitifolium*), another member of the arum family, is much taller than dasheen and grows in slightly drier conditions, but is otherwise similar. It is commonly grown in the West Indies, especially in Puerto Rico, and in West Africa.

Yam beans are leguminous plants with swollen tuberous storage roots; the seeds and pods are also edible. The best known yam bean, *Pachyrhizus tuberosus*, is native to tropical America, but is also grown in West Africa, in India, where it is called *sankalu*, and in Malaysia as *bengkuang*. The plant is a strong creeper and is grown on ridges. The fully-grown roots are tender and juicy, white and starchy. Only the young pods and seeds are cooked and eaten; they become poisonous as they grow older.

Oxalis tubers. *Oxalis* is a genus of some five hundred species which includes Wood sorrel (*O. acetosella*), of which the acid leaves may be eaten in moderation. The Bermuda buttercup or Cape sorrel (*O. pes-capres*), which carpets the orchards, orange groves and almond fields around the Mediterranean in early spring, was brought in from South Africa at the end of the 18th century. As late as the beginning of the 20th century, it was cultivated commercially on the Riviera, although the tubers, which are like very small, yellowish potatoes, are of no particular interest. Today the plant is a serious weed and its cultivation would be unthinkable.

Oka, **occa** or **oca** (*Oxalis tuberosa*) is a native of the South American Andes – Ecuador, Bolivia and Peru. It is an important food tuber in South America with the typical shamrock-shaped leaf of the genus and whitish or brownish tubers. It grows quite well in the European climate and is said to have gone wild in parts of France. The tubers are acid when fresh, and in the Andes they are dried for several days in the sun before use to dissipate the acid. Although oka was introduced into England in 1829, it has never become popular. *Larousse Gastronomique* suggests parboiling and sautéing it in butter. Leaves and shoots can also be eaten in moderation, but like any *Oxalis* should be watched for oxalic acid.

Ysaño or **añu** is a South American tuber (*Tropaeolum tuberosum*) closely related to the nasturtium (*T. majus*). A perennial climber, it is widely grown as a decorative flower, but there are mixed opinions about the culinary value of its knobbly yellow tubers. In Bolivia, they are claimed to be a delicacy if they are frozen after boiling, but another view is that they are just nasty.

Ulluco (*Ullucus tuberosus*) is another tuber from western South America. The plant is a half-hardy perennial which may be attractive to people who like uncommon vegetables. It has been grown in Britain. The small pink or yellow tubers are planted in the spring and lifted in the autumn after frost has killed the foliage.

....

Patra (India)

Pour boiling water over 100 g (4 oz) tamarind, leave it to cool and sieve the pulp from the seeds and fibre. Mix the pulp with 50 g (2 oz) *gur* (brown sugar), 150 g (5 oz) *besan* flour, 1 teaspoon powdered turmeric, 1 teaspoon powdered coriander, 2 teaspoons powdered chilli (to taste), and 1 teaspoon *garam masala. Add water to make a thick mixture of spreading consistency, and salt to taste. Cut out any thick stem and veins from 12 taro leaves (*arvi*), but otherwise keep them whole. Lay the first leaf glossy side down and spread a layer of the paste on the rough side. Put another leaf shiny side down on top and spread it. When you have a stack 6 leaves thick, interspersed with the *besan* spread, roll it up like a Swiss roll and secure it with thread. Repeat with the remaining 6 leaves. Steam the rolls for 35-45 minutes (pierce them to see if they are tender), then remove the rolls, cover them with a cloth and allow them to cool, but while they are still warm, cut them in slices 1 cm (½ in) thick. Deep fry the slices to a red-brown colour and serve them garnished with 2 tablespoons chopped green coriander leaves, 2 tablespoons grated coconut and wedges of lime or lemon. This is a well-known dish in Bombay – spicy, sweet-sour and unusual.

Curried Yam (Suram)

Peel the 1 kg (2 lb) elephant's foot yam, cut it into cubes and leave it to soak in salted water for 2 hours. Drain, dry and fry it. In a separate pan, fry together 1 teaspoon each of coriander, cumin and chilli gently until they are brown (but not burned). Add the yam, give it a turn and cool it with a dash of water. Add 25 g (1 oz) tamarind pulp or yoghurt when the yam is almost cooked. Sprinkle with chopped green coriander leaves before serving. Yam cubes may also be steamed, lightly browned in oil, then mixed with yoghurt, chopped green chillies and coriander leaves, seasoned with salt and a pinch of ground cumin seed, and served as a *raita* with curry.

[*Yam* – French: *ignarne* German: *Famwurzel* Italian: *igname* Spanish: *ñame*]

YAM BEAN. *See* yam.

YARD-LONG BEAN. *See* cowpea.

YAUTIA. *See* yam (yautia).

YEAST. Men used yeast for thousands of years without knowing it was composed of a mass of living organisms. Yeasts are single-celled, microscopic fungi. They commonly multiply by budding off daughters – a few kinds simply split in two like bacteria – but they also go in for sexual acts occasionally, so can form hybrids. To resist adversity (such as drying or too much alcohol), they can form *spores, for survival (not for multiplication). The atmosphere always has yeasts floating in it, and they are also introduced into the kitchen on fruit and vegetables. They drop into anything that is left uncovered.

Different species of yeast (and different strains within the same species) have individual characteristics. From a kitchen viewpoint, we can classify yeasts as wine yeasts, brewer's yeast, baker's yeast, wild yeasts and others. For rapid multiplication, yeasts need a good supply of air, but fermentation rather than growth is encouraged by the absence of air. Air is usually excluded during fermentation (and is often excluded naturally by the carbon dioxide that is produced), because air would encourage the bacteria that turn alcohol into acetic acid. It is worth noting that as fermentation is caused by enzymes made by the yeasts, the process can go on even when the yeasts are dead, though

treatment that kills yeast is likely also to destroy the enzymes. More heat than you can stand with your hand (the temperature for making 50°C or about 120°F) will quickly kill yeasts, even the spores, but they can stand being frozen, which is why yeast and bread dough can be kept for some time in the freezer. On the other hand, they need warmth to multiply – 25°C (77°F) is about right – and they prefer an acid medium of from pH 3.0-6.0; pH 5.3 is right for beer-making. Yeasts vary in their tolerance to alcohol (which they make themselves). It is no chance that man prizes yeasts that will thrive in a goodly amount of alcohol and calls the rest – the species which cannot hold their liquor – wild yeasts. Yeasts are inhibited by carbon dioxide gas under high pressure, a fact that is useful in the bulk storage of fruit juice in an unfermented state before filtration and bottling.

Bakers' yeast (*Saccharomyces cerevisiae*) can be bought fresh, as a compressed tan, clay-like substance, or as dried active yeast granules. Fresh yeast is not a pure culture, but contains fully active vegetative cells which will start to multiply immediately when mixed with warm sugary water at about 37°C (100°F). It will store well in the refrigerator for 10-14 days. If frozen, it should be used quickly after it has defrosted: it is most practical to package it for the freezer in 15-30 g (½-1 oz) lumps. For bread, 20 g (¾ oz) of yeast per 1 kg (2¼ lb) of flour is sufficient, although for fast, light results, more can be used. However, according to Elizabeth David, the more yeast that is used, the quicker the bread will dry and the less flavour it will have.

Active dry yeast has a considerable shelf life even at ordinary room temperature, but, being in an inactive state, takes a little longer to get going. This yeast should be softened in warm water or milk at about 43°C (110°F), but if it proves stubborn about behaving as its packet says it should, add a little sugar, glucose or honey and a squeeze of lemon to the liquid. For baking, fresh yeast is replaced by half of its weight of dried yeast.

Yeast cultures can be kept alive indefinitely by feeding them with sugar and starting up new bottles weekly with a bit of the old culture, as was once generally done and still is in out-of-the-way places. Such are the 'hops' used by Australian drovers, and these yeast stocks usually produce *sourdough bread.

For some reason, many people fight shy of using yeast, but it is easy to handle. The usual reason for failure is getting the dough too hot and so killing the yeast, or keeping it too cold, in which case the yeast hardly has a chance to function. Keep the dough nicely warm, like a baby, and the yeast should work. One touch of perversity is that yeast, like people, may become sluggish in very hot weather. If bread is heavier than usual during a heat-wave, add marginally more yeast than the recipe demands. And to test whether a yeast dough has finished its first rising, make a dent in the top of the dough with a finger tip. If the dent puffs back up, it should be left to rise further, until it does not spring back to the touch. Then it is ready to be punched down.

Brewers' yeast. There are two categories of brewers' yeast. One works mainly on the surface of the vat and is used for making most types of British beer, the other works more slowly and coolly on the bottom of the vat and is used to make lager and American beer. Serious home brewers must try to get the right type of yeast for the type of beer they wish to brew. Certainly never use ordinary bakers' yeast if you can help it, as the flavour will be very inferior (although some dried yeast packages give instructions for doing so.)

Wine yeast (*Saccharomyces ellipsoideus*). Until fairly recently, winemakers relied on the yeasts that occurred naturally on their vines; strains of yeast were associated with different types of wine. Today with more scientific control there is a tendency to introduce pure cultures of the strains required. Wine yeasts influence the taste of the wine (although a champagne yeast used on sugar and water will not make champagne). Ever since wine-making became legal in Britain, it has been possible to buy suitable strains of yeast for various styles of wine from shops catering for home wine enthusiasts. This has resulted in great improvement in flavour – you can even buy sherry yeasts which give the correct skin or *flor* on the surface of the vat. It is also possible now to increase the alcoholic strength of the drink, as one of the important differences between wine yeasts and other types is their ability to tolerate alcohol. Under special laboratory conditions, they have produced a concentration of up to 20%, but 10-14% is more normal. Wine yeasts come in powdered, granulated or tablet form, as well as in liquid yeast cultures.

Wild yeast (*Saccharomyces spiculatus*) and yeasts of the genera *Torula* and *Pichia*. The wild yeasts

are a nuisance to winemakers as they create bad flavours. They are usually quick off the mark, but luckily are quite sensitive to alcohol and are inhibited when the concentration reaches about 4%.They are much more sensitive to sulphur dioxide (*see* preservatives), than wine yeasts, so even though the number of wild yeast cells on one grape is often around 10,000,000, as compared with 100,000 of the wine yeasts, they are easy to control – 100 parts of sulphur dioxide per million is adequate. But this treatment of wine is frowned upon – there are legal limits to sulphur content in most countries. France allows up to 450 parts per million, but as little as 300 parts per million can be detected by taste in white wine. Another method of controlling wild yeasts is with alcohol. If the alcohol content of the must is brought up above the 4% mark by adding wine, then the wild yeasts will stop growing. Among other wild yeasts, some of the *Pichia* species are commonly seen growing on the surface of pickles, where they form a white skin or *flor* (as sherry yeasts form a *flor* on sherry). Though it is harmless, such a skin should be removed, because after a time it will create flavours in the pickles.

Yeasts in milk. There are usually yeasts in milk and they are sometimes responsible for creating unpleasant yeasty tastes in cottage cheese and yoghurt. They play a minor role in the microbiology of certain cheeses and are involved in the making of some sour milk products. An example is a yeast called *Saccharomyces taete*, which is necessary in making Swedish *rangmjölk* or *täte*, a sour milk product containing up to 0.5% alcohol. The correct souring of the milk depends on a bacterium called *Streptococcus lactis* which works in conjunction with the yeast, for the yeast will ferment milk sugar to alcohol only in the presence of lactic acid bacteria. Such symbiotic behaviour makes it far from simple to understand what goes on in foods made by the action of micro-organisms.

Health food yeasts. During World War II, many inmates of prison camps managed to stay alive by growing yeast, which is rich in protein, phosphorus, potassium and some of the B vitamins. Health food yeast is usually dried and dead (which it should be). It may be brewers' yeast or *Torula* yeast, which is even higher in nutrient value and more tolerable. Some yeasts are debittered to make them more palatable. It is usually recommended, that yeast be taken in orange juice in the hope that this will mask the taste, but I prefer to take it stirred into a cup of Marmite, which itself, being made of autolysed yeast, will marry tolerably with dried yeast in flavour. Yeast tablets are fairly useless, as you can rarely take enough for them to be effective.

Yeast nutrient. Yeasts require small amounts of nitrogenous material and minerals for proper growth so in some circumstances it is recommended to add a yeast nutrient to the culture. Yeast nutrient may be bought or it can be made up as follows:

Citric acid	130 g	(57%)
Ammonium sulphate	60 g	(26.3%)
Potassium phosphate	30 g	(13.2%)
Magnesium sulphate	8 g	(3.5%)

Use this at the rate of 3 g per litre (¼ to ½ oz per gallon).

[Yeast – French: *levure* German: *Hefe, Bärme* Italian: *lievito* Spanish: *levadura*]

YEAST EXTRACT has been made since the turn of the 20th century. It is not an extract in the usual sense of the word because it is not extracted from proteins and the yeast cells have been broken down. The breaking down can be done either by chemical treatment or biologically by autolysis, in effect salt-digestion by the yeast's own enzymes.

The simplest way of breaking down the yeast is by hydrolysis which is brought about by warming it with dilute hydrochloric acid. A 1-5% solution is used at a temperature of 30-100°C (86-212°F) for anything from 30 minutes to 2 hours – the various different manufacturers use different combinations, time, temperature and acid concentration. When hydrolysis of the proteins to amino acids is complete, the hydrochloric acid is neutralized with caustic soda to form common salt, but the mixture is left slightly acid because a slight sourness helps to mask the bitter taste of yeast, which most people find nasty. Careful filtration helps to take out even more of the yeasty bitterness. The clear liquid is concentrated by boiling it at 60°C (140°F) under reduced pressure until the extract will set to a paste on cooling. Flavourings such as celery are frequently included to make the result more palatable. A more modern chemical treatment which modifies the proteins less, is to digest yeast with ammonia under pressure for some 7 hours. The ammonia is then allowed to evaporate.

The autolytic process is more complex and may involve adding sugar, blood, starch, gum arabic, phosphates and other substances. These processes are usually trade secrets.

Yeast extracts contain useful amounts of Vitamin B_1, and B_2, and a number of amino acids, plus choline and other essential food substances that are found in yeast, but they are not a complete protein food. Yeast extracts such as the British Marmite are sold for use as spreads or flavourings, or to make hot savoury drinks.

YELLOWS. *See* sugar.

YERBA. *See* maté.

YOGHURT. This sour milk product has been introduced to almost the entire world in the last four decades. It may have originated in Central Asia, but is now traditional over a large area of Asia and south-eastern Europe, although for historical reasons Americans and Britons usually associate it with Bulgaria. Even the characteristic bacterium is called *Lactobacillus bulgaricus*. At the turn of this century, Elie Metchnikoff (1845-1916) the famous Russian microbiologist, proclaimed yoghurt to be almost the elixir of life. His theory was based partly on the longevity of tough, yoghurt-eating Bulgarians and partly on the scientific fact that the lactic acid in sour milk discourages putrefactive bacteria. Metchnikoff lived at a time when poisons from the putrefying contents of the human gut were blamed for ill health, a process of auto-intoxication. So the Victorians helped nature with frequent and massive doses of castor oil, cascara and Gregory powder, not to mention an occasional enema. As a result, survivors still suffer from constipation. In spite of his yoghurt, however, Metchnikoff lived to be only 71. The yoghurt bacterium does not survive in the human gut (although that of acidophilous milk does better) and auto-intoxication seems to have been over-rated as a source of illness. What is sure is that yoghurt is much more rapidly and easily digested than raw milk, and its mild acidity falls kindly on the stomach. In an hour, only 32% of raw milk is digested as against 91% of yoghurt, and the lactic acid content helps in the assimilation of calcium and phosphorus. Yoghurt is correctly made from sheep's, goat's or cow's whole milk, sometimes even from thin cream, but not, even in part, from reconstituted dried milk. It is a modern trick to add skim milk powder to give more body to the yoghurt. But then, the yoghurt of the supermarket does not have much likeness to the good yoghurt you can eat in Turkey. This is thick (it can be cut with a spoon) and never runny; it should be smooth, not grainy and with whey running out. It is even called 'sweet', although by its very nature it must contain some lactic acid. It should certainly never be very sour or bitter, although sour 'old' yoghurt is called for in some Indian recipes.

Making Yoghurt

l) Apparatus.There are many gadgets on the market, ranging from metal boxes lined with heat insulator and containing a set of pots (including a little one for the starter) to electric yoghurt makers in which temperature is maintained by a heating coil and thermostat. All that is traditionally necessary is a pot or bowl, which should hold 1-2 lt (1¾-3½ pt) of milk, a plate (or a sheet of cling film) big enough to cover it, and some wrapping to keep it warm. The wrapping may be a tin lined with cushions, a hay box or (as I use myself) an expanded polystyrene box of the type used for frozen foods. Wrapping in newspaper and then a blanket is a good makeshift. A vacuum flask is not recommended unless the yoghurt is to be turned out into a cloth after it has clabbered.

2) The starter. It is not necessary to buy a starter. A little taken from any pot of plain yoghurt will do as a starter, provided it contains live bacteria. Very little is needed – 1 teaspoon of starter per 1 lt (1¾ pt) of milk – and too much starter makes sour or grainy yoghurt. The starter should contain *Lactobacillus bulgaricus* and *Streptococcus thermophilus*, which both grow well at 40-45°C (104-113°F).This is more than the 'luke-warm' that is usually recommended. The temperature should be measured with a thermometer (after stirring the milk to get the heat even).The classic, though much less reliable, way is to dip in the knuckle of your little finger. When you can dip it in and count to ten slowly with some discomfort but without snatching it out with a scream, the temperature will be roughly right for yoghurt.

3) The milk. Sheep's milk and goat's milk are normally used in the Middle East, which has comparatively few cows. The milk should be brought nearly to the boil before use or alternatively may be boiled for a while to concentrate it by reduction to a creamier state.

4) Method. Pour the boiling milk into the bowl or pot (which should first, like the spoon you will use, be scalded with boiling water). Leave it to cool

until it reaches 45°C (113°F). Mix a teaspoonful or so smoothly with the starter, then pour it back into the milk and give a stir to distribute it evenly. Cover it with a plate and completely surround the pot with the insulation. Take a look after 5-6 hours and quickly wrap it up again if the milk has not clotted. Overnight is sometimes too long. When it has clotted, take it out of the wraps and put it preferably in a cool larder or, when it has cooled, in the bottom of the refrigerator.

5) Thickening. If the yoghurt is not thick enough, put it gently into a square of double muslin and hang it up to drip until it is as you want it. (Long draining makes yoghurt cheese or *labneh*, which is eaten with olive oil, Arab bread and black olives.) An alternative is carefully to make a well in the surface with a ladle; after some time, the well fills with watery whey, which can be spooned out. If necessary, you can repeat the process until the yoghurt is thick but it will still be almost undisturbed in the pot.

6) Troubles. There are three main reasons for failure. The first is failing to keep the pot warm enough. This happens if the insulation is insufficient or if you are trying to make yoghurt in too small a quantity. Try better insulation, a hot-water bottle or the airing cupboard. The next is using a dud yoghurt as a starter, it must contain living bacteria. Alternatively, you may have been killing the bacteria by putting them into milk that was too hot. Finally, you cannot use milk that contains antibiotics (which have been used to dose sick cows) or preservatives. Such things stop the organisms growing.

7) Cooking.Yoghurt is much used in the cooking of the region from the Balkans to India. Yoghurt made from goat's milk can be boiled (carefully) without it 'breaking', but cow's milk yoghurt needs something to stabilize it. Add a teaspoon of cornflour or of *besan flour and the white of an egg to every litre (1¾ pt) of yoghurt. Boil it warily, and stir it smoothly in one direction, a teaspoon of salt per litre (1¾ pt) is normally added as well.

Doogh (Iran)

One of the best refreshing drinks for hot weather. Beat 6 cups of yoghurt with about 10 cups of water and salt it very well (you need salt to replace what you have lost in sweating) – about 2 dessertspoons is normal for this quantity although it is added to taste. Chill thoroughly. I prefer to chill the yoghurt and to dilute it with soda water. Gassed, bottled doogh can be bought in Iran. Lebanese *ayran* or *'ayraan* and Indian *lassi* are similar.

....

Curd Curry (India)

This is delicious served as a soup, with rice if you like. Mix 4 cups of yoghurt with up to 8 cups water (depending on how thick you like it) and beat in 1-2 tablespoons *besan* flour. Chop and add a 2½ cm (1 in) piece of fresh ginger and 4 green chillies (powdered ginger and chilli powder can be used, but the taste is different). Put a tablespoonful of oil in a ladle, heat it and add 6 cloves, 2 sticks 5 cm (2 in) long of cinnamon, about 10 curry leaves, ½ teaspoon of asafoetida and a teaspoon of black mustard seed. When the mustard seeds begin to splutter immediately quench the whole ladle of goodies in the yoghurt mixture, which is then put on the heat. Add 1 teaspoon *gur* or dark brown sugar and salt to taste. Cook, stirring to begin with, until the soup is well thickened and the flavour has developed. Strain and serve garnished with chopped green coriander leaves if these are available. This is one of my favourite foods in hot weather. I use less water and the double quantity of *besan*, with a little powdered turmeric which slightly alters the taste and gives colour. Diced cucumber or okra can also be cooked in the soup.

....

Ab doogh khiar (Iran)

Finely chop 2 small cucumbers (ridge size), 3 spring onions, and a herb mixture (say, 2 sprigs each of mint, basil and savory). Also chop ½ cup raisins and ¼ cup walnuts. Mix with 4 cups thick yoghurt, season with salt and chill in the refrigerator. This dish is correctly served as a kind of salad, but makes a healthy lunch in summer.
[*Yoghurt* – French: *yaourt, yogourt* German: *Joghurt* Italian: *yog(h)urt* Spanish: *yogur*]

....

YOUNGBERRY. *See* raspberry.

YSAÑO. *See* yam (ysaño).

YUCA. *See* cassava.

....

Z

....

ZAMIKAND. *See* yam (elephant's foot).

ZAMPONE. A North Italian sausage for boiling. For this famous speciality, originally from around Modena, a boned pig's foot – correctly a forefoot – is stuffed with minced pork including some of the soft skin from the head and snout (as in *cotechino*), which gives it the splendidly soft, gelatinous texture that it has when cooked. *Zampone* is flavoured with salt, pepper and garlic, but there are fancy varieties such as *zampone al cedro* (which contains candied citron peel and sweet white wine). In Emilia, pieces of pig skin are cut into convenient shapes – squares, ovals, rounds – and stuffed with the *zampone* mixture. They have names like *bombonetti*, *cappelletti, monchi* and *vesicichette*. *Zampone* needs to be simmered for about 2 hours (some soak it first) and is served, cut in thick slices like *cotechino*, with lentils or as part of a *bollito misto* with a piquant sauce such as *salsa verde*. *Zampone* is food for cold weather.

ZAPOTE. *See* sapodilla.

ZEDOARY. A spice, the dried rhizome of a plant (*Curcuma zedoaria*) related to turmeric and ginger, which is native to South East Asia. The taste is something like musty camphor, and it is used in Malay and Indonesian cooking. Zedoary can be obtained in dried bits in some shops that specialize in exotic ingredients. It is usually sold under its Dutch name *kentjoer*.
[*Zedoary* – French: *zedoaire* German: *Zitwertwurzel* Italian: *zedoaria* Spanish: *cedoaria*]

ZEST. Originally the tough outer skin of the

walnut, but now used to denote the outer skin of citrus fruits, especially of lemon and orange, which contains the essential flavouring oils.

[*Zest* – French: *zeste* German: *Stückchen Orange – od Zitronenschale* Italian: *scarzetta* Spanish: *luquete*]

ZIGEUNER SPECK. *See* bacon.

ZINC (Zn). An essential trace metal. It is thought that 10 mg a day is the usual human requirement. Rich sources are oysters (270-600 parts per million) and herrings (700-1200). Wheatgerm and wheat bran are also rich in zinc, but it may not be absorbed efficiently from vegetable sources. Other sources are peanuts, liver, beef and mutton, cheese and cocoa, eggs and pulses. Although zinc deficiency is not common, it occurs in some communities. Zinc is lost in sweat, which is one reason why deficiency is more likely to occur in hot countries. In quantity, zinc salts are emetic. Metallic zinc is used as a coating for iron to stop rusting. This is known as galvanizing. As zinc is very easily dissolved by acids, it is important not to put acid substances in galvanized boilers and buckets. Brass can be an alloy of zinc and copper.

[*Zinc* – French: *zinc* German: *Zink* Italian: *zinco* Spanish: *zinc, cinc*]

ZITE. *See* pasta.

ZUCCHINI. *See* marrow.